PSYCHOLOGY

Lois Greenfield
ANTIGRAVITY
Chris Harrison, Aleksandr A. Semin

Two men trying to put on one pair of pajamas? Mimes fighting over a tablecloth? Contestants in a checkered taffy pull?

Well, it's art, so we really don't have to explain it. But we do know that this image caught our eye. What is it we liked? There's planned magic in this photo, a carefully mounted departure from convention that captures our approach to writing this book. We've worked hard to produce a text that is precise, organized—and just offbeat enough to be fun. Step inside and join us in our pajamas.

Lois Greenfield has been photographing dancers and dance movement since 1973. In the last three decades, her work has appeared in such diverse publications as *American Photographer, Dance Magazine, Elle, Esquire, Life,* the *New York Times, Newsweek, Rolling Stone, Vanity Fair, The Village Voice,* and *Vogue*. She has been featured in one-woman exhibitions in the United States, Europe, China, and most recently Japan. She has published two books, *Breaking Bounds: The Dance Photography of Lois Greenfield* (Chronicle Books, 1992) and *Airborne: The New Dance Photography of Lois Greenfield* (Chronicle Books, 1998). She currently lives in New York City.

PSYCHOLOGY

SECOND EDITION

DANIEL L. SCHACTER

HARVARD UNIVERSITY

DANIEL T. GILBERT

HARVARD UNIVERSITY

DANIEL M. WEGNER

HARVARD UNIVERSITY

WORTH PUBLISHERS

Senior Publisher: Catherine Woods
Executive Editor: Charles Linsmeier
Acquisitions Editor: Daniel DeBonis
Marketing Manager: Lindsay Johnson
Development Editor: Valerie Raymond
Media Editor: Christine Burak
Associate Managing Editor: Tracey Kuehn
Project Editor: Lisa Kinne
Photo Director: Ted Szczepanski
Photo Research: Donna Ranieri
Illustration Researcher: Lyndall Culbertson
Art Director and Cover Designer: Babs Reingold
Text Designers: Lissi Sigillo, Lyndall Culbertson, and Babs Reingold
Layout Designer: Lee Ann McKevitt
Illustration Coordinator: Janice Donnola
Illustrations: Matt Holt, Christy Krames, Don Stewart, and Todd Buck
Cover Photograph: Lois Greenfield
Production Manager: Sarah Segal
Composition: Macmillan Publishing Services
Printing and Binding: RR Donnelley

Chapter opening art credits: p. xxx, Lois Greefield; p. 38, John Rensten/Getty Images; p. 76, Adrianna Williams/Corbis; p. 124, Lucidio Studio Inc./Getty Images; p. 174, Lonny Kalfus/Getty Images; p. 218, Leland Bobbe; p. 262, Henrik Sorensen/Getty Images; p. 306, WIN-Initiative/Getty Images; p. 346, Mareen Fischinger/Getty Images; p. 388, bancoposta/Getty Images; p. 422, Eva Serrabassa/iStockphoto; p. 466, Jon Cartwright/Getty Images; p. 504, Seth Joel/Getty Images; p. 548, Lion Hecto/iStockphoto; p. 588, Mimi Haddon/Getty Images; p. 624, Patrick Siemer/Flickr/Getty Images

Library of Congress Project Control Number: 2010940234

ISBN-13: 978-1-4292-3719-2
ISBN-10: 1-4292-3719-8

Worth Publishers
41 Madison Avenue
New York, NY 10010
www.worthpublishers.com

To our children and their children

Hannah Schacter

Emily Schacter

Arlo Gilbert

Shona Gilbert

Daylyn Gilbert

Sari Gilbert

Kelsey Wegner

Haley Wegner

About the Authors

Daniel Schacter is William R. Kenan, Jr. Professor of Psychology at Harvard University. Dan received his BA degree from the University of North Carolina at Chapel Hill. He subsequently developed a keen interest in amnesic disorders associated with various kinds of brain damage. He continued his research and education at the University of Toronto, where he received his PhD in 1981. He taught on the faculty at Toronto for the next six years before joining the psychology department at the University of Arizona in 1987. In 1991, he joined the faculty at Harvard University. His research explores the relation between conscious and unconscious forms of memory and the nature of distortions and errors in remembering. Many of Schacter's studies are summarized in his 1996 book, *Searching for Memory: The Brain, The Mind, and The Past*, and his 2001 book, *The Seven Sins of Memory: How the Mind Forgets and Remembers*, both winners of the APA's William James Book Award. In 2009, Schacter received the Warren Medal from the Society of Experimental Psychologists for his research on true and false memories.

Daniel Gilbert is professor of psychology at Harvard University. After attending the Community College of Denver and completing his BA from the University of Colorado, Denver, he went on to earn his PhD from Princeton University. From 1985 to 1996, he taught at the University of Texas, Austin, and in 1996, he joined the faculty of Harvard University. He has received the American Psychological Association's Distinguished Scientific Award for an Early Career Contribution to Psychology and has won teaching awards that include the Phi Beta Kappa Teaching Prize and the Harvard College Professorship. His research focuses on how and how well people think about their emotional reactions to future events. He is the author of the international bestseller *Stumbling on Happiness*, which won the Royal Society's General Prize for best popular science book of the year, and he is the co-writer and host of the PBS television series *This Emotional Life*.

Daniel Wegner is professor of psychology at Harvard University. He received his BS in 1970 and PhD in 1974, both from Michigan State University. He began his teaching career at Trinity University in San Antonio, Texas, before his appointments at the University of Virginia in 1990 and then Harvard University in 2000. He is a Fellow of the American Association for the Advancement of Science, Fellow of the Society of Experimental Psychologists, and William James Fellow of the Association for Psychological Science. His research focuses on thought suppression and mental control, transactive memory in relationships and groups, and the experience of conscious will. His work in thought suppression and consciousness served as the basis of two popular books, *White Bears and Other Unwanted Thoughts* and *The Illusion of Conscious Will*, both of which were named *Choice* Outstanding Academic Books. His article "How to Think, Say, or Do Precisely the Worst Thing for Any Occasion" was selected for *The Best American Science Writing 2010*.

Brief Contents

Contents

Chapter **3** Neuroscience and Behavior 77

Preface

Why are you reading the preface? The book really gets going in about ten pages, so why are you here instead of there? Are you the kind of person who can't stand the idea of missing something? Are you trying to justify the cost of the book by consuming every word? Did you just open to this page out of habit? Are you starting to think you might have made a big mistake?

For as long as we can remember, the three of us have been asking questions like these about ourselves, about our friends, and about anyone else who didn't run away fast enough. Our curiosity about why people think, feel, and act as they do drew each of us into our first psychology course, and though we remember being swept away by the lectures, we don't remember anything about the textbooks. That's probably because our textbooks were little more than colorful encyclopedias of facts, names, and dates. Little wonder that we sold back our books the moment we finished our final exams.

When we became psychology professors, we did the things that psychology professors often do: We taught classes, we conducted research, and we wore sweater vests long after they stopped being fashionable. We also wrote popular books that people really liked to read, and that made us wonder why no one had ever written an introductory psychology textbook that students really liked to read. After all, psychology is the most interesting subject in the known universe, so why shouldn't a psychology textbook be the most interesting thing in a student's backpack? We couldn't think of a reason, so we sat down and wrote the book that we wished we'd been given as students. *Psychology* was published in 2008 and the reaction was astounding. We'd never written a textbook before so we didn't know exactly what to expect, but never in our wildest dreams did we imagine that we would *win the Pulitzer Prize*!

Which was good, because we didn't. But we did get unsolicited letters and e-mails from students all over the country who wrote just to tell us how much they liked our book. They liked the content because, as we may have mentioned, psychology is the most interesting subject in the known universe. But they also liked the fact that our textbook didn't *sound* like a textbook. It wasn't written in the scripted, stodgy voice of the announcer from the nature films we all saw in seventh-grade biology ("Behold the sea otter, nature's furry little scavenger"). Rather, it was written in *our* voices—the same voices in which we had written books for people who would stop reading them if they got bored. We made a conscious effort to tell the *story* of psychology—to integrate topics rather than just listing them, to illustrate ideas rather than just describing them. We realized that because science is such a complicated and serious business, some teachers might think that a science textbook should be complicated and serious too. We didn't see it that way. Writing is the art of making complicated things seem simple and making serious things seem fun. The students who wrote to us seemed to agree.

The first edition of our book was a hit—so why have we replaced it with a second edition? Two reasons. First, we got tired of being asked about the naked guy on the cover of the first edition. He's gone now and we're only going to say this one more time: No, he isn't one of us, and yes, he probably was a little cold. The second and somewhat more important reason for bringing out a new edition is that things change. Science changes (psychologists know all sorts of things about the mind and the brain that they didn't know just a few years ago), the world changes (when we wrote the first edition, no one had heard of an iPad or Barack Obama), and we change (our research and reading give us new perspectives on psychological issues, and our writing and teaching show us new ways to help students learn). With all of these changes happening around us and to us, we felt that our book should change as well.

Changes to the Second Edition

New Research

A textbook should give students a complete tour of the classics, of course, but it should also take them out dancing on the cutting edge. We want students to realize that psychology is not a museum piece—not just a collection of past events but also of current events—and that this young and evolving science has a place for them if they want it. So we've packed the second edition with information about what's happening in the field today. Not only have we included more than 700 new citations but we've featured some of the hottest new findings in the Hot Science boxes that you'll find in every chapter.

Chapter Number	Hot Science
1	How to Get Your Name in This Chapter, p. 21
2	Do Violent Movies Make Peaceful Streets?, p. 66
3	Mirror, Mirror, in My Brain, p. 81
	Establishing Causality in the Brain, p. 118
4	Expensive Taste, p. 168
5	The Mind Wanders, p. 182
6	Sleep on It, p. 230
7	Control of Learning: From the Laboratory to the Classroom, p. 287
	Even More Reasons to Sleep, p. 295
8	Fear Goggles, p. 315
9	Sudden Insight and the Brain, p. 379
10	The Breast and the Brightest, p. 411
	Big Brother Is Watching You, p. 413
11	Walk This Way, p. 438
12	Personality on the Surface, p. 476
13	The Eyes Have It, p. 512
	The Color of Expectations, p. 539
14	Autism and Childhood Disorders, p. 577
	Positive Psychology, p. 584
15	Happy Pills? Antidepressants for Ordinary Sadness, p. 611
16	This Is Your Brain on Placebos, p. 645

New Focus on Culture

Although we're all middle-aged White guys named Dan, we realize that not everyone else is. That's why this time around we've given special attention to cultural psychology, placing human behavior in the context of nations, ethnicities, religions, communities, and cultures. Culture influences just about everything we do—from how we perceive lines to how we long we will stand in them—and this edition celebrates the rich diversity of human beings throughout the text, and then especially in the Culture & Community boxes in many of the chapters.

Culture and Multicultural Experience

Culture and Multicultural Experience (*continued*)

The Psychology of Men and Women

New Organization

We've also rearranged our table of contents to better fit our changing sense of how psychology is best taught. For example, we've moved the chapter Social Psychology forward so that it can be closer to its cousin, Personality; we've moved Consciousness forward so that students will be better prepared to understand modern research on Memory and Learning; and we've clustered Psychological Disorders, Treatment of Psychological Disorders, and Stress and Health together to create a strong finish of clinically oriented material.

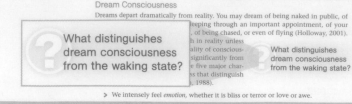

Dream Consciousness

Dreams depart dramatically from reality. You may dream of being naked in public, of ...eeping through an important appointment, of your ..., of being chased, or even of flying (Holloway, 2001). ...h in reality unless ...ality of conscious-...significantly from ...e five major char-...ss that distinguish ..., 1988).

> We intensely feel *emotion,* whether it is bliss or terror or love or awe.

KEY CONCEPT QUIZ

1. Which of the following is NOT a basic property of consciousness?
   a. intentionality
   b. disunity
   c. selectivity
   d. transience

2. Currently, unconscious processes are understood as
   a. a concentrated pattern of thought suppression.
   b. a hidden system of memories, instincts, and desires.
   c. a blank slate.
   d. unexperienced mental processes that give rise to thoughts and behavior.

3. The _____ unconscious is at work when subliminal and unconscious processes influence thought and behavior.
   a. minimal
   b. repressive
   c. dynamic
   d. cognitive

4. The cycle of sleep and waking is one of the major patterns of human life called
   a. the circadian rhythm.
   b. the sleep stages.
   c. the altered state of consciousness.
   d. subliminal perception.

5. Sleep needs _____ over the life span.
   a. decrease
   b. increase
   c. fluctuate
   d. remain the same

c. increased capacity for planning.
d. prevention of movement.

9. Psychoactive drugs influence consciousness by altering the effects of
   a. agonists.
   b. neurotransmitters.
   c. amphetamines.
   d. spinal neurons.

10. Tolerance to drugs involves
    a. larger doses being required over time to achieve the same effect.
    b. openness to new experiences.
    c. the initial attraction of drug use.
    d. the lessening of the painful symptoms that accompany withdrawal.

11. Drugs that heighten arousal and activity level by affecting the central nervous system are
    a. depressants.
    b. stimulants.
    c. narcotics.
    d. hallucinogens.

12. Alcohol expectancy refers to
    a. alcohol's initial effects of euphoria and reduced anxiety.
    b. the widespread acceptance of alcohol as a socially approved substance.
    c. alcohol leading people to respond in simple ways to complex situations.
    d. people's beliefs about how alcohol will influence them in particular situations.

New Pedagogy

Introductory psychology students are faced with absorbing the wide variety of facts, concepts, and applications of psychology. This challenge is made easier if the textbook supports their learning with thoughtful pedagogy to help students ask questions as they read about the ideas they encounter.

> *New cue questions* encourage critical thinking and help identify the most important concepts in every major section of the text.

> *New bulleted summaries* follow each major section to reinforce key concepts and make it easier to study for the test.

> *A new Key Concept Quiz* at the end of each chapter offers students the opportunity to test what they know.

> *New Critical Thinking Questions* are included at the end of each chapter, offering the opportunity to apply various concepts.

Emphasis on Practical Application and Debate

What would the facts and concepts of psychology be without real-world application? The special-topic boxes designed to bring psychology to life have been updated and retained for the second edition. The Real World boxes introduce practical applications of psychological science, and Where Do You Stand? boxes ask students to weigh in on a current debate.

Chapter Number	The Real World
1	Improving Study Skills, p. 11
	Joining the Club, p. 32
2	Oddsly Enough, p. 63
3	Brain Plasticity and Sensations in Phantom Limbs, p. 103
4	Multitasking, p. 132
	Cochlear Implants, p. 160
5	Drugs and the Regulation of Consciousness, p. 208
6	Deadly Misattributions, p. 250
7	Understanding Drug Overdoses, p. 267
8	Jeet Jet?, p. 332
9	Does Bilingualism Interfere with Cognitive Development?, p. 359
10	Look Smart, p. 397
11	When Mom's Away… , p. 441
12	Do Different Genders Lead to Different Personalities?, p. 478
13	Making the Move, p. 516
14	Suicide Risk and Prevention, p. 568
15	Types of Psychotherapists, p. 592
	Tales from the Madhouse, p. 607
16	Why Sickness Feels Bad: Psychological Effects of Immune Response, p. 633

Supplemental Resources and Media

PsychPortal

A comprehensive web resource for teaching and learning psychology

The PsychPortal website combines Worth Publishers' award winning media with an innovative platform for easy navigation. For students, it is the ultimate online study guide with rich interactive tutorials, videos, adaptive quizzing, and the full text in the eBook. For instructors, PsychPortal is a full course space where class documents can be posted, quizzes are easily assigned and graded, and students' progress can be assessed and recorded. Whether you are looking for the most effective study tools or a robust platform for an online course, PsychPortal is a powerful way to enhance an introductory psychology class.

> PsychPortal to Accompany *Psychology*, Second Edition, can be previewed and purchased at **www.yourpsychportal.com**
>
> *Psychology*, Second Edition, and PsychPortal can be ordered together with ISBN-10: 1429283068 / ISBN-13: 9781429283069. Individual components of PsychPortal may also be available for separate, stand-alone purchase.

PsychPortal for *Psychology*, Second Edition, includes all the following resources:

> **An interactive eBook** allows students to highlight, bookmark, and make their own notes, just as they would with a printed textbook. Google-style searching and in-text glossary definitions make the text ready for the digital age. *The interactive eBook for* Psychology, *Second Edition, can also be purchased online by visiting* **http://ebooks.bfwpub.com/schacter2e**

> **The Online Video Tool Kit for Introductory Psychology** includes more than 100 engaging video modules that instructors can easily assign and customize for student assessment. Videos cover classic experiments, current news footage, and

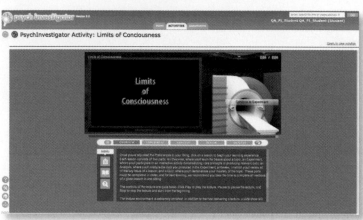

cutting-edge research, all of which are sure to spark discussion and encourage critical thinking. *The Online Video Tool Kit can also be purchased online by visiting **www.worthvideotoolkit.com***

> **PsychInvestigator: Laboratory Learning in Introductory Psychology** is a series of activities that model a virtual laboratory and are produced in association with Arthur Kohn, PhD, of Dark Blue Morning Productions. Students are introduced to core psychological concepts by a video host and then participate in activities that generate real data and lead to some startling conclusions! Like all activities in PsychPortal, PsychInvestigator activities can be assigned and automatically graded. *PsychInvestigator can also be purchased online by visiting **www.worthpi.com***

> The award-winning tutorials in Tom Ludwig's (Hope College) **PsychSim 5.0** and the new **Concepts in Action** provide an interactive, step-by-step introduction to key psychological concepts.

> **Focused Quizzing and Personalized Study Plans** allow students to focus their studying where it's needed the most. The Focused Quizzing engine produces a series of unique quizzes for students, and based on their performance, students receive individualized study recommendations in the form of a Personalized Study Plan. Students then have a rich variety of activities to build their comprehension of the chapter.

> **The Assignment Center** lets instructors easily construct and administer tests and quizzes from the book's Test Bank and course materials. Assignments can be automatically graded, and the results are recorded in a customizable grade book.

> **The *Scientific American* Newsfeed** delivers weekly articles, podcasts, and news briefs on the very latest developments in psychology from the first name in popular science journalism.

Additional Student Supplements

> **The Student Video Tool Kit for Introductory Psychology** is a DVD-based collection of more than 100 brief video clips (1 to 13 minutes each) and activities from PsychPortal. It gives students a fresh way to experience both the classic experiments at the heart of psychological science and cutting-edge research conducted by the field's most influential investigators.

> The **Psychology Book Companion Website** at **www.worthpublishers.com/schacter2e** is the home of Worth Publishers' free study aids and supplemental content. The site includes chapter outlines, online quizzes, interactive flashcards, and more.

> The **CourseSmart eBook** offers the complete text of *Psychology*, Second Edition, in an easy-to-use, flexible format. Students can choose to view the CourseSmart eBook online or download it to a personal computer or a portable media player, such as a smart phone or iPad. *The CourseSmart eBook for* Psychology, *Second Edition, can be previewed and purchased at **www.coursesmart.com***

> **Psych2Go** provides students with the opportunity to purchase podcasts of chapter reviews, quizzes, and flashcards in an easily downloadable format. *Find out more at **www.psych2go.com***

> The print **Study Guide** by Russell Frohardt of St. Edward's University is a portable resource, ideal for students on the go who want to rehearse their mastery of concepts from the text with the following features:
>   > "The Big Picture," a brief wrap-up of the chapter's main ideas and concepts
>   > Chapter Objectives, which also appear in the Instructor's Resources and Test Bank
>   > Chapter Overview, a fill-in-the-blank summary that is divided by major section
>   > Three 10-question "Quick Quizzes" per chapter
>   > "Hey, Guess What I Learned in Psychology Today," an essay question asking students to apply what they have learned
>   > "Things to Ponder," a section that helps students extend and apply knowledge and think about where the material might be going
>   > An answers section that includes in-depth explanations of complex topics
>   > Web Links and Suggested Readings for further investigation

> ***Pursuing Human Strengths: A Positive Psychology Guide*** by Martin Bolt of Calvin College is a perfect way to introduce students to the amazing field of positive psychology as well as their own personal strengths.

> ***The Critical Thinking Companion for Introductory Psychology*** by Jane S. Halonen of the University of West Florida and Cynthia Gray of Beloit College contains both a guide to critical thinking strategies as well as exercises in pattern recognition, practical problem solving, creative problem solving, scientific problem solving, psychological reasoning, and perspective-taking.

> Worth Publishers is proud to offer several readers of articles taken from the pages of *Scientific American*. Drawing on award-winning science journalism, the **Scientific American Reader to Accompany *Psychology*, Second Edition, by Daniel L. Schacter, Daniel T. Gilbert, and Daniel M. Wegner** features pioneering and cutting-edge research across the fields of psychology. Selected by the authors themselves, this collection provides further insight into the fields of psychology through articles written for a popular audience.

> ***Psychology and the Real World: Essays Illustrating Fundamental Contributions to Society*** is a superb collection of essays by major researchers that describe their landmark studies. Published in association with the not-for-profit FABBS Foundation, this engaging reader includes Elizabeth Loftus's own reflections on her study of false memories, Eliot Aronson on his cooperative classroom study, and Daniel Wegner on his study of thought suppression. A portion of all proceeds is donated to FABBS to support societies of cognitive, psychological, behavioral, and brain sciences.

Worth Publishers is pleased to offer cost-saving packages of *Psychology*, Second Edition, with our most popular supplements. Below is a list of some of the most popular combinations available for order through your local bookstore.

Psychology, 2nd Ed. & PsychPortal Access Card
ISBN-10: 1429283068/ISBN-13: 9781429283069

Psychology, 2nd Ed. & Study Guide
ISBN-10: 1429282657/ISBN-13: 9781429282659

Psychology, 2nd Ed. & iClicker
ISBN-10: 1429283033/ISBN-13: 9781429283038

Psychology, 2nd Ed. & *Scientific American* Reader
ISBN-10: 1429282665/ISBN-13: 9781429282666

Psychology, 2nd Ed. & *Psychology and the Real World*
ISBN-10: 1429283025/ISBN-13: 9781429283021

Course Management

> Worth Publishers supports multiple Course Management Systems with enhanced cartridges for upload into Blackboard, WebCT, Angel, Desire2Learn, Sakai, and Moodle. Cartridges are provided free upon adoption of *Psychology*, Second Edition, and can be downloaded at **www.bfwpub.com/lms**

Assessment

> The **Printed Test Bank** by Chad Galuska of the College of Charleston features over 200 multiple-choice, true/false, and essay questions per chapter to test students' factual and conceptual knowledge and address the teaching outcomes set by the American Psychological Association.

> The **Computerized Test Bank** powered by Diploma includes all the test bank items for the easy creation of tests and quizzes. With the accompanying grade book, you can record students' grades throughout a course, sort student records and view detailed analyses of test items, curve tests, generate reports, and add weights to grades.

> The **iClicker** Classroom Response System is a versatile polling system developed by educators for educators that makes class time more efficient and interactive. iClicker allows you to ask questions and instantly record your students' responses, take attendance, and gauge students' understanding and opinions. iClicker is available at a 10% discount when packaged with *Psychology*, Second Edition.

Presentation

> New **Interactive PowerPoint® Presentations** are another great way to introduce Worth's dynamic media into the classroom without lots of advance preparation. Each presentation covers a major topic in psychology and integrates Worth's high-quality videos and animations for an engaging teaching and learning experience. These interactive presentations are complimentary to adopters of *Psychology*, Second Edition, and are perfect for technology novices and experts alike.

> For teachers who want to promote interactive learning in the classroom, Worth Publishers is proud to offer **ActivePsych: Classroom Activities Projects and Video Teaching Modules.** ActivePsych includes a robust collection of videos and animations as well as two sets of activities created and class tested by veteran introductory psychology teachers. The materials cover the entire introductory psychology curriculum with 32 Flash®-based demonstrations to promote discussion and critical thinking as well as 22 PowerPoint®-based demonstrations designed to assess understanding and to be compatible with the iClicker classroom response system.

> The **Instructor's Resources** by Jeffrey Henriques of the University of Wisconsin-Madison features a variety of materials that are valuable to new and veteran teachers alike. In addition to background on the chapter reading and suggestions for in-class lectures, the manual is rich with activities to engage students in different modes of learning.

> The **Instructor's Resource CD-ROM** for *Psychology*, Second Edition, contains prebuilt PowerPoint® presentation slide sets for each chapter; all the figures, photos, and tables from the book; and an electronic version of the Instructor's Resources.

Video and DVD Resources

Worth Publisher's video collections—complimentary to adopters of *Psychology*, Second Edition—comprise over 300 unique video clips to enrich the classroom. These clips include clinical footage, interviews, animations, and news segments that vividly illustrate topics across the psychology curriculum.

> Instructor Video Tool Kit for *Introductory Psychology*, Volumes 1 and 2 (CD, DVD)
> Worth Digital Media Archive, First and Second Editions (CD, DVD)
> Psychology: The Human Experience Teaching Modules (DVD, VHS)
> The Many Faces of Psychology Video (DVD, VHS)
> *Scientific American* Frontiers Video Collection, Second and Third Editions (CD, DVD)

Acknowledgments

Despite what you might guess by looking at our photographs, we all found women who were willing to marry us. We thank Susan McGlynn, Marilynn Oliphant, and Toni Wegner for that particular miracle and also for their love and support during the years when we were busy writing this book.

Although ours are the names on the cover, writing a textbook is a team sport, and we were lucky to have an amazing group of professionals in our dugout. We greatly appreciate the contributions of Martin M. Antony, Mark Baldwin, Michelle A. Butler, Patricia Csank, Denise D. Cummins, Ian J. Deary, Howard Eichenbaum, Sam Gosling, Paul Harris, Catherine Myers, Shigehiro Oishi, Arthur S. Reber, Morgan T. Sammons, Dan Simons, Alan Swinkels, Richard M. Wenzlaff, and Steven Yantis.

We are grateful for the editorial, clerical, and research assistance we received from Clifford Robbins and Adrian Gilmore.

In addition, we would like to thank our core supplements authors. They provided insight into the role our book can play in the classroom and adeptly developed the materials to support it. Russ Frohardt, Chad Galuska, and Jeff Henriques, we appreciate your tireless work in the classroom and the experience you brought to the book's supplements.

We would like to thank the faculty who reviewed the manuscript. They showed a level of engagement we have come to expect from our best colleagues and students:

Eileen Achorn,
University of Texas at San Antonio

Jim Allen,
State University of New York, Geneseo

Randy Arnau,
University of Southern Mississippi

Kristin Biondolillo,
Arkansas State University

Stephen Blessing,
University of Tampa

Jeffrey Blum,
Los Angeles City College

Richard Bowen,
Loyola University of Chicago

Nicole Bragg,
Mt. Hood Community College

Michele Brumley,
Idaho State University

Josh Burk,
College of William and Mary

Richard Cavasina,
California University of Pennsylvania

Amber Chenoweth,
Kent State University

Stephen Chew,
Samford University

Chrisanne Christensen,
Southern Arkansas University

Jennifer Daniels,
University of Connecticut

Joshua Dobias,
University of New Hampshire

Dale Doty,
Monroe Community College

Valerie Farmer-Dugan,
Illinois State University

Diane Feibel,
University of Cincinnati-Raymond Walters College

Chad Galuska,
College of Charleston

Afshin Gharib,
Dominican University of California

Jeffrey Gibbons,
Christopher Newport University

Adam Goodie,
University of Georgia

Patricia Grace,
Kaplan University Online

Sarah Grison,
University of Illinois at Urbana-Champaign

Deletha Hardin,
University of Tampa

Jason Hart,
Christopher Newport University

Lesley Hathorn,
Metropolitan State College of Denver

Jacqueline Hembrook,
University of New Hampshire

Allen Huffcutt,
Bradley University

Mark Hurd,
College of Charleston

Linda Jackson,
Michigan State University

Lance Jones,
Bowling Green State University

Linda Jones,
Blinn College

Don Kates,
College of DuPage

Martha Knight-Oakley,
Warren Wilson College

Ken Koenigshofer,
Chaffey College

Neil Kressel,
William Patterson University

Josh Landau,
York College of Pennsylvania

Fred Leavitt,
California State University, East Bay

Tera Letzring,
Idaho State University

Ray Lopez,
University of Texas at San Antonio

Jeffrey Love,
Penn State University

Greg Loviscky,
Penn State University

Lynda Mae,
Arizona State University

Caitlin Mahy,
University of Oregon

Gregory Manley,
University of Texas at San Antonio

Karen Marsh,
University of Minnesota, Duluth

Robert Mather,
University of Central Oklahoma

Wanda McCarthy,
University of Cincinnati, Clermont College

Daniel McConnell,
University of Central Florida

Mignon Montpetit,
Illinois Wesleyan University

Todd Nelson, *California State University, Stanislaus*

Aminda O'Hare,
University of Kansas

Brady Phelps,
South Dakota State University

Raymond Phinney,
Wheaton College

Claire St. Peter Pipkin,
West Virginia University

Christy Porter,
College of William and Mary

Douglas Pruitt,
West Kentucky Community and Technical College

Elizabeth Purcell,
Greenville Technical College

Celia Reaves,
Monroe Community College

Diane Reddy,
University of Wisconsin-Milwaukee

Cynthia Shinabarger Reed,
Tarrant County College

David Reetz,
Hanover College

Tanya Renner,
Kapi'olani Community College

Wendy Rote,
University of Rochester

Larry Rudiger,
University of Vermont

Sharleen Sakai,
Michigan State University

Matthew Sanders,
Marquette University

Phillip Schatz,
Saint Joseph's University

Vann Scott,
Armstrong Atlantic State University

Colleen Seifert,
University of Michigan

Wayne Shebilske,
Wright State University

Elisabeth Sherwin,
University of Arkansas at Little Rock

Kenith Sobel,
University of Central Arkansas

Genevieve Stevens,
Houston Community College

Mark Stewart,
American River College

Holly Straub,
University of South Dakota

Mary Strobbe,
San Diego Miramar College

William Struthers,
Wheaton College

Lisa Thomassen,
Indiana University

John Wright,
Washington State University

Keith Young,
University of Kansas

Over 1,000 students have class-tested chapters of *Psychology* in various stages of development. Not only are we encouraged by the overwhelmingly positive responses to *Psychology*, but we are also pleased to incorporate these students' insightful and constructive comments. We learned a lot during the development the Second Edition of *Psychology* from the faculty who led our class testing efforts with students. We thank them for their time and insights, both of which were considerable.

They include:

Michele Baranczyk,
Kutztown University

David Baskind,
Delta College

Jennifer Bellingtier,
Hawkeye Community College

Wendi Born,
Baker University

Ellen Broom,
Texas Christian University

Mary Campa,
Skidmore College

Thomas Capo,
University of Maryland

Rachel Dinero,
Cazenovia College

Wendy Domjan,
University of Texas at Austin

Portia Dyrenforth,
Hobart and William Smith Colleges

Eli Finkel,
Northwestern University

Andy Gauler,
Florida State College at Jacksonville

Kendra Gilds,
Lane Community College

Tay Hack,
Angelo State College

Richard Hass,
University of Delaware

Matthew Isaak,
University of Louisiana at Lafayette

Norine Jalbert,
Western Connecticut State University

Deanna Julka,
University of Portland

Dannelle Larsen-Rife,
Dixie State College

Dianne Leader,
Georgia Institute of Technology

Sean Meegan,
University of Utah

Saaid Mendoza,
Amherst College

Todd Nelson,
California State University, Stanislaus

Bill Price,
North Country Community College

Nicole Rosa,
Bentley College

Jessica Salvatore,
Amherst College

Mike Serra,
Texas Tech University

Keith Shafritz,
Hofstra University

Lisa Sinclair,
University of Winnipeg

Karen Smith,
Truman State University

Meredith Stanford-Pollock,
University of Massachusetts, Lowell

Bob Swoap,
Warren Wilson College

Sandra Trafalis,
West Valley College

Mary Utley,
Drury University

Connie Varnhagen,
University of Alberta

Shelley Watson,
Laurentian University

We are especially grateful to the wonderful people at Worth Publishers. They include our publisher, Catherine Woods, who encouraged us at every stage of the project; our acquisitions editor, top dog, queso grande, and all around main man, Charles Linsmeier, who managed the project (and us) with intelligence, grace, and humor; our development editor for the first edition, Mimi Melek, who gave this edition a big head start; our development editor for the second edition, Valerie Raymond, who pushed us, prodded us, guided us, listened to us, and laughed at precisely the right moments; our associate managing editor Tracey Kuehn, project editor Lisa Kinne, production manager Sarah Segal, and editorial assistant Lukia Kliossis, who through some remarkable alchemy turned a manuscript into a book; our art director Babs Reingold, layout designer Lee Ann McKevitt, photo editor Ted Szczepanski, and photo researcher Donna Ranieri, who made that book an aesthetic delight; our media editor Christine Burak and production manager Stacey Alexander, who guided the development and creation of a superb supplements package; and our marketing manager Lindsay Johnson and associate director of market development Carlise Stembridge, who served as tireless public advocates for our vision. Thank you one and all. We look forward to working with you again.

Daniel L. Schacter   Daniel T. Gilbert   Daniel M. Wegner
                                                        Cambridge, 2010

1

Psychology: The Evolution of a Science

A lot was happening in 1860. Abraham Lincoln had just been elected president of the United States, the Pony Express had just begun to deliver mail between Missouri and California, and a woman named Anne Kellogg had just given birth to a child who would one day grow up to invent the cornflake. But none of this mattered very much to William James, a bright, taciturn, 18-year-old man who had no idea what to do with his life. He loved to paint and draw but worried that he wasn't talented enough to become a serious artist. He had enjoyed studying biology in school but doubted that a naturalist's salary would ever allow him to get married and have a family of his own. And so like many young people who are faced with difficult decisions about their futures, William abandoned his dreams and chose to do something in which he had little interest but of which his family heartily approved. Alas, within a few months of arriving at Harvard Medical School, his initial lack of interest in medicine blossomed into a troubling lack of enthusiasm, and so with a bit of encouragement from the faculty, he put his medical studies on hold to join a biological expedition to the Amazon. The adventure failed to focus his wandering mind (though he learned a great deal about leeches), and when he returned to medical school, both his physical and mental health began to deteriorate. It was clear to everyone that William James was not the sort of person who should be put in charge of a scalpel and a bag of drugs.

Had William become an artist, a biologist, or a physician, we would probably remember nothing about him today. Fortunately for us, he was a deeply confused young man who could speak five languages, and when he became so depressed that he was once again forced to leave medical school, he decided to travel around Europe, where at least he knew how to talk to people. And as he talked and listened, he learned about a new science called *psychology* (from a combination of the Greek *psyche*, which means "soul," and *logos*, which means "to study"), which was just beginning to develop.

▶ Over the years, many young people, like this happy pair, have turned to travel as they considered their next step in life. Thankfully, for the young William James, his travels led him to psychology.

MIKE HARRINGTON/GETTY IMAGES

▲ William James (1842–1910) was excited by the new field of psychology, which allowed him to apply a scientific approach to age-old questions about the nature of human beings.

As William read about psychology and talked with those who were developing it, he began to see that this new field was taking a modern, scientific approach to age-old questions about human nature—questions that had become painfully familiar to him during his personal search for meaning, but questions to which only poets and philosophers had ever before offered answers (Bjork, 1983; Simon, 1998). Excited about the new discipline, William returned to America and quickly finished his medical degree. But he never practiced medicine and never intended to do so. Rather, he became a professor at Harvard University and devoted the rest of his life to psychology. His landmark book—*The Principles of Psychology*—is still widely read and remains one of the most influential books ever written on the subject (James, 1890).

A lot has happened since then. Abraham Lincoln has become the face on a penny, the Pony Express has been replaced by e-mail and Twitter, and the Kellogg Company sells about $9 billion worth of cornflakes every year. If William James (1842–1910) were alive today, he would be amazed by all of these things. But he would probably be even more amazed by the intellectual advances that have taken place in the science that he helped create. Indeed, the sophistication and diversity of modern psychology are nothing short of staggering: Psychologists today are exploring perception, memory, creativity, consciousness, love, anxiety, addictions, and more. They use state-of-the-art technologies to examine what happens in the brain when people feel anger, recall a past experience, undergo hypnosis, or take an intelligence test. They examine the impact of culture on individuals, the origins and uses of language, the ways in which groups form and dissolve, and the similarities and differences between people from different backgrounds. Their research advances the frontiers of basic knowledge and has practical applications as well—from new treatments for depression and anxiety to new systems that allow organizations to function more effectively.

Psychology is *the scientific study of **mind** and **behavior**.* The **mind** refers to our *private inner experience,* the ever-flowing stream of consciousness that is made of perceptions, thoughts, memories, and feelings. **Behavior** refers to *observable actions of human beings and nonhuman animals,* the things that we do in the world, by ourselves or with others. As you will see in the chapters to come, psychology is an attempt to use scientific methods to address fundamental questions about mind and behavior that have puzzled people for millennia. The answers to these questions would have astonished William James. Let's take a look at some examples:

> *What are the bases of perceptions, thoughts, memories, and feelings, or our subjective sense of self?* For thousands of years, philosophers tried to understand how the objective, physical world of the body was related to the subjective, psychological world of the mind, and some philosophers even suggested that the pineal gland in the brain might function as the magic tunnel between these two worlds. Today, psychologists know that there is no magic tunnel, and no need for one, because all of our subjective experiences arise from the electrical and chemical activities of our brains. Our mental lives are nothing more or less than "how it feels to be a brain." (Of course, this is a bit like saying that becoming wealthy involves nothing more or less than making money: It makes something sound simple that isn't.)

 What are the bases of perceptions, thoughts, memories, and feelings, or our subjective sense of self?

As you will see throughout this book, some of the most exciting developments in psychological research focus on how our perceptions, thoughts, memories, and feelings are related to activity in the brain. Psychologists and neuroscientists are using new technologies to explore this relationship in ways that would have seemed like science fiction only 20 years ago. The technique known as *functional magnetic resonance*

imaging, or fMRI, allows scientists to "scan" a brain and see which parts are active when a person reads a word, sees a face, learns a new skill, or remembers a personal experience. William James was interested in how people acquire complex skills such as the ability to play the violin, and he wondered how the brain enabled great musicians to produce virtuoso performances. What William James could only ponder, modern psychologists can discover.

As one example, in a recent study, the brains of professional and novice pianists were scanned as they made complex finger movements like those involved in piano playing, and the results showed that professional pianists have *less* activity than novices in those parts of the brain that guide these finger movements (Krings et al., 2000). This result suggests that extensive practice at the piano changes the brains of professional pianists and that the regions controlling finger movements operate more efficiently than they do in novices. You'll learn more about this in Chapters 6 and 7 and see in the coming chapters how studies using fMRI and related techniques are beginning to transform many different areas of psychology.

> *How does the mind usually allow us to function effectively in the world?* Scientists sometimes say that form follows function; that is, if we want to understand *how* something works (e.g., an engine or a thermometer), we need to know what it is working *for* (e.g., powering vehicles or measuring temperature). As William James often noted, "Thinking is for doing," and the function of the mind is to help us do those things that sophisticated animals have to do in order to prosper, such as acquiring food, shelter, and mates. Psychological processes are said to be *adaptive,* which means that they promote the welfare and reproduction of organisms that engage in those processes.

How does the mind usually allow us to function effectively in the world?

For instance, perception allows us to recognize our families, see predators before they see us, and avoid stumbling into oncoming traffic. Language allows us to organize our thoughts and communicate them to others, which enables us to form social groups and cooperate. Memory allows us to avoid solving the same problems over again every time we encounter them and to keep in mind what we are doing and why. Emotions allow us to react quickly to events that have "life or death" significance, and they enable us to form strong social bonds. The list goes on and on, and as far as anyone can tell, there is no psychological equivalent of the body's appendix; that is, there's no thoroughly useless mental process that we'd all be better off without.

Given the adaptiveness of psychological processes, it is not surprising that those people with deficiencies in those processes often have a pretty tough time. The neurologist Antonio Damasio described the case of Elliot, a middle-aged husband and father with a good job, whose life was forever changed when surgeons discovered a tumor in the middle of his brain (Damasio, 1994). The surgeons were able to remove the tumor and save his life, and for a while Elliot seemed just fine. But then odd things began to happen. At first, Elliot seemed more likely than usual to make bad decisions (when he could make decisions at all), and as time went on, his bad decisions became truly dreadful ones. He couldn't prioritize tasks at work because he couldn't decide what to do first, and when he did, he got it wrong. Eventually he was fired, so he pursued a series of risky business ventures—all of which failed, and he lost his life's savings. His wife divorced him, he married again, and his second wife divorced him too.

So what ruined Elliot's life? The neurologists who tested Elliot were unable to detect any decrease in his cognitive functioning. His intelligence was intact, and his ability to speak, to think, and to solve logical problems was every bit as sharp as it ever was. But as they probed further, they made a startling discovery: Elliot was no longer able to experience emotions. For example, Elliot

psychology The scientific study of mind and behavior.

mind Our private inner experience of perceptions, thoughts, memories, and feelings.

behavior Observable actions of human beings and nonhuman animals.

▼ What good are emotions? Sometimes they just entertain us at the theater, but often they are adaptive and guide us to do what's good for us.

ADRIAN WEINBRECHT/GETTY IMAGES

didn't experience anxiety when he poured his entire bank account into a foolish business venture, he didn't experience any sorrow when his wives packed up and left him, and he didn't experience any regret or anger when his boss gave him the pink slip and showed him the door. Most of us have wished from time to time that we could be as stoic and unflappable as that; after all, who needs anxiety, sorrow, regret, and anger? The answer is that we all do. Emotions are adaptive because they function as signals that tell us when we are putting ourselves in harm's way. If you felt no anxiety when you thought about taking an upcoming exam, about borrowing your friend's car without permission, or about cheating on your taxes, you would probably make a string of poor decisions that would leave you without a degree and without a friend, except perhaps for your cellmate. Elliot didn't have those feelings, and he paid a big price for it. The ability of a basic psychological process (i.e., the experience of emotion) to perform its normally adaptive function was missing in poor Elliot's life.

> *Why does the mind occasionally function so ineffectively in the world?* The mind is an amazing machine that can do a great many things quickly. We can drive a car while talking to a passenger while recognizing the street address while remembering the name of the song that just came on the radio.

Why does the mind occasionally function so ineffectively in the world?

But like all machines, the mind often trades accuracy for speed and versatility. This can produce "bugs" in the system, such as when a doughnut-making machine occasionally spews out gobs of gooey mush rather than dozens of delicious doughnuts. Our mental life is just as susceptible to occasional malfunctions in our otherwise-efficient mental processing. One of the most fascinating aspects of psychology is that we are *all* prone to a variety of errors and illusions. Indeed, if thoughts, feelings, and actions were error free, then human behavior would be orderly, predictable, and dull, which it clearly is not. Rather, it is endlessly surprising, and its surprises often derive from our ability to do precisely the wrong thing at the wrong time.

For example, in two British airline crashes during the 1950s, pilots mistakenly shut down an engine that was operating perfectly normally after they became aware that another engine was failing (Reason & Mycielska, 1982, p. 5). Though the reasons for such catastrophic mental lapses are not well understood, they resemble far more mundane slips that we all make in our day-to-day lives. Consider a few examples from diaries of people who took part in a study concerning mental errors in everyday life (Reason & Mycielska, 1982, pp. 70–73):

> *I meant to get my car out, but as I passed the back porch on my way to the garage, I stopped to put on my boots and gardening jacket as if to work in the yard.*

> *I put some money into a machine to get a stamp. When the stamp appeared, I took it and said, "Thank you."*

> *On leaving the room to go to the kitchen, I turned the light off, although several people were there.*

If these lapses seem amusing, it is because, in fact, they are. But they are also potentially important as clues to human nature. For example, notice that the person who bought a stamp said, "Thank you," to the machine and not, "How do I find the subway?" In other words, the person did not just do *any* wrong thing; rather, he did something that would have been perfectly right in a real social interaction. As each of these examples suggest, people often operate on "autopilot," or behave automatically, relying on well-learned habits that they execute without really thinking. When we are not actively focused on what we are saying or doing, these habits may be triggered inappropriately. William James thought that the influence of habit could help explain the seemingly bizarre actions of "absentminded" people: "Very absent-minded persons," he wrote in *The Principles of Psychology*, "on going into their bedroom to dress for dinner have been known to take off one garment after another and finally get into bed."

James understood that the mind's mistakes are as instructive as they are intriguing, and modern psychology has found it quite useful to study them. Things that are whole and unbroken hum along nicely and do their jobs while leaving no clue about how they do them. Cars gliding down the expressway might as well be magic carpets as long as they are working properly because we have no idea what kind of magic is moving them along. It is only when automobiles break down that we learn about their engines, water pumps, and other fine pieces and processes that normally work together to produce the ride. Breakdowns and errors are not just about destruction and failure—they are pathways to knowledge. In the same way, understanding lapses, errors, mistakes, and the occasionally puzzling nature of human behavior provides a vantage point for understanding the normal operation of mental life and behavior. The story of Elliot, whose behavior broke down after he had brain surgery, is an example that highlights the role that emotions play in guiding normal judgment and behavior.

Psychology is exciting because it addresses fundamental questions about human experience and behavior, and the three questions we've just considered are merely the tip of the iceberg. Think of this book as a guide to exploring the rest of the iceberg. But before we don our parkas and grab our pick axes, we need to understand how the iceberg got here in the first place. To understand psychology in the 21st century, we need to become familiar with the psychology of the past.

nativism The philosophical view that certain kinds of knowledge are innate or inborn.

Psychology's Roots: The Path to a Science of Mind

When the young William James interrupted his medical studies to travel in Europe during the late 1860s, he wanted to learn about human nature. But he confronted a very different situation than a similarly curious student would confront today, largely because psychology did not yet exist as an independent field of study. As James cheekily wrote, "The first lecture in psychology that I ever heard was the first I ever gave." Of course, that doesn't mean no one had ever thought about human nature before. For 2,000 years, thinkers with scraggly beards and poor dental hygiene had pondered such questions, and in fact, modern psychology acknowledges its deep roots in philosophy. We will begin by examining those roots and then describe some of the early attempts to develop a scientific approach to psychology by relating the mind to the brain. Next, we'll see how psychologists divided into different camps or "schools of thought": *structuralists,* who tried to analyze the mind by breaking it down into its basic components, and *functionalists,* who focused on how mental abilities allow people to adapt to their environments.

Psychology's Ancestors: The Great Philosophers

The desire to understand ourselves is not new. Greek thinkers such as Plato (428 BC–347 BC) and Aristotle (384 BC–322 BC) were among the first to struggle with fundamental questions about how the mind works (Robinson, 1995). Greek philosophers debated many of the questions that psychologists continue to debate today. For example, are cognitive abilities and knowledge inborn, or are they acquired only through experience? Plato argued in favor of **nativism**, which maintains that *certain kinds of knowledge are innate or inborn.* Children in every culture figure out early on that sounds can have meanings that can be arranged into words, which then

? **What fundamental question has puzzled philosophers ever since humans began thinking about behavior?**

▼ Many current ideas in psychology can be traced to the theories of two Greek philosophers from the 4th century BC: Plato (left), who believed in nativism, and Aristotle (right), who was Plato's student and believed in empiricism.

GIANNI DAGLI ORTI/CORBIS

MANSELL/TIME LIFE PICTURES/GETTY IMAGES

can be arranged into sentences. Before a child is old enough to poop in the proper place, she has already mastered the fundamentals of language without any formal instruction. Is the propensity to learn language "hardwired"—that is, is it something that children are born with? Or does the ability to learn language depend on the child's experience? Aristotle believed that the child's mind was a *tabula rasa* (a blank slate) on which experiences were written, and he argued for **philosophical empiricism**, which holds that *all knowledge is acquired through experience*.

Although few modern psychologists believe that nativism or empiricism is entirely correct, the issue of just how much "nature" and "nurture" explain any given behavior is still a matter of controversy. In some ways, it is quite amazing that ancient philosophers were able to articulate so many of the important questions in psychology and offer many excellent insights into their answers without any access to scientific evidence. Their ideas came from personal observations, intuition, and speculation. Although they were quite good at arguing with one another, they usually found it impossible to settle their disputes because their approach provided no means of testing their theories. As you will see in Chapter 2, the ability to test a theory is the cornerstone of the scientific approach and the basis for reaching conclusions in modern psychology.

► How do young children learn about the world? Plato believed that certain kinds of knowledge are innate, whereas Aristotle believed that the mind is a blank slate on which experiences are written.

GEO MARTINEZ/FEATURE PICS

From the Brain to the Mind: The French Connection

We all know that the brain and the body are physical objects that we can see and touch and that the subjective contents of our minds—our perceptions, thoughts, and feelings—are not. Inner experience is perfectly real, but where in the world is it? The French philosopher René Descartes (1596–1650) argued that body and mind are fundamentally different things—that the body is made of a material substance, whereas the mind (or soul) is made of an immaterial or spiritual substance (**FIGURE 1.1**). But if the mind and the body are different things made of different substances, then how do they interact? How does the mind tell the body to put its foot forward, and when the body steps on a rusty nail, why does the mind say, "Ouch"? This is the problem of *dualism,* or how mental activity can be reconciled and coordinated with physical behavior.

Descartes suggested that the mind influences the body through a tiny structure near the bottom of the brain known as the pineal gland. He was largely alone in this view, as other philosophers at the time either rejected his explanation or offered alternative ideas. For example, the British philosopher Thomas Hobbes (1588–1679) argued that the mind and body aren't different things at all; rather, the mind *is* what the brain *does*. From Hobbes's perspective, looking for a place in the brain where the mind meets the body is like looking for the place in a television where the picture meets the flat panel display.

▼ FIGURE 1.1
René Descartes (1596–1650)
Descartes made contributions to many fields of inquiry, from physiology to philosophy. He is probably best known for his suggestion that the body and soul are fundamentally different.

LEONARD DE SELVA/CORBIS

The French physician Franz Joseph Gall (1758–1828) also thought that brains and minds were linked, but by size rather than by glands. He examined the brains of animals and of people who had died of disease, or as healthy adults, or as children, and observed that mental ability often increases with larger brain size and decreases with damage to the brain. These aspects of Gall's findings were generally accepted (and the part about brain damage still is today). But Gall went far beyond his evidence to develop a psychological theory known as **phrenology**, which held that *specific mental abilities and characteristics, ranging from memory to the capacity for happiness, are localized in specific regions of the brain* (**FIGURE 1.2**). The idea that different parts of the brain are specialized for specific psychological functions turned out to be right; as you'll learn later in the book, a part of the brain called the hippocampus is intimately involved in memory, just as a structure called the amygdala is intimately involved in fear. But phrenology took this idea to an absurd extreme. Gall asserted that the size of bumps or indentations on the skull reflected the size of the brain regions beneath them and that by feeling those bumps, one could tell whether a person was friendly, cautious, assertive, idealistic, and so on. What Gall didn't realize was that bumps on the skull do not necessarily reveal anything about the shape of the brain underneath.

Phrenology made for a nice parlor game and gave young people a good excuse for touching each other, but in the end it amounted to a series of strong claims based on weak evidence. Not surprisingly, his critics were galled (so to speak), and they ridiculed many of his proposals. Despite an initially large following, phrenology was quickly discredited (Fancher, 1979).

While Gall was busy playing bumpologist, other French scientists were beginning to link the brain and the mind in a more convincing manner. The biologist Pierre Flourens (1794–1867) was appalled by Gall's far-reaching claims and sloppy methods, so he conducted experiments in which he surgically removed specific parts of the brain from dogs, birds, and other animals and found (not surprisingly!) that their actions and movements differed from those of animals with intact brains.

The surgeon Paul Broca (1824–80) worked with a patient who had suffered damage to a small part of the left side of the brain (now known as Broca's area). The patient, Monsieur Leborgne, was virtually unable to speak and could utter only the single syllable "tan." Yet the patient understood everything that was said to him and was able to communicate using gestures. Broca had the crucial insight that damage to a specific part of the brain impaired a specific mental function, clearly demonstrating that the brain and mind are closely linked. This was important in the 19th century because at that time many people accepted Descartes' idea that the mind is separate from, but interacts with, the brain and the body. Broca and Flourens, then, were the first to demonstrate that the mind is grounded in a material substance; namely, the brain. Their work jump-started the scientific investigation of mental processes.

How did work involving patients with brain damage help demonstrate the mind-brain connection?

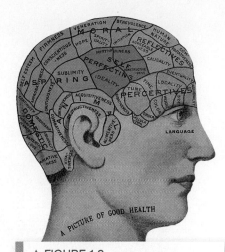

▲ **FIGURE 1.2**
Phrenology Franz Joseph Gall (1758–1828) developed a theory called phrenology, which suggested that psychological capacities (such as the capacity for friendship) and traits (such as cautiousness and mirth) were located in particular parts of the brain. The more of these capacities and traits a person had, the larger the corresponding bumps on the skull.

MARY EVANS PICTURE LIBRARY/ THE IMAGE WORKS

Structuralism: Applying Methods from Physiology to Psychology

In the middle of the 19th century, psychology benefited from the work of German scientists who were trained in the field of **physiology**, which is *the study of biological processes, especially in the human body.* Physiologists had developed methods that allowed them to measure such things as the speed of nerve impulses, and some of them had begun to use these methods to measure mental abilities. William James was drawn to the work of two such physiologists: Hermann von Helmholtz (1821–94) and Wilhelm Wundt (1832–1920). "It seems to me that perhaps the time has come for psychology to begin to be a science," wrote James in a letter written in 1867 during his visit to Berlin. "Helmholtz and a man called Wundt at Heidelberg are working at it." What attracted James to the work of these two scientists?

▲ Surgeon Paul Broca (1824–80) worked with a brain-damaged person who could comprehend but not produce spoken language. Broca suggested that the mind is grounded in the material processes of the brain.

THE GRANGER COLLECTION

▲ By measuring a person's reaction times to different stimuli, Hermann von Helmholtz (1821–94) estimated the length of time it takes a nerve impulse to travel to the brain.

HULTON ARCHIVE/GETTY IMAGES

philosophical empiricism The philosophical view that all knowledge is acquired through experience.

phrenology A now defunct theory that specific mental abilities and characteristics, ranging from memory to the capacity for happiness, are localized in specific regions of the brain.

physiology The study of biological processes, especially in the human body.

Helmholtz Measures the Speed of Responses

A brilliant experimenter with a background in both physiology and physics, Helmholtz had developed a method for measuring the speed of nerve impulses in a frog's leg, which he then adapted to the study of human beings. Helmholtz trained participants to respond when he applied a **stimulus**—*sensory input from the environment*—to different parts of the leg. He recorded his participants' **reaction time**, or *the amount of time taken to respond to a specific stimulus,* after applying the stimulus. Helmholtz found that people generally took longer to respond when their toe was stimulated than when their thigh was stimulated, and the difference between these reaction times allowed him to estimate how long it took a nerve impulse to travel to the brain. These results were astonishing to 19th-century scientists because at that time just about everyone thought that mental processes occurred instantaneously. When you move your hands in front of your eyes, you don't feel your hands move a fraction of a second before you see them. The real world doesn't appear like one of those late-night movies in which the video and the audio are off by just a fraction of a second. Scientists assumed that the neurological processes underlying mental events *must* be instantaneous for everything to be so nicely synchronized, but Helmholtz showed that this wasn't true. In so doing, he also demonstrated that reaction time could be a useful way to study the mind and the brain.

Wundt and the Development of Structuralism

Although Helmholtz's contributions were important, historians generally credit the official emergence of psychology to Helmholtz's research assistant, Wilhelm Wundt (Rieber, 1980). In 1867, Wundt taught at the University of Heidelberg what was probably the first course in physiological psychology, and this course led to the publication of his book *Principles of Physiological Psychology* in 1874. Wundt called the book "an attempt to mark out [psychology] as a new domain of science" (Fancher, 1979, p. 126). In 1879, at the University of Leipzig, Wundt opened the first laboratory ever to be exclusively devoted to psychological studies, and this event marked the official birth of psychology as an independent field of study. The new lab was full of graduate students carrying out research on topics assigned by Wundt, and it soon attracted young scholars from all over the world who were eager to learn about the new science that Wundt had developed.

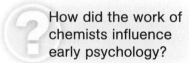 **How did the work of chemists influence early psychology?**

Wundt believed that scientific psychology should focus on analyzing **consciousness**, *a person's subjective experience of the world and the mind.* Consciousness encompasses a broad range of subjective experiences. We may be conscious of sights, sounds, tastes, smells, bodily sensations, thoughts, or feelings. As Wundt tried to figure out a way to study consciousness scientifically, he noted that chemists try to understand the structure of matter by breaking down natural substances into basic elements. So he

▶ Wilhelm Wundt (1832–1920), far right, founded the first laboratory devoted exclusively to psychology at the University of Leipzig in Germany.

and his students adopted an approach called **structuralism**, or *the analysis of the basic elements that constitute the mind.* This approach involved breaking consciousness down into elemental sensations and feelings, and you can do a bit of structuralism right now without leaving your chair.

Consider the contents of your own consciousness. At this very moment you may be aware of the meaning of these words, the visual appearance of the letters on the page, the key ring pressing uncomfortably against your thigh, your feelings of excitement or boredom (probably excitement), the smell of curried chicken salad, or the nagging question of whether the War of 1812 really deserves its own overture. At any given moment, all sorts of things are swimming in the stream of consciousness, and Wundt tried to analyze them in a systematic way using the method of **introspection**, which involves *the subjective observation of one's own experience.* In a typical experiment, observers (usually students) would be presented with a stimulus (usually a color or a sound) and then be asked to report their introspections. The observers would describe the brightness of a color or the loudness of a tone. They were asked to report on their "raw" sensory experience rather than on their interpretations of that experience. For example, an observer presented with this page would not report seeing words on the page (which counts as an interpretation of the experience), but instead might describe a series of black marks, some straight and others curved, against a bright white background. Wundt also attempted to carefully describe the feelings associated with elementary perceptions. For example, when Wundt listened to the clicks produced by a metronome, some of the patterns of sounds were more pleasant than others. By analyzing the relation between feelings and perceptual sensations, Wundt and his students hoped to uncover the basic structure of conscious experience.

Wundt tried to provide objective measurements of conscious processes by using reaction time techniques similar to those first developed by Helmholtz. Wundt used reaction times to examine a distinction between the perception and interpretation of a stimulus. His research participants were instructed to press a button as soon as a tone sounded. Some participants were told to concentrate on perceiving the tone before pressing the button, whereas others were told to concentrate only on pressing the button. Those people who concentrated on the tone responded about one tenth of a second more slowly than those told to concentrate only on pressing the button. Wundt reasoned that both fast and slow participants had to register the tone in consciousness (perception), but only the slower participants also had to interpret the significance of the tone and press the button. The faster research participants, focusing only on the response they were to make, could respond automatically to the tone because they didn't have to engage in the additional step of interpretation (Fancher, 1979). This type of experimentation broke new ground by showing that psychologists could use scientific techniques to disentangle even subtle conscious processes. In fact, as you'll see in later chapters, reaction time procedures have proven extremely useful in modern research.

Titchener Brings Structuralism to the United States

The pioneering efforts of Wundt's laboratory launched psychology as an independent science and profoundly influenced the field for the remainder of the 19th century. Many European and American psychologists journeyed to Leipzig to study with Wundt. Among the most eminent was the British-born Edward Titchener (1867–1927), who studied with Wundt for 2 years in the early 1890s. Titchener then came to the United States and set up a psychology laboratory at Cornell University (where, if you'd like to see it, his brain is still on display in the psychology department). Titchener brought some parts of Wundt's approach to America, but he also made some changes (Brock, 1993; Rieber, 1980). For instance, whereas Wundt emphasized the relationship between elements of consciousness, Titchener focused on identifying the basic elements themselves. In his textbook *An Outline of Psychology* (1896), Titchener put forward a list of more than 44,000 elemental qualities of conscious experience, most of them visual (32,820) or auditory (11,600) (Schultz & Schultz, 1987).

stimulus Sensory input from the environment.

reaction time The amount of time taken to respond to a specific stimulus.

consciousness A person's subjective experience of the world and the mind.

structuralism The analysis of the basic elements that constitute the mind.

introspection The subjective observation of one's own experience.

CARLA KROCH LIBRARY

▲ Edward Titchener (1867–1927) brought structuralism to America, setting up a psychology laboratory at Cornell University. Titchener studied under Wundt in Germany.

The influence of the structuralist approach gradually faded, due mostly to the introspective method. Science requires replicable observations—we could never determine the structure of DNA or the life span of a dust mite if every scientist who looked through a microscope saw something different. Alas, even trained observers provided conflicting introspections about their conscious experiences ("I see a cloud that looks like a duck"—"No, *I* think that cloud looks like a horse"), thus making it difficult for different psychologists to agree on the basic elements of conscious experience. Indeed, some psychologists had doubts about whether it was even possible to identify such elements through introspection alone. One of the most prominent skeptics was someone you've already met—a young man with a bad attitude and a useless medical degree named William James.

James and the Functional Approach

By the time James returned from his European tour, he was still inspired by the idea of approaching psychological issues from a scientific perspective. He received a teaching appointment at Harvard (primarily because the president of the university was a neighbor and family friend) and his position at Harvard enabled him to purchase laboratory equipment for classroom experiments. As a result, James taught the first course at an American university to draw on the new experimental psychology developed by Wundt and his German followers (Schultz & Schultz, 1987). These courses and experiments led James to write his masterpiece, *The Principles of Psychology* (James, 1890).

James agreed with Wundt on some points, including the importance of focusing on immediate experience and the usefulness of introspection as a technique (Bjork, 1983), but he disagreed with Wundt's claim that consciousness could be broken down into separate elements. James believed that trying to isolate and analyze a particular moment of consciousness (as the structuralists did) distorted the essential nature of consciousness. Consciousness, he argued, was more like a flowing stream than a bundle of separate elements. So James decided to approach psychology from a different perspective entirely, and he developed an approach known as **functionalism**: *the study of the purpose mental processes serve in enabling people to adapt to their environment.* In contrast to structuralism, which examined the structure of mental processes, functionalism set out to understand the functions those mental processes served. (See the Real World box for some strategies to enhance one of those functions—learning.)

James's thinking was inspired by the ideas in Charles Darwin's (1809–82) recently published book on biological evolution, *On the Origin of Species by Means of Natural Selection* (1859). Darwin proposed the principle of **natural selection**, which states that *the features of an organism that help it survive and reproduce are more likely than other features to be passed on to subsequent generations.* From this perspective, James reasoned, mental abilities must have evolved because they were adaptive—that is, because they helped people solve problems and increased their chances of survival. Like other animals, people have always needed to avoid predators, locate food, build shelters, and attract mates. Applying Darwin's principle of natural selection, James (1890) reasoned that consciousness must serve an important biological function and the task for psychologists was to understand what those functions are. Wundt and the other structuralists worked in laboratories, and James felt that such work was limited in its ability to tell us how consciousness functioned in the natural environment. Wundt, in turn, felt that James did not focus enough on new findings from the laboratory that he and the structuralists had begun to produce. Commenting on *The Principles of Psychology*, Wundt conceded that James was a topflight writer but disapproved of his approach: "It is literature, it is beautiful, but it is not psychology" (Bjork, 1983, p. 12).

How does functionalism relate to Darwin's theory of natural selection?

functionalism The study of the purpose mental processes serve in enabling people to adapt to their environment.

natural selection Charles Darwin's theory that the features of an organism that help it survive and reproduce are more likely than other features to be passed on to subsequent generations.

Improving Study Skills

By reading this book and taking this introductory course, you will learn a great deal about psychology, including a kind of insight that is applicable to everyday life: Psychology can help you to learn about psychology.

Psychologists have progressed a great deal in understanding how we remember and learn. We'll explore the science of memory and learning in Chapters 6 and 7, but here we focus on the practical implications of psychological research for everyday life: how you can use psychology to improve your study skills. Such knowledge should help you to perform your best in this course and others, but perhaps more importantly, it can help to prepare you for challenges you will face after graduation.

Psychologists have focused on mental strategies that can enhance your ability to *acquire* information, to *retain* it over time, and to *retrieve* what you have acquired and retained. Let's begin with the process of acquiring information—that is, transforming what you see and hear into an enduring memory. Our minds don't work like video cameras, passively recording everything that happens around us. To acquire information effectively, you need to actively manipulate it. One easy type of active manipulation is rehearsal: repeating to-be-learned information to yourself. You've probably tried this strategy already, but psychologists have found that some types of rehearsal are better than others. A particularly effective strategy is called *spaced rehearsal,* where you repeat information to yourself at increasingly long intervals. For example, suppose that you want to learn the name of a person you've just met named Eric. Repeat the name to yourself right away, wait a few seconds and think of it again, wait for a bit longer (maybe 30 seconds) and bring the name to mind once more, then rehearse the name again after a minute and once more after 2 or 3 minutes. Studies show that this type of rehearsal improves long-term learning more than rehearsing the name without any spacing between rehearsals (Landauer & Bjork, 1978). You can apply this technique to names, dates, definitions, and many other kinds of information, including concepts presented in this textbook.

Simple rehearsal can be beneficial, but one of the most important lessons from psychological research is that we acquire information most effectively when we think about its meaning and reflect on its significance. In fact, we don't even have to try to remember something if we think deeply enough about what we want to remember; the act of reflection itself will virtually guarantee good memory. For example, suppose that you want to learn the basic ideas behind Skinner's approach to behaviorism. Ask yourself the following kinds of questions: How did behaviorism differ from previous approaches in psychology? How would a behaviorist like Skinner think about psychological issues that interest you, such as whether a mentally disturbed individual should be held responsible for committing a crime, or what factors would contribute to your choice of a major subject or career path? In attempting to answer such questions, you will need to review what you've learned about behaviorism and then relate it to other things you already know about. It is much easier to remember new information when you can relate it to something you already know.

You'll also learn later in this book about techniques for visualizing information, first developed by the ancient Greeks, that modern psychological research has proven to be effective memory aids (Paivio, 1969). One such technique, known as the *method of loci,* involves "mentally depositing" information you wish to remember into familiar locations and then later searching through those locations to recall the information.

For example, suppose you want to remember the major contributions of Wundt, Freud, and Skinner to the development of psychology. You could use your current or former home as the location and imagine Wundt's reaction time apparatus lying on your bed, Freud's psychoanalysis couch sitting in your living room, and Skinner's rats running around your bathroom. Then when you need this information, you can "pull up" an image of your home and take a mental tour through it in order to see what's there. You can use this basic approach with a variety of familiar locations—a school building you know well, a shopping mall, and so forth—in order to remember many different kinds of information.

You can use each of the mental manipulations discussed here to help you remember and learn the material in this textbook and prepare for your tests:

- Think about and review the information you have acquired in class on a regular basis. Begin soon after class, and then try to schedule regular "booster" sessions.

- Don't wait until the last second to cram your review into one sitting; research shows that spacing out review and repetition leads to longer-lasting recall.

- Don't just look at your class notes or this textbook; test yourself on the material as often as you can. Research also shows that actively retrieving information you've acquired helps you to later remember that information more than just looking at it again.

- Take some of the load off your memory by developing effective note-taking and outlining skills. Students often scribble down vague and fragmentary notes during lectures, figuring that the notes will be good enough to jog memory later. But when the time comes to study, they've forgotten so much that their notes are no longer clear. Realize that you can't write down everything an instructor says, and try to focus on making detailed notes about the main ideas, facts, and people mentioned in the lecture.

- Organize your notes into an outline that clearly highlights the major concepts. The act of organizing an outline will force you to reflect on the information in a way that promotes retention and will also provide you with a helpful study guide to promote self-testing and review.

To follow up on these suggestions and find much more detailed information on learning and study techniques, see the Recommended Reading by Hermann, Raybeck, & Gruneberg (2002).

▼ Anxious feelings about an upcoming exam may be unpleasant, but as you've probably experienced yourself, they can motivate much-needed study.

SUPERSTUDIO/GETTY IMAGES

► G. Stanley Hall (1844–1924) contributed greatly to the growth of psychology in North America. He founded the continent's first psychology laboratory at Johns Hopkins University, the first academic journal devoted to psychology, and the first professional organization (the American Psychological Association).

THE GRANGER COLLECTION/NEW YORK

The rest of the world did not agree, and James's functionalist psychology quickly gained followers, especially in North America, where Darwin's ideas were influencing many thinkers. G. Stanley Hall (1844–1924), who studied with both Wundt and James, set up the first psychology research laboratory in North America at Johns Hopkins University in 1881. Hall's work focused on development and education and was strongly influenced by evolutionary thinking (Schultz & Schultz, 1987).

Hall believed that, as children develop, they pass through stages that repeat the evolutionary history of the human race. Thus, the mental capacities of a young child resemble those of our ancient ancestors, and children grow over a lifetime in the same way that a species evolves over aeons. Hall founded the *American Journal of Psychology* in 1887 (the first psychology journal in the United States), and he went on to play a key role in founding the American Psychological Association (the first national organization of psychologists in the United States), serving as its first president.

The efforts of James and Hall set the stage for functionalism to develop as a major school of psychological thought in North America. Psychology departments that embraced a functionalist approach started to spring up at many major American universities, and in a struggle for survival that would have made Darwin proud, functionalism became more influential than structuralism had ever been. By the time Wundt and Titchener died in the 1920s, functionalism was the dominant approach to psychology in North America.

ARNIE LEVIN/THE NEW YORKER COLLECTION/
CARTOONBANK.COM

"As I get older, I find I rely more and more on these sticky notes to remind me."

IN SUMMARY

○ Philosophers have pondered and debated ideas about human nature for millennia, but, given the nature of their approach, they did not provide empirical evidence to support their claims.

○ Some of the earliest successful efforts to develop a *science* linking mind and behavior came from the French scientists Pierre Flourens and Paul Broca, who showed that damage to the brain can result in impairments of behavior and mental functions. Hermann von Helmholtz furthered the science of the mind by developing methods for measuring reaction time.

○ Wilhelm Wundt, credited with the founding of psychology as a scientific discipline, created the first psychological laboratory and taught the first course in physiological psychology. His structuralist approach focused on analyzing the basic elements of consciousness. Wundt's student, Edward Titchener, brought structuralism to the United States.

○ William James emphasized the functions of consciousness and applied Darwin's theory of natural selection to the study of the mind, thus helping to establish functionalism and scientific psychology in the United States. Scientific psychology in America got a further boost from G. Stanley Hall, who established the first research laboratory, journal, and professional organization devoted to psychology.

The Development of Clinical Psychology

At about the same time that some psychologists were developing structuralism and functionalism in the laboratory, other psychologists working in the clinic were beginning to study patients with psychological disorders. They began to realize that one can often understand how something works by examining how it breaks, and their observations of mental disorders influenced the development of psychology.

The Path to Freud and Psychoanalytic Theory

The French physicians Jean-Martin Charcot (1825–93) and Pierre Janet (1859–1947) reported striking observations when they interviewed patients who had developed a condition known then as **hysteria**, or a *temporary loss of cognitive or motor functions, usually as a result of emotionally upsetting experiences.* Hysterical patients became blind, paralyzed, or lost their memories, even though there was no known physical cause of their problems. However, when the patients were put into a trancelike state through the use of hypnosis (an altered state of consciousness characterized by suggestibility), their symptoms disappeared: Blind patients could see, paralyzed patients could walk, and forgetful patients could remember. After coming out of the hypnotic trance, however, the patients forgot what had happened under hypnosis and again showed their symptoms. The patients behaved like two different people in the waking versus hypnotic states.

These peculiar disorders were ignored by Wundt, Titchener, and other laboratory scientists, who did not consider them a proper subject for scientific psychology (Bjork, 1983). But William James believed they had important implications for understanding the nature of the mind (Taylor, 2001). He thought it was important to capitalize on these mental disruptions as a way of understanding the normal operation of the mind. During our ordinary conscious experience we are only aware of a single "me" or "self," but the aberrations described by Charcot, Janet, and others suggested that the brain can create many conscious selves that are not aware of each other's existence (James, 1890, p. 400). These striking observations also fueled the imagination of a young physician from Vienna, Austria, who studied with Charcot in Paris in 1885. His name was Sigmund Freud (1856–1939).

After his visit to Charcot's clinic in Paris, Freud returned to Vienna, where he continued his work with hysteric patients. (The word *hysteria,* by the way, comes from the Latin word *hyster,* which means "womb." It was once thought that only women suffered from hysteria, which was thought to be caused by a "wandering womb.") Working with the physician Joseph Breuer (1842–1925), Freud began to make his own observations of hysterics and develop theories to explain their strange behaviors and symptoms. Freud theorized that many of the patients' problems could be traced to the effects of painful childhood experiences that the person could not remember, and he suggested that the powerful influence of these seemingly lost memories revealed the presence of an unconscious mind. According to Freud, the **unconscious** is *the part of the mind that operates outside of conscious awareness but influences conscious thoughts, feelings, and actions.* This idea led Freud to develop **psychoanalytic theory**, *an approach that emphasizes the importance of unconscious mental processes in shaping feelings, thoughts,*

How was Freud influenced by work with hysterics?

hysteria A temporary loss of cognitive or motor functions, usually as a result of emotionally upsetting experiences.

unconscious The part of the mind that operates outside of conscious awareness but influences conscious thoughts, feelings, and actions.

psychoanalytic theory Sigmund Freud's approach to understanding human behavior that emphasizes the importance of unconscious mental processes in shaping feelings, thoughts, and behaviors.

FREUD MUSEUM

◄ In this photograph, Sigmund Freud (1856–1939) sits by the couch reserved for his psychoanalytic patients.

and behaviors. From a psychoanalytic perspective, it is important to uncover a person's early experiences and to illuminate a person's unconscious anxieties, conflicts, and desires. Psychoanalytic theory formed the basis for a therapy that Freud called **psychoanalysis**, which focuses on *bringing unconscious material into conscious awareness*. During psychoanalysis, patients recalled past experiences ("When I was a toddler, I was frightened by a masked man on a black horse") and related their dreams and fantasies ("Sometimes I close my eyes and imagine not having to pay for this session"). Psychoanalysts used Freud's theoretical approach to interpret what their patients said.

In the early 1900s, Freud and a growing number of followers formed a psychoanalytic movement. Carl Gustav Jung (1875–1961) and Alfred Adler (1870–1937) were prominent in the movement, but both were independent thinkers, and Freud apparently had little tolerance for individuals who challenged his ideas. Soon enough, Freud broke off his relationships with both men so that he could shape the psychoanalytic movement himself (Sulloway, 1992). Psychoanalytic theory became quite controversial (especially in America) because it suggested that understanding a person's thoughts, feelings, and behavior required a thorough exploration of the person's early sexual experiences and unconscious sexual desires. In those days these topics were considered far too racy for scientific discussion.

Most of Freud's followers, like Freud himself, were trained as physicians and did not conduct psychological experiments in the laboratory (though early in his career, Freud did do some nice laboratory work on the sexual organs of eels). By and large, psychoanalysts did not hold positions in universities and developed their ideas in isolation from the research-based approaches of Wundt, Titchener, James, Hall, and others. One of the few times that Freud met with the leading academic psychologists was at a conference that G. Stanley Hall organized at Clark University in 1909. It was there that William James and Sigmund Freud met for the first time. Although James worked in an academic setting and Freud worked with clinical patients, both men believed that mental aberrations provide important clues into the nature of mind.

► This famous psychology conference, held in 1909 at Clark University, was organized by G. Stanley Hall and brought together many notable figures, such as William James and Sigmund Freud. Both men are circled, with James on the left.

Influence of Psychoanalysis and the Humanistic Response

Most historians consider Freud to be one of the two or three most influential thinkers of the 20th century, and the psychoanalytic movement influenced everything from literature and history to politics and art. Within psychology, psychoanalysis had its greatest impact on clinical practice, but that influence has been considerably diminished over the past 40 years.

This is partly because Freud's vision of human nature was a dark one, emphasizing limitations and problems rather than possibilities and potentials. He saw people as hostages to their forgotten childhood experiences and primitive sexual impulses, and the inherent pessimism of his perspective frustrated those psychologists who had a more optimistic view of human nature. In America, the years after World War II were positive, invigorating, and upbeat: Poverty and disease were being conquered by technology, the standard of living of ordinary Americans was on a sharp rise, and people were landing on the moon. The era was characterized by the accomplishments and not the foibles of the human mind, and Freud's viewpoint was out of step with the spirit of the times.

Why are Freud's ideas less influential today?

Freud's ideas were also difficult to test, and a theory that can't be tested is of limited use in psychology or other sciences. Though Freud's emphasis on unconscious processes has had an enduring impact on psychology, psychologists began to have serious misgivings about many aspects of Freud's theory.

It was in these times that psychologists such as Abraham Maslow (1908–70) and Carl Rogers (1902–87) pioneered a new movement called **humanistic psychology**, *an approach to understanding human nature that emphasizes the positive potential of human beings*. Humanistic psychologists focused on the highest aspirations that people had for themselves. Rather than viewing people as prisoners of events in

▲ Carl Rogers (1902–87) (left) and Abraham Maslow (1908–70) (right) introduced a positive, humanistic psychology in response to what they viewed as the overly pessimistic view of psychoanalysis.

their remote pasts, humanistic psychologists viewed people as free agents who have an inherent need to develop, grow, and attain their full potential. This movement reached its peak in the 1960s when a generation of "flower children" found it easy to see psychological life as a kind of blossoming of the spirit. Humanistic therapists sought to help people to realize their full potential; in fact, they called them "clients" rather than "patients." In this relationship, the therapist and the client (unlike the psychoanalyst and the patient) were on equal footing. In fact, the development of the humanistic perspective was one more reason why Freud's ideas eventually became less influential.

IN SUMMARY

○ Psychologists have often focused on patients with psychological disorders as a way of understanding human behavior. Clinicians such as Jean-Martin Charcot and Pierre Janet studied unusual cases in which patients acted like different people while under hypnosis, raising the possibility that each of us has more than one self.

○ Through his work with hysteric patients, Sigmund Freud developed psychoanalysis, which emphasized the importance of unconscious influences and childhood experiences in shaping thoughts, feelings, and behavior.

○ Happily, humanistic psychologists offered a more optimistic view of the human condition, suggesting that people are inherently disposed toward growth and can usually reach their full potential with a little help from their friends.

psychoanalysis A therapeutic approach that focuses on bringing unconscious material into conscious awareness to better understand psychological disorders.

humanistic psychology An approach to understanding human nature that emphasizes the positive potential of human beings.

The Search for Objective Measurement: Behaviorism Takes Center Stage

Our discussion of the development of clinical psychology into the 1960s took us a little ahead of ourselves—we need to turn our attention back a few decades to understand some other important developments.

The schools of psychological thought that had developed by the early 20th century—structuralism, functionalism, and psychoanalysis—differed substantially from one another. But they shared an important similarity: Each tried to understand the inner workings of the mind by examining conscious perceptions, thoughts, memories, and feelings or by trying to elicit previously unconscious material, all of which were reported by participants in experiments or patients in a clinical setting. In each case it proved difficult to establish with much certainty just what was going on in people's minds, due to the unreliable nature of the methodology. As the 20th century unfolded, a new approach developed as psychologists challenged the idea that psychology should focus on mental life at all. This new approach was called **behaviorism**, which advocated that psychologists should restrict themselves to *the scientific study of objectively observable behavior*. Behaviorism represented a dramatic departure from previous schools of thought.

How did behaviorism help psychology advance as a science?

Watson and the Emergence of Behaviorism

John Broadus Watson (1878–1958) believed that private experience was too idiosyncratic and vague to be an object of scientific inquiry. Science required replicable, objective measurements of phenomena that were accessible to all observers, and the introspective methods used by structuralists and functionalists were far too subjective for that. So instead of describing conscious experiences, Watson proposed that psychologists focus entirely on the study of behavior—what people *do,* rather than what people *experience*—because behavior can be observed by anyone and it can be measured objectively. Watson thought that a focus on behavior would put a stop to the endless philosophical debates in which psychologists were currently entangled, and it would encourage psychologists to develop practical applications in such areas as business, medicine, law, and education. The goal of scientific psychology, according to Watson, should be to predict and to control behavior in ways that benefit society.

Why would someone want to throw the mind out of psychology? This may seem excessive, until you notice that Watson studied the behavior of animals such as rats and birds. In such studies, inferring a mind is a matter of some debate. Shall we say that dogs have minds, for instance, but leave out pigeons? And if we include pigeons, what about worms? Animal behavior specialists staked out claims in this area. In 1908, Margaret Floy Washburn (1871–1939) published *The Animal Mind,* in which she reviewed what was then known about perception, learning, and memory in different animal species. She argued that nonhuman animals, much like human animals, have conscious mental experiences (Scarborough & Furumoto, 1987). Watson reacted to this claim with venom. Because we cannot ask pigeons about their private, inner experiences (well, we can *ask,* but they never tell us), Watson decided that the only way to understand how animals learn and adapt was to focus solely on their behavior, and he suggested that the study of human beings should proceed on the same basis.

Watson was influenced by the work of the Russian physiologist Ivan Pavlov (1849–1936), who carried out pioneering research on the physiology of digestion. In the course of this work, Pavlov noticed something interesting about the dogs he was studying (Fancher, 1979). Not only did the dogs salivate at the sight of food; they also salivated at the sight of the person who fed them. The feeders were not dressed in Alpo suits, so why should the mere sight of them trigger a basic digestive response in the

ARCHIVES OF THE HISTORY OF AMERICAN PSYCHOLOGY

▲ In 1894, Margaret Floy Washburn (1871–1939), a student of Edward Titchener at Cornell, became the first woman to receive a PhD degree in psychology. Washburn went on to a highly distinguished career, spent mainly in teaching and research at Vassar College in Poughkeepsie, New York. Washburn wrote an influential book, *The Animal Mind,* developed a theory of consciousness, and contributed to the development of psychology as a profession.

dogs? To answer this question, Pavlov developed a procedure in which he sounded a tone every time he fed the dogs, and after a while he observed that the dogs would salivate when they heard the tone alone. In Pavlov's experiments, the sound of the tone was a stimulus—sensory input from the environment—that influenced the salivation of the dogs, which was a **response**—*an action or physiological change elicited by a stimulus.* Watson and other behaviorists made these two notions the building blocks of their theories, which is why behaviorism is sometimes called "stimulus-response" or "S-R" psychology.

Watson applied Pavlov's techniques to human infants. In a famous and controversial study, Watson and his student Rosalie Rayner taught an infant known as "Little Albert" to have a strong fear of a harmless white rat (and other white furry animals and toys) that he had previously not feared. Why would they do such a thing? You'll learn more about this study in Chapter 7, but the short answer is this: Watson believed that human behavior is powerfully influenced by the environment, and the experiments with Little Albert provided a chance to demonstrate such influence at the earliest stage of life. Neither Watson nor later behaviorists believed that the environment was the *only* influence on behavior (Todd & Morris, 1992), but they did think it was the most important one. Consistent with that view, Watson became romantically involved with someone prominent in his environment: Rosalie Rayner. He refused to end the affair when confronted by colleagues, and the resulting scandal forced Watson to leave his position at Johns Hopkins University. He found work in a New York advertising agency, where he applied behaviorist principles to marketing and advertising (which certainly involves manipulating the environment to influence behavior!). Watson also wrote popular books that exposed a broad general audience to the behaviorist approach (Watson, 1924, 1928). The result of all these developments—Pavlov's work in the laboratory, Watson and Rayner's applications to humans, and Watson's practical applications to daily life—was that by the 1920s, behaviorism had become a dominant force in scientific psychology.

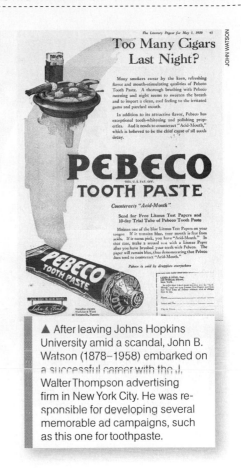

▲ After leaving Johns Hopkins University amid a scandal, John B. Watson (1878–1958) embarked on a successful career with the J. Walter Thompson advertising firm in New York City. He was responsible for developing several memorable ad campaigns, such as this one for toothpaste.

B. F. Skinner and the Development of Behaviorism

In 1926, Burrhus Frederick Skinner (1904–90) graduated from Hamilton College. Like William James, Skinner was a young man who couldn't decide what to do with his life. He aspired to become a writer, and his interest in literature led him indirectly to psychology. Skinner wondered whether a novelist could portray a character without understanding why the character behaved as he or she did, and when he came across Watson's books, he knew he had the answer. Skinner completed his PhD studies in psychology at Harvard (Wiener, 1996) and began to develop a new kind of behaviorism. In Pavlov's experiments, the dogs had been passive participants that stood around, listened to tones, and drooled. Skinner recognized that in everyday life, animals don't just stand there—they do something! Animals *act* on their environments in order to find shelter, food, or mates, and Skinner wondered if he could develop behaviorist principles that would explain how they *learned* to act in those situations.

Skinner built what he called a "conditioning chamber" but what the rest of the world would forever call a "Skinner box." The box has a lever and a food tray, and a hungry rat could get food delivered to the tray by pressing the lever. Skinner observed that when a rat was put in the box, it would wander around, sniffing and exploring, and would usually press the bar by accident, at which point a food pellet would drop into the tray. After that happened, the rate of bar pressing would increase dramatically and remain high until the rat was no longer hungry. Skinner saw evidence for what he called the principle of **reinforcement**, which states that *the consequences of a behavior determine whether it will be more or less likely to occur again.* The concept of reinforcement became the foundation for Skinner's new approach to behaviorism (see Chapter 7), which he formulated in a landmark book, *The Behavior of Organisms* (Skinner, 1938).

behaviorism An approach that advocates that psychologists restrict themselves to the scientific study of objectively observable behavior.

response An action or physiological change elicited by a stimulus.

reinforcement The consequences of a behavior that determine whether it will be more likely that the behavior will occur again.

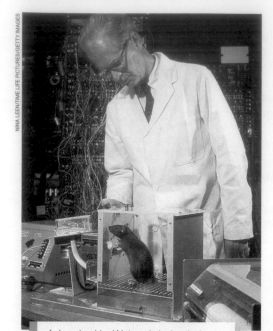

▲ Inspired by Watson's behaviorism, B. F. Skinner (1904–90) investigated the way an animal learns by interacting with its environment. Here, he demonstrates the "Skinner box," in which rats learn to press a lever to receive food.

Skinner set out to use his ideas about reinforcement to help improve the quality of everyday life. He was visiting his daughter's fourth-grade class when he realized that he might be able to improve classroom instruction by breaking a complicated task into small bits and then using the principle of reinforcement to teach children each bit (Bjork, 1993). He developed automatic devices known as "teaching machines" that did exactly that (Skinner, 1958). The teaching machine asked a series of increasingly difficult questions that built on the students' answers to the simpler ones. To learn a complicated math problem, for instance, students would first be asked an easy question about the simplest part of the problem. They would then be told whether the answer was right or wrong, and if a correct response was made, the machine would move on to a more difficult question. Skinner thought that the satisfaction of knowing they were correct would be reinforcing and help students learn.

If fourth graders and rats could be successfully trained, then why stop there? In the controversial books *Beyond Freedom and Dignity* (1971) and *Walden II* (1948/1986), Skinner laid out his vision of a utopian society in which behavior was controlled by the judicious application of the principle of reinforcement (Skinner, 1971). In those books he put forth the simple but stunning claim that our subjective sense of free will is an illusion and that when we think we are exercising free will, we are actually responding to present and past patterns of reinforcement. We do things in the present that have been rewarding in the past, and our sense of "choosing" to do them is nothing more than an illusion. In this, Skinner echoed the sentiments of the philosopher Benedict Spinoza (1632–1677), who several centuries earlier had noted that "men are deceived in thinking themselves free, a belief that consists only in this, that they are conscious of their actions and ignorant of the causes by which they are determined. As to their saying that human actions depend on the will, these are mere words without any corresponding idea" (1677/1982, p. 86).

Which of Skinner's claims provoked an outcry?

Skinner argued that his insights could be used to increase human well-being and solve social problems. Not surprisingly, that claim sparked an outcry from critics who believed that Skinner was giving away one of our most cherished attributes—free will—and calling for a repressive society that manipulated people for its own ends. The criticism even extended to *TV Guide*, which featured an interview with Skinner and called his ideas "the taming of mankind through a system of dog obedience schools for all" (Bjork, 1993, p. 201). Given the nature of Skinner's ideas, the critics' attacks were understandable—he had seriously underestimated how much people cherish the idea of free will—but in the sober light of hindsight, they were clearly overblown. Skinner did not want to turn society into a "dog obedience school" or strip people of their personal freedoms. Rather, he argued that an understanding of the principles by which behavior is generated could be used to increase the social welfare, which is precisely what happens when a government launches advertisements to encourage citizens to drink milk or quit smoking. The result of all the controversy, however, was that Skinner's fame reached a level rarely attained by psychologists. A popular magazine that listed the 100 most important people who ever lived ranked Skinner just 39 points below Jesus Christ (Herrnstein, 1977).

▶ Skinner's well-publicized questioning of such cherished notions as free will led to a rumor that he had raised his own daughter in a Skinner box. This urban legend, while untrue, likely originated from the climate-controlled, glass-encased crib that he invented to protect his daughter from the cold Minnesota winter. Skinner marketed the crib under various names, including the "Air-crib" and the "Heir Conditioner," but it failed to catch on with parents.

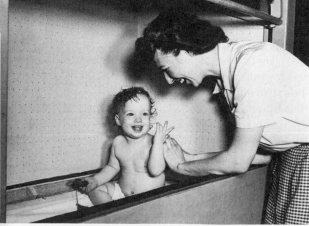

BETTMANN/CORBIS

IN SUMMARY

○ Behaviorism advocated the study of observable actions and responses and held that inner mental processes were private events that could not be studied scientifically. Ivan Pavlov and John B. Watson studied the association between a stimulus and a response and emphasized the importance of the environment in shaping behavior.

○ Influenced by Watson's behaviorism, B. F. Skinner developed the concept of reinforcement using a "Skinner box." He demonstrated that animals and humans repeat behaviors that generate pleasant results and avoid performing those that generate unpleasant results. Skinner extended Watson's contentions about the importance of the environment in shaping behavior by suggesting that free will is an illusion and that the principle of reinforcement can be used to benefit society.

illusions Errors of perception, memory, or judgment in which subjective experience differs from objective reality.

Return of the Mind: Psychology Expands

Watson, Skinner, and the behaviorists dominated psychology from the 1930s to the 1950s. The psychologist Ulric Neisser recalled the atmosphere when he was a student at Swarthmore in the early 1950s:

> Behaviorism was the basic framework for almost all of psychology at the time. It was what you had to learn. That was the age when it was supposed that no psychological phenomenon was real unless you could demonstrate it in a rat. (quoted in Baars, 1986, p. 275)

Behaviorism wouldn't dominate the field for much longer, however, and Neisser himself would play an important role in developing an alternative perspective. Why was behaviorism replaced? Although behaviorism allowed psychologists to measure, predict, and control behavior, it did this by ignoring some important things. First, it ignored the mental processes that had fascinated psychologists such as Wundt and James and, in so doing, found itself unable to explain some very important phenomena, such as how children learn language. Second, it ignored the evolutionary history of the organisms it studied and was thus unable to explain why, for example, a rat could learn to associate nausea with food much more quickly than it could learn to associate nausea with a tone or a light. As we will see, the approaches that ultimately replaced behaviorism met these kinds of problems head-on.

The Emergence of Cognitive Psychology

Even at the height of behaviorist domination, there were a few revolutionaries whose research and writings were focused on mental processes. One such group of psychologists focused on the study of **illusions**, that is, *errors of perception, memory, or judgment in which subjective experience differs from objective reality.* For example, if you measure the dark horizontal lines shown in **FIGURE 1.3** with a ruler, you'll see that they are of equal length. And yet, for most of us, the top line appears longer than the bottom one. As you'll learn in Chapter 4, this is because the surrounding vertical lines influence your perception of the horizontal lines. A similar visual illusion fired the imagination of a German psychologist named Max Wertheimer (1880–1943). In Wertheimer's experiment, a person was shown two lights that flashed quickly on a screen, one after the other. One light was flashed through a vertical slit, the other through a diagonal slit. When the time between two flashes was relatively long (one fifth of a second or more), an observer would see that it was just two lights

"What about that! His brain still uses the old vacuum tubes."

▼ FIGURE 1.3
The Mueller-Lyer Line Illusion Although they do not appear to be, these two horizontal lines are actually the same length. The Gestalt psychologists used illusions like this to show how the perception of a whole object or scene can influence judgments about its individual elements.

CULTURE & COMMUNITY

Why is it that most of us, but not all of us, see the top line in Figure 1.3 as longer than the bottom line? In the classic study, two groups of people classified culturally as European and non-European were asked to evaluate the length of the Mueller-Lyer lines (Segall, Campbell, & Herskovits, 1963). Europeans came to the wrong conclusion that the lines are of different lengths considerably more times than non-Europeans. The authors of the study inferred that people living in cities built of primarily rectangular shapes, as in European cities, see acute and obtuse angles drawn on paper as representative of 3-dimensional space. The non-Europeans in this study, primarily from rural hunting and gathering groups from southern Africa, did not make this mental leap, and so were more likely to see the lines as they truly are, of the same length.

CAROLINE PURSER/GETTY IMAGES

▲ The rectangular architecture so prominent in European cities such as London appears to influence how Europeans perceive lines and space, compared with non-Europeans such as rural Africans.

flashing in alternation. But when Wertheimer reduced the time between flashes to around one twentieth of a second, observers saw a single flash of light moving back and forth (Fancher, 1979; Sarris, 1989).

Wertheimer reasoned that the perceived motion could not be explained in terms of the separate elements that cause the illusion (the two flashing lights) but instead that the moving flash of light is perceived as a *whole* rather than as the sum of its two parts. This unified whole, which in German is called *Gestalt,* makes up the perceptual experience. Wertheimer's interpretation of the illusion led to the development of **Gestalt psychology,** *a psychological approach that emphasizes that we often perceive the whole rather than the sum of the parts.* In other words, the mind imposes organization on what it perceives, so people don't see what the experimenter actually shows them (two separate lights); instead they see the elements as a unified whole (one moving light).

Why might people not see what an experimenter actually showed them?

Another pioneer who focused on the mind was Sir Frederic Bartlett (1886–1969), a British psychologist interested in memory. He was dissatisfied with existing research and especially with the research of the German psychologist

Hermann Ebbinghaus (1850–1909), who had performed groundbreaking experiments on memory in 1885 that we'll discuss in Chapter 5. Serving as his own research subject, Ebbinghaus had tried to discover how quickly and how well he could memorize and recall meaningless information, such as the three-letter nonsense syllables *dap, kir,* and *sul.* Bartlett believed that it was more important to examine memory for the kinds of information people actually encounter in everyday life, and so he gave people stories to remember and carefully observed the kinds of errors they made when they tried to recall them some time later (Bartlett, 1932). Bartlett discovered many interesting things that Ebbinghaus could never have learned with his nonsense syllables. For example, he found that research participants often remembered what *should* have happened or what they *expected* to happen rather than what actually *did* happen. These and other errors led Bartlett to suggest that memory is not a photographic reproduction of past experience and that our attempts to recall the past are powerfully influenced by our knowledge, beliefs, hopes, aspirations, and desires.

Gestalt psychology A psychological approach that emphasizes that we often perceive the whole rather than the sum of the parts.

HOT SCIENCE

How to Get Your Name in This Chapter

There are hundreds of thousands of psychologists, and in the pages that follow you will learn about very few of them. That's because psychological science—like every other science—has been profoundly influenced by a small number of eminent people, such as William James, Sigmund Freud, and B. F. Skinner. What made these particular people so influential? Psychologist Dean Simonton (Simonton, 2000, 2002; Simonton & Song, 2009) has spent much of his career using mathematics to explore the history of science, and in the process he's discovered something interesting about the great psychologists.

Simonton began by taking a sample of the 54 most eminent psychologists born between 1801 and 1919. He then measured two things. First, he measured each psychologist's *scientific orientation* on a dimension that ran from *hard* to *soft.* Hard psychologists were those whose work emphasized observable behavior, quantitative analyses, and biological processes, whereas soft psychologists were those whose work emphasized subjective experience, qualitative analyses, and social processes. Next, Simonton measured each psychologist's *scientific impact* by counting how often he or she was mentioned in other people's books and articles. Finally, Simonton used a mathematical technique called correlation

(which you'll learn about in the next chapter) to uncover the relationship between orientation and impact.

As the accompanying figure shows, the results had two surprises. The first surprise was that the most impactful psychologists were the softest ones. Psychologists such as William James (who was best known as a philosopher) and Sigmund Freud (who had no laboratory and did no studies) were most frequently mentioned by others. The other surprise was that the second-most impactful psychologists were the hardest ones—people like B. F. Skinner, who did experiments and analyzed data—and that

these hard psychologists were much more impactful than those in the middle.

Why might soft psychologists be more impactful than hard psychologists? One possibility is that soft psychologists write books and articles that are more easily appreciated by general readers. It doesn't take any special training to read James, but you have to wade through a lot of graphs, numbers, and technical language to make sense of Skinner. Soft psychologists may have more impact simply because more people understand what they are saying.

What about the second surprise? Why are the softest and hardest psychologists both more impactful than those in the middle? One can only speculate, but Simonton suggests that "those who try to accommodate both sides of the division are ultimately obliged to satisfy neither and thereby undermine their influence in the long run." Apparently, if you want to be a famous psychologist it is better to be an extreme example of something than a moderate example of everything. The field of psychology is rapidly changing, and what was true of psychologists born in the 19th century may not be true of those born in the 20th and 21st, but these data do suggest that if you want to appear in a future edition of this textbook, you should write an essay or an equation—but not both.

Scientific impact (y-axis) vs. Scientific orientation (x-axis, from Soft to Hard)

▲ Jean Piaget (1896–1980) studied and theorized about the developing mental lives of children, a marked departure from the observations of external behavior dictated by the methods of the behaviorists.

Jean Piaget (1896–1980) was a Swiss psychologist who studied the perceptual and cognitive errors of children in order to gain insight into the nature and development of the human mind. For example, in one of his tasks, Piaget would give a 3-year-old child a large and a small mound of clay and tell the child to make the two mounds equal. Then Piaget would break one of the clay mounds into smaller pieces and ask the child which mound now had more clay. Although the amount of clay remained the same, of course, 3-year-old children usually said that the mound that was broken into smaller pieces was bigger, but by the age of 6 or 7, they no longer made this error. As you'll see in Chapter 11, Piaget theorized that younger children lack a particular cognitive ability that allows older children to appreciate the fact that the mass of an object remains constant even when it is divided. For Piaget, errors such as these provided key insights into the mental world of the child (Piaget & Inhelder, 1969).

The German psychologist Kurt Lewin (1890–1947) was also a pioneer in the study of thought at a time when thought had been banished from psychology. Lewin (1936) argued that one could best predict a person's behavior in the world by understanding the person's subjective experience of the world. A television soap opera is a meaningless series of unrelated physical movements unless one thinks about the characters' experiences—how Karen feels about Bruce, what Van was planning to say to Kathy about Emily, and whether Linda's sister, Nancy, will always hate their mother for meddling in her marriage. Lewin realized that it was not the stimulus, but rather the person's *construal* of the stimulus, that determined the person's subsequent behavior. A pinch on the cheek can be pleasant or unpleasant depending on who administers it, under what circumstances, and to which set of cheeks. Lewin used a special kind of mathematics called *topology* to model the person's subjective experience, and although his topological theories were not particularly influential, his attempts to model mental life and his insistence that psychologists study how people construe their worlds would have a lasting impact on psychology.

But, aside from a handful of pioneers such as these, psychologists happily ignored mental processes until the 1950s, when something important happened: the computer. The advent of computers had enormous practical impact, of course, but it also had an enormous conceptual impact on psychology. People and computers differ in important ways, but both seem to register, store, and retrieve information, leading psychologists to wonder whether the computer might be useful as a model for the human mind. Computers are information-processing systems, and the flow of information through their circuits is clearly no fairy tale. If psychologists could think of mental events—such as remembering, attending, thinking, believing, evaluating, feeling, and assessing—as the flow of information through the mind, then they might be able to study the mind scientifically after all. The emergence of the computer led to a reemergence of interest in mental processes all across the discipline of psychology, and it spawned a new approach called **cognitive psychology,** which is *the scientific study of mental processes, including perception, thought, memory, and reasoning.*

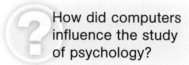

How did computers influence the study of psychology?

Technology and the Development of Cognitive Psychology

Although the contributions of psychologists such as Wertheimer, Bartlett, Piaget, and Lewin provided early alternatives to behaviorism, they did not depose it. That job required the army. During World War II, the military had turned to psychologists to help understand how soldiers could best learn to use new technologies, such as radar. Radar operators had to pay close attention to their screens for long periods while trying to decide whether blips were friendly aircraft, enemy aircraft, or flocks of wild geese in

cognitive psychology The scientific study of mental processes, including perception, thought, memory, and reasoning.

need of a good chasing (Ashcraft, 1998; Lachman, Lachman, & Butterfield, 1979). How could radar operators be trained to make quicker and more accurate decisions? The answer to this question clearly required more than the swift delivery of pellets to the radar operator's food tray. It required that those who designed the equipment think about and talk about cognitive processes, such as perception, attention, identification, memory, and decision making. Behaviorism solved the problem by denying it, and thus some psychologists decided to deny behaviorism and forge ahead with a new approach.

The British psychologist Donald Broadbent (1926–93) was among the first to study what happens when people try to pay attention to several things at once. For instance, Broadbent observed that pilots can't attend to many different instruments at once and must actively move the focus of their attention from one to another (Best, 1992). Broadbent (1958) showed that the limited capacity to handle incoming information is a fundamental feature of human cognition and that this limit could explain many of the errors that pilots (and other people) made. At about the same time, the American psychologist George Miller (1956) pointed out a striking consistency in our capacity limitations across a variety of situations—we can pay attention to, and briefly hold in memory, about seven (give or take two) pieces of information. Cognitive psychologists began conducting experiments and devising theories to better understand the mind's limited capacity, a problem that behaviorists had ignored.

As you have already read, the invention of the computer in the 1950s had a profound impact on psychologists' thinking. A computer is made of hardware (e.g., chips and disk drives today, magnetic tapes and vacuum tubes a half century ago) and software (stored on optical disks today and on punch cards a half century ago). If the brain is roughly analogous to the computer's hardware, then perhaps the mind was roughly analogous to a software program. This line of thinking led cognitive psychologists to begin writing computer programs to see what kinds of software could be made to mimic human speech and behavior (Newell, Shaw, & Simon, 1958).

Ironically, the emergence of cognitive psychology was also energized by the appearance of a book by B. F. Skinner called *Verbal Behavior,* which offered a behaviorist analysis of language (Skinner, 1957). A linguist at the Massachusetts Institute of Technology (MIT), Noam Chomsky (b. 1928), published a devastating critique of the book in which he argued that Skinner's insistence on observable behavior had caused him to miss some of the most important features of language. According to Chomsky, language relies on mental rules that allow people to understand and produce novel words and sentences. The ability of even the youngest child to generate new sentences that

▲ This Navy radar operator must focus his attention for long stretches of time, while making quick, important decisions. The mental processes involved in such tasks are studied by cognitive psychologists.

▲ Noam Chomsky's (b. 1928) critique of Skinner's theory of language signaled the end of behaviorism's dominance in psychology and helped spark the development of cognitive psychology.

◀ This 1950s computer was among the first generation of digital computers. Although different in many ways, computers and the human brain both process and store information, which led many psychologists at the time to think of the mind as a type of computer. Researchers currently adopt a more sophisticated view of the mind and the brain, but the computer analogy was helpful in the early days of cognitive psychology.

behavioral neuroscience An approach to psychology that links psychological processes to activities in the nervous system and other bodily processes.

cognitive neuroscience A field that attempts to understand the links between cognitive processes and brain activity.

he or she had never heard before flew in the face of the behaviorist claim that children learn to use language by reinforcement. Chomsky provided a clever, detailed, and thoroughly cognitive account of language that could explain many of the phenomena that the behaviorist account could not (Chomsky, 1959).

These developments during the 1950s set the stage for an explosion of cognitive studies during the 1960s. Cognitive psychologists did not return to the old introspective procedures used during the 19th century, but instead developed new and ingenious methods that allowed them to study cognitive processes. The excitement of the new approach was summarized in a landmark book, *Cognitive Psychology*, written by someone you met earlier in this chapter: Ulric Neisser (1967). His book provided a foundation for the development of cognitive psychology, which grew and thrived in years that followed.

What events set off the explosion of cognitive studies in the 1960s?

The Brain Meets the Mind: The Rise of Cognitive Neuroscience

If cognitive psychologists studied the software of the mind, they had little to say about the hardware of the brain. And yet, as any computer scientist knows, the relationship between software and hardware is crucial: Each element needs the other to get the job done. Our mental activities often seem so natural and effortless—noticing the shape of an object, using words in speech or writing, recognizing a face as familiar—that we fail to appreciate the fact that they depend on intricate operations carried out by the brain. This dependence is revealed by dramatic cases in which damage to a particular part of the brain causes a person to lose a specific cognitive ability. Recall that in the 19th century, the French physician Paul Broca described a patient who, after damage to a limited area in the left side of the brain, could not produce words—even though he could understand them perfectly well. As you'll see later in the book, damage to other parts of the brain can also result in syndromes that are characterized by the loss of specific mental abilities (e.g., prosopagnosia, in which the person cannot recognize human faces) or by the emergence of bizarre behavior or beliefs (e.g., Capgras syndrome, in which the person believes that a close family member has been replaced by an imposter). These striking—sometimes startling—cases remind us that even the simplest cognitive processes depend on the brain.

Karl Lashley (1890–1958), a psychologist who studied with John B. Watson, conducted a famous series of studies in which he trained rats to run mazes, surgically removed parts of their brains, and then measured how well they could run the maze again. Lashley hoped to find the precise spot in the brain where *learning* occurred. Alas, no one spot seemed to uniquely and reliably eliminate learning (Lashley, 1960). Rather, Lashley simply found that the more of the rat's brain he removed, the more poorly the rat ran the maze. Lashley was frustrated by his inability to identify a specific site of learning, but his efforts inspired other scientists to take up the challenge. They developed a research area called *physiological psychology*. Today, this area has grown into **behavioral neuroscience**, which *links psychological processes to activities in the nervous system and other bodily processes*. To learn about the relationship between brain and behavior, behavioral neuroscientists observe animals' responses as the animals perform specially constructed tasks, such as running through a maze to obtain food rewards. The neuroscientists can record electrical or chemical responses in the brain as the task is being performed or later remove specific parts of the brain to see how performance is affected.

Of course, experimental brain surgery cannot ethically be performed on human beings; thus psychologists who want to study the human brain often have had to rely on nature's cruel and inexact experiments. Birth defects, accidents, and illnesses often cause damage to particular brain regions, and if this damage disrupts a particular ability, then psychologists deduce that the region is involved in producing the ability.

▼ Karl Lashley (1890–1958) conducted experiments that he hoped would reveal a brain area that stores learned information. He removed different parts of animals' brains and observed the effects on the animals' behavior. Though he never found a specific area where learning is stored, his general approach had a major influence on behavioral neuroscience.

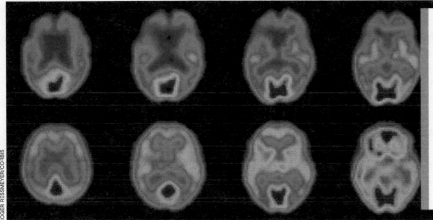

◄ FIGURE 1.4

PET Scans of Healthy and Alzheimer's Brains PET scans are one of a variety of brain-imaging technologies that psychologists use to observe the living brain. The four brain images on the top each come from a person suffering from Alzheimer's disease; the four on the bottom each come from a healthy person of similar age. The red and green areas reflect higher levels of brain activity compared to the blue areas, which reflect lower levels of activity. In each image, the front of the brain is on the top and the back of the brain is on the bottom. You can see that the patient with Alzheimer's disease, compared with the healthy person, shows more extensive areas of lowered activity toward the front of the brain.

For example, in Chapter 6 you'll learn about a patient whose memory was virtually wiped out by damage to a specific part of the brain, and you'll see how this tragedy provided scientists with remarkable clues about how memories are stored (Scoville & Milner, 1957). But in the late 1980s, technological breakthroughs led to the development of noninvasive "brain-scanning" techniques that made it possible for psychologists to watch what happens inside a human brain as a person performs a task

? What have we learned by watching the brain at work?

such as reading, imagining, listening, and remembering (**FIGURE 1.4**). Brain scanning is an invaluable tool because it allows us to observe the brain in action and to see which parts are involved in which operations (see Chapter 3).

For example, researchers used scanning technology to identify the parts of the brain in the left hemisphere that are involved in specific aspects of language, such as understanding or producing words (Peterson et al., 1989). Later scanning studies showed that people who are deaf from birth but who learn to communicate using American Sign Language (ASL) rely on regions in the right hemisphere (as well as the left) when using ASL. In contrast, people with normal hearing who learned ASL after puberty seemed to rely only on the left hemisphere when using ASL (Newman et al., 2002). These findings suggest that although both spoken and signed language usually rely on the left hemisphere, the right hemisphere also can become involved—but only for a limited period (perhaps until puberty). The findings also provide a nice example of how psychologists can now use scanning techniques to observe people with various kinds of cognitive capacities and use their observations to unravel the mysteries of the mind and the brain (**FIGURE 1.5**). In fact, there's a name for this area of research. **Cognitive neuroscience** is the *field that attempts to understand the links between cognitive processes and brain activity* (Gazzaniga, 2000).

The Adaptive Mind: The Emergence of Evolutionary Psychology

Psychology's renewed interest in mental processes and its growing interest in the brain were two developments that led psychologists away from behaviorism. A third development also pointed them in a different direction. Recall that one of behaviorism's key claims was that organisms are blank slates on which experience writes its lessons, and hence any one lesson should be as easily written as another. But in experiments conducted during the 1960s and 1970s, the psychologist John Garcia and his colleagues showed that rats can learn to associate nausea with the smell of food much more quickly than they can learn to associate nausea with a flashing light (Garcia, 1981). Why should this be? In the real world of forests, sewers, and garbage cans, nausea is usually caused by spoiled food and not by lightning, and although these particular rats had been born in a laboratory and had never left their cages, millions of years

▼ FIGURE 1.5

More Ways to Scan a Brain fMRI scanners produce more precise images than PET scans, allowing researchers to more accurately localize brain activity. fMRIs are also quicker at capturing images, allowing researchers to measure brain activity over briefer periods. Here, green areas of the brain were active when research participants remembered information presented visually, and red areas were active when they remembered information presented aurally. Yellow areas were active during both types of presentations.

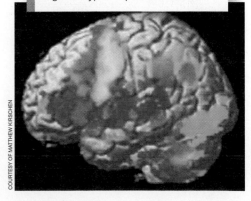

TIME LIFE PICTURES/GETTY IMAGES

▲ Today's evolutionary psychologists embrace Charles Darwin's (1809–82) ideas, just as William James did 100 years ago. Darwin's theories of evolution, adaptation, and natural selection have provided insight into why brains and minds work the way they do.

evolutionary psychology A psychological approach that explains mind and behavior in terms of the adaptive value of abilities that are preserved over time by natural selection.

of evolution had "prepared" their brains to learn the natural association more quickly than the artificial one. In other words, it was not only the rat's learning history but the rat's *ancestors'* learning histories that determined the rat's ability to learn. Although that fact was at odds with the behaviorist doctrine, it was the credo for a new kind of psychology.

Evolutionary psychology *explains mind and behavior in terms of the adaptive value of abilities that are preserved over time by natural selection.* Evolutionary psychology has its roots in Charles Darwin's theory of natural selection, which inspired William James's functionalist approach. But it is only since the publication in 1975 of *Sociobiology,* by the biologist E. O. Wilson, that evolutionary thinking has had an identifiable presence in psychology. That presence is steadily increasing (Buss, 1999; Pinker, 1997b; Tooby & Cosmides, 2000). Evolutionary psychologists think of the mind as a collection of specialized "modules" that are designed to solve the human problems our ancestors faced as they attempted to eat, mate, and reproduce over millions of years. According to evolutionary psychology, the brain is not an all-purpose computer that can do or learn one thing just as easily as it can do or learn another; rather, it is a computer that was built to do a few things well and everything else not at all. It is a computer that comes with a small suite of built-in applications that are designed to do the things that previous versions of that computer needed to have done.

Consider, for example, how evolutionary psychology treats the emotion of jealousy. All of us who have been in romantic relationships have been jealous, if only because we noticed our partner noticing someone else. Jealousy can be a powerful, overwhelming emotion that we might wish to avoid, but according to evolutionary psychology, it exists today because it once served an adaptive function. If some of our hominid ancestors experienced jealousy and others did not, then the ones who experienced it might have been more likely to guard their mates and aggress against their rivals and thus may have been more likely to reproduce their "jealous genes" (Buss, 2000).

Why might so many of us have inherited "jealous genes"?

Critics of the evolutionary approach point out that many current traits of people and other animals probably evolved to serve different functions than those they currently serve. For example, biologists believe that the feathers of birds probably evolved initially to perform such functions as regulating body temperature or capturing prey and only later served the entirely different function of flight. Likewise, people are reasonably adept at learning to drive a car, but nobody would argue that such an ability is the result of natural selection; the learning abilities that allow us to become skilled car drivers must have evolved for purposes other than driving cars.

Complications such as these have led the critics to wonder how evolutionary hypotheses can ever be tested (Coyne, 2000; Sterelny & Griffiths, 1999). We don't have a record of our ancestors' thoughts, feelings, and actions, and fossils won't provide much information about the evolution of mind and behavior. Testing ideas about the evolutionary origins of psychological phenomena is indeed a challenging task, but not an impossible one (Buss et al., 1998; Pinker, 1997b).

Start with the assumption that evolutionary adaptations should also increase reproductive success. So, if a specific trait or feature has been favored by natural selection, it should be possible to find some evidence of this in the numbers of offspring that are produced by the trait's bearers. Consider, for instance, the hypothesis that men tend to be tall because women prefer to mate with tall men. To investigate this hypothesis, researchers conducted a study in which they compared the numbers of offspring from short and tall men. They did their best to equate other factors that might affect the results, such as the level of education attained by short and tall men. Consistent with the evolutionary hypothesis, they found that tall men do indeed bear more offspring than short men (Pawlowski, Dunbar, & Lipowicz, 2000). This kind of study provides evidence that allows evolutionary psychologists to test their ideas. Not every evolutionary hypothesis can be tested, of course, but evolutionary psychologists are becoming increasingly inventive in their attempts.

IN SUMMARY

○ Psychologists such as Max Wertheimer, Frederic Bartlett, Jean Piaget, and Kurt Lewin defied the behaviorist doctrine and studied the inner workings of the mind. Their efforts, as well as those of later pioneers such as Donald Broadbent, paved the way for cognitive psychology to focus on inner mental processes such as perception, attention, memory, and reasoning.

○ Cognitive psychology developed as a field due to the invention of the computer, psychologists' efforts to improve the performance of the military, and Noam Chomsky's theories about language.

○ Cognitive neuroscience attempts to link the brain with the mind through studies of both brain-damaged and healthy people.

○ Evolutionary psychology focuses on the adaptive function that minds and brains serve and seeks to understand the nature and origin of psychological processes in terms of natural selection.

Beyond the Individual: Social and Cultural Perspectives

The picture we have painted so far may vaguely suggest a scene from some 1950s science-fiction film in which the protagonist is a living brain that thinks, feels, hopes, and worries while suspended in a vat of pink jelly in a basement laboratory. Although psychologists often do focus on the brain and the mind of the individual, they have not lost sight of the fact that human beings are fundamentally social animals who are part of a vast network of family, friends, teachers, and coworkers. Trying to understand people in the absence of that fact is a bit like trying to understand an ant or a bee without considering the function and influence of the colony or hive. People are the most important and most complex objects that we ever encounter; thus it is not surprising that our behavior is strongly influenced by their presence—or their absence. The two areas of psychology that most strongly emphasize these facts are social and cultural psychology.

"You're certainly a lot less fun since the operation."

The Development of Social Psychology

Social psychology is the study of *the causes and consequences of interpersonal behavior.* This broad definition allows social psychologists to address a remarkable variety of topics. Historians trace the birth of social psychology to an experiment conducted in 1895 by the psychologist and bicycle enthusiast Norman Triplett, who noticed that cyclists seemed to ride faster when they rode with others. Intrigued by this observation, he conducted an experiment that showed that children reeled in a fishing line faster when tested in the presence of other children than when tested alone. Triplett was not trying to improve the fishing abilities of American children, of course, but rather was trying to show that the mere presence of other people can influence performance on even the most mundane kinds of tasks.

How did historical events influence the development of social psychology? Social psychology's development began in earnest in the 1930s and was driven by several historical events. The rise of Nazism led many of Germany's most talented scientists to immigrate to America, and among them were psychologists such as Solomon Asch (1907–96) and Kurt Lewin. These psychologists had been strongly influenced by Gestalt psychology, which you'll recall held that "the whole is greater than the sum of its parts," and though the Gestaltists had been talking about the visual perception of objects, these psychologists felt that the phrase also captured a basic truth about the relationship between social groups and the individuals who constitute

social psychology A subfield of psychology that studies the causes and consequences of interpersonal behavior.

► Social psychology studies how the thoughts, feelings, and behaviors of individuals can be influenced by the presence of others. Members of the Reverend Sun Myung Moon's Unification Church are often married to one another in ceremonies of 10,000 people or more; in some cases couples don't know each other before the wedding begins. Social movements such as this have the power to sway individuals.

AHN YOUNG-JOON/AP PHOTO

them. Philosophers had speculated about the nature of sociality for thousands of years, and political scientists, economists, anthropologists, and sociologists had been studying social life scientifically for some time. But these German refugees were the first to generate theories of social behavior that resembled the theories generated by natural scientists, and more importantly, they were the first to conduct experiments to test their social theories. For example, Lewin (1936) adopted the language of midcentury physics to develop a "field theory" that viewed social behavior as the product of "internal forces" (such as personality, goals, and beliefs) and "external forces" (such as social pressure and culture), while Asch (1946) performed laboratory experiments to examine the "mental chemistry" that allows people to combine small bits of information about another person into a full impression of that person's personality.

Other historical events also shaped social psychology in its early years. For example, the Holocaust brought the problems of conformity and obedience into sharp focus, leading psychologists such as Asch (1956) and others to examine the conditions under which people can influence each other to think and act in inhuman or irrational ways. The civil rights movement and the rising tensions between African Americans and White Americans led psychologists such as Gordon Allport (1897–1967) to study stereotyping, prejudice, and racism and to shock the world of psychology by suggesting that prejudice was the result of a perceptual error that was every bit as natural and unavoidable as an optical illusion (Allport, 1954). Allport argued that the same perceptual processes that allow us to efficiently categorize elements of our social and physical world allow us to erroneously categorize entire groups of people. Social psychologists today study a wider variety of topics (from social memory to social relationships) and use a wider variety of techniques (from opinion polls to neuroimaging) than did their forebears, but this field of psychology remains dedicated to understanding the brain as a social organ, the mind as a social adaptation, and the individual as a social creature.

The Emergence of Cultural Psychology

North Americans and Western Europeans are sometimes surprised to realize that most of the people on the planet are members of neither culture. Although we're all more alike than we are different, there is nonetheless considerable diversity within the human species in social practices, customs, and ways of living. Culture refers to the values, traditions, and beliefs that are shared by a particular group of people. Although we usually think of culture in terms of nationality and ethnic groups, cultures can also be defined by age (youth culture), sexual orientation (gay culture), religion (Jewish culture), or occupation (academic culture). **Cultural psychology** is *the study of how cultures reflect and shape the psychological processes of their members* (Shweder & Sullivan, 1993). Cultural psychologists study a wide range of phenomena, ranging from visual perception to social interaction, as they seek to understand which of these phenomena are universal and which vary from place to place and time to time.

cultural psychology The study of how cultures reflect and shape the psychological processes of their members.

Perhaps surprisingly, one of the first psychologists to pay attention to the influence of culture was someone recognized today for pioneering the development of experimental psychology: Wilhelm Wundt. He believed that a complete psychology would have to combine a laboratory approach with a broader cultural perspective (Wundt, 1908). But Wundt's ideas failed to spark much interest from other psychologists, who had their hands full trying to make sense of results from laboratory experiments and formulating general laws of human behavior. Outside of psychology, anthropologists such as Margaret Mead (1901–78) and Gregory Bateson (1904–80) attempted to understand the workings of culture by traveling to far-flung regions of the world and carefully observing child-rearing patterns, rituals, religious ceremonies, and the like. Such studies revealed practices—some bizarre from a North American perspective—that served important functions in a culture, such as the painful ritual of violent body mutilation and bloodletting in mountain tribes of New Guinea, which initiates young boys into training to become warriors (Mead, 1935/1968; Read, 1965). Yet at the time, most anthropologists paid as little attention to psychology as psychologists did to anthropology.

How did anthropologists influence psychology in the 1980s?

Cultural psychology only began to emerge as a strong force in psychology during the 1980s and 1990s, when psychologists and anthropologists began to communicate with each other about their ideas and methods (Stigler, Shweder, & Herdt, 1990). It was then that psychologists rediscovered Wundt as an intellectual ancestor of this area of the field (Jahoda, 1993).

Physicists assume that $E - mc^2$ whether the m is located in Cleveland, Moscow, or the Orion Nebula. Chemists assume that water is made of hydrogen and oxygen and that it was made of hydrogen and oxygen in 1609 as well. The laws of physics and chemistry are assumed to be universal, and for much of psychology's history, the same assumption was made about the principles that govern human behavior (Shweder, 1991). *Absolutism* holds that culture makes little or no difference for most psychological phenomena—that "honesty is honesty and depression is depression, no matter where one observes it" (Segall, Lonner, & Berry, 1998, p. 1103). And yet, as any world traveler knows, cultures differ in exciting, delicious, and frightening ways, and things that are true of people in one culture are not necessarily true of people in another. *Relativism* holds that psychological phenomena are likely to vary considerably across cultures and should be viewed only in the context of a specific culture (Berry et al., 1992). Although depression is observed in nearly every culture, the symptoms associated with it vary dramatically from one place to another. For example, in Western cultures, depressed people tend to devalue themselves, whereas depressed people in Eastern cultures do not (Draguns, 1980).

Today, most cultural psychologists fall somewhere between these two extremes. Most psychological phenomena can be influenced by culture, some are completely determined

▼ The Namgay family from Shingkhey, Bhutan (left), and the Skeen family from Texas, U.S.A. (right), display their respective family possessions in these two photos, both taken in 1993. Cultural psychology studies the similarities and differences in psychological processes that arise between people living in different cultures.

by it, and others seem to be entirely unaffected. For example, the age of a person's earliest memory differs dramatically across cultures (MacDonald, Uesiliana, & Hayne, 2000),

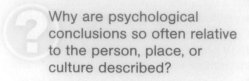

Why are psychological conclusions so often relative to the person, place, or culture described?

whereas judgments of facial attractiveness do not (Cunningham et al., 1995). As noted when we discussed evolutionary psychology, it seems likely that the most universal phenomena are those that are closely associated with the basic biology that all human beings share. Conversely, the least universal phenomena are those rooted in the varied socialization practices that different cultures evolve. Of course, the only way to determine whether a phenomenon is variable or constant across cultures is to design research to investigate these possibilities, and cultural psychologists do just that (Cole, 1996; Segall et al., 1998). We'll highlight the work of cultural psychologists at various points in the text in Culture & Community boxes like the one you read earlier in the chapter concerning cultural influences on the perception of a visual illusion.

IN SUMMARY

○ Social psychology recognizes that people exist as part of a network of other people and examines how individuals influence and interact with one another. Social psychology was pioneered by German émigrés, such as Kurt Lewin, who were motivated by a desire to address social issues and problems.

○ Cultural psychology is concerned with the effects of the broader culture on individuals and with similarities and differences among people in different cultures. Within this perspective, absolutists hold that culture has little impact on most psychological phenomena, whereas relativists believe that culture has a powerful effect.

○ Together, social and cultural psychology help expand the discipline's horizons beyond just an examination of individuals. These areas of psychology examine behavior within the broader context of human interaction.

The Profession of Psychology: Past and Present

If ever you find yourself on an airplane with an annoying seatmate who refuses to let you read your magazine, there are two things you can do. First, you can turn to the person and say in a calm and friendly voice, "Did you know that I am covered with strange and angry bacteria?" If that seems a bit extreme, you might instead try saying, "Did you know that I am a psychologist, and I'm forming an evaluation of you as you speak?," as this will usually shut them up without getting you arrested. The truth is that most people don't really know what psychology is or what psychologists do, but they do have some vague sense that it isn't wise to talk to one. Now that you've been briefly acquainted with psychology's past, let's consider its present by looking at psychology as a profession. We'll look first at the origins of psychology's professional organizations, next at the contexts in which psychologists tend to work, and finally at the kinds of training required to become a psychologist.

Psychologists Band Together: The American Psychological Association

You'll recall that when we last saw William James, he was wandering around the greater Boston area, expounding the virtues of the new science of psychology. In July 1892, James and five other psychologists traveled to Clark University to attend a meeting called by G. Stanley Hall. Each worked at a large university where they taught psychology courses, performed research, and wrote textbooks. Although they were too few to make up a jury or even a respectable hockey team, these seven men decided that it was time to form an organization that represented psychology as a profession, and on that day the American Psychological Association (APA) was born. The seven psychologists could scarcely have imagined that today their little club would have more than 150,000 members—approximately the population of a decent-sized city in the United States. Although all of the original members were employed by universities or colleges, today academic psychologists make up only 20% of the membership, while nearly 70% of the members work in clinical and health-related settings. Because the APA is no longer as focused on academic psychology as it once was, the American Psychological Society (APS) was formed in 1988 by 450 academic psychologists who wanted an organization that focused specifically on the needs of psychologists carrying out scientific research. The APS, renamed the Association for Psychological Science in 2006, grew quickly, attracting 5,000 members within six months; today it comprises nearly 12,000 psychologists.

The Growing Role of Women and Minorities

In 1892, the APA had 31 members, all of whom were White and all of whom were male. Today, about half of all APA members are women, and the percentage of non-White members continues to grow. Surveys of recent PhD recipients reveal a picture of increasing diversification in the field. The proportion of women receiving PhDs in psychology increased from only 15% in 1950 to 67% in 2004, and the proportion of minorities receiving PhDs in psychology grew from a very small number to 15% during that same period. Clearly, psychology is increasingly reflecting the diversity of American society.

◀ Mary Whiton Calkins (1863–1930), the first woman elected APA president, suffered from the sex discrimination that was common during her lifetime. Despite academic setbacks (such as Harvard University refusing to grant women an official PhD), Calkins went on to a distinguished career in research and teaching at Wellesley College.

WELLESLEY COLLEGE ARCHIVES–MARGARET CLAPP LIBRARY

The current involvement of women and minorities in the APA, and psychology more generally, can be traced to early pioneers who blazed a trail that others followed. In 1905, Mary Calkins (1863–1930) became the first woman to serve as president of the APA. Calkins became interested in psychology while teaching Greek at Wellesley College. She studied with William James at Harvard and later became a professor of psychology at Wellesley College, where she worked until retiring in 1929. In her presidential address to the APA, Calkins described her theory of the role of the "self" in psychological function. Arguing against Wundt's and Titchener's structuralist ideas that the mind can be dissected into components, Calkins claimed that the self is a single unit that cannot be broken down into individual parts. Calkins wrote four books and published over 100 articles during her illustrious career (Calkins, 1930; Scarborough & Furumoto, 1987; Stevens & Gardner, 1982). Today, women play leading roles in all areas of psychology. Some of the men who formed the APA might have been surprised by the prominence of women in the field today, but we suspect that William James, a strong supporter of Mary Calkins, would not be one of them.

How has the face of psychology changed as the field has evolved?

◀ Francis Cecil Sumner (1895–1954) was the first African American to hold a PhD in psychology, receiving his from Clark University in 1920. Sumner conducted research on race relations, equality, and the psychology of religion.

ARCHIVES OF THE HISTORY OF AMERICAN PSYCHOLOGY

THE REAL WORLD

Joining the Club

Once upon a time Western science was the hobby of wealthy European gentlemen. The pictures of the great figures in psychology's history you have seen in this chapter suggest that psychology likewise was once a narrow and exclusionary club. Fortunately, the face of this field has changed profoundly since its early days and continues to progress even now.

In fact, social changes have led to openness and diversity in psychology more swiftly and completely than in most other fields of study. In 2006, for example, while women were only poorly represented in engineering and the physical sciences, they received more than 71% of new PhD degrees in psychology (Burrelli, 2008). As you can see in the accompanying figure, although women are earning a growing proportion of PhDs in all fields, they are now a whopping majority in psychology. Meanwhile, psychology PhDs to Hispanic, African American, and Native American students have more than doubled from 1985 to 2005, and those to Asians and Pacific Islanders have tripled (National Science Board, 2008). It is now the future, and in this future, psychology is the science of everyone.

Signs of the openness of psychology are all around. Just take a look at some of the students in undergraduate psychology clubs, or *Psi Chi* (psychology's undergraduate and graduate student honorary society), or *Psi Beta* (the honorary society for community and junior college psychology students). Psychology students now are far more often women than men (77%; Planty et al., 2008), and there is substantial representation of minority groups in psychology everywhere you look. Like its clubs and honorary societies, the study of psychology is open and welcoming to people of any age, sex, sexual orientation, race, different ability, color, religion, or national or ethnic origin. Please join us!

▲ Psychology students smiling for the camera include (clockwise from left) Psi Chi from the University of Missouri, psychology clubs of Daytona State University and East Los Angeles College, and Psi Chi of Bradley University.

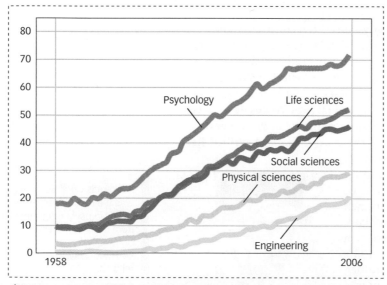

▲ The proportion of new PhDs earned by women has grown faster in psychology than in other fields (Burrelli, 2008).

▶ Kenneth B. Clark (1914–2005) studied the developmental effects of prejudice, discrimination, and segregation on children. In one classic study from the 1950s, he found that African American preschoolers preferred white dolls to black ones. Clark's research was cited by the U.S. Supreme Court in its decision for the landmark *Brown v. Board of Education* case that ended school segregation.

WILLIAM E. SAURO/NEW YORK TIMES CO./GETTY IMAGES

Just as there were no women at the first meeting of the APA, there weren't any non-White people either. The first member of a minority group to become president of the APA was Kenneth Clark (1914–2005), who was elected in 1970. Clark worked extensively on the self-image of African American children and argued that segregation of the races creates great psychological harm. Clark's conclusions had a large influence on public policy, and his research contributed to the Supreme Court's 1954 ruling (*Brown v. Board of Education*) to outlaw segregation in public schools (Guthrie, 2000). Clark's interest in psychology was sparked as an undergraduate at Howard University when he took a course from Francis Cecil Sumner (1895–1954), who was the first African American to receive a PhD in psychology (from Clark University, in 1920). Sumner's main interest focused on the education of African American youth (Sawyer, 2000).

What Psychologists Do: Research Careers

So what should you do if you want to become a psychologist—and what should you fail to do if you desperately want to avoid it? You can become "a psychologist" by a variety of routes, and the people who call themselves psychologists may hold a variety of different degrees. Typically, students finish college and enter graduate school in order to obtain a PhD (or doctor of philosophy) degree in some particular area of psychology (e.g., social, cognitive, developmental). During graduate school, students generally gain exposure to the field by taking classes and learn to conduct research by collaborating with their professors. Although William James was able to master every area of psychology because the areas were so small during his lifetime, today a student can spend the better part of a decade mastering just one.

After receiving a PhD, you can go on for more specialized research training by pursuing a postdoctoral fellowship under the supervision of an established researcher in their area or apply for a faculty position at a college or university or a research position in government or industry. Academic careers usually involve a combination of teaching and research, whereas careers in government or industry are typically dedicated to research alone.

The Variety of Career Paths

As you saw earlier, research is not the only career option for a psychologist. Most of the people who call themselves psychologists neither teach nor do research, but rather, they assess or treat people with psychological problems. Most of these *clinical psychologists* work in private practice, often in partnerships with other psychologists or with psychiatrists (who have earned an MD, or medical degree, and are allowed to prescribe medication). Other clinical psychologists work in

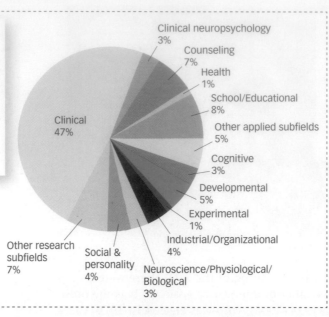

► FIGURE 1.6
The Major Subfields in Psychology Psychologists are drawn to many different subfields in psychology. Here are the percentages of people receiving PhDs in various subfields. Clinical psychology makes up almost half of the doctorates awarded in psychology.

Source: 2004 Graduate Study in Psychology. Compiled by APA Research Office.

hospitals or medical schools, some have faculty positions at universities or colleges, and some combine private practice with an academic job. Many clinical psychologists focus on specific problems or disorders, such as depression or anxiety, whereas others focus on specific populations, such as children, ethnic minority groups, or elderly adults (**FIGURE 1.6**).

Just over 10% of APA members are *counseling psychologists,* who assist people in dealing with work or career issues and changes or help people deal with common crises such as divorce, the loss of a job, or the death of a loved one. Counseling psychologists may have a PhD or an MA (master's degree) in counseling psychology or an MSW (Master of Social Work).

Psychologists are also quite active in educational settings. About 5% of APA members are *school psychologists,* who offer guidance to students, parents, and teachers. A similar proportion of APA members, known *as industrial/organizational psychologists,* focus on issues in the workplace. These psychologists typically work in business or industry and may be involved in assessing potential employees, finding ways to improve productivity, or helping staff and management to develop effective planning strategies for coping with change or anticipated future developments.

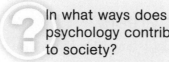 **In what ways does psychology contribute to society?** Even this brief and incomplete survey of the APA membership provides a sense of the wide variety of contexts in which psychologists operate. You can think of psychology as an international community of professionals devoted to advancing scientific knowledge; assisting people with psychological problems and disorders; and trying to enhance the quality of life in work, school, and other everyday settings.

IN SUMMARY

○ The American Psychological Association (APA) has grown dramatically since it was formed in 1892 and now includes over 150,000 members, working in clinical, academic, and applied settings. Psychologists are also represented by professional organizations such as the Association for Psychological Science (APS), which focuses on scientific psychology.

○ Through the efforts of pioneers such as Mary Calkins, women have come to play an increasingly important role in the field and are now as well represented as men. Minority involvement in psychology took longer, but the pioneering efforts of Francis Cecil Sumner, Kenneth B. Clark, and others have led to increased participation of minorities in psychology.

○ Psychologists prepare for research careers through graduate and postdoctoral training and work in a variety of applied settings, including schools, clinics, and industry.

WhereDoYouStand?

The Perils of Procrastination

As you've read in this chapter, the human mind and behavior are fascinating in part because they are not error free. The mind's mistakes interest us primarily as paths to achieving a better understanding of mental activity and behavior, but they also have practical consequences. Let's consider a malfunction that can have significant consequences in your own life: procrastination.

At one time or another, most of us have avoided carrying out a task or put it off to a later time. The task may be unpleasant, difficult, or just less entertaining than other things we could be doing at the moment. For college students, procrastination can affect a range of academic activities, such as writing a term paper or preparing for a test. Academic procrastination is not uncommon: Over 70% of college students report that they engage in some form of procrastination (Schouwenburg, 1995). Although it's fun to hang out with your friends tonight, it's not so much fun to worry for three days about your impending history exam or try to study at 4:00 a.m. the day of the test. Studying now, or at least a little bit each day, robs procrastination of its power over you.

Some procrastinators defend the practice by claiming that they tend to work best under pressure or by noting that as long as a task gets done, it doesn't matter all that much if it is completed just before the deadline. Is there any merit to such claims, or are they just feeble excuses for counterproductive behavior?

A study of 60 undergraduate psychology college students provides some intriguing answers (Tice & Baumeister, 1997). At the beginning of the semester, the instructor announced a due date for the term paper and told students that if they could not meet the date, they would receive an extension to a later date. About a month later, students completed a scale that measures tendencies toward procrastination. At that same time, and then again during the last week of class, students recorded health symptoms they had experienced during the past week, the amount of stress they had experienced during that week, and the number of visits they had made to a health care center during the previous month.

Students who scored high on the procrastination scale tended to turn in their papers late. One month into the semester, these procrastinators reported less stress and fewer symptoms of physical illness than did nonprocrastinators. But at the end of the semester, the procrastinators reported *more* stress and *more* health symptoms than did the nonprocrastinators and also reported more visits to the health center. The procrastinators also received lower grades on their papers and on course exams.

This study shows, then, that procrastination did have some benefits: Procrastinators tended to feel better early on, while they were procrastinating and their deadline was far in the future. But they paid a significant cost for this immediate relief: Procrastinators not only suffered more stress and health problems as they scrambled to complete their work near the deadline, but they also reported more stress and health symptoms across the entire semester. There was also no evidence to support the idea that procrastinators do their "best work under pressure," since their academic performance was worse than that of nonprocrastinators. Therefore, in addition to making use of the tips provided in the Real World box on increasing study skills (p. 11), it would seem wise to avoid procrastination in this course and others.

Where do you stand on procrastination? Calculate your procrastination score by rating the statements below on a scale of 1–5, where

1 = not at all;   4 = most of the time;

2 = incidentally;   5 = always

3 = sometimes;

How frequently last week did you engage in the following behaviors or thoughts?

1. Drifted off into daydreams while studying
2. Studied the subject matter that you had planned to do
3. Had no energy to study
4. Prepared to study at some point but did not get any further
5. Gave up when studying was not going well
6. Gave up studying early in order to do more pleasant things
7. Put off the completion of a task
8. Allowed yourself to be distracted from your work
9. Experienced concentration problems when studying
10. Interrupted studying for a while in order to do other things
11. Forgot to prepare things for studying
12. Did so many other things that there was insufficient time left for studying
13. Thought that you had enough time left, so that there was really no need to start studying

Chapter Review

KEY CONCEPT QUIZ

1. In the 1800s, French biologist Pierre Flourens and surgeon Paul Broca conducted research that demonstrated a connection between
   a. animals and humans.
   b. the mind and the brain.
   c. brain size and mental ability.
   d. skull indentations and psychological attributes.

2. What was the subject of the famous experiment conducted by Hermann von Helmholtz?
   a. reaction time
   b. childhood learning
   c. phrenology
   d. functions of specific brain areas

3. Wilhelm Wundt is credited with
   a. coining the phrase "philosophical empiricism."
   b. setting the terms for the nature-nurture debate.
   c. the founding of psychology as a scientific discipline.
   d. conducting the first psychological experiment.

4. Wundt and his students sought to analyze the basic elements that constitute the mind, an approach called
   a. consciousness.
   b. introspection.
   c. structuralism.
   d. objectivity.

5. William James and _____ helped establish functionalism as a major school of psychological thought in North America.
   a. G. Stanley Hall
   b. René Descartes
   c. Franz Joseph Gall
   d. Edward Titchener

6. The functional approach to psychology was inspired by
   a. Darwin's *On the Origin of Species by Means of Natural Selection.*
   b. James's *The Principles of Psychology.*
   c. Wundt's *Principles of Physiological Psychology.*
   d. Titchener's *An Outline of Psychology.*

7. To understand human behavior, French physicians Jean-Martin Charcot and Pierre Janet studied people
   a. who appeared to be completely healthy.
   b. with psychological disorders.
   c. with damage in particular areas of the brain.
   d. who had suffered permanent loss of cognitive and motor function.

8. Building on the work of Charcot and Janet, Sigmund Freud developed
   a. psychoanalytic theory.
   b. the theory of hysteria.
   c. humanistic psychology.
   d. physiological psychology.

9. Behaviorism involves the study of
   a. observable actions and responses.
   b. the potential for human growth.
   c. unconscious influences and childhood experiences.
   d. human behavior and memory.

10. The experiments of Ivan Pavlov and John Watson centered on
    a. perception and behavior.
    b. stimulus and response.
    c. reward and punishment.
    d. conscious and unconscious behavior.

11. Who developed the concept of reinforcement?
    a. B. F. Skinner
    b. Ivan Pavlov
    c. John Watson
    d. Margaret Floy Washburn

12. The study of mental processes such as perception and memory is called
    a. behavioral determinism.
    b. Gestalt psychology.
    c. social psychology.
    d. cognitive psychology.

13. The use of scanning techniques to observe the brain in action and to see which parts are involved in which operations helped the development of
    a. evolutionary psychology.
    b. cognitive neuroscience.
    c. cultural psychology.
    d. cognitive accounts of language formation.

14. Central to evolutionary psychology is the_____ function that minds and brains serve.
    a. emotional
    b. adaptive
    c. cultural
    d. physiological

15. Social psychology most differs from other psychological approaches in its emphasis on
    a. human interaction.
    b. behavioral processes.
    c. the individual.
    d. laboratory experimentation.

KEY TERMS

psychology (p. 2)
mind (p. 2)
behavior (p. 2)
nativism (p. 5)
philosophical empiricism (p. 6)
phrenology (p. 6)
physiology (p. 7)

stimulus (p. 8)
reaction time (p. 8)
consciousness (p. 8)
structuralism (p. 9)
introspection (p. 9)
functionalism (p. 10)
natural selection (p. 10)
hysteria (p. 13)

unconscious (p. 13)
psychoanalytic theory (p. 13)
psychoanalysis (p. 14)
humanistic psychology (p. 15)
behaviorism (p. 16)
response (p. 17)
reinforcement (p. 17)

illusions (p. 19)
Gestalt psychology (p. 20)
cognitive psychology (p. 22)
behavioral neuroscience (p. 24)
cognitive neuroscience (p. 25)
evolutionary psychology (p. 26)
social psychology (p. 27)
cultural psychology (p. 28)

CRITICAL THINKING QUESTIONS

1. William James thought Darwin's theory of natural selection might explain how mental abilities evolve, by conferring survival advantages on individuals who were better able to solve problems. How might a specific mental ability, such as the ability to recognize the facial expressions of others as signaling their emotional state, help an individual survive longer and produce more offspring?

2. Behaviorists explain behavior in terms of organisms learning to make particular responses that are paired with reinforcement (and to avoid responses that are paired with punishment). Evolutionary psychology focuses on how abilities are preserved over time if they contribute to an organism's ability to survive and reproduce. How might a proponent of each approach explain the fact that a rat placed in an unfamiliar environment will tend to stay in dark corners and avoid brightly lit open areas?

RECOMMENDED READINGS

Fancher, R. E. (1979). *Pioneers of psychology*. New York: Norton.

This engaging book examines the history of psychology by painting portraits of the field's pioneers, including many of the psychologists featured in this chapter. A great way to learn more about the history of psychology is by becoming familiar with the lives of its founders.

Hermann, D., Raybeck, D., & Gruneberg, M. (2002). *Improving memory and study skills*. Seattle: Hogrefe and Huber.

This excellent book offers a nice introduction to many aspects of cognitive psychology. More importantly, it offers several practical suggestions for improving memory, improving study habits, and mastering material that you are trying to learn.

James, W. (1890/1955). *The principles of psychology (1890/1955)*. New York: Holt.

Considered by many psychologists to be the "bible" of psychology, this masterpiece by William James is still exciting to read over a century after it was published. If you do have a chance to read it, you will understand why thousands of psychologists are so thankful that James bypassed a career in medicine for one in psychology.

Skinner, B. F. (1948/1986). *Walden II*. Englewood Cliffs, NJ: Prentice Hall.

Skinner's provocative novel describes a modern utopia in which scientific principles from behavioristic psychology are used to shape a model community. This controversial book raises intriguing questions about how knowledge from psychology could or should be used to influence day-to-day living in modern society.

American Psychological Association website: www.apa.org

Association for Psychological Science website: www.psychologicalscience.org

These websites provide a wealth of information about the APA and the APS and about news and research in all areas of psychology. Both sites have sections specially designed for students and contain many links to other useful and informative sites in psychology. An excellent way to learn about what is going on in the field today.

ANSWERS TO KEY CONCEPT QUIZ

1. b; 2. a; 3. c; 4. c; 5. a; 6. a; 7. b; 8. a; 9. a; 10. b; 11. a; 12. d; 13. b; 14. b; 15. a.

Need more help? Additional resources are located at the book's free companion Web site at:
www.worthpublishers.com/schacter

2

Methods in Psychology

Louise Hay is one of the bestselling authors of all time (Oppenheimer, 2008). One of her books, *You Can Heal Your Life*, has sold over 35 million copies, and her company is the world's largest publisher of self-help materials. Hay believes that everything that happens to us—including accident and disease—is a result of the thoughts we choose to think. She claims that she cured herself of cancer by changing her thoughts, and she says that others can learn this trick by buying her books, CDs, DVDs, and by attending her seminars. In a recent television interview, Hay explained why she's so sure that her technique works.

Interviewer:	How do you know what you're saying is right?
Hay:	Oh, my inner ding.
Interviewer:	Ding?
Hay:	My inner ding. It speaks to me. It feels right or it doesn't feel right. Happiness is choosing thoughts that make you feel good. It's really very simple.
Interviewer:	But I hear you saying that even if there were no proof for what you believed, or even if there were scientific evidence against it, it wouldn't change.
Hay:	Well, I don't believe in scientific evidence, I really don't. Science is fairly new. It hasn't been around that long. We think it's such a big deal, but it's, you know, it's just a way of looking at life.

Louise Hay says she doesn't "believe" in scientific evidence, but what could that mean? After all, if Hay's techniques really do cure cancer, then even she would have to expect cancer victims who practice her technique to have a higher rate of remission than cancer victims who don't. That isn't some strange, new, or exotic way of "looking at life." That's just plain, old-fashioned, common sense—exactly the kind of common sense that lies at the heart of science.

Science tells us that the only way to know for sure whether a claim is true is to go out, have a look, and see for ourselves. But that sounds easier than it is. For example, how would you go about looking to see whether Louise Hay's claims are true? Would you

▶ **Louise Hay** doesn't believe in scientific evidence and instead trusts her "inner ding."
MICHELE ASSELIN/CONTOUR BY GETTY IMAGES

empiricism The belief that accurate knowledge can be acquired through observation.

scientific method A set of principles about the appropriate relationship between ideas and evidence.

theory A hypothetical explanation of a natural phenomenon.

hypothesis A falsifiable prediction made by a theory.

go to one of her seminars and ask people in the audience whether or not they'd been healed? Would you examine the medical records of people who had and hadn't bought her books? Would you invite people to sign up for a class that teaches her techniques and then wait to see how many got cancer? All of these tests sound reasonable, but the fact is that none of them would be particularly informative. There are a few good ways to test claims like this one and a whole lot of bad ways, and in this chapter you will learn to tell one from the other. Scientists have developed powerful tools for determining when an inner ding is right and when it is wrong, and these tools are what make science unique. As the philosopher Bertrand Russell (1945, p. 527) wrote, "It is not *what* the man of science believes that distinguishes him, but *how* and *why* he believes it." (And that goes for women of science too!)

WE'LL START BY EXAMINING THE GENERAL PRINCIPLES THAT GUIDE scientific research and distinguish it from every other way of knowing. Next, we'll see that the methods of psychology are meant to answer two basic questions: *what* do people do, and *why* do they do it? Psychologists answer the first question by observing and measuring, and they answer the second question by looking for relationships between the things they measure. We'll see that scientific research allows us to draw certain kinds of conclusions and not others. Finally, we'll consider the unique ethical questions that confront scientists who study people and other animals.

Empiricism: How to Know Stuff

When ancient Greeks sprained their ankles, caught the flu, or accidentally set their togas on fire, they had to choose between two kinds of doctors: dogmatists (from *dogmatikos,* meaning "belief"), who thought that the best way to understand illness was to develop theories about the body's functions, and empiricists (from *empeirikos,* meaning "experience"), who thought that the best way to understand illness was to observe sick people. The rivalry between these two schools of medicine didn't last long because the people who went to see dogmatists tended to die a lot, which wasn't good for business. Today we use the word *dogmatism* to describe the tendency for people to cling to their assumptions and the word **empiricism** to describe *the belief that accurate knowledge can be acquired through observation.* The fact that we can answer questions about the natural world by examining it may seem obvious to you, but this obvious fact has only recently gained wide acceptance. For most of human history, people have trusted authority to answer important questions, and it is only in the last millennium (and especially in the past three centuries) that people have begun to trust their eyes and ears more than their elders.

▼ The 17th-century astronomer Galileo Galilei was excommunicated and sentenced to prison for sticking to his own observations of the solar system rather than accepting the teachings of the church. In 1597 he wrote to his friend and fellow astronomer Johannes Kepler, "What would you say of the learned here, who, replete with the pertinacity of the asp, have steadfastly refused to cast a glance through the telescope? What shall we make of this? Shall we laugh, or shall we cry?" As it turned out, the answer was *cry.*

BETTMANN/CORBIS

The Scientific Method

Empiricism is the essential element of the **scientific method**, which is *a set of principles about the appropriate relationship between ideas and evidence.* In essence, the scientific method suggests that when we have an idea about the world—about how bats navigate, or where the moon came from, or why people can't forget traumatic events— **What is the scientific method?** we should gather empirical evidence relevant to that idea and then modify the idea to fit with the evidence. Scientists usually refer to an idea of this kind as a **theory**, which is *a hypothetical* *explanation of a natural phenomenon.* We might theorize that bats navigate by making sounds and then listening for the echo, that the moon was formed when a small planet collided with the Earth, or that the brain responds to traumatic events by producing chemicals that facilitate memory. Each of these theories is an explanation of how something in the natural world works.

When scientists set out to develop a theory they start with the simplest one, and they refer to this as *the rule of parsimony*, which comes from the Latin word *parcere*, meaning "to spare." The rule of parsimony is often credited to the 14th-century logician William Ockham, who wrote "Plurality should only be posited when necessary," which is essentially the way people in the Middle Ages said, "Keep it simple, stupid." Ockham wasn't arguing that nature is simple or that complex theories are wrong. He was merely suggesting that it makes sense to *start* with the simplest theory possible and *then* make the theory more complicated only if we must. Part of what makes $E = mc^2$ such a good theory is that it has exactly three letters and one number.

Theories are ideas about how and why things work the way they do. So how do we decide if a theory is right? Most theories make predictions about what we should and should not be able to observe in the world. For example, if bats really do navigate by making sounds and then listening for echoes, then we should observe that deaf bats can't navigate. That "should statement" is technically known as a **hypothesis**, which is *a falsifiable prediction made by a theory*. The word *falsifiable* is a critical part of that definition. Some theories—such as "God created the universe"—do not specify what we should or should not observe if they are true, and thus no observations can falsify them. Because such theories do not give rise to hypotheses, they cannot be the subject of scientific investigation. That doesn't mean they're wrong. It just means that we can't judge them by using the scientific method.

So what *can* we find out when we use the scientific method? Albert Einstein once lamented that, "No amount of experimentation can ever prove me right, but a single experiment can prove me wrong." Why should that be? Well, just imagine what you could possibly learn about the navigation-by-sound theory if you observed a few bats. If you saw the deaf bats navigating every bit as well as the hearing bats, then the navigation-by-sound theory would instantly be proved wrong; but if you saw the deaf bats navigating more poorly than the hearing bats, your observation would be *consistent* with the navigation-by-sound theory but would not

Why can't evidence ever prove a theory right?

prove it. After all, even if you didn't see a deaf bat navigating perfectly today, it is still possible that someone else did, or that you will see one tomorrow. We can't observe every bat that has ever been and will ever be, which means that even if the theory wasn't disproved by your observation there always remains some chance that it will be disproved by some other observation. When evidence is consistent with a theory it increases our confidence in it, but it never makes us completely certain.

The scientific method suggests that the best way to learn the truth about the world is to develop theories, derive hypotheses from them, test those hypotheses by gathering evidence, and then use that evidence to modify the theories. But what exactly does "gathering evidence" entail?

The Art of Looking

For centuries, people rode horses. And for centuries when they got off their horses they sat around and argued about whether all four of a horse's feet ever leave the ground at the same time. Some said yes, some said no, and some said they really wished they could talk about something else. In 1877, Eadweard Muybridge invented a technique for taking photographs in rapid succession, and his photos showed that when horses gallop, all four feet leave the ground. And that was that. Never again did two riders have the pleasure of a flying horse debate because Muybridge had settled the matter, once and for all time.

▼ **Ibn al-Haytham (965–1039)** is considered by many to be the father of the scientific method. Classical thinkers like Euclid and Ptolemy believed that our eyes work by emitting rays that travel to the objects we see. Al-Haytham reasoned that if this were true, then when we open our eyes it should take longer to see something far away than something nearby. And guess what? It doesn't. And with that single observation, a centuries-old theory vanished—in the blink of an eye.

"Are you just pissing and moaning, or can you verify what you're saying with data?"

► As frames 2 and 3 of Eadweard Muybridge's historic photo show, horses can indeed fly, albeit briefly and only in coach.

EADWEARD MUYBRIDGE/CORBIS

But why did it take so long? After all, people had been watching horses gallop for quite a few years, so why did some say that they clearly saw the horse going airborne while others said that they clearly saw two hooves on the ground at all times? Because as wonderful as eyes may be, there are a lot of things they cannot see and a lot of things they see incorrectly. We can't see germs but they are very real. The Earth looks flat but it is very round. As Muybridge knew, we have to do more than just look if we want to know the truth about the world. Empiricism is the right approach, but to do it properly requires an **empirical method**, which is *a set of rules and techniques for observation.*

In many sciences, the word *method* refers primarily to technologies that enhance the powers of the senses. Biologists use microscopes and astronomers use telescopes because the phenomena they seek to explain are invisible to the naked eye. Human behavior, on the other hand, is relatively easy to observe, so you might expect psychology's methods to be relatively simple. In fact, the empirical challenges facing psychologists are among the most

What three things make people difficult to study?

daunting in all of modern science, thus psychology's empirical methods are among the most sophisticated in all of modern science. Three things make people especially difficult to study:

> *Complexity:* No galaxy, particle, molecule, or machine is as complicated as the human brain. Scientists can describe the birth of a star or the death of a cell in exquisite detail, but they can barely begin to say how the 500 million interconnected neurons that constitute the brain give rise to the thoughts, feelings, and actions that are psychology's core concerns.

> *Variability:* In almost all the ways that matter, one *E. coli* bacterium is pretty much like another. But people are as varied as their fingerprints. No two individuals ever do, say, think, or feel exactly the same thing under exactly the same circumstances, which means that when you've seen one, you've most definitely not seen them all.

> *Reactivity:* An atom of cesium-133 oscillates 9,192,631,770 times per second regardless of whether anyone is watching. But people often think, feel, and act one way when they are being observed and a different way when they are not. When people know they are being studied, they don't always behave as they otherwise would.

▼ Different people don't do exactly the same thing under exactly the same circumstances. Each one of the Maynard Sisters had a different reaction when *American Idol* judge Simon Cowell told them that they sang badly and looked like "overweight Jessica Simpsons."

A. RAPOPORT/PICTUREGROUP

AP PHOTO/ERIC JAMISON

The fact that human beings are complex, variable, and reactive presents a major challenge to the scientific study of their behavior, but psychologists have developed two kinds of methods that are designed to meet these challenges head-on: *methods of observation,* which allow them to determine what people do, and *methods of explanation,* which allow them to determine why people do it. We'll examine each of these two sets of methods in the sections that follow.

IN SUMMARY

○ Empiricism is the belief that the best way to understand the world is to observe it firsthand. It is only in the last few centuries that empiricism has come to prominence.

○ Empiricism is at the heart of the scientific method, which suggests that our theories about the world give rise to falsifiable hypotheses, and that we can thus make observations that test those hypotheses. The results of these tests can disprove our theories but cannot prove them.

○ Observation doesn't just mean "looking." It requires a method. The methods of psychology are special because more than most other natural phenomena, human beings are complex, variable, and reactive.

Observation: Discovering What People Do

To *observe* means to use one's senses to learn about the properties of an event (e.g., a storm or a parade) or an object (e.g., an apple or a person). For example, when you observe a round, red apple, your brain is using the pattern of light that is falling on your eyes to draw an inference about the apple's identity, shape, and color. That kind of informal observation is fine for buying fruit but not for doing science. Why? First, casual observations are notoriously unstable. The same apple may appear red in the daylight and crimson at night or spherical to one person and elliptical to another. Second, casual observations can't tell us about all of the properties that might interest us. No matter how long and hard you look, you will never be able to discern an apple's crunchiness or pectin content simply by watching it.

Luckily, scientists have devised techniques that allow them to overcome these problems. In the first section (Measurement), we'll see how psychologists design measures and use them to make measurements. In the second section (Descriptions), we'll see what psychologists do with their measurements once they've made them.

Measurement

For most of human history, people had no idea how old they were because there was no simple way to keep track of time. Or weight, or volume, or density, or temperature,

 What two things does measurement require?

or anything else, for that matter. Today we live in a world of tape measures and rulers, clocks and calendars, odometers, thermometers, and mass spectrometers. Measurement is the basis not just of science, but of modern life. But what does measurement require? Whether we want to measure the intensity of an earthquake, the distance between molecules, or the attitude of a registered voter, we must always do two things—*define* the property we wish to measure and then find a way to *detect* it.

Defining and Detecting

The last time you said, "Give me a second," you probably didn't know you were talking about atomic decay. Every unit of time has an **operational definition**, which is *a description of a property in concrete, measurable terms.* The operational definition of "a second" is *the*

empirical method A set of rules and techniques for observation.

operational definition A description of a property in concrete, measurable terms.

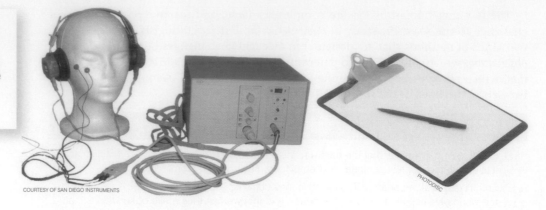

▶ FIGURE 2.1
Psychological Measures Psychological measures may take a variety of forms. An electromyograph (EMG) measures the electrical activity of the muscles in a person's face, and a questionnaire measures a person's preferences, attitudes, and beliefs.

COURTESY OF SAN DIEGO INSTRUMENTS

PHOTODISC

duration of 9,192,631,770 cycles of microwave light absorbed or emitted by the hyperfine transition of cesium-133 atoms in their ground state undisturbed by external fields (which takes roughly six seconds just to say). To actually count the cycles of light emitted as cesium-133 decays requires a **measure**, which is *a device that can detect the condition to which an operational definition refers*. A device known as a "cesium clock" can do just that, and when it counts 9,192,631,770 of them, a second has passed.

The steps we take to measure a physical property are the same steps we take to measure a psychological property. For example, if we wanted to measure a person's intelligence, or shyness, or happiness, we would have to start by developing an operational definition of that property—that is, by specifying some concrete, measurable event that indicates it. For example, we could define happiness as the frequency with which a person smiles, and we could then detect those smiles with an **electromyograph (EMG)**, which is *a device that measures muscle contractions under the surface of a person's skin* (see **FIGURE 2.1**). Having an operational definition that specifies a measurable event and a device that measures that event are the two keys to scientific measurement.

Validity, Reliability, and Power

There is nothing sacred about the way physicists define or detect a second, and if they wanted to they could define and detect it in some other way. Similarly, we could define happiness as the frequency with which a person smiles, or we could define it as a person's answer to the question, "How happy are you?" If we chose to define it in terms of smiling, we could measure those smiles with an EMG or we could ask trained observers to watch the person's face and count how many times he or she smiled. There are many ways to define and detect happiness, so which is the best way? Although there is no best way, some ways are clearly better than others. Good measures have three properties: validity, reliability, and power.

Validity refers to *the extent to which a measurement and a property are conceptually related*. For example, frequency of smiling is a valid way to define happiness because people all over the world tend to smile more often when they feel happy. On the other hand, the number of friends a person has would not be a valid way to define happiness. Happy people do have more friends, but there are many other reasons why people might have lots of friends. And while happiness changes instantly when a person breaks a bone or wins the lottery, number of friends does not. Number of friends may be vaguely related to happiness, but the two do not have a strong conceptual relationship, and the former really can't be taken as an indicator of the latter.

Good measures also have **reliability**, which is *the tendency for a measure to produce the same measurement whenever it is used to measure the same thing*. For example, if a person's facial muscles produced precisely the same electrical activity on

What are the three properties of a good measure?

measure A device that can detect the condition to which an operational definition refers.

electromyograph (EMG) A device that measures muscle contractions under the surface of a person's skin.

validity The extent to which a measurement and a property are conceptually related.

reliability The tendency for a measure to produce the same measurement whenever it is used to measure the same thing.

power The ability of a measure to detect the concrete conditions specified in the operational definition.

demand characteristics Those aspects of an observational setting that cause people to behave as they think they should.

naturalistic observation A technique for gathering scientific information by unobtrusively observing people in their natural environments.

two different occasions, then an EMG should produce precisely the same readings on those two occasions. If it produced different readings—that is, if it detected differences that did not actually exist—it would be unreliable. Similarly, good measures have **power**, which is *the ability of a measure to detect the concrete conditions specified in the operational definition.* If a person's facial muscles produced different amounts of electrical activity on two occasions, then an EMG should detect those differences and produce two different readings. If it produced the same reading—that is, if it failed to detect a difference that actually existed—then it would be powerless. Valid, reliable, and powerful measures consistently detect concrete conditions that are conceptually related to the property of interest when and only when those conditions actually exist (**FIGURE 2.2**).

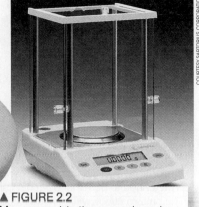

▲ **FIGURE 2.2**
Measures A bathroom scale and a laboratory balance both measure weight, but the balance is more likely to provide exactly the same measurement when it is used to weigh the same object twice (reliability) and more likely to provide different measurements when it is used to weigh two objects that differ by just a fraction of a gram (power). Not surprisingly, the bathroom scale sells for around $30 and the balance for around $3,000. Power and reliability don't come cheap.

Demand Characteristics

Once we have a valid, powerful, and reliable measure, then what do we do? The obvious answer is: Go measure something. But not so fast. Because people are reactive, measuring them can be tricky. While we are trying to measure how people behave, they may be trying to behave as they think we want them to or expect them to. **Demand characteristics** are *those aspects of an observational setting that cause people to behave as they think they should.* They are called demand characteristics because they seem to "demand" or require that people say and do things that they normally might not. When someone you love asks, "Do these jeans make me look fat?" the right answer is always no. If you've ever been asked this question, then you have experienced demand. Demand characteristics make it hard to measure behavior as it normally unfolds.

One way that psychologists avoid the problem of demand characteristics is by observing people without their knowledge. **Naturalistic observation** is *a technique*

How can demand characteristics be avoided?

for gathering information by unobtrusively observing people in their natural environments. For example, naturalistic observation has shown that the biggest groups leave the smallest tips in restaurants (Freeman et al., 1975), that hungry shoppers buy the most impulse items at the grocery store (Gilbert, Gill, & Wilson, 2002), that golfers are most likely to cheat when they play several opponents at once (Erffmeyer, 1984), that men do not usually approach the most beautiful woman at a singles' bar (Glenwick, Jason, & Elman, 1978), and that Olympic athletes smile more when they win the bronze rather than the silver medal (Medvec, Madey, & Gilovich, 1995). Each of these conclusions is the result of measurements

◄ This bar on 10th Avenue in New York City has a "one-way" mirror in its unisex restroom. Customers see their reflections in the restroom's mirror, and people who are walking down the street see the customers. Are the customers influenced by the fact that pedestrians may be watching them? Hard to say, but one observer did notice a suspiciously "high percentage of people who wash their hands" (Wolf, 2003).

CULTURE & COMMUNITY

Best place to fall on your face Robert Levine of California State University–Fresno sent his students to 23 large international cities for an observational study in the field. Their task was to observe helping behaviors in a naturalistic context. In two versions of the experiment, students pretended to be either blind or injured while trying to cross a street, while another student stood by to observe whether anyone would come to help. A third version involved a student dropping a pen to see if anyone would pick it up.

The results showed that people helped in all three events fairly evenly within cities, but there was a wide range of response between cities. Rio de Janeiro, Brazil, came out on top as the most helpful city in the study with an overall helping score of 93%. Kuala Lampur, Malaysia, came in last with a score of 40%, while New York City placed next to last with a score of 45%. On average, Latin American cities ranked as most helpful (Levine, Norenzayan, & Philbrick, 2001).

▲ When people feel anxious they tend to compress their lips involuntarily, as President Obama did during a difficult press conference in 2009. One way to avoid demand characteristics is to measure behaviors that people are unable or unlikely to control, such as facial expressions, blood pressure, reaction times, and so on.

made by psychologists who observed people who didn't know they were being observed. It seems unlikely that the same observations could have been made if the diners, shoppers, golfers, singles, and athletes had known that they were being scrutinized.

Unfortunately, naturalistic observation isn't always a viable solution to the problem of demand characteristics. First, some of the things psychologists want to observe simply don't occur naturally. For example, if we wanted to know whether people who have undergone sensory deprivation perform poorly on motor tasks, we would have to hang around the shopping mall for a very long time before a few dozen blindfolded people with earplugs just happened to wander by and start typing. Second, some of the things that psychologists want to observe can only be gathered from direct interaction with a person—for example, by administering a survey, giving tests, conducting an interview, or hooking someone up to a machine. If we wanted to know how often someone worried about dying, how accurately they could remember their high school graduation, how quickly they could solve a logic puzzle, or how much electrical activity their brain produced when they felt angry, then simply watching them from the bushes won't do.

Luckily, there are other ways to avoid demand characteristics. For instance, people are less likely to be influenced by demand characteristics when they cannot be identified as the originators of their actions, and psychologists often take advantage of this fact by allowing people to respond privately (e.g., by having them complete questionnaires when they are alone) or anonymously (e.g., by not collecting personal information, such as the person's name or address). Another technique that psychologists often use to avoid demand characteristics is to measure behaviors that are not susceptible to demand. For instance, a person's behavior can't be influenced by demand characteristics if that behavior isn't under the person's voluntary control. You may not want a psychologist to know that you are feeling sexually aroused, but you can't prevent your pupils from dilating, which is what they do when you experience arousal. Behaviors are also unlikely to be influenced by demand characteristics when people don't know that the demand and the behavior are related. For example, you may want a psychologist to believe that you are concentrating on a task, but you probably don't know that your blink rate slows when you are concentrating, thus you probably won't fake a slow blink.

One of the best ways to avoid demand characteristics is to keep the people who are being observed from knowing the true purpose of the observation. When people are "blind" to the purpose of an observation, they can't behave the way they think they should behave because they don't *know* how they should behave. For instance, if you didn't know

Why is it important for subjects to be "blind"?

that a psychologist was studying the effects of music on mood, you wouldn't feel obligated to smile when music was played. This is why psychologists typically don't reveal the true purpose of an observation to the people who are being observed until the study is over.

Of course, people are clever and curious, and when psychologists don't tell them the purpose of their observations, people generally try to figure it out for themselves. That's why psychologists sometimes use *cover stories,* or misleading explanations that are meant to keep people from discerning the true purpose of an observation. For example, if a psychologist wanted to know how music influenced your mood, he or she might falsely tell you that the purpose of the study was to determine how quickly people can do logic puzzles while music plays in the background. (We will discuss the ethical implications of deceiving people later in this chapter.) In addition, the psychologist might use *filler items,* or pointless measures that are designed to mislead you about the true purpose of the observation. So, for example, the psychologist might ask you a few questions whose answers are of real interest ("How happy are you right now?") as well as a few questions whose answers are not ("Do you like cats more or less than dogs?"). This makes it difficult for you to guess the true purpose of the observation from the nature of the questions you were asked.

Observer Bias

The people who are being observed aren't the only ones who can make measurement a bit tricky. When psychologists measure behavior, it is all too easy for them to see what they want to see or expect to see. This fact was demonstrated in a classic study

Why is it important for experimenters to be "blind"?

in which students in a psychology class were asked to measure the speed with which a rat learned to run through a maze (Rosenthal & Fode, 1963). Some students were told that their rat had been specially bred to be "maze-dull" (i.e., slow to learn a maze) and others were told that their rat had been specially bred to be "maze-bright" (i.e., quick to learn a maze). Although all the rats were actually the same breed, the students who *thought* they were measuring the speed of a maze-dull rat reported that their rats took longer to learn the maze than did the students who *thought* they were measuring the speed of a maze-bright rat. In other words, the measurements revealed precisely what the students expected them to reveal.

Why did this happen? First, *expectations can influence observations*. It is easy to make errors when measuring the speed of a rat, and expectations often determine the kinds of errors people make. Does putting one paw over the finish line count as "learning the maze"? If the rat falls asleep, should the stopwatch be left running or should the rat be awakened and given a second chance? If a rat runs a maze in 18.5 seconds, should that number be rounded up or rounded down before it is recorded in the log book? The answers to these questions may depend on whether one thinks the rat is bright or dull. The students who timed the rats probably tried to be honest, vigilant, fair, and objective, but their expectations influenced their observations in subtle ways that they could neither detect nor control. Second, *expectations can influence reality*. Students who expected their rats to learn quickly may have unknowingly done things to help that learning along—for example, by muttering, "Oh no!" when the bright rat looked the wrong direction or by petting the dull rat less affectionately. (We'll discuss these phenomena more extensively in Chapter 13.)

The New York Times

STOCK PRICES SLUMP $14,000,000,000 IN NATION-WIDE STAMPEDE TO UNLOAD; BANKERS TO SUPPORT MARKET TODAY

PREMIER ISSUES HARD HIT

Unexpected Torrent of Liquidation Again Rocks Markets.

DAY'S SALES 9,212,800

Nearly 3,000,000 Shares Are Traded In Final Hour—The Tickers Lag 167 Minutes.

NEW RALLY SOON BROKEN

Selling by Europeans and "Mob Psychology" Big Factors in Second Big Break.

◀ People's expectations can cause the phenomena they expect. In 1929, investors who expected the stock market to collapse sold their stocks and thereby caused the very crisis they feared. In this photo, panicked citizens stand outside the New York Stock Exchange the day after the crash, which the *New York Times* attributed to "mob psychology."

double-blind An observation whose true purpose is hidden from both the observer and the person being observed.

frequency distribution A graphical representation of measurements arranged by the number of times each measurement was made.

normal distribution A mathematically defined frequency distribution in which most measurements are concentrated around the middle.

mode The value of the most frequently observed measurement.

mean The average value of all the measurements.

median The value that is "in the middle"–i.e., greater than or equal to half the measurements and less than or equal to half the measurements.

Observers' expectations, then, can have a powerful influence on both their observations and on the behavior of those whom they observe. Psychologists use many techniques to avoid these influences, and one of the most common is the **double-blind** observation, which is *an observation whose true purpose is hidden from both the observer and the person being observed.* For example, if the students had not been told which rats were bright and which were dull, then they wouldn't have *had* any expectations about their rats, thus their expectations couldn't have influenced their measurements. That's why it is common practice in psychology to keep the observers as blind as the participants. For example, measurements are often made by research assistants who do not know what is being studied or why, and who thus don't have any expectations about what the people being observed will or should do. Indeed, many modern studies are carried out by the world's blindest experimenter—a computer—which can present information to people and measure their responses without having any expectations whatsoever.

Descriptions

You now know how to operationally define a property, how to design a valid, reliable, and powerful measure of that property, and how to use that measure while avoiding demand characteristics and observer bias. So where does that leave you? With a big page filled with numbers, and if you are like most people, a big page filled with numbers just doesn't seem very informative. Psychologists feel the same way, and that's why they have two techniques for making sense of big pages full of numbers: graphic representations and descriptive statistics.

Graphic Representations

If a picture is worth a thousand words, then it is worth ten thousand digits. As you'll learn in Chapter 4, vision is our most sophisticated sense, and human beings typically find it easier to understand things when they are represented visually than numerically or verbally. Psychologists are people too, and they often create graphic representations of the measurements they collect. The most common kind is the **frequency distribution**, which is *a graphic representation of measurements arranged by the number of times each measurement was made.* **FIGURE 2.3** shows a pair of frequency distributions that represent the hypothetical performances of a group of men and women who took a test of fine motor skill (i.e., the ability to manipulate things with their hands). Every possible test score is shown on the horizontal axis. The number of times (or the *frequency* with which) each score was observed is shown on the vertical axis. Although a frequency distribution can have any shape, a common shape is the *bell curve,* which is technically known as the *Gaussian distribution* or the **normal distribution**, which is *a mathematically defined frequency distribution in which most measurements are concentrated around the middle.* The mathematical definition of the normal distribution isn't important. (Well, to you anyway. To mathematicians it is more important than breathing.) What is important is what you can easily see for yourself: The normal distribution is symmetrical (i.e., the left half is a mirror image of the right half), has a peak in the middle, and trails off at both ends.

The picture in Figure 2.3 reveals in a single optical gulp what a page full of numbers never can. For instance, the shape of the distributions instantly tells you that most people have moderate motor skills, and that only a few have exceptionally good or exceptionally bad motor skills. You can also see that the distribution of men's scores is displaced a bit to the left of the distribution of women's scores, which instantly tells you that women tend to have somewhat better motor skills than men. And finally, you can see that the two distributions have a great deal of overlap, which tells you that although women tend to have better motor skills than men, there are still plenty of men who have better motor skills than plenty of women.

What is a frequency distribution?

▲ On average, men are taller than women, but there are still many women (like Katie Holmes) who are taller than many men (like her husband, Tom Cruise).

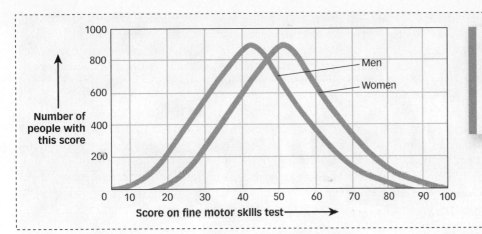

◀ FIGURE 2.3
Frequency Distributions This graph shows how a hypothetical group of men and women scored on a test of motor skill. Test scores are listed along the horizontal axis, and the frequency with which each score was obtained is represented along the vertical axis.

Descriptive Statistics

A frequency distribution depicts every measurement and thus provides a full and complete picture of those measurements. But sometimes a full and complete picture is just TMI.* When we ask a friend how she's been, we don't want her to show us a frequency distribution of her self-rated happiness on each day of the previous six months. We want a brief summary statement that captures the essential information that such a graph would provide—for example, "I'm doing pretty well," or, "I've been having some ups and downs lately." In psychology, brief summary statements that capture the essential information from a frequency distribution are called *descriptive statistics*. There are two important kinds of descriptive statistics: those that describe the *central tendency* of a frequency distribution and those that describe the *variability* in a frequency distribution.

What are the two major kinds of descriptive statistics?

Descriptions of *central tendency* are statements about the value of the measurements that *tend* to lie near the *center* or midpoint of the frequency distribution. When a friend says that she's been "doing pretty well," she is describing the central tendency (or approximate location of the midpoint) of the frequency distribution of her happiness. The three most common descriptions of central tendency are the **mode** (*the value of the most frequently observed measurement*), the **mean** (*the average value of all the measurements*), and the **median** (*the value that is "in the middle"– i.e., greater than or equal to half the measurements and less than or equal to half the measurements*). **FIGURE 2.4** shows how each of these descriptive statistics is calculated. When you hear a descriptive statistic such as "the average American college student sleeps 8.3 hours per day," you are hearing about the mean of a frequency distribution.

In a normal distribution, the mean, median, and mode all have the same value, but when the distribution is not normal, these three descriptive statistics can differ. For example, imagine that you measured the net worth of 40 college professors, and Bill Gates.

*Our publisher thinks you need a bunch of middle-aged professors to tell you this means "too much information," so there, we told you. LOL.

▼ FIGURE 2.4
Some Descriptive Statistics This frequency distribution shows the scores of 15 individuals on a seven-point test. Descriptive statistics include measures of central tendency (such as the mean, median, and mode) and measures of variability (such as the range and the standard deviation).

• Mode = 3 because there are five 3s and only three 2s, two 1s, two 4s, one 5, one 6, and one 7.

• Mean = 3.27 because (1 + 1 + 2 + 2 + 2 + 3 + 3 + 3 + 3 + 3 + 4 + 4 + 5 + 6 + 7)/15 = 3.27

• Median = 3 because 10 scores are ≥ 3 and 10 scores are ≤ 3

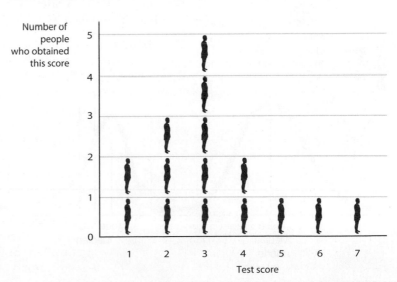

▶ When Bill Gates walks into a room he dramatically increases the mean income of the people in it, but doesn't much change the median, and does nothing to the mode. Microsoft is working on a fix for that.

The frequency distribution of your measurements would not be normal, but *positively skewed*. As you can see in **FIGURE 2.5**, the mode and the median of a positively skewed distribution are much lower than the mean because the mean is more strongly influenced by the value of a single extreme measurement (which, in case you've been sleeping for the last few years, would be the net worth of Bill Gates). When distributions become skewed, the mean gets dragged off toward the tail, the mode stays home at the hump, and the median goes to live between the two. When distributions are skewed, a single measure of central tendency can paint a misleading picture of the measurements. For example, the average net worth of the people you measured is probably about a billion dollars each, but that statement makes the college professors sound a whole lot richer than they are. You could provide a much better description of the net worth of the people you measured if you also mentioned that the median net worth is $300,000 and that the modal net worth is $288,000. Indeed, you should always be suspicious when you hear some new fact about "the average person" but don't hear anything about the shape of the frequency distribution.

Whereas descriptions of central tendency are statements about the location of the measurements in a frequency distribution, descriptions of variability are statements about the extent to which the measurements differ from each other. When a friend says that she has been "having some ups and downs lately," she is offering a brief summary statement that describes how measurements of her happiness taken at different times tend to differ from one another. The simplest

What are two measures of variability?

▼ FIGURE 2.5
Skewed Distributions When a frequency distribution is normal (a), the mean, median, and mode are all the same, but when it is positively skewed (b) or negatively skewed (c) these three measures of central tendency are quite different.

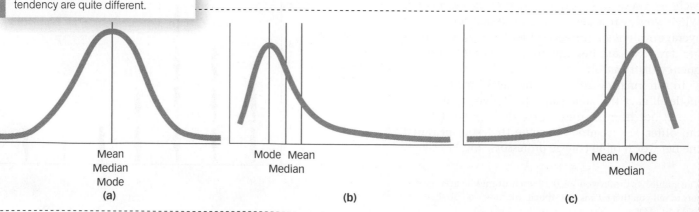

Mean	Mode Mean	Mean Mode
Median	Median	Median
Mode		
(a)	**(b)**	**(c)**

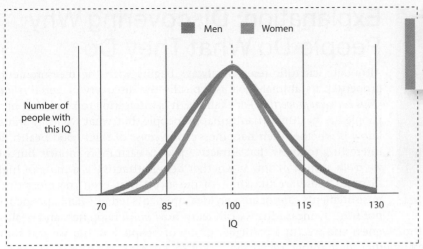

■ Men ■ Women

Number of people with this IQ

70   85   100   115   130

IQ

◄ FIGURE 2.6
IQ of Men and Women Men and women have the same average IQ, but men are more variable than women.

description of variability is the **range**, which is *the value of the largest measurement in a frequency distribution minus the value of the smallest measurement*. When the range is small, the measurements don't vary as much as when the range is large. The range is easy to compute, but like the mean it can be dramatically affected by a single measurement. If you said that the net worth of people you had measured ranged from $40,000 to $40,000,000,000, a listener might get the impression that these people were all remarkably different from each other when, in fact, they were all quite similar save for one rich guy from Seattle.

Other descriptions of variability aren't quite as susceptible to this problem. For example, the **standard deviation** is *a statistic that describes the average difference between the measurements in a frequency distribution and the mean of that distribution*. In other words, on average, how far are the measurements from the center of the distribution? As **FIGURE 2.6** shows, two frequency distributions can have the same mean, but very different ranges and standard deviations. For example, studies show that men and women have the same mean IQ, but that men have a larger range and standard deviation, which is to say that a man is more likely than a woman to be much more or much less intelligent than the average person of his or her own gender.

range The value of the largest measurement in a frequency distribution minus the value of the smallest measurement.

standard deviation A statistic that describes the average difference between the measurements in a frequency distribution and the mean of that distribution.

IN SUMMARY

○ Measurement involves defining a property in terms of a concrete condition, and then constructing a measure that can detect that condition. A good measure is valid (the concrete conditions it measures are conceptually related to the property of interest), is reliable (it produces the same measurement whenever it is used to measure the same thing), and is powerful (it can detect the concrete conditions when they actually exist).

○ When people know they are being observed, they may behave as they think they should. Demand characteristics are features of a setting that suggest to people that they should behave in a particular way. Psychologists try to reduce or eliminate demand characteristics by observing participants in their natural habitats or by hiding their expectations from the participant. Observer bias is the tendency for observers to see what they expect to see or cause others to behave as they expect them to behave. Psychologists try to eliminate observe bias by making double-blind observations.

○ Psychologists often describe the measurements they make with a graphic representation called a frequency distribution, which often has a special shape known as the normal distribution. They also describe their measurements with descriptive statistics, the most common of which are descriptions of central tendency (such as the mean, median, and mode) and descriptions of variability (such as the range and the standard deviation).

▲ It doesn't hurt to be a redhead—or does it? In fact, studies show that redheads are more sensitive to pain than are brunettes or blondes. Does red hair cause pain sensitivity? Does pain sensitivity cause red hair? We'll give you the answer in a few pages. (Now you have something to live for.)

Explanation: Discovering Why People Do What They Do

Although scientific research always begins with the measurement of properties, its ultimate goal is typically the discovery of *causal relationships between properties*. For example, it is interesting to know that happy people are healthier than unhappy people, but what we *really* want to know is whether their happiness is the *cause* of their good health. It is interesting to know that attractive people earn more money, but what we *really* want to know is whether being attractive is a *cause* of higher income. These are the kinds of questions that even the most careful measurements cannot answer. Measurements tell us *what* happened, but not *why*. By measuring we can learn how *much* happiness and health or attractiveness and wealth a particular group of people has, but we still cannot tell whether these things are related, and if so, whether one causes the other.

As you are about to see, scientists have developed some clever ways of using their measurements to answer these questions. In the first section (Correlation) we'll examine techniques that can tell us whether two things are related. In the second section (Causation), we'll examine techniques that can tell us whether the relationship between two things is causal. In the third section (Drawing Conclusions) we'll see what kinds of conclusions these techniques do—and do not—allow us to draw.

Correlation

If you insult someone, they probably won't give you the time of day. If you have any doubt about this, you can demonstrate it by standing on a street corner, insulting a few people as they walk by ("Hello there, stupid ugly freak . . ."), not insulting others ("Hello there, Sir or Madam . . ."), and then asking everyone for the time of day (". . . could you please tell me what time it is?"). If you did this, the results of your investigation would probably look a lot like those shown in **TABLE 2.1**. Specifically, every person who was not insulted would give you the time of day, and every person who was insulted would refuse. Results such as these would probably convince you that being insulted *causes* people to refuse requests from the people who insulted them. You would conclude that two events—being insulted by someone and refusing to do that person a favor—have a causal relationship. But on what basis did you draw that conclusion? How did you manage to use measurement to tell you not only about *how much* insulting and refusing had occurred, but also about the *relationship* between insulting and refusing?

Patterns of Variation

Measurements can only tell us about properties of objects and events, but we can learn about the relationships between objects and events by comparing the *patterns of variation in a series of measurements*. When you performed your imaginary study of insults and requests, you did three things:

How can we tell if two variables are correlated?

> First, you measured a pair of **variables**, which are *properties whose values can vary across individuals or over time*. (When you took your first algebra course you were probably horrified to learn that everything you'd been taught in grade school about

TABLE 2.1

Hypothetical Data of the Relationship between Insults and Favors		
Participant	**Treatment**	**Response**
1	Insulted	Refused
2	Insulted	Refused
3	Not insulted	Agreed
4	Not insulted	Agreed
5	Insulted	Refused
6	Insulted	Refused
7	Not insulted	Agreed
8	Not insulted	Agreed
9	Insulted	Refused
10	Insulted	Refused
11	Not insulted	Agreed
12	Not insulted	Agreed
13	Insulted	Refused
14	Insulted	Refused
15	Not insulted	Agreed
16	Not insulted	Agreed
17	Insulted	Refused
18	Insulted	Refused
19	Not insulted	Agreed
20	Not insulted	Agreed

the distinction between letters and numbers was a lie, that mathematical equations could contain *X*s and *Y*s as well as 7s and 4s, and that the letters are called *variables* because they can have different values under different circumstances. Same idea here.) You measured one variable whose value could vary from *not insulted* to *insulted,* and you measured a second variable whose value could vary from *refused* to *agreed.*

> Second, you did this again. And then again. And then again. That is, you made a *series* of measurements rather than making just one.

> Third and finally, you tried to discern a pattern in your series of measurements. If you look at the second column of Table 2.1, you will see that it contains values that vary as your eyes move down the column. That column has a particular *pattern of variation.* If you compare the third column with the second, you will notice that the patterns of variation in the two columns are synchronized. This synchrony is known as a *pattern of covariation* or a **correlation** (as in "co-relation"). Two variables are said to "covary" or to "be correlated" when *variations in the value of one variable are synchronized with variations in the value of the other.* As the table shows, whenever the value in the second column varies from *not insulted* to *insulted,* the value in the third column varies from *agreed* to *refused.*

By looking for synchronized patterns of variation, we can use measurement to discover the relationships between variables. Indeed, this is the only way anyone has *ever* discovered the relationship between variables, which is why most of the facts you know about the world can be thought of as correlations. For example, you know that adults are generally taller than children, but this is just a shorthand way of saying that as the value of *age* varies from *young* to *old,* the value of *height* varies from *short* to *tall.* You know that people who eat a pound of spinach every day generally live longer than people who eat a pound of bacon every day, but this is just a shorthand way of saying that as the value of *daily food intake* varies from *spinach* to *bacon,* the value of *longevity* varies from *high* to *low.* As these statements suggest, correlations are the fundamental building blocks of knowledge.

variable A property whose value can vary across individuals or over time.

correlation Two variables are said to "be correlated" when variations in the value of one variable are synchronized with variations in the value of the other.

◄ When children line up by age, they also tend to line up by height. The pattern of variation in age (from youngest to oldest) is synchronized with the pattern of variation in height (from shortest to tallest).

PETER TURNLEY/CORBIS

Correlations not only describe the past, but also allow us to predict the future. Given the correlation between diet and longevity, can you predict how long a person will live if she eats a pound of bacon every day? Answer: probably not as long as she would have lived if she'd instead eaten a pound of spinach every day. Given the correlation between height and age, can you predict how tall Walter will be on his next birthday? Answer: probably taller if he is turning 21 than if he is turning 2. As you can see, when two variables are correlated, knowledge of the value of one variable (diet or age) allows us to make predictions about the value of the other variable (longevity or height).

Every correlation can be described in two equally reasonable ways. A positive correlation describes a relationship between two variables in "more-more" or "less-less" terms. When we say that *more spinach* is associated with *more longevity* or that *less spinach* is associated with *less longevity,* we are describing a positive correlation. A negative correlation describes a relationship between two variables in "more-less" or "less-more" terms. When we say that *more bacon* is associated with *less longevity* or that *less bacon* is associated with *more longevity,* we are describing a negative correlation. How we choose to describe any particular correlation is usually just a matter of simplicity and convenience.

What's the difference between a positive and a negative correlation?

correlation coefficient A measure of the direction and strength of a correlation, which is signified by the letter *r*.

Measuring Correlation

The hypothetical variables shown in Table 2.1 are perfectly correlated; that is, each and every time *not insulted* changes to *insulted, agreed* also changes to *refused,* and there are no exceptions to this rule. This perfect correlation allows you to make an extremely confident prediction about how pedestrians will respond to a request after being insulted. But perfect correlations are so rare in everyday life that we had to make up a hypothetical study just to show you one. There really *is* a correlation between age and height, and if we predict that a child will be shorter than an adult we will be right more often than we are wrong. But we *will* be wrong in some instances because there are *some* tall kids and *some* short adults. So how much confidence should we have in predictions based on correlations?

Statisticians have developed a way to estimate just how accurate a particular prediction is likely to be by measuring the *strength* of the correlation on which it is based. The **correlation coefficient** is *a measure of the direction and strength of a correlation,* and

> How can correlations be measured?

it is symbolized by the letter *r* (as in "relationship"). Like most measures, the correlation coefficient has a limited range. What does that mean? Well, if you were to measure the number of hours of sunshine per day in your hometown, that number could range from 0 to 24. Numbers such as –7 and 36.8 would be meaningless. Similarly, the value of *r* can range from –1 to 1, and numbers outside that range are meaningless. What, then, do the numbers *inside* that range mean?

> ❯ If every time the value of one variable increases by a fixed amount the value of the second variable also increases by a fixed amount, then the relationship between the variables is called a *perfect positive correlation* and *r* = 1. For example, if every increase in age of 1 year were associated with an increase in height of .3 inches, then age and height would be *perfectly positively correlated.*

> ❯ If every time the value of one variable increases by a fixed amount the value of the second variable *decreases* by a fixed amount, then the relationship between the variables is called a *perfect negative correlation* and *r* = −1. For example, if every increase in age of 1 year were associated with a decrease in height of .3 units, then age and height would be *perfectly negatively correlated.*

> ❯ If every time the value of one variable increases by a fixed amount the value of the second variable does not increase or decrease systematically, then the two variables are said to be *uncorrelated* and *r* = 0. For example, if increases in age of 1 year were sometimes associated with increases in height, were sometimes associated with decreases in height, and were sometimes associated with no change in height, then age and height would be uncorrelated.

The correlations shown in **FIGURE 2.7a** and **b** are illustrations of perfect correlations—that is, they show patterns of variation that are perfectly synchronized and

▼ FIGURE 2.7

Three Kinds of Correlations This figure illustrates pairs of variables that have (a) a perfect positive correlation (*r* = +1), (b) a perfect negative correlation (*r* = −1), and (c) no correlation (*r* = 0).

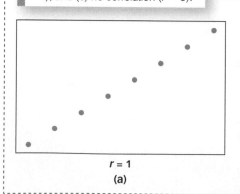

r = 1

(a)

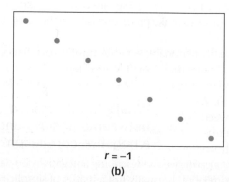

r = −1

(b)

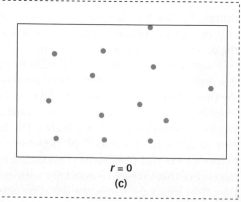

r = 0

(c)

without exceptions. Such correlations are extremely rare in real life. It may be true that the older you are the taller you tend to be, but it's not as though height increases exactly .3 inches for every year you live. Age and height are *positively* correlated (i.e., as one increases, the other also increases), but they are also *imperfectly* correlated, thus *r* will lie somewhere between 0 and 1. But where? That depends on how many exceptions there are to the "*X* more years = *Y* more inches" rule. If there are just a few exceptions, then *r* will be much closer to 1 than to 0. But as the number of exceptions increases, then the value of *r* will begin to move toward 0.

What does it mean for a correlation to be strong?

FIGURE 2.8 shows four cases in which two variables are positively correlated but have different numbers of exceptions, and as you can see, the number of exceptions changes the value of *r* quite dramatically. Two variables can have a perfect correlation (*r* = 1), a strong correlation (for example, *r* = .90), a moderate correlation (for example, *r* = .70), or a weak correlation (for example, *r* = .30). The correlation coefficient, then, is a measure of both the *direction* and *strength* of the relationship between two variables. The sign of *r* (plus or minus) tells us the direction of the relationship and the absolute value of *r* (between 0 and 1) tells us about the number of exceptions and hence about how confident we can be when using the correlation to make predictions.

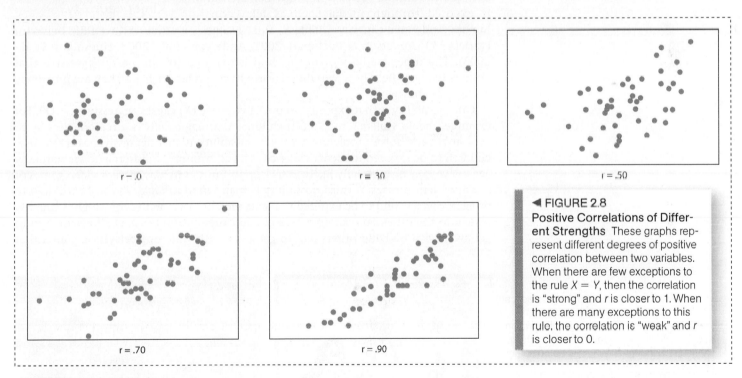

◀ FIGURE 2.8
Positive Correlations of Different Strengths These graphs represent different degrees of positive correlation between two variables. When there are few exceptions to the rule *X* = *Y*, then the correlation is "strong" and *r* is closer to 1. When there are many exceptions to this rule, the correlation is "weak" and *r* is closer to 0.

Causation

If you watched a cartoon in which a moving block collided with a stationary block, which then went careening off the screen, your brain would instantly make a very reasonable assumption, namely, that the moving block was the *cause* of the stationary block's motion (Heider & Simmel, 1944; Michotte, 1963). In fact, studies show that infants make such assumptions long before they have had a chance to learn anything about cartoons, blocks, collisions, or causality (Oakes & Cohen, 1990). For human beings, detecting causes and effects is as natural as sucking, sleeping, pooping, and howling, which is what led the philosopher Immanuel Kant (1781/1965) to suggest that people come into the world with cause-detectors built into their brains.

natural correlation A correlation observed in the world around us.

third-variable correlation The fact that two variables are correlated only because each is causally related to a third variable.

matched samples A technique whereby the participants in two groups are identical in terms of a third variable.

But those cause-detectors don't work perfectly. Sometimes we see causal relationships that don't actually exist: For centuries, people held superstitious beliefs such as "solar eclipses cause birth defects" or "human sacrifices bring rain," and in fact, many still do. Just as we see causal relationships that don't exist, we sometimes fail to see causal relationships that do exist: It is only in the past century or so that surgeons have made it a practice to wash their hands before operating because before that, no one seemed to notice that dirty hands caused infections. Because our built-in cause-detectors are imperfect, we need a scientific method for discovering causal relationships. As you'll see, we've got one. But before learning about it, let's explore a bit more the problem it is meant to solve.

The Third-Variable Problem

We observe correlations all the time—between automobiles and pollution, between bacon and heart attacks, between sex and pregnancy. **Natural correlations** are *the correlations we observe in the world around us,* and although such observations can tell us *whether* two variables have a relationship, they cannot tell us what *kind* of relationship these variables have. For example, many studies have found a positive correlation between the amount of violence to which a child is exposed through media such as television, movies, and video games (variable X) and the aggressiveness of the child's behavior (variable Y) (Anderson & Bushman, 2001; Anderson et al., 2003; Huesmann et al., 2003). The more media violence a child is exposed to, the more aggressive that child is likely to be. These variables clearly have a relationship—they are positively correlated—but why?

Why can't we use natural correlations to infer causality?

One possibility is that exposure to media violence (X) causes aggressiveness (Y). For example, media violence may teach children that aggression is a reasonable way to vent anger and solve problems. A second possibility is that aggressiveness (Y) causes children to be exposed to media violence (X). For example, children who are naturally aggressive may be especially likely to seek opportunities to play violent video games or watch violent movies. A third possibility is that a *third variable* (Z) causes children to be aggressive (Y) and to be exposed to media violence (X), neither of which is causally related to the other. For example, lack of adult supervision (Z) may allow children to get away with bullying others and to get away with watching television shows that

▶ It isn't always easy to accurately detect causal relationships. For centuries, people sacrificed their enemies without realizing that doing so doesn't actually cause rain, and they smoked cigarettes without realizing that doing so actually does cause illness.

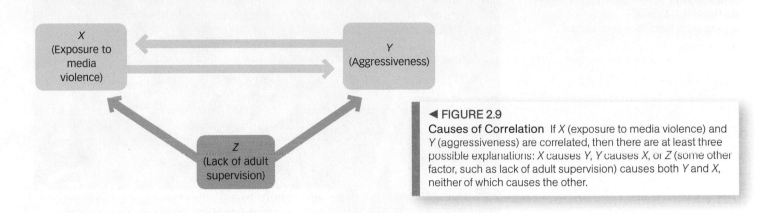

◄ FIGURE 2.9
Causes of Correlation If X (exposure to media violence) and Y (aggressiveness) are correlated, then there are at least three possible explanations: X causes Y, Y causes X, or Z (some other factor, such as lack of adult supervision) causes both Y and X, neither of which causes the other.

adults would normally not allow. If so, then being exposed to media violence (X) and behaving aggressively (Y) may not be causally related to each other at all and may instead be the independent effects of a lack of adult supervision (Z). In other words, the relation between aggressiveness and exposure to media violence may be a case of **third-variable correlation**, which means that *two variables are correlated only because each is causally related to a third variable.* **FIGURE 2.9** shows three possible causes of any correlation.

What is third-variable correlation?

How can we determine by simple observation which of these three possibilities best describes the relationship between exposure to media violence and aggressiveness? Take a deep breath. The answer is: *We can't.* When we observe a natural correlation, the possibility of third-variable correlation can never be dismissed. Don't take this claim on faith. Let's try to dismiss the possibility of third-variable correlation and you'll see why such efforts are always doomed to fail.

The most straightforward way to determine whether a third variable, such as lack of adult supervision (Z), causes exposure to media violence (X) and aggressive behavior (Y) is to eliminate differences in adult supervision (Z) among a group of children and see if the correlation between exposure (X) and aggressiveness (Y) is eliminated too. For example, we could observe children using the **matched samples technique**, which is *a technique whereby the participants in two groups are identical in terms of a third variable.* (See **FIGURE 2.10**.) For instance, we could measure only children who are supervised by an adult exactly X% of the time, thus ensuring that every child who was

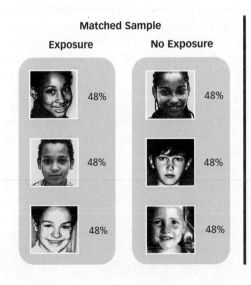

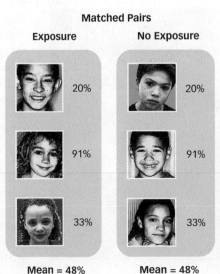

◄ FIGURE 2.10
Matched Sample and Pairs Both the matched samples technique (a) and the matched pairs technique (b) ensure that children in the Exposure and No Exposure groups have the same amount of adult supervision on average, and thus any differences we observe between the groups can't be due to differences in adult supervision.

matched pairs A technique whereby each participant is identical to one other participant in terms of a third variable.

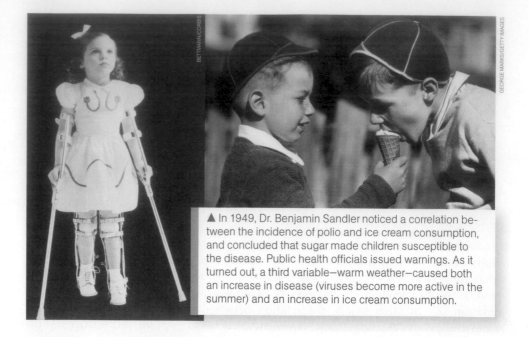

▲ In 1949, Dr. Benjamin Sandler noticed a correlation between the incidence of polio and ice cream consumption, and concluded that sugar made children susceptible to the disease. Public health officials issued warnings. As it turned out, a third variable—warm weather—caused both an increase in disease (viruses become more active in the summer) and an increase in ice cream consumption.

exposed to media violence had exactly the same amount of adult supervision as every child who was not exposed. Alternatively, we could observe children using the **matched pairs technique**, which is *a technique whereby each participant is identical to one other participant in terms of a third variable*. We could measure children who have different amounts of adult supervision, but we could make sure that for every child we measure who is exposed to media violence and is supervised X or Y% of the time, we also observe a child who is not exposed to media violence and is supervised X or Y% of the time, thus ensuring that children who are and are not exposed to media violence have the same amount of adult supervision *on average*. Regardless of which technique we used, we would know that children who were and were not exposed had equal amounts of adult supervision on average. So if those who were exposed are on average more aggressive than those who were not exposed, we can be sure that lack of adult supervision was not the cause of this difference.

What's the difference between matched samples and matched pairs?

Although both the matched samples and matched pairs techniques can be useful, neither eliminates the possibility of third-variable correlation entirely. Why? Because even if we used these techniques to dismiss a *particular* third variable (such as lack of adult supervision), we would not be able to dismiss *all* third variables. For example, as soon as we finished making these observations, it might suddenly occur to us that emotional instability (Z) could cause children to gravitate toward violent television or video games (X) and to behave aggressively (Y). Emotional instability would be a new third variable and we would have to design a new test to investigate whether it explains the correlation between exposure and aggression. Unfortunately, we could keep dreaming up new third variables all day long without ever breaking a sweat, and every time we dreamed one up, we would have to rush out and do a new test using matched samples or matched pairs to determine

▼ Here's the answer you've been waiting for. Redheads are especially sensitive to pain because a mutation in the MCR-1 gene causes both pain sensitivity and red hair.

whether *this* third variable was the cause of the correlation between exposure and aggressiveness.

Are you starting to see the problem? Because there are an infinite number of third variables, there are an infinite number of reasons why X and Y might be correlated. And because we can't perform an infinite number of studies with matched samples or matched pairs, we can never be absolutely sure that the correlation we observe between X and Y is evidence of a causal relationship between them. The **third-variable problem** refers to the fact that *a causal relationship between two variables cannot be inferred from the naturally occurring correlation between them because of the ever-present possibility of third-variable correlation.* In other words, if we care about causality, then naturally occurring correlations just won't tell us what we really want to know. But there is a technique that will!

Experimentation

The matched pairs and matched samples techniques eliminate a single difference between two groups—for example, the difference in adult supervision between groups of children who were and were not exposed to media violence. The problem is they only eliminate one difference and countless others remain.

What are the two main features of an experiment?

If we could just find a technique that eliminated *all* of these countless differences then we *could* conclude that exposure and aggression are causally related. If exposed kids were more aggressive than unexposed kids, and if the two groups didn't differ in *any* way except for that exposure, then we could be sure that their level of exposure had caused their level of aggression.

In fact, scientists have a technique that does exactly that. It is called an **experiment**, which is *a technique for establishing the causal relationship between variables.* The best way to understand how experiments eliminate the countless differences between groups is by examining their two key features: *manipulation* and *random assignment.*

Manipulation

The most important thing to know about experiments is that you already know the most important thing about experiments because you've been doing them all your life. Imagine that you are surfing the web on a laptop when all of a sudden you lose your wireless connection. You suspect that another device—say, your roommate's new cell phone—has somehow bumped you off the network. What would you do to test your suspicion? Observing a natural correlation wouldn't be much help. You could carefully note when you did and didn't have a connection and when your roommate did and didn't use his cell phone, but even if you observed a correlation between these two variables you still couldn't conclude that the cell phone was *causing* your connection to fail. After all, if your roommate was afraid of loud noises and called his mommy for comfort whenever there was an electrical storm, and if that storm somehow zapped your wireless connection, then the storm (Z) would be the cause of both your roommate's cell phone usage (X) and your connectivity problem (Y).

◀ Experiments are the best way to establish causal relationships—and to win the Nobel Prize, as Dr. Elizabeth Blackburn did in 2009 for her discovery of how chromosomes protect themselves during cell division.

third-variable problem The fact that a causal relationship between two variables cannot be inferred from the naturally occurring correlation between them because of the ever-present possibility of third-variable correlation.

experiment A technique for establishing the causal relationship between variables.

▲ How do you determine whether eating 60 hotdogs will make you sick? You eat them one day, don't eat them the next day, and then see which day you barf. *That's* manipulation! BTW, world champion Joey Chestnut ate 60 hot dogs in 12 minutes by folding them up. *That's* manipulation too!

AP PHOTO/HENNY RAY ABRAMS

manipulation The creation of an artificial pattern of variation in a variable in order to determine its causal powers.

independent variable The variable that is manipulated in an experiment.

experimental group The group of people who are treated in a particular way, as compared to the control group, in an experiment.

control group The group of people who are not treated in the particular way that the experimental group is treated in an experiment.

dependent variable The variable that is measured in a study.

self-selection A problem that occurs when anything about a person determines whether he or she will be included in the experimental or control group.

So how could you test your suspicion? Well, rather than *observing* the correlation between cell phone usage and connectivity, you could try to *create* a correlation by intentionally making a call on your roommate's cell phone, hanging up, making another call, hanging up again, and observing changes in your laptop's connectivity as you did so. If you observed that "connection off" only occurred in conjunction with "cell phone on" then you could conclude that your roommate's cell phone was the *cause* of your failed connection, and you could sell the phone on eBay and then lie about it when asked. The technique you intuitively used to solve the third-variable problem in this case was an experiment, and it included one of the hallmarks of experimentation—**manipulation**—which is *the creation of an artificial pattern of variation in a variable in order to determine its causal powers.*

Manipulation is a critical ingredient in an experiment. Up until now, we have approached science like polite dinner guests, taking what we were offered and making the best of it. Nature offered us children who differed in how much violence they were exposed to and who differed in how aggressively they behaved, and we dutifully measured the natural patterns of variation in these two variables and computed their correlations. The problem with this approach is that when all was said and done, we still didn't know what we really wanted to know, namely, whether these variables had a causal relationship. No matter how many matched samples or matched pairs we observed, there was always another third variable that we hadn't yet dismissed. Experiments solve this problem. Rather than *measuring* exposure and *measuring* aggression and then computing the correlation between these two naturally occurring variables, experiments require that we *manipulate* exposure in exactly the same way that you manipulated your roommate's cell phone. In essence, we need to systematically switch exposure on and off in a group of children and then watch to see whether aggression goes on and off too.

There are many ways to do this. For example, we might ask some children to participate in an experiment, then have half of them play violent video games for an hour and make sure the other half does not (see **FIGURE 2.11**). At the end of the study we could measure the children's aggression and compare the measurements across the two groups. When we compared these measurements, we would essentially be computing the correlation between a variable that we manipulated (exposure) and a variable that we measured (aggression). Because we *manipulated* rather than *measured* exposure, we would never have to ask whether a third variable (such as lack of adult supervision) caused kids to experience different levels of exposure. After all, we already *know* what caused that to happen. *We* did!

Doing an experiment, then, involves three critical steps (and several technical terms):

> First, we perform a manipulation. We call *the variable that is manipulated* the **independent variable** because it is under our control, and thus it is "independent" of what the participant says or does. When we manipulate an independent variable (such as exposure to media violence), we create at least two groups of participants: an **experimental group**, which is *the group of people who are treated in a particular way,* such as being exposed to media violence, and a **control group**, which is *the group of people who are not treated in this particular way.*

> Second, having manipulated one variable (exposure), we now measure the other variable (aggression). We call *the variable that is measured* the **dependent variable** because its value "depends" on what the person being measured says or does.

> Third and finally, we check to see whether our manipulation produced changes in the variable we measured.

What are the three main steps in doing an experiment?

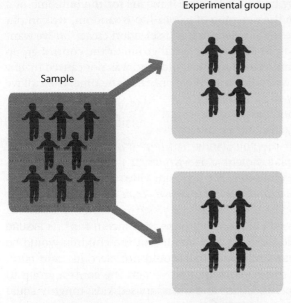

Experimental group

Exposed to media violence?	Aggression
Yes	High
Yes	High
Yes	High
Yes	High

Exposed to media violence?	Aggression
No	Low
No	Low
No	Low
No	Low

Sample

Control group

◄ FIGURE 2.11
Manipulation The independent variable is exposure to media violence and the dependent variable is aggression. Manipulation of the independent variable results in an experimental group and a control group. When we compare the behavior of participants in these two groups, we are actually computing the correlation between the independent variable and the dependent variable.

Random Assignment

When we have manipulated an independent variable and measured a dependent variable, we've done one of the two things that experimentation requires. The second thing is a little less intuitive but equally important.

Imagine that we began our exposure and aggression experiment by finding a group of children and asking each child whether he or she would like to be in the experimental group or the control group. Imagine that half the children said that they'd like to play violent video games and the other half said they would rather not. Imagine that we let the children do what they wanted to do, measured aggression some time later, and found that the children who had played the violent video games were more aggressive than those who had not. Would this experiment allow us to conclude that playing violent video games causes aggression? Definitely not. But *why* not? After all, we switched exposure on and off like a cell phone, and we watched to see whether aggression went on and off too. So where did we go wrong?

We went wrong when we let the children decide for themselves whether or not they would play violent video games. After all, children who ask to play such games are probably different in many ways from those who ask not to. They may be older, or stronger, or smarter. Or younger, or weaker, or dumber. Or less often supervised or more often supervised. The list of possible differences goes on and on. The whole point of doing an experiment was to divide children into two groups that differed *in only one way,* namely, in terms of their exposure to media violence. The moment we allowed the children to select their own groups, the two groups differed in countless ways, and any of those countless differences could have been a third variable that was responsible for any differences we observed in their measured aggression. **Self-selection** is *a problem that occurs when anything about a person determines whether he or she will be included in the experimental or control group.* Just as we cannot allow nature to decide which of the children in our study is exposed to media violence, we cannot allow the children to decide either. Okay, then who decides?

The answer to this question is a bit spooky: *No one does.* If we want to be sure that there is one and only one difference between the children who are and are not exposed to media violence, then their inclusion in these groups must be *randomly determined.* If you flipped a coin and a friend asked what had *caused* it to land heads up, you

Why can't we allow people to select the condition of the experiment in which they will participate?

▼ There is no evidence that Louise Hay's techniques can cure cancer. But even if cancer victims who bought her books *did* show a higher rate of remission than those who didn't, there would *still* be no evidence because buyers are self-selected and thus may differ from non-buyers in countless ways.

JETTA PRODUCTIONS/GETTY IMAGES

▲ Do strawberries taste better when dipped in chocolate? If you dip the big juicy ones and don't dip the small dry ones, then you won't know if the chocolate is what made the difference. But if you randomly assign some to be dipped and others not to be dipped, and if the dipped ones taste better on average, then you will have demonstrated scientifically what every 3-year-old already knows.

would correctly say that *nothing* had. This is what it means for the outcome of a coin flip to be random. Because the outcome of a coin flip is random, we can put coin flips to work for us to solve the problem that self-selection creates. If we want to be sure that a child's inclusion in the experimental group or the control group was not caused by nature, was not caused by the child, and was not caused by *any* of the countless third variables we could name if we only had the time, then all we have to do is let it be caused by the outcome of a coin flip—which itself has no cause! For example, we could walk up to each child in our experiment, flip a coin, and, if the coin lands

Why is random assignment so useful and important?

heads up, assign the child to play violent video games. If the coin lands heads down, then we could assign the child to play no violent video games. **Random assignment** is *a procedure that uses a random event to assign people to the experimental or control group.*

What would happen if we assigned children to groups with a coin flip? As **FIGURE 2.12** shows, the first thing we would expect is that about half the children would be assigned to play violent video games and about half would not. Second—and *much more important*—we could expect the experimental group and the control group to have roughly equal numbers of supervised kids and unsupervised kids, roughly equal numbers of emotionally stable and unstable kids, roughly equal numbers of big kids and small kids, of active kids, fat kids, tall kids, funny kids, and kids with blue hair named Larry who can't stand to eat spinach. In other words, we could expect the two groups to have roughly equal numbers of kids who are anything-you-can-ever-name-and-everything-you-can't! Because the kids in the two groups will be the same *on average* in terms of height, weight, emotional stability, adult supervision, and every other variable in the known universe *except the one we manipulated*, we can be sure that the variable we manipulated (exposure) caused any changes in the variable we measured (aggression). Because exposure was the *only* difference between the two groups of children when we started the experiment, it *must* be the cause of any differences in aggression we observe at the end of the experiment.

Significance

random assignment A procedure that uses a random event to assign people to the experimental or control group.

Random assignment is a powerful tool, but like a lot of tools, it doesn't work every time you use it. If we randomly assigned children to watch or not watch televised violence, we could expect the two groups to have roughly equal numbers of supervised

▶ **FIGURE 2.12**
Random Assignment
Children with adult supervision are shown in orange and those without adult supervision are shown in blue. The independent variable is exposure to media violence and the dependent variable is aggression. Random assignment ensures that participants in the experimental and the control groups are on average equal in terms of all possible third variables. In essence, it ensures that there is no correlation between a third variable and the dependent variable.

Sample

Experimental group

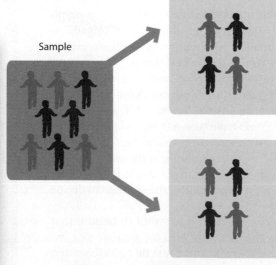

Exposed to media violence?	Adult supervision?	Aggression
Yes	Yes	High
Yes	No	High
Yes	Yes	High
Yes	No	High

Exposed to media violence?	Adult supervision?	Aggression
No	Yes	Low
No	No	Low
No	Yes	Low
No	No	Low

Control group

and unsupervised kids, rich kids and poor kids, tall kids and short kids, and so on. The key word in that sentence is *roughly*. When you flip a coin 100 times, you can expect it to land heads up *roughly* 50 times. But every once in a while, 100 coin flips will produce 80 heads, or 90 heads, or even 100 heads, by sheer chance alone. This does not happen often, of course, but it does happen. Because random assignment is achieved by using a randomizing device such as a coin, every once in a long while the coin will assign more unsupervised, emotionally disturbed kids to play violent video games and more supervised, emotionally undisturbed kids to play none. When this happens, random assignment has failed—and when random assignment fails, the third-variable problem rises up out of its grave like a guy with a hockey mask and a grudge. When random assignment fails, we cannot conclude that there is a causal relationship between the independent and dependent variables.

How can we tell when random assignment has failed? Unfortunately, we can't tell for sure. But we can calculate the *odds* that random assignment has failed each time we use it. It isn't important for you to know how to do this calculation, but it is important for you to understand how psychologists interpret its results. Psychologists perform this calculation every time they do an experiment, and they do not accept the results

▲ Some things just won't stay dead. Jason is one example. The third-variable problem is another.

THE REAL WORLD

Oddsly Enough

A recent Gallup survey found that 53% of college graduates believe in extrasensory perception, or ESP. Very few psychologists share that belief. What makes them such a skeptical lot is their understanding of the laws of probability.

Consider the case of The Truly Amazing Coincidence. One night you dream that a panda is piloting an airplane over the Indian Ocean, and the next day you tell a friend, who says, "Wow, I had exactly the same dream!" One morning you wake up humming an old Radiohead tune (probably "Paranoid Android") and an hour later you hear it playing in the mall. You and your roommate are sitting around watching television when suddenly you turn to each other and say in perfect unison, "Want pizza?" Coincidences like these might make anyone believe in supernatural mental weirdness.

Well, not anyone. The Nobel laureate Luis Alverez was reading the newspaper one day and a particular story got him thinking about an old college friend whom he hadn't seen in years. A few minutes later, he turned the page and was shocked to see the very same friend's obituary. But before concluding that he had an acute case of ESP, Alvarez decided to use probability theory to determine just how amazing this coincidence really was.

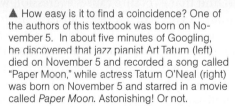

▲ How easy is it to find a coincidence? One of the authors of this textbook was born on November 5. In about five minutes of Googling, he discovered that jazz pianist Art Tatum (left) died on November 5 and recorded a song called "Paper Moon," while actress Tatum O'Neal (right) was born on November 5 and starred in a movie called *Paper Moon*. Astonishing! Or not.

First he estimated the number of friends an average person has, and then he estimated how often an average person thinks about each of those friends. With these estimates in hand, he did a few simple calculations and determined the likelihood that someone would think about a friend five minutes before learning about that friend's death. The odds were astonishing. In a country the size of the United States, for example, Alvarez predicted that this amazing coincidence should happen to 10 people every day (Alvarez, 1965). Another

Nobel laureate disagreed. He put the number closer to 80 people a day (Charpak & Broch, 2004)!

"In 10 years there are 5 million minutes," says statistics professor Irving Jack. "That means each person has plenty of opportunity to have some remarkable coincidences in his life" (Neimark, 2004). For example, 250 million Americans dream for about two hours every night (that's a half billion hours of dreaming!), so it isn't surprising that two people sometimes have the same dream, or that we sometimes dream about something that actually happens the next day. As mathematics professor John Allen Paulos put it, "In reality, the most astonishingly incredible coincidence imaginable would be the complete absence of all coincidence."

If all of this seems surprising to you, then you are not alone. Research shows that people routinely underestimate the likelihood of coincidences happening by chance (Diaconis & Mosteller, 1989; Falk & McGregor, 1983; Hintzman, Asher, & Stern, 1978). If you want to profit from this fact, assemble a group of 24 or more people and bet anyone that at least two of the people share a birthday. The odds are in your favor, and the bigger the group, the better the odds. In fact, in a group of 35, the odds are 85%. Happy fleecing!

internal validity The characteristic of an experiment that establishes the causal relationship between variables.

external validity A property of an experiment in which the variables have been operationally defined in a normal, typical, or realistic way.

of those experiments unless the calculation tells them that there is less than a 5% chance that random assignment failed. In other words, the calculation must allow us to be 95% certain that random assignment succeeded before we can accept the results of our experiment.

When the odds that random assignment failed are less than 5%, an experimental result is said to be *statistically significant*. You've already learned about descriptive statistics, such as the mean, median, mode, range, and standard deviation. There is another kind of statistics—called *inferential statistics*—that tells scientists what kinds of conclusions or inferences they can draw from observed differences between the experimental and control groups. For example, p (for "probability") is an inferential statistic that tells psychologists the likelihood that random assignment failed in a particular experiment. When psychologists report that $p < .05$, they are saying that according to the inferential statistics they calculated, the odds that random assignment failed are less than 5%, and thus the differences between the experimental and control groups were unlikely to have been caused by a third variable.

Drawing Conclusions

If we applied all the techniques discussed so far, we could design an experiment that had a very good chance (better than 95%, to be exact!) of establishing the causal relationship between two variables. That experiment would be said to have **internal validity**, which is *the characteristic of an experiment that establishes the causal relationship between variables*. When we say that an experiment is internally valid, we mean that everything *inside* the experiment is working exactly as it must in order for us to draw conclusions about causal relationships. But what exactly are those conclusions? If our imaginary experiment revealed a difference between the aggressiveness of children in the exposed and unexposed groups, then we could conclude that media violence *as we defined it* caused aggression *as we defined it* in the people *whom we studied*. Notice the phrases in italics. Each corresponds to an important restriction on the kinds of conclusions we can draw from an experiment, so let's consider each in turn.

Representative Variables

Whether an experiment shows that exposure to media violence causes aggression will depend in part on how these variables are defined. We are probably more likely to find that exposure causes aggression when we define exposure as "watching two hours of gory axe murders" rather than "watching 10 minutes of football," or when we define aggression as "interrupting another person" rather than "smacking someone with a tire iron." As you'll recall from our discussion of operational definitions, there are many ways to define the independent and dependent variables in an experiment, and how they are defined will have a huge impact on whether a manipulation of the former causes measurable changes in the latter. So what is the *right* way to define these variables?

One answer is that we should define them in an experiment as they are defined in the real world. **External validity** is *a property of an experiment in which variables have been operationally defined in a normal, typical, or realistic way*. It seems pretty clear that the kind of aggressive behavior that concerns teachers and parents lies somewhere between an interruption and an assault, and that the kind of media violence to which children are typically exposed lies somewhere between sports and torture. If the goal of an experiment is to determine whether the kinds of media violence to which children are typically exposed causes the kinds of aggression with which societies are typically concerned, then external validity is essential. When variables are defined in an experiment as they typically are in the real world, we say that the variables are *representative* of the real world.

▲ Does piercing make a person more or less attractive? The answer, of course, depends entirely on how you operationally define *piercing*.

External validity sounds like such a good idea that you may be surprised to learn that most psychology experiments are externally *in*valid—and that most psychologists don't mind. The reason for this is that psychologists are rarely trying to learn about the real world by creating tiny replicas of it in their laboratories. Rather, they are usu-
Why is external validity not always important?
ally trying to learn about the real world by using experiments to test theories and hypotheses, and externally invalid experiments can often do that splendidly (Mook, 1983).

Consider first an example from physics. Physicists have a theory stating that heat is the result of the rapid movement of molecules. This theory gives rise to a hypothesis, namely, that when the molecules that constitute an object are slowed, the object should become cooler. Now imagine that a physicist tested this hypothesis by performing an experiment in which a laser was used to slow the movement of the molecules in a rubber ball, whose temperature was then measured. Would you criticize this experiment by saying, "Sorry, but your experiment teaches us nothing about the real world because in the real world, no one actually uses lasers to slow the movement of the molecules in rubber balls"? Let's hope not. The physicist's theory (molecular motion causes heat) led to a hypothesis about *what would happen in the laboratory* (slowing the molecules in a rubber ball should cool it), and thus the events that the physicist manipulated and measured in the laboratory served to test the theory. Similarly, a well thought out theory about the causal relationship between exposure to media violence and aggression should lead to hypotheses about how children in a laboratory will behave after watching Road Runner cartoons or *A Nightmare on Elm Street*, and thus their reaction to these forms of media violence should serve to test the theory. If the children who watched cartoons were more likely to push and shove in the lunch line, for example, then any theory that says that media violence cannot influence aggression has just been proved wrong.

In short, theories allow us to generate hypotheses about what can, must, or will happen under particular circumstances, and experiments are usually meant to create these circumstances, test the hypotheses, and thereby provide evidence for or against the theories that generated them. Experiments are not meant to be miniature versions of everyday life, and thus external invalidity is not necessarily a problem (see the Hot Science box on the next page).

Representative People

Our imaginary experiment on exposure to media violence and aggression would allow us to conclude that exposure as we defined it caused aggression as we defined it in the people *whom we studied*. That last phrase represents another important restriction on the kinds of conclusions we can draw from experiments.

Who are the people whom psychologists study? Psychologists rarely observe an entire **population**, which is *a complete collection of people*, such as the population of human beings (about 6.8 billion), the population of Californians (about 37 million), or the population of people with Down syndrome (about 1 million). Rather, they observe a **sample**, which is *a*
What is the difference between a population and a sample?
partial collection of people drawn from a population. How big can a sample be? The size of a population is signified by the uppercase letter N, the size of a sample is signified by the lowercase letter n, and so $0 < n < N$.

In some cases, $n = 1$. For example, sometimes a single individual is so remarkable that he or she deserves close study, and when psychologists study them they are using the **case method**, which is *a method of gathering scientific knowledge by studying a single individual*. We can learn a lot about memory by studying someone like Akira Haraguchi, who can recite the first 100,000 digits of pi; about consciousness by studying someone like Henry Molaison, whose ability to look backward and forward in time was destroyed by damage to his brain; about intelligence and creativity by

population The complete collection of participants who might possibly be measured.

sample The partial collection of people drawn from a population.

case method A method of gathering scientific knowledge by studying a single individual.

▲ Jay Greenburg is not a typical 14-year-old. According to the *New York Times*, the London Symphony Orchestra's recent recording of Greenburg's 5th Symphony reveals a "gift for drama and for lyricism, expressed in sophisticated colors and textures."

studying someone like 14-year-old Jay Greenburg, whose musical compositions have been recorded by the Julliard String Quartet and the London Symphony Orchestra. Cases such as these are interesting in their own right, but they also provide important insights into how the rest of us work.

Of course, most of the psychological studies you will read about in the other chapters of this book included samples of ten, a hundred, a thousand, or a few thousand people. So how do psychologists decide which people to include in their samples? One way to select a sample from a population is by **random sampling**, which is *a technique for choosing participants that ensures that every member of a population has an equal chance of being included in the sample*. When we randomly sample participants from a population, the sample is said to be *representative* of the population. This allows us to *generalize* from the sample to the population—that is, to conclude that what we observed in our sample would also have been observed if we had measured the entire population. You probably already have solid intuitions about the importance of random sampling. For example, if you stopped at a farm stand to buy a bag of cherries and the farmer offered to let you taste a few that he had handpicked from the bag, you'd be reluctant to generalize from that sample to the population of cherries in the bag. But if the farmer invited you to pull a few cherries from the bag at random, you'd probably be willing to take those cherries as representative of the cherry population.

Random sampling sounds like such a good idea that you might be surprised to learn that most psychological studies involve non-random samples—and that most psychologists don't mind. Indeed, virtually every participant in every psychology experiment you will ever read about was a volunteer, and most were college students who

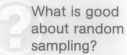

What is good about random sampling?

HOT SCIENCE

Do Violent Movies Make Peaceful Streets?

In 2000, the American Medical Association and five other public health organizations issued a joint statement warning about the risks of exposure to media violence. They cited evidence from psychological experiments in which children and young adults who were exposed to violent movie clips showed a sharp increase in aggressive behavior immediately afterwards. They noted that "well over 1000 studies . . . point overwhelmingly to a causal connection between media violence and aggressive behavior."

Given the laboratory results, we might expect to see a correlation in the real world between the number of people who see violent movies in theaters and the number of violent crimes. When economists Gordon Dahl and Stefano Della Vigna (2009) analyzed crime statistics and box office statistics, they found just such a correlation—except that it was negative! In other words, on evenings when more people went to the theatre to watch violent movies there were *fewer* violent crimes. Why? The researchers suggested that violent movies are especially appealing to the people who are most likely to commit violent crimes. Because those people are busy watching movies for a few hours, violent crime drops. In other words, blood-and-bullet movies take criminals off the street by luring them to the theater!

Laboratory experiments clearly show that exposure to media violence *can* cause aggression. But as the movie theater data remind us, experiments are a tool for establishing the causal relationships between variables and are not meant to be miniature versions of the real world, where things are ever so much more complex.

▲ One thing we know about the people who went to see the movie *American Gangster* is that for 2 hours and 37 minutes they didn't shoot anybody.

◄ Non-random sampling can lead to errors. In the presidential election of 1948, the *Chicago Tribune* mistakenly predicted that Thomas Dewey would beat Harry Truman. Why? Because polling was done by telephone, and Dewey Republicans were more likely to have telephones than were Truman Democrats. In the presidential election of 2004, exit polls mistakenly predicted that John Kerry would beat George Bush. Why? Because polling was done by soliciting voters as they left the polls, and Kerry supporters were more willing to stop and talk.

random sampling A technique for choosing participants that ensures that every member of a population has an equal chance of being included in the sample.

were significantly younger, smarter, healthier, wealthier, and Whiter than the average Earthling. Why do psychologists sample non-randomly? Convenience. Even if there were an alphabetized list of all the world's human inhabitants from which we could randomly choose our research participants, how would we find the 72-year-old Bedouin woman whose family roams the desert so that we could measure the electrical activity in her brain while she watched cartoons? How would we convince the 3-week-old infant in New Delhi to complete a lengthy questionnaire about his political beliefs? Most psychology experiments are conducted by professors and graduate students at colleges and universities in the Western Hemisphere, and as much as they might *like* to randomly sample the population of the planet, the practical truth is that they are pretty much stuck studying the folks who volunteer for their studies.

So how can we learn *anything* from psychology experiments? Isn't the failure to randomly sample a fatal flaw? No, it's not, and there are three reasons why. First,

Why is the failure to sample randomly not always a problem?

sometimes the similarity of a sample and a population doesn't matter. If one pig flew over the Statue of Liberty just one time, it would instantly disprove the traditional theory of porcine locomotion. It wouldn't matter if all swine flew; it would only matter that one did. Similarly, in psychology it often doesn't matter if *everyone* does something as long as *someone* does it. Most people can't recite the first 100,000 digits of pi from memory, but Akira Haraguchi can—and when he did this in 2006, psychologists learned something important about the nature of human memory. An experimental result can be illuminating even when the sample isn't typical of the population.

Second, when the ability to generalize an experimental result *is* important, psychologists perform new experiments that use the same procedures on different samples. For example, after measuring how some American children behaved after playing violent video games, we could replicate our experiment with Japanese children, or with teenagers, or with adults. In essence, we could treat the attributes of our sample, such as culture and age, as independent variables, and we could do experiments to determine whether these attributes influenced our dependent variable. If the results of our study were replicated in numerous non-random samples, we could be more confident (though never completely confident) that the results would generalize to the population at large.

Third, sometimes the similarity of the sample and the population is a reasonable assumption. Instead of asking, "Do I have a compelling reason to believe that my sample is representative of the population?" we might ask, "Do I have a compelling reason not to?" For example, few of us would be willing to take an experimental medicine if a non-random sample of seven participants took it and died. Indeed, we would probably refuse the medicine even if the seven participants were

▼ This mouse died after drinking the green stuff. Want to drink the green stuff? Why not? You're not a mouse, are you?

"Hi. You've been randomly selected to participate in a sex survey upstairs in 15 minutes."

mice. Although these non-randomly sampled participants were different from us in many ways (including tails and whiskers), most of us would be willing to generalize from their experience to ours because we know that even mice share enough of our basic biology to make it a good bet that what harms them can harm us too. By this same reasoning, if a psychology experiment demonstrated that some American children behaved violently after playing violent video games, we might ask whether there is a compelling reason to suspect that Ecuadorian college students or middle-aged Australians would behave any differently. If the answer was yes, then experiments would provide a way for us to investigate that possibility.

IN SUMMARY

○ To determine whether two variables are causally related, we must first determine whether they are related at all. This can be done by measuring each variable many times and then comparing the patterns of variation within each series of measurements. If the patterns covary, then the variables are correlated. Correlations allow us to predict the value of one variable from knowledge of the value of the other. The direction and strength of a correlation are measured by the correlation coefficient (r).

○ Even when we observe a correlation between two variables, we can't conclude that they are causally related because there are an infinite number of "third variables" that might be causing them both. Experiments solve this third-variable problem by manipulating an independent variable, randomly assigning participants to the experimental and control groups that this manipulation creates, and measuring a dependent variable. These measurements are then compared across groups. If inferential statistics show that there was less than a 5% chance that random assignment failed, then differences in the measurements across groups are assumed to have been caused by the manipulation.

○ An internally valid experiment establishes a causal relationship between variables as they were operationally defined and among the participants whom they included.

○ When an experiment mimics the real world it is externally valid. But most psychology experiments are not attempts to mimic the real world, but to test hypotheses derived from theories.

The Ethics of Science: First, Do No Harm

Somewhere along the way, someone probably told you that it isn't nice to treat people like objects. And yet, it may seem that psychologists do just that—creating situations that cause people to feel fearful or sad, to do things that are embarrassing or immoral, and to learn things about themselves and others that they might not really want to know. Don't be fooled by appearances. The fact is that psychologists go to great lengths to protect the well-being of their research participants, and they are bound by a code of ethics that is as detailed and demanding as the professional codes that bind physicians, lawyers, and accountants. That code requires that psychologists show respect for people, for animals, and for the truth. Let's examine each of these obligations in turn.

Respecting People

During World War II, Nazi doctors performed truly barbaric experiments on human subjects (see Where Do You Stand? at the end of the chapter). When the war ended, the international community developed the Nuremberg Code of 1947 and then the Declaration of Helsinki in 1964, both of which spelled out rules for the ethical treatment of human subjects. Unfortunately, not everyone obeyed them. For example, from 1932 until 1972, the U.S. Public Health Service conducted the infamous "Tuskegee Experiment" in which 399 African American men with syphilis were denied treatment so that researchers could observe the progression of the disease. As one journalist noted, the government "used human beings as laboratory animals in a long and inefficient study of how long it takes syphilis to kill someone" (Coontz, 2008).

In 1974, Congress created the National Commission for the Protection of Human Subjects of Biomedical and Behavioral Research. In 1979, the U.S. Department of Health, Education and Welfare released what came to be known as the Belmont Report, which described three basic principles that all research involving human subjects should follow. First, research should show *respect for persons* and their right to make decisions for and about themselves without undue influence or coercion. Second, research should be *beneficent*, which means that it should attempt to maximize benefits and reduce risks to the participant. Third, research should be *just*, which means that it should distribute benefits and risks equally to participants without prejudice toward particular individuals or groups.

What are three features of ethical research?

The specific ethical code that psychologists follow incorporates these basic principles and expands them. (You can find the American Psychological Association's *Ethical Principles of Psychologists and Codes of Conduct* at http://www.apa.org/ethics/code/index.aspx.) Here are a few of the most important rules that govern the conduct of psychological research:

> *Informed consent:* Participants may not take part in a psychological study unless they have given **informed consent**, which is *a written agreement to participate in a study made by an adult who has been informed of all the risks that participation may entail.* This doesn't mean that the person must know everything about the study (e.g., the hypothesis), but it does mean that the person must know about anything that might potentially be harmful or painful. If people cannot give informed consent (e.g., because they are minors or are mentally incapable), then informed consent must be obtained from their legal guardians. And even after people give informed consent, they always have the right to withdraw from the study at any time without penalty.

> *Freedom from coercion:* Psychologists may not coerce participation. Coercion not only means physical and psychological coercion but monetary coercion as well. It is unethical to offer people large amounts of money to persuade them to do something that they might otherwise decline to do. College students may be invited to participate in studies as part of their training in psychology, but they are ordinarily offered the option of learning the same things by other means.

informed consent A written agreement to participate in a study made by an adult who has been informed of all the risks that participation may entail.

◀ The man at this bar is upset. He just saw another man slip a drug into a woman's drink and he is alerting the bartender. What he doesn't know is that all the people at the bar are actors and that he is being filmed for the television show *What Would You Do?* Was it ethical for ABC to put this man in such a stressful situation without his consent? And how did men who didn't alert the bartender feel when they turned on their televisions months later and were confronted by their own shameful behavior?

debriefing A verbal description of the true nature and purpose of a study.

> *Protection from harm:* Psychologists must take every possible precaution to protect their research participants from physical or psychological harm. If there are two equally effective ways to study something, the psychologist must use the safer method. If no safe method is available, the psychologist may not perform the study.

> *Risk-benefit analysis:* Although participants may be asked to accept small risks, such as a minor shock or a small embarrassment, they may not even be *asked* to accept large risks, such as severe pain, psychological trauma, or any risk that is greater than the risks they would ordinarily take in their everyday lives. Furthermore, even when participants are asked to take small risks, the psychologist must first demonstrate that these risks are outweighed by the social benefits of the new knowledge that might be gained from the study.

> *Deception:* Psychologists may only use deception when it is justified by the study's scientific, educational, or applied value and when alternative procedures are not feasible. They may never deceive participants about any aspect of a study that could cause them physical or psychological harm or pain.

> *Debriefing:* If a participant is deceived in any way before or during a study, the psychologist must provide a **debriefing**, which is *a verbal description of the true nature and purpose of a study*. If the participant was changed in any way (e.g., made to feel sad), the psychologist must attempt to undo that change (e.g., ask the person to do a task that will make them happy) and restore the participant to the state he or she was in before the study.

> *Confidentiality:* Psychologists are obligated to keep private and personal information obtained during a study confidential.

These are just some of the rules that psychologists must follow. But how are those rules enforced? Almost all psychology studies are done by psychologists who work at colleges and universities. These institutions have institutional review boards (IRBs) that are composed of instructors and researchers, university staff, and laypeople from the community (e.g., business leaders or members of the clergy). If the research is federally funded (as most research is) then the law requires that the IRB include at least one non-scientist and one person who is not affiliated with the institution. A psychologist may conduct a study only after the IRB has reviewed and approved it.

As you can imagine, the code of ethics and the procedure for approval are so strict that many studies simply cannot be performed anywhere, by anyone, at any time. For example, psychologists would love to know how growing up without exposure to language affects a person's subsequent ability to speak and think, but they cannot ethically manipulate that variable in an experiment. They can only study the natural correlations between language exposure and speaking ability, and thus may never be able to firmly establish the causal relationships between these variables. Indeed, there are many questions that psychologists will never be able to answer definitively because doing so would require unethical experiments that violate basic human rights.

Respecting Animals

Of course, not all research participants have human rights because not all research participants are human. Some are chimpanzees, rats, pigeons, or other nonhuman animals. The American Psychological Association's code specifically describes the special rights of these nonhuman participants, and some of the more important ones are these:

What steps must psychologists take to protect nonhuman subjects?

> All procedures involving animals must be supervised by psychologists who are trained in research methods and experienced in the care of laboratory animals and who are responsible for ensuring appropriate consideration of the animal's comfort, health, and humane treatment.

> Psychologists must make reasonable efforts to minimize the discomfort, infection, illness, and pain of animals.

> Psychologists may use a procedure that subjects an animal to pain, stress, or privation only when an alternative procedure is unavailable and when the procedure is justified by the scientific, educational, or applied value of the study.

> Psychologists must perform all surgical procedures under appropriate anesthesia and must minimize an animal's pain during and after surgery.

"I don't usually volunteer for experiments, but I'm kind of a puzzle freak."

All good—but good enough? Some people don't think so. For example, the philosopher Peter Singer (1975) has argued that all creatures capable of feeling pain have the same fundamental rights, and that treating nonhumans differently than humans is a form of "species-ism" that is every bit as abhorrent as racism or sexism. Singer's philosophy has inspired groups such as People for the Ethical Treatment of Animals to call for an end to all research involving nonhuman animals. Unfortunately, it has also inspired some groups to attack psychologists who do such research. As two researchers (Ringach & Jentsch, 2009) recently reported:

> We have seen our cars and homes firebombed or flooded, and we have received letters packed with poisoned razors and death threats via e-mail and voicemail. Our families and neighbors have been terrorized by angry mobs of masked protesters who throw rocks, break windows, and chant that "you should stop or be stopped" and that they "know where you sleep at night." Some of the attacks have been cataloged as attempted murder. Adding insult to injury, misguided animal-rights militants openly incite others to violence on the Internet, brag about the resulting crimes, and go as far as to call plots for our assassination "morally justifiable."

Where do most people stand on this issue? A recent Gallup poll showed that about two thirds of Americans consider it morally acceptable to use nonhuman animals in research and would reject a governmental ban on such research (Kiefer, 2004; Moore, 2003). Indeed, most Americans eat meat, wear leather, and support the rights of hunters, which is to say that most Americans see a sharp distinction between animal and human rights. Science is not in the business of resolving moral controversies and every individual must draw his or her own conclusions about this issue. But it is worth noting that only a small percentage of psychological studies involve animals, and that only a small percentage of those studies cause the animals any harm or pain. Psychologists mainly study people, and when they do study animals, they mainly study their behavior.

◄ Some people consider it unethical to use animals for clothing or research. Others see an important distinction between these two purposes.

Respecting Truth

Institutional review boards ensure that data are collected ethically. But once the data are collected, who ensures that they are ethically analyzed and reported? No one does. Psychology, like all sciences, works on the honor system. No authority is charged with monitoring what psychologists do with the data they've collected, and no authority is charged with checking to see if the claims they make are true. You may find that a bit odd. After all, we don't use the honor system in stores ("Take the television set home and pay us next time you're in the neighborhood"), banks ("I don't need to look up your account, just tell me how much money you want to withdraw"), or courtrooms ("If you say you're innocent, well then, that's good enough for me"), so why would we expect it to work in science? Are scientists more honest than everyone else?

The honor system doesn't work because scientists are especially honest, but because science is a community enterprise. When scientists claim to have discovered something important, other scientists don't just applaud; they start studying it too. When the physicist Jan Hendrik Schön announced in 2001 that he had produced a molecular-scale transistor, other physicists were deeply impressed—that is, until they tried to replicate his work and discovered that Schön had fabricated his data (Agin, 2007). Schön lost his job and his doctoral degree was revoked, but the important point is that such frauds can't last long because one scientist's conclusion is the next scientist's research question. This doesn't mean that all frauds are eventually uncovered, but it does mean that the important ones are. The psychologist who fraudulently claims to have shown that chimps are smarter than goldfish may never get caught because no one is likely to follow up on such an obvious finding, but the psychologist who fraudulently claims to have shown the opposite will soon have a lot of explaining to do.

What exactly are psychologists on their honor to do? At least three things. First, when they write reports of their studies and publish them in scientific journals, psychologists are obligated to report truthfully on what they did and what they found. They can't fabricate results (e.g., claiming to have performed studies that they never really performed) or "fudge" results (e.g., changing records of data that were actually collected), and they can't mislead by omission (e.g., by reporting only the results that confirm their hypothesis and saying nothing about the results that don't). Second, psychologists are obligated to share credit fairly by including as co-authors of their reports the other people who contributed to the work, and by mentioning in their reports the other scientists who have done related work. And third, psychologists are obligated to share their data. The American Psychological Association's code of conduct states that "psychologists do not withhold the data on which their conclusions are based from other competent professionals who seek to verify the substantive claims through reanalysis." The fact that anyone can check up on anyone else is part of why the honor system works as well as it does.

What are psychologists expected to do when they report the results of their research?

▲ Ethical reporting of research is not only an issue for scientists. Christie Whitman was Administrator of the Environmental Protection Agency in 2003 when the agency wrote a scientific report and then removed references to studies showing that global warming is caused by human activity (Revkin & Seelye, 2003). Whitman denied that there was anything wrong with the way the report was written, but many scientists did not agree.

REUTERS/LARRY DOWNING

IN SUMMARY

○ Institutional review boards ensure that the rights of human beings who participate in scientific research are based on the principles of respect for persons, beneficence, and justice.

○ Psychologists are obligated to uphold these principles by getting informed consent from participants, not coercing participation, protecting participants from harm, weighing benefits against risks, avoiding deception, and keeping information confidential.

○ Psychologists are obligated to respect the rights of animals and treat them humanely. Most people are in favor of using animals in scientific research.

○ Psychologists are obligated to tell the truth about their studies, to share credit appropriately, and to grant others access to their data.

WhereDoYouStand?

The Morality of Immoral Experiments

Is it wrong to benefit from someone else's wrongdoing? Although this may seem like an abstract question for moral philosophers, it is a very real question that scientists must ask when they consider the results of unethical experiments. During World War II, Nazi doctors conducted barbaric medical studies on prisoners in concentration camps. They placed prisoners in decompression chambers and then dissected their living brains in order to determine how altitude affects pilots. They irradiated and chemically mutilated the reproductive organs of men and women in order to find inexpensive methods for the mass sterilization of "racially inferior" people. They infected prisoners with streptococcus and tetanus in order to devise treatments for soldiers who had been exposed to these bacteria. And in one of the most horrible experiments, prisoners were immersed in tanks of ice water so that the doctors could discover how long pilots would survive if they bailed out over the North Sea. The prisoners were frozen, thawed, and frozen again until they died. During these experiments, the doctors carefully recorded the prisoners' physiological responses.

These experiments were hideous. But the records of these experiments remain, and in some cases they provide valuable information that could never be obtained ethically. For example, because researchers cannot perform controlled studies that would expose volunteers to dangerously cold temperatures, there is still controversy among doctors about the best treatment for hypothermia. In 1988, Dr. Robert Pozos, a physiologist at the University of Minnesota Medical School, who had spent a lifetime studying hypothermia, came across an unpublished report written in 1945 titled "The Treatment of Shock from Prolonged Exposure to Cold, Especially in Water." The report described the results of the horrible freezing experiments performed on prisoners at the Dachau concentration camp, and it suggested that contrary to the conventional medical wisdom, rapid rewarming (rather than slow rewarming) might be the best way to treat hypothermia.

Should the Nazi medical studies have been published so that modern doctors might more effectively treat hypothermia? Many scientists and ethicists thought they should. "The prevention of a death outweighs the protection of a memory. The victims' dignity was irrevocably lost in vats of freezing liquid forty years ago. Nothing can change that," argued bioethicist Arthur Caplan. Others disagreed. "I don't see how any credence can be given to the work of unethical investigators," wrote Dr. Arnold Relman, editor of the *New England Journal of Medicine*. "It goes to legitimizing the evil done," added Abraham Foxman, national director of the Anti-Defamation League (Siegel, 1988). The debate about this issue continues (Caplan, 1992). If we use data that were obtained unethically, are we rewarding those who collected it and legitimizing their actions? Or can we condemn such investigations but still learn from them? Where do you stand?

Chapter Review

KEY CONCEPT QUIZ

1. The belief that accurate knowledge can be acquired through observation is
   a. parsimony.
   b. dogmatism.
   c. empiricism.
   d. scientific research.

2. Which of the following is the best definition of a hypothesis?
   a. empirical evidence
   b. a scientific investigation
   c. a falsifiable prediction
   d. a theoretical idea

3. The methods of psychological investigation take _____ into account because when people know they are being studied, they don't always behave as they otherwise would.
   a. reactivity
   b. complexity
   c. variability
   d. sophistication

4. When a measure produces the same measurement whenever it is used to measure the same thing, it is said to have
   a. validity.
   b. reliability.
   c. power.
   d. concreteness.

5. Aspects of an observational setting that cause people to behave as they think they should are called
   a. observer biases.
   b. reactive conditions.
   c. natural habitats.
   d. demand characteristics.

6. In a double-blind observation
   a. the participants know what is being measured.
   b. people are observed in their natural environments.
   c. the purpose is hidden from both the observer and the person being observed.
   d. only objective, statistical measures are recorded.

7. Which of the following describes the average value of all the measurements in a particular distribution?
   a. mean
   b. median
   c. mode
   d. range

8. What does a correlation coefficient show?
   a. the value of one specific variable
   b. the direction and strength of a correlation
   c. the efficiency of the relevant research method
   d. the degree of natural correlation

9. When two variables are correlated, what keeps us from concluding that one is the cause and the other is the effect?
   a. the possibility of third-variable correlation
   b. random assignment of control groups
   c. the existence of false positive correlation
   d. correlation strength is impossible to measure accurately

10. A researcher administers a questionnaire concerning attitudes toward global warming to people of both genders and of all ages who live all across the country. The dependent variable in the study is the _____ of the participants.
    a. age
    b. gender
    c. attitudes toward global warming
    d. geographic location

11. The characteristic of an experiment that allows conclusions about causal relationships to be drawn is called
    a. external validity.
    b. internal validity.
    c. random assignment.
    d. self-selection.

12. An experiment that operationally defines variables in a realistic way is said to be
    a. externally valid.
    b. controlled.
    c. operationally defined.
    d. statistically significant.

13. What are psychologists ethically required to do when reporting research results?
    a. to report findings truthfully
    b. to share credit for research
    c. to make data available for further research
    d. All of the above.

KEY TERMS

empiricism (p. 40)
scientific method (p. 40)
theory (p. 40)
hypothesis (p. 41)
empirical method (p. 42)
operational definition (p. 43)
measure (p. 44)
electromyograph (EMG) (p. 44)
validity (p. 44)
reliability (p. 44)

power (p. 45)
demand characteristics (p. 45)
naturalistic observation (p. 45)
double-blind (p. 48)
frequency distribution (p. 48)
normal distribution (p. 48)
mode (p. 49)
mean (p. 49)
median (p. 49)
range (p. 51)
standard deviation (p. 51)
variable (p. 52)

correlation (p. 53)
correlation coefficient (p. 54)
natural correlation (p. 56)
third-variable correlation (p. 57)
matched samples technique (p. 57)
matched pairs technique (p. 58)
third-variable problem (p. 59)
experiment (p. 59)
manipulation (p. 60)
independent variable (p. 60)
experimental group (p. 60)

control group (p. 60)
dependent variable (p. 60)
self-selection (p. 61)
random assignment (p. 62)
internal validity (p. 64)
external validity (p. 64)
population (p. 65)
sample (p. 65)
case method (p. 65)
random sampling (p. 66)
informed consent (p. 69)
debriefing (p. 70)

CRITICAL THINKING QUESTIONS

1. A good theory gives rise to testable hypotheses—predictions about what can and should happen. And yet, when we actually go out and test these hypotheses, the results can prove the theory wrong, but they can never prove it right. Why?

2. Demand characteristics are those aspects of a research setting that cause participants to behave as they think the researcher wants or expects them to behave. Suppose you wanted to know whether people are more likely to cheat when they feel sad than when they feel happy. People rarely cheat when they think someone is watching them, so how could you test this hypothesis in a way that minimized demand characteristics?

3. A newspaper article recently reported that couples who live together before marriage are less likely to stay married than are couples who don't live together before marriage. The article suggested that people who want to have long-lasting marriages should therefore avoid living together beforehand. Is that conclusion reasonable? How else could you explain this correlation?

RECOMMENDED READINGS

Miller, A. J. (1986). *The obedience experiments: A case study of controversy in social science.* New York: Praeger.

An examination of the most controversial psychology experiment ever conducted: Stanley Milgram's study of obedience (which you will read more about in Chapter 13).

Shermer, M. (2002). *Why people believe weird things: Pseudoscience, superstition, and other confusions of our time.* New York: Holt.

One of the world's best-known skeptics explains how to tell science from pseudoscience.

Sobel, D. (1995). *Longitude: The true story of a lone genius who solved the greatest scientific problem of his time.* New York: Walker.

In the 18th century, thousands of people died at sea because no one knew how to measure longitude. This is the story of the man who solved the measurement problem that stumped geniuses from Newton to Galileo.

ANSWERS TO KEY CONCEPT QUIZ

1. c; 2. c; 3. a; 4. b; 5. d; 6. c; 7. a; 8. b; 9. a; 10. c; 11. b; 12. a; 13. d.

Need more help? Additional resources are located at the book's free companion Web site at:
www.worthpublishers.com/schacter

3

Neuroscience and Behavior

It was an unusual night, even for the late shift in the hospital emergency room. Seventeen-year-old David saw people who weren't there and 75-year-old Betty saw, but didn't recognize, her own husband.

David was brought in by some fellow members of his gang. They told the doctors that David had become frantic, believing he saw members of a rival gang sneaking up on him. At first David's friends listened to his warnings and searched for their rivals. After repeated scares and false alarms, they decided David had gone crazy. The doctors didn't find any problems with David's eyes. Instead, they discovered he was suffering from hallucinations—a side effect of abusing methamphetamine (McKetin et al., 2006). David's prolonged crystal meth habit had altered the normal functioning of some chemicals in his brain, distorting his perception of reality and "fooling" his brain into perceiving things that were not actually there. After David stopped taking the drug, the hallucinations disappeared.

The second patient, Betty, had fainted earlier in the day. After she was revived, Betty no longer recognized her husband, George, or their two sons. She insisted it was just a problem with her eyes and had the family bring her to the emergency room for examination. The doctor who examined Betty's eyes found her vision to be perfectly normal. A brain scan showed that Betty had suffered a stroke that damaged a small area on the right side of her brain. Doctors diagnosed Betty with a rare disorder called *prosopagnosia*, which is an inability to recognize familiar faces (Duchaine et al., 2006; Kleinschmidt & Cohen, 2006; Yin, 1970)—a result of the brain damage caused by her stroke.

David and Betty both complained of problems with their vision, but their symptoms were actually caused by disorders in the brain. Our ability to perceive the world around us and recognize familiar people depends not only on information we take in through our senses but, perhaps more importantly, on the interpretation of this information performed by the brain.

▼ Betty and David both complained of problems with their vision, but their symptoms were actually caused by disorders in the brain. Brain disorders, whether caused by taking drugs or suffering from a stroke, can produce bizarre and sometimes dangerous distortions of perception.

HOMESTUDIO/DREAMSTIME.COM

IN THIS CHAPTER, WE'LL CONSIDER HOW THE BRAIN WORKS, what happens when it doesn't, and how both states of affairs determine behavior. First, we'll introduce you to the basic unit of information processing in the brain, the neuron. The electrical and chemical activities of neurons are the starting point of all behavior, thought, and emotion. Next, we'll consider the anatomy of the central nervous system, focusing especially on the brain, including its overall organization, key structures that perform different functions, and its evolutionary development. Finally, we'll discuss methods that allow us to study the brain and clarify our understanding of how it works. These include methods that examine the damaged brain and methods for scanning the living and healthy brain.

Neurons: The Origin of Behavior

An estimated 1 billion people watch the final game of World Cup soccer every four years. That's a whole lot of people, but to put it in perspective, it's still only 16% of the estimated 6.5 billion people currently living on Earth. A more impressive number might be the 30 billion viewers who tune in to watch any of the World Cup action over the course of the tournament. But a really, really big number is inside your skull right now, helping you make sense of these big numbers you're reading about. There are approximately *100 billion* cells in your brain that perform a variety of tasks to allow you to function as a human being.

Humans have thoughts, feelings, and behaviors that are often accompanied by visible signals. Consider how you might feel on your way to meet a good friend. An observer might see a smile on your face or notice how fast you are walking; internally, you might mentally rehearse what you'll say to your friend and feel a surge of happiness as you approach her. But all those visible and experiential signs are produced by an underlying invisible physical component coordinated by the activity of your brain cells. The anticipation you have, the happiness you feel, and the speed of your feet are the result of information processing in your brain. In a way, all of your thoughts, feelings, and behaviors spring from cells in the brain that take in information and produce some kind of output trillions of times a day. These cells are **neurons**, *cells in the nervous system that communicate with one another to perform information-processing tasks.*

In this section, we'll look at how neurons were discovered, what their components are, and how they are specialized for different types of information processing.

Discovery of How Neurons Function

During the 1800s, scientists began to turn their attention from studying the mechanics of limbs, lungs, and livers to studying the harder-to-observe workings of the brain. Philosophers wrote poetically about an "enchanted loom" that mysteriously wove a tapestry of behavior, and many scientists confirmed the metaphor (Corsi, 1991). To these scientists, the brain looked as though it were composed of a continuously connected lattice of fine threads, leading to the conclusion that it was one big woven web of material.

However, in the late 1880s, a Spanish physician named Santiago Ramón y Cajal (1852–1934) learned about a new technique for staining neurons in the brain (DeFelipe & Jones, 1988). The stain highlighted the appearance of entire cells, revealing that they came in different shapes and sizes (see **FIGURE 3.1**). Cajal (1937) recalls in his autobiography that during an 1887 visit to Madrid a colleague showed Cajal some samples stained with the new technique, and his imagination was immediately captured by the idea that it could provide important new insights into the nature and structure of the nervous system. Using this technique, Cajal was the first to see that each neuron was composed of a body with many threads extending outward toward other neurons. Surprisingly, he also saw that the threads of each neuron did not actually touch other neurons. Cajal (1937, p. 325) recalled that these observations stimulated a burst of creative thinking: "As new facts appeared in my preparations, ideas boiled up and jostled each other in my mind." Cajal arrived at the fundamental insight that neurons are the information-processing units of the brain and that even though he saw gaps between neurons, they had to communicate in some way (Rapport, 2005).

▼ FIGURE 3.1
Golgi-Stained Neurons Santiago Ramón y Cajal used a Golgi stain to highlight the appearance of neurons.

ALFRED PASIEKA/PETER ARNOLD

Components of the Neuron

Cajal discovered that neurons are complex structures composed of three basic parts: the cell body, the dendrites, and the axon (see **FIGURE 3.2**). Like cells in all organs of the body, neurons have a **cell body** (also called the *soma*), the largest component of the neuron that *coordinates the information-processing tasks and keeps the cell alive*. Functions such as protein synthesis, energy production, and metabolism take place here. The cell body contains a *nucleus*; this structure houses chromosomes that contain your DNA, or the genetic blueprint of who you are. The cell body is surrounded by a porous cell membrane that allows molecules to flow into and out of the cell.

Unlike other cells in the body, neurons have two types of specialized extensions of the cell membrane that allow them to communicate: dendrites and axons. **Dendrites** *receive information from other neurons and relay it to the cell body*. The term *dendrite* comes from the Greek word for "tree"; indeed, most neurons have many dendrites that look like tree branches. The **axon** *transmits information to other neurons, muscles, or glands*. Each neuron has a single axon that sometimes can be very long, even stretching up to a meter from the base of the spinal cord down to the big toe.

In many neurons, the axon is covered by a **myelin sheath**, *an insulating layer of fatty material*. The myelin sheath is composed of **glial cells**, which are *support cells found in the nervous system*. Although there are 100 billion neurons busily processing information in your brain, there are 10 to 50 times that many glial cells serving a variety of functions.

neurons Cells in the nervous system that communicate with one another to perform information-processing tasks.

cell body The part of a neuron that coordinates information-processing tasks and keeps the cell alive.

dendrite The part of a neuron that receives information from other neurons and relays it to the cell body.

axon The part of a neuron that transmits information to other neurons, muscles, or glands.

myelin sheath An insulating layer of fatty material.

glial cells Support cells found in the nervous system.

▼ FIGURE 3.2
Components of a Neuron A neuron is made up of three parts: a cell body that houses the chromosomes with the organism's DNA and maintains the health of the cell; dendrites that receive information from other neurons; and an axon that transmits information to other neurons, muscles, and glands.

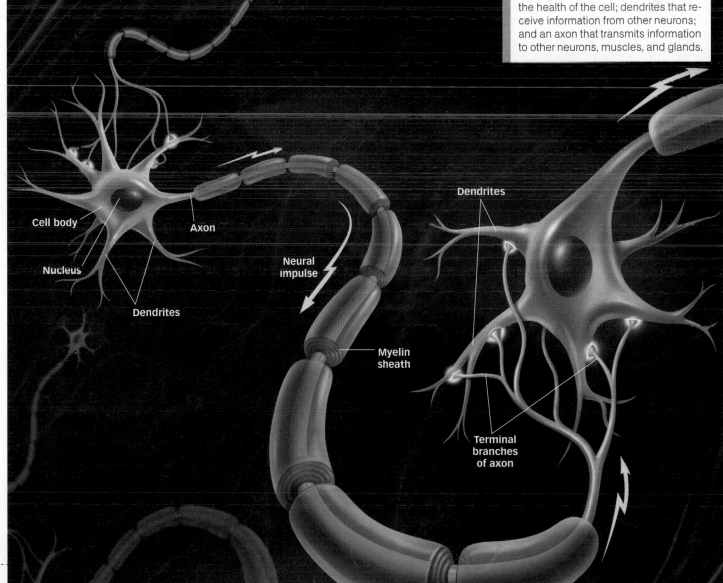

Cell body

Axon

Nucleus

Dendrites

Neural impulse

Dendrites

Myelin sheath

Terminal branches of axon

synapse The junction or region between the axon of one neuron and the dendrites or cell body of another.

Some glial cells digest parts of dead neurons, others provide physical and nutritional support for neurons, and others form myelin to help the axon transmit information more efficiently. Imagine for a minute the pipes coming from the water heater in the basement, leading upstairs to heat a house. When those pipes are wrapped in insulation, they usually perform their task more efficiently: The water inside stays hotter, the heater works more effectively, and so on. Myelin performs this same function for an axon: An axon insulated with myelin can more efficiently transmit signals to other neurons, organs, or muscles. In fact, with *demyelinating diseases*, such as multiple sclerosis, the myelin sheath deteriorates, slowing the transmission of information from one neuron to another (Schwartz & Westbrook, 2000). This leads to a variety of problems, including loss of feeling in the limbs, partial blindness, and difficulties in coordinated movement and cognition (Butler, Corboy, & Filley, 2009).

As you'll remember, Cajal observed that the dendrites and axons of neurons do not actually touch each other. There's a small gap between the axon of one neuron and the dendrites or cell body of another. This gap is part of the **synapse**: *the junction or region between the axon of one neuron and the dendrites or cell body of another* (see **FIGURE 3.3**). Many of the 100 billion neurons in your brain have a few thousand synaptic junctions, so it should come as no shock that most adults have between 100 trillion and 500 trillion synapses. As you'll read shortly, the transmission of information across the synapse is fundamental to communication between neurons, a process that allows us to think, feel, and behave.

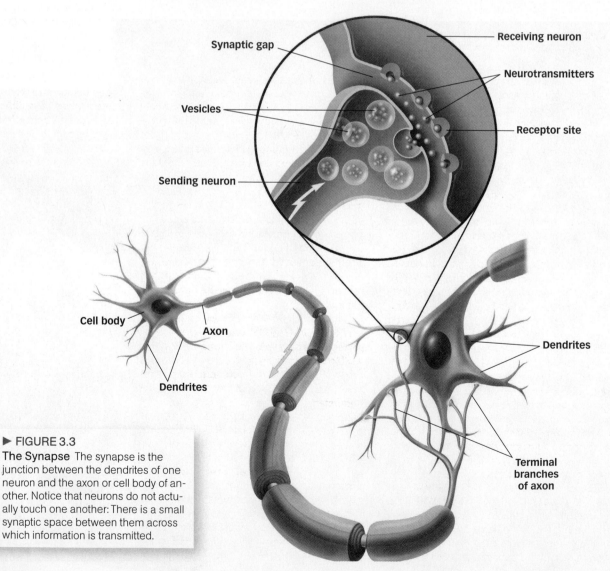

▶ FIGURE 3.3
The Synapse The synapse is the junction between the dendrites of one neuron and the axon or cell body of another. Notice that neurons do not actually touch one another: There is a small synaptic space between them across which information is transmitted.

Major Types of Neurons

There are three major types of neurons, each performing a distinct function: sensory neurons, motor neurons, and interneurons. **Sensory neurons** *receive information from the external world and convey this information to the brain via the spinal cord.* They have specialized endings on their dendrites that receive signals for light, sound, touch, taste, and smell. In our eyes, sensory neurons' endings are sensitive to light. **Motor neurons** *carry signals from the spinal cord to the muscles to produce movement.* These neurons often have long axons that can stretch to muscles at our extremities. However, most of the nervous system is composed of the third type of neuron, **interneurons**, which *connect sensory neurons, motor neurons, or other interneurons.* Some interneurons carry information from sensory neurons into the nervous system, others carry information from the nervous system to motor neurons, and still others perform a variety of information-processing functions within the nervous system. Interneurons work together in small circuits to perform simple tasks, such as identifying the location of a sensory signal, and much more complicated ones, such as recognizing a familiar face. (See the Hot Science box below.)

How do the three types of neurons work together to transmit information?

sensory neurons Neurons that receive information from the external world and convey this information to the brain via the spinal cord.

motor neurons Neurons that carry signals from the spinal cord to the muscles to produce movement.

interneurons Neurons that connect sensory neurons, motor neurons, or other interneurons.

HOT SCIENCE

Mirror, Mirror, in My Brain

One of the most exciting recent advances in neuroscience is the discovery of the mirror-neuron system. Mirror neurons are found in the frontal lobe (near the motor cortex) and in the parietal lobe (Rizzolatti & Craighero, 2004). They have been identified in birds, monkeys, and humans, and their name reflects the function they serve. Mirror neurons are active when an animal performs a behavior, such as reaching for or manipulating an object and are also activated when another animal *observes* this animal performing the behavior. This kind of mirroring holds intriguing implications for understanding the brain's role in complex social behavior (Iacoboni, 2009).

A recent study on mirror neurons used fMRI to monitor the brains of humans as they watched each of three presentations (Iacoboni et al., 2005). Sometimes participants saw a hand making grasping motions but without a context. Sometimes they saw only the context, coffee cups or scrubbing sponges, but no hands making motions to go with them. Other times they saw hand motions in two different contexts, either grasping and moving a coffee cup to drink or cleaning dishes with a sponge.

The participants' mirror neurons responded more strongly when actions were embedded in a context. This suggests that the same set of neurons involved in action recognition are also involved in understanding the intentions of others. Mirror neurons are active when watching someone perform a behavior, such as grasping in midair. But they are more highly activated when that behavior has some purpose or context, such as grasping a cup to take a drink. Subsequent fMRI studies show that the activity of brain regions that contain mirror neurons is related to recognizing the goal someone has in carrying out an action, and the outcome of the action, rather than to the particular movements a person makes while performing that action (Hamilton & Grafton, 2006, 2008). Recognizing another person's intentions means that the observer has inferred something about that person's goals, wants, or wishes ("Oh, she must be thirsty").

Why is this interesting? These results suggest a possible inborn neural basis for empathy. Grasping the intentions of another person—indeed, having your brain respond in kind as another person acts—is critical to smooth social interaction. It allows us to understand other people's possible motivations and anticipate their future actions. In fact, these are the kinds of skills that people suffering from autism severely lack. Autism is a developmental disorder characterized by impoverished social interactions and communication skills (Frith, 2001). Psychologists who study autism focus on trying to understand the nature of the disorder and devising ways to help autistic people cope with and function in human society. Recent evidence indicates that although autistic children can recognize the actions that another person is performing (e.g., grasping an object), they have difficulties understanding the intention behind the action (e.g., grasping an object in order to eat it)—just what we would expect if autistic individuals have impairments in their mirror neurons (Rizzolati, Fabbri-Destro, & Cattaneo, 2009). Research on mirror neurons may therefore offer one avenue for better understanding the origin and prognosis of this disorder (Iacoboni & Dapretto, 2006; Rizzolati et al., 2009).

▲ When one animal observes another engaging in a particular behavior, some of the same neurons become active in the observer as well as in the animal exhibiting the behavior. These mirror neurons seem to play an important role in social behavior.

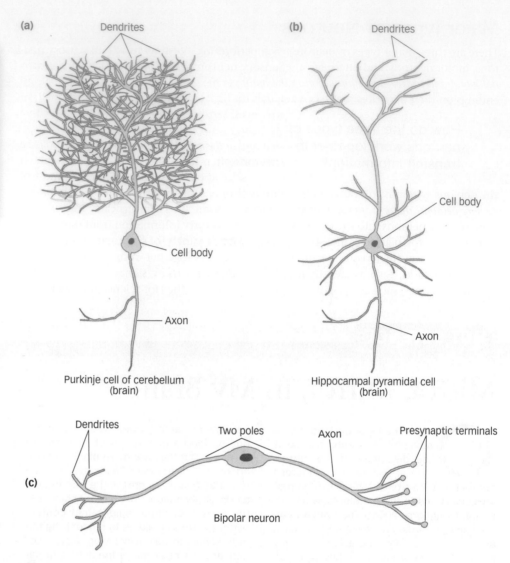

FIGURE 3.4

Neurons Neurons have an axon, and at least one dendrite. The size and shape of neurons vary considerably, however. (a) The Purkinje cell has an elaborate treelike assemblage of dendrites. (b) Pyramidal cells have a triangular cell body and a single, long dendrite with many smaller dendrites. (c) Bipolar cells have only one dendrite and a single axon.

(a) Dendrites

Cell body

Axon

Purkinje cell of cerebellum
(brain)

(b) Dendrites

Cell body

Axon

Hippocampal pyramidal cell
(brain)

(c) Dendrites — Two poles — Axon — Presynaptic terminals

Bipolar neuron

Neurons Specialized by Location

Besides specialization for sensory, motor, or connective functions, neurons are also somewhat specialized depending on their location (see **FIGURE 3.4**). For example, *Purkinje cells* are a type of interneuron that carries information from the cerebellum to the rest of the brain and spinal cord. These neurons have dense, elaborate dendrites that resemble bushes. *Pyramidal cells*, found in the cerebral cortex, have a triangular cell body and a single, long dendrite among many smaller dendrites. *Bipolar cells*, a type of sensory neuron found in the retinas of the eye, have a single axon and a single dendrite. The brain processes different types of information, so a substantial amount of specialization at the cellular level has evolved to handle these tasks.

IN SUMMARY

○ Neurons are the building blocks of the nervous system. They process information received from the outside world, they communicate with one another, and they send messages to the body's muscles and organs.

○ Neurons are composed of three major parts: the cell body, dendrites, and the axon.

  ○ The cell body contains the nucleus, which houses the organism's genetic material.

  ○ Dendrites receive sensory signals from other neurons and transmit this information to the cell body.

Continued

○ Each neuron has only one axon, which carries signals from the cell body to other neurons or to muscles and organs in the body.

○ Neurons don't actually touch: They are separated by a small gap, which is part of the synapse across which signals are transmitted from one neuron to another.

○ Glial cells provide support for neurons, usually in the form of the myelin sheath, which coats the axon to facilitate the transmission of information. In demyelinating diseases, the myelin sheath deteriorates.

○ Neurons are differentiated according to the functions they perform. The three major types of neurons include sensory neurons, motor neurons, and interneurons. Examples of sensory neurons and interneurons are, respectively, bipolar neurons and Purkinje and pyramidal cells.

resting potential The difference in charge between the inside and outside a neuron's cell membrane.

The Electrochemical Actions of Neurons: Information Processing

Our thoughts, feelings, and actions depend on neural communication, but how does it happen? The communication of information within and between neurons proceeds in two stages—*conduction* and *transmission*. The first stage is the conduction of an electric signal over relatively long distances within neurons, from the dendrites, to the cell body, then throughout the axon. The second stage is the transmission of electric signals between neurons over the synapse. Together, these stages are what scientists generally refer to as the *electrochemical action* of neurons.

Electric Signaling: Conducting Information within a Neuron

As you'll recall, the neuron's cell membrane is porous: It allows small electrically charged molecules, called *ions*, to flow in and out of the cell. If you imagine using a strainer while you're preparing spaghetti, you'll get the idea. The mesh of the strainer cradles your dinner, but water can still seep in and out of it. Just as the flow of water out of a strainer enhances the quality of pasta, the flow of molecules across a cell membrane enhances the transmission of information in the nervous system.

The Resting Potential: The Origin of the Neuron's Electrical Properties

Neurons have a natural electric charge called the **resting potential**, which is *the difference in electric charge between the inside and outside of a neuron's cell membrane* (Kandel, 2000). The resting potential is similar to the difference between the "+" and "−" poles of a battery, and just like a battery, resting potential creates the environment for a possible electrical impulse. When first discovered by biologists in the 1930s, the resting potential was measured at about about −70 millivolts, or roughly 1/200 of the charge of an AA battery (Stevens, 1971).

The resting potential arises from the difference in concentrations of ions inside and outside the neuron's cell membrane (see **FIGURE 3.5a** on the next page). Ions can carry a positive (+) or a negative (−) charge. In the resting state, there is a high concentration of a positively charged ion, potassium (K^+), as well as negatively charged protein ions (A^-), *inside* the neuron's cell membrane compared to outside it. By contrast, there is a high concentration of positively charged sodium ions (Na^+) and negatively charged chloride ions (Cl^-) *outside* the neuron's cell membrane. Since both the inside and

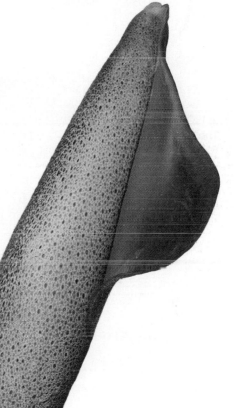

◀ Biologists Alan Hodgkin and Andrew Huxley discovered the resting potential in the summer of 1939, while studying marine invertebrates—sea creatures that lack a spine, such as clams, squid, and lobsters (Stevens, 1971). Hodgkin and Huxley worked with the squid giant axon because it is 100 times larger than the biggest axon in humans. They inserted a thin wire into the squid axon so that it touched the jellylike fluid inside. Then they placed another wire just outside the axon in the watery fluid that surrounds it. They found a substantial difference between the electric charges inside and outside the axon, which they called the resting potential.

MAREVISION/AGEFOTOSTOCK/PHOTOLIBRARY

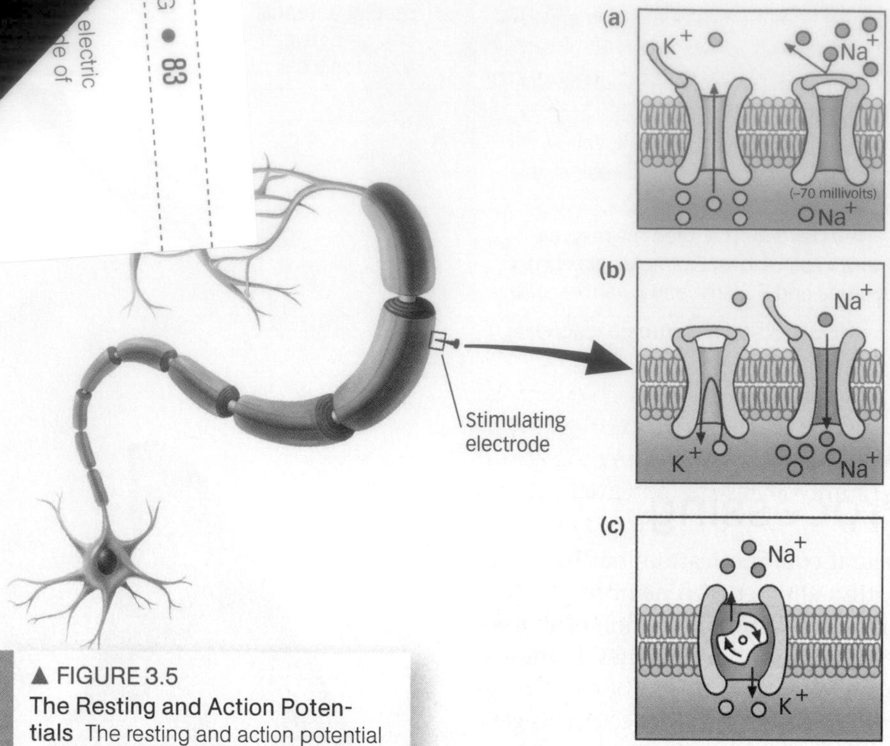

(a) **The Resting Potential** In the resting state K⁺ molecules flow freely across the cell membrane, but Na⁺ molecules are kept out, creating a difference in electric charge between the inside and outside of a neuron's cell membrane. The inside of the neuron has a charge of about −70 millivolts relative to the outside, which is the potential energy that will be used to generate the action potential.

(b) **The Action Potential** Electric stimulation of the neuron shuts down the K⁺ channels and opens the Na⁺ channels, allowing Na⁺ to rush in and increase the positive charge inside the axon relative to the outside, triggering the action potential.

(c) The imbalance in ions from the action potential is reversed by an active chemical "pump" in the cell membrane that moves Na⁺ outside the axon and moves K⁺ inside the axon. The neuron can now generate another action potential.

Stimulating electrode

▲ FIGURE 3.5
The Resting and Action Potentials The resting and action potential neurons have a natural electric charge called a resting potential. Electric stimulation causes an action potential.

the outside of the neuron contain one positively and one negatively charged ion, you might think that the positive and negative charges would simply cancel each other out, so that the resting potential is neither positive nor negative. But we've already noted that the resting potential is negative. Why is this so?

The behavior of the K⁺ ion provides the key to understanding this seemingly odd state of affairs. Raising the concentration of K⁺ in the fluid outside the neuron to match the concentration of K⁺ inside the neuron causes the resting potential to disappear. This simple test confirms that differences in K⁺ concentration are the basis of the resting potential (Dowling, 1992).

The concentration of K⁺ inside and outside an axon is controlled by channels in the axon membrane that allow molecules to flow in and out of the neuron. In the resting state, the channels that allow K⁺ molecules to flow freely across the cell membrane are open, while channels that allow the flow of Na⁺ and the other ions noted earlier are generally closed. Because, as you just learned, there is a naturally higher concentration of K⁺ molecules *inside* the neuron, some K⁺ molecules move out of the neuron through the open channels, leaving the inside of the neuron with a charge of about −70 millivolts relative to the outside.

As an example of this process, imagine a field trip to the zoo. Many zoos have turnstiles that allow only one person at a time to enter. The most eager children rush through the turnstiles to see the lions and tigers and bears, while parents hover outside, deciding where to meet later and who's got the sunscreen. With many children on one side of the turnstile, a greater concentration of parents is left on the opposite side. This is like the many small K⁺ ions that move outside the neuron, leaving the other large negatively charged ions inside the neuron, which produces a resting potential across the cell membrane (Figure 3.5a).

The Action Potential: Sending Signals Across the Neuron

The neuron maintains its resting potential most of the time. However, the biologists working with the squid giant axon (see photo) noticed that they could produce a signal by stimulating the axon with a brief electric shock, which resulted in the conduction of a large electric impulse down the length of the axon (Hausser, 2000; Hodgkin & Huxley, 1939). This electric impulse is called an **action potential**, which is *an electric*

action potential An electric signal that is conducted along a neuron's axon to a synapse.

refractory period The time following an action potential during which a new action potential cannot be initiated.

signal that is conducted along the length of a neuron's axon to the synapse (see **FIGURE 3.5b**). The action potential occurs only when the electric shock reaches a certain level, or *threshold*. When the shock was below this threshold, the researchers recorded only tiny signals, which dissipated rapidly. When the shock reached the threshold, a much larger signal, the action potential, was observed. Interestingly, increases in the electric shock above the threshold did *not* increase the strength of the action potential. The action potential is *all or none*: Electric stimulation below the threshold fails to produce an action potential, whereas electric stimulation at or above the threshold always produces the action potential. The action potential always occurs with exactly the same characteristics and at the same magnitude regardless of whether the stimulus is at or above the threshold. The biologists working with the squid giant axon observed another surprising property of the action potential: They measured it at a charge of about +40 millivolts, which is well above zero. This suggests that the mechanism driving the action potential could not simply be the loss of the –70 millivolt resting potential because this would have only brought the charge back to zero. So why does the action potential reach a value above zero?

> Why is an action potential an all-or-nothing event?

The action potential occurs when there is a change in the state of the axon's membrane channels. Remember, during the resting potential, only the K^+ channels are open. However, when an electric charge is raised to the threshold value, the K^+ channels briefly shut down, and other channels that allow the flow of a *positively* charged ion, Na^+, are opened. We've seen already that Na^+ is typically much more concentrated outside the axon than inside. When the Na^+ channels open, those positively charged ions flow inside, increasing the positive charge inside the axon relative to that outside. This flow of Na^+ into the axon pushes the action potential to its maximum value of +40 millivolts.

After the action potential reaches its maximum, the membrane channels return to their original state, and K^+ flows out until the axon returns to its resting potential. This leaves a lot of extra Na^+ ions inside the axon and a lot of extra K^+ ions outside the axon. During this period where the ions are imbalanced, the neuron cannot initiate another action potential, so it is said to be in a **refractory period,** *the time following an action potential during which a new action potential cannot be initiated*. The imbalance in ions eventually is reversed by an active chemical "pump" in the cell membrane that moves Na^+ outside the axon and moves K^+ inside the axon (the pump does not operate during the action potential).

Earlier, we described how the action potential occurs at one point in the neuron. But how does this electric charge move down the axon? When an action potential is generated at the beginning of the axon, it spreads a short distance, which generates an action potential at a nearby location on the axon (see Figure 3.5). That action potential also spreads, initiating an action potential at another nearby location, and so on, thus transmitting the charge down the length of the axon. This simple mechanism ensures that the action potential travels the full length of the axon and that it achieves its full intensity at each step, regardless of the distance traveled.

The myelin sheath, which is made up of glial cells that coat and insulate the axon, facilitates the transmission of the action potential. Myelin doesn't cover the entire axon; rather, it clumps around the axon with little break points between clumps, looking kind of like sausage links. These breakpoints are called the *nodes of Ranvier*, after French pathologist Louis-Antoine Ranvier, who discovered them (see **FIGURE 3.6**). When an electric current passes down the length of a myelinated axon, the charge seems to "jump" from node to node rather than having to traverse the entire axon (Poliak & Peles, 2003). This process is called *saltatory conduction*, and it helps speed the flow of information down the axon.

▼ FIGURE 3.6
Myelin and Nodes of Ranvier Myelin is formed by a type of glial cell, and it wraps around a neuron's axon to speed the transmission of the action potential along the length of the axon. Breaks in the myelin sheath are called the nodes of Ranvier. The electric impulse jumps from node to node, thereby speeding the conduction of information down the axon.

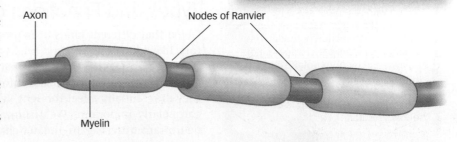

Axon

Nodes of Ranvier

Myelin

terminal buttons Knoblike structures that branch out from an axon.

neurotransmitters Chemicals that transmit information across the synapse to a receiving neuron's dendrites.

receptors Parts of the cell membrane that receive the neurotransmitter and initiate or prevent a new electric signal.

Chemical Signaling: Transmission between Neurons

When the action potential reaches the end of an axon, you might think that it stops there. After all, the synaptic space between neurons means that the axon of one neuron and the neighboring neuron's dendrites do not actually touch one another. However, the electric charge of the action potential takes a form that can cross the relatively small synaptic gap by relying on a bit of chemistry.

Axons usually end in **terminal buttons**, which are *knoblike structures that branch out from an axon.* A terminal button is filled with tiny *vesicles*, or "bags," that contain **neurotransmitters**, *chemicals that transmit information across the synapse to a receiving neuron's dendrites.* The dendrites of the receiving neuron contain **receptors**, *parts of the cell membrane that receive neurotransmitters and either initiate or prevent a new electric signal.*

> How does a neuron communicate with another neuron?

As K$^+$ and Na$^+$ flow across a cell membrane, they move the sending neuron, or *presynaptic neuron*, from a resting potential to an action potential. The action potential travels down the length of the axon to the terminal buttons, where it stimulates the release of neurotransmitters from vesicles into the synapse. These neurotransmitters float across the synapse and bind to receptor sites on a nearby dendrite of the receiving neuron, or *postsynaptic neuron*. A new electric potential is initiated in that neuron, and the process continues down that neuron's axon to the next synapse and the next neuron. This electrochemical action, called *synaptic transmission* (see **FIGURE 3.7**), allows neurons to communicate with one another and ultimately underlies your thoughts, emotions, and behavior.

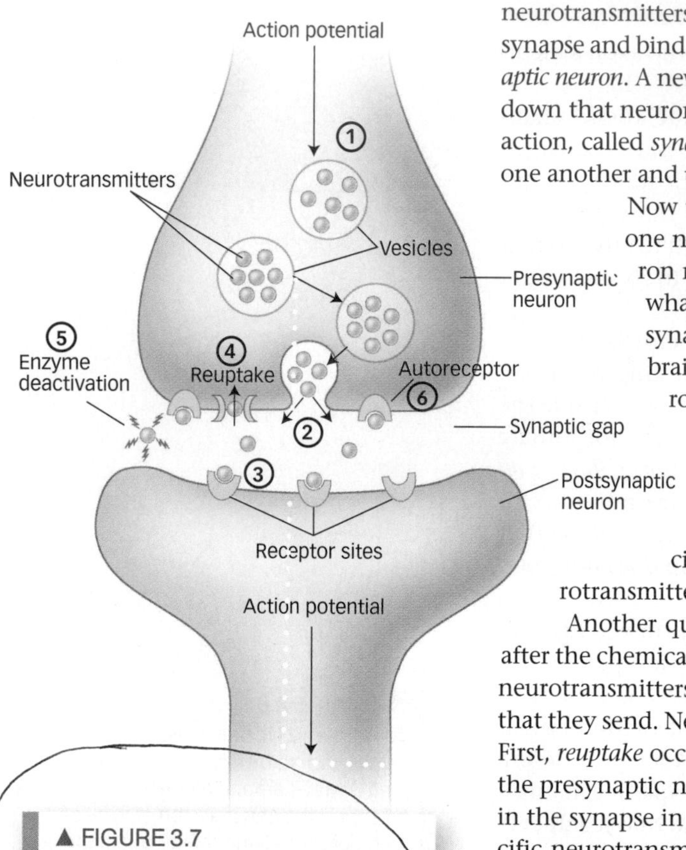

Now that you understand the basic process of how information moves from one neuron to another, let's refine things a bit. You'll recall that a given neuron may make a few thousand synaptic connections with other neurons, so what tells the dendrites which of the neurotransmitters flooding into the synapse to receive? One answer is that neurons tend to form pathways in the brain that are characterized by specific types of neurotransmitters; one neurotransmitter might be prevalent in one part of the brain, whereas a different neurotransmitter might be prevalent in a different part of the brain.

A second answer is that neurotransmitters and receptor sites act like a lock-and-key system. Just as a particular key will only fit in a particular lock, so, too, will only some neurotransmitters bind to specific receptor sites on a dendrite. The molecular structure of the neurotransmitter must "fit" the molecular structure of the receptor site.

Another question is: What happens to the neurotransmitters left in the synapse after the chemical message is relayed to the postsynaptic neuron? Something must make neurotransmitters stop acting on neurons; otherwise, there'd be no end to the signals that they send. Neurotransmitters leave the synapse through three processes (Figure 3.7). First, *reuptake* occurs when neurotransmitters are reabsorbed by the terminal buttons of the presynaptic neuron's axon. Second, neurotransmitters can be destroyed by enzymes in the synapse in a process called *enzyme deactivation*; specific enzymes break down specific neurotransmitters. Finally, neurotransmitters can bind to the receptor sites called *autoreceptors* on the presynaptic neurons. Autoreceptors detect how much of a neurotransmitter has been released into a synapse and signal the neuron to stop releasing the neurotransmitter when an excess is present.

▲ FIGURE 3.7

Synaptic Transmission (1) The action potential travels down the axon and (2) stimulates the release of neurotransmitters from vesicles. (3) The neurotransmitters are released into the synapse, where they float to bind with receptor sites on a dendrite of a postsynaptic neuron, initiating a new action potential. The neurotransmitters are cleared out of the synapse by (4) reuptake into the sending neuron, (5) being broken down by enzymes in the synapse, or (6) binding to autoreceptors on the sending neuron.

Types and Functions of Neurotransmitters

Given that different kinds of neurotransmitters can activate different kinds of receptors, like a lock and key, you might wonder how many types of neurotransmitters are floating across synapses in your brain right now. Today we know that some 60 chemicals play a role in transmitting information throughout the brain and body and that they differentially affect thought, feeling, and behavior, but a few major classes seem particularly important. We'll summarize those here, and you'll meet some of these neurotransmitters again, in later chapters.

> **Acetylcholine (ACh),** *a neurotransmitter involved in a number of functions, including voluntary motor control,* was one of the first neurotransmitters discovered. Acetylcholine is found in neurons of the brain and in the synapses where axons connect to muscles and body organs, such as the heart. Acetylcholine activates muscles to initiate motor behavior, but it also contributes to the regulation of attention, learning, sleeping, dreaming, and memory (Gais & Born, 2004; Hasselmo, 2006; Wrenn et al., 2006). These are rather broad effects on a variety of important behaviors, but here are some specific examples. Alzheimer's disease, a medical condition involving severe memory impairments (Salmon & Bondi, 2009), is associated with the deterioration of Ach-producing neurons. Like acetylcholine, other neurotransmitters in the brain affect a range of behaviors.

> **Dopamine** is *a neurotransmitter that regulates motor behavior, motivation, pleasure, and emotional arousal.* Because of its role in basic motivated behaviors, such as seeking pleasure or associating actions with rewards, dopamine plays a role in drug addiction (Baler & Volkow, 2006). High levels of dopamine have been linked to schizophrenia (Winterer & Weinberger, 2004), while low levels have been linked to Parkinson's disease.

> **Glutamate** is *a major excitatory neurotransmitter involved in information transmission throughout the brain.* This means that glutamate enhances the transmission of information. Too much glutamate can overstimulate the brain, causing seizures. **GABA (gamma-aminobutyric acid),** in contrast, is *the primary inhibitory neurotransmitter in the brain.* Inhibitory neurotransmitters stop the firing of neurons, an activity that also contributes to the function of the organism. Too little GABA, just like too much glutamate, can cause neurons to become overactive.

> **Norepinephrine,** *a neurotransmitter that influences mood and arousal,* is particularly involved in states of vigilance, or a heightened awareness of dangers in the environment (Ressler & Nemeroff, 1999). Similarly, **serotonin** is *involved in the regulation of sleep and wakefulness, eating, and aggressive behavior* (Dayan & Huys, 2009; Kroeze & Roth, 1998). Because both neurotransmitters affect mood and arousal, low levels of each have been implicated in mood disorders (Tamminga et al., 2002).

> **Endorphins** *are chemicals that act within the pain pathways and emotion centers of the brain* (Keefe et al., 2001). The term *endorphin* is a contraction of *endogenous morphine,* and that's a pretty apt description. Morphine is a synthetic drug that has a calming and pleasurable effect; an endorphin is an internally produced substance that has similar properties, such as dulling the experience of pain and elevating moods. The "runner's high" experienced by many athletes as they push their bodies to painful limits of endurance can be explained by the release of endorphins in the brain (Boecker et al., 2008).

acetylcholine (ACh) A neurotransmitter involved in a number of functions, including voluntary motor control.

dopamine A neurotransmitter that regulates motor behavior, motivation, pleasure, and emotional arousal.

glutamate A major excitatory neurotransmitter involved in information transmission throughout the brain.

GABA (gamma-aminobutyric acid) The primary inhibitory neurotransmitter in the brain.

norepinephrine A neurotransmitter that influences mood and arousal.

serotonin A neurotransmitter that is involved in the regulation of sleep and wakefulness, eating, and aggressive behavior.

endorphins Chemicals that act within the pain pathways and emotion centers of the brain.

Each of these neurotransmitters affects thought, feeling, and behavior in different ways, so normal functioning involves a delicate balance of each. Even a slight imbalance—too much of one neurotransmitter or not enough of another—can dramatically affect behavior. These imbalances sometimes occur naturally: The brain doesn't produce enough serotonin, for example, which contributes to depressed or anxious moods. Other times a person may actively seek to cause imbalances. People who smoke, drink alcohol, or take drugs, legal or not, are altering the balance of neurotransmitters in their brains. The drug LSD, for example, is structurally very similar to serotonin, so it binds very easily with serotonin receptors in the brain, producing similar effects on thoughts, feelings, or behavior. In the next section, we'll look at how some drugs are able to "trick" receptor sites in just this way.

How do neurotransmitters create the feeling of a "runner's high"?

▼ Shaun White won the gold medal in men's snowboarding at the Vancouver 2010 Olympics. When athletes like White engage in these kinds of extreme sports, they may experience subjective highs that result from the release of endorphins—chemical messengers acting in emotion and pain centers that elevate mood and dull the experience of pain.

REUTERS/MIKE BLAKE

How Drugs Mimic Neurotransmitters

Many drugs that affect the nervous system operate by increasing, interfering with, or mimicking the manufacture or function of neurotransmitters (Cooper, Bloom, & Roth, 2003; Sarter, 2006). **Agonists** are *drugs that increase the action of a neurotransmitter*. **Antagonists** are *drugs that block the function of a neurotransmitter*. Some drugs alter a step in the production or release of the neurotransmitter, whereas others have a chemical structure so similar to a neurotransmitter that the drug is able to bind to that neuron's receptor. If, by binding to a receptor, a drug activates the neurotransmitter, it is an agonist; if it blocks the action of the neurotransmitter, it is an antagonist (see **FIGURE 3.8**).

How does giving patients L-dopa alleviate symptoms of Parkinson's disease?

For example, a drug called L-dopa has been developed to treat Parkinson's disease, a movement disorder characterized by tremors and difficulty initiating movement and caused by the loss of neurons that use the neurotransmitter dopamine. Dopamine is created in neurons by a modification of a common molecule called L-dopa. Ingesting L-dopa will elevate the amount of L-dopa in the brain and spur the surviving neurons to produce more dopamine. In other words, L-dopa acts as an agonist for dopamine. The use of L-dopa has been reasonably successful in the alleviation of Parkinson's disease symptoms (Muenter & Tyce, 1971; Schapira et al., 2009). However, the effectiveness of L-dopa typically decreases when used over a long period of time, so that many long-time users experience some symptoms of the disease. The actor Michael J. Fox, who was diagnosed with Parkinson's disease in 1991 and takes L-dopa, describes in his recent memoir the simple act of trying to brush his teeth:

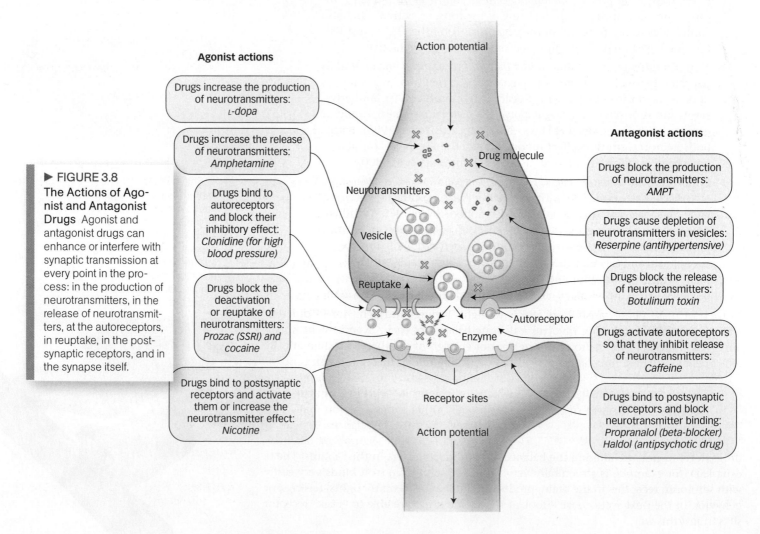

► FIGURE 3.8
The Actions of Agonist and Antagonist Drugs Agonist and antagonist drugs can enhance or interfere with synaptic transmission at every point in the process: in the production of neurotransmitters, in the release of neurotransmitters, at the autoreceptors, in reuptake, in the postsynaptic receptors, and in the synapse itself.

Agonist actions

Drugs increase the production of neurotransmitters:
L-dopa

Drugs increase the release of neurotransmitters:
Amphetamine

Drugs bind to autoreceptors and block their inhibitory effect:
Clonidine (for high blood pressure)

Drugs block the deactivation or reuptake of neurotransmitters:
Prozac (SSRI) and cocaine

Drugs bind to postsynaptic receptors and activate them or increase the neurotransmitter effect:
Nicotine

Antagonist actions

Drugs block the production of neurotransmitters:
AMPT

Drugs cause depletion of neurotransmitters in vesicles:
Reserpine (antihypertensive)

Drugs block the release of neurotransmitters:
Botulinum toxin

Drugs activate autoreceptors so that they inhibit release of neurotransmitters:
Caffeine

Drugs bind to postsynaptic receptors and block neurotransmitter binding:
Propranalol (beta-blocker)
Haldol (antipsychotic drug)

Action potential

Drug molecule

Neurotransmitters

Vesicle

Reuptake

Autoreceptor

Enzyme

Receptor sites

Action potential

Grasping the toothpaste is nothing compared to the effort it takes to coordinate the two-handed task of wrangling the toothbrush and strangling out a line of paste onto the bristles. By now, my right hand has started up again, rotating at the wrist in a circular motion, perfect for what I'm about to do. My left hand guides my right hand up to my mouth, and once the back of the Oral-B touches the inside of my upper lip, I let go. It's like releasing the tension on a slingshot and compares favorably to the most powerful state-of-the-art electric toothbrush on the market. With no off switch, stopping means seizing my right wrist with my left hand, forcing it down to the sink basin, and shaking the brush loose as though disarming a knife-wielding attacker. (Fox, 2009, pp. 2–3)

Some unexpected evidence also highlights the central role of dopamine in regulating movement and motor performance. In 1982, six people ranging in age from 25 to 45 from the San Francisco Bay area were admitted to emergency rooms with a bizarre set of symptoms: paralysis, drooling, and an inability to speak (Langston, 1995). A diagnosis of advanced Parkinson's disease was made, as these symptoms are consistent with the later stages of this degenerative disease. It was unusual for six fairly young people to come down with advanced Parkinson's at the same time in the same geographical area. In fact, none of the patients had Parkinson's, but they were all heroin addicts. These patients thought they were ingesting a synthetic form of heroin (called MPPP), but instead they had ingested a close derivative called MPTP, which unfortunately had the effects of destroying dopamine-producing neurons in an area of the brain crucial for motor performance. Hence, these "frozen addicts" exhibited paralysis and masklike expressions. The patients experienced a remarkable recovery after they were given L-dopa. In fact, it was later discovered that chemists who had worked with MPTP early in their careers later developed Parkinson's disease. Just as L-dopa acts as an agonist by enhancing the production of dopamine, drugs such as MPTP act as antagonists by destroying dopamine-producing neurons.

Many other drugs, including some street drugs, alter the actions of neurotransmitters. Let's look at a few more examples.

Methamphetamine affects pathways for dopamine, serotonin, and norepinephrine at the neuron's synapses, making it difficult to interpret exactly how it works. But the combination of its agonist and antagonist effects alters the functions of neurotransmitters that help us perceive and interpret visual images. Think back to David in the chapter opening vignette: His paranoid hallucinations were induced by his crystal meth habit. In David's case, it led to hallucinations that called his eyesight, and his sanity, into question.

Amphetamine is a popular drug that stimulates the release of norepinephrine and dopamine. In addition, both amphetamine and *cocaine* prevent the reuptake of norepinephrine and dopamine. The combination of increased release of norepinephrine and dopamine and prevention of their reuptake floods the synapse with those neurotransmitters, resulting in increased activation of their receptors. Both of these drugs therefore are strong agonists, although the psychological effects of the two drugs differ somewhat because of subtle distinctions in where and how they act on the brain. Norepinephrine and dopamine play a critical role in mood control, such that increases in either neurotransmitter result in euphoria, wakefulness, and a burst of energy. However, norepinephrine also increases heart rate. An overdose of amphetamine or cocaine can cause the heart to contract so rapidly that heartbeats do not last long enough to pump blood effectively, leading to fainting and sometimes to death.

But it doesn't take an overdose to produce some striking effects on behavior in recreational drug users. Consider, for example, a recent study that examined the ability of men and women who reported using cocaine regularly, at least once per month, to recognize facial expressions. Compared with participants who reported using cocaine less than once per month, and with a control group who said they had never used cocaine, the regular recreational users had no difficulty recognizing facial expressions such as happiness, disgust, and surprise. But the regular users were much less accurate than the other participants in recognizing expressions of fear (Kemmis et al., 2007; see **FIGURE 3.9** on the next page). Intriguingly, it has also been found that the size of a

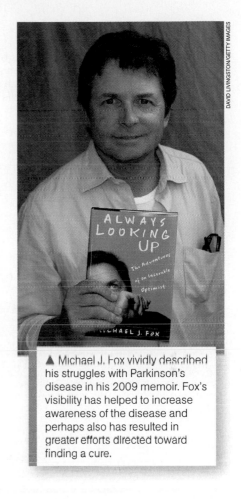

DAVID LIVINGSTON/GETTY IMAGES

▲ Michael J. Fox vividly described his struggles with Parkinson's disease in his 2009 memoir. Fox's visibility has helped to increase awareness of the disease and perhaps also has resulted in greater efforts directed toward finding a cure.

agonists Drugs that increase the action of a neurotransmitter.

antagonists Drugs that block the function of a neurotransmitter.

▶ FIGURE 3.9
Recognition of Facial Expressions by Cocaine Users Regular users of cocaine recognized facial expressions of fear less accurately than did occasional cocaine users or nonusers, but had little or no difficulty correctly recognizing facial expressions of anger, sadness, disgust, surprise, or happiness.

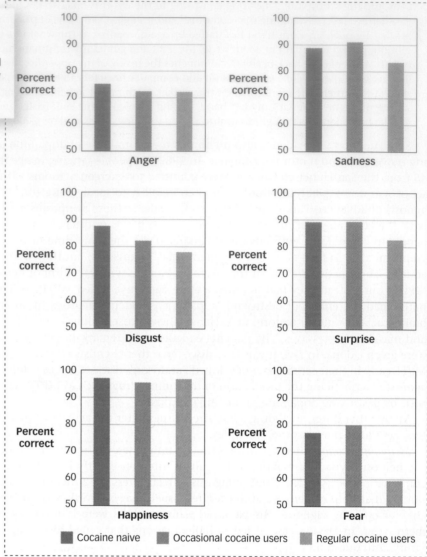

brain structure known as the amygdala, which plays an important role in recognizing expressions of fear (see p. 99), is reduced in regular cocaine users (Makris et al., 2004). Researchers are debating the reasons why this happens, but such abnormalities in brain and behavior shouldn't be surprising given the effects of a potent agonist like cocaine on neurotransmitter function.

Prozac, a drug commonly used to treat depression, is another example of a neurotransmitter agonist. Prozac blocks the reuptake of the neurotransmitter *serotonin*, making it part of a category of drugs called *selective serotonin reuptake inhibitors*, or *SSRIs* (Wong, Bymaster, & Engelman, 1995). Patients suffering from clinical depression typically have reduced levels of serotonin in their brains. By blocking reuptake, more of the neurotransmitter remains in the synapse longer and produces greater activation of serotonin receptors. Serotonin elevates mood, which can help relieve depression (Mann, 2005).

An antagonist with important medical implications is a drug called *propranalol*, one of a class of drugs called *beta-blockers* that obstruct a receptor site for norepinephrine in the heart. Because norepinephrine cannot bind to these receptors, heart rate slows down, which is helpful for disorders in which the heart beats too fast or irregularly. Beta-blockers are also prescribed to reduce the agitation, racing heart, and nervousness associated with stage fright (Mills & Dimsdale, 1991; for additional discussion of anti-anxiety and anitdepression drug treatments, see Chapter 15).

IN SUMMARY

○ The conduction of an electric signal within a neuron happens when the resting potential is changed by an electric impulse called an action potential.

○ The neuron's resting potential is due to differences in the K^+ concentrations inside and outside the cell membrane, resulting from open potassium channels that allow K^+ to flow outside the membrane together with closed channels for Na^+ and other ions.

○ If electric signals reach a threshold, this initiates an action potential, an all-or-none signal that moves down the entire length of the axon. The action potential occurs when sodium channels in the axon membrane open and potassium channels close, allowing the Na^+ ions to flow inside the axon. After the action potential has reached its maximum, the sodium channels close and the potassium channels open, allowing K^+ to flow out of the axon, returning the neuron to its resting potential. For a brief refractory period, the action potential cannot be re-initiated. Once it is initiated, the action potential spreads down the axon, jumping across the nodes of Ranvier to the synapse.

○ Communication between neurons takes place through synaptic transmission, where an action potential triggers release of neurotransmitters from the terminal buttons of the sending neuron's axon, which travel across the synapse to bind with receptors in the receiving neuron's dendrite.

○ Neurotransmitters bind to dendrites based on existing pathways in the brain and specific receptor sites for neurotransmitters. Neurotransmitters leave the synapse through reuptake, through enzyme deactivation, and by binding to autoreceptors.

○ Some of the major neurotransmitters are acetylcholine (ACh), dopamine, glutamate, GABA, norepinephrine, serotonin, and endorphins.

○ Drugs can affect behavior by acting as agonists, that is, by facilitating or increasing the actions of neurotransmitters, or as antagonists by blocking the action of neurotransmitters. Recreational drug use can have an effect on brain function.

The Organization of the Nervous System

We've seen how individual neurons communicate with each other. What's the bigger picture? Neurons work by forming circuits and pathways in the brain, which in turn influence circuits and pathways in other areas of the body. Without this kind of organization and delegation, neurons would be churning away with little purpose. Neurons are the building blocks that form *nerves,* or bundles of axons and the glial cells that support them. The **nervous system** *is an interacting network of neurons that conveys electrochemical information throughout the body.* In this section, we'll look at the major divisions and components of the nervous system.

Divisions of the Nervous System

There are two major divisions of the nervous system: the central nervous system and the peripheral nervous system (see **FIGURE 3.10** on the next page). The **central nervous system (CNS)** *is composed of the brain and spinal cord.* The central nervous system receives sensory information from the external world, processes and coordinates this information, and sends commands to the skeletal and muscular systems for action. At the top of the CNS rests the brain, which contains structures that support the most complex perceptual, motor, emotional, and cognitive functions of the nervous system. The spinal cord branches down from the brain; nerves that process sensory information and relay commands to the body connect to the spinal cord.

The **peripheral nervous system (PNS)** *connects the central nervous system to the body's organs and muscles.* The peripheral nervous system is itself composed of two major subdivisions, the somatic nervous system and the autonomic nervous system.

nervous system An interacting network of neurons that conveys electrochemical information throughout the body.

central nervous system (CNS) The part of the nervous system that is composed of the brain and spinal cord.

peripheral nervous system (PNS) The part of the nervous system that connects the central nervous system to the body's organs and muscles.

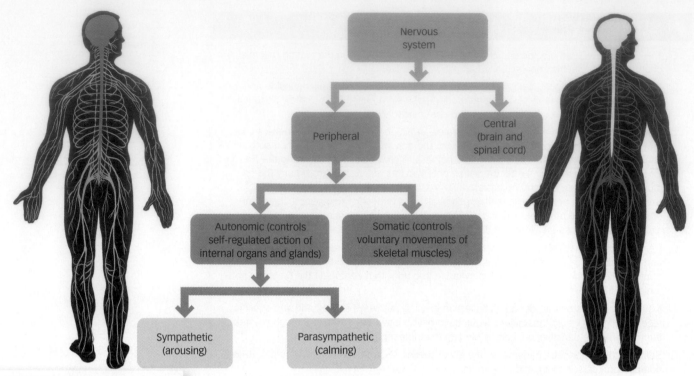

▲ FIGURE 3.10
The Human Nervous System The nervous system is organized into the peripheral and central nervous systems. The peripheral nervous system is further divided into the autonomic and somatic nervous systems.

somatic nervous system A set of nerves that conveys information into and out of the central nervous system.

autonomic nervous system (ANS) A set of nerves that carries involuntary and automatic commands that control blood vessels, body organs, and glands.

sympathetic nervous system A set of nerves that prepares the body for action in threatening situations.

parasympathetic nervous system A set of nerves that helps the body return to a normal resting state.

The **somatic nervous system** is *a set of nerves that conveys information into and out of the central nervous system.* Humans have conscious control over this system and use it to perceive, think, and coordinate their behaviors. For example, reaching for your morning cup of coffee involves the elegantly orchestrated activities of the somatic nervous system: Information from the receptors in your eyes travels to your brain, registering that a cup is on the table; signals from your brain travel to the muscles in your arm and hand; feedback from those muscles tells your brain that the cup has been grasped; and so on.

In contrast, the **autonomic nervous system (ANS)** is *a set of nerves that carries involuntary and automatic commands that control blood vessels, body organs, and glands.* As suggested by its name, this system works on its own to regulate bodily systems, largely outside of conscious control. The ANS has two major subdivisions, the sympathetic nervous system and the parasympathetic nervous system. Each exerts a different type of control on the body. The **sympathetic nervous system** is *a set of nerves that prepares the body for action in threatening situations* (see **FIGURE 3.11**). For example, imagine that you are walking alone late at night and frightened by footsteps behind you in a dark alley. Your sympathetic nervous system kicks into action at this point: It dilates your pupils to let in more light, increases your heart rate and respiration to pump more oxygen to muscles, diverts blood flow to your brain and muscles, and activates sweat glands to cool your body. To conserve energy, the sympathetic nervous system inhibits salivation and bowel movements, suppresses the body's immune responses, and suppresses responses to pain and injury. The sum total of these fast, automatic responses is that they increase the likelihood that you can escape.

What triggers the increase in your heart rate when you feel threatened?

The **parasympathetic nervous system** *helps the body return to a normal resting state.* When you're far away from your would-be attacker, your body doesn't need to remain on red alert. Now the parasympathetic nervous system kicks in to reverse the effects of the sympathetic nervous system and return your body to its normal state. The parasympathetic nervous system generally mirrors the connections of the sympathetic nervous system. For example, the parasympathetic nervous system constricts your pupils, slows your heart rate and respiration, diverts blood flow to your digestive system, and decreases activity in your sweat glands.

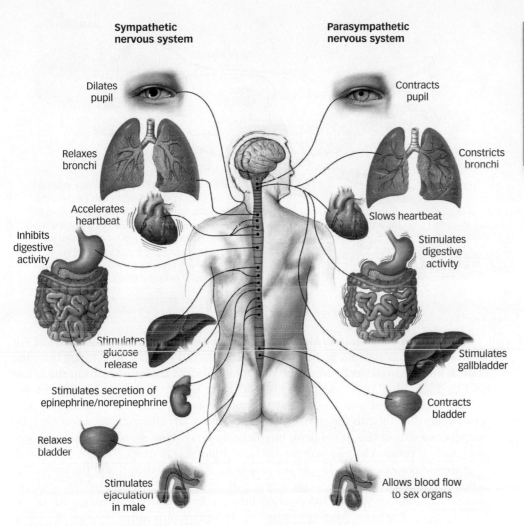

Sympathetic nervous system

Parasympathetic nervous system

Dilates pupil

Contracts pupil

Relaxes bronchi

Constricts bronchi

Accelerates heartbeat

Slows heartbeat

Inhibits digestive activity

Stimulates digestive activity

Stimulates glucose release

Stimulates gallbladder

Stimulates secretion of epinephrine/norepinephrine

Contracts bladder

Relaxes bladder

Stimulates ejaculation in male

Allows blood flow to sex organs

◀ FIGURE 3.11
Sympathetic and Parasympathetic Systems The autonomic nervous system is composed of two subsystems that complement each other. Activation of the sympathetic system serves several aspects of arousal, whereas the parasympathetic nervous system returns the body to its normal resting state.

As you might imagine, the sympathetic and parasympathetic nervous systems coordinate to control many bodily functions. One example is sexual behavior. In men, the parasympathetic nervous system engorges the blood vessels of the penis to produce an erection, but the sympathetic nervous system is responsible for ejaculation. In women, the parasympathetic nervous system produces vaginal lubrication, but the sympathetic nervous system underlies orgasm. In both men and women, a successful sexual experience depends on a delicate balance of these two systems; in fact, anxiety about sexual performance can disrupt this balance. For example, sympathetic nervous system activation caused by anxiety can lead to premature ejaculation in males and lack of lubrication in females.

Components of the Central Nervous System

Compared to the many divisions of the peripheral nervous system, the central nervous system may seem simple. After all, it has only two elements: the brain and the spinal cord. But those two elements are ultimately responsible for most of what we do as humans.

The spinal cord often seems like the brain's poor relation: The brain gets all the glory and the spinal cord just hangs around, doing relatively simple tasks. Those tasks, however, are pretty important: keeping you breathing, responding to pain, moving your muscles, allowing you to walk. What's more, without the spinal cord, the brain would not be able to put any of its higher processing into action.

What important functions does the spinal cord perform on its own?

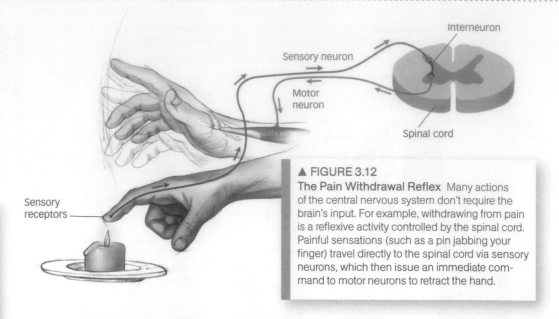

▲ FIGURE 3.12
The Pain Withdrawal Reflex Many actions of the central nervous system don't require the brain's input. For example, withdrawing from pain is a reflexive activity controlled by the spinal cord. Painful sensations (such as a pin jabbing your finger) travel directly to the spinal cord via sensory neurons, which then issue an immediate command to motor neurons to retract the hand.

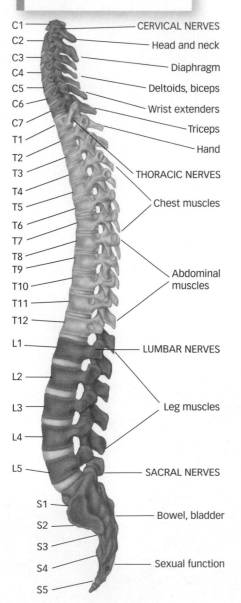

▼ FIGURE 3.13
Regions of the Spinal Cord The spinal cord is divided into four main sections, each of which controls different parts of the body. Damage higher on the spinal cord usually portends greater impairment.

Do you need your brain to tell you to pull your hand away from a hot stove? For some very basic behaviors such as this, the spinal cord doesn't need input from the brain at all. Connections between the sensory inputs and motor neurons in the spinal cord mediate **spinal reflexes**, *simple pathways in the nervous system that rapidly generate muscle contractions*. If you touch a hot stove, the sensory neurons that register pain send inputs directly into the spinal cord (see **FIGURE 3.12**). Through just a few synaptic connections within the spinal cord, interneurons relay these sensory inputs to motor neurons that connect to your arm muscles and direct you to quickly retract your hand.

More elaborate tasks require the collaboration of the spinal cord and the brain. The peripheral nervous system communicates with the central nervous system through nerves that conduct sensory information into the brain, carry commands out of the brain, or both. The brain sends commands for voluntary movement through the spinal cord to motor neurons, whose axons project out to skeletal muscles and send the message to contract. Damage to the spinal cord severs the connection from the brain to the sensory and motor neurons that are essential to sensory perception and movement. The location of the spinal injury often determines the extent of the abilities that are lost. As you can see in **FIGURE 3.13**, different regions of the spinal cord control different systems of the body. Patients with damage at a particular level of the spinal cord lose sensations of touch and pain in body parts below the level of the injury as well as a loss of motor control of the muscles in the same areas. A spinal injury higher up the cord usually predicts a much poorer prognosis, such as quadriplegia (the loss of sensation and motor control over all limbs), breathing through a respirator, and lifelong immobility.

The late actor Christopher Reeve, who starred as Superman in four *Superman* movies, damaged his spinal cord in a horseback riding accident in 1995, resulting in loss of sensation and motor control in all of his body parts below the neck. Despite great efforts

▶ The human brain weighs only three pounds and isn't much to look at, but its accomplishments are staggering.

over several years, Reeve made only modest gains in his motor control and sensation, highlighting the extent to which we depend on communication from the brain through the spinal cord to the body, and showing how difficult it is to compensate for the loss of these connections (Edgerton et al., 2004). Sadly, Christopher Reeve died at age 52 in 2004 from complications due to his paralysis. On a brighter note, researchers are making progress in understanding the nature of spinal cord injuries and how to treat them by focusing on how the brain changes in response to injury (Blesch & Tuszynski, 2008; Dunlop, 2008), a process that is closely related to the concept of brain plasticity that we will examine later in this chapter (p. 102).

spinal reflexes Simple pathways in the nervous system that rapidly generate muscle contractions.

IN SUMMARY

○ Neurons make up nerves, which in turn form the human nervous system.

○ The nervous system is divided into the peripheral and the central nervous systems.

○ The peripheral nervous system connects the central nervous system with the rest of the body, and it is itself divided into the somatic nervous system and the autonomic nervous system.

○ The somatic nervous system, which conveys information into and out of the central nervous system, controls voluntary muscles, whereas the autonomic nervous system automatically controls the body's organs.

○ The autonomic nervous system is further divided into the sympathetic and parasympathetic nervous systems, which complement each other in their effects on the body. The sympathetic nervous system prepares the body for action in threatening situations, and the parasympathetic nervous system returns it to its normal state.

○ The central nervous system is composed of the spinal cord and the brain. The spinal cord can mediate some basic behaviors such as spinal reflexes without input from the brain.

Structure of the Brain

The human brain, weighing in at about three pounds, is really not much to look at. You already know that its neurons and glial cells are busy humming away, giving you potentially brilliant ideas, consciousness, and feelings. But which neurons in which parts of the brain control which functions? To answer that question, neuroscientists had to find a way of describing the brain that allows researchers to communicate with one another. It can be helpful to talk about areas of the brain from "bottom to top," noting how the different regions are specialized for different kinds of tasks. In general, simpler functions are performed at the "lower levels" of the brain, whereas more complex functions are performed at successively "higher" levels (see **FIGURE 3.14**). Or, as you'll see shortly, the brain can also be approached in a "side-by-side" fashion: Although each side of the brain is roughly analogous, one half of the brain specializes in some tasks that the other half doesn't. Although these divisions make it easier to understand areas of the brain and their functions, keep in mind that none of these structures or areas in the brain can act alone: They are all part of one big, interacting, interdependent whole.

Let's look first at the divisions of the brain, and the responsibilities of each part, moving from the bottom to the top. Using this view, we can divide the brain into three parts: the hindbrain, the midbrain, and the forebrain (see Figure 3.14).

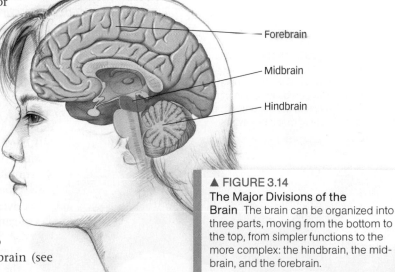

Forebrain

Midbrain

Hindbrain

▲ FIGURE 3.14
The Major Divisions of the Brain The brain can be organized into three parts, moving from the bottom to the top, from simpler functions to the more complex: the hindbrain, the midbrain, and the forebrain.

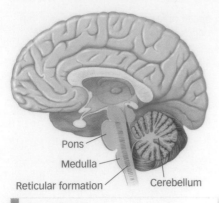

Pons

Medulla

Reticular formation   Cerebellum

▲ FIGURE 3.15

The Hindbrain The hindbrain coordinates information coming into and out of the spinal cord and controls the basic functions of life. It includes the medulla, the reticular formation, the cerebellum, and the pons.

The Hindbrain

If you follow the spinal cord from your tailbone to where it enters your skull, you'll find it difficult to determine where your spinal cord ends and your brain begins. That's because the spinal cord is continuous with the **hindbrain**, *an area of the brain that coordinates information coming into and out of the spinal cord*. The hindbrain looks like a stalk on which the rest of the brain sits, and it controls the most basic functions of life: respiration, alertness, and motor skills. There are three anatomical structures that make up the hindbrain: the medulla, the cerebellum, and the pons (see **FIGURE 3.15**).

The **medulla** is *an extension of the spinal cord into the skull that coordinates heart rate, circulation, and respiration*. Inside the medulla is a small cluster of neurons called the **reticular formation**, which *regulates sleep, wakefulness, and levels of arousal*. In one early experiment, researchers stimulated the reticular formation of a sleeping cat. This caused the animal to awaken almost instantaneously and remain alert. Conversely, severing the connections between the reticular formation and the rest of the brain caused the animal to lapse into an irreversible coma (Moruzzi & Magoun, 1949). The reticular formation maintains the same delicate balance between alertness and unconsciousness in humans. In fact, many general anesthetics work by reducing activity in the reticular formation, rendering patient unconscious.

▶ The cerebellum, which helps us to maintain balance while walking, needs to be functioning normally in order to pass a roadside sobriety test.

HUTCHINGS STOCK PHOTOGRAPHY/CORBIS

Behind the medulla is the **cerebellum**, *a large structure of the hindbrain that controls fine motor skills*. *Cerebellum* is Latin "little brain," and the structure does look like a small replica of the brain. The cerebellum orchestrates the proper sequence movements when we ride a bike, play the piano, or maintain balance while walking and running. It contributes to the "fine tuning" of behavior, smoothing our actions to allow their graceful execution rather than initiating the actions (Smetacek, 2002). The initiation of behavior involves other areas of the brain; as you'll recall, different brain systems interact and are interdependent with one another.

Which part of the brain helps to orchestrate movements that keep you steady on your bike?

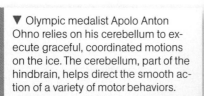

▼ Olympic medalist Apolo Anton Ohno relies on his cerebellum to execute graceful, coordinated motions on the ice. The cerebellum, part of the hindbrain, helps direct the smooth action of a variety of motor behaviors.

AP PHOTO/KEVORK DJANSEZIAN

The last major area of the hindbrain is the **pons**, *a structure that relays information from the cerebellum to the rest of the brain*. *Pons* means "bridge" in Latin. Although the detailed functions of the pons remain poorly understood, it essentially acts as a "relay station" or bridge between the cerebellum and other structures in the brain.

The Midbrain

Sitting on top of the hindbrain is the *midbrain*, which is relatively small in humans. As you can see in **FIGURE 3.16**, the midbrain contains two main structures: the tectum and the tegmentum.

The **tectum** *orients an organism in the environment*. The tectum receives stimulus input from the eyes, ears, and skin and moves the organism in a coordinated way toward the stimulus. For example, when you're studying in a quiet room and you hear a *click* behind and to the right of you, your body will swivel and orient to the direction of the sound; this is your tectum in action.

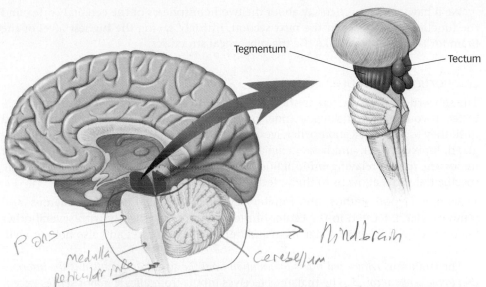

◄ FIGURE 3.16
The Midbrain The midbrain is important for orientation and movement. It includes structures such as the tectum and tegmentum.

[Handwritten annotations: Pons, Medulla, reticular info, Cerebellum, Midbrain]

The **tegmentum** is *involved in movement and arousal;* it also helps to orient an organism toward sensory stimuli. The midbrain may be relatively small, but it is a central location of neurotransmitters involved in arousal, mood, and motivation and the brain structures that rely on them (White, 1996).

You could survive if you had only a hindbrain and a midbrain. The structures in the hindbrain would take care of all the bodily functions necessary to sustain life, and the structures in the midbrain would orient you toward or away from pleasurable or threatening stimuli in the environment. But this wouldn't be much of a life. To understand where the abilities that make us fully human come from, we need to consider the last division of the brain.

The Forebrain

When you appreciate the beauty of a poem, detect the sarcasm in a friend's remark, plan to go skiing next winter, or notice the faint glimmer of sadness on a loved one's face, you are enlisting the forebrain. The *forebrain* is the highest level of the brain—literally and figuratively—and controls complex cognitive, emotional, sensory, and motor functions (see **FIGURE 3.17**). The forebrain itself is divided into two main sections: the cerebral cortex and the subcortical structures.

The **cerebral cortex** is *the outermost layer of the brain, visible to the naked eye, and divided into two hemispheres.* The **subcortical structures** are *areas of the forebrain housed under the cerebral cortex near the very center of the brain.*

hindbrain An area of the brain that coordinates information coming into and out of the spinal cord.

medulla An extension of the spinal cord into the skull that coordinates heart rate, circulation, and respiration.

reticular formation A brain structure that regulates sleep, wakefulness, and levels of arousal.

cerebellum A large structure of the hindbrain that controls fine motor skills.

pons A brain structure that relays information from the cerebellum to the rest of the brain.

tectum A part of the midbrain that orients an organism in the environment.

tegmentum A part of the midbrain that is involved in movement and arousal.

cerebral cortex The outermost layer of the brain, visible to the naked eye and divided into two hemispheres.

subcortical structures Areas of the forebrain housed under the cerebral cortex near the very center of the brain.

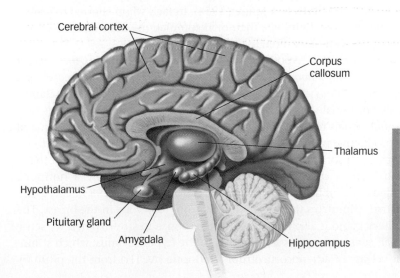

◄ FIGURE 3.17
The Forebrain The forebrain is the highest level of the brain and is critical for complex cognitive, emotional, sensory, and motor functions. The forebrain is divided into two parts: the cerebral cortex and the underlying subcortical structures. These include the thalamus, hypothalamus, pituitary gland, amygdala, and hippocampus. The corpus callosum connects the two hemispheres of the brain.

limbic system A group of forebrain structures including the hypothalamus, the amygdala, and the hippocampus, which are involved in motivation, emotion, learning, and memory.

thalamus A subcortical structure that relays and filters information from the senses and transmits the information to the cerebral cortex.

hypothalamus A subcortical structure that regulates body temperature, hunger, thirst, and sexual behavior.

pituitary gland The "master gland" of the body's hormone-producing system, which releases hormones that direct the functions of many other glands in the body.

We'll have much more to say about the two hemispheres of the cerebral cortex and the functions they serve in the next section, fittingly saving the highest level of the brain for last. First, we'll examine the subcortical structures.

Subcortical Structures

The subcortical structures are nestled deep inside the brain, where they are quite protected. If you imagine sticking an index finger in each of your ears and pushing inward until they touch, that's about where you'd find the thalamus, hypothalamus, pituitary gland, limbic system, and basal ganglia. Each of these subcortical structures plays an important role in relaying information throughout the brain, as well as performing specific tasks that allow us to think, feel, and behave as humans.

Thalamus, Hypothalamus, and Pituitary Gland. The thalamus, hypothalamus, and pituitary gland, located in the center of the brain, interact closely with several other brain structures: They relay signals to and from these structures and also help to regulate them.

The **thalamus** *relays and filters information from the senses and transmits the information to the cerebral cortex.* The thalamus receives inputs from all the major senses except smell, which has direct connections to the cerebral cortex.

The thalamus acts as a kind of computer server in a networked system, taking in multiple inputs and relaying them to a variety of locations (Guillery & Sherman, 2002). However, unlike the mechanical operations of a computer—"send input A to location B"—the thalamus actively filters sensory information, giving more weight to some inputs and less weight to others. The thalamus also closes the pathways of incoming sensations during sleep, providing a valuable function in *not* allowing information to pass to the rest of the brain.

How is the thalamus like a computer?

The **hypothalamus**, located below the thalamus (*hypo-* is Greek for "under"), *regulates body temperature, hunger, thirst, and sexual behavior.* Although the hypothalamus is a tiny area of the brain, clusters of neurons in the hypothalamus oversee a wide range of basic behaviors, keeping body temperature, blood sugar levels, and metabolism within an optimal range for normal human functioning. Lesions to some areas of the hypothalamus result in overeating, whereas lesions to other areas leave an animal with no desire for food at all, highlighting that the hypothalamus plays a key role in regulating food intake (Berthoud & Morrison, 2008). Also, when you think about sex, messages from your cerebral cortex are sent to the hypothalamus to trigger the release of hormones. Finally, electric stimulation of the hypothalamus in cats can produce hissing and biting, whereas stimulation of other areas in the hypothalamus can produce what appears to be intense pleasure for an animal (Siegel et al., 1999). Researchers James Olds and Peter Milner found that a small electric current delivered to a certain region of a rat's hypothalamus was extremely rewarding for the animal (Olds & Milner, 1954). In fact, when allowed to press a bar attached to the electrode to initiate their own stimulation, rats would do so several thousand times an hour, often to the point of exhaustion!

Located below the hypothalamus is the **pituitary gland**, *the "master gland" of the body's hormone-producing system, which releases hormones that direct the functions of many other glands in the body.* The hypothalamus sends hormonal signals to the pituitary gland, which in turn sends hormonal signals to other glands to control stress, digestive activities, and reproductive processes. For example, when a baby suckles its mother's breast, sensory neurons in her breast send signals to her hypothalamus, which then signals her pituitary gland to release a hormone called *oxytocin* into the bloodstream (McNeilly et al., 1983). Oxytocin, in turn, stimulates the release of milk from reservoirs in the breast. The pituitary gland is also involved in the response to stress. When we sense a threat, sensory neurons send signals to the hypothalamus, which stimulates the release of adrenocorticotropic hormone (ACTH) from the pituitary

▼ FIGURE 3.18
The Limbic System The limbic system includes the hippocampus and the amygdala, as well as the hypothalamus. These structures are involved in motivation, emotion, learning, and memory.

Hypothalamus

Pituitary gland

Amygdala

Hippocampus

gland. ACTH, in turn, stimulates the adrenal glands (above the kidneys) to release hormones that activate the sympathetic nervous system (Selye & Fortier, 1950). As you read earlier in this chapter, the sympathetic nervous system prepares the body to either meet the threat head-on or flee from the situation.

The Limbic System

The hypothalamus also is part of the **limbic system**, a group of forebrain structures including the hypothalamus, the amygdala, and the hippocampus, which are involved in motivation, emotion, learning, and memory (Maclean, 1970; Papex, 1937). (See **FIGURE 3.18**.) The limbic system is where the subcortical structures meet the cerebral cortex.

The **hippocampus** (from the Latin for "sea horse," due to its shape) is *critical for creating new memories and integrating them into a network of knowledge so that they can be stored indefinitely in other parts of the cerebral cortex.* Patients with damage to the hippocampus can acquire new information and keep it in awareness for a few seconds, but as soon as they are distracted, they forget the information and the experience that produced it (Scoville & Milner, 1957; Squire, 2009). This kind of disruption is limited to everyday memory for facts and events that we can bring to consciousness; memory of learned habitual routines or emotional reactions remains intact (Squire, Knowlton, & Musen, 1993). As an example, people with damage to the hippocampus can remember how to drive and talk, but they cannot recall where they have recently driven or a conversation they have just had. You will read more about the hippocampus and its role in creating, storing, and combining memories in Chapter 6.

The **amygdala** (from the Latin for "almond," also due to its shape), *located at the tip of each horn of the hippocampus, plays a central role in many emotional processes, particularly the formation of emotional memories* (Aggleton, 1992). The amygdala attaches significance to previously neutral events that are associated with fear, punishment, or reward (LeDoux, 1992). As an example, think of the last time something scary or unpleasant happened to you: A car came barreling toward you as you started walking into an intersection or a ferocious dog leapt out of an alley as you passed by. Those stimuli—a car or a dog—are fairly neutral; you don't have a panic attack every time you walk by a used car lot. The emotional significance attached to events involving those stimuli is the work of the amygdala (McGaugh, 2006). When we are in emotionally arousing situations, the amygdala stimulates the hippocampus to remember many details surrounding the situation (Kensinger & Schacter, 2005). For example, people

Why are you likely to remember details of a traumatic event?

who lived through the terrorist attacks of September 11, 2001 remember vivid details about where they were, what they were doing, and how they felt when they heard the news, even years later (Hirst et al., 2009). In particular, the amygdala seems to be especially involved in encoding events as *fearful* (Adolphs et al., 1995; Sigurdsson et al., 2007). We'll have more to say about the amygdala's role in emotion and motivated behavior in Chapter 8. For now, keep in mind that a group of neurons the size of a lima bean buried deep in your brain help you to laugh, weep, or shriek in fright when the circumstances call for it.

The Basal Ganglia. There are several other structures in the subcortical area, but we'll consider just one more. The **basal ganglia** are *a set of subcortical structures that directs intentional movements.* The basal ganglia are located near the thalamus and hypothalamus; they receive input from the cerebral cortex and send outputs to the motor centers in the brain stem (see **FIGURE 3.19**). One part of the basal ganglia, the *striatum*, is involved in the control of posture and movement. As we saw in the excerpt from Michael J. Fox's book, patients who suffer from Parkinson's disease typically show symptoms of uncontrollable shaking and sudden jerks of the limbs and are unable to initiate a sequence of movements to achieve a specific goal. This happens because the dopamine-producing neurons in the substantia nigra (found in the tegmentum of the midbrain) have become

hippocampus A structure critical for creating new memories and integrating them into a network of knowledge so that they can be stored indefinitely in other parts of the cerebral cortex.

amygdala A part of the limbic system that plays a central role in many emotional processes, particularly the formation of emotional memories.

basal ganglia A set of subcortical structures that directs intentional movements.

▼ FIGURE 3.19
The Basal Ganglia The basal ganglia are a group of subcortical brain structures that direct intentional movement. They receive input from the cerebral cortex and send output to the motor centers in the brain stem.

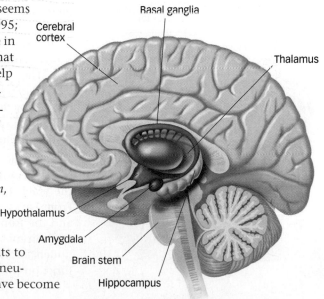

Basal ganglia

Cerebral cortex

Thalamus

Hypothalamus

Amygdala

Brain stem

Hippocampus

DONNA RANIERI

► Crumpling a newspaper allows the same amount of surface area to fit into a much smaller space, just like the wrinkles and folds in the cortex allow a great deal of brain power to fit inside the human skull.

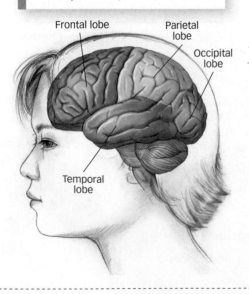

DONNA RANIERI

▼ FIGURE 3.20
Cerebral Cortex and Lobes The four major lobes of the cerebral cortex are the occipital lobe, the parietal lobe, the temporal lobe, and the frontal lobe.

Frontal lobe

Parietal lobe

Occipital lobe

Temporal lobe

damaged (Dauer & Przedborski, 2003). The undersupply of dopamine then affects the striatum in the basal ganglia, which in turn leads to the visible behavioral symptoms of Parkinson's.

So, what's the problem in Parkinson's—the jerky movements, the ineffectiveness of the striatum in directing behavior, the botched interplay of the substantia nigra and the striatum, or the underproduction of dopamine at the neuronal level? The answer is "all of the above." This unfortunate disease provides a nice illustration of two themes regarding the brain and behavior. First, invisible actions at the level of neurons in the brain can produce substantial effects at the level of behavior. Second, the interaction of hindbrain, midbrain, and forebrain structures shows how the various regions are interdependent.

The Cerebral Cortex

Our tour of the brain has taken us from the very small (neurons) to the somewhat bigger (major divisions of the brain) to the very large: the cerebral cortex. The cortex is the highest level of the brain, and it is responsible for the most complex aspects of perception, emotion, movement, and thought (Fuster, 2003). It sits over the rest of the brain, like a mushroom cap shielding the underside and stem, and it is the wrinkled surface you see when looking at the brain with the naked eye.

The smooth surfaces of the cortex—the raised part—are called *gyri* (*gyrus* if you're talking about just one), and the indentations or fissures are called *sulci* (*sulcus* when singular). Sulci and gyri represent a triumph of evolution. The cerebral cortex occupies roughly the area of a newspaper page. Fitting that much cortex into a human skull is a tough task. But if you crumple a sheet of newspaper, you'll see that the same surface area now fits compactly into a much smaller space. The cortex, with its wrinkles and folds, holds a lot of brainpower in a relatively small package that fits comfortably inside the human skull (see **FIGURE 3.20**).

The functions of the cerebral cortex can be understood at three levels: the separation of the cortex into two hemispheres, the functions of each hemisphere, and the role of specific cortical areas.

Organization across Hemispheres. The first level of organization divides the cortex into the left and right hemispheres. The two hemispheres are more or less symmetrical in their appearance and, to some extent, in their functions. However, each hemisphere controls the functions of the opposite side of the body. This is called *contralateral control*, meaning that your right cerebral hemisphere perceives stimuli from and controls movements on the left side of your body, whereas your left cerebral hemisphere perceives stimuli from and controls movement on the right side of your body (see **FIGURE 3.21**).

The cerebral hemispheres are connected to each other by *commissures*, bundles of axons that make possible communication between parallel areas of the cortex in each half. The largest of these commissures is the **corpus callosum**, which *connects large areas of the cerebral cortex on each side of the brain and supports communication of information across the hemispheres.* This means that information received in the right hemisphere, for example, can pass across the corpus callosum and be registered, virtually instantaneously, in the left hemisphere.

Organization within Hemispheres. The second level of organization in the cerebral cortex distinguishes the functions of the different regions within each hemisphere of the brain. Each hemisphere of the cerebral cortex is divided into four areas, or *lobes*: From back to front, these are the occipital lobe, the parietal lobe, the temporal lobe, and the frontal lobe, as shown in Figure 3.20. We'll examine the functions of these lobes in more detail later, noting how scientists have used a variety of techniques to understand the operations of the brain. For now, here's a brief overview of the main functions of each lobe.

The **occipital lobe**, located at the back of the cerebral cortex, *processes visual information*. Sensory receptors in the eyes send information to the thalamus, which in turn sends information to the primary areas of the occipital lobe, where simple features of the stimulus are extracted, such as the location and orientation of an object's edges (see p. 141 in Chapter 4 for more details). These features are then processed into a more complex "map" of the stimulus onto the occipital cortex, leading to comprehension of what's being seen. As you might imagine, damage to the primary visual areas of the occipital lobe can leave a person with partial or complete blindness. Information still enters the eyes, which work just fine. But without the ability to process and make sense of the information at the level of the cerebral cortex, the information is as good as lost (Zeki, 2001).

The **parietal lobe**, located in front of the occipital lobe, carries out functions that include *processing information about touch*. The parietal lobe contains the *somatosensory cortex*, a strip of brain tissue running from the top of the brain down to the sides (see **FIGURE 3.22**). Within each hemisphere, the somatosensory cortex represents the skin areas on the contralateral surface of the body. Each part of the somatosensory cortex maps onto a particular part of the body. If a body area is more sensitive, a larger part of the somatosensory cortex is devoted to it. For example, the part of the somatosensory cortex that corresponds to the lips and tongue is larger than the area corresponding to the feet. The somatosensory cortex can be illustrated as a distorted figure, called a *homunculus* ("little man"), in which the body parts are rendered according to how much of the somatosensory cortex is devoted to them (Penfield & Rasmussen, 1950). Directly in front of the somatosensory cortex, in the frontal lobe, is a parallel strip of brain tissue called the *motor cortex*. Like the somatosensory cortex, different parts of the motor cortex correspond to different body parts. The motor cortex initiates voluntary movements and sends messages to the basal ganglia, cerebellum, and spinal cord. The motor and somatosensory cortices, then, are like sending and receiving areas of the cerebral cortex, taking in information and sending out commands as the case might be.

Corpus callosum

◄ **FIGURE 3.21**
Cerebral Hemispheres Top view of the brain with part of the right cerebral hemisphere pulled away to expose the corpus callosum.

CAROL DONNER/PHOTOTAKE

corpus callosum A thick band of nerve fibers that connects large areas of the cerebral cortex on each side of the brain and supports communication of information across the hemispheres.

occipital lobe A region of the cerebral cortex that processes visual information.

parietal lobe A region of the cerebral cortex whose functions include processing information about touch.

▼ **FIGURE 3.22**
Somatosensory and Motor Cortices The motor cortex, a strip of brain tissue in the frontal lobe, represents and controls different skin and body areas on the contralateral side of the body. Directly behind the motor cortex, in the parietal lobe, lies the somatosensory cortex. Like the motor cortex, the somatosensory cortex represents skin areas of particular parts on the contralateral side of the body.

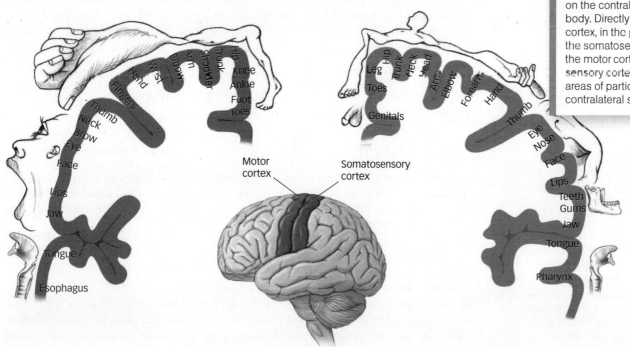

Motor cortex

Somatosensory cortex

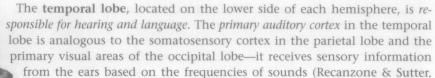

▶ The homunculus is a rendering of the body in which each part is shown in proportion to how much of the somatosensory cortex is devoted to it.

THE BRITISH MUSEUM, NATURAL HISTORY

The **temporal lobe**, located on the lower side of each hemisphere, is *responsible for hearing and language*. The *primary auditory cortex* in the temporal lobe is analogous to the somatosensory cortex in the parietal lobe and the primary visual areas of the occipital lobe—it receives sensory information from the ears based on the frequencies of sounds (Recanzone & Sutter, 2008). Secondary areas of the temporal lobe then process the information into meaningful units, such as speech and words. The temporal lobe also houses the visual association areas that interpret the meaning of visual stimuli and help us recognize common objects in the environment (Martin, 2007).

The **frontal lobe**, which sits behind the forehead, has *specialized areas for movement, abstract thinking, planning, memory, and judgment*. As you just read, it contains the motor cortex, which coordinates movements of muscle groups throughout the body. Other areas in the frontal lobe coordinate thought processes that help us manipulate information and retrieve memories, which we can use to plan our behaviors and interact socially with others. In short, the frontal cortex allows us to do the kind of thinking, imagining, planning, and anticipating that sets humans apart from most other species (Schoenemann, Sheenan, & Glotzer, 2005; Stuss & Benson, 1986; Suddendorf & Corballis, 2007).

What types of thinking occur in the frontal lobe?

Organization within Specific Lobes. The third level of organization in the cerebral cortex involves the representation of information within specific lobes in the cortex. There is a hierarchy of processing stages from primary areas that handle fine details of information all the way up to **association areas**, which are *composed of neurons that help provide sense and meaning to information registered in the cortex*. For example, neurons in the primary visual cortex are highly specialized—some detect features of the environment that are in a horizontal orientation, others detect movement, and still others process information about human versus nonhuman forms. The association areas of the occipital lobe interpret the information extracted by these primary areas—shape, motion, and so on—to make sense of what's being perceived; in this case, perhaps a large cat leaping toward your face. Similarly, neurons in the primary auditory cortex register sound frequencies, but it's the association areas of the temporal lobe that allow you to turn those noises into the meaning of your friend screaming, "Look out for the cat!!" Association areas, then, help stitch together the threads of information in the various parts of the cortex to produce a meaningful understanding of what's being registered in the brain. Neurons in the association areas are usually less specialized and more flexible than neurons in the primary areas. As such, they can be shaped by learning and experience to do their job more effectively. This kind of shaping of neurons by environmental forces allows the brain flexibility, or "plasticity," our next topic.

Brain Plasticity

The cerebral cortex may seem like a fixed structure, one big sheet of neurons designed to help us make sense of our external world. Remarkably, though, sensory cortices are not fixed. They can adapt to changes in sensory inputs, a quality researchers call *plasticity* (i.e., "the ability to be molded"). As an example, if you lose your middle finger in an accident, the part of the somatosensory area that represents that finger is initially unresponsive (Kaas, 1991). After all, there's no longer any sensory input going from that location to that part of the brain. You might expect the "left middle finger neurons" of the somatosensory cortex to wither away. However, over time, that area in the somatosensory cortex becomes responsive to stimulation of the fingers *adjacent* to the missing

What does it mean to say that the brain is plastic?

temporal lobe A region of the cerebral cortex responsible for hearing and language.

frontal lobe A region of the cerebral cortex that has specialized areas for movement, abstract thinking, planning, memory, and judgment.

association areas Areas of the cerebral cortex that are composed of neurons that help provide sense and meaning to information registered in the cortex.

finger. The brain is plastic: Functions that were assigned to certain areas of the brain may be capable of being reassigned to other areas of the brain to accommodate changing input from the environment (Feldman, 2009). This suggests that sensory inputs "compete" for representation in each cortical area. (See the Real World box for a striking illustration of "phantom limbs.")

THE REAL WORLD

Brain Plasticity and Sensations in Phantom Limbs

Long after a limb is amputated, many patients continue to experience sensations where the missing limb would be, a phenomenon called *phantom limb syndrome*. Patients can feel their missing limbs moving, even in coordinated gestures such as shaking hands. Some even report feeling pain in their phantom limbs. Why does this happen? Some evidence suggests that phantom limb syndrome may arise in part because of plasticity in the brain.

Researchers stimulated the skin surface in various regions around the face, torso, and arms while monitoring brain activity in amputees and non-amputated volunteers (Ramachandran & Blakeslee, 1998; Ramachandran, Rodgers-Ramachandran, & Stewart, 1992). Brain-imaging techniques displayed the somatosensory cortical areas activated when the skin was stimulated. This allowed the researchers to map how touch is represented in the somatosensory cortex for different areas of the body. For example, when the face was touched, the researchers could determine which areas in the somatosensory cortex were most active; when the torso was stimulated, they could see which areas responded; and so on.

Brain scans of the amputees revealed that stimulating areas of the face and upper

▶ Mapping Sensations in Phantom Limbs (a) Researchers lightly touch an amputee's face with a cotton swab, eliciting sensations in the "missing" hand. (b) Touching different parts of the cheek can even result in sensations in particular fingers or the thumb of the missing hand.

Cotton swab

Amputee

Thumb

Ball of thumb

Index finger

Pinkie finger

(a)

(b)

arm activated an area in the somatosensory cortex that previously would have been activated by a now-missing hand. The face and arm were represented in the somatosensory cortex in an area adjacent to where the person's hand—now amputated—would have been represented. Stimulating the face or arm produced phantom limb sensations in the amputees; they reported "feeling" a sensation in their missing limbs.

Brain plasticity can explain these results (Pascual-Leone et al., 2005). The cortical representations for the face and the upper arm normally lie on either side of the representation for the hand. The somatosensory areas for the face and upper arm were larger in amputees and had taken over the part of the cortex normally representing the hand. Indeed, the new face and arm representations were now contiguous with each other, filling in the space occupied by the hand representation. Some of these new mappings were quite concise. For example, in some amputees, when specific areas of the facial skin were activated, the patient reported sensations in just *one finger* of the phantom hand!

This and related research suggest one explanation for a previously poorly understood phenomenon. How can a person "feel" something that isn't there? Brain plasticity, an adaptive process through which the brain reorganizes itself, offers an answer (Flor, Nikolajsen, & Jensen, 2006). The brain established new mappings that led to novel sensations.

This idea also has practical implications for dealing with the pain that can result from phantom limbs (Ramachandran & Altschuler, 2009). Researchers have used a "mirror box" to teach patients a new mapping to increase voluntary control over their phantom limbs. For example, a patient would place his intact right hand and phantom left hand in the mirror box such that when looking at the mirror, he sees his right hand reflected on the left—where he has placed his phantom—creating the illusion the phantom has been restored. The phantom hand thus appears to respond to motor commands given by the patient, and with practice the patient can become better at "'moving" the phantom in response to voluntary commands. As a result, when feeling the excrutiating pain associated with a clenched phantom hand, the patient can now voluntarily unclench the hand and reduce the pain. This therapeutic approach based on brain plasticity has been applied successfully to a variety of patient populations (Ramachandran & Altschuler, 2009).

▼ A mirror box creates the illusion that the phantom limb has been restored.

Plasticity doesn't only occur to compensate for missing digits or limbs, however. An extraordinary amount of stimulation of one finger can result in that finger "taking over" the representation of the part of the cortex that usually represents other, adjacent fingers (Merzenich et al., 1990). For example, concert pianists have highly developed cortical areas for finger control: The continued input from the fingers commands a larger area of representation in the somatosensory cortices in the brain. Consistent with this observation, recent research indicates greater plasticity within the motor cortex of professional musicians compared with nonmusicians, perhaps reflecting an increase in the number of motor synapses as a result of extended practice (Rosenkranz, Williamon, & Rothwell, 2007). Similar findings have been obtained with quilters (who may have highly developed areas for the thumb and forefinger, which are critical to their profession) and taxi drivers (who have overdeveloped brain areas in the hippocampus that are used during spatial navigation; Maguire, Woollett, & Spiers, 2006).

Plasticity is also related to a question you might not expect to find in a psychology text: How much exercise have you been getting lately? While we expect that you are spending countless happy hours reading this text, we also hope that you've been finding enough time for physical exercise. A large of number of studies in rats and other nonhuman animals indicate that physical exercise can increase the number of synapses and even promote the development of new neurons in the hippocampus (Hillman, Erickson, & Kramer, 2008; van Praag, 2009). Recent studies with people have begun to document beneficial effects of cardiovascular exercise on aspects of brain function and cognitive performance (Colcombe et al., 2004, 2006). Though these effects tend to be seen most clearly in older adults (OK, so it's time for your textbook authors to get on a treadmill), benefits have also been documented throughout the life span (Hillman et al., 2008). In fact, some researchers believe that this kind of activity-dependent brain plasticity is relevant to treating spinal cord injuries (which as we saw have a devastating impact on people's lives), because understanding how to maximize plasticity through exercise and training may help to guide rehabilitation efforts (Dunlop, 2008). It should be clear by now that the plasticity of the brain is not just an interesting theoretical idea; it has potentially important applications to everyday life.

▶ Everyday forms of exercise, such as running, can benefit not only your heart but also your brain.

MARK ANDERSEN/GETTY IMAGES

IN SUMMARY

○ The brain can be divided into the hindbrain, midbrain, and forebrain.

○ The hindbrain generally coordinates information coming into and out of the spinal cord with structures such as the medulla, the reticular formation, the cerebellum, and the pons. These structures respectively coordinate breathing and heart rate, regulate sleep and arousal levels, coordinate fine motor skills, and communicate this information to the cortex.

○ The midbrain, with the help of structures such as the tectum and tegmentum, generally coordinates functions such as orientation to the environment and movement and arousal toward sensory stimuli.

○ The forebrain generally coordinates higher-level functions, such as perceiving, feeling, and thinking. The forebrain houses subcortical structures, such as the thalamus, hypothalamus, limbic system (including the hippocampus and amygdala), and basal ganglia; all these structures perform a variety of functions related to motivation and emotion. Also in the forebrain, the cerebral cortex, composed of two hemispheres with four lobes each (occipital, parietal, temporal, and frontal), performs tasks that help make us fully human: thinking, planning, judging, perceiving, and behaving purposefully and voluntarily.

○ Neurons in the brain can be shaped by experience and the environment, making the human brain amazingly plastic.

The Development and Evolution of Nervous Systems

The human brain is surprisingly imperfect. Why? Far from being a single, elegant machine—the enchanted loom the philosophers wrote so poetically about—the human brain is instead a system comprised of many distinct components that have been added at different times during the course of evolution. The human species has retained what worked best in earlier versions of the brain, then added bits and pieces to get us to our present state through evolution.

To understand the organization of the nervous system it is helpful to consider both its development in the uterus and its evolution over time. The first approach reveals how the nervous system develops and changes within each member of a species, whereas the second approach reveals how the nervous system in humans evolved and adapted from other species. Both approaches help us understand how the human brain came to be the way it is.

Prenatal Development of the Central Nervous System

The nervous system is the first major bodily system to take form in an embryo (Moore, 1977). It begins to develop within the third week after fertilization, when the embryo is still in the shape of a sphere. Initially, a ridge forms on one side of the sphere and then builds up at its edges to become a deep groove. The ridges fold together and fuse to enclose the groove, forming a structure called the *neural tube*. The tail end of the neural tube will remain a tube, and as the embryo grows larger, it forms the basis of the spinal cord. The tube expands at the opposite end, so that by the fourth week the three basic levels of the brain are visible; during the fifth week, the forebrain and hindbrain further differentiate into subdivisions. During the seventh week and later, the forebrain expands considerably to form the cerebral hemispheres.

What are the stages of development of the embryonic brain?

As the embryonic brain continues to grow, each subdivision folds onto the next one and begins to form the structures easily visible in the adult brain (see **FIGURE 3.23**): The hindbrain forms the cerebellum and medulla, the midbrain forms the tectum and the

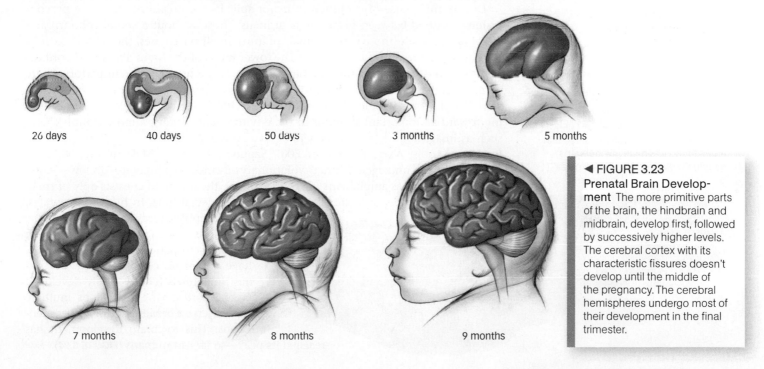

26 days   40 days   50 days   3 months   5 months

7 months   8 months   9 months

◀ FIGURE 3.23
Prenatal Brain Development The more primitive parts of the brain, the hindbrain and midbrain, develop first, followed by successively higher levels. The cerebral cortex with its characteristic fissures doesn't develop until the middle of the pregnancy. The cerebral hemispheres undergo most of their development in the final trimester.

tegmentum, and the forebrain subdivides further, separating the thalamus and hypothalamus from the cerebral hemispheres. Over time, the cerebral hemispheres undergo the greatest development, ultimately covering almost all the other subdivisions of the brain.

The *ontogeny* of the brain—how it develops within a given individual—is pretty remarkable. In about half the time it takes you to complete a 15-week semester, the basic structures of the brain are in place and rapidly developing, eventually allowing a newborn to enter the world with a fairly sophisticated set of abilities. In comparison, the *phylogeny* of the brain—how it developed within a particular species—is a much slower process. However, it, too, has allowed humans to make the most of the available brain structures, enabling us to perform an incredible array of tasks.

Evolutionary Development of the Central Nervous System

The central nervous system evolved from the very simple one found in simple animals to the elaborate nervous system in humans today. Even the simplest animals have sensory neurons and motor neurons for responding to the environment (Shepherd, 1988). For example, single-celled protozoa have molecules in their cell membrane that are sensitive to food in the water. These molecules trigger the movement of tiny threads called *cilia,* which help propel the protozoa toward the food source. The first neurons appeared in simple invertebrates, such as jellyfish; the sensory neurons in the jellyfish's tentacles can feel the touch of a potentially dangerous predator, which prompts the jellyfish to swim to safety. If you're a jellyfish, this simple neural system is sufficient to keep you alive.

The first central nervous system worthy of the name, though, appeared in flatworms. The flatworm has a collection of neurons in the head—a simple kind of brain—that includes sensory neurons for vision and taste and motor neurons that control feeding behavior. Emerging from the brain are a pair of tracts that form a spinal cord. They are connected by *commissures,* neural fibers that cross between the left and right side of the nervous system to allow communication between neurons at symmetrical positions on either side of the body. The tracts are also connected by smaller collections of neurons called *ganglia,* which integrate information and coordinate motor behavior in the body region near each ganglion.

During the course of evolution, a major split in the organization of the nervous system occurred between invertebrate animals (those without a spinal column) and vertebrate animals (those with a spinal column). In all vertebrates, the central nervous system is organized into a hierarchy: The lower levels of the brain and spinal cord execute simpler functions, while the higher levels of the nervous system perform more complex functions. As you saw earlier, in humans, reflexes are accomplished in the spinal cord. At the next level, the midbrain executes the more complex task of orienting toward an important stimulus in the environment. Finally, a more complex task, such as imagining what your life will be like 20 years from now, is performed in the forebrain (Addis, Wong, & Schacter, 2007; Szpunar, Watson, & McDermott, 2007).

The forebrain undergoes further evolutionary advances in vertebrates. In lower vertebrate species such as amphibians (frogs and newts), the forebrain consists only of small clusters of neurons at the end of the neural tube. In higher vertebrates, including reptiles, birds, and mammals, the forebrain is much larger, and it evolves in two different patterns. Reptiles and birds have almost no cerebral cortex. By contrast, mammals have a highly developed cerebral cortex, which develops multiple areas that serve a broad range of higher mental functions. This forebrain development has reached its peak—so far—in humans (**FIGURE 3.24**).

▼ Flatworms don't have much of a brain, but then again, they don't need much of a brain. The rudimentary brain areas found in simple invertebrates eventually evolved into the complex brain structures found in humans.

BLICKWINKEL/ALAMY

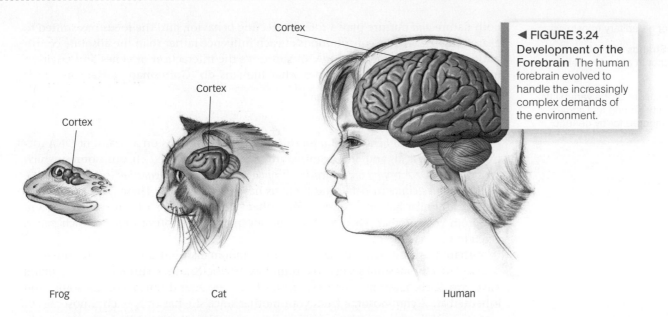

Cortex

Cortex

Cortex

◄ FIGURE 3.24
Development of the Forebrain The human forebrain evolved to handle the increasingly complex demands of the environment.

Frog   Cat   Human

The human brain, then, is not so much one remarkable thing; rather, it is a succession of extensions from a quite serviceable foundation. Like other species, humans have a hindbrain, and like those species, it performs important tasks to keep us alive. For some species, that's sufficient. All flatworms need to do to ensure their species' survival is eat, reproduce, and stay alive a reasonable length of time. But as the human brain evolved, structures in the midbrain and forebrain developed to handle the increasingly complex demands of the environment. The forebrain of a bullfrog is about as differentiated as it needs to be to survive in a frog's world. The human forebrain, however, shows substantial refinement, which allows for some remarkable, uniquely human abilities: self-awareness, sophisticated language use, social interaction, abstract reasoning, imagining, and empathy, among others.

There is intriguing evidence that the human brain evolved more quickly than the brains of other species (Dorus et al., 2004). Researchers compared the sequences of 200 brain-related genes in mice, rats, monkeys, and humans and discovered a collection of genes that evolved more rapidly among primates. What's more, they found that this evolutionary process was more rapid along the lineage that led to humans. That is, primate brains evolved quickly compared to those of other species, but the brains of the primates who eventually became humans evolved even more rapidly. These results suggest that in addition to the normal adaptations that occur over the process of evolution, the genes for human brains took particular advantage of a variety of mutations (changes in a gene's DNA) along the evolutionary pathway (Vallender, Mekel-Bobrov, & Lahn, 2008). These results also suggest that the human brain is still evolving—becoming bigger and more adapted to the demands of the environment (Evans et al., 2005; Mekel-Bobrov et al., 2005).

Are our brains still evolving?

Genes may direct the development of the brain on a large, evolutionary scale, but they also guide the development of an individual and, generally, the development of a species. Let's take a brief look at how genes and the environment contribute to the biological bases of behavior.

Genes and the Environment

You may have heard the phrase "nature vs. nurture." Do these twin influences grapple with each other for supremacy in directing a person's behavior? This suggests that either genetics ("nature") or the environment ("nurture") played a major role in producing particular behaviors, personality traits, psychological disorders, or pretty much any other thing that a human does. The emerging picture from current research is that

▼ If, as recent evidence suggests, the human brain is continuing to evolve, is this our future?

PARAMOUNT PICTURES/PHOTOFEST

gene The unit of hereditary transmission.

chromosomes Strands of DNA wound around each other in a double-helix configuration.

heritability A measure of the variability of behavioral traits among individuals that can be accounted for by genetic factors.

both nature *and* nurture play a role in directing behavior, and the focus has shifted to examining the relative contributions of each influence rather than the absolute contributions of either influence alone. In short, it's the interaction of genes and environmental influences that determines what humans do (Gottesman & Hanson, 2005; Rutter & Silberg, 2002).

What are Genes?

A **gene** is *the unit of hereditary transmission*. Genes are sections on a strand of DNA (deoxyribonucleic acid) and are organized into large threads called **chromosomes**, which are *strands of DNA wound around each other in a double-helix configuration* (see **FIGURE 3.25**). Chromosomes come in pairs, and humans have 23 pairs each. These pairs of chromosomes are similar but not identical: You inherit one of each pair from your father and one from your mother. There's a twist, however: The selection of *which* of each pair is given to you is random.

Perhaps the most striking example of this random distribution is the determination of sex. The chromosomes that determine sex are the X and Y chromosomes; females have two X chromosomes, whereas males have one X and one Y chromosome. You inherited an X chromosome from your mother since she has only X chromosomes to give. Your biological sex, therefore, was determined by whether you received an additional X chromosome or a Y chromosome from your father.

There is considerable variability in the genes that individual offspring receive. Nonetheless, children share a higher proportion of their genes with their parents than with more distant relatives or with nonrelatives. Children share half their genes with each parent, a quarter of their genes with their grandparents, an eighth of their genes with cousins, and so on. The probability of sharing genes is called *degree of relatedness*. The most genetically related people are *monozygotic twins* (also called *identical twins*), who develop from the splitting of a single fertilized egg and therefore share 100% of their genes. *Dizygotic twins* (*fraternal twins*) develop from two separate fertilized eggs and share 50% of their genes, the same as any two siblings born separately. Many researchers have tried to determine the relative influence of genetics on behavior. One way to do this is to compare a trait shown by monozygotic twins with that same trait among dizygotic twins. This type of research usually enlists twins who were raised in the same household, so that the impact of their environment—their socioeconomic status, access to education, parental child-rearing practices, environmental stressors—remains relatively constant. Finding that monozygotic twins have a higher prevalence of a specific trait suggests a genetic influence (Boomsma, Busjahn, & Peltonen, 2002).

As an example, the likelihood that the dizygotic twin of a person who has schizophrenia (a mental disorder we'll discuss in greater detail in Chapter 14) will *also* develop schizophrenia is 27%. However, this statistic rises to 50% for monozygotic twins. This observation suggests a substantial genetic influence on the likelihood of developing schizophrenia. Monozygotic twins share 100% of their genes, and if one assumes environmental influences are relatively consistent for both members of the twin pair,

▶ **FIGURE 3.25**
Genes, Chromosomes, and Their Recombination The cell nucleus houses chromosomes, which are made up of double-helix strands of DNA. Every cell in our bodies has 23 pairs of chromosomes. Genes are segments on a strand of DNA with codes that make us who we are.

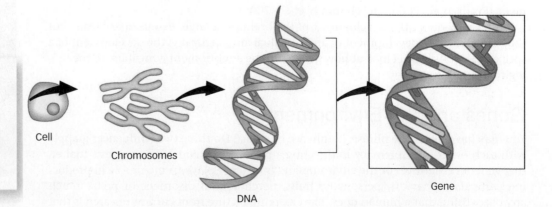

Cell

Chromosomes

DNA

Gene

▲ Monozygotic twins (left) share 100% of their genes in common, while dizygotic twins (right) share 50% of their genes, the same as other siblings. Studies of monozygotic and dizygotic twins help researchers estimate the relative contributions of genes and environmental influences on behavior.

the 50% likelihood can be traced to genetic factors. That sounds scarily high . . . until you realize that the remaining 50% probability must be due to environmental influences. In short, genetics can contribute to the development, likelihood, or onset of a variety of traits. But a more complete picture of genetic influences on behavior must always take the environmental context into consideration. Genes express themselves within an environment, not in isolation.

The Role of Environmental Factors

Genes set the range of possibilities that can be observed in a population, but the characteristics of any individual within that range are determined by environmental factors and experience. Genetically, it's possible for humans to live comfortably 12,000 feet above sea level. The residents of La Paz, Bolivia, have done so for centuries. But chances are *you* wouldn't enjoy gasping for breath on a daily basis. Your environmental experiences have made it unlikely for you to live that way, just as the experience and environment of the citizens of La Paz have made living at high altitude quite acceptable. Genetically, you and the Bolivians come from the same species, but the range of genetic capabilities you share is not expressed in the same way. What's more, neither you nor a Bolivian can breathe underwater in Lake Titicaca, which is also 12,000 feet above sea level. The genetic capabilities that another species might enjoy, such as breathing underwater, are outside the range of *your* possibilities, no matter how much you might desire them.

With these parameters in mind, behavioral geneticists use calculations based on relatedness to compute the heritability of behaviors (Plomin et al., 2001). **Heritability** is *a measure of the variability of behavioral traits among individuals that can be accounted for by genetic factors*. Heritability is calculated as a proportion, and its numerical value (index) ranges from 0 to 1.00. A heritability of 0 means that genes do not contribute to individual differences in the behavioral trait; a heritability of 1.00 means that genes are the *only* reason for the individual differences. As you might guess, scores of 0 or 1.00 occur so infrequently that they serve more as theoretical limits than realistic values; almost nothing in human behavior is completely due to the environment or owed *completely* to genetic inheritance. Scores between 0 and 1.00, then, indicate that individual differences are caused by varying degrees of genetic and environmental contributions—a little stronger influence of genetics here, a little stronger influence of the environment there, but each always within the context of the other (Moffitt, 2005; Zhang & Meaney, 2010).

For human behavior, almost all estimates of heritability are in the moderate range, between .30 and .60. For example, a heritability index of .50 for intelligence indicates that half of the variability in intelligence test scores is attributable to genetic influences and the remaining half is due to environmental influences. Smart parents often (but not always) produce smart

"The title of my science project is 'My Little Brother: Nature or Nurture.'"

children; genetics certainly plays a role. But smart and not-so-smart children attend good or not-so-good schools, practice their piano lessons with more or less regularity, study or not study as hard as they might, have good and not-so-good teachers and role models, and so on. Genetics is only half the story in intelligence. Environmental influences also play a significant role in predicting the basis of intelligence (see Chapter 10).

Heritability has proven to be a theoretically useful and statistically sound concept in helping scientists understand the relative genetic and environmental influences on behavior. However, there are four important points about heritability to bear in mind.

Are abilities, such as intelligence and memory, inherited through our genes?

First, remember that *heritability is an abstract concept*: It tells us nothing about the *specific* genes that contribute to a trait. Second, *heritability is a population concept*: It tells us nothing about an individual. Heritability provides guidance for understanding differences across individuals in a population rather than abilities within an individual.

Third, *heritability is dependent on the environment*. Just as behavior occurs within certain contexts, so do genetic influences. For example, intelligence isn't an unchanging quality: People are intelligent within a particular learning context, a social setting, a family environment, a socioeconomic class, and so on. Heritability, therefore, is meaningful only for the environmental conditions in which it was computed, and heritability estimates may change dramatically under other environmental conditions. Finally, *heritability is not fate*. It tells us nothing about the degree to which interventions can change a behavioral trait. Heritability is useful for identifying behavioral traits that are influenced by genes, but it is not useful for determining how individuals will respond to particular environmental conditions or treatments.

IN SUMMARY

- Examining the development of the nervous system over the life span of an individual—its ontogeny—and across the time within which a species evolves—its phylogeny—presents further opportunities for understanding the human brain.

- The nervous system is the first system that forms in an embryo, starting as a neural tube, which forms the basis of the spinal cord. The neural tube expands on one end to form the hindbrain, midbrain, and forebrain, each of which folds onto the next structure.

- Within each of these areas, specific brain structures begin to differentiate. The forebrain shows the greatest differentiation, and in particular, the cerebral cortex is the most developed in humans.

- Nervous systems evolved from simple collections of sensory and motor neurons in simple animals, such as flatworms, to elaborate centralized nervous systems found in mammals.

  - The evolution of the human nervous system can be thought of as a process of refining, elaborating, and expanding structures present in other species.

  - Reptiles and birds have almost no cerebral cortex. By contrast, mammals have a highly developed cerebral cortex.

  - The human brain appears to have evolved more quickly compared to other species to become adapted to a more complex environment.

- The gene, or the unit of hereditary transmission, is built from strands of DNA in a double-helix formation that is organized into chromosomes.

- Humans have 23 pairs of chromosomes—half come from each parent.

  - A child shares 50% of his or her genes with each parent.

  - Monozygotic twins share 100% of their genes, while dizygotic twins share 50%, the same as any other siblings. Because of their genetic relatedness, twins are often participants in genetic research.

- The study of genetics indicates that both genes and the environment work together to influence behavior. Genes set the range of variation in populations within a given environment, but they do not predict individual characteristics; experience and other environmental factors play a crucial role as well.

Investigating the Brain

So far, you've read a great deal about the nervous system: how it's organized, how it works, what its components are, and what those components do. But one question remains largely unanswered—*how* do we know all of this? Anatomists can dissect a human brain and identify its structures, but they cannot determine which structures play a role in producing which behaviors by dissecting a nonliving brain.

Scientists use a variety of methods to understand how the brain affects behavior. Let's consider three of the main ones: testing people with brain damage and observing their deficits, studying electrical activity in the brain during behavior, and conducting brain scans while people perform various tasks. Studying people with brain damage highlights a theme illustrated many times in this book: To better understand the normal operation of a process, it is instructive to understand what happens when that process fails. Observing the behavioral problems that result from damage to certain areas of the brain enables researchers to identify the functions of those areas. The second approach, studying the brain's electrical activity, has a long history and has produced a wealth of information about which neurons fire when behavior is enacted. The modern extensions of that technique are the various ways that the brain can be scanned, mapped, and coded using a variety of sophisticated instruments, which is the third approach we'll consider. Let's examine each of these ways of investigating the brain.

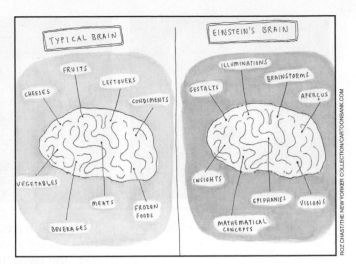

Learning about Brain Organization by Studying the Damaged Brain

Remember Betty, the 75-year-old grandmother at the beginning of this chapter admitted to the emergency room because she couldn't recognize her own husband? She had suffered a stroke from a blood clot that deprived her brain of oxygen and caused the death of neurons in the afflicted area. Betty's stroke affected part of the association area in her temporal lobe, where complex visual objects are identified. Betty's occipital lobe, the main area where visual processing takes place, was unaffected, so Betty could see her husband and two sons, but because of the damage to her temporal lobe, she could not recognize them.

Much research in neuroscience correlates the loss of specific perceptual, motor, emotional, or cognitive functions with specific areas of brain damage (Andrewes, 2001; Kolb & Whishaw, 2003). By studying these instances, neuroscientists can theorize about the functions those brain areas normally perform. The modern history of neuroscience can be dated to the work of Paul Broca (see Chapter 1). In 1861, Broca described a patient who had lost the capacity to produce spoken language (but not the ability to understand language) due to damage in a small area in the left frontal lobe. In 1874, Carl Wernicke (1848–1905) described a patient with an impairment in language comprehension (but not the ability to produce speech) associated with damage to an area in the upper-left temporal lobe. These areas were named, respectively, *Broca's area* and *Wernicke's area,* and they provided the earliest evidence that the brain locations for speech production and speech comprehension are separate and that for most people, the left hemisphere is critical to producing and understanding language (Young, 1990).

How have brain disorders been central to our study of specific areas of the brain?

The Emotional Functions of the Frontal Lobes

As you've already seen, the human frontal lobes are a remarkable evolutionary achievement. However, psychology's first glimpse at some functions of the frontal lobes came from a rather unremarkable fellow; so unremarkable, in fact, that a single event in his

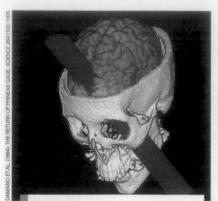

▲ **FIGURE 3.26**

Phineas Gage Phineas Gage's traumatic accident allowed researchers to investigate the functions of the frontal lobe and its connections with emotion centers in the subcortical structures. The likely path of the metal rod through Gage's skull is reconstructed here.

life defined his place in the annals of psychology's history (Macmillan, 2000). Phineas Gage was a muscular 25-year-old railroad worker. On September 13, 1848, in Cavendish, Vermont, he was packing an explosive charge into a crevice in a rock when the powder exploded, driving a 3-foot, 13-pound iron rod through his head at high speed (Harlow, 1848). As **FIGURE 3.26** shows, the rod entered through his lower left jaw and exited through the middle top of his head. Incredibly, Gage lived to tell the tale. But his personality underwent a significant change.

Before the accident, Gage had been mild mannered, quiet, conscientious, and a hard worker. After the accident, however, he became irritable, irresponsible, indecisive, and given to profanity. The sad decline of Gage's personality and emotional life nonetheless provided an unexpected benefit to psychology. His case study was the first to allow researchers to investigate the hypothesis that the frontal lobe is involved in emotion regulation, planning, and decision making. Furthermore, because the connections between the frontal lobe and the subcortical structures of the limbic system were affected, scientists were able to better understand how the amygdala, hippocampus, and related brain structures interacted with the cerebral cortex (Damasio, 2005).

The Distinct Roles of the Left and Right Hemispheres

You'll recall that the cerebral cortex is divided into two hemispheres, although typically the two hemispheres act as one integrated unit. Sometimes, though, disorders can threaten the ability of the brain to function, and the only way to stop them is with radical methods. This is sometimes the case with patients who suffer from severe, intractable epilepsy. Seizures that begin in one hemisphere cross the corpus callosum (the thick band of nerve fibers that allows the two hemispheres to communicate) to the opposite hemisphere and start a feedback loop that results in a kind of firestorm in the brain. To alleviate the severity of the seizures, surgeons can sever the corpus callosum in a procedure called a *split-brain procedure*. The result is that a seizure that starts in one hemisphere is isolated in that hemisphere since there is no longer a connection to the other side. This procedure helps the patients with epilepsy but also produces some unusual, if not unpredictable, behaviors.

The Nobel laureate Roger Sperry (1913–94) was intrigued by the observation that the everyday behavior of patients who had their corpus collosum servered did not seem to be affected by the operation. Did this mean that the corpus callosum played no role at all in behavior? Sperry thought that this conclusion was premature, reasoning that casual observations of everyday behaviors could easily fail to detect impairments that might be picked up by sensitive tests. To evaluate this idea experimentally, Sperry and his colleagues first showed that cats in whom the corpus callosum had been cut did not transfer learning

from one hemisphere to the other (Sperry, 1964). Later, they designed several experiments that investigated the behaviors of human split-brain patients and in the process revealed a great deal about the independent functions of the left and right hemispheres (Sperry, 1964). Normally, any information that initially enters the left hemisphere is also registered in the right hemisphere and vice versa: The information comes in and travels across the corpus callosum, and both hemispheres understand what's going on. But in a split-brain patient, information entering one hemisphere stays there. Without an intact corpus callosum, there's no way for that information to reach the other hemisphere. Sperry and his colleagues used this understanding of lateralized perception in a series of experiments. For example, they had patients look at a spot in the center of a screen and then projected a stimulus on one side of the screen, isolating the stimulus to one hemisphere.

The hemispheres themselves are specialized for different kinds of tasks. You just learned about Broca's and Wernicke's areas, which revealed that language processing is largely a left-hemisphere activity. So imagine that some information came into the left hemisphere of a split-brain patient, and she was asked to verbally describe what it was. No problem: The left hemisphere has the information, it's the "speaking" hemisphere, so the patient should have no difficulty verbally describing what she saw. But suppose the patient was asked to reach behind a screen with her left hand and pick up the object she just saw. Remember that the hemispheres exert contralateral control over the body, meaning that the left hand is controlled by the right hemisphere. But this patient's right hemisphere has no clue what the object was because that information was received in the left hemisphere and was unable to travel to the right hemisphere! So, even though the split-brain patient saw the object and could verbally describe it, she would be unable to use the right hemisphere to perform other tasks regarding that object, such as correctly selecting it from a group with her left hand (see **FIGURE 3.27**).

Of course, information presented to the right hemisphere would produce complementary deficits. In this case, a patient might be presented with a familiar object in her left hand (such as a key), be able to demonstrate that she knew what it was (by twisting and turning the key in midair), yet be unable to verbally describe what she was holding. In this case, the information in the right hemisphere is unable to travel to the left hemisphere, which controls the production of speech.

Furthermore, suppose a split-brain person was shown the unusual face in **FIGURE 3.28** on the next page. This is called a *chimeric face*, and it is assembled from half-face components of the full faces also shown in the figure. When asked to indicate which face was presented, a split-brain person would indicate that she saw *both* faces because information about the face on the left is recorded in the right hemisphere and information about the face on the right is recorded in the left hemisphere (Levy, Trevarthen, & Sperry, 1972).

These split-brain studies reveal that the two hemispheres perform different functions and can work together seamlessly as long as the corpus callosum is intact. Without a way to transmit information from one hemisphere to the other, information gets "stuck" in the hemisphere it initially entered and we become acutely aware of the different functions of each hemisphere. Of course, a split-brain patient can adapt to this by simply moving her eyes a little so that the same information independently enters both hemispheres. Split-brain studies have continued over the past few decades and continue to play an important role in shaping our understanding of how the brain works (Gazzaniga, 2006).

▲ Roger Wolcott Sperry (1913–94) received the Nobel Prize in Physiology in 1981 for his pioneering work investigating the independent functions of the cerebral hemispheres.

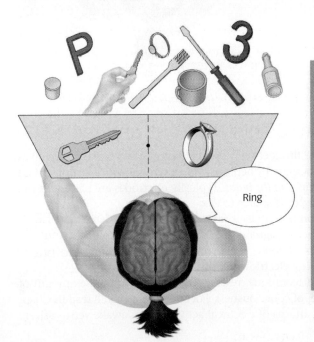

◄ FIGURE 3.27

Split-Brain Experiment When a split-brain patient is presented with the picture of a ring on the right and that of a key on the left side of a screen, she can verbalize *ring* but not *key* because the left hemisphere "sees" the ring and language is usually located in the left hemisphere. This patient would be able to choose a key with her left hand from a set of objects behind a screen. She would not, however, be able to pick out a ring with her left hand since what the left hemisphere "sees" is not communicated to the left side of her body.

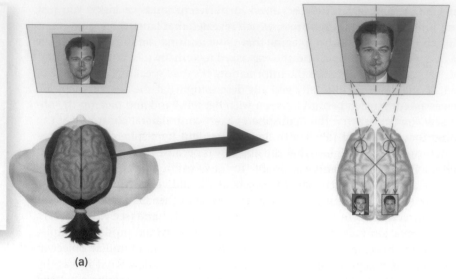

(a)

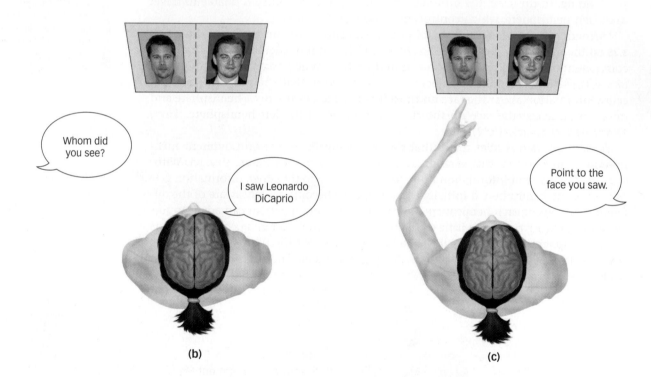

(b)

(c)

Listening to the Brain: Single Neurons and the EEG

A second approach to studying the link between brain structures and behavior involves recording the pattern of electrical activity of neurons. An **electroencephalograph (EEG)** is *a device used to record electrical activity in the brain.* Typically electrodes are placed on the outside of the head, and even though the source of electrical activity in synapses and action potentials is far removed from these wires, the electric signals can be amplified several thousand times by the EEG. This provides a visual record of the underlying electrical activity, as shown in **FIGURE 3.29.** Using this technique, researchers can determine the amount of brain activity during different states of consciousness. For example, as you'll read in Chapter 5, the brain shows distinctive patterns of electrical activity when awake versus asleep;

How does the EEG record electrical activity in the brain?

electroencephalograph (EEG) A device used to record electrical activity in the brain.

in fact, there are even different brain-wave patterns associated with different stages of sleep. EEG recordings allow researchers to make these fundamental discoveries about the nature of sleep and wakefulness (Dement, 1978). The EEG can also be used to examine the brain's electrical activity when awake individuals engage in a variety of psychological functions, such as perceiving, learning, and remembering.

A different approach to recording electrical activity resulted in a more refined understanding of the brain's division of responsibilities, even at a cellular level. Nobel laureates David Hubel and Torsten Wiesel used a technique that inserted electrodes into the occipital lobes of anesthetized cats and observed the patterns of action potentials of individual neurons (Hubel, 1988). Hubel and Wiesel amplified the action potential signals through a loudspeaker so that the signals could be heard as clicks as well as seen on an oscilloscope. While flashing lights in front of the animal's eye, Hubel and Wiesel recorded the resulting activity of neurons in the occipital cortex. What they discovered was not much of anything: Most of the neurons did not respond to this kind of general stimulation. This was frustrating to them—Hubel (1988, p. 69) recalled years later that "we tried everything short of standing on our heads to get it to fire"—but then they began to notice something interesting.

Nearing the end of what seemed like a failed set of experiments, they projected a glass slide that contained a black dot in front of the cat's eyes and heard a brisk flurry of clicks as the neurons in the cat's occipital lobe fired away! Observing carefully, they realized that the firing did not have anything to do with the black dot, but instead was produced by a faint but sharp shadow cast by the edge of the glass slide. They discovered that neurons in the primary visual cortex are activated whenever a contrast between light and dark occurs in part of the visual field, seen particularly well when the visual stimulus was a thick line of light against a dark background. In this case, the shadow caused by the edge of the slide provided the kind of contrast that prompted particular neurons to respond. They then found that each neuron responded vigorously only when presented with a contrasting edge at a particular orientation. Since then, many studies have shown that neurons in the primary visual cortex represent particular features of visual stimuli, such as contrast, shape, and color (Zeki, 1993).

These neurons in the visual cortex are known as *feature detectors* because they selectively respond to certain aspects of a visual image. For example, some neurons fire only when detecting a vertical line in the middle of the visual field, other neurons fire when a line at a 45-degree angle is perceived, and still others in response to wider lines, horizontal lines, lines in the periphery of the visual field, and so on (Livingstone & Hubel, 1988). The discovery of this specialized function for neurons was a huge leap forward in our understanding of how the visual cortex works. Feature detectors identify basic dimensions of a stimulus ("slanted line . . . other slanted line . . . horizontal line"); those dimensions are then combined during a later stage of visual processing to allow recognition and perception of a stimulus ("Oh, it's a letter *A*").

Other studies have identified a variety of features that are detected by sensory neurons. For example, some visual processing neurons in the temporal lobe are activated only when detecting faces (Kanwisher, 2000; Perrett, Rolls, & Caan, 1982). These neurons lie in the same area of the temporal cortex that was damaged in Betty's stroke. Neurons in this area are specialized for processing faces; damage to this area results in an inability to perceive faces. These complementary observations—showing that the type of function that is lost or altered when a brain area is damaged corresponds to the kind of information processed by neurons in that cortical area—provide the most compelling evidence linking the brain to behavior.

▲ **FIGURE 3.29**
EEG The electroencephalograph (EEG) records electrical activity in the brain. Many states of consciousness, such as wakefulness and stages of sleep, are characterized by particular types of brain waves.

▲ David Hubel (left, b. 1926) and Torsten Wiesel (right, b. 1924) received the Nobel Prize in Physiology in 1981 for their work on mapping the visual cortex.

Brain Imaging: From Visualizing Structure to Watching the Brain in Action

The third major way that neuroscientists can peer into the workings of the human brain has only become possible within the past several decades. EEG readouts give an overall picture of a person's level of consciousness, and single-cell recordings shed light on the actions of particular clumps of neurons. The ideal of neuroscience, however, has been the ability to see the brain in operation while behavior is being enacted. This goal has been steadily achieved thanks to a wide range of *neuroimaging techniques* that use advanced technology to create images of the living, healthy brain (Posner & Raichle, 1994; Raichle & Mintun, 2006). *Structural brain imaging* provides information about the basic structure of the brain and allows clinicians or researchers to see abnormalities in brain structure. *Functional brain imaging*, in contrast, provides information about the acivity of the brain when people perform various kinds of cognitive or motor tasks.

Structural Brain Imaging

One of the first neuroimaging techniques developed was the *computerized axial tomography (CT) scan*. In a CT scan, a scanner rotates a device around a person's head and takes a series of x-ray photographs from different angles. Computer programs then combine these images to provide views from any angle. CT scans show different densities of tissue in the brain. For example, the higher-density skull looks white on a CT scan, the cortex shows up as gray, and the least dense fissures and ventricles in the brain look dark (see **FIGURE 3.30**). CT scans are used to locate lesions or tumors, which typically appear darker since they are less dense than the cortex.

Magnetic resonance imaging (MRI) involves applying brief but powerful magnetic pulses to the head and recording how these pulses are absorbed throughout the brain. For very short periods, these magnetic pulses cause molecules in the brain tissue to twist slightly and then relax, which releases a small amount of energy. Differently charged molecules respond differently to the magnetic pulses, so the energy signals reveal brain structures with different molecular compositions. Magnetic resonance imaging produces pictures of soft tissue at a better resolution than a CT scan, as you can see in Figure 3.30. These techniques give psychologists a clearer picture of the structure of the brain and can help localize brain damage (as when someone suffers a stroke), but they reveal nothing about the functions of the brain.

Functional Brain Imaging

Two newer functional-brain-imaging techniques show researchers much more than just the structure of the brain by allowing us to actually watch the brain in action. These techniques rely on the fact that activated brain areas demand more energy for their neurons to work. This energy is supplied through increased blood flow to the

▶ FIGURE 3.30
Structural Imaging Techniques (CT and MRI) CT (left) and MRI (right) scans are used to provide information about the structure of the brain and can help to spot tumors and other kinds of damage. Each scan shown here provides a snapshot of a single slice in the brain. Note that the MRI scan provides a clearer, higher–resolution image than the CT scan (see the text for further discussion of how these images are constructed and what they depict).

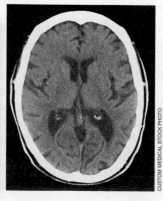

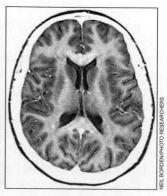

activated areas. Functional-imaging techniques can detect such changes in blood flow. In *positron emission tomography (PET)*, a harmless radioactive substance is injected into a person's bloodstream. Then the brain is scanned by radiation detectors as the person performs perceptual or cognitive tasks, such as reading or speaking. Areas of the brain that are activated during these tasks demand more energy and greater blood flow, resulting in a higher amount of the radioactivity in that region. The radiation detectors record the level of radioactivity in each region, producing a computerized image of the activated areas (see **FIGURE 3.31**). Note that PET scans differ from CT scans and MRIs in that the image produced shows activity in the brain while the person performs certain tasks. So, for example, a PET scan of a person speaking would show activation in Broca's area in the left frontal lobe.

For psychologists, the most widely used functional-brain-imaging technique nowadays is *functional magnetic resonance imaging (fMRI)*, which detects the twisting of hemoglobin molecules in the blood when they are exposed to magnetic pulses. Hemoglobin is the molecule in the blood that carries oxygen to our tissues, including the brain. When active neurons demand more energy and blood flow, oxygenated hemoglobin concentrates in the active areas. fMRI detects the oxygenated hemoglobin and provides a picture of the level of activation in each brain area (see Figure 3.31). Just as MRI was a major advance over CT scans, *functional MRI* represents a similar leap in our ability to record the brain's activity during behavior. Both fMRI and PET allow researchers to localize changes in the brain very accurately. However, fMRI has a couple of advantages over PET. First, fMRI does not require any exposure to a radioactive substance. Second, fMRI can localize changes in brain activity across briefer periods than PET, which makes it more useful for analyzing psychological processes that occur extremely quickly, such as reading a word or recognizing a face. With PET, researchers often have to use experimental designs different from those they would use in the psychological laboratory in order to adapt to the limitations of PET technology. With fMRI, researchers can design experiments that more closely resemble the ones they carry out in the psychological laboratory.

> **What does an fMRI track in an active brain?**

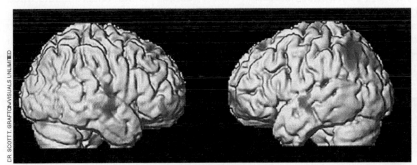

Gesture Preparation

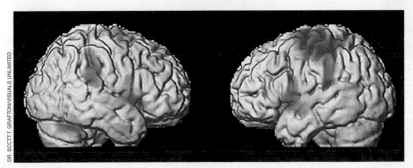

Gesture Production

◄ **FIGURE 3.31**

Functional-Imaging Techniques (PET and fMRI) PET and fMRI scans provide information about the functions of the brain by revealing which brain areas become more or less active in different conditions. The PET scan (directly above) shows areas in the left hemisphere (Broca's area, left; lower parietal-upper temporal area, right) that become active when people hold in mind a string of letters for a few seconds. The fMRI scans (all views to the left) show several different regions in both hemispheres that become active when someone is thinking about a gesture (top) and performing a gesture (bottom).

Insights from Functional Imaging

PET and fMRI provide remarkable insights into the types of information processing that take place in specific areas of the brain. For example, when a person performs a simple perceptual task, such as looking at a circular checkerboard, the primary visual areas are activated. As you have read, when the checkerboard is presented to the left visual field, the right visual cortex shows activation, and when the checkerboard is

HOT SCIENCE

Establishing Causality in the Brain

Sometimes the best way to learn about something is to see what happens when it breaks, and the human brain is no exception. Scientists have studied the effects of brain damage for centuries, and those studies reveal a lot about how the brain normally works so well. As you read in Chapter 1, in the middle of the 19th century, a French surgeon named Paul Broca observed that people who had lost their ability to speak often had damage in a particular spot on the left side of their brains. Broca suggested that this region might control speech production but not other functions such as the ability to understand speech. As it turned out, he was right, which is why this brain region is now known as Broca's area.

Scientists have learned a lot about the brain by studying the behavior of people whose brains are defective or have been damaged by accidents. But the problem with studying brain-damaged patients, of course, is the problem with studying any naturally occurring variable: Brain damage may be related to particular patterns of behavior, but that relationship may or may not be causal. Experimentation is the premiere method for establishing causal relationships between variables, but scientists cannot ethically cause brain damage in human beings, thus they have not been able to establish causal relationships between particular kinds of brain damage and particular patterns of behavior.

Until now. Scientists have recently discovered a way to mimic brain damage with a benign technique called *transcranial magnetic stimulation* (or TMS) (Barker, Jalinous, & Freeston, 1985; Hallett, 2000). If you've ever held a magnet under a piece of paper and used it to drag a pin across the paper's surface, you know that magnetic fields can pass through insulating material. The human skull is no exception. TMS delivers a magnetic pulse that passes through the skull and deactivates neurons in the cerebral cortex for a short period. Researchers can direct TMS pulses to particular brain regions—essentially turning them "off"—and then measure temporary changes in the way a person moves, sees, thinks, remembers, speaks, or feels. By manipulating the state of the brain, scientists can perform experiments that establish causal relationships.

For example, in an early study using TMS, scientists discovered that magnetic stimulation of the visual cortex temporarily impairs a person's ability to detect the motion of an object without impairing the person's ability to recognize that object (Beckers & Zeki, 1995). This intriguing discovery suggests that motion perception and object recognition are accomplished by different parts of the brain, but moreover, it establishes that activity in the visual cortex *causes* motion perception. More recent research has revealed that applying TMS to the specific part of the visual cortex responsible for motion perception also impairs the accuracy with which people reach for moving objects (Schenk et al., 2005) or for stationary objects when there is motion in the background of a visual scene (Whitney et al., 2007). These findings indicate that the visual motion area plays a crucial role in guiding actions when we're responding to motion in the visual environment.

For the first time in human history, the causal relationships between particular brain regions and particular behaviors have been unequivocally established. Rather than relying on observational studies of brain-damaged patients or the snapshots provided by fMRI or PET scans, researchers can now manipulate brain activity and measure its effects. Scientists have also recently begun to combine TMS with fMRI, allowing them to localize precisely where in the brain TMS is having its effect (Caparelli, 2007). Studies suggest that TMS has no harmful side effects (Anand & Hotson, 2002; Pascual-Leone et al., 1993), and this new tool has begun to revolutionize the study of how our brains create our thoughts, feelings, and actions.

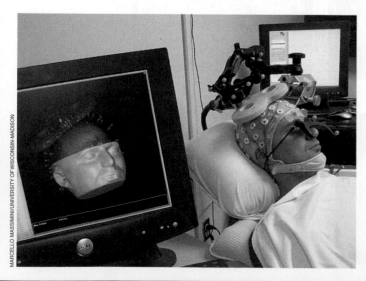

◀ Transcranial magnetic stimulation activates and deactivates regions of the brain with a magnetic pulse, temporarily mimicking brain damage.

MARCELLO MASSIMINI/UNIVERSITY OF WISCONSIN-MADISON

presented to the right visual field, the left visual cortex shows activation (Fox et al., 1986). Similarly, when people look at faces, fMRI reveals strong activity in a region located near the border of the temporal and occipital lobes called the *fusiform gyrus* (Kanwisher, McDermott, & Chun, 1997). When this structure is damaged, people experience problems with recognizing faces, as Betty did in the opening vignette. Finally, when people perform a task that engages emotional processing, for example, looking at sad pictures, researchers observe significant activation in the amygdala, which you learned earlier is linked with emotional arousal (Phelps, 2006). There is also increased activation in parts of the frontal lobe that are involved in emotional regulation, in fact, in the same areas that were most likely damaged in the case of Phineas Gage (Wang et al., 2005).

As you may have noticed, then, the most modern brain-imaging techniques confirm what studies of brain damage from over 100 years ago suspected. When Broca and Wernicke reached their conclusions about language production and language comprehension, they had little more to go on than some isolated cases and good hunches. PET scans have since confirmed that different areas of the brain are activated when a person is listening to spoken language, reading words on a screen, saying words out loud, or thinking of related words. This suggests that different parts of the brain are activated during these related but distinct functions. Similarly, it was pretty clear to the physician who examined Phineas Gage that the location of Gage's injuries played a major role in his drastic change in personality and emotionality. fMRI scans have since confirmed that the frontal lobe plays a central role in regulating emotion. It's always nice when independent methods—in these instances, very old case studies and very recent technology—arrive at the same conclusions (see also the Hot Science box for a description of a technique that provides complementary information to fMRI by temporarily interfering with the functioning of specific brain regions). As you'll also see at various points in the text, brain-imaging techniques such as fMRI are also revealing new and surprising findings, such as the insights described in the Where Do You Stand? box. Although the human brain still holds many mysteries, researchers are developing increasingly sophisticated ways of unraveling them.

IN SUMMARY

○ There are three major approaches to studying the link between the brain and behavior.

○ Observing how perceptual, motor, intellectual, and emotional capacities are affected following brain damage. By carefully relating specific psychological and behavioral disruptions to damage in particular areas of the brain, researchers can better understand how the brain area normally plays a role in producing those behaviors.

○ Examining global electrical activity in the brain and the activity patterns of single neurons. The patterns of electrical activity in large brain areas can be examined from outside the skull using the electroencephalograph (EEG). Single-cell recordings taken from specific neurons can be linked to specific perceptual or behavioral events, suggesting that those neurons represent particular kinds of stimuli or control particular aspects of behavior.

○ Using brain imaging to scan the brain as people perform different perceptual or intellectual tasks. Correlating energy consumption in particular brain areas with specific cognitive and behavioral events suggests that those brain areas are involved in specific types of perceptual, motor, cognitive, or emotional processing.

WhereDoYouStand?

Brain Death

A story shrouded in mystery follows the memory of Andreas Vesalius (1514–64), a Belgian physician regarded as one of the founders of modern anatomy. According to the story, Vesalius conducted an autopsy in 1564 in front of a large crowd in Madrid, Spain. When the cadaver's chest was opened, the audience saw that the man's heart was still beating! The possibility that the patient was still alive created a scandal that forced Vesalius to leave Spain, where he was serving as the imperial physician at the time. He died during his exodus in a shipwreck, on a pilgrimage to Jerusalem under the pressures of the Spanish Inquisition.

We may never know whether this story is accurate. However, it raises a question related to the brain and behavior that is still fiercely debated today. In Vesalius's time, if a patient didn't appear to be breathing, was generally unresponsive, or gave no strong evidence of a heartbeat, the person could safely be considered dead (despite the occasional misdiagnosis). Modern resuscitative techniques can keep the heart, lungs, and other organs functioning for days, months, or even years, so physicians have identified measures of brain function that allow them to decide more definitively when someone is dead.

In 1981, the President's Commission for the Study of Ethical Problems in Medicine and Biomedical and Behavioral Research defined brain death as the *irreversible loss of all functions of the brain*. Contrary to what you may think, brain death is not the same as being in a coma or being unresponsive to stimulation. Indeed, even a flat-line EEG does not indicate that all brain functions have stopped; the reticular formation in the hindbrain, which generates spontaneous respiration and heartbeat, may still be active.

Brain death came to the forefront of national attention during March 2005 in the case of Terri Schiavo, a woman who had been kept alive on a respirator for nearly 15 years in a Florida nursing home. She died on March 31, 2005, after the feeding tube that sustained her was removed. A person like Schiavo is commonly referred to as brain dead, but such an individual is more accurately described as being in a *persistent vegetative state*. In fact, people in a persistent vegetative state are still considered to be alive by some. Respiration is controlled by structures in the hindbrain, such as the medulla, and will continue as long as this area is intact. A heartbeat does not require input from any area of the brain, so the heart will continue to beat as long it continues to receive oxygen, either by intact respiration or if the patient is artificially ventilated. Also, a patient who is brain dead may continue to have muscle spasms, twitches, or even sit up. This so-called *Lazarus reflex* is coordinated solely by the spinal cord.

Terri Schiavo's parents thought she had a substantial level of voluntary consciousness; they felt that she appeared to smile, cry, and turn toward the source of a voice. Terri's parents hired physicians who claimed that she had a primitive type of consciousness. However, neurologists who specialize in these cases emphasized that these responses could be automatic reflexes supported by circuits in the thalamus and midbrain. These neurologists considered Schiavo to be in a persistent vegetative state; they failed to see conclusive evidence of consciousness or voluntary behavior.

Terri's husband, Michael, agreed with the neurologists and asked the courts to remove the feeding tube that kept her alive, a decision a Florida court accepted. Nonetheless, Florida Governor Jeb Bush decreed in 2003 that doctors retain Terri's feeding tube and continue to provide medical care. Eventually, the court again ordered her feeding tube removed, and this time it was not replaced, resulting in her death.

Where do you stand on this issue? Should Terri Schiavo have been kept alive indefinitely? The definition of brain death includes the term "irreversible," suggesting that as long as *any* component of the brain can still function—with or without the aid of a machine—the person should be considered alive. But does a persistent vegetative state qualify as "life"? Is a simple consensus of qualified professionals—doctors, nurses, social workers, specialists—sufficient to decide whether someone is "still living" or at least "still living enough" to maintain whatever treatments may be in place? How should the wishes of family members be considered? For that matter, should the wishes of lawmakers and politicians play a role at all? What is your position on these questions of the brain and the ultimate behavior: staying alive?

After you've considered your answers to these questions, consider this: A recent study found evidence that a person diagnosed as being in a vegetative state showed intentional mental activity (Owen et al., 2006). Researchers used fMRI to observe the patterns of brain activity in a 25-year-old woman with severe brain injuries as the result of a traffic accident. When the researchers spoke ambiguous sentences ("The creak came from a beam in the ceiling") and unambiguous sentences ("There was milk and sugar in his coffee"), fMRI revealed that the activated areas in the woman's brain were comparable to those areas activated in the brains of normal volunteers. What's more, when the woman was instructed to imagine playing a game of tennis and then imagine walking through the rooms of her house, the areas of her brain that showed activity were again indistinguishable from those brain areas in normal, healthy volunteers.

The researchers suggest that these findings are evidence for, at least, conscious understanding of spoken commands and, at best, a degree of intentionality in an otherwise vegetative person. The patient's brain activity while "playing tennis" and "walking through her house" revealed that she could both understand the researchers' instructions and willfully complete them. A more recent fMRI study that used these and related mental imagery tasks in a much larger sample found evidence for willful modulation of brain activity in 5 of 54 patients with disorders of consciousness (Monti et al., 2010). Other recent fMRI studies have revealed evidence of normal cerebral responses to language and complex sounds in two out of three patients in a vegetative state (Fernandez-Espejo et al., 2008), and stronger emotional responding to familiar than to unfamiliar voices in a single patient (Eickhoff et al., 2008). Although it's too early to tell how these and other research findings may impact decisions regarding the brain and when life ends (Laureys et al., 2006), scientists and physicians are now engaged in intensive discussions concerning their ethical and clinical implications (Bernat, 2009; Monti, Coleman, & Owen, 2009).

Chapter Review

KEY CONCEPT QUIZ

1. Which of the following is NOT a function of a neuron?
   a. processing information
   b. communicating with other neurons
   c. nutritional provision
   d. sending messages to body organs and muscles

2. Signals from other neurons are received and relayed to the cell body by
   a. the nucleus.
   b. dendrites.
   c. axons.
   d. glands.

3. Signals are transmitted from one neuron to another
   a. across a synapse.
   b. through a glial cell.
   c. by the myelin sheath.
   d. in the cell body.

4. Which type of neuron receives information from the external world and conveys this information to the brain via the spinal cord?
   a. sensory neuron
   b. motor neuron
   c. interneuron
   d. axon

5. An electric signal that is conducted along the length of a neuron's axon to the synapse is called
   a. a resting potential.
   b. an action potential.
   c. a node of Ranvier.
   d. an ion.

6. The chemicals that transmit information across the synapse to a receiving neuron's dendrites are called
   a. vesicles.
   b. terminal buttons.
   c. postsynaptic neurons.
   d. neurotransmitters.

7. The _____ automatically controls the organs of the body.
   a. autonomic nervous system
   b. parasympathetic nervous system
   c. sympathetic nervous system
   d. somatic nervous system

8. Which part of the hindbrain coordinates fine motor skills?
   a. the medulla
   b. the cerebellum
   c. the pons
   d. the tegmentum

9. What part of the brain is involved in movement and arousal?
   a. the hindbrain
   b. the midbrain
   c. the forebrain
   d. the reticular formation

10. The _____ regulates body temperature, hunger, thirst, and sexual behavior.
    a. cerebral cortex
    b. pituitary gland
    c. hypothalamus
    d. hippocampus

11. What explains the apparent beneficial effects of cardiovascular exercise on aspects of brain function and cognitive performance?
    a. the different sizes of the somatosensory cortices
    b. the position of the cerebral cortex
    c. specialization of association areas
    d. neuron plasticity

12. During the course of embryonic brain growth, the _____ undergoes the greatest development.
    a. cerebral cortex
    b. cerebellum
    c. tectum
    d. thalamus

13. The first true central nervous system appeared in
    a. flatworms.
    b. jellyfish.
    c. protozoa.
    d. early primates.

14. Genes set the _____ in populations within a given environment.
    a. individual characteristics
    b. range of variation
    c. environmental possibilities
    d. behavioral standards

15. Identifying the brain areas that are involved in specific types of motor, cognitive, or emotional processing is best achieved through
    a. recording patterns of electrical activity.
    b. observing psychological disorders.
    c. psychosurgery.
    d. brain imaging.

KEY TERMS

neurons (p. 78)
cell body (p. 79)
dendrite (p. 79)
axon (p. 79)
myelin sheath (p. 79)
glial cell (p. 79)
synapse (p. 80)
sensory neurons (p. 81)
motor neurons (p. 81)
interneurons (p. 81)
resting potential (p. 83)
action potential (p. 84)
refractory period (p. 85)
terminal buttons (p. 86)
neurotransmitters (p. 86)
receptors (p. 86)

acetylcholine (ACh) (p. 87)
dopamine (p. 87)
glutamate (p. 87)
GABA (gamma-aminobutyric
   acid) (p. 87)
norepinephrine (p. 87)
serotonin (p. 87)
endorphins (p. 87)
agonists (p. 88)
antagonists (p. 88)
nervous system (p. 91)
central nervous system (CNS)
   (p. 91)
peripheral nervous system
   (PNS) (p. 91)
somatic nervous system
   (p. 92)

autonomic nervous system
   (ANS) (p. 92)
sympathetic nervous system
   (p. 92)
parasympathetic nervous
   system (p. 92)
spinal reflexes (p. 94)
hindbrain (p. 96)
medulla (p. 96)
reticular formation (p. 96)
cerebellum (p. 96)
pons (p. 96)
tectum (p. 96)
tegmentum (p. 97)
cerebral cortex (p. 97)
subcortical structures (p. 97)
thalamus (p. 98)

hypothalamus (p. 98)
pituitary gland (p. 98)
limbic system (p. 99)
hippocampus (p. 99)
amygdala (p. 99)
basal ganglia (p. 99)
corpus callosum (p. 100)
occipital lobe (p. 101)
parietal lobe (p. 101)
temporal lobe (p. 102)
frontal lobe (p. 102)
association areas (p. 102)
gene (p. 108)
chromosomes (p. 108)
heritability (p. 109)
electroencephalograph (EEG)
   (p. 114)

CRITICAL THINKING QUESTIONS

1. In this chapter, you read about the various functions of different areas of the human cerebral cortex. Reptiles and birds have almost no cerebral cortex, while mammals such as rats and cats do have a cerebral cortex, but their frontal lobes are proportionately much smaller than the frontal lobes of humans and other primates.

   How might this explain the fact that only humans have developed complex language, computer technology, and calculus?

2. Different parts of the human cerebral cortex specialize in processing different types of information: The occipital lobe processes visual information, the parietal lobe processes information about touch, the temporal lobe is responsible for hearing and language, and the frontal lobe is involved in planning and judgment.

   Suppose a toddler is playing with the remote control and accidentally pushes the big red button, at which point her favorite cartoon disappears from the television screen. How would the different parts of her cortex encode information about this event so that she may learn not to make the same mistake twice?

3. In Chapter 2, you learned about the difference between correlation and causation, and that even if two events are correlated, it does not necessarily mean that one causes the other. In this chapter, you read about techniques such as fMRI and PET, which researchers can use to measure blood flow or activity in different regions while people perform particular tasks.

   Suppose a researcher designs an experiment in which participants view words on a screen and are asked to pronounce each word aloud, while the researcher uses fMRI to examine brain activity. First, what areas of the brain would you expect to show activity on fMRI while participants complete this task? Second, can the researcher now safely conclude that those brain areas are required for humans to perform word pronunciation?

RECOMMENDED READINGS

Damasio, A. (2005). *Descartes' error: Emotion, reason, and the human brain*. New York: Penguin.

Emotion and reason seem like competing forces in directing our behavior: One force wants to feel good, while the other wants to think things through. Antonio Damasio, a distinguished neuroscientist, considers how emotion and reason relate to each other and how both cooperate to allow the brain to function efficiently.

Johnson, S. (2004). *Mind wide open: Your brain and the neuroscience of everyday life*. New York: Scribner.

Steven Johnson is a science writer who synthesizes scholarly research for a popular audience. In this book, he explores a range of findings related to neuroscience, including techniques for studying the brain (such as MRI), the purposes and functions of brain structures (such as the amygdala), and the meaning behind what the brain does and why it does it.

LeDoux, J. (2002). *The synaptic self: How our brains become who we are*. New York: Viking.

Joseph LeDoux is a neuroscientist who studies how cortical and subcortical structures direct behavior. In this book, he takes us on a journey from a basic understanding of what neurons are to a proposal that our synaptic connections make us who we are: Personality, self, and related concepts stem from the interwoven connections that make up our brains.

Lehrer, J. (2007). *Proust was a neuroscientist*. New York: Houghton Mifflin Harcourt.

Jonah Lehrer is a thoughtful and engaging science writer who has written a unique book that examines how non-scientists—including a novelist such as Proust—have in some sense anticipated later discoveries in neuroscience. His discussions of Proust's remarkably insightful observations concerning memory, based on the novelist's search for his own childhood experiences, are the centerpiece of a book that tries to tighten the links between science and art.

Ramachandran, V. S., & Blakeslee, S. (1998). *Phantoms in the brain: Probing the mysteries of the human mind*. New York: Morrow.

Vilayanur Ramachandran is a leading theorist in understanding how the brain produces the mind. Susan Blakeslee is a *New York Times* science writer. Together they explore the sometimes bizarre world of the usual and not-so-usual workings of the brain. This book is a good survey of several topics discussed in the current chapter and a nice introduction to some related ideas.

ANSWERS TO KEY CONCEPT QUIZ

1. c; 2. b; 3. a; 4. a; 5. b; 6. d; 7. a; 8. b; 9. b; 10. c; 11. d; 12. a; 13. a; 14. b; 15. d.

Need more help? Additional resources are located at the book's free companion Web site at:
www.worthpublishers.com/schacter

4

Sensation and Perception

N is sort of . . . rubbery . . . smooth, L is sort of the consistency of watery paint . . . Letters also have vague personalities, but not as strongly as numerals do.
—Julieta

The letter A is blue, B is red, C is kind of a light gray, D is orange. . . .
—Karen

I hear a note by one of the fellows in the band and it's one color. I hear the same note played by someone else and it's a different color. When I hear sustained musical tones, I see just about the same colors that you do, but I see them in textures.
—Jazz musician Duke Ellington (George, 1981, p. 226)

Basically, i taste words.
—Amelia

T hese comments are not from a recent meeting of the Slightly Odd Society. They're the remarks of otherwise perfectly normal people describing what seem to be perfectly bizarre experiences except to them—they think these experiences are quite commonplace and genuine. After all, if you can't trust Duke Ellington, an internationally acclaimed jazz composer and bandleader, who can you trust? Perhaps Stevie Wonder? Eddie Van Halen? Franz Liszt, the classical composer? Richard Feynman, the Nobel Prize–winning physicist? Take your pick because these and many other notable people have at least one thing in common: Their perceptual worlds seem to be quite different from most of ours.

▼ What do these people have in common? Duke Ellington, Stevie Wonder, Eddie Van Halen, and Franz Liszt are all musicians, but Richard Feynman was a physicist. All of these people are men, but that has little to do with it. Some are living; some are dead. In fact, all of these people have fairly well-documented experiences of synesthesia, the experience of one sense that is evoked by a different sense.

METRONOME/GETTY IMAGES
EVERETT KENNEDY BROWN/EPA/CORBIS
MARK DAVIS/GETTY IMAGES
W. & D. DOWNEY/GETTY IMAGES
SHELLEY GAZIN/CORBIS

synesthesia The perceptual experience of one sense that is evoked by another sense.

THESE UNUSUAL PERCEPTUAL EVENTS ARE VARIETIES OF **synesthesia,** *the perceptual experience of one sense that is evoked by another sense* (Hubbard & Ramachandran, 2003). For some synesthetes, musical notes evoke the visual sensation of color. Other people with synesthesia see printed letters (**FIGURE 4.1**) or numbers in specific, consistent colors (always seeing the digit 2 as pink and 3 as green, for example). Still others experience specific tastes when certain sounds are heard.

For those of us who don't experience synesthesia, the prospect of tasting sounds or hearing colors may seem unbelievable or the product of some hallucinogenic experience. Indeed, for many years scientists dismissed synesthesia as either a rare curiosity or a case of outright faking. But recent research indicates that synesthesia is far more common than previously believed. Synesthesia was once thought to occur in as few as one in every 25,000 people, but it is now clear that some forms of synesthesia are not as rare as others and may be found in as many as one in every 100 people (Hubbard & Ramachandran, 2005). The experience of seeing colors evoked by sounds or of seeing letters in specific colors is much more common among synesthetes than, say, a smell evoked by touching a certain shape.

Recent research has documented the psychological and neurobiological reality of synesthesia. For example, a synesthete who sees the digits 2 and 4 as pink and 3 as green will find it easier to pick out a 2 among a bunch of 3s than among a bunch of 4s, whereas a nonsynesthete will perform these two tasks equally well (Palmieri, Ingersoll, & Stone, 2002). Brain-imaging studies also show that in some synesthetes, areas of the brain involved in processing colors are more active when they hear words that evoke color than when they hear tones that don't evoke color; no such differences are seen among people in a control group (Mattingly, 2009; Nunn, Gregory, & Brammer, 2002).

So, synesthesia is neither an isolated curiosity nor the result of faking. In fact, it may indicate that in some people, the brain is "wired" differently than in most, so that brain regions for different sensory modalities cross-activate one another (Ramachandran & Hubbard, 2003; Rouw & Scholte, 2007). Whatever the ultimate explanations for these fascinating phenomena, this recent wave of research, and related work we'll consider later in the chapter, shows that synesthesia can shed new light on how the brain is organized and how we sense and perceive the world.

In this chapter we'll explore key insights into the nature of sensation and perception. These experiences are basic to survival and reproduction; we wouldn't last long without the ability to accurately make sense of the world around us. Indeed, research on sensation and perception is the basis for much of psychology, a pathway toward understanding more complex cognition and behavior such as memory, emotion, motivation, or decision making. Yet sensation and perception also sometimes reveal various kinds of illusions that you might see at a science fair or in a novelty shop—reminders that the act of perceiving the world is not as simple or straightforward as it might seem.

We'll look at how physical energy in the world around us is encoded by our senses, sent to the brain, and enters conscious awareness. Vision is predominant among our senses; correspondingly, we'll devote a fair amount of space to understanding how the visual system works. Then we'll discuss how we perceive sound waves as words or music or noise, followed by the body senses, emphasizing touch, pain, and balance. We'll end with the chemical senses of smell and taste, which together allow you to savor the foods you eat. But before doing any of that, we will provide a foundation for examining all of the sensory systems by reviewing how psychologists measure sensation and perception in the first place.

▼ FIGURE 4.1
Synesthesia Most of us see letters printed in black as they appear in (a). Some people with synesthesia link their perceptions of letters with certain colors and perceive letters as printed in different colors, as shown in (b). In synesthesia, brain regions for different sensory modalities cross-activate one another.

A B C D E

(a) Usual appearance

A B C D E

(b) Appearance to a person with synesthesia

Our Senses Encode the Information Our Brains Perceive

From the vantage point of our own consciousness, sensation and perception appear to be one seamless event. Information comes in from the outside world, gets registered and interpreted, and triggers some kind of action: no breaks, no balks, just one continuous process. Psychologists know, however, that sensation and perception are two separate activities. **Sensation** is *simple stimulation of a sense organ*. It is the basic registration of light, sound, pressure, odor, or taste as parts of your body interact with the physical world. After a sensation registers in your central nervous system, **perception** takes place at the level of your brain: It is *the organization, identification, and interpretation of a sensation in order to form a mental representation*.

As an example, your eyes are coursing across these sentences right now. The sensory receptors in your eyeballs are registering different patterns of light reflecting off the page. Your brain, however, is integrating and processing that light information into the meaningful perception of words, such as *meaningful*, *perception*, and *words*. Your eyes—the sensory organ—aren't really seeing words; they're simply encoding different lines, curves, and patterns of ink on a page. Your brain—the perceptual organ—is transforming those lines and curves into a coherent mental representation of words and concepts.

If all of this sounds a little peculiar, it's because from the vantage point of your conscious experience, it *seems* as if you're reading words directly; again, sensation and perception feel like one single event. If you think of the discussion of brain damage in Chapter 3, however, you'll recall that sometimes a person's eyes can work just fine, yet the individual is still "blind" to faces she has seen for many years. Damage to the visual-processing centers in the brain can interfere with the interpretation of information coming from the eyes: The senses are intact, but perceptual ability is compromised. Sensation and perception are related—but separate—events.

What role does the brain play in what we see and hear? We all know that we have five senses: vision, hearing, touch, taste, and smell. Arguably, we possess several more senses besides these five. Touch, for example, encompasses distinct body senses, including sensitivity to pain and temperature, joint position and balance, and even the state of the gut. Despite the variety of our senses, they all depend on the process of **transduction**, which occurs *when many sensors in the body convert physical signals from the environment into encoded neural signals sent to the central nervous system*.

In vision, light reflected from surfaces provides the eyes with information about the shape, color, and position of objects. In audition, vibrations (from vocal cords or a guitar string, perhaps) cause changes in air pressure that propagate through space to a listener's ears. In touch, the pressure of a surface against the skin signals its shape, texture, and temperature. In taste and smell, molecules dispersed in the air or dissolved in saliva reveal the identity of substances that we may or may not want to eat. In each case physical energy from the world is converted to neural energy inside the central nervous system (see **TABLE 4.1** on the next page). We've already seen that synesthetes experience a mixing of these perceptions; however, even during synesthesia the

sensation Simple stimulation of a sense organ.

perception The organization, identification, and interpretation of a sensation in order to form a mental representation.

transduction What takes place when many sensors in the body convert physical signals from the environment into encoded neural signals sent to the central nervous system.

◀ You can enjoy a tempting ice cream sundae even if you do not know that its sweet taste depends on a complex process of transduction, in which molecules dissolved in saliva are converted to neural signals processed by the brain.

FOTOFLARE/ISTOCKPHOTO

TABLE 4.1

Transduction

The five senses convert physical energy from the world into neural energy, which is sent to the brain.

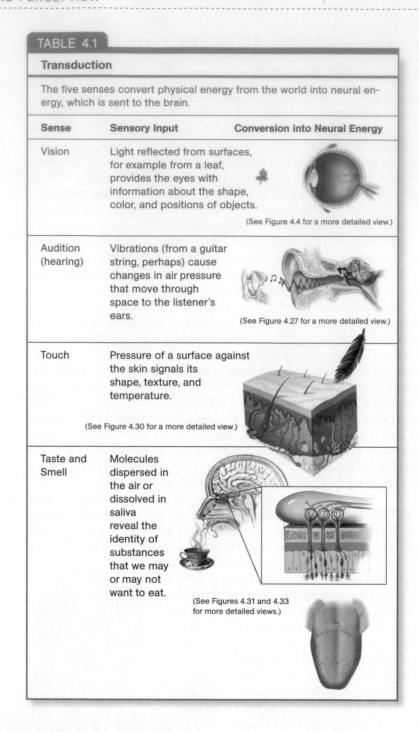

Sense	Sensory Input	Conversion into Neural Energy
Vision	Light reflected from surfaces, for example from a leaf, provides the eyes with information about the shape, color, and positions of objects.	(See Figure 4.4 for a more detailed view.)
Audition (hearing)	Vibrations (from a guitar string, perhaps) cause changes in air pressure that move through space to the listener's ears.	(See Figure 4.27 for a more detailed view.)
Touch	Pressure of a surface against the skin signals its shape, texture, and temperature.	(See Figure 4.30 for a more detailed view.)
Taste and Smell	Molecules dispersed in the air or dissolved in saliva reveal the identity of substances that we may or may not want to eat.	(See Figures 4.31 and 4.33 for more detailed views.)

processes of transduction that begin those perceptions are the same. Despite "hearing colors," your eyes simply can't transduce sound waves, no matter how long you stare at your stereo speakers!

Psychophysics

It's intriguing to consider the possibility that our basic perceptions of sights or sounds might differ fundamentally from those of other people. One reason we find synesthetes fascinating is because their perceptual experiences are so different from most of ours. But we won't get very far in understanding such differences by simply relying on casual self-reports. As you learned in Chapter 2, to understand a behavior researchers must first *operationalize* it, and that involves finding a reliable way to measure it.

Any type of scientific investigation requires objective measurements. Measuring the physical energy of a stimulus, such as the wavelength of a light, is easy enough: You can probably buy the necessary instruments online to do that yourself. But how do you quantify a person's private, subjective *perception* of that light? It's one thing to know that a flashlight produces "100 candlepower" or gives off "8,000 lumens," but it's another matter entirely to measure a person's psychological experience of that light energy.

The structuralists, led by Wilhelm Wundt and Edward Titchener, tried using introspection to measure perceptual experiences (see Chapter 1). They failed miserably at this task. After all, you can describe your experience to another person in words, but that person cannot know directly what you perceive when you look at a sunset. You both may call the sunset "orange" and "beautiful," but neither of you can directly perceive the other's experience of the same event. Evoked memories and emotions intertwine with what you are hearing, seeing, and smelling, making your perception of an event—and therefore your experience of that event—unique.

? Why isn't it enough for a psychophysicist to measure only the strength of a stimulus?

Given that perception is different for each of us, how could we ever hope to measure it? This question was answered in the mid-1800s by the German scientist and philosopher Gustav Fechner (1801–87). Fechner developed an approach to measuring sensation and perception called **psychophysics**: *methods that measure the strength of a stimulus and the observer's sensitivity to that stimulus* (Fechner, 1860). In a typical psychophysics experiment, researchers ask people to make a simple judgment—whether or not they saw a flash of light, for example. The psychophysicist then relates the measured stimulus, such as the brightness of the light flash, to each observer's yes-or-no response.

Measuring Thresholds

Psychophysicists begin the measurement process with a single sensory signal to determine precisely how much physical energy is required to evoke a sensation in an observer.

Absolute Threshold

The simplest quantitative measurement in psychophysics is the **absolute threshold**, *the minimal intensity needed to just barely detect a stimulus*. A *threshold* is a boundary. The doorway that separates the inside from the outside of a house is a threshold, as is the boundary between two psychological states ("awareness" and "unawareness," for example). In finding the absolute threshold for sensation, the two states in question are *sensing* and *not sensing* some stimulus. **TABLE 4.2** lists the approximate sensory thresholds for each of the five senses.

To measure the absolute threshold for detecting a sound, for example, an observer sits in a soundproof room wearing headphones linked to a computer. The experimenter presents a pure tone (the sort of sound made by striking a tuning fork) using the computer to vary the loudness or the length of time each tone lasts and recording how often the observer reports hearing that tone under each condition. The outcome of such an experiment is graphed in **FIGURE 4.2** on the next page. Notice from the shape of the curve that the transition from *not*

psychophysics Methods that measure the strength of a stimulus and the observer's sensitivity to that stimulus.

absolute threshold The minimal intensity needed to just barely detect a stimulus.

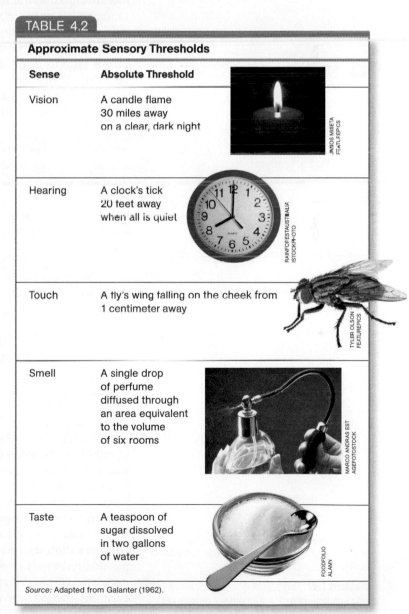

TABLE 4.2		
Approximate Sensory Thresholds		
Sense	**Absolute Threshold**	
Vision	A candle flame 30 miles away on a clear, dark night	
Hearing	A clock's tick 20 feet away when all is quiet	
Touch	A fly's wing falling on the cheek from 1 centimeter away	
Smell	A single drop of perfume diffused through an area equivalent to the volume of six rooms	
Taste	A teaspoon of sugar dissolved in two gallons of water	

Source: Adapted from Galanter (1962).

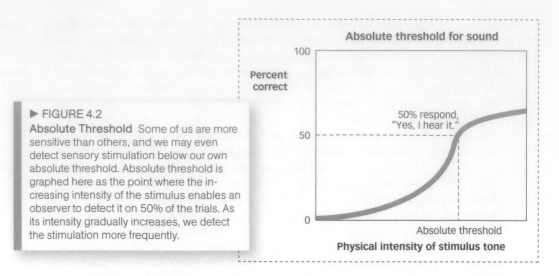

Absolute threshold for sound

Percent correct

50% respond, "Yes, I hear it."

Absolute threshold

Physical intensity of stimulus tone

▶ FIGURE 4.2

Absolute Threshold Some of us are more sensitive than others, and we may even detect sensory stimulation below our own absolute threshold. Absolute threshold is graphed here as the point where the increasing intensity of the stimulus enables an observer to detect it on 50% of the trials. As its intensity gradually increases, we detect the stimulation more frequently.

hearing to *hearing* is gradual rather than abrupt. Investigators typically define the absolute threshold as the loudness required for the listener to say she or he has heard the tone on 50% of the trials.

If we repeat this experiment for many different tones, we can observe and record the thresholds for tones ranging from very low pitch to very high. It turns out that people tend to be most sensitive to the range of tones corresponding to human conversation. If the tone is low enough, such as the lowest note on a pipe organ, most humans cannot hear it at all; we can only feel it. If the tone is high enough, we likewise cannot hear it, but dogs and many other animals can.

Difference Thresholds

The absolute threshold is useful for assessing how sensitive we are to faint stimuli, but most everyday perception involves detecting differences among stimuli that are well above the absolute threshold. Most people are pretty adept at noticing that a couch is red, but they're likely to want to know if the couch is redder than the drapes they're considering. Similarly, parents can usually detect their own infant's cry from the cries of other babies, but it's probably more useful to be able to differentiate the "I'm hungry" cry from the "I'm cranky" cry from the "Something is biting my toes" cry. In short, the human perceptual system excels at detecting *changes* in stimulation rather than the simple onset or offset of stimulation.

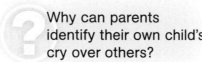 Why can parents identify their own child's cry over others?

As a way of measuring this difference threshold, Fechner proposed the **just noticeable difference**, or **JND**, *the minimal change in a stimulus that can just barely be detected.* The JND is not a fixed quantity; rather, it depends on how intense the stimuli being measured are and on the particular sense being measured. Consider measuring the JND for a bright light. An observer in a dark room is shown a light of fixed intensity, called the *standard* (S), next to a comparison light that is slightly brighter or dimmer than the standard. When S is very dim, observers can see even a very small difference in brightness between the two lights: The JND is small. But if S is bright, a much larger increment is needed to detect the difference: The JND is larger.

In fact, the just noticeable difference can be calculated for each sense. It is roughly proportional to the magnitude of the standard stimulus. This relationship was first noticed in 1834 by a German physiologist named Ernst Weber, who taught at the University of Leipzig around the time that Fechner was a student there and likely influenced Fechner's thinking (Watson, 1978). Fechner applied Weber's insight directly to psychophysics, resulting in a formal relationship called **Weber's law**, which states that *the just noticeable difference of a stimulus is a constant proportion despite variations in intensity.* As an example, the JND for weight is about 2–3%. If you picked up a one-ounce envelope, then a two-ounce envelope, you'd probably notice the difference between them. But if

just noticeable difference (JND) The minimal change in a stimulus that can just barely be detected.

Weber's law The just noticeable difference of a stimulus is a constant proportion despite variations in intensity.

you picked up a twenty-pound package, then a twenty-pound, one-ounce package, you'd probably detect no difference at all between them. In fact, you'd probably need about a twenty-and-a-half-pound package to detect a JND. When calculating a difference threshold, it is the proportion between stimuli that is important; the measured size of the difference, whether in brightness, loudness, or weight, is irrelevant.

signal detection theory An observation that the response to a stimulus depends both on a person's sensitivity to the stimulus in the presence of noise and on a person's response criterion.

Signal Detection

Measuring absolute and difference thresholds requires a critical assumption: that a threshold exists! But much of what scientists know about biology suggests that such a discrete, all-or-none change in the brain is unlikely. Humans don't suddenly and rapidly switch between perceiving and not perceiving; in fact, recall that the transition from *not sensing* to *sensing* is gradual (see Figure 4.2). The very same physical stimulus, such as a dim light or a quiet tone, presented on several different occasions, may be perceived by the same person on some occasions but not on others. Remember, an absolute threshold is operationalized as perceiving the stimulus 50% of the time . . . which means the other 50% of the time it might go undetected.

Our accurate perception of a sensory stimulus, then, can be somewhat haphazard. Whether in the psychophysics lab or out in the world, sensory signals face a lot of competition, or *noise,* which refers to all the other stimuli coming from the internal and external environment. Memories, moods, and motives intertwine with what you are seeing, hearing, and smelling at any given time. This internal "noise" competes with your ability to detect a stimulus with perfect, focused attention. Other sights, sounds, and smells in the world at large also compete for attention; you rarely have the luxury of attending to just one stimulus apart from everything else. As a consequence of noise, you may not perceive everything that you sense, and you may even perceive things that you haven't sensed. Think of the last time you had a hearing test. You no doubt missed some of the quiet beeps that were presented, but you also probably said you heard beeps that weren't really there.

? How accurate and complete are our perceptions of the world? ·

An approach to psychophysics called **signal detection theory** holds that *the response to a stimulus depends both on a person's sensitivity to the stimulus in the presence of noise and on a person's decision criterion.* That is, observers consider the sensory evidence evoked by the stimulus and compare it to an internal decision criterion (Green & Swets, 1966; Macmillan & Creelman, 2005). If the sensory evidence exceeds the criterion, the observer responds by saying, "Yes, I detected the stimulus," and if it falls short of the criterion, the observer responds by saying, "No, I did not detect the stimulus."

Signal detection theory allows researchers to quantify an observer's response in the presence of noise. In a signal detection experiment, a stimulus, such as a dim light, is randomly presented or not. If you've ever taken an eye exam that checks your peripheral vision, you have an idea about this kind of setup: Lights of varying intensity are flashed at various places in the visual field, and your task is to respond anytime you see one. Observers in a signal detection experiment must decide whether they saw the light or not. If the light is presented and the observer correctly responds, "Yes," the outcome is a *hit.* If the light is presented and the observer says, "No," the result is a *miss.* However, if the light is *not* presented and the observer nonetheless says it was, a *false alarm* has occurred. Finally, if the light is *not* presented and the observer responds, "No," a *correct rejection* has occurred: The observer accurately detected the absence of the stimulus.

▼ Cluttered environments such as this promenade in Venice Beach, California, present our visual system with a challenging signal detection task.

ERNST WRBA/ALAMY

Signal detection theory is a more sophisticated approach than was used in the early days of establishing absolute thresholds because it explicitly takes into account observers' response tendencies, such as liberally saying "Yes" when there is any hint of a stimulus or conservatively reserving identifications only for obvious instances of the stimulus. Signal detection theory proposes a way to measure *perceptual sensitivity*—how effectively the perceptual system represents sensory events—separately from the observer's decision-making strategy. Even when one person says "Yes" much more often than another, both may be equally accurate in distinguishing between the presence or absence of a stimulus. Although the purely conservative and liberal strategies represent two poles on a long continuum of possible decision criteria, signal detection theory has practical applications at home, school, work, and even while driving.

For example, a radiologist may have to decide whether a mammogram shows that a patient has breast cancer. The radiologist knows that certain features, such as a mass of a particular size and shape, are associated with the presence of cancer. But noncancerous features can have a very similar appearance to cancerous ones. The radiologist may decide on a strictly liberal criterion and check every possible case of cancer with a biopsy. This decision strategy

THE REAL WORLD

Multitasking

By one estimate, using a cell phone while driving makes having an accident four times more likely (McEvoy et al., 2005). In response to highway safety experts and statistics such as this, state legislatures are passing laws that restrict, and sometimes ban, using mobile phones while driving. You might think that's a fine idea . . . for everyone else on the road. But surely *you* can manage to punch in a number on a phone, carry on a conversation, or maybe even text-message while simultaneously driving in a safe and courteous manner. Right? In a word, *wrong*.

The issue here is *selective attention*, or perceiving only what's currently relevant to you. Perception is an active, moment-to-moment exploration for relevant or interesting information, not a passive receptacle for whatever happens to come along. Talking on a cell phone while driving demands that you juggle two independent sources of sensory input—vision and audition—at the same time. This kind of *multitasking* creates problems when you need to react suddenly while driving. Researchers have tested experienced drivers in a highly realistic driving simulator, measuring their response times to brake lights and stop signs while they listened to the radio or carried on phone conversations about a political issue, among other tasks (Strayer, Drews, & Johnston, 2003).

These experienced drivers reacted significantly more slowly during phone conversations than during the other tasks. This is because a phone conversation requires memory retrieval, deliberation, and planning what to say and often carries an emotional stake in the conversation topic. Tasks such as listening to the radio require far less attention.

The tested drivers became so engaged in their conversations that their minds no longer seemed to be in the car. Their slower braking response translated into an increased stopping distance that, depending on the driver's speed, would have resulted in a rear-end collision. Whether the phone was handheld or hands-free made little difference, and similar results have been obtained in field studies of actual driving (Horrey & Wickens, 2006). This suggests that laws requiring drivers to use hands-free phones may have little effect on reducing accidents. Even after extensive practice at driving while using a hands-free cell phone in a simulator, the distruptive effects of cell phone use were still observed (Cooper & Strayer, 2008). The situation is even worse when text messaging is involved: Compared with a no-texting control condition, when either sending or receiving a text message in the simulator drivers spent dramatically less time looking at the road, had a much harder time staying in their lane, missed numerous lane changes, and had greater difficulty maintaining an appropriate distance behind the car ahead of them (Hosking, Young, & Regan, 2009).

Other researchers have measured brain activity using fMRI while people were shifting attention between visual and auditory information. The strength of visual and auditory brain activity was affected: When attention was directed to audition, activity in visual areas decreased compared to when attention was directed to vision (Shomstein & Yantis, 2004). It was as if the participants could adjust a mental "volume knob" to regulate the flow of incoming information according to which task they were attending to at the moment. Interestingly, people who report that they multitask frequently in everyday life have difficulty in laboratory tasks that require focusing attention in the face of distractions compared with individuals who do not multitask much in daily life (Ophir, Nass, & Wagner, 2009).

So how well do we multitask in several thousand pounds of metal hurtling down the highway? Experienced drivers can handle divided attention to a degree, yet most of us have to acknowledge that we have had close calls due to driving while distracted. Unless you have two heads with one brain each—one to talk and one to concentrate on driving—you would do well to keep your eyes on the road and not on the phone.

Superior temporal lobe   Fusiform gyrus

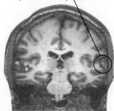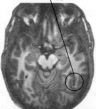

SHOMSTEIN & YANTIS, 2004

▲ **Shifting Attention** Participants received fMRI scans as they performed tasks that required them to shift their attention between visual and auditory information. (a) When focusing on auditory information, a region in the superior (upper) temporal lobe involved in auditory processing showed increased activity (yellow/orange). (b) In striking contrast, a visual region, the fusiform gyrus, showed decreased activity when participants focused on auditory information (blue).

minimizes the possibility of missing a true cancer but leads to many false alarms. A strictly conservative criterion will cut down on false alarms but will miss some treatable cancers.

As another example, imagine that police are on the lookout for a suspected felon who they have reason to believe will be at a crowded soccer match. Although the law enforcement agency provided a fairly good description—6'0", sandy brown hair, beard, glasses—there are still thousands of people to scan. Rounding up all men between 5'5" and 6'5" would probably produce a hit (the felon is caught) but at the expense of an extraordinary number of false alarms (many innocent people are detained and questioned).

These different types of errors have to be weighed against one another in setting the decision criterion. Signal detection theory offers a practical way to choose among criteria that permit decision makers to take into account the consequences of hits, misses, false alarms, and correct rejections (McFall & Treat, 1999; Swets, Dawes, & Monahan, 2000). (For an example of a common everyday task that can interfere with signal detection, see the Real World box.)

Sensory Adaptation

When you walk into a bakery, the aroma of freshly baked bread overwhelms you, but after a few minutes the smell fades. If you dive into cold water, the temperature is shocking at first, but after a few minutes you get used to it. When you wake up in the middle of the night for a drink of water, the bathroom light blinds you, but after a few minutes you no longer squint.

What conditions have you already adapted to today? Sounds? Smells?

These are all examples of **sensory adaptation**, the observation that *sensitivity to prolonged stimulation tends to decline over time as an organism adapts to current conditions*. Imagine that while you are studying in a quiet room, your neighbor in the apartment next door turns on the stereo. That gets your attention, but after a few minutes the sounds fade from your awareness as you continue your studies. But remember that our perceptual systems emphasize *change* in responding to sensory events: When the music stops, you notice.

Sensory adaptation is a useful process for most organisms. Imagine what your sensory and perceptual world would be like without it. When you put on your jeans in the morning, the feeling of rough cloth against your bare skin would be as noticeable hours later as it was in the first few minutes. The stink of garbage in your apartment when you first walk in would never dissipate. If you had to constantly be aware of how your tongue feels while it is resting in your mouth, you'd be driven to distraction. Our sensory systems respond more strongly to changes in stimulation than to constant stimulation. A stimulus that doesn't change usually doesn't require any action; your car probably emits a certain hum all the time that you've gotten used to. But a change in stimulation often signals a need for action. If your car starts making different kinds of noises, you're not only more likely to notice them, but you're also more likely to do something about it.

sensory adaptation Sensitivity to prolonged stimulation tends to decline over time as an organism adapts to current conditions.

IN SUMMARY

○ Sensation and perception are critical to survival. Sensation is the simple stimulation of a sense organ, whereas perception organizes, identifies, and interprets sensation at the level of the brain.

○ All of our senses depend on the process of transduction, which converts physical signals from the environment into neural signals carried by sensory neurons into the central nervous system.

○ In the 19th century, researchers developed psychophysics, an approach to studying perception that measures the strength of a stimulus and an observer's sensitivity to that stimulus. Psychophysicists have developed procedures for measuring an observer's absolute threshold, or the smallest intensity needed to just barely detect a stimulus, and the just noticeable difference (JND), or the smallest change in a stimulus that can just barely be detected.

○ Signal detection theory allows researchers to distinguish between an observer's perceptual sensitivity to a stimulus and criteria for making decisions about the stimulus.

○ Sensory adaptation occurs because sensitivity to lengthy stimulation tends to decline over time.

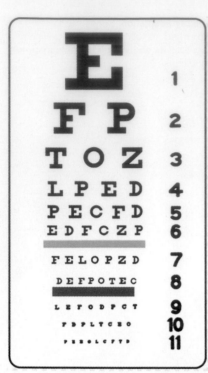

▲ The Snellen chart is commonly used to measure visual acuity. Chances are good you've seen one yourself on more than one occasion.

Vision I: How the Eyes and the Brain Convert Light Waves to Neural Signals

You might be proud of your 20/20 vision, even if it is corrected by glasses or contact lenses. *20/20* refers to a measurement associated with a Snellen chart, named after Hermann Snellen (1834–1908), the Dutch ophthalmologist who developed it as a means of assessing **visual acuity**, *the ability to see fine detail;* it is the smallest line of letters that a typical person can read from a distance of 20 feet. But if you dropped into the Birds of Prey Ophthalmologic Office, your visual pride would wither. Hawks, eagles, owls, and other raptors have much greater visual acuity than humans; in many cases, about eight times greater, or the equivalent of 20/2 vision. Your sophisticated visual system has evolved to transduce visual energy in the world into neural signals in the brain. Humans have sensory receptors in their eyes that respond to wavelengths of light energy. When we look at people, places, and things, patterns of light and color give us information about where one surface stops and another begins. The array of light reflected from those surfaces preserves their shapes and enables us to form a mental representation of a scene (Rodieck, 1998). Understanding vision, then, starts with understanding light.

Sensing Light

Visible light is simply the portion of the electromagnetic spectrum that we can see, and it is an extremely small slice. You can think about light as waves of energy. Like ocean waves, light waves vary in height and in the distance between their peaks, or *wavelengths,* as **TABLE 4.3** shows. There are three properties of light waves, each of which has a physical dimension that produces a corresponding psychological dimension.

> The *length* of a light wave determines its hue, or what humans perceive as color.

> The intensity or *amplitude* of a light wave—how high the peaks are—determines what we perceive as the brightness of light.

> *Purity* is the number of distinct wavelengths that make up the light. Purity corresponds to what humans perceive as saturation, or the richness of colors (see **FIGURE 4.3**).

visual acuity The ability to see fine detail.

retina Light-sensitive tissue lining the back of the eyeball.

accommodation The process by which the eye maintains a clear image on the retina.

TABLE 4.3	
Properties of Light Waves	
Physical Dimension	**Psychological Dimension**
Length	Hue or what we perceive as color
Amplitude	Brightness
Purity	Saturation or richness of color

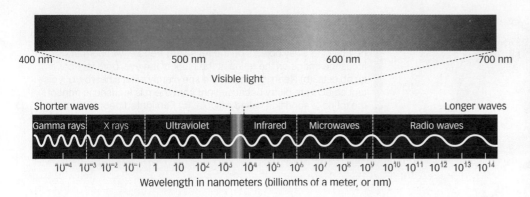

Electromagnetic Spectrum The sliver of light waves visible to humans as a rainbow of colors from violet-blue to red is bounded on the short end by ultraviolet rays, which honeybees can see, and on the long end by infrared waves, upon which night-vision equipment operates. Someone wearing night-vision goggles, for example, can detect another person's body heat in complete darkness. Light waves are minute, but the scale along the bottom of this chart offers a glimpse of their varying lengths, measured in nanometers (nm; 1 nm = 1 billionth of a meter).

In other words, light doesn't need a human to have the properties it does: Length, amplitude, and purity are properties of the light waves themselves. What humans perceive from those properties are color, brightness, and saturation.

The Human Eye

Eyes have evolved as specialized organs to detect light. **FIGURE 4.4** shows the human eye in cross-section. Light that reaches the eyes passes first through a clear, smooth outer tissue called the *cornea*, which bends the light wave and sends it through the *pupil*, a hole in the colored part of the eye. This colored part is the *iris*, which is a translucent, doughnut-shaped muscle that controls the size of the pupil and hence the amount of light that can enter the eye.

Immediately behind the iris, muscles inside the eye control the shape of the *lens* to bend the light again and focus it onto the **retina**, *light-sensitive tissue lining the back of the eyeball*. The muscles change the shape of the lens to focus objects at different distances, making the lens flatter for objects that are far away or rounder for nearby objects. This is called **accommodation**, *the process by which the eye maintains a clear image on the retina*. **FIGURE 4.5a** (on the next page) shows how accommodation works.

If your eyeballs are a little too long or a little too short, the lens will not focus images properly on the retina. If the eyeball is too long, images are focused in front of the retina, leading to nearsightedness (*myopia*), which is shown in **FIGURE 4.5b**. If the eyeball is too short, images are focused behind the retina, and the result is farsightedness (*hyperopia*), as shown in **FIGURE 4.5c**.

How do eyeglasses actually correct vision?

Eyeglasses, contact lenses, and surgical procedures can correct either condition. For example, eyeglasses and contacts both provide an additional lens to help focus light more appropriately, and procedures such as LASIK physically reshape the eye's existing lens.

Light reflected from a surface enters the eyes via the transparent **cornea**, bending to pass through the **pupil** at the center of the colored **iris**.

Muscles to move eye

Behind the iris, the thickness and shape of the **lens** adjust to focus light on the **retina**, where the image appears upside down and backward. Vision is clearest at the **fovea**.

Light-sensitive receptor cells in the **retinal surface**, excited or inhibited by spots of lights, influence the specialized neurons that signal the brain's visual centers through their bundled axons, which make up the **optic nerve**. The optic nerve creates the **blind spot**.

Anatomy of the Human Eye Light reflected from a surface enters the eye via the transparent cornea, bending to pass through the pupil at the center of the colored iris. Behind the iris, the thickness and shape of the lens adjust to focus the light on the retina, where the image appears upside down and backward. Basically, this is how a camera lens works. Light-sensitive receptor cells in the retinal surface, excited or inhibited by spots of light, influence the specialized neurons that convey nerve impulses to the brain's visual centers through their axons, which make up the optic nerve.

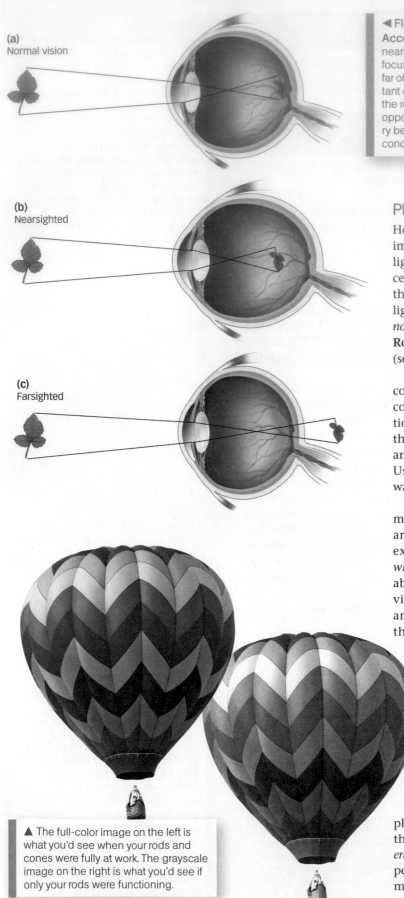

(a)
Normal vision

(b)
Nearsighted

(c)
Farsighted

▲ The full-color image on the left is what you'd see when your rods and cones were fully at work. The grayscale image on the right is what you'd see if only your rods were functioning.

MIKE SONNENBERG/ISTOCKPHOTO

◀ FIGURE 4.5
Accommodation Inside the eye, the lens changes shape to focus nearby or faraway objects on the retina. (a) People with normal vision focus the image on the retina at the back of the eye, both for near and far objects. (b) Nearsighted people see clearly what's nearby, but distant objects are blurry because light from them is focused in front of the retina, a condition called myopia. (c) Farsighted people have the opposite problem: Distant objects are clear, but those nearby are blurry because their point of focus falls beyond the surface of the retina, a condition called hyperopia.

Phototransduction in the Retina

How does a wavelength of light become a meaningful image? The retina is the interface between the world of light outside the body and the world of vision inside the central nervous system. Two types of *photoreceptor cells* in the retina contain light-sensitive pigments that transduce light into neural impulses. **Cones** *detect color, operate under normal daylight conditions, and allow us to focus on fine detail.* **Rods** *become active under low-light conditions for night vision* (see **FIGURE 4.6**).

Rods are much more sensitive photoreceptors than cones, but this sensitivity comes at a cost. Because all rods contain the same photopigment, they provide no information about color and sense only shades of gray. Think about this the next time you wake up in the middle of the night and make your way to the bathroom for a drink of water. Using only the moonlight from the window to light your way, do you see the room in color or in shades of gray?

Rods and cones differ in several other ways as well, most notably in their numbers. About 120 million rods are distributed more or less evenly around each retina except in the very center, the **fovea**, *an area of the retina where vision is the clearest and there are no rods at all.* The absence of rods in the fovea decreases the sharpness of vision in reduced light, but it can be overcome. For example, when amateur astronomers view dim stars through their telescopes at night, they know to look a little off to the side of the target so that the image will fall not on the rod-free fovea but on some other part of the retina that contains many highly sensitive rods.

In contrast to rods, each retina contains only about 6 million cones, which are densely packed in the fovea and much more sparsely distributed over the rest of the retina, as you can see in Figure 4.6. This distribution of cones directly affects visual acuity and explains why objects off to the side, in your *peripheral vision,* aren't so clear. The light reflecting from those peripheral objects has a difficult time landing in the fovea, making the resulting image less clear. The more fine detail

What are the major differences between rods and cones?

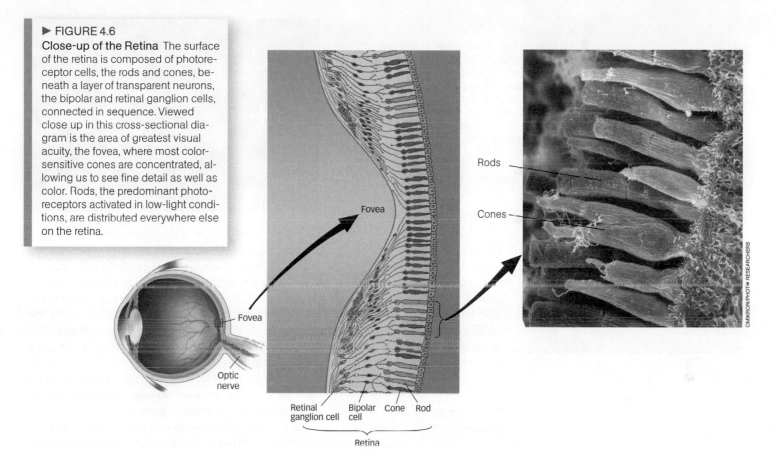

► FIGURE 4.6

Close-up of the Retina The surface of the retina is composed of photoreceptor cells, the rods and cones, beneath a layer of transparent neurons, the bipolar and retinal ganglion cells, connected in sequence. Viewed close up in this cross-sectional diagram is the area of greatest visual acuity, the fovea, where most color-sensitive cones are concentrated, allowing us to see fine detail as well as color. Rods, the predominant photoreceptors activated in low-light conditions, are distributed everywhere else on the retina.

encoded and represented in the visual system, the clearer the perceived image. The process is analogous to the quality of photographs taken with a six-megapixel digital camera versus a two-megapixel camera.

The retina is thick with cells. As seen in Figure 4.6, the photoreceptor cells (rods and cones) form the innermost layer. The middle layer contains *bipolar cells,* which collect neural signals from the rods and cones and transmit them to the outermost layer of the retina, where neurons called *retinal ganglion cells* (RGCs) organize the signals and send them to the brain.

The bundled RGC axons—about 1.5 million per eye—form the *optic nerve,* which leaves the eye through a hole in the retina. Because it contains neither rods nor cones and therefore has no mechanism to sense light, this hole in the retina creates a **blind spot**, which is *a location in the visual field that produces no sensation on the retina*. Try the demonstration in **FIGURE 4.7** on the next page to find the blind spot in each of your own eyes.

cones Photoreceptors that detect color, operate under normal daylight conditions, and allow us to focus on fine detail.

rods Photoreceptors that become active under low-light conditions for night vision.

fovea An area of the retina where vision is the clearest and there are no rods at all.

blind spot A location in the visual field that produces no sensation on the retina because the corresponding area of the retina contains neither rods nor cones and therefore has no mechanism to sense light.

◄ The image on the left was taken at a higher resolution than the image on the right. The difference in quality is analogous to light falling on the fovea versus not.

► FIGURE 4.7

Blind Spot Demonstration To find your blind spot, close your left eye and stare at the cross with your right eye. Hold the book 6 to 12 inches (15 to 30 centimeters) away from your eyes and move it slowly toward and away from you until the dot disappears. The dot is now in your blind spot and so is not visible. At this point the vertical lines may appear as one continuous line because the visual system fills in the area occupied by the missing dot. To test your left-eye blind spot, turn the book upside down and repeat with your right eye closed.

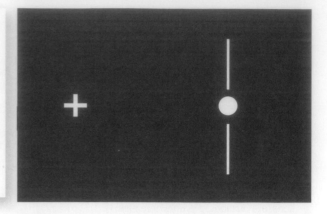

receptive field The region of the sensory surface that, when stimulated, causes a change in the firing rate of that neuron.

Receptive Fields

Each axon in the optic nerve originates in an individual retinal ganglion cell (RGC), as shown at the bottom of **FIGURE 4.8**. Most RGCs respond to input not from a single retinal cone or rod but from an entire patch of adjacent photoreceptors lying side by side, or laterally, in the retina. A particular RGC will respond to light falling anywhere within that small patch, which is called its **receptive field**, *the region of the sensory surface that, when stimulated, causes a change in the firing rate of that neuron.* Although we'll focus on vision here, the general concept of receptive fields applies to all sensory systems. For example, the cells that connect to the touch centers of the brain have receptive fields, which are the part of the skin that, when stimulated, causes that cell's response to change in some way.

A given RGC responds to a spot of light projected anywhere within a small, roughly circular patch of retina (Kuffler, 1953). Most receptive fields contain either a central excitatory zone surrounded by a doughnut-shaped inhibitory zone, which is called an *on-center cell,* or a central inhibitory zone surrounded by an excitatory zone, which is called an *off-center cell* (see **FIGURE 4.9**). The doughnut-shaped regions represent patches of retina, as if the top of the diagram in Figure 4.8 were tilted forward so we could look at the cones end-on.

Think about the response of an on-center retinal ganglion cell when its receptive field is stimulated with spots of light of different sizes (Figure 4.9*a*). A small spot shining on the central excitatory zone increases the RGC's firing rate. When the spot exactly fills the excitatory zone, it elicits the strongest response, whereas light falling on the surrounding inhibitory zone elicits the weakest response or none at all. The response of an off-center cell, shown in Figure 4.9*b*, is just the opposite. A small spot shining on the central inhibitory zone elicits a weak response, and a spot shining on the surrounding excitatory zone elicits a strong response in the RGC.

The retina is organized in this way to detect edges—abrupt transitions from light to dark or vice versa. Edges are of supreme importance in vision. They define the shapes of objects, and anything that highlights such boundaries improves our ability to see an object's shape, particularly in low-light situations.

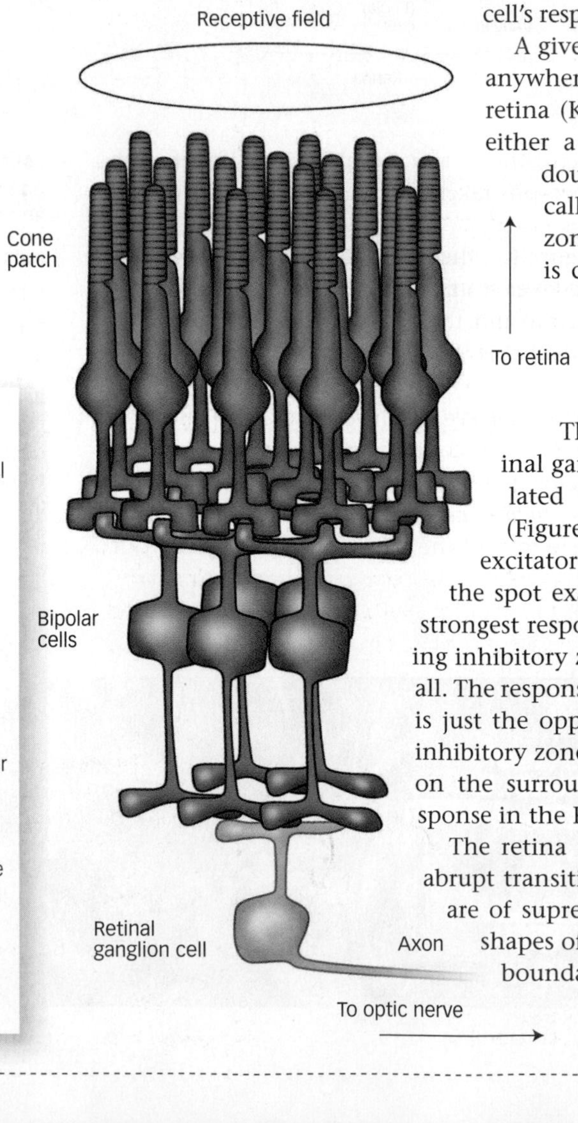

Receptive field

Cone patch

To retina

► FIGURE 4.8

Receptive Field of a Retinal Ganglion Cell The axon of a retinal ganglion cell, shown at the bottom of the figure, joins with all other RGC axons to form the optic nerve. Moving back toward the surface of the retina in this side view, each RGC connects to a cluster of five or six bipolar cells. The responses conveyed to the ganglion cell by each bipolar cell depend on the combination of excitatory or inhibitory signals transduced by the larger group of photoreceptors connected to that bipolar cell. The entire grouping, from photoreceptors to RGC, forms a receptive field, shown at the top of the figure. The RGC responds to a spot of light falling on any or all of the photoreceptors within its receptive field as a result of lateral inhibition.

Bipolar cells

Retinal ganglion cell

Axon

To optic nerve

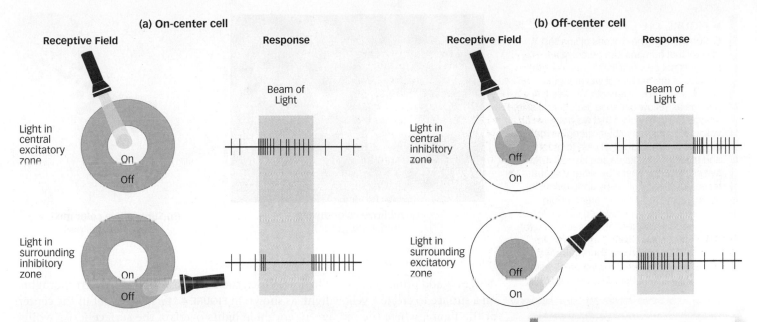

(a) On-center cell

Receptive Field   Response

Light in central excitatory zone

On
Off

Beam of Light

Light in surrounding inhibitory zone

On
Off

(b) Off-center cell

Receptive Field   Response

Light in central inhibitory zone

Off
On

Beam of Light

Light in surrounding excitatory zone

Off
On

Perceiving Color

We thrill to the burst of colors during a fireworks display, "ooh" and "aah" at nature's palette during sunset, and marvel at the vibrant hues of a peacock's tail feathers. Color indeed adds zest to the visual world, but it also offers fundamental clues to an object's identity. A black banana or blue lips are color-coded calls to action—to avoid or sound the alarm, as the case might be.

Seeing Color

Sir Isaac Newton pointed out around 1670 that color is not something "in" light. In fact, color is nothing but our perception of wavelengths (see Table 4.3) from the spectrum of visible light (see Figure 4.3). We perceive the shortest visible wavelengths as deep purple. As wavelengths increase, the color perceived changes gradually and continuously to blue, then green, yellow, orange, and, with the longest visible wavelengths, red. This rainbow of hues and accompanying wavelengths is called the *visible spectrum,* illustrated in **FIGURE 4.10**.

You'll recall that all rods contain the same photopigment, which makes them ideal for low-light vision but bad at distinguishing colors. Cones, by contrast, contain any one of three types of pigment. Each cone absorbs light over a range of wavelengths, but its pigment type is especially sensitive to visible wavelengths that correspond to red (long-wavelength), green (medium-wavelength), or blue (short-wavelength) light. Red, green, and blue are the primary colors of light; color perception results from different combinations of the three basic elements in the retina that respond to the wavelengths corresponding to the three primary colors of light. For example, lighting

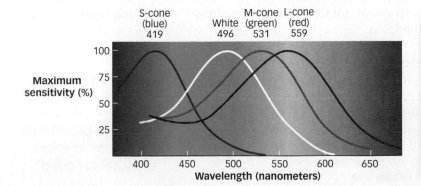

S-cone (blue) 419   White 496   M-cone (green) 531   L-cone (red) 559

Maximum sensitivity (%)

100
75
50
25

400   450   500   550   600   650

Wavelength (nanometers)

◀ FIGURE 4.10
Seeing in Color We perceive a spectrum of color because objects selectively absorb some wavelengths of light and reflect others. Color perception corresponds to the summed activity of the three types of cones. Each type is most sensitive to a narrow range of wavelengths in the visible spectrum—short (bluish light), medium (greenish light), or long (reddish light). Rods, represented by the white curve, are most sensitive to the medium wavelengths of visible light but do not contribute to color perception.

Color Mixing The millions of shades of color that humans can perceive are products not only of a light's wavelength but also of the mixture of wavelengths a stimulus absorbs or reflects. We see a ripe banana as yellow because the banana skin reflects the light waves that we perceive as yellow but absorbs the wavelengths that we perceive as shades of blue to green and those that make us see red. (a) Additive color mixing works by increasing the reflected wavelengths—by adding light to stimulate the red, blue, or green photo-pigments in the cones. When all visible wavelengths are present, we see white. (b) Subtractive color mixing removes wavelengths, thus absorbing light waves we see as red, blue, or yellow. When all visible wavelengths are absorbed, we see black.

(a) **Additive color mixing**
(red, blue, green)

(b) **Subtractive color mixing**
(red, blue, yellow)

FRITZ GORO, LIFE MAGAZINE. 1971, TIME WARNER, INC.

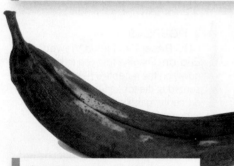

▲ Color can guide behavior: What does the black on the banana say to you?

MARK HERREID/SHUTTERSTOCK.COM

designers add primary colors of light together, such as shining red and green spotlights on a surface to create a yellow light, as shown in **FIGURE 4.11a**. Notice that in the center of the figure, where the red, green, and blue lights overlap, the surface looks white. This demonstrates that a white surface really is reflecting all visible wavelengths of light. Increasing light to create color in this way is called *additive color mixing*.

As you may have discovered for yourself when mixing paints, you can re-create any color found in nature simply by mixing only three colors: red, blue, and yellow. This *subtractive color mixing* works by removing light from the mix, such as when you combine yellow and red to make orange or blue and yellow to make green, shown in **FIGURE 4.11b**. The darker the color, the less light it reflects, which is why black surfaces reflect no light.

Trichromatic Color Representation in the Cones

Light striking the retina causes a specific pattern of response in the three cone types (Schnapf, Kraft, & Baylor, 1987). One type responds best to short-wavelength (bluish) light, the second type to medium-wavelength (greenish) light, and the third type to long-wavelength (reddish) light. Researchers refer to them as S-cones, M-cones, and L-cones, respectively (see Figure 4.10).

This **trichromatic color representation** means that *the pattern of responding across the three types of cones provides a unique code for each color.* Researchers can "read out" the wavelength of the light entering the eye by working backward from the relative firing rates of the three types of cones (Gegenfurtner & Kiper, 2003). A genetic disorder in which one of the cone types is missing—and, in some very rare cases, two or all three—causes a *color deficiency*. This trait is sex-linked, affecting men much more often than women.

Color deficiency is often referred to as *color blindness,* but in fact, people missing only one type of cone can still distinguish many colors, just not as many as someone who has the full complement of three cone types. Like synesthetes, people whose vision is color deficient often do not realize that they experience color differently from others.

Trichromatic color representation is well established as the first step of encoding color in the visual system (Abromov & Gordon, 1994). Sensory adaptation helps to explain the second step.

Color-Opponent Representation into the Brain

Recall that sensory adaptation occurs because our sensitivity to prolonged stimulation tends to decline over time. Just like the rest of your body, cones need an occasional break too. Staring too long at one color fatigues the cones that respond to that color, producing a form of sensory adaptation that results in a *color afterimage*. To demonstrate this effect for yourself, follow these instructions for **FIGURE 4.12**:

trichromatic color representation The pattern of responding across the three types of cones that provides a unique code for each color.

color-opponent system Pairs of visual neurons that work in opposition.

area V1 The part of the occipital lobe that contains the primary visual cortex.

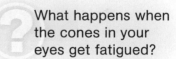

What happens when the cones in your eyes get fatigued?

> Stare at the small cross between the two color patches for about 1 minute. Try to keep your eyes as still as possible.

> After a minute, look at the lower cross. You should see a vivid color aftereffect that lasts for a minute or more. Pay particular attention to the colors in the afterimage.

Were you puzzled that the red patch produces a green afterimage and the green patch produces a red afterimage? This result reveals something important about color perception. The explanation stems from the **color-opponent system**, where *pairs of visual neurons work in opposition:* red-sensitive cells against green-sensitive (as in Figure 4.12) and blue-sensitive cells against yellow-sensitive (Hurvich & Jameson, 1957).

It may be that opponent pairs evolved to enhance color perception by taking advantage of excitatory and inhibitory stimulation. Red-green cells are excited (they increase their firing rates) in response to wavelengths corresponding to red and inhibited (they decrease their firing rates) in response to wavelengths corresponding to green. Blue-yellow cells increase their firing rate in response to blue wavelengths (excitatory) and decrease their firing rate in response to yellow wavelengths (inhibitory). The color pairs are linked to each other as opposites.

How does the color-opponent system explain color aftereffects?

The color-opponent system explains color aftereffects. When you view a color, let's say, green, the cones that respond most strongly to green become fatigued over time. Fatigue leads to an imbalance in the inputs to the red-green color-opponent neurons, beginning with the retinal ganglion cells: The weakened signal from the green-responsive cones leads to an overall response that emphasizes red. A similar explanation can be made for other color aftereffects; find a bright blue circle of color and get ready to make your roommate see yellow spots!

The Visual Brain

We have seen that a great deal of visual processing takes place within the retina itself, including the encoding of simple features such as spots of light, edges, and color. More complex aspects of vision, however, require more powerful processing, and that enlists the brain.

Streams of action potentials containing information encoded by the retina travel to the brain along the optic nerve. Half of the axons in the optic nerve that leave each eye come from retinal ganglion cells that code information in the right visual field, whereas the other half code information in the left visual field. These two nerve bundles link to the left and right hemispheres of the brain, respectively (see **FIGURE 4.13**). The optic nerve travels from each eye to the *lateral geniculate nucleus* (*LGN*), located in the thalamus. As you will recall from Chapter 3, the thalamus receives inputs from all of the senses except smell. From there the visual signal travels to the back of the brain, to a location called **area V1**, the *part of the occipital lobe that contains the primary visual cortex.* Here the information is systematically mapped into a representation of the visual scene. There are about 30 to 50 brain areas specialized for vision, located mainly in the occipital lobe at the back of the brain and in the temporal lobes on the sides of the brain (Orban, Van Essen, & Vanduffel, 2004; Van Essen, Anderson, & Felleman, 1992).

▲ **FIGURE 4.12**
Color Afterimage Demonstration Follow the accompanying instructions in the text, and sensory adaptation will do the rest. When the afterimage fades, you can get back to reading the chapter.

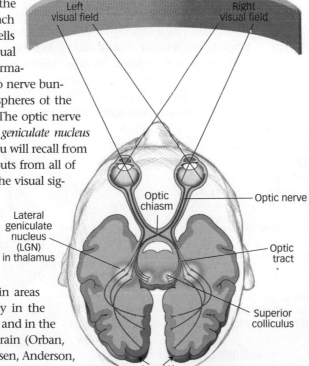

Left visual field

Right visual field

Optic chiasm

Optic nerve

Lateral geniculate nucleus (LGN) in thalamus

Optic tract

Superior colliculus

Area V1

◀ FIGURE 4.13
Visual Pathway from Eye through Brain Objects in the right visual field stimulate the left half of each retina, and objects in the left visual field stimulate the right half of each retina. The optic nerves, one exiting each eye, are formed by the axons of retinal ganglion cells emerging from the retina. Just before they enter the brain at the optic chiasm, about half the nerve fibers from each eye cross. The left half of each optic nerve, representing the right visual field, runs through the brain's left hemisphere via the thalamus, and the right halves, representing the left visual field, travel this route through the right hemisphere. So information from the right visual field ends up in the left hemisphere and information from the left visual field ends up in the right hemisphere.

Stimulus   Neuron's responses

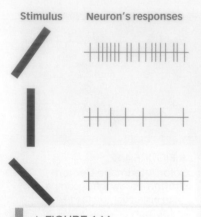

▲ FIGURE 4.14
Single-Neuron Feature Detectors Area V1 contains neurons that respond to specific orientations of edges. Here a single neuron's responses are recorded (above) as the monkey views bars at different orientations (above right). This neuron fires continuously when the bar is pointing to the right at 45 degrees, less often when it is vertical, and not at all when it is pointing to the left at 45 degrees.

Neural Systems for Perceiving Shape

One of the most important functions of vision involves perceiving the shapes of objects; our day-to-day lives would be a mess if we couldn't distinguish individual shapes from one another. Imagine not being able to reliably differentiate between a warm doughnut with glazed icing and a straight stalk of celery and you'll get the idea; breakfast could become a traumatic experience if you couldn't distinguish shapes. Perceiving shape depends on the location and orientation of an object's edges. It is not surprising, then, that area V1 is specialized for encoding edge orientation.

As you read in Chapter 3, neurons in the visual cortex selectively respond to bars and edges in specific orientations in space (Hubel & Weisel, 1962, 1998). In effect, area V1 contains populations of neurons, each "tuned" to respond to edges oriented at each position in the visual field. This means that some neurons fire when an object in a vertical orientation is perceived, other neurons fire when an object in a horizontal orientation is perceived, still other neurons fire when objects in a diagonal orientation of 45 degrees are perceived, and so on (see **FIGURE 4.14**). The outcome of the coordinated response of all these feature detectors contributes to a sophisticated visual system that can detect where a doughnut ends and celery begins. We'll probe further into how the responses of feature detectors are coordinated when we discuss the role of attention in visual processing on p. 144, but let's first examine an important distinction that provides a foundation for that discussion.

Pathways for What, Where, and How

In Chapter 3 you learned how brain researchers have used transcranial magnetic stimulation (TMS) to demonstrate that a person who can recognize what an object is may not be able to perceive that the object is moving. This observation implies that one brain system identifies people and things and another tracks their movements, or guides our movements in relation to them. Two functionally distinct pathways, or *visual streams*, project from the occipital cortex to visual areas in other parts of the brain (see **FIGURE 4.15**):

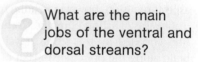

What are the main jobs of the ventral and dorsal streams?

> The *ventral* ("below") *stream* travels across the occipital lobe into the lower levels of the temporal lobes and includes brain areas that represent an object's shape and identity—in other words, what it is. The damage caused by Betty's stroke that you read about in Chapter 3 interrupted this "what pathway" (Tanaka, 1996). As a result, Betty could not recognize familiar faces even though she could still see them.

▶ FIGURE 4.15
Visual Streaming One interconnected visual system forms a pathway that courses from the occipital visual regions into the lower temporal lobe. This ventral pathway enables us to identify what we see. Another interconnected pathway travels from the occipital lobe through the upper regions of the temporal lobe into the parietal regions. This dorsal pathway allows us to locate objects, to track their movements, and to move in relation to them.

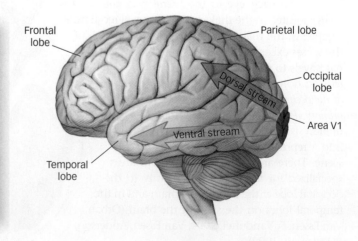

> The *dorsal* ("above") *stream* travels up from the occipital lobe to the parietal lobes (including some of the middle and upper levels of the temporal lobes), connecting with brain areas that identify the location and motion of an object—in other words, where it is. Because the dorsal stream allows us to perceive spatial relations, researchers originally dubbed it the "where pathway" (Ungerleider & Mishkin, 1982). Neuroscientists later argued that because the dorsal stream is crucial for guiding movements, such as aiming, reaching, or tracking with the eyes, the "where pathway" should more appropriately be called the "how pathway" (Milner & Goodale, 1995)

Some of the most dramatic evidence for two distinct visual streams comes from studying the impairments that result from brain injury. A patient known as D. F. suffered permanent brain damage following exposure to toxic levels of carbon monoxide (Goodale et al., 1991). A large region of the lateral occipital cortex was destroyed, an area in the ventral stream that is very active when people recognize objects. D. F.'s ability to recognize objects by sight was greatly impaired, although her ability to recognize objects by touch was normal. This suggests that the *visual representation* of objects, and not D. F.'s *memory* for objects, was damaged. Like Betty's inability to recognize familiar faces, D. F.'s brain damage belongs to a category called **visual-form agnosia,** *the inability to recognize objects by sight* (Goodale & Milner, 1992, 2004).

Oddly, although D. F. could not recognize objects visually, she could accurately *guide* her actions by sight. D. F. was shown a display board with a slot in it, as in **FIGURE 4.16**. The researchers could adjust the orientation of the slot. In one version of the task, shown at the left in the figure, they asked D. F. to report the orientation of the slot by holding her hand up at the same angle as the slot. D. F. performed very poorly at this task, almost randomly, suggesting that she did not have a reliable representation of visual orientation.

In another version of the task, shown at the right in Figure 4.16, D. F. was asked to insert a flat block into the slot, as if she were posting a letter into a mail slot. Now she performed the task almost perfectly! The paradox is that D. F.'s explicit or conscious understanding of what she was seeing was greatly impaired, but her ability to use this very same information nonconsciously to guide her movements remained intact. When D. F. was scanned with fMRI, researchers found that she showed normal activation of regions within the dorsal stream during guided movement (James et al., 2003).

Other patients with brain damage to the parietal section of the dorsal stream have difficulty using vision to guide their reaching and grasping movements, a condition termed *optic ataxia* (Perenin & Vighetto, 1988). However, these patients' ventral streams are intact, meaning they recognize what objects are. We can conclude from these two patterns of impairment that the ventral and dorsal visual streams are functionally distinct; it is possible to damage one while leaving the other intact.

Still, the two streams must work together during visual perception in order to integrate "what" and "where," and researchers are starting to examine how they interact.

visual-form agnosia The inability to recognize objects by sight.

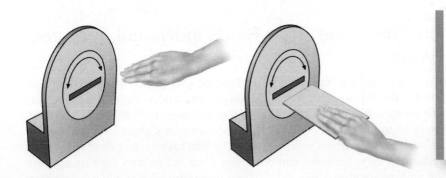

◄ FIGURE 4.16
Testing Visual-Form Agnosia When researchers asked patient D. F. to orient her hand to match the angle of the slot in the testing apparatus, as shown at the left, she was unable to comply. Asked to insert a card into the slot at various angles, as shown at the right, however, D. F. accomplished the task virtually to perfection.

One intriguing possibility is suggested by recent fMRI research indicating that some regions within the dorsal stream are sensitive to properties of an object's identity, responding differently, for example, to line drawings of the same object in different sizes or viewed from different vantage points (Konen & Kastner, 2008). The sensitivity of some regions within the dorsal stream to aspects of object identity may allow the dorsal and ventral streams to exchange information and thus promote integration of "what" and "where" (Farivar, 2009; Konen & Kastner, 2008).

IN SUMMARY

○ Light passes through several layers in the eye to reach the retina, which links the world of light outside the body and the world of vision inside the central nervous system. Two types of photoreceptor cells in the retina—cones, which operate under normal daylight conditions and sense color, and rods, which are active under low-light conditions for night vision—transduce light into neural impulses.

○ The retina contains several layers, and the outermost consists of retinal ganglion cells (RGCs) that collect and send signals to the brain. A particular RGC will respond to light falling anywhere within a small patch that constitutes its receptive field.

○ Light striking the retina causes a specific pattern of response in each of three cone types that are critical to color perception: short-wavelength (bluish) light, medium-wavelength (greenish) light, and long-wavelength (reddish) light. The overall pattern of response across the three cone types results in a unique code for each color, known as its trichromatic color representation.

○ Information encoded by the retina travels to the brain along the optic nerve, which connects to the lateral geniculate nucleus in the thalamus and then to the primary visual cortex, area V1, in the occipital lobe.

○ Two functionally distinct pathways project from the occipital lobe to visual areas in other parts of the brain. The ventral stream travels into the lower levels of the temporal lobes and includes brain areas that represent an object's shape and identity. The dorsal stream goes from the occipital lobes to the parietal lobes, connecting with brain areas that identify the location and motion of an object.

Vision II: Recognizing What We Perceive

Our journey into the visual system has already revealed how it accomplishes some pretty astonishing feats. But the system needs to do much more in order for us to be able to interact effectively with our visual worlds. Let's now consider how the system links together individual visual features into whole objects, allows us to recognize what those objects are, organizes objects into visual scenes, and detects motion and change in those scenes. Along the way we'll see that studying visual errors and illusions provides key insights into how these processes work, and we'll also revisit the intriguing world of synesthesia.

Attention: The "Glue" That Binds Individual Features into a Whole

As we've seen, specialized feature detectors in different parts of the visual system analyze each of the multiple features of a visible object—orientation, color, size, shape, and so forth. But how are different features combined into single, unified objects? What allows us to perceive so easily and correctly that the man in the photo is wearing a red shirt and the woman is wearing a yellow shirt? Why don't we see free-floating patches of red and yellow, or even incorrect combinations, such as the man wearing a yellow shirt and the woman wearing a red shirt? These questions refer to what researchers

▼ We correctly combine features into unified objects, so, for example, we see that the man is wearing a red shirt and the woman is wearing a yellow shirt.

FUSE/PUNCHSTOCK

call the **binding problem** in perception, which concerns *how features are linked together so that we see unified objects in our visual world rather than free-floating or miscombined features* (Treisman, 1998, 2006).

Illusory Conjunctions: Perceptual Mistakes

In everyday life, we correctly combine features into unified objects so automatically and effortlessly that it may be difficult to appreciate that binding is ever a problem at all. However, researchers have discovered errors in binding that reveal important clues about how the process works. One such error is known as an **illusory conjunction**, *a perceptual mistake where features from multiple objects are incorrectly combined*. In a pioneering study of illusory conjunctions, Treisman and Schmidt (1982) briefly showed study participants visual displays in which black digits flanked colored letters, then instructed them to first report the black digits and second to describe the colored letters. Participants frequently reported illusory conjunctions, claiming to have seen, for example, a blue A or a red X instead of the red A and the blue X that had actually been shown (see **FIGURE 4.17**). These illusory conjunctions were not just the result of guessing; they occurred more frequently than other kinds of errors, such as reporting a letter or color that was not present in the display (Figure 4.17). Illusory conjunctions look real to the participants, who were just as confident they had seen them as they were about the actual colored letters they perceived correctly.

> How does the study of Illusory conjunctions help in understanding the role of attention in feature binding?

Why do illusory conjunctions occur? Treisman and her colleagues have tried to explain them by proposing a **feature integration theory** (Treisman, 1998, 2006; Treisman & Gelade, 1980; Treisman & Schmidt, 1982), which holds that *focused attention is not required to detect the individual features that comprise a stimulus, such as the color, shape, size, and location of letters, but is required to bind those individual features together.* From this perspective, attention provides the "glue" necessary to bind features together, and illusory conjunctions occur when it is difficult for participants to pay full attention to the features that need to be glued together. For example, in the experiments we just considered, participants were required to process the digits that flank the colored letters, thereby reducing attention to the letters and allowing illusory conjunctions to occur. When experimental conditions are changed so that participants can pay full attention to the colored letters, and they are able to correctly bind their features together, illusory conjunctions disappear (Treisman, 1998; Treisman & Schmidt, 1982.

Feature integration theory also helps to explain some striking effects observed when people search for targets in displays containing many items. When searching through a display containing green Xs and Os (see **FIGURE 4.18** on the next page), it does not require much focused attention to spot a target item defined by a unique feature such as a red X. The red X seems to simply "pop out" of the display, and people can find it just as quickly when there are many other nontarget items in the display as when there are only a few nontarget items in the display. But when searching through a display of green Xs and red Os, a target red X is no longer

binding problem How features are linked together so that we see unified objects in our visual world rather than free-floating or miscombined features.

illusory conjunction A perceptual mistake where features from multiple objects are incorrectly combined.

feature integration theory The idea that focused attention is not required to detect the individual features that comprise a stimulus but is required to bind those individual features together.

◄ FIGURE 4.17
Illusory Conjunctions Illusory conjunctions occur when features such as color and shape are combined incorrectly. For example, when participants are shown a red A and blue X, they sometimes report seeing a blue A and red X. Other kinds of errors, such as a misreported letter (e.g., reporting "T" when no T was presented) or misreported color (reporting "green" when no green was presented) occur rarely, indicating that illusory conjunctions are not the result of guessing (based on Robertson, 2003).

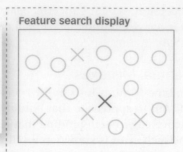
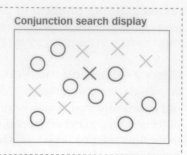

Feature search display   **Conjunction search display**

► FIGURE 4.18

Visual Search If you are asked to try to find the red X in these displays, it is very easy to find when the red X differs from the surrounding items in either color or shape (feature search); the target just pops out at you. It is harder to find the red X when it is surrounded by both red Os and green Xs (conjunction search), because focused attention is now required to spot the target (based on Robertson, 2003.)

defined by a unique feature in relation to the nontarget items; instead, it contains a conjunction of two features, "X" like the green Xs and "red" like the red Os. Now the red X requires focused attention to pick out, and it takes more time to find when the display contains many nontargets than when it contains few nontargets (Treisman, 1998; Treisman & Gelade, 1980; Figure 4.18).

The Role of the Parietal Lobe

The binding process makes use of feature information processed by structures within the ventral visual stream, the "what pathway" (Seymour et al., 2010; see Figure 4.15). But because binding involves linking together features processed in distinct parts of the ventral stream at a particular spatial location, it also depends critically on the parietal lobe in the dorsal stream, the "where pathway" (Robertson, 1999). For example, Treisman and others studied a patient, R. M., who had suffered strokes that destroyed both his left and right parietal lobes. Though many aspects of his visual function were intact, he had severe problems attending to spatially distinct objects. When presented with stimuli such as those in Figure 4.17, R. M. perceived an abnormally large number of illusory conjunctions, even when he was given as long as 10 seconds to look at the displays (Friedman-Hill, Robertson, & Treisman, 1995; Robertson, 2003). More recent studies of similar patients suggest that damage to the upper and posterior portions of the parietal lobe is likely to produce problems with focused attention, resulting in binding problems and increased illusory conjunctions (Braet & Humphreys, 2009; McCrea, Buxbaum, & Coslett, 2006). Neuroimaging studies indicate that these same parietal regions are activated in healthy individuals when they perform the kind of visual feature binding that patients with parietal lobe damage are unable to perform (Shafritz, Gore, & Marois, 2002), as well as when they search for conjunction features (Corbetta et al., 1995; Donner et al., 2002).

These findings fit nicely with recent TMS studies in which researchers attempted to temporarily "turn off" the posterior parietal lobe while participants performed a feature binding task involving colors and letters. Applying TMS during the task resulted in an increased number of illusory conjunctions but not in other kinds of perceptual errors (Braet & Humphreys, 2009). When TMS was applied to the occipital lobe, it had no effect on illusory conjunctions (Braet & Humphreys, 2009). Interestingly, the effects of parietal TMS on illusory conjunctions were seen mainly when TMS was applied after presentation of the target item, suggesting that the attentional process supported by the parietal region serves to "lock-in" or consolidate perceived features. These findings help to refine the original suggestion from feature integration theory that feature binding depends critically on attentional processes (Treisman, 1998).

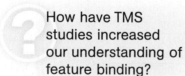

How have TMS studies increased our understanding of feature binding?

Binding and Attention in Synesthesia

Although it is unlikely that Stevie Wonder or Eddie Van Halen keeps up with research on feature binding, the findings and ideas we've just considered turn out to be highly relevant to an experience they share: synesthesia. We considered examples of synesthesia at the outset of this chapter, such as consistently perceiving particular letters in a particular color (see Figure 4.1). Some researchers have characterized synesthesia as an instance of atypical feature binding. Normal binding of colors and letters, for example, is a reponse to actual features of the external stimulus, but in synesthesia, the color feature is not present in the external stimulus.

Surprisingly, recent research shows that some of the same processes involved in normal feature binding also occur in synesthesia. fMRI studies of synesthetic individuals have revealed that the parietal lobe regions that we've already seen are implicated in normal binding of color and shape and become active during the experience of letter-color synesthesia (Weiss, Zilles, & Fink, 2005). Further, applying TMS to these parietal regions interferes with synesthetic perceptions (Esterman et al., 2006; Muggleton et al., 2007). Consistent with the idea that parietal activity is related to attentional processes needed for binding, other experiments have shown that synesthetic bindings, such as seeing a particular digit in a particular color, depend on attention (Mattingly, 2009; Robertson, 2003; Sagiv, Heer, & Robertson, 2006). For instance, when dots are quickly presented to a synesthetic individual together with digits (e.g., "7") that induce a synesthetic perception of green, the synesthete names the color of the dots more quickly when they are green than when they are orange—that is, when the dot color matches the color of the synesthetic perception. But when synesthetes are instructed to ignore the numbers, there is little difference in the amount of time taken to name the color of the green and orange dots, suggesting that attention is required to bind the synesthetic color to the digit (Robertson, 2003; Sagiv, Heer, & Robertson, 2006). Although our perceptual experiences differ substantially from those of synesthetes, they rely on the same basic mechanisms of feature binding.

Recognizing Objects by Sight

Take a quick look at the letters in the accompanying illustration. Even though they're quite different from one another, you probably effortlessly recognized them as all being examples of the letter G. Now consider the same kind of demonstration using your best friend's face. Your friend might have long hair, but one day she decides to get it cut dramatically short. Suppose one day your friend gets a dramatic new haircut—or adds glasses, hair dye, or a nose ring. Even though your friend now looks strikingly different, you still recognize that person with ease. Just like the variability in Gs, you somehow are able to extract the underlying features of the face that allow you to accurately identify your friend.

This thought exercise may seem trivial, but it's no small perceptual feat. If the visual system were somehow stumped each time a minor variation occurred in an object being perceived, the inefficiency of it all would be overwhelming. We'd have to effortfully process information just to perceive our friend as the same person from one meeting to another, not to mention laboring through the process of knowing when a G is really a G. In general, though, object recognition proceeds fairly smoothly, in large part due to the operation of the feature detectors we discussed earlier.

How do feature detectors help the visual system get from a spatial array of light hitting the eye to the accurate perception of an object in different circumstances, such as your friend's face? Some researchers argue for a *modular view:* that specialized brain areas, or modules, detect and represent faces or houses or even body parts. Using fMRI to examine visual processing in healthy young adults, researchers found a subregion in the temporal lobe that responds most strongly to faces compared to just about any other object category, while a nearby area responds most strongly to buildings and landscapes (Kanwisher, McDermott, & Chun, 1997). This view suggests we not only have feature detectors to aid in visual perception but also "face detectors," "building detectors," and possibly other types of neurons specialized for particular types of object perception (Downing et al., 2006; Kanwisher & Yovel, 2006).

Psychologists and researchers who argue for a more *distributed representation* of object categories challenge the modular view. Researchers have shown that although a subregion in the temporal lobes does respond more to faces than to any other category, parts of the brain outside this area may also be involved in face recognition. In this view, it is

▼ A quick glance and you recognize all these letters as G, but their varying sizes, shapes, angles, and orientations ought to make this recognition task difficult. What is it about the process of object recognition that allows us to perform this task effortlessly?

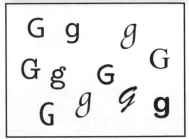

▶ Our visual systems allows us to identify people as the same individual even when they change such features as their hair style, hair color, or jewelry. Despite the extreme changes between these actors in their natural state and as they appeared in the movie *Avatar*, can you tell that the same individuals are shown in each of the two photos?

the pattern of activity across multiple brain regions that identifies any viewed object, including faces (Haxby et al., 2001). Each of these views explains some data better than the other one, and researchers are continuing to debate their relative merits.

Another perspective on this issue is provided by experiments designed to measure precisely where seizures originate; these experiments have also provided insights on how single neurons in the human brain respond to objects and faces (Quiroga et al., 2005). Electrodes were placed in the temporal lobes of people who suffer from epilepsy. Then the volunteers were shown photographs of faces and objects as the researchers recorded their neural responses. The researchers found that neurons in the temporal lobe respond to specific objects viewed from multiple angles and to people wearing different clothing and facial expressions and photographed from various angles. In some cases, the neurons also respond to the words for the objects they prefer. For example, a neuron that responded to photographs of the Sydney Opera House also responded when the words *Sydney Opera* were displayed but not when the words *Eiffel Tower* were displayed (Quiroga et al., 2005).

Taken together, these experiments demonstrate the principle of **perceptual constancy**: *Even as aspects of sensory signals change, perception remains consistent.* Think back once again to our discussion of difference thresholds early in this chapter. Our perceptual systems are sensitive to relative differences in changing stimulation and make allowances for varying sensory input. This general principle helps explain why you still recognize your friend despite changes in hair color or style or the addition of facial jewelry. It's not as though your visual perceptual system responds to a change with, "Here's a new and unfamiliar face to perceive." Rather, it's as though it responds with, "Interesting . . . here's a deviation from the way this face usually looks." Perception is sensitive to changes in stimuli, but perceptual constancies allow us to notice the differences in the first place.

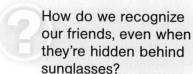

How do we recognize our friends, even when they're hidden behind sunglasses?

Principles of Perceptual Organization

Before object recognition can even kick in, the visual system must perform another important task: to group the image regions that belong together into a representation of an object. The idea that we tend to perceive a unified, whole object rather than a collection of separate parts is the foundation of Gestalt psychology, which you read about in Chapter 1. Gestalt principles characterize many aspects of human perception. Among the foremost are the Gestalt *perceptual grouping rules,* which govern how the features and regions of things fit together (Koffka, 1935). Here's a sampling:

> *Simplicity:* A basic rule in science is that the simplest explanation is usually the best. This is the idea behind the Gestalt grouping rule of *Pragnanz,* which translates as "good form." When confronted with two or more possible interpretations of an object's shape, the visual system tends to select the simplest or most likely interpretation (see **FIGURE 4.19***a*).

perceptual constancy A perceptual principle stating that even as aspects of sensory signals change, perception remains consistent.

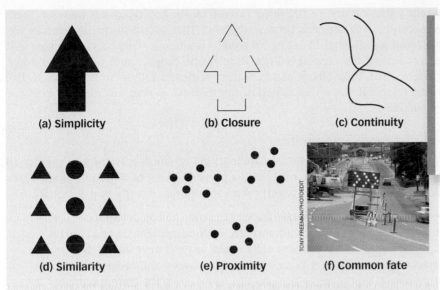

(a) Simplicity (b) Closure (c) Continuity

(d) Similarity (e) Proximity (f) Common fate

TONY FREEMAN/PHOTOEDIT

◄ **FIGURE 4.19**
Perceptual Grouping Rules Principles first identified by Gestalt psychologists and now supported by experimental evidence demonstrate that the brain is predisposed to impose order on incoming sensations. One neural strategy for perception involves responding to patterns among stimuli and grouping like patterns together.

> *Closure:* We tend to fill in missing elements of a visual scene, allowing us to perceive edges that are separated by gaps as belonging to complete objects (see **FIGURE 4.19b**).

> *Continuity:* Edges or contours that have the same orientation have what the Gestaltists called "good continuation," and we tend to group them together perceptually (see **FIGURE 4.19c**).

> *Similarity:* Regions that are similar in color, lightness, shape, or texture are perceived as belonging to the same object (see **FIGURE 4.19d**).

> *Proximity:* Objects that are close together tend to be grouped together (see **FIGURE 4.19e**).

> *Common fate:* Elements of a visual image that move together are perceived as parts of a single moving object (see **FIGURE 4.19f**).

Separating Figure from Ground

Perceptual grouping is a powerful aid to our ability to recognize objects by sight. Grouping involves visually separating an object from its surroundings. In Gestalt terms, this means identifying a *figure* apart from the (back)*ground* in which it resides. For example, the words on this page are perceived as figural: They stand out from the ground of the sheet of paper on which they're printed. Similarly, your instructor is perceived as the figure against the backdrop of all the other elements in your classroom. You certainly can perceive these elements differently, of course: The words *and* the paper are all part of a thing called "a page," and your instructor *and* the classroom can all be perceived as "your learning environment." Typically, though, our perceptual systems focus attention on some objects as distinct from their environments.

Size provides one clue to what's figure and what's ground: Smaller regions are likely to be figures, such as tiny letters on a big paper. Movement also helps: Your instructor is (we hope) a dynamic lecturer, moving around in a static environment. Another critical step toward object recognition is *edge assignment*. Given an edge, or boundary, between figure and ground, which region does that edge belong to? If the edge belongs to the figure, it helps define the object's shape, and the background continues behind the edge. Sometimes, though, it's not easy to tell which is which.

Edgar Rubin (1886–1951), a Danish psychologist, capitalized on this ambiguity in developing a famous illusion called the *Rubin vase* or, more generally, a *reversible figure-ground relationship*. You can view this "face-vase" illusion in **FIGURE 4.20** in two ways, either as a vase on a black background or as a pair of silhouettes facing each other. Your

▼ **FIGURE 4.20**
Ambiguous Edges Here's how Rubin's classic reversible figure-ground illusion works: Fixate your eyes on the center of the image, and your perception will alternate between a vase and facing silhouettes, even as the sensory stimulation remains constant.

template A mental representation that can be directly compared to a viewed shape in the retinal image.

monocular depth cues Aspects of a scene that yield information about depth when viewed with only one eye.

visual system settles on one or the other interpretation and fluctuates between them every few seconds. This happens because the edge that would normally separate figure from ground is really part of neither: It equally defines the contours of the vase as it does the contours of the faces. Evidence from fMRIs shows, quite nicely, that when people are seeing the Rubin image as a face, there is greater activity in the face-selective region of the temporal lobe we discussed earlier than when they are seeing it as a vase (Hasson et al., 2001).

Theories of Object Recognition

Researchers have proposed two broad explanations of object recognition, one based on the object as a whole and the other on its parts. Each set of theories has strengths and weaknesses, making object recognition an active area of study in psychology.

> According to *image-based object recognition* theories, an object you have seen before is stored in memory as a **template**, *a mental representation that can be directly compared to a viewed shape in the retinal image* (Tarr & Vuong, 2002). Shape templates are stored along with name, category, and other associations to that object. Your memory compares its templates to the current retinal image and selects the template that most closely matches the current image. For example, supermarket scanners use a form of template matching to identify the bar codes on grocery labels. Image-based theories are widely accepted, yet they do not explain everything about object recognition. For one thing, the time it takes to recognize a familiar object does not depend on its current orientation relative to the object's standard orientation: You can quickly recognize that a cup is a cup even when it is tilted on its side. Correctly matching images to templates suggests that you'd have to have one template for cups in a normal orientation, another template for cups on their side, another for cups upside down, and so on. This makes for an unwieldy and inefficient system and therefore one that is unlikely to be effective, yet seeing a cup on its side rarely perplexes anyone for long.

What is an important difference between template and parts-based theories of object recognition?

> *Parts-based object recognition* theories propose instead that the brain deconstructs viewed objects into a collection of parts (Marr & Nishihara, 1978). One important parts-based theory contends that objects are stored in memory as structural descriptions: mental inventories of object parts along with the spatial relations among those parts (Biederman, 1987). The parts inventories act as a sort of "alphabet" of geometric elements called *geons* that can be combined to make objects, just as letters are combined to form words (see **FIGURE 4.21**). Parts-based object recognition does not

▶ FIGURE 4.21
An Alphabet of Geometric Elements Parts-based theory holds that objects such as those shown in (b) are made up of simpler three-dimensional components called geons, shown in (a), much as letters combine to form different words.

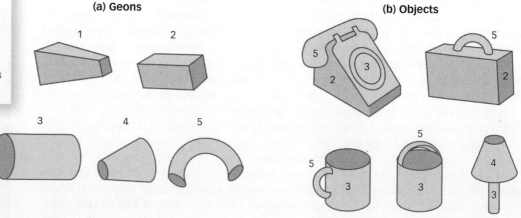

(a) Geons

(b) Objects

require a template for every view of every object, and so avoids some of the pitfalls of image-based theories. But parts-based object recognition does have major limitations. Most importantly, it allows for object recognition only at the level of categories and not at the level of the individual object. Parts-based theories offer an explanation for recognizing an object such as a face, for example, but are less effective at explaining how you distinguish between your best friend's face and a stranger's face.

As you can see, there are strengths and weaknesses of both image-based and parts-based explanations of object recognition. Researchers are developing hybrid theories that attempt to exploit the strengths of each approach (Peissig & Tarr, 2007).

Perceiving Depth and Size

Objects in the world are arranged in three dimensions—length, width, and depth—but the retinal image contains only two dimensions, length and width. How does the brain process a flat, two-dimensional retinal image so that we perceive the depth of an object and how far away it is? The answer lies in a collection of *depth cues* that change as you move through space. Monocular and binocular depth cues all help visual perception (Howard, 2002).

Monocular Depth Cues

Monocular depth cues are *aspects of a scene that yield information about depth when viewed with only one eye.* These cues rely on the relationship between distance and size. Even with one eye closed, the retinal image of an object you're focused on grows smaller as that object moves farther away and larger as it moves closer. Our brains routinely use these differences in retinal image size, or *relative size,* to perceive distance.

This works particularly well in a monocular depth cue called *familiar size.* Most adults, for example, fall within a familiar range of heights (perhaps five to seven feet tall), so retinal image size alone is usually a reliable cue to how far away they are. Our visual system automatically corrects for size differences and attributes them to differences in distance. **FIGURE 4.22** demonstrates how strong this mental correction for familiar size is.

In addition to relative size and familiar size, there are several more monocular depth cues, such as

> *Linear perspective,* which describes the phenomenon that parallel lines seem to converge as they recede into the distance (see **FIGURE 4.23a** on the next page).

◀ FIGURE 4.22
Familiar Size and Relative Size When you view images of people, such as the people in the left-hand photo, or of things you know well, the object you perceive as smaller appears farther away. With a little image manipulation, you can see in the right-hand photo that the relative size difference projected on your retinas is far greater than you perceive. The image of the person in the blue vest is exactly the same size in both photos.

binocular disparity The difference in the retinal images of the two eyes that provides information about depth.

▶ FIGURE 4.23

Pictorial Depth Cues Visual artists rely on a variety of monocular cues to make their work come to life. You can rely on cues such as (a) linear perspective, (b) texture gradient, (c) interposition, and (d) relative height in an image to infer distance, depth, and position, even if you're wearing an eye patch.

(a)

(b)

(c)

(d)

▼ FIGURE 4.24

Binocular Disparity We see the world in three dimensions because our eyes are a distance apart and the image of an object falls on the retinas of each eye at a slightly different place. In this two-object scene, the images of the square and the circle fall on different points of the retina in each eye. The disparity in the positions of the circle's retinal images provides a compelling cue to depth.

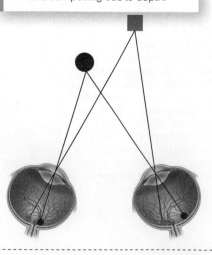

> *Texture gradient,* which arises when you view a more or less uniformly patterned surface because the size of the pattern elements, as well as the distance between them, grows smaller as the surface recedes from the observer (see **FIGURE 4.23b**).

> *Interposition,* which occurs when one object partly blocks another (see **FIGURE 4.23c**). You can infer that the block*ing* object is closer than the block*ed* object. However, interposition by itself cannot provide information about how far apart the two objects are.

> *Relative height in the image* depends on your field of vision (see **FIGURE 4.23d**). Objects that are closer to you are lower in your visual field, while faraway objects are higher.

Binocular Depth Cues

We can also obtain depth information through **binocular disparity**, *the difference in the retinal images of the two eyes that provides information about depth.* Because our eyes are slightly separated, each registers a slightly different view of the world.

Your brain computes the disparity between the two retinal images to perceive how far away objects are, as shown in **FIGURE 4.24**. Viewed from above in the figure, the images of the more distant square and the closer circle each fall at different points on each retina.

Binocular disparity as a cue to depth perception was first discussed by Sir Charles Wheatstone in 1838. Wheatstone went on to invent the stereoscope, essentially a holder for a pair of photographs or drawings taken from two horizontally displaced locations (Wheatstone did not lack for original ideas—he also invented the accordion and an early telegraph and coined the term *microphone*). When viewed, one by

◀ The View-Master has been a popular toy for decades. It is based on the principle of binocular disparity: Two images taken from slightly different angles produce a stereoscopic effect.

each eye, the pairs of images evoked a vivid sense of depth. The View-Master toy is the modern successor to Wheatstone's invention, and 3-D movies are based on this same idea.

Illusions of Depth and Size

We all are vulnerable to *illusions,* which, as you'll remember from Chapter 1, are errors of perception, memory, or judgment in which subjective experience differs from objective reality (Wade, 2005). The relation between size and distance has been used to create elaborate illusions that depend on fooling the visual system about how far away objects are. All these illusions depend on the same principle: When you view two objects that project the same retinal image size, the object you perceive as farther away will be perceived as larger. One of the most famous illusions is the *Ames room,* constructed by the American ophthalmologist Adelbert Ames in 1946. The room is trapezoidal in shape rather than square: Only two sides are parallel (see **FIGURE 4.25a**). A person standing in one corner of an Ames room is physically twice as far away from the viewer as a person standing in the other corner. But when viewed with one eye through the small peephole placed in one wall, the Ames room looks square because the shapes of the windows and the flooring tiles are carefully crafted to *look* square from the viewing port (Ittelson, 1952).

What does the Ames room tell us about how the brain can be fooled?

The visual system perceives the far wall as perpendicular to the line of sight so that people standing at different positions along that wall appear to be at the same distance, and the viewer's judgments of their sizes are based directly on retinal image size. As a result, a person standing in the right corner appears to be much larger than a person standing in the left corner (see **FIGURE 4.25b**).

▼ FIGURE 4.25
The Amazing Ames Room (a) A diagram showing the actual proportions of the Ames room reveals its secrets. The sides of the room form a trapezoid with parallel sides but a back wall that's way off square. The uneven floor makes the room's height in the far back corner shorter than the other. Add misleading cues such as specially designed windows and flooring and position the room's occupants in each far corner and you're ready to lure an unsuspecting observer. (b) Looking into the Ames room through the viewing port with only one eye, the observer infers a normal size-distance relationship—that both people are the same distance away. But the different image sizes they project on the retina leads the viewer to conclude, based on the monocular cue of familiar size, that one person is very small and the other very large.

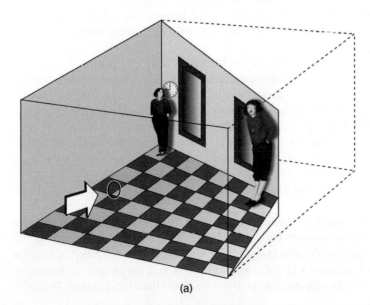

(a)

(b)

apparent motion The perception of movement as a result of alternating signals appearing in rapid succession in different locations.

Perceiving Motion and Change

You should now have a good sense of how we see what and where objects are, a process made substantially easier when the objects stay in one place. But real life, of course, is full of moving targets; objects change position over time. Birds fly and horses gallop, rain and snow fall, trees bend in the wind. Understanding how we perceive motion and why we sometimes fail to perceive change can bring us closer to appreciating how visual perception works in everyday life.

Motion Perception

To sense motion, the visual system must encode information about both space and time. The simplest case to consider is an observer who does not move trying to perceive an object that does.

As an object moves across an observer's stationary visual field, it first stimulates one location on the retina, and then a little later it stimulates another location on the retina. Neural circuits in the brain can detect this change in position over time and respond to specific speeds and directions of motion (Emerson, Bergen, & Adelson, 1992). A region in the middle of the temporal lobe referred to as *MT* (part of the dorsal stream we discussed earlier) is specialized for the visual perception of motion (Born & Bradley, 2005; Newsome & Paré, 1988), and brain damage in this area leads to a deficit in normal motion perception (Zihl, von Cramon, & Mai, 1983).

Of course, in the real world, rarely are you a stationary observer. As you move around, your head and eyes move all the time, and motion perception is not as simple. The motion-perception system must take into account the position and movement of your eyes, and ultimately of your head and body, in order to perceive the motions of objects correctly and allow you to approach or avoid them. The brain accomplishes this by monitoring your eye and head movements and "subtracting" them from the motion in the retinal image.

Motion perception, like color perception, operates in part on opponent processes and is subject to sensory adaptation. A motion aftereffect called the *waterfall illusion* is analogous to color aftereffects. If you stare at the downward rush of a waterfall for several seconds, you'll experience an upward motion aftereffect when you then look at stationary objects near the waterfall such as trees or rocks. What's going on here?

The process is similar to seeing green after staring at a patch of red. Motion-sensitive neurons are connected to motion detector cells in the brain that encode motion in opposite directions. A sense of motion comes from the difference in the strength of these two opposing sensors. If one set of motion detector cells is fatigued through adaptation to motion in one direction, then the opposing sensor will take over. The net result is that motion is perceived in the opposite direction. Evidence from fMRIs indicates that when people experience the waterfall illusion while viewing a stationary stimulus, there is increased activity in region MT, which plays a key role in motion perception (Tootell et al., 1995).

The movement of objects in the world is not the only event that can evoke the perception of motion. The successively flashing lights of a Las Vegas casino sign can evoke a strong sense of motion, exactly the sort of illusion that inspired Max Wertheimer to investigate the *phi phenomenon,* discussed in Chapter 1. Recall, too, the Gestalt grouping rule of *common fate:* People perceive a series of flashing lights as a whole, moving object (see Figure 4.19f). This *perception of movement as a result of alternating signals appearing in rapid succession in different locations* is called **apparent motion.**

> **How can flashing lights on a casino sign give the impression of movement?**

Video technology and animation depend on apparent motion. A sequence of still images sample the continuous motion in the original scene. In the case of motion pictures, the sampling rate is 24 frames per second (fps). A slower sampling rate would produce a much choppier sense of motion; a faster sampling rate would be a waste of resources because we would not perceive the motion as any smoother than it appears at 24 fps.

▼ Want a powerful demonstration of apparent motion? Take a stroll down the Las Vegas strip.

VISIONS OF AMERICA/JOE SOHM/GETTY IMAGES

Change Blindness and Inattentional Blindness

Motion involves a change in an object's position over time, but objects in the visual environment can change in ways that do not involve motion (Rensink, 2002). You might walk by the same clothing store window every day and notice when a new suit or dress is on display or register surprise when you see a friend's new haircut. Intuitively, we feel that we can easily detect changes to our visual environment. However, our comfortable intuitions have been challenged by experimental demonstrations of **change blindness**, which occurs *when people fail to detect changes to the visual details of a scene* (Rensink, 2002; Simons & Rensink, 2005). Strikingly, change blindness occurs even when major details of a scene are changed—changes that we incorrectly believe that we could not miss (Beek, Levin, & Angelone, 2007). For example, Levin and Simons (1997) showed participants a movie in which a young blond man sits at a desk, gets up and walks away from the desk, and exits from the room. The scene then shifts outside the room, where the young man makes a phone call. This all sounds straightforward, but unknown to the participants, the man sitting at the desk is not the same person as the man who makes the phone call. Although both are young, blond, and wearing glasses, they are clearly different people. Still, two-thirds of the participants failed to notice the change.

It's one thing to create change blindness by splicing a film, but does change blindness also occur in live interactions? Simons and Levin (1998) tested this idea by having an experimenter ask a person on a college campus for directions. While they were talking, two men walked between them holding a door that hid a second experimenter (see **FIGURE 4.26**). Behind the door, the two experimenters traded places, so that when the men carrying the door moved on, a different person was asking for directions than the one who had been there just a second or two earlier. Remarkably, only 7 of 15 participants reported noticing this change.

How can a failure of focused attention explain change blindness?

Although it is surprising that people can be blind to such dramatic changes, these findings once again illustrate the importance of focused attention for visual perception. We saw earlier that focused attention is critical for binding together the features of objects; experiments on change detection indicate that it is also necessary for detecting changes to objects and scenes (Rensink, 2002; Simons & Rensink, 2005). Change blindness is most likely to occur when people fail to focus attention on

change blindness When people fail to detect changes to the visual details of a scene.

(a)

(b)

(c)

(d)

◀ FIGURE 4.26

Change Blindness The white-haired man was giving directions to one experimenter (a), who disappeared behind the moving door (b), only to be replaced by another experimenter (c). Like many other people, the man failed to detect a seemingly obvious change.

From: Simons, D. J., & Levin, D. T. (1998). Failure to detect changes to people during a real-world interaction. *Psychonomic Bulletin & Review, 5*(4), 644-649. Figure provided by Daniel Simons.

▲ College students who were using their cell phones while walking through campus failed to notice the unicycling clown more frequently than students who were not using their cell phones.

the changed object (even though the object is registered by the visual system) and is reduced for items that draw attention to themselves (Rensink, O'Regan, & Clark, 1997). Focused attention selects and binds together only some of the many visual features in the environment, and those bound features are the ones that comprise our conscious visual experience.

The role of focused attention in conscious visual experience is also dramatically illustrated by the closely related phenomenon of **inattentional blindness**, which involves *a failure to perceive objects that are not the focus of attention*. Imagine the following scenario. You are watching a circle of people passing around a basketball, somebody dressed in a gorilla costume walks through the circle, and the gorilla stops to beat his chest before moving on. It seems inconceivable that you would fail to notice the gorilla, right? Think again. Simons and Chabris (1999) filmed such a scene, using two teams of three players each who passed the ball to one another as the costumed gorilla made his entrance and exit. Participants watched the film and were asked to track the movement of the ball by counting the number of passes made by one of the teams. With their attention focused on the moving ball, approximately half the participants failed to notice the chest-beating gorilla (for related observations, see the discussion of divided attention in Chapter 6).

These findings have interesting implications for a world in which many of us are busy texting and talking on our cell phones while carrying on other kinds of everyday business. We've already seen that using cell phones has negative effects on driving (see The Real World: Multitasking). Hyman and colleagues (2010) asked whether cell phone use contributes to inattentional blindness in everyday life. They recruited a clown to ride a unicycle in the middle of a large square in the middle of the campus at Western Washington University. On a pleasant afternoon, the researchers asked 151 students who had just walked through the square whether they saw the clown. Seventy-five percent of the students who were using cell phones failed to notice the clown, compared with less than 50% who were not using cell phones. Using cell phones draws on focused attention, resulting in increased inattentional blindness and emphasizing again that our conscious experience of the visual environment is restricted to those features or objects selected by focused attention.

IN SUMMARY

○ Illusory conjunctions occur when features from separate objects are mistakenly combined. According to feature integration theory, attention provides the "glue" necessary to bind features together. The parietal lobe is important for attention and contributes to feature binding, both in normal perception and synesthetic perception.

○ Some regions in the occipital and temporal lobes respond selectively to specific object categories, supporting the modular view that specialized brain areas represent particular classes of objects.

○ The principle of perceptual constancy holds that even as sensory signals change, perception remains consistent. Gestalt principles of perceptual grouping, such as simplicity, closure, and continuity, govern how the features and regions of things fit together.

○ Image-based and parts-based theories each explain some but not all features of object recognition.

○ Depth perception depends on monocular cues, such as familiar size and linear perspective; binocular cues, such as retinal disparity; and motion-based cues, such as motion parallax, which is based on the movement of the head over time.

○ We experience a sense of motion through the differences in the strengths of output from motion-sensitive neurons. These processes can give rise to illusions such as apparent motion.

○ Change blindness and inattentional blindness occur when we fail to notice visible and even salient features of our environment, emphasizing that our conscious visual experience depends on focused attention.

inattentional blindness A failure to perceive objects that are not the focus of attention.

Audition: More Than Meets the Ear

Vision is based on the spatial pattern of light waves on the retina. The sense of hearing, by contrast, is all about *sound waves*—changes in air pressure unfolding over time. Plenty of things produce sound waves: the collision of a tree hitting the forest floor, the impact of two hands clapping, the vibration of vocal cords during a stirring speech, the resonance of a bass guitar string during a thrash metal concert. Except for synesthetes who "hear colors," understanding most people's auditory experience requires understanding how we transform changes in air pressure into perceived sounds.

Sensing Sound

Striking a tuning fork produces a *pure tone,* a simple sound wave that first increases air pressure and then creates a relative vacuum. This cycle repeats hundreds or thousands of times per second as sound waves propagate outward in all directions from the source.

Just as there are three dimensions of light waves corresponding to three dimensions of visual perception, so, too, there are three physical dimensions of a sound wave. Frequency, amplitude, and complexity determine what we hear as the pitch, loudness, and quality of a sound (see **TABLE 4.4**).

> The *frequency* of the sound wave, or its wavelength, depends on how often the peak in air pressure passes the ear or a microphone, measured in cycles per second, or hertz (abbreviated Hz). Changes in the physical frequency of a sound wave are perceived by humans as changes in **pitch**, *how high or low a sound is.*

> The *amplitude* of a sound wave refers to its height, relative to the threshold for human hearing (which is set at zero decibels, or dBs). Amplitude corresponds to **loudness**, or *a sound's intensity.* To give you an idea of amplitude and intensity, the rustling of leaves in a soft breeze is about 20 dB, normal conversation is measured at about 40 dB, shouting produces 70 dB, a Slayer concert is about 130 db, and the sound of the space shuttle taking off one mile away registers at 160 dB or more. That's loud enough to cause permanent damage to the auditory system and is well above the pain threshold; in fact, any sounds above 85 decibels can be enough to cause hearing damage, depending on the length and type of exposure.

pitch How high or low a sound is.

loudness A sound's intensity.

▲ Foo Fighters star Dave Grohl has revealed that his deafness is causing problems in his marriage. "I'm virtually deaf . . . my wife asks me where we should go for dinner, and it sounds like the schoolteacher from the TV show *Charlie Brown*!"

TABLE 4.4

Properties of Sound Waves

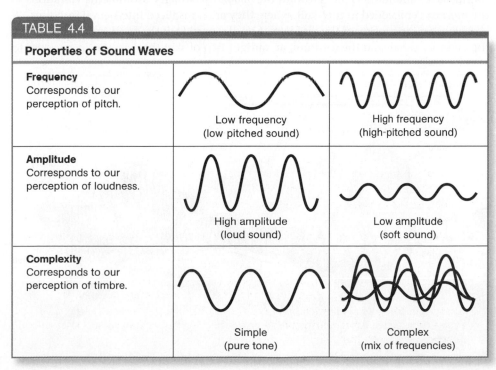

Frequency Corresponds to our perception of pitch.	Low frequency (low pitched sound) / High frequency (high-pitched sound)
Amplitude Corresponds to our perception of loudness.	High amplitude (loud sound) / Low amplitude (soft sound)
Complexity Corresponds to our perception of timbre.	Simple (pure tone) / Complex (mix of frequencies)

timbre A listener's experience of sound quality or resonance.

> Differences in the *complexity* of sound waves, or their mix of frequencies, correspond to **timbre**, *a listener's experience of sound quality or resonance.* Timbre (pronounced "TAM-ber") offers us information about the nature of sound. The same note played at the same loudness produces a perceptually different experience depending on whether it was played on a flute versus a trumpet, a phenomenon due entirely to timbre. Many "natural" sounds also illustrate the complexity of wavelengths, such as the sound of bees buzzing, the tonalities of speech, or the babbling of a brook. Unlike the purity of a tuning fork's hum, the drone of cicadas is a clamor of overlapping sound frequencies.

Why does one note sound so different on a flute and a trumpet?

Of the three dimensions of sound waves, frequency provides most of the information we need to identify sounds. Amplitude and complexity contribute texture to our auditory perceptions, but it is frequency that carries their meaning. Sound-wave frequencies blend together to create countless sounds, just as different wavelengths of light blend to create the richly colored world we see.

Moreover, sound-wave frequency is as important for audition as spatial perception is for vision. Changes in frequency over time allow us to identify the location of sounds, an ability that can be crucial to survival and also allow us to understand speech and appreciate music, skills that are valuable to our cultural survival. The focus in our discussion of hearing, then, is on how the auditory system encodes and represents sound-wave frequency (Kubovy, 1981).

"The ringing in your ears—I think I can help."

The Human Ear

How does the auditory system convert sound waves into neural signals? The process is very different from the visual system, which is not surprising, given that light is a form of electromagnetic radiation whereas sound is a physical change in air pressure over time: Different forms of energy require different processes of transduction. The human ear is divided into three distinct parts, as shown in **FIGURE 4.27**. The *outer ear* collects sound waves and funnels them toward the *middle ear,* which transmits the vibrations to the *inner ear,* embedded in the skull, where they are transduced into neural impulses.

The outer ear consists of the visible part on the outside of the head (called the *pinna*); the auditory canal; and the eardrum, an airtight flap of skin that vibrates in response to

▶ **FIGURE 4.27**

Anatomy of the Human Ear The pinna funnels sound waves into the auditory canal to vibrate the eardrum at a rate that corresponds to the sound's frequency. In the middle ear, the ossicles pick up the eardrum vibrations, amplify them, and pass them along by vibrating a membrane at the surface of the fluid-filled cochlea in the inner ear. Here fluid carries the wave energy to the auditory receptors that transduce it into electrochemical activity, exciting the neurons that form the auditory nerve, leading to the brain.

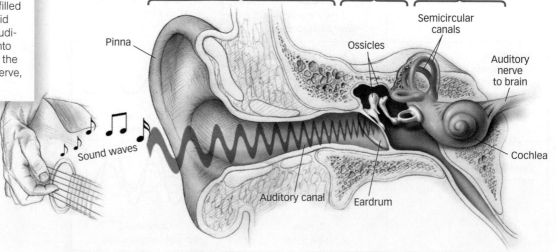

sound waves gathered by the pinna and channeled into the canal. The middle ear, a tiny, air-filled chamber behind the eardrum, contains the three smallest bones in the body, called *ossicles*. Named for their appearance as hammer, anvil, and stirrup, the ossicles fit together into a lever that mechanically transmits and intensifies vibrations from the eardrum to the inner ear.

The inner ear contains the spiral-shaped **cochlea** (Latin for "snail"), *a fluid-filled tube that is the organ of auditory transduction*. The cochlea is divided along its length by the **basilar membrane**, *a structure in the inner ear that undulates when vibrations from the ossicles reach the cochlear fluid* (see **FIGURE 4.28**). Its wavelike movement stimulates thousands of tiny **hair cells**, *specialized auditory receptor neurons embedded in the basilar membrane*. The hair cells then release neurotransmitter molecules, initiating a neural signal in the auditory nerve that travels to the brain. You might not want to think that the whispered "I love you" that sends chills up your spine got a kick start from lots of little hair cells wiggling around, but the mechanics of hearing are what they are!

How do hair cells in the ear enable us to hear?

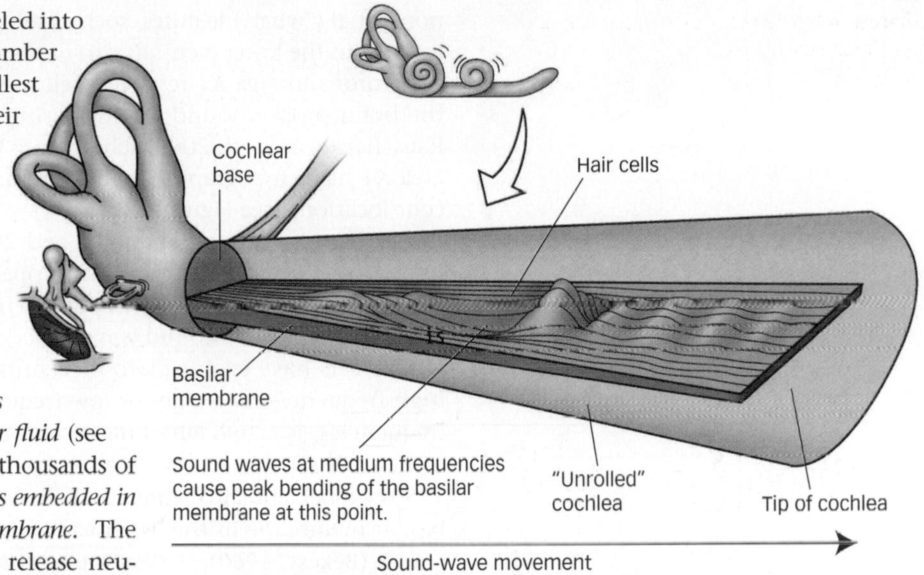

Cochlear base

Hair cells

Basilar membrane

"Unrolled" cochlea

Tip of cochlea

Sound waves at medium frequencies cause peak bending of the basilar membrane at this point.

Sound-wave movement

▲ **FIGURE 4.28**
Auditory Transduction Inside the cochlea, shown here as though it were uncoiling, the basilar membrane undulates in response to wave energy in the cochlear fluid. Waves of differing frequencies ripple varying locations along the membrane, from low frequencies at its tip to high frequencies at the base, and bend the embedded hair cell receptors at those locations. The hair-cell motion generates impulses in the auditory neurons, whose axons form the auditory nerve that emerges from the cochlea.

Perceiving Pitch

From the inner ear, action potentials in the auditory nerve travel to the thalamus and ultimately to the contralateral ("opposite side"; see Chapter 3) hemisphere of the cerebral cortex. This is called **area A1**, *a portion of the temporal lobe that contains the primary auditory cortex* (see **FIGURE 4.29**). For most of us, the auditory areas in the left hemisphere analyze sounds related to language and those in the right hemisphere specialize in rhythmic sounds and music. There is also evidence that the auditory cortex is composed of two distinct streams, roughly analogous to the dorsal and ventral streams of the visual system. Spatial ("where") auditory features, which allow you to locate the source of a sound in space, are handled by areas toward the back (caudal) part of the auditory cortex, whereas

cochlea A fluid-filled tube that is the organ of auditory transduction.

basilar membrane A structure in the inner ear that undulates when vibrations from the ossicles reach the cochlear fluid.

hair cells Specialized auditory receptor neurons embedded in the basilar membrane.

area A1 A portion of the temporal lobe that contains the primary auditory cortex.

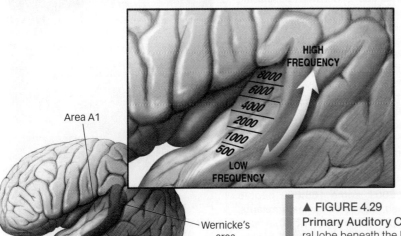

Area A1

HIGH FREQUENCY

8000
6000
4000
2000
1000
500

LOW FREQUENCY

Wernicke's area

Secondary auditory cortex

Temporal lobe

▲ **FIGURE 4.29**
Primary Auditory Cortex Area A1 is folded into the temporal lobe beneath the lateral fissure in each hemisphere. The left hemisphere auditory areas govern speech in most people. (inset) A1 cortex has a topographic organization, with lower frequencies mapping toward the front of the brain and higher frequencies toward the back, mirroring the organization of the basilar membrane along the cochlea (see Figure 4.28).

nonspatial ("what") features, such as temporal aspects of the acoustic signal, are handled by areas in the lower (ventral) part of the auditory cortex (Recanzone & Sutter, 2008).

Neurons in area A1 respond well to simple tones, and successive auditory areas in the brain process sounds of increasing complexity (Schreiner, Read, & Sutter, 2000; Rauschecker & Scott, 2009; Schreiner & Winer, 2007). Like area V1 in the visual cortex, area A1 has a topographic organization: Similar frequencies activate neurons in adjacent locations (see Figure 4.29, inset). A young adult with normal hearing ideally can detect sounds between about 20 and 20,000 Hz, although the ability to hear at the upper range decreases with age; an upper limit of about 16,000 Hz may be more realistic. The human ear is most sensitive to frequencies around 1,000 to 3,500 Hz. But how is the frequency of a sound wave encoded in a neural signal?

Our ears have evolved two mechanisms to encode sound-wave frequency, one for high frequencies and one for low frequencies. The **place code**, used mainly for high frequencies, is active when *the cochlea encodes different frequencies at different locations along the basilar membrane*. In a series of experiments carried out from the 1930s to the 1950s, Nobel laureate Georg von Békésy (1899–1972) used a microscope to observe the basilar membrane in the inner ear of cadavers that had been donated for medical research (Békésy, 1960). Békésy found that the movement of the basilar membrane resembles a traveling wave (see Figure 4.28). The wave's shape depends on the frequency

THE REAL WORLD

Cochlear Implants

Ten days after Natalie was born, she developed a persistent high fever. Her pediatrician's diagnosis was meningitis, an inflammation of the lining around the brain and spinal cord. Natalie spent several weeks in the hospital, at times close to death. Finally, the fever broke and Natalie seemed to recover fully.

During the next several months, Natalie's parents grew increasingly concerned because she was not responding to sound. They took her to a pediatric audiologist for assessment and learned that the meningitis had damaged the hair cells in Natalie's cochleas. The damage was irreversible.

Broadly speaking, hearing loss has two main causes. *Conductive hearing loss* arises because the eardrum or ossicles are damaged to the point that they cannot conduct sound waves effectively to the cochlea. The cochlea itself, however, is normal, making this a kind of "mechanical problem" with the moving parts of the ear: the hammer, anvil, stirrup, or eardrum. In many cases, medication or surgery can correct the problem. Sound amplification from a hearing aid also can improve hearing through conduction via the bones around the ear directly to the cochlea.

Sensorineural hearing loss is caused by damage to the cochlea, the hair cells, or the auditory nerve. This was Natalie's affliction, rare in an infant but commonly experienced by people as they grow older. Sensorineural

hearing loss can be heightened in people regularly exposed to high noise levels (such as rock musicians or jet mechanics). Simply amplifying the sound does not help because the hair cells can no longer transduce sound waves. In these cases a *cochlear implant* may offer some relief.

A cochlear implant is an electronic device that replaces the function of the hair cells (Waltzman, 2006). The external parts of the device include a microphone, a small speech processor the size of an iPod (worn on a belt), and an external transmitter worn behind the ear. The implanted parts include a receiver just inside the skull and a thin wire containing electrodes inserted into the cochlea to stimulate the auditory nerve. Sound picked up by the microphone is transformed into electric signals by the speech processor, which is essentially a small computer. The signal is transmitted to the implanted receiver, which activates the electrodes in the cochlea.

Cochlear implants are now in routine use and can improve hearing to the point where speech can be understood. According to the Food and Drug Administration, as of April 2009, some 188,000 people worldwide had received cochlear implants, including approximately 41,500 adults and 25,500 children in the United States. Young infants like Natalie, who have not yet learned to speak, are especially vulnerable because they may miss the critical period for language learning (see Chapter

7). Without auditory feedback during this time, normal speech is nearly impossible to achieve, but early use of cochlear implants has been associated with improved speech and language skills for deaf children (Hay-McCutcheon et al., 2008). Efforts are under way to introduce cochlear implants to children as early as 12 months or younger to maximize their chances of normal language development (DesJardin, Eisenberg, & Hodapp, 2006).

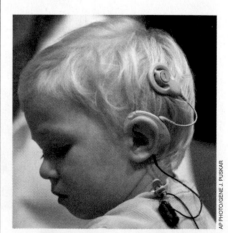

▲ A microphone picks up sounds and sends them to a small speech-processing computer worn on the user's belt or behind the ear. The electric signals from the speech processor are transmitted to an implanted receiver, which sends the signals via electrodes to the cochlea, where the signals directly stimulate the auditory nerve.

of the stimulating pitch. When the frequency is low, the wide, floppy tip (*apex*) of the basilar membrane moves the most; when the frequency is high, the narrow, stiff end (*base*) of the membrane moves the most.

The movement of the basilar membrane causes hair cells to bend, initiating a neural signal in the auditory nerve. Axons fire the strongest in the hair cells along the area of the basilar membrane that moves the most; in other words, the place of activation on the basilar membrane contributes to the perception of sound. The place code works best for relatively high frequencies that resonate at the basilar membrane's base and less well for low frequencies that resonate at the tip because low frequencies produce a broad traveling wave and therefore an imprecise frequency code.

How does the frequency of a sound wave relate to what we hear?

A complementary process handles lower frequencies. A **temporal code** *registers low frequencies via the firing rate of action potentials entering the auditory nerve.* Action potentials from the hair cells are synchronized in time with the peaks of the incoming sound waves (Johnson, 1980). If you imagine the rhythmic *boom-boom-boom* of a bass drum, you can probably also imagine the *fire-fire-fire* of action potentials corresponding to the beats. This process provides the brain with very precise information about pitch that supplements the information provided by the place code.

However, individual neurons can produce action potentials at a maximum rate of only about 1,000 spikes per second, so the temporal code does not work as well as the place code for high frequencies. (Imagine if the action potential has to fire in time with the *rat-a-tat-a-tat-a-tat* of a snare drum roll!) Like trichromatic representation and opponent processes in color processing, the place code and the temporal code work together to cover the entire range of pitches that people can hear. (For research on how to combat hearing loss, see the Real World box.)

place code The cochlea encodes different frequencies at different locations along the basilar membrane.

temporal code The cochlea registers low frequencies via the firing rate of action potentials entering the auditory nerve.

Localizing Sound Sources

Just as the differing positions of our eyes give us stereoscopic vision, the placement of our ears on opposite sides of the head gives us stereophonic hearing. The sound arriving at the ear closer to the sound source is louder than the sound in the farther ear, mainly because the listener's head partially blocks sound energy. This loudness difference decreases as the sound source moves from a position directly to one side (maximal difference) to straight ahead (no difference).

Another cue to a sound's location arises from timing: Sound waves arrive a little sooner at the near ear than at the far ear. The timing difference can be as brief as a few microseconds, but together with the intensity difference, it is sufficient to allow us to perceive the location of a sound. When the sound source is ambiguous, you may find yourself turning your head from side to side to localize it. By doing this, you are changing the relative intensity and timing of sound waves arriving in your ears and collecting better information about the likely source of the sound.

IN SUMMARY

○ Perceiving sound depends on three physical dimensions of a sound wave: The frequency of the sound wave determines the pitch; the amplitude determines the loudness; and differences in the complexity, or mix, of frequencies determines the sound quality or timbre.

○ Auditory perception begins in the ear, which consists of an outer ear that funnels sound waves toward the middle ear, which in turn sends the vibrations to the inner ear, which contains the cochlea. Action potentials from the inner ear travel along an auditory pathway through the thalamus to the contralateral primary auditory cortex, area A1, in the temporal lobe.

○ Auditory perception depends on both a place code and a temporal code, which together cover the full range of pitches that people can hear. Our ability to localize sound sources depends critically on the placement of our ears on opposite sides of the head.

The Body Senses: More Than Skin Deep

Vision and audition provide information about the world at a distance. By responding to light and sound energy in the environment, these "distance" senses allow us to identify and locate the objects and people around us. In comparison, the body senses, also called *somatosenses* (*soma* from the Greek for "body"), are up close and personal. **Haptic perception** results from our *active exploration of the environment by touching and grasping objects with our hands*. We use sensory receptors in our muscles, tendons, and joints as well as a variety of receptors in our skin to get a feel for the world around us (see **FIGURE 4.30**).

▶ This rather unimposing geodesic dome sits on the floor of the Exploratorium, a world-renowned science museum in San Francisco. Called the Tactile Dome, it was created in 1971 by August Coppola (brother of director Francis Ford Coppola and father of actor Nicolas Cage) and Carl Day, who wanted to create an environment in which only haptic perception could be used. The inside of the dome is pitch black; visitors must crawl, wiggle, slide, and otherwise navigate the unfamiliar terrain using only their sense of touch. How would you feel being in that environment for an hour or so?

© EXPLORATORIUM

▼ FIGURE 4.30

Touch Receptors Specialized sensory neurons form distinct groups of haptic receptors that detect pressure, temperature, and vibrations against the skin. Touch receptors respond to stimulation within their receptive fields, and their long axons enter the brain via the spinal or cranial nerves. Pain receptors populate all body tissues that feel pain: They are distributed around bones and within muscles and internal organs as well as under the skin surface. Both types of pain receptors—the fibers that transmit immediate, sharp pain sensations quickly and those that signal slow, dull pain that lasts and lasts—are free nerve endings.

Touch

Four types of receptors located under the skin's surface enable us to sense pressure, texture, pattern, or vibration against the skin (see Figure 4.30). The receptive fields of these specialized cells work together to provide a rich tactile (from Latin, "to touch") experience when you explore an object by feeling it or attempting to grasp it. In addition, *thermoreceptors,* nerve fibers that sense cold and warmth, respond when your skin temperature changes. All these sensations blend seamlessly together in perception, of course, but detailed physiological studies have successfully isolated the parts of the touch system (Johnson, 2002).

Touch begins with the transduction of skin sensations into neural signals. Like cells in the retina of each eye, touch receptors have receptive fields with central excitatory zones surrounded by doughnut-shaped inhibitory zones that, when stimulated, cause that cell's response to change. The representation of touch in the brain follows a topographic scheme, much as vision and hearing do. Think back to the homunculus you read about in Chapter 3; you'll recall that different locations on the body project sensory signals to different locations in the somatosensory cortex in the parietal lobe.

There are three important principles regarding the neural representation of the body's surface. First, there is contralateral organization: The left half of the body is represented in the right half of the brain and vice versa. Second, just as more of the visual brain is devoted to foveal vision where acuity is greatest, more of the tactile brain is devoted to parts of the skin surface that have greater spatial resolution. Regions such as the fingertips

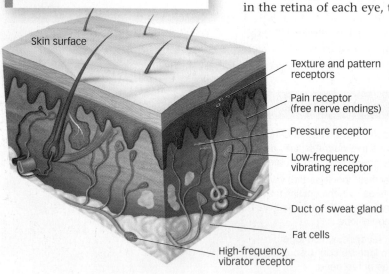

Skin surface

Texture and pattern receptors

Pain receptor (free nerve endings)

Pressure receptor

Low-frequency vibrating receptor

Duct of sweat gland

Fat cells

High-frequency vibrator receptor

and lips are very good at discriminating fine spatial detail, whereas areas such as the lower back are quite poor at that task. These perceptual abilities are a natural consequence of the fact that the fingertips and lips have a relatively dense arrangement of touch receptors and a large topographical representation

Why might discriminating spatial detail be important for fingertips and lips?

in the somatosensory cortex; comparatively, the lower back, hips, and calves have a relatively small representation (Penfield & Rasmussen, 1950). Third, there is mounting evidence for a distinction between "what" and "where" pathways in touch analogous to similar distinctions we've already considered for vision and audition. The "what" system for touch provides information about the properties of surfaces and objects; the "where" system provides information about a location in external space that is being touched or a location on the body that is being stimulated (Lederman & Klatzky, 2009). fMRI evidence suggests that the "what" and "where" touch pathways involve areas in the lower and upper parts of the parietal lobe, respectively (Reed, Klatzky, & Halgren, 2005).

Touch information can have a powerful effect on our decisions and judgments. For example, recent research has shown that merely touching an object that we don't already own can increase our feeling of ownership and lead us to value the object more highly than when we view it but don't touch it (Peck & Shu, 2009); the longer we touch an object, the more highly we value it (Wolf, Arkes, & Muhanna, 2008). You might keep this "mere touch" effect in mind next time you are in a shop and considering buying an expensive item. Retailers are probably aware of this effect: During the 2003 holiday shopping season the office of the Illinois state attorney general warned shoppers to be cautious in stores that encouraged them to touch the merchandise (Peck & Shu, 2009).

▲ Be warned for your next shopping trip: Touching the merchandise can lead us to value it more highly than just looking at it.

Pain

Does the possibility of a life free from pain seem appealing? Although pain is arguably the least pleasant of sensations, this aspect of touch is among the most important for survival: Pain indicates damage or potential damage to the body. Without the ability to feel pain, we might ignore infections, broken bones, or serious burns. Congenital insensitivity to pain, a rare inherited disorder that specifically impairs pain perception, is more of a curse than a blessing: Children who experience this disorder often mutilate themselves (biting into their tongues, for example, or gouging their skin while scratching) and are at increased risk of dying during childhood (Nagasako, Oaklander, & Dworkin, 2003).

Tissue damage is transduced by pain receptors, the free nerve endings shown in Figure 4.30. Researchers have distinguished between fast-acting *A-delta fibers,* which transmit the initial sharp pain one might feel right away from a sudden injury, and slower *C fibers,* which transmit the longer-lasting, duller pain that persists after the initial injury. If you were running barefoot outside and stubbed your toe against a rock, you would first feel a sudden stinging pain transmitted by A-delta fibers that would die down quickly, only to be replaced by the throbbing but longer-lasting pain carried by C fibers. Both the A-delta and C fibers are impaired in cases of congenital insensitivity to pain, which is one reason why the disorder can be life threatening.

As you'll remember from Chapter 3, the pain withdrawal reflex is coordinated by the spinal cord. No brainpower is required when you touch a hot stove; you retract your hand almost instantaneously. But neural signals for pain—such as wrenching your elbow as you brace yourself from falling—travel to two distinct areas in the brain and evoke two distinct psychological experiences (Treede et al., 1999). One pain pathway sends signals to the somatosensory cortex, identifying where the pain is occurring and what sort of pain it is (sharp, burning, dull). The second pain pathway sends

haptic perception The active exploration of the environment by touching and grasping objects with our hands.

▲ Aron Ralston was hiking in a remote canyon in Utah when tragedy struck. A 1,000-pound boulder pinned him in a three-foot-wide space for 5 days, eventually leaving him no choice but to amputate his own arm with a pocketknife. He then applied a tourniquet, rappelled down the canyon, and hiked out to safety. These and similar stories illustrate that the extent of an injury is not perfectly correlated with the amount of pain felt. Although self-amputation is undoubtedly excruciating, luckily in this case it was not debilitating.

signals to the motivational and emotional centers of the brain, such as the hypothalamus and amygdala, and to the frontal lobe. This is the aspect of pain that is unpleasant and motivates us to escape from or relieve the pain.

Pain typically feels as if it comes from the site of the tissue damage that caused it. If you burn your finger, you will perceive the pain as originating there. But we have pain receptors in many areas besides the skin—around bones and within muscles and internal organs as well. When pain originates internally, in a body organ, for example, we actually feel it on the surface of the body. This kind of **referred pain** occurs when *sensory information from internal and external areas converges on the same nerve cells in the spinal cord*. One common example is a heart attack: Victims often feel pain radiating from the left arm rather than from inside the chest.

Pain intensity cannot always be predicted solely from the extent of the injury that causes the pain (Keefe, Abernathy, & Campbell, 2005). For example, *turf toe* sounds like the mildest of ailments; it is pain at the base of the big toe as a result of bending or pushing off repeatedly, as a runner or football player might do during a sporting event. This small-sounding injury in a small area of the body can nonetheless sideline an athlete for a month with considerable pain. On the other hand, you've probably heard a story or two about someone treading bone-chilling water for hours on end, or dragging their shattered legs a mile down a country road to seek help after a tractor accident, or performing some other incredible feat despite searing pain and extensive tissue damage. Pain type and pain intensity show a less-than-perfect correlation, a fact that has researchers intrigued.

Some recent evidence indicates subjective pain intensity may differ among ethnic groups. A study that examined responses to various kinds of experimentally induced pain, including heat pain and cold pain, found that compared to White young adults, African American young adults had a lower tolerance for several kinds of pain and rated the same pain stimuli as more intense and unpleasant (Campbell, Edward, & Fillingim, 2005).

One influential account of pain perception is known as **gate-control theory**, which holds that *signals arriving from pain receptors in the body can be stopped, or gated, by interneurons in the spinal cord via feedback from two directions* (Melzack & Wall, 1965). Pain can be gated by the skin receptors, for example, by rubbing the affected area. Rubbing your stubbed toe activates neurons that "close the gate" to stop pain signals

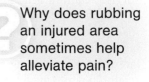

Why does rubbing an injured area sometimes help alleviate pain?

from traveling to the brain. Pain can also be gated from the brain by modulating the activity of pain-transmission neurons. This neural feedback is elicited not by the pain itself, but rather by activity deep within the thalamus.

The neural feedback comes from a region in the midbrain called the *periaqueductal gray* (PAG). Under extreme conditions, such as high stress, naturally occurring endorphins can activate the PAG to send inhibitory signals to neurons in the spinal cord that then suppress pain signals to the brain, thereby modulating the experience of pain. The PAG is also activated through the action of opiate drugs, such as morphine.

A different kind of feedback signal can *increase* the sensation of pain. This system is activated by events such as infection and learned danger signals. When we are quite ill, what might otherwise be experienced as mild discomfort can feel quite painful. This pain facilitation signal presumably evolved to motivate people who are ill to rest and avoid strenuous activity, allowing their energy to be devoted to healing.

Although some details of gate-control theory have been challenged, a key concept underlying the theory—that perception is a two-way street—has broad implications. The senses feed information, such as pain sensations, to the brain, a pattern termed *bottom-up control* by perceptual psychologists. The brain processes this sensory data into perceptual information at successive levels to support movement, object recognition, and eventually more complex cognitive tasks, such as memory and planning. But

referred pain Feeling of pain when sensory information from internal and external areas converges on the same nerve cells in the spinal cord.

gate-control theory A theory of pain perception based on the idea that signals arriving from pain receptors in the body can be stopped, or *gated*, by interneurons in the spinal cord via feedback from two directions.

there is ample evidence that the brain exerts plenty of control over what we sense as well. Visual illusions and the Gestalt principles of filling in, shaping up, and rounding out what isn't really there provide some examples. This kind of *top-down control* also explains the descending pain pathway initiated in the midbrain.

Body Position, Movement, and Balance

It may sound odd, but one aspect of sensation and perception is knowing where parts of your body are at any given moment. Your body needs some way to sense its position in physical space other than moving your eyes to constantly visually check the location of your limbs. Sensations related to position, movement, and balance depend on stimulation produced within our bodies. Receptors in the muscles, tendons, and joints signal the position of the body in space, whereas information about balance and head movement originates in the inner ear.

Sensory receptors provide the information we need to perceive the position and movement of our limbs, head, and body. These receptors also provide feedback about whether we are performing a desired movement correctly and how resistance from held objects may be influencing the movement. For example, when you swing a baseball bat, the weight of the bat affects how your muscles move your arm as well as the change in sensation when the bat hits the ball. Muscle, joint, and tendon feedback about how your arms actually moved can be used to improve performance through learning.

Maintaining balance depends primarily on the **vestibular system**, *the three fluid-filled semicircular canals and adjacent organs located next to the cochlea in each inner ear* (see Figure 4.27). The semicircular canals are arranged in three perpendicular orientations and studded with hair cells that detect movement of the fluid when the head moves or accelerates. This detected motion enables us to maintain our balance, or the position of our bodies relative to gravity. The movements of the hair cells encode these somatic sensations (Lackner & DiZio, 2005).

Vision also helps us keep our balance. If you see that you are swaying relative to a vertical orientation, such as the contours of a room, you move your legs and feet to keep from falling over. Psychologists have experimented with this visual aspect of balance by placing people in rooms that can be tilted forward and backward (Bertenthal, Rose, & Bai, 1997; Lee & Aronson, 1974). If the room tilts enough—particularly when small children are tested—people will topple over as they try to compensate for what their visual system is telling them. When a mismatch between the information provided by visual cues and vestibular feedback occurs, motion sickness can result. Remember this discrepancy the next time you try reading in the back seat of a moving car!

Why is it so hard to stand on one foot with your eyes closed?

◄ Hitting a ball with a bat or racket provides feedback as to where your arms and body are in space as well as to how the resistance of these objects affects your movement and balance. Successful athletes, such as Serena Williams, have particularly well-developed body senses.

AP PHOTO/RICK RYCROFT

IN SUMMARY

○ Touch is represented in the brain according to a topographic scheme in which locations on the body project sensory signals to locations in the somatosensory cortex, a part of the parietal lobe.

○ The experience of pain depends on signals that travel along two distinct pathways. One sends signals to the somatosensory cortex to indicate the location and type of pain, and another sends signals to the emotional centers of the brain that result in unpleasant feelings that we wish to escape. The experience of pain varies across individuals, which is explained by bottom-up and top-down aspects of gate-control theory.

○ Balance and acceleration depend primarily on the vestibular system but are also influenced by vision.

vestibular system The three fluid-filled semicircular canals and adjacent organs located next to the cochlea in each inner ear.

The Chemical Senses: Adding Flavor

Somatosensation is all about physical changes in or on the body: Vision and audition sense energetic states of the world—light and sound waves—and touch is activated by physical changes in or on the body surface. The last set of senses we'll consider share a chemical basis to combine aspects of distance and proximity. The chemical senses of *olfaction* (smell) and *gustation* (taste) respond to the molecular structure of substances floating into the nasal cavity as you inhale or dissolving in saliva. Smell and taste combine to produce the perceptual experience we call *flavor*.

Smell

Olfaction is the least understood sense and the only one directly connected to the forebrain, with pathways into the frontal lobe, amygdala, and other forebrain structures (recall from Chapter 3 that the other senses connect first to the thalamus). This mapping indicates that smell has a close relationship with areas involved in emotional and social behavior. Smell seems to have evolved in animals as a signaling sense for the familiar—a friendly creature, an edible food, or a sexually receptive mate.

Countless substances release odors into the air, and some of their *odorant molecules* make their way into our noses, drifting in on the air we breathe. Situated along the top of the nasal cavity shown in **FIGURE 4.31** is a mucous membrane called the *olfactory epithelium,* which contains about 10 million **olfactory receptor neurons (ORNs),** *receptor cells that initiate the sense of smell.* Odorant molecules bind to sites on these specialized receptors, and if enough bindings occur, the ORNs send action potentials into the olfactory nerve (Dalton, 2003).

Each olfactory neuron has receptors that bind to some odorants but not to others, as if the receptor is a lock and the odorant is the key (see Figure 4.31). Groups of ORNs

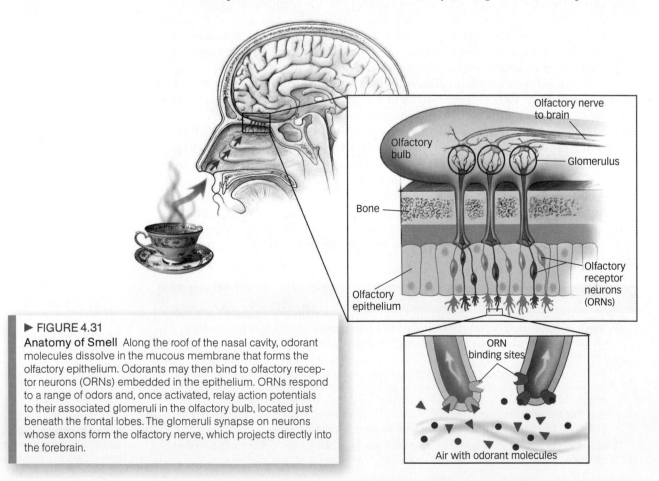

► FIGURE 4.31

Anatomy of Smell Along the roof of the nasal cavity, odorant molecules dissolve in the mucous membrane that forms the olfactory epithelium. Odorants may then bind to olfactory receptor neurons (ORNs) embedded in the epithelium. ORNs respond to a range of odors and, once activated, relay action potentials to their associated glomeruli in the olfactory bulb, located just beneath the frontal lobes. The glomeruli synapse on neurons whose axons form the olfactory nerve, which projects directly into the forebrain.

send their axons from the olfactory epithelium into the **olfactory bulb**, *a brain structure located above the nasal cavity beneath the frontal lobes*. Humans possess about 350 different ORN types that permit us to discriminate among some 10,000 different odorants through the unique patterns of neural activity each odorant evokes. This setup is similar to our ability to see a vast range of colors based on only a small number of retinal cell types or to feel a range of skin sensations based on only a handful of touch receptor cell types.

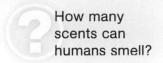

How many scents can humans smell?

The axons of all ORNs of a particular type converge at a site called a *glomerulus* within the olfactory bulb; thus, humans have about 350 glomeruli. Different odorant molecules produce varied patterns of activity (Rubin & Katz, 1999). A given odorant may strongly activate some glomeruli, moderately activate others, and have little effect on still others. The genetic basis for this olfactory coding was worked out in large part by Linda Buck and Richard Axel (1991), who were awarded a Nobel Prize in 2004 for their efforts.

Some dogs have as many as 100 times more ORNs than humans do, producing a correspondingly sharpened ability to detect and discriminate among millions of odors. Nevertheless, humans are sensitive to the smells of some substances in extremely small concentrations. For example, a chemical compound that is added to natural gas to help detect gas leaks can be sensed at a concentration of just 0.0003 part per million. By contrast, acetone (nail polish remover), something most people regard as pungent, can be detected only if its concentration is 15 parts per million or greater.

The olfactory bulb sends outputs to various centers in the brain, including the parts that are responsible for controlling basic drives, emotions, and memories. This explains why smells can have immediate, strongly positive or negative effects on us. If the slightest whiff of an apple pie baking brings back fond memories of childhood or the unexpected sniff of vomit mentally returns you to a particularly bad party you once attended, you've got the idea. Thankfully, sensory adaptation is at work when it comes to smell, just as it is with the other senses. Whether the associations are good or bad, after just a few minutes the smell fades. Smell adaptation makes sense: It allows us to detect new odors that may require us to act, but after that initial evaluation has occurred, it may be best to reduce our sensitivity to allow us to detect other smells. Evidence from fMRIs indicates that experience with a smell can modify odor perception by changing how specific parts of the brain involved in olfaction respond to that smell (Li et al., 2006).

This observation suggests that our experience of smell is determined not only by bottom-up influences, such as odorant molecules binding to sites on ORNs, but also by top-down influences, such as our previous experiences with an odor (Gottfried, 2008). Consistent with this idea, people rate the identical odor as more pleasant when it is paired with an appealing verbal label such as "cheddar cheese" rather than an unappealing one such as "body odor" (de Araujo et al., 2005; Herz & von Clef, 2001). fMRI evidence indicates that brain regions involved in coding the pleasantness of an experience, such as the orbitofrontal cortex, respond more strongly to the identical odor when people think it is cheddar cheese than when they think it is a body odor (de Araujo et al., 2005; see the Hot Science box on the next page for a related finding concerning taste perception).

Smell may also play a role in social behavior. Humans and other animals can detect odors from **pheromones**, *biochemical odorants emitted by other members of its species that can affect the animal's behavior or physiology*. Parents can distinguish the smell of their own children from other people's children. An infant can identify the smell of its mother's breast from the smell of other mothers. Pheromones also play a role in reproductive behavior in insects and in several mammalian species, including mice, dogs, and primates (Brennan & Zufall, 2006). Can the same thing be said of human reproductive behavior?

Studies of people's preference for the odors of individuals of the opposite sex have produced mixed results, with no consistent tendency for people to prefer them over other pleasant odors. Recent research, however, has provided a link between sexual orientation

olfactory receptor neurons (ORNs) Receptor cells that initiate the sense of smell.

olfactory bulb A brain structure located above the nasal cavity beneath the frontal lobes.

pheromones Biochemical odorants emitted by other members of its species that can affect an animal's behavior or physiology.

HOT SCIENCE

Expensive Taste

In 2008, the publication of a book titled *The Wine Trials* (Goldstein & Herschkowitsch, 2008) ruffled the feathers of more than a few wine connoisseurs. The book was based on a paper in which the authors and several colleagues analyzed the results of 6,175 observations gathered during 17 blind wine tastings organized by lead author and food critic Robin Goldstein (Goldstein et al., 2008). In a blind wine tasting, drinkers sample wines from a wide range of prices ($1.65 to $150 in the Goldstein tastings), but both the taster and the person serving the wine are blind concerning the identity of the wine and its price. The sample of tasters ranged in age from 21 to 88 years of age, and each taster rated each wine on a 1–4 scale, where 1 = "Bad," 2 = "Okay," 3 = "Good," and 4 = "Great." The study revealed a weak and slightly negative correlation between price and ratings, suggesting that, if anything, tasters liked the more expensive wines slightly *less* than the more inexpensive ones.

Though these findings will not encourage ordinary wine drinkers to spend a large amount of money on their next wine purchase, they leave open the question of whether knowing a wine's price affects enjoyment of it. Similar to olfaction (see p. 166), our experience of taste is partly determined by bottom-up influences, such as the patterns of activity in the five taste receptor types that are evoked by food molecules, but it is also influenced by top-down factors, such as knowing what brand we are eating or drinking. For example, when people know that they are drinking either Pepsi or Coke, their subjective preferences and brain activity differ markedly from when they do not know which of the two beverages they are drinking (McClure et al., 2004).

To investigate the effects of price knowledge on the enjoyment of wine and associated brain activity, researchers used fMRI to scan 20 participants while they drank different wines or a control solution (Plassman et al., 2008). The participants were told that they would be sampling five different cabernet sauvignons, that the different wines would be identified by their price, and that they should rate how much they liked each wine. The participants did not know, however, that only three different wines were actually presented and that two critical wines were presented twice. One critical wine was presented once at its actual price ($5) and once marked up to a high price ($45); the other critical wine was also presented once at its actual price ($90) and once at a marked-down price ($10). This design allowed the researchers to compare ratings and brain activity for the identical wine when participants thought it was expensive or cheap.

Results revealed that during scanning, participants reported liking both wines better when they were accompanied by a high price than by a low price. For the fMRI analysis, the researchers focused on the activity of the medial orbitofrontal cortex (mOFC), a part of the brain located deep inside the frontal lobe that is known to be involved in coding the pleasantness of an experience; the level of mOFC activity was closely correlated with subjective ratings of taste pleasantness in a previous fMRI study (Kringelbach et al., 2003). As shown in the accompanying figure, there was greater mOFC activity for both wines in the high-price condition than in the low-price condition.

These results demonstrate clearly that taste experience and associated neural activity can be influenced by top-down influences such as price knowledge. The results should provide some comfort to wine drinkers who are willing to pay for expensive brands. Even if they can't tell the difference from cheaper brands under blind tasting conditions, just knowing that they're drinking an expensive wine should make for an enjoyable experience.

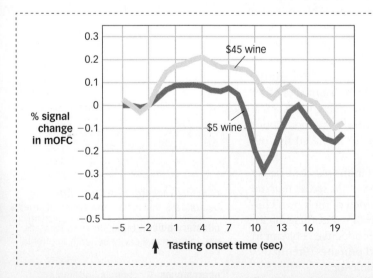

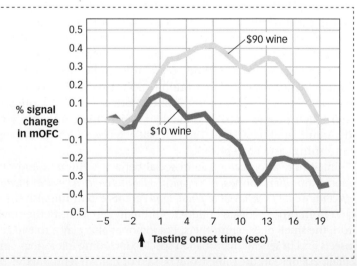

Heterosexual women	Homosexual men	Heterosexual men

AND

Hypothalamus

◀ FIGURE 4.32
Smell and Social Behavior In a PET study, heterosexual women, homosexual men, and heterosexual men were scanned as they were presented with each of several odors. During the presentation of a testosterone-based odor (referred to in the figure as AND), there was significant activation in the hypothalamus for heterosexual women (left) and homosexual men (center) but not for heterosexual men (right) (Savic et al., 2005).

IVANKA SAVIC, HA BERGLUND, AND PER LINDSTROM

and responses to odors that may constitute human pheromones. Researchers used positron emission tomography (PET) scans to study the brain's response to two odors, one related to testosterone, which is produced in men's sweat, and the other related to estrogen, which is found in women's urine. The testosterone-based odor activated the hypothalamus (a part of the brain that controls sexual behavior; see Chapter 3) in heterosexual women but not in heterosexual men, whereas the estrogen-based odor activated the hypothalamus in heterosexual men but not in women. Strikingly, homosexual men responded to the two chemicals in the same way as women did: The hypothalamus was activated by the testosterone- but not estrogen-based odor (Savic, Berglund, & Lindstrom, 2005; see **FIGURE 4.32**). Other common odors unrelated to sexual arousal were processed similarly by all three groups. A follow-up study with lesbian women showed that their responses to the testosterone- and estrogen-based odors were largely similar to those of heterosexual men (Berglund, Lindstrom, & Savic, 2006). Taken together, the two studies suggest that some human pheromones are related to sexual orientation.

Taste

One of the primary responsibilities of the chemical sense of taste is identifying things that are bad for you—as in "poisonous and lethal." Many poisons are bitter, and we avoid eating things that nauseate us for good reason, so taste aversions have a clear adaptive significance. Some aspects of taste perception are genetic, such as an aversion to extreme bitterness, and some are learned, such as an aversion to a particular food that once caused nausea. In either case, the direct contact between a tongue and possible foods allows us to anticipate whether something will be harmful or palatable.

Why is the sense of taste an evolutionary advantage?

The tongue is covered with thousands of small bumps, called *papillae*, which are easily visible to the naked eye. Within each papilla are hundreds of **taste buds**, *the organ of taste transduction* (see **FIGURE 4.33** on the next page). Most of our mouths contain between 5,000 and 10,000 taste buds fairly evenly distributed over the tongue, roof of the mouth, and upper throat (Bartoshuk & Beauchamp, 1994; Halpern, 2002). Each taste bud contains 50 to 100 taste receptor cells. Taste perception fades with age: On average, people lose half their taste receptors by the time they turn 20. This may help to explain why young children seem to be "fussy eaters," since their greater number of taste buds brings with it a greater range of taste sensations.

The human eye contains millions of rods and cones, the human nose contains some 350 different types of olfactory receptors, but the taste system contains just five main types of taste receptors, corresponding to five primary taste sensations: salt, sour, bitter, sweet, and umami (savory). The first four are quite familiar, but *umami* may not be. In fact, perception researchers are still debating its existence. The umami receptor was discovered by Japanese scientists who attributed it to the tastes evoked by foods containing a high concentration of protein, such as meats and cheeses (Yamaguchi, 1998). If you're a meat eater and you savor the feel of a steak topped with butter or a cheeseburger as it sits in your mouth, you've got an idea of the umami sensation.

LESLIE BANKS/ISTOCKPHOTO.COM

▲ Fussy eater or just too many taste buds? Our taste perception declines with age: We lose about half of our taste receptors by the time we're 20 years old. That can make childhood a time of either savory delight or a sensory overload of taste.

taste buds The organ of taste transduction.

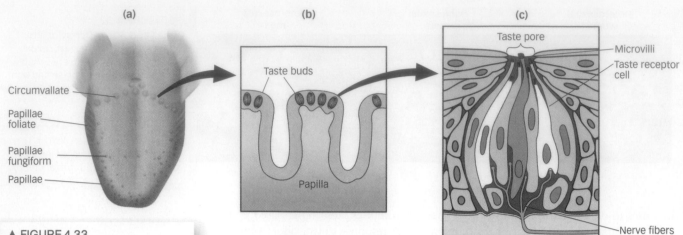

(a)

Circumvallate

Papillae foliate

Papillae fungiform

Papillae

(b)

Taste buds

Papilla

(c)

Taste pore

Microvilli

Taste receptor cell

Nerve fibers

▲ FIGURE 4.33

A Taste Bud (a) Taste buds stud the bumps (papillae) on your tongue, shown here, as well as the back, sides, and roof of the mouth. (b) Each taste bud contains a range of receptor cells that respond to varying chemical components of foods called tastants. Tastant molecules dissolve in saliva and stimulate the microvilli that form the tips of the taste receptor cells. (c) Each taste bud contacts the branch of a cranial nerve at its base.

Each taste bud contains several types of taste receptor cells whose tips, called *microvilli,* react with *tastant molecules* in food. Salt taste receptors are most strongly activated by sodium chloride—table salt. Sour receptor cells respond to acids, such as vinegar or lime juice. Bitter and sweet taste receptors are more complex. Some 50 to 80 distinct binding sites in bitter receptors are activated by an equal number of different bitter-tasting chemicals. Sweet receptor cells likewise can be activated by a wide range of substances in addition to sugars.

Although umami receptor cells are the least well understood, researchers are homing in on their key features (Chandrashekar et al., 2006). They respond most strongly to glutamate, an amino acid in many protein-containing foods. Recall from Chapter 3, glutamate acts as a neurotransmitter; in fact, it's a major excitatory neurotransmitter. The food additive *monosodium glutamate* (MSG), which is often used to flavor Asian foods, particularly activates umami receptors. Some people develop headaches or allergic reactions after eating MSG.

Of course, the variety of taste experiences greatly exceeds the five basic receptors discussed here. Any food molecules dissolved in saliva evoke specific, combined patterns of activity in the five taste receptor types. Although we often think of taste as the primary source for flavor, in fact, taste and smell collaborate to produce this complex perception. As any wine connoisseur will attest, the full experience of a wine's flavor cannot be appreciated without a finely trained sense of smell. Odorants from substances outside your mouth enter the nasal cavity via the nostrils, and odorants in the mouth enter through the back of the throat. This is why wine aficionados are taught to pull air in over wine held in the mouth: It allows the wine's odorant molecules to enter the nasal cavity through this "back door." (The taste of wine can also be influenced by cognitive factors, as illustrated in the Hot Science box.)

You can easily demonstrate the contribution of smell to flavor by tasting a few different foods while holding your nose, preventing the olfactory system from detecting their odors. If you have a head cold, you probably already know how this turns out. Your favorite spicy burrito or zesty pasta probably tastes as bland as can be.

Taste experiences also vary widely across individuals. About 50% of people report a mildly bitter taste in caffeine, saccharine, certain green vegetables, and other substances, while roughly 25% report no bitter taste. Members of the first group are called *tasters* and members of the second group are called *nontasters*. The remaining 25% of people are *supertasters*, who report that such substances, especially dark green vegetables, are extremely bitter, to the point of being inedible (Bartoshuk, 2000). Children start out as tasters or supertasters, which could help explain their early tendency toward fussiness in food preference. However, some children grow

"We would like to be genetically modified to taste like Brussels sprouts."

up to become nontasters. Because supertasters tend to avoid fruits and vegetables that contain tastes they experience as extremely bitter, they may be at increased health risk for diseases such as colon cancer. On the other hand, because they also tend to avoid fatty, creamy foods, they tend to be thinner and may have decreased risk of cardiovascular disease (Bartoshuk, 2000). There is evidence that genetic factors contribute to individual differences in taste perception (Kim et al., 2003), but much remains to be learned about the specific genes that are involved (Hayes et al., 2008; Reed, 2008).

IN SUMMARY

○ Our experience of smell, or olfaction, is associated with odorant molecules binding to sites on specialized olfactory receptors, which converge at the glomerulus within the olfactory bulb. The olfactory bulb in turn sends signals to parts of the brain that control drives, emotions, and memories, which helps to explain why smells can have immediate and powerful effects on us.

○ Smell is also involved in social behavior, as illustrated by pheromones, which are related to reproductive behavior and sexual responses in several species.

○ Sensations of taste depend on taste buds, which are distributed across the tongue, roof of the mouth, and upper throat and on taste receptors that correspond to the five primary taste sensations of salt, sour, bitter, sweet, and umami.

○ Taste experiences vary widely across individuals and, like olfactory experiences, depend in part on cognitive influences.

ALUMA IMAGES/MASTERFILE/RADIUS IMAGES

▲ Taste and smell both contribute to what we perceive as flavor. This is why "smelling" the bouquet of a wine is an essential part of the wine-tasting ritual. The experience of wine tasting is also influenced by cognitive factors, such as knowledge of a wine's price.

| WhereDoYouStand? |

Perception and Persuasion

We're used to seeing advertisements that feature exciting, provocative, or sexual images to sell products. In television commercials these images are accompanied by popular music that advertisers hope will evoke an overall mood favorable to the product. The notion is that the sight and sound of exciting things will become associated with what might be an otherwise drab product. This form of advertising is known as *sensory branding* (Lindstrom, 2005). The idea is to exploit all the senses to promote a product or a brand.

Sensory branding goes beyond sight and sound by enlisting smell, taste, and touch as well as vision and hearing. You probably recognize the distinctive aroma of a newly opened can of Play-Doh or a fresh box of Crayola crayons. Their scents are unmistakable, but they're also somewhat inadvertent: Play-Doh was first sold in 1956 and Crayola crayons appeared in 1903, both long before there was any thought given to marketing as a total sensory experience.

Sensory branding is a much more intentional approach to marketing. That new-car smell you anticipate while you take a test drive? Actually, it's a manufactured fragrance sprayed into the car, carefully tested to evoke positive feelings among potential buyers. Bang and Olufsen, a Danish high-end stereo manufacturer, carefully designed its remote control units to have a certain distinctive "feel" in a user's hand. Singapore Airlines, which has consistently been rated "the world's best airline," has actually patented the smell of their airplane cabins (it's called Stefan Floridian Waters).

Another form of advertising that has grown dramatically in recent years is product placement: Companies pay to have their products appear prominently in motion pictures and television productions. Do you notice when the star of a film drinks a can of a well-known beverage or drives a particular model of automobile in a car chase? Although viewers may not notice or even be aware of the product, advertisers believe that product placement benefits their bottom lines.

Video technology has advanced even to the point where products can be placed in motion pictures after the fact. Princeton Video, using its L-VIS (live-video insertion) system, placed a Snackwell's cookie box on the kitchen counter of a *Bewitched* rerun from the 1960s, long before the Snackwell's brand existed (Wenner, 2004)! Currently, there's a wave of interest in developing product placement advertising for multiplayer online games, even to the extent that ads can be tailored to specific users based on their preferences and previous buying habits.

Is there any harm in marketing that bombards the senses or even sneaks through to perception undetected? Advertising is a business, and like any business it is fueled by innovation in search of a profit. Perhaps these recent trends are simply the next clever step to get potential buyers to pay attention to a product message. On the other hand, is there a point when "enough is enough"? Do you want to live in a world where every sensory event is trademarked, patented, or test-marketed before reaching your perceptual system? Does the phrase "Today's sunset was brought to you by the makers of . . ." cause you alarm? Where do you stand?

Chapter Review

KEY CONCEPT QUIZ

1. Sensation involves _____ , while perception involves _____ .
   a. organization, coordination
   b. stimulation, interpretation
   c. identification, translation
   d. comprehension, information

2. What process converts physical signals from the environment into neural signals carried by sensory neurons into the central nervous system?
   a. representation
   b. identification
   c. propagation
   d. transduction

3. The smallest intensity needed to just barely detect a stimulus is called
   a. proportional magnitude.
   b. absolute threshold.
   c. just noticeable difference.
   d. Weber's law.

4. The world of light outside the body is linked to the world of vision inside the central nervous system by the
   a. cornea.
   b. lens.
   c. retina.
   d. optic nerve.

5. Light striking the retina, causing a specific pattern of response in the three cone types, leads to our ability to see
   a. motion.
   b. colors.
   c. depth.
   d. shadows.

6. In which part of the brain is the primary visual cortex, where encoded information is systematically mapped into a representation of the visual scene?
   a. the thalamus
   b. the lateral geniculate nucleus
   c. the fovea
   d. area V1

7. Our ability to visually combine details so that we perceive unified objects is explained by
   a. feature integration theory.
   b. illusory conjunction.
   c. synesthesia.
   d. ventral and dorsal streaming.

8. The idea that specialized brain areas represent particular classes of objects is
   a. the modular view.
   b. attentional processing.
   c. distributed representation.
   d. neuron response.

9. The principle of _____ holds that even as sensory signals change, perception remains consistent.
   a. apparent motion
   b. signal detection
   c. perceptual constancy
   d. closure

10. Image-based and parts-based theories both involve the problem of
    a. motion detection.
    b. object identification.
    c. separating figure from ground.
    d. judging proximity.

11. What kind of cues are relative size and linear perspective?
    a. motion-based
    b. binocular
    c. monocular
    d. template

12. What does the frequency of a sound wave determine?
    a. pitch
    b. loudness
    c. sound quality
    d. timbre

13. The placement of our ears on opposite sides of the head is crucial to our ability to
    a. localize sound sources.
    b. determine pitch.
    c. judge intensity.
    d. recognize complexity.

14. The location and type of pain we experience is indicated by signals sent to
    a. the amygdala.
    b. the spinal cord.
    c. pain receptors.
    d. the somatosensory cortex.

15. What best explains why smells can have immediate and powerful effects?
    a. the involvement in smell of brain centers for emotions and memories
    b. the vast number of olfactory receptor neurons we have
    c. our ability to detect odors from pheromones
    d. the fact that different odorant molecules produce varied patterns of activity

KEY TERMS

synesthesia (p. 126)
sensation (p. 127)
perception (p. 127)
transduction (p. 127)
psychophysics (p. 129)
absolute threshold (p. 129)
just noticeable difference (JND) (p. 130)
Weber's law (p. 130)
signal detection theory (p. 131)

sensory adaptation (p. 133)
visual acuity (p. 134)
retina (p. 135)
accommodation (p. 135)
cones (p. 136)
rods (p. 136)
fovea (p. 136)
blind spot (p. 137)
receptive field (p. 138)

trichromatic color representation (p. 140)
color-opponent system (p. 141)
area V1 (p. 141)
visual-form agnosia (p. 143)
binding problem (p. 145)
illusory conjunction (p. 145)
feature integration theory (p. 145)

perceptual constancy (p. 148)
template (p. 150)
monocular depth cues (p. 151)
binocular disparity (p. 152)
apparent motion (p. 154)
change blindness (p. 155)
inattentional blindness (p. 156)
pitch (p. 157)
loudness (p. 157)
timbre (p. 158)

CRITICAL THINKING QUESTIONS

1. Sensory adaptation refers to the fact that sensitivity to prolonged stimulation tends to decline over time. According to the theory of natural selection, inherited characteristics that provide a survival advantage tend to spread throughout the population across generations.

   Why might sensory adaptation have evolved? What survival benefits might it confer to a small animal trying to avoid predators? To a predator trying to hunt prey?

2. When visual light (light waves with particular length, amplitude, and purity) reaches the retina, it is transduced by rods and cones into visual signals, interpreted by the brain as color, brightness, and saturation.

   Many people (including about 5% of all males) inherit a common type of color blindness, in which the cones that normally process green light are mildly deficient; these people have difficulty distinguishing red from green. Unfortunately, in the United States, traffic signals use red and green lights to indicate whether cars should stop or go through an intersection. Why do drivers with red-green color blindness not risk auto accidents every time they approach an intersection?

3. Color perception and motion perception both rely partially on opponent processing, which is why we fall prey to illusions such as color aftereffects and the waterfall illusion.

   How might the concept of aftereffects account for "sea legs," in which a person who has been on a small boat for a few hours has trouble walking on land—because the ground seems to be rising and falling as if the person were still on the boat?

RECOMMENDED READINGS

Cytowic, R. (2003). *The man who tasted shapes.* Cambridge: MIT Press.

Richard Cytowic is a neurologist and author who offers insights on synesthesia. Interspersed with first-person accounts of synesthetic experiences are Cytowic's views on how and why the brain developed as it did and the implications of that evolutionary process for the mind, behavior, and social interaction.

Enns, J. T. (2004). *The thinking eye, the seeing brain.* New York: Norton.

James Enns offers a tour through the visual system, focusing both on sensations in the eye and perception in the brain. This is a fine summary of the key points mentioned in the current chapter and a nice starting point for branching out to other topics in the science of vision.

Goodale, M., & Milner, D. (2004). *Sight unseen.* Oxford, UK: Oxford University Press.

Melvyn Goodale and David Milner explore conscious and unconscious vision in this intriguing book. Their arguments from studies of brain damage and neuroscience lead to the proposal of dual systems in visual perception.

Livingstone, M. S. (2008). *Vision and art: The biology of seeing.* New York: Abrams.

Margaret Livingstone is a neuroscientist who has done important research on the neurobiology of the visual system. Here she discusses how our eyes and brains work together to allow us to perceive and appreciate visual art, discussing painters ranging from da Vinci to Monet and Warhol.

Illusions

http://www.philomel.com/phantom_words/description.html

http://www.faculty.ucr.edu/~rosenblu/VSMcGurk.html

http://www.psychologie.tudresden.de/i1/kaw/diverses%20Material/
www.illusionworks.com/html/hall_of_illusions.html

Visual illusions trick the eye and the brain, and they're admittedly fun to demonstrate and intriguing in their operation. However, there are other types of sensory and perceptual illusions that you may find interesting. Visit some of these websites for demonstrations and more information.

Need more help? Additional resources are located at the book's free companion Web site at:
www.worthpublishers.com/schacter

ANSWERS TO KEY CONCEPT QUIZ

1. b; 2. d; 3. b; 4. c; 5. b; 6. d; 7. a; 8. a; 9. c; 10. b; 11. c; 12. a; 13. a; 14. d; 15. a.

5

Consciousness

nconsciousness is something you don't really appreciate until you need it. Belle Riskin needed it one day on an operating table, when she awoke just as doctors were pushing a breathing tube down her throat. She felt she was choking, but she couldn't see, breathe, scream, or move. Unable even to blink an eye, she couldn't signal to the surgeons that she was conscious. "I was terrified. Why is this happening to me? Why can't I feel my arms? I could feel my heart pounding in my head. It was like being buried alive, but with somebody shoving something down your throat," she explained later. "I knew I was conscious, that something was going on during the surgery. I had just enough awareness to know I was being intubated" (Groves, 2004).

How could this happen? Anesthesia for surgery is supposed to leave the patient unconscious, "feeling no pain," and yet in this case—and in about one in a thousand other operations (Sandin et al., 2000)—the patient regains consciousness at some point and even remembers the experience. Some patients remember pain; others remember the clink of surgical instruments in a pan or the conversations of doctors and nurses. This is *not* how modern surgery is supposed to go, but the problem arises because muscle-relaxing drugs are used to keep the patient from moving involuntarily and making unhelpful contributions to the operation. Then, when the drugs that are given to induce unconsciousness fail to do the job, the patient with extremely relaxed muscles is unable to show or tell doctors that there is a problem.

Waking up in surgery sounds pretty rough all by itself, but this could cause additional complications. The conscious patient could become alarmed and emotional during the operation, spiking blood pressure and heart rate to dangerous levels. Awareness also might lead to later emotional problems. Fortunately, new methods of monitoring wakefulness by measuring the electrical activity of the brain are being developed. One system uses sensors attached to the person's head and gives readings on a scale from 0 (no electrical activity signaling consciousness in the brain) to 100 (fully alert), providing a kind of "consciousness meter." Anesthesiologists using this index deliver anesthetics to keep the patient in the recommended range of 40 to 65 for general anesthesia during surgery; they have found that this system reduces postsurgical reports of consciousness and memory for the surgical experience (Sigl & Chamoun, 1994). One of these devices in the operating room might have helped Belle Riskin settle into the unconsciousness she so dearly needed.

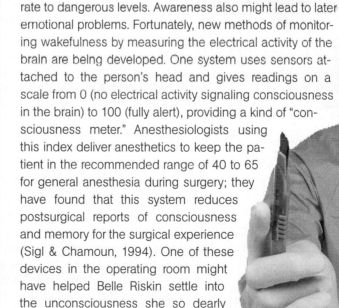

▶ When it's time for surgery, it's great to be unconscious.

consciousness A person's subjective experience of the world and the mind.

phenomenology How things seem to the conscious person.

problem of other minds The fundamental difficulty we have in perceiving the consciousness of others.

MOST OF THE TIME, OF COURSE, CONSCIOUSNESS IS SOMETHING we cherish. How else could we experience a favorite work of art; the familiar strains of an oldie on the radio; the taste of a sweet, juicy peach; or the touch of a loved one's hand? **Consciousness** is *a person's subjective experience of the world and the mind.* Although you might think of consciousness as simply "being awake," the defining feature of consciousness is *experience,* which you have when you're not awake but experiencing a vivid dream. Conscious experience is essential to what it means to be human. The anesthesiologist's dilemma in trying to monitor Belle Riskin's consciousness is a stark reminder, though, that it is impossible for one person to experience another's consciousness. Your consciousness is utterly private, a world of personal experience that only you can know.

How can this private world be studied? We'll begin by examining consciousness directly, trying to understand what it is like and how it compares with the mind's *un*conscious processes. Then we'll examine its altered states: the departures from normal, everyday waking that occur during altered states such as sleep and dreams, intoxication with alcohol and other drugs, and hypnosis and meditation. Like the traveler who learns the meaning of *home* by roaming far away, we can learn the meaning of consciousness by exploring its exotic variations.

Conscious and Unconscious: The Mind's Eye, Open and Closed

What does it feel like to be you right now? It probably feels as though you are somewhere inside your head, looking out at the world through your eyes. You can feel your hands on this book, perhaps, and notice the position of your body or the sounds in the room when you orient yourself toward them. If you shut your eyes, you may be able to imagine things in your mind, even though all the while thoughts and feelings come and go, passing through your imagination. But where are "you," really? And how is it that this theater of consciousness gives you a view of some things in your world and your mind but not others? The theater in your mind doesn't have seating for more than one, making it difficult to share what's on our mental screen with our friends, a researcher, or even ourselves in precisely the same way a second time. We'll look first at the difficulty of studying consciousness directly, examine the nature of consciousness (what it is that can be seen in this mental theater), and then explore the unconscious mind (what is *not* visible to the mind's eye).

"We keep this section closed off."

The Mysteries of Consciousness

Other sciences, such as physics, chemistry, and biology, have the great luxury of studying *objects,* things that we all can see. Psychology studies objects, too, looking at people and their brains and behaviors, but it has the unique challenge of also trying to make sense of *subjects.* A physicist is not concerned with what it is like to be a neutron, but psychologists hope to understand what it is like to be a human, that is, grasping the subjective perspectives of the people that they study. Psychologists hope to include an understanding of **phenomenology,** *how things seem to the conscious person,* in their understanding of mind and behavior. After all, consciousness is an extraordinary human property that could well be unique to us. But including phenomenology in psychology brings up mysteries pondered by great thinkers almost since the beginning of thinking. Let's look at two of the more vexing mysteries of consciousness: the problem of other minds and the mind/body problem.

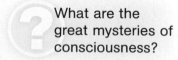

What are the great mysteries of consciousness?

The Problem of Other Minds

One great mystery is called the **problem of other minds,** *the fundamental difficulty we have in perceiving the consciousness of others.* How do you know that anyone else is conscious? They tell you that they are conscious, of course, and are often willing to describe in depth how they feel, how they think, what they are experiencing, and how good or how bad it all is. But perhaps they are just *saying* these things. There is no clear way to distinguish a conscious person from someone who might do and say all the same things as a conscious person but who is *not* conscious. Philosophers have called this hypothetical nonconscious person a "zombie," in reference to the living-yet-dead creatures of horror films (Chalmers, 1996). A philosopher's zombie could talk about experiences ("The lights are so bright!") and even seem to react to them (wincing and turning away) but might not be having any inner experience at all. No one knows whether there could be such a zombie, but then again, because of the problem of other minds, none of us will ever know for sure that another person is *not* a zombie.

Even the "consciousness meter" used by anesthesiologists falls short. It certainly doesn't give the anesthesiologist any special insight into what it is like to be the patient on the operating table; it only predicts whether patients will *say* they were conscious. We simply lack the ability to directly perceive the consciousness of others. In short, you are the only thing in the universe you will ever truly know what it is like to be.

The problem of other minds also means there is no way you can tell if another person's experience of anything is at all like yours. Although you know what the color red looks like to you, for instance, you cannot know whether it looks the same to other people. Maybe they're seeing what you see as blue and just *calling* it red in a consistent way. If their inner experience "looks" blue, but they say it looks hot and is the color of a tomato, you'll never be able to tell that their experience differs from yours. Of course, most people have come to trust each other in describing their inner lives, reaching the general assumption that other human minds are pretty much like their own. But they don't know this for a fact, and they can't know it directly.

How do people perceive other minds? Researchers conducting a large online survey asked people to compare the minds of 13 different targets, such as a baby, chimp, robot, man, and woman, on 18 different mental capacities, such as feeling pain, pleasure, hunger, and consciousness (see **FIGURE 5.1**) (Gray, Gray, & Wegner, 2007). Respondents who were judging the mental capacity to feel pain, for example, compared pairs of targets: Is a frog or a dog more able to feel pain? Is a baby or a robot more able to feel pain? Is a 7-week-old fetus or a man in a persistent vegetative state more able to feel pain? When the researchers examined all the comparisons on the different mental capacities with

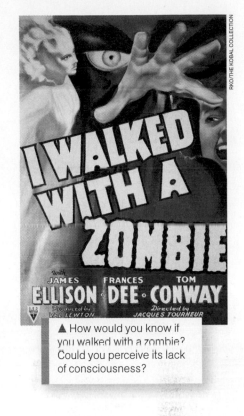

▲ How would you know if you walked with a zombie? Could you perceive its lack of consciousness?

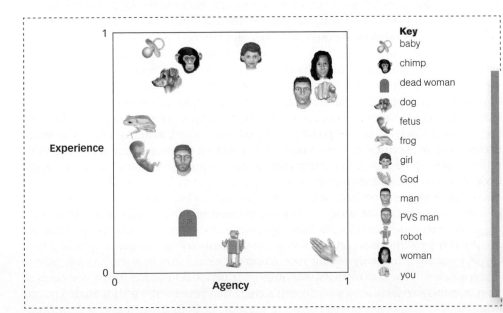

Key
baby
chimp
dead woman
dog
fetus
frog
girl
God
man
PVS man
robot
woman
you

◄ **FIGURE 5.1**
Dimensions of Mind Perception When participants judged the mental capacities of 13 targets, two dimensions of mind perception were discovered (Gray et al., 2007). Participants perceived minds as varying in the capacity for experience (such as abilities to feel pain or pleasure) and in the capacity for agency (such as abilities to plan or exert self-control). They perceived normal adult humans (male, female, or "you," the respondent) to have minds on both dimensions, whereas other targets were perceived to have reduced experience or agency. The man in a persistent vegetative state ("PVS man"), for example, was judged to have only some experience and very little agency.

mind/body problem The issue of how the mind is related to the brain and the body.

the computational technique of factor analysis (see Chapter 10,) they found two dimensions of mind perception. People judge minds according to the capacity for *experience* (such as the ability to feel pain, pleasure, hunger, consciousness, anger, or fear) and the capacity for *agency* (such as the ability for self-control, planning, memory, or thought). As shown in Figure 5.1, respondents rated some targets as having little experience or agency (the dead person), others as having experiences but little agency (the baby), and yet others as having both experience and agency (adult humans). Still others were perceived to have agency without experiences (the robot, God). The perception of minds, then, involves more than just whether something has a mind. People appreciate that minds both have experiences and act as agents that perform actions.

Ultimately, the problem of other minds is a problem for psychological science. As you'll remember from Chapter 2, the scientific method requires that any observation made by one scientist should, in principle, be available for observation by any other scientist. But if other minds aren't observable, how can consciousness be a topic of scientific study? One radical solution is to eliminate consciousness from psychology entirely and follow the other sciences into total objectivity by renouncing the study of *anything* mental. This was the solution offered by behaviorism, and it turned out to have its own shortcomings, as you saw in Chapter 1. Despite the problem of other minds, modern psychology has embraced the study of consciousness. The astonishing richness of mental life simply cannot be ignored.

The Mind/Body Problem

Another mystery of consciousness is the **mind/body problem**, *the issue of how the mind is related to the brain and body*. French philosopher and mathematician René Descartes (1596–1650) is famous for proposing, among other things, that the human body is a machine made of physical matter but that the human mind or soul is a separate entity made of a "thinking substance." He suggested that the mind has its effects on the brain and body through the pineal gland, a small structure located near the center of the brain (see **FIGURE 5.2**). In fact, the pineal gland is not even a nerve structure but rather is an endocrine gland quite poorly equipped to serve as a center of human consciousness. We now know that, far from the tiny connection between mind and brain in the pineal gland that was proposed by Descartes, the mind and brain are connected everywhere to each other. In other words, "the mind is what the brain does" (Minsky, 1986, p. 287).

But Descartes was right in pointing out the difficulty of reconciling the physical body with the mind. Most psychologists assume that mental events are intimately tied to brain events, such that every thought, perception, or feeling is associated with a particular pattern of activation of neurons in the brain (see Chapter 3). Thinking about a particular duck, for instance, occurs with a unique array of neural connections and activations. If the neurons repeat that pattern, then you must be thinking of the duck; conversely, if you think of the duck, the brain activity occurs in that pattern.

One telling set of studies, however, suggests that the brain's activities *precede* the activities of the conscious mind. The electrical activity in the brains of volunteers was measured using sensors placed on their scalps as they repeatedly decided when to move a hand (Libet, 1985). Participants were also asked to indicate exactly when they consciously chose to move by reporting the position of a dot moving rapidly around the face of a clock just at the point of the decision (**FIGURE 5.3***a*). As a rule, the brain begins to show electrical activity around half a second before a voluntary action (535 milliseconds, to be exact). This makes sense since brain activity certainly seems to be necessary to get an action started.

What this experiment revealed, though, was that the brain also started to show electrical activity before the person's conscious decision to move. As shown in **FIGURE 5.3***b*, these studies found that the brain becomes active more than 300 milliseconds before participants report that they are consciously trying to move. The feeling that you are consciously willing your actions, it seems, may be a result rather than a cause of your brain activity. Although your personal intuition is that you *think* of an action and *then* do it, these experiments suggest that your brain is getting started before *either* the thinking or the doing, preparing the way for both thought and action. Quite

▼ FIGURE 5.2

Seat of the Soul Descartes imagined that the seat of the soul—and consciousness—might reside in the pineal gland located in the ventricles of the brain. This original drawing from Descartes (1662) shows the pineal gland (H) nicely situated for a soul, right in the middle of the brain.

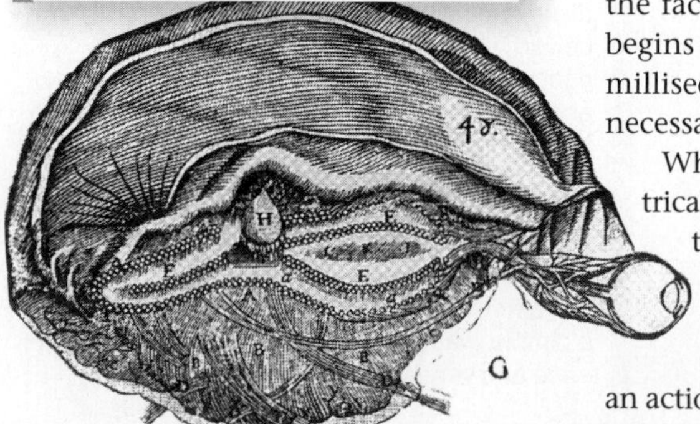

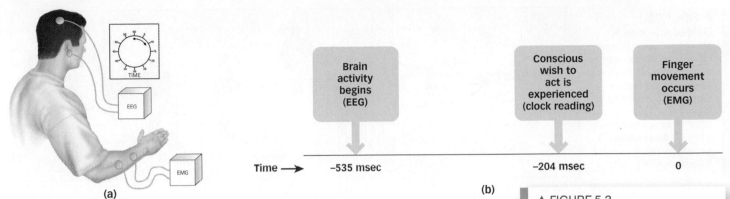

(a)

| Brain activity begins (EEG) | Conscious wish to act is experienced (clock reading) | Finger movement occurs (EMG) |

Time ⟶   −535 msec   −204 msec   0

(b)

▲ FIGURE 5.3
The Timing of Conscious Will (a) In Benjamin Libet's experiments, the participant was asked to move fingers at will while simultaneously watching a dot move around the face of a clock to mark the moment at which the action was consciously willed. Meanwhile, EEG sensors timed the onset of brain activation and EMG sensors timed the muscle movement. (b) The experiment showed that brain activity (EEG) precedes the willed movement of the finger (EMG) but that the reported time of consciously willing the finger to move follows the brain activity.

simply, it may appear to us that our minds are leading our brains and bodies, but the order of events may be the other way around (Haggard & Tsakiris, 2009; Wegner, 2002).

? What comes first: brain activity or thinking?

Consciousness has its mysteries, but psychologists like a challenge. Although researchers may not be able to see the consciousness of others or know exactly how consciousness arises from the brain, this does not prevent them from collecting people's reports of conscious experiences and learning how these reports reveal the nature of consciousness. We'll consider that topic next.

The Nature of Consciousness

How would you describe your own consciousness? Researchers examining people's descriptions suggest that consciousness has four basic properties (intentionality, unity, selectivity, and transience), that it occurs on different levels, and that it includes a range of different contents. Let's examine each of these points in turn.

Four Basic Properties

The first property of consciousness is *intentionality,* the quality of being directed toward an object. Consciousness is always *about* something. Psychologists have tried to measure the relationship between consciousness and its objects, examining the size and duration of the relationship. How long can consciousness be directed toward an object, and how many objects can it take on at one time? Researchers have found that conscious attention is limited. Despite all the lush detail you see in your mind's eye, the kaleidoscope of sights and sounds and feelings and thoughts, the object of your consciousness at any one moment is just a small part of all of this (see **FIGURE 5.4**). To describe how this limitation works, psychologists refer to three other properties of consciousness: unity, selectivity, and transience.

▼ FIGURE 5.4
Bellotto's Dresden and Close-up The people on the bridge in the distance look very finely detailed in *View of Dresden with the Frauenkirche at Left,* by Bernardo Bellotto (1720–80) (left). However, when you examine the detail closely (right), you find that the people are made of brushstrokes merely *suggesting* people—an arm here, a torso there. Consciousness produces a similar impression of "filling in," as it seems to consist of extreme detail even in areas that are peripheral (Dennett, 1991).

▶ FIGURE 5.5
Divided Attention Research participants presented with two different games (A and B) could easily follow each game separately. When participants tried to follow the action in the two different games simultaneously (C), they performed remarkably poorly (Neisser & Becklen, 1975).

(a)

(b)

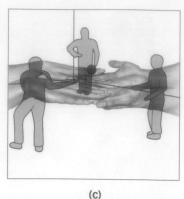

(c)

The second basic property of consciousness is *unity,* or resistance to division. This property becomes clear when you try to attend to more than one thing at a time. You may wishfully think that you can study and watch TV simultaneously, for example, but research suggests not. One study had research participants divide their attention by reacting to two games superimposed on a television screen (see **FIGURE 5.5**). They had to push one button when one person slapped another's hands in the first game and push another button when a ball was passed in the second game. The participants were easily able to follow one game at a time, but their performance took a nosedive when they tried to follow both simultaneously. Their error rate when attending to the two tasks was eight times greater than when attending to either task alone (Neisser & Becklen, 1975). Your attempts to study, in other words, could seriously interfere with a full appreciation of your TV show.

Why shouldn't you study and watch TV at the same time?

The third property of consciousness is *selectivity,* the capacity to include some objects but not others. This property is shown through studies of **dichotic listening,** *in which people wearing headphones are presented with different messages in each ear.* Research participants were instructed to repeat aloud the words they heard in one ear while a different message was presented to the other ear (Cherry, 1953). As a result of focusing on the words they were supposed to repeat, participants noticed little of the second message, often not even realizing that at some point it changed from English to German! So, consciousness *filters out* some information. At the same time, participants did notice when the voice in the unattended ear changed from a male's to a female's, suggesting that the selectivity of consciousness can also work to *tune in* other information.

How does consciousness decide what to filter in and what to tune out? The conscious system is most inclined to select information of special interest to the person. For example, in what has come to be known as the **cocktail party phenomenon,** *people tune in one message even while they filter out others nearby.* In the dichotic listening situation, for example, research participants are especially likely to notice if their own name is spoken into the unattended ear (Moray, 1959). Perhaps you, too, have noticed how abruptly your attention is diverted from whatever conversation you are having when someone else within earshot at the party mentions your name. Selectivity is not only a property of waking consciousness, however; the mind works this way in other states. People are more sensitive to their own name than others' names, for example, even during sleep (Oswald, Taylor, & Triesman, 1960). This is why when you are trying to wake someone, it is best to use the person's name (particularly if you want to sleep with that person again).

The fourth and final basic property of consciousness is *transience,* or the tendency to change. Consciousness wiggles and fidgets like that toddler in the seat behind you on the airplane. The mind wanders not just sometimes, but incessantly, from one "right now" to the next "right now" and then on to the next (Wegner, 1997). William James, whom you met way back in Chapter 1, famously described consciousness as a stream: "Consciousness . . . does not appear to itself chopped up in bits. Such words as

▼ Participants in a dichotic listening experiment hear different messages played to the right and left ear and may be asked to "shadow" one of the messages by repeating it aloud.

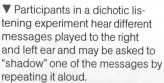

'chain' or 'train' do not describe it. . . . It is nothing jointed; it flows. A 'river' or a 'stream' are the metaphors by which it is most naturally described" (James, 1890, Vol. 1, p. 239). Books written in the "stream of consciousness" style, such as James Joyce's *Ulysses,* illustrate the whirling, chaotic, and constantly changing flow of consciousness. Here's an excerpt:

> I wished I could have picked every morsel of that chicken out of my fingers it was so tasty and browned and as tender as anything only for I didn't want to eat everything on my plate those forks and fishslicers were hallmarked silver too I wish I had some I could easily have slipped a couple into my muff when I was playing with them then always hanging out of them for money in a restaurant for the bit you put down your throat we have to be thankful for our mangy cup of tea itself as a great compliment to be noticed the way the world is divided in any case if its going to go on I want at least two other good chemises for one thing and but I dont know what kind of drawers he likes none at all I think didn't he say yes and half the girls in Gibraltar never wore them either naked as God made them that Andalusian singing her Manola she didn't make much secret of what she hadnt yes and the second pair of silkette stockings is laddered after one days wear I could have brought them back to Lewers this morning and kicked up a row and made that one change them only not to upset myself and run the risk of walking into him and ruining the whole thing and one of those kidfitting corsets Id want advertised cheap in the Gentlewoman with elastic gores on the hips he saved the one I have but thats no good what did they say they give a delightful figure line 11/6 obviating that unsightly broad appearance across the lower back to reduce flesh my belly is a bit too big Ill have to knock off the stout at dinner or am I getting too fond of it (1994, p. 741)

The stream of consciousness may flow in this way partly because of the limited capacity of the conscious mind. We humans can hold only so much information in mind, after all, so when more information is selected, some of what is currently there must disappear. As a result, our focus of attention keeps changing. The stream of consciousness flows so inevitably that it even changes our perspective when we view a constant object like a Necker Cube (see **FIGURE 5.6**).

Levels of Consciousness

Consciousness can also be understood as having levels, ranging from minimal consciousness to full consciousness to self consciousness. These levels of consciousness would probably all register as "conscious" on that wakefulness meter for surgery patients you read about at the beginning of the chapter. The levels of consciousness that psychologists distinguish are not a matter of degree of overall brain activity but instead involve different qualities of awareness of the world and of the self.

In its minimal form, consciousness is just a connection between the person and the world. When you sense the sun coming in through the window, for example, you might turn toward the light. Such **minimal consciousness** is *consciousness that occurs when the mind inputs sensations and may output behavior* (Armstrong, 1980). This level of consciousness is a kind of sensory awareness and responsiveness, something that could even happen when someone pokes you during sleep and you turn over. Something seems to register in your mind, at least in the sense that you experience it, but you may not think at all about having had the experience. It could be that animals or, for that matter, even plants can have this minimal level of consciousness. But because of the problem of other minds and the notorious reluctance of animals and plants to talk to us, we can't know for sure that they *experience* the things that make them respond. At least in the case of humans, we can safely assume that there is something it "feels like" to be them and that when they're awake, they are at least minimally conscious.

Human consciousness is often more than minimal, of course, but what exactly gets added? Consider the glorious feeling of waking up on a spring morning as rays of sun stream across your pillow. It's not just that you are having this experience; being fully conscious means that you are also *aware* that you are having this experience. The critical ingredient that accompanies **full consciousness** is that you *know and are able to report your mental state.* That's a subtle distinction; being fully conscious means that you are aware of

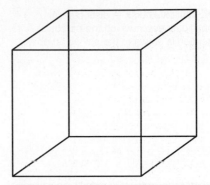

▲ FIGURE 5.6
The Necker Cube This cube has the property of reversible perspective in that you can bring one or the other of its two square faces to the front in your mind's eye. Although it may take awhile to reverse the figure at first, once people have learned to do it, they can reverse it regularly, about once every 3 seconds (Gomez et al., 1995). The stream of consciousness flows even when the target is a constant object.

dichotic listening A task in which people wearing headphones hear different messages presented to each ear.

cocktail party phenomenon A phenomenon in which people tune in one message even while they filter out others nearby.

minimal consciousness A low-level kind of sensory awareness and responsiveness that occurs when the mind inputs sensations and may output behavior.

full consciousness Consciousness in which you know and are able to report your mental state.

self-consciousness A distinct level of consciousness in which the person's attention is drawn to the self as an object.

having a mental state while you are experiencing the mental state itself. When you have a hurt leg and mindlessly rub it, for instance, your pain may be minimally conscious. After all, you seem to be experiencing pain because you have acted and are indeed rubbing your leg. It is only when you realize that it hurts, though, that the pain becomes fully conscious. Full consciousness involves not only thinking about things but also thinking about the fact that you are thinking about things (Jaynes, 1976) (see the Hot Science box).

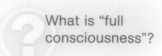 **What is "full consciousness"?**

Full consciousness involves a certain consciousness of oneself; the person notices the self in a particular mental state ("Here I am, reading this sentence"). However, this is not quite the same thing as *self*-consciousness. Sometimes consciousness is entirely flooded with the self ("Not only am I reading this sentence, but I have a blemish on the end of my nose today that makes me feel like guiding a sleigh"). Self-consciousness focuses on the self to the exclusion of almost everything else. William James (1890) and other theorists have suggested that **self-consciousness** is yet another distinct level of consciousness in which *the person's attention is drawn to the self as an object* (Morin, 2005). Most people report experiencing such self-consciousness when they are embarrassed; when they find themselves the focus of attention in a group; when someone focuses a camera on them; or when they are deeply introspective about their thoughts, feelings, or personal qualities.

HOT SCIENCE

The Mind Wanders

Yes, the mind wanders. Ideally, it doesn't wander so much that it can't finish this paragraph. But it does tend to come and go over time, not only changing topics as it goes, but sometimes simply "zoning out." You've no doubt had experiences of reading and suddenly realizing that you have not even been processing what you read. Even while your eyes are dutifully following the lines of print, at some point you begin to think about something else—and only later catch yourself having wandered.

Our minds most often wander when we are engaged in automated, repetitive tasks or in tasks that are so difficult we can't even follow what's going on (Smallwood & Schooler, 2006). And this happens a lot. For one study of mindwandering, students reading passages from *War and Peace* were asked to push a button each time they noticed their thoughts straying (Schooler, Reichle, & Halpern, 2005). In 45 minutes of reading, they averaged more than five reported zone-outs. And this included only the times that they *noticed*. When other readers doing this task were additionally stopped every two to four minutes and probed for whether their minds were wandering at that time, they usually reported one or more added instances of being "caught" wandering beyond those they reported spontaneously. Sometimes the mind wanders and we don't even know this is happening.

◄ When the bus driver's mind wandered, the bus wandered too.

AP PHOTO/TOBY TALBOT

Knowing that our minds are wandering would seem to be important. A Green Mountain Transit bus driver in Barre, Vermont, probably didn't know his mind was wandering, for example, when he ran his bus into a line of traffic stopped for a construction zone ("Bus driver charged with interstate bus crash," 2009). To avoid bus crashes and other calamities, we need to know when our minds are wandering. A lack of awareness of wandering may in fact be one of the reasons that driving under the influence of alcohol can be so dangerous. To test alcohol effects, researchers ran the *War and Peace* reading study again, this time with people who had been served vodka and cranberry juice before reading (Sayette, Reichle, & Schooler, 2009). These readers reported less mindwandering than did readers who were sober. However, they were actually wandering more, but were unaware of it. Students reading after drinking who were repeatedly probed to see if they were wandering were caught far more often than were those who didn't drink. And on a follow-up quiz, the drinkers had also forgotten much more of the text. When alcohol or other distractions make the mind wander, we may remain blissfully unaware of our inattention. Best not to be driving a bus at this time.

Self-consciousness brings with it a tendency to evaluate yourself and notice your shortcomings. Looking in a mirror, for example, is all it takes to make people evaluate themselves—thinking not just about their looks but also about whether they are good or bad in other ways. People go out of their way to avoid mirrors when they've done something they are ashamed of (Duval & Wicklund, 1972). Self-consciousness can certainly spoil a good mood, so much so that a tendency to be chronically self-conscious is associated with depression (Pyszczynski, Holt, & Greenberg, 1987). However, because it makes people self-critical, the self-consciousness that results when people see their own mirror images can make them briefly more helpful, more cooperative, and less aggressive (Gibbons, 1990). Perhaps everyone would be a bit more civilized if mirrors were held up for them to see themselves as objects of their own scrutiny.

Most animals can't follow this path to civilization. The typical dog, cat, or bird seems mystified by a mirror, ignoring it or acting as though there is some other critter back there. However, chimpanzees that have spent time with mirrors sometimes behave in ways that suggest they recognize themselves in a mirror. To examine this, researchers painted an odorless red dye over the eyebrow of an anesthetized chimp and then watched when the awakened chimp was presented with a mirror (Gallup, 1977b). If the chimp interpreted the mirror image as a representation of some other chimp with an unusual approach to cosmetics, we would expect it just to look at the mirror or perhaps to reach toward it. But the chimp reached toward its *own eye* as it looked into the mirror—not the mirror image—suggesting that it recognized the image as a reflection of itself.

Versions of this experiment have now been repeated with many different animals, and it turns out that, like humans, animals such as chimpanzees and orangutans (Gallup, 1997a), possibly dolphins (Reiss & Marino, 2001), and maybe even elephants (Plotnik, de Waal, & Reiss, 2006) and magpies (Prior, Schwartz, & Güntürkün, 2008) recognize their own mirror images. Dogs, cats, monkeys, and gorillas have been tested, too, but don't seem to know they are looking at themselves. Even humans don't have self-recognition right away. Infants don't recognize themselves in mirrors until they've reached about 18 months of age (Lewis & Brooks-Gunn, 1979). The experience of self-consciousness, as measured by self-recognition in mirrors, is limited to a few animals and to humans only after a certain stage of development.

Conscious Contents

What's on your mind? For that matter, what's on everybody's mind? One way to learn what is on people's minds is to ask them, and much research has called on people simply to *think aloud.* A more systematic approach is the *experience sampling technique,* in which people are asked to report their conscious experiences at particular times. Equipped with electronic beepers or called on cell phones, for example, participants are asked to record their current thoughts when asked at random times throughout the day (Csikszentmihalyi & Larson, 1987).

Experience sampling studies show that consciousness is dominated by the immediate environment, what is seen, felt, heard, tasted, and smelled—all are at the forefront of the mind. Much of consciousness beyond this orientation to the environment turns

▲ Self-consciousness is a curse and a blessing. Looking in a mirror can make people evaluate themselves on deeper attributes such as honesty as well as superficial ones such as looks.

▼ A chimpanzee tried to wipe off the red dye on its eyebrow in the Gallup experiment. This suggests that some animals recognize themselves in the mirror.

Dilbert

OKAY, LET ME THINK ALOUD FOR A MINUTE.

THE COST WILL BE $3,000...LOSING FOCUS...MONKEYS ARE FUNNY...MY TONGUE IS DIGESTING IN MY MOUTH.

THAT DIDN'T HELP AS MUCH AS I HAD HOPED.

©SCOTT ADAMS/DIST. BY UNITED FEATURES SYNDICATE, INC.

mental control The attempt to change conscious states of mind.

thought suppression The conscious avoidance of a thought.

rebound effect of thought suppression The tendency of a thought to return to consciousness with greater frequency following suppression.

TABLE 5.1

What's on Your Mind? College Students' Current Concerns

Current Concern Category	Example	Frequency of Students Who Mentioned the Concern
Family	Gain better relations with immediate family	40%
Roommate	Change attitude or behavior of roommate	29%
Household	Clean room	52%
Friends	Make new friends	42%
Dating	Desire to date a certain person	24%
Sexual intimacy	Abstaining from sex	16%
Health	Diet and exercise	85%
Employment	Get a summer job	33%
Education	Go to graduate school	43%
Social activities	Gain acceptance into a campus organization	34%
Religious	Attend church more	51%
Financial	Pay rent or bills	8%
Government	Change government policy	14%

to the person's *current concerns,* or what the person is thinking about repeatedly (Klinger, 1975). **TABLE 5.1** shows the results of a Minnesota study where 175 college students were asked to report their current concerns (Goetzman, Hughes, & Klinger, 1994). The researchers sorted the concerns into the categories shown in the table. Keep in mind that these concerns are ones the students didn't mind reporting to psychologists; their private preoccupations may have been different and probably far more interesting.

Think for a moment about your own current concerns. What topics have been on your mind the most in the past day or two? Your mental "to do" list may include things you want to get, keep, avoid, work on, remember, and so on (Little, 1993). Items on the list often pop into mind, sometimes even with an emotional punch ("The test in this class is tomorrow!"). People in one study had their skin conductance level (SCL) measured to assess their emotional responses (Nikula, Klinger, & Larson-Gutman, 1993). SCL sensors attached to their fingers indicated when their skin became moist—a good indication that they were thinking about something distressing. Once in a while, SCL would rise spontaneously, and at these times the researchers quizzed the participants about their conscious thoughts. These emotional moments, compared to those when SCL was normal, often corresponded with a current concern popping into mind. Thoughts that are not emotional all by themselves can still come to mind with an emotional bang when they are topics of our current concern.

Current concerns do not seem all that concerning, however, during *daydreaming,* a state of consciousness in which a seemingly purposeless flow of thoughts comes to mind. When thoughts drift along this way, it may seem as if you are just wasting time. The brain, however, is active even when there is no specific task at hand. This mental work done in daydreaming was examined in an fMRI study of people resting in the scanner (Mason et al., 2007). Usually, people in brain-scanning studies don't have time to daydream much because they are kept busy with mental tasks—scans

▼ One concern on many students' minds is diet and exercise to keep in shape.

AP PHOTO/MARY ANN CHASTAIN

cost money and researchers want to get as much data as possible for their bucks. But when people are *not* busy, they still show a widespread pattern of activation in many areas of the brain—now known as the *default network* (Gusnard & Raichle, 2001). The study by Mason et al. (2007) revealed that this network became activated whenever people worked on a mental task that they knew so well that they could daydream while doing it (see **FIG-URE 5.7**). The areas of the default network are known to be involved in thinking about social life, about the self, and about the past and future—all the usual haunts of the daydreaming mind (Mitchell, 2006).

What part of the brain is active during daydreaming?

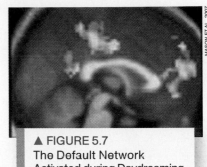

▲ FIGURE 5.7
The Default Network Activated during Daydreaming An fMRI scan shows that many areas, known as the default network, are active when the person is not given a specific mental task to perform during the scan (Mason et al., 2007).

The current concerns that populate consciousness can sometimes get the upper hand, transforming daydreams or everyday thoughts into rumination and worry. Thoughts that return again and again, or problem-solving attempts that never seem to succeed, can come to dominate consciousness. When this happens, people may exert **mental control**, *the attempt to change conscious states of mind*. For example, someone troubled by a recurring worry about the future ("What if I can't get a decent job when I graduate?") might choose to try not to think about this because it causes too much anxiety and uncertainty. Whenever this thought comes to mind, the person engages in **thought suppression**, the *conscious avoidance of a thought*. This may seem like a perfectly sensible strategy because it eliminates the worry and allows the person to move on to think about something else.

Or does it? The great Russian novelist Fyodor Dostoevsky (1863–1955) remarked on the difficulty of thought suppression: "Try to pose for yourself this task: not to think of a polar bear, and you will see that the cursed thing will come to mind every minute." Inspired by this observation, Daniel Wegner and his colleagues gave people this exact task in the laboratory (1987). Participants were asked to try not to think about a white bear for 5 minutes while they recorded all their thoughts aloud into a tape recorder. In addition, they were asked to ring a bell if the thought of a white bear came to mind. On average, they mentioned the white bear or rang the bell (indicating the thought) more than once per minute. Thought suppression simply didn't work and instead produced a flurry of returns of the unwanted thought. What's more, when some research participants later were specifically asked to change tasks and deliberately *think* about a white bear, they became oddly preoccupied with it. A graph of their bell rings in **FIGURE 5.8** shows that these participants had the white bear come to mind far more often than did people who had only been asked to think about the bear from the outset, with no prior suppression. This **rebound effect of thought suppression**,

"Are you not thinking what I'm not thinking?"

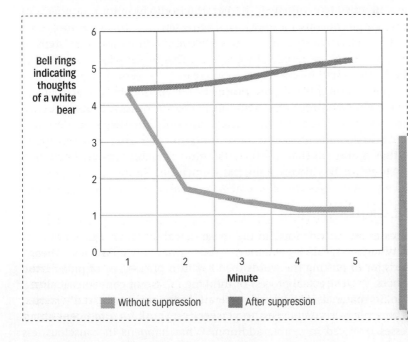

◀ FIGURE 5.8
Rebound Effect Research participants were first asked to try not to think about a white bear, and then they were asked to think about it and to ring a bell whenever it came to mind. Compared to those who were simply asked to think about a bear without prior suppression, those people who *first* suppressed the thought showed a rebound of increased thinking (Wegner et al., 1987).

▶ Go ahead, look away from the book for a minute and try not to think about a white bear.

the tendency of a thought to return to consciousness with greater frequency following suppression, suggests that attempts at mental control may be difficult indeed. The act of trying to suppress a thought may itself cause that thought to return to consciousness in a robust way.

As with thought suppression, other attempts to "steer" consciousness in any direction can result in mental states that are precisely the opposite of those desired. How ironic: Trying to consciously achieve one task may produce precisely the opposite outcome! These ironic effects seem most likely to occur when the person is distracted or under stress. People who are distracted while they are trying to get into a good mood, for example, tend to become sad (Wegner, Erber, & Zanakos, 1993), and those who are distracted while trying to relax actually become more anxious than those who are not trying to relax (Wegner, Broome, & Blumberg, 1997). Likewise, an attempt not to overshoot a golf putt, undertaken during distraction, often yields the unwanted overshot (Wegner, Ansfield, & Pilloff, 1998). The theory of **ironic processes of mental control** proposes that such *ironic errors occur because the mental process that monitors errors can itself produce them* (Wegner, 1994a, 2009). In the attempt not to think of a white bear, for instance, a small part of the mind is ironically *searching* for the white bear.

This ironic monitoring process is not present in consciousness. After all, trying *not* to think of something would be useless if monitoring the progress of suppression required keeping that target in consciousness. For example, if trying not to think of a white bear meant that you consciously kept repeating to yourself, "No white bear! No white bear!" then you've failed before you've begun: That thought is present in consciousness even as you strive to eliminate it. Rather, the ironic monitor is a process of the mind that works *outside* of consciousness, making us sensitive to all the things we do not want to think, feel, or do so that we can notice and consciously take steps to regain control if these things come back to mind. As this unconscious monitoring whirs along in the background, it unfortunately increases the person's sensitivity to the very thought that is unwanted. Ironic processes are mental functions that are needed for effective mental control—they help in the process of banishing a thought from consciousness—but they can sometimes yield the very failure they seem designed to overcome. Ironic effects of mental control arise from processes that work outside of consciousness, so they remind us that much of the mind's machinery may be hidden from our view, lying outside the fringes of our experience.

The Unconscious Mind

Many mental processes are unconscious, in the sense that they occur without our experience of them. When we speak, for instance, "We are not really conscious either of the search for words, or of putting the words together into phrases, or of putting the phrases into sentences. . . . The actual process of thinking . . . is not conscious at all . . . only its preparation, its materials, and its end result are consciously perceived" (Jaynes, 1976). Just to put the role of consciousness in perspective, think for a moment about the mental processes involved in simple addition. What happens in consciousness

ironic processes of mental control Mental processes that can produce ironic errors because monitoring for errors can itself produce them.

dynamic unconscious An active system encompassing a lifetime of hidden memories, the person's deepest instincts and desires, and the person's inner struggle to control these forces.

repression A mental process that removes unacceptable thoughts and memories from consciousness.

between hearing a problem ("What's 4 plus 5?") and thinking of the answer ("9")? Probably nothing—the answer just appears in the mind. But this is a piece of calculation that must take at least a bit of thinking. After all, at a very young age you may have had to solve such problems by counting on your fingers. Now that you don't have to do that anymore (. . . right?), the answer seems to pop into your head automatically, by virtue of a process that doesn't require you to be aware of any underlying steps and, for that matter, doesn't even *allow* you to be aware of the steps. The answer just suddenly appears.

In the early part of the 20th century, when structuralist psychologists, such as Wilhelm Wundt, believed that introspection was the best method of research (see Chapter 1), research volunteers trained in describing their thoughts tried to discern what happens in such cases—when a simple problem brings to mind a simple answer (e.g., Watt, 1905). They drew the same blank you probably did. Nothing conscious seems to bridge this gap, but the answer comes from somewhere, and this emptiness points to the unconscious mind. To explore these hidden recesses, we can look at the classical theory of the unconscious introduced by Sigmund Freud and then at the modern cognitive psychology of unconscious mental processes.

▲ There are no conscious steps between hearing an easy problem ("What's 4 plus 5?") and thinking of the answer—unless you have to count on your fingers.

Freudian Unconscious

The true champion of the unconscious mind was Sigmund Freud. As you read in Chapter 1, Freud's psychoanalytic theory viewed conscious thought as the surface of a much deeper mind made up of unconscious processes. Far more than just a collection of hidden processes, Freud described a **dynamic unconscious**—*an active system encompassing a lifetime of hidden memories, the person's deepest instincts and desires, and the person's inner struggle to control these forces.* The dynamic unconscious might contain hidden sexual thoughts about one's parents, for example, or destructive urges aimed at a helpless infant—the kinds of thoughts people keep secret from others and may not even acknowledge to themselves. According to Freud's theory, the unconscious is a force to be held in check by **repression**, *a mental process that removes unacceptable thoughts and memories from consciousness and keeps them in the unconscious.* Without repression, a person might think, do, or say every unconscious impulse or animal urge, no matter how selfish or immoral. With repression, these desires are held in the recesses of the dynamic unconscious.

Freud looked for evidence of the unconscious mind in speech errors and lapses of consciousness, or what are commonly called "Freudian slips." Forgetting the name of

What do Freudian slips tell us about the unconscious mind?

someone you dislike, for example, is a slip that seems to have special meaning. Freud believed that errors are not random and instead have some surplus meaning that may appear to have been created by an intelligent unconscious mind, even though the person consciously disavows them. For example, in the heat of his successful 2008 campaign for the presidency, Barack Obama slipped by referring to "my Muslim faith" in a televised interview. He is not Muslim and noted this immediately, but reporters seemed to agree with Freud, wondering at length what this slip might mean for the real loyalties of the unusually African American candidate.

Did Obama's slip mean anything? One experiment revealed that slips of speech can indeed be prompted by a person's pressing concerns (Motley & Baars, 1979). Research participants in one group were told they might receive minor electric shocks, whereas those in another group heard no mention of this. Each person was then asked to read quickly through a series of word pairs, including *shad bock*. Those in the group warned about shock more often slipped in pronouncing this pair, blurting out *bad shock*.

▼ Barack Obama slipped in a televised interview with George Stephanopoulos, referring to "my Muslim faith." Obama is a member of the United Church of Christ.

cognitive unconscious The mental processes that give rise to a person's thoughts, choices, emotions, and behavior even though they are not experienced by the person.

subliminal perception A thought or behavior that is influenced by stimuli that a person cannot consciously report perceiving.

Unlike errors created in experiments such as this one, many of the meaningful errors Freud attributed to the dynamic unconscious were not predicted in advance and so seem to depend on clever after-the-fact interpretations. Such interpretations can be wrong. Suggesting a pattern to a series of random events is quite clever, but it's not the same as scientifically predicting and explaining when and why an event should happen. Anyone can offer a reasonable, compelling explanation for an event after it has already happened, but the true work of science is to offer testable hypotheses that are evaluated based on reliable evidence. Freud's book *The Psychopathology of Everyday Life* (Freud, 1901/1938) suggests not so much that the dynamic unconscious produces errors but that Freud himself was a master at finding meaning in errors that might otherwise have seemed random. Obama's slip didn't mean he was considering changing religions, after all, but rather that reporters were motivated for political reasons to interpret his gaffe as especially meaningful.

A Modern View of the Cognitive Unconscious

Modern psychologists share Freud's interest in the impact of unconscious mental processes on consciousness and on behavior. However, rather than Freud's vision of the unconscious as a teeming menagerie of animal urges and repressed thoughts, the current study of the unconscious mind views it as the factory that builds the products of conscious thought and behavior (Kihlstrom, 1987; Wilson, 2002). The **cognitive unconscious** includes *all the mental processes that are not experienced by a person but that give rise to the person's thoughts, choices, emotions, and behavior.*

One indication of the cognitive unconscious at work is when the person's thought or behavior is changed by exposure to information outside of consciousness. This happens in **subliminal perception**, when *thought or behavior is influenced by stimuli that a person cannot consciously report perceiving.* Worries about the potential of subliminal influence were first provoked in 1957, when a marketer, James Vicary, claimed he had increased concession sales at a New Jersey theater by flashing the words "Eat Popcorn" and "Drink Coke" briefly on-screen during movies. It turns out his story was a hoax, and many attempts to increase sales using similar methods have failed. But the very idea of influencing behavior outside of consciousness created a wave of alarm about insidious "subliminal persuasion" that still concerns people (Epley, Savitsky, & Kachelski, 1999; Pratkanis, 1992).

Subliminal perception does occur, but the degree of influence it has on behavior is not very large (Dijksterhuis, Aarts, & Smith, 2005). One set of studies examined whether beverage choices could be influenced by brief visual exposures to thirst-related words (Strahan, Spencer, & Zanna, 2002). Research volunteers were asked to perform a computer task that involved deciding whether each of 26 letter strings was a word or not. This ensured that they would be looking intently at the screen when, just before each letter string appeared, a target was shown that could not be consciously perceived: A word was flashed for 16 milliseconds just off the center of the screen, followed by a row of *x*'s in that spot to mask any visual memory of the word. For half the participants, this subliminal word was thirst related (such as *thirst* and *dry*) and for the other half it was unrelated (such as *pirate* and *won*). When the volunteers afterward were given a choice of free coupons toward the purchase of possible new sports beverages *Super-Quencher* ("the best thirst-quenching beverage ever developed") and *PowerPro* ("the best electrolyte-restoring beverage ever developed"), those who had been subliminally exposed to thirst words more often chose Super-Quencher (see **FIGURE 5.9**).

There are two important footnotes to this research. First, the influence of the subliminal persuasion was primarily found for people who reported already being thirsty when the experiment started. The subliminal exposure to

▼ Do people in a movie theater need any subliminal messages to get them to eat popcorn? Probably not. Would subliminal messages make them more likely to eat popcorn? Maybe, but not much.

WALTER DARAN/TIME LIFE PICTURES/GETTY IMAGES

thirst words had little effect on people who didn't feel thirsty, suggesting that Vicary's "Drink Coke" campaign, even if it had actually happened, would not have drawn people out to the lobby unless they were already inclined to go. Second, the researchers also conducted a study in which other participants were shown the target words at a slower speed (300 milliseconds) so the words could be seen and consciously recognized. Their conscious perception of the thirst words had effects just like subliminal perception. Subliminal influences might be worrisome because they can change behavior without our conscious awareness but not because they are more powerful in comparison to conscious influences.

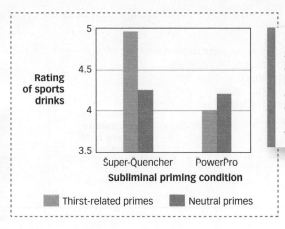

◀ FIGURE 5.9
Subliminal Influence Preference for a thirst-quenching beverage, "Super-Quencher," increased relative to another sports drink, "PowerPro," among people subliminally primed with thirst words (Strahan et al., 2002).

Unconscious influences on behavior are not limited to cases of subliminal persuasion—they can happen when you are merely reminded of an idea in passing. For example, the thought of getting old can make a person walk more slowly. John Bargh and his colleagues discovered this by having college students complete a survey that

What's an example of an idea that had an unconscious influence on you?

called for them to make sentences with various words (1996). The students were not informed that most of the words were commonly associated with aging (Florida, gray, wrinkled), and even afterward they didn't report being aware of this trend. In this case, the "aging" idea wasn't presented subliminally, just not very noticeably. As these research participants left the experiment, they were clocked as they walked down the hall. Compared with those not exposed to the aging-related words, these people walked more slowly! Just as with subliminal perception, a passing exposure to ideas can influence actions without conscious awareness.

The unconscious mind can be a kind of "mental butler," taking over background tasks that are too tedious, subtle, or bothersome for consciousness to trifle with (Bargh & Chartrand, 1999; Bargh & Morsella, 2008; Bower, 1999). Psychologists have long debated just how smart this mental butler might be. Freud attributed great intelligence to the unconscious, believing that it harbors complex motives and inner conflicts and that it expresses these in an astonishing array of thoughts and emotions, as well as psychological disorders (see Chapter 14). Contemporary cognitive psychologists wonder whether the unconscious is so smart, however, and point out that some unconscious processes even seem downright stupid (Loftus & Klinger, 1992). For example, the unconscious processes that underlie the perception of subliminal visual stimuli do not seem able to understand the combined meaning of word pairs, although they can understand single words. To the *conscious* mind, for example, a word pair such as *enemy loses* is somewhat positive—it is good to have your enemy lose. However, subliminal presentations of this word pair make people think of negative things, as though the unconscious mind is simply adding together the unpleasantness of the single words *enemy* and *loses* (Greenwald, 1992). Perhaps the mental butler is not all that bright.

In some cases, however, the unconscious mind can make better decisions than the conscious mind. Participants in an experiment were asked to choose which of three hypothetical people with many different qualities they would prefer to have as a roommate (Dijksterhuis, 2004). One candidate was objectively better, with more positive qualities, and participants given 4 minutes to make a *conscious decision* tended to choose this one.

A second group was asked for an *immediate decision* as soon as the information display was over and a third group was encouraged to reach an *unconscious decision*. This group was allowed the same 4 minutes of time after the display ended to give their answer (as the conscious group had been given), but during this interval their

▼ Choosing a roommate can be like playing the lottery: You win some, you lose some, and then you lose some more.

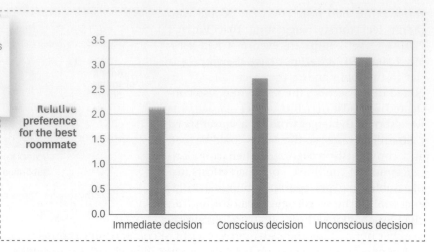

► FIGURE 5.10

Decisions People making roommate decisions who had some time for unconscious deliberation chose better roommates than those who thought about the choice consciously or those who made snap decisions (Dijksterhuis, 2004).

conscious minds were occupied with solving a set of anagrams. As you can see in **FIGURE 5.10**, the unconscious decision group showed a stronger preference for the good roommate than did the immediate decision or conscious decision groups. Unconscious minds seemed *better able* than conscious minds to sort out the complex information and arrive at the best choice. You sometimes can end up more satisfied with decisions you make after just "going with your gut" than with the decisions you consciously agonize over.

IN SUMMARY

○ Consciousness is a mystery of psychology because other people's minds cannot be perceived directly and because the relationship between mind and body is perplexing.

○ Consciousness has four basic properties: intentionality, unity, selectivity, and transience. It can also be understood in terms of levels: minimal consciousness, full consciousness, and self-consciousness.

○ Conscious contents can include current concerns, daydreams, and unwanted thoughts.

○ Unconscious processes are sometimes understood as expressions of the Freudian dynamic unconscious, but they are more commonly viewed as processes of the cognitive unconscious that create our conscious thought and behavior.

○ The cognitive unconscious is at work when subliminal perception and unconscious decision processes influence thought or behavior without the person's awareness.

Sleep and Dreaming: Good Night, Mind

What's it like to be asleep? Sometimes it's like nothing at all. Sleep can produce a state of unconsciousness in which the mind and brain apparently turn off the functions that create experience: The theater in your mind is closed. But this is an oversimplification because the theater actually seems to reopen during the night for special shows of bizarre cult films—in other words, dreams.

Dream consciousness involves a transformation of experience that is so radical it is commonly considered an **altered state of consciousness**— *a form of experience that departs significantly from the normal subjective experience of the world and the mind.* Such altered states can be accompanied by changes in thinking, disturbances in the sense of time, feelings of the loss of control, changes in emotional expression, alterations in body image and sense

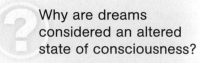

Why are dreams considered an altered state of consciousness?

of self, perceptual distortions, and changes in meaning or significance (Ludwig, 1966). The world of sleep and dreams, the two topics in this section, provides two unique perspectives on consciousness: a view of the mind without consciousness and a view of consciousness in an altered state.

Sleep

Consider a typical night. As you begin to fall asleep, the busy, task-oriented thoughts of the waking mind are replaced by wandering thoughts and images, odd juxtapositions, some of them almost dreamlike. This presleep consciousness is called the *hypnagogic state*. On some rare nights you might experience a *hypnic jerk,* a sudden quiver or sensation of dropping, as though missing a step on a staircase. (No one is quite sure why these happen, but there is no truth to the theory that you are actually levitating and then fall.) Eventually, your presence of mind goes away entirely. Time and experience stop, you are unconscious, and in fact there seems to be no "you" there to have experiences. But then come dreams, whole vistas of a vivid and surrealistic consciousness you just don't get during the day, a set of experiences that occur with the odd prerequisite that there is nothing "out there" you are actually experiencing. More patches of unconsciousness may occur, with more dreams here and there. And finally, the glimmerings of waking consciousness return again in a foggy and imprecise form as you enter postsleep consciousness (the *hypnopompic state*) and then awake, often with bad hair.

Sleep Cycle

190 - 214

The sequence of events that occurs during a night of sleep is part of one of the major rhythms of human life, the cycle of sleep and waking. This **circadian rhythm** is *a naturally occurring 24-hour cycle*—from the Latin *circa,* "about," and *dies,* "day." Even people who are sequestered in underground buildings without clocks ("time-free environments") and are allowed to sleep when they want to tend to have a rest-activity cycle of about 25.1 hours (Aschoff, 1965). This slight deviation from 24 hours is not easily explained (Lavie, 2001), but it seems to underlie the tendency many people have to want to stay up a little later each night and wake up a little later each day. We're 25.1-hour people living in a 24-hour world.

The sleep cycle is far more than a simple on/off routine, however, as many bodily and psychological processes ebb and flow in this rhythm. In 1929 researchers made EEG (electroencephalograph) recordings of the human brain for the first time (Berger, 1929; see Chapter 3). Before this, many people had offered descriptions of their night-time experiences, and researchers knew that there are deeper and lighter periods of sleep, as well as dream periods. But no one had been able to measure much of anything about sleep without waking up the sleeper and ruining it. The EEG recordings revealed a regular pattern of changes in electrical activity in the brain accompanying the circadian cycle. During waking, these changes involve alternation between high-frequency activity (called *beta waves*) during alertness and lower-frequency activity (*alpha waves*) during relaxation.

The largest changes in EEG occur during sleep. These changes show a regular pattern over the course of the night that allowed sleep researchers to identify five sleep stages (see **FIGURE 5.11** on the next page). In the first stage of sleep, the EEG moves to frequency patterns even lower than alpha waves (*theta waves*). In the second stage of sleep, these patterns are interrupted by short bursts of activity called *sleep spindles* and *K complexes,* and the sleeper becomes somewhat more difficult to awaken. The deepest stages of sleep are 3 and 4, known as slow-wave sleep, in which the EEG patterns show activity called *delta waves*.

During the fifth sleep stage, **REM sleep,** *a stage of sleep characterized by rapid eye movements and a high level of brain activity,* EEG patterns become high-frequency saw-tooth waves, similar to beta waves, suggesting that the mind at this time is as active as it is during waking (see Figure 5.11). Using an **electrooculograph (EOG),** *a device to*

altered states of consciousness Forms of experience that depart from the normal subjective experience of the world and the mind.

circadian rhythm A naturally occurring 24-hour cycle.

REM sleep A stage of sleep characterized by rapid eye movements and a high level of brain activity.

electrooculograph (EOG) An instrument that measures eye movements.

▶ FIGURE 5.11
EEG Patterns during the Stages of Sleep The waking brain shows high-frequency beta wave activity, which changes during drowsiness and relaxation to lower-frequency alpha waves. Stage 1 sleep shows lower-frequency theta waves, which are accompanied in Stage 2 by irregular patterns called sleep spindles and K complexes. Stages 3 and 4 are marked by the lowest frequencies, delta waves. During REM sleep, EEG patterns return to higher-frequency sawtooth waves that resemble the beta waves of waking.

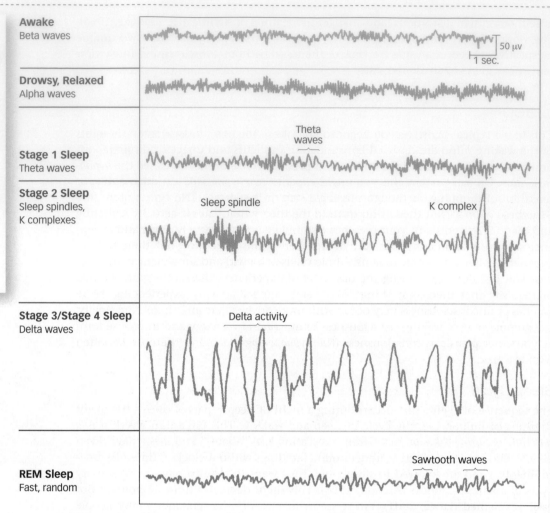

Awake
Beta waves

50 µv
1 sec.

Drowsy, Relaxed
Alpha waves

Stage 1 Sleep
Theta waves

Theta waves

Stage 2 Sleep
Sleep spindles,
K complexes

Sleep spindle

K complex

Stage 3/Stage 4 Sleep
Delta waves

Delta activity

REM Sleep
Fast, random

Sawtooth waves

measure eye movements, during sleep, researchers found that sleepers wakened during REM periods reported having dreams much more often than those wakened during non-REM periods (Aserinsky & Kleitman, 1953). During REM sleep, the pulse quickens, blood pressure rises, and there are telltale signs of sexual arousal. At the same time, measurements of muscle movements indicate that the sleeper is very still, except for a rapid side-to-side movement of the eyes. (Watch someone sleeping and you may be able to see the REMs through their closed eyelids. But be careful doing this with strangers down at the bus depot.)

▶ *Dreamers,* by Albert Joseph Moore (1879/1882). Without measuring REM sleep, it's hard to know whether Moore's "Dreamers" are actually dreaming.

Although many people believe that they don't dream much (if at all), some 80% of people awakened during REM sleep report dreams. If you've ever wondered whether dreams actually take place in an instant or whether they take as long to happen as the events they portray might take, the analysis of REM sleep offers an answer. Sleep researchers William Dement and Nathaniel Kleitman (1957) woke volunteers either 5 minutes or 15 minutes after the onset of REM sleep and asked them to judge, on the basis of the events in the remembered dream, how long they had been dreaming. Sleepers in 92 of 111 cases were correct, suggesting that dreaming occurs in "real time." The discovery of REM sleep has offered many insights into dreaming, but not all dreams occur in REM periods. Some dreams are also reported in other sleep stages (non-REM sleep, also called *NREM sleep*) but not as many—and the dreams that occur at these times are described as less wild than REM dreams and more like normal thinking.

Putting EEG and REM data together produces a picture of how a typical night's sleep progresses through cycles of sleep stages (see **FIGURE 5.12**). In the first hour of the night, you fall all the way from waking to the fourth and deepest stage of sleep, the stage marked by delta waves. These slow waves indicate a general synchronization of neural firing, as though the brain is doing one thing at this time rather than many—the neuronal equivalent of "the wave" moving through the crowd at a stadium, as lots of individuals move together in synchrony. You then return to lighter sleep stages, eventually reaching REM and dreamland. Note that although REM sleep is lighter than that of lower stages, it is deep enough that you may be difficult to awaken. You then continue to cycle between REM and slow-wave sleep stages every 90 minutes or so throughout the night. Periods of REM last longer as the night goes on, and lighter sleep stages predominate between these periods, with the deeper slow-wave stages 3 and 4 disappearing halfway through the night. Although you're either unconscious or dream-conscious at the time, your brain and mind cycle through a remarkable array of different states each time you have a night's sleep.

What are the stages in a typical night's sleep?

▲ REM sleep discoverer Nathaniel Kleitman as a participant in his own sleep experiment with REM and EEG measurement electrodes in place.

WILLIAM VANDIVERT

Sleep Needs and Deprivation

How much do people sleep? The answer depends on the age of the sleeper (Dement, 1999). Newborns will sleep 6 to 8 times in 24 hours, often totaling more than 16 hours. Their napping cycle gets consolidated into "sleeping through the night," usually sometime between 9 and 18 months, but sometimes even later. The typical 6-year-old child might need 11 or 12 hours of sleep, and the progression to less sleep then continues into adulthood, when the average is about 7 to 7½ hours per night. With aging, people can get along with even a bit less sleep than that. Over a whole lifetime, we get about 1 hour of sleep for every 2 hours we are awake.

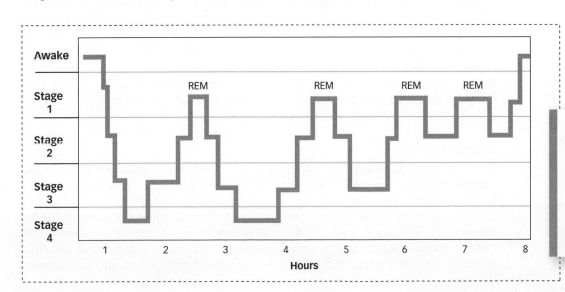

◀ FIGURE 5.12
Stages of Sleep during the Night Over the course of the typical night, sleep cycles into deeper stages early on and then more shallow stages later. REM periods become longer in later cycles, and the deeper slow-wave sleep of stages 3 and 4 disappears halfway through the night.

▲ Sleep deprivation can often be diagnosed without the help of any psychologists or brain-scanning equipment.

This is a lot of sleeping. Could we tolerate less? The world record for staying awake belongs to Randy Gardner, who at age 17 stayed up for 264 hours and 12 minutes in 1965 for a science project. When Randy finally did go to sleep, he slept only 14 hours and 40 minutes and awakened essentially recovered (Dement, 1978).

Feats like this one suggest that sleep might be expendable. This is the theory behind the classic "all-nighter" that you may have tried on the way to a rough exam. But it turns out that this theory is mistaken. Robert Stickgold and his colleagues (2000) found that when people learning a difficult perceptual task are kept up all night after they finished practicing the task, their learning of the task is wiped out. Even after two nights of catch-up sleep, they show little indication of their initial training on the task. Sleep following learning appears to be essential for memory consolidation (see Hot Science: Sleep On It, p. 230 in Chapter 6). It is as though memories normally deteriorate unless sleep occurs to help keep them in place. Studying all night may help you cram for the exam, but it won't make the material stick—which pretty much defeats the whole point.

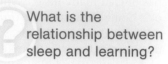

What is the relationship between sleep and learning?

Sleep turns out to be a necessity rather than a luxury in other ways as well. At the extreme, sleep loss can be fatal. When rats are forced to break Randy Gardner's human waking record and stay awake even longer, they have trouble regulating their body temperature and lose weight although they eat much more than normal. Their bodily systems break down and they die, on average, in 21 days (Rechsthaffen et al., 1983). Shakespeare called sleep "nature's soft nurse," and it is clear that even for healthy young humans, a few hours of sleep deprivation each night can have a cumulative detrimental effect: reducing mental acuity and reaction time, increasing irritability and depression, and increasing the risk of accidents and injury (Coren, 1997).

Some studies have deprived people of different sleep stages selectively by waking them whenever certain stages are detected. Studies of REM sleep deprivation indicate that this part of sleep is important psychologically, as memory problems and excessive aggression are observed in both humans and rats after only a few days of being wakened whenever REM activity starts (Ellman et al., 1991). The brain must value something about REM sleep because REM deprivation causes a rebound of more REM sleep the next night (Brunner et al., 1990). Deprivation from slow-wave sleep (in stages 3 and 4), in turn, has more physical effects, with just a few nights of deprivation leaving people feeling tired, fatigued, and hypersensitive to muscle and bone pain (Lentz et al., 1999).

It's clearly dangerous to neglect the need for sleep. But why would we have such a need in the first place? Insects don't seem to sleep, but most "higher" animals do, including fish and birds. Giraffes sleep less than 2 hours daily, whereas brown bats snooze for almost 20 hours. These variations in sleep needs, and the very existence of a need, are hard to explain. Is the restoration that happens during the unconsciousness of sleep something that simply can't be achieved during consciousness? Sleep is, after all, potentially costly in the course of evolution. The sleeping animal is easy prey, so the habit of sleep would not seem to have developed so widely across species unless it had significant benefits that made up for this vulnerability. Theories of sleep have not yet determined why the brain and body have evolved to need these recurring episodes of unconsciousness.

insomnia Difficulty in falling asleep or staying asleep.

sleep apnea A disorder in which the person stops breathing for brief periods while asleep.

somnambulism (sleepwalking) Occurs when the person arises and walks around while asleep.

narcolepsy A disorder in which sudden sleep attacks occur in the middle of waking activities.

Sleep Disorders

In answer to the question, "Did you sleep well?," comedian Stephen Wright said, "No, I made a couple of mistakes." Sleeping well is something everyone would love to do, but for many people, sleep disorders are deeply troubling. Disorders that plague sleep include insomnia, sleep apnea, somnambulism, narcolepsy, sleep paralysis, nightmares, and night terrors. Perhaps the most common sleep disorder is **insomnia**, *difficulty in falling asleep or staying asleep*. About 15% of adults complain of severe or frequent insomnia, and another 15% report having mild or occasional insomnia

(Bootzin et al., 1993). Although people often overestimate their insomnia, the distress caused even by the perception of insomnia can be significant. There are many causes of insomnia, including anxiety associated with stressful life events, so insomnia may sometimes be a sign of other emotional difficulties.

Insomnia can be exacerbated by worry about insomnia (Borkevec, 1982). No doubt you've experienced some nights on which sleeping was a high priority, such as before a class presentation or an important interview, and you've found that you were unable to fall asleep. The desire to sleep initiates an ironic process of mental control—a heightened sensitivity to signs of sleeplessness—and this sensitivity interferes with sleep. In fact, participants in an experiment who were instructed to go to sleep quickly became hypersensitive and had more difficulty sleeping than those who were not instructed to hurry (Ansfield, Wegner, & Bowser, 1996). The paradoxical solution for insomnia in some cases, then, may be to give up the pursuit of sleep and instead find something else to do.

"I can't sleep. I think I'll get up and solve all my problems."

Giving up on trying so hard to sleep is probably better than another common remedy—the use of sleeping pills. Although sedatives can be useful for brief sleep problems associated with emotional events, their long-term use is not effective. To begin with, most sleeping pills are addictive. People become dependent on the pills to sleep and may need to increase the dose over time to achieve the same effect. Even in short-term use, sedatives can interfere with the normal sleep cycle. Although they promote sleep, they reduce the proportion of time spent in REM and slow-wave sleep (Nishino, Mignot, & Dement, 1995), robbing people of dreams and their deepest sleep stages. As a result, the quality of sleep achieved with pills may not be as high as without, and there may be side effects such as grogginess and irritability during the day. Finally, stopping the treatment suddenly can produce insomnia that is worse than before.

What are some problems caused by sleeping pills?

Sleep apnea is *a disorder in which the person stops breathing for brief periods while asleep*. A person with apnea usually snores, as apnea involves an involuntary obstruction of the breathing passage. When episodes of apnea occur for over 10 seconds at a time and recur many times during the night, they may cause many awakenings and sleep loss or insomnia. Apnea occurs most often in middle-age overweight men (Partinen, 1994) and may go undiagnosed because it is not easy for the sleeper to notice. Bed partners may be the ones who finally get tired of the snoring and noisy gasping for air when the sleeper's breathing restarts, or the sleeper may eventually seek treatment because of excessive sleepiness during the day. Therapies involving weight loss, drugs, or surgery may solve the problem.

Another sleep disorder is **somnambulism**, commonly called sleepwalking, which occurs when *a person arises and walks around while asleep*. Sleepwalking is more common in children, peaking around the age of 11 or 12, with as many as 25% of children experiencing at least one episode (Empson, 1984). Sleepwalking tends to happen early in the night, usually in slow-wave sleep, and sleepwalkers may awaken during their walk or return to bed without waking, in which case they will probably not remember the episode in the morning. The sleepwalker's eyes are usually open in a glassy stare, although walking with hands outstretched is uncommon except in cartoons. Sleepwalking is not usually linked to any additional problems and is only problematic in that sleepwalkers can hurt themselves. People who walk while they are sleeping do not tend to be very coordinated and can trip over furniture or fall down stairs. After all, they're sleeping. Contrary to popular belief, it is safe to wake sleepwalkers or lead them back to bed.

Is it safe to wake a sleepwalker?

There are other sleep disorders that are less common. **Narcolepsy** is *a disorder in which sudden sleep attacks occur in the middle of waking activities*. Narcolepsy involves the intrusion of a dreaming state of sleep (with REM) into waking and is often accompanied by

▲ Sleepwalkers in cartoons have their arms outstretched and eyes closed, but that's just for cartoons. A real-life sleepwalker usually walks normally with eyes open, sometimes with a glassy look.

unrelenting excessive sleepiness and uncontrollable sleep attacks lasting from 30 seconds to 30 minutes. This disorder appears to have a genetic basis, as it runs in families, and can be treated effectively with medication. **Sleep paralysis** is *the experience of waking up unable to move* and is sometimes associated with narcolepsy. This eerie experience usually lasts only a few moments, happens in hypnagogic or hypnopompic sleep, and may occur with an experience of pressure on the chest (Hishakawa, 1976). **Night terrors** (or sleep terrors) are *abrupt awakenings with panic and intense emotional arousal*. These terrors, which occur mainly in boys ages 3 to 7, happen most often in NREM sleep early in the sleep cycle and do not usually have dream content the sleeper can report.

To sum up, there is a lot going on when we close our eyes for the night. Humans follow a pretty regular sleep cycle, going through five stages of NREM and REM sleep during the night. Disruptions to that cycle, either from sleep deprivation or sleep disorders, can produce consequences for waking consciousness. But something else happens during a night's sleep that affects our consciousness, both while asleep and when we wake up. It's dreaming, and we'll look at what psychologists know about dreams next.

Dreams

Pioneering sleep researcher William C. Dement (1959) said, "Dreaming permits each and every one of us to be quietly and safely insane every night of our lives." Indeed, dreams do seem to have a touch of insanity about them. We experience crazy things in dreams, but even more bizarre is the fact that we are the writers, producers, and directors of the crazy things we experience. Just what are these experiences, and how can the experiences be explained?

Dream Consciousness

Dreams depart dramatically from reality. You may dream of being naked in public, of falling from a great height, of sleeping through an important appointment, of your teeth being loose and falling out, of being chased, or even of flying (Holloway, 2001). These things don't happen much in reality unless you have a very bad life. The quality of consciousness in dreaming is also altered significantly from waking consciousness. There are five major characteristics of dream consciousness that distinguish it from the waking state (Hobson, 1988).

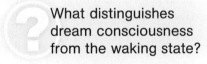 What distinguishes dream consciousness from the waking state?

> We intensely feel *emotion*, whether it is bliss or terror or love or awe.

> Dream *thought* is illogical: The continuities of time, place, and person don't apply. You may find you are in one place and then another, for example, without any travel in between—or people may change identity from one dream scene to the next.

> *Sensation* is fully formed and meaningful; visual sensation is predominant, and you may also deeply experience sound, touch, and movement (although pain is very uncommon).

> Dreaming occurs with *uncritical acceptance*, as though the images and events were perfectly normal rather than bizarre.

> We have *difficulty remembering* the dream after it is over. People often remember dreams only if they are awakened during the dream and even then may lose recall for the dream within just a few minutes of waking. If waking memory were this bad, you'd be standing around half-naked in the street much of the time, having forgotten your destination, clothes, and lunch money.

"Frank! Frank, honey, wake up! Your lamp—it's humongous!"

Not all of our dreams are fantastic and surreal, however. Far from the adventures in nighttime insanity storied by Freud, dreams are often ordinary (Domhoff, 2007). We often dream about mundane topics that reflect prior waking experiences or "day residue." Current conscious concerns pop up (Nikles et al., 1998), along with images from the recent past. A dream may even incorporate sensations experienced during sleep, as when sleepers in one study were led to dream of water when drops were sprayed on their faces during REM sleep (Dement & Wolpert, 1958). The day residue does not usually include episodic memories, that is, complete daytime events replayed in the mind. Rather, dreams that reflect the day's experience tend to single out sensory experiences or objects from waking life. After watching a badminton tournament one evening, for example, you might dream about shuttlecocks darting through the air. One study had research participants play the computer game Tetris and found that participants often reported dreaming about the Tetris geometrical figures falling down—even though they seldom reported dreams about being in the experiment or playing the game (Stickgold et al., 2001). Even severely amnesic patients who couldn't recall playing the game at all reported Tetris-like images appearing in their dreams (Stickgold et al., 2000). The content of dreams takes snapshots from the day rather than retelling the stories of what you have done or seen. This means that dreams often come without clear plots or storylines, and so they may not make a lot of sense.

Some of the most memorable dreams are nightmares, and these frightening dreams can wake up the dreamer (Levin & Nielsen, 2009). One set of daily dream logs from college undergraduates suggested that the average student has about 24 nightmares per year (Wood & Bootzin, 1990), although some people may have them as often as every night. Children have more nightmares than adults, and people who have experienced traumatic events are inclined to have nightmares that relive those events. Following the 1989 earthquake in the San Francisco Bay Area, for example, college students who had experienced the quake reported more nightmares than those who had not and often reported that the dreams were about the quake (Wood et al., 1992). This effect of trauma may not only produce dreams of the traumatic event: When police officers experience "critical incidents" of conflict and danger, they tend to have more nightmares in general (Neylan et al., 2002).

▲ *The Nightmare*, by Henry Fuseli (1790). Fuseli depicts not only a mare in this painting but also an incubus—an imp perched on the dreamer's chest that is traditionally associated with especially horrifying nightmares.

Dream Theories

Dreams are puzzles that cry out to be solved. How could you *not* want to make sense out of these experiences? Although dreams may be fantastic and confusing, they are emotionally riveting, filled with vivid images from your own life, and they seem very real. The search for dream meaning goes all the way back to biblical figures, who interpreted dreams and looked for prophecies in them. In the Old Testament, the prophet Daniel (a favorite of the three Daniels who authored this book) curried favor with King Nebuchadnezzar of Babylon by interpreting the king's dream. The question of what dreams mean has been burning since antiquity, mainly because the meaning of dreams is usually far from obvious.

In the first psychological theory of dreams, Freud (1900/1965) proposed that dreams are confusing and obscure because the dynamic unconscious creates them precisely *to be* confusing and obscure. According to Freud's theory, dreams represent wishes, and some of these wishes are so unacceptable, taboo, and anxiety producing that the mind can only express them in disguised form. Freud believed that many of the most unacceptable wishes are sexual, so he interpreted a dream of a train going into a tunnel as symbolic of sexual intercourse. According to Freud, the **manifest content** of a dream, *a dream's apparent topic or superficial meaning*, is a smoke screen for its **latent content**, *a dream's true underlying meaning*. For example, a dream about a tree burning down in the park across the street from where a friend once lived (the manifest content) might represent a camouflaged wish for the death of the friend (the latent content). In this case, wishing for the death of a friend is unacceptable, so it is disguised as a tree on fire. The problem with Freud's approach is that there are an infinite number of potential interpretations of any dream and finding the correct one is a matter of guesswork—and of convincing the dreamer that one interpretation is superior to the others.

sleep paralysis The experience of waking up unable to move.

night terrors (or sleep terrors) Abrupt awakenings with panic and intense emotional arousal.

manifest content A dream's apparent topic or superficial meaning.

latent content A dream's true underlying meaning.

CULTURE & COMMUNITY

What do dreams mean to us around the world? A recent study (Morewedge & Norton, 2009) assessed how people from three different cultures evaluate their dreams. Participants were asked to rate different theories of dreaming on a scale of 1 (do not agree at all) to 7 (agree completely).

A significant majority of students from the United States, South Korea, and India agreed with the Freudian theory that dreams have meanings. Only small percentages believed the other options, that dreams: provide a means to solve problems, promote learning, or are by-products of unrelated brain activity.

The accompanying figure illustrates the findings across all three cultural groups. It appears that in many parts of the world, people have an intuition that dreams contain something deep and relevant.

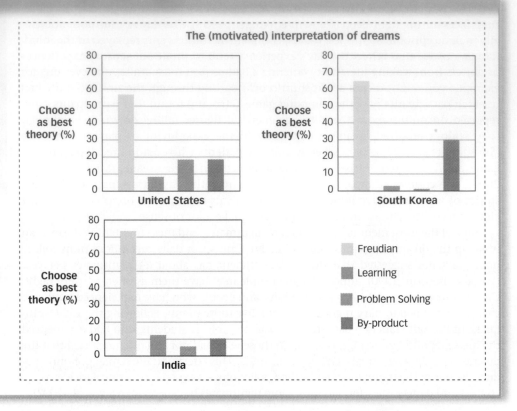

Although dreams may not represent elaborately hidden wishes, there is evidence that they do feature the return of suppressed thoughts. Researchers asked volunteers to think of a personal acquaintance and then to spend 5 minutes before going to bed writing down whatever came to mind (Wegner, Wenzlaff, & Kozak, 2004). Some participants were asked to suppress thoughts of this person as they wrote, others were asked to focus on thoughts of the person, and yet others were asked just to write freely about anything. The next morning, participants wrote dream reports. Overall, all participants mentioned dreaming more about the person they had named than about other people. But they most often dreamed of the person they named if they were in the group that had been assigned to suppress thoughts of the person the night before. This finding suggests that Freud was right to suspect that dreams harbor unwanted thoughts. Perhaps this is why actors dream of forgetting their lines, travelers dream of getting lost, and football players dream of fumbling the ball.

> **What is the evidence that we dream about our suppressed thoughts?**

Another key theory of dreaming is the **activation-synthesis model** (Hobson & McCarley, 1977). This theory proposes that *dreams are produced when the mind attempts to make sense of random neural activity that occurs in the brain during sleep.* During waking consciousness, the mind is devoted to interpreting lots of information that arrives through the senses. You figure out that the odd noise you're hearing during class is your cell phone vibrating, for example, or you realize that the strange smell in the hall outside your room must be from burned popcorn. In the dream state, the mind doesn't have access to external sensations, but it keeps on doing what it usually does: interpreting information. Because that information now comes from neural activations that occur without the continuity provided by the perception of reality, the brain's interpretive mechanisms can run free. This might be why, for example, a person in a

activation-synthesis model The theory that dreams are produced when the brain attempts to make sense of activations that occur randomly during sleep.

dream can sometimes change into someone else. There is no actual person being perceived to help the mind keep a stable view. In the mind's effort to perceive and give meaning to brain activation, the person you view in a dream about a grocery store might seem to be a clerk but then change to be your favorite teacher when the dream scene moves to your school. The great interest people have in interpreting their dreams the next morning may be an extension of the interpretive activity they've been doing all night.

The Freudian theory and the activation-synthesis theory differ in the significance they place on the meaning of dreams. In Freud's theory, dreams begin with meaning, whereas in the activation-synthesis theory, dreams begin randomly—but meaning can be added as the mind lends interpretations in the process of dreaming. Dream research has not yet sorted out whether one of these theories or yet another might be the best account of the meaning of dreams.

The Dreaming Brain

What happens in the brain when we dream? Several studies have made fMRI scans of people's brains during sleep, focusing on the areas of the brain that show changes in activation during REM periods. These studies show that the brain changes that occur during REM sleep correspond clearly with certain alterations of consciousness that occur in dreaming. **FIGURE 5.13** shows some of the patterns of activation and deactivation found in the dreaming brain (Schwartz & Maquet, 2002).

In dreams there are heights to look down from, dangerous people lurking, the occasional monster, some minor worries, and at least once in a while that major exam you've forgotten about until you walk into class. These themes suggest that the brain areas responsible for fear or emotion somehow work overtime in dreams, and it turns out that this is clearly visible in fMRI scans. The amygdala is involved in responses to threatening or stressful events, and indeed the amygdala is quite active during REM sleep.

The typical dream is also a visual wonderland, with visual events present in almost all dreams. However, there are fewer auditory sensations, even fewer tactile sensations, and almost no smells or tastes. This dream "picture show" doesn't involve actual perception, of course, just the imagination of visual events. It turns out that the areas of the brain responsible for visual perception are *not* activated during dreaming, whereas the visual association areas in the occipital lobe that are responsible for visual imagery *do* show activation (Braun et al., 1998). Your brain is smart enough to realize that it's not really seeing bizarre images but acts instead as though it's imagining bizarre images.

During REM sleep, the prefrontal cortex shows relatively less arousal than it usually does during waking consciousness. What does this mean for the dreamer? As a rule, the prefrontal areas are associated with planning and executing actions, and often dreams seem to be unplanned and rambling. Perhaps this is why dreams often don't have very sensible storylines—they've been scripted by an author whose ability to plan is inactive.

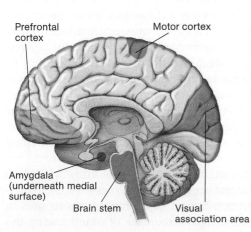

(a)

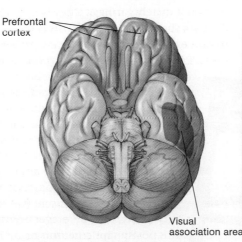

(b)

◄ FIGURE 5.13
Brain Activation and Deactivation during REM Sleep Brain areas shaded red are activated during REM sleep; those shaded blue are deactivated. (a) The medial view shows the activation of the amygdala, the visual association areas, the motor cortex, and the brain stem and the deactivation of the prefrontal cortex. (b) The ventral view shows the activation of other visual association areas and the deactivation of the prefrontal cortex (Schwartz & Maquet, 2002).

Another odd fact of dreaming is that while the eyes are moving rapidly, the body is otherwise very still. During REM sleep, the motor cortex is activated, but spinal neurons running through the brain stem inhibit the expression of this motor activation (Lai & Siegal, 1999). This turns out to be a useful property of brain activation in dreaming; otherwise, you might get up and act out every dream! Patients suffering from one rare sleep disorder, in fact, lose the normal muscular inhibition accompanying REM sleep and so act out their dreams, thrashing around in bed or stalking around the bedroom (Mahowald & Schenck, 2000). People who are moving during sleep are probably not dreaming. The brain specifically inhibits movement during dreams, perhaps to keep us from hurting ourselves.

IN SUMMARY

- ○ Sleep and dreaming present a view of the mind with an altered state of consciousness.
- ○ During a night's sleep, the brain passes in and out of five stages of sleep; most dreaming occurs in the REM sleep stage.
- ○ Sleep needs decrease over the life span, but being deprived of sleep and dreams has psychological and physical costs.
- ○ Sleep can be disrupted through disorders that include insomnia, sleep apnea, somnambulism, narcolepsy, sleep paralysis, and night terrors.
- ○ In dreaming, the dreamer uncritically accepts changes in emotion, thought, and sensation but poorly remembers the dream on awakening.
- ○ Theories of dreaming include Freud's psychoanalytic theory and more current views such as the activation-synthesis model.
- ○ fMRI studies of the brain in dreaming reveal activations associated with visual activity, reductions of other sensations, increased sensitivity to emotions such as fear, lessened capacities for planning, and the prevention of movement.

Drugs and Consciousness: Artificial Inspiration

The author of the anti-utopian novel *Brave New World*, Aldous Huxley, once wrote of his experiences with the drug mescaline. His essay "The Doors of Perception" described the intense experience that accompanied his departure from normal consciousness. He described "a world where everything shone with the Inner Light, and was infinite in its significance. The legs, for example, of a chair—how miraculous their tubularity, how supernatural their polished smoothness! I spent several minutes—or was it several centuries?—not merely gazing at those bamboo legs, but actually *being* them" (Huxley, 1954).

Being the legs of a chair? This is better than being a seat cushion, but it sounds like an odd experience. Still, many people seek out such experiences, often through using drugs. **Psychoactive drugs** are *chemicals that influence consciousness or behavior by altering the brain's chemical message system.* You read about several such drugs in Chapter 3 when we explored the brain's system of neurotransmitters. And you will read about them in a different light when we turn to their role in the treatment of psychological disorders in Chapter 14. Whether these drugs are used for entertainment, for treatment, or for other reasons, they each exert their influence either by increasing the activity of a neurotransmitter (the agonists) or decreasing its activity (the antagonists).

Some of the most common neurotransmitters are serotonin, dopamine, gamma-aminobutyric acid (GABA), and acetylcholine. Drugs alter these neural connections by preventing the bonding of neurotransmitters to sites in the postsynaptic neuron or by inhibiting the reuptake of or enhancing the

BRENT MADISON

▲ The seat of consciousness.

bonding and transmission of neurotransmitters. Different drugs can intensify or dull transmission patterns, creating changes in brain electrical activities that mimic natural operations of the brain. For example, a drug such as Valium (benzodiazepine) induces sleep but prevents dreaming and so creates a state similar to slow-wave sleep, that is, what the brain naturally develops several times each night. Other drugs prompt patterns of brain activity that do not occur naturally, however, and their influence on consciousness can be dramatic. Like Huxley experiencing himself becoming the legs of a chair, people using drugs can have experiences unlike any they might find in normal waking consciousness or even in dreams. To understand these altered states, let's explore how people use and abuse drugs and examine the major categories of psychoactive drugs.

psychoactive drug A chemical that influences consciousness or behavior by altering the brain's chemical message system.

drug tolerance The tendency for larger doses of a drug to be required over time to achieve the same effect.

Drug Use and Abuse

Why do children sometimes spin around until they get dizzy and fall to the ground? There is something strangely attractive about states of consciousness that depart from the norm, and people throughout history have sought out these altered states by dancing, fasting, chanting, meditating, and ingesting a bizarre assortment of chemicals to intoxicate themselves (Tart, 1969). People pursue altered consciousness even when there are costs, from the nausea that accompanies dizziness to the life-wrecking obsession with a drug that can come with addiction. In this regard, the pursuit of altered consciousness can be a fatal attraction.

Often, drug-induced changes in consciousness begin as pleasant and spark an initial attraction. Researchers have measured the attractiveness of psychoactive drugs by seeing how much laboratory animals will work to get them. In one study researchers allowed rats to intravenously administer cocaine to themselves by pressing a lever (Bozarth & Wise, 1985). Rats given free access to cocaine increased their use over the course of the 30-day study. They not only continued to self-administer at a high rate but also occasionally binged to the point of giving themselves convulsions. They stopped grooming themselves and eating until they lost on average almost a third of their body weight. About 90% of the rats died by the end of the study. Rats do show more attraction to sweets such as sugar or saccharine than they do to cocaine (Lenoir et al., 2007), but their interest in cocaine is deadly serious.

What is the allure of altered consciousness?

Rats are not tiny little humans, of course, so such research is not a firm basis for understanding human responses to cocaine. But these results do make it clear that cocaine is addictive and that the consequences of such addiction can be dire. Studies of self-administration of drugs in laboratory animals show that animals will work to obtain not only cocaine but also alcohol, amphetamines, barbiturates, caffeine, opiates (such as morphine and heroin), nicotine, phencyclidine (PCP), MDMA (ecstasy), and THC (tetrahydrocannabinol, the active ingredient in marijuana). There are some psychoactive drugs that animals won't work for (such as mescaline or the anti-psychotic drug phenothiazine), suggesting that these drugs have less potential for causing addiction (Bozarth, 1987).

People usually do not become addicted to a psychoactive drug the first time they use it. They may experiment a few times, then try again, and eventually find that their tendency to use the drug increases over time due to several factors, such as drug tolerance, physical dependence, and psychological dependence. **Drug tolerance** is *the tendency for larger drug doses to be required over time to achieve the same effect.* Physicians who prescribe morphine to control pain in their patients are faced with tolerance problems because steadily greater amounts of the drug may be needed to dampen the same pain. With increased tolerance comes the

"At this point, we know it's addictive."

danger of drug overdose; recreational users find they need to use more and more of a drug to produce the same high. But then, if a new batch of heroin or cocaine is more concentrated than usual, the "normal" amount the user takes to achieve the same high can be fatal.

What problems can arise in drug withdrawal?

Self-administration of addictive drugs can also be prompted by withdrawal symptoms, which result when drug use is abruptly discontinued. Some withdrawal symptoms signal *physical dependence,* when pain, convulsions, hallucinations, or other unpleasant symptoms accompany withdrawal. People who suffer from physical dependence seek to continue drug use to avoid getting physically ill. A common example is the "caffeine headache" some people complain of when they haven't had their daily jolt of java. Other withdrawal symptoms result from *psychological dependence,* a strong desire to return to the drug even when physical withdrawal symptoms are gone. Drugs can create an emotional need over time that continues to prey on the mind, particularly in circumstances that are reminders of the drug. Some ex-smokers report longing wistfully for an after-dinner smoke, for example, even years after they've successfully quit the habit.

Drug addiction reveals a human frailty: our inability to look past the immediate consequences of our behavior. Although we would like to think that our behavior is guided by a rational analysis of future consequences, more typically occasions when we "play first, pay later" lead directly to "let's just play a lot right now." There is something intensely inviting about the prospect of a soon-to-be-had pleasure and something pale, hazy, and distant about the costs this act might bring at some future time. For example, given the choice of receiving $1 today or $2 a week later, most people will take the $1 today. However, if the same choice is to be made for some date a year in the future (when the immediate pleasure of today's windfall is not so strong), people choose to wait and get the $2 (Ainslie, 2001). The immediate satisfaction associated with taking most drugs may outweigh a rational analysis of the later consequences that can result from taking those drugs, such as drug addiction.

The psychological and social problems stemming from addiction are major. For many people, drug addiction becomes a way of life, and for some, it is a cause of death. Like the cocaine-addicted rats in the study noted earlier (Bozarth & Wise, 1985), some people become so attached to a drug that their lives are ruled by it. However, this is not always the end of the story. This ending is most well known because the addict becomes a recurrent, visible social problem, "publicized" through repeated crime and repeated appearances in prisons and treatment programs. But a life of addiction is not the only possible endpoint of drug use. Stanley Schachter (1982) suggested that the visibility of addiction is misleading and that in fact many people overcome addictions. He found that 64% of a sample of people who had a history of cigarette smoking had quit successfully, although many had to try again and again to achieve their success. One study of soldiers who became addicted to heroin in Vietnam found that 3 years after their return, only 12% remained addicted (Robins et al., 1980). The return to the attractions and obligations of normal life, as well as the absence of the familiar places and faces associated with their old drug habit, made it possible for returning soldiers to successfully quit. Although addiction is dangerous, it may not be incurable.

It may not be accurate to view all recreational drug use under the umbrella of "addiction." Many people at this point in the history of Western society, for example, would not call the repeated use of caffeine an addiction, and some do not label the use of alcohol, tobacco, or marijuana in this way. In other times and places, however, each of these has been considered a terrifying addiction worthy of prohibition and public censure. In the early 17th century, for example, tobacco use was punishable by death in Germany, by castration in Russia, and by decapitation in China (Corti,

▶ The antique coffee maker, a sight that warms the hearts of caffeine lovers around the world.

INTERFOTO/ALAMY

1931). Not a good time to be traveling around waving a cigar. By contrast, cocaine, heroin, marijuana, and amphetamines have each been popular and even recommended as medicines at several points throughout history, each without any stigma of addiction attached (Inciardi, 2001).

Although addiction has a certain meaning here and now, this meaning is open to interpretation (Cherry, Dillon, & Rugh, 2002). Indeed, the concept of addiction has been extended to many human pursuits, giving rise to such terms as "sex addict," "gambling addict," "workaholic," and, of course, "chocoholic." Societies react differently at different times, with some uses of drugs ignored, other uses encouraged, others simply taxed, and yet others subjected to intense prohibition (see the Real World box on p. 208). Rather than viewing *all* drug use as a problem, it is important to consider the costs and benefits of such use and to establish ways to help people choose behaviors that are informed by this knowledge (Parrott et al., 2004).

"Hi, my name is Barry, and I check my E-mail two to three hundred times a day."

Types of Psychoactive Drugs

Four in five North Americans use caffeine in some form every day, but not all psychoactive drugs are this familiar. To learn how both the well-known and lesser-known drugs influence the mind, let's consider several broad categories of drugs: depressants, stimulants, narcotics, hallucinogens, and marijuana. **TABLE 5.2** summarizes what is known about the potential dangers of these different types of drugs.

Depressants

Depressants are *substances that reduce the activity of the central nervous system*. The most commonly used depressant is alcohol, and others include barbiturates, benzodiazepines, and toxic inhalants (such as glue or gasoline). Depressants have a sedative or calming effect, tend to induce sleep in high doses, and can arrest breathing in extremely high doses. Depressants can produce both physical and psychological dependence.

TABLE 5.2

Dangers of Drugs

| | Dangers | | |
| Drug | Overdose | Physical Dependence | Psychological Dependence |
	(Can taking too much cause death or injury?)	(Will stopping use make you sick?)	(Will you crave it when you stop using it?)
Depressants			
Alcohol	X	X	X
Benzodiazepines/Barbiturates	X	X	X
Toxic inhalants	X	X	X
Stimulants			
Amphetamines	X	X	X
MDMA (ecstasy)	X		?
Nicotine	X	X	X
Cocaine	X	X	X
Narcotics (opium, heroin, morphine, methadone, codeine)	X	X	X
Hallucinogens (LSD, mescaline, psilocybin, PCP, ketamine)	X		?
Marijuana			?

depressants Substances that reduce the activity of the central nervous system.

Alcohol. Alcohol is "king of the depressants," with its worldwide use beginning in prehistory, its easy availability in most cultures, and its widespread acceptance as a socially approved substance. Fifty-one percent of Americans over 12 years of age report having had a drink in the past month, and 23% have binged on alcohol (over five drinks in succession) in that time. Young adults (ages 18 to 25) have even higher rates, with 62% reporting a drink last month and 42% reporting a binge (*Health, United States,* 2008).

Alcohol's initial effects, euphoria and reduced anxiety, feel pretty positive. As it is consumed in greater quantities, drunkenness results, bringing slowed reactions, slurred speech, poor judgment, and other reductions in the effectiveness of thought and action. The exact way in which alcohol influences neural mechanisms is still not understood, but like other depressants, alcohol increases activity of the neurotransmitter GABA (De Witte, 1996). As you read in Chapter 3, GABA normally inhibits the transmission of neural impulses, so one effect of alcohol is as a disinhibitor—a chemical that lets transmissions occur that otherwise would be held in check. But there are many contradictions. Some people using alcohol become loud and aggressive, others become emotional and weepy, others become sullen, and still others turn giddy—and the same person can experience each of these effects in different circumstances. How can one drug do this? Two theories have been offered to account for these variable effects: *expectancy theory* and *alcohol myopia.*

> **?** Why do people experience being drunk differently?

Expectancy theory suggests that *alcohol effects are produced by people's expectations of how alcohol will influence them in particular situations* (Marlatt & Rohsenow, 1980). So, for instance, if you've watched friends or family drink at weddings and notice that this often produces hilarity and gregariousness, you could well experience these effects yourself should you drink alcohol on a similarly festive occasion. Seeing people getting drunk and fighting in bars, in turn, might lead to aggression after drinking.

The expectancy theory has been tested in studies that examine the effects of actual alcohol ingestion independent of the *perception* of alcohol ingestion. In experiments using a **balanced placebo design**, *behavior is observed following the presence or absence of an actual stimulus and also following the presence or absence of a placebo stimulus.* In such a study, participants are given drinks containing alcohol or a substitute liquid, and some people in each group are led to believe they had alcohol and others are led to believe they did not. People told they are drinking alcohol when they are not, for instance, might get a touch of vodka on the plastic lid of a cup to give it the right odor when the drink inside is merely tonic water. These experiments often show that the belief that one has had alcohol can influence behavior as strongly as the ingestion of alcohol itself (Goldman, Brown, & Christiansen, 1987). You may have seen people at parties getting rowdy after only one beer—perhaps because they expected this effect rather than because the beer actually had this influence.

Another approach to the varied effects of alcohol is the theory of **alcohol myopia**, which proposes that *alcohol hampers attention, leading people to respond in simple ways to complex situations* (Steele & Josephs, 1990). This theory recognizes that life is filled with complicated pushes and pulls, and our behavior is often a balancing act. Imagine that you are really attracted to someone who is dating your friend. Do you make your feelings known or focus on your friendship? The myopia theory holds that when you drink alcohol, your fine judgment is impaired. It becomes hard to appreciate the subtlety of these different options, and the inappropriate response is to veer full tilt one way or the other. So, alcohol might lead you to make a wild pass at your friend's date or perhaps just cry in your beer over your timidity—depending on which way you happened to tilt in your myopic state.

In one study on the alcohol myopia theory, men, half of whom were drinking alcohol, watched a video showing an unfriendly woman and then were asked how acceptable it would be for a man to act sexually aggressive toward a woman (Johnson, Noel, & Sutter-Hernandez, 2000). The unfriendly woman seemed to remind them that sex was out of the question, and indeed, men who were drinking alcohol and had seen

---

expectancy theory The idea that alcohol effects can be produced by people's expectations of how alcohol will influence them in particular situations.

balanced placebo design A study design in which behavior is observed following the presence or absence of an actual stimulus and also following the presence or absence of a placebo stimulus.

alcohol myopia A condition that results when alcohol hampers attention, leading people to respond in simple ways to complex situations.

stimulants Substances that excite the central nervous system, heightening arousal and activity levels.

this video were no more likely to think sexual advances were acceptable than men who were sober. However, when the same question was asked of a group of men who had seen a video of a *friendly* woman, those who were drinking were more inclined to recommend sexual overtures than those who were not, even when these overtures might be unwanted. Apparently, alcohol makes the complicated decisions involved in relationships seem simple ("Gee, she was so friendly")—and potentially open to serious misjudgments.

Both the expectancy and myopia theories suggest that people using alcohol will often go to extremes (Cooper, 2006). In fact, it seems that drinking is a major contributing factor to social problems that result from extreme behavior. Drinking while driving is a main cause of auto accidents, for example, contributing to 32% of U.S. crash fatalities in 2006 (Dept. of Transportation (US), 2008). A survey of undergraduates revealed that alcohol contributes to as many as 90% of rapes and 95% of violent crimes on campus (Wechsler et al., 1994). Of the binge drinkers in the student sample, 41% reported that they had had unplanned sex due to drinking, and 22% said their drinking led to unprotected sex.

Barbiturates, Benzodiazepines, and Toxic Inhalants. Compared to alcohol, the other depressants are much less popular but still are widely used and abused. Barbiturates such as Seconal or Nembutal are prescribed as sleep aids and as anesthetics before surgery. Benzodiazepines such as Valium and Xanax are also called minor tranquilizers and are prescribed as antianxiety drugs. These drugs are prescribed by physicians to treat anxiety or sleep problems, but they are dangerous when used in combination with alcohol because they can cause respiratory depression—and it's never good to stop breathing. Physical dependence is possible since withdrawal from long-term use can produce severe symptoms (including convulsions), and psychological dependence is common as well. Finally, toxic inhalants are perhaps the most alarming substances in this category (Kurtzman, Otsuka, & Wahl, 2001). These drugs are easily accessible even to children in the vapors of glue, gasoline, or propane. Sniffing or "huffing" these vapors can promote temporary effects that resemble drunkenness, but overdoses are sometimes lethal, and continued use holds the potential for permanent brain damage (Fornazzari et al., 1983).

Stimulants

The **stimulants** are *substances that excite the central nervous system, heightening arousal and activity levels.* They include caffeine, amphetamines, nicotine, cocaine, modafinil, and ecstasy (MDMA), and sometimes have a legitimate pharmaceutical purpose. Amphetamines (also called "speed"), for example, were originally prepared for medicinal uses and as diet drugs; however, amphetamines such as Methedrine and Dexedrine are widely abused, causing insomnia, aggression, and paranoia with long-term use. Stimulants increase the levels of dopamine and norepinephrine in the brain, thereby inducing higher levels of activity in the brain circuits that depend on these neurotransmitters. As a result, they increase alertness and energy in the user, often producing a euphoric sense of confidence and a kind of agitated motivation to get things done. Stimulants produce physical and psychological dependence, and their withdrawal symptoms involve depressive effects such as fatigue and negative emotions.

Ecstasy is an amphetamine derivative also known as MDMA, "X," or "e." It is a stimulant, but it has added effects somewhat like those of hallucinogens (we'll talk about those shortly). Ecstasy is particularly known for making users feel empathic and close to those around them. It is used often as a party drug to enhance the group feeling at dances or raves, but it has unpleasant side effects such as causing jaw clenching and interfering with the regulation of body temperature. The rave culture has popularized pacifiers and juices as remedies for these problems, but users remain highly

▼ People will often endure significant inconveniences to maintain their addictions.

JEFF GREENBERG/THE IMAGE WORKS

▲ Coca-Cola has been a popular product for more than 100 years. In the early days, one of the fatigue-relieving ingredients was a small amount of cocaine.

susceptible to heatstroke and exhaustion. Although ecstasy is not as likely as some other drugs to cause physical or psychological dependence, it nonetheless can lead to some dependence. What's more, the impurities sometimes found in "street" pills are also dangerous (Parrott, 2001). Ecstasy's potentially toxic effect on serotonin-activated neurons in the human brain is under intense debate, and a good deal of research attention is being devoted to studying the effects of this drug on humans.

Cocaine is derived from leaves of the coca plant, which has been cultivated by indigenous peoples of the Andes for millennia and chewed as a medication. Yes, the urban legend is true: *Coca-Cola* contained cocaine until 1903 and still may use coca leaves (with cocaine removed) as a flavoring—although the company's not telling (*Pepsi-Cola* never contained cocaine and is probably made from something brown). Sigmund Freud tried cocaine and wrote effusively about it for a while. Cocaine (usually snorted) and crack cocaine (smoked) produce exhilaration and euphoria and are seriously addictive, both for humans and the rats you read about earlier in this chapter. Withdrawal takes the form of an unpleasant "crash," cravings are common, and antisocial effects like those generated by amphetamines—aggressiveness and paranoia—are frequent with long-term use. Although cocaine has enjoyed popularity as a "party drug," its extraordinary potential to create dependence should be taken very seriously.

Nicotine is something of a puzzle. This is a drug with almost nothing to recommend it to the newcomer. It usually involves inhaling smoke that doesn't smell that great, at least at first, and there's not much in the way of a "high" either—at best, some dizziness or a queasy feeling. So why do people do it? Tobacco use is motivated far more by the unpleasantness of quitting than by the pleasantness of using. The positive effects people report from smoking—relaxation and improved concentration, for example—come chiefly from relief from withdrawal symptoms (Baker, Brandon, & Chassin, 2004). The best approach to nicotine is never to get started.

Narcotics

Opium, which comes from poppy seeds, and its derivatives heroin, morphine, methadone, and codeine (as well as prescription drugs such as Demerol and Oxycontin), are known as **narcotics** or **opiates,** *drugs derived from opium that are capable of relieving pain.* Narcotics induce a feeling of well-being and relaxation that is enjoyable but can also induce stupor and lethargy. The addictive properties of narcotics are powerful, and long-term use produces both tolerance and dependence. Because these drugs are often administered with hypodermic syringes, they also introduce the danger of diseases such as HIV when users share syringes. Unfortunately, these drugs are especially alluring because they are external mimics of the brain's own internal relaxation and well-being system.

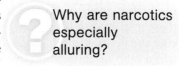

Why are narcotics especially alluring?

The brain produces endorphins or endogenous opioids, which are neurotransmitters that are closely related to opiates. As you learned in Chapter 3, endorphins play a role in how the brain copes internally with pain and stress. These substances reduce the experience of pain naturally. When you exercise for a while and start to feel your muscles burning, for example, you may also find that there comes a time when the pain eases—sometimes even *during* the exercise. Endorphins are secreted in the pituitary gland and other brain sites as a response to injury or exertion, creating a kind of natural remedy (like the so-called runner's high) that subsequently reduces pain and increases feelings of well-being. When people use narcotics, the brain's endorphin receptors are artificially flooded, however, reducing receptor effectiveness and possibly also depressing the production of endorphins. When external administration of narcotics stops, withdrawal symptoms are likely to occur.

narcotics or opiates Highly addictive drugs derived from opium that relieve pain.

Hallucinogens

The drugs that produce the most extreme alterations of consciousness are the **hallucinogens**, *drugs that alter sensation and perception, often causing hallucinations.* These include LSD (lysergic acid diethylamide), or acid; mescaline; psilocybin; PCP (phencyclidine); and ketamine (an animal anesthetic). Some of these drugs are derived from plants (mescaline from peyote cactus, psilocybin or "shrooms" from mushrooms) and have been used by people since ancient times. For example, the ingestion of peyote plays a prominent role in some Native American religious practices. The other hallucinogens are largely synthetic. LSD was first made by chemist Albert Hofman in 1938, leading to a rash of experimentation that influenced popular culture in the 1960s. Timothy Leary, at the time a Harvard psychology professor, championed the use of LSD to "turn on, tune in, and drop out"; the Beatles sang of *Lucy in the sky with diamonds* (denying, of course, that this might be a reference to LSD); and the wave of interest led many people to experiment with hallucinogens.

The experiment was not a great success. These drugs produce profound changes in perception. Sensations may seem unusually intense, objects may seem to move or change, patterns or colors may appear, and these perceptions may be accompanied by exaggerated emotions ranging from blissful transcendence to abject terror. These are the "I've-become-the-legs-of-a-chair!" drugs. But the effects of hallucinogens are dramatic and unpredictable, creating a psychological roller-coaster ride that some people find intriguing but others find deeply disturbing. Hallucinogens are the main class of drugs that animals *won't* work to self-administer, so it is not surprising that in humans these drugs are unlikely to be addictive. Hallucinogens do not induce significant tolerance or dependence, and overdose deaths are rare. Although hallucinogens still enjoy a marginal popularity with people interested in experimenting with their perceptions, they have been more a cultural trend than a dangerous attraction.

▲ Psychedelic art and music of the 1960s were inspired by some visual and auditory effects of drugs such as LSD.

Marijuana

The *leaves and buds of the hemp plant* contain THC, the active ingredient in **marijuana**. When smoked or eaten, either as is or in concentrated form as *hashish,* this drug produces an intoxication that is mildly hallucinogenic. Users describe the experience as euphoric, with heightened senses of sight and sound and the perception of a rush of ideas. Marijuana affects judgment and short-term memory and impairs motor skills and coordination—making driving a car or operating heavy equipment a poor choice during its use ("Where did I leave the darn bulldozer?"). Researchers have found that receptors in the brain that respond to THC (Stephens, 1999) are normally activated by a neurotransmitter called *anandamide* that is naturally produced in the brain (Wiley, 1999). Anandamide is involved in the regulation of mood, memory, appetite, and pain perception and has been found temporarily to stimulate overeating in laboratory animals, much as marijuana does in humans (Williams & Kirkham, 1999). Some chemicals found in dark chocolate also mimic anandamide, although very weakly, perhaps accounting for the well-being some people claim they enjoy after a "dose" of chocolate.

The addiction potential of marijuana is not strong, as tolerance does not seem to develop, and physical withdrawal symptoms are minimal. Psychological dependence is possible, however, and some people do become chronic users. Marijuana use has been widespread throughout the world for recorded history, both as a medicine for pain and/or nausea and as a recreational drug, but its use

? What are the risks of marijuana use?

remains controversial. Laws vary across the United States and Canada, with a number of states and provinces reducing penalties for the cultivation or possession of marijuana for medical use. The U.S. government classifies marijuana as a "Schedule I Controlled Substance," recognizing no medical use and maintaining that marijuana has the same high potential for abuse as heroin—but has recently announced that federal prosecution under the law is "unlikely to be an efficient use of limited federal resources" (Fields & Scheck, 2009). The marijuana story is in flux, but right now the greatest danger of marijuana is that its use is illegal.

hallucinogens Drugs that alter sensation and perception and often cause visual and auditory hallucinations.

marijuana The leaves and buds of the hemp plant.

THE REAL WORLD

Drugs and the Regulation of Consciousness

Why does everyone have an opinion about drug use? Given that it's not possible to perceive what happens in anyone else's mind, why does it matter so much to us what people do to their own consciousness? Is consciousness something that governments should be able to legislate—or should people be free to choose their own conscious states (McWilliams, 1993)? After all, how can a "free society" justify regulating what people do inside their own heads?

Individuals and governments alike answer these questions by pointing to the costs of drug addiction, both to the addict and to the society that must "carry" unproductive people, pay for their welfare, and often even take care of their children. Drug users appear to be troublemakers and criminals, the culprits behind all those "drug-related" shootings, knifings, robberies, and petty thefts you see in the news day after day. Widespread anger about the drug problem surfaced in the form of the "War on Drugs," a federal government program born in the Nixon years that focused on drug use as a criminal offense and attempted to stop drug use through the imprisonment of users.

Drug use did not stop with 40 years of the War on Drugs, though, and instead, prisons filled with people arrested for drug use. From 1990 to 2007, the number of drug offenders in state and federal prisons increased from 179,070 to 348,736—a jump of 94% (Bureau of Justice Statistics, 2008)—not because of a measurable increase in drug use, but because of the rapidly increasing use of imprisonment for drug offenses. Many people who were being prevented from ruining their lives with drugs were instead having their lives ruined by prison. Like the failed policy of alcohol Prohibition from 1920 to 1933 (Trebach & Zeese, 1992), the policy of the drug war seemed to be causing more harm than it was preventing.

What can be done? The new policy of the Obama administration is to wind down the "war" mentality and instead focus on reducing the harm that drugs cause (Fields, 2009). This **harm reduction approach** *is a response to high-risk behaviors that focuses on reducing the harm such behaviors have on people's lives* (Marlatt, 1998). Harm reduction originated in the Netherlands and England with tactics such as eliminating criminal penalties for some drug use or providing intravenous drug users with sterile syringes to help them avoid contracting HIV and other infections from shared needles (Des Jarlais et al., 2009). Harm reduction may even involve providing drugs for addicts to reduce the risks of poisoning and overdose they face when they get impure drugs of unknown dosage from criminal suppliers. A harm reduction idea for alcoholics, in turn, is to allow moderate drinking; the demand to be cold sober might keep many alcoholics on the street and away from any treatment at all (Marlatt et al., 1993). Harm reduction strategies may not always find public support because they challenge the popular idea that the solution to drug and alcohol problems must always be prohibition: stopping use entirely.

The mistaken belief in prohibition is fueled, in part, by the worry that drug use turns people into criminals and causes psychological disorders. A key study that followed 101 children as they grew from the age of 3 to 18 did not confirm this theory (Shedler & Block, 1990). Personality assessments given to participants showed that those who were frequent drug users at 18 indeed were the most irresponsible, inconsiderate, irritable, rebellious, low in self-esteem, and so on. However, the adjustment problems of the frequent users were *already present* in early childhood, long before they started using drugs. Some other factor (a poor family environment as a child, perhaps) caused both their adjustment problems *and* their frequent drug use. As you read in Chapter 2, a third variable can be at work in producing a correlation. It may be that allowing some limited forms of drug use—and instead focusing greater attention on reducing harm—would not create the problems we fear.

▲ In the Netherlands, marijuana use is not prosecuted. The drug is sold in "coffee shops" to those over 18.

Harm reduction seems to be working in the Netherlands. The Netherlands Ministry of Justice (1999) reported that the decriminalization of marijuana there in 1979 has not led to increased use and that the use of other drugs remains at a level far below that of other European countries and the United States. A comparison of drug users in Amsterdam and San Francisco revealed that the city in which marijuana is criminalized—San Francisco—had higher rates of drug use for both marijuana and other drugs (Reinarman, Cohen, & Kaal, 2004). Separating the markets in which people buy marijuana and alcohol from those in which they get "hard" drugs such as heroin, cocaine, or methamphetamine may create a social barrier that reduces interest in the hard drugs. There may be solutions that find a middle ground between prohibition and deregulation as a way of reducing harm. Former President Jimmy Carter expressed it this way: "Penalties against drug use should not be more damaging to an individual than the use of the drug itself" (Carter, 1977).

◀ There are many reasons that U.S. prisons are overcrowded—this country has the highest incarceration rate in the world. Treating drug abuse as a crime that requires imprisonment is one of the reasons.

IN SUMMARY

○ Psychoactive drugs influence consciousness by altering the brain's chemical messaging system and intensifying or dulling the effects of neurotransmitters.

○ Drug tolerance can result in overdose, and physical and psychological dependence can lead to addiction.

○ Major types of psychoactive drugs include depressants, stimulants, narcotics, hallucinogens, and marijuana.

○ The varying effects of alcohol, a depressant, are explained by theories of alcohol expectancy and alcohol myopia.

harm reduction approach A response to high-risk behaviors that focuses on reducing the harm such behaviors have on people's lives.

hypnosis An altered state of consciousness characterized by suggestibility and the feeling that one's actions are occurring involuntarily.

Hypnosis: Open to Suggestion

You may have never been hypnotized, but you have probably heard or read about it. Its wonders are often described with an air of amazement, and demonstrations of stage hypnosis make it seem very powerful and mysterious. When you think of hypnosis, you may envision people down on all fours acting like farm animals or perhaps "regressing" to early childhood and talking in childlike voices. Some of what you might think is true, but many of the common beliefs about hypnosis are false. **Hypnosis** is *an altered state of consciousness characterized by suggestibility and the feeling that one's actions are occurring involuntarily.* In other words, it is mainly a state of mind in which people follow instructions readily and feel that their actions are things that are happening to them rather than things they are doing (Lynn, Rhue, & Weekes, 1990).

▲ As you gaze at this magazine cover, you are getting sleepy… very sleepy…

Induction and Susceptibility

The essence of hypnosis is in leading people to expect that certain things will happen to them that are outside their conscious will (Wegner, 2002). To induce hypnosis, then, a hypnotist may ask the person to be hypnotized to sit quietly and focus on some item (such as a spot on the wall) and then suggest to the person what effects hypnosis will have (for example, "Your eyelids are slowly closing" or "Your arms are getting heavy"). These are "suggestions," ideas the hypnotist mentions to the volunteer about what the volunteer will do. Some of these ideas seem to cause the actions— just thinking about their eyelids slowly closing, for instance, may make many people shut their eyes briefly or at least blink. Just as you may find yawning contagious when you see someone else yawning, many different behaviors can be made more common just by concentrating on them. In hypnosis, a series of behavior suggestions can induce in some people a state of mind that makes them susceptible to even very unusual suggestions, such as getting down on all fours and sniffing in the corner.

Not everyone is equally hypnotizable. Susceptibility varies greatly, such that while some hypnotic "virtuosos" are strongly influenced, most people are only moderately influenced, and some people are entirely unaffected.

What makes someone easy to hypnotize? Susceptibility is not easily predicted by a person's personality traits, so tests of hypnotic susceptibility are made up of a series of suggestions in a standard hypnotic induction. One of the best indicators of a person's susceptibility is the person's own judgment. So, if you think you might be hypnotizable, you may well be (Hilgard, 1965). People with active, vivid imaginations, or who are easily absorbed in activities such as watching a movie, are also somewhat more prone to be good candidates for hypnosis (Sheehan, 1979; Tellegen & Atkinson, 1974).

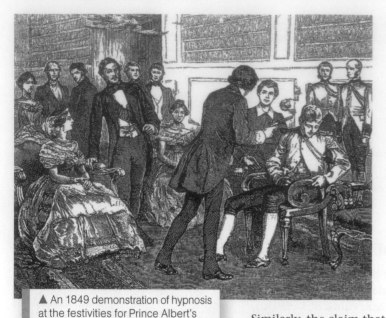

▲ An 1849 demonstration of hypnosis at the festivities for Prince Albert's birthday. A pistol is discharged near the face of a young man in a trance, and he does not even flinch.

Hypnotic Effects

From watching stage hypnotism, you might think that the major effect of hypnosis is making people do peculiar things. In fact, there are some impressive demonstrations. At the 1849 festivities for Prince Albert of England's birthday, for example, a hypnotized guest was asked to ignore any loud noises and then didn't even flinch when a pistol was fired near his face. The real effects of hypnosis are often clouded, however, by extravagant claims—that hypnotized people can perform extraordinary physical stunts, for example, or that they can remember things they have forgotten in normal consciousness.

Hypnotists often claim that their volunteers can perform great feats not possible when the volunteers are fully conscious. One of the claims for superhuman strength involves asking a hypnotized person to become "stiff as a board" and lie unsupported with shoulders on one chair and feet on another. However, many people can do this without hypnosis. Similarly, the claim that people will perform extreme actions when hypnotized fails to take into account that people will also perform these actions when they are simply under a lot of social pressure. Some early studies reported, for instance, that hypnotized people could be led to throw what they thought was a flask of acid in an experimenter's face (Rowland, 1939; Young, 1948). In further examinations of this phenomenon, participants who were not hypnotized were asked to *simulate* being hypnotized (Orne & Evans, 1965). They were instructed to be so convincing in faking their hypnosis that they would fool the experimenter. These people, just like the hypnotized participants, threw what they thought was acid in the experimenter's face! Clearly, hypnotic induction was not a necessary requirement to produce this behavior in the research participants.

Other strong claims for hypnosis have arisen because of the extraordinary agreeableness of many hypnotized people. When a susceptible person under hypnosis is asked to go back in time to childhood, for example, the person may become remarkably childlike, even to the point of babbling like an infant or breaking down in tears. One young man whose first language was Japanese but who was raised speaking English from the age of 8 reverted to Japanese spontaneously when under hypnosis; it was suggested that he was only 3 years old (Hilgard, 1986). Such cases have made psychologists wonder whether there is true "hypnotic age regression" or whether such cases are matters of playacting. (After all, does the hypnotized person who barks like a dog actually *become* a dog?) It turns out that the mental abilities of adults who have been age-regressed in hypnosis do not truly revert to early developmental stages or show childlike ways of thinking (Nash, 1987).

Hypnosis also has been touted as a cure for lost memory. The claim that hypnosis helps people to unearth memories that they are not able to retrieve in normal consciousness, however, seems to have surfaced because hypnotized people often make up memories to satisfy the hypnotist's suggestions. For example, Paul Ingram, a sheriff's deputy accused of sexual abuse by his daughters in the 1980s, was asked by interrogators in session after session to relax and imagine having committed the crimes. He emerged from these sessions having confessed to dozens of horrendous acts of "satanic ritual abuse." These confessions were called into question, however, when independent investigator Richard Ofshe used the same technique to ask Ingram about a crime that Ofshe had simply made up out of thin

▼ A hypnotist stands on a subject who has been rendered "stiff as a board" by hypnosis.

HULTON-DEUTSCH COLLECTION/CORBIS

air, something of which Ingram had never been accused. Ingram produced a three-page handwritten confession, complete with dialogue (Ofshe, 1992). Still, prosecutors in the case accepted Ingram's guilty plea, and he was only released in 2003 after a public outcry and years of work on his defense. After a person claims to remember something, even under hypnosis, it is difficult to convince others that the memory was false (Loftus & Ketchum, 1994).

Hypnosis can also undermine memory. People susceptible to hypnosis can be led to experience **posthypnotic amnesia**, *the failure to retrieve memories following hypnotic suggestions to forget.* Ernest Hilgard (1986) taught a hypnotized person the populations of some remote cities, for example, and then suggested that he forget the study session. The person was quite surprised after the session at being able to give the census figures correctly. (Asked how he knew the answers, the individual decided he might have learned them from a TV program.) Such amnesia can then be reversed in subsequent hypnosis.

However, research does *not* find that people can retrieve through hypnosis memories that were not originally lost through hypnosis. Instead, hypnotized people try to report memories in line with the hypnotist's questioning. In one study, 27 hypnotizable research volunteers were given suggestions during hypnosis that they had been awakened by loud noises in the night a week before. After hypnosis, 13 of them—roughly 50%—reported that they had been awakened by loud noises (Laurence & Perry, 1983). Hypnosis does not enhance the accuracy of memory and instead only increases the person's *confidence* in false memory reports (Kihlstrom, 1985).

Although all the preceding claims for hypnosis are somewhat debatable, one well-established effect is **hypnotic analgesia**, *the reduction of pain through hypnosis in people who are hypnotically susceptible.* For example, one study (see **FIGURE 5.14**) found that for pain induced in volunteers in the laboratory, hypnosis was more effective than morphine, diazepam (Valium), aspirin, acupuncture, or placebos (Stern et al., 1977). For people who are hypnotically susceptible, hypnosis can be used to control pain in surgeries and dental procedures, in some cases more effectively than any form of anesthesia (Druckman & Bjork, 1994; Kihlstrom, 1985). Evidence for pain control supports the idea that hypnosis is a different state of consciousness and not entirely a matter of skillful role-playing on the part of highly motivated people.

▲ Stage hypnotists often perform an induction on a whole audience and then bring some of the more susceptible members onstage for further demonstrations.

Why do some argue that hypnosis is indeed a different state of consciousness?

posthypnotic amnesia The failure to retrieve memories following hypnotic suggestions to forget.

hypnotic analgesia The reduction of pain through hypnosis in people who are susceptible to hypnosis.

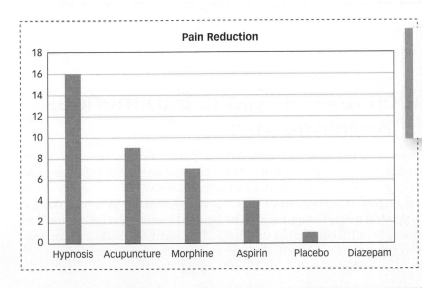

Pain Reduction

◀ FIGURE 5.14

Hypnotic Analgesia The degree of pain reduction reported by people using different techniques for the treatment of laboratory-induced pain. Hypnosis wins. From Stern et al., 1977.

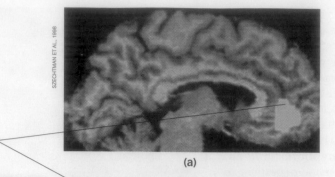

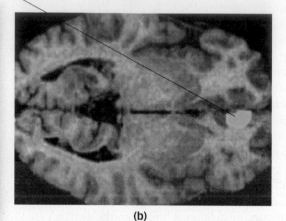

SZECHTMAN ET AL., 1998

Right anterior
cingulate cortex

(a)

(b)

▶ FIGURE 5.15
Brain Activity during Hypnosis
Researchers found right anterior cingulate cortex activation in hypnotized research participants both when they were hearing a target sentence and when they were following the suggestion to hallucinate the sentence. The right anterior cingulate cortex is involved in the regulation of attention. The brain is viewed here in two cross-sectional scans: (a) upright and (b) horizontal. From Szechtman et al., 1998.

The conscious state of hypnosis is accompanied by unique patterns of brain activation. In one study, researchers prescreened highly hypnotizable people for their ability to hallucinate during hypnosis (Szechtman et al., 1998). After a standard hypnotic induction, these participants were tested in a PET (positron emission tomography) scanner while performing each of three tasks: perception, imagination, and hypnotic hallucination. For the perception task, participants heard a recording of the sentence, "The man did not speak often, but when he did, it was worth hearing what he had to say." For the imagination task, they were asked to imagine hearing this line again. For the hypnotic hallucination task, they listened as the hypnotist suggested that the tape was playing once more (although it was not). The researchers expected this last suggestion to prompt an auditory hallucination of the line, and participants indeed reported thinking they heard it.

The PET scan revealed that the right anterior cingulate cortex, an area involved in the regulation of attention, was just as active while the participants were hallucinating as when they were actually hearing the line. However, there was less activation in this brain area when participants were merely imagining the sentence. **FIGURE 5.15** shows where the right anterior cingulate area was activated in the hypnotizable participants both during hearing and hallucinating. This pattern of activation was not found in people who were not highly hypnotizable. The researchers concluded that hypnosis stimulated the brain to register the hallucinated voice as real rather than as imagined.

IN SUMMARY

○ Hypnosis is an altered state of consciousness characterized by suggestibility.

○ Although many claims for hypnosis overstate its effects, hypnosis can create the experience that one's actions are occurring involuntarily, create analgesia, and even change brain activations in ways that suggest that hypnotic experiences are more than imagination.

Meditation and Religious Experiences: Higher Consciousness

Some altered states of consciousness occur without hypnosis, without drugs, and without other external aids. In fact, the altered states of consciousness that occur naturally or through special practices such as meditation can provide some of the best moments in life. Abraham Maslow (1962) described these "peak experiences" as special states of mind in which you feel fully alive and glad to be human. Sometimes these come from simple pleasures—a breathtaking sunset or a magical moment of personal creativity— and other times they can arise through meditative or religious experiences.

Meditation

Meditation is *the practice of intentional contemplation.* Techniques of meditation are associated with a variety of religious traditions and are also practiced outside religious contexts. The techniques vary widely. Some forms of meditation call for attempts to clear the mind of thought, others involve focusing on a single thought (for example, thinking about a candle flame), and still others involve concentration on breathing or on a mantra, a repetitive sound such as *om*. At a minimum, the techniques have in common a period of quiet.

Why would someone meditate? The time spent meditating can be restful and revitalizing, and according to meditation enthusiasts, the

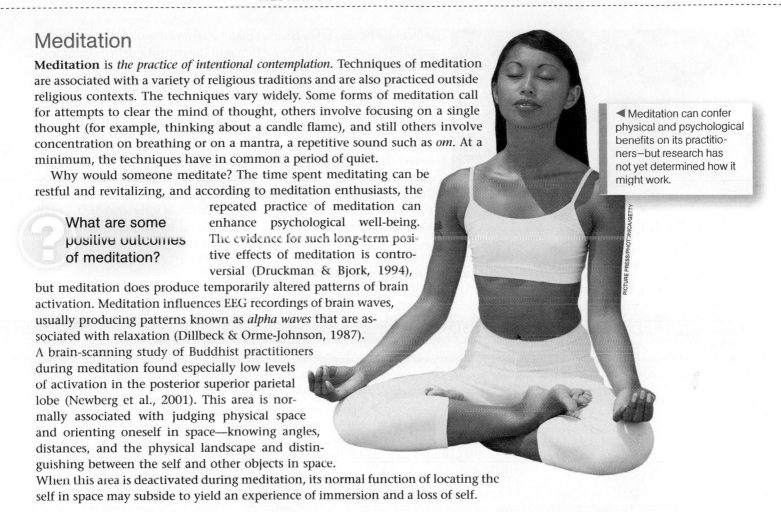

◄ Meditation can confer physical and psychological benefits on its practitioners—but research has not yet determined how it might work.

PICTURE PRESS/PHOTONICA/GETTY

What are some positive outcomes of meditation?

repeated practice of meditation can enhance psychological well-being. The evidence for such long-term positive effects of meditation is controversial (Druckman & Bjork, 1994), but meditation does produce temporarily altered patterns of brain activation. Meditation influences EEG recordings of brain waves, usually producing patterns known as *alpha waves* that are associated with relaxation (Dillbeck & Orme-Johnson, 1987). A brain-scanning study of Buddhist practitioners during meditation found especially low levels of activation in the posterior superior parietal lobe (Newberg et al., 2001). This area is normally associated with judging physical space and orienting oneself in space—knowing angles, distances, and the physical landscape and distinguishing between the self and other objects in space. When this area is deactivated during meditation, its normal function of locating the self in space may subside to yield an experience of immersion and a loss of self.

Ecstatic Religious Experiences

In some religious traditions, people describe personal experiences of altered consciousness—feelings of ecstasy, rapture, conversion, or mystical union. Members of a religious group may "speak in tongues," or the celebrants may go into trances, report seeing visions, or feel as though they are possessed by spirits. These altered states may happen during prayer or worship or without any special religious activity. Over 40% of one sample of Americans reported having a profound experience of this kind at least once in their lives (Greeley, 1975), and altered states of consciousness of one sort or another are associated with religious practices around the world (Bourguignon, 1968).

Like meditation, certain brain activation patterns are associated with ecstatic religious experiences. Some people who experience religious fervor show the same type of brain activation that occurs in some cases of epilepsy. Several prophets, saints, and founders of religions have been documented as having epilepsy—St. Joan of Arc, for ex-

What is the relationship between religious fervor and epilepsy?

ample, had symptoms of epilepsy accompanying the religious visions that inspired her and her followers (Saver & Rabin, 1997). Similar symptoms occurred to St. Paul on the road to Damascus when he fell to the ground and suffered three days of blindness; the prophet Mohammed described falling episodes accompanied by religious visions; and Joseph Smith, who founded Mormonism, reported lapses of consciousness and speech arrest (Trimble, 2007). People asked to describe what it is like to have a seizure, in turn, sometimes report feeling what they call a religious "aura." One patient described his seizures as consisting of feelings of incredible contentment, detachment, and fulfillment, accompanied by the visualization of a bright light and soft music;

GAHAN WILSON/THE NEW YORKER COLLECTION/ CARTOONBANK.COM

"Nothing happens next. This is it."

meditation The practice of intentional contemplation.

▲ **Speaking in Tongues** Part of worship in some churches involves being "filled with the Holy Spirit" and speaking in tongues. This usually means speaking in no recognizable language—although members of each congregation tend to have their own style and so sound alike.

sometimes he also saw a bearded man he assumed was Jesus Christ (Morgan, 1990). Surgery to remove a tumor in the patient's right anterior temporal lobe eliminated the seizures but also stopped his religious ecstasies. Cases such as this suggest the right anterior temporal lobe might be involved when people without epilepsy experience profound religious feelings. The special moments of connection that people feel with God or the universe may depend on the way in which brain activation promotes a religious state of consciousness.

The states of religious ecstasy and meditation are just two of the intriguing varieties of experience that consciousness makes available to us. Our consciousness ranges from the normal everyday awareness of walking, thinking, or gazing at a picture to an array of states that are far from normal or everyday—sleep, dreams, drug intoxication, hypnosis, and beyond. These states of mind stand as a reminder that the human mind is not just something that students of psychology can look at and study. The mind is something each of us looks *through* at the world and at ourselves.

IN SUMMARY

○ Meditation and religious ecstasy can be understood as altered states of consciousness.

○ Meditation involves contemplation that may focus on a specific thought, sound, or action, or it may be an attempt to avoid any focus.

○ The practice of meditation promotes relaxation in the short term, but the long-term benefits claimed by enthusiasts have not been established.

○ Ecstatic religious experiences may have a basis in the same brain region—the right anterior temporal lobe—associated with some forms of epilepsy.

WhereDoYouStand?

Between NORML and MADD: What Is Acceptable Drug Use?

Where is the line between drug use and abuse, between acceptable chemical alteration of consciousness and over-the-top, drug-crazed insanity? Some people think the line is drawn too strictly—organizations such as NORML (National Organization for the Reform of Marijuana Laws) lobby for the legalization of marijuana. Others think the line is too loose—MADD (Mothers Against Drunk Driving) asks bars and restaurants to end "happy hours" that promote alcohol consumption. At the extremes, some people advocate the legalization of cocaine and heroin (for instance, Jenny Tonge, member of the British Parliament), and others propose to fight caffeine addiction (for example, Rosemarie Ives, mayor of Redmond, Washington).

Drug use is a controversial topic, and whenever it comes up, you may find yourself face-to-face with people who have very strong opinions. Talking with some people about drugs and alcohol may feel like talking with interrogators under a bright light down at the police station, and you may find yourself taking sides that do not reflect how you really feel. On the other hand, people you know who drink or use drugs may make you feel like a stick-in-the-mud if you don't always approve of what they're doing. Where do you stand? Should people be legally allowed to use psychoactive drugs and if yes, which ones? What about alcohol? Should there be restrictions on when or where these substances are used? For a legal drug, how old should a person be to use it?

Chapter Review

KEY CONCEPT QUIZ

1. Which of the following is NOT a basic property of consciousness?
   a. intentionality
   b. disunity
   c. selectivity
   d. transience

2. Currently, unconscious processes are understood as
   a. a concentrated pattern of thought suppression.
   b. a hidden system of memories, instincts, and desires.
   c. a blank slate.
   d. unexperienced mental processes that give rise to thoughts and behavior.

3. The _____ unconscious is at work when subliminal and unconscious processes influence thought and behavior.
   a. minimal
   b. repressive
   c. dynamic
   d. cognitive

4. The cycle of sleep and waking is one of the major patterns of human life called
   a. the circadian rhythm.
   b. the sleep stages.
   c. the altered state of consciousness.
   d. subliminal perception.

5. Sleep needs _____ over the life span.
   a. decrease
   b. increase
   c. fluctuate
   d. remain the same

6. During dreaming, the dreamer _____ changes in emotion, thought, and sensation.
   a. is skeptical of
   b. is completely unconscious of
   c. uncritically accepts
   d. views objectively

7. Which explanation of dreams proposes that they are produced when the mind attempts to make sense of random neural activity that occurs in the brain during sleep?
   a. Freud's psychoanalytic theory
   b. the activation-synthesis model
   c. the cognitive unconscious model
   d. the manifest content framework

8. fMRI studies of the dreaming brain reveal all of the following EXCEPT
   a. increased sensitivity to emotions.
   b. activations associated with visual activity.
   c. increased capacity for planning.
   d. prevention of movement.

9. Psychoactive drugs influence consciousness by altering the effects of
   a. agonists.
   b. neurotransmitters.
   c. amphetamines.
   d. spinal neurons.

10. Tolerance to drugs involves
    a. larger doses being required over time to achieve the same effect.
    b. openness to new experiences.
    c. the initial attraction of drug use.
    d. the lessening of the painful symptoms that accompany withdrawal.

11. Drugs that heighten arousal and activity level by affecting the central nervous system are
    a. depressants.
    b. stimulants.
    c. narcotics.
    d. hallucinogens.

12. Alcohol expectancy refers to
    a. alcohol's initial effects of euphoria and reduced anxiety.
    b. the widespread acceptance of alcohol as a socially approved substance.
    c. alcohol leading people to respond in simple ways to complex situations.
    d. people's beliefs about how alcohol will influence them in particular situations.

13. Hypnosis has been proven to have
    a. an effect on physical strength.
    b. a positive effect on memory retrieval.
    c. an analgesic effect.
    d. an age-regression effect.

14. Meditation and religious ecstasy are altered states of consciousness that occur
    a. with the aid of drugs.
    b. through hypnosis.
    c. naturally or through special practices.
    d. as a result of dreamlike brain activity.

KEY TERMS

consciousness (p. 176)

phenomenology (p. 176)

problem of other minds (p. 177)

mind/body problem (p. 178)

dichotic listening (p. 180)

cocktail party phenomenon (p. 180)

minimal consciousness (p. 181)

full consciousness (p. 181)

self-consciousness (p. 182)

mental control (p. 185)

thought suppression (p. 185)

rebound effect of thought suppression (p. 185)

ironic processes of mental control (p. 186)

dynamic unconscious (p. 187)

repression (p. 187)

cognitive unconscious (p. 188)

subliminal perception (p. 188)

altered state of consciousness (p. 190)

circadian rhythm (p. 191)

REM sleep (p. 191)

electrooculograph (EOG) (p. 191)

insomnia (p. 194)

sleep apnea (p. 195)

somnambulism (p. 195)

narcolepsy (p. 195)

sleep paralysis (p. 196)

night terrors (p. 196)

manifest content (p. 197)

latent content (p. 197)

activation-synthesis model (p. 198)

psychoactive drugs (p. 200)

drug tolerance (p. 201)

depressants (p. 203)

expectancy theory (p. 204)

balanced placebo design (p. 204)

alcohol myopia (p. 204)

stimulants (p. 205)

narcotics or opiates (p. 206)

hallucinogens (p. 207)

marijuana (p. 207)

harm reduction approach (p. 208)

hypnosis (p. 209)

posthypnotic amnesia (p. 211)

hypnotic analgesia (p. 211)

meditation (p. 213)

CRITICAL THINKING QUESTIONS

1. Freud theorized that dreams represent unacceptable or anxiety-producing wishes that the mind can only express in disguised form. A different theory of dreaming, the activation-synthesis model, proposes that dreams are produced when the mind attempts to make sense of random neural activity that occurs in the brain during sleep.

   Suppose a man is expecting a visit from his mother-in-law; the night before her arrival, he dreams that he comes home from work to find that his mother-in-law has driven a bus through the living room window of his house. How might Freud have interpreted such a dream? How might the activation-synthesis model interpret such a dream?

2. Alcohol has many effects that can differ from person to person and from situation to situation. Expectancy theory suggests that alcohol's effects are affected by people's

expectations of how alcohol will influence them. The theory of alcohol myopia proposes that alcohol hampers attention, leading people to respond in simple ways to complex situations.

   Which one of these theories views a person's response to alcohol as being (at least partially) learned, through a process similar to observational learning?

3. Psychoactive drugs are chemicals that, when ingested, influence consciousness or behavior by altering the brain's chemical message system. Stimulant drugs can influence brain activity and often produce a sense of euphoria and well-being. Meditation is the practice of internal contemplation, and it can also temporarily influence brain activity and enhance the sense of well-being.

   Why do you think many cultures view psychoactive drugs as dangerous but meditation as healthful?

RECOMMENDED READINGS

Blackmore, S. (2011). *Consciousness: An introduction* (2nd ed.) New York: Oxford University Press.

Susan Blackmore is the sort of writer whom you might expect would show up every few weeks with her hair freshly dyed in a new pattern of rainbow colors, and in fact this is exactly what she does. Her book blends philosophy, psychology, and neuroscience in a clear, enjoyable, and yes, colorfully written introduction to the field of consciousness.

Hobson, A. (2004). *Dreaming: An introduction to the science of sleep.* New York: Oxford University Press.

Hobson asks whether we go insane when we go to sleep—and then answers the question with a careful and fascinating study of the content of dreams and its relation to the activation of brain areas in sleep and dreaming.

Wegner, D. M. (1994b). *White bears and other unwanted thoughts: Suppression, obsession, and the psychology of mental control.* New York: Guilford Press.

Why it is that we have so much trouble controlling our own minds? This book describes the initial experiments in which people were asked to try to stop thinking about a white bear—and found they could not.

Wegner, D. M. (2002). *The illusion of conscious will.* Cambridge, MA: MIT Press.

This book describes how it is that we come to believe that we consciously will our own actions and examines along the way such anomalies as phantom limbs, Ouija board spelling, spirit possession, and hypnosis.

Zeman, A. (2002). *Consciousness: A user's guide.* New Haven, CT: Yale University Press.

The author is a neurologist, and his wide-ranging interests in everything from Shakespeare to the architecture of the brain make for exhilaratingly broad reading—and a high-level introduction to the science of consciousness.

ANSWERS TO KEY CONCEPT QUIZ

1. b; 2. d; 3. d; 4. a; 5. a; 6. c; 7. b; 8. c; 9. b; 10. a; 11. b; 12. d; 13. c; 14. c.

Need more help? Additional resources are located at the book's free companion Web site at:
www.worthpublishers.com/schacter

6

Memory

--------------------------------○--------------------------------

Jill Price was 12 years old when she began to suspect that she possessed an unusually good memory. Studying for a seventh-grade science final on May 30th, her mind drifted and she became aware that she could recall vividly everything she had been doing on May 30th of the previous year. A month later, something similar happened: Enjoying vanilla custards at Paradise Cove near Los Angeles with her friend Kathy, Jill recalled that they had done the same thing precisely a year earlier. Expecting that Kathy would recall the episode as easily as she did, Jill was surprised when Kathy replied blankly: "We did?"

Remembering specifics of events that occurred a year ago may not seem so extraordinary—you can probably recall what you did for your last birthday, or where you spent last Thanksgiving—but can you recall the details of what you did exactly 1 year ago today? Or what you did a week, a month, 6 months, or 6 years before that day? Probably not—but Jill Price can.

As she grew older, Jill's memory flashes became even more frequent. Now in her mid-40s, Jill can recall clearly and in great detail what has happened to her *every single day since early 1980* (Price & Davis, 2008). This is not just Jill's subjective impression. Dr. James McGaugh, a well-known memory researcher based at the University of California-Irvine, and his colleagues tested Jill's memory over a period of a few years and came up with some shocking results (Parker et al., 2006). For example, they asked Jill to recall the dates of each Easter from 1980 to 2003, which is a pretty tough task considering that Easter can fall on any day between March 22nd and April 15th. Even though she had no idea that she would be asked this question, Jill recalled the correct dates quickly and easily; Nobody else the researchers tested came close. When Jill was asked about the dates of public events that had occurred years earlier (Rodney King beating? OJ Simpson verdict? Bombing at Atlanta Olympics?), she rattled off the correct answers without a hitch (March 3, 1991; October 3, 1995; July 26, 1996). The researchers also asked Jill about the details of what she had been doing on various randomly chosen dates, and they checked Jill's recall against her personal diary. Again, Jill answered quickly and accurately: *July 1, 1986?*—"I see it all, that day, that month, that summer. Tuesday. Went with (friend's name) to (restaurant name)." *October 3, 1987?*—"That was a Saturday. Hung out at the apartment all weekend, wearing a sling—hurt my elbow." *April 27, 1994?*—"That was Wednesday. That was easy for me because I knew where I was exactly. I was down in Florida. I was summoned to come down and to say goodbye to my Grandmother who they all thought was dying but she ended up living" (Parker et al., 2006, pp. 39–40).

Can you recall the day of the week and exactly what you were doing on, say, July 1, 2003, October 3, 2007, or April 27, 2009? One thing is for certain: None of your textbook authors can.

▶ Jill Price can accurately remember just about everything that has happened to her during the past 30 years, as confirmed by her diary, but Jill's extraordinary memory is more of a curse than a blessing.
ROBERT HANASHIRO/USA TODAY

Researchers still don't understand all the reasons why Jill Price can remember her past so much more fully than the rest of us, but Jill's memory is a gift we'd all love to have—right? Not necessarily. Here's what Jill has to say about her ability: "Most have called it a gift but I call it a burden. I run my entire life through my head every day and it drives me crazy!!!" (Parker et al., 2006, p. 35).

MEMORY *IS THE ABILITY TO STORE AND RETRIEVE INFORMATION OVER TIME.* Even though few of us possess the extraordinary memory abilities of a Jill Price, each of us has a unique identity that is intricately tied to the things we have thought, felt, done, and experienced. Memories are the residue of those events, the enduring changes that experience makes in our brains and leaves behind when it passes. If an experience passes without leaving a trace, it might just as well not have happened. But as Jill's story suggests, remembering all that has happened is not necessarily a good thing, either—a point we'll explore more fully later in the chapter.

The ease with which someone like Jill can instantly remember her past shouldn't blind us from appreciating how complex that act of remembering really is. Because memory is so remarkably complex, it is also remarkably fragile (Schacter, 1996). We all have had the experience of forgetting something we desperately wanted to remember or of remembering something that never really happened. Why does memory serve us so well in some situations and play such cruel tricks on us in other cases? When can we trust our memories and when should we view them skeptically? Is there just one kind of memory, or are there many? These are among the questions that psychologists have asked and answered.

As you've seen in other chapters, the mind's mistakes provide key insights into its fundamental operation, and there is no better illustration of this than in the realm of memory. In this chapter, we will consider the three key functions of memory: **encoding,** *the process by which we transform what we perceive, think, or feel into an enduring memory;* **storage,** *the process of maintaining information in memory over time;* and **retrieval,** *the process of bringing to mind information that has been previously encoded and stored.* We'll then examine several different kinds of memory and focus on the ways in which errors, distortions, and imperfections can reveal the nature of memory itself.

Encoding: Transforming Perceptions into Memories

Bubbles P., a professional gambler with no formal education, who spent most of his time shooting craps at local clubs or playing high-stakes poker, had no difficulty rattling off 20 numbers, in either forward or backward order, after just a single glance (Ceci, DeSimone, & Johnson, 1992). Most people can listen to a list of numbers and then repeat them from memory—as long as the list is no more than about seven items long (try it for yourself using **FIGURE 6.1**).

How did Bubbles accomplish his astounding feats of memory? For at least 2,000 years, people have thought of memory as a recording device that makes exact copies of information that comes in through our senses, and then stores those copies for later use. This idea is simple and intuitive. It is also completely incorrect. Memories are made by combining information we *already* have in our brains with new information that comes in through our senses. In this way memory is like cooking; starting from a recipe but improvising along the way, we add old information to new information, mix, shake, bake, and out pops a memory. Memories are *constructed,* not recorded, and encoding is the process by which we transform what we perceive, think, or feel into an

How is making a memory like following a recipe?

28
691
0473
87454
902481
5742296
64719304
356718485
1028834729
472082742 64
731093435138

▲ **FIGURE 6.1**
Digit Memory Test How many digits can you remember? Start on the first row and cover the rows below it with a piece of paper. Study the numbers in the row for 1 second and then cover that row back up again. After a couple of seconds, try to repeat the numbers. Then uncover the row to see if you were correct. If so, continue down to the next row, using the same instructions, until you can't recall all the numbers in a row. The number of digits in the last row you can remember correctly is your digit span. Bubbles P. could remember 20 random numbers, or about 5 rows deep. How did you do?

enduring memory. Let's look at three types of encoding processes—elaborative encoding, visual imagery encoding, and organizational encoding—and then consider the possible survival value of encoding for our ancestors.

Elaborative Encoding

Memories are a combination of old and new information, so the nature of any particular memory depends as much on the old information already in our memories as it does on the new information coming in through our senses. In other words, how we remember something depends on how we think about it at the time. For example, as a professional gambler, Bubbles found numbers unusually meaningful, and so when he saw a string of digits, he tended to think about their meanings. He might have thought about how they related to his latest bet at the racetrack or to his winnings after a long night at the poker table. Whereas you might try to memorize the string 22061823 by saying it over and over, Bubbles would think about betting $220 at 6 to 1 odds on horse number 8 to place 2nd in the 3rd race. Indeed, when Bubbles was tested with materials other than numbers—faces, words, objects, or locations—his memory performance was no better than average.

How do old memories influence new memories?

In one study, researchers presented participants with a series of words and asked them to make one of three types of judgments (Craik & Tulving, 1975). *Semantic judgments* required the participants to think about the meaning of the words ("Is *hat* a type of clothing?"), *rhyme judgments* required the participants to think about the sound of the words ("Does *hat* rhyme with *cat*?"), and *visual judgments* required the participants to think about the appearance of the words ("Is *HAT* written uppercase or lowercase?"). The type of judgment task influenced how participants thought about each word— what old information they combined with the new—and had a powerful impact on their memories (**FIGURE 6.2**). Those participants who made semantic judgments (i.e., had thought about the meaning of the words) had much better memory for the words than did participants who had thought about how the word looked or sounded. The results of these and many other studies have shown that long-term retention is greatly enhanced by **elaborative encoding**, which is *the process of actively relating new information to knowledge that is already in memory* (Brown & Craik, 2000).

Have you ever wondered why you can remember 20 experiences (your last summer vacation, your 16th birthday party, your first day at college) but not 20 digits? The reason is that most of the time we think of the meaning behind our experiences, and so we elaboratively encode them without even trying to (Craik & Tulving, 1975).

So where does this elaborative encoding take place? What's going on in the brain when this type of information processing occurs? Studies reveal that elaborative encoding is uniquely associated with increased activity in the lower left part of the

memory The ability to store and retrieve information over time.

encoding The process by which we transform what we perceive, think, or feel into an enduring memory.

storage The process of maintaining information in memory over time.

retrieval The process of bringing to mind information that has been previously encoded and stored.

elaborative encoding The process of actively relating new information to knowledge that is already in memory.

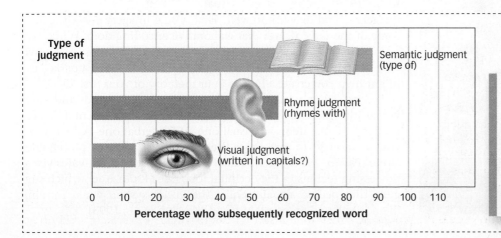

Type of judgment

Semantic judgment (type of)

Rhyme judgment (rhymes with)

Visual judgment (written in capitals?)

0   10   20   30   40   50   60   70   80   90   100   110
Percentage who subsequently recognized word

◄ FIGURE 6.2
Levels of Processing Elaborative encoding enhances subsequent retention. Thinking about a word's meaning (making a semantic judgment) results in deeper processing—and better memory for the word later—than merely attending to its sound (rhyme judgment) or shape (visual judgment). (From Craik & Tulving, 1975)

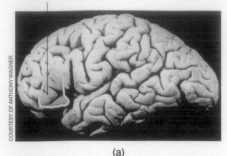

Lower left frontal lobe

(a)

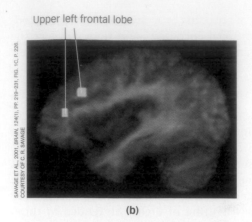

Upper left frontal lobe

(b)

SAVAGE ET AL., 2001, BRAIN, 124(1), PP. 219–231, FIG. 1C, P. 226. COURTESY OF C. R. SAVAGE

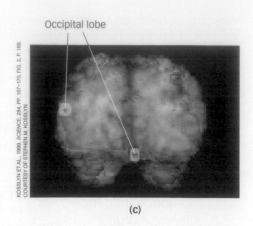

Occipital lobe

(c)

KOSSLYN ET AL., 1999, SCIENCE, 284, PP. 167–170, FIG. 2, P. 168. COURTESY OF STEPHEN M. KOSSLYN

▲ FIGURE 6.3
Brain Activity during Different Types of Judgments fMRI studies reveal that different parts of the brain are active during different types of judgments: (a) During semantic judgments, the lower left frontal lobe is active; (b) during organizational judgments, the upper left frontal lobe is active; and (c) during visual judgments, the occipital lobe is active.

frontal lobe and the inner part of the left temporal lobe (**FIGURE 6.3a**) (Demb et al., 1995; Kapur et al., 1994; Wagner et al., 1998). In fact, the amount of activity in each of these two regions during encoding is directly related to whether people later remember an item. The more activity there is in these areas, the more likely the person will remember the information.

Visual Imagery Encoding

In Athens in 477 BC, the Greek poet Simonides had just left a banquet when the ceiling collapsed and killed all the people inside. Simonides was able to name every one of the dead simply by visualizing each chair around the banquet table and recalling the person who had been sitting there. Simonides wasn't the first, but he was among the most proficient, to use **visual imagery encoding**, *the process of storing new information by converting it into mental pictures*.

If you wanted to use Simonides' method to create an enduring memory, you could simply convert the information that you wanted to remember into a visual image and then "store it" in a familiar location. For instance, if you were going to the grocery store and wanted to remember to buy Coke, popcorn, and cheese dip, you could use the rooms in your house as locations and imagine your living room flooded in Coke, your bedroom pillows stuffed with popcorn, and your bathtub as a greasy pond of cheese dip. When you arrived at the store, you could then take a "mental walk" around your house and "look" into each room to remember the items you needed to purchase.

Numerous experiments have shown that visual imagery encoding can substantially improve memory. In one experiment, participants who studied lists of words by creating visual images of them later recalled twice as many items as participants who just mentally repeated the words (Schnorr & Atkinson, 1969). Why does visual imagery encoding work so well? First, visual imagery encoding does some of the same things that elaborative encoding does: When you create a visual image, you relate incoming information to knowledge already in memory. For example, a visual image of a parked car might help you create a link to your memory of your first kiss.

Second, when you use visual imagery to encode words and other verbal information, you end up with two different mental "placeholders" for the items—a visual one and a verbal one—which gives you more ways to remember them than just a verbal placeholder alone (Paivio, 1971, 1986). Visual imagery encoding activates visual processing regions in the occipital lobe (see **FIGURE 6.3c**), which suggests that people actually enlist the visual system when forming memories based on mental images (Kosslyn et al., 1993).

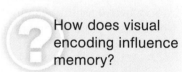
How does visual encoding influence memory?

▶ No one remembers how the Greek poet Simonides actually looked, but his memory improvement method, which uses visual images to encode new information, has never been forgotten.

COURTESY THE NUREMBERG CHRONICLES, MORSE LIBRARY, BELOIT COLLEGE

Organizational Encoding

Have you ever ordered dinner with a group of friends and watched in amazement as your server took the order without writing anything down? To find out how this is done, one researcher spent 3 months working in a restaurant where waitresses routinely wrote down orders but then left the check at the customer's table before proceeding to the kitchen and *telling* the cooks what to make (Stevens, 1988). The researcher wired each waitress with a microphone and asked her to think aloud, that is, to say what she was thinking as she walked around all day doing her job. The researcher found that as soon as the waitress left a customer's table, she immediately began *grouping* or *categorizing* the orders into hot drinks, cold drinks, hot foods, and cold foods. The waitresses grouped the items into a sequence that matched the layout of the kitchen, first placing drink orders, then hot food orders, and finally cold food orders. The waitresses remembered their orders by relying on **organizational encoding**, *the process of categorizing information according to the relationships among a series of items.*

For example, suppose you had to memorize the words *peach, cow, chair, apple, table, cherry, lion, couch, horse, desk*. The task seems difficult, but if you organize the items into three categories—fruit (*peach, apple, cherry*), animals (*cow, lion, horse*), and furniture (*chair, table, couch, desk*)—the task becomes much easier. Studies have shown that instructing people to sort items into categories like this is an effective way to enhance their subsequent recall of those items (Mandler, 1967). Even more complex organizational schemes have been used, such as the hierarchy in **FIGURE 6.4** (Bower et al., 1969). People can improve their recall of individual items by organizing them into multiple-level categories, all the way from a general category such as *animals*, through intermediate categories such as *birds* and *songbirds*, down to specific examples such as *wren* and *sparrow*.

> Why might mentally organizing the material for an exam enhance your retrieval of that material?

Just as elaborative and visual imagery encoding activate distinct regions of the brain, so, too, does organizational encoding. As you can see in Figure 6.3*b*, organizational encoding activates the upper surface of the left frontal lobe (Fletcher, Shallice, & Dolan, 1998; Savage et al., 2001). Different types of encoding strategies appear to rely on different areas of brain activation.

> ▼ Ever wonder how a server remembers who ordered the pizza and who ordered the fries without writing anything down? Some have figured out how to use organizational encoding.
>
> JEFF GREENBERG/ALAMY

visual imagery encoding The process of storing new information by converting it into mental pictures.

organizational encoding The process of categorizing information according to the relationships among a series of items.

Encoding of Survival-Related Information

Encoding new information is critical to many aspects of everyday life—prospects for attaining your degree would be pretty slim without this ability—and the survival of our ancestors likely depended on encoding and later remembering such things as the source of food and water or where a predator appeared (Nairne & Pandeirada, 2008; Sherry & Schacter, 1987).

Animals
— Birds
  — Waterfowl
    Duck
    Goose
    Swan
  — Songbirds
    Wren
    Sparrow
    Warbler
    Finch
— Mammals
  — Horses
    Arabian
    Pinto
    Mustang
  — Dogs
    Collie
    Shepherd
    Terrier
    Dachshund
  — Cats
    Manx
    Siamese
    Persian

◄ FIGURE 6.4
Organizing Words into a Hierarchy Organizing words into conceptual groups and relating them to one another—such as in this example of a hierarchy—makes it easier to reconstruct the items from memory later (Bower et al., 1969). Keeping track of the 17 items in this example can be facilitated by remembering the hierarchical groupings they fall under.

Recent experiments have addressed these ideas by examining encoding of survival-related information. The experiments were motivated by an evolutionary perspective based on Darwin's principle of natural selection: that the features of an organism that help it survive and reproduce are more likely than other features to be passed on to subsequent generations (see Chapter 1). Therefore, memory mechanisms that help us to survive and reproduce should be preserved by natural selection, and our memory systems should be built in a way that allows us to remember especially well encoded information that is relevant to our survival.

To test this idea, the researchers gave participants three different encoding tasks (Nairne, Thompson, & Pandeirada, 2007):

> In the *survival encoding* condition, participants were asked to imagine that they were stranded in the grasslands of a foreign land without any survival materials and that over the next few months they would need supplies of food and water and also need to protect themselves from predators. The researchers then showed participants randomly chosen words (e.g., *stone, meadow, chair*) and asked them to rate on a 1–5 scale how relevant each item would be to survival in the hypothetical situation.

> In the *moving encoding* condition, a second group of participants were asked to imagine that they were planning to move to a new home in a foreign land, and to rate on a 1–5 scale how useful each item might be in helping them to set up a new home. This task is similar in many respects to the survival encoding task, except that it does not involve thinking about survival.

> Finally, in the *pleasantness encoding* condition, a third group was shown the same words and asked to rate on a 1–5 scale the pleasantness of each word. They used a pleasantness encoding task taken from previous research that was proven to involve deep, elaborative encoding of the kind that we have already seen is beneficial to later retention.

The findings, displayed in **FIGURE 6.5**, show that participants recalled more words after the survival encoding task than after either the moving or pleasantness tasks. In later studies, the researchers found that survival encoding resulted in higher levels of recall than several other non-survival encoding tasks involving either elaborative encoding, imagery encoding, or organizational encoding (Nairne, Pandeirada, & Thompson, 2008). Exactly what about survival encoding produces such high levels of memory? Survival encoding draws on elements of elaborative, imagery, and organizational encoding, which may give it an advantage over any one of the other three. Alternatively, perhaps thinking about information with regard to its survival value is more interesting or emotionally arousing than other kinds of encoding.

▼ FIGURE 6.5

Survival Encoding Enhances Later Recall What does a pouncing cougar that may threaten our survival have to do with recall? Nairne, Thompson, and Pandeirada (2007) showed that people recall more words after survival encoding (a). Ratings of how relevant the words are to each task were highest for the pleasantness condition and did not differ between survival and moving conditions (b); response times for encoding judgments did not differ for survival and moving conditions, but were slightly faster in the pleasantness condition. The point of these latter two findings is that the survival recall advantage cannot be attributed to differences in relevance or response time.

DON JOHNSTON/ALL CANADA PHOTOS/GETTY IMAGES

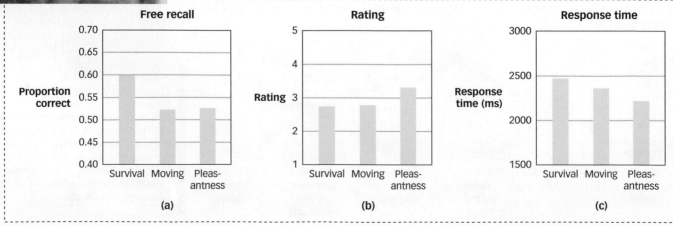

Free recall

Proportion correct

(a) Survival, Moving, Pleasantness

Rating

Rating

(b) Survival, Moving, Pleasantness

Response time

Response time (ms)

(c) Survival, Moving, Pleasantness

IN SUMMARY

○ Encoding is the process by which we transform into a lasting memory the information our senses take in. Most instances of spectacular memory performance reflect the skillful use of encoding strategies rather than so-called photographic memory. Memory is influenced by the type of encoding we perform regardless of whether we consciously intend to remember an event or a fact.

○ Elaborative encoding, visual imagery encoding, and organizational encoding all increase memory, but they use different parts of the brain to accomplish that.

○ Encoding information with respect to its survival value is a particularly effective method for increasing subsequent recall, perhaps because our memory systems have evolved in a way that allows us to remember especially well information that is relevant to our survival.

sensory memory A type of storage that holds sensory information for a few seconds or less.

Storage: Maintaining Memories over Time

Encoding is the process of turning perceptions into memories. But one of the hallmarks of a memory is that you can bring it to mind on Tuesday, not on Wednesday, and then bring it to mind again on Thursday. So where are our memories when we aren't using them? Clearly, those memories are stored in some form in your brain. As pointed out earlier, *storage is the process of maintaining information in memory over time*. There are three major kinds of memory storage—sensory, short-term, and long-term. As these names suggest, the three kinds of storage are distinguished primarily by the amount of time over which a memory is retained.

Sensory Storage

Sensory memory *holds sensory information for a few seconds or less*. In a series of classic experiments, research participants were asked to remember rows of letters (Sperling, 1960). In one version of the procedure, participants viewed three rows of four letters each, as shown in **FIGURE 6.6**. The researcher flashed the letters on a screen for just 1/20th of a second. When asked to remember all 12 of the letters they had just seen, participants recalled fewer than half (Sperling, 1960). There were two possible explanations for this: Either people simply couldn't encode all the letters in such a brief period of time, or they had encoded the letters but forgotten them while trying to recall everything they had seen.

To test the two ideas, the researchers relied on a clever trick. Just after the letters disappeared from the screen, a tone sounded that cued the participants to report the letters in a particular row. A *high tone* cued participants to report the contents of the top row, a *medium* tone cued participants to report the contents of the middle row, and a *low* tone cued participants to report the contents of the bottom row. When asked to report only a single row, people recalled almost all of the letters in that row! Because the tone sounded *after* the letters disappeared from the screen, the researchers concluded that people could have recalled the same number of letters from *any* of the rows had they been asked to. Participants had no way of knowing which of the three rows would be cued, so the researchers inferred that virtually all the letters had been encoded. In fact, if the tone was substantially delayed, participants couldn't perform the task; the information had slipped away from their sensory memories. Like the afterimage of a flashlight, the 12 letters flashed on a screen are visual icons, a lingering trace stored in memory for a very short period.

▼ FIGURE 6.6
Iconic Memory Test When a grid of letters is flashed on screen for only 1/20th of a second, it is difficult to recall individual letters. But if prompted to remember a particular row immediately after the grid is shown, research participants will do so with high accuracy. Sperling used this procedure to demonstrate that although iconic memory stores the whole grid, the information fades away too quickly for a person to recall everything (Sperling, 1960).

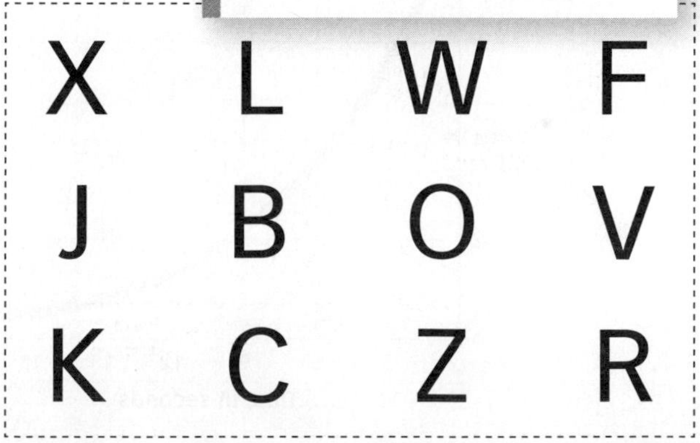

X	L	W	F
J	B	O	V
K	C	Z	R

Because we have more than one sense, we have more than one kind of sensory memory. **Iconic memory** is *a fast-decaying store of visual information*. A similar storage area serves as a temporary warehouse for sounds. **Echoic memory** is *a fast-decaying store of auditory information*. When you have difficulty understanding what someone has just said, you

> **How long is information held in iconic and echoic memory before it decays?**

probably find yourself replaying the last few words—listening to them echo in your "mind's ear," so to speak. When you do that, you are accessing information that is being held in your echoic memory store. The hallmark of both the iconic and echoic memory stores is that they hold information for a very short time. Iconic memories usually decay in about a second or less, and echoic memories usually decay in about five seconds (Darwin, Turvey, & Crowder, 1972). These two sensory memory stores are a bit like doughnut shops: The products come in, they sit briefly on the shelf, and then they are discarded. If you want one, you have to grab it fast.

Short-Term Storage and Working Memory

A second kind of memory storage is **short-term memory**, which *holds nonsensory information for more than a few seconds but less than a minute*. For example, if someone tells you a telephone number, you can usually repeat it back with ease—but only for a few seconds. In one study, research participants were given consonant strings to remember, such as DBX and HLM. After seeing each string, participants were asked to count backward from 100 by 3s for varying amounts of time and were then asked to recall the strings (Peterson & Peterson, 1959). As shown in **FIGURE 6.7**, memory for the consonant strings declined rapidly, from approximately 80% after a 3-second delay to less than 20% after a 20-second delay. These results suggest that information can be held in the short-term memory store for about 15 to 20 seconds.

What if 15 to 20 seconds isn't enough time? What if we need the information for a while longer? We can use a trick that allows us to get around the natural limitations of our short-term memories. **Rehearsal** is *the process of keeping information in short-term memory by mentally repeating it*. If someone gives you a telephone number and you don't have a pencil, you say it over and over

> **Why is it helpful that local phone numbers are only seven digits long?**

to yourself until you find one. Each time you repeat the number, you are "reentering" it into short-term memory, giving it another 15 to 20 seconds of shelf life.

Short-term memory is limited in how *long* it can hold information, and also limited in how *much* information it can hold. Not only can most people keep approximately seven numbers in short-term memory, but if they put more new numbers in, then old numbers begin to fall out (Miller, 1956). Short-term memory isn't limited to numbers, of course: it can also hold about seven letters or seven words—even though those seven words contain many more than seven letters. In fact, short-term memory can hold about seven *meaningful items* at once (Miller, 1956). Therefore, one way to increase storage is to group several letters into a single meaningful item. **Chunking** involves *combining small pieces of information into larger clusters or chunks*. Waitresses who use organizational encoding (p. 223) to organize customer orders into groups are essentially chunking the information, giving themselves less to remember.

Short-term memory was originally conceived of as a kind of "place" where information is kept for a limited amount of time. As a result, researchers did not pay much attention to the operation and processes that we use to manipulate information in short-term memory, nor did they say much about how the system is used to help us carry out cognitive tasks. A more dynamic

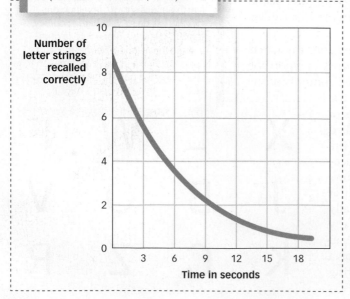

▼ **FIGURE 6.7**
The Decline of Short-Term Memory A 1959 experiment showed how quickly short-term memory fades without rehearsal. On a test for memory of three-letter strings, research participants were highly accurate when tested a few seconds after exposure to each string, but if the test was delayed another 15 seconds, people barely recalled the strings at all (Peterson & Peterson, 1959).

model of a limited-capacity memory system has been developed and refined over the past few decades. **Working memory** refers to *active maintenance of information in short-term storage* (Baddeley & Hitch, 1974). It differs from the traditional view that short-term memory is simply a place to hold information and instead includes the operations and processes we use to work with information in short-term memory.

Working memory includes subsystems that store and manipulate visual images or verbal information, as well as a central executive that coordinates the subsystems (Baddeley, 2001). If you wanted to keep the arrangement of pieces on a chessboard in mind as you contemplated your next move, you'd be relying on working memory. Working memory includes the visual representation of the positions of the pieces, your mental manipulation of the possible moves, and your awareness of the flow of information into and out of memory, all stored for a limited amount of time. In short, the working memory model acknowledges both the limited nature of this kind of memory storage and the activities that are commonly associated with it.

Research conducted in the context of this model has taught us that working memory plays an important role in many aspects of our cognitive lives. For example, studies of neurological patients with damage to the verbal subsystem of working memory reveal that not only do they have problems holding onto strings of digits and letters for a few seconds, they also have difficulties learning novel words, suggesting a link between this part of the working memory system and the ability to learn language (Baddeley, 2001; Gathercole, 2008). Brain-imaging studies indicate that the central executive component of working memory depends on regions within the frontal lobe that are important for controlling and manipulating information on a wide range of cognitive tasks (Baddeley, 2001). This research has had practical implications too: Children who score low on working memory tasks have difficulty learning new information and performing well in the classroom (Alloway et al., 2009).

Long-Term Storage

The artist Franco Magnani was born in Pontito, Italy, in 1934. In 1958, he left his village to see the rest of the world, and he settled in San Francisco in the 1960s. Soon after arriving, Magnani began to suffer from a strange illness. Every night he experienced feverish dreams of Pontito, in which he recalled the village in vivid detail. The dreams soon penetrated his waking life in the form of overpowering recollections, and Magnani decided that the only way to rid himself of these images was to capture them on canvas. For the next 20 years, he devoted much of his time to painting in exquisite detail his memories of his beloved village. Many years later, photographer Susan Schwartzenberg went to Pontito, armed with a collection of Magnani's paintings, and photographed each scene from the perspective of the paintings. As you can see in the images, the correspondence between the paintings and the photographs was striking (Sacks, 1995; Schacter, 1996).

Many years intervened between Magnani's visual perception and artistic reconstruction of the village, suggesting that very detailed information can sometimes be stored for a very long time. In contrast to the time-limited sensory memory and short-term memory stores, **long-term memory** *holds information for hours, days, weeks, or years.* In contrast to both sensory and short-term memory, long-term memory has no known capacity limits (see **FIGURE 6.8** on the next page). For example, most people can recall 10,000 to 15,000 words in their native language, tens of thousands of facts ("The capital of France is Paris" and "$3 \times 3 = 9$"), and an untold number of personal experiences.

iconic memory A fast-decaying store of visual information.

echoic memory A fast-decaying store of auditory information.

short-term memory A type of storage that holds nonsensory information for more than a few seconds but less than a minute.

rehearsal The process of keeping information in short-term memory by mentally repeating it.

chunking Combining small pieces of information into larger clusters or chunks that are more easily held in short-term memory.

working memory Active maintenance of information in short-term storage.

long-term memory A type of storage that holds information for hours, days, weeks, or years.

▼ Even years after leaving home in Pontito, Italy, painter Franco Magnani was able to create a near-perfect reproduction of what he'd seen there. Magnani's painting (left), based on a memory of a place he hadn't seen for years, is remarkably similar to the photograph Susan Schwartzenberg took of the actual scene (right).

© FRANCO MAGNANI

SUSAN SCHWARTZENBERG. © EXPLORATORIUM. WWW.EXPLORATORIUM.EDU

KEVIN MAZUR/WIREIMAGE/GETTY IMAGES

▶ FIGURE 6.8
The Flow of Information through the Memory System Information moves through several stages of memory as it gets encoded, stored, and made available for later retrieval.

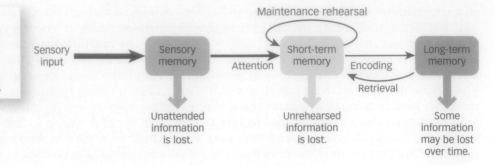

Just think of all the song lyrics you can recite by heart, and you'll understand that you've got a lot of information tucked away in long-term memory!

Amazingly, people can recall items from long-term memory even if they haven't thought of them for years. For example, researchers have found that even 50 years after graduation, people can accurately recognize about 90% of their high school classmates from yearbook photographs (Bahrick, 2000). The feat is the more remarkable when you consider that most of this information had probably not been accessed for years before the experiment.

The Role of the Hippocampus as Index

Where is long-term memory located in the brain? The clues to answering this question come from patients who are unable to store long-term memories. Not everyone has the same ability to encode information into long-term memory. In 1953, a 27-year-old man, known then by the initials HM, suffered from intractable epilepsy (Scoville & Milner, 1957). In a desperate attempt to stop the seizures, HM's doctors removed parts of his temporal lobes, including the hippocampus and some surrounding regions (**FIGURE 6.9**). After the operation, HM could converse easily, use and understand language, and perform well on intelligence tests—but he could not remember anything that happened to him *after* the operation. HM could repeat a telephone number with no difficulty, suggesting that his short-term memory store was just fine (Corkin, 1984, 2002; Hilts, 1995; Squire, 2009). But after information left the short-term store, it was gone forever. For example, he would often forget that he had just eaten a meal or fail to recognize the hospital staff who helped him on a daily basis. HM now lacked the ability to hang on to the new memories he created. Studies of HM and others have shown that the hippocampal region of the brain is critical for putting new information into the long-term store. When this region is damaged, patients suffer from a condition known as **anterograde amnesia**, which is *the inability to transfer new information from the short-term store into the long-term store.*

Some amnesic patients also suffer from **retrograde amnesia**, which is *the inability to retrieve information that was acquired before a particular date, usually the date of an injury or operation.* The fact that HM had much worse anterograde than retrograde amnesia suggests that the hippocampal region is not the site of long-term memory; indeed,

▲ Bruce Springsteen can count on his fans to know the words to almost all his songs.

▶ FIGURE 6.9
The Hippocampus Patient (left) HM had his hippocampus and adjacent structures of the medial temporal lobe (indicated by the shaded area) surgically removed to stop his epileptic seizures. As a result, he could not remember things that happened after the surgery. (right) Henry Molaison, better known to the world as patient HM, passed away on December 2, 2008, at the age of 82 at a nursing home near Hartford, Connecticut. Henry participated in countless memory experiments after he became amnesic in 1953, and in so doing made fundamental contributions to our understanding of memory and the brain.

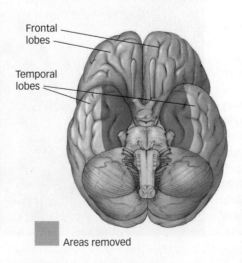

Frontal lobes

Temporal lobes

■ Areas removed

research has shown that different aspects of a single memory—its sights, sounds, smells, emotional content—are stored in different places in the cortex (Damasio, 1989; Schacter, 1996; Squire & Kandel, 1999). Psychologists now believe that the hippocampal region acts as a kind of "index" that links together all of these otherwise separate bits and pieces so that we remember them as one memory (Schacter, 1996; Squire, 1992; Teyler & DiScenna, 1986). Over time, this index may become less necessary. Going back to our cooking analogy, you can think of the hippocampal-region index like a printed recipe. The first time you make a pie, you need the recipe to help you retrieve all the ingredients and then mix them together in the right amounts. As you bake more and more pies, though, you don't need to rely on the printed recipe anymore. Similarly, although the hippocampal-region index is critical when a new memory is first formed, it may become less important as the memory ages. Scientists are still debating the extent to which the hippocampal region helps us to remember details of our old memories (Bayley et al., 2005b; Kirwan et al., 2008; Moscovitch et al., 2006), but the notion of the hippocampus as an index explains why people like HM *cannot* make new memories and why they *can* remember old ones.

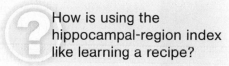

How is using the hippocampal-region index like learning a recipe?

Memory Consolidation

The idea that the hippocampus becomes less important over time for maintaining memories is related to the concept of **consolidation**, *a process by which memories become stable in the brain* (McGaugh, 2000). Shortly after encoding, memories exist in a fragile state in which they can be easily disrupted; once consolidation has occurred, they are more resistant to disruption. One type of consolidation operates over seconds or minutes. For example, when someone experiences a head injury in a car crash and later cannot recall what happened during the few seconds or minutes before the crash—but can recall other events normally—the head injury probably prevented consolidation of short-term memory into long-term memory. Another type of consolidation occurs over much longer periods of time—days, weeks, months, and years—and likely involves transfer of information from the hippocampus to more permanent storage sites in the cortex. The operation of this longer-term consolidation process is seen in the retrograde amnesia of patients with hippocampal damage who can recall memories from childhood relatively normally, but are impaired when recalling experiences that occurred just a few years prior to the time they became amnesic (Kirwan et al., 2008).

How does a memory become consolidated? The act of recalling a memory, thinking about it, and talking about it with others probably contributes to consolidation (Moscovitch et al., 2006). And though you may not be aware of it, consolidation gets a boost from something that you do effortlessly every night: sleep. As explained in the Hot Science box (p. 230), mounting evidence gathered during the past decade indicates that sleep plays an important role in memory consolidation.

Many researchers have long believed that a fully consolidated memory becomes a permanent fixture in the brain, more difficult to get rid of than a tenured professor. But another line of research that has developed rapidly in recent years suggests that things are not so simple. Experiments have shown that even seemingly consolidated *memories can again become vulnerable to disruption when they are recalled, thus requiring them to be consolidated again.* This process is called **reconsolidation** (Nader & Hardt, 2009). Evidence for reconsolidation mainly comes from experiments with rats showing that when animals are cued to retrieve a new memory that was acquired a day earlier, giving the animal a drug (or an electrical shock) that prevents initial consolidation will cause forgetting (Nader, Shafe, & LeDoux, 2000; Sara, 2000). Critically, if the animal is not actively retrieving the memory, the same drug (or shock) has no effect when given a day after initial encoding. This finding is surprising because it was once thought that when memories are consolidated, drugs or shock that prevent initial consolidation no longer have any impact. To the contrary, it appears that each time they are retrieved, memories

anterograde amnesia The inability to transfer new information from the short-term store into the long-term store.

retrograde amnesia The inability to retrieve information that was acquired before a particular date, usually the date of an injury or operation.

consolidation The process by which memories become stable in the brain.

reconsolidation Memories can become vulnerable to disruption when they are recalled, requiring them to become consolidated again.

LEE DAVID/FOCUS FEATURES/THE KOBAL COLLECTION

▲ The film *Eternal Sunshine of the Spotless Mind* builds on the premise that erasing some memories might be a good idea.

become vulnerable to disruption and have to be reconsolidated. In other words, memories are not given permanent "tenure" after all (we're hoping professors won't suffer the same fate). Evidence of reconsolidation raises the intriguing possibility that it might be possible one day to eliminate painful memories by reminding individuals of traumatic experiences and injecting the right drug while the memory is held in mind (Brunet et al., 2008). Indeed, recent research with humans has shown that something like this happens as a result of reactivating a fear memory (being shocked in the presence of a particular object) a day after the memory was acquired. Adding nonfearful information to the reactivated memory (re-presenting the object without shock) a few minutes later——when the memory is vulnerable to reconsolidation—resulted in long-lasting reduction of fear responses to the object, whereas adding nonfearful information to the reactivated memory six hours later—when the memory is no longer vulnerable to reconsolidation—did not have a long-lasting effect (Schiller et al., 2010). While the possibility of selectively erasing painful memories makes for good entertainment in movies such as *Eternal Sunshine of the Spotless Mind,* research into reconsolidation is already beginning to turn such seemingly fanciful ideas into scientific reality.

HOT SCIENCE

Sleep on It

Thinking about pulling an all-nighter before your next big test? Here's reason to reconsider: We spend nearly one-third of our lives sleeping, and our minds don't simply shut off when we sleep (see Chapter 5). In fact, sleep may be as important to our memories as wakefulness.

Psychologists have long been interested in the relationship between sleep and memory. Nearly a century ago, Jenkins and Dallenbach (1924) reported that recall of recently learned information is greater immediately after sleeping than after the same amount of time spent awake. But Jenkins and Dallenbach did not think that sleep played an active role in strengthening or consolidating memory. They argued instead that being asleep passively protects us from encountering information that interferes with our ability to remember. As is explained later in the chapter (see p. 244), your ability to recall what happened yesterday can be impaired by new information that overwrites or confuses the earlier information. When you're asleep, you are not exposed to potentially interfering information, and so your memories may be protected compared with an equivalent period of wakefulness. However, during the past few years, evidence has accumulated that sleep plays an active role in memory

consolidation, doing more than simply protecting us from waking interference (Diekelmann, Wilhelm, & Born, 2009; Ellenbogen, Payne, & Stickgold, 2006).

Gais et al. (2007) provided evidence on this point by using fMRI to measure brain activity when people recalled recently studied words after sleep or sleep deprivation. In the first session, all participants were scanned during the evening while they studied a list of 90 word pairs, followed immediately by a test in which the first word of the pair was presented and they were instructed to recall the other word. Half the participants were assigned to a sleep group that had two nights of normal sleep before going into the scanner again and receiving another recall test for the pairs they had studied during the first session. The other participants were assigned to a sleep deprivation group that stayed up the first night (playing games and watching films in the lab) and then had a recovery night's sleep before going into the scanner for the recall test so that they would not be fatigued during recall testing.

The number of items recalled on the first test did not differ between the two groups, but participants in the sleep group recalled more items on the second test than did participants in the sleep deprivation group. Most important, brain activity differed

between the two groups. In the sleep group there was greater activity in the hippocampus during correct recall of words on the second test as compared with the first test; there was no such difference in the sleep deprivation group. Further, on the second test, the hippocampus showed stronger interactions with a region in the frontal lobe for the sleep group than the sleep deprivation group. When brought back for a third test six months later, this frontal region again showed increased activity in the sleep group, but now the hippocampus was no longer engaged during correct recall.

What does it all mean? The evidence is consistent with the idea that sleep contributes to memory consolidation by (1) increasing hippocampal involvement in recall a couple of days later and (2) facilitating interaction of the hippocampus with the frontal lobe, such that the hippocampus is later less centrally involved in recall. Other recent studies indicate that sleep selectively enhances the consolidation of memories that reflect the meaning or gist of an experience (Payne et al., 2009), as well as emotionally important memories (Payne et al., 2008), suggesting that sleep helps us to remember what's important and to discard what's trivial. So, when you find yourself nodding off after hours of studying for your exam, the science is on the side of a good night's sleep.

Memories, Neurons, and Synapses

We've already discussed parts of the brain that are related to memory storage, but exactly where in these regions are memories stored? You might be tempted to think they're in neurons, but that isn't where you'd find them. Research suggests that memories are in the *spaces* between neurons. You'll recall from Chapter 3 that a *synapse* is

Why are the spaces between neurons so important to memory?

the small space between the axon of one neuron and the dendrite of another, and neurons communicate by sending neurotransmitters across these synapses. As it turns out, sending a neurotransmitter across a synapse isn't like sending a toy boat across a pond because the act of sending actually *changes* the synapse. Specifically, it strengthens the connection between the two neurons, making it easier for them to transmit to each other the next time. This is why researchers sometimes say, "Cells that fire together wire together" (Hebb, 1949).

The idea that the connections between neurons are strengthened by their communication, making communication easier the next time, provides the neurological basis for long-term memory, and much of what we know about this comes from the tiny sea slug *Aplysia*. The story of *Aplysia* and memory is closely linked with the work of neuroscientist Eric Kandel, who won the Nobel Prize in 2000 for his work with the creature. When Kandel first became interested in *Aplysia* back in the late 1950s, there were only two researchers in the entire world studying the tiny slug. But *Aplysia* was attractive to Kandel because it is relatively uncomplicated, having an extremely simple nervous system consisting of only 20,000 neurons (compared to roughly 100 billion in the human brain), and Kandel followed his intuition that he should make a bold switch to studying *Aplysia* (Kandel, 2006).

When an experimenter stimulates *Aplysia*'s tail with a mild electric shock, the slug immediately withdraws its gill, and if the experimenter does it again a moment later, *Aplysia* withdraws its gill even more quickly. If the experimenter comes back an hour later and shocks *Aplysia*, the withdrawal of the gill happens as slowly as it did the first time, as if *Aplysia* can't "remember" what happened an hour earlier (Abel et al., 1995). But if the experimenter shocks *Aplysia* over and over, it does develop an enduring "memory" that can last for days or even weeks. Research suggests that this long-term storage involves the growth of new synaptic connections between neurons (Abel et al., 1995; Kandel, 2006; Squire & Kandel, 1999). So, learning in *Aplysia* is based on changes involving the synapses for both short-term storage (enhanced neurotransmitter release) and long-term storage (growth of new synapses). Any experience that results in memory produces physical changes in the nervous system—even if you are a slug.

If you're something more complex than a slug—say, a mammal or your roommate—a similar process of synaptic strengthening happens in the hippocampus, which we've seen is an area crucial for storing new long-term memories. In the early 1970s, researchers applied a brief electrical stimulus to a neural pathway in a rat's hippocampus (Bliss & Lømo, 1973). They found that the electrical current produced a stronger connection between synapses that lay along the pathway and that the strengthening lasted for hours or even weeks. They called this **long-term potentiation**, more commonly known as **LTP**, which is *a process whereby communication across the synapse between neurons strengthens the connection, making further communication easier*. Long-term potentiation has a number of properties that indicate to researchers that it plays an important role in long-term memory storage: It occurs in several pathways within the hippocampus; it can be induced rapidly; and it can last for a long time. In fact, drugs that block LTP can turn rats into rodent versions of patient HM: The animals have great difficulty remembering where they've been recently and become easily lost in a maze (Bliss, 1999; Morris et al., 1986).

So how does LTP take place? What's going on in the neurons in the hippocampus to produce these stronger synaptic connections? The primary agent is a neural

▲ The sea slug *Aplysia californica* is useful to researchers because it has an extremely simple nervous system that can be used to investigate the mechanisms of short- and long-term memory.

long-term potentiation (LTP) A process whereby communication across the synapse between neurons strengthens the connection, making further communication easier.

▼ Nobel Prize–winning neuroscientist Eric Kandel became convinced to take a risk and study the tiny sea slug *Aplysia* based in part on a lesson he had learned from his wife regarding their recent marriage, which encouraged him to trust his intuition: "Denise was confident that our marriage would work, so I took a leap of faith and went ahead. I learned from that experience that there are many situations in which one cannot decide on the basis of cold facts alone—because the facts are often insufficient. One ultimately has to trust one's unconscious, one's instincts, one's creative urge. I did this again in choosing *Aplysia*" (Kandel, 2006, p. 149).

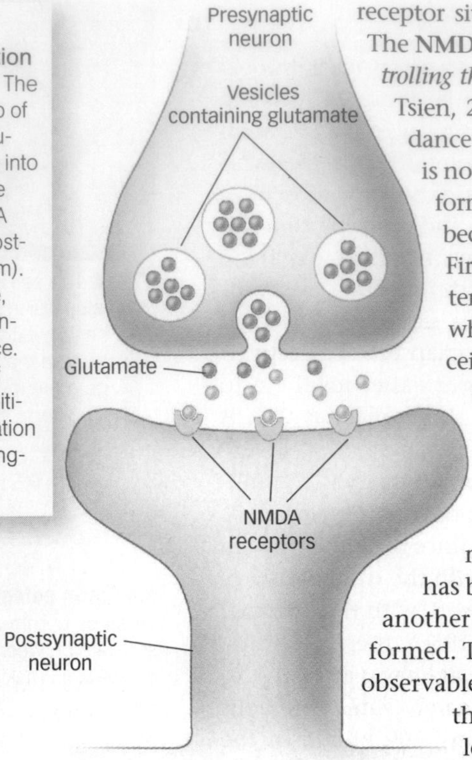

▶ FIGURE 6.10
Long-Term Potentiation in the Hippocampus The presynaptic neuron (top of figure) releases the neurotransmitter glutamate into the synapse. Glutamate then binds to the NMDA receptor sites on the postsynaptic neuron (bottom). At about the same time, excitation in the postsynaptic neuron takes place. The combined effect of these two processes initiates long-term potentiation and the formation of long-term memories.

Presynaptic neuron

Vesicles containing glutamate

Glutamate

NMDA receptors

Postsynaptic neuron

receptor site called NMDA, known more formally as *N*-methyl-D-aspartate. The **NMDA receptor** *influences the flow of information between neurons by controlling the initiation of LTP in most hippocampal pathways* (Bliss, 1999; Li & Tsien, 2009). Here's how it works: The hippocampus contains an abundance of NMDA receptors, more so than in other areas of the brain. This is not surprising because the hippocampus is intimately involved in the formation of long-term memories. But for these NMDA receptors to become activated, two things must happen at roughly the same time. First, the presynaptic, or "sending," neuron releases a neurotransmitter called *glutamate* (a major excitatory neurotransmitter in the brain), which attaches to the NMDA receptor site on the postsynaptic, or "receiving," neuron. Second, excitation takes place in the postsynaptic neuron. Together, these two events initiate LTP, which in turn increases synaptic connections by allowing neurons that fire together to wire together (**FIGURE 6.10**).

Let's step back and look at the big picture for a minute. It's easy to say that humans and other animals can form long-term memories. We can tell from a person's behavior that information has been stored and is able to be called up again and acted on. But it's another matter to understand *how* and *why* long-term memories are formed. The neural research on LTP and NMDA receptors helps us link an observable mental phenomenon ("Look! The squirrel remembered where the nuts were! She went right back to the correct tree!") with the biological underpinnings that produce it. More work remains to be done in this area to conclusively show how LTP leads to the formation of long-term memories, but the implications of this line of research are considerable. For example, recent progress in understanding the workings of NMDA receptors may have implications for coming up with more effective treatments for Alzheimer's disease, a disease that produces severe deficits in memory and other aspects of cognition in over 4 million older Americans (Li & Tsien, 2009; see Chapter 11 for further discussion of aspects of Alzheimer's disease).

IN SUMMARY

○ There are several different types of memory storage:
  ○ Sensory memory holds information for a second or two.
  ○ Short-term or working memory retains information for about 15 to 20 seconds.
  ○ Long-term memory stores information for anywhere from minutes to years or decades.
○ The hippocampus and nearby structures play an important role in long-term memory storage, as shown by the severe amnesia of patients such as HM. The hippocampus also is important for memory consolidation, the process that makes memories increasingly resistant to disruption over time. Sleep contributes importantly to memory consolidation.
○ Memory storage depends on changes in synapses, and long-term potentiation (LTP) increases synaptic connections.

NMDA receptor A receptor site on the hippocampus that influences the flow of information between neurons by controlling the initiation of long-term potentiation.

retrieval cue External information that helps bring stored information to mind.

encoding specificity principle The idea that a retrieval cue can serve as an effective reminder when it helps re-create the specific way in which information was initially encoded.

Retrieval: Bringing Memories to Mind

There is something fiendishly frustrating about piggy banks. You can put money in them, you can shake them around to assure yourself that the money is there, but you can't easily get the money out. If memories were like pennies in a piggy bank, stored but inaccessible, what would be the point of saving them in the first place? Retrieval is the process of bringing to mind information that has been previously encoded and stored, and it is perhaps the most important of all memory processes (Roediger, 2000; Schacter, 2001a).

Retrieval Cues: Reinstating the Past

One of the best ways to retrieve information from *inside* your head is to encounter information *outside* your head that is somehow connected to it. The information outside your head is called a **retrieval cue**, which is *external information that is associated with stored information and helps bring it to mind*. Retrieval cues can be incredibly effective. How many times have you said something like, "I *know* who starred in *Pirates of the Caribbean*, but I just can't remember it"?, only to have a friend give you a hint ("Wasn't he in *Alice in Wonderland*?"), which instantly brings the answer to mind ("Johnny Depp!").

In one experiment, undergraduates studied lists of words, such as *table, peach, bed, apple, chair, grape,* and *desk* (Tulving & Pearlstone, 1966). Later, the students were asked to write down all the words from the list that they could remember. When they were absolutely sure that they had emptied their memory stores of every last word that was in them, the experimenters again asked the students to remember the words on the list, but this time, the experimenters provided retrieval cues, such as "furniture" or "fruit." The students who were sure that they had done all the remembering they possibly could were suddenly able to remember more words (Tulving & Pearlstone, 1966). These results suggest that information is sometimes *available* in memory even when it is momentarily *inaccessible* and that retrieval cues help us bring inaccessible information to mind.

Hints are one kind of retrieval cue, but they are not the only kind. The **encoding specificity principle** states that *a retrieval cue can serve as an effective reminder when it helps re-create the specific way in which information was initially encoded* (Tulving & Thomson, 1973). External contexts often make powerful retrieval cues (Hockley, 2008). For example, in one study divers learned some words on land and some other words underwater; they recalled the words best when they were tested in the same dry or wet environment in which they had initially learned them because the environment itself served

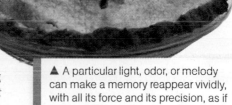

▲ A particular light, odor, or melody can make a memory reappear vividly, with all its force and its precision, as if a window opened on the past.

DENISE KAPPA/DREAMSTIME.COM

CULTURE & COMMUNITY

Is language a factor in memory retrieval? A study from Cornell University indicates that it is. In a memory retrieval experiment, bilingual Russian American college students were asked to relate memories that came to mind after hearing prompt words (Marian & Neisser, 2000). They were queried about four different stages of their lives. One part of the interview was conducted in English, and the other part was conducted in Russian. Participants were able to recall more events that took place in Russia when interviewed in Russian than in English, whereas they were able to recall more events that took place in the United States when interviewed in English than in Russian. Like other forms of context discussed in this section that are known to influence remembering, such as our moods or the external environment, this study shows that language can serve as a contextual cue that plays a significant role in determining what will be remembered.

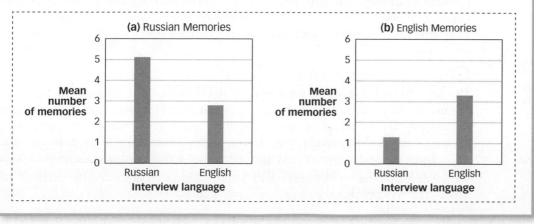

as a retrieval cue (Godden & Baddeley, 1975). Recovering alcoholics often experience a renewed urge to drink when visiting places in which they once drank because these places serve as retrieval cues. There may even be some wisdom to finding a seat in a classroom, sitting in it every day, and then sitting in it again when you take the test because the feel of the chair and the sights you see may help you remember the information you learned while you sat there.

? Why might it be a good idea to sit in the same seat for an exam that you sat in during lecture?

Retrieval cues need not be external contexts—they can also be inner states. **State-dependent retrieval** is *the tendency for information to be better recalled when the person is in the same state during encoding and retrieval.* For example, retrieving information when you are in a sad or happy mood increases the likelihood that you will retrieve sad or happy episodes (Eich, 1995), which is part of the reason it is so hard to "look on the bright side" when you're feeling low. Similarly, you'd probably expect a fellow student who studied for an exam while drunk to perform poorly, and you would probably be right—but only if he made the mistake of taking the exam while sober! Studies of state-dependent retrieval suggest that if the student studied while drunk, he would probably perform poorly the next day, but he'd perform better if he'd had a six-pack instead of Cheerios for breakfast (Eich, 1980; Weissenborn, 2000). Why should that be? Because a person's physiological or psychological state at the time of encoding is associated with the information that is encoded. For example, being in a good mood affects patterns of electrical activity in parts of the brain responsible for semantic processing, suggesting that mood has a direct influence on semantic encoding (Kiefer et al., 2007). If the person's state at the time of retrieval matches the person's state at the time of encoding, the state itself serves as a retrieval cue—a bridge that connects the moment at which we experience something to the moment at which we remember it. Retrieval cues can even be thoughts themselves, as when one thought calls to mind another, related thought (Anderson et al., 1976).

The encoding specificity principle makes some unusual predictions. For example, you learned earlier that making semantic judgments about a word (e.g., "What does *orange* mean?") usually produces more durable memory for the word than does making rhyme judgments (e.g., "What rhymes with *orange*?"). So if you were asked to think of a word that rhymes with *brain* and your friend was asked to think about what *brain* means, we would expect your friend to remember the word better the next day if we simply asked you both, "Hey, what was that word you saw yesterday?" However, if instead of asking that question, we asked you both, "What was that word that rhymed with *train*?" we would expect you to remember it better than your friend did (Fisher & Craik, 1977). This is a fairly astounding finding. Semantic judgments almost always yield better memory than rhyme judgments. But in this case, the typical finding is turned upside down because the retrieval cue matched your encoding context better than it matched your friend's. The principle of **transfer-appropriate processing** states that *memory is likely to transfer from one situation to another when the encoding context of the situations match* (Morris, Bransford, & Franks, 1977; Roediger, Weldon, & Challis, 1989).

Consequences of Retrieval

The act of retrieval provides a window on the contents of memory; only by retrieving information can we tell what we have encoded and retained. But retrieval doesn't merely provide a readout of what is in memory; it also changes the state of the memory system in important ways. In this respect, human memory differs substantially from computer memory. Simply retrieving a file from my computer doesn't have any effect on the likelihood that the file will open again in the future. Not so with human memory.

state-dependent retrieval The tendency for information to be better recalled when the person is in the same state during encoding and retrieval.

transfer-appropriate processing The idea that memory is likely to transfer from one situation to another when the encoding context of the situations match.

Retrieval Can Improve Subsequent Memory

Psychologists have known for some time that the act of retrieval can strengthen a retrieved memory, making it easier to remember that information at a later time (Bjork, 1975). Does this finding surprise you? Probably not. We've known since the time of Ebbinghaus (1885/1964) that repeating an item usually improves memory for that item, so the act of retrieval might boost subsequent memory simply because the information is repeated, resulting in the same benefit you would receive from studying the information twice instead once. Makes sense, right? Wrong. It turns out that retrieving information from memory has different effects than studying it again. This point was made dramatically in an experiment where participants studied brief stories and then either studied them again or were given a test that required retrieving the stories (Roediger & Karpicke, 2006). Participants were then given a final recall test for the stories either 5 minutes, 2 days, or 1 week later. As shown in **FIGURE 6.11**, at the 5-minute delay, studying the stories twice resulted in slightly higher recall than studying and retrieving them. Critically, the opposite occurred at the 2-day and 1-week delays: Retrieval produced much higher levels of recall than did an extra study exposure. A subsequent experiment using foreign vocabulary items also revealed that retrieval of the items produced a much bigger benefit on a delayed vocabulary test than did further study (Karpicke & Roediger, 2008).

These findings are especially important to college students, who are frequently preparing for exams that rely on memory. A clear implication of research on the benefits of retrieval for long-term retention is that students should spend more time testing themselves on the to-be-learned material rather than simply studying it over and over. You might think that this would be obvious to college students, given the amount of time spent preparing for exams—but it's not. In Karpicke and Roediger's (2008) study of vocabulary learning, students made predictions about how well they would do with additional study or retrieval trials, and their predictions were totally unrelated to their actual performance! We'll explore further some of the educational implications of these effects of retrieval on learning in Chapter 7.

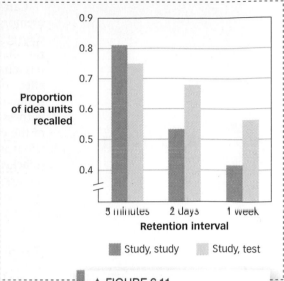

▲ FIGURE 6.11
Memory Testing Benefits Long-Term Retention With a five-minute retention interval, the study-study condition results in slightly higher recall. But the results change dramatically with retention intervals of 2 days and 1 week: at these longer delays, the study-test condition yields much higher levels of recall than does the study-study condition (Roediger & Karpicke, 2006).

Retrieval Can Impair Subsequent Memory

As much as retrieval can help memory, that's not always the case. **Retrieval-induced forgetting** is *a process by which retrieving an item from long-term memory impairs subsequent recall of related items* (Anderson, 2003; Anderson, Bjork, & Bjork, 1994).

Let's see how a typical experiment on retrieval-induced forgetting works (Anderson et al., 1994). Participants first studied word pairs consisting of a category name and an example from that category (e.g., fruit-orange, fruit-apple, tree-elm, tree-birch). Then they practiced recalling some of the items from a few of the studied categories by retrieving the target in response to category cue and the initial letters of the target. As an example, for the fruit category participants would practice recalling "orange" to the cue "fruit or___," but would not practice recalling "apple." The general idea is that while they are practicing recall of "orange," participants are trying to suppress the competitor "apple." For other categories (e.g., trees), no retrieval practice was given for any of the studied pairs. Later, the participants were given a final test for all the words they initially studied. Not surprisingly, on this final test participants remembered words that they practiced (e.g., orange) better than words from categories that they did not practice (e.g., elm). But what happened on the final test to the items such as "apple" that were not practiced, and which participants presumably had to suppress while they practiced recall of related items? These items were recalled most poorly of all, indicating that retrieving the similar target items (e.g., orange) caused subsequent forgetting of the related but suppressed items (e.g., apple). In fact, even if you don't successfully retrieve the target, the act of suppressing the competitors while you attempt to retrieve the target still reduces your ability to retrieve the competitors at a later time (Storm et al., 2006).

retrieval-induced forgetting A process by which retrieving an item from long-term memory impairs subsequent recall of related items.

Can you think of any examples of how retrieval-induced forgetting could impact memory in everyday life? Here are two. First, retrieval-induced forgetting can occur during conversations: When a speaker selectively talks about some aspects of memories shared with a listener and doesn't mention related information, the listener later has a harder time remembering the omitted events (Cue, Koppel, & Hirst, 2007). This effect occurs even for memories as important as the events of September 11, 2001 (Coman, Manier, & Hirst, 2009). Second, retrieval-induced forgetting can affect eyewitness memory. When witnesses to a staged crime are questioned about some details of the crime scene, their ability to later recall related details that they were not asked about is impaired compared with witnesses who were not questioned at all initially (MacLeod, 2002; Shaw, Bjork, & Handal, 1995). These findings suggest that initial interviews with eyewitnesses should be as complete as possible in order to avoid potential retrieval-induced forgetting of significant details that are not probed during an interview (MacLeod & Saunders, 2008).

Separating the Components of Retrieval

Before leaving the topic of retrieval, let's look at how the process actually works. There is reason to believe that *trying* to recall an incident and *successfully* recalling one are fundamentally different processes that occur in different parts of the brain (Moscovitch, 1994; Schacter, 1996). For example, regions in the left frontal lobe show heightened activity when people *try* to retrieve information that was presented to them earlier (Oztekin, Curtis, & McElree, 2009; Squire et al., 1992; Tulving et al., 1994). Many psychologists believe that this activity reflects the mental effort that people put forth when they struggle to dredge up the past event (Lepage et al., 2000). However, *successfully* remembering a past experience tends to be accompanied by activity in the hippocampal region (see **FIGURE 6.12**; Eldridge et al., 2000; Giovanello, Schnyer, & Verfaellie, 2004; Schacter et al., 1996a). Further, successful recall also activates parts of the brain that play a role in processing the sensory features of an experience. For instance, recall of previously heard sounds is accompanied by activity in the auditory cortex (the upper part of the temporal lobe), whereas recall of previously seen pictures is accompanied by activity in the visual cortex (in the occipital lobe) (Wheeler, Petersen, & Buckner, 2000). Although retrieval may seem like a single process, brain studies suggest that separately identifiable processes are at work.

 How is brain activity different when *trying* to recall versus *successfully* recalling?

Once we appreciate this important point, we can use it to better understand how the brain handles complex memory processes, including one we just discussed: retrieval-induced forgetting. Recent fMRI evidence indicates that during the retrieval practice phase of a retrieval-induced forgetting paradigm, regions within the frontal

▶ FIGURE 6.12
PET Scans of Successful and Unsuccessful Recall When people successfully remembered words they saw earlier in an experiment, achieving high levels of recall on a test, the hippocampus showed increased activity. When people tried but failed to recall words they had seen earlier, achieving low levels of recall on a test, the left frontal lobe showed increased activity (Schacter et al., 1996a).

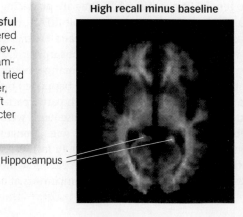
High recall minus baseline

Hippocampus

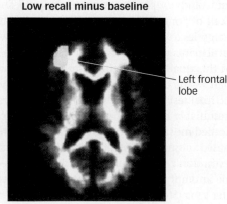
Low recall minus baseline

Left frontal lobe

lobe that are involved in retrieval effort play a role in suppressing competitors, whereas the hippocampal region is associated with successful recall (Kuhl et al., 2007; Wimber et al., 2009). However, when hippocampal activity during retrieval practice signals successful recall of an unwanted competitor, frontal lobe mechanisms are recruited that help to suppress the competitor. Though this process results in retrieval-induced forgetting, there's also a benefit: Once the competitor is suppressed, the frontal lobe no longer has to work as hard at controlling retrieval, ultimately making it easier to recall the target item (Kuhl et al., 2007). In Chapter 12 (see Figure 12.4), you'll see that successful suppression of an unwanted memory causes reduced activity in the hippocampus (Anderson et al., 2004). These findings make sense once we understand the specific roles played by particular brain regions in the retrieval process.

IN SUMMARY

○ Whether we remember a past experience depends on whether retrieval cues are available to trigger recall. Retrieval cues are effective when they help reinstate how we encoded an experience. Moods and inner states can serve as retrieval cues.

○ Retrieving information from memory has consequences for later remembering. Retrieval improves subsequent memory of the retrieved information, as exemplified by the beneficial effect of testing on later recall. However, retrieval can impair subsequent remembering of related information that is not retrieved.

○ Retrieval can be separated into the effort we make while trying to remember what happened in the past and the successful recovery of stored information. Neuroimaging studies suggest that trying to remember activates the left frontal lobe, whereas successful recovery of stored information activates the hippocampus and regions in the brain related to sensory aspects of an experience.

Multiple Forms of Memory: How the Past Returns

In 1977, the neurologist Oliver Sacks interviewed a young man named Greg who had a tumor in his brain that wiped out his ability to remember day-to-day events. One thing Greg could remember was his life during the 1960s in New York's Greenwich Village, years before the tumor formed, when Greg's primary occupation seemed to be attending rock concerts by his favorite band, The Grateful Dead. Greg's memories of those Dead concerts stuck with him over the following years, when he was living in a long-term care hospital and interviewed regularly by Dr. Sacks. In 1991, Dr. Sacks took Greg to a Dead concert at New York's Madison Square Garden, wondering whether such a momentous event might jolt his memory into action. "That was fantastic," Greg told Dr. Sacks as they left the concert. "I will always remember it. I had the time of my life." But when Dr. Sacks saw Greg the next morning and asked him whether he recalled the previous night's Dead concert at the Garden, Greg drew a blank: "No, I've never been to the Garden" (Sacks, 1995, pp. 76–77).

Although Greg was unable to make new memories, some of the new things that happened to him seemed to leave a mark. For example, Greg did not recall learning that his father had died, but he did seem sad and withdrawn for years after hearing the news. Similarly, HM could not make new memories after his surgery, but if he played a game in which he had to track a moving target, his performance gradually improved with each round (Milner, 1962). Greg could not consciously remember hearing about his father's death, and HM could not consciously remember playing the tracking game, but both showed clear signs of having been permanently changed by experiences that they so rapidly forgot. In other words, these patients *behaved* as though they were re-membering things while claiming to remember nothing at all. This suggests that there must be several kinds of memory, some of which are accessible to conscious recall, and some that we cannot consciously access (Eichenbaum & Cohen, 2001; Schacter & Tulving, 1994; Schacter, Wagner, & Buckner, 2000; Squire & Kandel, 1999).

Explicit and Implicit Memory

The fact that people can be changed by past experiences without having any aware-ness of those experiences suggests that there must be at least two different classes of memory (**FIGURE 6.13**). **Explicit memory** occurs *when people consciously or intention-ally retrieve past experiences*. Recalling last summer's vacation, incidents from a novel you just read, or facts you studied for a test all involve explicit memory. Indeed, any-time you start a sentence with, "I remember . . .," you are talking about an explicit memory. **Implicit memory** occurs when *past experiences influence later behavior and performance, even though people are not trying to recollect them and are not aware that they are remembering them* (Graf & Schacter, 1985; Schacter, 1987). Implicit memories are not consciously recalled, but their presence is "implied" by our actions. Greg's persis-tent sadness after his father's death, even though he had no conscious knowledge of the event, is an example of implicit memory.

So is HM's improved performance on a track-ing task that he didn't consciously remember doing. So is the ability to ride a bike or tie your shoelaces or play guitar: You may know how to do these things, but you probably can't de-scribe how to do them. Such knowledge reflects a particular kind of implicit memory called **procedural memory**, which refers to *the gradual acquisition of skills as a result of practice, or "knowing how" to do things*.

> **What type of memory is it when you just "know how" to do something?**

One of the hallmarks of procedural memory is that the things you remember are automatically translated into actions. Sometimes you can explain how it is done ("Put one finger on the third fret of the E string, one finger . . .") and sometimes you can't ("Get on the bike and . . . well, uh . . . just balance"). The fact that people who have amnesia can acquire new procedural memories suggests that the hippocampal struc-tures that are usually damaged in these patients may be necessary for explicit memory, but they aren't needed for implicit procedural memory. In fact, it appears that brain regions outside the hippocampal area (including areas in the motor cortex) are in-volved in procedural memory. Chapter 7 discusses this evidence further, where you will also see that procedural memory is crucial for learning various kinds of motor, perceptual, and cognitive skills.

Not all implicit memories are procedural or "how to" memories. For example, in one experiment, college students were asked to study a long list of words, including items such as *avocado, mystery, climate, octopus,* and *assassin* (Tulving, Schacter, & Stark, 1982). Later, explicit memory was tested by showing participants some of these words

► **FIGURE 6.13**
Multiple Forms of Memory Explicit and implicit memories are distinct from each other. Thus, a person with amnesia may lose explicit memory yet display implicit memory for material that she or he cannot consciously recall learning.

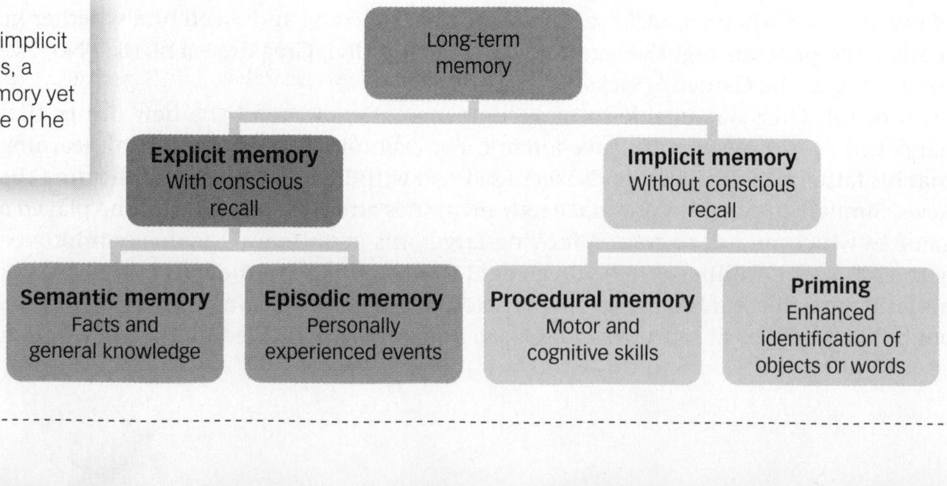

along with new ones they hadn't seen and asking them which words were on the list. To test implicit memory, participants received word fragments and were asked to come up with a word that fit the fragment. Try the test yourself:

ch– – – – nk   o–t–p– –   –og–y– – –   –l–m–te

You probably had difficulty coming up with the answers for the first and third fragments (*chipmunk, bogeyman*) but had little problem coming up with answers for the second and fourth (*octopus, climate*). Seeing *octopus* and *climate* on the original list made those words more accessible later, during the fill-in-the-blanks test. This is an example of **priming**, which refers to *an enhanced ability to think of a stimulus, such as a word or object, as a result of a recent exposure to the stimulus*

How does priming make memory more efficient?

(Tulving & Schacter, 1990). Just as priming a pump makes water flow more easily, priming the memory system makes some information more accessible. In the fill-in-the-blanks experiment, people showed priming for studied words even when they failed to consciously remember that they had seen them earlier. This suggests that priming is an example of implicit, not explicit, memory.

A truly stunning example of this point comes from a study by Mitchell (2006) in which participants first studied black-and-white line drawings depicting everyday objects. Later, the participants were shown fragmented versions of the drawings that are difficult to identify; some of them depicted objects that had been studied earlier in the experiment, whereas others depicted new objects that had not been studied. Mitchell found that participants correctly identified more fragmented drawings of studied than new objects, and identified more studied objects than did participants in a control group who had never seen the pictures—a clear demonstration of priming (see **FIGURE 6.14**). Here's the stunning part: The fragmented drawing test was given 17 years after presentation of the study list! By that time, participants had little or no explicit memory of having seen the drawings, and some had no recollection that they had ever participated in the experiment! "I'm sorry—I really don't remember this experiment at all," said one 36-year-old man who showed a strong priming effect. A 36-year-old female who showed even more priming stated simply, "Don't remember anything about it." (Mitchell, 2006, p. 929). These observations confirm that priming is an example of implicit memory, and also that priming can persist over very long periods of time.

As such, you'd expect amnesic patients such as HM and Greg to show priming. In fact, many experiments have shown that amnesic patients can show substantial priming effects—often as large as healthy, nonamnesic people—even though they have no explicit memory for the items they studied. These and other similar results suggest that priming, like procedural memory, does not require the hippocampal structures that are damaged in cases of amnesia (Schacter & Curran, 2000).

If the hippocampal region isn't required for procedural memory and priming, what parts of the brain are involved? Experiments have revealed that priming is associated with *reduced* activity in various regions of the cortex that are activated when people perform an unprimed task. For instance, when research participants are shown the word stem *mot___* or *tab___* and are asked to provide the first word that comes to mind, parts of the occipital lobe involved in visual processing and parts of the frontal lobe involved in word retrieval become active. But if people perform the same task after being primed by seeing *motel* and *table*, there's less activity in these same regions (Buckner et al., 1995; Schott et al., 2005). Something similar happens when people see pictures of everyday objects on two different occasions. On the second exposure to a picture, there's less activity in parts of the visual cortex that were activated by seeing the picture initially. Priming seems to make it easier for parts of the cortex that are involved in perceiving a word or object to identify the item after a recent exposure to it (Schacter, Dobbins, & Schnyer, 2004; Wiggs & Martin, 1998). This suggests that the brain "saves" a bit of processing time after priming (see **FIGURE 6.15** on the next page).

explicit memory The act of consciously or intentionally retrieving past experiences.

implicit memory The influence of past experiences on later behavior, even without an effort to remember them or an awareness of the recollection.

procedural memory The gradual acquisition of skills as a result of practice, or "knowing how" to do things.

priming An enhanced ability to think of a stimulus, such as a word or object, as a result of a recent exposure to the stimulus.

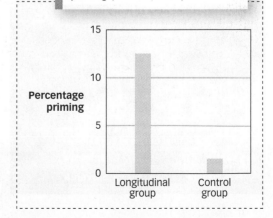

▼ FIGURE 6.14
Long-Term Priming of Visual Objects Participants who viewed drawings of common objects, and 17 years later were given a test in which they tried to identify the objects from fragmented drawings (longitudinal group), showed a strong priming effect; by contrast, participants who had not seen the drawing 17 years earlier (control group) showed nonsignificant priming (Mitchell, 2006).

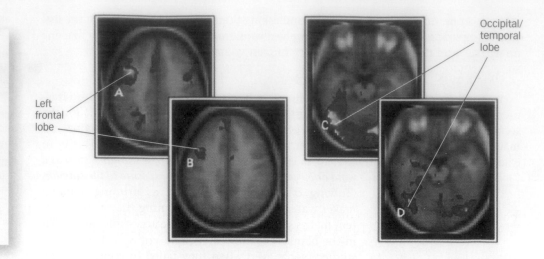

D. L. SCHACTER & R. L. BUCKNER, 1998, PRIMING AND THE BRAIN, NEURON, 20, PP. 185–195.

▶ **FIGURE 6.15**
Primed and Unprimed Processing of Stimuli Priming is associated with reduced levels of activation in the cortex on a number of different tasks. In each pair of fMRIs, the images on the upper left (A, C) show brain regions in the frontal lobe (A) and occipital/temporal lobe (C) that are active during an unprimed task (in this case, providing a word response to a visual word cue). The images on the lower right within each pair (B, D) show reduced activity in the same regions during the primed version of the same task.

Neuroimaging studies also indicate that different brain systems are involved in two distinct forms of priming: *perceptual priming,* which reflects implicit memory for the sensory features of an item (e.g., the visual characteristics of a word or picture), and *conceptual priming,* which reflects implicit memory for the meaning of a word or how you would use an object. fMRI studies indicate that perceptual priming depends primarily on regions toward the back of the brain, such as the visual cortex, whereas conceptual priming depends more on regions toward the front of the brain, such as the frontal lobes (Wig, Buckner, & Schacter, 2009). There is also some evidence that perceptual priming is associated primarily with the right cerebral hemisphere, whereas conceptual priming is associated with the left hemisphere (Schacter, Wig, & Stevens, 2007).

Semantic and Episodic Memory

Consider these two questions: (1) Why do we celebrate on July 4th? and (2) What is the most spectacular Fourth of July celebration you've ever seen? Every American knows the answer to the first question (we celebrate the signing of the Declaration of Independence on July 4, 1776), but we all have our own answers to the second. Although both of these questions required you to search your long-term memory and explicitly retrieve information that was stored there, one required you to dredge up a fact that every American schoolchild knows and that is not part of your personal autobiography, and one required you to revisit a particular time and place—or episode—from your personal past. These memories are called *semantic* and *episodic* memories, respectively (Tulving, 1972, 1983, 1998). **Semantic memory** is *a network of associated facts and concepts that make up our general knowledge of the world,* whereas **episodic memory** is *the collection of past personal experiences that occurred at a particular time and place.*

Episodic memory is special because it is the only form of memory that allows us to engage in "mental time travel," projecting ourselves into the past and revisiting events that have happened to us. This ability allows us to connect our pasts and our presents and construct a cohesive story of our lives. People who have amnesia can usually travel back in time and revisit episodes that occurred before they became amnesic, but they are unable to revisit episodes that happened later. For example, Greg couldn't travel back to any time after 1969 because that's when he stopped being able to create new episodic memories. But can people with amnesia create new semantic memories?

What form of memory uses "mental time travel"?

Researchers have studied three young adults who suffered damage to the hippocampus during birth as a result of difficult deliveries that interrupted the oxygen supply to their brains (Brandt et al., 2009; Vargha-Khadem et al.,

▼ This contestant on the game show *Who Wants to Be a Millionaire?* is consulting her semantic memory in order to answer the question. The answer is B: Bulgaria.

THE PHOTO WORKS

1997). Their parents noticed that the children could not recall what happened during a typical day, had to be constantly reminded of appointments, and often became lost and disoriented. In view of their hippocampal damage, you might also expect that each of the three would perform poorly in school and might even be classified as learning disabled. Remarkably, however, all three children learned to read, write, and spell; developed normal vocabularies; and acquired other kinds of semantic knowledge that allowed them to perform well in school. Based on this evidence, researchers have concluded that the hippocampus is not necessary for acquiring new *semantic* memories.

Episodic Memory and Imagining the Future

We've already seen that episodic memory allows us to travel backward in time, but it turns out that episodic memory also plays a role in allowing to us to travel forward in time. An amnesic patient known by the initials K.C. provided an early clue. K.C. could not recollect any specific episodes from his past, and when asked to imagine a future episode—such as what he might do tomorrow—he reported a complete "blank" (Tulving, 1985). Consistent with this observation, more recent findings from hippocampal amnesics reveal that they have difficulty imagining new experiences, such as sunbathing on a sandy beach (Hassabis et al., 2007). Something similar happens with aging. When asked either to recall episodes that actually occurred in their pasts or imagine new episodes that might occur in their futures, elderly adults provided fewer details about what happened, or what might happen, than did college students (Addis, Wong, & Schacter, 2008). Consistent with these findings, neuroimaging studies reveal that a network of brain regions known to be involved in episodic memory—including the hippocampus—shows similarly increased activity when people remember the past and imagine the future (Addis, Wong, & Schacter, 2007; Okuda et al., 2003; Szpunar, Watson, & McDermott, 2007; see **FIGURE 6.16**).

Taken together, these observations strongly suggest that we rely heavily on episodic memory to envision the future (Schacter, Addis, & Buckner, 2008). Episodic memory is well-suited to the task, because it is a flexible system that allows us to recombine elements of past experience in new ways, so that we can mentally "try out" different versions of what might happen (Schacter & Addis, 2007; Suddendorf & Corballis, 2007). For example, when you imagine having a difficult conversation with a friend that will take place in a couple of days, you can draw on past experiences to envisage different ways in which the conversation might unfold, and hopefully avoid saying things that, based on past experience, are likely to make the situation worse. As we'll discuss later, however, this flexibility of episodic memory might also be responsible for some kinds of memory errors (see p. 256).

semantic memory A network of associated facts and concepts that make up our general knowledge of the world.

episodic memory The collection of past personal experiences that occurred at a particular time and place.

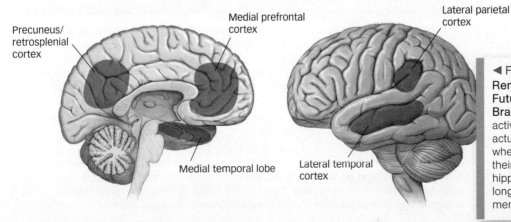

◄ FIGURE 6.16
Remembering the Past and Imagining the Future Depend on a Common Network of Brain Regions A common brain network is activated when people remember episodes that actually occurred in their personal pasts and when they imagine episodes that might occur in their personal futures. This network includes the hippocampus, a part of the medial temporal lobe long known to play an important role in episodic memory (Schacter, Addis, & Bucknew, 2007).

▲ Clark's nutcracker shows a remarkable ability to remember thousands of seed-hiding spots months after storing the seeds. Researchers are debating whether this type of memory indicates an ability for humanlike episodic memory.

Do Animals Have Episodic Memory?

Thinking about episodic memory as mental time travel raises an intriguing question: Can monkeys, rats, birds, or other nonhuman animals revisit their pasts as people do? Or can they project themselves into the future? We know that animals *behave* as though they can retrieve information acquired during specific past episodes. Monkeys act as though they are recalling objects they've seen only once during experimental tests (Zola & Squire, 2000). Rats seem to remember places they've visited recently in a maze (Olton & Samuelson, 1976). And birds that store food (such as Clark's nutcracker) can store as many as 30,000 seeds in 5,000 locations during the fall and then retrieve them all the next spring (Kamil & Jones, 1997; Shettleworth, 1995). Such food-storing behavior also suggests that the animals are planning for the future.

But do these smart pet tricks involve the same kind of mental time travel that we all do when we relive the July 4th picnic when Uncle Harry spilled barbecue sauce all over Aunt Norma, or envisage what might happen when those two get together at next year's celebration? Or are the episodic memories of animals more similar to the kinds of memory available to people who have amnesia; for example, are they simply implicit procedural memories?

It's difficult to say. Explicit memories, as well as future imaginings, always have a subjective component: When information "comes to mind," it *feels* like something. Animals cannot tell us whether they are having this subjective experience, and we can never tell by watching them whether they are actually having that experience or just behaving as though they are. Some researchers believe that even birds possess abilities closely related to episodic memory (Clayton & Russell, 2009). Food-storing scrub jays act as though they can recall what type of food they've stored (a worm or a peanut), where they stored it (on one side of a storage tray or another), and when they stored it (hours or days prior to a test) (Clayton & Dickinson, 1998). They also act as though they can plan for the future. When given a choice between storing food in an empty location that they've learned will not contain food the next morning, versus a location they've learned will contain food, they choose the empty location—suggesting that they're engaging in a type of mental time travel that allows them to anticipate being hungry and plan tomorrow's breakfast accordingly (Raby et al., 2007)!

Other researchers remain skeptical that demonstrations of highly detailed memories or future planning in birds or other animals truly signal the presence of mental time travel (Suddendorf & Corballis, 2007; Tulving, 1998). Human episodic memory involves a conscious experience of the self at different points in time. Does a scrub jay project itself backward in time when the bird recalls where and when it stored a worm or a peanut, or does it imagine being hungry the next day when it stores food in an empty location? No one knows for sure. The only reason we are so confident that other *people* engage in mental time travel is that they tell us they do. Because animals can't talk, it seems likely that we will never have a definitive answer to this intriguing question.

IN SUMMARY

○ Long-term memory consists of several different forms. Explicit memory is the act of consciously or intentionally retrieving past experiences, whereas implicit memory refers to the unconscious influence of past experiences on later behavior and performance, such as procedural memory and priming. Procedural memory involves the acquisition of skills as a result of practice, and priming is a change in the ability to recognize or identify an object or a word as the result of past exposure to it.

○ People who have amnesia are able to retain implicit memory, including procedural memory and priming, but they lack explicit memory.

○ Episodic memory is the collection of personal experiences from a particular time and place; it allows us both to recollect the past and imagine the future. Semantic memory is a networked, general, impersonal knowledge of facts, associations, and concepts. Animals possess extensive memory abilities, but it is still a matter of debate as to whether they can engage in the "mental time travel" characteristic of human episodic memory.

Memory Failures: The Seven Sins of Memory

transience Forgetting what occurs with the passage of time.

You probably haven't given much thought to breathing today, and the reason is that from the moment you woke up, you've been doing it effortlessly and well. But the moment breathing fails, you are reminded of just how important it is. Memory is like that. Every time we see, think, notice, imagine, or wonder, we are drawing on our ability to use information stored in our brains, but it isn't until this ability fails that we become acutely aware of just how much we should treasure it. Like a lot of human behavior, we can better understand how a process works correctly by examining what happens when it works incorrectly. We've seen in other contexts how an understanding of foibles and errors of human thought and action reveals the normal operation of various behaviors. Such memory errors—the "seven sins" of memory—cast similar illumination on how memory normally operates and how often it operates well (Schacter, 1999, 2001b). We'll discuss each of the seven sins in detail below.

1. Transience

On March 6, 2007, I. Lewis "Scooter" Libby, former Chief of Staff to Vice-President Dick Cheney, was convicted of perjury, making false statements, and obstruction of justice during an FBI investigation into whether members of the Bush administration had unlawfully disclosed the identity of a CIA agent to the media a couple of years earlier. According to Libby's defense team, any misstatements he might have made in response to FBI questioning were the result of faulty memory, not an intention to deceive. Libby's case received massive media attention, and resulted in a national debate about how much and what kind of forgetting is plausible for important events like those Libby claimed to forget. Indeed, the case stimulated experimental research showing that people sometimes have mistaken intuitions about what factors influence forgetting of important events (Kassam et al., 2009).

Despite the controversy over forgetting in the Libby case, one thing is certain: memories can and do degrade with time. The culprit here is **transience**: *forgetting what occurs with the passage of time*. Transience occurs during the storage phase of memory, after an experience has been encoded and before it is retrieved. You've already seen the workings of transience—rapid forgetting—in sensory storage and short-term storage. Transience also occurs in long-term storage, as was first illustrated in the late 1870s by Hermann Ebbinghaus, a German philosopher who measured his own memory for lists of nonsense syllables at different delays after studying them (Ebbinghaus, 1885/1964). Ebbinghaus charted his recall of nonsense syllables over time, creating the forgetting curve shown in **FIGURE 6.17**. Ebbinghaus noted a rapid drop-off in retention during the first few tests, followed by a slower rate of forgetting on later tests—a general pattern

▲ I. Lewis "Scooter" Libby was convicted of perjury and obstructing justice, but claimed that forgetting and related memory problems were responsible for any misstatements he made.

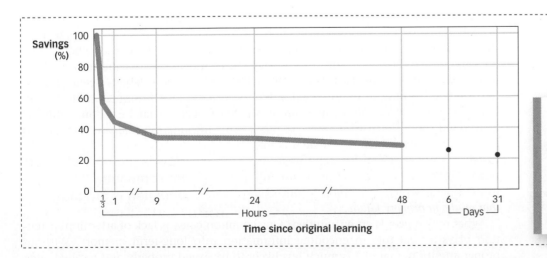

◀ FIGURE 6.17
The Curve of Forgetting Hermann Ebbinghaus measured his retention at various delay intervals after he studied lists of nonsense syllables. Retention was measured in percent savings, that is, the percentage of time needed to relearn the list compared to the time needed to learn it initially.

▲ Hermann Ebbinghaus (1850–1909), a German philosopher and psychologist, conducted some of the first scientific studies of memory. Ebbinghaus trained himself to memorize lists of nonsense syllables, then kept track of how long he could retain the information. Ebbinghaus's research revealed a great deal about the nature of remembering and forgetting.

confirmed by many subsequent memory researchers (Wixted & Ebbesen, 1991). So, for example, when English speakers were tested for memory of Spanish vocabulary acquired during high school or college courses 1 to 50 years previously, there was a rapid drop-off in memory during the first three years after the students' last class, followed by tiny losses in later years (Bahrick, 1984, 2000). In all these studies, memories didn't fade at a constant rate as time passed; most forgetting happened soon after an event occurred, with increasingly less forgetting as more time passed.

With the passage of time, the quality of our memories also changes. At early time points on the forgetting curve—minutes, hours, and days—memory preserves a relatively detailed record, allowing us to reproduce the past with reasonable if not perfect accuracy. But with the passing of time, we increasingly rely on our general memories for what usually happens and attempt to reconstruct the details by inference and even sheer guesswork. Transience involves a gradual switch from specific to more general memories (Brewer, 1996; Eldridge, Barnard, & Bekerian, 1994; Thompson et al., 1996). In one early study, British research participants read a brief Native American folktale that had odd imagery and unfamiliar plots in it, and then recounted it as best they could after a delay (Bartlett, 1932). The readers made interesting but understandable errors, often eliminating details that didn't make sense to them or adding elements to make the story more coherent. As the specifics of the story slipped away, the general meaning of the events stayed in memory but usually with elaborations and embellishments that were consistent with the readers' worldview. Because the story was unfamiliar to the readers, they raided their stores of general information and patched together a reasonable recollection of what *probably* happened.

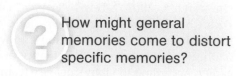

How might general memories come to distort specific memories?

Yet another way that memories can be distorted is by interference from other memories. For example, if you carry out the same activities at work each day, by the time Friday rolls around, it may be difficult to remember what you did on Monday because later activities blend in with earlier ones. This is an example of **retroactive interference**, which occurs when *later learning impairs memory for information acquired earlier* (Postman & Underwood, 1973). **Proactive interference**, in contrast, refers to situations in which *earlier learning impairs memory for information acquired later*. If you use the same parking lot each day at work or at school, you've probably gone out to find your car and then stood there confused by the memories of having parked it on previous days.

off the mark.com
by Mark Parisi

"THE PERSISTENCE OF MEMORY" TYPIFIES DALI'S EARLY WORK. NOW LET'S TAKE A LOOK AT A PIECE FROM HIS LATER YEARS...

THE PERPETUITY OF FORGETFULNESS

2. Absentmindedness

The great cellist Yo-Yo Ma put his treasured $2.5 million instrument in the trunk of a taxicab in Manhattan and then rode to his destination. After a 10-minute trip, he paid the driver and left the cab, forgetting his cello. Minutes later, Ma realized what he had done and called the police. Fortunately, they tracked down the taxi and recovered the instrument within hours (Finkelstein, 1999). But how had the celebrated cellist forgotten about something so important that had occurred only 10 minutes earlier? Transience is not a likely culprit. As soon as Mr. Ma realized what he'd done with his instrument, he recalled where he had put it. This information had not disappeared from his memory (which is why he was able to tell the police where the cello was). Instead, Yo-Yo Ma was a victim of **absentmindedness**, which is *a lapse in attention that results in memory failure.*

How is memory affected for someone whose attention is divided?

retroactive interference Situations in which information learned later impairs memory for information acquired earlier.

proactive interference Situations in which information learned earlier impairs memory for information acquired later.

absentmindedness A lapse in attention that results in memory failure.

What makes people absentminded? One common cause is lack of attention. Attention plays a vital role in encoding information into long-term memory. Without proper attention, material is much less likely to be stored properly and recalled later.

In studies of "divided attention," research participants are given materials to remember, such as a list of words, a story, or a series of pictures. At the same time, they are required to perform an additional task that draws their attention away from the material. For example, in one study, participants listened to lists of 15 words for a later memory test (Craik et al., 1996). They were allowed to pay full attention to some of the lists, but while they heard other lists, they simultaneously viewed a visual display containing four boxes and pressed different keys to indicate where an asterisk was appearing and disappearing. On a later test, participants recalled far fewer words from the list they had heard while their attention was divided.

What happens in the brain when attention is divided? In one study, volunteers tried to learn a list of word pairs while researchers scanned their brains with positron emission tomography (PET) (Shallice et al., 1994). Some people simultaneously performed a task that took little attention (they moved a bar the same way over and over), whereas other people simultaneously performed a task that took a great deal of attention (they moved a bar over and over but in a novel, unpredictable way each time). The researchers observed less activity in the participants' lower left frontal lobe when their attention was divided. As you saw earlier, greater activity in the lower left frontal region during encoding is associated with better memory. Dividing attention, then, prevents the lower left frontal lobe from playing its normal role in elaborative encoding, and the result is absentminded forgetting. More recent research using fMRI has shown that divided attention also leads to less hippocampal involvement in encoding (Kensinger, Clarke, & Corkin, 2003; Uncapher & Rugg, 2008). Given the importance of the hippocampus to episodic memory, this finding may help to explain why absentminded forgetting is sometimes so extreme, as when we forget where we put our keys or glasses only moments earlier.

▶ Yo-Yo Ma with his $2.5 million cello. The famous cellist lost it when he absentmindedly forgot that he'd placed the instrument in a taxicab's trunk minutes earlier.

TED THAI/GETTY IMAGES

Another common cause of absentmindedness is forgetting to carry out actions that we planned to do in the future. On any given day, you need to remember the times and places that your classes meet, you need to remember with whom and where you are having lunch, you need to remember which grocery items to pick up for dinner, and you need to remember which page of this book you were on when you fell asleep. In other words, you have to remember to remember, and this is called **prospective memory**, or *remembering to do things in the future* (Einstein & McDaniel, 1990, 2005).

Failures of prospective memory are a major source of absentmindedness. Avoiding these problems often requires having a cue available at the moment you need to remember to carry out an action. For example, air traffic controllers must sometimes postpone an action, such as granting a pilot's request to change altitude, but remember to carry out that action a few minutes later when conditions change. In a simulated air traffic control experiment, researchers provided controllers with electronic

CHRISTINA KENNEDY/GETTY IMAGES

◀ Talking on a cell phone while driving is a common occurrence of divided attention in everyday life; texting is even worse. This can be dangerous, and an increasing number of states have banned the practice.

prospective memory Remembering to do things in the future.

▲ Many people rely on memory aids such as calendars—and, more recently, personal digital assistants (PDAs)—to help them remember to perform a particular activity in the future.

signals to remind them to carry out a deferred request 1 minute later. The reminders were made available either during the 1-minute waiting period or at the time the controller needed to act on the deferred request. The controllers' memory for the deferred action improved only when the reminder was available at the time needed for retrieval. Providing the reminder during the waiting period did not help (Vortac, Edwards, & Manning, 1995). An early reminder, then, is no reminder at all.

3. Blocking

Have you ever tried to recall the name of a famous movie actor or a book you've read—and felt that the answer was "on the tip of your tongue," rolling around in your head *somewhere* but just out of reach it at the moment? This tip-of-the-tongue experience is a classic example of **blocking**, which is *a failure to retrieve information that is available in memory even though you are trying to produce it*. The sought-after information has been encoded and stored, and a cue is available that would ordinarily trigger recall of it. The information has not faded from memory, and you aren't forgetting to retrieve it. Rather, you are experiencing a full-blown retrieval failure, which makes this memory breakdown especially frustrating. It seems absolutely clear that you should be able to produce the information you seek, but the fact of the matter is that you can't. Researchers have described the tip-of-the-tongue state, in particular, as "a mild torment, something like [being] on the brink of a sneeze" (Brown & McNeill, 1966, p. 326).

Studies have found that when people are in tip-of-the-tongue states, they often know something about the item they can't recall, such as the meaning of a word (Schwartz, 2002). When experimenters induced tip-of-the-tongue states by playing participants theme songs from 1950s and 1960s television shows and asking for the names of the shows, people who were blocked on *The Munsters* often came up with the similarly themed *The Addams Family*. Likewise, some of those who blocked on *Leave It to Beaver* thought of *Dennis the Menace* (Riefer, Kevari, & Kramer, 1995) (**FIGURE 6.18**). If these titles mean anything at all to you, then you are either middle-aged or watching too much Nick-at-Nite.

Blocking occurs especially often for the names of people and places (Cohen, 1990; Semenza, 2009; Valentine, Brennen, & Brédart, 1996). Why? Because their links to related concepts and knowledge are weaker than for common names. That somebody's last name is Baker doesn't tell us much about the person, but saying that he *is* a baker does. To illustrate this point, researchers showed people pictures of cartoon and comic strip characters, some with descriptive names that highlight key features of

▶ FIGURE 6.18

Blocking Suppose you were asked to name a classic television comedy from hearing the show's theme music. The tip-of-the-tongue experience might cause you to block the Munsters, pictured on the left, for their close counterparts the Addams Family, on the right.

the character (e.g., Grumpy, Snow White, Scrooge) and others with arbitrary names (e.g., Aladdin, Mary Poppins, Pinocchio) (Brédart & Valentine, 1998). Even though the two types of names were equally familiar to participants in the experiment, they blocked less often on the descriptive names than on the arbitrary names.

Why is Snow White's name easier to remember than Mary Poppins's?

Although it's frustrating when it occurs, blocking is a relatively infrequent event for most of us. However, it occurs more often as we grow older, and it is a very common complaint among people in their 60s and 70s (Burke et al., 1991; Schwartz, 2002). Even more striking, some brain-damaged patients live in a nearly perpetual tip-of-the-tongue state (Semenza, 2009). One patient could recall the names of only 2 of 40 famous people when she saw their photographs, compared to 25 out of 40 for healthy volunteers in the control group (Semenza & Zettin, 1989). Yet she could still recall correctly the occupations of 32 of these people—the same number as healthy people could recall. This case and similar ones have given researchers important clues about what parts of the brain are involved in retrieving proper names. Name blocking usually results from damage to parts of the left temporal lobe on the surface of the cortex, most often as a result of a stroke. In fact, studies that show strong activation of regions within the temporal lobe when people recall proper names support this idea (Damasio et al., 1996; Tempini et al., 1998).

4. Memory Misattribution

Shortly after the devastating 1995 bombing of the federal building in Oklahoma City, police set about searching for two suspects they called John Doe 1 and John Doe 2. John Doe 1 turned out to be Timothy McVeigh, who was quickly apprehended and later convicted of the crime and sentenced to death. John Doe 2, who had supposedly accompanied McVeigh when he rented a van from Elliott's Body Shop two days before the bombing, was never found. In fact, John Doe 2 had never existed; he was a product of the memory of Tom Kessinger, a mechanic at Elliott's Body Shop who was present when McVeigh rented the van. The day after, two other men had also rented a van in Kessinger's presence. The first man, like McVeigh, was tall and fair. The second man was shorter and stockier, was dark-haired, wore a blue-and-white cap, and had a tattoo beneath his left sleeve—a match to the description of John Doe 2. Tom Kessinger had confused his recollections of men he had seen on separate days in the same place. He was a victim of **memory misattribution:** *assigning a recollection or an idea to the wrong source* (**FIGURE 6.19**).

Memory misattribution errors are some of the primary causes of eyewitness misidentifications. The memory researcher Donald Thomson was accused of rape based on the victim's detailed recollection of his face, but he was eventually cleared when it

blocking A failure to retrieve information that is available in memory even though you are trying to produce it.

memory misattribution Assigning a recollection or an idea to the wrong source.

◄ FIGURE 6.19
Memory Misattribution In 1995, the Murrah Federal Building in Oklahoma City was bombed in an act of terrorism. The police sketch shows "John Doe 2," who was originally thought to have been culprit Timothy McVeigh's partner in the bombing. It was later determined that the witness had confused his memories of different men whom he had encountered at Elliott's Body Shop on different days.

DAVID GLASS/AP PHOTO

FBI/THE OKLAHOMAN/AP PHOTO

Doonesbury

source memory Recall of when, where, and how information was acquired.

false recognition A feeling of familiarity about something that hasn't been encountered before.

▼ We may end up re-telling the same old story to a bored listener when our destination memory fails.

turned out he had an airtight alibi. At the time of the rape, Thomson was giving a live television interview on the subject of distorted memories! The victim had been watching the show just before she was assaulted and misattributed her memory of Thomson's face to the rapist (Schacter, 1996; Thomson, 1988).

Part of memory is knowing where our memories came from. This is known as **source memory**: *recall of when, where, and how information was acquired* (Johnson, Hashtroudi, & Lindsay, 1993; Mitchell & Johnson, 2009; Schacter, Harbluk, & McLachlan, 1984). People sometimes correctly recall a fact they learned earlier or accurately recognize a person or object they have seen before but misattribute the source of this knowledge—just as happened to Tom Kessinger and the rape victim in the Donald Thomson incident (Davies, 1988). Such misattribution could be the cause of déjà vu experiences, where you suddenly feel that you have been in a situation before even though you can't recall any details. A present situation that is similar to a past experience may trigger a general sense of familiarity that is mistakenly attributed to having been in the exact situation previously (Brown, 2004; Reed, 1988).

? What can explain a déjà vu experience?

Have you ever told someone a story or joke, only to have them tell you—or eventually realize yourself—that you had already told them what you thought you were communicating for the first time? Although source memory errors are common in everyday life, we may be even more prone to mistakes in remembering who we have told something before, a process called destination memory (Gopie & MacLeod, 2009). Recent experiments directly comparing source and destination memory revealed that participants made more errors when trying to remember who they told an interesting fact, compared with trying to remember who told them an interesting fact. The effect seems to occur because when we are telling someone else a fact or a story, we are focused primarily on our own thoughts, resulting in a weak association between the fact and the person with whom we are communicating (Gopie & MacLeod, 2009).

Patients with damage to the frontal lobes are especially prone to memory misattribution errors (Schacter et al., 1984; Shimamura & Squire, 1987). This is probably because the frontal lobes play a significant role in effortful retrieval processes, which are required to dredge up the correct source of a memory. These patients sometimes produce bizarre misattributions. In 1991, a British photographer in his mid-40s known as MR was overcome with feelings of familiarity about people he didn't know. He kept asking his wife whether each new passing stranger was "somebody"—a screen actor, television newsperson, or local celebrity. MR's feelings were so intense that he often could not resist approaching strangers and asking whether they were indeed famous celebrities. When given formal tests, MR recognized the faces of actual celebrities as accurately as did healthy volunteers in the control group. But MR also "recognized" more than 75% of unfamiliar faces, whereas healthy controls hardly ever did. Neurological exams revealed that MR suffered from multiple sclerosis, which had caused damage to his frontal lobes (Ward et al., 1999). Psychologists call the type of memory misattribution made by MR **false recognition**, which is *a feeling of familiarity about something that hasn't been encountered before.*

The subjective experience for patient MR, as in everyday déjà vu experiences, is characterized by a strong sense of familiarity without any recall of associated details. Other neurological patients exhibit a recently discovered type of memory misattribution called déjà vecu. Here, patients feel strongly—but mistakenly—that they have already lived through an experience and remember the details of what happened (Moulin et al., 2005). For example, when watching television, one patient was certain that he recalled seeing each show before, even when he watching an entirely new episode. When this patient went shopping, he constantly thought it was unnecessary to buy needed items because he remembered having done so already. Although the basis of this strange disorder is not well understood, it probably involves disruption to parts of the temporal lobe that normally generate a subjective feeling of remembering (Moulin et al., 2005).

But we are all vulnerable to memory misattribution. Take the following test and there is a good chance that you will experience false recognition for yourself. First, study the two lists of words presented in **TABLE 6.1** by reading each word for about 1 second. When you are done, return to the paragraph you were reading for more instructions, but don't look back at the table!

Now, try to recognize which of the following words appeared on the list you just studied: *taste, bread, needle, king, sweet, thread.* If you think that *taste* and *thread* were on the lists you studied, you're right. And if you think that *bread* and *king* weren't on those lists, you're also right. But if you think that *needle* or *sweet* appeared on the lists, you're dead wrong.

Most people make exactly the same mistake, claiming with confidence that they saw *needle* and *sweet* on the list. This occurs because all the words in the lists are associated with *needle* or *sweet*. Seeing each word in the study list activates related words. Because *needle* and *sweet* are related to all of the associates, they become more activated than other words—so highly activated that only minutes later, people swear that they actually studied the words (Deese, 1959; Gallo, 2006; Roediger & McDermott, 1995, 2000). In fact, brain-scanning studies using PET and fMRI show that many of the same brain regions are active during false recognition and true recognition, including the hippocampus (Cabeza et al., 2001; Schacter et al., 1996b; Slotnick & Schacter, 2004) (**FIGURE 6.20**). It is possible, however, to reduce or avoid false recognition by presenting distinctive information, such as a picture of *thread*, and encouraging participants to require specific recollections of seeing the picture before they say "yes" on a recognition test (Schacter, Israel, & Racine, 1999). Even patients with frontal

TABLE 6.1

False Recognition

Sour	Thread
Candy	Pin
Sugar	Eye
Bitter	Sewing
Good	Sharp
Taste	Point
Tooth	Prick
Nice	Thimble
Honey	Haystack
Soda	Pain
Chocolate	Hurt
Heart	Injection
Cake	Syringe
Tart	Cloth
Pie	Knitting

▼ FIGURE 6.20

Hippocampal Activity during True and False Recognition Many brain regions show similar activation during true and false recognition, including the hippocampus. The figure shows results from an fMRI study of true and false recognition of visual shapes (Slotnick & Schacter, 2004). (a) A plot showing the activity level in the strength of the fMRI signal from the hippocampus over time. This shows that after a few seconds, there is comparable activation for true recognition of previously studied shapes (red line) and false recognition of similar shapes that were not presented (yellow line). Both true and false recognition show increased hippocampal activity compared with correctly classifying unrelated shapes as new (purple line). (b) A region of the left hippocampus.

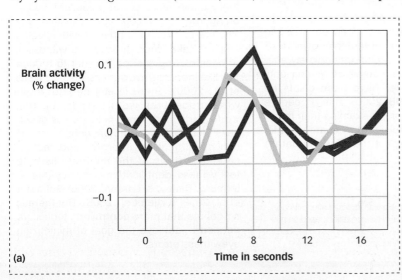

Brain activity (% change) / Time in seconds

(a)

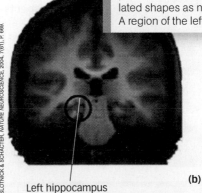

SLOTNICK & SCHACTER, *NATURE NEUROSCIENCE*, 2004, 7(61), P. 669.

Left hippocampus

(b)

lobe damage can reduce false recognition when they are encouraged to rely on distinctive information when making recognition decisions (Hwang et al., 2007). Unfortunately, we do not always demand specific recollections before we say that we encountered a word in an experiment or—more importantly—make a positive identification of a suspect. When people experience a strong sense of familiarity about a person, object, or event but lack specific recollections, a potentially dangerous recipe for memory misattribution is in place. Understanding this point may be a key to reducing the dangerous consequences of misattribution in eyewitness testimony (see the Real World box).

THE REAL WORLD

Dangerous Misattributions

On July 25, 1984, a 9-year-old girl was found dead in the woods near Baltimore after being brutally beaten and sexually assaulted. A witness identified 23-year-old Kirk Bloodsworth as the killer, based on a sketch police generated from five other witness accounts. Although Bloodsworth passionately maintained his innocence, a jury convicted him of first-degree murder and the judge sentenced him to death. After Bloodsworth spent 2 years on death row, the sentence was reduced to life in prison on an appeal. In 1993, DNA testing revealed that Bloodsworth was not the source of incriminating semen stains in the victim's underwear. He was released from prison after serving 9 years, later received a full pardon, and returned to his quiet life as a crab fisherman (Chebium, 2000; Connors et al., 1997; Wells et al., 1998). The witness's memory misattribution cost Bloodsworth a decade of his life, and his mother did not live to see him freed: She died of a heart attack several months before his release.

Bloodsworth is not alone. The first 40 cases in which DNA evidence led to the release of wrongfully imprisoned individuals revealed that 36 of the convictions—90%— were based partly or entirely on mistaken eyewitness identification (Wells et al., 1998). Fifty separate eyewitnesses were involved in these cases; they were all confident in their memories but seriously mistaken. These statistics are especially troubling because eyewitness testimony is frequently relied on in the courtroom: Each year more than 75,000 criminal trials are decided on the basis of eyewitness testimony (Ross et al., 1994, p. 918). Common lineup identification practices may often promote misattribution because people are encouraged to rely on general familiarity (Wells et al., 1998, 2000). In standard lineup procedures, witnesses are shown several suspects; after seeing all of them, they attempt to identify the culprit. Under these conditions, witnesses tend to rely on "relative judgments": They choose the person who, relative to the others in the lineup, looks most like the suspect. The problem is that even when the suspect is *not in* the lineup, witnesses still tend to choose the person who looks most like the suspect. Witnesses rely on general similarities between a face in a lineup and the actual culprit, even when they lack specific recollections of the culprit. There are ways to minimize reliance on relative judgments. For example, witnesses can be asked to make a "thumbs-up or thumbs-down" decision about each suspect immediately after seeing each face instead of waiting until all suspects' faces have been displayed (Wells et al., 1998, 2000). This procedure encourages people to examine their memories more carefully and evaluate whether the pictured suspect matches the details

of their recollections, sometimes (but not always) resulting in more accurate witness identification (Gronlund et al., 2009).

One encouraging development is that law enforcement officials are listening to what psychologists have to say about the construction of lineups and other identification procedures that could promote inaccurate identification. In early 1998, then-Attorney General Janet Reno formed a working group of psychologists, police, and attorneys to develop guidelines for collecting eyewitness evidence. This group eventually published a set of guidelines based on rigorous psychological studies that provide law enforcement officials with specific steps to take when questioning witnesses or constructing lineups in order to reduce the likelihood of eyewitness errors (Wells et al., 2000). There is still debate about what procedures work best in the real world, particularly since field studies of witness identification in actual criminal cases can be difficult to interpret and require careful analysis of the methods used to test witness identification accuracy (Mecklenburg, Bailey, & Larsen, 2008; Schacter et al., 2008; Turtle et al., 2008). But there is no debate that more controlled studies are needed to achieve the goal of minimizing eyewitness errors.

◀ Kirk Bloodsworth spent 9 years behind bars for a crime he didn't commit. He was released after DNA evidence led to the reversal of his conviction based on mistaken eyewitness testimony. Here he holds up the book that tells his story, by author and attorney Tim Junkin.

5. Suggestibility

On October 4, 1992, an El Al cargo plane crashed into an apartment building in a southern suburb of Amsterdam, killing 39 residents and all four members of the airline crew. The disaster dominated news in the Netherlands for days as people viewed footage of the crash scene and read about the catastrophe. Ten months later, Dutch psychologists asked a simple question of university students: "Did you see the television film of the moment the plane hit the apartment building?" Fifty-five percent answered "yes." (Crombag et al., 1996). All of this might seem perfectly normal except for one key fact: There was no television film of the moment when the plane actually crashed. The researchers had asked a suggestive question that implied that television film of the crash had been shown. Respondents may have viewed television film of the post-crash scene, and they may have read, imagined, or talked about what might have happened when the plane hit the building, but they most definitely did not see it. The suggestive question led participants to misattribute information from these or other sources to a film that did not exist. **Suggestibility** is the *tendency to incorporate misleading information from external sources into personal recollections*.

▲ In 1992, an El Al cargo plane crashed into an apartment building in a suburb of Amsterdam. When Dutch psychologists asked students if they'd seen the television film of the plane crashing, most said they had. In fact, no such footage exists (Crombag, Wagenaar, & Van Koppen, 1996).

Research evidence of suggestibility abounds. For example, in one study, Elizabeth Loftus and her colleagues showed participants a videotape of an automobile accident involving a white sports car (Loftus, 1975; Loftus et al., 1978). Some participants were then asked how fast the car was going when it passed the barn. Nearly 20% of these individuals later recalled seeing a barn in the videotape—even though there was no barn (participants who weren't asked about a barn almost never recalled seeing one). Misleading suggestions do not eliminate the original memory (Berkerian & Bowers, 1983; McCloskey & Zaragoza, 1985). Instead, they cause participants to make source memory errors: They have difficulty recollecting whether they actually saw a yield sign or only learned about it later.

suggestibility The tendency to incorporate misleading information from external sources into personal recollections.

If misleading details can be implanted in people's memories, is it also possible to suggest entire episodes that never occurred? Could you be convinced, for example, that you had once been lost in a shopping mall as a child or spilled a bowl of punch at a wedding—even though these events never actually happened? The answer seems to be "yes" (Loftus, 1993, 2003). In one study, the research participant, a teenager named Chris, was asked by his older brother, Jim, to try to remember the time Chris had been lost in a shopping mall at age 5. He initially recalled nothing, but after several days, Chris produced a detailed recollection of the event. He recalled that he "felt so scared I would never see my family again" and remembered that a kindly old man wearing a flannel shirt found him crying (Loftus, 1993, p. 532). But according to Jim and other family members, Chris was never lost in a shopping mall. Of 24 participants in a larger study on implanted memories, approximately 25% falsely remembered being lost as a child in a shopping mall or in a similar public place (Loftus & Pickrell, 1995).

◀ In a classic experiment by Elizabeth Loftus, people were shown a video-tape of a car at a stop sign. Those who later received a misleading suggestion that the car had stopped at a yield sign often claimed they had seen the car at a yield sign (Loftus, Miller, & Burns, 1978).

Other researchers have also successfully implanted false memories of childhood experiences in a significant minority of participants (Hyman & Billings, 1998; Hyman & Pentland, 1996). In one study, college students were asked about several childhood events that, according to their parents, actually happened. But they were also asked about an event that never happened. For instance, the students were asked if they remembered a wedding reception they attended when they were 5, running around with some other kids and bumping into a table and spilling the punch bowl on the parents of the bride. Students remembered nearly all of the true events and initially reported no memory for the false events. However, with repeated probing, approximately 20% to 40% of the participants in different experimental conditions eventually came to describe some memory of the false event.

People develop false memories in response to suggestions for some of the same reasons memory misattribution occurs. We do not store all the details of our experiences in memory, making us vulnerable to accepting suggestions about what might have happened or should have happened. In addition, visual imagery plays an important role in constructing false memories (Goff & Roediger, 1998). Asking people to imagine an event like spilling punch all over the bride's parents at a wedding increases the likelihood that they will develop a false memory of it (Hyman & Pentland, 1996).

Why can childhood memories be influenced by suggestion?

Suggestibility played an important role in a controversy that arose during the 1980s and 1990s concerning the accuracy of childhood memories that people recall during psychotherapy. One highly publicized example involved a woman named Diana Halbrooks (Schacter, 1996). After a few months in psychotherapy, she began recalling disturbing incidents from her childhood—for example, that her mother had tried to kill her and that her father had abused her sexually. Although her parents denied that these events had ever occurred, her therapist encouraged her to believe in the reality of her memories. Had Halbrooks retrieved terrible memories of events that had actually occurred, or were the memories inaccurate, perhaps the result of suggestive probing during psychotherapy?

In the early 1990s, more and more American families found themselves coping with similar issues. Educated middle-class women (and some men) entered psychotherapy for depression or related problems, only to emerge with recovered memories of previously forgotten childhood sexual abuse, typically perpetrated by fathers and sometimes by mothers. Families and psychologists were split by these controversies. Patients believed their memories were real, and many therapists supported those beliefs, but accused parents contended that the alleged abuses had never happened and that they were instead the products of false memories.

Several kinds of evidence suggest that many recovered memories are inaccurate (Loftus & Davis, 2006; McNally & Geraerts, 2009). First, some people have recovered highly implausible memories of being abused repeatedly during bizarre practices in satanic cults, and yet there is no proof of these practices or even that the cults exist (Pendergrast, 1995; Wright, 1994). Second, a number of the techniques used by psychotherapists to try to pull up forgotten childhood memories are clearly suggestive. A survey of 145 therapists in the United States revealed that approximately 1 in 3 tried to help patients remember childhood sexual abuse by using hypnosis or by encouraging them to imagine incidents that might or might not have actually happened (Poole et al., 1995). Yet research has shown that imagining past events and hypnosis can help create false memories (Garry et al., 1996; Hyman & Pentland, 1996; McConkey, Barnier, & Sheehan, 1998). Third, some individuals who claim to have recovered memories of trauma, including childhood abuse and alien abductions, also show unusually high rates of false memories on laboratory tests (Clancy et al., 2000, 2002). While some recovered memories—especially those that people remember on their own—are probably accurate (Gleaves et al., 2004), those recovered using techniques such as visualization that are known to create false memories in the lab are suspect. Consistent with this idea, recent studies show that spontaneously recovered memories are corroborated by other people at about the same rate as the memories of individuals who never forgot their abuse, whereas memories recovered in response to suggestive therapeutic techniques are virtually never corroborated by others (McNally & Geraerts, 2009).

A growing number of patients eventually retracted their recovered memories after leaving therapy or returning to their families (McHugh et al., 2004). This is just what happened to Diana Halbrooks: She stopped therapy and eventually came to realize that the "memories" she had recovered were inaccurate. By the end of the 1990s, the number of new cases of disputed recovered memories of childhood sexual abuse had slowed to a trickle (McHugh et al., 2004). This probably occurred, at least in part, because some of the therapists who had been using suggestive procedures stopped doing so (McNally, 2003).

6. Bias

In 2000, the outcome of a very close presidential race between George W. Bush and Al Gore was decided by the Supreme Court 5 weeks after the election had taken place.

The day after the election (when the result was still in doubt), supporters of Bush and Gore were asked to predict how happy they would be after the outcome of the election was determined (Wilson, Meyers, & Gilbert, 2003). These same respondents reported how happy they felt with the outcome on the day after Al Gore conceded. And 4 months later, the participants recalled how happy they had been right after the election was decided.

Bush supporters, who eventually enjoyed a positive result (their candidate took office), were understandably happy on the day after the Supreme Court's decision. However, their retrospective accounts *over*estimated how happy they were at the time. Conversely, Gore supporters were not pleased with the outcome. But when polled 4 months after the election was decided, Gore supporters *under*estimated how happy they actually were at the time of the result. In both groups, recollections of happiness were at odds with existing reports of their actual happiness at the time (Wilson et al., 2003).

▲ How happy do you think you'd be if the candidate you supported won an election? Do you think you'd accurately remember your level of happiness if you recalled it several months later? Chances are good that bias in the memory process would alter your recollection of your previous happiness. Indeed, 4 months after they heard the outcome of the 2000 presidential election, Bush supporters overestimated how happy they were, while Gore supporters underestimated how happy they were.

These results illustrate the problem of **bias**, which is *the distorting influences of present knowledge, beliefs, and feelings on recollection of previous experiences.* Sometimes what people remember from their pasts says less about what actually happened than about what they think, feel, or believe now. Researchers have also found that our current moods can bias our recall of past experiences (Bower, 1981; Buchanan, 2007; Eich, 1995). So, in addition to helping you recall actual sad memories (as you saw earlier in this chapter), a sad mood can also bias your recollections of experiences that may not have been so sad. *Consistency bias* is the bias to reconstruct the past to fit the present. One researcher asked people in 1973 to rate their attitudes toward a variety of controversial social issues, including legalization of marijuana, women's rights, and aid to minorities (Marcus, 1986). They were asked to make the same rating again in 1982 and also to indicate what their attitudes had been in 1973. Researchers found that partici-

How does your current outlook color your memory of a past event?

pants' recollections of their 1973 attitudes in 1982 were more closely related to what they believed in 1982 than to what they had actually said in 1973.

Whereas consistency bias exaggerates the similarity between past and present, *change bias* is the tendency to exaggerate differences between what we feel or believe now and what we felt or believed in the past. In other words, *change biases* also occur. For example, most of us would like to believe that our romantic attachments grow stronger over time. In one study, dating couples were asked, once a year for 4 years, to assess the present quality of their relationships and to recall how they felt in past years (Sprecher, 1999). Couples who stayed together for the 4 years recalled that the strength of their love had increased since they last reported on it. Yet their actual ratings at the time did not show any increases in love and attachment. Objectively, the couples did not love each other more today than yesterday. But they did from the subjective perspective of memory.

bias The distorting influences of present knowledge, beliefs, and feelings on recollection of previous experiences.

A special case of change bias is *egocentric bias,* the tendency to exaggerate the change between present and past in order to make ourselves look good in retrospect. For example, students sometimes remember feeling more anxious before taking an exam than they actually reported at the time (Keuler & Safer, 1998), and blood donors sometimes recall being more nervous about giving blood than they actually were (Breckler, 1994). In both cases, change biases color memory and make people feel that they behaved more bravely or courageously than they actually did. Similarly, when college students tried to remember high school grades and their memories were checked against actual transcripts, they were highly accurate for grades of A (89% correct) and extremely inaccurate for grades of D (29% correct) (Bahrick, Hall, & Berger, 1996). The same kind of egocentric bias occurs with memory for college grades: 81% of errors inflated the actual grade, and this bias was evident even when participants were asked about their grades soon after graduation (Bahrick, Hall, & DaCosta, 2008). People were remembering the past as they wanted it to be rather than the way it was.

7. Persistence

The artist Melinda Stickney-Gibson awoke in her apartment to the smell of smoke. She jumped out of bed and saw black plumes rising through cracks in the floor. Raging flames had engulfed the entire building, and there was no chance to escape except by jumping from her third-floor window. Shortly after she crashed to the ground, the building exploded into a brilliant fireball. Although she survived the fire and the fall, Melinda became overwhelmed by memories of the fire. When Melinda sat down in front of a blank canvas to start a new painting, her memories of that awful night intruded. Her paintings, which were previously bright, colorful abstractions, became dark meditations that included only black, orange, and ochre—the colors of the fire (Schacter, 1996).

Melinda Stickney-Gibson's experiences illustrate memory's seventh and most deadly sin: **persistence,** or *the intrusive recollection of events that we wish we could forget.* Melinda's experience is far from unique: Persistence frequently occurs after disturbing or traumatic incidents, such as the fire that destroyed her home. Although being able to quickly call up memories is usually considered a good thing, in the case of persistence, that ability mutates into an unwelcome burden.

Controlled laboratory studies have revealed that emotional experiences tend to be better remembered than nonemotional ones. For instance, memory for unpleasant pictures, such as mutilated bodies, or pleasant ones, such as attractive men and women, is more accurate than for emotionally neutral pictures, such as household objects (Ochsner, 2000). Emotional arousal seems to focus our attention on the central features of an event. In one experiment, people who viewed an emotionally arousing sequence of slides involving a bloody car accident remembered more of the central themes and fewer peripheral details than people who viewed a nonemotional sequence (Christianson & Loftus, 1987).

Intrusive memories are undesirable consequences of the fact that emotional experiences generally lead to more vivid and enduring recollections than nonemotional experiences do. One line of evidence comes from the study of **flashbulb memories**, which are *detailed recollections of when and where we heard about shocking events* (Brown & Kulick, 1977). For example, most Americans can recall exactly where they were and how they

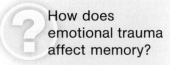 **How does emotional trauma affect memory?**

heard about the September 11, 2001, terrorist attacks on the World Trade Center and the Pentagon—almost as if a mental flashbulb had gone off automatically and recorded the event in long-lasting and vivid detail (Kvavilashvili et al., 2009). Several studies have shown that flashbulb memories are not always entirely accurate, but they are generally better remembered than mundane news events from the same time (Larsen, 1992; Neisser & Harsch, 1992). Enhanced retention of flashbulb memories is partly attributable to the emotional arousal elicited by events such as the September 11th terrorist attacks, and partly attributable to the fact that we tend to talk and think a lot about these experiences. Recall that elaborative encoding enhances memory: When we talk about

▲ The way each member of this happy couple recalls earlier feelings toward the other depends on how each currently views their relationship.

ANDERSEN ROSS/PHOTOLIBRARY

persistence The intrusive recollection of events that we wish we could forget.

flashbulb memories Detailed recollections of when and where we heard about shocking events.

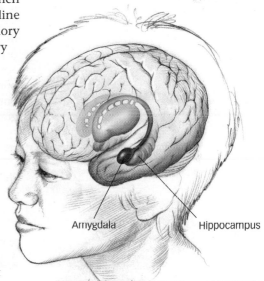

◄ Some events are so emotionally charged, such as the Kennedy assassination and the terrorist attack on the World Trade Center, that we form unusually detailed memories of when and where we heard about them. These flashbulb memories generally persist much longer than memories for more ordinary events.

flashbulb experiences, we elaborate on them and thus further increase the memorability of those aspects of the experience that we discuss (Hirst et al., 2009).

Why do our brains succumb to persistence? A key player in the brain's response to emotional events is a small, almond-shaped structure called the amygdala, shown in **FIGURE 6.21.** The amygdala influences hormonal systems that kick into high gear when we experience an arousing event; these stress-related hormones, such as adrenaline and cortisol, mobilize the body in the face of threat—and they also enhance memory for the experience. Damage to the amygdala does not result in a general memory deficit. Patients with amygdala damage, however, do not remember emotional events any better than nonemotional events (Cahill & McGaugh, 1998).

For example, consider what happened when people viewed a series of photographic slides that began with a mother walking her child to school and later included an emotionally arousing event: the child being hit by a car. When tested later, the research participants remembered the arousing event better than the mundane ones. But patients with amygdala damage remembered the mundane and emotionally arousing events equally well (Cahill & McGaugh, 1998). PET and fMRI scans show that when healthy people view a slide sequence that includes an emotionally arousing event, the level of activity in their amygdalas at the time they see it is a good predictor of their subsequent memory for the slide. When there is heightened activity in the amygdala as people watch emotional events, there's a better chance that they will recall those events on a later test (Cahill et al., 1996; Kensinger & Schacter, 2005, 2006). And when people are given a drug that interferes with the amygdala-mediated release of stress hormones, their memory for the emotional sections is no better than their memory for the mundane sections.

In many cases, there are clear benefits to forming strong memories for highly emotional events—particularly those that are life-threatening. In the case of persistence, though, such memories may be too strong—strong enough to interfere with other aspects of daily life.

Are the Seven Sins Vices or Virtues?

You may have concluded that evolution burdened us with an extremely inefficient memory system that is so prone to error that it often jeopardizes our well-being. Not so. The seven sins are the price we pay for the many benefits that memory provides, the occasional result of the normally efficient operation of the human memory system (Schacter, 2001b).

Consider transience, for example. Wouldn't it be great to remember all the details of every incident in your life, no matter how much time had passed? Not necessarily. Do you remember the words of Jill Price, a woman we discussed earlier in this chapter who has this ability? Commenting on her own memory, Jill complained that, "I run my entire life through my head every day and it drives me crazy!!!" (Parker et al., 2006, p. 35)

▲ FIGURE 6.21
The Amygdala's Influence on Memory The amygdala, located next to the hippocampus, responds strongly to emotional events. Patients with amygdala damage are unable to remember emotional events any better than nonemotional ones (Cahill & McGaugh, 1998).

It is helpful and sometimes important to forget information that isn't current, like an old phone number. If we didn't gradually forget information over time, our minds would be cluttered with details that we no longer need (Bjork & Bjork, 1988). Information that is used infrequently is less likely to be needed in the future than information that is used more frequently over the same period (Anderson & Schooler, 1991, 2000).

How are we better off with imperfect memories?

Memory, in essence, makes a bet that when we haven't used information recently, we probably won't need it in the future. We win this bet more often than we lose it, making transience an adaptive property of memory. But we are acutely aware of the losses—the frustrations of forgetting—and are never aware of the wins. This is why people are often quick to complain about their memories: The drawbacks of forgetting are painfully evident, but the benefits of forgetting are hidden.

Similarly, absentmindedness and blocking can be frustrating, but they are side effects of our memory's usually successful attempt to sort through incoming information, preserving details that are worthy of attention and recall, and discarding those that are less worthy.

Memory misattribution and suggestibility both occur because we often fail to recall the details of exactly when and where we saw a face or learned a fact. This is because memory is adapted to retain information that is most likely to be needed in the environment in which it operates. We seldom need to remember all the precise contextual details of every experience. Our memories carefully record such details only when we think they may be needed later, and most of the time we are better off for it. Further, we often use memories to anticipate possible future events. As discussed earlier, memory is flexible, allowing us to recombine elements of past experience in new ways, so that we can mentally "try out" different versions of what might happen. But this very flexibility—a strength of memory—may sometimes produce misattribution errors in which elements of past experience are miscombined (Schacter & Addis, 2007). Bias skews our memories so that we depict ourselves in an overly favorable light—but it can produce the benefit of contributing to our overall sense of contentment. Holding positive illusions about ourselves can lead to greater psychological well-being (Taylor, 1989). Although persistence can cause us to be haunted by traumas that we'd be better off forgetting, overall, it is probably adaptive to remember threatening or traumatic events that could pose a threat to survival.

Although each of the seven sins can cause trouble in our lives, they have an adaptive side as well. You can think of the seven sins as costs we pay for benefits that allow memory to work as well as it does most of the time.

IN SUMMARY

○ Memory's mistakes can be classified into seven "sins."

○ *Transience* is reflected by a rapid decline in memory followed by more gradual forgetting. With the passing of time, memory switches from detailed to general. Both decay and interference contribute to transience. *Absentmindedness* results from failures of attention, shallow encoding, and the influence of automatic behaviors, and is often associated with forgetting to do things in the future. *Blocking* occurs when stored information is temporarily inaccessible, as when information is on the tip of the tongue.

○ *Memory misattribution* happens when we experience a sense of familiarity but don't recall, or mistakenly recall, the specifics of when and where an experience occurred. Misattribution can result in eyewitness misidentification or false recognition. Patients suffering from frontal lobe damage are especially susceptible to false recognition. *Suggestibility* gives rise to implanted memories of small details or entire episodes. Suggestive techniques such as hypnosis or visualization can promote vivid recall of suggested events, and therapists' use of suggestive techniques may be responsible for some patients' false memories of childhood traumas. *Bias* reflects the influence of current knowledge, beliefs, and feelings on memory or past experiences. Bias can lead us to make the past consistent with the present, exaggerate changes between past and present, or remember the past in a way that makes us look good.

Continued

○ *Persistence* reflects the fact that emotional arousal generally leads to enhanced memory, whether we want to remember an experience or not. Persistence is partly attributable to the operation of hormonal systems influenced by the amygdala. Although each of the seven sins can cause trouble in our lives, they have an adaptive side as well.

○ You can think of the seven sins as costs we pay for benefits that allow memory to work as well as it does most of the time.

WhereDoYouStand?

The Mystery of Childhood Amnesia

As you have seen, transience is a pervasive characteristic of memory. Nonetheless, you can easily recall many experiences from different times in your life, such as last summer's job or vacation, the sights and sounds of a favorite concert, or the most exciting sporting event you've ever attended. But there is one period of time from which you likely have few or no memories: the first few years of your life. This lack of memory for our early years is called *childhood amnesia* or *infantile amnesia*.

Psychoanalyst Sigmund Freud was one of the first psychologists to comment on childhood amnesia (see Chapter 1). In 1905, he described a "peculiar amnesia which, in the case of most people, though by no means all, hides the earliest beginnings of their childhood up to their sixth or eighth year" (Freud, 1905/1953, p. 174). Freud's assessments of childhood amnesia were based on observations of individual patients from his psychoanalytic practice.

In the 1930s and 1940s, psychologists carried out systematic studies in which they asked large samples of individuals to report their earliest memories with the dates when they occurred. Contrary to Freud's suggestion that most people cannot remember childhood experiences prior to their sixth or eighth year, these studies revealed that, on average, an individual's earliest memory dates to about 3½ years of age (Dudycha & Dudycha, 1933; Waldfogel, 1948). Later studies suggested that women report slightly earlier first memories (3.07 years of age) than men (3.4 years) (Howes, Siegel, & Brown, 1993).

Try to recall your own earliest memory. As you mentally search for it, you may encounter a problem that has troubled researchers: How do you know the exact time when your recollection took place? Memory for dates is notoriously poor, so it is often difficult to determine precisely when your earliest memory occurred (Friedman, 1993). To address this problem, researchers asked people about memories for events that have clearly definable dates, such as the birth of a younger sibling, the death of a loved one, or a family move (Sheingold & Tenney, 1982; Usher & Neisser, 1993). In one study, researchers asked individuals between 4 and 20 years old to recall as much as they could about the birth of a younger sibling (Sheingold & Tenney, 1982). Participants who were at least 3 years old at the time of the birth remembered it in considerable detail, whereas participants who were younger than 3 years old at the time of the birth remembered little or nothing. A more recent study found that individuals can recall events surrounding the birth of a sibling that occurred when they were about 2.4 years old; some people even showed evidence of recall from ages 2.0 to 2.4 years, although these memories were very sketchy (Eacott & Crawley, 1998).

It is difficult to draw firm conclusions from these kinds of studies. On the one hand, they suggest that people can come up with memories from earlier in life than was previously thought. On the other hand, memories of early events may be based on family conversations that took place long after the events occurred. An adult or a child who remembers having ice cream in the hospital as a 3-year-old when his baby sister was born may be recalling what his parents told him after the event. Consistent with this idea, cross-cultural studies have turned up an interesting finding. Individuals from cultures that emphasize talking about the past, such as North American culture, tend to report earlier first memories than individuals from cultures that place less emphasis on talking about the past, such as Korean and other Asian cultures (MacDonald, Uesiliana, & Hayne, 2000; Mullen, 1994).

Recent research has examined whether the events that people say they remember from early childhood really are *personal recollections*, which involve conscious re-experiencing of some aspect of the event, or whether people *just know* about these events (perhaps from family photos and discussions), even though they don't truly possess personal recollections (Multhaup, Johnson, & Tetirick, 2005). Several experiments revealed that personal recollections tend to emerge later than memories based on "just knowing," with the transition from mostly "know" memories to mostly "recollect" memories occurring at 4.7 years of age.

Some events in your personal history are personal recollections. In other words, you actually remember the occurrence of the event. Personal recollections are ones in which you can become consciously aware again of some aspects of the event, of what happened, or of what you experienced at the time. Perhaps you have an image of the event or can re-experience some specific details.

Other events from your past are ones that you know happened but are not personal recollections. In other words, you know the event occurred, but you cannot consciously recollect any aspect of what happened or of what you experienced at the time. Instead, your knowledge of the event is based on an external source of information, perhaps your parents and/or other family members, friends, pictures, photo albums, diaries, or family stories. To find out about your own "recollected" versus "known" memories, complete the items listed on the next page from the 2005 study by Multhaup et al.

Continued

Instructions	Event	Recollect	Know	Age	Don't Know
Please label each of the events listed as a personal "recollection" or as an event that you "know" happened but that is not a personal memory. If you neither "recollect" nor "know" the event (perhaps because you never experienced it), please label it as "don't know." For each event you "recollect" or "know," indicate your age at the time the event occurred, as best you can determine, with the year followed by month (e.g., 4.0 is 4 years old exactly, 4.6 is 4½ years old, 4.9 is 4¾, and so forth).	You read your first book with chapters.	❑	❑	❑	❑
	You went to your first sleepover.	❑	❑	❑	❑
	You saw your first movie in a movie theater.	❑	❑	❑	❑
	You took your first swimming lesson.	❑	❑	❑	❑
	You joined your first organized sports team.	❑	❑	❑	❑
	You learned to write in cursive.	❑	❑	❑	❑
	You stopped taking naps.	❑	❑	❑	❑
	You learned to spell your name.	❑	❑	❑	❑
	You went to an amusement park for the first time.	❑	❑	❑	❑
	You were toilet trained.	❑	❑	❑	❑
	Your first permanent tooth came in.	❑	❑	❑	❑
	You learned to ride a bicycle (two wheels, no training wheels).	❑	❑	❑	❑
	You slept in a bed instead of a crib.	❑	❑	❑	❑

(Items are sampled from experiments 1 and 2 of Multhaup et al., 2005, p. 172.)

Chapter Review

KEY CONCEPT QUIZ

1. Encoding is the process
   a. by which we transform what we perceive, think, or feel into an enduring memory.
   b. of maintaining information in memory over time.
   c. of bringing to mind information that has been previously stored.
   d. through which we recall information previously learned but forgotten.

2. What is the process of actively relating new information to knowledge that is already in memory?
   a. spontaneous encoding
   b. organization encoding
   c. elaborative encoding
   d. visual imagery encoding

3. Our human ancestors depended on the encoding of
   a. organizational information.
   b. reproductive mechanisms.
   c. survival-related information.
   d. pleasantness conditions.

4. What kind of memory storage holds information for a second or two?
   a. retrograde memory
   b. working memory
   c. short-term memory
   d. sensory memory

5. The process by which memories become stable in the brain is called
   a. consolidation.
   b. long-term memory.
   c. iconic memory.
   d. hippocampal indexing.

6. Long-term potentiation occurs through
   a. the interruption of communication between neurons.
   b. the strengthening of synaptic connections.
   c. the reconsolidation of disrupted memories.
   d. sleep.

7. The increased likelihood of recalling a sad memory when you are in a sad mood is an illustration of
   a. the encoding specificity principle.
   b. state-dependent retrieval.
   c. transfer-appropriate processing.
   d. memory accessibility.

8. Which of the following statements regarding the consequences of memory retrieval is false?
   a. Retrieval-induced forgetting can affect eyewitness memory.
   b. The act of retrieval can strengthen a retrieved memory.
   c. Retrieval can impair subsequent memory.
   d. Retrieval boosts subsequent memory through the repetition of information.

9. Neuroimaging studies suggest that *trying* to remember activates the
   a. right frontal lobe.
   b. hippocampal region.
   c. occipital lobe.
   d. upper temporal lobe.

10. The act of consciously or intentionally retrieving past experiences is
    a. priming.
    b. procedural memory.
    c. implicit memory.
    d. explicit memory.

11. People who have amnesia are able to retain all of the following except
    a. explicit memory.
    b. implicit memory.
    c. procedural memory.
    d. priming.

12. Remembering a family reunion that you attended as a child illustrates
    a. semantic memory.
    b. procedural memory.
    c. episodic memory.
    d. perceptual priming.

13. The rapid decline in memory, followed by more gradual forgetting, is reflected by
    a. chunking.
    b. blocking.
    c. absentmindedness.
    d. transience.

14. Eyewitness misidentification or false recognition is most likely a result of
    a. memory misattribution.
    b. suggestibility.
    c. bias.
    d. retroactive interference.

15. The fact that emotional arousal generally leads to enhanced memory is supported by
    a. egocentric bias.
    b. persistence.
    c. proactive interference.
    d. source memory.

KEY TERMS

memory (p. 220)

encoding (p. 220)

storage (p. 220)

retrieval (p. 220)

elaborative encoding (p. 221)

visual imagery encoding
(p. 222)

organizational encoding
(p. 223)

sensory memory (p. 225)

iconic memory (p. 226)

echoic memory (p. 226)

short-term memory (p. 226)

rehearsal (p. 226)

chunking (p. 226)

working memory (p. 227)

long-term memory (p. 227)

anterograde amnesia
(p. 228)

retrograde amnesia (p. 228)

consolidation (p. 229)

reconsolidation (p. 229)

long-term potentiation (LTP)
(p. 231)

NMDA receptor (p. 232)

retrieval cue (p. 233)

encoding specificity principle
(p. 233)

state-dependent retrieval
(p. 234)

transfer-appropriate processing
(p. 234)

retrieval-induced forgetting
(p. 235)

explicit memory (p. 238)

implicit memory (p. 238)

procedural memory (p. 238)

priming (p. 239)

semantic memory (p. 240)

episodic memory (p. 240)

transience (p. 243)

retroactive interference
(p. 244)

proactive interference
(p. 244)

absentmindedness (p. 244)

prospective memory
(p. 245)

blocking (p. 246)

memory misattribution
(p. 247)

source memory (p. 248)

false recognition (p. 249)

suggestibility (p. 251)

bias (p. 253)

persistence (p. 254)

flashbulb memories (p. 254)

CRITICAL THINKING QUESTIONS

1. Elaborative encoding involves actively relating new information to facts you already know; visual imagery encoding involves storing new information by converting it into mental pictures.

   How might you use both kinds of encoding to help store a new fact, such as the date of a friend's birthday that falls on, say, November 1st?

2. Retrieval cues are "hints" that help bring stored information to mind. How does this explain the fact that most students prefer multiple-choice exams to fill-in-the-blank exams?

3. Transience, absentmindedness, and blocking are three of the seven "sins" of memory, and deal with ways that memories can be temporarily or permanently lost.

   Suppose that, mentally consumed by planning for a psychology test the next day, you place your keys in an unusual spot, and later forget where you put them. Is this more likely to reflect the "memory sin" of transience, absentmindedness, or blocking?

4. Misattribution, suggestibility, and bias are three memory "sins" that involve memories that are not forgotten but are distorted.

   When researchers ask romantically involved couples to rate their relationships, and then ask again 2 months later, those couples whose relationships have since soured tend to recall their initial ratings as more negative than they really were. Is this more likely to reflect the "memory sin" of misattribution, suggestibility, or bias?

RECOMMENDED READINGS

Brainerd, C. J., & Reyna, V. F. (2005). *The science of false memory.* New York: Oxford University Press.

Written by two of the leading researchers into the nature of false memories, this volume provides a readable summary of what we know about false memories and how they differ from true memories.

Kandel, E. R. (2006). *In search of memory.* New York: W.W. Norton.

A readable book that combines autobiography and an accessible account of the neurobiology of memory, written by the winner of a 2000 Nobel Prize.

Luminet, O., & Curci, A. (Eds.). (2009). *Flashbulb memories.* New York: Psychology Press.

A fascinating collection of chapters concerning vivid, seemingly unforgettable memories of various kinds of emotionally arousing events.

McNally, R. J. (2003). *Remembering trauma.* Cambridge, MA: Harvard University Press.

This is the single most comprehensive source concerning traumatic memories. McNally explains the characteristics and origins of traumatic memories and also provides a useful discussion of the controversy concerning the accuracy of repressed and recovered traumatic memories.

Schacter, D. L. (2001). *The seven sins of memory.* New York and Boston: Houghton Mifflin.

This book provides a more in-depth treatment of memory's seven sins than that provided in this chapter, including many more examples of how the seven sins affect us in everyday life.

Wearing, D. (2006). *Forever today.* London: Corgi Books.

Clive Wearing is a gifted musician who also has the dubious distinction of having one of the most severe cases of amnesia ever documented. His memory lasts for about 7 seconds, making every experience seem new to him. His wife, Deborah, wrote a book about their relationship and the challenges associated with coping with this kind of brain damage.

ANSWERS TO KEY CONCEPT QUIZ

1. a; 2. c; 3. c; 4. d; 5. a; 6. b; 7. b; 8. d; 9. a; 10. d; 11. a; 12. c; 13. d; 14. a; 15. b.

Need more help? Additional resources are located at the book's free companion Web site at:
www.worthpublishers.com/schacter

7

Learning

J
ennifer, a 45-year-old career military nurse, lived quietly in a rural area of the United States with her spouse of 21 years and their two children before she served 19 months abroad during the Iraq war. In Iraq, she provided care to American and international soldiers as well as to Iraqi civilians, prisoners, and militant extremists.

Jennifer served 4 months of her assignment in the Abu Ghraib prison hospital near Baghdad, where she witnessed many horrifying events. The prison was the target of relentless mortar fire, resulting in numerous deaths and serious casualties, including bloody injuries and loss of limbs. Jennifer worked 12- to 14-hour shifts, trying to avoid incoming fire while at the same time tending to some of the most gruesomely wounded cases. She frequently encountered the smell of burnt flesh and the sight of "young, mangled bodies" as part of her daily duties (Feczer & Bjorklund, 2009, p. 285).

This repetitive trauma took a toll on Jennifer, and when she returned home, it became evident that she had not left behind her war experiences; Jennifer thought about them repeatedly and they profoundly influenced her reactions to many aspects of everyday life. The sight of blood or the smell of cooking meat made her sick to her stomach, to the point that she had to stop eating meat. The previously innocent sound of a helicopter approaching, which in Iraq signaled that new wounded bodies were about to arrive, now created in Jennifer heightened feelings of fear and anxiety. She regularly awoke from nightmares concerning the most troubling aspects of her Iraq experiences, such as tending to soldiers with multiple amputations. In the words of the authors who described her case, Jennifer was "forever changed" by her Iraq experiences (Feczer & Bjorklund, 2009). And that is one reason why Jennifer's story is a compelling, though disturbing, introduction to the topic of learning.

Much of what happened to Jennifer after she returned home reflects the operation of a kind of learning based on association. Sights, sounds, and smells in Iraq had become associated with negative emotions in a way that created an enduring bond, so that encountering similar sights, sounds, and smells at home elicited similarly intense negative feelings.

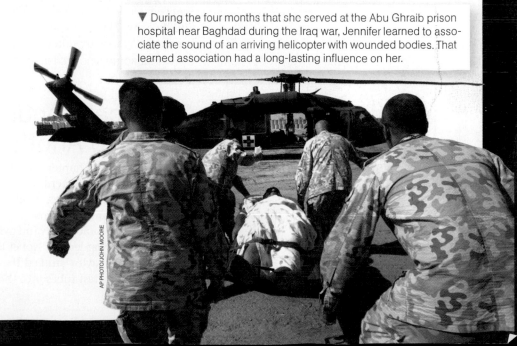

▼ During the four months that she served at the Abu Ghraib prison hospital near Baghdad during the Iraq war, Jennifer learned to associate the sound of an arriving helicopter with wounded bodies. That learned association had a long-lasting influence on her.

AP PHOTO/JOHN MOORE

LEARNING IS SHORTHAND FOR A COLLECTION OF DIFFERENT TECHNIQUES, procedures, and outcomes that produce changes in an organism's behavior. Learning psychologists have identified and studied as many as 40 different kinds of learning. However, there is a basic principle at the core of all of them. **Learning** involves *the acquisition of new knowledge, skills, or responses from experience that result in a relatively permanent change in the state of the learner*. This definition emphasizes these key ideas:

> Learning is based on experience.

> Learning produces changes in the organism.

> These changes are relatively permanent.

Think about Jennifer's time in Iraq and you'll see all of these elements: Experiences such as the association between the sound of an approaching helicopter and the arrival of wounded bodies changed the way Jennifer responded to certain situations in a way that lasted for years.

As you'll recall from Chapter 1, a sizable chunk of psychology's history was devoted to a single dominant viewpoint. Behaviorism, with its insistence on measuring only observable, quantifiable behavior and its dismissal of mental activity as irrelevant and unknowable, was the major outlook of most psychologists working from the 1930s through the 1950s. This was also the period during which most of the fundamental work on learning theory took place.

You might find the intersection of behaviorism and learning theory a bit surprising. After all, at one level learning seems abstract: Something intangible happens to you, and you think or behave differently thereafter. It seems logical that you'd need to explain that transformation in terms of a change in mental outlook. However, most behaviorists argued that learning's "permanent change in experience" could be demonstrated equally well in almost any organism: rats, dogs, pigeons, mice, pigs, or humans. From this perspective, behaviorists viewed learning as a purely behavioral, eminently observable activity that did not necessitate any mental activity.

As you'll see shortly, in many ways the behaviorists were right. Much of what we know about how organisms learn comes directly from the behaviorists' observations of behaviors. However, the behaviorists also overstated their case. There are some important cognitive considerations—that is, elements of mental activity—that need to be addressed in order to understand the learning process. In the first two sections of this chapter, we'll discuss the development and basic principles of two major approaches to learning: classical conditioning and operant conditioning. We'll then move on to see that some important kinds of learning occur simply by watching others, and that such observational learning plays an important role in the cultural transmission of behavior. Finally, we'll discover that some kinds of learning can occur entirely outside of awareness.

Classical Conditioning: One Thing Leads to Another

You'll recall from Chapter 1 that American psychologist John B. Watson kick-started the behaviorist movement, arguing that psychologists should "never use the terms *consciousness, mental states, mind, content, introspectively verifiable, imagery*, and the like" (Watson, 1913, p. 166). Watson's firebrand stance was fueled in large part by the work of a Russian physiologist, Ivan Pavlov (1849–1936).

Pavlov was awarded the Nobel Prize in Physiology in 1904 for his work on the salivation of dogs. Pavlov studied the digestive processes of laboratory animals by surgically implanting test tubes into the cheeks of dogs to measure their salivary responses

"Perhaps, Dr. Pavlov, he could be taught to seal envelopes."

to different kinds of foods. Serendipitously, however, his explorations into spit and drool revealed the mechanics of one form of learning, which came to be called classical conditioning. **Classical conditioning** occurs *when a neutral stimulus produces a response after being paired with a stimulus that naturally produces a response.* In his classic experiments, Pavlov showed that dogs learned to salivate to neutral stimuli such as a bell or a tone after that stimulus had been associated with another stimulus that naturally evokes salivation, such as food.

The Development of Classical Conditioning: Pavlov's Experiments

Pavlov's basic experimental setup involved cradling dogs in a harness to administer the foods and to measure the salivary response, as shown in **FIGURE 7.1**. He noticed that dogs that previously had been in the experiment began to produce a kind of "anticipatory" salivary response as soon as they were put in the harness, before any food was presented. Pavlov and his colleagues regarded these responses as annoyances at first because they interfered with collecting naturally occurring salivary secretions. In reality, the dogs were behaving in line with the four basic elements of classical conditioning:

> When the dogs were initially presented with a plate of food, they began to salivate. No surprise here—placing food in front of most animals will launch the salivary process. Pavlov called the presentation of food an **unconditioned stimulus (US)**, or *something that reliably produces a naturally occurring reaction in an organism.*

> He called the dogs' salivation an **unconditioned response (UR)**, or *a reflexive reaction that is reliably produced by an unconditioned stimulus.*

> Pavlov soon discovered that he could make the dogs salivate to stimuli that don't usually make animals salivate, such as the sound of a buzzer. In various experiments, Pavlov paired the presentation of food with the sound of a buzzer, the ticking of a metronome, the humming of a tuning fork, or the flash of a light (Pavlov, 1927). Sure enough, he found that the dogs salivated to the sound of a buzzer, the ticking of a metronome, the humming of a tuning fork, or the flash of a light, each of which had become a **conditioned stimulus (CS)**, or *a stimulus that is initially neutral and produces no reliable response in an organism* (see **FIGURE 7.2** on the next page).

> Nothing in nature would make a dog salivate to the sound of a buzzer. However, when the conditioned stimulus (CS), in this case the sound of a buzzer, is paired over time with the unconditioned stimulus (US), or the food, the animal will learn to associate food with the sound and eventually the CS is sufficient to produce a response, or salivation. This response resembles the UR, but Pavlov called it the **conditioned response (CR)**, or *a reaction that resembles an unconditioned response but is produced by a conditioned stimulus.* In this example, the dogs' salivation (CR) was eventually prompted by the sound of the buzzer (CS) alone because the sound of the buzzer and the food (US) had been associated so often in the past. Technically, though, the salivation is not a UR (the naturally occurring, reflexive reaction to the presentation of food) because it is produced instead by the CS (the sound of the buzzer). As you can imagine, a range of stimuli might be used as a CS, and as we noted earlier, several different stimuli became the CS in Pavlov's experiment.

learning Experience that results in a relatively permanent change in the state of the learner.

classical conditioning When a neutral stimulus produces a response after being paired with a stimulus that naturally produces a response.

unconditioned stimulus (US) Something that reliably produces a naturally occurring reaction in an organism.

unconditioned response (UR) A reflexive reaction that is reliably produced by an unconditioned stimulus.

conditioned stimulus (CS) A stimulus that is initially neutral and produces no reliable response in an organism.

conditioned response (CR) A reaction that resembles an unconditioned response but is produced by a conditioned stimulus.

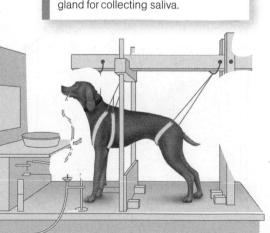

▼ FIGURE 7.1
Pavlov's Apparatus for Studying Classical Conditioning Pavlov presented auditory stimuli to the animals using a bell or a tuning fork. Visual stimuli could be presented on the screen. The inset shows a close-up of the tube inserted in the dog's salivary gland for collecting saliva.

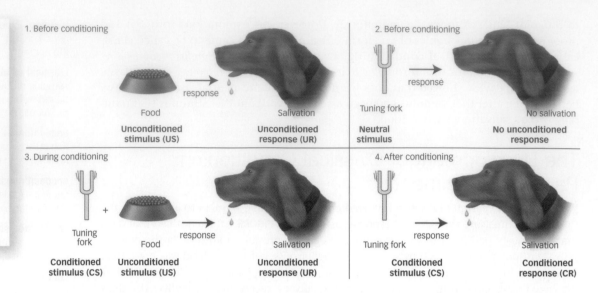

► FIGURE 7.2
The Elements of Classical Conditioning In classical conditioning, a previously neutral stimulus (such as the sound of a tuning fork) is paired with an unconditioned stimulus (such as the presentation of food). After several trials associating the two, the conditioned stimulus (the sound) alone can produce a conditioned response.

1. Before conditioning

Food
Unconditioned stimulus (US)
response
Salivation
Unconditioned response (UR)

2. Before conditioning

Tuning fork
Neutral stimulus
response
No salivation
No unconditioned response

3. During conditioning

Tuning fork + Food
Conditioned stimulus (CS) **Unconditioned stimulus (US)**
response
Salivation
Unconditioned response (UR)

4. After conditioning

Tuning fork
Conditioned stimulus (CS)
response
Salivation
Conditioned response (CR)

Consider your own dog (or cat). You probably think you have the only dog that can tell time because she always knows when dinner's coming and gets prepared, stopping short of pulling up a chair and tucking a napkin into her collar. It's as though she has one eye on the clock every day, waiting for the dinner hour. Sorry to burst your bubble, but your dog is no clock-watching wonder hound. Instead, the presentation of food (the US) has become associated with a complex CS—your getting up, moving into the kitchen, opening the cabinet, working the can opener—such that the CS alone signals to your dog that food is on the way and therefore initiates the CR of her getting ready to eat.

? Why do some dogs seem to know when it's dinnertime?

The Basic Principles of Classical Conditioning

When Pavlov's findings first appeared in the scientific and popular literature (Pavlov, 1923a, 1923b), they produced a flurry of excitement because psychologists now had demonstrable evidence of how conditioning produced learned behaviors. This was the kind of behaviorist psychology John B. Watson was proposing: An organism experiences events or stimuli that are observable and measurable, and changes in that organism can be directly observed and measured. Dogs learned to salivate to the sound of a buzzer, and there was no need to resort to explanations about why it had happened, what the dog wanted, or how the animal thought about the situation. In other words, there was no need to consider the mind in this classical-conditioning paradigm, which appealed to Watson and the behaviorists. Pavlov also appreciated the significance of his discovery and embarked on a systematic investigation of the mechanisms of classical conditioning. Let's take a closer look at some of these principles. (As the Real World box shows, these principles help explain how drug overdoses occur.)

Acquisition

Remember when you first got your dog? Chances are she didn't seem too smart, especially the way she stared at you vacantly as you went into the kitchen, not anticipating that food was on the way. That's because learning through classical conditioning requires some period of association between the CS and US. This period is called **acquisition**, or *the phase of classical conditioning when the CS and the US*

DENNIS THE MENACE

"I think Mom's using the can opener."

are presented together. During the initial phase of classical conditioning, typically there is a gradual increase in learning: It starts low, rises rapidly, and then slowly tapers off, as shown on the left side of **FIGURE 7.3** on the next page. Pavlov's dogs gradually increased their amount of salivation over several trials of pairing a tone with the presentation of food, and similarly, your dog eventually learned to associate your kitchen preparations with the subsequent appearance of food. After learning has been established, the CS by itself will reliably elicit the CR.

acquisition The phase of classical conditioning when the CS and the US are presented together.

THE REAL WORLD

Understanding Drug Overdoses

All too often, police are confronted with a perplexing problem: the sudden death of addicts from a drug overdose. These deaths are puzzling for at least three reasons: The victims are often experienced drug users; the dose taken is usually not larger than what they usually take; and the deaths tend to occur in unusual settings. Experienced drug users are just that: experienced! So, you'd think that the chances of an overdose would be *lower* than usual.

Classical conditioning provides some insight into how these deaths occur. First, when classical conditioning takes place, the CS is more than a simple bell or tone: It also includes the overall *context* within which the conditioning takes place. Indeed, Pavlov's dogs often began to salivate even as they approached the experimental apparatus. Second, many CRs are compensatory reactions to the US. Heroin, for example, slows down a person's breathing rate, so the body responds with a compensatory reaction that speeds up breathing in order to maintain a state of balance or homeostasis, a critically important CR.

These two finer points of classical conditioning help explain the seeming paradox of fatal heroin overdoses in experienced drug users (Siegel, 1984, 2005). When the drug is injected, the entire setting (the drug paraphernalia, the room, the lighting, the addict's usual companions) functions as the CS, and the addict's brain reacts to the heroin by secreting neurotransmitters that counteract its effects. Over time, this protective physiological response becomes part of the CR, and like all CRs, it occurs in the presence of the CS but prior to the actual administration of the drug. These compensatory physiological reactions are also what make drug abusers take increasingly larger doses to achieve the same effect;

ultimately, these reactions produce *drug tolerance*, discussed in Chapter 5.

Based on these principles of classical conditioning, taking drugs in a new environment can be fatal for a longtime drug user. If an addict injects the usual dose in a setting that is sufficiently novel or where heroin has never been taken before, the CS is now altered, so that the physiological compensatory CR that usually serves a protective function either does not occur or is substantially decreased (Siegel et al., 2000). As a result, the addict's usual dose becomes an overdose and death often results. Intuitively, addicts may stick with the crack houses, opium dens, or "shooting galleries" with which they're familiar for just this reason. This effect has also been shown experimentally: Rats that have had extensive experience with morphine in one setting were much more likely to survive dose increases in that same setting than in a novel one (Siegel, 1976; Siegel et al., 2000). This same basic effect occurs with a variety of drugs. For

example, college students show less tolerance for the intoxicating effects of alcohol when they consume it in the presence of a novel cue (a peppermint-flavored drink) than a familiar one (a beer-flavored drink) (Siegel, 2005).

Understanding these principles has also led to treatments for drug addicts. For example, the brain's compensatory response to a drug, when elicited by the familiar contextual cues ordinarily associated with drug taking that constitute the CS, can be experienced by the addict as withdrawal symptoms. In *cue exposure therapies*, an addict is exposed to drug-related cues without being given the usual dose of the drug itself, eventually resulting in extinction of the association between the contextual cues and the effects of the drug. After such treatment, encountering familiar drug-related cues will no longer result in the compensatory response linked to withdrawal symptoms, thereby making it easier for a recovering addict to remain abstinent (Siegel, 2005).

◀ Although opium dens and crack houses may be considered blight, it is often safer for addicts to use drugs there. The environment becomes part of the addict's CS, so ironically, busting crack houses may contribute to more deaths from drug overdose when addicts are pushed to use drugs in new situations.

AP PHOTO/CHRIS GARDNER

► FIGURE 7.3

Acquisition, Extinction, and Spontaneous Recovery In classical conditioning, the CS is originally neutral and produces no specific response. After several trials pairing the CS with the US, the CS alone comes to elicit the salivary response (the CR). Learning tends to take place fairly rapidly and then levels off as stable responding develops. In extinction, the CR diminishes quickly until it no longer occurs. A rest period, however, is typically followed by spontaneous recovery of the CR. In fact, a well-learned CR may show spontaneous recovery after more than one rest period even though there have been no additional learning trials.

▼ Some people desire money to the extent that they hoard it and value it more than the things it can buy. Multibillionaire Ingvar Kamprad, founder of the Swedish furniture company Ikea and ranked the fifth richest individual in the world by Forbes in 2009, drives an old Volvo, flies economy class, and dines at cheap restaurants. Such people may be showing the effects of second-order conditioning.

Second-Order Conditioning

After conditioning has been established, a phenomenon called **second-order conditioning** can be demonstrated: *conditioning where the stimulus that functions as the US is actually the CS from an earlier procedure in which it acquired its ability to produce learning.* For example, in an early study Pavlov repeatedly paired a new CS, a black square, with the now reliable tone. After a number of training trials, his dogs produced a salivary response to the black square even though the square itself had never been directly associated with the food.

Second-order conditioning helps explain why some people desire money to the point that they hoard it and value it even more than the objects it purchases. Money is initially used to purchase objects that produce gratifying outcomes, such as an expensive car. Although money is not directly associated with the thrill of a drive in a new sports car, through second-order conditioning, money can become linked with this type of desirable quality.

Extinction

After Pavlov and his colleagues had explored the process of acquisition extensively, they turned to the next logical question: What would happen if they continued to present the CS (tone) but stopped presenting the US (food)? Repeatedly presenting the CS without the US produces exactly the result you might imagine. As shown on the right side of the first panel in Figure 7.3, behavior declines abruptly and continues to drop until eventually the dog ceases to salivate to the sound of the tone. This process is called **extinction**, *the gradual elimination of a learned response that occurs when the US is no longer presented.* The term was introduced because the conditioned response is "extinguished" and no longer observed.

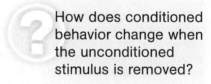

How does conditioned behavior change when the unconditioned stimulus is removed?

Spontaneous Recovery

Having established that he could produce learning through conditioning and then extinguish it, Pavlov wondered if this elimination of conditioned behavior was permanent. Is a single session of extinction sufficient to knock out the CR completely, or is there some residual change in the dog's behavior so that the CR might reappear?

To explore this question, Pavlov extinguished the classically conditioned salivation response and then allowed the dogs to have a short rest period. When they were brought back to the lab and presented with the CS again, they displayed **spontaneous recovery**, *the tendency of a learned behavior to recover from extinction after a rest period*. This phenomenon is shown in the middle panel in Figure 7.3. Notice that this recovery takes place even though there have not been any additional associations between the CS and US. Some spontaneous recovery of the conditioned response even takes place in what is essentially a second extinction session after another period of rest (see the right-hand panel in Figure 7.3). Clearly, extinction had not completely wiped out the learning that had been acquired. The ability of the CS to elicit the CR was weakened, but it was not eliminated.

Generalization and Discrimination

Do you think your dog will be stumped, unable to anticipate the presentation of her food, if you get a new can opener? Will a whole new round of conditioning need to be established with this modified CS?

Probably not. It wouldn't be very adaptive for an organism if each little change in the CS-US pairing required an extensive regimen of new learning. Rather, the phenomenon of **generalization** tends to take place, in which *the CR is observed even though the CS is slightly different from the original one used during acquisition*. This means that the conditioning "generalizes" to stimuli that are similar to the CS used during the original training. As you might expect, the more the new stimulus changes, the less conditioned responding is observed. If you replaced the can opener with an electric can opener, your dog would probably show a much weaker conditioned response (Pearce, 1987; Rescorla, 2006).

How can a change in can opener affect a conditioned dog's response?

When an organism generalizes to a new stimulus, two things are happening. First, by responding to the new stimulus used during generalization testing, the organism demonstrates that it recognizes the similarity between the original CS and the new stimulus. Second, by displaying *diminished* responding to that new stimulus, it also tells us that it notices a difference between the two stimuli. In the second case, the organism shows **discrimination**, or *the capacity to distinguish between similar but distinct stimuli*.

Conceptually, generalization and discrimination are two sides of the same coin. The more organisms show one, the less they show the other, and training can modify the balance between the two.

Conditioned Emotional Responses: The Case of Little Albert

Before you conclude that classical conditioning is merely a sophisticated way to train your dog, let's revisit the larger principles of Pavlov's work. Classical conditioning demonstrates that durable, substantial changes in behavior can be achieved simply by setting up the proper conditions. By skillfully associating a naturally occurring US with an appropriate CS, an organism can learn to perform a variety of behaviors, often after relatively few acquisition trials. There is no reference to an organism's *wanting* to learn the behavior, *willingness* to do it, *thinking* about the situation, or *reasoning* through the available options. We don't need to consider internal and cognitive explanations to demonstrate the effects of classical conditioning: The stimuli, the eliciting circumstances, and the resulting behavior are there to be observed by one and all.

It was this kind of simplicity that appealed to behaviorists. In fact, Watson and his followers thought that it was possible to develop general explanations of pretty much *any* behavior of *any* organism based on classical-conditioning principles. As a step in that direction, Watson embarked on a controversial study with his research assistant Rosalie Rayner (Watson & Rayner, 1920). To support his contention that even complex behaviors

second-order conditioning Conditioning where the US is a stimulus that acquired its ability to produce learning from an earlier procedure in which it was used as a CS.

extinction The gradual elimination of a learned response that occurs when the US is no longer presented.

spontaneous recovery The tendency of a learned behavior to recover from extinction after a rest period.

generalization A process in which the CR is observed even though the CS is slightly different from the original one used during acquisition.

discrimination The capacity to distinguish between similar but distinct stimuli.

▲ John Watson and Rosalie Rayner show Little Albert an unusual bunny mask. Why doesn't the mere presence of these experimenters serve as a conditioned stimulus in itself?

were the result of conditioning, Watson enlisted the assistance of 9-month-old "Little Albert." Albert was a healthy, well-developed child, and, by Watson's assessment, "stolid and unemotional" (Watson & Rayner, 1920, p. 1). Watson wanted to see if such a child could be classically conditioned to experience a strong emotional reaction—namely, fear.

Watson presented Little Albert with a variety of stimuli: a white rat, a dog, a rabbit, various masks, and a burning newspaper. Albert's reactions in most cases were curiosity or indifference, and he showed no fear of any of the items. Watson also established that something *could* make him afraid. While Albert was watching Rayner, Watson unexpectedly struck a large steel bar with a hammer, producing a loud noise. Predictably, this caused Albert to cry, tremble, and be generally displeased.

Watson and Rayner then led Little Albert through the acquisition phase of classical conditioning. Albert was presented with a white rat. As soon as he reached out to touch it, the steel bar was struck. This pairing occurred again and again over several trials. Eventually, the sight of the rat alone caused Albert to recoil in terror, crying and clamoring to get away from it. In this situation, a US (the loud sound) was paired with a CS (the presence of the rat) such that the CS all by itself was sufficient to produce the CR (a fearful reaction). Little Albert also showed stimulus generalization. The sight of a white rabbit, a seal-fur coat, and a Santa Claus mask produced the same kinds of fear reactions in the infant.

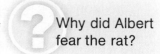 **Why did Albert fear the rat?**

What was Watson's goal in all this? First, he wanted to show that a relatively complex reaction could be conditioned using Pavlovian techniques. Second, he wanted to show that emotional responses such as fear and anxiety could be produced by classical conditioning and therefore need not be the product of deeper unconscious processes or early life experiences as Freud and his followers had argued (see Chapter 1). Instead, Watson proposed that fears could be learned, just like any other behavior. Third, Watson wanted to confirm that conditioning could be applied to humans as well as to other animals. This study was controversial in its cavalier treatment of a young child, especially given that Watson and Rayner did not follow up with Albert or his mother during the ensuing years (Harris, 1979). Modern ethical guidelines that govern the treatment of research participants make sure that this kind of study could not be conducted today. At the time, however, it was consistent with a behaviorist view of psychology.

The kind of conditioned fear responses that were at work in Little Albert's case were also important in the chapter-opening case of Jennifer, who experienced fear and anxiety when hearing the previously innocent sound of an approaching helicopter as a result of her experiences in Iraq. Indeed, a therapy that has proven effective in dealing with such trauma-induced fears is based directly on principles of classical conditioning: Patients are repeatedly exposed to conditioned stimuli associated with their trauma in a safe setting in an attempt to extinguish the conditioned fear response (Bouton, 1988; Rothbaum & Schwartz, 2002). However, conditioned emotional responses include much more than just fear and anxiety responses. Advertisers, for example, understand that conditioned emotional responses can include various kinds of positive emotions that they would like potential customers to associate with their products, which may be why attractive women are commonly involved in ads for products geared toward young males, including beer and sports cars. Even the warm and fuzzy feeling that envelopes you when hearing a song on the radio that you used to listen to with a former boyfriend or girlfriend represents a type of conditioned emotional response.

A Deeper Understanding of Classical Conditioning

As a form of learning, classical conditioning could be reliably produced, it had a simple set of principles, and it had applications to real-life situations. In short, classical conditioning offered a good deal of utility for psychologists who sought to understand the mechanisms underlying learning, and it continues to do so today.

Like a lot of strong starters, though, classical conditioning has been subjected to deeper scrutiny in order to understand exactly how, when, and why it works. Let's examine three areas that give us a closer look at the mechanisms of classical conditioning: the cognitive, neural, and evolutionary elements.

The Cognitive Elements of Classical Conditioning

As we've seen, Pavlov's work was a behaviorist's dream come true. In this view, conditioning is something that *happens to* a dog, a rat, or a person, apart from what the organism thinks about the conditioning situation. However, eventually someone was bound to ask an important question: *Why didn't Pavlov's dogs salivate to Pavlov?* After all, he was instrumental in the arrival of the CS. If Pavlov delivered the food to the dogs, why didn't they form an association with him? Indeed, if Watson was present whenever the unpleasant US was sounded, why didn't Little Albert come to fear *him*?

Maybe classical conditioning isn't such an unthinking, mechanical process as behaviorists originally had assumed (Rescorla, 1966, 1988). Somehow, Pavlov's dogs were sensitive to the fact that Pavlov was not a *reliable* indicator of the arrival of food. Pavlov was linked with the arrival of food, but he was also linked with other activities that had nothing to do with food, including checking on the apparatus, bringing the dog from the kennel to the laboratory, and standing around and talking with his assistants. These observations suggest that perhaps cognitive components are involved in classical conditioning after all.

Robert Rescorla and Allan Wagner (1972) were the first to theorize that classical conditioning only occurs when an animal has learned to set up an *expectation*. The sound of a tone, because of its systematic pairing with food, served to set up this cognitive state for the laboratory dogs; Pavlov, because of the lack of any reliable link with food, did not. In fact, in situations such as this, many responses are actually being conditioned. When the tone sounds, the dogs also wag their tails, make begging sounds, and look toward the food source (Jenkins et al., 1978). In short, what is really happening is something like the situation shown in **FIGURE 7.4**.

The *Rescorla-Wagner model* introduced a cognitive component that accounted for a variety of classical-conditioning phenomena that were difficult to understand from a simple behaviorist point of view. For example, the model predicted that conditioning would be easier when the CS was an *unfamiliar* event than when it was familiar. The reason is that familiar events, being familiar, already have expectations associated with them, making new conditioning difficult. In short, classical conditioning might appear to be a primitive and unthinking process, but it is actually quite sophisticated and incorporates a significant cognitive element.

How does the role of expectation in conditioning challenge behaviorist ideas?

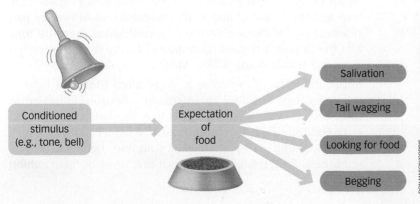

Conditioned stimulus (e.g., tone, bell) → Expectation of food → Salivation / Tail wagging / Looking for food / Begging

DON MASON/CORBIS

◀ FIGURE 7.4
Expectation in Classical Conditioning In the Rescorla-Wagner model of classical conditioning, a CS serves to set up an expectation. The expectation in turn leads to an array of behaviors associated with the presence of the CS.

The Role of Consciousness. One issue that arises from this cognitive view of classical conditioning concerns the role of consciousness. In the Rescorla-Wagner model, the cognitive elements are not necessarily conscious. Rather, they likely reflect the operation of nonconscious associative mechanisms that do more than just record co-occurrences of events—they link those co-occurrences to prior experiences, generating an expectation. Also, most of the research related to the Rescorla-Wagner model involved nonhuman animals, so the model leaves open some important questions that are especially relevant to people: What role does conscious awareness play in classical conditioning? Is awareness of the relationship between the CS and US necessary in order for conditioning to occur? Or can conditioning occur even without awareness of the CS-US relation? These questions have been addressed using two procedures for conditioning eyeblink responses that, on the surface, seem to be very similar to one another, yet have unexpectedly produced strikingly different results that initially puzzled researchers:

> In *delay conditioning*, the CS is a tone that is followed immediately by the US, a puff of air, which elicits an eyeblink response. Importantly, the tone and air puff overlap in time—the air puff follows the tone, but the tone remains on when the air puff is delivered. Then, the tone and air puff end at the same time. After a few pairings of the tone and air puff, conditioning occurs and the tone alone elicits an eyeblink response.

> *Trace conditioning* uses the identical procedures, with one difference: In trace conditioning, there is a brief interval of time after the tone ends and the air puff is delivered (see **FIGURE 7.5**).

During the late 1990s, experiments revealed that amnesic patients—who, as you recall from Chapter 6, lack explicit memory of recent experiences—showed normal delay conditioning of eyeblink responses compared with non-amnesic control subjects. However, the amnesics failed to show trace conditioning (Clark & Squire, 1998; McGlinchey-Berroth et al., 1997). Intact delay conditioning in amnesic patients makes sense in light of findings indicating that amnesic patients often exhibit intact implicit memory (Chapter 6). Several researchers have suggested that classical conditioning draws on implicit but not explicit memory (Eichenbaum & Cohen, 2001; Squire & Kandel, 1999). But why would amnesics exhibit impaired trace conditioning?

Clark and Squire (1998) tried to solve this puzzle. They studied both delay and trace conditioning in healthy volunteers, and after each procedure gave participants a true-false test with questions that probed their awareness of the contingency between the tone and the air puff, such as, "I believe the tone predicted when the air puff would come." Participants who scored significantly above chance on this test were classified as "aware"; those who did not score significantly above chance were classified as "unaware." Clark and Squire found that only aware participants showed trace conditioning, whereas both aware and unaware participants showed delay conditioning.

These findings suggest a solution to the puzzle of why amnesics showed delay but not trace conditioning: Delay conditioning does not require awareness of the contingency between the tone and the air puff, whereas trace conditioning does. Critically, none of the amnesic patients Clark and Squire tested showed awareness of the contingency between the tone and the air puff. Later studies revealed that informing participants in advance about the relationship between the tone and the air puff increased the amount of trace conditioning but not delay conditioning (Clark, Manns, & Squire, 2002).

Implications for Patients in a Vegetative State. In light of these findings, consider an intriguing question addressed in more recent work: Would patients in a vegetative state exhibit trace conditioning? As we discussed in Chapter 3, though such patients exhibit no overt signs of voluntary behavior or consciousness, fMRI studies have shown that some of them exhibit

▼ FIGURE 7.5

Delay and Trace Conditioning Clark and Squire (1998) compared delay and trace conditioning. During delay conditioning, the CS (a tone) was presented for either 700 msec (A) or 1250 msec (B), and then remained on for 100 msec while the US (an air puff) was presented. During trace conditioning, the CS was presented for 250 msec (C and D), and was followed by a blank "trace" interval of either 500 msec (C) or 1000 msec (D) before presentation of the US for 100 msec. Trace conditioning depended on awareness of the relationship between the US and CS, whereas delay conditioning did not.

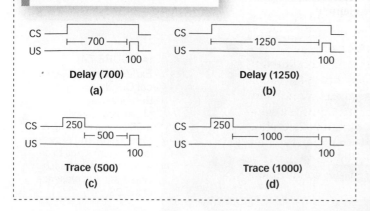

brain activity that may reflect conscious processing of spoken stimuli. Researchers examined trace conditioning in 22 patients with a diagnosis of either vegetative state or a related condition called a minimally conscious state (these patients occasionally exhibit overt behavior by responding appropriately to a command). They used a standard trace conditioning procedure in which the CS (a tone) was followed a half-second later by the US (an air puff), and assessed conditioned responses by measuring changes in the activity of eye muscles (Bekinschtein et al., 2009). Strikingly, both vegetative state and minimally conscious patients showed robust trace conditioning. In contrast, subjects who were rendered unconscious by the administration of anesthesia showed no trace conditioning.

Given evidence that trace conditioning depends on awareness of the contingency between the CS and the US, the researchers argued that trace conditioning in the vegetative state reflects some degree of conscious processing in these patients. Alternatively, the researchers acknowledged that they might have demonstrated a type of trace conditioning that occurs without conscious processing. Though more research needs to be done to sort out this issue, it is clear that comparing trace and delay conditioning can teach us a lot about the role of conscious awareness in learning.

Implications for Understanding Schizophrenia. Conditioning procedures are being used to study the relationship between hallucinations and reality, as often occurs in patients with schizophrenia (see Chapter 14). Studies with rats have shown that, not surprisingly, pairing a rewarding stimulus such as a sugar solution with nausea will cause the animals to reduce their subsequent intake of sugar. More remarkably, though, if the rats are exposed to the sugar paired with a tone, and are later made to feel nauseous in the presence of only the tone, then they subsequently behave as if the sugar had been present when they felt nauseous—they reduce their subsequent consumption of sugar (Holland, 1981, 2005). McDannald and Schoenbaum (2009) suggest that this occurs because the rats experience something like a sensory hallucination of the sugar when the tone is played, perhaps analogous to what is observed in human disorders of reality testing. Importantly, with repeated training, this "hallucination" of the sugar reward seems to disappear: The rats learn that the tone signals an upcoming reward but no longer confuse the tone with the reward itself, suggesting that they eventually develop a more abstract expectation about what is about to happen. Based on these ideas, McDannald and Schoenbaum (2009) proposed using conditioning procedures to test hypotheses concerning impaired reality testing in schizophrenia.

The Neural Elements of Classical Conditioning

Pavlov saw his research as providing insights into how the brain works. After all, he was trained in medicine, not psychology, and was a bit surprised when psychologists became excited by his findings. Recent research has clarified some of what Pavlov hoped to understand about conditioning and the brain.

A series of pioneering experiments conducted across several decades by Richard Thompson and his colleagues focused on eyeblink conditioning in the rabbit, and showed convincingly that the cerebellum is critical for both delay and trace conditioning (Thompson, 2005). Studies of patients with lesions to the cerebellum supported these findings (Daum et al., 1993). As you learned in Chapter 3, the cerebellum is part of the hindbrain and plays an important role in motor skills and learning.

In contrast to the cerebellum, the hippocampus is important for trace conditioning but not delay conditioning. Some of the supporting evidence for this point comes from Thompson's rabbit studies (Thompson, 2005), as well as the studies we just considered in which amnesic patients—who typically have damage to the hippocampus—exhibited intact delay conditioning along with impaired trace conditioning. Rounding out the picture, more recent neuroimaging findings in healthy young adults show greater hippocampal activation during trace than delay conditioning, together with similar amounts of activation in the cerebellum during the two types of conditioning (Cheng et al., 2008).

In addition to eyeblink conditioning, fear conditioning has been extensively studied. In Chapter 3, you saw that the amygdala plays an important role in the experience of emotion, including fear and anxiety. So, it should come as no surprise that the amygdala, particularly an area known as the *central nucleus,* is also critical for emotional conditioning.

Consider a rat who is conditioned to a series of CS-US pairings where the CS is a tone and the US is a mild electric shock. When rats experience sudden painful stimuli in nature, they show a defensive reaction, known as *freezing,* where they crouch down and sit motionless. In addition, their autonomic nervous systems go to work: Heart rate and blood pressure increase, and various hormones associated with stress are released. When fear conditioning takes place, these two components—one behavioral and one physiological—occur, except that now they are elicited by the CS.

The central nucleus of the amygdala plays a role in producing both of these outcomes through two distinct connections with other parts of the brain. If connections linking the amygdala to the midbrain are disrupted, the rat does not exhibit the behavioral freezing response. If the connections between the amygdala and the hypothalamus are severed, the autonomic responses associated with fear cease (LeDoux et al., 1988). Hence, the action of the amygdala is an essential element in fear conditioning, and its links with other areas of the brain are responsible for producing specific features of conditioning. The amygdala is involved in fear conditioning in people as well as rats and other animals (Phelps & LeDoux, 2005; Olsson & Phelps, 2007).

? What is the role of the amygdala in fear conditioning?

The Evolutionary Elements of Classical Conditioning

In addition to this cognitive component, evolutionary mechanisms also play an important role in classical conditioning. As you learned in Chapter 1, evolution and natural selection go hand in hand with adaptiveness: Behaviors that are adaptive allow an organism to survive and thrive in its environment. In the case of classical conditioning, psychologists began to appreciate how this type of learning could have adaptive value. Much research exploring this adaptiveness has focused on conditioned food aversions.

Consider this example: A psychology professor was once on a job interview in Southern California, and his hosts took him to lunch at a Middle Eastern restaurant. Suffering from a case of bad hummus, he was up all night long, and developed a lifelong aversion to hummus.

On the face of it, this looks like a case of classical conditioning, but there are several peculiar aspects to this case. The hummus was the CS, a bacterium or some other source of toxicity was the US, and the resulting nausea was the UR. The UR (the nausea) became linked to the once-neutral CS (the hummus) and became a CR (an aversion to hummus). However, all of the psychologist's hosts also ate the hummus, yet none of them reported feeling ill. It's not clear, then, what the US was; it couldn't have been anything that was actually in the food. What's more, the time between the hummus and the distress was several hours; usually a response follows a stimulus fairly quickly. Most baffling, this aversion was cemented with a single acquisition trial. Usually it takes several pairings of a CS and US to establish learning.

These peculiarities are not so peculiar from an evolutionary perspective. Any species that forages or consumes a variety of foods needs to develop a mechanism by which it can learn to avoid any food that once made it ill. To have adaptive value, this mechanism should have several properties:

► Under certain conditions, people may develop food aversions. This serving of hummus looks inviting and probably tastes delicious, but at least one psychologist avoids it like the plague.

> There should be rapid learning that occurs in perhaps one or two trials. If learning takes more trials than this, the animal could die from eating a toxic substance.

> Conditioning should be able to take place over very long intervals, perhaps up to several hours. Toxic substances often don't cause illness immediately, so the organism would need to form an association between food and the illness over a longer term.

> The organism should develop the aversion to the smell or taste of the food rather than its ingestion. It's more adaptive to reject a potentially toxic substance based on smell alone than it is to ingest it.

> Learned aversions should occur more often with novel foods than familiar ones. It is not adaptive for an animal to develop an aversion to everything it has eaten on the particular day it got sick. Our psychologist friend didn't develop an aversion to the Coke he drank with lunch or the scrambled eggs he had for breakfast that day; however, the sight and smell of hummus do make him uneasy.

John Garcia and his colleagues illustrated the adaptiveness of classical conditioning in a series of studies with rats (Garcia & Koelling, 1966). They used a variety of CSs (visual, auditory, tactile, taste, and smell) and several different USs (injection of a toxic substance, radiation) that caused nausea and vomiting hours later. The researchers found weak or no conditioning when the CS was a visual, auditory, or tactile stimulus, but a strong food aversion developed with stimuli that have a distinct taste and smell.

This research had an interesting application. It led to the development of a technique for dealing with an unanticipated side effect of radiation and chemotherapy: Cancer patients who experience nausea from their treatments often develop aversions to foods they ate before the therapy. Broberg and Bernstein (1987) reasoned that, if the findings with rats generalized to humans, a simple technique should minimize the negative consequences of this effect. They gave their patients an unusual food (coconut- or root-beer–flavored candy) at the end of the last meal before undergoing treatment. Sure enough, the conditioned food aversions that the patients developed were overwhelmingly for one of the unusual flavors and not for any of the other foods in the meal. Other than any root beer or coconut fanatics among the sample, patients were spared developing aversions to more common foods that they are more likely to eat.

How has cancer patients' discomfort been eased by our understanding of food aversions?

Studies such as these suggest that evolution has provided each species with a kind of **biological preparedness**, *a propensity for learning particular kinds of associations over others,* so that some behaviors are relatively easy to condition in some species but not others. For example, the taste and smell stimuli that produce food aversions in rats do not work with most species of birds. Birds depend primarily on visual cues for finding food and are relatively insensitive to taste and smell. However, as you might guess, it is relatively easy to produce a food aversion in birds using an unfamiliar visual stimulus as the CS, such as a brightly colored food (Wilcoxon, Dragoin, & Kral, 1971). Indeed, most researchers agree that conditioning works best with stimuli that are biologically relevant to the organism (Domjan, 2005). (See the Culture & Community box on the next page.)

biological preparedness A propensity for learning particular kinds of associations over others.

◀ Rats can be difficult to poison because of learned taste aversions, which are an evolutionarily adaptive element of classical conditioning. Here a worker tries his best in the sewers of France.

BOYER/ROGER VIOLLET/GETTY IMAGES

CULTURE & COMMUNITY

Is it possible that humans have an innate ability to understand geometry? In a study (Dehaene et al., 2006) of the Munduruku, an isolated indigenous tribe located in the Amazon, Munduruku children and adults were compared to American children and adults on their basic comprehension of geometric shapes. In each test, the participants identified which figure among the series of six images presented to them did *not* belong in the group. Each series tested basic geometric concepts like parallels, shapes, distance, and symmetry.

All participants performed well above the level of chance, and only American adults showed a significant advantage. Before this study, it was largely believed that people must "learn" geometry through cultural interventions like maps, mathematical tools, or the terms used in geometry. In contrast, this study provides evidence that core knowledge of geometry is a universal intuition of the human mind.

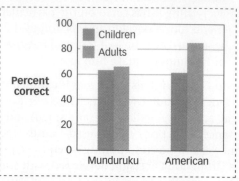

IN SUMMARY

○ Classical conditioning can be thought of as an exercise in pairing a neutral stimulus with a meaningful event or stimulus. Ivan Pavlov's initial work paired a neutral tone (a conditioned stimulus) with a meaningful act: the presentation of food to a hungry animal (an unconditioned stimulus). As he and others demonstrated, the pairing of a CS and US during the acquisition phase of classical conditioning eventually allows the CS all by itself to elicit a response called a conditioned response (CR).

○ Classical conditioning was embraced by behaviorists such as John B. Watson, who viewed it as providing a foundation for a model of human behavior. As a behaviorist, Watson believed that no higher-level functions, such as thinking or awareness, needed to be invoked to understand behavior.

○ Later researchers showed, however, the underlying mechanism of classical conditioning turned out to be more complex (and more interesting) than the simple association between a CS and a US. Researchers discovered that even simple species set up expectations and are sensitive to the degree to which the CS functions as a genuine predictor of the US, indicating that classical conditioning involves some degree of cognition. One form of classical conditioning—trace conditioning—appears to depend on awareness of the contingency between CS and US.

○ Different parts of the brain are involved in different types of classical conditioning: the cerebellum in delay conditioning, the hippocampus in trace conditioning, and the amygdala in fear conditioning.

○ The evolutionary aspects of classical conditioning show that each species is biologically predisposed to acquire particular CS-US associations based on its evolutionary history. In short, classical conditioning is not an arbitrary mechanism that merely forms associations. Rather, it is a sophisticated mechanism that evolved precisely because it has adaptive value.

Operant Conditioning: Reinforcements from the Environment

The study of classical conditioning is the study of behaviors that are *reactive*. Most animals don't voluntarily salivate or feel spasms of anxiety; rather, these animals exhibit these responses involuntarily during the conditioning process. In fact, these reflexlike behaviors make up only a small portion of our behavioral repertoires. The remainder are behaviors that we voluntarily perform, behaviors that modify and change the environment around us. We engage in these voluntary behaviors in order to obtain rewards and avoid punishment; understanding them is essential to developing a complete picture of learning. Because classical conditioning has little to say about these voluntary behaviors, we turn now to a different form of learning: **operant conditioning**, *a type of learning in which the consequences of an organism's behavior determine whether it will be repeated in the future.* The study of operant conditioning is the exploration of behaviors that are *active.*

operant conditioning A type of learning in which the consequences of an organism's behavior determine whether it will be repeated in the future.

law of effect The principle that behaviors that are followed by a "satisfying state of affairs" tend to be repeated and those that produce an "unpleasant state of affairs" are less likely to be repeated.

The Development of Operant Conditioning: The Law of Effect

The study of how active behavior affects the environment began at about the same time as classical conditioning. In fact, Edward L. Thorndike (1874–1949) first examined active behaviors back in the 1890s, before Pavlov published his findings. Thorndike's research focused on *instrumental behaviors*, that is, behavior that required an organism to *do* something, solve a problem, or otherwise manipulate elements of its environment (Thorndike, 1898). For example, Thorndike completed several experiments using a puzzle box, which was a wooden crate with a door that would open when a concealed lever was moved in the right way (see **FIGURE 7.6**). A hungry cat placed in a puzzle box would try various behaviors to get out—scratching at the door, meowing loudly, sniffing the inside of the box, putting its paw through the openings—but only one behavior opened the door and led to food: tripping the lever in just the right way. After this happened, Thorndike placed the cat back in the box for another round. Don't get the wrong idea. Thorndike probably *really liked* cats. Far from teasing them, he was after an important behavioral principle.

Fairly quickly, the cats became quite skilled at triggering the lever for their release. Notice what's going on. At first, the cat enacts any number of likely (but ultimately ineffective) behaviors, but only one behavior leads to freedom and food. Over time, the ineffective behaviors become less and less frequent, and the one instrumental behavior (going right for the latch) becomes more

What is the relationship between behavior and reward?

frequent (see **FIGURE 7.7** on the next page). From these observations, Thorndike developed the **law of effect**, which states that *behaviors that are followed by a "satisfying state of affairs" tend to be repeated and those that produce an "unpleasant state of affairs" are less likely to be repeated.*

The circumstances that Thorndike used to study learning were very different from those in studies of classical conditioning. Remember that in classical-conditioning experiments, the US occurred on every training trial no matter what the animal did. Pavlov delivered food to the dog whether it salivated or not. But in Thorndike's work, the behavior of the animal determined what happened next. If the behavior was "correct" (i.e., the latch was triggered), the animal was rewarded with food. Incorrect

▼ FIGURE 7.6

Thorndike's Puzzle Box In Thorndike's original experiments, food was placed just outside the door of the puzzle box, where the cat could see it. If the cat triggered the appropriate lever, it would open the door and let the cat out.

YALE UNIVERSITY LIBRARY

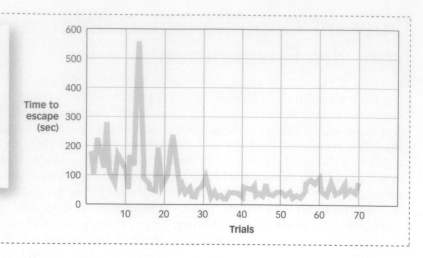

► FIGURE 7.7
The Law of Effect Thorndike's cats displayed trial-and-error behavior when trying to escape from the puzzle box. They made lots of irrelevant movements and actions until, over time, they discovered the solution. Once they figured out what behavior was instrumental in opening the latch, they stopped all other ineffective behaviors and escaped from the box faster and faster.

operant behavior Behavior that an organism produces that has some impact on the environment.

reinforcer Any stimulus or event that functions to increase the likelihood of the behavior that led to it.

punisher Any stimulus or event that functions to decrease the likelihood of the behavior that led to it.

behaviors produced no results and the animal was stuck in the box until it performed the correct behavior. Although different from classical conditioning, Thorndike's work resonated with most behaviorists at the time: It was still observable, quantifiable, and free from explanations involving the mind (Galef, 1998).

B. F. Skinner: The Role of Reinforcement and Punishment

Several decades after Thorndike's work, B. F. Skinner (1904–90) coined the term **operant behavior** to refer to *behavior that an organism produces that has some impact on the environment.* In Skinner's system, all of these emitted behaviors "operated" on the environment in some manner, and the environment responded by providing events that either strengthened those behaviors (i.e., they *reinforced* them) or made them less likely to occur (i.e., they *punished* them). Skinner's elegantly simple observation was that most organisms do *not* behave like a dog in a harness, passively waiting to receive food no matter what the circumstances. Rather, most organisms are like cats in a box, actively engaging the environment in which they find themselves to reap rewards (Skinner, 1938, 1953).

In order to study operant behavior scientifically, Skinner developed a variation on Thorndike's puzzle box. The *operant chamber,* or *Skinner box,* as it is commonly called, shown in **FIGURE 7.8**, allows a researcher to study the behavior of small organisms in a controlled environment.

Skinner's approach to the study of learning focused on *reinforcement* and *punishment.* These terms, which have commonsense connotations, turned out to be rather difficult to define. For example, some people love roller coasters, whereas others find them horrifying; the chance to go on one will be reinforcing for one group but punishing for another. Dogs can be trained with praise and a good belly rub—procedures that are nearly useless for most cats. Skinner settled on a "neutral" definition that would characterize each term by its effect on behavior. Therefore, a **reinforcer** is *any stimulus or event that functions to increase the likelihood of the behavior that led to it,* whereas a **punisher** is *any stimulus or event that functions to decrease the likelihood of the behavior that led to it.*

Whether a particular stimulus acts as a reinforcer or a punisher depends in part on whether it increases or decreases the likelihood of a behavior. Presenting food is usually reinforcing, producing an increase in the behavior that led to it; removing food is often punishing, leading to a decrease in the behavior. Turning on an electric shock is typically punishing (and decreases the behavior that led to it); turning it off is rewarding (and increases the behavior that led to it).

▼ FIGURE 7.8
Skinner Box In a typical Skinner box, or *operant conditioning chamber,* a rat, pigeon, or other suitably sized animal is placed in this environment and observed during learning trials that use operant conditioning principles.

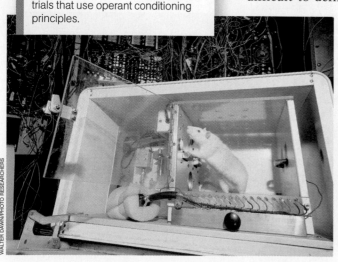

WALTER DAWN/PHOTO RESEARCHERS

To keep these possibilities distinct, Skinner used the term *positive* for situations in which a stimulus was presented and *negative* for situations in which it was removed. Consequently, there is *positive reinforcement* (where a rewarding stimulus is presented) and *negative reinforcement* (where an unpleasant stimulus is removed), as well as *positive punishment* (where an unpleasant stimulus is administered) and *negative punishment* (where a rewarding stimulus is removed). Here the words *positive* and *negative* mean, respectively, something that is *added* or something that is *taken away*, but do not mean "good" or "bad" as they do in everyday speech. As you can see from **TABLE 7.1**, positive and negative reinforcement increase the likelihood of the behavior and positive and negative punishment decrease the likelihood of the behavior.

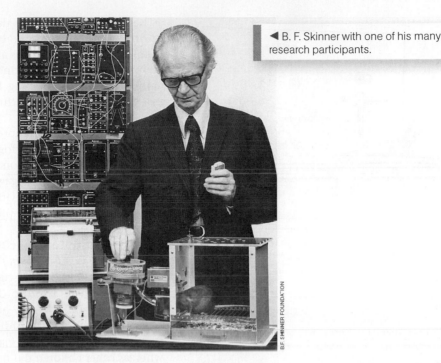

◄ B. F. Skinner with one of his many research participants.

These distinctions can be confusing at first; after all, "negative reinforcement" and "punishment" both sound like they should be "bad" and produce the same type of behavior. However, negative reinforcement, for example, involves something pleasant; it's the *removal* of something unpleasant, like a shock, and the absence of a shock is indeed pleasant.

? Why is reinforcement more constructive than punishment in learning desired behavior?

Reinforcement is generally more effective than punishment in promoting learning. There are many reasons (Gershoff, 2002), but one reason is this: Punishment signals that an unacceptable behavior has occurred, but it doesn't specify what should be done instead. Spanking a young child for starting to run into a busy street certainly stops the behavior—which, in this case, is probably a good idea. But it doesn't promote any kind of learning about the *desired* behavior.

TABLE 7.1		
Reinforcement and Punishment		
	Increases the Likelihood of Behavior	**Decreases the Likelihood of Behavior**
Stimulus is presented	Positive reinforcement	Positive punishment
Stimulus is removed	Negative reinforcement	Negative punishment

Primary and Secondary Reinforcement and Punishment

Reinforcers and punishers often gain their functions from basic biological mechanisms. A pigeon who pecks at a target in a Skinner box is usually reinforced with food pellets, just as an animal who learns to escape a mild electric shock has avoided the punishment of tingly paws. Food, comfort, shelter, or warmth are examples of *primary reinforcers* because they help satisfy biological needs. However, the vast majority of reinforcers or punishers in our daily lives have little to do with biology: Handshakes, verbal approval, an encouraging grin, a bronze trophy, or money all serve powerful reinforcing functions, yet none of them taste very good or help keep you warm at night. The point is, we learn to perform a lot of behaviors based on reinforcements that have little or nothing to do with biological satisfaction.

▼ Negative reinforcement involves the removal of something unpleasant from the environment. When Daddy stops the car, he gets a reward: His little monster stops screaming. However, from the perspective of the child, this is positive reinforcement. The child's tantrum results in something positive added to the environment—stopping for a snack.

"Oh, not bad. The light comes on, I press the bar, they write me a check. How about you?"

These *secondary reinforcers* derive their effectiveness from their associations with primary reinforcers through classical conditioning. For example, money starts out as a neutral CS that, through its association with primary USs like acquiring food or shelter, takes on a conditioned emotional element. Flashing lights, originally a neutral CS, acquire powerful negative elements through association with a speeding ticket and a fine.

Sometimes the presentation of rewards can cause exactly the opposite effect: a decrease in performing the behavior. Extrinsic reinforcement—rewards that come from external sources—don't always capture the reasons why people engage in behavior in the first place. Many times people engage in activities for intrinsic rewards, such as the pure pleasure of simply doing the behavior.

Can rewards backfire?

The **overjustification effect** happens *when external rewards undermine the intrinsic satisfaction of performing a behavior.* In one study, nursery school children were given colored pens and paper and were asked to draw whatever they wanted (Lepper & Greene, 1978). For a young child, this is a pretty satisfying event: The pleasures of drawing and creative expression are rewarding all by themselves. Some children, though, received a "Good Player Award" for their efforts at artwork, whereas other children did not. As you may have guessed, the Good Players spent more time at the task than the other children. As you may not have guessed, when the experimenters stopped handing out the Good Player certificates to the first group, the amount of time the children spent drawing dropped significantly below that of the group that never received any external reinforcements.

This was a case of *over*justification, or too much reinforcement. The children who received the extrinsic reinforcement of the certificate came to view their task as one that gets rewards. The children who didn't receive the extrinsic reinforcement continued to perform the task for its own sake. When the extrinsic rewards were later removed, children in the first group found little reason to continue engaging in the task. Other researchers have found that when people are paid for tasks such as writing poetry, drawing, or finding solutions to economic and business problems, they tend to produce *less* creative solutions when monetary rewards are offered (Amabile, 1996). You'll see more about extrinsic rewards in the next chapter on

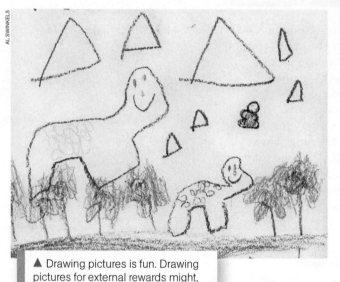

▲ Drawing pictures is fun. Drawing pictures for external rewards might, oddly enough, make drawing pictures seem like much less fun.

motivation and you can weigh in on these issues in the Where Do You Stand? box at the end of this chapter.

The Basic Principles of Operant Conditioning

After establishing how reinforcement and punishment produced learned behavior, Skinner and other scientists began to expand the parameters of operant conditioning. This took the form of investigating some phenomena that were well known in classical conditioning (such as discrimination, generalization, and extinction) as well as some practical applications, such as how best to administer reinforcement or how to produce complex learned behaviors in an organism. Let's look at some of these basic principles of operant conditioning.

Discrimination, Generalization, and the Importance of Context

We all take off our clothes at least once a day, but usually not in public. We scream at rock concerts but not in libraries. We say, "Please pass the gravy," at the dinner table but not in a classroom. Although these observations may seem like nothing more than common sense, Thorndike was the first to recognize the underlying message: Learning takes place *in contexts,* not in the free range of any plausible situation. As Skinner rephrased it later, most behavior is under *stimulus control,* which develops when a particular response only occurs when an appropriate discriminative stimulus is present. Skinner (1972) discussed this process in terms of a "three-term contingency": In the presence of a *discriminative stimulus* (classmates drinking coffee together in Starbucks), a *response* (joking comments about a psychology professor's increasing waistline and receding hairline) produces a *reinforcer* (laughter among classmates). The same response in a different context—the professor's office—would most likely produce a very different outcome.

Stimulus control, perhaps not surprisingly, shows both discrimination and generalization effects similar to those we saw with classical conditioning. To demonstrate this, researchers used either a painting by the French Impressionist Claude Monet or one of Pablo Picasso's paintings from his Cubist period for the discriminative stimulus (Watanabe, Sakamoto, & Wakita, 1995). Participants in the experiment were only reinforced if they responded when the appropriate painting was presented. After training, the participants discriminated appropriately; those trained with the Monet painting responded when other paintings by Monet were presented and those trained with a Picasso painting reacted when other Cubist paintings by Picasso were shown. And as you might expect, Monet-trained participants did not react to Picassos and Picasso-trained participants did not respond to Monets. What's more, the research participants showed that they could generalize *across* painters as long as they were from the same artistic tradition. Those trained with Monet responded appropriately when shown paintings by Auguste Renoir (another French Impressionist), and the Picasso-trained participants responded to artwork by Cubist painter Henri Matisse, despite never having seen these paintings before. If these results don't seem particularly startling to you, it might help to know that the research participants were pigeons who were trained to key-peck to these various works of art. Stimulus control, and its ability to foster stimulus discrimination and stimulus generalization, is effective even if the stimulus has no meaning to the respondent.

▲ In research on stimulus control, participants trained with Picasso paintings, such as the one on the left, responded to other paintings by Picasso or even to paintings by other Cubists. Participants trained with Monet paintings, such as the one on the right, responded to other paintings by Monet or by other French Impressionists. Interestingly, the participants in this study were pigeons.

Extinction

As in classical conditioning, operant behavior undergoes extinction when the reinforcements stop. Pigeons cease pecking at a key if food is no longer presented following the behavior. You wouldn't put more money into a vending machine if it failed to give you its promised candy bar or soda. Warm smiles that are greeted with scowls and frowns will quickly disappear. On the surface, extinction of operant behavior looks like that of classical conditioning: The response rate drops off fairly rapidly and, if a rest period is provided, spontaneous recovery is typically seen.

However, there is an important difference. In classical conditioning, the US occurs on every trial no matter what the organism does. In operant conditioning, the reinforcements only occur when the proper response has been made, and they don't always occur even then. Not every trip into the forest produces nuts for a squirrel, auto salespeople don't sell to everyone who takes a test drive, and researchers run many experiments that do not work out and never get published. Yet these behaviors don't weaken and gradually extinguish. In fact, they typically become stronger and more resilient. Curiously, then, extinction is a bit more complicated in operant conditioning than in classical conditioning because it depends in part on how often reinforcement is received. In fact, this principle is an important cornerstone of operant conditioning that we'll examine next.

overjustification effect Circumstances when external rewards can undermine the intrinsic satisfaction of performing a behavior.

▲ Students cramming for an exam often show the same kind of behavior as pigeons being reinforced under a fixed interval schedule.

BRAND X PICTURES/JUPITERIMAGES

Schedules of Reinforcement

Skinner was intrigued by the apparent paradox surrounding extinction, and in his autobiography, he described how he began studying it (Skinner, 1979). He was laboriously rolling ground rat meal and water to make food pellets to reinforce the rats in his early experiments. It occurred to him that perhaps he could save time and effort by not giving his rats a pellet for every bar press but instead delivering food on some intermittent schedule. The results of this hunch were dramatic. Not only did the rats continue bar pressing but they also shifted the rate and pattern of bar pressing depending on the timing and frequency of the presentation of the reinforcers. Unlike classical conditioning, where the sheer *number* of learning trials was important, in operant conditioning the *pattern* with which reinforcements appeared was crucial.

Skinner explored dozens of what came to be known as *schedules of reinforcement* (Ferster & Skinner, 1957) (see **FIGURE 7.9**). The two most important are *interval schedules,* based on the time intervals between reinforcements, and *ratio schedules,* based on the ratio of responses to reinforcements.

Interval Schedules. Under a **fixed interval schedule (FI),** *reinforcers are presented at fixed time periods, provided that the appropriate response is made.* For example, on a 2-minute fixed interval schedule, a response will be reinforced, but only after 2 minutes have expired since the last reinforcement. Rats and pigeons in Skinner boxes produce predictable patterns of behavior under these schedules. They show little responding right after the presentation of reinforcement, but as the next time interval draws to a close, they show a burst of responding. Many undergraduates behave exactly like this. They do relatively little work until just before the upcoming exam, then engage in a burst of reading and studying.

Under a **variable interval schedule (VI),** a *behavior is reinforced based on an average time that has expired since the last reinforcement.* For example, on a 2-minute variable interval schedule, responses will be reinforced every 2 minutes *on average* but not after each 2-minute period. Variable interval schedules typically produce steady, consistent responding because the time until the next reinforcement is less predictable. Variable interval schedules are not encountered that often in real life, although one example might be radio promotional giveaways, such as tickets to rock concerts. The reinforcement—getting the tickets—might average out to once an hour across the span of the

▼ FIGURE 7.9

Reinforcement Schedules Different schedules of reinforcement produce different rates of responding. These lines represent the amount of responding that occurs under each type of reinforcement. The black slash marks indicate when reinforcement was administered. Notice that ratio schedules tend to produce higher rates of responding than do interval schedules, as shown by the steeper lines for fixed ratio and variable ratio reinforcement.

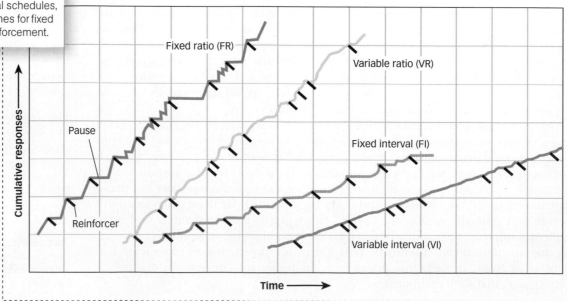

broadcasting day, but the presentation of the reinforcement is variable: It might come early in the 10:00 o'clock hour, later in the 11:00 o'clock hour, immediately into the 12:00 o'clock hour, and so on.

How does a radio station use scheduled reinforcements to keep you listening?

Both fixed interval schedules and variable interval schedules tend to produce slow, methodical responding because the reinforcements follow a time scale that is independent of how many responses occur. It doesn't matter if a rat on a fixed interval schedule presses a bar 1 time during a 2-minute period or 100 times: The reinforcing food pellet won't drop out of the shoot until 2 minutes have elapsed, regardless of the number of responses.

▲ Radio station promotions and giveaways often follow a variable interval schedule of reinforcement.

Ratio Schedules. Under a **fixed ratio schedule (FR)**, *reinforcement is delivered after a specific number of responses have been made.* One schedule might present reinforcement after every fourth response, a different schedule might present reinforcement after every 20 responses; the special case of presenting reinforcement after *each* response is called *continuous reinforcement,* and it's what drove Skinner to investigate these schedules in the first place. Notice that, in each example, the ratio of reinforcements to responses, once set, remains fixed.

How do ratio schedules work to keep you spending your money?

There are many situations in which people, sometimes unknowingly, find themselves being reinforced on a fixed ratio schedule:

Book clubs often give you a "freebie" after a set number of regular purchases, pieceworkers get paid after making a fixed number of products, and some credit card companies return to their customers a percent of the amount charged. When a fixed ratio schedule is operating, it is possible, in principle, to know exactly when the next reinforcer is due. A laundry pieceworker on a 10-response fixed ratio schedule who has just washed and ironed the ninth shirt knows that payment is coming after the next shirt is done.

◄ These pieceworkers in a textile factory get paid following a fixed ratio schedule: They receive payment after some set number of shirts have been sewn.

Under a **variable ratio schedule (VR)**, *the delivery of reinforcement is based on a particular average number of responses.* For example, if a laundry worker was following a 10-response variable ratio schedule instead of a fixed ratio schedule, she or he would still be paid, on average, for every 10 shirts washed and ironed but not for *each* tenth shirt. Slot machines in a modern casino pay off on variable ratio schedules that are determined by the random number generator that controls the play of the machines. A casino might advertise that they pay off on "every 100 pulls on average," which could be true. However, one player might hit a jackpot after 3 pulls on a slot machine, whereas another player might not hit until after 80 pulls. The ratio of responses to reinforcements is variable, which probably helps casinos stay in business.

Not surprisingly, variable ratio schedules produce slightly higher rates of responding than fixed ratio schedules primarily because the organism never knows when the next reinforcement is going to appear. What's more, the higher the ratio, the higher the response rate tends to be; a 20-response variable ratio schedule will produce considerably more responding than a 2-response variable ratio schedule. When schedules of reinforcement provide **intermittent reinforcement**, *when only some of the responses made are followed by reinforcement,* they produce behavior that is much more resistant to extinction than a continuous reinforcement schedule. One way to think about this effect is to recognize that the more irregular and intermittent a schedule is, the more difficult it becomes for an organism to detect when it has actually been placed on extinction.

fixed interval schedule (FI) An operant conditioning principle in which reinforcements are presented at fixed time periods, provided that the appropriate response is made.

variable interval schedule (VI) An operant conditioning principle in which behavior is reinforced based on an average time that has expired since the last reinforcement.

fixed ratio schedule (FR) An operant conditioning principle in which reinforcement is delivered after a specific number of responses have been made.

variable ratio schedule (VR) An operant conditioning principle in which the delivery of reinforcement is based on a particular average number of responses.

intermittent reinforcement An operant conditioning principle in which only some of the responses made are followed by reinforcement.

For example, if you've just put a dollar into a soda machine that, unbeknownst to you, is broken, no soda comes out. Because you're used to getting your sodas on a continuous reinforcement schedule—one dollar produces one soda—this abrupt change in the environment is easily noticed and you are unlikely to put additional money into the machine: You'd quickly show extinction. However, if you've put your dollar into a slot machine that, unbeknownst to you, is broken, do you stop after one or two plays? Almost certainly not. If you're a regular slot player, you're used to going for many plays in a row without winning anything, so it's difficult to tell that anything is out of the ordinary. Under conditions of intermittent reinforcement, all organisms will show considerable resistance to extinction and continue for many trials before they stop responding. The effect has even been observed in infants (Weir et al., 2005).

This relationship between intermittent reinforcement schedules and the robustness of the behavior they produce is called the **intermittent-reinforcement effect**, *the fact that operant behaviors that are maintained under intermittent reinforcement schedules resist extinction better than those maintained under continuous reinforcement.* In one extreme case, Skinner gradually extended a variable ratio schedule until he managed to get a pigeon to make an astonishing 10,000 pecks at an illuminated key for one food reinforcer! Behavior maintained under a schedule like this is virtually immune to extinction.

▲ Slot machines in casinos pay out following a variable ratio schedule. This helps explain why some gamblers feel incredibly lucky, whereas others (like this chap) can't believe they can play a machine for so long without winning a thing.

Shaping through Successive Approximations

Have you ever been to AquaLand and wondered how the dolphins learn to jump up in the air, twist around, splash back down, do a somersault, and then jump through a hoop, all in one smooth motion? Well, they don't. Wait—of course they do; you've seen them. It's just that they don't learn to do all those complex aquabatics in *one* smooth motion. Rather, elements of their behavior get shaped over time until the final product looks like one smooth motion.

Skinner noted that the trial-by-trial experiments of Pavlov and Thorndike were rather artificial. Behavior rarely occurs in fixed frameworks where a stimulus is presented and then an organism has to engage in some activity or another. We are continuously acting and behaving, and the world around us reacts in response to our actions. Most of our behaviors, then, are the result of **shaping**, or *learning that results from the reinforcement of successive steps to a final desired behavior.* The outcomes of one set of behaviors shape the next set of behaviors, whose outcomes shape the next set of behaviors, and so on.

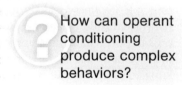

How can operant conditioning produce complex behaviors?

Skinner realized the potential power of shaping one day in 1943 when he was working on a wartime project sponsored by General Mills in a lab on the top floor of a flour mill where pigeons frequently visited (Peterson, 2004). In a lighthearted moment, Skinner and his colleagues decided to see whether they could teach the pigeons to

▼ B. F. Skinner shaping a dog named Agnes. In the span of 20 minutes, Skinner was able to use reinforcement of successive approximations to shape Agnes's behavior. The result was a pretty neat trick: to wander in, stand on hind legs, and jump.

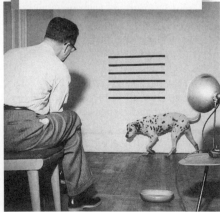

1 Minute

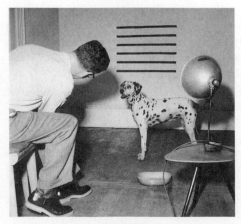

4 Minutes

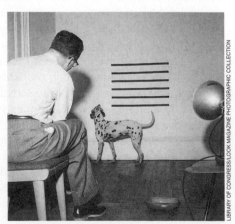

8 Minutes

"bowl" by swiping with their beaks at a ball that Skinner had placed in a box along with some pins. Nothing worked until Skinner decided to reinforce any response even remotely related to a swipe, such as merely looking at the ball. "The result amazed us", Skinner recalled. "In a few minutes the ball was caroming off the walls of the box as if the pigeon had been a champion squash player" (Skinner, 1958, p. 94). Skinner applied this insight in his later laboratory research. For example, he noted that if you put a rat in a Skinner box and wait for it to press the bar, you could end up waiting a very long time: Bar pressing just isn't very high in a rat's natural hierarchy of responses. However, it is relatively easy to "shape" bar pressing. Watch the rat closely: If it turns in the direction of the bar, deliver a food reward. This will reinforce turning toward the bar, making such a movement more likely. Now wait for the rat to take a step toward the bar before delivering food; this will reinforce moving toward the bar. After the rat walks closer to the bar, wait until it touches the bar before presenting the food. Notice that none of these behaviors is the final desired behavior—reliably pressing the bar. Rather, each behavior is a *successive approximation* to the final product, or a behavior that gets incrementally closer to the overall desired behavior. In the dolphin example—and indeed, in many instances of animal training in which relatively simple animals seem to perform astoundingly complex behaviors—you can think through how each smaller behavior is reinforced until the overall sequence of behavior gets performed reliably.

Superstitious Behavior

Everything we've discussed so far suggests that one of the keys to establishing reliable operant behavior is the correlation between an organism's response and the occurrence of reinforcement. In the case of continuous reinforcement, when every response is followed by the presentation of a reinforcer, there is a one-to-one, or perfect, correlation. In the case of intermittent reinforcement, the correlation is weaker (i.e., not every response is met with the delivery of reinforcement), but it's not zero. As you read in Chapter 2, however, just because two things are correlated (that is, they tend to occur together in time and space) doesn't imply that there is causality (that is, the presence of one reliably causes the other to occur).

Skinner (1948) designed an experiment that illustrates this distinction. He put several pigeons in Skinner boxes, set the food dispenser to deliver food every 15 seconds, and left the birds to their own devices. Later he returned and found the birds engaging in odd, idiosyncratic behaviors, such as pecking aimlessly in a corner or turning in circles. He referred to these behaviors as "superstitious" and offered a behaviorist analysis of their occurrence. The pigeons, he argued, were simply repeating behaviors that had been accidentally reinforced. A pigeon that just happened to have pecked

> How would a behaviorist explain superstitions?

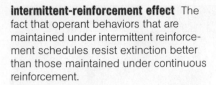

intermittent-reinforcement effect The fact that operant behaviors that are maintained under intermittent reinforcement schedules resist extinction better than those maintained under continuous reinforcement.

shaping Learning that results from the reinforcement of successive steps to a final desired behavior.

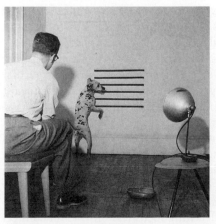

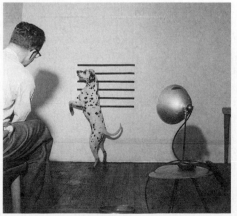

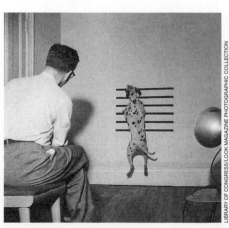

12 Minutes

16 Minutes

20 Minutes

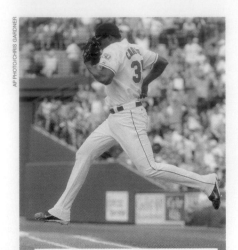

▲ People believe in many different superstitions and engage in all kinds of superstitious behaviors. Many major league baseball players, for example, maintain a superstition of not stepping on the baselines when they enter or leave the field, as illustrated by former Baltimore Orioles pitcher Daniel Cabrera. Skinner thought superstitions resulted from the unintended reinforcement of inconsequential behavior.

randomly in the corner when the food showed up had connected the delivery of food to that behavior. Because this pecking behavior was "reinforced" by the delivery of food, the pigeon was likely to repeat it. Now pecking in the corner was more likely to occur, and it was more likely to be reinforced 15 seconds later when the food appeared again. For each pigeon, the behavior reinforced would most likely be whatever the pigeon happened to be doing when the food was first delivered. Skinner's pigeons acted as though there was a causal relationship between their behaviors and the appearance of food when it was merely an accidental correlation.

Although some researchers questioned Skinner's characterization of these behaviors as "superstitious" (Staddon & Simmelhag, 1971), later studies have shown that reinforcing adults or children using schedules in which reinforcement is not contingent on their responses can produce seemingly superstitious behavior. One particularly provocative report suggests that superstitious conditioning might be a good model for understanding the formation of delusions in chronic drug users (Freeman et al., 2009). The researchers observed that delusions, like superstitious behaviors, are based on mistaken beliefs regarding causal relationships. It seems that people, like pigeons, behave as though there's a correlation between their responses and reward when in fact the connection is merely accidental (Bloom et al., 2007; Mellon, 2009; Ono, 1987; Wagner & Morris, 1987). Such findings should not be surprising to sports fans. Baseball players who enjoy several home runs on a day when they happened not to have showered are likely to continue that tradition, laboring under the belief that the accidental correlation between poor personal hygiene and a good day at bat is somehow causal. This "stench causes home runs" hypothesis is just one of many examples of human superstitions (Gilbert et al., 2000; Radford & Radford, 1949).

A Deeper Understanding of Operant Conditioning

Like classical conditioning, operant conditioning also quickly proved to be a powerful approach to learning. But B. F. Skinner, like Watson before him, was satisfied to observe an organism perform a learned behavior; he didn't look for a deeper explanation of mental processes (Skinner, 1950). In this view, an organism behaved in a certain way as a response to stimuli in the environment, not because there was any wanting, wishing, or willing by the animal in question. However, some research on operant conditioning digs deeper into the underlying mechanisms that produce the familiar outcomes of reinforcement. Like we did earlier in the chapter with classical conditioning, let's examine three elements that expand our view of operant conditioning: the cognitive, neural, and evolutionary elements of operant conditioning.

The Cognitive Elements of Operant Conditioning

Edward Chace Tolman (1886–1959) was one of the first researchers to question Skinner's strictly behaviorist interpretation of learning, and was the strongest early advocate of a cognitive approach to operant learning. Tolman argued that there was more to learning than just knowing the circumstances in the environment (the properties of the stimulus) and being able to observe a particular outcome (the reinforced response). Instead, Tolman proposed that an animal established a means-ends relationship. That is, the conditioning experience produced knowledge or a belief that, in this particular situation, a specific reward (the end state) will appear if a specific response (the means to that end) is made. (For an example of one aspect of the reward [being ready for the test] given the response [decision to study], see the Hot Science box.)

Tolman's means-ends relationship may remind you of the Rescorla-Wagner model of classical conditioning. Rescorla argued that the CS functions by setting up an expectation about the arrival of a US—and "expectations" most certainly involve cognitive processes. In both Rescorla's and Tolman's theories, the stimulus does not directly evoke a response; rather, it establishes an internal cognitive state, which then produces the behavior. These cognitive theories of learning focus less on the S-R connection and more on what happens in the organism's mind when faced with the stimulus.

▲ Edward Chace Tolman advocated a cognitive approach to operant learning and provided evidence that in maze learning experiments, rats develop a mental picture of the maze, which he called a cognitive map.

During the 1930s and 1940s, Tolman and his students conducted studies that focused on *latent learning* and *cognitive maps,* two phenomena that strongly suggest that simple stimulus-response interpretations of operant learning behavior are inadequate.

Latent Learning and Cognitive Maps. In **latent learning**, *something is learned but it is not manifested as a behavioral change until sometime in the future.* Latent learning can easily be established in rats and occurs without any obvious reinforcement, a finding that posed a direct challenge to the then-dominant behaviorist position that all learning required some form of reinforcement (Tolman & Honzik, 1930a).

Tolman gave three groups of rats access to a complex maze every day for over 2 weeks. The control group never received any reinforcement for navigating the maze.

latent learning A condition in which something is learned but it is not manifested as a behavioral change until sometime in the future.

HOT SCIENCE

Control of Learning: From the Laboratory to the Classroom

It's the night before the final exam in your introductory psychology course. You've put in a lot of time reviewing your course notes and the material in this textbook, and you feel that you have learned most of it pretty well. You are coming down the home stretch with little time left, and you've got to decide whether to devote those precious remaining minutes to studying psychological disorders or social psychology. How do you make that decision? What are its potential consequences? Recent research in cognitive psychology has shown that people's judgments about what they have learned play a critical role in guiding further study and learning (Metcalfe, 2009).

An important part of learning involves assessing how well we know something and how much more time we need to devote to studying it. Experimental evidence reveals that these subjective assessments—which psychologists refer to as "judgments of learning" (JOLs)—are related to learning: People typically devote more time to studying items that they judge they have not learned well (Son & Metcalfe, 2000). However, this relationship might simply reflect the fact that items that are difficult to learn require more study time than easier items, rather than showing that JOLs have a causal effect on how people approach the learning task.

Metcalfe and Finn (2008) provided evidence for a causal effect by taking advantage of an illusion that influences JOLs. The illusion occurs when people are given lists of word pairs. Some pairs are studied three times on Trial 1, given an initial test, and

then studied one more time on Trial 2 before a final test (3-1 condition); other pairs are studied once on Trial 1, given an initial test, and then studied three times on Trial 2 before a final test (1-3 condition).

You should not be surprised to find out that on the final test, people recalled the same number of pairs from the 3-1 and 1-3 condtions; after all, they studied all the word pairs the same number of times. Thus the items in the two conditions were learned equally well. Further, participants made their JOLs about each word pair on the final study presentation of Trial 2—at a time when items from the 3-1 and 1-3 conditions should have been equally well learned. Strikingly, though, the participants' JOLs were higher at the end of Trial 2 in the 3-1 condition than the 1-3 condition. This illusion occurred because JOLs were influenced by the fact that participants recalled more items on the initial test in the 3-1 condition than in the 1-3 condition (remember, the initial test followed three exposures to the list in the 3-1 condition versus only one exposure to the list in the 1-3 condition).

This manipulation then allowed the experimenters to examine whether JOLs influenced how much time people devoted to each pair when the pairs in the two conditions were learned equally well (even though participants didn't think that they were). Critically, Metcalfe and Finn found evidence for a causal effect: The participants chose to devote more time to studying pairs from the 1-3 condition, which they thought were less well learned, than pairs from the 3-1 condition, which they thought were better learned.

The fact that JOLs have a causal effect on how people study is especially important because—as illustrated by the experiment we just considered—JOLs are sometimes inaccurate. For example, after reading and re-reading a chapter or article in preparation for a test, the material will likely feel quite familiar, and that feeling may convince you that you've learned the material well enough that you don't need to study it further. However, the feeling of familiarity can be misleading. Although we think it reflects a deep understanding of the material, it may instead be a manifestation of a low-level process such as perceptual priming (see Chapter 6) that may not reflect either comprehension or the kind of learning that will be required to perform well on an exam (Bjork & Bjork, 2011). One way to avoid being fooled by such such misleading subjective impressions is to test yourself from time to time when studying for an exam under conditions similar to those that will occur during the exam. As we saw in Chapter 6, testing oneself improves later learning of the target material more than simply restudying it.

So, if you are preparing for the final exam in this course and need to decide whether to devote more time to studying psychological disorders or social psychology, try to exert control over learning by testing yourself on material from the two chapters; you can use the results of those tests to help you decide which chapter requires further work. We can exert control over learning, but we also need to be aware of the possible pitfalls in attempting to exercise that control.

cognitive map A mental representation of the physical features of the environment.

They were simply allowed to run around until they reached the goal box at the end of the maze. In **FIGURE 7.10** you can see that over the 2 weeks of the study, this group (in green) got a little better at finding their way through the maze but not by much. A second group of rats received regular reinforcements; when they reached the goal box, they found a small food reward there. Not surprisingly, these rats showed clear learning, as can be seen in blue in Figure 7.10. A third group was treated exactly like the control group for the first 10 days and then rewarded for the last 7 days. This group's behavior (in orange) was quite striking. For the first 10 days, they behaved like the rats in the control group. However, during the final 7 days, they behaved a lot like the rats in the second group that had been reinforced every day. Clearly, the rats in this third group had learned a lot about the maze and the location of the goal box during those first 10 days even though they had not received any reinforcements for their behavior. In other words, they showed evidence of latent learning.

These results suggested to Tolman that beyond simply learning "start here, end here," his rats had developed a sophisticated mental picture of the maze. Tolman called this a **cognitive map**, or *a mental representation of the physical features of the environment*. Beyond simply learning "start here, end here," Tolman thought that the rats had developed a mental picture of the maze, more along the lines of "make two lefts, then a right, then a quick left at the corner." He devised several experiments to test this idea (Tolman & Honzik, 1930b; Tolman, Ritchie, & Kalish, 1946).

? What are "cognitive maps" and why are they a challenge to behaviorism?

Further Support for Cognitive Explanations. One simple experiment provided support for Tolman's theories and wreaked havoc with the noncognitive explanations offered by staunch behaviorists. Tolman trained a group of rats in the maze shown in **FIGURE 7.11a.** As you can see, rats run down a straightaway, take a left, a right, a long right, and then end up in the goal box at the end of the maze. Because we're looking at it from above, we can see that the rat's position at the end of the maze, relative to the starting point, is "diagonal to the upper right." Of course, all the rat in the maze sees are the next set of walls and turns until it eventually reaches the goal box. Nonetheless, rats learned to navigate this maze without error or hesitation after about four nights. Clever rats. But they were more clever than you think.

After they had mastered the maze, Tolman changed things around a bit and put them in the maze shown in **FIGURE 7.11b.** The goal box was still in the same place relative to the start box. However, many alternative paths now spoked off the main platform, and the main straightaway that the rats had learned to use was blocked. Most behaviorists would predict that the rats in this situation—running down a familiar path only to find it blocked—would show stimulus generalization and pick the next closest path, such as one immediately adjacent to the straightaway. This was not what Tolman observed. When faced with the blocked path, the rats instead ran all the way down the path that led directly to the goal box. The rats had formed a sophisticated cognitive map of their environment and behaved in a way that suggested they were successfully following that map after the conditions had changed. Latent learning and cognitive maps suggest that operant conditioning involves much more than an animal responding to a stimulus. Tolman's experiments strongly suggest that there is a cognitive component, even in rats, to operant learning.

In a more recent study, Blake et al. (2006) measured how responses in a monkey's auditory cortex changed when a tone was associated with a reward. They found that changes in the neural response to the tone in the auditory cortex, as well as behavioral evidence of learning, occurred only when monkeys developed what the researchers called a "cognitive association" between the tone and reward; mere exposure to the tone and reward failed to produce learning or changes in the auditory cortex.

▼ FIGURE 7.10

Latent Learning Rats in a control group that never received any reinforcement (in green) improved at finding their way through the maze over 17 days but not by much. Rats that received regular reinforcements (in blue) showed fairly clear learning; their error rate decreased steadily over time. Rats in the latent learning group (in orange) were treated exactly like the control group rats for the first 10 days and then like the regularly rewarded group for the last 7 days. Their dramatic improvement on day 12 shows that these rats had learned a lot about the maze and the location of the goal box even though they had never received reinforcements. Notice also that on the last 7 days, these latent learners actually seem to make *fewer* errors than their regularly rewarded counterparts.

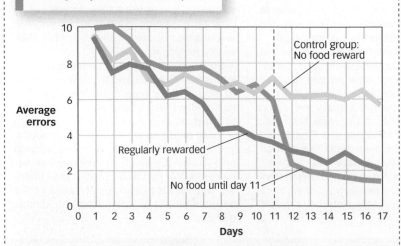

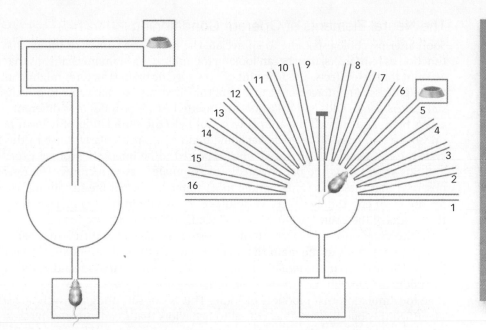

(a) Apparatus used in preliminary training   (b) Apparatus used in test trial

◄ FIGURE 7.11
Cognitive Maps (a) Rats trained to run from a start box to a goal box in the maze on the left mastered the task quite readily. When these rats were then placed in the maze on the right (b), in which the main straightaway had been blocked, they did something unusual. Rather than simply backtrack and try the next closest runway (i.e., those labeled 8 or 9 in the figure), which would be predicted by stimulus generalization, the rats typically chose runway 5, which led most directly to where the goal box had been during their training. The rats had formed a cognitive map of their environment and so knew where they needed to end up, spatially, compared to where they began.

Learning to Trust: For Better or Worse. Cognitive factors also played a key role in an experiment examining learning and brain activity (using fMRI) in people who played a "trust" game with a fictional partner (Delgado, Frank, & Phelps, 2005). On each trial, a participant could either keep a $1 reward or transfer the reward to a partner, who would receive $3. The partner could then either keep the $3 or share half of it with the participant—so, when playing with a partner who was willing to share the reward, the participant would be better off transferring the money, but when playing with a partner who did not share, the participant would be better off keeping the reward in the first place. Participants in such experiments typically find out who is trustworthy on the basis of trial-and-error learning during the game, transferring more money to partners who reinforce them by sharing.

In the study by Delgado et al., participants were given detailed descriptions of their partners that either portrayed the partners as trustworthy, neutral, or suspect. Even though during the game itself the sharing behavior of the three types of partners did not differ—they each reinforced participants to the same extent through sharing—the participants' cognitions about their partners had powerful effects. Partcipants transferred more money to the "trustworthy" partner than to the others, essentially ignoring the trial-by-trial feedback that would ordinarily shape their playing behavior, and thus reducing the amount of reward they received. Highlighting the power of the cognitive effect, signals in a part of the brain that ordinarily distinguishes between positive and negative feedback were evident only when participants played with the neutral partner—these feedback signals were absent when participants played with the "trustworthy" partner and reduced when participants played with the suspect partner.

These kinds of effects might help us to understand otherwise perplexing real-life cases such as that of the con artist Bernard Madoff, who in March 2009 pleaded guilty to swindling numerous investors out of billions of dollars in a highly publicized case that attracted worldwide attention. Madoff had been the chairman of the NASDAQ stock exchange and seemed to his investors an extremely trustworthy figure with whom one could safely invest money. Those powerful cognitions might have caused investors to miss danger signals that otherwise would have led them to learn about the true nature of Madoff's operation. If so, the result was one of the most expensive failures of learning in modern history.

▼ Bernard Madoff, shown here leaving a court hearing in March 2009, pleaded guilty to fraud after swindling billions of dollars from investors who trusted him.

AFP PHOTO/TIMOTHY A. CLARY/NEWSCOM

The Neural Elements of Operant Conditioning

Soon after psychologists came to appreciate the range and variety of things that could function as reinforcers, they began looking for underlying brain mechanisms that might account for these effects. The first hint of how specific brain structures might contribute to the process of reinforcement came from the discovery of what came to be called *pleasure centers*. James Olds and his associates inserted tiny electrodes into different parts of a rat's brain and allowed the animal to control electric stimulation of its own brain by pressing a bar. They discovered that some brain areas, particularly those in the limbic system (see Chapter 3), produced what appeared to be intensely positive experiences: The rats would press the bar repeatedly to stimulate these structures. The researchers observed that these rats would ignore food, water, and other life-sustaining necessities for hours on end simply to receive stimulation directly in the brain. They then called these parts of the brain "pleasure centers" (Olds, 1956) (see **FIGURE 7.12**).

In the years since these early studies, researchers have identified a number of structures and pathways in the brain that deliver rewards through stimulation (Wise, 1989, 2005). The neurons in the *medial forebrain bundle,* a pathway that meanders its way from the midbrain through the *hypothalamus* into the *nucleus accumbens,* are the most susceptible to stimulation that produces pleasure. This is not surprising as psychologists have identified this bundle of cells as crucial to behaviors that clearly involve pleasure, such as eating, drinking, and engaging in sexual activity. Second, the neurons all along this pathway and especially those in the nucleus accumbens itself are all *dopaminergic;* that is, they secrete the neurotransmitter *dopamine*. Remember from Chapter 3 that higher levels of dopamine in the brain are usually associated with positive emotions. During recent years, several competing hypotheses about the precise role of dopamine have emerged, including the idea that dopamine is more closely linked with the expectation of reward than with reward itself (Fiorillo, Newsome, & Schultz, 2008; Schultz, 2006, 2007), or that dopamine is more closely associated with wanting or even craving something rather than simply liking it (Berridge, 2007).

▼ FIGURE 7.12
Pleasure Centers in the Brain The nucleus accumbens, medial forebrain bundle, and hypothalamus are all major pleasure centers in the brain.

Nucleus accumbens
Hypothalamus
Pituitary gland
Medial forebrain bundle
Amygdala
Hippocampus

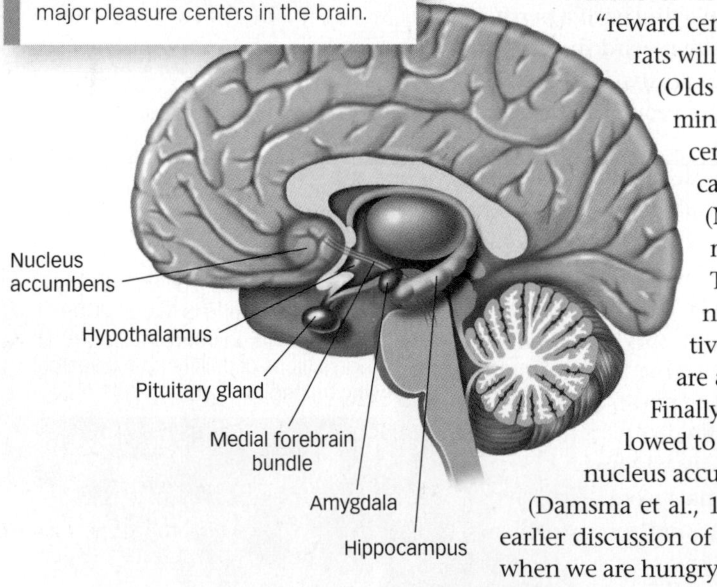

Whichever view turns out to be correct, researchers have found good support for a "reward center" in which dopamine plays a key role. First, as you've just seen, rats will work to stimulate this pathway at the expense of other basic needs (Olds & Fobes, 1981). However, if drugs that block the action of dopamine are administered to the rats, they cease stimulating the pleasure centers (Stellar, Kelley, & Corbett, 1983). Second, drugs such as cocaine, amphetamine, and opiates activate these pathways and centers (Moghaddam & Bunney, 1989), but dopamine-blocking drugs dramatically diminish their reinforcing effects (White & Milner, 1992). Third, fMRI studies (see Chapter 3) show increased activity in the nucleus accumbens in heterosexual men looking at pictures of attractive women (Aharon et al., 2001) and in individuals who believe they are about to receive money (Cooper et al., 2009; Knutson et al., 2001). Finally, rats given primary reinforcers such as food or water or who are allowed to engage in sexual activity show increased dopamine secretion in the nucleus accumbens—but only if the rats are hungry, thirsty, or sexually aroused (Damsma et al., 1992). This last finding is exactly what we might expect given our earlier discussion of the complexities of reinforcement. After all, food tastes a lot better when we are hungry and sexual activity is more pleasurable when we are aroused. These biological structures underlying rewards and reinforcements probably evolved to ensure that species engaged in activities that helped survival and reproduction.

The Evolutionary Elements of Operant Conditioning

As you'll recall, classical conditioning has an adaptive value that has been fine-tuned by evolution. Not surprisingly, we can also view operant conditioning from an evolutionary perspective. This viewpoint grew out of a set of curious observations from the early days of conditioning experiments. Several behaviorists who were using simple T mazes like the one shown in **FIGURE 7.13** to study learning in rats discovered that if a rat found food in one arm of the maze on the first trial of the day, it typically ran down the *other* arm on the very next trial. A staunch behaviorist wouldn't expect the rats to behave this way. After all, the rats in these experiments were hungry and they had just been reinforced for turning in a particular direction. According to operant conditioning, this should *increase* the likelihood of turning in that same direction, not reduce it. With additional trials the rats eventually learned to go to the arm with the food, but they had to learn to overcome this initial tendency to go "the wrong way." How can we explain this?

What was puzzling from a behaviorist perspective makes sense when viewed from an evolutionary perspective. Rats are foragers, and like all foraging species, they have evolved a highly adaptive strategy for survival. They move around in their environment looking for food. If they find it somewhere, they eat it (or store it) and then go somewhere else for more. If they do not find food, they forage in another part of the environment. So, if the rat just found food in the *right* arm of a T maze, the obvious place to look next time is the *left* arm. The rat knows that there isn't any more food in the right arm because it just ate the food it found there! Indeed, foraging animals such as rats have well-developed spatial representations that allow them to search their environment efficiently. If given the opportunity to explore a complex environment like the multi-arm maze shown in **FIGURE 7.14,** rats will systematically go from arm to arm collecting food, rarely returning to an arm they have previously visited (Olton & Samuelson, 1976).

What explains a rat's behavior in a T maze?

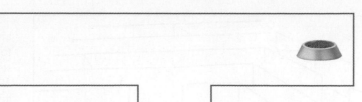
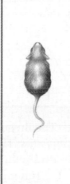

▲ FIGURE 7.13
A Simple T Maze When rats find food in the right arm of a typical T maze, on the next trial, they will often run to the *left* arm of the maze. This contradicts basic principles of operant conditioning: If the behavior of running to the right arm is reinforced, it should be more likely to occur again in the future. However, this behavior is perfectly consistent with a rat's evolutionary preparedness. Like most foraging animals, rats explore their environments in search of food and seldom return to where food has already been found. Quite sensibly, if food has already been found in the right arm of the T maze, the rat will search the left arm next to see if *more* food is there.

Start

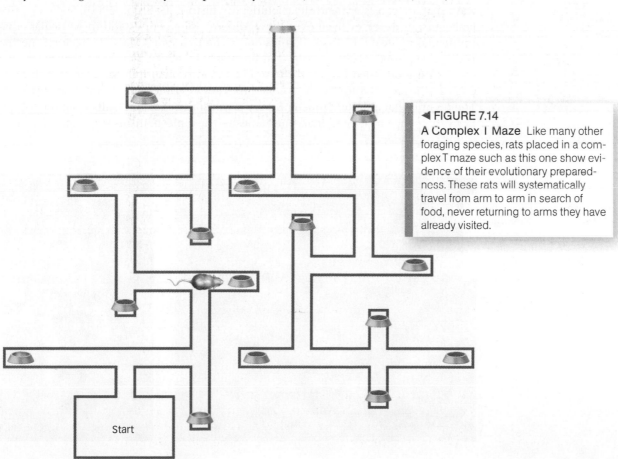

◄ FIGURE 7.14
A Complex T Maze Like many other foraging species, rats placed in a complex T maze such as this one show evidence of their evolutionary preparedness. These rats will systematically travel from arm to arm in search of food, never returning to arms they have already visited.

Start

BY KAZ WWW.CARTOONSTOCK.COM–"YOU ARE HERE"

YOU ARE HERE

Two of Skinner's former students, Keller Breland and Marian Breland, were among the first researchers to discover that it wasn't just rats in T mazes that presented a problem for behaviorists (Breland & Breland, 1961). The Brelands pointed out that psychologists and the organisms they study often seemed to "disagree" on what the organisms should be doing. Their argument was simple: When this kind of dispute develops, the animals are always right, and the psychologists had better rethink their theories.

The Brelands, who made a career out of training animals for commercials and movies, often used pigs because pigs are surprisingly good at learning all sorts of tricks. However, they discovered that it was extremely difficult to teach a pig the simple task of dropping coins in a box. Instead of depositing the coins, the pigs persisted in rooting with them as if they were digging them up in soil, tossing them in the air with their snouts and pushing them around. The Brelands tried to train raccoons at the same task, with different but equally dismal results. The raccoons spent their time rubbing the coins between their paws instead of dropping them in the box.

Having learned the association between the coins and food, the animals began to treat the coins as stand-ins for food. Pigs are biologically predisposed to root out their food, and raccoons have evolved to clean their food by rubbing it with their paws. That is exactly what each species of animal did with the coins.

The Brelands' work shows that each species, including humans, is biologically predisposed to learn some things more readily than others and to respond to stimuli in ways that are consistent with its evolutionary history (Gallistel, 2000). Such adaptive behaviors, however, evolved over extraordinarily long periods and in particular environmental contexts. If those circumstances change, some of the behavioral mechanisms that support learning can lead an organism astray. Raccoons that associated coins with food failed to follow the simple route to obtaining food by dropping the coins in the box; "nature" took over and they wasted time rubbing the coins together. The point is that although much of every organism's behavior results from predispositions sharpened by evolutionary mechanisms, these mechanisms sometimes can have ironic consequences.

► The misbehavior of organisms: Pigs are biologically predisposed to root out their food, just as raccoons are predisposed to wash their food. Trying to train either species to behave differently can prove to be an exercise in futility.

JOHN WILKINSON ECOSCENE/CORBIS

JOE MCDONALD/VISUALS UNLIMITED

IN SUMMARY

○ Operant conditioning, as developed by B. F. Skinner, is a process by which behaviors are reinforced and therefore become more likely to occur, where complex behaviors are shaped through reinforcement, and where the contingencies between actions and outcomes are critical in determining how an organism's behaviors will be displayed.

○ Like Watson, Skinner tried to explain behavior without considering cognitive, neural, or evolutionary mechanisms. However, as with classical conditioning, this approach turned out to be incomplete.

○ Operant conditioning has clear cognitive components: Organisms behave as though they have expectations about the outcomes of their actions and adjust their actions accordingly. Cognitive influences can sometimes override the trial-by-trial feedback that usually influences learning.

○ Studies with both animals and people highlight the operation of a neural reward center that impacts learning.

○ The associative mechanisms that underlie operant conditioning have their roots in evolutionary biology. Some things are relatively easily learned and others are difficult; the history of the species is usually the best clue as to which will be which.

observational learning A condition in which learning takes place by watching the actions of others.

Observational Learning: Look at Me

Four-year-old Rodney and his 2-year-old sister Margie had always been told to keep away from the stove, and that's good advice for any child and many an adult. Being a mischievous imp, however, Rodney decided one day to heat up a burner and place his hand over it until the singeing of his flesh led him to recoil, shrieking in pain. Rodney was more scared than hurt, really—and no one hearing this story doubts that he learned something important that day. But little Margie, who stood by watching these events unfold, *also* learned the same lesson. Rodney's story is a behaviorist's textbook example: The administration of punishment led to a learned change in his behavior. But how can we explain Margie's learning? She received neither punishment nor reinforcement—indeed, she didn't even have direct experience with the wicked appliance—yet it's arguable that she's just as likely to keep her hands away from stoves in the future as Rodney is.

Margie's is a case of **observational learning**, in which *learning takes place by watching the actions of others*. Observational learning challenges behaviorism's reinforcement-based explanations of classical and operant conditioning, but there is no doubt that this type of learning produces changes in behavior. In all societies, appropriate social behavior is passed on from generation to generation largely through observation (Bandura, 1965). The rituals and behaviors that are a part of our culture are acquired by each new generation, not only through deliberate training of the young but also through young people observing the patterns of behaviors of their elders and also each other (Flynn & Whiten, 2008). Tasks such as using chopsticks or learning to operate a TV's remote control are more easily acquired if we watch these activities being carried out before we try ourselves. Even complex motor tasks, such as performing surgery, are learned in part through extensive observation and imitation of models. And anyone who is about to undergo surgery is grateful for observational learning. Just the thought of a generation of surgeons acquiring their surgical techniques using the trial-and-error techniques studied by Thorndike or the shaping of successive approximations that captivated Skinner would make any of us very nervous.

? Why might a younger sibling appear to learn faster than a first-born?

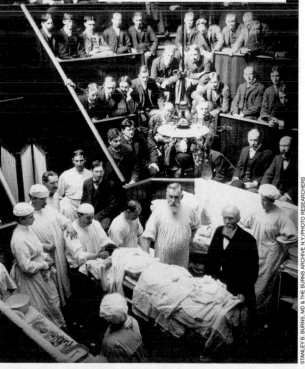

▼ Observational learning plays an important role in surgical training, as illustrated by the medical students observing famed German surgeon Vincenz Czerny (beard and white gown) perform stomach surgery in 1901 at a San Francisco hospital.

STANLEY B. BURNS, MD & THE BURNS ARCHIVE N.Y./PHOTO RESEARCHERS

diffusion chain A process in which individuals initially learn a behavior by observing another individual perform that behavior, and then serve as a model from which other individuals learn the behavior.

Observational Learning in Humans

In a series of studies that have become landmarks in psychology, Albert Bandura and his colleagues investigated the parameters of observational learning (Bandura, Ross, & Ross, 1961; for additional discussion of Bandura's work, see Chapter 13). The researchers escorted individual preschoolers into a play area, where they found a number of desirable toys that 4-year-olds typically like. An adult *model,* someone whose behavior might serve as a guide for others, was then led into the room and seated in the opposite corner, where there were several other toys, including a Bobo doll, which is a large inflatable plastic toy with a weighted bottom that allows it to bounce back upright when knocked down. The adult played quietly for a bit but then started aggressing toward the Bobo doll, knocking it down, jumping on it, hitting it with the mallet, kicking it around the room, and yelling "Pow!" and "Kick him!" When the children who observed these actions were later allowed to play with a variety of toys, including a child-size Bobo doll, they were more than twice as likely to interact with it in an aggressive manner as a group of children who hadn't observed the aggressive model.

? What did the Bobo doll experiment show about children and aggressive behavior?

So what? Kids like to break stuff, and after all, Bobo dolls are made to be punched. Although that's true, as **FIGURE 7.15** shows, the degree of imitation that the children showed was startling. In fact, the adult model purposely used novel behaviors such as hitting the doll with a toy mallet or throwing it up in the air so that the researchers could distinguish aggressive acts that were clearly the result of observational learning. The children in these studies also showed that they were sensitive to the consequences of the actions they observed. When they saw the adult models being punished for behaving aggressively, the children showed considerably less aggression. When the children observed a model being rewarded and praised for aggressive behavior, they displayed an increase in aggression (Bandura, Ross, & Ross, 1963). The observational learning seen in Bandura's studies has implications for social learning and cultural transmission of behaviors, norms, and values (Bandura, 1977, 1994).

▼ FIGURE 7.15

Beating Up Bobo Children who were exposed to an adult model who behaved aggressively toward a Bobo doll were likely to behave aggressively themselves. This behavior occurred in the absence of any direct reinforcement. Observational learning was responsible for producing the children's behaviors.

Recent research with children has shown that observational learning is well suited to seeding behaviors that can spread widely across a culture through a process called a **diffusion chain**, where *individuals initially learn a behavior by observing another individual perform that behavior, and then serve as a model from which other individuals learn the behavior* (Flynn, 2008; Flynn & Whiten, 2008). Experiments investigating the operation of diffusion chains in preschool-aged children have used a procedure in which a child (B) observes an adult model (A) performing a target act, such as using a novel tool to obtain a reward. Then, person B serves as a model for another child, C, who watches B perform the target act, followed by child D observing C perform the target act, and so forth. The evidence to date indicates that children can learn how to use a novel tool by observing an adult model use that tool, and more importantly, can then serve as effective models for other children to learn how to use the tool. Initial studies of diffusion chains showed that behaviors such as novel tool use could be spread accurately across 10 children (Flynn & Whiten, 2008; Horner et al., 2006), and more recent work indicates faithful tranmission of tool use across a diffusion chain comprised of 20 children (Hopper et al., in press). These findings of transmission across multiple "cultural generations" (Hopper et al., in press) underscore that observational learning is well suited for transmission through a diffusion chain, and thus a potentially powerful means of influencing our culture.

▲ Coaches rely on observational learning when they demonstrate techniques to athletes.

Observational learning is important in many domains of everyday life. Sports provide a good example. Coaches in just about all sports rely on observational learning when they demonstrate to players critical techniques and skills, and athletes also have numerous opportunities to observe other athletes perform. Studies of varsity and recreational-level athletes in both team and individual sports indicate that they all report relying heavily on observational learning to improve their performance of critical skills in their respective sports, with varsity athletes reporting an even greater reliance on observational learning than recreational atheles (Wesch, Law, & Hall, 2007). But can merely observing a skill result in an improvement in performing that skill, without actually practicing it? A number of studies have shown that observing someone else perform a motor task, ranging from reaching for a target to pressing a sequence of keys, can produce robust learning in the observer—in fact, observational learning sometimes results in just as much learning as practicing the task itself (Heyes & Foster, 2002; Mattar & Gribble, 2005; Vinter & Perruchet, 2002).

HOT SCIENCE

Even More Reasons to Sleep

Sleep has so much going for it, and yet here's something more. Observational learning can be enhanced by simply closing your eyes and going to sleep. We saw in Chapter 6 that sleep facilitates the consolidation of episodic memories, and other studies indicate that sleep can also facilitate consolidation of motor skills (Walker & Stickgold, 2006). To investigate effects on observational learning, researchers showed participants a video in which a hand performs a fingertapping task involving one of three different sequences (Van Der Werf et al., 2009). To prevent participants from subtly practicing the task while observing, the researchers required them to press two keys spaced apart on a keyboard using two of the fingers required for the tapping task.

Participants who went to sleep shortly after the observational learning period (which occurred in the evening) showed significant improvements when tested 12 or 24 hours later on the exact sequence they had observed compared with another sequence they had not observed. In contrast, participants who did not sleep within 12 hours of watching the video (which they saw in the morning) showed no benefits when performing the observed sequence compared with one they had not observed.

The researchers conducted a follow-up experiment to rule out the possibility that the effects of sleep were due to watching the video in the evening instead of the morning: Participants who were tested immediately after observational learning without sleeping—either in the morning or in the evening—showed no benefit on performance. In this case, going to sleep soon after viewing the video was *necessary* in order to benefit from observational learning. If this effect generalizes to other instances of observational learning, coaches may want to consider hauling beds, hammocks, or cots to practices in which they demonstrate techniques to their players.

Observational Learning in Animals

Humans aren't the only creatures capable of learning through observing. A wide variety of species learn by observing. In one study, for example, pigeons watched other pigeons get reinforced for either pecking at the feeder or stepping on a bar. When placed in the box later, the pigeons tended to use whatever technique they had observed other pigeons using earlier (Zentall, Sutton, & Sherburne, 1996).

In an interesting series of studies, researchers showed that laboratory-raised rhesus monkeys that had never seen a snake would develop a fear of snakes simply by observing the fear reactions of other monkeys (Cook & Mineka, 1990; Mineka & Cook, 1988). In fact, the fear reactions of these lab-raised monkeys were so authentic and pronounced that they could function as models for still *other* lab-raised monkeys, creating a kind of observational learning "chain." These results also support our earlier discussion of how each species has evolved particular biological predispositions for specific behaviors. Virtually every rhesus monkey raised in the wild has a fear of snakes, which strongly suggests that such a fear is one of this species' predispositions. This research also helps to explain why some phobias that humans suffer from, such as a fear of heights (acrophobia) or enclosed spaces (claustrophobia), are so common, even in people who have never had unpleasant experiences in these contexts (Mineka & Ohman, 2002). The fears may emerge not from specific conditioning experiences but from observing and learning from the reactions of others.

One of the most important questions about observational learning in animals concerns whether monkeys and chimpanzees can learn to use tools by observing tool use in others, which we've already seen can be accomplished by young children. In one of the first controlled studies to examine this issue, chimpanzees observed a model (the experimenter) use a metal bar shaped like a T to pull items of food toward them (Tomasello et al., 1987). Compared with a group that did not observe any tool use, these chimpanzees showed more learning when later performing the task themselves. However, the researchers noted that the chimpanzees hardly ever used the tool in the exact same way that the model did. So, in a later experiment, they introduced a novel twist (Nagell, Olguin, & Tomasello, 1993). In one condition, a model used a rake in its normal position (with the teeth pointed to the ground) to capture a food reward, which was rather inefficient because the teeth were widely spaced and the food sometimes slipped between them. In a second condition, the model flipped over the rake, so that the teeth were pointed up and the flat edge of the rake touched the ground—a more effective procedure for capturing the food. Both groups who observed tool use performed better when trying to obtain the food themselves than did a control group who did not observe a model use the tool. However, the chimpanzees who observed the more efficient procedure did not use it any more often than did those who observed the less efficient procedure; the two groups performed identically. By contrast, 2-year old children exposed to the same conditions used the rake in the exact same way that each of the models did in the two observational learning conditions. The chimpanzees seemed only to be learning that the tool could be used to obtain food, whereas the children learned something specific about how to use the tool.

The chimpanzees in these studies had been raised by their mothers in the wild. In a related study, the researchers asked whether chimpanzees who had been raised in environments that also included human contact could learn to imitate the exact actions performed by a model (Tomasello, Savage-Rumbaugh, & Kruger, 1993). The answer was a resounding "yes": Chimpanzees raised in a more human-like environment showed more specific observational learning than did those who had been reared by their mothers, performing similarly to human children. This finding led Tomasello et al. (1993) to put forth what they termed the "enculturation hypothesis": being raised in a human culture has a profound effect on the cognitive abilities of chimpanzees, especially their ability to understand the intentions of others when performing tasks such as using tools, which in turn increases their observational learning capacities. Others have criticized the hypothesis (Bering, 2004), noting that there is relatively little evidence in support of it beyond the results of the Tomasello et al. (1993) study.

However, more recent research has found something similar in capuchin monkeys, who are known for their tool use in the wild, such as employing branches or stone hammers to crack open nuts (Boinski, Quatrone, & Swartz, 2000; Fragaszy et al., 2004) or using stones to dig up buried roots (Moura & Lee, 2004). Fredman and Whiten (2008) studied monkeys who had been reared in the wild by their mothers, or by human families in Israel as part of a project to train the monkeys to aid quadriplegics. A model demonstrated two ways of using a screwdriver to gain access to a food reward hidden in a box. Some monkeys observed the model poke through a hole in the center of the box, whereas others watched him pry open the lid at the rim of the box (see **FIGURE 7.16**). A control group did not observe any use of the tool. Both mother-reared and human-reared monkeys showed evidence of observational learning compared with the controls, but the human-reared monkeys carried out the exact action they had observed more often than the mother-reared monkeys.

While this evidence implies that there is a cultural influence on the cognitive processes that support observational learning, the researchers noted that the effects on observational learning could be attributed to any number of influences on the human-reared monkeys, including more experience with tools, more attention to a model's behavior, or as originally suggested by Tomasello et al. (1993), increased sensitivity to the intentions of others. Thus, more work is needed to understand the exact nature of those processes (Bering, 2004; Tomasello & Call, 2004).

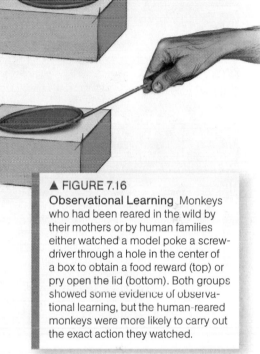

▲ FIGURE 7.16
Observational Learning Monkeys who had been reared in the wild by their mothers or by human families either watched a model poke a screwdriver through a hole in the center of a box to obtain a food reward (top) or pry open the lid (bottom). Both groups showed some evidence of observational learning, but the human-reared monkeys were more likely to carry out the exact action they watched.

Neural Elements of Observational Learning

Observational learning involves a neural component as well. As you read in Chapter 3, *mirror neurons* are a type of cell found in the brains of primates (including humans). Mirror neurons fire when an animal performs an action, such as when a monkey reaches for a food item. More importantly, however, mirror neurons also fire when an animal watches someone *else* perform the same specific task (Rizzolatti & Craighero, 2004). Although this "someone else" is usually a fellow member of the same species, some research suggests that mirror neurons in monkeys also fire when they observe humans performing an action (Fogassi et al., 2005). For example, monkeys' mirror neurons fired when they observed humans grasping for a piece of food, either to eat it or to place it in a container.

Mirror neurons, then, may play a critical role in the imitation of behavior as well as the prediction of future behavior (Rizzolatti, 2004). Mirror neurons are thought to be represented in specific subregions in the frontal and parietal lobes, and there is evidence that individual subregions respond most strongly to observing certain kinds of actions (see **FIGURE 7.17**). If appropriate neurons fire when another organism is seen performing an action, it could indicate an awareness of intentionality, or that the animal is anticipating a likely course of future actions. Although the exact functions of mirror neurons continue to be debated (Hickok, 2009), both of these elements—rote imitation of well-understood behaviors and an awareness of how behavior is likely to unfold—contribute to observational learning.

? What do mirror neurons do?

Studies of observational learning in healthy adults have shown that watching someone else perform a task engages some of the same brain regions that are activated when people actually perform the task themselves. Do you consider yourself a good dancer? Have you ever watched someone who is a good dancer—a friend or maybe a celebrity on *Dancing with the Stars*—in the hopes of improving your own dance floor moves? In a recent fMRI study, participants performed two tasks for several days prior to scanning: practicing dance sequences to unfamiliar techno-dance songs, and watching music videos containing other dance sequences accompanied by unfamiliar techno-dance songs (Cross et al., 2009). They were then scanned while viewing videos of sequences that they had previously danced or watched, as well as videos of untrained sequences.

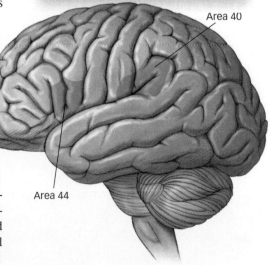

▼ FIGURE 7.17
Mirror Neuron System Regions in the frontal lobe (area 44) and parietal lobe (area 40) are thought to be part of the mirror neuron system in humans.

Area 40

Area 44

▲ Observing skilled dancers, such as Nicole Scherzinger and Derek Hough on *Dancing with the Stars*, engages many of the same brain regions as does actual dance practice, and can produce significant learning.

Analysis of the fMRI data revealed that in comparison with the untrained sequences, viewing the previously danced or watched sequences recruited a largely similar brain network, including regions considered to be part of the mirror-neuron system, as well as a couple of brain regions that showed more activity for previously danced than watched videos. The results of a surprise dancing test given to participants after the conclusion of scanning showed that performance was better on sequences previously watched than on the untrained sequences, demonstrating significant observational learning, but was best of all on the previously danced sequences (Cross et al., 2009). So, while watching *Dancing in the Stars* might indeed improve your dancing skills, practicing on the dance floor should help even more.

Related evidence indicates that observational learning of some motor skills relies on the motor cortex, which is known to be critical for motor learning. For example, when participants watch another individual engage in a task that involves making a complex reaching movement, significant observational learning occurs (Mattar & Gribble, 2005). To examine whether the observational learning depends on the motor cortex, researchers applied transcranial magnetic stimulation, or "TMS," to the motor cortex just after participants observed performance of the reaching movement (as you learned in Chapter 3, TMS results in a temporary disruption in the function of the brain region to which it is applied). Strikingly, applying TMS to the motor cortex greatly reduced the amount of observational learning, whereas applying TMS to a control region outside the motor cortex had no effect on observational learning (Brown, Wilson, & Gribble, 2009).

These findings indicate that some kinds of observational learning are grounded in brain regions that are essential for action. When one organism patterns its actions on another organism's behaviors, learning is speeded up and potentially dangerous errors—think of Margie, who won't burn her hand on the stove—are prevented.

IN SUMMARY

○ Observational learning is based on cognitive mechanisms such as attention, perception, memory, or reasoning. But observational learning also has roots in evolutionary biology and for the most basic of reasons: It has survival value. Observational learning is an important process by which species gather information about the world around them.

○ Observational learning has important social and cultural consequences, as it appears to be well suited for transmission of novel behaviors across individuals. Chimpanzees and monkeys can benefit from observational learning, especially those reared in settings that include humans.

○ The mirror-neuron system becomes active during observational learning, and many of the same brain regions are active during observation and performance of a skill. Observational learning is closely tied to parts of the brain that are involved in action.

Implicit Learning: Under the Wires

It's safe to assume that people are sensitive to the patterns of events that occur in the world around them. Most people don't stumble through life thoroughly unaware of what's going on. Okay, maybe your roommate does. But people usually are attuned to linguistic, social, emotional, or sensorimotor events in the world around them so much so that they gradually build up internal representations of those patterns that were acquired without explicit awareness. This process is often called **implicit learning**, or *learning that takes place largely independent of awareness of both the process and the products of information acquisition*. Because it occurs without awareness, implicit learning is knowledge that sneaks in "under the wires." As an example we've already seen, delay conditioning does not require awareness of the contingency between the CS and US, whereas trace conditioning does.

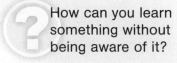

How can you learn something without being aware of it?

Some forms of learning start out explicitly but become more implicit over time. When you first learned to drive a car, for example, you probably devoted a lot of attention to the many movements and sequences that needed to be carried out simultaneously ("step lightly on the accelerator while you push the turn indicator and look in the rearview mirror while you turn the steering wheel"). That complex interplay of motions is now probably quite effortless and automatic for you. Explicit learning has become implicit over time. These distinctions in learning might remind you of similar distinctions in memory and for good reason. In Chapter 6, you read about the differences between *implicit* and *explicit* memories. Do im-

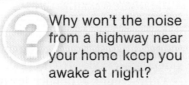
How are learning and memory linked?

plicit and explicit learning mirror implicit and explicit memory? It's not that simple, but it is true that learning and memory are inextricably linked. Learning produces memories, and conversely, the existence of memories implies that knowledge was acquired, that experience was registered and recorded in the brain, or that learning has taken place.

In this section, we'll consider evidence showing that some basic learning processes in humans do not require an awareness on the part of the learner.

Habituation: A Simple Case of Implicit Learning

One very basic form of implicit learning is known as **habituation**, *a general process in which repeated or prolonged exposure to a stimulus results in a gradual reduction in responding*. If you've ever lived under the flight path of your local airport, near railroad tracks, or by a busy highway, you've probably noticed the deafening roar as a Boeing 737 made its way toward the landing strip, the clatter of a train speeding down the track, or the sound of traffic when you first moved in. You probably also noticed that, after a while, the roar wasn't quite so deafening anymore and that eventually you ignored the sounds of the planes, trains, or automobiles in your vicinity. This welcome reduction in responding reflects the operation of habituation.

Habituation is considered a form of implicit learning in part because it occurs even in the simplest organisms that do not have the brain structures necessary for explicit learning, such as the hippocampus (Eichenbaum, 2008; Squire & Kandel, 1999). For example, in Chapter 6 you learned about the tiny sea slug *Aplysia*, studied in detail by Nobel Prize winner Eric Kandel (Kandel, 2006). Kandel and his colleagues showed clearly that *Aplysia* exhibits habituation. In rats, which can

▲ Living near a busy highway can be unpleasant. Most people who live near major highways become habituated to the sound of traffic.

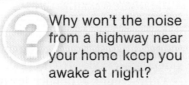
Why won't the noise from a highway near your home keep you awake at night?

exhibit both explicit and implicit learning, habituation is unaffected by lesions to the hippocampus, which impair explicit learning (Lee, Hunsaker, & Kesner, 2005).

Even in human beings, habituation can occur in the absence of explicit learning or memory. Consider a study in which two amnesic patients exhibited a form of implicit learning related to habituation in an experiment that explored how appetite changes as a function of experience (Higgs et al., 2008). Fifteen minutes after eating sandwiches to the point that they felt full, both amnesic patients and healthy control subjects indicated less desire for, and liking of, those sandwiches than they had prior to eating them. They also expressed less desire to eat the sandwiches than other foods that they had sampled lightly 15 minutes earlier. But the amnesic patients had no explicit memory that they had eaten any sandwiches 15 minutes earlier! Clearly, their reduction in liking and desire was based on implicit learning.

Habituation is an extremely simple form of learning. Although an experience results in a change in the state of the learner, this kind of change usually doesn't last very long. In most cases of habituation, a person will exhibit the original reaction if enough time has gone by. If you lived near an airport and had habituated to the sounds of the jets, when you return home from a 2-week vacation the roar of the jets will probably be just as loud as ever. A week after eating sandwiches, amnesics and controls would presumably revert to rating them as they had prior to eating. However, implicit learning can last for long periods of time and can occur for much more complex behaviors.

implicit learning Learning that takes place largely without awareness of the process or the products of information acquisition.

habituation A general process in which repeated or prolonged exposure to a stimulus results in a gradual reduction in response.

Cognitive Approaches to Implicit Learning

Interest in implicit learning among psychologists was sparked when researchers began to investigate how children learned language and social conduct (Reber, 1967). Most children, by the time they are 6 or 7 years old, are linguistically and socially fairly sophisticated. Yet most children reach this state with very little explicit awareness that they have learned something and with equally little awareness of what it was they have actually learned. As an example, although children are often given explicit rules of social conduct ("Don't chew with your mouth open"), they learn how to behave in a civilized way through experience. They're probably not aware of when or how they learned a particular course of action and may not even be able to state the general principle underlying their behavior. Yet most kids have learned not to eat with their feet, to listen when they are spoken to, and not to kick the dog.

To investigate implicit learning in the laboratory, early studies showed research participants 15 or 20 letter strings and asked them to memorize them. The letter strings, which at first glance look like nonsense syllables, were actually formed using a complex set of rules called an *artificial grammar* (see **FIGURE 7.18**). Participants were not told anything about the rules, but with experience, they gradually developed a vague, intuitive sense of the "correctness" of particular letter groupings. These letter groups became familiar to the participants, and they processed these letter groupings more rapidly and efficiently than the "incorrect" letter groupings (Reber, 1967, 1996).

Take a look at the letter strings shown in Figure 7.18. The ones on the left are "correct" and follow the rules of the artificial grammar; the ones on the right all violated the rules. The differences are pretty subtle, and if you haven't been through the learning phase of the experiment, both sets look a lot alike. In fact, each nongrammatical string only has a single letter violation. Research participants are asked to classify new letter strings based on whether they follow the rules of the grammar. People turn out to be quite good at this task (usually they get between 60 and 70% correct), but they are unable to provide much in the way of explicit awareness of the rules and regularities that they are using. The experience is like when you come across a sentence with a grammatical error—you are immediately aware that something is wrong and you can certainly make the sentence grammatical. But unless you are a trained linguist, you'll probably find it difficult to articulate which rules of English grammar were violated or which rules you used to repair the sentence.

Why are tasks learned implicitly difficult to explain to others?

Other studies of implicit learning have used a *serial reaction time* task (Nissen & Bullemer, 1987). Here research participants are presented with five small boxes on a computer screen. Each box lights up briefly, and when it does, the person is asked to press the button that is just underneath that box as quickly as possible. As with the artificial grammar task, the sequence of lights appears to be random, but in fact it follows a pattern. Research participants eventually get faster with practice as they learn to anticipate which box is most likely to light up next. But, if asked, they are generally unaware that there is a pattern to the lights.

Implicit learning has some characteristics that distinguish it from explicit learning. For example, when asked to carry out implicit tasks, people differ relatively little from one another, but on explicit tasks, such as conscious problem solving, they show large individual-to-individual differences (Reber, Walkenfeld, & Hernstadt, 1991). Implicit learning also seems to be unrelated to IQ: People with high scores on standard intelligence tests are no better at implicit-learning tasks, on average, than those whose scores are more modest (Reber & Allen, 2000). Implicit learning changes little across the life span. Researchers discovered well-developed implicit learning of complex, rule-governed auditory patterns in 8-month-old infants (Saffran, Aslin, & Newport, 1996). Infants heard streams of speech that contained experimenter-defined nonsense words. For example, the infants might hear a sequence such as "bidakupadotigolabubidaku," which contains the nonsense word *bida*. The infants weren't given any explicit clues

▼ FIGURE 7.18

Artificial Grammar and Implicit Learning These are examples of letter strings formed by an artificial grammar. Research participants are exposed to the rules of the grammar and are later tested on new letter strings. Participants show reliable accuracy at distinguishing the valid, grammatical strings from the invalid, nongrammatical strings even though they usually can't explicitly state the rule they are following when making such judgments. Using an artificial grammar is one way of studying implicit learning (Reber, 1996).

Grammatical Strings	Nongrammatical Strings
VXJJ	VXTJJ
XXVT	XVTVVJ
VJTVXJ	VJTTVTV
VJTVTV	VJTXXVJ
XXXXVX	XXXVTJJ

as to which sounds were "words" and which were not, but after several repetitions, the infants showed signs that they had learned the novel words. Infants tend to prefer novel information, and they spent more time listening to novel nonsense words that had not been presented earlier than to the nonsense words such as *bida* that had been presented. Remarkably, the infants in this study were as good at learning these sequences as college students. At the other end of the life span, researchers have found that implicit-learning abilities extend well into old age and that they decline more slowly than explicit-learning abilities (Howard & Howard, 1997).

Implicit learning is remarkably resistant to various disorders that are known to affect explicit learning. A group of patients suffering from various psychoses were so severely impaired that they could not solve simple problems that college students had little difficulty with. Yet these patients were able to solve an artificial grammar learning task about as well as college students (Abrams & Reber, 1988). Other studies have found that profoundly amnesic patients not only show normal implicit memories but also display virtually normal implicit learning of artificial grammar (Knowlton, Ramus, & Squire, 1992). In fact, these patients made accurate judgments about novel letter strings even though they had essentially no explicit memory of having been in the learning phase of the experiment! In contrast, several studies have shown that dyslexic children, who fail to acquire reading skills despite normal intelligence and good educational opportunities, exhibit deficits in implicit learning of artificial grammars (Pavlidou, Williams, & Kelly, 2009) and motor and spatial sequences on the serial reaction time task (Bennett et al., 2008; Orban, Lungu, & Doyon, 2008; Stoodley et al., 2008). These findings suggest that problems with implicit learning play an important role in developmental dyslexia and need to be taken into account when developing remedial programs (Stoodley et al., 2008).

▲ Implicit learning, which is involved in acquiring and retaining the skills needed to ride a bicycle, tends to be less affected by age than explicit learning.

Implicit and Explicit Learning Use Distinct Neural Pathways

The fact that patients suffering amnesia show intact implicit learning strongly suggests that the brain structures that underlie implicit leaning are distinct from those that underlie explicit learning. As we learned in Chapter 6, amnesic patients are characterized by lesions to the hippocampus and nearby structures in the medial temporal lobe; accordingly, these regions are not necessary for implicit learning (Bayley, Frascino, & Squire, 2005a). What's more, it appears that distinct regions of the brain may be activated depending on how people approach a task.

For example, in one study, participants saw a series of dot patterns, each of which looked like an array of stars in the night sky (Reber et al., 2003). Actually, all the stimuli were constructed to conform to an underlying prototypical dot pattern. The dots, however, varied so much that it was virtually impossible for a viewer to guess that they all had this common structure. Before the experiment began, half of the participants were told about the existence of the prototype; in other words, they were given instructions that encouraged explicit processing. The others were given standard implicit-learning instructions: They were told nothing other than to attend to the dot patterns.

The participants were then scanned as they made decisions about new dot patterns, attempting to categorize them into those that conformed to the prototype and those that did not. Interestingly,

? What technology shows that implicit and explicit learning are associated with separate structures of the brain?

both groups performed equally well on this task, correctly classifying about 65% of the new dot patterns. However, the brain scans revealed that the two groups were making these decisions using very different parts of their brains (see **FIGURE 7.19** on the next page). Participants who were given the explicit instructions showed *increased* brain activity in the prefrontal

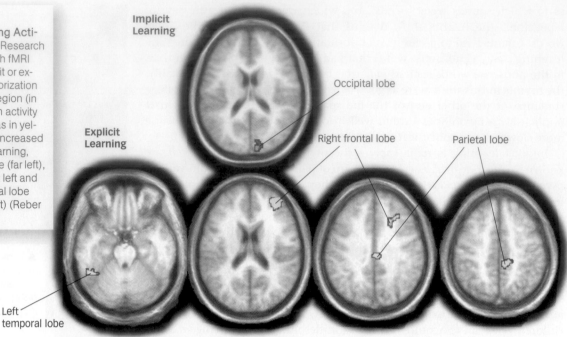

▶ FIGURE 7.19

Implicit and Explicit Learning Activate Different Brain Areas Research participants were scanned with fMRI while engaged in either implicit or explicit learning about the categorization of dot patterns. The occipital region (in blue) showed decreased brain activity after implicit learning. The areas in yellow, orange, and red showed increased brain activity during explicit learning, including the left temporal lobe (far left), right frontal lobe (second from left and second from right), and parietal lobe (second from right and far right) (Reber et al., 2003).

cortex, parietal cortex, hippocampus, and a variety of other areas known to be associated with the processing of explicit memories. Those given the implicit instructions showed *decreased* brain activation primarily in the occipital region, which is involved in visual processing. This finding suggests that participants recruited distinct brain structures in different ways depending on whether they were approaching the task using explicit or implicit learning.

Other studies have begun to pinpoint the brain regions that are involved in two of the most commonly used implicit-learning tasks, artificial grammar learning and sequence learning on the serial reaction time task. Several fMRI studies have shown that Broca's area—which, as you learned in Chapter 3, plays a key role in language production—is turned on during artificial grammar learning (Forkstam et al., 2006; Petersson, Forkstam, & Ingvar, 2004). Further, activating Broca's area by applying electrical stimulation to the nearby scalp enhances implicit learning of artificial grammar, most likely by facilitating acquisition of grammatical rules (De Vries et al., in press). In contrast, the motor cortex appears critical for sequence learning on the serial reaction time task. When the motor cortex was temporarily disabled by the application of a recently developed type of TMS that lasts for a long time, so that participants can perform the task without having TMS constantly applied while they are doing so, sequence learning was abolished (Wilkinson et al., 2010).

IN SUMMARY

○ Implicit learning is a process that detects, learns, and stores patterns without the application of explicit awareness on the part of the learner.

○ Simple behaviors such as habituation can reflect implicit learning, but complex behaviors, such as language use or socialization, can also be learned through an implicit process.

○ Tasks that have been used to document implicit learning include artificial grammar and serial reaction time tasks.

○ Implicit and explicit learning differ from each other in a number of ways: There are fewer individual differences in implicit than explicit learning, psychotic and amnesic patients with explicit-learning problems can exhibit intact implicit learning, and neuroimaging studies indicate that implicit and explicit learning recruit distinct brain structures, sometimes in different ways.

WhereDoYouStand?

Learning for Rewards or for Its Own Sake?

The principles of operant conditioning and the merits of reinforcement have more than found their way into mainstream culture. The least psychology-savvy parent intuitively understands that rewarding a child's good behavior should make that behavior more likely to occur in the future; the "law of effect" may mean nothing to this parent, but the principle and the outcome are readily appreciated nonetheless. And what parent wouldn't want the best for her or his child? If reward shapes good behavior, then more reward must be the pathway to exemplary behavior, often in the form of good grades, high test scores, and overall clean living. So, bring on the rewards!

Maybe, maybe not. As you learned earlier in this chapter, the *overjustification effect* predicts that sometimes too much external reinforcement for performing an intrinsically rewarding task can undermine future performance. Rewarding a child for getting good grades or high test scores might backfire: The child may come to see the behavior as directed toward the attainment of rewards rather than for its own satisfying outcomes. In short, learning should be fun for its own sake, not because new toys, new clothes, or cash are riding on a set of straight A's.

Many parents seem to think differently. You probably have friends whose parents shower them with gifts whenever a report card shows improvement; in fact, you may have experienced this yourself. Nobody objects to a little recognition now and then, and it's nice to know that others appreciate your hard work. In fact, if you'd like to know the many, many others who'll appreciate your hard work, pay a visit to www.rewardsforgrades.com. It's a website that lists organizations that will give students external reinforcements for good grades, high test scores, perfect school attendance, and other behaviors that students are usually expected to produce just because they're students. Krispy Kreme offers a free doughnut for each A, Blockbuster gives free kids' movie rentals, Chick-fil-A rewards honor roll membership and perfect attendance with free kids' meals, and Limited Too offers a $5 discount on merchandise if you present a report card "with passing grades" (which, in many school districts, might mean all D's).

Before you get too excited by visions of a "grades for junk food" scam, you should know that there are often age limits on these offers. However, if you're a precocious fourth grader reading this textbook, feel free to cash in on the goods. Or if you happen to be enrolled at Wichita State University, you already might be familiar with the Cash for Grades initiative (www.cashforgrades.com). The proposal is that an 8%-per-credit-hour increase to student fees would be used to then reward good student performance: $624 to a student with a 3.5 GPA at the end of a semester, $804 for straight A's.

Where do you stand on this issue? Is this much ado about nothing or too much of a good thing? Some proponents of rewarding good academic performance argue that it mirrors the real world that, presumably, academic performance is preparing students to enter. After all, in most jobs, better performance is reinforced with better salaries, so why not model that in the school system? On the other hand, shouldn't the search for knowledge be reward enough? Is the subtle shift away from wanting to learn for its own sake to wanting to learn for a doughnut harmful in the long run?

Chapter Review

KEY CONCEPT QUIZ

1. In classical conditioning, a conditioned stimulus is paired with an unconditioned stimulus to produce
   a. a neutral stimulus.
   b. a conditioned response.
   c. an unconditioned response.
   d. another conditioned stimulus.

2. What occurs when a conditioned stimulus is no longer paired with an unconditioned stimulus?
   a. generalization
   b. spontaneous recovery
   c. extinction
   d. acquisition

3. What did Watson and Rayner seek to demonstrate about behaviorism through the Little Albert experiment?
   a. Conditioning involves a degree of cognition.
   b. Classical conditioning has an evolutionary component.
   c. Behaviorism alone cannot explain human behavior.
   d. Even sophisticated behaviors such as emotion are subject to classical conditioning.

4. Which part of the brain is involved in the classical conditioning of fear?
   a. the amygdala   c. the hippocampus
   b. the cerebellum   d. the hypothalamus

5. After having a bad experience with a particular type of food, people can develop a lifelong aversion to the food. This suggests that conditioning has a(n) _____ aspect.
   a. cognitive   c. neural
   b. evolutionary   d. behavioral

6. Which of the following is NOT an accurate statement concerning operant conditioning?
   a. Actions and outcomes are critical to operant conditioning.
   b. Operant conditioning involves the reinforcement of behavior.
   c. Complex behaviors cannot be accounted for by operant conditioning.
   d. Operant conditioning has associative mechanisms with roots in evolutionary behavior.

7. Which of the following mechanisms have no role in Skinner's approach to behavior?
   a. cognitive
   b. neural
   c. evolutionary
   d. all of the above

8. Latent learning provides evidence for a cognitive element in operant conditioning because
   a. it occurs without any obvious reinforcement.
   b. it requires both positive and negative reinforcement.
   c. it points toward the operation of a neural reward center.
   d. it depends on a stimulus-response relationship.

9. Activity of neurons in the _____ contributes to the process of reinforcement.
   a. hippocampus
   b. pituitary gland
   c. medial forebrain bundle
   d. parietal lobe

10. Which of the following mechanisms does NOT help form the basis of observational learning?
    a. attention
    b. perception
    c. punishment
    d. memory

11. Neural research indicates that observational learning is closely tied to brain areas that are involved in
    a. memory.
    b. vision.
    c. action.
    d. emotion.

12. What kind of learning takes place largely independent of awareness of both the process and the products of information acquisition?
    a. latent learning
    b. implicit learning
    c. observational learning
    d. conscious learning

13. The process in which repeated or prolonged exposure to a stimulus results in a gradual reduction in responding is called
    a. habituation.
    b. explicit learning.
    c. serial reaction time.
    d. delay conditioning.

14. Which of the following statements about implicit learning is inaccurate?
    a. Some forms of learning start out explicitly but become more implicit over time.
    b. Implicit learning occurs even in the simplest organisms.
    c. People with high scores on intelligence tests are more adept at implicit-learning tasks.
    d. Children learn language and social conduct largely through implicit learning.

15. Responding to implicit instructions results in decreased brain activation in which part of the brain?
    a. the hippocampus
    b. the parietal cortex
    c. the prefrontal cortex
    d. the occipital region

KEY TERMS

learning (p. 264)
classical conditioning (p. 265)
unconditioned stimulus (US) (p. 265)
unconditioned response (UR) (p. 265)
conditioned stimulus (CS) (p. 265)
conditioned response (CR) (p. 265)
acquisition (p. 266)

second-order conditioning (p. 268)
extinction (p. 268)
spontaneous recovery (p. 269)
generalization (p. 269)
discrimination (p. 269)
biological preparedness (p. 275)
operant conditioning (p. 277)
law of effect (p. 277)
operant behavior (p. 278)
reinforcer (p. 278)

punisher (p. 278)
overjustification effect (p. 280)
fixed interval schedule (FI) (p. 282)
variable interval schedule (VI) (p. 282)
fixed ratio schedule (FR) (p. 283)
variable ratio schedule (VR) (p. 283)
intermittent reinforcement (p. 283)

intermittent-reinforcement effect (p. 284)
shaping (p. 284)
latent learning (p. 287)
cognitive map (p. 288)
observational learning (p. 293)
diffusion chain (p. 295)
implicit learning (p. 298)
habituation (p. 299)

CRITICAL THINKING QUESTIONS

1. Little Albert was exposed to the sight of a rat paired with a distressing loud noise; with repeated pairings of the rat and the noise, he began to show a CR to the rat—crying and trembling.
   Many people break into a cold sweat at the mere sound of a dentist's drill. How might this reaction be explained as a conditioned emotional response? [Hint: Assuming that human babies aren't born with a natural fear of drill sounds, then the cold sweat is a learned response (CR). What are the CS and US?]

2. In operant conditioning, a reinforcer is a stimulus or event that increases the likelihood of the behavior that led to it, and a punisher is a stimulus or event that decreases the likelihood of the behavior that led to it.

   Suppose you are the mayor of a suburban town and you want to institute some new policies to decrease the number of drivers who speed on residential streets. How might you use punishment to decrease the behavior you desire (speeding)? How might you use reinforcement to increase the behavior you desire (safe driving)? Based on the principles of operant conditioning you read about in this section, which approach do you think might be most fruitful?

3. In fixed ratio (FR) schedules, reinforcement is delivered after a specific number of responses have been made. In variable ratio (VR) schedules, reinforcement is delivered after an average number of responses on average. Both FR and VR are examples

of intermittent reinforcement schedules, because only some responses are followed by reinforcement, and they are both more resistant to extinction than continuous reinforcement schedules, in which a reinforcement is delivered after every response.

Imagine you own an insurance company and you want to encourage your salespeople to sell as much merchandise as possible. You decide to give them bonuses, based on the number of items sold. How might you set up a system of bonuses using an FR schedule? Using a VR schedule? Which system do you think would encourage your salespeople to work harder, in terms of making more sales?

4. Observational learning takes place when one individual watches and learns from the actions of others. By contrast, in classical conditioning, learning takes place when an individual directly experiences the consequences (US) associated with a stimulus or event (CS).

Monkeys can be classically conditioned to fear objects such as snakes or flowers if those objects are paired with an aversive US, such as an electric shock. Monkeys can also learn to fear snakes through observational learning if they see another monkey reacting with fear to the sight of a snake. But monkeys cannot be trained to fear flowers through observational learning—no matter how many times they watch another monkey who has been conditioned to fear the same flower. How does the principle of biological preparedness account for this finding?

5. In habituation, repeated or prolonged exposure to a stimulus that initially evoked a response results in a gradual reduction of that response.

How might psychologists use the concept of habituation to explain the fact that today's action movies tend to show much more graphic violence than movies of the 1980s, which in turn tended to show more graphic violence than movies of the 1950s?

RECOMMENDED READINGS

Animal Training at SeaWorld. http://www.seaworld.org/animalinfo/info-books/training/how animals learn.htm.

This website offers a glimpse at the operant conditioning techniques used to train Shamu, porpoises, and the occasional squid or two. There are solid, research-based discussions of the principles of reinforcement, observational learning, and other concepts in this chapter.

Bandura, A. (1986). *Social foundations of thought and action: A social cognitive theory*. Englewood Cliffs, NJ: Prentice Hall.

This book is a classic statement of Albert Bandura's ideas on the origins of human functioning. Drawing from the beginnings of observational learning, Bandura sketches an elegant and comprehensive theory of how behavior develops and the determinants that shape it.

Buckley, K. W. (1989). *Mechanical man: John Broadus Watson and the beginnings of behaviorism*. New York: Guilford Press.

There are many biographies of Watson available; Kerry Buckley's is one of the best. Buckley is a historian specializing in the history of psychology, and he has published numerous scholarly works on Watson's life and ideas.

Rutherford, A. (2009). *Beyond the box: B.F. Skinner's technology of behavior from laboratory to life, 1950s–1970s*. Toronto: University of Toronto Press.

Rutherford, a historian of psychology, has written an engaging account of attempts by Skinner and his followers to develop and apply a behavior technology based on operant principles. She considers a variety of contexts where these technologies were used, including prisons and psychiatric wards, as well as Skinner's attempts to use operant principles to raise his own children.

Skinner, B. F. (1971). *Beyond freedom and dignity*. New York: Bantam Books.

This book, reprinted by Hackett Publishing in 2002, is largely considered Skinner's definitive statement on humankind and its behavior. Skinner argues that most of society's problems can be better addressed by reshaping the environment following the principles of operant conditioning. Outmoded concepts such as "freedom" and "human dignity" should be abandoned in favor of developing more effective cultural practices. A controversial book when it first appeared, it remains so today.

Todes, D. P. (2000). *Pavlov: Exploring the animal machine*. New York: Oxford University Press.

This overview of Pavlov's life and work is part of the Oxford *Portraits in Science* series, a set of titles that provides easy access to information about key scientists in all disciplines. This title should provide a bit more background about Pavlov's discoveries and the events in his life that helped shape his work.

ANSWERS TO KEY CONCEPT QUIZ

1. b; 2. c; 3. d; 4. a; 5. b; 6. c; 7. d; 8. a; 9. c; 10. c; 11. c; 12. b; 13. a; 14. c; 15. d.

Need more help? Additional resources are located at the book's free companion Web site at: **www.worthpublishers.com/schacter**

8

Emotion and Motivation

eonardo is 5 years old and cute as a button. He can do many of the things that other 5-year-olds can do—solve puzzles, build towers of blocks, and play guessing games with grown-ups. But unlike other 5 year olds, Leonardo has never been proud of his abilities, angry at his mother, or bored with his lessons. That's because Leonardo has a condition that makes him unable to experience emotions of any kind. He has never felt joy or sorrow, delight or despair, shame, envy, annoyance, excitement, gratitude, or regret. He has never laughed or cried.

Leonardo's condition has had a profound impact on his life. For example, because he doesn't experience emotions, he isn't motivated to do things that bring most children pleasure, such as eating cookies or playing hide-and-seek or watching Saturday morning cartoons. And because he doesn't feel, he doesn't have any intuitions about what others are feeling, which can make social interaction a challenge. His mother has spent years teaching him how to make the facial expressions that indicate emotions such as surprise and sadness, and how to detect those facial expressions in others. Leonardo now knows that he should smile when someone says something nice to him and that he should raise his eyebrow once in a while to show interest in what people are saying. Leonardo is a quick learner, and he's gotten so good at this that when strangers interact with him they find it hard to believe that deep down inside he is feeling nothing at all.

So when Leonardo's mother smiles at him, he always smiles back. And yet, she is keenly aware that Leonardo is merely making the faces he was taught to make and that he doesn't really love her.

▲ **Leonardo** is a typical 5-year-old in some ways—but not all.

ALEX CAO/JUPITERIMAGES

But that's okay. Although Leonardo cannot return her affection, Dr. Cynthia Breazeal still considers him one of the greatest robots she's ever designed (Breazeal, 2009).

► Leonardo and his "mom," MIT Professor Cynthia Breazeal.

YES, LEONARDO IS A MACHINE. HE CAN SEE AND HEAR, he can remember and reason. But despite his adorable smile and knowing wink, he can't feel a thing, and that makes him infinitely different than us. Our ability to love and to hate, to be amused and annoyed, to feel elated and devastated, is an essential element of our humanity, and a person who could not feel these things would seem a lot like a robot to the rest of us. But what exactly are these things we call emotions and why are they so essential? In this chapter we will explore these questions. We'll start by discussing the nature of emotions and seeing how they relate to the states of our bodies and our brains. Next we'll see how people express their emotions, and how they use those expressions to communicate with each other. Finally, we'll examine the essential role that emotions play in motivation—how they inform us, and how they compel us do everything from making war to making love.

Emotional Experience: The Feeling Machine

"I never realized they had feelings."

Leonardo doesn't know what love feels likes and there's no way to teach him, because trying to describe the feeling of love to someone who has never experienced it is a bit like trying to describe the color green to someone who was born blind. We could tell Leonardo what causes the feeling ("It happens whenever I see Marilynn") and we could tell him about its consequences ("I breathe hard and say goofy stuff"), but in the end these descriptions would miss the point because the essential feature of love—like the essential feature of all emotions—is the *experience*. It *feels* like something to love, and what it feels like is love's defining attribute.

What Is Emotion?

How can we study something whose defining attribute defies description? Psychologists have developed a clever technique that capitalizes on the fact that although people can't always say what an emotional experience feels like ("Love is ... um ... uh ..."),

◀ It is almost impossible not to feel something when you look at this photograph, and it is almost impossible to say exactly what you are feeling.

they usually can say how similar one experience is to another ("Love is more like happiness than like anger"). By asking people to rate the similarity of dozens of emotional experiences, psychologists have been able to use a technique known as *multidimensional scaling* to create a map of those experiences. The mathematics behind this technique is complex, but the logic is simple. If you drew up a list of the distances between a half-dozen U.S. cities, handed the list to a friend, and challenged her to turn those distances into a map, your friend would have to draw a map of the United States (see **FIGURE 8.1**). Why? Because there is no other map that allows every city to appear at precisely the right distance from every other.

The same technique can be used to generate a map of the emotional landscape. If you listed the similarity of a large number of emotional experiences (assigning smaller "distances" to those that feel similar and larger "distances" to those that feel dissimilar) and then challenged a friend to incorporate them into a map, your friend would be forced to draw a map like the one shown in **FIGURE 8.2** on

? Why do psychologists use *multidimensional scaling*?

the next page. This is the unique map that allows every emotional experience to be precisely the right "distance" from every other. What good is this map? As it turns out, maps don't just show how close things are to each other: They also reveal the *dimensions* on which those things vary. For example, the map in Figure 8.2 reveals that emotional experiences differ on two dimensions called *valence* (how positive or negative the experience is) and *arousal* (how active or passive the experience is). Research shows that all emotional experiences can be described by their unique coordinates on this two-dimensional map (Russell, 1980; Watson & Tellegen, 1985).

▼ FIGURE 8.1
From Distances to Maps Knowing the distances between things—like cities, for example—allows us to draw a map that reveals the dimensions on which they vary.

	Chicago	LA	SF	Omaha	Phoenix	Boston
Chicago	0	1749	1863	433	1447	856
LA	1749	0	344	1318	367	2605
SF	1863	344	0	1432	658	2708
Omaha	433	1318	1432	0	1029	1288
Phoenix	1447	367	658	1029	0	2290
Boston	856	2605	2708	1288	2299	0

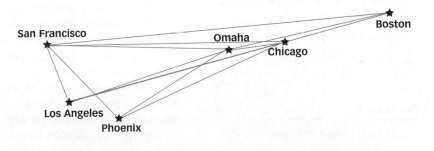

AP PHOTO/STEPHEN MORTON

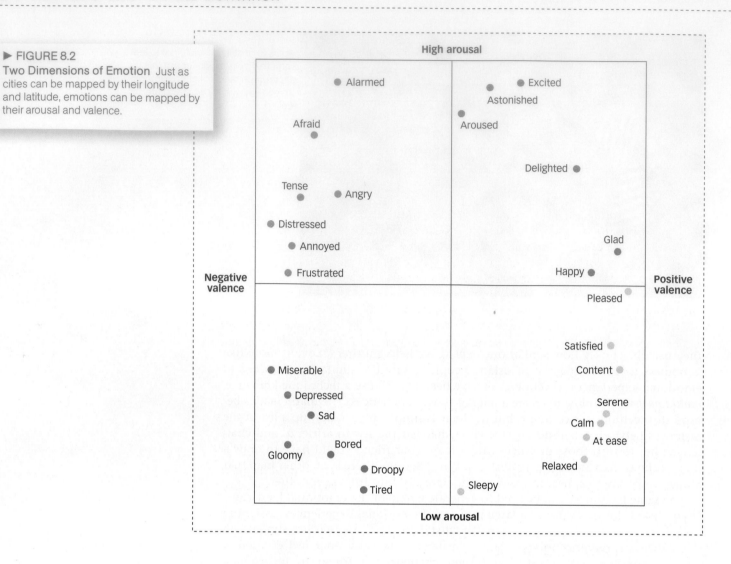

This map of emotional experience suggests that any definition of emotion must include two things: first, the fact that emotional experiences are always good or bad, and second, the fact that these experiences are associated with characteristic levels of bodily arousal. As such, **emotion** can be defined as *a positive or negative experience that is associated with a particular pattern of physiological activity*. As you are about to see, the first step in understanding emotion involves understanding how experience and physiological activity are related.

The Emotional Body

You probably think that if you walked into your kitchen right now and saw a bear nosing through the cupboards, you would feel fear, your heart would start to pound, and the muscles in your legs would prepare you for running. Presumably away. But in the late 19th century, William James suggested that the events that produce an emotion might actually happen in the opposite order: First you see the bear, then your heart starts pounding and your leg muscles contract, and *then* you experience fear, which is nothing more or less than your experience of your physiological response. As James (1884) wrote, "Bodily changes follow directly the perception of the exciting fact. . . . And feeling of the same changes as they occur *is* the emotion" (pp. 189–190). For James, each unique emotional experience was the result of a unique pattern of physiological responses, and he suggested that without all the heart pounding and muscle clenching, there would be no experience of emotion at all. Psychologist Carl Lange

emotion A positive or negative experience that is associated with a particular pattern of physiological activity.

James-Lange theory A theory which asserts that stimuli trigger activity in the autonomic nervous system, which in turn produces an emotional experience in the brain.

Cannon-Bard theory A theory which asserts that a stimulus simultaneously triggers activity in the autonomic nervous system and emotional experience in the brain.

two-factor theory A theory which asserts that emotions are inferences about the causes of physiological arousal.

suggested something similar at about the same time; thus this idea is now known as the **James-Lange theory** of emotion, which asserts that *stimuli trigger activity in the autonomic nervous system, which in turn produces an emotional experience in the brain*. According to this theory, emotional experience is the consequence—and not the cause—of our physiological reactions to objects and events in the world.

But James's former student, Walter Cannon, disagreed, and together with *his* student, Philip Bard, Cannon proposed an alternative to James's theory. The **Cannon-Bard theory** of emotion suggested that *a stimulus simultaneously triggers activity in the autonomic nervous system and emotional experience in the brain* (Bard, 1934; Cannon, 1927). Canon favored his own theory over the James-Lange theory for several reasons. First, the autonomic nervous system reacts too slowly to account for the rapid onset of emotional experience. For example, a blush is an autonomic response to embarrassment that takes 15 to 30 seconds to occur, and yet one can feel embarrassed long before that, so how could the blush be the cause of the feeling? Second, people often have difficulty accurately detecting changes in their own autonomic activity, such as their heart rates. If people cannot detect increases in their heart rates, then how can they experience those increases as an emotion? Third, if nonemotional stimuli—such as temperature—can cause the same pattern of autonomic activity that emotional stimuli do, then why don't people feel afraid when they get a fever? Finally, Cannon argued that there simply weren't enough unique patterns of autonomic activity to account for all the unique emotional experiences people have. If many different emotional experiences are associated with the same pattern of autonomic activity, then how could that pattern of activity be the sole determinant of the emotional experience?

These are all good questions, and about 30 years after Cannon asked them, psychologists Stanley Schachter and Jerome Singer supplied some answers (Schachter & Singer, 1962). James and Lange were right, they claimed, to equate emotion with the perception of one's bodily reactions. But Cannon and Bard were right, they claimed, to note that there are not nearly enough distinct bodily reactions to account for the wide variety of emotions that human beings can experience. Whereas James and Lange had suggested that different emotions are *different experiences* of *different patterns* of bodily activity, Schachter and Singer claimed that different emotions are merely *different interpretations* of *a single pattern* of bodily activity, which they called "undifferentiated physiological arousal" (see **FIGURE 8.3**).

Schachter and Singer's **two-factor theory** of emotion claimed that *emotions are inferences about the causes of physiological arousal*. When you see a bear in your kitchen, your heart begins to pound. Your brain quickly scans the environment, looking for a reasonable explanation for all that pounding, and notices, of all things, a bear. Having noticed both a bear and a pounding heart, your brain then

▲ England's Prince William blushes with embarrassment as he arrives at his hotel and finds a throng of adoring fans. Because the experience of embarrassment precedes blushing by up to 30 seconds, it is unlikely that blushing is the cause of the experience.

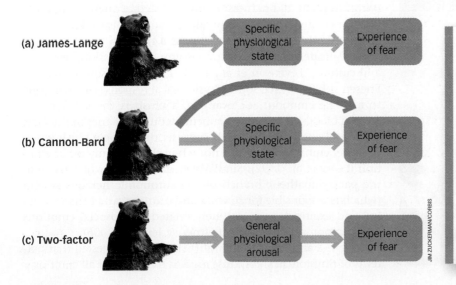

(a) James-Lange → Specific physiological state → Experience of fear

(b) Cannon-Bard → Specific physiological state → Experience of fear

(c) Two-factor → General physiological arousal → Experience of fear

◄ FIGURE 8.3
Classic Theories of Emotion Classic theories make different claims about the origins of emotion. (a) The James-Lange theory suggests that stimuli trigger specific physiological states, which are then experienced as emotions. (b) The Cannon-Bard theory suggests that stimuli trigger both specific physiological states and emotional experiences independently. (c) The two-factor theory suggests that stimuli trigger general physiological arousal whose cause the brain interprets, and this interpretation leads to emotional experience.

appraisal An evaluation of the emotion-relevant aspects of a stimulus.

does what brains do so well: It puts two and two together, makes a logical inference, and interprets your arousal as fear. In other words, when you are physiologically aroused in the presence of something you think should scare you, you label that arousal as *fear*. But if you have precisely the same bodily response in the presence of something that you think should delight you, then you label that arousal as *excitement*. According to Schachter and Singer, people have the same physiological reaction to all emotional stimuli, but they interpret that reaction differently on different occasions.

> **?** How did the *two-factor theory* of emotion expand on earlier theories?

Schachter and Singer tested their theory by giving participants an injection of epinephrine, which causes increases in blood pressure, heart rate, blood flow to the brain, blood sugar levels, and respiration. Participants then interacted with another person who, unbeknownst to them, was a confederate of the experimenter and had been instructed to act in a particular way. Schachter and Singer predicted that those participants who experienced epinephrine-induced arousal, but who hadn't been informed of the injection's effects, would seek an explanation for their arousal—and that the confederate's behavior would supply it. In fact, that's what happened. When the confederate acted goofy, the participants concluded that they themselves were feeling *happy*; when the confederate acted nasty, they concluded that they themselves were feeling *angry*.

How has the two-factor model fared in the last half century? One of the model's claims has fared very well. Research has shown that when people are aroused—say, by having them ride an exercise bike in the laboratory—they subsequently find attractive people more attractive, annoying people more annoying, and funny cartoons funnier, as if they were interpreting their exercise-induced arousal as attraction, annoyance, or amusement (Byrne et al., 1975; Dutton & Aron, 1974; Zillmann, Katcher, & Milavsky, 1972). In fact, these effects occur even when people merely *think* they're aroused—for example, when they hear an audiotape of a rapidly beating heart and are led to believe that the heartbeat they're hearing is their own (Valins, 1966). It appears that the two-factor model is right when it suggests that people make inferences about the causes of their arousal and that these inferences influence their emotional experience (Lindquist & Barrett, 2008).

However, research has not been so kind to the model's claim that all emotional experiences are merely different interpretations of the same bodily state. For example,

► Research shows that when people exercise, they sometimes misattribute their arousal to the attractiveness of those around them.

researchers measured participants' physiological reactions as they experienced six different emotions and found that anger, fear, and sadness each produced a higher heart rate than disgust; that fear and disgust produced higher galvanic skin response (sweating) than did sadness or anger; and that anger produced a larger increase in finger temperature than did fear (Ekman, Levenson, & Friesen, 1983) (see **FIGURE 8.4**). These findings have been replicated across different age groups, professions, genders, and cultures (Levenson et al., 1991, 1992, Levenson, Ekman, & Friesen, 1990). In fact, some physiological responses seem unique to a single emotion. For example, a blush is the result of increased blood volume in the subcutaneous capillaries in the face, neck, and chest, and research suggests that people blush when they feel embarrassment but not when they feel any other emotion (Leary et al., 1992). Similarly, certain patterns of activity in the parasympathetic branch of the autonomic nervous system (which is responsible for slowing and calming rather than speeding and exciting) seem uniquely related to prosocial emotions such as compassion (Oately, Keltner, & Jenkins, 2006).

So James and Lange were right when they suggested that patterns of physiological response are not the same for all emotions.

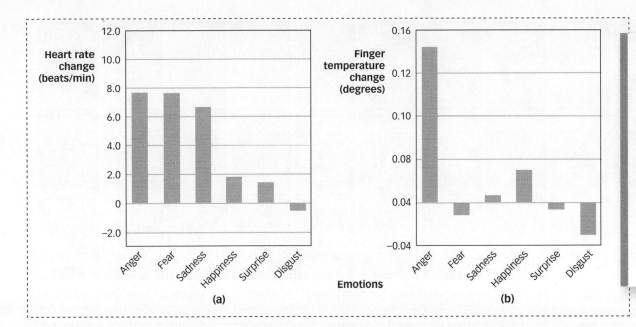

AP PHOTO/DAVID LONGSTREATH

◄ **FIGURE 8.4**
The Physiology of Emotion Contrary to the claims of the two-factor theory, different emotions do seem to have different underlying patterns of physiological arousal. (a) Anger, fear, and sadness all produce higher heart rates compared to happiness, surprise, and disgust. (b) Anger produces a much larger increase in finger temperature than any other emotion.

But Cannon and Bard were right when they suggested that people are not perfectly sensitive to these patterns of response, which is why people must sometimes make inferences about what they are feeling. Our bodily activity and our mental activity are both the causes and the consequences of our emotional experience. The precise nature of their interplay is not yet fully understood, but as you are about to see, much progress has been made over last few decades by following the trail of emotion from the beating heart to the living brain.

The Emotional Brain

The psychologist Heinrich Klüver and the physician Paul Bucy were studying the effects of hallucinogenic drugs in rhesus monkeys when they made an accidental discovery that Klüver would later call "the most striking behavior changes ever produced by a brain operation in animals" (Klüver, 1951, p. 151). After doing some brain surgery on a monkey named Aurora, they noticed that she would eat just about anything and have sex with just about anyone—as though she could no longer distinguish between good and bad food or good and bad mates. But the most striking thing about Aurora was that she did all this with an extraordinary lack of fear. She was eerily calm when being handled by experimenters or being confronted by snakes, both of which rhesus monkeys typically find alarming (Klüver & Bucy, 1937, 1939).

What explained this behavior? It turned out that during surgery, Klüver and Bucy had accidentally damaged a brain structure called the amygdala, which plays a special role in producing emotions such as fear. Before an animal can feel fear, its brain must first decide that there is something to be afraid of. This decision is called an **appraisal**, which is *an evaluation of the emotion-relevant aspects of a stimulus* (Arnold, 1960; Ellsworth & Scherer, 2003; Lazarus, 1984; Roseman, 1984; Roseman & Smith, 2001; Scherer, 1999, 2001). Many studies have shown that the amygdala is critical to making these appraisals. For example, some researchers performed an operation on monkeys so that

▼ The tourist and the tiger have something in common. Each has an amygdala that is trying to decide whether the other is a threat.

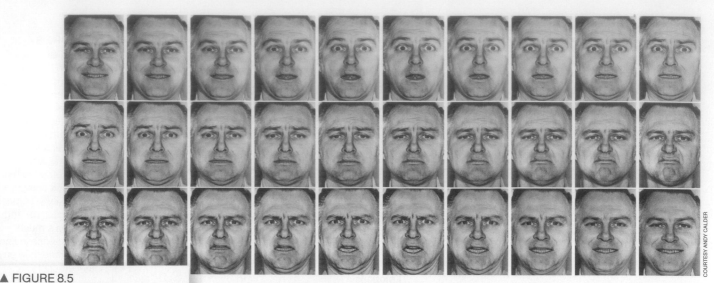

COURTESY ANDY CALDER

▲ **FIGURE 8.5**
Emotion Recognition and the Amygdala Facial expressions of emotion were morphed into a continuum that ran from happiness to surprise to fear to sadness to disgust to anger and back to happiness. This sequence was shown to a patient with bilateral amygdala damage and to a group of 10 people without brain damage. Although the patient's recognition of happiness, sadness, and surprise was generally in line with that of the undamaged group, her recognition of anger, disgust, and fear was impaired. (Calder et al., 1996)

information entering the monkey's left eye could be transmitted to the amygdala but information entering the monkey's right eye could not (Downer, 1961). When these monkeys were allowed to see a threatening stimulus with only their left eye, they responded with fear and alarm, but when they were allowed to see the threatening stimulus with only their right eye, they were calm and unruffled. These results suggest that if visual information doesn't reach the amygdala, then its emotional significance cannot be assessed. Research on human beings has reached a similar conclusion. For example, normal people have superior memory for emotionally evocative words such as *death* or *vomit,* but people whose amygdalae are damaged (LaBar & Phelps, 1998) or who take drugs that temporarily impair neurotransmission in the amygdala (van Stegeren et al., 1998) do not (see **FIGURE 8.5**).

The amygdala is an extremely fast and sensitive "threat detector" that is activated even when potentially threatening stimuli (such as fearful faces) are shown at speeds so fast that people are unaware of having seen them (Whalen et al., 1998). Psychologist Joseph LeDoux (2000) mapped the route that information about a stimulus takes through the brain and found that it is transmitted simultaneously along two distinct routes: the "fast pathway," which goes from the thalamus directly to the amygdala,

▶ **FIGURE 8.6**
The Fast and Slow Pathways of Fear According to Joseph LeDoux, information about a stimulus takes two routes simultaneously: the "fast pathway" (shown in pink), which goes from the thalamus directly to the amygdala, and the "slow pathway" (shown in green), which goes from the thalamus to the cortex and then to the amygdala. Because the amygdala receives information from the thalamus before it receives information from the cortex, people can be afraid of something before they know what it is.

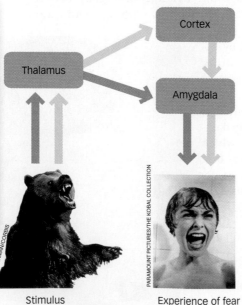

Thalamus

Cortex

Amygdala

Stimulus

Experience of fear

JIM ZUCKERMAN/CORBIS

PARAMOUNT PICTURES/THE KOBAL COLLECTION

and the "slow pathway," which goes from the thalamus to the cortex and *then* to the amygdala (see **FIGURE 8.6**). This means that while the cortex is slowly using the information to conduct a full-scale investigation of the stimulus's identity and importance ("This seems to be an animal . . . probably a mammal . . . perhaps a member of the genus *Ursus* . . ."), the amygdala has already received the information directly from the thalamus and is making one very fast and very simple decision: "Is this a threat?" If the amygdala's answer to that question is "yes," it initiates the neural processes that ultimately produce the bodily reactions and conscious experience that we call fear.

The cortex takes much longer to process this information, but when it finally does, it sends a signal to the amygdala. That signal can tell the amygdala to maintain the state of fear

("We've now analyzed all the data up here, and sure enough, that thing is a bear—and bears bite!") or decrease it ("Relax, it's just some guy in a bear costume"). When experimental subjects are instructed to *experience* emotions such as happiness, sadness, fear, and anger, they show increased activity in the amygdala and decreased activity in the cortex (Damasio et al., 2000), but when they are asked to *inhibit* these emotions, they show increased cortical activity and decreased amygdala activity (Ochsner Bunge, Gross, & Gabrieli, 2002). In a sense, the amygdala presses the emotional gas pedal and the cortex then hits the brakes. That's why both adults with cortical damage and children (whose cortices are not well developed) have difficulty inhibiting their emotions (Stuss & Benson, 1986).

How do the limbic system and cortex interact?

Studies of the brain confirm what psychologists have long suspected: Emotion is a primitive system that prepares us to react rapidly and on the basis of little information to things that are relevant to our survival and well-being. (See the Hot Science box.) While our newly acquired cortex identifies a stimulus, considers what it knows about it, and carefully plans a response, our ancient amygdala does what it has done so well for all those millennia before the cortex evolved: It makes a split-second decision about the significance of the objects and events in our environment and, when necessary, prepares our hearts and our legs to get our butts out of the woods.

HOT SCIENCE

Fear Goggles

Have you ever been so angry that you couldn't see straight? You may think this is just a figure of speech, but psychologists have recently discovered that our emotions can actually affect our vision. Bruno Bocanegra and René Zeelenberg (2009) showed participants either neutral faces or fearful faces for 70 milliseconds, and then showed them a set of black and white lines and asked them to quickly decide whether the lines were vertical or horizontal. What the researchers discovered was that seeing fearful faces made participants better at detecting the orientation of the lines—but only when the lines were thick (or had "low spatial frequency"). When the lines were thin (or had "high spatial frequency"), the fearful faces had exactly the opposite effect: They made participants worse at detecting the orientation of the lines.

Okay. That's weird. Why should fear make us better at detecting thick lines and worse at detecting thin lines? As it turns out, the visual information that is critical to making the split-second decisions that ensure our survival—the decision to freeze, or run, or fight—typically has low spatial frequency. High spatial frequency information allows us to see fine detail, but you really don't need to be able to count a tiger's teeth when he's lunging toward you. You just need to see that something big

is coming your way, and the dental exam can wait. Nature designed our brains so that the experience of fear momentarily enhances our ability to see what matters and momentarily diminishes our tendency to be distracted by unimportant details.

Now if someone could just figure out how to keep the tigers from seeing us.

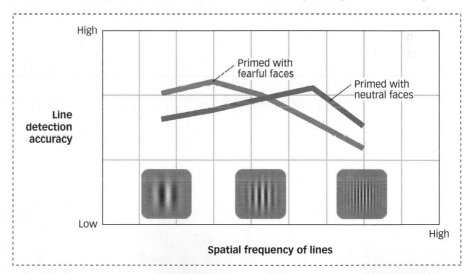

▲ Low spatial frequency information (left) tells you that something big is coming, and high spatial frequency information (right) tells you exactly what it is.

S.R. MAGLIONE/SHUTTERSTOCK

emotion regulation The use of cognitive and behavioral strategies to influence one's emotional experience.

reappraisal Changing one's emotional experience by changing the meaning of the emotion-eliciting stimulus.

emotional expression Any observable sign of an emotional state.

The Regulation of Emotion

We may not care whether we have cereal or eggs for breakfast, whether we play cricket or cards this afternoon, or whether we spend a few minutes thinking about hedgehogs, earwax, or the War of 1812. But we always care whether we are feeling happy or fearful, angry or relaxed, joyful or disgusted. Because we care so much about our emotional experiences, we work hard to have some and avoid others. **Emotion regulation** refers to *the cognitive and behavioral strategies people use to influence their own emotional experience.* Although there are occasionally times when people feel a bit too chipper for their own good and seek ways to "cheer down" (Erber, Wegner, & Therriault, 1996; Michaela et al., 2009; Parrott, 1993), emotion regulation is typically an attempt to cheer up—to turn negative emotions into positive ones.

Nine out of 10 people report that they attempt to regulate their emotional experience at least once a day (Gross, 1998), and they describe more than a thousand different strategies for doing so (Parkinson & Totterdell, 1999). Some of these are behavioral strategies (e.g., avoiding situations that trigger unwanted emotions, doing distracting activities, or taking drugs) and some are cognitive strategies (e.g., trying not to think about the cause of the unwanted emotion or recruiting memories that trigger the desired emotion). Research suggests that one of the most effective strategies for emotion regulation is **reappraisal**, which involves *changing one's emotional experience by changing the meaning of the emotion-eliciting stimulus* (Ochsner et al., 2009).

For example, participants in one study who watched a circumcision that was described as a joyous religious ritual had slower heart rates, had lower skin conductance levels, and reported less distress than did participants who watched the circumcision but did not hear the same description (Lazarus & Alfert, 1964). In another study, participants' brains were scanned as they saw photos that induced negative emotions, such as a photo of a woman crying during a funeral. Some participants were then asked to reappraise the picture, for example, by imagining that the woman in the photo was at a wedding rather than a funeral. The results showed that when participants initially saw the photo, their amygdalae became active. But as they reappraised the picture, several key areas of the cortex became active, and moments later, their amygdalae were deactivated (Ochsner et al., 2002). In other words, participants consciously and willfully turned down the activity of their own amygdalae simply by thinking about the photo in a different way.

The Roman emperor Marcus Aurelius wrote two millennia ago, "If you are distressed by anything external, the pain is not due to the thing itself, but to your estimate of it; and this you have the power to revoke at any moment." Is that true? As you will learn in Chapter 15, therapists often attempt to alleviate depression and distress by helping people find new ways to think about the events that happen to them. Indeed, reappraisal appears to be important for both mental and physical health (Davidson, Putnam, &

▶ Shooting heroin and singing in church would seem to have little in common, but both can be forms of emotion regulation. (We recommend trying singing first.)

Larson, 2000), and the inability to reappraise events lies at the heart of psychiatric disorders, such as depression (Gross & Munoz, 1995). Nonetheless, the way we see the world is not entirely under our control, so while reappraisal can be a useful strategy for regulating emotions, it is not a panacea for all that ails us.

IN SUMMARY

○ Emotional experiences are difficult to describe, but psychologists have identified their two underlying dimensions: arousal and valence.

○ Psychologists have spent more than a century trying to understand how emotional experience and physiological activity are related. The James-Lange theory suggests that a stimulus causes a physiological reaction, which leads to an emotional experience; the Cannon-Bard theory suggests that a stimulus causes both an emotional experience and a physiological reaction simultaneously; and Schachter and Singer's two-factor theory suggests that a stimulus causes undifferentiated physiological arousal about which people draw inferences. None of these theories are entirely right, but each has elements that are supported by research.

○ Emotions are produced by the complex interaction of limbic (see Figure 3.18) and cortical structures (see Figure 3.20). Information about a stimulus is sent simultaneously to the amygdala (which makes a quick appraisal of the stimulus's goodness or badness) and the cortex (which does a slower and more comprehensive analysis of the stimulus). In some instances, the amygdala will trigger an emotional experience that the cortex later inhibits.

○ People care about their emotional experiences and use many strategies to regulate them. Reappraisal involves changing the way one thinks about an object or event, and it is one of the most effective strategies for emotion regulation.

Emotional Communication: Msgs w/o Wrds

Leonardo the robot may not be able to feel, but boy oh boy, can he smile. And wink. And nod. Indeed, one of the reasons why people who interact with him find it so hard to think of him as a machine is that Leonardo *expresses* emotions that he doesn't actually have. An **emotional expression** is *an observable sign of an emotional state,* and while robots have to be taught to exhibit them, human beings do it naturally.

©FARDAD FARIDI/COURTESY PERSONAL ROBOTS GROUP, M.I.T. MEDIA LAB

◄ Leonardo's face is capable of expressing a wide range of emotions (Breazeal, 2003).

universality hypothesis The hypothesis that emotional expressions have the same meaning for everyone.

Our emotional states influence just about everything we do. For example, they influence the way we talk—from intonation and inflection to loudness and duration—and research shows that listeners can infer our emotional states from vocal cues alone with

Why are we "walking, talking advertisements" of our inner states?

better-than-chance accuracy (though vocal signs of anger, happiness, and sadness are somewhat easier to recognize than are vocal signs of fear and disgust; Banse & Scherer, 1996; Frick, 1985). Observers can also estimate our emotional states from the direction of our gaze, out gait, our posture, and even from a brief touch on the arm (Dittrich et al., 1996; Hertenstein et al., 2009; Keltner & Shiota, 2003; Wallbott, 1998). In some sense, we are walking, talking advertisements for what's going on inside us.

But no part of the body is more exquisitely designed for communicating emotion than the face. Underneath every face lie 43 muscles that are capable of creating more than 10,000 unique configurations, which enable a face to convey information about its owner's emotional state with an astonishing degree of subtlety and specificity (Ekman, 1965). Psychologists Paul Ekman and Wallace Friesen (1978) spent years cataloguing the muscle movements of which the human face is capable. They isolated 46 unique movements, which they called *action units,* and they gave each one a number and a name, such as "cheek puffer" and "dimpler" and "nasolabial deepener" (all of which, coincidentally enough, are also the names of heavy metal bands). Research has shown that combinations of these action units are reliably related to specific emotional states (Davidson et al., 1990). For example, when we feel happy, our *zygomatic major* (a muscle that pulls our lip corners up) and our *obicularis oculi* (a muscle that crinkles the outside edges of our eyes) produce a unique facial expression that psychologists describe as "action units 6 and 12" and that the rest of us simply call smiling (Ekman & Friesen, 1982; Frank, Ekman, & Friesen, 1993; Steiner, 1986).

▲ On September 19, 1982, Scott Fahlman posted a message to an Internet user's group that read, "I propose the following character sequence for joke markers: :-) Read it sideways." And so the emoticon was born. Fahlman's smile (above right) is a sign of happiness, whereas his emoticon is a symbol.

COURTESY OF SCOTT FAHLMAN

Communicative Expression

Why are our emotions written all over our faces? In 1872, Charles Darwin published a book titled *The Expression of the Emotions in Man and Animals,* in which he speculated about the evolutionary significance of emotional expression. Darwin noticed that human and nonhuman animals share certain facial and postural expressions, and he suggested that these expressions were meant to communicate information about internal states. Such communications could be quite useful. For example, if a dominant animal could bare its teeth and communicate the message, "I am angry at you," and if a subordinate animal could lower its head and communicate the message, "I am afraid of you," then the two could establish a pecking order without actually spilling any blood. Darwin suggested that emotional expressions are a convenient way for one animal to let another animal know how it is feeling and hence how it is prepared to act. In this sense, emotional expressions are a bit like the words of a nonverbal language.

► According to Charles Darwin, both human and nonhuman animals use facial expressions to communicate information about their internal states.

© WILLIAM H. CALVIN/WILLIAMCALVIN.ORG

ANDREAS GEBERT/DPA/NEWSCOM

The Universality of Expression

Of course, a language only works if everybody speaks the same one, and that fact led Darwin to develop the **universality hypothesis**, which suggests that *emotional expressions have the same meaning for everyone.* In other words, every human being naturally expresses happiness with a smile, and every human being naturally understands that a smile signifies happiness. Two lines of evidence suggest that Darwin was largely correct.

First, people are quite accurate at judging the emotional expressions of members of other cultures (Ekman & Friesen, 1971; Elfenbein & Ambady, 2002; Frank & Stennet, 2001; Haidt & Keltner, 1999). Not only do Chileans, Americans, and Japanese all recognize a smile as a sign of happiness and a frown as a sign of sadness, but so do members of preliterate cultures. In the 1950s, researchers took photographs of people expressing anger, disgust, fear, happiness, sadness, and surprise (see **FIGURE 8.7**) and showed them to members of the South Fore, a people who lived a Stone Age existence in the highlands of Papua New Guinea and who had had little contact with the outside world. The researchers discovered that the Fore could recognize the emotional expressions of Americans about as accurately as Americans could, and vice versa. The one striking exception to this rule was that the Fore had trouble distinguishing expressions of surprise from expressions of fear, perhaps because for people who live in the wild, surprises are rarely pleasant.

The second line of evidence in favor of the universality hypothesis is that people who have never seen a human face make the same facial expressions as those who have.

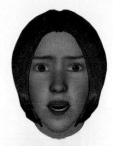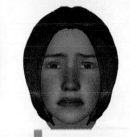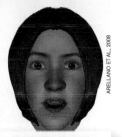

▲ FIGURE 8.7
Six Basic Emotions These computer-generated faces are displaying anger, disgust, fear, happiness, sadness, and surprise. The universality hypothesis suggests that no matter who you are or where you live, you will be able to identify the emotion in each face. Adapted from Arellano, Varona, & Perales, 2008.

(?) **Why are some facial expressions universal?**

For instance, congenitally blind people make all the facial expressions associated with the six emotions mentioned above (Galati, Scherer, & Ricci-Bitt, 1997; Matsumoto & Willingham, 2009). And 2-day-old infants (who have had virtually no exposure to human faces) react to sweet tastes with a smile and to bitter tastes with an expression of disgust (Steiner, 1973, 1979). In short, a good deal of evidence suggests that the facial displays of at least six emotions—*anger, disgust, fear, happiness, sadness,* and *surprise*—are universal. Recent evidence suggests that some other emotions, such as embarrassment, amusement, guilt, or shame, may have a universal pattern of facial expression as well (Keltner, 1995; Keltner & Buswell, 1996; Keltner & Haidt, 1999; Keltner & Harker, 1998).

The Cause and Effect of Expression

Members of different cultures seem to express many emotions in the same ways—but why? After all, they don't speak the same languages, so why do they smile the same smiles and frown the same frowns? The answer is that words are *symbols,* but facial expressions are *signs.* Symbols are arbitrary designations that have no causal relationship with the things they symbolize. English speakers use the word *cat* to indicate a particular animal, but there is nothing about felines that actually causes this particular sound to pop out of our mouths, and we aren't surprised when other human beings make different sounds—such as *popoki* or *gatto*—to indicate the same thing. In contrast, facial expressions are not arbitrary symbols of emotion. They are signs of emotion

▲ Why is Stevie Wonder smiling? Perhaps it's the 25 Grammy Awards he's won since 1974. Research shows that people who are born blind express emotion on their faces in the same ways that sighted people do.

because signs are *caused* by the things they signify. The feeling of happiness *causes* the contraction of the zygomatic major; thus that contraction is a sign of that feeling in the same way a footprint in the snow is a sign that someone walked there.

Of course, just as a symbol ("bat") can have more than one meaning ("wooden club" or "flying mammal"), so, too, can a sign. Is the man in the photo at left feeling joy or sorrow? In fact, these two emotions often produce rather similar facial expressions—so how do we tell them apart? The answer is context. When someone says, "The centerfielder hit the ball with the bat," the sentence provides a context that tells us that *bat* means "club" and not "mammal." Similarly, the context in which a facial expression occurs often tells us what that expression means (Aviezer et al., 2008; Meeren, Heijnsbergen, & de Gelder, 2005). If you turn to page 324 you will see the photo to the left in context, and you won't have any trouble knowing what the man is feeling. In fact, if you now return to the photo to the left, it will be very difficult for you to see his expression.

Emotional experiences can cause emotional expressions. But interestingly, it also works the other way around. The **facial feedback hypothesis** (Adelmann & Zajonc, 1989; Izard, 1971; Tomkins, 1981) suggests that *emotional expressions can cause the emotional experiences they signify.* For instance, people feel happier when they are asked to make the sound of a long *e* or to hold a pencil in their teeth (both of which cause contraction of the zygomatic major) than when they are asked to make the sound of a long *u* or to hold a pencil in their lips (Strack, Martin, & Stepper, 1988; Zajonc, 1989) (see **FIGURE 8.8**). Some researchers believe that this happens because the muscle contractions of a smile change the temperature of the brain, which in turn brings about a pleasant affective state (Zajonc, 1989); but most think that smiles and happiness become strongly associated through experience, with one generally bringing about the other. These expression-causes-emotion effects are not limited to the face. For example, people who are asked to make a fist rate themselves as more assertive (Schubert & Koole, 2009) and people who are asked to extend their middle fingers rate others as more hostile (Chandler & Schwarz, 2009). (The odds seem pretty good that others would rate them as more hostile too).

The fact that emotional expressions can cause the emotional experiences they signify may help explain why people are generally so good at recognizing the emotional expressions of others. Many studies show that people unconsciously mimic other people's body postures and facial expressions (Chartrand & Bargh, 1999; Dimberg, 1982). When we see someone smile (or even when we read about someone smiling), our zygomatic major contracts ever so slightly (Foroni & Semin, 2009). The tendency to "ape" the facial expressions of our interaction partners is so natural that, yes, even apes do it (Davila Ross, Menzler, & Zimmermann, 2008).

What purpose does this mimicry serve? It appears that its main function is to help us figure out what others are feeling. Because of the expression-causes-emotion effect, when we mimic someone's facial expression, we also feel their emotions. That's why we find it difficult to recognize other people's emotions when we are unable to make a facial expression (Niedenthal et al., 2005) or when we are unable

Why do emotional expressions cause emotional experience?

▲ Is this man feeling happy or sad? See page 324.

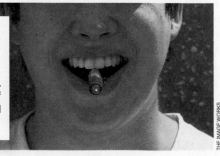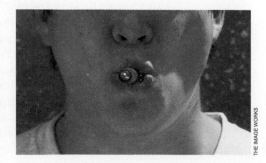

▶ FIGURE 8.8
The Facial Feedback Hypothesis Research shows that people who hold a pen with their teeth feel happier than those who hold a pen with their lips. These two postures cause contraction of the muscles associated with smiling and frowning, respectively.

to experience emotions ourselves (Hussey & Safford, 2009; Pitcher et al., 2008). For example, people with amygdala damage have trouble experiencing fear and anger and are typically poor at recognizing the expressions of those emotions in others (Adolphs, Russell, & Tranel, 1999). And as you might expect, people who are naturally good at figuring out what others are feeling tend to be natural mimics (Sonnby-Borgstrom, Jonsson, & Svensson, 2003), and their mimicry seems to pay off: Negotiators who mimic the facial expressions of their opponents earn more money than those who don't (Maddux, Mullen, & Galinsky, 2008).

Deceptive Expression

Given how important emotional expressions are, it's no wonder people have learned to use them to their advantage. Because you can control most of the muscles in your face, you don't have to display the emotion you are actually feeling. When your roommate makes a sarcastic remark about your haircut, you may make the facial expression for contempt (accompanied, perhaps, by a reinforcing hand gesture), but when your boss makes the same remark, you probably swallow hard and display a pained smile. Your expressions are moderated by your knowledge that it is permissible to show contempt for your peers but not for your superiors. **Display rules** are *norms for the control of emotional expression* (Ekman, 1972; Ekman & Friesen, 1968), and following them requires using several techniques:

> *Intensification* involves exaggerating the expression of one's emotion, as when a person pretends to be more surprised by a gift than she really is.

> *Deintensification* involves muting the expression of one's emotion, as when the loser of a contest tries to look less distressed than he really is.

> *Masking* involves expressing one emotion while feeling another, as when a poker player tries to look distressed rather than delighted as she examines a hand with four aces.

> *Neutralizing* involves feeling an emotion but displaying no expression, as when a judge tries not to betray his leanings while lawyers are making their arguments (see **FIGURE 8.9**).

Although people in different cultures all use the same techniques, they use them in the service of different display rules. For example, in one study, Japanese and American college students watched an unpleasant film of car accidents and amputations (Ekman, 1972; Friesen, 1972). When the students

How does emotional expression differ across cultures?

didn't know that the experimenters were observing them, Japanese and American students made similar expressions of disgust, but when they realized that they were being observed, the Japanese students (but not the American students) masked their disgust with pleasant expressions. Many Asian societies have a cultural norm against displaying negative emotions in the presence of a respected person, and people in these societies may mask or neutralize their expressions. The fact that different cultures have different display rules may also help explain the fact that people are better at recognizing the facial expressions of people from their own cultures (Elfenbein & Ambady, 2002).

Our attempts to obey our culture's display rules don't always work out so well. Darwin (1899/2007) noted that "those muscles of the face which are least obedient to the will, will sometimes alone betray a slight and passing emotion" (p. 64). Anyone who has ever watched the loser of a beauty pageant congratulate the winner knows that voices, bodies, and faces are "leaky" instruments that often betray a person's emotional state even when he or she is pretending to feel something else. For example, even when people smile bravely to mask their disappointment, their faces tend to express small bursts of disappointment that last just 1/5 to 1/25 of a second (Porter & ten Brinke, 2008). These "micro-expressions" happen so quickly that they are almost impossible to detect with the naked eye.

facial feedback hypothesis The hypothesis that emotional expressions can cause the emotional experiences they signify.

display rules Norms for the control of emotional expression.

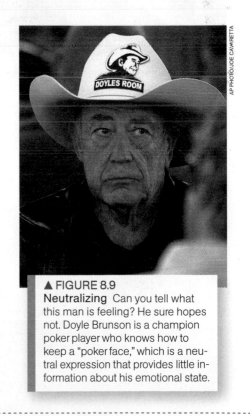

▲ FIGURE 8.9
Neutralizing Can you tell what this man is feeling? He sure hopes not. Doyle Brunson is a champion poker player who knows how to keep a "poker face," which is a neutral expression that provides little information about his emotional state.

Four other features that are more readily observable seem to distinguish between sincere and insincere facial expressions (Ekman, 2003a):

> *Morphology:* Certain facial muscles tend to resist conscious control, and for a trained observer, these so-called *reliable muscles* are quite revealing. For example, the zygomatic major raises the corners of the mouth, and this happens when people smile spontaneously or when they force themselves to smile. But only a genuine, spontaneous smile engages the obicularis oculi, which crinkles the corners of the eyes (see **FIGURE 8.10**).

> *Symmetry:* Sincere expressions are a bit more symmetrical than insincere expressions. A slightly lopsided smile is less likely to be genuine than is a perfectly even one.

> *Duration:* Sincere expressions tend to last between a half second and 5 seconds, and expressions that last for shorter or longer periods are more likely to be insincere.

> *Temporal patterning:* Sincere expressions appear and disappear smoothly over a few seconds, whereas insincere expressions tend to have more abrupt onsets and offsets.

▼ FIGURE 8.10
Crinkle Eyes Can you tell which of the two finalists in the 1986 Miss America pageant just won? Check out their eyes. Only one woman is showing the telltale "corner crinkle" that signifies genuine happiness. The winner is on the right, but don't feel too bad for the loser on the left. Her name is Halle Berry and she went on to have a pretty good acting career.

Our emotions don't just leak on our faces: They leak all over the place. Research has shown that many aspects of our verbal and non-verbal behavior are altered when we tell a lie (DePaulo et al., 2003). For example, liars speak more slowly, take longer to respond to questions, and respond in less detail than do those who are telling the truth. Liars are also less fluent, less engaging, more uncertain, more tense, and less pleasant than truth-tellers. Oddly enough, one of the telltale signs of a liar is that his or her performances tend to be just a bit too good. A liar's speech lacks the little imperfections that are typical of truthful speech, such as superfluous detail ("I noticed that the robber was wearing the same shoes that I saw on sale last week at Bloomingdale's and I found myself wondering what he paid for them"), spontaneous correction ("He was six feet tall . . . well, no, actually more like six-two"), and expressions of self-doubt ("I think he had blue eyes, but I'm really not sure").

Given the reliable differences between sincere and insincere expressions, you might think that people would be quite good at telling

▶ President Barack Obama wipes away the tears he shed while singing a hymn with his wife. Crying is very difficult to control and thus provides reliable information about the intensity of a person's emotions.

one from the other. In fact, studies show that human lie detection ability is pretty close to dreadful. Although trained professionals can learn to do it fairly well (Ekman & O'Sullivan, 1991; Ekman, O'Sullivan, & Frank, 1999), under most conditions ordinary people do barely better than chance (De-Paulo, Stone, & Lassiter, 1985; Ekman, 1992; Zuckerman, DePaulo, & Rosenthal, 1981; Zuckerman & Driver, 1985). One reason for this is that people have a strong bias toward believing that others are sincere, which explains why people tend to mistake liars for truth-tellers more often than they mistake truth-tellers for liars (Gilbert, 1991).

A second reason why people are such poor lie detectors is that they don't seem to know which pieces of information to attend to and which to ignore. People seem to think that certain things—such as whether a person speaks quickly or averts her gaze—are associated with lying when, in fact, they are not, and people seem to think that certain other things—such as talking too little or repeating words—are not associated with lying when, in fact, they are. To add insult to injury, people are bad lie detectors who don't even know how bad they are. The correlation between a person's ability to detect lies and the person's confidence in that ability is essentially zero (DePaulo et al., 1997).

When people can't do something well (e.g., adding numbers or picking up 10-ton rocks), they typically turn the job over to machines (see

What is the problem with lie detecting machines?

FIGURE 8.11). Can machines detect lies better than we can? The answer is yes, but that's not saying much. The most widely used lie detection machine is the *polygraph,* which measures a variety of physiological responses that are associated with stress, which people often feel when they are afraid of being caught in a lie. In fact, the machine is so widely used by governments and businesses that the National Research Council recently met to consider all the scientific evidence on its validity. After much study, it concluded that the polygraph can indeed detect lies at a rate that is significantly better than chance (National Research Council, 2003). However, it also concluded that "almost a century of research in scientific psychology and physiology provides little basis for the expectation that a polygraph test could have extremely high accuracy" (p. 212).

CULTURE & COMMUNITY

Is it what you say or how you say it? We can learn a lot about people by paying attention both to what they say and to how they say it. But recent evidence (Ishii, Reyes, & Kitayama, 2003) suggests that some cultures place more of an emphasis on one of these than on the other.

Subjects heard a voice pronouncing pleasant or unpleasant words (such as *pretty* or *complaint*) in either a pleasant or an unpleasant tone of voice. On some trials, subjects were told to ignore the word and to classify the pleasantness of the voice; on other trials, subjects were told to ignore the voice and classify the pleasantness of the word.

Which of these kinds of information was more difficult to ignore? It depended on the subject's nationality. American subjects found it relatively easy to ignore the speaker's tone of voice but relatively difficult to ignore the pleasantness of the word being spoken. Japanese subjects, on the other hand, found it relatively easy to ignore the pleasantness of the word, but relatively difficult to ignore the speaker's tone of voice.

It seems that, in America, what you say matters more than how you say it, but in Japan, just the opposite is true.

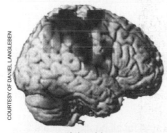

Right side

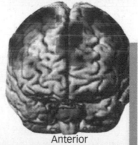

Left side

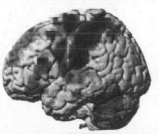

Anterior

◄ **FIGURE 8.11**

Lie Detection Machines Some researchers hope to replace the polygraph with accurate machines that measure changes in blood flow in the brain and the face. As the top panel shows, some areas of the brain are more active when people tell lies than when they tell the truth (shown in red), and some are more active when people tell the truth than when they tell lies (shown in blue) (Langleben et al., 2005). The bottom panel shows images taken by a thermal camera that detects the heat caused by blood flow to different parts of the face. The images show a person's face before (left) and after (right) telling a lie (Pavlidis, Eberhardt, & Levine, 2002). Although neither of these new techniques is extremely accurate, that could soon change.

Why? Because while the polygraph is better than chance, its error rate is still quite high. For example, imagine that 10 of the 10,000 people coming through a particular airport are terrorists. If we hooked them all up to a polygraph, all 10,000 people would proclaim their innocence. Given the machine's error rate, if we were to make the polygraph sensitive enough to catch 8 of the 10 terrorists in a lie, then we would also mistakenly "catch" 1,598 innocent people. On the other hand, if we made the polygraph so insensitive that it mistakenly caught only 39 innocent people, then it would only catch 2 of the 10 real terrorists. And these numbers assume that the terrorists don't know how to fool the polygraph, which is something that people can, in fact, be trained to do. No wonder the National Research Council warned, "Given its level of accuracy, achieving a high probability of identifying individuals who pose major security risks in a population with a very low proportion of such individuals would require setting the test to be so sensitive that hundreds, or even thousands, of innocent individuals would be implicated for every major security violator correctly identified" (p. 6). In short, neither people nor machines are particularly good at lie detection, which is why lying remains such a popular sport.

▶ This Pakistani man is being led away from the scene of a Taliban suicide-bombing that killed his father.

IN SUMMARY

○ The voice, the body, and the face all communicate information about a person's emotional state.

○ Darwin suggested that these emotional expressions are the same for all people and are universally understood, and research suggests that this is generally true.

○ Emotions cause expressions, but expressions can also cause emotions.

○ Emotional mimicry allows people to experience and hence identify the emotions of others.

○ Not all emotional expressions are sincere because people use display rules to help them decide which emotions to express.

○ Different cultures have different display rules, but people enact those rules using the same techniques.

○ There are reliable differences between sincere and insincere emotional expressions and between truthful and untruthful utterances, but people are generally poor at determining when an expression is sincere or an utterance is truthful. The polygraph can distinguish true from false utterances with better-than-chance accuracy, but its error rate is troublingly high.

motivation The purpose for or psychological cause of an action.

Motivation: Getting Moved

Leonardo is a robot and so he does what he is programmed to do—nothing more and nothing less. Leonardo doesn't care about anything, doesn't value anything, doesn't desire anything. He has no wants or urges. He can learn, but he cannot yearn. Because he doesn't have emotions, he isn't motivated in the same way that human beings are. **Motivation** refers to *the purpose for or psychological cause of an action,* and it is no coincidence that the words *emotion* and *motivation* share a common linguistic root that means "to move." Unlike robots, human beings act because their emotions move them, and emotions do this in two different ways: First, emotions provide people with *information* about the world, and second, emotions are the *objectives* toward which people strive. Let's examine each of these in turn.

The Function of Emotion

In the old sci-fi film *Invasion of the Body Snatchers,* a young couple suspects that most of the people they know have been kidnapped by aliens and replaced with replicas. This sort of bizarre belief is a common story device in bad movies, but it is also the primary symptom of Capgras syndrome (see **FIGURE 8.12**). People who suffer from this syndrome typically believe that one or more of their family members are imposters. As one Capgras sufferer told her doctor, "He looks exactly like my father, but he really isn't. He's a nice guy, but he isn't my father. . . . Maybe my father employed him to take care of me, paid him some money so he could pay my bills" (Hirstein & Ramachandran, 1997, p. 438).

This person's dad had not been body-snatched, of course, nor had he hired his own stand-in. Rather, the person had sustained damage to the neural connections between her temporal lobe (where faces are identified) and her limbic system (where emotions are generated). As a result, when she saw her father's face, she recognized it, but because this information was not transmitted to her limbic system, she didn't feel the warm emotions that her father's face once produced. Her father "looked right" but didn't "feel right," and so she concluded that the man before her was an imposter (see Figure 8.12).

◀ In 1956's *Invasion of the Body Snatchers*, little Jimmy Grimaldi tells the nurse and the doctor that his mother has been replaced by a replica. Their response? Chill him out with drugs and send him home to be eaten by aliens.

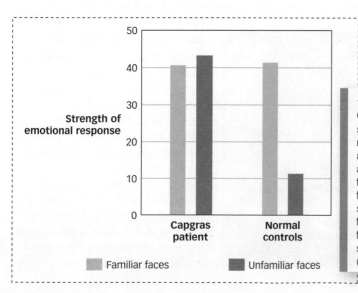

◀ **FIGURE 8.12**
Capgras Syndrome This graph shows the emotional responses (as measured by skin conductance) of a patient with Capgras syndrome and a group of control participants to a set of familiar and unfamiliar faces. Although the controls have stronger emotional responses to the familiar than to the unfamiliar faces, the Capgras patient has similar emotional responses to both (Hirstein & Ramachandran, 1997).

Strength of emotional response

Capgras patient   Normal controls

Familiar faces   Unfamiliar faces

STEVE/JASON/OBR/NATIONAL PHOTO GROUP

▲ When we try to make a decision, we often ask how we "feel" about it. If we couldn't feel, then we wouldn't know which alternative to choose. Without emotions, Rihanna would just stand there until someone gave her a Grammy for Best Hot Pink Stiletto.

People with Capgras syndrome use their emotional experience as information about the world, and this is something that the rest of us do all the time. For example, people report having better lives when they are asked the question on a sunny day rather than a rainy day. Why? Because people feel happier on sunny days, and they use their happiness as information about the quality of their lives (Schwarz & Clore, 1983). People who are in good moods believe that they have a higher probability of winning a lottery than do people who are in bad moods. Why? Because people use their moods as information about the likelihood of succeeding at a task (Isen & Patrick, 1983). We all know that satisfying lives and bright futures make us feel good—so when we feel good, we conclude that our lives must be satisfying and our futures must be bright. Because the world influences our emotions, our emotions can provide information about the world (Schwarz, Mannheim, & Clore, 1988).

This information isn't just useful. It is critical. When neurologist Antonio Damasio was asked to examine a patient with an unusual form of brain damage, he asked the patient to choose between two dates for an appointment. It sounds like a simple decision, but for the next half hour, the patient enumerated reasons for and against each of the two possible dates, completely unable to decide in favor of one option or the other (Damasio, 1994). The problem wasn't any impairment of the patient's ability to think or reason. On the contrary, he could think and reason all too well. What he couldn't do was feel. The patient's injury had left him unable to experience emotion; thus when he entertained one option ("If I come next Tuesday, I'll have to cancel my lunch with Fred"), he didn't feel any better or any worse than when he entertained another ("If I come next Wednesday, I'll have to get up early to catch the bus"). And because he *felt* nothing when he thought about an option, he couldn't decide which was better. Studies show that when patients with this particular kind of brain damage are given the opportunity to gamble, they make a lot of reckless bets because they don't feel the twinge of anxiety that tells most of us that we're about to do something stupid. On the other hand, under certain conditions these patients make excellent investors, precisely because they are willing to take risks that others will not (Shiv et al., 2005).

? Why do we need emotions to help us make decisions?

The first function of emotions, then, is to provide us with information. The second function is to give us something to *do* with that information. People naturally prefer to experience positive rather than negative emotions; thus happiness, satisfaction, pleasure, and joy are often the goals, the ends, and the objectives toward which our behavior is aimed. The **hedonic principle** is *the claim that people are motivated to experience pleasure and avoid pain*. This claim has a long history. The ancient Greek philosopher Aristotle (350 BC) argued that the hedonic principle explained everything there was to know about human motivation: It "is a first principle, for it is for the sake of this that we all do all that we do." Yes, we want many things, from peace and prosperity to health and security, but the *reason* we want them is that they make us feel good. "Are these things good for any other reason except that they end in pleasure, and get rid of and avert pain?," asked Aristotle's teacher, Plato (380 BC). "Are you looking to any other standard but pleasure and pain when you call them good?" Plato and Aristotle were suggesting that pleasure isn't just good— it is what good *means*.

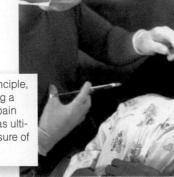

► According to the hedonic principle, this woman would not be visiting a U.S. military dentist unless the pain of having her tooth extracted was ultimately outweighed by the pleasure of having had it done.

AP PHOTO/PAT ROQUE

According to the hedonic principle, then, our emotional experience can be thought of as a gauge that ranges from bad to good, and our primary motivation—perhaps even our *sole* motivation—is to keep the needle on the gauge as close to *good* as possible. Even when we voluntarily do things that tilt the needle in the opposite direction, such as letting the dentist drill our teeth or waking up early for a boring class, we are doing these things because we believe that they will nudge the needle toward *good* in the future and keep it there longer.

hedonic principle The notion that all people are motivated to experience pleasure and avoid pain.

The Conceptualization of Motivation

The hedonic principle sets the stage for an understanding of motivation but leaves many questions unanswered. For example, if our primary motivation is to keep the needle on *g*, so to speak, then which things push the needle in that direction and which things push it away? And where do these things get the power to push our needle around, and exactly how do they do the pushing? The answers to such questions lie in two concepts that have played an unusually important role in the history of psychology: *instincts* and *drives*.

Instincts

When a newborn baby is given a drop of sugar water, it smiles, and when it is given a check for $10,000, it acts like it couldn't care less. By the time the baby goes to college, these responses pretty much reverse. It seems clear that nature endows us with certain motivations and that experience endows us with others. William James (1890) called the natural tendency to seek a particular goal an *instinct,* which he defined as "the faculty of acting in such a way as to produce certain ends, without foresight of the ends, and without previous education in the performance" (p. 383). According to James, nature hardwired penguins, parrots, puppies, and people to want certain things without training and to execute the behaviors that produce these things without thinking. He and other psychologists of his time tried to make a list of what those things were.

Unfortunately, in just a few decades, psychology's list of instincts had grown preposterously long, coming to include some rather exotic entries such as "the instinct to be secretive" and "the instinct to grind one's teeth" (both of which were contributed by James himself). In his 1924 survey of the burgeoning literature on instinct, sociologist Luther Bernard counted 5,759 instincts and concluded that after three decades of list-making, the term seemed to be suffering from "a great variety of usage and the almost universal lack of critical standards" (Bernard, 1924, p. 21). Furthermore, some psychologists began to worry that explaining the fact that people befriend each other by claiming that people have an "affiliation instinct" wasn't much of an explanation at all. When Aristotle explained the downhill movement of water and the upward movement of fire by claiming that the former had "gravity" and the latter had "levity," it didn't take long for his fellow philosophers to catch on to the fact that Aristotle had merely named these tendencies and not really explained them (Ayres, 1921; Dunlap, 1919; Field, 1921).

By 1930, the concept of instinct had fallen out of fashion. Not only did it fail to explain anything, but it also flew in the face of American psychology's hot new trend: behaviorism. Behaviorists rejected the concept of instinct on two grounds. First, they believed that behavior should be explained by the external stimuli that evoke it and not by the hypothetical internal states on which it depends. John Watson (1913) had written that "the time seems to have come when psychology must discard all reference to consciousness" (p. 163), and behaviorists saw instincts as just the sort of unnecessary "internal talk" that Watson forbade. Second, behaviorists wanted nothing to do with the notion of inherited behavior because they believed that all complex behavior was learned. Because instincts were inherited tendencies that resided inside the organism, behaviorists considered them doubly repugnant.

▼ All animals are born with instincts. In the annual "running of the bulls" in Pamplona, Spain, no one has to teach the bulls to chase the runners, and no one has to teach the runners to flee.

AP PHOTO/LALO R. VILLAR

▲ Michigan gets cold in the winter. Luckily, both Governor Jennifer Granholm and her thermostat are homeostatic devices. The thermostat senses the room's temperature and adjusts the furnace when necessary. The governor senses her body temperature and adjusts the thermostat when necessary. Voters sense the economy and adjust the governor when necessary.

Drives

But within a few decades, some of Watson's younger followers began to realize that the strict prohibition against the mention of internal states made certain phenomena difficult to explain. For example, if all behavior is a response to an external stimulus, then why does a rat that is sitting still in its cage at 9:00 a.m. start wandering around and looking for food by noon? Nothing in the cage has changed, so why has the rat's behavior changed? What visible, measurable external stimulus is the wandering rat responding to? The obvious answer is that the rat is responding to something inside itself, which meant that Watson's young followers—the "new behaviorists" as they called themselves—were forced to look inside the rat to explain its wandering. How could they do that without talking about the "thoughts" and "feelings" that Watson had forbidden them to mention?

They began by noting that bodies are a bit like thermostats. When thermostats detect that the room is too cold, they send signals that initiate corrective actions such as turning on a furnace. Similarly, when bodies detect that they are underfed, they send signals that initiate corrective actions such as eating. **Homeostasis** is *the tendency for a system to take action to keep itself in a particular state,* and two of the new behaviorists, Clark Hull and Kenneth Spence, suggested that rats, people, and thermostats are all homeostatic mechanisms. To survive, an organism needs to maintain precise levels of nutrition, warmth, and so on, and when these levels depart from an optimal point, the organism receives a signal to take corrective action. That signal is called a **drive**, which is *an internal state caused by physiological needs.* According to Hull and Spence, it isn't food per se that organisms find rewarding; it is the reduction of the drive for food. Hunger is a drive, a drive is an internal state, and when organisms eat, they are attempting to change their internal state.

In what ways is the human body like a thermostat?

Although the words *instinct* and *drive* are no longer widely used in psychology, the concepts remain part of the modern conception of motivation. The concept of instinct reminds us that nature endows organisms with a tendency to seek certain things, and the concept of drive reminds us that this seeking is initiated by an internal state. The psychologist William McDougall (1930) called the study of motivation "hormic psychology," which is a term derived from the Greek word for "urge," and people clearly do have urges—some of which they acquire through experience and some of which they do not—that motivate them to take certain actions. What kinds of urges do we have, and what kinds of actions do we take to satisfy them?

Basic Motivations

Abraham Maslow (1954) attempted to organize the list of human urges—or, as he called them, *needs*—in a meaningful way (see **FIGURE 8.13**). He noted that some needs (such as the need to eat) must be satisfied before others (such as the need to have friends), and he built a hierarchy of needs that had the most immediate needs at the bottom and the most deferrable needs at the top. Maslow suggested that, as a rule, people will not experience a need until all the needs below it are met. So when people are hungry or thirsty or exhausted, they will not seek intellectual fulfillment or moral clarity, which is to say that philosophy is a luxury of the well fed. Although many aspects of Maslow's theory have failed to win empirical support (e.g., a person on a hunger strike may value her principles more than her physical needs; see Wahba & Bridwell,

Why do some motivations take precedence over others?

homeostasis The tendency for a system to take action to keep itself in a particular state.

drive An internal state generated by departures from physiological optimality.

1976), the idea that some needs take precedence over others is clearly right. And although there are exceptions, the needs that typically take precedence are those we share with other mammals and that are related to our common biology. Two of these biological needs—the need for food and the need for sex—are among the most powerful and well studied, so let's see how they work.

Motivation for Food

Animals convert matter into energy by eating, and they are driven to do this by an internal state called hunger. But what is hunger and where does it come from? At every moment, your body is sending signals to your brain about its current energy state. If your body needs energy, it sends an *orexigenic* signal to tell your brain to switch hunger on, and if your body has sufficient energy, it sends an *anorexigenic* signal to tell your brain to switch hunger off (Gropp et al., 2005). No one knows precisely what these signals are or how they are sent and received, but research has identified a variety of candidates.

For example, *ghrelin* is a hormone that is produced in the stomach, and it appears to be a signal that tells the brain to switch hunger on (Inui, 2001; Nakazato et al., 2001). When people are injected with ghrelin, they become intensely hungry and eat about 30% more than usual (Wren et al., 2001). Interestingly, ghrelin also binds to neurons in the hippocampus and temporarily improves learning and memory (Diano et al., 2006) so that we become just a little bit better at locating food when our bodies need it most. *Leptin* is a chemical secreted by fat cells, and it appears to be a signal that tells the brain to switch hunger off. It seems to do this by making food less rewarding (Farooqi et al., 2007). People who are born with a leptin deficiency have trouble controlling their appetites (Montague et al., 1997). For example, in 2002, medical researchers reported on the case of a 9-year-old girl who weighed 200 pounds, but after just a few leptin injections, she reduced her food intake by 84% and attained normal weight (Farooqi et al., 2002). Some researchers think the idea that chemicals turn hunger and off is far too simple, and they argue that there is no general state called hunger but rather that there are many different hungers, each of which is a response to a unique nutritional deficit and each of which is switched on by a unique chemical messenger (Rozin & Kalat, 1971). For example, rats that are deprived of protein will seek proteins while turning down fats and carbohydrates, suggesting that they are experiencing a specific "protein hunger" and not a general hunger (Rozin, 1968).

Whether hunger is one signal or many, the primary receiver of these signals is the hypothalamus. Different parts of the hypothalamus receive different signals (see **FIGURE 8.14**). The *lateral hypothalamus* receives orexigenic signals, and when it is destroyed, animals sitting in a cage full of food will starve themselves to death. The *ventromedial hypothalamus* receives anorexigenic signals, and when it is destroyed, animals will gorge themselves to the point of illness and obesity (Miller, 1960; Steinbaum & Miller, 1965). These two structures were once thought to be the "hunger center" and "satiety center" of the brain, but recent research has shown that this view is far too simple (Woods et al., 1998). Hypothalamic structures play an important role in turning hunger on and off, but the precise way in which they execute these functions is complex and remains poorly understood (Stellar & Stellar, 1985).

? What purpose does hunger serve?

◄ **FIGURE 8.13**
Maslow's Hierarchy of Needs Human beings are motivated to satisfy a variety of needs. Psychologist Abraham Maslow thought these needs formed a hierarchy, with physiological needs forming a base and self-actualization needs forming a pinnacle. He suggested that people don't experience higher needs until the needs below them have been met.

Need for self-actualization

Esteem needs

Belongingness and love needs

Safety and security needs

Physiological needs

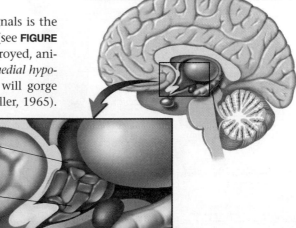

▼ **FIGURE 8.14**
Hunger, Satiety, and the Hypothalamus The hypothalamus comprises many parts. In general, the lateral hypothalamus receives the signals that turn hunger on and the ventromedial hypothalamus receives the signals that turn hunger off

Lateral hypothalamus

Ventromedial hypothalamus

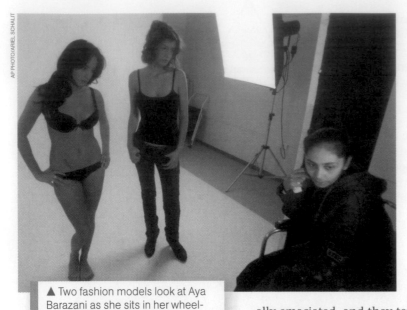

▲ Two fashion models look at Aya Barazani as she sits in her wheelchair. Aya suffers from anorexia. All three women are taking part in a photo shoot for a publicity campaign to convince modeling agencies not to feature malnourished women.

▼ Times have changed. People today are often astonished to see that ads once promised to help young women *gain* weight to become popular.

Eating Disorders

Feelings of hunger tell us when to eat and when to stop. But for the 10 to 30 million Americans who have eating disorders, eating is a much more complicated affair (Hoek & van Hoeken, 2003). For instance, **bulimia nervosa** is *a disorder characterized by binge eating followed by purging*. People with bulimia typically ingest large quantities of food in a relatively short period and then take laxatives or induce vomiting to purge the food from their bodies. These people are caught in a cycle: They eat to ease negative emotions such as sadness and anxiety, but then concern about weight gain leads them to experience negative emotions such as guilt and self-loathing, and these emotions then lead them to purge.

Anorexia nervosa is *a disorder characterized by an intense fear of being fat and severe restriction of food intake*. People with anorexia tend to have a distorted body image that leads them to believe they are fat when they are actually emaciated, and they tend to be high-achieving perfectionists who see their severe control of eating as a triumph of will over impulse. Contrary to what you might expect, people with anorexia have extremely *high* levels of ghrelin in their blood, which suggests that their bodies are trying desperately to switch hunger on but that hunger's call is being suppressed, ignored, or overridden (Ariyasu et al., 2001). Like most eating disorders, anorexia strikes more women than men, and 40% of newly identified cases of anorexia are among females who are 15 to 19 years old.

Anorexia may have both cultural and biological causes. For example, women with anorexia typically believe that thinness equals beauty, and it isn't hard to understand why. The average American woman is 5′4″ tall and weighs 140 pounds, but the average American fashion model is 5′11″ tall and weighs 117 pounds. Indeed, most college-age women report wanting to be thinner than they are (Rozin, Trachtenberg, & Cohen, 2001), and nearly one in five reports being *embarrassed* to be seen buying a chocolate bar (Rozin, Bauer, & Catanese, 2003). But anorexia is not just "vanity run amok" (Striegel-Moore & Bulik, 2007). Many researchers believe that there are as-yet-undiscovered biological and/or genetic components to the illness as well. For example, although anorexia primarily affects women, men have a sharply increased risk of becoming anorexic if they have a female twin who has the disorder (Procopio & Marriott, 2007), suggesting that anorexia may have something to do with prenatal exposure to female hormones.

? What causes anorexia?

Bulimia and anorexia are problems for many people. But America's most pervasive eating-related problem is obesity. Since 1999, Americans have collectively gained more than a billion pounds (Kolbert, 2009). The average American man is now 17 pounds heavier and the average American woman is now 19 pounds heavier than they were in the 1970s. The proportion of overweight children has doubled, the proportion of overweight teens has tripled, and a full 40% of American women are now too heavy to enlist in the military. In 1991, no state had an obesity rate higher than 20%. By 2008, only one state (Colorado) had an obesity rate of 20% or less (see **FIGURE 8.15**).

Obesity is defined as having a body mass index (or BMI) of 30 or greater. **TABLE 8.1** allows you to compute your body mass index, and the odds are that you won't like what you learn. Although BMI is a better predictor of mortality for some people than for others (Romero-Corral et al., 2006; van Dis et al., 2009), most researchers agree that an extremely high BMI is unhealthy. Every year, obesity-related illnesses cost our nation about $147 billion (Finkelstein et al., 2009) and about 3 million lives (Allison et al., 1999).

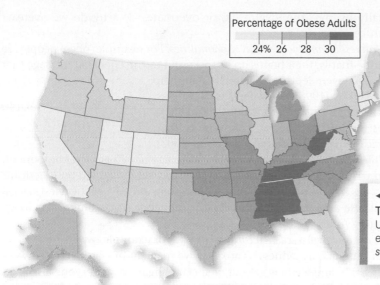

Percentage of Obese Adults

24% 26 28 30

bulimia nervosa An eating disorder characterized by binge eating followed by purging.

anorexia nervosa An eating disorder characterized by an intense fear of being fat and severe restriction of food intake.

◀ FIGURE 8.15
The Geography of Obesity This 2008 map of U.S. obesity rates shows that obesity is a problem everywhere, but especially in the Southeast.
Source: http://www.nytimes.com/2009/08/11/health/11stat.html

In addition to these physical risks, obese people tend to be viewed negatively by others, have lower self-esteem, and have a lower quality of life (Hebl & Heatherton, 1997; Kolotkin, Meter, & Williams, 2001). Obese women earn about 7% less than their non-obese counterparts (Lempert, 2007), and the stigma of obesity is so powerful that average-weight people are viewed negatively if they even have a relationship with someone who is obese (Hebl & Mannix, 2003). All of this is terribly unfair, of course. As one scientist noted, we need to declare "a war on obesity, not the obese" (Friedman, 2003).

TABLE 8.1

Body Mass Index Table

	Normal						Overweight					Obese										Extreme Obesity														
BMI	19	20	21	22	23	24	25	26	27	28	29	30	31	32	33	34	35	36	37	38	39	40	41	42	43	44	45	46	47	48	49	50	51	52	53	54
Height (Inches)	Body Weight (pounds)																																			
58	91	96	100	105	110	115	119	124	129	134	138	143	148	153	158	162	167	172	177	181	186	191	196	201	205	210	215	220	224	229	234	239	244	248	253	258
59	94	99	104	109	114	119	124	128	133	138	143	148	153	158	163	169	173	178	183	188	193	198	203	308	212	217	222	227	232	237	242	247	252	257	262	267
60	97	102	107	112	116	123	128	133	138	143	148	153	156	163	168	174	179	184	189	194	199	204	209	215	220	225	230	235	240	245	250	256	261	266	271	278
61	100	108	111	116	122	127	132	137	143	148	153	156	164	169	174	180	186	190	195	201	206	211	217	222	227	232	238	243	248	254	259	264	269	275	280	285
62	104	109	115	120	126	131	138	142	147	153	158	164	169	175	180	186	191	196	202	207	213	218	224	229	235	240	248	251	258	262	267	273	278	264	289	295
63	107	113	118	124	130	135	141	148	152	158	163	169	175	180	188	191	197	203	208	214	220	225	231	237	242	248	254	260	265	270	278	282	287	293	299	304
64	110	118	122	128	134	140	145	151	157	163	169	174	180	188	192	197	204	209	215	221	227	232	238	244	250	258	262	267	273	279	285	291	298	302	308	314
65	114	120	128	132	138	144	150	156	162	168	174	180	186	192	193	204	210	218	222	228	234	240	246	252	258	264	270	278	282	288	294	300	308	312	318	324
66	118	124	130	138	142	148	155	161	167	173	179	186	192	198	204	210	216	223	229	235	241	247	253	260	266	272	278	284	291	297	303	309	315	322	328	334
67	121	127	134	140	146	153	159	166	172	178	185	191	198	204	211	217	223	230	238	242	249	256	261	268	274	280	287	293	299	308	312	319	325	331	338	344
68	125	131	138	144	151	158	164	171	177	184	190	197	203	210	216	223	230	236	243	249	256	262	269	278	282	289	295	302	303	315	322	328	335	341	348	354
69	128	135	142	149	155	162	169	178	182	189	195	203	209	218	223	230	236	243	250	257	263	270	277	284	291	297	304	311	318	324	331	338	345	351	358	365
70	132	139	146	153	160	167	174	181	188	195	202	209	216	222	229	236	243	250	257	264	271	278	285	292	299	308	313	320	327	334	341	348	355	362	369	378
71	138	143	150	157	166	172	179	186	193	200	208	215	222	229	235	243	250	257	265	272	279	288	293	301	308	315	322	329	338	343	351	358	365	372	379	388
72	140	147	154	162	169	177	184	191	199	208	213	221	228	235	242	250	258	265	272	279	287	294	302	309	316	324	331	338	346	353	361	368	375	383	390	397
73	144	151	159	166	174	182	189	197	204	212	219	227	236	242	250	257	266	272	280	288	295	302	310	318	326	333	340	348	355	363	371	378	388	393	401	408
74	148	155	163	171	179	188	194	202	210	218	225	233	241	249	258	264	272	280	287	295	303	311	319	328	334	342	350	358	365	373	381	389	398	404	412	420
75	152	160	166	178	184	192	200	208	216	224	232	240	248	256	264	272	279	287	295	303	311	319	327	335	343	351	359	367	375	383	391	399	407	415	423	431
76	158	164	172	180	189	197	205	213	221	230	238	246	254	263	271	279	287	295	304	312	320	328	338	344	353	361	369	377	385	394	402	410	418	428	436	443

Source: Adapted from National Institutes of Health, 1998, *Clinical Guidelines on the Identification, Evaluation, and Treatment of Overweight and Obesity in Adults: The Evidence Report.* This and other information about overweight and obesity can be found at www.nhlbi.nih.gov/guidelines/obesity/ob_home.htm.

metabolism The rate at which energy is used by the body.

We don't typically overbreathe, overdrink, or overmate—so why do we overeat? There are at least three reasons.

First, *overeating can result from biochemical abnormalities.* For example, obese people are often leptin-resistant—that is, their brains do not respond to the chemical message that shuts hunger off—and even leptin injections don't help them (Friedman & Halaas, 1998; Heymsfield et al., 1999). For such people, the urge to eat is incredibly compelling, and they can't "just decide" to stop eating any more than you could just decide to stop breathing (Friedman, 2003). Obesity is also highly heritable (Allison et al., 1996) and may have a genetic component, which may explain why a disproportionate amount of the weight gained by Americans in the past few decades has been gained by those who were already the heaviest (Flegal & Troiano, 2000). These people may have a genetic tendency to become obese in response to the changing American diet.

? Why do people overeat?

Second, *we often eat even when we aren't really hungry.* For example, we may eat to reduce negative emotions such as sadness or anxiety, we may eat out of habit ("I always have ice cream at night"), and we may eat out of social obligation ("Everyone else is ordering dessert") (Herman, Roth, & Polivy, 2003). Sometimes we eat simply because the clock tells us that we should (Schachter & Gross, 1968), which is why people with amnesia will happily eat a second lunch shortly after finishing an unremembered first one (Rozin et al., 1998). (See the Real World box.)

Third, *nature designed us to overeat.* For most of our evolutionary history, the main food-related problem facing our ancestors was starvation, and we evolved two strategies to avoid it. First, we developed a strong attraction to foods that provide large amounts of energy per bite—in other words, foods that are calorically rich—which is why most of us prefer hamburgers and milkshakes to celery and water. Second, we developed an ability to store excess food energy in the form of

THE REAL WORLD

Jeet Jet?

In 1923, a reporter for the *New York Times* asked the British mountaineer George Leigh Mallory why he wanted to climb Mount Everest. Mallory replied: "Because it's there."

Apparently, that's also the reason why we eat. Brian Wansink and colleagues (2005) wondered whether the amount of food people eat is influenced by the amount of food they see in front of them. So they invited participants to their laboratory, sat them down in front of a large bowl of tomato soup, and told them to eat as much as they wanted. In one condition of the study, a server came to the table and refilled the participant's bowl whenever it got down to about a quarter full. In another condition, the bowl was not refilled by a server. Rather, unbeknownst to the participants, the bottom of the bowl was connected by a long tube to a large vat of soup, so whenever the participant ate from the bowl it would slowly and almost imperceptibly refill itself.

▲ Researcher Brian Wansink and his bottomless bowl of soup.

What the researchers found was sobering. Participants who unknowingly ate from a "bottomless bowl" consumed a whopping 73% more soup than those who ate from normal bowls—and yet, they didn't think they had consumed more and they didn't report feeling any more full.

It seems that we find it easier to keep track of what we are eating than how much, and this can cause us to overeat even when we are trying our best to do just the opposite. For instance, one study showed that diners at an Italian restaurant often chose to eat butter on their bread rather than dipping it in olive oil because they thought that doing so would reduce the number of calories per slice. And they were right. What they didn't realize, however, is that they would unconsciously compensate for this reduction in calories by eating 23% more bread during the meal (Wansink & Linder, 2003).

This and other research suggests that one of the best ways to reduce our waists is simply to count our bites.

fat, which enabled us to eat more than we needed when food was plentiful and then live off our reserves when food was scarce. We are beautifully engineered for a world in which food is generally low-cal and scarce, and the problem is that we don't live in that world anymore. Instead, we live in a world in which the calorie-laden miracles of modern technology—from chocolate cup-cakes to sausage pizzas—are inexpensive and readily available. As two researchers recently wrote, "We evolved on the savannahs of Africa; we now live in Candy-land" (Power & Schulkin, 2009). To make matters worse, many of Candyland's foods tend to be high in saturated fat, which has the paradoxical effect of making the brain *less* sensitive to some of the chemical messengers that tell us to stop eating (Benoit et al., 2009).

It is all too easy to overeat and become overweight or obese, and it is all too difficult to reverse course. The human body resists weight loss in two ways. First, when we gain weight, we experience an increase in both the size and the number of fat cells in our bodies (usually in our abdomens if we are male and in our thighs and buttocks if we are female). But when we lose weight, we experience a decrease in the size of our fat cells but no decrease in their number. Once our bodies have added a fat cell, that cell is pretty much there to stay. It may become thinner when we diet, but it is unlikely to die.

? **Why is dieting so difficult and ineffective?**

Second, our bodies respond to dieting by decreasing our **metabolism**, which is *the rate at which energy is used.* When our bodies sense that we are living through a famine (which is what they conclude when we refuse to feed them), they find more efficient ways to turn food into fat—a great trick for our ancestors but a real nuisance for us. Indeed, when rats are overfed, then put on diets, then overfed again and put on diets again, they gain weight faster and lose it more slowly the second time around, which suggests that with each round of dieting, their bodies become increasingly efficient at converting food to fat (Brownell et al., 1986). The bottom line is that avoiding obesity is easier than overcoming it.

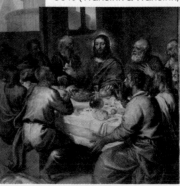

◀ Idris Lewis and his wife both fit into the pants he used to wear in 2009 when he weighed 364 pounds. Unfortunately, dieting rarely works. Most people who lose significant amounts of weight regain most or all of it within a year (Polivy & Herman, 2002).

BEN BIRCHALL/PA WIRE URN: 7606032/AP IMAGES

▼ One reason why obesity rates are rising is that "normal portions" keep getting larger. When researchers analyzed 52 depictions of "The Last Supper" that were painted between the years 1000 and 1800, they found that the average plate size increased by 66% (Wansink & Wansink, 2010).

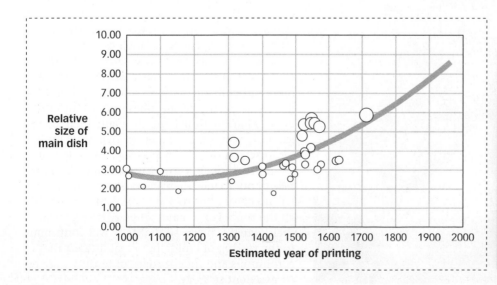

SCALA/ART RESOURCE, NY

Relative size of main dish

Estimated year of printing

"Come back, young man. He needs a booster shot."

Motivation for Sex

Food motivates us because it is essential to our survival. But sex is also essential to our survival—or at least to the survival of our DNA—thus evolution has ensured that a desire for sex is wired deep into the brain of almost every one of us. In some ways, that wiring scheme is simple: Glands secrete hormones that travel through the blood to the brain and stimulate sexual desire. But which hormones, which parts of the brain, and what triggers the launch in the first place?

A hormone called dihydroepiandosterone (DHEA) seems to be involved in the initial onset of sexual desire. Both males and females begin producing this slow-acting hormone at about the age of 6, which may explain why boys and girls both experience their initial sexual interest at about the age of 10 despite the fact that boys reach puberty much later than girls. Two other hormones have more gender-specific effects. Both males and females produce testosterone and estrogen, but males produce more of the former and females produce more of the latter. As you will learn in Chapter 11, these two hormones are largely responsible for the physical and psychological changes that characterize puberty. But are they also responsible for the waxing and waning of sexual desire in adults?

The answer appears to be yes—as long as those adults are rats. Testosterone increases the sexual desire of male rats by acting on a particular area of the hypothalamus, and estrogen increases the sexual desire of female rats by acting on a different area of the hypothalamus. Lesions to these areas reduce sexual motivation in the respective genders, and when testosterone or estrogen is applied to these areas, sexual motivation increases. In short, testosterone regulates sexual desire in male rats and estrogen regulates both sexual desire and fertility in female rats.

The story for human beings is far more interesting. The females of most mammalian species—for example, dogs, cats, and rats—have little or no interest in sex except when their estrogen levels are high, which happens when they are ovulating (i.e., when they are "in estrus" or "in heat"). In other words, estrogen regulates both ovulation and sexual interest in these mammals. But female human beings can be interested in sex at any point in their monthly cycles. Although the level of estrogen in a woman's body changes dramatically over the course of her monthly menstrual cycle, studies suggest that sexual desire changes little, if at all. Somewhere in the course of our evolution, it seems, women's sexual interest became independent of their ovulation.

Why don't female humans show clear signs of ovulation?

Some theorists have speculated that the advantage of this independence was that it made it more difficult for males to know whether a female was in the fertile phase of her monthly cycle. Male mammals often guard their mates jealously when their mates are ovulating but go off in search of other females when their mates are not. If a male cannot use his mate's sexual receptivity to tell when she is ovulating, then he has no choice but to stay around and guard her all the time. For females who are trying to keep their mates at home so that they will contribute to the rearing of children, sexual interest that is continuous and independent of fertility may be an excellent strategy.

▼ The red coloration on the female gelada's chest (left) indicates that she is in estrus and amenable to sex. The sexual interest of a female human being (right) is not limited to a particular time in her monthly cycle.

If estrogen is not the hormonal basis of women's sex drives, then what is? Two pieces of evidence suggests that the answer is testosterone—the same hormone that drives male sexuality. First, when women are given testosterone, their sex drives increase. Second, men naturally have more testosterone than women do, and they clearly have a stronger sex drive. Men are more likely than women to think about sex, have sexual fantasies, seek sex and sexual variety (whether positions or partners), masturbate, want sex at an early point in a relationship, sacrifice other things for sex, have permissive attitudes toward sex, and complain about low sex drive in their partners (Baumeister, Cantanese, & Vohs, 2001). All of this suggests that testosterone is the hormonal basis of sex drive in both men and women.

human sexual response cycle The stages of physiological arousal during sexual activity.

Sexual Activity

Men and women may have different levels of sexual drive, but their physiological responses during sex are fairly similar. Prior to the 1960s, data on human sexual behavior consisted primarily of people's answers to questions about their sex lives—and you may have noticed that this is a topic about which people don't always tell the truth. William Masters and Virginia Johnson changed all that by conducting groundbreaking studies in which they actually measured the physical responses of many hundreds of volunteers as they masturbated or had sex in the laboratory (Masters & Johnson, 1966). Their work led to many discoveries, including a better understanding of the **human sexual response cycle**, which refers to *the stages of physiological arousal during sexual activity* (see **FIGURE 8.16**). Human sexual response has four phases:

> During the *excitement phase*, muscle tension and blood flow increase in and around the sexual organs, heart and respiration rates increase, and blood pressure rises. Both men and women may experience erect nipples and a "sex flush" on the skin of the upper body and face. A man's penis typically becomes erect or partially erect and his testicles draw upward, while a woman's vagina typically becomes lubricated and her clitoris becomes swollen.

> During the *plateau phase,* heart rate and muscle tension increase further. A man's urinary bladder closes to prevent urine from mixing with semen, and muscles at the base of his penis begin a steady rhythmic contraction. A man's Cowper gland may secrete a small amount of lubricating fluid (which often contains enough sperm to cause pregnancy). A woman's clitoris may withdraw slightly, and her vagina may become more lubricated. Her outer vagina may swell, and her muscles may tighten and reduce the diameter of the opening of the vagina.

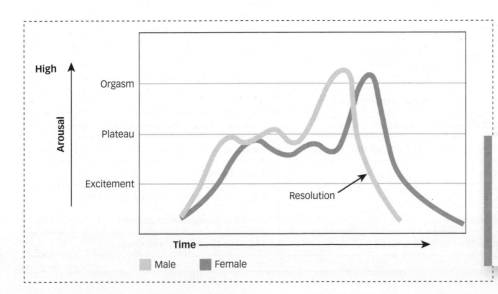

◄ FIGURE 8.16
The Human Sexual Response Cycle The pattern of the sexual response cycle is quite similar for men and for women. Both men and women go through the excitement, plateau, orgasm, and resolution phases, though the timing of their response may differ.

> During the *orgasm* phase, breathing becomes extremely rapid and the pelvic muscles begin a series of rhythmic contractions. Both men and women experience quick cycles of muscle contraction of the anus and lower pelvic muscles, and women often experience uterine and vaginal contractions as well. During this phase, men ejaculate about two to five milliliters of semen (depending on how long it has been since their last orgasm and how long they were aroused prior to ejaculation). Ninety-five percent of heterosexual men and 69% of heterosexual women reported having an orgasm during their last sexual encounter (Richters et al., 2006), though roughly 15% of women never experience orgasm, less than half experience orgasm from intercourse alone, and roughly half report having "faked" an orgasm at least once (Wiederman, 1997). The frequency with which women have orgasms seems to have a relatively large genetic component (Dawood et al., 2005). When men and women do have orgasms, they typically experience them as intensely pleasurable.

> During the *resolution phase,* muscles relax, blood pressure drops, and the body returns to its resting state. Most men and women experience a *refractory period,* during which further stimulation does not produce excitement. This period may last from minutes to days and is typically longer for men than for women.

People have sex for many different reasons. Although sex is necessary for reproduction, the vast majority of sexual acts are not meant to produce babies. Research on college students (Meston & Buss, 2007) suggests that people have sex for four general reasons: *physical attraction* ("The person had beautiful eyes"), as a *means to an end* ("I wanted to be popular"), to increase *emotional connection* ("I wanted to communicate at a deeper level"), and to *alleviate insecurity* ("It was the only way my partner would spend time with me"). Although men are more likely than women to report having sex for purely physical reasons, **TABLE 8.2** shows that men and women don't differ dramatically in their most frequent responses. It is worth noting that not all sex is motivated by reasons like these: About half of college-age women and a quarter of college-age men report having unwanted sexual activity in a dating relationship (O'Sullivan & Allegeier, 1998). We will have much more to say about sexual attraction and relationships in Chapter 13.

? Why do people have sex?

TABLE 8.2

Reasons for Sex

Top Ten Reasons Why Men and Women Report Having Sex

	Women	Men
1	I was attracted to the person.	I was attracted to the person.
2	I wanted to experience the physical pleasure.	It feels good.
3	It feels good.	I wanted to experience the physical pleasure.
4	I wanted to show my affection to the person.	It's fun.
5	I wanted to express my love for the person.	I wanted to show my affection to the person.
6	I was sexually aroused and wanted the release.	I was sexually aroused and wanted the release.
7	I was "horny."	I was "horny."
8	It's fun.	I wanted to express my love for the person.
9	I realized I was in love.	I wanted to achieve an orgasm.
10	I was "in the heat of the moment."	I wanted to please my partner.

Source: Meston & Buss, 2007.

Psychological Motivations

So is life nothing more than the pursuit of ice cream and orgasms? To be sure, eating and sex are fundamental motivations, but most of us care about a few other things as well. We may crave kisses of both the romantic and chocolate variety, but we also crave friendship and respect, security and certainty, wisdom and meaning. In addition to the biological motivations that we share with all mammals, we also have psychological motivations that make us unique.

For example, all animals strive to stay alive, but only human beings realize that this striving is ultimately in vain and that death is life's inevitable end. We and we alone know that every breath we take brings us just a little bit closer to our own demise. Some psychologists have suggested that this knowledge creates a sense of "existential terror" and that much of our behavior is merely an attempt to manage it. According to *terror management theory,* one of the ways that people cope with their existential terror is by developing a *cultural worldview*—a shared set of beliefs about what is good and right and true (Greenberg, Solomon, & Arndt, 2008; Solomon et al., 2004). These beliefs allow people to see themselves as more than mortal animals because they inhabit a world of meaning in which they can achieve symbolic immortality (e.g., by leaving a great legacy or having children) and perhaps even literal immortality (e.g., by being pious and earning a spot in the afterlife). According to this theory, our cultural worldview is a shield that buffers us against the anxiety that knowledge of our own mortality creates.

Terror management theory gives rise to the **mortality-salience hypothesis**, which is *the prediction that people who are reminded of their own mortality will work to reinforce their cultural worldviews.* In the last 20 years, this hypothesis has been supported by nearly 400 studies. The results show that when people are reminded of death (often in very subtle ways, such as by flashing the word "death" for just a few milliseconds in a laboratory, or by stopping people on a street corner that happens to be near a graveyard), they are more likely to praise and reward those who share their cultural worldviews, derogate and punish those who don't, value their spouses and defend their countries, feel disgusted by "animalistic" behaviors such as breast-feeding, and so on. All of these responses are presumably ways of shoring up one's cultural worldview and thereby defending against the anxiety that reminders of one's own mortality naturally elicit. The motivation to avoid the anxiety associated with death is just one of dozens perhaps even hundreds of psychological motives that researchers have identified (Fiske, 2009; Shah & Gardner, 2008). We are motivated to like ourselves (Kwan et al., 2008; Sedikides & Gregg, 2008), to know ourselves (North & Swann, 2009; Swann et al., 2003), to belong to groups (Leary et al., 2008), to control our fates (Thompson et al., 2008), to achieve our goals (Conroy et al., 2009), and so on. Indeed, the list of psychological motives is so long that it is hard to tell when it will end. Is there a sensible way to organize this list?

> **How do people deal with knowledge of death?**

mortality-salience hypothesis The prediction that people who are reminded of their own mortality will work to reinforce their cultural worldviews.

▼ Miranda Patterson and Scott Amelor made an unusual decision when they decided to get married in a graveyard. Studies show that most people feel anxious when they think about death, which motivates them to do a variety of things to alleviate that anxiety.

AP PHOTO/JEFF ROBERSON

intrinsic motivation A motivation to take actions that are themselves rewarding.

extrinsic motivation A motivation to take actions that are not themselves rewarding but that lead to reward.

Kinds of Motivation

Without Carolus Linnaeus, there would be no *Homo sapiens*. Linnaeus was the 18th-century Swedish naturalist who developed the classification system, or "taxonomy," by which all living things are described. For example, he decided that your genus would be called *Homo* and your species would be called *sapiens*. Before Linnaeus, biologists had a long list of plants and animals. His organizational scheme brought order to the list and made modern biology possible.

Psychology needs its own Linnaeus. As of now, there is no widely accepted taxonomy of human motivations, and this makes it difficult for psychologists to develop theories about where motivations come from and how they operate. Nonetheless, psychologists have made some initial progress by identifying several of the key dimensions on which motivations differ.

Intrinsic vs. Extrinsic

Taking a psychology exam is not like eating a French fry. One makes you tired and the other makes you fat, one requires that you move your lips and the other requires that you don't, and so on. But the key difference between these activities is that one is a means to an end and one is an end in itself. An **intrinsic motivation** is *a motivation to take actions that are themselves rewarding.* When we eat a French fry because it tastes good, exercise because it feels good, or listen to music because it sounds good, we are intrinsically motivated. These activities don't *have* a payoff because they *are* a payoff. Conversely, an **extrinsic motivation** is *a motivation to take actions that lead to reward.* When we floss our teeth so we can avoid gum disease (and get dates), when we work hard for money so we can pay our rent (and get dates), and when we take an exam so we can get a college degree (and get money to get dates), we are extrinsically motivated. None of these things directly brings pleasure, but all may lead to pleasure in the long run.

Extrinsic motivation gets a bad rap. Americans tend to believe that people should "follow their hearts" and "do what they love," and we feel sorry for students who choose courses just to please their parents and for parents who choose jobs just to earn a pile of money. But the fact is that our ability to engage in behaviors that are unrewarding in the present because we believe they will bring greater rewards in the future is one of our species' most significant talents, and no other species can do it quite as well as we can (Gilbert, 2006). In research on the

? Why should people delay gratification?

ability to delay gratification (Ayduk et al., 2007; Mischel et al., 2004), people are typically faced with a choice between getting something they want right now (e.g., a scoop of ice cream) or waiting and getting more of what they want later (e.g., two scoops of ice cream). Waiting for ice cream is a lot like taking an exam or flossing: It isn't much

▶ Nobody shovels snow for fun, but rather, as a means to an end.

AFP PHOTO/STAN HONDA/NEWSCOM

fun, but you do it because you know you will reap greater rewards in the end. Studies show that 4-year-old children who can delay gratification are judged to be more intelligent and socially competent 10 years later and that they have higher SAT scores when they enter college (Mischel, Shoda, & Rodriguez, 1989). In fact, the ability to delay gratification is a better predictor of a child's grades in school than is the child's IQ (Duckworth & Seligman, 2005). Apparently there is something to be said for extrinsic motivation.

There is a lot to be said for intrinsic motivation too. People work harder when they are intrinsically motivated, they enjoy what they do more, and they do it more creatively. Both kinds of motivation have advantages, which is why many of us try to build lives in which we are both intrinsically and extrinsically motivated by the same activity—lives in which we are paid the big bucks for doing exactly what we like to do best. Who hasn't fantasized about becoming an artist or an athlete or Kanye's personal party planner? Alas, research suggests that it is difficult to get paid for doing what you love and still end up loving what you do because extrinsic rewards can undermine intrinsic interest (Deci, Koestner, & Ryan, 1999; Henderlong & Lepper, 2002). For example, in one study, college students who were intrinsically interested in a puzzle either were paid to complete it or completed it for free, and those who were paid were less likely to play with the puzzle later on (Deci, 1971). In a similar study, children who enjoyed drawing with Magic Markers were either promised or not promised an award for using them, and those who were promised the award were less likely to use the markers later (Lepper, Greene, & Nisbett, 1973). It appears that under some circumstances people take rewards to indicate that an activity isn't inherently pleasurable ("If they had to pay me to do that puzzle, it couldn't have been a very fun one"); thus rewards can cause people to lose their intrinsic motivation.

Why do rewards sometimes backfire?

Just as rewards can undermine intrinsic motivation, punishments can create it. In one study, children who had no intrinsic interest in playing with a toy suddenly gained an interest when the experimenter threatened to punish them if they touched it (Aronson, 1963). College students who had no intrinsic motivation to cheat on a test were more likely to do so if the experimenter explicitly warned against it (Wilson & Lassiter, 1982). Threats can suggest that a forbidden activity is desirable, and they can also have the paradoxical consequence of promoting the very behaviors they are meant to discourage. For example, when a group of day-care centers got fed up with parents who arrived late to pick up their children, some of them instituted a financial penalty for tardiness. As **FIGURE 8.17** shows, the financial penalty caused an *increase* in late arrivals (Gneezy & Rustichini, 2000). Why? Because parents are intrinsically motivated to fetch their kids and they generally do their best to be on time. But when the day-care centers imposed a fine for

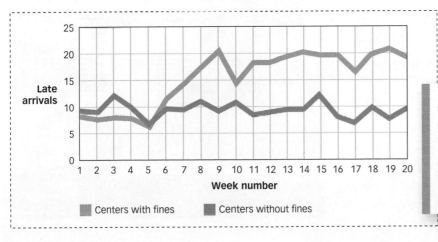

Late arrivals (y-axis)

Week number (x-axis) 1 2 3 4 5 6 7 8 9 10 11 12 13 14 15 16 17 18 19 20

■ Centers with fines   ■ Centers without fines

◀ FIGURE 8.17
When Threats Backfire Threats can cause behaviors that were once intrinsically motivated to become extrinsically motivated. Day-care centers that instituted fines for late-arriving parents saw an increase in the number of parents who arrived late.

conscious motivation A motivation of which one is aware.

unconscious motivation A motivation of which one is not aware.

need for achievement The motivation to solve worthwhile problems.

approach motivation A motivation to experience positive outcomes.

avoidance motivation A motivation not to experience negative outcomes.

late arrival, the parents became extrinsically motivated to fetch their children—and because the fine wasn't particularly large, they decided to pay a small financial penalty in order to leave their children in day care for an extra hour. When threats and rewards change intrinsic motivation into extrinsic motivation, unexpected consequences can follow.

Conscious vs. Unconscious

When prizewinning artists or scientists are asked to explain their achievements, they typically say things like, "I wanted to liberate color from form" or "I wanted to cure diabetes." They almost never say, "I wanted to exceed my father's accomplishments, thereby proving to my mother that I was worthy of her love." People clearly have **conscious motivations**, which are *motivations of which people are aware*, but they also have **unconscious motivations**, which are *motivations of which people are not aware* (Aarts, Custers, & Marien, 2008; Bargh et al., 2001; Hassin, Bargh, & Zimerman, 2009).

For example, psychologists David McClelland and John Atkinson argued that people vary in their **need for achievement**—which is *the motivation to solve worthwhile problems* (McClelland et al., 1953). They argued that this basic motivation is unconscious and thus must be measured with special techniques such as the *Thematic Apperception Test*, which presents people with a series of drawings and asks them to tell stories about them. The amount of "achievement-related imagery" in the person's story ostensibly reveals the person's unconscious need for achievement. (You'll learn more about these sorts of tests in Chapter 12.) Although there has been much controversy about the validity and reliability of measures such as these (Lilienfeld, Wood, & Garb, 2000; Tuerlinckx, De Boeck, & Lens, 2002), research shows that a person's responses on this test reliably predict the person's behavior in certain circumstances. For example, they can predict a child's grades in school (Khalid, 1991). Research also suggests that this motivation can be "primed" in much the same way that thoughts and feelings can be primed. For example, when words such as *achievement* are presented on a computer screen so rapidly that people cannot consciously perceive them, those people will work especially hard to solve a puzzle (Bargh et al., 2001) and will feel especially unhappy if they fail (Chartrand & Kay, 2006).

> **What makes people conscious of their motivations?**

What determines whether we are conscious of our motivations? Most actions have more than one motivation, and Robin Vallacher and Daniel Wegner have suggested that the ease or difficulty of performing the action determines which of these motivations we will be aware of (Vallacher & Wegner, 1985, 1987). When actions are easy

► Michael Phelps is clearly high—in need for achievement, that is—which helped him win eight gold medals at the 2008 Olympics.

AP PHOTO/NATI HARNIK

(e.g., screwing in a light bulb), we are aware of our most *general motivations* (e.g., to be helpful), but when actions are difficult (e.g., wrestling with a light bulb that is stuck in its socket), we are aware of our more specific motivations (e.g., to get the threads aligned). Vallacher and Wegner argue that people are usually aware of the general motivations for their behavior and only become aware of their more specific motivations when they encounter problems. For example, participants in an experiment drank coffee either from a normal mug or from a mug that had a heavy weight attached to the bottom, which made the mug difficult to manipulate. When asked what they were doing, those who were drinking from the normal mug explained that they were "satisfying needs," whereas those who were drinking from the weighted mug explained that they were "swallowing" (Wegner et al., 1984).

Approach vs. Avoidance

The poet James Thurber (1956) wrote "All men should strive to learn before they die/ what they are running from, and to, and why." The hedonic principle describes two conceptually distinct motivations: a motivation to "run to" pleasure and a motivation to "run from" pain. These motivations are what psychologists call an **approach motivation**, which is *a motivation to experience a positive outcome,* and an **avoidance motivation**, which is *a motivation not to experience a negative outcome.* Pleasure is not just the lack of pain, and pain is not just the lack of pleasure. They are independent experiences that occur in different parts of the brain (Davidson et al., 1990; Gray, 1990).

Research suggests that, all else being equal, avoidance motivations tend to be more powerful than approach motivations. Most people will turn down a chance to bet on a coin flip that would pay them $10 if it came up heads but would require them to pay $8 if it came up tails because they believe that the pain of losing $8 will be more intense than the pleasure of winning $10 (Kahneman & Tversky, 1979). Because people expect losses to have more powerful emotional consequences than equal-size gains, they will take more risks to avoid a loss than to achieve a gain. When participants are told that a disease is expected to kill 600 people and that one vaccine will definitely save 400 people, whereas another has a one-third chance of saving 600 people and a two-thirds chance of saving no one, they typically say that the government should play it safe and use the first vaccine. But when people are told that one vaccine will definitely allow 200 people to die, whereas the other has a one-third chance of letting no one die and a two-thirds chance of letting 600 people die, they say that the government should gamble and use the second vaccine (Tversky & Kahneman, 1981). If you whip out your calculator, you will quickly see that these are just two ways of describing the same thing—and yet when the vaccines are described in terms of the number of lives lost instead of the number of lives gained, most people are ready to take a big risk in order to avoid the horrible loss of 600 human lives.

On average, avoidance motivation is stronger than approach motivation, but the relative strength of these two tendencies does differ somewhat from person to person. **TABLE 8.3** on the next page shows a series of questions that have been used to measure the relative strength of a person's approach and avoidance tendencies (Carver & White, 1994). Research shows that people who are described by the high-approach items are happier when rewarded than those who are not, and that those who are described by the high-avoidance items are more anxious when threatened than those who are not (Carver, 2006). Just as some people seem to be more responsive to rewards than to punishments (and vice versa), some people tend to think about their behavior as attempts to get reward rather than to avoid punishment (and vice versa). People who have a *promotion focus* tend to think in terms of achieving gains whereas people who have a *prevention focus* tend to think in terms of avoiding losses. In one study, participants were given an anagram task. Some were told that they would be paid $4 for the experiment, but they could earn an extra dollar by finding 90% or more of all the possible words. Others were told that they would be paid $5 for the experiment,

TABLE 8.3

BIS/BAS

To what extent do each of these items describe you? The items in red measure the strength of your avoidance tendency and the items in green measure the strength of your approach tendency.

- Even if something bad is about to happen to me, I rarely experience fear or nervousness. (LOW AVOIDANCE)

- I go out of my way to get things I want. (HIGH APPROACH)

- When I'm doing well at something, I love to keep at it. (HIGH APPROACH))

- I'm always willing to try something new if I think it will be fun. (HIGH APPROACH)

- When I get something I want, I feel excited and energized. (HIGH APPROACH)

- Criticism or scolding hurts me quite a bit. (HIGH AVOIDANCE)

- When I want something, I usually go all-out to get it. (HIGH APPROACH)

- I will often do things for no other reason than that they might be fun. (HIGH APPROACH)

- If I see a chance to get something I want, I move on it right away. (HIGH APPROACH)

- I feel pretty worried or upset when I think or know somebody is angry at me. (HIGH AVOIDANCE)

- When I see an opportunity for something I like, I get excited right away. (HIGH APPROACH)

- I often act on the spur of the moment. (HIGH APPROACH)

- If I think something unpleasant is going to happen, I usually get pretty "worked up." (HIGH AVOIDANCE)

- When good things happen to me, it affects me strongly. (HIGH APPROACH)

- I feel worried when I think I have done poorly at something important. (HIGH AVOIDANCE)

- I crave excitement and new sensations. (HIGH APPROACH)

- When I go after something, I use a "no holds barred" approach. (HIGH APPROACH)

- I have very few fears compared to my friends. (LOW AVOIDANCE)

- It would excite me to win a contest. (HIGH APPROACH)

- I worry about making mistakes. (HIGH AVOIDANCE)

▶ People are motivated to avoid losses and achieve gains, but whether an outcome is seen as a loss or a gain often depends on how it is described. Smart retailers refer to price discrepancies such as this one as a "cash discount" rather than a "credit card surcharge."

MICHAEL BROWN/GETTY IMAGES

but they could avoid losing a dollar by not missing more than 10% of all the possible words. People who had a promotion focus performed better in the first case than in the second, but people who had a prevention focus performed better in the second case than in the first (Shah, Higgins, & Friedman, 1998). Similarly, people with a high need for achievement tend to be somewhat more motivated by their hope for success, whereas people with a low need for achievement tend to be somewhat more motivated by their fear of failure.

IN SUMMARY

○ Emotions motivate us indirectly by providing information about the world, but they also motivate us directly.

○ The hedonic principle suggests that people approach pleasure and avoid pain and that this basic motivation underlies all others. All organisms are born with some motivations and acquire others through experience.

○ When the body experiences a deficit, we experience a drive to remedy it. Biological motivations generally take precedence over psychological motivations. An example of a biological motivation is hunger, which is the result of a complex system of physiological processes, and problems with this system can lead to eating disorders and obesity, both of which are difficult to overcome. Another example of a biological motivation is sexual interest. Men and women experience roughly the same sequence of physiological events during sex, they engage in sex for most of the same reasons, and both have sex drives that are regulated by testosterone. An example of a psychological motivation is terror management. Knowledge of their own mortality makes people anxious, and they develop and maintain cultural worldviews to alleviate that anxiety.

○ People have many motivations that can be classified in many ways. Intrinsic motivations can be undermined by extrinsic rewards and punishments. People tend to be aware of their more general motivations unless difficulty with the production of action forces them to be aware of their more specific motivations. Avoidance motivations are generally more powerful than approach motivations, but this is truer for some people than for others.

WhereDoYouStand?

Here Comes the Bribe

Americans prize their right to vote. They talk about it, they sing about it, and they die for it. They just don't use it very much.

The U.S. Census Bureau estimates that about 60% of American citizens who are eligible to vote in a presidential election actually do so, and the numbers are significantly lower for "off-year" elections. Everyone seems to agree that this is a problem, including the people who don't vote, so what can be done? Government officials and social scientists have investigated numerous ways to increase voter turnout, and some of their efforts have had modest effects, but none have come close to solving the problem. And yet not all countries have this problem. Belgium, for instance, has a voter turnout rate close to 100% because for the better part of a century, failing to vote in Belgium has been illegal. (If you failed to vote in Belgium, don't worry; this only applies to Belgians.) Belgians who fail to vote may be fined, and if they fail to vote several times in a row, they may be "legally disenfranchised," which makes it difficult for them to get a job. Although some people have suggested that America should join the long list of countries that have compulsory voting, Americans generally don't like the threat of punishment.

But they sure do love the possibility of reward—and that's what led Arizona ophthalmologist Mark Osterloh to propose the Arizona Voter Reward Act, which would have awarded $1 million to a randomly selected voter in every election. As soon as Osterloh announced his idea, principled people lined up against it. "People should not go vote because they might win a lottery," said Curtis Gans, the director of the Center for the Study of the American Electorate in Washington. "We need to rekindle the religion of civic duty, and that is a hard job, but we should not make voting crassly commercial" (Archibold, 2006). An editorial in Arizona's *Yuma Sun* newspaper stated: "A jackpot is not the right motivator for voting. . . . People should vote because they want to and because they think it is important. . . . Bribing people to vote is a superficial approach that will have no beneficial outcome to the process, except to make some people feel good that the turnout numbers are higher" (Editorial, 2006). Nonetheless, 185,902 of Osterloh's fellow Arizonans thought his idea had merit, and they signed their names to get his measure on the ballot.

In November 2006, Arizonans defeated the measure by a sound margin, but Osterloh wasn't dejected. "I believe somebody is eventually going to bring this back and get this approved somewhere around the world, and it's going to spread," he said days after the election. "If anybody has a better idea of how to get people to vote, let me know and I will support it" (Rotstein, 2006).

Should our government motivate people to vote with extrinsic rewards or punishments? We know where Arizonans stand on this issue. How about you?

Chapter Review

KEY CONCEPT QUIZ

1. Emotions can be described by their location on the two dimensions of
   a. motivation and scaling.
   b. arousal and valence.
   c. stimulus and reaction.
   d. pain and pleasure.

2. Which theorists claimed that that a stimulus simultaneously causes both an emotional experience and a physiological reaction?
   a. Cannon and Bard
   b. James and Lange
   c. Schacter and Singer
   d. Klüver and Bucy

3. Which brain structure is most directly involved in the rapid appraisal of whether a stimulus is good or bad?
   a. the cortex
   b. the hypothalamus
   c. the amygdala
   d. the thalamus

4. Through _____, we change an emotional experience by changing the meaning of the emotion-eliciting stimulus.
   a. deactivation
   b. appraisal
   c. valence
   d. reappraisal

5. Which of the following does NOT provide any support for the universality hypothesis?
   a. Congenitally blind people make the facial expressions associated with the basic emotions.
   b. Infants only days old react to sweet tastes with smiles and to bitter tastes with expressions of disgust.
   c. Robots have been engineered to exhibit emotional expressions.
   d. Researchers have discovered that isolated people living a Stone Age existence with little contact with the outside world recognize the emotional expressions of people with contemporary lifestyles.

6. _____ is the idea that emotional expressions can cause emotional experiences.
   a. A display rule
   b. Expressional deception
   c. The universality hypothesis
   d. The facial feedback hypothesis

7. Two friends have asked you to help them settle a disagreement. You hear each side of the story and have an emotional response to one viewpoint, but you don't express it. This is an example of which display rule?
   a. deintensification
   b. masking
   c. neutralizing
   d. intensification

8. Insincere expressions tend to appear and disappear abruptly. What concept explains this?
   a. temporal patterning
   b. duration
   c. symmetry
   d. morphology

9. Which of the following statements is inaccurate?
   a. Certain facial muscles are reliably engaged by sincere facial expressions.
   b. Even when people smile bravely to mask disappointment, their faces tend to express small bursts of disappointment.
   c. Studies show that human lie detection ability is extremely good.
   d. The polygraph machines detect lies at a rate better than chance, but their error rate is still quite high.

10. The hedonic principle states that
    a. emotions provide people with information.
    b. people are motivated to experience pleasure and avoid pain.
    c. people use their moods as information about the likelihood of succeeding at a task.
    d. motivations are acquired solely through experience.

11. According to the early psychologists, an unlearned tendency to seek a particular goal is called
    a. an instinct.
    b. a drive.
    c. a motivation.
    d. a corrective action.

12. According to Maslow, the most basic of our needs is the need for
    a. self-actualization.
    b. esteem.
    c. safety and security.
    d. belongingness and love.

13. Which of the following is a primarily psychological motivation?
    a. hunger
    b. sexual interest
    c. terror management
    d. nutrition

14. Which of the following statements is true?
    a. Men and women engage in sex for many of the same reasons.
    b. Boys and girls experience initial sexual interest at different ages.
    c. The sequence of physiological arousal for men and women differs.
    d. The human male sex drive is regulated by testosterone while the human female sex drive is regulated by estrogen.

15. Which of the following activities is most likely the result of extrinsic motivation?
    a. completing a crossword puzzle
    b. pursuing a career as a musician
    c. having ice cream for dessert
    d. flossing one's teeth

KEY TERMS

CRITICAL THINKING QUESTIONS

1. More than two millennia ago, Roman emperor Marcus Aurelius wrote, "If you are distressed by anything external, the pain is not due to the thing itself, but to your estimate of it; and this you have the power to revoke at any moment." Does research support this claim? What about your personal experience? Have you ever had a painful emotion that you were able to revoke?

2. Whereas there is a rich variety of human languages across the globe, evidence suggests that facial displays of at least six primary emotions—anger, disgust, fear, happiness, sadness, and surprise—are universal. How can you explain this?

3. The hedonic principle is the notion that all people are motivated to experience pleasure and avoid pain. According to Aristotle, all other motivations rest on this one. If this is true, then how can you explain war?

RECOMMENDED READINGS

Ekman, P. (2007). *Emotions revealed: Recognizing faces and feelings to improve communication and emotional life* (2nd ed.). New York: Times Books.

Psychologist Paul Ekman explains the roots of our emotions and their expressions and answers such questions as: How does our body signal to others whether we are slightly sad or anguished, peeved or enraged? Can we learn to distinguish between a polite smile and the genuine thing? Can we ever truly control our emotions? A fascinating and fun book, packed with unique exercises and photographs.

Kessler, D. (2009). *The end of overeating: Taking control of the insatiable American appetite.* New York: Rodale Books.

Kessler explains how the desire to eat is stimulated by combinations of salt, fat, and sugar, and how the American food industry uses this knowledge to promote overeating. Why are McNuggets so soft? Because the less you chew, the more you eat. Somebody knows you better than you know yourself, and this book lets you fight back.

Westen, D. (2008). *The political brain: The role of emotion in deciding the fate of the nation.* Washington, PublicAffairs.

Dissecting everything from electoral outcomes to campaign advertisements, psychologist Drew Westen shows that Americans don't vote with their heads but with their hearts. President Clinton called it "the most interesting, informative book on politics I've read in many years."

ANSWERS TO KEY CONCEPT QUIZ

1. b; 2. a; 3. c; 4. d; 5. c; 6. d; 7. c; 8. a; 9. c; 10. b; 11. a; 12. c; 13. c; 14. a; 15. d.

Need more help? Additional resources are located at the book's free companion Web site at:
www.worthpublishers.com/schacter

9

Language and Thought

An English boy named Christopher showed an amazing talent for languages. By the age of 6, he had learned French from his sister's schoolbooks; he acquired Greek from a textbook in only 3 months. His talent was so prodigious that grown-up Christopher could converse fluently in 16 languages. When tested on English-French translations, he scored as well as a native French speaker. Presented with a made-up language, he figured out the complex rules easily, even though advanced language students found them virtually impossible to decipher (Smith & Tsimpli, 1995).

If you've concluded that Christopher is extremely smart, perhaps even a genius, you're wrong. His scores on standard intelligence tests are far below normal. He fails simple cognitive tests that 4-year-old children pass with ease, and he cannot even learn the rules for simple games like tic-tac-toe. Despite his dazzling talent, Christopher lives in a halfway house because he does not have the cognitive capacity to make decisions, reason, or solve problems in a way that would allow him to live independently.

▶ Christopher absorbed languages quickly from textbooks, yet he completely failed simple tests of other cognitive abilities.

ROMAN SIGAEV/ISTOCKPHOTO

CHRISTOPHER'S STRENGTHS AND WEAKNESSES OFFER COMPELLING EVIDENCE THAT COGNITION is composed of distinct abilities. People who learn languages with lightning speed are not necessarily gifted at decision making or problem solving. People who excel at reasoning may have no special ability to master languages. In this chapter, you will learn about five key higher cognitive functions: acquiring and using language, forming concepts and categories, making decisions, solving problems, and reasoning. We excel at these functions compared with other animals, and they help define who we are as a species. We'll learn about each of these abilities by examining evidence that reveals their unique psychological characteristics, and we'll learn about their distinct neural underpinnings by considering patients with brain lesions as well as neuroimaging studies. But despite clear differences among them, these five cognitive abilities share something important in common: They are critical to our functioning in just about all aspects of our everyday existence—including work, school, and personal relationships—and as we've already seen with Christopher, impairment of these cognitive abilities can result in major and lasting disruptions to our lives.

Language and Communication: From Rules to Meaning

Most social species have systems of communication that allow them to transmit messages to each other. Honeybees communicate the location of food sources by means of a "waggle dance" that indicates both the direction and distance of the food source from the hive (Kirchner & Towne, 1994; Von Frisch, 1974). Vervet monkeys have three different warning calls that uniquely signal the presence of their main predators: a leopard, an eagle, and a snake (Cheney & Seyfarth, 1990). A leopard call provokes them to climb higher into a tree; an eagle call makes them look up into the sky. Each different warning call conveys a particular meaning and functions like a word in a simple language.

Language is *a system for communicating with others using signals that are combined according to rules of grammar and convey meaning.* **Grammar** is *a set of rules that specify how the units of language can be combined to produce meaningful messages.* Language allows individuals to exchange information about the world, coordinate group action, and form strong social bonds.

Human language may have evolved from signaling systems used by other species. However, three striking differences distinguish human language from vervet monkey yelps, for example. First, the complex structure of human language distinguishes it from simpler signaling systems. Most humans can express a wider range of ideas and concepts than are found in the communications of other species, and humans can generate an essentially infinite number of novel sentences, whereas animals do not have anything like this capacity.

Second, humans use words to refer to intangible things, such as *unicorn* or *democracy*. These words could not have originated as simple alarm calls. Third, we use language to name, categorize, and describe things to ourselves when we think, which influences how knowledge is organized in our brains. It's doubtful that honeybees consciously think, *I'll fly north today to find more honey so the queen will be impressed!*

In this section, we'll examine the elements of human language that contribute to its complex structure, the ease with which we acquire language despite this complexity, and

What are the distinctions between human language and animal communication?

▼ Honeybees communicate with each other about the location of food by doing a waggle dance that indicates the direction and distance of food from the hive.

HANS REINHARD/CORBIS

DON FARRALL/GETTY IMAGES

how both biological and environmental influences shape language acquisition and use. We'll also look at startling disorders that reveal how language is organized in the brain and at researchers' attempts to teach apes human language. Finally, we'll consider the long-standing puzzle of how language and thought are related.

The Complex Structure of Human Language

Compared with other forms of communication, human language is a relatively recent evolutionary phenomenon, emerging as a spoken system no more than 1 to 3 million years ago and as a written system as little as 6,000 years ago. There are approximately 4,000 human languages, which linguists have grouped into about 50 language families (Nadasdy, 1995). Despite their differences, all of these languages share a basic structure involving a set of sounds and rules for combining those sounds to produce meanings.

What do all languages have in common?

Basic Characteristics

The smallest units of sound that are recognizable as speech rather than as random noise are **phonemes**. These building blocks of spoken language differ in how they are produced. For example, when you say *ba,* your vocal cords start to vibrate as soon as you begin the sound, but when you say *pa,* there is a 60-millisecond lag between the time you start the *p* sound and the time your vocal cords start to vibrate. *B* and *p* are classified as separate phonemes in English because they differ in the way they are produced by the human speaker.

Every language has **phonological rules** that *indicate how phonemes can be combined to produce speech sounds.* For example, the initial sound *ts* is acceptable in German but not in English. Typically, people learn these phonological rules without instruction, and if the rules are violated, the resulting speech sounds so odd that we describe it as speaking with an accent.

Phonemes are combined to make **morphemes**, *the smallest meaningful units of language* (see **FIGURE 9.1**). For example, your brain recognizes the *pe* sound you make at the beginning of *pat* as a speech *sound,* but it carries no particular meaning. The morpheme *pat,* on the other hand, is recognized as an element of speech that carries meaning.

language A system for communicating with others using signals that are combined according to rules of grammar and convey meaning.

grammar A set of rules that specify how the units of language can be combined to produce meaningful messages.

phoneme The smallest unit of sound that is recognizable as speech rather than as random noise.

phonological rules A set of rules that indicate how phonemes can be combined to produce speech sounds.

morphemes The smallest meaningful units of language.

▼ FIGURE 9.1
Units of Language A sentence—the largest unit of language—can be broken down into progressively smaller units: phrases, morphemes, and phonemes. In all languages, phonemes and morphemes form words, which can be combined into phrases and ultimately into sentences.

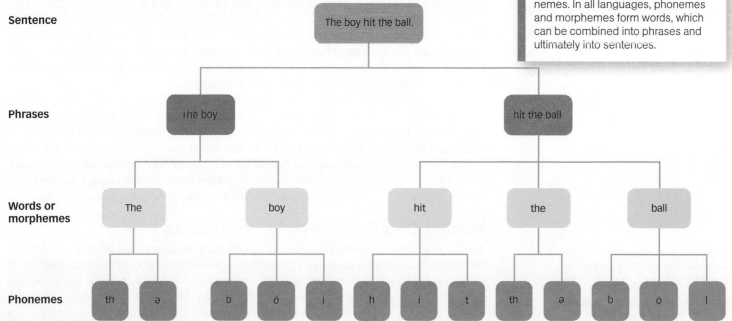

Sentence	The boy hit the ball.	
Phrases	The boy	hit the ball
Words or morphemes	The boy	hit the ball
Phonemes	th ə b ȯ i	h i t th ə b ȯ l

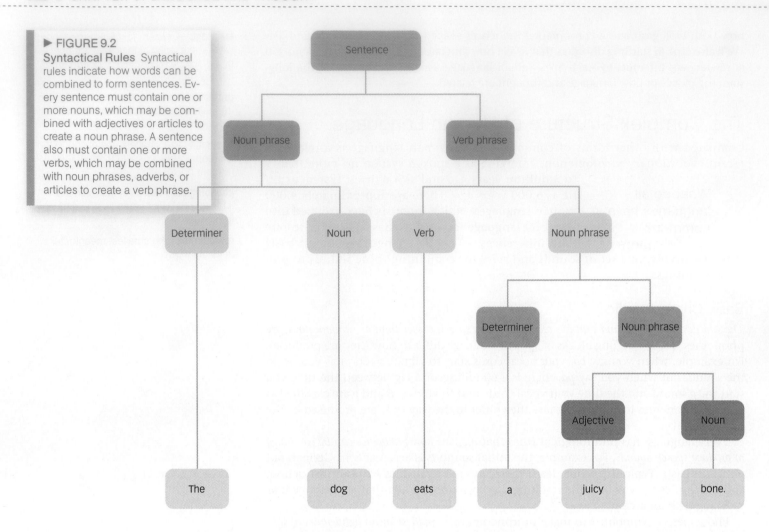

► FIGURE 9.2
Syntactical Rules Syntactical rules indicate how words can be combined to form sentences. Every sentence must contain one or more nouns, which may be combined with adjectives or articles to create a noun phrase. A sentence also must contain one or more verbs, which may be combined with noun phrases, adverbs, or articles to create a verb phrase.

All languages have grammar rules that generally fall into two categories: rules of morphology and rules of syntax. **Morphological rules** *indicate how morphemes can be combined to form words.* Some morphemes—content morphemes and function morphemes—can stand alone as words. *Content morphemes* refer to things and events (e.g., "cat," "dog," "take"). *Function morphemes* serve grammatical functions, such as tying sentences together ("and," "or," "but") or indicating time ("when"). About half of the morphemes in human languages are function morphemes, and it is the function morphemes that make human language grammatically complex enough to permit us to express abstract ideas rather than simply to verbally point to real objects in the here and now.

Content and function morphemes can be combined and recombined to form an infinite number of new sentences, which are governed by syntax. **Syntactical rules** *indicate how words can be combined to form phrases and sentences.* A simple syntactical rule in English is that every sentence must contain one or more nouns, which may be combined with adjectives or articles to create noun phrases (see **FIGURE 9.2**). A sentence also must contain one or more verbs, which may be combined with adverbs or articles to create verb phrases. So, the utterance "dogs bark" is a full sentence while "the big gray dog over by the building" is not.

Meaning: Deep Structure vs. Surface Structure

Sounds and rules are critical ingredients of human language that allow us to convey meaning. A sentence can be constructed in a way that obeys syntactical and other rules, yet is entirely lacking in meaning or *semantics,* as in the famous example provided by the linguist Noam Chomsky (1957, p. 15): "Colorless green ideas sleep furiously." Though we wouldn't be breaking any grammatical rules by uttering such a sentence, we could expect to elicit head scratches and strange looks from any nearby

morphological rules A set of rules that indicate how morphemes can be combined to form words.

syntactical rules A set of rules that indicate how words can be combined to form phrases and sentences.

listeners. Language usually conveys meaning quite well, but everyday experience shows us that misunderstandings can occur. These errors sometimes result from differences between the deep structure of sentences and their surface structure (Chomsky, 1957). **Deep structure** refers to *the meaning of a sentence*. **Surface structure** refers to *how a sentence is worded*. The sentences "The dog chased the cat" and "The cat was chased by the dog" mean the same thing (they have the same deep structure) even though on the surface their structures are different.

To generate a sentence, you begin with a deep structure (the meaning of the sentence) and create a surface structure (the particular words) to convey that meaning. When you comprehend a sentence, you do the reverse, processing the surface structure in order to extract the deep structure. After the deep structure is extracted, the surface structure is usually forgotten (Jarvella, 1970, 1971). In one study, researchers played tape-recorded stories to volunteers and then asked them to pick the sentences they had heard (Sachs, 1967). Participants frequently confused sentences they heard with sentences that had the same deep structure but a different surface structure. For example, if they heard the sentence "He struck John on the shoulder," they often mistakenly claimed they had heard "John was struck on the shoulder by him." In contrast, they rarely misidentified "John struck him on the shoulder" because this sentence has a different deep structure from the original sentence.

? Is the meaning or wording of a sentence typically more memorable?

Language Development

Language is a complex cognitive skill, yet we can carry on complex conversations with playmates and family before we begin school. Three characteristics of language development are worth bearing in mind. First, children learn language at an astonishingly rapid rate. The average 1-year-old has a vocabulary of 10 words. This tiny vocabulary expands to over *10,000* words in the next 4 years, requiring the child to learn, on average, about six or seven new words *every day*. Second, children make few errors while learning to speak, and as we'll see shortly, the errors they do make usually result from applying, but overgeneralizing, grammatical rules they've learned. This is an extraordinary feat. There are over 3 *million* ways to rearrange the words in any 10-word sentence, but only a few of these arrangements will be both grammatically correct and meaningful (Bickerton, 1990). Third, children's *passive mastery* of language develops faster than their *active mastery*. At every stage of language development, children understand language better than they speak.

Distinguishing Speech Sounds

At birth, infants can distinguish among all of the contrasting sounds that occur in all human languages. Within the first 6 months of life, they lose this ability, and, like their parents, can only distinguish among the contrasting sounds in the language they hear being spoken around them. For example, two distinct sounds in English are the *l* sound and the *r* sound, as in *lead* and *read*. These sounds are not distinguished in Japanese; instead, the *l* and *r* sounds fall within the same phoneme. Japanese adults cannot hear the difference between these two phonemes, but American adults can distinguish between them easily—and so can Japanese infants.

? What language ability do babies have that adults do not?

In one study, researchers constructed a tape of a voice saying "la-la-la" or "ra-ra-ra" repeatedly (Eimas et al., 1971). They rigged a pacifier so that whenever an infant sucked on it, a tape player that broadcast the "la-la" tape was activated. When the *la-la* sound began playing in response to their sucking, the babies were delighted and kept sucking on the pacifier to keep the *la-la* sound playing. After a while, they began to lose interest, and sucking frequency declined to about half of its initial rate. At this point, the experimenters switched the tape so that the voice now said "ra-ra-ra" repeatedly. The Japanese infants began sucking again with vigor, indicating that they could hear the difference between the old, boring *la* sound and the new, interesting *ra* sound.

deep structure The meaning of a sentence.

surface structure How a sentence is worded.

▲ In this videotaped test, the baby watches an animated toy animal while a single speech sound is repeated. After a few repetitions, the sound changes and then the display changes, and then they both change again. If the baby switches her attention when the sound changes, she is anticipating the new display, which demonstrates that she can discriminate between the sounds.

Infants can distinguish among speech sounds, but they cannot produce them reliably, relying mostly on cooing, cries, laughs, and other vocalizations to communicate. Between the ages of about 4 and 6 months, they begin to babble speech sounds. Regardless of the language they hear spoken, all infants go through the same babbling sequence. For example, *d* and *t* appear in infant babbling before *m* and *n*. Even deaf babies babble sounds they've never heard, and they do so in the same order as hearing babies do (Ollers & Eilers, 1988). This is evidence that babies aren't simply imitating the sounds they hear and suggests that babbling is a natural part of the language development process. Deaf babies don't babble as much, however, and their babbling is delayed relative to hearing babies (11 months rather than 6).

In order for vocal babbling to continue, however, babies must be able to hear themselves. In fact, delayed babbling or the cessation of babbling merits testing for possible hearing difficulties. Babbling problems can lead to speech impairments, but they do not necessarily prevent language acquisition. Deaf infants whose parents communicate using American Sign Language (ASL) begin to babble with their hands at the same age that hearing children begin to babble vocally—between 4 and 6 months (Petitto & Marentette, 1991). Their babbling consists of sign language syllables that are the fundamental components of ASL.

Language Milestones

At about 10 to 12 months of age, babies begin to utter (or sign) their first words. By 18 months, they can say about 50 words and can understand several times more than that. Toddlers generally learn nouns before verbs, and the nouns they learn first are names for everyday, concrete objects (e.g., chair, table, milk) (see **TABLE 9.1**). At about this time, their vocabularies undergo explosive growth. By the time the average child begins school, a vocabulary of 10,000 words is not unusual. By fifth grade, the average child knows the meanings of 40,000 words. By college, the average student's vocabulary is about 200,000 words. **Fast mapping**, in which *children map a word onto an underlying concept after only a single exposure,* enables them to learn at this rapid pace (Kan & Kohnert, 2008; Mervis & Bertrand, 1994). This astonishingly easy process contrasts dramatically with the effort required later to learn other concepts and skills, such as arithmetic or writing.

▼ Deaf infants who learn sign language from their parents start babbling with their hands around the same time that hearing infants babble vocally.

Around 24 months, children begin to form two-word sentences, such as "more milk" or "throw ball." Such sentences are referred to as **telegraphic speech** because they are *devoid of function morphemes and consist mostly of content words.* Yet despite the absence of function words, such as prepositions or articles, these two-word sentences tend to be grammatical; the words are ordered in a manner consistent with the syntactical rules of the language children are learning to speak. So, for example, toddlers will say "throw ball" rather than "ball throw" when they want you to throw the ball to them and "more milk" rather than "milk more" when they want you to give them more milk. With these seemingly primitive expressions, 2-year-olds show that they have already acquired an appreciation of the syntactical rules of the language they are learning.

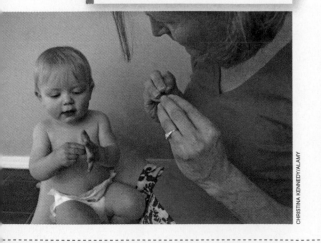

TABLE 9.1

Language Milestones

Average Age	Language Milestones
0–4 months	Can tell the difference between speech sounds (phonemes). Cooing, especially in response to speech.
4–6 months	Babbles consonants.
6–10 months	Understands some words and simple requests.
10–12 months	Begins to use single words.
12–18 months	Vocabulary of 30–50 words (simple nouns, adjectives, and action words).
18–24 months	Two-word phrases ordered according to syntactic rules. Vocabulary of 50–200 words. Understands rules.
24–36 months	Vocabulary of about 1,000 words. Production of phrases and incomplete sentences.
36–60 months	Vocabulary grows to more than 10,000 words; production of full sentences; mastery of grammatical morphemes (such as -ed for past tense) and function words (such as the, and, but). Can form questions and negations.

The Emergence of Grammatical Rules

Evidence of the ease with which children acquire grammatical rules comes from some interesting errors that children make while forming sentences. If you listen to average 2- or 3-year-old children speaking, you may notice that they use the correct past-tense versions of common verbs, as in the expressions "I ran" and "You ate." By the age of 4 or 5, the same children will be using incorrect forms of these verbs, saying such things as "I runned" or "You eated"—forms most children are unlikely to have ever heard (Prasada & Pinker, 1993). The reason is that very young children memorize the particular sounds (i.e., words) that express what they want to communicate. But as children acquire the grammatical rules of their language, they tend to *overgeneralize*. For example, if a child overgeneralizes the rule that past tense is indicated by -*ed*, then *run* becomes *runned* or even *ranned* instead of *ran*.

These errors show that language acquisition is not simply a matter of imitating adult speech. Instead, children acquire grammatical rules by listening to the speech around them and using the rules to create verbal forms they've never heard. They manage this without explicit awareness of the grammatical rules they've learned. In fact, few children or adults can articulate the grammatical rules of their native language, yet the speech they produce obeys these rules.

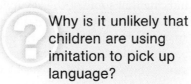 **Why is it unlikely that children are using imitation to pick up language?**

By about 3 years of age, children begin to generate complete simple sentences that include function words (e.g., "Give me *the* ball" and "That belongs *to* me"). The sentences increase in complexity over the next 2 years. By 4 to 5 years of age, many aspects of the language acquisition process are complete. As children continue to mature, their language skills become more refined, with added appreciation of subtler communicative uses of language, such as humor, sarcasm, or irony.

Language Development and Cognitive Development

Language development typically unfolds as a sequence of steps in which one milestone is achieved before moving on to the next. Nearly all infants begin with one-word utterances before moving on to telegraphic speech and then to simple sentences that include function morphemes. It's hard to find solid evidence of infants launching immediately into speaking in sentences—even though you may occasionally hear reports

fast mapping The fact that children can map a word onto an underlying concept after only a single exposure.

telegraphic speech Speech that is devoid of function morphemes and consists mostly of content words.

of such feats from proud parents, including possibly your own! This orderly progression could result from general cognitive development that is unrelated to experience with a specific language (Shore, 1986; Wexler, 1999). For example, perhaps infants begin with one- and then two-word utterances because their short-term memories are so limited that initially they can only hold in mind a word or two; additional cognitive development might be necessary before they have the capacity to put together a simple sentence. By contrast, the orderly progression might depend on experience with a specific language, reflecting a child's emerging knowledge of that language (Bates & Goodman, 1997; Gillette et al., 1999).

These two possibilities are difficult to tease apart, but recent research has begun to do so using a novel strategy: examining the acquisition of English by internationally adopted children who did not know any English prior to adoption (Snedeker, Geren, & Shafto, 2007). According to government statistics, there were just over 12,000 international adoptions to the United States in 2009 and in the range of 15,000–23,000 yearly during the preceding decade (U.S. Department of State, 2009). While most of those adoptees are infants or toddlers, a significant proportion are preschoolers. Studying the acquisition of English in such an older population provides a unique opportunity to explore the relationship between language development and cognitive development. If the orderly sequence of milestones that characterizes the acquisition of English by infants is a by-product of general cognitive development, then different patterns should be observed in older internationally adopted children, who are more advanced cognitively than infants. However, if the milestones of language development are critically dependent on experience with a specific language—English—then language learning in older adopted children should show the same orderly progression as seen in infants.

Why are studies of internationally adopted children especially useful?

The researchers examined preschoolers ranging from 2½ to 5½ years old, 3 to 18 months after they were adopted from China (Snedeker et al., 2007). They did so by mailing materials to parents, who periodically recorded language samples in their homes and also completed questionnaires concerning specific features of language observed in their children. These data were compared to similar data obtained from monolingual infants. The main result was clear-cut: Language acquisition in preschool-aged adopted children showed the same orderly progression of milestones that characterizes infants. These children began with one-word utterances before moving on to simple word combinations. Further, their vocabulary, just like that of infants, was initially dominated by nouns and they produced few function morphemes. These results indicate that some of the key milestones of language development depend on experience with English. However, the adopted children did add new words to their vocabularies more quickly than infants did, perhaps reflecting an influence of general cognitive development. Overall, though, the main message from this study is that observed shifts in early language development reflect specific characteristics of language learning rather than general limitations of cognitive development.

MARVIN JOSEPH/WASHINGTON POST/GETTY IMAGES

▲ Chinese preschoolers who are adopted by English-speaking parents progress through the same sequence of linguistic milestones as do infants born into English-speaking families, suggesting that these milestones reflect experience with English rather than general cognitive development.

Theories of Language Development

We know a good deal about how language develops, but what underlies the process? The language acquisition process has been the subject of considerable controversy and (at times) angry exchanges among scientists coming from three different approaches: behaviorist, nativist, and interactionist.

Behaviorist Explanations

According to B. F. Skinner's behaviorist explanation of language learning, we learn to talk in the same way we learn any other skill: through reinforcement, shaping, extinction, and the other basic principles of operant conditioning that you learned about in Chapter 7 (Skinner, 1957). As infants mature, they begin to vocalize. Those vocalizations that are not reinforced gradually diminish, and those that are reinforced remain in the developing child's repertoire. So, for example, when an infant gurgles "prah," most parents are pretty indifferent. However, a sound that even remotely resembles "da-da" is likely to be reinforced with smiles, whoops, and cackles of "Goooood baaaaaby!" by doting parents. Maturing children also imitate the speech patterns they hear. Then parents or other adults shape those speech patterns by reinforcing those that are grammatical and ignoring or punishing those that are ungrammatical. "I no want milk" is likely to be squelched by parental clucks and titters, whereas "No milk for me, thanks" will probably be reinforced.

The behavioral explanation is attractive because it offers a simple account of language development, but the theory cannot account for many fundamental characteristics of language development (Chomsky, 1986; Pinker, 1994; Pinker & Bloom, 1990).

> First, parents don't spend much time teaching their children to speak grammatically. In one well-documented study, researchers found that parents typically respond more to the truth content of their children's statements than to the grammar (Brown & Hanlon, 1970). So, for example, when a child expresses a sentiment such as "Nobody like me," his or her mother will respond with something like "Why do you think that?" or "I like you!" rather than "Now, listen carefully and repeat after me: Nobody likes me."

> Second, children generate many more grammatical sentences than they ever hear. This shows that children don't just imitate; they learn the rules for generating sentences. You'll recall that the same deep structure can generate a multitude of surface structures. It's highly unlikely that each of those separate surface structures was heard, reinforced, and learned by the developing child and much more likely that children simply acquire the ability to generate grammatical sentences.

> Third, as you read earlier in this chapter, the errors children make when learning to speak tend to be overgeneralizations of grammatical rules. The behaviorist explanation would not predict these overgeneralizations if children were learning through trial and error or simply imitating what they hear. That is, it would be difficult to overgeneralize if language development consisted solely of reinforced individual sentences or phrases.

Nativist Explanations

The study of language and cognition underwent an enormous change in the 1950s, when linguist Noam Chomsky published a blistering reply to the behaviorist approach. According to Chomsky, language-learning capacities are built into the brain, which is specialized to rapidly acquire language through simple exposure to speech. Chomsky and others have argued that humans have a particular ability for language that is separate from general intelligence. This **nativist theory** holds that *language development is best explained as an innate, biological capacity.* According to Chomsky, the human brain is equipped with a **language acquisition device (LAD)**—*a collection of processes that facilitate language learning.* Language processes naturally emerge as the infant matures, provided the infant receives adequate input to maintain the acquisition process.

Christopher's story is consistent with the nativist view of language development—his genius for language acquisition, despite his low overall intelligence, indicates that language capacity can be distinct from other mental capacities. Other individuals show the opposite pattern: People with normal or nearly normal intelligence can find certain aspects of human language difficult or impossible to learn. This condition is known as **genetic dysphasia**, *a syndrome characterized by an inability to learn the grammatical structure of language despite having otherwise normal intelligence.* Genetic dysphasia tends to run in families, and a single dominant gene has been implicated in its transmission (Gontier, 2008; Gopnik, 1990a, 1990b; Vargha-Khadem et al., 2005). Consider some sentences generated by children with the disorder:

She remembered when she hurts herself the other day.
Carol is cry in the church.

nativist theory The view that language development is best explained as an innate, biological capacity.

language acquisition device (LAD) A collection of processes that facilitate language learning.

genetic dysphasia A syndrome characterized by an inability to learn the grammatical structure of language despite having otherwise normal intelligence.

"Got idea. Talk better. Combine words. Make sentences."

▲ Immigrants who learn English as a second language are more proficient if they start to learn English before puberty rather than after.

Notice that the ideas these children are trying to communicate are intelligent. Their problems with grammatical rules persist even if they receive special language training. When asked to describe what she did over the weekend, one child wrote, "On Saturday I watch TV." Her teacher corrected the sentence to "On Saturday, I watch*ed* TV," drawing attention to the *-ed* rule for describing past events. The following week, the child was asked to write another account of what she did over the weekend. She wrote, "On Saturday I wash myself and I watched TV and I went to bed." Notice that although she had memorized the past-tense forms *watched* and *went*, she could not generalize the rule to form the past tense of another word (*washed*).

As predicted by the nativist view, studies of people with genetic dysphasia suggest that normal children learn the grammatical rules of human language with ease in part because they are "wired" to do so. This biological predisposition to acquire language explains why newborn infants can make contrasts among phonemes that occur in all human languages—even phonemes they've never heard spoken. If we learned language through imitation, as behaviorists theorized, infants would only distinguish the phonemes they'd actually heard. The nativist theory also explains why deaf babies babble speech sounds they have never heard and why the pattern of language development is similar in children throughout the world. These characteristics of language development are just what would be expected if our biological heritage provided us with the broad mechanics of human language.

Also consistent with the nativist view is evidence that language can be acquired only during a restricted period of development, as has been observed with songbirds. If young songbirds are prevented from hearing adult birds sing during a particular period in their early lives, they do not learn to sing. A similar mechanism seems to affect human language learning, as illustrated by the tragic case of Genie (Curtiss, 1977). At the age of 20 months, Genie was tied to a chair by her parents and kept in virtual isolation. Her father forbade Genie's mother and brother to speak to her, and he himself only growled and barked at her. She remained in this brutal state until the age of 13. Genie's life improved substantially, and she received years of language instruction. But it was too late. Her language skills remained extremely primitive. She developed a basic vocabulary and could communicate her ideas, but she could not grasp the grammatical rules of English.

Similar cases have been reported, with a common theme: Once puberty is reached, acquiring language becomes extremely difficult (Brown, 1958). Data from studies of language acquisition in immigrants support this conclusion. In one study, researchers found that the proficiency with which immigrants spoke English depended not on how long they'd lived in the United States, but on their age at immigration (Johnson & Newport, 1989). Those who arrived as children were the most proficient, whereas among those who immigrated after puberty, proficiency showed a significant decline regardless of the number of years in their new country. More recent work using fMRI shows that acquiring a second language early in childhood (between 1 and 5 years of age) results in very different representation of that language in the brain than does acquiring that language much later (after 9 years of age; Bloch et al., 2009).

Interactionist Explanations

Nativist theories are often criticized because they do not explain *how* language develops; they merely explain why. A complete theory of language acquisition requires an explanation of the processes by which the innate, biological capacity for language combines with environmental experience. The interactionist approach is that although infants are born with an innate ability to acquire language, social interactions play a crucial role in language. Interactionists point out that parents tailor their verbal interactions with children in ways that simplify the language acquisition process: They speak slowly, enunciate clearly, and use simpler sentences than they do when speaking with adults (Bruner, 1983; Farrar, 1990).

How does the interactionist theory of language acquisition differ from behaviorist and nativist theories?

Further evidence of the interaction of biology and experience comes from a fascinating study of deaf children's creation of a new language (Senghas, Kita, & Ozyurek, 2004). Prior to about 1980, deaf children in Nicaragua stayed at home and usually had little contact with other deaf individuals. In 1981, some deaf children began to attend a new vocational school. At first, the school did not teach a formal sign language, and none of the children had learned to sign at home, but the children gradually began to communicate using hand signals that they invented.

Over the past 25 years, their sign language has developed considerably, and researchers have studied this new language for the telltale characteristics of languages that have evolved over much longer periods. For instance, mature languages typically break down experience into separate components. When we describe something in motion, such as a rock rolling down a hill, our language separates the type of movement (rolling) and the direction of movement (down). If we simply made a gesture, however, we would use a single continuous downward movement to indicate this motion. This is exactly what the first children to develop the Nicaraguan sign language did. But younger groups of children, who have developed the sign language further, use separate signs to describe the direction and the type of movement—a defining characteristic of mature languages. That the younger children did not merely copy the signs from the older users suggests that a predisposition exists to use language to dissect our experiences. Thus, their acts of creation nicely illustrate the interplay of nativism (the predisposition to use language) and experience (growing up in an insulated deaf culture).

▲ A group of deaf children in Nicaragua created their own sign language, complete with grammatical rules, without receiving formal instruction. The language has evolved and matured over the past 25 years.

SUSAN MEISELAS/MAGNUM

Language Development and the Brain

As the brain matures, specialization of specific neurological structures takes place, and this allows language to develop (Kuhl & Rivera-Gaxiola, 2008). In early infancy, language processing is distributed across many areas of the brain. But language processing gradually becomes more and more concentrated in two areas, Broca's area and Wernicke's area, sometimes referred to as the language centers of the brain. As the brain matures, these areas become increasingly

How does language processing change in the brain as the child matures?

specialized for language, so much so that damage to them results in a serious condition called **aphasia**, defined as *difficulty in producing or comprehending language.*

Broca's area is located in the left frontal cortex; it is involved in the production of the sequential patterns in vocal and sign languages (see **FIGURE 9.3** on the next page). As you saw in Chapter 1, Broca's area is named after French physician Paul Broca, who first reported on speech problems resulting from damage to a specific area of the left frontal cortex (Broca, 1861, 1863). Patients with this damage, resulting in *Broca's aphasia,* understand language relatively well, although they have increasing comprehension difficulty as grammatical structures get more complex. But their real struggle is with speech production: Typically, they speak in short, staccato phrases that consist mostly of content morphemes (e.g., *cat, dog*). Function morphemes (e.g., *and, but*) are usually missing and grammatical structure is impaired. A person with the condition might say something like "Ah, Monday, uh, Casey park. Two, uh, friends, and, uh, 30 minutes."

Wernicke's area, located in the left temporal cortex, is involved in language comprehension (whether spoken or signed). German neurologist Carl Wernicke first described

aphasia Difficulty in producing or comprehending language.

▶ FIGURE 9.3
Broca's and Wernicke's Areas Neuroscientists study people with brain damage in order to better understand how the brain normally operates. When Broca's area is damaged, patients have a hard time producing sentences. When Wernicke's area is damaged, patients can produce sentences, but they tend to be meaningless.

Broca's area

Wernicke's area

the area that bears his name after observing speech difficulty in patients who had sustained damage to the left posterior temporal cortex (Wernicke, 1874). Patients with *Wernicke's aphasia* differ from those with Broca's aphasia in two ways: They can produce grammatical speech, but it tends to be meaningless, and they have considerable difficulty comprehending language. A patient suffering from Wernicke's aphasia might say something like, "Feel very well. In other words, I used to be able to work cigarettes. I don't know how. Things I couldn't hear from are here."

In normal language processing, Wernicke's area is highly active when we make judgments about word meaning, and damage to this area impairs comprehension of spoken and signed language, although the ability to identify nonlanguage sounds is unimpaired. For example, Japanese can be written using symbols that, like the English alphabet, represent speech sounds, or by using pictographs that, like Chinese pictographs, represent ideas. Japanese patients who suffer from Wernicke's aphasia encounter difficulties in writing and understanding the symbols that represent speech sounds but not pictographs.

As important as Broca's and Wernicke's areas are for language, they are not the entire story (for additional insight into brain and language in relation to bilingualism, see the Real World box). Four kinds of evidence indicate that the right cerebral hemisphere also contributes to language processing—especially to language comprehension (Jung-Beeman, 2005). First, when words are presented to the right hemisphere of healthy participants using divided visual field techniques (see Chapter 3), the right hemisphere shows some capacity for processing meaning. Second, patients with damage to the right hemisphere sometimes have subtle problems with language comprehension. Third, a number of neuroimaging studies have revealed evidence of right-hemisphere activation during language tasks. Fourth, and most directly related to language development, some children who have had their entire left hemspheres removed during adolescence as a treatment for epilepsy can recover many of their language abilities.

Can Other Species Learn Human Language?

The human vocal tract and the extremely nimble human hand are better suited to human language than are the throats and paws of other species. Nonetheless, attempts have been made to teach nonhuman animals, particularly apes, to communicate using human language.

Early attempts to teach apes to speak failed dismally because their vocal tracts cannot accommodate the sounds used in human languages (Hayes & Hayes, 1951). Later attempts to teach apes human language have met with more success—including teaching them to use American Sign Language and computer-monitored keyboards that display geometric symbols that represent words. Allen and Beatrix Gardner were the first to use ASL with apes (Gardner & Gardner, 1969). The Gardners worked with a young female chimpanzee named Washoe as though she were a deaf child, signing to her regularly, rewarding her correct efforts at signing, and assisting her acquisition of signs by manipulating her hands in a process referred to as "molding." In 4 years, Washoe learned approximately 160 words and could construct simple sentences, such as "More fruit." She also formed novel word constructions such as "water bird" for "duck." After a fight with a rhesus monkey, she signed, "dirty monkey!" This constituted a creative use of the term because she had only been taught the use of "dirty" to refer to soiled objects.

Other chimpanzees were immersed in ASL in a similar fashion, and Washoe and her companions were soon signing to each other, creating a learning environment conducive to language acquisition. One of Washoe's cohorts, a chimpanzee named Lucy, learned to sign "drink fruit" for watermelon. When Washoe's second infant died, her caretakers arranged for her to adopt an infant chimpanzee named Loulis.

▼ Allen and Beatrix Gardner used sign language to teach the female chimpanzee Washoe about 160 words. Washoe could also construct simple sentences and combine words in novel ways.

CHIMPANZEE & HUMAN COMMUNICATION INSTITUTE, CENTRAL WASHINGTON UNIVERSITY

THE REAL WORLD

Does Bilingualism Interfere with Cognitive Development?

Question: What do you call someone who speaks more than one language?

Answer: A polyglot

Question: What do you call someone who speaks only one language?

Answer: An American.

In most of the world, bilingualism is the norm, not the exception. In fact, nearly half of the world's population grows up speaking more than one language (Bialystok & Hakuta, 1994; Hakuta, 1986, 1999). Despite this, bilingualism is the source of considerable controversy in the American educational system. In recent years, many states have passed laws and many courts have issued rulings outlawing bilingual educational environments, and well-meaning authorities have discouraged parents from raising their children bilingually. These well-intentioned actions have been based on the assumption that bilingualism slows or interferes with normal cognitive development. Because much of our conceptual learning occurs verbally, the fear is that communicating with children in more than one language might hinder the proper acquisition and retrieval of crucial conceptual knowledge as well as slow the development of language skills. Is there any evidence for these assumptions?

In the United States, we are used to seeing street signs in English only, but in many countries multiple languages are used.

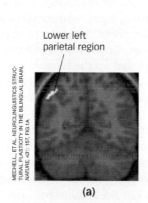

Lower left parietal region

MECHELLI, ET AL. NEUROLINGUISTICS STRUCTURAL PLASTICITY IN THE BILINGUAL BRAIN. NATURE, 43.: 157, FIG.1A

(a)

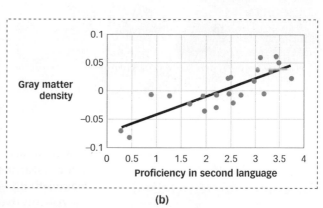

Gray matter density

Proficiency in second language

(b)

Bilingualism Alters Brain Structure Learning a second language early in life increases the density of gray matter in the brain. (a) A view of the lower left parietal region; has denser gray matter in bilinguals relative to monolinguals. (b) As proficiency in a second language increases, so does the density of gray matter in the lower parietal region. People who acquired a second language earlier in life were also found to have denser gray matter in this region. Interestingly, this area corresponds to the same area that is activated during verbal fluency tasks (Mechelli et al., 2004).

Early studies of bilingual children seemed to support this assumption. When compared with monolingual children, bilingual children performed more slowly when processing language, and their IQ scores were lower. A reexamination of these studies, however, revealed several crucial flaws. First, the tests were given in English even when that was not the child's primary language. Second, the bilingual participants were often first- or second-generation immigrants whose parents were not proficient in English. Finally, the bilingual children came from lower socioeconomic backgrounds than the monolingual children (Andrews, 1982).

Later studies controlled for these factors, revealing a very different picture of bilingual children's cognitive skills. The available evidence concerning language acquisition indicates that bilingual and monolingual children do not differ significantly in the course and rate of many aspects of their language development (Nicoladis & Genesee, 1997). In fact, middle-class participants who are fluent in two languages have been found to score higher than monolingual participants on measures of cognitive functioning, including cognitive flexibility and analytic reasoning (Bialystok, 1999, 2009; Campbell & Sais, 1995). These studies have revealed some disadvantages, however. Bilinguals tend to have a smaller vocabulary in each language than their monolingual peers (Portocarrero, Burright, & Donovick, 2007); they also process language more slowly than monolinguals and can sometimes take longer to formulate sentences (Bialystock, 2009; Taylor & Lambert, 1990).

Recent research on the brains of bilingual individuals indicates that when first learning a new language, there are marked differences in the brain regions engaged when reading words in the second language as compared to the first language, with much greater activity in the frontal lobe for second than first language words, probably reflecting great cognitive effort to read the newly learned words (Stein et al., 2009). However, these differences are reduced after just a few months of experiences with the second language, suggesting that the first and second languages come to depend increasingly on a shared brain network as second language proficiency increases (Stein et al., 2009). Further, learning a second language produces lasting changes in a part of the left parietal lobe that is involved in language (Mechelli et al., 2004). The gray matter in this region is denser in bilinguals than in monolinguals, and the increased density is most pronounced in those individuals who are most proficient in using their second language. Thus, rather than broadly impairing language development or cognitive development, learning a second language seems to increase the ability of the left parietal lobe to handle linguistic demands.

THE GREAT APE TRUST ORGANIZATION

▲ Kanzi, a young male chimpanzee, learned hundreds of words and word combinations through a keyboard system as he watched researchers try to teach his mother.

In a few months, young Loulis, who was not exposed to human signers, learned 68 signs simply by watching Washoe communicate with the other chimpanzees. People who have observed these interactions and are themselves fluent in ASL report little difficulty in following the conversations (Fouts & Bodamer, 1987). One such observer, a *New York Times* reporter who spent some time with Washoe, reported, "Suddenly I realized I was conversing with a member of another species in my native tongue."

Other researchers have taught bonobo chimpanzees to communicate using a geometric keyboard system (Savage-Rumbaugh, Shanker, & Taylor, 1998). Their star pupil, Kanzi, learned the keyboard system by watching researchers try to teach his mother. Like Loulis, young Kanzi picked up the language relatively easily (his mother never did learn the system), suggesting that like humans, birds, and other species, apes experience a critical period for acquiring communicative systems.

Kanzi has learned hundreds of words and has combined them to form thousands of word combinations. Also like human children, his passive mastery of language appears to exceed his ability to produce language. In one study, researchers tested 9-year-old Kanzi's understanding of 660 spoken sentences. The grammatically complex sentences asked him to perform simple actions, such as "Go get the balloon that's in the microwave" and "Pour the Perrier into the Coke." Some sentences were also potentially misleading, such as "Get the pine needles that are in the refrigerator," when there were pine needles in clear view on the floor. Impressively, Kanzi correctly carried out 72% of the 660 requests (Savage-Rumbaugh & Lewin, 1996).

These results indicate that apes can acquire sizable vocabularies, string words together to form short sentences, and process sentences that are grammatically complex. Their skills are especially impressive because human language is hardly their normal means of communication. Research with apes also suggests that the neurological "wiring" that allows us to learn language overlaps to some degree with theirs (and perhaps with other species').

Equally informative are the limitations apes exhibit when learning, comprehending, and using human language.

What do studies of apes and language teach us about humans and language?

The first limitation is the size of the vocabularies they acquire. As mentioned, Washoe's and Kanzi's vocabularies number in the hundreds, but an average 4-year-old human child has a vocabulary of approximately 10,000 words. The second limitation is the type of words they can master, primarily names for concrete objects and simple actions. Apes (and several other species) have the ability to map arbitrary sounds or symbols onto objects and actions, but learning, say, the meaning of the word *economics* would be difficult for Washoe or Kanzi. In other words, apes can learn signs for concepts they understand, but their conceptual repertoire is smaller and simpler than that of humans.

The third and perhaps most important limitation is the complexity of grammar that apes can use and comprehend. Apes can string signs together, but their constructions rarely exceed three or four words, and when they do, they are rarely grammatical. Comparing the grammatical structures produced by apes with those produced by human children highlights the complexity of human language as well as the ease and speed with which we generate and comprehend it.

Language and Thought: How Are They Related?

Language is such a dominant feature of our mental world that it is tempting to equate language with thought. Some theorists have even argued that language is simply a means of expressing thought. The **linguistic relativity hypothesis** maintains that *language shapes the nature of thought*. This idea was championed by Benjamin Whorf, an engineer who studied language in his spare time and was especially interested in Native American languages (1956). The most frequently

TOM CHALKLEY/THE NEW YORKER COLLECTION/CARTOONBANK.COM

"He says he wants a lawyer."

cited example of linguistic relativity comes from the Inuit in Canada. Their language has many different terms for frozen white flakes of precipitation, for which we use the word *snow*. Whorf believed that because they have so many terms for snow, the Inuit perceive and think about snow differently than do English speakers.

Whorf has been criticized for the anecdotal nature of his observations (Pinker, 1994), and some controlled research has cast doubt on Whorf's hypothesis. Eleanor Rosch (1973) studied the Dani, an isolated agricultural tribe living in New Guinea. They have only two terms for colors that roughly refer to "dark" and "light." If Whorf's hypothesis were correct, you would expect the Dani to have problems perceiving and learning different shades of color. But in Rosch's experiments, they learned shades of color just as well as people who have many more color terms in their first language. More recent evidence shows that language may influence color processing (Roberson et al., 2004). Researchers compared English children with African children from a cat-

▲ The Inuit in Canada use many different terms for snow, leading Benjamin Whorf to propose that they think about snow differently than do English speakers.

How does language influence our understanding of color?

tle-herding tribe in Namibia known as the Himba. The English have 11 basic color terms, but the Himba, who are largely isolated from the outside world, have only five. For example, they use the term *serandu* to refer to what English speakers would call red, pink, or orange.

Researchers showed a series of colored tiles to each child and then asked the child to choose that color from an array of 22 different colors. The youngest children, both English and Himba, who knew few or no color names, tended to confuse similar colors. But as the children grew and acquired more names for colors, their choices increasingly reflected the color terms they had learned. English children made fewer errors matching tiles that had English color names; Himba children made fewer errors for tiles with color names in Himba. These results reveal that language can indeed influence how children think about colors.

Similar effects have been observed in adults. Consider the 20 blue rectangles shown in **FIGURE 9.4**, which you'll easily see change gradually from lightest blue on the left to darkest blue on the right. What you might not know is that in Russian, there are different words

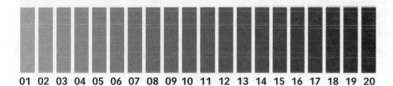

01 02 03 04 05 06 07 08 09 10 11 12 13 14 15 16 17 18 19 20

◄ **FIGURE 9.4**
Language Affects How We Think About Color Unlinke English, the Russian language has different words for light blue and dark blue. Russian speakers asked to pick which of the two bottom squares matched the color of the single square above responded more quickly when one of the bottom squares was called "goluboy" (light blue) and the other was called "siniy" (dark blue) than when both were referred to by the same name. English speakers took about the same amount of time.

WINAWER ET AL, PNAS V 104-19 2007 7780-7785? 2007 NATIONAL ACADEMY OF SCIENCES, USA

linguistic relativity hypothesis The proposal that language shapes the nature of thought.

for light blue ("goluboy") and dark blue ("siniy"). Researchers investigated whether Russian speakers would respond differently to patches of blue when they fell into different linguistic categories rather than into the same linguistic category (Winawer et al., 2007). Both Russian and English speakers on average classified rectangles 1–8 as "light blue" and 9–20 as "dark blue," but only Russian speakers use different words to refer to the two classes of blue. In the experimental task, participants were shown three blue squares, as in the lower part of Figure 9.4, and were asked to pick which of the two bottom squares matched the colors of the top square. Russian speakers responded more quickly when one of the bottom squares was "goluboy" and the other was "siniy" than when both bottom squares were "goluboy" or both were "siniy," whereas English speakers took about the same amount of time to respond in the two conditions (Winawer et al., 2007). As with children, language can affect how adults think about colors.

In another study exploring the relationship between language and thought, researchers looked at the way people think about time. In English, we often use spatial terms: We look *forward* to a promising future or move a meeting *back* to fit our schedule (Casasanto & Boroditsky, 2008). We also use these terms to describe horizontal spatial relations, such as taking three steps *forward* or two steps *back* (Boroditsky, 2001). In contrast, speakers of Mandarin (Chinese) often describe time using terms that refer to a vertical spatial dimension: Earlier events are referred to as "up," and later events as "down." To test the effect of this difference, researchers showed English speakers and Mandarin speakers either a horizontal or vertical display of objects and then asked them to make a judgment involving time, such as whether March comes before April (Boroditsky, 2001). English speakers were faster to make the time judgments after seeing a horizontal display, whereas for Mandarin speakers the opposite was true. When English speakers learned to use Mandarin spatial terms, their time judgments were also faster after seeing the vertical display! This result nicely shows another way in which language can influence thought.

Bear in mind, though, that either thought or language ability can be severely impaired while the capacity for the other is spared, as illustrated by the dramatic case of Christopher that you read earlier in this chapter—and as we'll see again in the next section. These kinds of observations have led some researchers to suggest that Whorf was only "half right" in his claims about the effect of language on thought (Regier & Kay, 2009).

IN SUMMARY

○ Human language is characterized by a complex organization—from phonemes to morphemes to phrases and finally to sentences.

○ Each of these levels of human language is constructed and understood according to grammatical rules that are acquired early in development, even without being taught explicitly. Instead, children appear to be biologically predisposed to process language in ways that allow them to extract these grammatical rules from the language they hear.

○ Our abilities to produce and comprehend language depend on distinct regions of the brain, with Broca's area critical for language production and Wernicke's area critical for comprehension.

○ Nonhuman primates can learn new vocabulary and construct simple sentences, but there are significant limitations on the size of their vocabularies and the grammatical complexity they can handle.

○ Recent studies on color processing and time judgments point to an influence of language on thought. However, it is also clear that language and thought are to some extent separate.

Concepts and Categories: How We Think

In October 2000, a 69-year old man known by the initials JB went for a neurological assessment because he was having difficulty understanding the meaning of words, even though he still performed well on many other perceptual and cognitive tasks. In 2002, as his problems worsened, he began participating in a research project concerned with the role of language in naming, recognizing, and classifying colors (Haslam et al., 2007). As the researchers observed JB over the next 15 months, they documented that his color language deteriorated dramatically; he had great difficulty naming colors and could not even match objects with their typical colors (e.g., strawberry and red, bananna and yellow). Yet even as his language deteriorated, JB could still classify colors normally, sorting color patches into groups of green, yellow, red, and blue in the exact same manner that healthy participants did. JB retained an intact concept of colors despite the decline of his language ability—a finding that suggests that we need to look at factors in addition to language in order to understand concepts (Haslam et al., 2007).

Concept refers to a *mental representation that groups or categorizes shared features of related objects, events, or other stimuli.* A concept is an abstract representation, description, or definition that serves to designate a class or category of things. The brain organizes our concepts about the world, classifying them into categories based on shared similarities. Our category for "dog" may be something like "small, four-footed animal with fur that wags its tail and barks." Our category for "bird" may be something like "small, winged, beaked creature that flies." We form these categories in large part by noticing similarities among objects and events that we experience in everyday life. For example, your concept of a chair might include such features as sturdiness, relative flatness, an object that you can sit on. That set of attributes defines a category of objects in the world—desk chairs, recliner chairs, flat rocks, bar stools, and so on—that can all be described in that way.

> **concept** A mental representation that groups or categorizes shared features of related objects, events, or other stimuli.

? Why are concepts useful to us?

Concepts are fundamental to our ability to think and make sense of the world. We'll first compare various theories that explain the formation of concepts and then consider studies that link the formation and organization of concepts to the brain. As with other aspects of cognition, we can gain insight into how concepts are organized by looking at some instances in which they are rather disorganized. We'll encounter some unusual disorders that help us understand how concepts are organized in the brain.

Psychological Theories of Concepts and Categories

Early psychological theories described concepts as rules that specify the necessary and sufficient conditions for membership in a particular category. A necessary condition is something that must be true of the object in order for it to belong to the category. For example, suppose you were trying to determine whether an unfamiliar animal was a dog. It is necessary that the creature be a mammal; otherwise it doesn't belong to the category "dog" because all dogs are mammals. A sufficient condition is something that, if it is true of the object, proves that it belongs to the category. Suppose someone told you that the creature was a German shepherd and you know that a German shepherd is a type of dog. "German shepherd" is a sufficient condition for membership in the category "dog."

Most natural categories, however, cannot be so easily defined in terms of this classical approach of necessary and sufficient conditions. For example, what is your definition of "dog"? Can you come up with a rule of "dogship" that includes all dogs and excludes all nondogs? Most people can't, but they still use the term *dog* intelligently, easily classifying objects as dogs or nondogs. Three theories seek to explain how people perform these acts of categorization.

"Attention, everyone! I'd like to introduce the newest member of our family."

▶ There is family resemblance between family members despite the fact that there is no defining feature that they all have in common. Instead, there are shared common features. Someone who also shares some of those features may be categorized as belonging to the family.

Family Resemblance Theory

Eleanor Rosch put aside necessity and sufficiency to develop a theory of concepts based on **family resemblance**—that is, *features that appear to be characteristic of category members but may not be possessed by every member* (Rosch, 1973, 1975; Rosch & Mervis, 1975; Wittgenstein, 1953/1999). For example, you and your brother may have your mother's eyes, although you and your sister may have your father's high cheekbones. There is a strong family resemblance between you, your parents, and your siblings despite the fact that there is no necessarily defining feature that you all have in common. Similarly, many members of the "bird" category have feathers and wings, so these are the characteristic features. Anything that has these features is likely to be classified as a bird because of this "family resemblance" to other members of the "bird" category. **FIGURE 9.5** illustrates family resemblance theory.

▶ FIGURE 9.5
Family Resemblance Theory The family resemblance here is unmistakable, even though no two Smith brothers share all the family features. The prototype is brother 9. He has it all: brown hair, large ears, large nose, mustache, and glasses.

Prototype Theory

Building on the idea of family resemblance, Rosch also proposed that psychological categories (those that we form naturally) are best described as organized around a **prototype**, which is *the "best" or "most typical member" of the category*. A prototype possesses most (or all) of the most characteristic features of the category. For North Americans, the prototype of the "bird" category would be something like a wren: a small

Properties	Generic bird	Wren	Blue heron	Golden eagle	Domestic goose	Penguin
Flies regularly	✓	✓	✓	✓		
Sings	✓	✓	✓			
Lays eggs	✓	✓	✓	✓	✓	✓
Is small	✓	✓				
Nests in trees	✓	✓				

◄ **FIGURE 9.6**
Critical Features of a Category
We tend to think of a generic bird as possessing a number of critical features, but not every bird possesses all of those features. In North America, a wren is a "better example" of a bird than a penguin or an ostrich.

animal with feathers and wings that flies through the air, lays eggs, and migrates (see **FIGURE 9.6**). If you lived in Antarctica, your prototype of a bird might be a penguin: a small animal that has flippers, swims, and lays eggs. According to *prototype theory*, if your prototypical bird is a robin, then a canary would be considered a better example of a bird than would an ostrich because a canary has more features in common with a robin than an ostrich does. People make category judgments by comparing new instances to the category's prototype. This contrasts with the classical approach to concepts in which something either is or is not an example of a concept (i.e., it either does or does not belong in the category "dog" or "bird").

"Don't panic. It's only a prototype."

Exemplar Theory

In contrast to prototype theory, **exemplar theory** holds that *we make category judgments by comparing a new instance with stored memories for other instances of the category* (Medin & Schaffer, 1978). Imagine that you're out walking in the woods, and from the corner of your eye you spot a four-legged animal that might be a wolf or a coyote but that reminds you of your cousin's German shepherd. You figure it must be a dog and continue to enjoy your walk rather than fleeing in a panic. You probably categorized this new animal as a dog because it bore a striking resemblance to other dogs you've encountered; in other words, it was a good example (or an *exemplar*) of the category "dog." Exemplar theory does a better job than prototype theory in accounting for certain aspects of categorization, especially in that we recall not only what a *prototypical* dog looks like but also what *specific* dogs look like. **FIGURE 9.7** on the next page illustrates the difference between prototype theory and exemplar theory.

family resemblance theory Members of a category have features that appear to be characteristic of category members but may not be possessed by every member.

prototype The "best" or "most typical" member of a category.

exemplar theory A theory of categorization that argues that we make category judgments by comparing a new instance with stored memories for other instances of the category.

▶ FIGURE 9.7
Prototype Theory and Exemplar Theory
According to prototype theory, we classify new objects by comparing them to the "prototype" (or most typical) member of a category. According to exemplar theory, we classify new objects by comparing them to all category members.

Exemplars

Prototype

Exemplar Theory

Prototype Theory

New stimulus

Concepts, Categories, and the Brain

Studies that have attempted to link concepts and categories to the brain have helped to make sense of the theories we just considered. For example, in one set of studies (Marsolek, 1995), participants classified prototypes faster when the stimuli were presented to the right visual field, meaning that the left hemisphere received the input first (see Chapter 3 for a discussion of how the two hemispheres of the brain receive input from the outside world). In contrast, participants classified previously seen exemplars faster when images were presented to the left visual field (meaning that the right hemisphere received the input first). These results suggest a role for both exemplars and prototypes: The left hemisphere is primarily involved in forming prototypes and the right hemisphere is mainly active in recognizing exemplars.

How do prototypes and exemplars relate to each other?

More recently, researchers using neuroimaging techniques have also concluded that we use both prototypes and exemplars when forming concepts and categories. The visual cortex is involved in forming prototypes, whereas the prefrontal cortex and basal ganglia are involved in learning exemplars (Ashby & Ell, 2001; Ashby & O'Brien, 2005). This evidence suggests that exemplar-based learning involves analysis and decision making (prefrontal cortex), whereas prototype formation is a more holistic process involving image processing (visual cortex).

Some of the most striking evidence linking concepts and categories with the brain originated in a pioneering study conducted over 20 years ago in which two neuropsychologists worked with a brain-damaged patient who could not recognize a variety of human-made objects or retrieve any information about them—but his knowledge of living things and foods was perfectly normal (Warrington & McCarthy, 1983). In the following year, the two neuropsychologists reported four brain-damaged patients who exhibited the reverse pattern: They could recognize information about human-made objects, but their ability to recognize information about living things and foods was severely impaired (Warrington & Shallice, 1984). Over 100 similar cases have since been reported (Martin & Caramazza, 2003). These unusual cases became the basis for a syndrome called **category-specific deficit**, *an inability to recognize objects that belong to a particular category though the ability to recognize objects outside the category is undisturbed.*

Category-specific deficits like these have been observed even when the brain trauma that produces them occurs shortly after birth. Two researchers reported the case of Adam, a 16-year-old boy who suffered a stroke a day after he was born (Farah & Rabinowitz, 2003). Adam has severe difficulty recognizing faces and other biological objects. When shown a picture of a cherry, he identified it as "a Chinese yo-yo." When shown a picture of a mouse, he identified it as an owl. He made errors like these on 79% of the animal pictures and 54% of the plant pictures he was shown. In contrast, he made errors only 15% of the time when identifying pictures of nonliving things, such as spatulas, brooms, and cigars. What's so important about this case? The fact that 16-year-old Adam exhibited category-specific deficits despite suffering his stroke when he was only 1 day old strongly suggests that the brain is "prewired" to organize perceptual and sensory inputs into broad-based categories, such as living and nonliving things.

The type of category-specific deficit suffered depends on where the brain is damaged. Deficits usually result when an individual suffers a stroke or other trauma to areas in the left hemisphere of the cerebral cortex (Martin & Caramazza, 2003). Damage to the front part of the left temporal lobe results in difficulty identifying humans, damage to the lower left temporal lobe results in difficulty identifying animals, and damage to the region where the temporal lobe meets the occipital and parietal lobes impairs the ability to retrieve names of tools (Damasio et al., 1996). Similarly, when healthy people undertake the same task, imaging studies have demonstrated that the same regions of the brain are more active during naming of tools than animals and vice versa, as shown in **FIGURE 9.8** (Martin, 2007; Martin & Chao, 2001).

How do particular brain regions develop category preferences for objects such as tools or animals? One possibility is that these preferences develop from the specific visual experiences that individuals have during the course of their lives. An alternative possibility is suggested by the study of Adam that we just considered: The brain may be "prewired" such that particular regions respond more strongly to some categories than others. A recent study tested these ideas by examining the activity of category-preferential regions

category-specific deficit A neurological syndrome that is characterized by an inability to recognize objects that belong to a particular category though the ability to recognize objects outside the category is undisturbed.

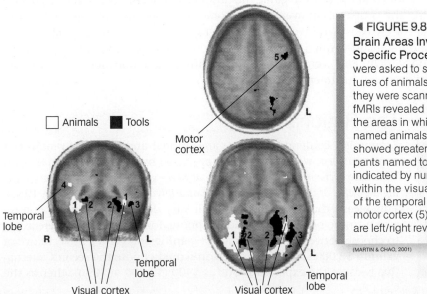

◀ FIGURE 9.8
Brain Areas Involved in Category-Specific Processing Participants were asked to silently name pictures of animals and tools while they were scanned with fMRI. The fMRIs revealed greater activity in the areas in white when participants named animals, and areas in black showed greater activity when participants named tools. Specific regions indicated by numbers include areas within the visual cortex (1, 2), parts of the temporal lobe (3, 4), and the motor cortex (5). Note that the images are left/right reversed.

(MARTIN & CHAO, 2001)

in adults who had been blind since birth (Mahon et al., 2009). While in the fMRI scanner, blind and sighted individuals each heard a series of words, including some words that referred to animals and others that referred to tools. For each word, participants made a judgment about the size of the corresponding object. The critical finding was that category-preferential regions showed highly similar patterns of activity in the blind and sighted individuals. In both groups, for example, regions in the visual cortex and temporal lobe responded to animals and tools in much the same manner as shown in

What is the role of vision in category-specific organization?

Figure 9.8. These results provide compelling evidence that category-specific organization of visual regions does not depend on an individual's visual experience. The category-specific organization could conceivably have arisen from interactions with objects that blind individuals have had involving senses other than vision, such as touch (Peelen & Kastner, 2009). However, when combined with the observations of Adam, the simplest explanation may be that category-specific brain organization is innately determined (Mahon et al., 2009).

IN SUMMARY

○ We organize knowledge about objects, events, or other stimuli by creating concepts, prototypes, and exemplars.

○ We acquire concepts using three theories: family resemblance theory, which states that items in the same category share certain features, if not all; prototype theory, which uses the most "typical" member of a category to assess new items; and exemplar theory, which states that we compare new items with stored memories of other members of the category.

○ Neuroimaging studies have shown that prototypes and exemplars are processed in different parts of the brain.

○ Studies of people with cognitive and visual deficits have shown that the brain organizes concepts into distinct categories, such as living things and human-made things, and also suggest that visual experience is not necessary for the development of such categories.

▼ People don't always make rational choices. When a lottery jackpot is larger than usual, more people will buy lottery tickets, thinking that they might well "win big." However, more people buying lottery tickets reduces the likelihood of any one person's winning the lottery. Ironically, people have a better chance at winning a lottery with a relatively small jackpot.

Decision Making: Rational and Otherwise

We use categories and concepts to guide the hundreds of decisions and judgments we make during the course of an average day. Some decisions are easy—what to wear, what to eat for breakfast, and whether to walk, ride a bicycle, or drive to class—and some are more difficult—which car to buy, which apartment to rent, who to hang out with on Friday night, and even which job to take after graduation. Some decisions are made based on sound judgments. Others are not.

The Rational Ideal

Economists contend that if we are rational and are free to make our own decisions, we will behave as predicted by **rational choice theory:** *We make decisions by determining how likely something is to happen, judging the value of the outcome, and then multiplying the two* (Edwards, 1955). This means that our judgments will vary depending on the value we assign to the possible outcomes. Suppose, for example, you were asked to choose between a 10% chance of gaining $500 and a 20% chance of gaining $2,000. The rational person would choose the second alternative because the expected payoff is $400 ($2,000 × 20%), whereas the first offers an expected gain of only $50($500 × 10%). Selecting the option with the highest expected value seems so straightforward that many economists accepted the basic ideas in rational choice theory. But how well does this theory describe decision making in our everyday lives? In many cases, the answer is "not very well."

The Irrational Reality

Is the ability to classify new events and objects into categories always a useful skill? Alas, no. These strengths of human decision making can turn into weaknesses when certain tasks inadvertently acti-

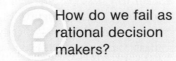

How do we fail as rational decision makers?

vate these skills. In other words, the same principles that allow cognition to occur easily and accurately can pop up to bedevil our decision making.

Judging Frequencies and Probabilities

Consider the following list of words:

> *block table block pen telephone block disk glass table block telephone block watch table candy*

You probably noticed that the words *block* and *table* occurred more frequently than the other words did. In fact, studies have shown that people are quite good at estimating *frequency*, or simply the number of times something will happen. This skill matters quite a bit when it comes to decision making. In contrast, we perform poorly on tasks that require us to think in terms of *probabilities*, or the likelihood that something will happen.

Even with probabilities, however, performance varies depending on how the problem is described. In one experiment, 100 physicians were asked to predict the incidence of breast cancer among women whose mammogram screening tests showed possible evidence of breast cancer. The physicians were told to take into consideration the rarity of breast cancer (1% of the population at the time the study was done) and radiologists' record in diagnosing the condition (correctly recognized only 79% of the time and falsely diagnosed almost 10% of the time). Of the 100 physicians, 95 estimated the probability that cancer was present to be about *75%!* The correct answer was 8%. The physicians apparently experienced difficulty taking so much information into account when making their decision (Eddy, 1982). Similar dismal results have been reported with a number of medical screening tests (Hoffrage & Gigerenzer, 1996; Windeler & Kobberling, 1986).

However, dramatically different results were obtained when the study was repeated using *frequency* information instead of *probability* information. Stating the problem as "10 out of every 1,000 women actually have breast cancer" instead of "1% of women actually have breast cancer" led 46% of the physicians to derive the right answer, compared to only 8% who came up with the right answer when the problem was presented using probabilities (Hoffrage & Gigerenzer, 1998). This finding suggests at a minimum that when seeking advice—even from a highly skilled decision maker—make sure that your problem is described using frequencies rather than probabilities.

Availability Bias

Take a look at the list of names in **FIGURE 9.9.** Now look away from the book and estimate the number of male names and female names in the figure. Did you notice that some of the women on the list are famous and none of the men are? Was your estimate off because you thought the list contained more women's than men's names (Tversky & Kahneman, 1973, 1974)? The reverse would have been true if you had looked at a list with the names of famous men and unknown women because people typically fall prey to **availability bias**, in which *items that are more readily available in memory are judged as having occurred more frequently.*

rational choice theory The classical view that we make decisions by determining how likely something is to happen, judging the value of the outcome, and then multiplying the two.

availability bias Items that are more readily available in memory are judged as having occurred more frequently.

▼ FIGURE 9.9
Availability Bias Looking at this list of names, estimate the number of women's and men's names.

Jennifer Aniston	Robert Kingston
Judy Smith	Gilbert Chapman
Frank Carson	Gwyneth Paltrow
Elizabeth Taylor	Martin Mitchell
Daniel Hunt	Thomas Hughes
Henry Vaughan	Michael Drayton
Agatha Christie	Julia Roberts
Arthur Hutchinson	Hillary Clinton
Jennifer Lopez	Jack Lindsay
Allan Nevins	Richard Gilder
Jane Austen	George Nathan
Joseph Litton	Britney Spears

heuristic A fast and efficient strategy that may facilitate decision making but does not guarantee that a solution will be reached.

algorithm A well-defined sequence of procedures or rules that guarantees a solution to a problem.

conjunction fallacy When people think that two events are more likely to occur together than either individual event.

The availability bias affects our estimates because memory strength and frequency of occurrence are directly related. Frequently occurring items are remembered more easily than *infrequently* occurring items, so you naturally conclude that items for which you have better memory must also have been more frequent. Unfortunately, better memory in this case was not due to greater *frequency*, but to greater *familiarity*.

Shortcuts such as the availability bias are sometimes referred to as **heuristics**: *fast and efficient strategies that may facilitate decision making but do not guarantee that a solution will be reached.* Heuristics are mental shortcuts, or "rules of thumb," that are often—but not always—effective when approaching a problem (Swinkels, 2003). In contrast, an **algorithm** is *a well-defined sequence of procedures or rules that guarantees a solution to a problem.* Consider, for example, two approaches to constructing a Power-Point presentation involving features you rarely use, such as inserting movies and complex animations: (1) You try to remember what you did the last time you tried to do a similar presentation; (2) You follow a set of step-by-step directions that you wrote down the last time you did something similar, which tells you exactly how to insert movies and build complex animations.

The first procedure is an intelligent heuristic that may be successful, but you could continue searching your memory until you finally run out of time or patience. The second strategy is a series of well-defined steps that, if properly executed, will guarantee a solution.

The Conjunction Fallacy

The availability bias illustrates a potential source of error in human cognition. Unfortunately, it's not the only one.

Consider the following description:

> Linda is 31 years old, single, outspoken, and very bright. In college, she majored in philosophy. As a student, she was deeply concerned with issues of discrimination and social justice and also participated in antinuclear demonstrations.
> Which state of affairs is more probable?
>
> **a.** Linda is a bank teller.
> **b.** Linda is a bank teller and is active in the feminist movement.

In one study, 89% of participants rated option **b** as more probable than option **a** (Tversky & Kahneman, 1983), although that's logically impossible. Let's say there's a 20% chance that Linda is a bank teller; after all, there are plenty of occupations she might hold. Independently, let's say there's also a 20% chance that she's active in the feminist movement; she probably has lots of interests. The joint probability that *both* things are true simultaneously is the product of their separate probabilities. In other words, the 20% chance that she's a teller multiplied by the 20% chance that she's in the feminist movement produces a 4% chance that both things are true at the same time (.20 × .20 = .04, or 4%). The combined probability of events is always less than the independent probability of each event; therefore, it's always *more* probable that any one state of affairs is true than is a set of events simultaneously.

This is called the **conjunction fallacy** because *people think that two events are more likely to occur together than either individual event.* The fallacy is that with more and more pieces of information, people think there's a higher probability that all are true. Actually, the probability diminishes rapidly. Based on her description, do you think Linda also voted for the liberal candidate in the last election? Do you think she also writes poetry? Do you think she's also signed her name to fair-housing petitions? With each additional bit of information, you probably think you're getting a better and better description of Linda, but as you can see in **FIGURE 9.10**, the likelihood of all those events being true *at the same time* is very small.

▼ FIGURE 9.10
The Conjunction Fallacy People often think that with each additional bit of information, the probability that all the facts are simultaneously true of a person increases. In fact, the probability decreases dramatically. Notice how the intersection of all these possibilities is much smaller than the area of any one possibility alone.

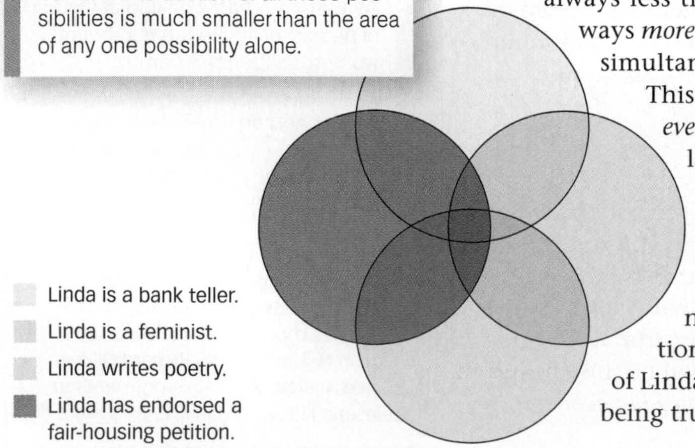

- Linda is a bank teller.
- Linda is a feminist.
- Linda writes poetry.
- Linda has endorsed a fair-housing petition.

Representativeness Heuristic

Think about the following situation:

A panel of psychologists wrote 100 descriptions based on interviews with engineers and lawyers. THE DESCRIPTIONS CAME FROM 70 ENGINEERS AND 30 LAWYERS. You will be shown a random selection of these descriptions. Read each and then pause and decide if it is more likely that the person is an engineer or a lawyer. Note your decision and read on.

1. Jack enjoys reading books on social and political issues. During the interview, he displayed particular skill at argument.
2. Tom is a loner who enjoys working on mathematical puzzles during his spare time. During the interview, his speech remained fairly abstract and his emotions were well controlled.
3. Harry is a bright man and an avid racquetball player. During the interview, he asked many insightful questions and was very well spoken.

Research participants were shown a series of descriptions like these and asked after each one to judge the likelihood that the person described was a lawyer or an engineer (Kahneman & Tversky, 1973). Remember, of the descriptions, 70 were engineers and 30 were lawyers. If participants took this proportion into consideration, their judgments should have reflected the fact that there were more than twice as many engineers as lawyers. But researchers found that people didn't use this information and based their judgments solely on how closely the description matched their concepts of lawyers and engineers. So, the majority of participants thought descriptions such as 1 were more likely to be lawyers, those like 2 were more likely to be engineers, and those like 3 could be either.

Consider participants' judgments about Harry. His description doesn't sound like a lawyer's or an engineer's, so most people said he was *equally likely* to hold either occupation. But the pool contains more than twice as many engineers as lawyers, so it is far *more* likely that he is an engineer. People seem to ignore information about *base rate*, or the existing probability of an event, basing their judgments on similarities to categories. Researchers call this the **representativeness heuristic**—*making a probability judgment by comparing an object or event to a prototype of the object or event* (Kahneman & Tversky, 1973). Thus, the probability judgments were skewed toward the participants' prototypes of lawyer and engineer. The greater the similarity, the more likely they were judged to be members of that category despite the existence of much more useful base rates.

Heuristics such as availability, representativeness, or the conjunction fallacy highlight both the strengths and weaknesses of the way we think. We are very good at forming categories based on prototypes and making classification judgments on the basis of similarity to prototypes. Judging probabilities is not our strong suit. As we saw earlier in this chapter, the human brain easily processes frequency information, and decision-making performance can usually be improved if probability problems are re-framed using frequencies.

Framing Effects

You've seen that, according to rational choice theory, our judgments will vary depending on the value we place on the expected outcome. So how effective are we at assigning value to our choices? Studies show that **framing effects**, which occur when *people give different answers to the same problem depending on how the problem is phrased (or framed)*, can influence the assignment of value.

Why does a 70% success rate sound better than a 30% failure rate?

For example, if people are told that a particular drug has a 70% effectiveness rate, they're usually pretty impressed: 70% of the time the drug cures what ails you sounds like a good deal. Tell them instead that a drug has a 30% failure rate—30% of the time it does no good—and they typically perceive it as risky, potentially harmful, something

representativeness heuristic A mental shortcut that involves making a probability judgment by comparing an object or event to a prototype of the object or event.

framing effects When people give different answers to the same problem depending on how the problem is phrased (or framed).

▶ Worth the cost? Sports teams sometimes try to justify their investment in an expensive player who is underperforming, an example of a sunk-cost effect. Erick Dampier is a highly paid basketball player, but his performance has not always lived up to his salary

GARRETT W. ELLWOOD/NBAE VIA GETTY IMAGES

to be avoided. Notice that the information is the same: A 70% effectiveness rate means that 30% of the time, it's ineffective. The way the information is framed, however, leads to substantially different conclusions (Tversky & Kahneman, 1981).

One of the most striking framing effects is the **sunk-cost fallacy**, which occurs when *people make decisions about a current situation based on what they have previously invested in the situation*. Imagine waiting in line for 3 hours, paying $100 for a ticket to the Warped Tour to see your favorite bands, and waking on the day of the outdoor concert to find that it's bitterly cold and rainy. If you go, you'll feel miserable. But you go anyway, reasoning that the $100 you paid for the ticket and the time you spent in line will have been wasted if you stay home.

Notice that you have two choices: (1) Spend $100 and stay comfortably at home or (2) spend $100 and endure many uncomfortable hours in the rain. The $100 is gone in either case; it's a sunk cost, irretrievable at the moment of your decision. But the way you framed the problem created a problem: Because you invested time and money, you feel obligated to follow through, even though it's something you no longer want. If you can turn off this feeling and ask, "Would I rather spend $100 to be comfortable or spend it to be miserable?," the smart choice is clear: Stay home and listen to the podcast!

Even the National Basketball Association (NBA) is guilty of a sunk-cost fallacy. Coaches should play their most productive players and keep them on the team longer. But they don't. The most *expensive* players are given more time on court and are kept on the team longer than cheaper players, even if the costly players are not performing up to par (Staw & Hoang, 1995). Coaches act to justify their team's investment in an expensive player rather than recognize the loss. Framing effects can be costly!

Why Do We Make Decision-Making Errors?

As you have seen, everyday decision making seems riddled with errors and shortcomings. Our decisions vary wildly depending on how a problem is presented (e.g., frequencies versus probabilities or framed in terms of losses rather than savings), and we seem to be prone to fallacies, such as the sunk-cost fallacy or the conjunction fallacy. Psychologists have developed several explanations for why everyday decision making suffers from these failings. We'll review two of the most influential theories—prospect theory and the frequency format hypothesis.

Prospect Theory

According to a totally rational model of inference, people should make decisions that maximize value; in other words, they should seek to increase what psychologists and economists call *expected utility*. We face decisions like this every day. If you are making a decision that involves money and money is what you value, then you should choose the outcome that is likely to bring you the most money. When deciding which of two apartments to rent, you'd compare the monthly expenses for each and choose the one that leaves more money in your pocket.

As you have seen, however, people often make decisions that are inconsistent with this simple principle. The question is, why? To explain these effects, Amos Tversky and Daniel Kahneman (1992) developed **prospect theory**, which argues that *people choose to take on risk when evaluating potential losses and avoid risks when evaluating potential gains*. These decision processes take place in two phases.

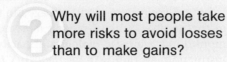

Why will most people take more risks to avoid losses than to make gains?

> First, people simplify available information. So, in a task like choosing an apartment, they tend to ignore a lot of potentially useful information because apartments differ in so many ways (the closeness of restaurants, the presence of a swimming pool, the color of the carpet, and so forth). Comparing each apartment on each factor is simply too much work; focusing only on differences that matter is more efficient.

> In the second phase, people choose the prospect that they believe offers the best value. This value is personal and may differ from an objective measure of "best value." For example, you might choose the apartment with higher rent because you can walk to eight great bars and restaurants.

Prospect theory makes other assumptions that account for people's choice patterns. One assumption, called the *certainty* effect, suggests that when making decisions, people give greater weight to outcomes that are a sure thing. When deciding between playing a lottery with an 80% chance of winning $4,000 or receiving $3,000 outright, most people choose the $3,000, even though the expected value of the first choice is $200 more ($4,000 × 80% = $3,200)! Apparently, people weigh certainty much more heavily than expected payoffs when making choices.

Prospect theory also assumes that in evaluating choices, people compare them to a reference point. For example, suppose you're still torn between two apartments. The $400 monthly rent for apartment A is discounted $10 if you pay before the fifth of the month. A $10 surcharge is tacked onto the $390 per month rent for apartment B if you pay after the fifth of the month. Although the apartments are objectively identical in terms of cost, different reference points may make apartment A seem psychologically more appealing than B.

Prospect theory also assumes that people are more willing to take risks to avoid losses than to achieve gains. Given a choice between a definite $300 rebate on your first month's rent or spinning a wheel that offers an 80% chance of getting a $400 rebate, you'll most likely choose the lower sure payoff over the higher potential payoff ($400 × 80% = $320). However, given a choice between a sure fine of $300 for damaging an apartment or a spinning of a wheel that has an 80% chance of a $400 fine, most people will choose the higher potential loss over the sure loss. This asymmetry in risk preferences shows that we are willing to take on risk if we think it will ward off a loss, but we're risk-averse if we expect to lose some benefits.

Frequency Format Hypothesis

According to the **frequency format hypothesis**, *our minds evolved to notice how frequently things occur, not how likely they are to occur* (Gigerenzer, 1996; Gigerenzer & Hoffrage, 1995). Thus, we interpret, process, and manipulate information about frequency with comparative ease because that's the way quantitative information usually occurs in natural circumstances. For example, the 20 men, 15 women, 5 dogs, 13 cars, and 2 bicycle accidents you encountered on the way to class came in the form of frequencies, not probabilities or percentages. Probabilities and percentages are, evolutionarily speaking, recent developments, emerging in the mid-17th century (Hacking, 1975). Millennia passed before humans developed these cultural notions, and years of schooling are needed to competently use them as everyday cognitive tools. Thus, our susceptibility to errors when dealing with probabilities is not surprising.

sunk-cost fallacy A framing effect in which people make decisions about a current situation based on what they have previously invested in the situation.

prospect theory The proposal that people choose to take on risk when evaluating potential losses and avoid risks when evaluating potential gains.

frequency format hypothesis The proposal that our minds evolved to notice how frequently things occur, not how likely they are to occur.

In contrast, people can track frequencies virtually effortlessly and flawlessly (Hasher & Zacks, 1984). We are also remarkably good at recognizing how often two events occur together (Mandel & Lehman, 1998; Spellman, 1996; Waldmann, 2000). Infants as young as 6 months of age can tell the difference between displays that differ in the number of items present (Starkey, Spelke, & Gelman, 1983, 1990). Frequency monitoring is a basic biological capacity rather than a skill learned through formal instruction. According to the frequency format hypothesis, presenting statistical information in frequency format rather than probability format results in improved performance because it capitalizes on our evolutionary strengths (Gigerenzer & Hoffrage, 1995; Hertwig & Gigerenzer, 1999).

Decision Making and the Brain

A patient identified as "Elliot" (whom you met briefly in Chapter 1) was a successful businessman, husband, and father prior to developing a brain tumor. After surgery, his intellectual abilities seemed intact, but he was unable to differentiate between important and unimportant activities and would spend hours at mundane tasks. He lost his job and got involved in several risky financial ventures that bankrupted him. He had no difficulty discussing what had happened, but his descriptions were so detached and dispassionate that it seemed as though his abstract intellectual functions had become dissociated from his social and emotional abilities.

Research confirms that this interpretation of Elliot's downfall is right on track. In one study, researchers looked at how healthy volunteers differed from people with prefrontal lobe damage on a gambling task that involves risky decision making (Bechara et al., 1994, 1997). Four decks of cards were placed face down, and participants were required to make 100 selections of cards that specified an amount of play money they could win or lose. Two of the decks usually provided large payoffs or large losses, whereas the other two provided smaller payoffs and losses. While playing the game, the participants' galvanic skin responses (GSR) were recorded to measure heightened emotional reactions.

The performance of players with prefrontal lobe damage mirrored Elliot's real-life problems: They selected cards equally from the riskier and the safer decks, leading most to eventually go bankrupt. At first, the healthy volunteers also selected from each deck equally, but they gradually shifted to choosing primarily from the safer decks. This difference in strategy occurred even though both groups showed strong emotional reactions to big gains and losses, as measured by their comparable GSR scores. The two groups differed in one important way. As the game progressed, the healthy participants began to show anticipatory emotional reactions when they even *considered* choosing a card from the risky deck. Their GSR scores jumped dramatically even before they were able to say that some decks were riskier than others (Bechara et al., 1997). The patients with prefrontal damage didn't show these anticipatory feelings when they were thinking about selecting a card from the risky deck. Apparently their emotional reactions did not guide their thinking, and so they continued to make risky decisions, as shown in **FIGURE 9.11.**

Further studies of these patients suggest that their risky decision making grows out of insensitivity to the future consequences of their behavior (Naqvi, Shiv, & Bechara, 2006). Unable to think beyond immediate consequences, they could not shift their choices in response to a rising rate of losses or a declining rate of rewards (Bechara, Tranel, & Damasio, 2000). Interestingly, substance-dependent individuals, such as alcoholics and cocaine addicts, act the same way. Most perform as poorly on the gambling task as do patients with prefrontal damage (Bechara et al., 2001). More recent work has extended these impairments on the gambling task across cultures to Chinese adolescents with binge-drinking problems (Johnson et al., 2008).

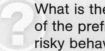 What is the relationship of the prefrontal cortex to risky behavior?

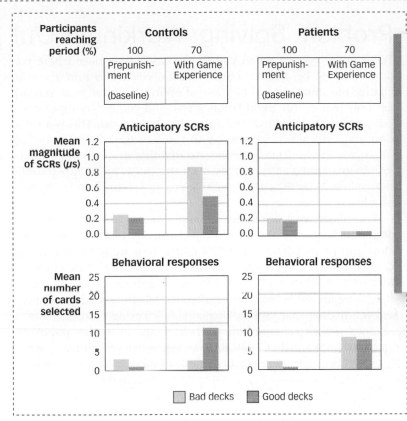

After Bechara et al., 1997.

◄ FIGURE 9.11

The Neuroscience of Risky Decision Making In a study of risky decision making, researchers compared healthy controls' choices to those made by people with damage to the prefrontal cortex. Participants played a game in which they selected a card from one of four decks. Two of the decks were made up of riskier cards, that is, cards that provided large payoffs or large losses. The other two contained "safer" cards—those with much smaller payoffs and losses. At the beginning of the game, both groups chose cards from the two decks with equal frequency. Over the course of the game, the healthy controls avoided the bad decks and they showed large emotional responses (SCRs, or skin conductance responses) when they even considered choosing a card from a "risky" deck. Patients with prefrontal brain damage, on the other hand, continued to choose cards from the two decks with equal frequency and showed no evidence of emotional learning. These participants eventually went bankrupt.

Neuroimaging studies of healthy individuals have provided evidence that fits well with the earlier studies of patients with damage to the prefrontal cortex: When performing the gambling task, an area in the prefrontal cortex is activated when participants need to make risky decisions as compared to safe decisions (Fukui et al., 2005; Lawrence et al., 2009). Indeed, the activated region is in the part of the prefrontal cortex that is typically damaged in patients who perform poorly on the gambling task, and greater activation in this region is correlated with better task performance in healthy individuals (Fukui et al., 2005; Lawrence et al., 2009). Taken together, the neuroimaging and lesion studies show clearly that aspects of risky decision making depend critically on the contributions of the prefrontal cortex.

IN SUMMARY

○ Human decision making often departs from a completely rational process, and the mistakes that accompany this departure tell us a lot about how the human mind works.

○ The values we place on outcomes weigh so heavily in our judgments that they sometimes overshadow objective evidence. When people are asked to make probability judgments, they will turn the problem into something they know how to solve, such as judging memory strength, judging similarity to prototypes, or estimating frequencies. This can lead to errors of judgment.

○ When a problem fits their mental algorithms, people show considerable skill at making appropriate judgments. In making a judgment about the probability of an event, performance can vary dramatically.

○ Because we feel that avoiding losses is more important than achieving gains, framing effects can affect our choices. Emotional information also strongly influences our decision making, even when we are not aware of it. Although this influence can lead us astray, it often is crucial for making decisions in everyday life.

○ The prefrontal cortex plays an important role in decision making, and patients with prefrontal damage make more risky decisions than do non-brain-damaged indiviuals.

▶ Even though it may not be easy to put together this Lego model, having instructions for assembly makes it a well-defined problem.

CORBIS COLLECTION/ALAMY

Problem Solving: Working It Out

You have a problem when you find yourself in a place where you don't want to be. In such circumstances, you try to find a way to change the situation so that you end up in a situation you *do* want. Let's say that it's the night before a test, and you are trying to study but just can't settle down and focus on the material. This is a situation you don't want. So, you try to think of ways to help yourself focus. You might begin with the material that most interests you or providing yourself with rewards, such as a music break or trip to the refrigerator. If these activities enable you to get down to work, your problem is solved.

Two major types of problems complicate our daily lives. The first and most frequent is the *ill-defined problem,* one that does not have a clear goal or well-defined solution paths. Your study block is an ill-defined problem: Your goal isn't clearly defined (i.e., "somehow get focused"), and the solution path for achieving the goal is even less clear (i.e., there are many ways to gain focus). Most everyday problems— being a "better person," finding that "special someone," achieving "success"—are ill defined. In contrast, a *well-defined problem* is one with clearly specified goals and clearly defined solution paths. Examples include following a clear set of directions to get to school, solving simple algebra problems, or playing a game of chess.

Means-Ends Analysis

In 1945, a German psychologist named Karl Duncker reported some important studies of the problem-solving process. He presented people with ill-defined problems and asked them to "think aloud" while solving them (Duncker, 1945). Based on what people said about how they solve problems, Duncker described problem solving in terms of **means-ends analysis**, which is *a process of searching for the means or steps to reduce the differences between the current situation and the desired goal.* This process usually took the following steps:

1. Analyze the goal state (i.e., the desired outcome you want to attain).
2. Analyze the current state (i.e., your starting point, or the current situation).
3. List the differences between the current state and the goal state.
4. Reduce the list of differences by
   • Direct means (a procedure that solves the problem without intermediate steps).
   • Generating a subgoal (an intermediate step on the way to solving the problem).
   • Finding a similar problem that has a known solution.

Consider, for example, one of Duncker's problems:

A patient has an inoperable tumor in his abdomen. The tumor is inoperable because it is surrounded by healthy but fragile tissue that would be severely damaged during surgery. How can the patient be saved?

The *goal state* is a patient without the tumor and with undamaged surrounding tissue. The *current state* is a patient with an inoperable tumor surrounded by fragile tissue. The *difference* between these two states is the tumor. A *direct-means solution* would be to destroy the tumor with x-rays, but the required x-ray dose would destroy the fragile surrounding tissue and possibly kill the patient. A *subgoal* would be to modify the x-ray machine to deliver a weaker dose. After this subgoal is achieved, a direct-means solution could be to deliver the weaker dose to the patient's abdomen. But this solution won't work either: The weaker dose wouldn't damage the healthy tissue but also wouldn't kill the tumor.

So, what to do? Find a similar problem that has a known solution. Let's see how this can be done.

means-ends analysis A process of searching for the means or steps to reduce differences between the current situation and the desired goal.

Analogical Problem Solving

When we engage in **analogical problem solving**, we attempt to *solve a problem by finding a similar problem with a known solution and applying that solution to the current problem.* Consider the following story:

> An island surrounded by bridges is the site of an enemy fortress. The massive fortification is so strongly defended that only a very large army could overtake it. Unfortunately, the bridges would collapse under the weight of such a huge force. So, a clever general divides the army into several smaller units and sends the units over different bridges, timing the crossings so that the many streams of soldiers converge on the fortress at the same time and the fortress is taken.

Does this story suggest a solution to the tumor problem? It should. Removing a tumor and attacking a fortress are very different problems, but the two problems are analogous because they share a common structure: The *goal state* is a conquered fortress and with undamaged surrounding bridges. The *current state* is an occupied fortress surrounded by fragile bridges. The *difference* between the two states is the occupying enemy. The *solution* is to divide the required force into smaller units that are light enough to spare the fragile bridges and send them down the bridges simultaneously so that they converge on the fortress. The combined units will form an army strong enough to take the fortress (see **FIGURE 9.12**).

This analogous problem of the island fortress suggests the following direct-means solution to the tumor problem:

> Surround the patient with x-ray machines and simultaneously send weaker doses that converge on the tumor. The combined strength of the weaker x-ray doses will be sufficient to destroy the tumor, but the individual doses will be weak enough to spare the surrounding healthy tissue.

Did this solution occur to you after reading the fortress story? In studies that have used the tumor problem, only 10% of participants spontaneously generated the correct solution. This percentage rose to 30% if participants read the island fortress problem or other analogous story. However, the success climbed dramatically to 75% among participants who had a chance to read more than one analogous problem or were given a deliberate hint to use the solution to the fortress story (Gick & Holyoak, 1980).

Why was the fortress problem so ineffective by itself? Problem solving is strongly affected by superficial similarities between problems, and the relationship between the tumor and fortress problems lies deep in their structure (Catrambone, 2002).

Why are analogies useful in problem solving?

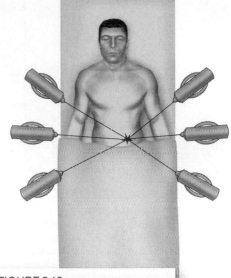

▲ FIGURE 9.12
Analogical Problem Solving Just as smaller, lighter battalions can reach the fortress without damaging the bridges, so can many small x-ray doses get to the tumor without harming the delicate surrounding tissue. In both cases, the additive strength achieves the objective.

Creativity and Insight

Analogical problem solving shows us that successfully solving a problem often depends on learning the principles underlying a particular type of problem and also that solving lots of problems improves our ability to recognize certain problem types and generate effective solutions. Some problem solving, however, seems to involve brilliant flashes of insight and creative solutions that have never before been tried. Creative and insightful solutions often rely on restructuring a problem so that it turns into a problem you already know how to solve.

Genius and Insight

Consider the exceptional mind of the mathematician Friedrich Gauss (1777–1855). One day, Gauss's elementary school teacher asked the class to add up the numbers 1 through 10. While his classmates laboriously worked their sums, Gauss had a flash of insight that caused the answer to occur to him immediately.

analogical problem solving Solving a problem by finding a similar problem with a known solution and applying that solution to the current problem.

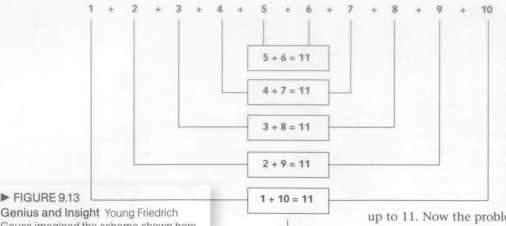

$$1 + 2 + 3 + 4 + 5 + 6 + 7 + 8 + 9 + 10$$

$$5 + 6 = 11$$

$$4 + 7 = 11$$

$$3 + 8 = 11$$

$$2 + 9 = 11$$

$$1 + 10 = 11$$

$$5 \times 11 = 55$$

► **FIGURE 9.13**

Genius and Insight Young Friedrich Gauss imagined the scheme shown here and quickly reduced a laborious addition problem to an easy multiplication task. Gauss's early insight led him to realize later an intriguing truth: This simple solution generalizes to number series of any length.

After Wertheimer, 1945/1982.

Gauss imagined the numbers 1 through 10 as weights lined up on a balance beam, as shown in **FIGURE 9.13**. Starting at the left, each "weight" increases by 1. In order for the beam to balance, each weight on the left must be paired with a weight on the right. You can see this by starting at the middle and noticing that $5 + 6 = 11$, then moving outward, $4 + 7 = 11$, $3 + 8 = 11$, and so on. This produces five number pairs that add up to 11. Now the problem is easy. Multiply. Gauss's genius lay in restructuring the problem in a way that allowed him to notice a very simple and elegant solution to an otherwise tedious task—a procedure, by the way, that generalizes to series of any length.

According to Gestalt psychologists, insights such as these reflect a spontaneous restructuring of a problem. A sudden flash of insight contrasts with incremental problem-solving procedures in which one gradually gets closer and closer to a solution. Early researchers studying insight found that people were more likely to solve a non-insight problem if they felt they were gradually getting "warmer" (incrementally closer to the solution). But whether someone felt "warm" did not predict the likelihood of their solving an insight problem (Metcalfe & Wiebe, 1987). The solution for an insight problem seemed to appear out of the blue, regardless of what the participant felt.

What is the role of the unconscious in flashes of insight?

Later research, however, suggests that sudden insightful solutions may actually result from unconscious incremental processes (Bowers et al., 1990). In one study, research participants were shown paired, three-word series like those in **FIGURE 9.14** and asked to find a fourth word that was associated with the three words in each series. However, only one series in each pair had a common associate. Solvable series were termed *coherent,* whereas those with no solution were called *incoherent.*

Even if participants couldn't find a solution, they could reliably decide, more than by chance alone, which of the pairs was coherent. However, if insightful solutions actually occur in a sudden, all-or-nothing manner, their performance should have been no better than chance. Thus, the findings suggest that even insightful problem solving is an incremental process—one that occurs outside of conscious awareness. The process works something like this: The pattern of clues that constitute a problem unconsciously activates relevant information in memory. Activation then spreads through the memory network, recruiting additional relevant information (Bowers et al., 1990). When sufficient information has been activated, it crosses the threshold of awareness and we experience a sudden flash of insight into the problem's solution.

Finding a connection between the words *strawberry* and *traffic* might take some time, even for someone motivated to figure out how they are related. But if the word *strawberry* activates *jam* in long-term memory (see Chapter 6) and the activation spreads from *strawberry* to *traffic,* the solution to the puzzle may suddenly spring into awareness without the thinker knowing how it got there. What would seem like a sudden insight would really result from an incremental process that consists of activation spreading through memory, adding new information as more knowledge is activated. Nonetheless, studies of brain activity during problem solving reveal striking differences between problems solved by sudden insight and those solved by using more deliberate strategies (see the Hot Science box).

▼ **FIGURE 9.14**

Insightful Solutions Are Really Incremental Participants were asked to find a fourth word that was associated with the other three words in each series. Even if they couldn't find a solution, they could reliably choose which series of three words were solvable and which were not. Try to solve these.

After Bowers et al., 1990.

Coherent	Incoherent
Playing	Still
Credit	Pages
Report	Music
Blank	Light
White	Folk
Lines	Head
ticket	Town
Shop	Root
Broker	Car
Magic	House
Plush	Lion
Floor	Butter
Base	Swan
Snow	Army
Dance	Mask
Gold	Noise
Stool	Foam
Tender	Shade

Solutions: Card, paper, pawn, carpet, ball, bar

HOT SCIENCE

Sudden Insight and the Brain

The "Aha!" moment that accompanies a sudden flash of insight is a compelling experience, one that highlights that solving a problem based on insight *feels* radically different from solving it through step-by-step analysis or trial and error. This difference in subjective experience suggests that something different is going on in the brain when we solve a problem using insight instead of analytic strategies. Recent studies have provided evidence that this is so, and have also revealed clues as to why some people rely more on insight while others rely more on analytic strategies (Kounios & Beeman, 2009).

To examine brain activity associated with insight, researchers used a procedure called *compound remote associates* that is similar in some respects to the three-word problems displayed in Figure 9.14. Each compound remote associates problem consists of three words, such as *crab, pine,* and *sauce*. Sometimes people solve these problems with a flash of insight: the solution word (*apple!*) suddenly pops into their minds, seemingly out of nowhere. Other times, people solve the problem by using analytic strategies that involve trying out different alternatives generating a compound word for *crab* and then assessing whether they fit *pine* and *sauce. Crabgrass,* works, but grass doesn't work with *pine* and *sauce. Crabapple?* Problem solved.

Participants are instructed to press a button the moment a solution comes to mind, then describe whether they arrived at the solution via insight or through an analytic strategy. In an initial study, researchers used the electroencephalograph (EEG; see Chapter 3) to measure brain electrical activity as participants attempted to solve the problems. What they observed was striking: Beginning about one-third of a second before participants came up with a solution, there was a sudden and dramatic burst of high-frequency electrical activity (40 cycles-per-second or gamma-band) for problems solved via insight as compared with problems solved via analytic strategies (Jung-Beeman et al., 2004). This activity was centered over the front part of the right temporal lobe, slightly above the right ear. The researchers then performed a similar study using fMRI to measure brain activity, and found that this right temporal area was the only region in the entire brain that showed greater activity for insight solutions compared with solutions based on analytic strategies.

While these findings demonstrate clearly that brain activity differs for solutions based on insight versus analytic strategies, they leave open a critical question: Why do people solve some problems with insight and others with analytic strategies? The great French scientist Louis Pasteur once stated that "Chance favors only the prepared mind." Inspired by this observation, the researchers asked whether brain activity occurring just before presentation of a problem influenced whether that problem was solved via insight or analytic strategies (Kounios et al., 2006). It did. In the moments before a problem was solved with an insight solution, there was increased activity deep in the frontal lobes, in a part of the brain known as the anterior cingulate, which controls cognitive processes such as the ability to switch attention from one thing to another. The researchers suggested that this increased activity in the anterior cingulate allowed participants to attend to and detect associations that were only weakly activated, perhaps at a subconscious level, and that facilitate sudden insight.

A related study with the compound remote associates task revealed that when people were in a positive mood, they solved more problems with insight than people who were in a less positive mood (Subramaniam et al., 2009). Moreover, as shown in the figure, positive mood was associated with heightened activity in the anterior cingulate during the moments before a problem was presented—suggesting that being in a positive mood helps to prepare the brain for sudden insight by "turning on" the anterior cingulate and thereby increasing one's ability to detect associations that aid problem solution.

The same research team also asked whether brain activity prior to problem solving provides clues about which individuals are more likely to rely on insight over analytic strategies to solve compound remote associates (Kounios et al., 2008). Using EEG to measure resting brain activity, they found that insight problem solvers showed more resting activity in the right cerebral hemisphere than did analytic problem solvers, which is consistent with other research linking creativity with right-hemisphere activity (Folley & Park, 2005; Howard-Jones et al., 2005).

The results of these studies suggest that the familiar image of a light bulb going off in your head when you experience an "Aha!" moment is on the mark: Those moments are indeed accompanied by something like an electrical power surge in the brain, and are preceded by specific types of electrical activity patterns. It seems likely that future research will tell us much more about how to turn on the mental light bulb and keep it burning bright.

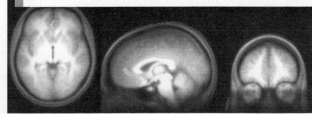

▶ Being in a positive mood was associated with increased activity in the anterior cingulate (yellow coloring) in the moments before people solved a problem via sudden insight.

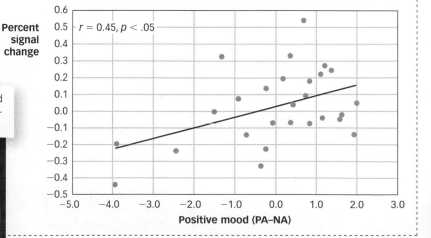

$r = 0.45, p < .05$

Percent signal change (y-axis)

Positive mood (PA–NA) (x-axis)

► FIGURE 9.15

Functional Fixedness and the Candle Problem How can you use these objects—a box of matches, thumbtacks, and a candle—to mount the candle on the wall so that it illuminates the room? Give this problem some thought before you check the answer in Figure 9.18 on page 382.

Functional Fixedness

If insight is a simple incremental process, why isn't its occurrence more frequent? In the research discussed previously, participants produced insightful solutions only 25% of the time. Insight is rare because problem solving (like decision making) suffers from framing effects. In problem solving, framing tends to limit the types of solutions that occur to us.

Functional fixedness—*the tendency to perceive the functions of objects as fixed*—is a process that constricts our thinking. Look at **FIGURES 9.15** and **9.16** and see if you can solve the problems before reading on. In Figure 9.15, your task is to illuminate a dark room using the following objects: some thumbtacks, a box of matches, and a candle. In Figure 9.16, you're holding a string hanging from the ceiling and without letting go of it and using the items on the table, you're expected to reach another string too far away to grasp.

Difficulty solving these problems derives from our tendency to think of the objects only in terms of their normal, typical, or "fixed" functions. We don't think to use the matchbox for a candleholder because boxes typically hold matches, not candles. Similarly, using the hammer as a pendulum weight doesn't spring to mind because hammers are typically used to pound things. Did functional fixedness prevent you from solving these problems? (The solutions are shown in **FIGURES 9.18** and **9.19.**)

Sometimes framing limits our ability to generate a solution. Before reading on, look at **FIGURE 9.17.** Without lifting your pencil from the page, try to connect all nine dots with only four straight lines.

To solve this problem, you must allow the lines you draw to extend outside the imaginary box that surrounds the dots (see **FIGURE 9.20**). This constraint does not reside in the problem but in the mind of the problem solver (Kershaw & Ohlsson, 2004). Despite the apparent sudden flash of insight that seems to yield a solution to problems of this type, research indicates that the thought processes people use when solving even this type of insight problem are best described as an incremental, means-ends analysis (MacGregor, Ormerod, & Chronicle, 2001).

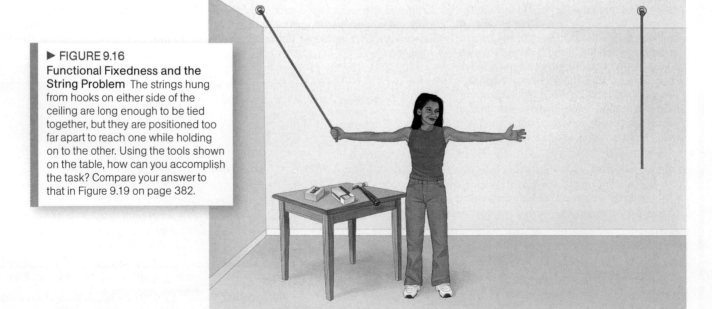

► FIGURE 9.16

Functional Fixedness and the String Problem The strings hung from hooks on either side of the ceiling are long enough to be tied together, but they are positioned too far apart to reach one while holding on to the other. Using the tools shown on the table, how can you accomplish the task? Compare your answer to that in Figure 9.19 on page 382.

IN SUMMARY

○ Like concept formation and decision making, problem solving is a process in which new inputs (in this case, problems) are interpreted in terms of old knowledge. Problems may be ill defined or well defined, leading to more or less obvious solutions.

○ The solutions we generate depend as much on the organization of our knowledge as they do on the objective characteristics of the problems. Means-end analysis and analogical problem solving offer pathways to effective solutions, although we often frame things in terms of what we already know and already understand.

○ Sometimes, as in the case of functional fixedness, that knowledge can restrict our problem-solving processes, making it difficult to find solutions that should be easy to find.

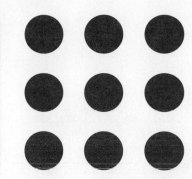

▲ FIGURE 9.17
The Nine-Dot Problem Connect all nine dots with four straight lines without lifting your pencil from the paper. Compare your answer to those in Figure 9.20 on page 383.

Transforming Information: How We Reach Conclusions

Reasoning is *a mental activity that consists of organizing information or beliefs into a series of steps to reach conclusions.* Not surprisingly, sometimes our reasoning seems sensible and straightforward, and other times it seems a little off. Consider some reasons offered by people who filed actual insurance accident claims (www.swapmeetdave.com):

> "I left for work this morning at 7:00 a.m. as usual when I collided straight into a bus. The bus was 5 minutes early."

> "Coming home, I drove into the wrong house and collided with a tree I don't have."

> "My car was legally parked as it backed into another vehicle."

> "The indirect cause of the accident was a little guy in a small car with a big mouth."

> "Windshield broke. Cause unknown. Probably voodoo."

When people like these hapless drivers argue with you in a way that seems inconsistent or poorly thought out, you may accuse them of being "illogical." Logic is a system of rules that specifies which conclusions follow from a set of statements. To put it another way, if you know that a given set of statements is true, logic will tell you which other statements *must* also be true. If the statement "Jack and Jill went up the hill" is true, then according to the rules of logic, the statement "Jill went up the hill" must also be true. To accept the truth of the first statement while denying the truth of the second statement would be a contradiction. Logic is a tool for evaluating reasoning, but it should not be confused with the process of reasoning itself. Equating logic and reasoning would be like equating carpenter's tools (logic) with building a house (reasoning).

Practical, Theoretical, and Syllogistic Reasoning

Earlier in the chapter, we discussed decision making, which often depends on reasoning with probabilities. Practical reasoning and theoretical reasoning also allow us to make decisions (Walton, 1990). **Practical reasoning** is *figuring out what to do, or reasoning directed toward action.* Means-ends analysis is one kind of practical reasoning. An example is figuring out how to get to a concert across town if you don't have a car. In contrast, **theoretical reasoning** (sometimes also called *discursive reasoning*) is *reasoning directed toward arriving at a belief.* We use theoretical reasoning when we try to determine which beliefs follow logically from other beliefs.

Suppose you asked your friend Bruce to take you to a concert, and he said that his car wasn't working. You'd undoubtedly find another way to get to the concert. If you

functional fixedness The tendency to perceive the functions of objects as fixed.

reasoning A mental activity that consists of organizing information or beliefs into a series of steps to reach conclusions.

practical reasoning Figuring out what to do, or reasoning directed toward action.

theoretical reasoning Reasoning directed toward arriving at a belief.

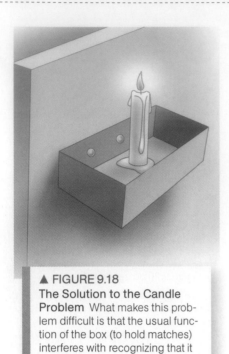

▲ FIGURE 9.18
The Solution to the Candle Problem What makes this problem difficult is that the usual function of the box (to hold matches) interferes with recognizing that it can be tacked to the wall to serve as a candleholder.

then spied him drive into the concert parking lot, you might reason: "Bruce told me his car wasn't working. He just drove into the parking lot. If his car wasn't working, he couldn't drive it here. So, either he suddenly fixed it, or he was lying to me. If he was lying to me, he's not much of a friend." Notice the absence of an action-oriented goal. Theoretical reasoning is just a series of inferences concluding in a belief—in this case, about your so-called friend's unfriendliness!

If you concluded from these examples that we are equally adept at both types of reasoning, experimental evidence suggests you're wrong. People generally find figuring out what to do easier than deciding which beliefs follow logically from other beliefs. In cross-cultural studies, this tendency to respond practically when theoretical reasoning is sought has been demonstrated in individuals without schooling. Consider, for example, this dialogue between a Nigerian rice farmer, a member of the preliterate Kpelle people, and an American researcher (Scribner, 1975, p. 155):

Experimenter: All Kpelle men are rice farmers. Mr. Smith (this is a Western name) is not a rice farmer. Is he a Kpelle man?

Participant: I don't know the man in person. I have not laid eyes on the man himself.

Experimenter: Just think about the statement.

Participant: If I know him in person, I can answer that question, but since I do not know him in person, I cannot answer that question.

Experimenter: Try and answer from your Kpelle sense.

Participant: If you know a person, if a question comes up about him, you are able to answer. But if you do not know a person, if a question comes up about him, it's hard for you to answer it.

As this excerpt shows, the participant does not seem to understand that the problem can be resolved with theoretical reasoning. Instead, he is concerned with retrieving and verifying facts, a strategy that does not work for this type of task.

A very different picture emerges when members of preliterate cultures are given tasks that require practical reasoning. One well-known study of rural Kenyans illustrates a typical result (Harkness, Edwards, & Super, 1981). The problem describes a dilemma in which a boy must decide whether to obey his father and give the family

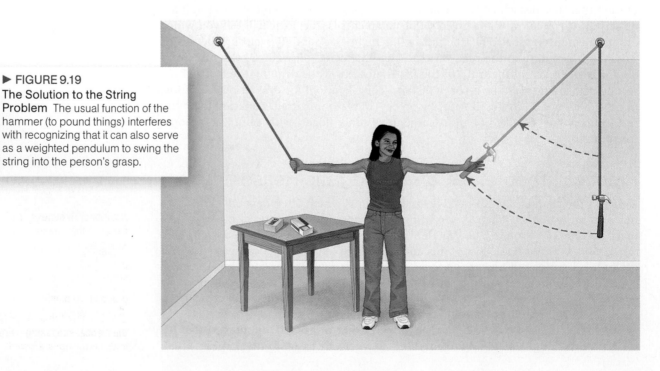

► FIGURE 9.19
The Solution to the String Problem The usual function of the hammer (to pound things) interferes with recognizing that it can also serve as a weighted pendulum to swing the string into the person's grasp.

some of the money he has earned, even though his father previously promised that the boy could keep it all. After hearing the dilemma, the participants were asked what the boy should do. Here is a typical response from a villager:

> A child has to give you what you ask for just in the same way as when he asks for anything you give it to him. Why then should he be selfish with what he has? A parent loves his child and maybe the son refused without knowing the need of helping his father. . . . By showing respect to one another, friendship between us is assured, and as a result this will increase the prosperity of our family.

This preliterate individual had little difficulty understanding this practical problem. His response is intelligent, insightful, and well reasoned. A principal finding from this kind of cross-cultural research is that the appearance of competency on reasoning tests depends more on whether the task makes sense to participants than on their problem-solving ability.

What have cross-cultural studies shown us about reasoning tests?

Educated individuals in industrial societies are prone to similar failures in reasoning, as illustrated by **belief bias**, in which *people's judgments about whether to accept conclusions depend more on how believable the conclusions are than on whether the arguments are logically valid* (Evans, Barston, & Pollard, 1983).

For example, in **syllogistic reasoning**, we assess *whether a conclusion follows from two statements that we assume to be true*. Consider the two following syllogisms, evaluate the argument, and ask yourself whether or not the conclusions must be true if the statements are true:

Syllogism 1

Statement 1: No cigarettes are inexpensive.

Statement 2: Some addictive things are inexpensive.

Conclusion: Some addictive things are not cigarettes.

Syllogism 2

Statement 1: No addictive things are inexpensive.

Statement 2: Some cigarettes are inexpensive.

Conclusion: Some cigarettes are not addictive.

If you're like most people, you probably concluded that the reasoning is valid in Syllogism 1 but flawed in Syllogism 2. Indeed, researchers found that nearly 100% of participants accepted the first conclusion as valid, but fewer than half accepted the second (Evans, Barston, & Pollard, 1983). But notice that the syllogisms are in exactly the same form. This form of syllogism is valid, so both conclusions are valid. Evidently, the believability of the conclusions influences people's judgments.

Reasoning and the Brain

Research using fMRI provides novel insights into belief biases on reasoning tasks. In *belief-laden* trials, participants were scanned while they reasoned about syllogisms that could be influenced by knowledge affecting the believability of the conclusions. In *belief-neutral* trials, syllogisms contained obscure terms whose meaning was unknown to participants, as in the following example:

Syllogism 3

Statement 1: No codes are highly complex.

Statement 2: Some quipu are highly complex.

Conclusion: No quipu are codes.

Belief-neutral reasoning activated different brain regions than did belief-laden reasoning (as shown in **FIGURE 9.21** on the next page). Activity in a part of the left

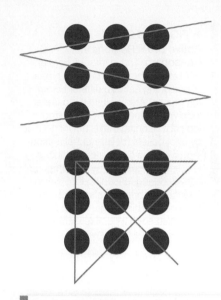

▲ FIGURE 9.20
Two Solutions to the Nine-Dot Problem Solving this problem requires "thinking outside the box," that is, going outside the imaginary box implied by the dot arrangement. The limiting box isn't really there; it is imposed by the problem solver's perceptual set.

belief bias People's judgments about whether to accept conclusions depend more on how believable the conclusions are than on whether the arguments are logically valid.

syllogistic reasoning Determining whether a conclusion follows from two statements that are assumed to be true.

▶ FIGURE 9.21

Active Brain Regions in Reasoning These images from an fMRI study show that different types of reasoning activate different brain regions. (a) Areas within the parietal lobe were especially active during logical reasoning that is not influenced by prior beliefs (belief-neutral reasoning), whereas (b) an area within the left temporal lobe showed enhanced activity during reasoning that was influenced by prior beliefs (belief-laden reasoning). This suggests that people approach each type of reasoning problem in a different way.

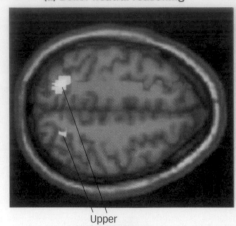
(a) Belief-neutral reasoning

Upper parietal lobe

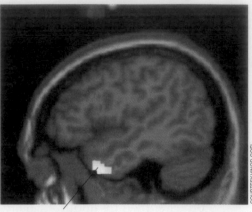
(b) Belief-laden reasoning

Front left temporal lobe

COURTESY VINOD GOEL

temporal lobe involved in retrieving and selecting facts from long-term memory increased during belief-laden reasoning. In contrast, that part of the brain showed little activity and parts of the parietal lobe involved in mathematical reasoning and spatial representation showed greater activity during belief-neutral reasoning (Goel & Dolan, 2003). This evidence suggests that participants took different approaches to the two types of reasoning tasks, relying on previously encoded memories in belief-laden reasoning and on more abstract thought processes in belief-neutral reasoning. These findings fit with other results from neuroimaging studies indicating that there is no single "reasoning center" in the brain; different types of reasoning tasks call on distinct processes that are associated with different brain regions (Goel, 2007).

IN SUMMARY

○ The success of human reasoning depends on the content of the argument or scenario under consideration. People seem to excel at practical reasoning while stumbling when theoretical reasoning requires evaluation of the truth of a set of arguments.

○ Belief bias describes a distortion of judgments about conclusions of arguments, causing people to focus on the believability of the conclusions rather than on the logical connections between the premises.

○ Neuroimaging provides evidence that different brain regions are associated with different types of reasoning.

○ We can see here and elsewhere in the chapter that some of the same strategies that earlier helped us to understand perception, memory, and learning—carefully examining errors and trying to integrate information about the brain into our psychological analyses—are equally helpful in understanding thought and language.

WhereDoYouStand?

Choosing a Mate

Perhaps the most important decision that we make as adults is who to marry. Your spouse is a partner in all of your most valued and intimate human activities: bearing and raising children, acquiring and sharing wealth, and providing emotional sustenance. If divorce rates are considered, however, it appears that we are not very good at making this type of decision. According to the National Center for Health Statistics, 43% of first marriages in the United States end in separation or divorce within 15 years (Bramlett & Mosher, 2001). Projections indicate that the proportion could be as high as 50% for people now in their early 40s (Kreider & Fields, 2002).

Why is choosing a mate such a difficult decision? It may be that mate choice constitutes the ultimate "ill-defined" problem. There are no clearly specified decision-making procedures that will ensure a satisfactory outcome. The desired goal itself (the "perfect spouse" or "perfect marriage") may be difficult to specify precisely, may change as a function of age, and perhaps most importantly may be defined differently by the two parties involved. A large body of research indicates that men and women value different characteristics in prospective mates. Research by more than 50 scientists studying more than 10,000 individuals inhabiting 33 countries shows that women prefer male mates who possess good financial prospects, favorable social status, and ambition, while men prefer female mates who possess physical attractiveness and good health (Buss, 1994; Buss et al., 1990).

The most frequent explanation for this virtually universal sex-linked difference is that men and women, with respect to reproductive success, have confronted different adaptive problems over evolutionary history (Buss, 1994; Buss & Schmitt, 1993). The different adaptive problems between the genders concern parental investment, which researchers define as any investment of time, energy, or risk that an animal makes to enhance the survival and eventual reproduction of an offspring (Krebs & Davies 1991; Trivers, 1972a). Among mammals, females typically invest more in childbearing and child-rearing than males do. Females carry the offspring within their bodies, undergo the risks of childbirth, nurse the infant, and care for their offspring until they are old enough to care for themselves. The reproductive cost for females is therefore greater than for males. This means that reproductive success in females is limited by access to resources, while reproductive success in males is limited by access to potential mates.

Where do you stand on the issue of choosing a mate? Do you think that we should take this type of evolutionary analysis seriously? If so, does this mean that we are "prisoners of biology"? We don't think so—while we are affected by our evolutionary history, we are not constrained by it. For example, one study found that Hungarian women did not cook mates with resources as frequently as females in other nations (Bereczkei et al., 1997). Since the collapse of Communism in Hungary, there are still relatively few men with an income sufficient enough to maintain a family. The researchers speculate that, because of this, females in this culture have shifted their attention to cues other than those referring to resources when seeking mates, such as physical attractiveness or compatibility of values (Bereczkei et al., 1997). Understanding mating decisions clearly requires us to take into account social and cultural factors as well as cognitive and evolutionary ones.

Chapter Review

KEY CONCEPT QUIZ

1. The combining of words to form phrases and sentences is governed by
   a. phonological rules
   b. morphological rules.
   c. structural rules.
   d. syntactical rules.

2. Which of the following statements about language development is inaccurate?
   a. Language acquisition is largely a matter of children imitating adult speech.
   b. Deep structure refers to the meaning of a sentence, while surface structure refers to how it is constructed.
   c. By the time the average child begins school, a vocabulary of 10,000 words is not unusual.
   d. Children's passive mastery of language develops faster than their active mastery.

3. Language development as an innate, biological capacity is explained by
   a. fast mapping.   c. nativist theory.
   b. behaviorism.   d. interactionist explanations.

4. A collection of processes that facilitate language learning is referred to as
   a. phonological rules.
   b. dysphasia.
   c. a language acquisition device.
   d. grammatical generalizations.

5. Damage to the brain region called Broca's area results in
   a. failure to comprehend language.
   b. difficulty in producing grammatical speech.
   c. the reintroduction of infant babbling.
   d. difficulties in writing.

6. The linguistic relativity hypothesis maintains that
   a. language and thought are separate cognitive phenomena.
   b. words have different meanings to different cultures.
   c. human language is too complex for nonhuman animals to acquire.
   d. language shapes the nature of thought.

7. The "most typical" member of a category is a(n)
   a. prototype.
   b. exemplar.
   c. concept.
   d. definition.

8. Which theory of how we form concepts is based on our judgment of features that appear to be characteristic of category members but may not be possessed by every member?
   a. prototype theory
   b. family resemblance theory
   c. exemplar theory
   d. heuristic theory

9. The inability to recognize objects that belong to a particular category though the ability to recognize objects outside the category is undisturbed is called
   a. category-preferential organization.
   b. cognitive-visual deficit.
   c. a category-specific deficit.
   d. aphasia.

10. Making use of which of the following would most likely lead to a solution to a problem?
    a. rational choice theory
    b. probability
    c. a heuristic
    d. an algorithm

11. People give different answers to the same problem depending on how the problem is phrased because of
    a. the availability bias.
    b. the conjunction fallacy.
    c. the representativeness heuristic.
    d. framing effects.

12. The view that people choose to take on risk when evaluating potential losses and avoid risks when evaluating potential gains describes
    a. expected utility.
    b. the frequency format hypothesis.
    c. prospect theory.
    d. the sunk-cost fallacy.

13. People with damage to the prefrontal cortex are prone to
    a. heightened anticipatory emotional reactions.
    b. risky decision making.
    c. galvanic skin response.
    d. extreme sensitivity to behavioral consequences.

14. Miranda decides on a goal, analyzes her current situation, lists the differences between her current situation and her goal, then settles on strategies to reduce those differences. Miranda is engaging in
    a. means-end analysis.
    b. analogical problem solving.
    c. capitalizing on insight.
    d. functional fixedness.

15. What kind of reasoning is aimed at deciding on a course of action?
    a. theoretical
    b. belief
    c. syllogistic
    d. practical

KEY TERMS

language (p. 348)

grammar (p. 348)

phoneme (p. 349)

phonological rules (p. 349)

morphemes (p. 349)

morphological rules (p. 350)

syntactical rules (p. 350)

deep structure (p. 351)

surface structure (p. 351)

fast mapping (p. 352)

telegraphic speech (p. 352)

nativist theory (p. 355)

language acquisition device (LAD) (p. 355)

genetic dysphasia (p. 355)

aphasia (p. 357)

linguistic relativity hypothesis (p. 360)

concept (p. 363)

family resemblance theory (p. 364)

prototype (p. 364)

exemplar theory (p. 365)

category-specific deficit (p. 367)

rational choice theory (p. 368)

availability bias (p. 369)

heuristic (p. 370)

algorithm (p. 370)

conjunction fallacy (p. 370)

representativeness heuristic (p. 371)

framing effects (p. 371)

sunk-cost fallacy (p. 372)

prospect theory (p. 373)

frequency format hypothesis (p. 373)

means-ends analysis (p. 376)

analogical problem solving (p. 377)

functional fixedness (p. 380)

reasoning (p. 381)

practical reasoning (p. 381)

theoretical reasoning (p. 381)

belief bias (p. 383)

syllogistic reasoning (p. 383)

CRITICAL THINKING QUESTIONS

1. To create a sentence, you have to change the deep structure of an idea into the surface structure of a sentence. The one receiving the message translates the surface structure of the sentence back into the deep structure of the idea.

   With surface structure so important to communication, why are we able to communicate effectively when we quickly forget the surface structure of sentences? Why might this forgetfulness of the surface structure be an evolutionary benefit?

2. In this chapter you read about how deaf children at a school in Nicaragua developed their own sign language. Explain how this supports the interactionist explanation of language development.

3. According to rational choice theory, people evaluate all options when making a decision and choose the alternative with the greatest benefit to them. However, psychological research shows us that this is not always the case. Indeed, we are often forced to make decisions without all the information present. In these conditions, we are often fooled into making a different decision than we normally would because of how the options are presented to us.

   Think to a recent election. How might some political candidates use the conjunction fallacy, framing effects, or prospect theory to influence voters' evaluations of their opponents or their opponents' views?

RECOMMENDED READINGS

Ariely, D. (2008). *Predictably irrational: The hidden forces that shape our decisions.* New York: Harper Collins.

Ariely combines psychology and economics to study how the mind influences economic decisions. In this engaging book, he draws on both psychological and economic experiments to explore why our decisions often seem to be irrational.

Cummins, D. D., & Allen, C. A. (2000). *The evolution of mind.* New York: Oxford University Press.

This anthology contains entertaining and informative papers written by psychologists, anthropologists, ethologists, and philosophers that utilize new ideas about biological functions to illuminate puzzling questions of human cognitive evolution.

Dawes, R. M. (2001). *Everyday irrationality: How pseudo scientists, lunatics, and the rest of us systematically fail to think rationally.* Boulder, CO: Westview Press.

An informal and humorous commentary on our society based on rigorous psychological research undertaken by Daniel Kahneman, Amos Tversky, Richard Thaler, and other pioneering researchers of human cognition.

Leighton, J. P., & Sternberg, R. J. (Eds.). (2003). *The nature of reasoning.* Cambridge, MA: Cambridge University Press.

This handy collection of current theory and research on the psychology of reasoning not only presents the state of the science but also charts new directions. This is a comprehensive account of what is known about reasoning in psychology and cognitive science.

Pinker, S. (1994). *The language instinct.* New York: Morrow.

A provocative, entertaining, and skillfully written book on language and language development by a professor who specializes in language research.

ANSWERS TO KEY CONCEPT QUIZ

1. d; 2. a; 3. c; 4. c; 5. b; 6. d; 7. a; 8. b; 9. c; 10. d; 11. d; 12. c; 13. b; 14. a; 15. d.

Need more help? Additional resources are located at the book's free companion Web site at: www.worthpublishers.com/schacter

10 Intelligence

When Anne McGarrah died in 2006 at the age of 57, she had lived more years than she could count. That's because Anne couldn't count at all. Like most people with Williams syndrome, she couldn't add three and seven, couldn't make change for a dollar, and couldn't distinguish right from left. Her retardation was so severe that she was unable to care for herself or hold a full-time job. So what did she do with her time?

"I love to read. Biographies, fiction, novels, different articles in newspapers, articles in magazines, just about anything. I just read a book about a young girl—she was born in Scotland—and her family who lived on a farm. . . . I love listening to music. I like a little bit of Beethoven, but I specifically like Mozart and Chopin and Bach. I like the way they develop their music—it's very light, it's very airy, and it's very cheerful music. I find Beethoven depressing." (Finn, 1991, p. 54)

Although people with Williams syndrome are often unable to tie their own shoes or make their own beds, they typically have gifts for speech and music that anyone would envy. Williams syndrome is caused by the absence of 20 genes on chromosome 7, and no one knows why this tiny genetic glitch so profoundly impairs a person's general cognitive abilities and yet leaves them with a talent for music and language.

▼ People with Williams syndrome have a distinct "elfin" facial appearance and diminished cognitive abilities. But they often have unusual gifts for music and language.

BONNIE WELLER/PHILADELPHIA INQUIRER/NEWSCOM

intelligence The ability to direct one's thinking, adapt to one's circumstances, and learn from one's experiences.

WAS ANNE MCGARRAH INTELLIGENT? IT SEEMS ODD TO SAY that someone is intelligent when she can't do simple addition. But it seems equally odd to say that someone is unintelligent when she can articulate the difference between baroque counterpoint and 19th-century romanticism. In a world of Albert Einsteins and Homer Simpsons, we'd have no trouble distinguishing the geniuses from the dullards. But ours is a world of people like Anne McGarrah and people like us—people who are sometimes brilliant, typically competent, and occasionally dimmer than broccoli. Which forces us to ask the hard question: What exactly *is* intelligence? About 20 years ago, 52 scientific experts came together to answer this very question, and they concluded that **intelligence** is *the ability to direct one's thinking, adapt to one's circumstances, and learn from one's experiences* (Gottfredson, 1997). As you will see, that definition captures much of what scientists and laypeople mean when they use that term.

Psychologists have been studying intelligence for more than a century, and in this chapter we will examine the progress they've made on several fronts. First, we will discuss what intelligence is and how it can be measured. Second, we will ask whether intelligence is a single ability or a collection of different abilities that may or may not be measured by standard intelligence tests. Third, we will discuss the origins of intelligence and see how genes and environments work together to influence it. Fourth, we will ask whether some groups of people are more intelligent than others, and if so, why? Fifth and finally, we will see how intelligence can be improved.

How Can Intelligence Be Measured?

Few things are more dangerous than a man with a mission. In the 1920s, psychologist Henry Goddard administered intelligence tests to arriving immigrants at Ellis Island and concluded that the overwhelming majority of Jews, Hungarians, Italians, and Russians were "feebleminded." Goddard also used his tests to identify feebleminded American families (whom, he claimed, were largely responsible for the nation's social problems) and suggested that the government should segregate them in isolated colonies and "take away from these people the power of procreation" (Goddard, 1913, p. 107). The United States subsequently passed laws restricting the immigration of people from Southern and Eastern Europe, and 27 states passed laws requiring the sterilization of "mental defectives."

From Goddard's day to our own, intelligence tests have been used to rationalize prejudice and discrimination against people of different races, religions, and nationalities. Although intelligence testing has achieved many notable successes, its history is marred by more than its share of fraud and disgrace (Chorover, 1980; Lewontin, Rose, & Kamin, 1984). But the fact that intelligence tests have occasionally been used to further detestable ends is especially ironic because, as we are about to see, such tests were developed for the most noble of purposes: to help underprivileged children succeed in school.

▼ When immigrants arrived at Ellis Island in the 1920s, they were given intelligence tests, which supposedly revealed whether they were "feebleminded."

NATIONAL PARK SERVICE

The Intelligence Quotient

At the end of the 19th century, France instituted a sweeping set of education reforms that made a primary school education available to children of every social class, and suddenly French classrooms were filled with a diverse mix of children who differed dramatically in their readiness to learn. The French government called on psychologist Alfred Binet and physician Theodore Simon to develop a test that would allow educators to develop remedial programs for those children who lagged behind their peers. "Before these children could be educated," Binet (1909) wrote, "they had to be selected. How could this be done?"

Why were intelligence tests originally developed?

Binet and Simon worried that if teachers were allowed to do the selecting, then the remedial classrooms would be filled with poor children, and that if parents were allowed to do the selecting, then the reme-dial classrooms would be empty. So they set out to develop an objective test that would provide an unbiased measure of a child's ability. They began, sensibly enough, by looking for tasks that the best students in a class could perform and that the worst students could not—in other words, tasks that could distinguish the best and worst students and thus predict a fu-ture child's success in school. The tasks they tried included solving logic problems, remembering words, copying pictures, dis-tinguishing edible and inedible foods, making rhymes, and answering questions such as, "When anyone has offended you and asks you to excuse him, what ought you to do?" Binet and Simon settled on 30 of these tasks and assembled them into a test that they claimed could measure a child's "natural intelligence." What did they mean by that phrase?

▲ Alfred Binet (left, 1857–1911) and Theodore Simon (right, 1872–1961) developed the first intel-ligence test to identify children who needed remedial education.

> We here separate natural intelligence and instruction . . . by disregarding, insofar as possible, the degree of instruction which the subject possesses. . . . We give him noth-ing to read, nothing to write, and submit him to no test in which he might succeed by means of rote learning. In fact, we do not even notice his inability to read if a case occurs. It is simply the level of his natural intelligence that is taken into account. (Binet, 1905)

Binet and Simon designed their test to measure a child's *aptitude* for learning inde-pendent of the child's prior educational *achievement*, and it was in this sense that they called theirs a test of "natural intelligence." They suggested that teachers could use their test to estimate a child's "mental level" simply by computing the average test score of children in different age groups and then finding the age group whose average test score was most like that of the child's. For example, a child who was 10 years old but whose score was about the same as the score of the average 8-year-old was considered to have the mental level of an 8-year-old and thus to need remedial education.

How do the two kinds of intelligence quotients differ?

German psychologist William Stern (1914) suggested that this mental level could be thought of as a child's *mental age* and that the best way to determine whether a child was developing normally was to examine the ratio of the child's mental age to the child's physical age. American psychologist Lewis Terman (1916) formalized this

▶ The magazine columnist Marilyn vos Savant is said to have the world's highest measured IQ. The relatively stupid guy standing next to her is her husband, Dr. Robert Jarvik, who invented the artificial heart.

comparison with the intelligence quotient or **ratio IQ,** which *is a statistic obtained by dividing a person's mental age by the person's physical age and then multiplying the quotient by 100*. Thus, a 10-year-old child whose test score was about the same as the average 10-year-old child's test score would have a ratio IQ of 100 because $(10/10) \times 100 = 100$. But a 10-year-old child whose test score was about the same as the average 8-year-old child's test score would have a ratio IQ of 80 because $(8/10) \times 100 = 80$.

The ratio of a person's mental and physical ages seems like a handy way to talk about his or her intelligence—until you actually stop and think about it. For example, a 6-year-old who performs like the average 12-year-old will have a ratio IQ of 200. That makes a certain amount of sense because a 6-year-old who can do algebra is pretty darn smart. But a 30-year-old who performs like the average 60-year-old will also have a ratio IQ of 200. That doesn't make much sense because it means that a perfectly ordinary 30-year-old need only maintain his or her mental abilities for a few decades to be labeled a genius.

As a result of anomalies such as this, researchers devised a new measure called the **deviation IQ,** which is a *statistic obtained by dividing a person's test score by the average test score of people in the same age group and then multiplying the quotient by 100*. According to this formula, a person who scored the same as the average person his or her age would have a deviation IQ of 100. The good thing about the deviation IQ is that a 30-year-old cannot become a genius simply by getting older. The bad thing about the deviation IQ is that it does not allow comparisons between people of different ages. A 5-year-old and a 65-year-old might both have a deviation IQ of 120 because they both outscored their peers, but this does not mean that they are equally intelligent. To solve this problem, modern researchers compute the ratio IQ for children and the deviation IQ for adults. **FIGURE 10.1** shows the percentage of people who typically score at each level of IQ on a standard intelligence test.

▶ FIGURE 10.1
The Normal Curve of Intelligence Deviation IQ scores produce a normal curve. This chart shows the percentage of people who score in each range of IQ.

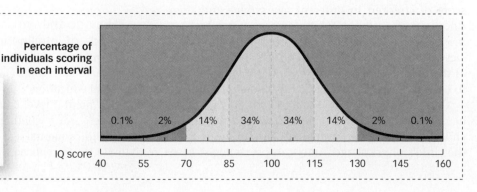

The Logic of Intelligence Testing

Binet and Simon's test did a good job of predicting a child's performance in school, and intelligence is one of the factors that contributes to that performance. But surely there are others. Affability, motivation, intact hearing, doting parents—all of these seem likely to influence a child's scholastic performance. Binet and Simon's test identified students who were likely to perform poorly in school, but was it a test of intelligence?

As you learned in Chapter 2, measurement always requires that we generate an operational definition of the property we wish to measure. To design an intelligence test, we begin with the assumption that a *property* called intelligence leads people to experience a wide variety of *consequences* such as getting good grades in school, becoming a group leader, earning a large income, finding the best route to the gym, or inventing a greaseless burrito. Because it would be highly impractical to actually measure these consequences, we instead devise an easily administered set of tasks (e.g., a geometric puzzle) and questions (e.g., "*Butterfly* is to *caterpillar* as *woman* is to ____") whose successful completion is known to be correlated with those consequences. Now, instead of measuring the consequences (which is difficult to do), we can simply give people our test (which is easy to do). We could call this "an intelligence test" as long as we understand that what we mean by that phrase is "a measurement of a person's performance on tasks that are correlated with the consequences that intelligence produces." In other words, intelligence tests do not "measure" intelligence in the same way that thermometers measure temperature. Rather, they measure the ability to answer questions and perform tasks that are highly correlated with the ability to get good grades, solve real-world problems, and so on.

Finding such questions and tasks isn't easy, and since Binet and Simon's day, psychologists have worked hard to construct intelligence tests that can predict the consequences of intelligence. Today the most widely used intelligence tests are the *Stanford-Binet* (a test that is based on Binet and Simon's original test but that has been modified and updated many times, most notably by Lewis Terman and his colleagues at Stanford University) and the *WAIS* (the Wechsler Adult Intelligence Scale). Both tests require respondents to answer a variety of questions and solve a variety of problems. For example, the WAIS's 13 subtests involve seeing similarities and differences, drawing inferences, working out and applying rules, remembering and manipulating material, constructing shapes, articulating the meaning of words, recalling general knowledge, explaining practical actions in everyday life, working with numbers, attending to details, and so forth. Only 3 of the 13 tests require the examinee to write anything down, and none requires writing words. Some sample problems are shown in **TABLE 10.1** on the next page.

ratio IQ A statistic obtained by dividing a person's mental age by the person's physical age and then multiplying the quotient by 100 (see *deviation IQ*).

deviation IQ A statistic obtained by dividing a person's test score by the average test score of people in the same age group and then multiplying the quotient by 100 (see *ratio IQ*).

◀ At a singles event in Chicago, Mary Kravenas quickly raises her hand and answers "yes" to the question, "Is your IQ greater than your eyeglass prescription?" Does that question count as a test of intelligence?

AP PHOTO/STACIE FREUDENBERG

TABLE 10.1

The Wechsler Adult Intelligence Scale III

WAIS-III Subtest	Questions and Tasks
Vocabulary	The test taker is asked to tell the examiner what certain words mean. For example, *chair* (easy), *hesitant* (medium), and *presumptuous* (hard).
Similarities	The test taker is asked what 19 pairs of words have in common. For example: In what way are an apple and a pear alike? In what way are a painting and a symphony alike?
Information	The test taker is asked several general knowledge questions. These cover people, places, and events. For example: How many days are in a week? What is the capital of France? Name three oceans. Who wrote *The Inferno*?
Comprehension	The test taker is asked questions about everyday life problems, aspects of society, and proverbs. For example: Why do we put food in a refrigerator? Why do people require driving licenses? What does it mean to say "a bird in the hand is worth two in the bush"?
Picture completion	The test taker is asked to spot the missing element in a series of color drawings. For example: Spokes might be missing from one wheel in a picture of a bicycle; in a picture of a person, the person's jacket could be missing a buttonhole.
Block design	The test taker is shown two-dimensional patterns made up of red and white squares and triangles and is asked to reproduce these patterns using cubes with red and white faces.
Matrix reasoning	The test taker is asked to add a missing element to a pattern so that it progresses logically. For example, which of the four symbols at the bottom goes in the empty cell of the table?
Picture arrangement	The test taker is given a series of cartoon drawings and asked to put them in an order that tells a logical story.
Arithmetic	The test taker is asked to solve arithmetic problems, progressing from easy to difficult ones.
Digit span	The test taker is asked to repeat a sequence of numbers. Sequences run from two to nine numbers in length. In the second part of this test, the sequences must be repeated in reversed order. An easy example is to repeat 3-7-4. A harder one is 3-9-1-7-4-5-3-9.
Letter-number sequencing	The examiner reads a series of alternate letters and numbers. The test taker is asked to repeat them, putting the numbers first and in numerical order, followed by the letters in alphabetical order. For example, he or she would repeat "W-4-G-8-L-3" as "3-4-8-G-L-W."
Digit symbol coding	The test taker is asked to write down the number that corresponds to a code for a given symbol (for example, a cross, a circle, and an upside-down T) and does as many as he or she can in 90 seconds.
Symbol search	The test taker is asked to indicate whether one of a pair of abstract symbols is contained in a list of abstract symbols. There are many of these lists, and the test taker does as many as he or she can in 2 minutes.

The Consequences of Intelligence

You've probably heard people say things like, "IQ tests don't predict anything important." That's absolutely true—as long as you don't think grades, jobs, money, health, or longevity are important. The fact is that intelligence test scores are highly correlated with just about every outcome that human beings care about.

For example, the correlation between a person's score on a standard intelligence test and his or her academic performance is roughly $r = .5$ across a wide range of people and

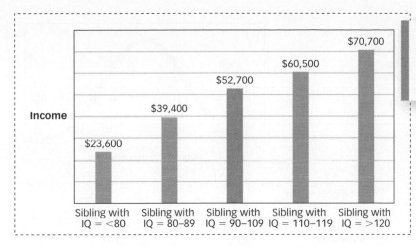

◀ FIGURE 10.2
Income and Intelligence among Siblings This graph shows the average annual salary of a person who has an IQ of 90–109 (shown in pink) and of his or her siblings who have higher or lower IQs (shown in blue).

situations. An intelligence test score is also the best predictor of the number of years of education an individual will receive, which is in part why these scores also predict a

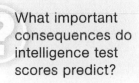

What important consequences do intelligence test scores predict?

person's occupational status and income (Nyborg & Jensen, 2001). For example, a person's score on an intelligence test taken in early adulthood correlates about $r = .4$ with the person's later occupational status (Jencks, 1979). One study of siblings with significantly different IQs found that the less intelligent sibling earned about half of what the more intelligent sibling earned (Murray, 2002) (see **FIGURE 10.2**). There is also a strong correlation between the average intelligence score of a nation and its overall economic status (Lynn & Vanhanen, 2002). Clearly, it pays to be smart.

Intelligence tests scores are also among the best predictors of how well employees perform in their jobs (Hunter & Hunter, 1984), and job performance correlates more highly with intelligence ($r = .53$) than with factors such as performance during a job interview ($r = .14$) or education ($r = .10$). The conclusion to be drawn from almost a century of research on the topic is that "for hiring employees without previous experience in the job, the most valid measure of future performance and learning is general mental ability" (Schmidt & Hunter, 1998, p. 252) (see the Real World box on p. 397).

Intelligence test scores predict a wide variety of other important consequences—from how likely people are to commit crimes to how long people are likely to live (Deary et al., 2008; Der, Batty, & Deary, 2009; Gottfredson & Deary, 2004; Leon et al., 2009; Richards et al., 2009; Rushton & Templer, 2009; Whalley & Deary, 2001). One study identified 320 people with extremely high intelligence test scores at age 13 and followed them for 10 years (Lubinski et al., 2001). Not only were they 50 times more likely than the general population to get graduate degrees and 500 times more likely than the general population to obtain a perfect score on the Graduate Record Examination, but at a time when fewer than a quarter of their peers had completed an undergraduate degree they had already published scientific studies in peer-reviewed journals and stories in leading literary magazines, obtained prestigious scholastic fellowships, written operas, developed successful commercial products, and obtained patents (**FIGURE 10.3** on the next page).

Intelligence test scores also predict people's performance on basic cognitive tasks. For instance, when people are briefly exposed to a pair of vertical lines and are

◀ Intelligence is highly correlated with income. Ken Jennings has won more money on television game shows than any other human being—a whopping $3,623,414.

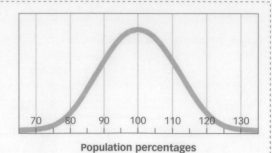

▶ FIGURE 10.3
Life Outcomes and Intelligence People with lower intelligence test scores typically have poorer life outcomes. This chart shows the percentage of people at different levels of IQ who experience the negative life outcomes listed in the leftmost column.

Population percentages

IQ					
Total population distribution	5	20	50	20	5
Unemployed more than 1 month out of year (men)	12	10	7	7	2
Divorced in 5 years	21	22	23	15	9
Lives in poverty	30	16	6	3	2
Ever incarcerated (men)	7	7	3	1	0
Chronic welfare recipient (mothers)	31	17	8	2	0
High school dropout	55	35	6	.4	0

asked to determine which is longer, people with high intelligence test scores require less time to get the right answer (Deary & Stough, 1996; Grudnick & Kranzler, 2001; Nettleback & Lally, 1976). The same is true when people attempt to distinguish between colors or between tones (Acton & Schroeder, 2001). People with high intelligence test scores also have faster and less variable reactions to almost any kind of stimulus (Deary, Der, & Ford, 2001), and researchers are beginning to discover neural differences between more and less intelligent people that may account for these differences in speed (Luders et al., 2009; Neubauer & Fink, 2009; Waiter et al., 2009). Interestingly, intelligence test scores also seem to be fairly good predictors of a person's political and religious attitudes: The more intelligent people are, the more likely they are to be liberal and atheistic (Deary, Batty, & Gale, 2008; Lynn, Harvey, & Nyborg, 2009; Reeve, Heggestad, & Lievens, 2009; Stankov, 2009). All in all, intelligence tests scores are excellent predictors of a remarkable range of important consequences. IQ clearly matters.

IN SUMMARY

○ *Intelligence* is a mental ability that enables people to direct their thinking, adapt to their circumstances, and learn from their experiences.

○ Intelligence tests measure responses that are known to be correlated with consequential behaviors that are thought to be made possible by intelligence.

○ Intelligence tests produce a score known as an *intelligence quotient* or IQ. *Ratio IQ* is the ratio of a person's mental to physical age and *deviation IQ* is the deviation of a person's test score from the average score of his or her peers.

○ Intelligence test scores predict a person's academic performance, job performance, health, wealth, attitudes, and even basic cognitive abilities.

Is Intelligence One Ability or Many?

During the 1990s, Michael Jordan won the National Basketball Association's Most Valuable Player award five times, led the Chicago Bulls to six league championships, and had the highest regular season scoring average in the history of the game. The Associated Press named him the second-greatest athlete of the century, and ESPN named him the first. So when Jordan quit professional basketball in 1993 to join professional baseball, he was as surprised as anyone to find that he—well, there's really no way to say this nicely—sucked. One of his teammates lamented that Jordan "couldn't hit a curveball with an ironing board," and a major-league manager called him "a disgrace to the game" (Wulf, 1994). Given his lackluster performance, it's no wonder that Jordan gave up baseball after just one season and returned to basketball, where he led his team to three consecutive championships.

Michael Jordan's brilliance on the basketball court and his mediocrity on the baseball field proved beyond all doubt that these two sports require different abilities that are not necessarily possessed by the same individual. But if basketball and baseball require different abilities, then what does it mean to say that someone is the greatest athlete of the century? Is *athleticism* a meaningless abstraction? The science of intelligence has grappled with a similar question for more than a hundred years. As we have seen, intelligence test scores predict important outcomes, from academic success to longevity. But is that because they measure a real property of the human mind, or is intelligence just a meaningless abstraction?

▲ Michael Jordan was an extraordinary basketball player and a mediocre baseball player. So was he or wasn't he a great athlete?

PATRICK MURPHY-RACEY/SPORTS ILLUSTRATED/GETTY IMAGES

THE REAL WORLD

Look Smart

Your interview is in 30 minutes. You've checked your hair twice, eaten your weight in breath mints, combed your résumé for typos, and rehearsed your answers to all the standard questions. Now you have to dazzle them with your intelligence whether you've got it or not. Because intelligence is one of the most valued of all human traits, we are often in the business of trying to make others think we're smart regardless of whether that's true. So we make clever jokes and drop the names of some of the longer books we've read in the hope that prospective employers, prospective dates, prospective customers, and prospective in-laws will be appropriately impressed.

But are we doing the right things, and if so, are we getting the credit we deserve? Research shows that ordinary people are, in fact, reasonably good judges of other people's intelligence (Borkenau & Liebler, 1995). For example, observers can look at a pair of photographs and reliably determine which of the two people in them is smarter (Zebrowitz et al., 2002). When observers watch 1-minute videotapes of different people engaged in social interactions, they can accurately estimate which person has the highest IQ—even if they see the videos without sound (Murphy, Hall, & Colvin, 2003).

▲ Wahad Mehood is interviewing for a job as a petroleum engineer with EPC Global. Studies show that when a job candidate holds an interviewer's gaze, the interviewer is more likely to consider the candidate to be intelligent. And the interviewer is right!

People base their judgments of intelligence on a wide range of cues, from physical features (being tall and attractive) to dress (being well groomed and wearing glasses) to behavior (walking and talking quickly). And yet, none of these cues is actually a reliable indicator of a person's intelligence. The reason why people are such good judges of intelligence is that in addition to all these useless cues, they also take into account one very useful cue: eye gaze. As it turns out, intelligent people hold the gaze of their conversation partners both when they are speaking and when they are listening, and observers know this, which is what enables them to accurately estimate a person's intelligence despite their mythical beliefs about the informational value of spectacles and neckties (Murphy et al., 2003). All of this is especially true when the observers are women (who tend to be better judges of intelligence) and the people being observed are men (whose intelligence tends to be easier to judge).

The bottom line? Breath mints are fine and a little gel on the cowlick certainly can't hurt, but when you get to the interview, don't forget to stare.

A Hierarchy of Abilities

Charles Spearman was a student of Wilhelm Wundt (who founded the first experimental psychology laboratory), and he set out to answer precisely this question. Spearman invented a technique known as **factor analysis**, which is *a statistical technique that explains a large number of correlations in terms of a small number of underlying factors.* (We'll get into a bit more detail about this in the next section.) Although Spearman's technique was complex, his reasoning was simple: If there really is a single, general ability called intelligence that enables people to perform a variety of intelligent behaviors, then those who have this ability should do well at just about everything and those who lack it should do well at just about nothing. In other words, if intelligence is a single, general ability, then there should be a very strong positive correlation between people's performances on all kinds of tests.

To find out if there was, Spearman (1904) measured how well school-age children could discriminate small differences in color, auditory pitch, and weight, and he then correlated these scores with the children's grades in different academic subjects as well as with their teachers' estimates of their intellectual ability. His research revealed two things. First, it revealed that most of these measures were indeed positively correlated: Children who scored high on one measure—for example, distinguishing the musical note C# from D—tended to score high on the other measures—for example, solving algebraic equations. Some psychologists have called this finding "the most replicated result in all of psychology" (Deary, 2000, p. 6), and in fact, even *mice* show a strong positive correlation between performances on different kinds of cognitive tests (Matzel et al., 2003). Second, Spearman's research revealed that although different measures were positively correlated, they were not perfectly correlated: The child who had the very highest score on one measure didn't necessarily have the very highest score on *every* measure. Spearman combined these two facts into a **two-factor theory of intelligence**, which suggested that *every task requires a combination of a general ability* (g) *and skills that are specific to the task* (s).

► Dr. Olufunmilayo Olopade received a so-called "genius award" from the MacArthur Foundation for her work in molecular genetics. Spearman's two-factor theory of intelligence suggests that because she's a brilliant scientist we should expect her to be a competent (though not necessarily brilliant) musician.

AP PHOTO/CHARLES REX ARBOGAST

As sensible as Spearman's conclusions were, not everyone agreed with them. Louis Thurstone (1938) noticed that while scores on most tests were indeed positively correlated, scores on one kind of verbal test were more highly correlated with scores on another kind of verbal test than they were with scores on perceptual tests. Thurstone took this "clustering of correlations" to mean that there was actually no such thing as *g* and that there were instead a few stable and independent mental abilities such as perceptual ability, verbal ability, and numerical ability, which he called the *primary mental abilities*. These primary mental abilities were neither general like *g* (for example, a person might have strong verbal abilities and weak numerical abilities) nor specific like *s* (for example, a person who had strong verbal abilities tended both to speak and read well). In essence, Thurstone argued that just as we have games called *baseball* and *basketball* but no game called *athletics,* so we have abilities such as verbal ability and perceptual ability but no general ability called intelligence. **TABLE 10.2** shows the primary mental abilities that Thurstone identified.

? How was the debate between Spearman and Thurstone resolved?

factor analysis A statistical technique that explains a large number of correlations in terms of a small number of underlying factors.

two-factor theory of intelligence Spearman's theory suggesting that every task requires a combination of a general ability (which he called *g*) and skills that are specific to the task (which he called *s*).

TABLE 10.2

Thurstone's Primary Mental Abilities

Primary Mental Ability	Description
Word fluency	Ability to solve anagrams and to find rhymes, etc.
Verbal comprehension	Ability to understand words and sentences
Number	Ability to make mental and other numerical computations
Space	Ability to visualize a complex shape in various orientations
Memory	Ability to recall verbal material, learn pairs of unrelated words, etc.
Perceptual speed	Ability to detect visual details quickly
Reasoning	Ability to induce a general rule from a few instances

The debate among Spearman, Thurstone, and other mathematical giants was quite technical, and it raged for half a century as psychologists hotly debated the existence of *g*. But in the 1980s, a new mathematical technique called *confirmatory factor analysis* brought the debate to a quiet close by revealing that Spearman and Thurstone had each been right in his own way. Specifically, this new technique showed that the correlations between scores on different mental ability tests are best described by a three-level hierarchy (see **FIGURE 10.4**) with a *general factor* (like Spearman's *g*) at the top, *specific factors* (like Spearman's *s*) at the bottom, and a set of factors called *group factors* (like Thurstone's *primary mental abilities*) in the middle (Gustafsson, 1984). A reanalysis of massive amounts of data collected over 60 years from more than 130,000 healthy adults, schoolchildren, infants, college students, people with learning disabilities, and people with mental and physical illnesses has shown that almost every study done over the past half century results in a three-level hierarchy of this kind (Carroll, 1993). This hierarchy suggests that people have a very general ability called intelligence, which is made up of a small set of middle-level abilities, which are made up of a large set of specific abilities that are unique to particular tasks. Although this resolution to a hundred years of disagreement is not particularly exciting, it appears to have the compensatory benefit of being true.

▼ **FIGURE 10.4**
A Three-Level Hierarchy Most intelligence test data are best described by a three-level hierarchy with general intelligence (*g*) at the top, specific abilities (*s*) at the bottom, and a small number of middle-level abilities (*m*) (sometimes called group factors) in the middle.

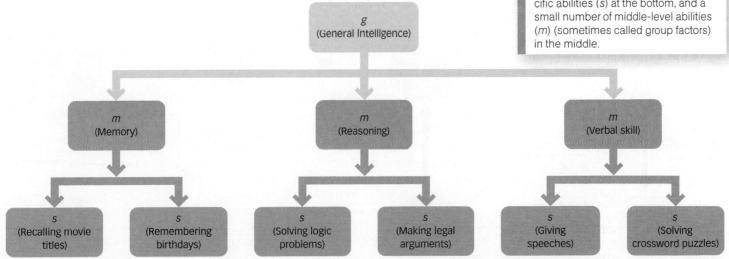

fluid intelligence The ability to see abstract relationships and draw logical inferences.

crystallized intelligence The ability to retain and use knowledge that was acquired through experience.

The Middle-Level Abilities

Michael Jordan played basketball much better than baseball, but he played both sports much better than most people can. His specific abilities allowed him to be more successful at one sport than another, but his general ability allowed him to outperform 99.9% of the world's population on both the court and the field. It is easy to see that Michael Jordan had both specific abilities (dribbling) and a general ability (athleticism), but it is not so easy to say precisely what his middle-level abilities were. Should we draw a distinction between speed and power, between guile and patience, or between the ability to work with a team or perform as an individual? Should we describe his athleticism as a function of 3 middle-level abilities or 4? Or 6? Or 92?

Similar questions arise when we consider intelligence. Most psychologists agree that there are very specific mental abilities as well as a very general mental ability and that one of the important challenges is to describe the middle-level abilities that lie between them. Some psychologists have taken a *data-based approach* to this problem by starting with people's responses on intelligence tests and then looking to see what kinds of independent clusters these responses form. Other psychologists have taken a *theory-based approach* to this problem by starting with a broad survey of human abilities and then looking to see which of these abilities intelligence tests measure—or fail to measure. These approaches have led to rather different suggestions about the best way to describe the middle-level abilities that constitute intelligence.

The Data-Based Approach

One way to determine the nature of the middle-level abilities is to start with the data and go where they lead us. Just as Spearman and Thurstone did, we could compute the correlations between the performances of a large number of people on a large number of tests and then see how those correlations cluster. For example, imagine that we tested how quickly and well a large group of people could (a) balance teacups, (b) understand Shakespeare, (c) swat flies, and (d) sum the whole numbers between one and a thousand. Now imagine that we computed the correlation between scores on each of these tests and observed a pattern of correlations like the one shown in **FIGURE 10.5a**. What would this pattern tell us?

This pattern suggests that a person who can swat flies well can also balance teacups well and that a person who can understand Shakespeare well can also sum numbers well, but that a person who can swat flies well and balance teacups well may or may not be able to sum numbers or understand Shakespeare well. From this pattern, we could conclude that there are two middle-level abilities (shown in **FIGURE 10.5b**), which we might call "physical coordination" (the ability

How do patterns of correlation reveal the middle-level abilities?

▼ FIGURE 10.5
Patterns of Correlation Can Reveal Middle-Level Abilities The pattern of correlations shown in (a) suggests that these four specific abilities can be thought of as instances of the two middle-level abilities—physical coordination and academic skill—shown in (b).

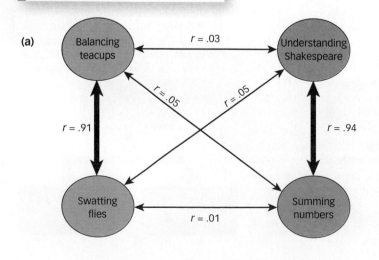

(a)

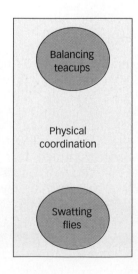
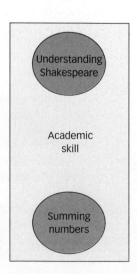

(b)

Jim Lash (left) has Alzheimer's disease, and Josh Roberts (right) has a form of autism known as Asperger's syndrome. Alzheimer's impairs fluid intelligence more than crystallized intelligence and autism does the opposite.

that allows people to swat flies and balance teacups well) and "academic skill" (the ability that allows people to understand Shakespeare and sum numbers well). This pattern suggests that different specific abilities such as fly swatting and teacup balancing are made possible by a single middle-level ability and that this middle-level ability is unrelated to the other middle-level ability, which enables people to sum numbers and understand Shakespeare. As this example reveals, simply by examining the pattern of correlations between different tests, we can divine the nature and number of the middle-level abilities.

In the real world, of course, there are more than four tests. So what kinds of patterns do we observe when we calculate the correlations between the tests of mental ability that psychologists actually use? This is precisely what psychologist John Carroll set out to discover in his landmark analysis of intelligence test scores from nearly 500 studies conducted over a half century (Carroll, 1993). Carroll found that the pattern of correlations among these tests suggested the existence of eight independent middle-level abilities: *memory and learning, visual perception, auditory perception, retrieval ability, cognitive speediness, processing speed, crystallized intelligence,* and *fluid intelligence.*

Although most of the abilities on this list are self-explanatory, the last two are not. **Fluid intelligence** is *the ability to see abstract relationships and draw logical inferences,* and **crystallized intelligence** is *the ability to retain and use knowledge that was acquired through experience* (Horn & Cattell, 1966). If we think of the brain as an information-processing device, then crystallized intelligence refers to the "information" part and fluid intelligence refers to the "processing" part (Salthouse, 2000). Whereas crystallized intelligence is generally assessed by tests of vocabulary, factual information, and so on, fluid intelligence is generally assessed by tests that pose novel, abstract problems that must be solved under time pressure, such as Raven's Progressive Matrices Test, shown in **FIGURE 10.6**.

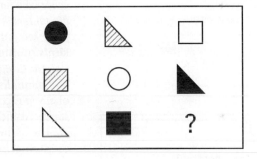

Which of these shapes correctly completes the above pattern?

▲ FIGURE 10.6
Raven's Progressive Matrices Test This item from Raven's Progressive Matrices Test measures nonverbal reasoning abilities and is unlikely to be culturally biased.

The Theory-Based Approach

The data-based approach attempts to discover the middle-level abilities by analyzing people's responses to questions on intelligence tests. The good thing about this approach is that its conclusions are based on hard evidence. But the bad thing about this approach is that it is incapable of discovering any middle-level ability that intelligence tests didn't already measure (Stanovich, 2009). For example, no intelligence test asks people to find three new uses for an origami fish or to answer the question, "What is the question you thought you'd be asked but weren't?" As a result, the scores from these tests may be incapable of revealing the middle-level abilities such as imagination or creativity. Are there middle-level abilities to which the data-based approach is blind?

? What are the advantages of a theory-based approach to intelligence?

▲ Won Park is an origami master who can fold dollar bills into astounding shapes. Some researchers believe that "creative intelligence" is quite different from the "analytic intelligence" that intelligence tests are designed to measure.

Psychologist Robert Sternberg believes there are. He suggests that there are three kinds of intelligence, which he calls *analytic intelligence, creative intelligence,* and *practical intelligence.* Analytic intelligence is the ability to identify and define problems and to find strategies for solving them; creative intelligence is the ability to generate solutions that other people do not; and practical intelligence is the ability to apply and implement these solutions in everyday settings. According to Sternberg, standard intelligence tests typically confront people with clearly defined problems that have one right answer and then supply all the information needed to solve them. These kinds of problems require (and thus serve to measure) analytic intelligence. But everyday life confronts people with situations in which they must formulate the *problem,* find the information needed to solve it, and then choose among multiple acceptable solutions. These situations require (and thus serve to measure) practical intelligence. Some studies suggest that these different kinds of intelligence are independent. For example, workers at milk-processing plants develop complex strategies for efficiently combining partially filled cases of milk, and not only do they outperform highly educated white-collar workers, but their performance is also unrelated to their scores on intelligence tests, suggesting that practical and analytic intelligence are not the same thing (Scribner, 1984). Sternberg has argued that tests of practical intelligence are better than tests of analytic intelligence at predicting a person's job performance, though such claims have been criticized (Brody, 2003; Gottfredson, 2003).

Psychologist Howard Gardner also believes that standard intelligence tests fail to measure some important human abilities. His observations of ordinary people, people with brain damage, **prodigies** (*people of normal intelligence who have an extraordinary ability*), and **savants** (*people of low intelligence who have an extraordinary ability*) have led him to conclude that there are eight distinct kinds of intelligence: *linguistic, logical-mathematical, spatial, musical, bodily-kinesthetic, interpersonal, intrapersonal,* and *naturalistic.* Although there are few data to confirm the existence or independence of these eight abilities, Gardner's suggestions are intriguing. Moreover, he argues that standard intelligence tests measure only the first three of these abilities because they are the abilities most valued by Western culture, but that other cultures may conceive of intelligence differently.

How does the concept of intelligence differ across cultures?

For instance, the Confucian tradition emphasizes the ability to behave properly, the Taoist tradition emphasizes humility and self-knowledge, and the Buddhist tradition emphasizes determination and mental effort (Yang & Sternberg, 1997). Westerners regard people as intelligent when they speak quickly and often, but

"I don't have to be smart, because someday I'll just hire lots of smart people to work for me."

▶ The 5-year-old who drew the picture on the left is a savant—a "low-functioning" autistic child with a mental age of about 3 years. The picture on the right was drawn by a typical 5-year-old.

Africans regard people as intelligent when they are deliberate and quiet (Irvine, 1978). Unlike Western societies, many African and Asian societies conceive of intelligence as including social responsibility and cooperativeness (Azuma & Kashiwagi, 1987; Serpell, 1974; White & Kirkpatrick, 1985), and the word for *intelligence* in Zimbabwe, *ngware,* means to be wise in social relationships. Definitions of intelligence may even differ within a culture: Californians of Latino ancestry are more likely to equate intelligence with social competence while Californians of Asian ancestry are more likely to equate it with cognitive skill (Okagaki & Sternberg, 1993). Some researchers take all this to mean that different cultures have radically different conceptualizations of intelligence, but others are convinced that what appear to be differences in the conceptualization of intelligence are really just differences in language. They argue that every culture values the ability to solve important problems and that what really distinguishes cultures is the *kinds* of problems that are considered to be important.

One of the most important kinds of problems in any culture is an emotional problem. How do you tell a friend that she talks too much without hurting her feelings? How do you cheer yourself up after failing a test? How do you know whether you are feeling anxious or angry? Psychologists John Mayer and Peter Salovey define **emotional intelligence** as *the ability to reason about emotions and to use emotions to enhance reasoning* (Mayer, Roberts, & Barsade, 2008; Salovey & Grewal, 2005). Emotionally intelligent people know what kinds of emotions a particular event will trigger, they can identify, describe, and manage their emotions, they know how to use their emotions to improve their decisions, and they can identify other people's emotions from facial expressions and tones of voice. Furthermore, they do all this quite easily, which is why emotionally intelligent people show *less* neural activity when solving emotional problems than emotionally unintelligent people do (Jausovec & Jausovec, 2005; Jausovec, Jausovec, & Gerlic, 2001).

All of these skills turn out to be quite important, especially when it comes to social relationships. Emotionally intelligent children have better social skills and more friends (Eisenberg et al., 2000; Mestre et al., 2006; Schultz, Izard, & Bear, 2004); emotionally intelligent students are judged to be more competent in their interactions (Brackett et al., 2006); emotionally intelligent adults have better romantic relationships (Brackett, Warner, & Bosco, 2005) and better workplace relationships (Elfenbein et al., 2007; Lopes et al., 2006). Given all this, it isn't surprising that emotionally intelligent people tend to be happier (Brackett & Mayer, 2003; Brackett et al., 2006) and more satisfied with their lives (Ciarrochi, Chan, & Caputi, 2000; Mayer, Caruso, & Salovey, 1999).

▲ Unlike Americans, Africans describe people as intelligent when they are deliberate and quiet. *Thought is hallowed in the lean oil of solitude,* wrote Nigerian poet Wole Soyinka, who won the Nobel Prize in Literature in 1986.

prodigy A person of normal intelligence who has an extraordinary ability.

savant A person of low intelligence who has an extraordinary ability.

emotional intelligence The ability to reason about emotions and to use emotions to enhance reasoning.

1.

COURTESY OF DANIEL GILBERT

Emotion	Select one:
a. Happy	○
b. Angry	○
c. Fearful	○
d. Sad	○

2.

Tom felt worried when he thought about all the work he needed to do. He believed he could handle it—if only he had the time. When his supervisor brought him an additional project, he felt _____. (Select the best choice.)

Emotion	Select one:
a. Frustrated and anxious	○
b. Content and calm	○
c. Ashamed and accepting	○
d. Sad and guilty	○

◄ Two items from a test of emotional intelligence. Item 1 (left) measures the accuracy with which a person can read emotional expressions and Item 2 (right) measures the ability to predict emotional responses to external events. The correct answer to both questions is A.
Source: Mayer et al., 2008

fraternal twins (also called dizygotic twins) Twins who develop from two different eggs that were fertilized by two different sperm (see *identical twins*).

identical twins (also called monozygotic twins) Twins who develop from the splitting of a single egg that was fertilized by a single sperm (see *fraternal twins*).

The data-based and theory-based approaches identify many of the core competencies that constitute intelligence. It isn't entirely clear how many of these there are or what they should be called, but it *is* clear that some people have a lot more of them than others. So what makes smart people so smart? We'll tackle that question next.

IN SUMMARY

○ People who score well on one test of mental ability *usually* score well on others, which suggests that there is a property called *g* (general intelligence).

○ People who score well on one test of mental ability don't *always* score well on others, which suggests that there are properties called *s* (specific abilities).

○ Research reveals that between *g* and *s* are several *middle-level abilities*.

○ The *data-based approach* suggests that there are eight middle-level abilities.

○ The *theory-based approach* suggests that there may be middle-level abilities, such as imagination or creativity, which standard intelligence tests don't measure. Non-Western cultures may include measures of social responsibility and cooperation in their definitions of intelligence.

Where Does Intelligence Come From?

No one knows where the Latin phrase *nihil est in intellectu quod non prius fuerit in sensu* originated, but philosophers have been repeating it for about 700 years (Cranefield, 1970). In English it means, "There is nothing in the intellect that was not first in the senses," which is to say that everything we know and think is the product of our experience with the world. Of course, not all philosophers believed this. In 1764, Gottfried Leibniz wrote, "There is nothing in the intellect that was not first in the senses—except for the intellect," which is a clever way of saying that a baby's mind is not a formless blob of clay that gets molded by experience, but a well-formed vessel that was designed by millions of years of evolution and into which individual experience is poured. Leibniz's view has prevailed among modern scientists, who think of human beings as the joint product of nature and of nurture—of the innate characteristics with which they are endowed and of the experiences they subsequently have. As you will see, both nature and nurture have a profound influence on intelligence.

▲ Sir Francis Galton (1822–1911) studied the physical and psychological traits that appeared to run in families. In his book *Hereditary Genius*, he concluded that intelligence was largely inherited.

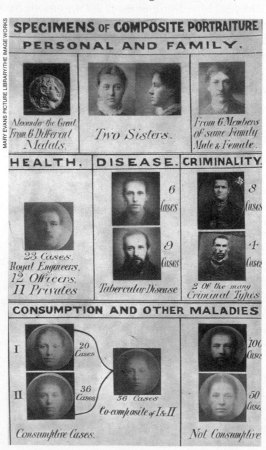

Genetic Influences on Intelligence

The notion that intelligence is "in the blood" has been with us for a long time. For example, in *The Republic,* the philosopher Plato suggested that some people are born to rule, others to be soldiers, and others to be tradesmen. But it wasn't until late in the 19th century that this suggestion became the subject of scientific inquiry. Sir Francis Galton was a half cousin of Charles Darwin, and his contributions to science ranged from meteorology to fingerprinting. Late in life, Galton (1869) became interested in the origins of intelligence. He did careful genealogical studies of eminent families and collected measurements from over 12,000 people that ranged from head size to the ability to discriminate tones. As the title of his book *Hereditary Genius* suggests, he concluded that intelligence was inherited. Was he right?

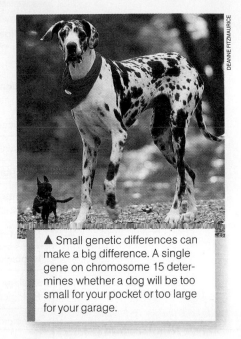

▲ Small genetic differences can make a big difference. A single gene on chromosome 15 determines whether a dog will be too small for your pocket or too large for your garage.

Studying Relatives

The fact that intelligence appears to "run in families" isn't very good evidence of this genetic influence. After all, brothers and sisters share genes, but they share many other

Why are the intelligence test scores of relatives so similar?

things as well. They typically grow up in the same house, go to the same schools, read many of the same books, and have many of the same friends. Members of a family may have similar levels of intelligence because they share genes, environments, or both. To separate the influence of genes and environments, we need to examine the intelligence test scores of people who share genes but not environments (e.g., biological siblings who are separated at birth and raised by different families), people who share environments but not genes (e.g., adopted siblings who are raised together), and people who share both (e.g., biological siblings who are raised together).

There are several kinds of siblings with different degrees of genetic relatedness. When siblings have the same biological parents but different birthdays, they share on average 50% of their genes. **Fraternal twins** (also called *dizygotic twins*) are *twins who develop from two different eggs that were fertilized by two different sperm* and although they happen to have the same birthday, they are merely siblings who shared a womb and they, too, share on average 50% of their genes. **Identical twins** (also called *monozygotic twins*) are *twins who develop from the splitting of a single egg that was fertilized by a single sperm,* and unlike other siblings, they are genetic copies of each other, sharing 100% of their genes.

These different degrees of genetic relatedness allow psychologists to assess the influence that genes have on intelligence. Studies show that the intelligence test scores of identical twins are strongly correlated ($r = .86$) when the twins are raised in the same household, but they are also strongly correlated ($r = .78$) when they are raised in different households—for example, when they are separated at birth and adopted by different families. In fact, as you'll notice from **TABLE 10.3** on the next page, identical twins who are raised apart have more similar intelligence scores than do fraternal twins who are raised together.

What this means is that people who share all their genes have similar intelligence test scores regardless of whether they share their environments. Indeed, the correlation between the intelligence test scores of identical twins who have never met is about the same as the correlation between the intelligence test scores of a single person who has taken the test twice! By comparison, the intelligence test scores of unrelated people raised in the same household—for example, two siblings, one or both of whom were adopted—are correlated only modestly—about $r = .26$ (Bouchard & McGue, 2003). These patterns of correlation suggest that genes play an important role in determining intelligence. This shouldn't surprise us. Intelligence is in part a function of how well a brain works, and given that brains are designed by genes it would be quite remarkable if genes *didn't* play a role in determining a person's intelligence. Indeed, a mere 20 genes on a single chromosome are all that separates you from a person with Williams syndrome.

▼ Tamara Rabi and Adrian Scott were 20 years old when they met in a McDonald's parking lot in New York. "I'm just standing there looking at her," Adriana recalled. "It was a shock. I saw me" (Gootman, 2003). The two soon discovered that they were twins who had been separated at birth and adopted by different families.

TABLE 10.3

Intelligence Test Correlations between People with Different Relationships

Relationship	Shared Home?	% Shared Genes	Correlation between Intelligence Test Scores (*r*)
Twins Identical twins (*n* = 4,672)	Yes	100%	.86
Identical twins (*n* = 93)	No	100%	.78
Fraternal twins (*n* = 5,533)	Yes	50%	.60
Parents and Children Parent-biological child (*n* = 8,433)	Yes	50%	.42
Parent-biological child (*n* = 720)	No	50%	.24
Nonbiological parent-adopted child (*n* = 1,491)	Yes	0%	.19
Siblings Biological siblings (2 parents in common) (*n* = 26,473)	Yes	50%	.47
Nonbiological siblings (no parents in common) (*n* = 714)	Yes	0%	.32
Biological siblings (2 parents in common) (*n* = 203)	No	50%	.24

Source: Plomin et al., 2001a, p. 168.

heritability coefficient A statistic (commonly denoted as h^2) that describes the proportion of the difference between people's scores that can be explained by differences in their genes.

shared environment Those environmental factors that are experienced by all relevant members of a household (see *nonshared environment*).

Heritability

Exactly how powerful is the influence of genes? The **heritability coefficient** (commonly denoted as h^2) is *a statistic that describes the proportion of the difference between people's scores that can be explained by differences in their genes*. When the data from numerous studies of children and adults are analyzed together, the heritability of intelligence is roughly .5, which is to say that about 50% of the difference between people's intelligence test scores is due to genetic differences between them (Plomin & Spinath, 2004).

This fact may tempt you to conclude that half your intelligence is due to your genes and half is due to your experiences, but that's not right. To understand why, consider the rectangles in **FIGURE 10.7**. These rectangles clearly differ in size, and if you were asked to say what percentage of that difference was due to differences in the rectangles' heights and what percentage was due to differences in the rectangles' widths, you would correctly say that 100% of the difference in their sizes was due to differences in their widths and 0% was due to differences in their heights (which are, after all, identical). Good answer. Now, if you were asked to say how much of rectangle A's size was due to its height and how much was due to its width, you would correctly say, "That's a dumb question." It is a dumb question because a rectangle's size is a product of *both* its height and its width and it can't be "due" to one more or less than the other.

Similarly, if you measured the intelligence of all the people at a baseball game and were then asked to say what percentage of the difference in their intelligences was due to differences in their genes and what percentage was due to differences in their experiences, you could reasonably guess that about 50% of the difference was due to each of these factors. That's what the heritability coefficient of .5 suggests. But if you were next asked to say how much of the intelligence of the annoying guy with the bad haircut in Row 17, Seat 4 was due to genes and how much was due to experiences, you

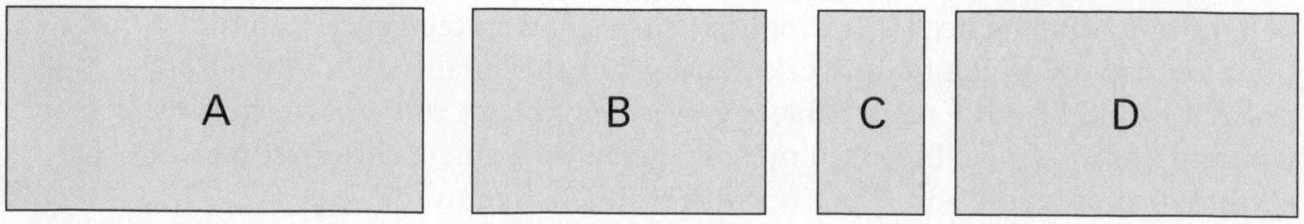

► FIGURE 10.7
How to Ask a Dumb Question
These four rectangles differ in size. How much of the difference in their sizes is due to differences in their widths and how much is due to differences in their heights? Answer: 100% and 0%, respectively. Now, how much of rectangle A's size is due to width and how much is due to height? Answer: That's a dumb question.

A   B   C   D

could only reply, "That's a dumb question." It is a dumb question because the intelligence of a single person is a product of both genes and experience and cannot be "due" to one of these things more than another.

The heritability coefficient tells us why people in a particular group differ from one another; thus its value can change depending on the particular group of people we measure. For example, the heritability of intelligence among wealthy children is about .72 and among poor children about .10 (Turkheimer et al., 2003). How can that be? Well, if we assume that wealthy children have fairly similar environments—that is, if they all have nice homes with books, plenty of free time, ample nutrition, and so on—then all the differences in their intelligence must be due to the one and only factor that distinguishes them from each other, namely, their genes. Conversely, if we assume that poor children have fairly different environments—that is, some have books and free time and ample nutrition while others have some or none of these—then the difference in their intelligences may be due to either of the factors that distinguish them, namely, their genes and their environments. The heritability coefficient can also depend on the age of the people being measured and is typically larger among adults than among children (see **FIGURE 10.8**), which suggests that the environments of any pair of 65-year-olds tend to be more similar than the environments of any pair of 3-year-olds. In short, when people have identical experiences, then the difference in their intelligences must be due to the difference in their genes, and when people have identical genes, then the difference in their intelligences must be due to the difference in their experiences. It may seem paradoxical, but in a science-fictional world of perfect clones, the heritability of intelligence (and of everything else) would be zero.

Does this imply that in a science-fictional world of individuals who lived in exactly the same kinds of houses and received exactly the same kinds of meals, educations, parental care, and so on, the heritability coefficient would be 1? Not likely. Two unrelated people who live in the same household will have *some* but not *all* of their experiences in common. The **shared environment** refers to *those environmental factors that are experienced by all relevant*

> **Why is h^2 higher among wealthy kids than among poor kids?**

▲ A river separates one of the richest and one of the poorest neighborhoods in Mumbai, India. Research suggests that intelligence is more heritable in wealthy than in poor neighborhoods.

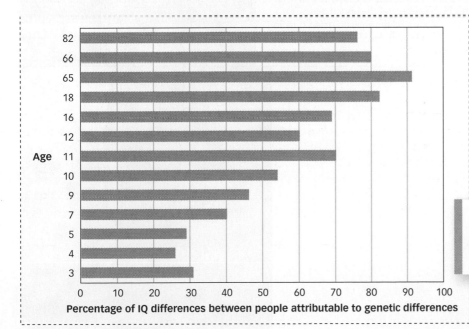

Age

Percentage of IQ differences between people attributable to genetic differences

◀ FIGURE 10.8
Age and Heritability of Intelligence The heritability of intelligence generally increases with the age of the sample measured.

Contrary to what you might think, as siblings get older their intelligence test scores become more similar, not less.

members of a household. For example, siblings raised in the same household have about the same level of affluence, the same number and type of books, the same diet, and so on. The **nonshared environment** refers to *those environmental factors that are not experienced by all relevant members of a household.* Siblings raised in the same household may have very different friends and teachers and may contract different illnesses. This may be why the correlation between the IQ scores of siblings decreases as the age difference between them increases (Sundet, Eriksen, & Tambs, 2008). Being raised in the same household is only a rough measure of the similarity of two people's experiences (Turkheimer & Waldron, 2000); thus studies of twins may overestimate the influence of genes and underestimate the influence of experiences (Nisbett, 2009). As psychologist Eric Turkheimer (2000, p. 162) notes, "The appropriate conclusion [to draw from twin studies] is not so much that the family environment does not matter for development, but rather that the part of the family environment that is shared by siblings does not matter. What does matter is the individual environments of children, their peers, and the aspects of their parenting that they do not share."

Environmental Influences on Intelligence

Americans believe that every individual should have an equal chance to succeed in life, and one of the reasons why we bristle when we hear about genetic influences on intelligence is that we mistakenly believe that our genes are our destinies—that "genetic" is a synonym for "unchangeable" (Pinker, 2003). In fact, traits that are strongly influenced by genes may also be strongly influenced by the environment. Height is a heritable trait, which is why tall parents tend to have tall children; and yet, the average height of Korean boys has increased by more than seven inches in the last 50 years simply because of changes in nutrition (Nisbett, 2009). In 1848, 25% of all Dutch men were rejected by the military because they were less than 5 feet 2 inches, but today the average Dutch man is over 6 feet tall (Max, 2006). Genes may explain why two people who have the same diet differ in height—that is, why Chang-sun is taller than Kwan-ho and why Thijs is taller than Daan—but they do not dictate how tall any of these boys will actually grow up to be.

? In what ways is intelligence like height?

At 7 feet, Pieter Gijselaar is taller than most of his friends—but not *that* much taller. The Dutch government recently adjusted building codes so that doors must now be 7 feet, 6.5 inches high.

nonshared environment Those environmental factors that are not experienced by all relevant members of a household (see *shared environment*).

Is intelligence like height? Alfred Binet (1909) thought so:

A few modern philosophers . . . assert that an individual's intelligence is a fixed quantity that cannot be increased. We must protest and react against this brutal pessimism. . . . With practice, training, and above all method, we manage to increase our attention, our memory, our judgment, and literally to become more intelligent than we were before.

Was Binet right? It depends on whether we are talking about relative or absolute intelligence. *Relative intelligence* is generally stable over time. For example, **TABLE 10.4** shows the results of six studies in which people were given intelligence tests many years apart. The large correlations between the two tests tell us that the people who got the best (or worst) scores when the test was administered the first time tended to get the best (or worst) scores when it was administered the second time. Indeed, studies show that those who are most intelligent at age 11 are likely to be most intelligent at age 80 (Deary et al., 2000, 2004, 2008).

On the other hand, as **FIGURE 10.9** shows, an individual's *absolute intelligence* can change considerably over time, just as Binet suspected (Owens, 1966; Schaie, 1996, 2005; Schwartzman, Gold, & Andres, 1987). Studies show that intelligence tends to increase between adolescence and middle age and to decline thereafter. The sharpest decrease occurs in old age (Kaufman, 2001; Salthouse, 1996a, 2000; Schaie, 2005), and may be due to a general slowing of the brain's processing speed (Salthouse, 1996b; Zimprich & Martin, 2002). Age-related declines are more evident in some domains than in others. For example, on tests that measure vocabulary, general information, and verbal reasoning, people show only small changes from the ages of 18 to 70, but on tests that are timed, have abstract material, involve making new memories, or require reasoning about spatial relationships, most people show marked declines in performance after middle age (Avolio & Waldman, 1994; Lindenberger & Baltes, 1997; Rabbit et al., 2004; Salthouse, 2001). Absolute intelligence tends to decrease across the individual's life span but, oddly enough, it tends to *increase* across generations. The *Flynn Effect* refers to the accidental discovery by the philosopher James Flynn that the average intelligence test score has been rising by about .3% every year, which is to say that the average person today scores about 15 IQ points higher than the average person did just 50 years ago (Dickens & Flynn, 2001; Flynn, 1984, 1987). Most of the improvement has come in areas such as abstract reasoning, spatial relations, and comprehension. Some researchers have suggested that these improvements are the result of better nutrition (Lynn, 2009) or better parenting and schooling (Neisser, 1998), and some have suggested that they are a result of the fact that the least intelligent people in each generation are being left out of the mating game (Mingroni, 2007).

TABLE 10.4			
The Stability of Intelligence Test Scores over Time			
Study	**Mean Initial Age (Years)**	**Mean Follow-up Age (Years)**	**Correlation (*r*)**
1	2	9	.56
2	14	42	.68
3	19	61	.78
4	25	65	.78
5	30	43	.64–.79
6	50	70	.90

Source: Adapted from Deary, 2000.

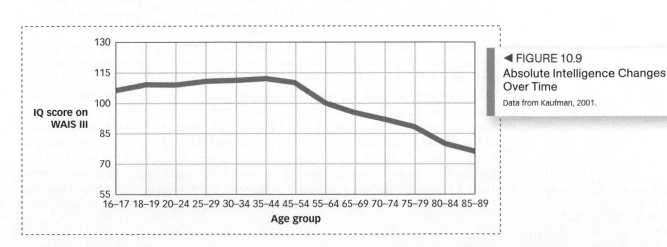

◄ FIGURE 10.9
Absolute Intelligence Changes Over Time
Data from Kaufman, 2001.

► 105-year-old Khatijah (front row, second from right) sits with five generations of her family. The Flynn Effect suggests that intelligence is increasing across generations.

AP PHOTO/BINSAR BAKKARA

Josh

95   100   105

Jason

▲ **FIGURE 10.10**
Genes and Environment
Genes may establish the range in which a person's intelligence *may* fall, but environment determines the point in that range at which the person's intelligence *will* fall. Even though Jason's genes give him a better chance to be smart than do Josh's, differences in their diets could easily cause Josh to have a higher IQ than Jason.

Others (and that includes Flynn himself) believe that the industrial and technological revolutions have changed the nature of daily living such that people now spend more and more time solving precisely the kinds of abstract problems that intelligence tests include—and as we all know, practice makes perfect (Flynn, 2009; Neisser, 1998). In other words, these scientists argue, people today score better than their grandparents did because modern life is becoming more like an IQ test!

All of these studies of change over the life span and across generations clearly show that intelligence is not "a fixed quantity that cannot be increased." Genes may determine the *range* in which a person's IQ is *likely* to fall, but environments determine the exact *point* in that range at which the person's IQ actually *will* fall (see **FIGURE 10.10**). Intelligence can and does change—so what kinds of things can and do change it?

Economics

Perhaps money can't buy love, but it sure can buy intelligence. One of the best predictors of a person's intelligence is the material wealth of the family in which he or she was raised—what scientists call *socioeconomic status* or SES. Studies suggest that being raised in a high-SES family rather than a low-SES family is worth between 12 and 18 IQ points (Nisbett, 2009; van IJzendoorn, Juffer, & Klein Poelhuis, 2005). For example, one study compared the IQs of siblings from low-SES families. One of the siblings was adopted and raised by an upper-middle-class family and one of the siblings was not. On average, the sibling who had been adopted had an IQ of about 109 and the sibling who had not

Why are wealthier people more intelligent?

been adopted had an average IQ of 95 (Schiff et al., 1978). Although the siblings had similar genes, they ended up with dramatically different IQs simply because one was raised by wealthier parents.

Exactly how does SES influence intelligence? One way is by influencing the structure of the brain itself. Low-SES children have poorer nutrition and medical care, they experience greater daily stress, and they are more likely to be exposed to environmental toxins such as air pollution and lead—all of which can impair brain development (Chen, Cohen, & Miller, 2010; Evans, 2004; Hackman & Farah, 2008). Low-SES children are also less likely to be breast-fed, and breast-feeding is known to enhance IQ by about 6 points (Anderson, Johnstone, & Remley, 1999; Kramer et al., 2008) (see the Hot Science box). The fact that low SES can impair a child's brain development may explain why children who experience poverty in early childhood are less intelligent than those who experience poverty in middle or late childhood (Duncan et al., 1998).

SES has biological effects, but it also has cultural effects. For example, research shows that children who grow up in more intellectually stimulating environments tend to be more intelligent. In one study, infants who had been abandoned at birth were randomly assigned to live either with foster parents or to live in the much less intellectually stimulating environment of a state-run orphanage (Nelson et al., 2007). A few years later, the children who had been raised by foster parents had IQs that were about eight points higher than those who had been raised in the orphanage. Intellectual stimulation matters, and high-SES parents are more likely to provide

HOT SCIENCE

The Breast and the Brightest

Scientists have been studying the effects of numerous intelligence-enhancing drugs. Although the jury is still out on most of them, one has now been conclusively shown to increase both academic performance and measured intelligence—and to have a variety of other health benefits to boot. What's the name of this mystery molecule? Mother's milk.

Researchers have known for some time that babies who are breast-fed grow up to have higher IQs than do babies who are formula-fed (Anderson et al., 1999). The problem is that almost all of the studies showing this effect are observational—that is, they show that children whose mothers *elected* to breast-feed end up being more intelligent than children whose mothers *elected* not to. As you learned in Chapter 2, this is a methodological problem called *self-selection*, and it has kept researchers from knowing whether breast-feeding is actually the *cause* of increased intelligence.

▲ These women are among the 3,738 Filipino mothers who came together in 2006 to set a world's record for simultaneous breast-feeding. A new study shows that breast-feeding leads to increased intelligence. For the babies, that is.

But recently, a group of researchers completed a clever study that seems to have settled the matter (Kramer et al., 2008). First, the researchers located several maternity hospitals. Next, they randomly selected half of these hospitals and paid them a visit. During their visits they spoke with new mothers and promoted breast-feeding. The visits worked: Mothers in the visited hospitals were seven times more likely than mothers in the unvisited hospitals to exclusively breast-feed their babies. Finally, the researchers sat back and waited for the babies to grow.

Six years later, the researchers measured the intelligence of nearly 14,000 children who had been born in either a visited or an unvisited hospital. They found that children who had been born in a visited hospital had significantly higher IQs than those who had been born in an unvisited hospital. What's more, the teachers of those children (who didn't know that they'd been breast-fed) gave them higher marks in a variety of subjects.

The jury is in: You can make kids smart with milk from the start. However, scientists still don't know the cause of bad rhymes.

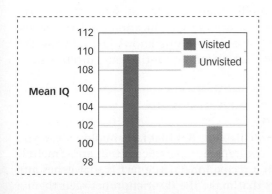

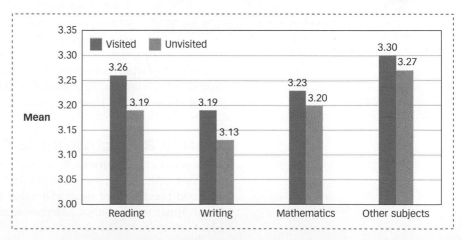

it (Nisbett, 2009). High-SES parents are more likely to read to their children and to connect what they are reading to the outside world ("Billy has a rubber ducky. Who do you know who has a rubber ducky?") (Heath, 1983; Lareau, 2003). When high-SES parents talk to their children, they tend to ask stimulating questions ("Do you think a ducky likes to eat grass?"), whereas low-SES parents tend to give instructions ("Please put your ducky away") (Hart & Risley, 1995). By the age of 3, the average high-SES child has heard 30 million different words, while the average low-SES child has heard only 10 million different words, and as a result, the high-SES child knows 50% more words than his or her low-SES counterpart. These differences in the intellectual richness of the home environment may explain why children from low-SES families show a decrease in intelligence during the summer when school is not in session, whereas children from high-SES families do not (Burkham et al., 2004; Cooper et al., 1996). Clearly, poverty is the enemy of intelligence.

Education

Alfred Binet believed that if poverty was intelligence's enemy, then education was its friend. And he was right. The correlation between the amount of formal education a person receives and his or her intelligence is quite large—somewhere in the range of $r = .55$ to $.90$ (Ceci, 1991; Neisser et al., 1996). One reason why this correlation is so large is that smart people tend to stay in school, but the other reason is that school makes people smarter (Ceci & Williams, 1997, p. 1052). When schooling is delayed because

How much influence does education have on intelligence?

of war, political strife, or the simple lack of qualified teachers, children show a measurable decline in intelligence (Nisbett, 2009). Indeed, children born in the first 9 months of a calendar year typically start school an entire year earlier than those born in the last 3 months of the same year, and sure enough, people with late birthdays tend to have lower intelligence test scores than people with early birthdays (Baltes & Reinert, 1969).

Does this mean that anyone can become a genius just by showing up for class? Unfortunately not. Although education reliably increases intelligence, its impact is small, and some studies suggest that it tends to enhance test-taking ability more than general cognitive ability and that its effects vanish within a few years (Perkins & Grotzer, 1997). In other words, education seems to produce increases in intelligence that are smaller, narrower, and shorter-lived than we would like. That might mean that education can't change intelligence all that much, or it might mean that education is potentially very powerful but that modern schools aren't very good at providing it. Research leans toward the latter conclusion. Although most experiments in education—from magnet schools and charter schools to voucher systems and Head Start programs—have failed to produce substantial intellectual gains for students, a few have been quite successful (Nisbett, 2009), which shows that education *can* increase intelligence substantially even if it usually doesn't. No one knows just how big the impact of an optimal education could be, but it seems clear that our current educational system is less than optimal.

▲ Although their school was burned by attackers in 2006, the students at the Girls High School of Mondrawet in Afghanistan continue to attend. Studies show that education increases intelligence.

Genes and Environments

Both genes and environment influence intelligence. But that fact shouldn't lead you to think of genes and environments as two separate ingredients that are somehow blended together like flour and sugar in a recipe for IQ. The fact is that genes and environments interact in complex ways that make the distinction between them a bit murky.

For example, imagine a gene that made people enjoy the smell of library dust or that made them unusually sensitive to the glare produced by television sets. People who had such a gene might well read more books and thus end up being smarter. Would their increased intelligence be due to their genes or to their environments? Well, if they hadn't had those genes, then they wouldn't have gone to the library, but if they hadn't gone to the library, then they wouldn't have gotten smarter. The fact is that genes can exert some of their most powerful influences not by changing the structure of a person's brain, but by changing the person's environment (Dickens & Flynn, 2001; Nisbett, 2009; Plomin et al., 2001a). A gene that made someone sociable might lead her to have good relationships with peers, which might lead her to stay in school longer, which might lead her to become smarter. Would we call such a gene a "sociability gene" or an "intelligence gene" (Posthuma & de Geus, 2006)? Would we attribute that person's intelligence to her genes or to the environment that her genes enabled her to create? As these questions suggest, genes and environments are not independent influences on intelligence, and the clear difference between nature and nurture is not as clear as it might first appear (see the Hot Science Box).

How might genes exert their influence on intelligence?

HOT SCIENCE

Big Brother Is Watching You

If you've ever been told that you were lucky to have a big brother or sister, here's yet another reason to doubt it: First-born children tend to be more intelligent than their later-born siblings (Sulloway, 2007). Scientists used to think that this had something to do with gestational biology—that a "used" womb was a poorer environment for brain development than a "new" womb was. But a recent discovery suggests that first-borns are indeed smarter—but not because they were born first.

First-born children are typically the oldest children in their families. If Kyle was born before Ethan and the two were raised together, then Kyle would be both the first-born child and the oldest child. On the other hand, if Kyle died, then Ethan—the second-born child—would now be the oldest child in the family. If being born first makes people more intelligent, then we would expect Ethan to be as intelligent as the average second-born child. On the other hand, if being the oldest child in the family makes people more intelligent, then we would expect Ethan to be as intelligent as the average first-born child. So which is it?

As the accompanying figure shows, when a first-born child dies in infancy and the second-born child becomes the oldest, that second-born child ends up being just as intelligent as the average first-born child (Kristensen & Bjerkedal, 2007). When

both a first-born and second-born child die in infancy, then the third-born child ends up being just as intelligent as the average first-born child. Why should being oldest matter? Many psychologists believe that the advantage of being the oldest lies in the fact that for a little while at least, oldest children don't have to share their parents with anyone else, and thus they have a richer intellectual environment than their younger siblings do (Hertwig, Davis, & Sulloway, 2002; Zajonc, 1997, 2001).

Clearly, intelligence isn't about being *born* first; it is about being *raised* first. If you are the oldest child in your family, that's good news. If you aren't, then don't get any bright ideas.

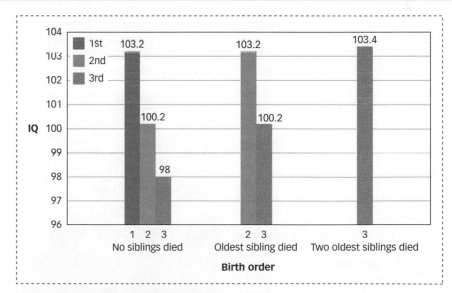

▲ **First-Born and First-Raised** Later-born children are just as intelligent as first-born children—but only when their older siblings die in infancy, thus making them the oldest child in the family. This suggests that the effect of birth order on intelligence is not biological.

Data from Kristensen & Bjerkedal, 2007.

IN SUMMARY

○ Both genes and environments influence intelligence.

○ The heritability coefficient (h^2) tells us what portion of the difference between the intelligence scores of different people is attributable to differences in their genes.

○ Relative intelligence is generally stable over time, but absolute intelligence changes.

○ SES has a powerful influence on intelligence, and education has a moderate influence.

Are Some Groups More Intelligent Than Others?

In the early 1900s, Stanford professor Lewis Terman improved on Binet and Simon's work and produced the intelligence test now known as the Stanford-Binet. Among the things his test revealed was that Whites performed much better than non-Whites. "Are the inferior races really inferior, or are they merely unfortunate in their lack of opportunity to learn?" he asked, and then answered unequivocally: "Their dullness seems to be racial, or at least inherent in the family stocks from which they come." He went on to suggest that "children of this group should be segregated into separate classes . . . [because] they cannot master abstractions but they can often be made into efficient workers" (Terman, 1916).

A century later, these sentences make us cringe, and it is difficult to decide which of Terman's claims is the most repugnant. Is it the claim that a person's intelligence is a product of his or her genes? Is it the claim that members of some racial groups score better than others on intelligence tests? Is it the claim that one race is genetically superior to another? If all of these claims seem repugnant to you, then you may be surprised to learn that virtually all scientists agree that intelligence *is* influenced by genes and that some groups *do* perform better than others on intelligence tests. These are the plain and simple facts. However, Terman's final claim—that differences in genes are the *reason* why some groups outperform others—is not a fact. Indeed, it is a provocative conjecture that has been the subject of both passionate and acrimonious debate. What does science have to tell us about it?

Let's be clear about one thing: Between-group differences in intelligence are not inherently troubling. No one is troubled by the possibility that Nobel laureates are on average more intelligent than shoe salesmen, and that includes the shoe salesmen. But most of us are extremely troubled by the possibility that people of one gender, race, or nationality may be more intelligent than people of another because intelligence is a valuable commodity and it just doesn't seem fair for a few groups to corner the market by accidents of birth or geography.

But fair or not, the fact is that some groups routinely outscore others on intelligence tests. Whites routinely outscore Latinos, who routinely outscore Blacks (Neisser et al., 1996; Rushton, 1995). Women routinely outscore men on tests that require rapid access to and use of semantic information, production and comprehension of complex prose, fine motor skills, and perceptual speed of verbal intelligence, and men routinely outscore women on

► Research suggests that men tend to outperform women in abstract mathematical and scientific domains and women tend to outperform men on production and comprehension of complex prose. Sonya Kovalevsky (1850–91), who was regarded as one of the greatest mathematicians of her time, wrote: "It seems to me that the poet must see what others do not see, must look deeper than others look. And the mathematician must do the same thing. As for myself, all my life I have been unable to decide for which I had the greater inclination, mathematics or literature."

THE GRANGER COLLECTION

tests that require transformations in visual or spatial memory, certain motor skills, spatiotemporal responding, and fluid reasoning in abstract mathematical and scientific domains (Halpern, 1997; Halpern et al., 2007). Indeed, group differences in performance on intelligence tests "are among the most thoroughly documented findings in psychology" (Suzuki & Valencia, 1997, p. 1104). Although the average difference between groups is considerably less than the average difference within groups, Terman was right when he suggested that some groups perform better than others on intelligence tests. But do group differences in intelligence test *scores* reflect group differences in *actual intelligence*?

"I don't know anything about the bell curve, but I say heredity is everything."

Group Differences in Scores

No test is perfect. Might the imperfections of intelligence tests give one group an advantage over another? There is little doubt that the earliest intelligence tests did exactly that by asking questions whose answers were more likely to be known by members of one group (usually White Europeans) than by members of another. When Binet and Simon asked students, "When anyone has offended you and asks you to excuse him, what ought you to do?," they were looking for answers such as "Accept the apology graciously," and the answer "Demand three goats" would have been counted as wrong. But intelligence tests have come a long way in a century, and one would have to look hard to find questions on a modern intelligence test that have the same blatant cultural bias that Binet and Simon's test did (Suzuki & Valencia, 1997). Moreover, group differences emerge even on those portions of intelligence tests that measure nonverbal skills, such as Raven's Progressive Matrices Test (see Figure 10.6). It would be difficult to argue that the large differences between the average scores of different groups is due entirely—or even largely—to a cultural bias in IQ tests.

> **How might intelligence testing disadvantage one group more than another?**

Of course, even when test *questions* are unbiased, testing *situations* may not be. For example, studies show that African American students perform more poorly on tests if they are asked to report their race at the top of the answer sheet because doing so causes them to feel anxious about confirming racial stereotypes (Steele & Aronson, 1995) and anxiety naturally interferes with test performance (Reeve et al., 2009). European American students do not show the same effect when asked to report their race. When Asian American

◄ These high school juniors in South Carolina are taking the SAT. When people are anxious about the possibility of confirming a racial or gender stereotype, their test performance can suffer.

women are reminded of their gender, they perform unusually poorly on tests of mathematical skill, presumably because they are aware of stereotypes suggesting that women can't do math. But when the same women are instead reminded of their ethnicity, they perform unusually *well* on such tests, presumably because they are aware of stereotypes suggesting that Asians are especially good at math (Shih, Pittinsky, & Ambady, 1999). Indeed, when women read an essay suggesting that mathematical ability is strongly influenced by genes, they perform more poorly on subsequent math tests (Dar-Nimrod & Heine, 2006). Findings such as these remind us that the situation in which intelligence tests are administered can affect members of different groups differently and may cause group differences in performance that do not reflect group differences in actual intelligence.

Group Differences in Intelligence

Biases in the testing situation may explain some of the between-group differences in intelligence test scores, but probably not all. If we assume that some of these differences reflect real differences in the abilities that intelligence tests are meant to measure, then what accounts for these ability differences?

There is broad agreement among scientists that environment plays a major role. For example, African American children have lower birth weights, poorer diets, higher rates of chronic illness, poorer medical care, attend worse schools, and are three times more likely than European American children to live in single-parent households (Acevedo-Garcia et al., 2007; National Center for Health Statistics, 2004). Given the vast

How can environmental factors help explain between-group differences in intelligence?

differences between the SES of European Americans and African Americans, it isn't very surprising that African Americans score on average 10 points lower on IQ tests than do European Americans. Do genes play any role in this difference? So far, scientists have not found a single fact that requires such a conclusion—but they have found several facts that make such a conclusion difficult to accept. For example, the average African American has about 20% European genes, but those who have more are no smarter than those who have fewer, which is not what we'd expect if European genes

▶ Millionaire Robert Graham opened the Repository for Germinal Choice in 1980 to collect sperm from Nobel laureates and mathematical prodigies and allow healthy young women to be inseminated with it. His so-called "genius factory" produced more than 200 children but closed after his death in 1999.

ERIC MYER PHOTOGRAPHY INC.

made people smart (Loehlin, 1973; Scarr et al., 1977). Similarly, African American children and mixed-race children have different amounts of European genes, and yet, when they are adopted into middle-class families, their IQs don't differ (Moore, 1986). These facts do not rule out the possibility that between-group differences in intelligence are caused by genetic differences, but they do make that possibility unlikely.

What would it take to prove that behavioral and psychological differences between groups have a genetic origin? It would take the kind of evidence that scientists often find when they study the *physical* differences between groups. For example, people who have hepatitis C are often given a prescription for antiviral drugs, and European Americans typically benefit more from this treatment than African Americans do. Although physicians once thought this was because European Americans were more likely to *take* the medicine they were given, scientists have recently discovered a gene that makes people unresponsive to these antiviral drugs—and guess what? African Americans are much more likely than European Americans to have that gene (Ge et al., 2009). This kind of clear-cut evidence of genetic differences between groups is exactly what's lacking in the debate on the causes of between-group differences in intelligence. Although scientists have discovered some genes that are weakly associated with intelligence (Burdick et al., 2006), they have not found these genes to be more prevalent in one group than another. Until that happens, psychologists are unlikely to embrace genetic explanations of between-group differences in intelligence. Indeed, some experts, like psychologist Richard Nisbett, believe the debate is all but over: "Genes account for none of the difference in IQ between blacks and whites; measurable environmental factors plausibly account for all of it" (Nisbett, 2009, p. 118).

IN SUMMARY

○ Some groups outscore others on intelligence tests because (a) testing situations impair the performance of some groups more than others and (b) some groups live in less healthful and stimulating environments.

○ There is no compelling evidence to suggest that between-group differences in intelligence are due to genetic differences.

Improving Intelligence

Education can increase intelligence, but it is expensive and time consuming. Not surprisingly, then, scientists are looking for cheaper, quicker, and more effective ways to boost the national IQ. *Cognitive enhancers* are drugs that produce improvements in the psychological processes that underlie intelligent behavior. For example, stimulants such as Ritalin (methylphenidate) and Adderall (mixed amphetamine salts) can enhance cognitive performance (Elliott et al., 1997; Halliday et al., 1994; McKetin et al., 1999), which is why there has been an increase in their use by healthy students over the past few years. A recent survey suggests that almost 7% of students in U. S. universities have used prescription stimulants for cognitive enhancement, and that on some campuses the number is as high as 25% (McCabe et al., 2005). These drugs improve people's ability to focus attention, manipulate information in working memory, and flexibly control responses (Sahakian & Morein-Zamir, 2007). Cognitive performance can also be enhanced by a new class of drugs called ampakines (Ingvar et al., 1997). Modafinil is one such drug, and it has been shown to improve short-term memory and planning abilities in healthy, young volunteers (Turner et al., 2003).

How might your children enhance their intelligence?

Although everyone worries about the abuse of these drugs, the distinction between enhancing cognition by taking drugs and enhancing it by other means is not crystal clear. As one distinguished group of scientists (Greely et al., 2008) recently concluded, "Drugs may seem distinctive among enhancements in that they bring about their effects by altering brain function, but in reality so does any intervention that enhances cognition. Recent research has identified beneficial neural changes engendered by exercise, nutrition and sleep, as well as instruction and reading." In other words, if both drugs and exercise enhance cognition by altering the way the brain functions, then what's the difference between them? Other scientists believe this question will soon be moot because cognitive enhancement will be achieved not by altering the brain's chemistry in college, but by altering its basic structure at birth. By manipulating the genes that guide hippocampal development, scientists have created a strain of "smart mice" that have extraordinary memory and learning abilities, leading the researchers to conclude that "genetic enhancement of mental and cognitive attributes such as intelligence and memory in mammals is feasible" (Tang et al., 1999, p. 64). Although no one has yet developed a safe and powerful "smart pill" or "smart gene therapy," many experts believe that this will happen in the next few years (Farah et al., 2004; Rose, 2002; Turner & Sahakian, 2006). Clearly, we are about to enter a brave new world.

What kind of world will it be? Intelligent people tend to have better health, longer lives, better jobs, and higher incomes than unintelligent people, so it isn't unreasonable to suggest that the more intelligence we have, the better off we will be. But is it possible to have too much of a good thing? Psychologists who study the people who have more than their fair share of IQ points suggest the answer is no. Books and movies often portray the "tortured genius" who is misunderstood, friendless, and depressed, but research shows that gifted children are generally as well-adjusted as their peers, and that any special social or emotional problems they have stem from a lack of appropriate scholastic opportunities (Garland & Zigler, 1999; Neihart, 1999). Although extraordinary intelligence doesn't seem to make a person's life worse, it also doesn't necessarily make it better. For instance, profoundly gifted children are no more likely than moderately intelligent children to become major contributors to the fields in which they work (Richert, 1997; Terman & Oden, 1959). No one knows why the gifts of childhood don't always ripen into the fruits of adulthood. Perhaps there is a natural limit on how much intelligence can influence life outcomes, or perhaps the educational system fails to help profoundly gifted children make the best use of their talents (Robinson & Clinkenbeard, 1998; Winner, 2000).

So will a world of gifted people be a better world? The answer may depend in part on the kinds of gifts that cognitive enhancement produces. For example, naturally gifted people are rarely gifted in all departments. Rather, they tend to have gifts in very specialized domains such as math, language, or music. More than 95% of gifted children show a sharp disparity between their mathematical and verbal abilities (Achter, Lubinski, & Benbow, 1996). Because gifted children tend to be "single-gifted," they also tend to be single-minded, displaying a "rage to master" the domain in which they excel. As one expert noted, "one cannot tear these children away from activities in their area of giftedness, whether they involve an instrument, a computer, a sketch pad, or a math book. These children . . . can focus so intently on work in this domain that they lose sense of the outside world" (Winner, 2000, p. 162). Some research suggests that one of the things that most clearly distinguishes gifted children is the sheer amount of time they spend engaged in their domain of excellence (Ericsson & Charness, 1999). Part of nature's gift, then, may be the capacity for passionate devotion to a single activity. It isn't clear whether efforts to increase intelligence by artificial means will produce people who are smarter in general or people who have specific talents and passions. In the coming years, we're certain to find out.

IN SUMMARY

○ Human intelligence can be temporarily increased by cognitive enhancers such as Ritalin and Adderall, and nonhuman intelligence has been permanently increased by genetic manipulation.

○ Gifted children tend to be as well-adjusted as their peers and no more successful than moderately intelligent children.

○ Gifted children tend to be gifted in a single domain, and they tend to be passionately interested in that domain.

WhereDoYouStand?

Making Kids Smart or Making Smart Kids?

Once upon a time, babies were a surprise. Until the day they were born, no one knew if Mom would deliver a girl, a boy, or perhaps one of each. Advances in medicine such as amniocentesis and ultrasound technology have allowed parents to look inside the womb and learn about the gender and health of their fetuses long before they meet them. Now parents can do more than just look. For example, IVF (in vitro fertilization) involves creating dozens of human embryos in the laboratory, using PGD (pre-implantation genetic diagnosis) to determine which have genetic abnormalities, and then implanting only the normal embryos in a woman's womb. Gene therapy involves replacing the faulty sections of an embryo's DNA with healthy sections. These and other techniques may be used to reduce a couple's chances of having a child with a devastating illness such as Tay-Sachs, early-onset Alzheimer's, sickle-cell disease, hemophilia, neurofibromatosis, muscular dystrophy, and Fanconi's anemia. But in the not too distant future they may also enable a couple to increase the odds that their baby will have the traits they value—such as intelligence.

If in the coming years scientists find genes or gene complexes that are directly related to intelligence, IVF and gene therapy will provide methods of increasing a couple's chances of having an intelligent—and perhaps even an extraordinarily intelligent—child. Those who oppose the selection or manipulation of embryos fear that there is no bright line that separates repairing or selecting genes that cause disease and repairing or de-selecting genes that cause normal intelligence. "Today it's early-onset Alzheimer's" that we use PGD to avoid, said Jeffrey Kahn, director of the University of Minnesota's Center for Bioethics. "Tomorrow it could easily be intelligence, or a good piano player or many other things we might be able to identify the genetic factors for" (Tanner, February 7, 2002). This could ultimately lead to a lot of interesting people never being born. As Shannon Brownlee (2002) of the New America Foundation noted, "Today, Tom Sawyer and Huck Finn would have been diagnosed with attention-deficit disorder and medicated. Tomorrow, they might not be allowed out of the petri dish."

People on the other side of this debate wonder what the fuss is about. After all, people can already select their offspring for high IQ by mating with the smartest partners they can find. And once their babies are born, most parents will work hard to enhance their children's intelligence by giving them everything from carrots to cello lessons. Science writer Ron Bailey predicted that "parents will someday use PGD to screen embryos for desirable traits such as tougher immune systems, stronger bodies, and smarter brains. What horrors do such designer babies face? Longer, healthier, smarter, and perhaps even happier lives? It is hard to see any ethical problem with that" (Bailey, 2002).

Should parents be allowed to use PGD or gene therapy to increase the intelligence of their children? Where do you stand?

Chapter Review

KEY CONCEPT QUIZ

1. Which of the following abilities is not an accepted feature of intelligence?
   a. the ability to direct one's thinking
   b. the ability to adapt to one's circumstances
   c. the ability to care for oneself
   d. the ability to learn from one's experiences

2. Intelligence tests
   a. were first developed to help children who lagged behind their peers.
   b. were developed to measure aptitude rather than educational achievement.
   c. have been used for detestable ends.
   d. all of the above

3. Intelligence tests have been shown to be predictors of
   a. academic performance.
   b. health.
   c. attitudes.
   d. all of the above.

4. People who score well on one test of mental ability usually score well on others, suggesting that
   a. tests of mental ability are perfectly correlated.
   b. intelligence cannot be measured meaningfully.
   c. there is a general ability called intelligence.
   d. intelligence is genetic.

5. The two-factor theory suggests that intelligence is a combination of general ability and
   a. factor analysis.
   b. specific abilities.
   c. primary mental abilities.
   d. creative intelligence.

6. Most scientists now believe that intelligence is best described
   a. as a set of group factors.
   b. by a two-factor framework.
   c. as a single, general ability.
   d. by a three-level hierarchy.

7. Standard intelligence tests typically measure
   a. analytic intelligence.
   b. practical intelligence.
   c. creative intelligence.
   d. all of the above.

8. Intelligence is influenced by
   a. genes alone.
   b. genes and environment.
   c. environment alone.
   d. neither genes nor environment.

9. The heritability coefficient is a statistic that describes how much of the difference between different people's intelligence scores can be explained by
   a. the nature of the specific test.
   b. differences in their environment.
   c. differences in their genes.
   d. their age at the time of testing.

10. Relative intelligence _____ over time; absolute intelligence _____ over time.
    a. changes; is generally stable
    b. is generally stable; changes
    c. is generally stable; is generally stable
    d. changes; changes

11. A person's socioeconomic status has a(n) _____ effect on intelligence.
    a. powerful
    b. negligible
    c. unsubstantiated
    d. unknown

12. Which of the following statements is false?
    a. Modern intelligence tests have a very strong cultural bias.
    b. Testing situations can impair the performance of some groups more than others.
    c. Test performance can suffer if the test taker is concerned about confirming a racial or gender stereotype.
    d. Some ethnic groups perform better than others on intelligence tests.

13. On which of the following does broad agreement exist among scientists?
    a. Differences in the intelligence test scores of different ethnic groups are clearly due to genetic differences between those groups.
    b. Differences in the intelligence test scores of different ethnic groups are caused in part by factors such as low birth weight and poor diet that are more prevalent in some groups than in others.
    c. Differences in the intelligence test scores of different ethnic groups always reflect real differences in intelligence.
    d. Genes that are strongly associated with intelligence have been found to be more prevalent in some ethnic groups than in others.

14. Gifted children tend to
    a. be equally gifted in several domains.
    b. be gifted in a single domain.
    c. lose their special talent in adulthood.
    d. change the focus of their interests relatively quickly.

KEY TERMS

CRITICAL THINKING QUESTIONS

1. Intelligence tests have been used to rationalize prejudice
   and discrimination, and their results can be influenced by
   features of the testing situation. On the other hand, they are
   excellent predictors of success in life. Given this, do you support or oppose giving intelligence tests to children in school?

2. Scientists have not found any convincing evidence to suggest
   that genes are responsible for the average difference between
   the intelligence test scores of different ethnic groups. Should
   they even look for such evidence, and if they found it, how
   and why would it matter?

3. There are many ways to improve intelligence, from educational to pharmaceutical. Are any of these methods more
   legitimate than others? If scientists developed an "intelligence
   pill," would you support or oppose allowing people to take it?

RECOMMENDED READINGS

Deary, I. J. (2001). *Intelligence: A very short introduction*. Oxford,
UK: Oxford University Press.

This is a short, accessible, and lively introduction to many of
the important issues in the study of intelligence by one of the
leading scientists in the area. Each chapter deals with a different topic, such as whether there are several different types
of intelligence, whether intelligence differences are caused by
genes or the environment, the biological basis of intelligence
differences, and whether intelligence declines or increases as
we grow older.

Herrnstein, R. J., & Murray, C. (1994). *The bell curve*. New York:
Free Press.

National Review wrote, "Our intellectual landscape has been
disrupted by the equivalent of an earthquake." And it was true.

The Bell Curve was one of the most controversial books of the
second half of the 20th century. It examined the influence of
intelligence on life outcomes and discussed the stratification of
American society on the basis of intelligence differences. But
what made it so controversial was its claim that between-group
differences in intelligence are largely genetic. Find out for
yourself what the debate was about.

Nisbett, R. E. (2009). *Intelligence and how to get it*. New York:
Norton.

According to the *New York Times*, this book "offers a meticu-
lous and eye-opening critique of hereditarianism . . . its real
value lies in Nisbett's forceful marshaling of the evidence . . .
which stresses the importance of nonhereditary factors in
determining I.Q."

ANSWERS TO KEY CONCEPT QUIZ

1. c; 2. c; 3. d; 4. c; 5. b; 6. d; 7. a; 8. b; 9. c; 10. b; 11. a; 12. a;
13. b; 14. b.

**Need more help? Additional resources are located
at the book's free companion Web site at:**
www.worthpublishers.com/schacter

11

Development

His mother called him Adi and showered him with affection, but his father was not so kind. As his sister later recalled, "Adi challenged my father to extreme harshness and got his sound thrashing every day. . . . How often on the other hand did my mother caress him and try to obtain with her kindness where the father could not succeed with harshness." Although his father wanted him to become a civil servant, Adi's true love was art, and his mother quietly encouraged that gentler interest. Adi was just 18 years old when his mother was diagnosed with terminal cancer, and he was heartbroken when she died. Even her physician remarked that, "in all my career, I have never seen anyone so prostrate with grief."

But Adi had little time for grieving. As he wrote, "Poverty and hard reality compelled me to make a quick decision. I was faced with the problem of somehow making my own living." Adi resolved to make his living as an artist. He moved to the city and applied to art school, but he was flatly rejected. Motherless and penniless, Adi wandered the city streets for 5 long years, sleeping on park benches, living in homeless shelters, and eating in soup kitchens, while trying desperately to sell his sketches and watercolors. Ten years later, Adi had achieved the fame he so desired, and today his paintings are sought by collectors, who pay significant sums to acquire them.

The largest collection of Adi's work is owned by the U.S. government, which keeps the pieces locked in a room in Washington, DC, and never allows them to be displayed. The curator of the collection, Marylou Gjernes, once remarked, "I often looked at them and wondered, 'What if? What if he had been accepted into art school? Would World War II have happened?'" Why would the curator ask such a question? Because while the artist's mother called him Adi, the rest of us know him as Adolf Hitler.

► One of Adi's paintings, *Village Scene*, sold at auction in 2006 for almost $20,000.

WHY IS IT SO DIFFICULT TO IMAGINE THE GREATEST mass murderer of the 20th century as a gentle child who loved to draw, as a compassionate adolescent who cared for his ailing mother, or as a dedicated young adult who suffered cold and hunger for the sake of beauty? After all, none of us began as the people we are now, and few of us will end up that way. From birth to infancy, from childhood to adolescence, from young adulthood to old age, one of the most obvious facts about human beings is that they change over time. Their development includes both dramatic transformations and striking consistencies in the way they look, think, feel, and act. **Developmental psychology** is *the study of continuity and change across the life span,* and in the last century, developmental psychologists have discovered some amazing things about this metamorphosis.

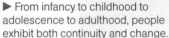
▶ From infancy to childhood to adolescence to adulthood, people exhibit both continuity and change.

We'll start where it all starts by examining the 9-month period between conception and birth, and we'll see how prenatal events set the stage for everything to come. Next, we'll examine childhood, during which children must learn how to think about the world and their relationship to it, to understand and bond with others, to tell the difference between right and wrong. Next, we'll examine the relatively modern invention called adolescence, the stage at which children become both independent and sexual creatures. Finally, we'll examine adulthood, the stage at which people typically leave their parents, find mates, have children, and grow old—with some surprising results.

Prenatality: A Womb with a View

You probably calculate your age by counting your birthdays, but the fact is that when you were born, you were already 9 months old. The *prenatal stage* of development ends with birth, but it begins 9 months earlier when about 200 million sperm begin a hazardous journey from a woman's vagina, through her uterus, and on to her fallopian tubes. Many of these sperm have defects that prevent them from swimming vigorously enough to make progress, and others get stuck in the spermatazoidal equivalent of a traffic jam in which too many sperm are on the same road, headed in the same direction at the same time. Of those that manage to make their way through the uterus, many take a wrong turn and end up in the fallopian tube that does not contain an egg. A mere 200 or so of the original 200 million sperm manage to find the correct fallopian tube and get close enough to an egg to release digestive enzymes that erode the egg's protective outer layer. As soon as one of these sperm manages to penetrate the coating, the egg quickly releases a chemical that seals the coating and keeps all the remaining sperm from entering. After triumphing over massive odds, the one successful sperm sheds its tail and fertilizes the egg. In about 12 hours, the nuclei of the sperm and the egg merge, and the prenatal development of a unique human being begins.

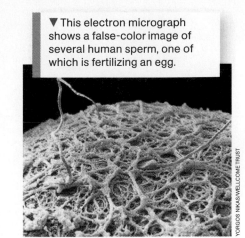

▼ This electron micrograph shows a false-color image of several human sperm, one of which is fertilizing an egg.

YORGOS NIKAS/WELLCOME TRUST

Prenatal Development

A **zygote** is *a fertilized egg that contains chromosomes from both a sperm and an egg.* From the first moment of its existence, a zygote has one thing in common with the person it will ultimately become: gender. Each human sperm cell and each human egg cell contain 23 *chromosomes* that contain *genes,* which provide the blueprint for all biological development. One of these chromosomes (the 23rd) can come in two variations: X or Y. Some sperm carry an X chromosome, others carry a Y chromosome. If the egg is fertilized by a sperm that carries a Y chromosome, then the zygote is male; if the egg is fertilized by a sperm that carries an X chromosome, the zygote is female.

The 2-week period that begins at conception is known as the **germinal stage**, and it is during this stage that the one-celled zygote begins to divide—into two cells that divide into four, which then divide into eight, and so on. By the time of birth, the zygote has divided into trillions of cells, each of which contains exactly one set of 23 chromosomes from the sperm and one set of 23 chromosomes from the egg. During the germinal stage, the zygote migrates back down the fallopian tube and implants itself in the wall of the uterus. This is a difficult journey, and about half of all zygotes do not complete it, either because they are defective or because they implant themselves in an inhospitable part of the uterus. Male zygotes are especially unlikely to complete this journey and no one understands why (though some of us suspect that it's because male zygotes are especially unwilling to stop and ask for directions).

> **?** What are the three prenatal stages?

When the zygote implants itself on the uterine wall, a new stage of development begins. The **embryonic stage** is *a period that lasts from the second week until about the eighth week* (see **FIGURE 11.1**). During this stage, the zygote continues to divide and its cells begin to differentiate. The zygote at this stage is known as an *embryo,* and although it is just an inch long, it already has a beating heart and other body parts, such as arms and legs. Embryos that have one X chromosome and one Y chromosome begin to produce a hormone called testosterone, which masculinizes their reproductive organs, and embryos that have two X chromosomes do not. Without testosterone, the embryo continues developing as a female.

developmental psychology The study of continuity and change across the life span.

zygote A fertilized egg that contains chromosomes from both a sperm and an egg.

germinal stage The 2-week period of prenatal development that begins at conception.

embryonic stage The period of prenatal development that lasts from the second week until about the eighth week.

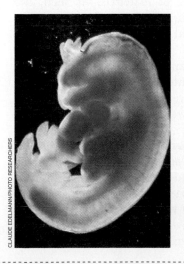

CLAUDE EDELMANN/PHOTO RESEARCHERS

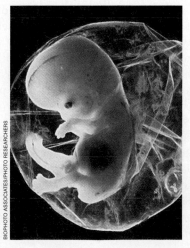

BIOPHOTO ASSOCIATES/PHOTO RESEARCHERS

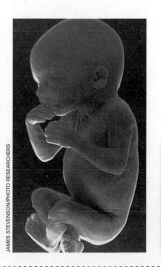

JAMES STEVENSON/PHOTO RESEARCHERS

◄ FIGURE 11.1
Human beings undergo amazing development in the 9 months of prenatal development. These images show an embryo at 30 days, an embryo at 8 to 9 weeks, and a fetus at 5 months.

The **fetal stage** is *a period that lasts from the ninth week until birth.* The embryo at this stage is known as a *fetus,* and it has a skeleton and muscles that make it capable of movement. During the last 3 months of the fetal stage, the size of the fetus increases rapidly. It develops a layer of insulating fat beneath its skin, and its digestive and respiratory systems mature. The cells that ultimately become the brain divide very quickly around the third and fourth week after conception, and this process is more or less complete by 6 months. During the fetal stage, these brain cells begin to generate axons and dendrites (which permit communication with other brain cells). They also begin to undergo a process (described in Chapter 3) known as **myelination**, which is *the formation of a fatty sheath around the axons of a neuron.* Just as plastic sheathing insulates a wire, myelin insulates a brain cell and prevents the leakage of neural signals that travel along the axon. This process starts during the fetal stage but doesn't end for years; the myelination of the cortex, for example, continues into adulthood.

Although the brain undergoes rapid and complex growth during the fetal period, at birth it is nowhere near its adult size. Whereas a newborn chimpanzee's brain is nearly 60% of its adult size, a newborn human's brain is only 25% of its adult size, which is to say that 75% of the brain's development occurs outside the womb. Why are human beings born with such underdeveloped brains when other primates are not?

Why are human beings born with underdeveloped brains?

There are at least two reasons. First, the human brain has nearly tripled in size in just 2 million years of evolution, and bigger brains require bigger heads to house them. If a newborn's head were closer to its adult size, the baby could not pass through its mother's birth canal. Second, one of our species' greatest talents is its ability to adapt to a wide range of novel environments that differ in terms of climate, social structure, and so on. Rather than arriving in the world with a fully developed brain that may or may not meet the requirements of its environment, human beings arrive with brains that do much of their developing *within* the very environments in which they will function. The fact that our underdeveloped brains are specifically shaped by the unique social and physical environment into which we are born allows us to be exceptionally adaptable.

Prenatal Environment

It is natural to assume that genes influence development from the moment of conception and that the environment influences development from the moment of birth. But that's not so. The womb is an environment that influences development in a multitude of ways (Coe & Lubach, 2008; Wadhwa, Sandman, & Garite, 2001). For example, the *placenta* is the organ that physically links the bloodstreams of the mother and the developing embryo or fetus and permits the exchange of materials. As such, the foods a woman eats during pregnancy can affect her fetus. The children of mothers who received insufficient nutrition during pregnancy tend to have both physical problems (Stein et al., 1975) and psychological problems, most notably an increased risk of schizophrenia and antisocial personality disorder (Neugebauer, Hoek, & Susser, 1999; Susser, Brown, & Matte, 1999). The foods a woman eats during pregnancy can also shape her child's food preferences: Infants tend to like the foods and spices that their mothers ate while they were in utero (Mennella, Johnson, & Beauchamp, 1995).

How does the uterine environment affect the unborn child?

But it isn't just food that affects the fetus. Almost anything a woman eats, drinks, inhales, injects, or otherwise comes into contact with can pass through the placenta. *Agents that damage the process of development* are called **teratogens**, which literally means "monster makers." Teratogens include environmental poisons such as lead in the water, paint dust in the air, or mercury in fish, but the most common teratogen is alcohol. **Fetal alcohol syndrome** *is a developmental disorder that stems from heavy alcohol use by the mother during pregnancy,* and children with FAS have a variety of

fetal stage The period of prenatal development that lasts from the ninth week until birth.

myelination The formation of a fatty sheath around the axons of a neuron.

teratogens Agents that damage the process of development, such as drugs and viruses.

fetal alcohol syndrome A developmental disorder that stems from heavy alcohol use by the mother during pregnancy.

distinctive facial features, brain abnormalities, and cognitive deficits (Carmichael Olson et al., 1997; Streissguth et al., 1999). Some studies suggest that light drinking does not harm the fetus, but at present there is no medical consensus about what constitutes a "safe" amount (Warren & Hewitt, 2009).

Tobacco is another common teratogen, and there is no debate about its effects. Babies whose mothers smoke have lower birth weights (Horta et al., 1997) and are more likely to have perceptual and attentional problems in childhood (Fried & Watkinson, 2000). Even secondhand smoke can lead to reduced birth weight and deficits in attention and learning (Makin, Fried, & Watkinson, 1991; Windham, Eaton, & Hopkins, 1999). The embryo is more vulnerable to teratogens than is the fetus, but structures such as the central nervous system remain vulnerable throughout the entire prenatal period. Some researchers estimate that if all pregnant women in America quite smoking, there would be an 11% reduction in stillbirths and a 5% reduction in newborn deaths (March of Dimes, 2010).

▲ This child has some of the telltale facial features associated with FAS: short eye openings, a flat midface, a flat ridge under the nose, a thin upper lip, and an underdeveloped jaw.

The prenatal environment is rich with chemicals, but it is also rich with information. Unlike an automobile, which operates only after it has been fully assembled, the human brain is operating even as it is being built, and research shows that the developing fetus can sense stimulation and learn from it. Wombs are dark because only the brightest light can filter through the mother's abdomen, but they are not quiet. The fetus can hear its mother's heartbeat, the gastrointestinal sounds associated with her digestion, and her voice. Newborns suck a nipple more vigorously when they hear the sound of their mother's voice than when they hear the voice of a female stranger (Querleu et al., 1984), suggesting that they are more familiar with the former than the latter. Newborns whose mothers read aloud from *The Cat in the Hat* during their pregnancies reacted as though the story was familiar (DeCasper & Spence, 1986). Indeed, newborn babies even seem to cry in the melody of their mother's native language—French newborns with a rising melody and German newborns with a falling melody (Mampe et al., 2009). Clearly, the fetus is listening.

What can a fetus hear?

IN SUMMARY

○ Developmental psychology studies continuity and change across the life span.

○ The prenatal stage of development begins when a sperm fertilizes an egg, producing a zygote. The zygote, which contains chromosomes from both the egg and the sperm, develops into an embryo at 2 weeks and then into a fetus at 8 weeks.

○ The fetal environment has important physical and psychological influences on the fetus. In addition to the food a pregnant woman eats, teratogens, or agents that impair fetal development, can affect the fetus. Some of the most common teratogens are tobacco and alcohol.

○ Although the fetus cannot see much in the womb, it can hear sounds and become familiar with those it hears often, such as its mother's voice.

Infancy and Childhood: Becoming a Person

Newborns may appear to be capable of little more than squalling and squirming, but in the last decade, researchers have discovered that they are actually more sophisticated than most people suspected. **Infancy** is *the stage of development that begins at birth and lasts between 18 and 24 months*, and as you will see, much more happens during this stage than meets the untrained eye.

infancy The stage of development that begins at birth and lasts between 18 and 24 months.

Perceptual and Motor Development

New parents like to stand around the crib and make goofy faces at the baby because they think the baby will be amused. In fact, newborns have a rather limited range of vision. The level of detail that a newborn can see at a distance of 20 feet is roughly equivalent to the level of detail that an adult can see at 600 feet (Banks & Salapatek, 1983). On the other hand, when visual stimuli are close enough, newborns are quite responsive. How do we know what newborns are seeing? In one study, newborns were shown a circle with diagonal stripes over and over again. The babies stared a lot at first, and then less and less on each subsequent presentation. Recall from Chapter 7 that *habituation* is the tendency for organisms to respond less intensely to a stimulus as the frequency of exposure to that stimulus increases, and babies habituate just like the rest of us do. So what happened when the researchers rotated the circle 90 degrees? The newborns once again stared intently, indicating that they had noticed the change in the circle's orientation (Slater, Morison, & Somers, 1988).

What do babies notice most?

Newborns are even more attentive to social stimuli. For example, newborns in one study were shown a circle, a circle with scrambled facial features, or a circle with a regular face. When the circle was moved across their fields of vision, the newborns tracked the circle by moving their heads and eyes—and they tracked the circle with the regular face longer than they tracked the others (Johnson et al., 1991). But newborns do more than merely track social stimuli. Researchers in one study stood close to some newborns while sticking out their tongues and stood close to other newborns while pursing their lips. Newborns in the first group stuck out their own tongues more often than those in the second group did, and newborns in the second group pursed their lips more often than those in the first group did (Meltzoff & Moore, 1977). Indeed, newborns have been shown to mimic facial expressions in their very first *hour* of life (Reissland, 1988).

▲ Infants mimic the facial expressions of adults. And vice versa.

Although infants can use their eyes right away, they must spend considerably more time learning how to use most of their other parts. **Motor development** is *the emergence of the ability to execute physical actions* such as reaching, grasping, crawling, and walking. Infants are born with a small set of **reflexes**, which are *specific patterns of motor response that are triggered by specific patterns of sensory stimulation.* For example, the *rooting reflex* is the tendency for infants to move their mouths toward any object that touches their cheek, and the *sucking reflex* is the tendency to suck any object that enters their mouths. These two reflexes allow newborns to find their mother's nipple and begin feeding—a behavior so vitally important that nature took no chances and hardwired it into every one of us. Interestingly, these and other reflexes that are present at birth seem to disappear in the first few months as children learn to execute more sophisticated motor behavior.

▼ Some children develop motor skills earlier than others.

The development of these more sophisticated behaviors tends to obey two general rules. The first is the **cephalocaudal rule** (or the "top-to-bottom" rule), which describes *the tendency for motor skills to emerge in sequence from the head to the feet.* Infants tend to gain control over their heads first, their arms and trunks next, and their legs last. A young baby who is placed on her stomach may lift her head and may even lift her chest by using her arms for support, but she typically has little control over her legs. The second rule is the **proximodistal rule** (or the "inside-to-outside" rule), which describes *the tendency for motor skills to emerge in sequence from the center to the periphery.* Babies learn to control their trunks before their elbows and knees, and they learn to control their elbows and knees before their hands and feet (see **FIGURE 11.2**).

In what order do infants learn to use parts of their bodies?

Motor skills generally emerge in an orderly sequence but not on a strict timetable. Rather, the timing of these skills is influenced by many factors, such as the baby's incentive for reaching, body weight, muscular development, and general level of activity.

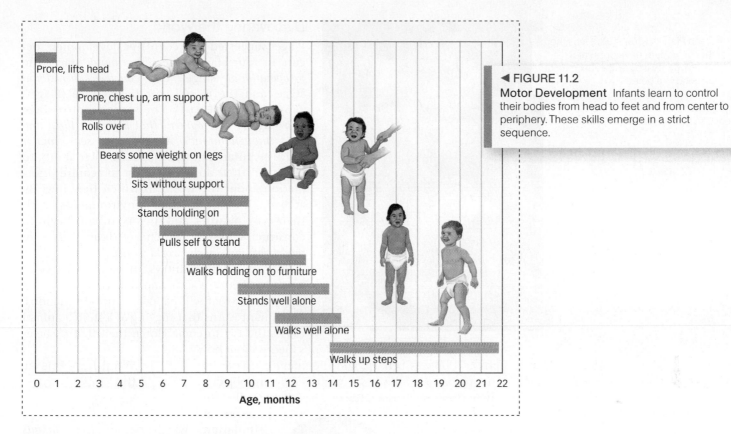

◀ FIGURE 11.2
Motor Development Infants learn to control their bodies from head to feet and from center to periphery. These skills emerge in a strict sequence.

In one study, babies who had visually stimulating mobiles hanging above their cribs began reaching for objects 6 weeks earlier than babies who did not (White & Held, 1966). Furthermore, different infants seem to acquire the same skill in different ways. By closely following the development of four infants, one study examined how children learn to reach (Thelen et al., 1993). Two of the infants were especially energetic and initially produced large circular movements of both arms. To reach accurately, these infants had to learn to dampen these large circular movements by holding their arms rigid at the elbow and swiping at an object. The other two infants were less energetic and did not produce large, circular movements. Thus, their first step in learning to reach involved learning to lift their arms against the force of gravity and extend them forward. Detailed observations such as these suggest that while all infants learn skills such as reaching, different infants accomplish this goal in different ways (Adolph & Avoilio, 2000) .

Cognitive Development

Infants can see and move. But can they think? In the first half of the 20th century, a Swiss biologist named Jean Piaget became interested in this question. He noticed that

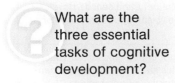 **What are the three essential tasks of cognitive development?**

when confronted with difficult problems—Does the big glass have more liquid in it than the small glass? Can Billy see what you see?—children of the same age made precisely the same mistakes. And as they aged, they stopped making these mistakes at precisely the same time. This led Piaget to suspect that children move through discrete stages of **cognitive development**, which is *the emergence of the ability to think and understand*. Between infancy and adulthood, children must come to understand (a) how the physical world works, (b) how their minds represent it, and (c) how other minds represent it. These are the three essential tasks of cognitive development, so let's see how children master them.

motor development The emergence of the ability to execute physical action.

reflexes Specific patterns of motor response that are triggered by specific patterns of sensory stimulation.

cephalocaudal rule The "top-to-bottom" rule that describes the tendency for motor skills to emerge in sequence from the head to the feet.

proximodistal rule The "inside-to-outside" rule that describes the tendency for motor skills to emerge in sequence from the center to the periphery.

cognitive development The emergence of the ability to think and understand.

▶ Jean Piaget (1896–1980) was the father of modern developmental psychology, as well as the last man to look good in a beret.

FARRELL GREHAN/CORBIS

▶ During the sensorimotor stage, infants explore with their hands and mouths, learning important lessons about the physical world such as, "If you whack Jell-o hard enough, you can actually wear it as a hat."

MICHAEL HAGEDORN/CORBIS

Discovering the World

Piaget suggested that cognitive development occurs in four stages: the *sensorimotor* stage, the *preoperational* stage, the *concrete operational* stage, and the *formal operational* stage (Piaget, 1954) (see **TABLE 11.1**). The **sensorimotor stage** is *a stage of development that begins at birth and lasts through infancy*. As the word *sensorimotor* suggests, infants at this stage use their ability to *sense* and their ability to *move* to acquire information about the world in which they live. By actively exploring their environments with their eyes, mouths, and fingers, infants begin to construct **schemas**, which are *theories about or models of the way the world works*.

As every scientist knows, the key advantage of having a theory is that one can use it to predict and control what will happen in novel situations. If an infant learns that tugging at a stuffed animal causes the toy to come closer, then that observation is incorporated into the infant's theory about how physical objects behave, and the infant can later use that theory when he or she wants a different object to come closer, such as a rattle or a ball. Piaget called this process **as-**

What happens at the sensorimotor stage?

similation, which occurs when *infants apply their schemas in novel situations*. Of course, if the infant tugs the tail of the family cat, the cat is likely to sprint in the opposite direction. Infants' theories about the world ("Things come closer if I pull them") are occasionally disconfirmed; thus infants must occasionally adjust their schemas in light of their new experiences ("Aha! *Inanimate* things come closer when I pull them"). Piaget called this process **accommodation**, which occurs when *infants revise their schemas in light of new information*.

TABLE 11.1	
Piaget's Four Stages of Cognitive Development	
Stage	**Characteristics**
Sensorimotor (Birth–2 years)	Infant experiences world through movement and senses, develops schemas, begins to act intentionally, and shows evidence of understanding object permanence.
Preoperational (2–6 years)	Child acquires motor skills but does not understand conservation of physical properties. Child begins this stage by thinking egocentrically but ends with a basic understanding of other minds.
Concrete operational (6–11 years)	Child can think logically about physical objects and events and understands conservation of physical properties.
Formal operational (11 years and up)	Child can think logically about abstract propositions and hypotheticals.

What kinds of schemas do infants develop, apply, and adjust? Piaget suggested that infants do not have—and hence must acquire—some very basic understandings about the physical world. For example, when you put a pair of socks in a drawer, you know that the socks exist even after you close the drawer, and you would be quite surprised if you opened the drawer a moment later and found it empty. But according to Piaget, this would not surprise an infant because infants do not have a theory of **object permanence**, which is *the idea that objects continue to exist even when they are not visible.* Piaget noted that in the first few months of life, infants act as though objects stop existing the moment they are out of sight. For instance, he observed that a 2-month-old infant will track a moving object with her eyes, but once the object leaves her visual field, she will not search for it.

When do children acquire a theory of object permanence?

Was Piaget right? Recent research suggests that when infants are tested in other ways, they demonstrate a sense of object permanence much earlier than Piaget realized (Shinskey & Munakata, 2005). For instance, in one study, babies were shown a miniature drawbridge that flipped up and down (see **FIGURE 11.3**). Once the babies got used to this, they watched as a box was placed behind the drawbridge—in its path but out of their sight. Some infants then saw a *possible* event: The drawbridge began to flip and then suddenly stopped, as if impeded by the box that the infants could not see. Other infants saw an *impossible* event: The drawbridge began to flip and then continued, as if unimpeded by the box. What did infants do? Four-month-old infants stared longer at the impossible event than at the possible event, suggesting that they were puzzled by it (Baillargeon, Spelke, & Wasserman, 1985). The only thing that could have made it puzzling, of course, was the existence of an unseen box (Fantz, 1964).

Studies such as these suggest that infants have some understanding of object permanence by the time they are just 4 months old. For example, what do infants see when they look at the line labeled A in **FIGURE 11.4** on the next page? Adults see a continuous blue line that is being obstructed by the solid orange block in front of it. Do infants see line A as continuous and obstructed, or do they see it as two blue objects on either side of an orange object? Studies show that when infants are allowed to become familiar with line A, they are subsequently more surprised by line C than by line B—despite the fact that line C actually *looks* more like line A than does line B (Kellman & Spelke, 1983). This suggests that infants see line A as a continuous line.

Infants clearly do not think of the world only in terms of its visible parts, and at some level they must "know" that objects continue to exist even when they are out of

"You mustn't pull the cat's tail so hard it tugs the head inside, sweetie!"

sensorimotor stage A stage of development that begins at birth and lasts through infancy in which infants acquire information about the world by sensing it and moving around within it.

schemas Theories about or models of the way the world works.

assimilation The process by which infants apply their schemas in novel situations.

accommodation The process by which infants revise their schemas in light of new information.

object permanence The idea that objects continue to exist even when they are not visible.

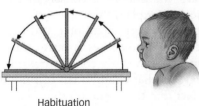
Habituation

Possible event

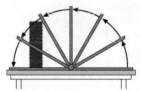

Impossible event

(a)

60
50
40
Looking time (seconds) 30
20
10
0

Impossible event

Possible event

Habituation trials   **Test trials**

(b)

◀ FIGURE 11.3
The Impossible Event (a) In the habituation trials, infants watched a drawbridge flip back and forth with nothing in its path until they grew bored. Then a box was placed behind the drawbridge and the infants were shown one of two events: In the possible event, the box kept the drawbridge from flipping all the way over; in the impossible event, it did not. (b) The graph shows the infants' "looking time" during the habituation and the test trials. During the test trials, their interest was reawakened by the impossible event but not by the possible event (Baillargeon, Spelke, & Wasserman, 1985).

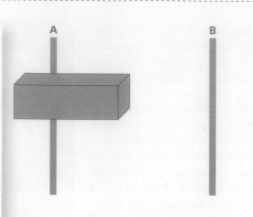

▶ FIGURE 11.4
Object Permanence Do infants see line A as continuous or broken? Infants who are shown line A are subsequently more interested when they are shown line C than line B. This indicates that they consider C more novel than B, which suggests that the infants saw line A as continuous and not broken (Kellman & Spelke, 1983).

sight (Wang & Baillargeon, 2008). Although infants seem to have a better understanding of the physical world than Piaget suspected, it is still not clear just how much they know or how and when they come to know it. As Piaget (1927/1977) wrote: "The child's first year of life is unfortunately still an abyss of mysteries for the psychologist. If only we could know what is going on in a baby's mind while observing him in action, we could certainly understand everything there is to psychology."

Discovering the Mind

The long period following infancy is called **childhood**, which is *the stage of development that begins at about 18 to 24 months and lasts until adolescence, which begins between 11 and 14 years*. According to Piaget, childhood consists of two stages. The first is a **preoperational stage**, which is *the stage of development that begins at about 2 years and ends at about 6 years*, during which the child learns about physical or "concrete" objects. The second is the **concrete operational stage**, which is *the stage of development that begins at about 6 years and ends at about 11 years*, during which the child learns how various actions or "operations" can affect or transform those objects.

The difference between these stages is illustrated by an experiment in which Piaget showed children a row of cups and asked them to place an egg in each. Preoperational children were able to do this, and afterward they readily agreed that there were just as many eggs as there were cups. Then Piaget removed the eggs and spread them out in a long line that extended beyond the row of cups. Preoperational children incorrectly claimed that there were now more eggs than cups,

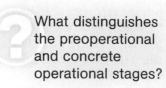

What distinguishes the preoperational and concrete operational stages?

pointing out that the row of eggs was longer than the row of cups and hence there must be more of them. Concrete operational children, on the other hand, correctly reported that the number of eggs did not change when they were spread out in a longer line. They understood that *quantity* is a property of a set of concrete objects that does not change when an operation such as *spreading out* alters the set's appearance (Piaget, 1954). Piaget called the child's insight **conservation**, which is *the notion that the quantitative properties of an object are invariant despite changes in the object's appearance*.

Why don't preoperational children seem to grasp the notion of conservation? Piaget suggested that children have several tendencies that explain their mistakes. For instance, *centration* is the tendency to focus on just one property of an object to the exclusion of all others. Whereas adults can consider several properties at once, children focus on the length of the line of eggs without simultaneously considering the amount of space between each egg. Piaget also suggested that children fail to think about *reversibility*. That is, they do not consider the fact that the operation that made the line of eggs longer could be reversed: The eggs could be repositioned more closely together, and the line would become shorter.

But the main reason why preoperational children do not fully grasp the notion of conservation is that they do not fully grasp the fact that they have *minds* and that these minds contain *mental representations* of the world. As adults, we all distinguish between the subjective and the objective, between appearances and realities, between things in the mind and things in the world. We realize that things aren't always as they seem— that a wagon can *be* red but *look* gray at dusk, a highway can *be* dry but *look* wet in the heat. We make a distinction between the way things *are* and the way we *see* them. But preoperational children don't make this distinction so easily. When something *looks* gray or wet, they tend to assume it *is* gray or wet. As children develop into the concrete operational stage, they begin to realize that the way the world *appears* is not necessarily the way the world really *is*. Once children understand that brains represent—and hence

▲ When preoperational children are shown two equal-size glasses filled with equal amounts of liquid, they correctly say that neither glass "has more." But when the contents of one glass are poured into a taller, thinner glass, they incorrectly say that the taller glass now "has more." Concrete operational children don't make this mistake because they recognize that operations such as pouring change the appearance of the liquid but not its actual volume.

can misrepresent—objects in the world, they are in a better position to solve a variety of problems that require them to ignore an object's subjective appearance while attempting to understand its objective properties (cf. Deák, 2006).

For instance, concrete operational children can understand that when a ball of clay is rolled, stretched, or flattened, it is still the same amount of clay despite the fact that it looks larger in one form than in another. They can understand that when water is poured from a short, wide beaker into a tall, thin cylinder, it is still the same amount of water despite the fact that the water level in the cylinder is higher. They can understand that when a sponge is painted gray to look like a rock, it is still a sponge despite its mineral appearance. Once children can make a distinction between objects and their mental representation of objects, between an object's properties and an object's appearance, they can begin to understand that some operations change what an object *looks* like without changing what the object *is* like.

Children at the concrete operational stage can solve a variety of physical problems. But it isn't until they move on to the **formal operational stage**, which is *the stage of development that begins around the age of 11 and lasts through adulthood,* that they can solve

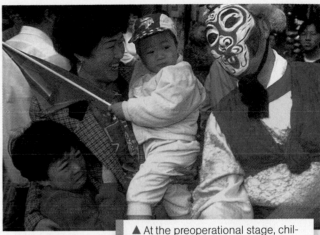

▲ At the preoperational stage, children generally do not distinguish between the way things look and the way things are. They do not realize that when a friendly adult wears a scary mask, he is still a friendly adult.

> **What is the essential feature of the formal operational stage?**

nonphysical problems with similar ease. Childhood ends when formal operations begin, and people who move on to this stage (and Piaget believed that some people never did) are able to reason systematically about abstract concepts such as *liberty* and *love* and about events that will happen, that might have happened, and that never happened. There are no concrete objects in the world to which words such as *liberty* or *love* refer, and yet people at the formal operational stage can think and reason about such concepts in a systematic way. The ability to generate, consider, reason about, or otherwise operate on abstract objects is the hallmark of formal operations.

Discovering Other Minds

As children develop, they discover their own minds, but they also discover the minds of others. Because preoperational children don't fully grasp the fact that they have minds that mentally represent objects, they also don't fully grasp the fact that other people have minds that may mentally represent the same objects in different ways. Hence, they generally expect others to see the world as they do. **Egocentrism** is *the failure to understand that the world appears differently to different observers.* When 3-year-old children are asked what a person on the opposite side of a table is seeing, they typically claim that the other person sees what they see.

Perceptions and Beliefs. Just as 3-year-old children have trouble understanding that others may not see what they see, so, too, do they have trouble understanding that others may not know what they know. In one study using the *false belief test,* children saw a puppet named Maxi deposit some chocolate in a cupboard and then leave the room. A second puppet arrived a moment later, found the chocolate, and moved it to a different cupboard. The children were then asked where Maxi would look for the chocolate when he returned—in the first cupboard where he had initially put it or in the second cupboard where the children knew it was currently. Most 5-year-olds realized that Maxi would search the first cupboard because, after all, Maxi had not seen the chocolate being moved. But 3-year-olds typically claimed that Maxi would look in the second cupboard because, after all, that's where *the children* knew the chocolate really was (Wimmer & Perner, 1983). Children all over the world begin to pass the *false belief test* somewhere between the ages of 4 to 6 (Callaghan et al., 2005), and no one yet understands why children in some cultures pass it earlier than children in others (Liu et al., 2008). Much younger children can pass certain versions of the false belief

> **What does the false belief test show?**

childhood The stage of development that begins at about 18 to 24 months and lasts until adolescence.

preoperational stage The stage of development that begins at about 2 years and ends at about 6 years, in which children have a preliminary understanding of the physical world.

concrete operational stage The stage of development that begins at about 6 years and ends at about 11 years, in which children learn how various actions or "operations" can affect or transform "concrete" objects.

conservation The notion that the quantitative properties of an object are invariant despite changes in the object's appearance.

formal operational stage The stage of development that begins around the age of 11 and lasts through adulthood, in which people can solve nonphysical problems.

egocentrism The failure to understand that the world appears differently to different observers.

test (Baillargeon, Scott, & He, 2010; Onishi & Baillargeon, 2005; Southgate, Senju, & Csibra, 2007), though they may not do it the same way that older children do, namely, by understanding that their beliefs and other people's beliefs are not always the same (Apperly & Butterfill, 2009).

Egocentrism colors children's understandings of others, and it can also color their understanding of themselves. Researchers showed young children an M&M's box and then opened it, revealing that it contained pencils instead of candy. Then the researchers closed the box and asked, "When I first showed you the box all closed up like this, what did you think was inside?" Although most 5-year-olds said, "M&M's," most 3-year-olds said, "Pencils" (Gopnik & Astington, 1988). For the 3-year-old child, a past self is like another person; thus the past self must have known then what the child knows now. Only when the child understands the concept of mental representation can she understand that different people—including herself at different times—sometimes have different beliefs. Although we all ultimately achieve this insight, research suggests that even adults have trouble believing that others see the world differently than they do (Birch & Bloom, 2007). It seems that egocentrism goes away, but that it doesn't go very far.

Desires and Emotions. Different people have different perceptions and beliefs. They also have different desires and emotions. Do children understand that these aspects of other people's mental lives may also differ from their own? Surprisingly, even very young children (who cannot understand that others have different perceptions or beliefs) seem to understand that other people have different desires. For example, a 2-year-old who likes dogs can understand that other children don't and can correctly predict that other children will avoid dogs that the child herself would approach. When 18-month-old toddlers see an adult express disgust while eating a food that the toddlers enjoy, they hand the adult a different food, as if they understand that different people have different tastes (Repacholi & Gopnik, 1997).

Do children understand emotions better than beliefs?

In contrast, children take quite a long time to understand that other people may have emotional reactions unlike their own. When 5-year-olds hear a story in which Little Red Riding Hood knocks on her grandmother's door, unaware that a wolf is inside waiting to devour her, they realize that Little Red Riding Hood does not know what they know; nonetheless, they expect Little Red Riding Hood to feel what they feel, namely, afraid (Bradmetz & Schneider, 2004; DeRosnay et al., 2004; Harris et al., 1989). When asked where Maxi will look for the chocolate that was moved while Maxi was out of the room, they correctly say that he will look in the original location, but they incorrectly say that Maxi feels sad. It is only at about 6 years of age that children come to understand that because they and others have different knowledge, they and others may also experience different emotions in the same situation.

Theory of Mind. Clearly, children have a whole lot to learn about how the mind works—and most of them eventually do. The vast majority of children ultimately come to understand that they and others have minds and that these minds represent the world in different ways. Once children understand these things, they are said to have acquired a **theory of mind**, which is *the idea that human behavior is guided by mental representations.*

But two groups of children lag far behind their peers in acquiring this understanding. *Autism* is a relatively rare disorder that affects approximately 1 in 2,500 children (Frith, 2003). Children with autism typically have difficulty communicating with other people and making friends, and some psychologists have suggested that

Which children have special difficulty acquiring a theory of mind?

▲ Because children are egocentric, they think that others see what they see. When small children are told to hide, they sometimes cover their eyes. Because they cannot see themselves, they think that others can't see them either.

COURTESY OF DANIEL GILBERT

"You're five. How could you possibly understand the problems of a five-and-a-half-year-old?"

MICHAEL MASLIN/THE NEW YORKER COLLECTION/CARTOONBANK.COM

this is because autistic children fail to acquire a theory of mind. Although children with autism are typically normal—and sometimes far *better* than normal—on most intellectual dimensions (Dawson et al., 2007), they have difficulty understanding the inner life of other people. Specifically, they do not seem to understand that other people can have false beliefs (Baron-Cohen, Leslie, & Frith, 1985; Senju et al., 2009), belief-based emotions (Baron-Cohen, 1991), or self-conscious emotions such as embarrassment and shame (Heerey, Keltner, & Capps, 2003). Research has shown that until children acquire a theory of mind, they are not generally susceptible to the phenomenon of "contagious yawning" (Platek et al., 2003), and people with autism are especially unlikely to "catch" other people's yawns (Senju et al., 2007).

The second group of children who lag behind their peers in acquiring a theory of mind are deaf children whose parents do not know sign language. These children are slow to learn to communicate because they do not have ready access to any form of conventional language, and this restriction seems to slow the development of their understanding of other minds. Like children with autism, they display difficulties in understanding false beliefs even at 5 or 6 years of age (DeVilliers, 2005; Peterson & Siegal, 1999). Just as learning a spoken language seems to help hearing children acquire a theory of mind, so does learning a sign language help deaf children do the same (Pyers & Senghas, 2009).

The age at which children acquire a theory of mind appears to be influenced by a variety of factors, such as the number of siblings the child has, the frequency with which the child engages in pretend play, whether the child has an imaginary companion, and the socioeconomic status of the child's family. But of all the factors researchers have studied, language seems to be the most important (Astington & Baird, 2005). Children's language skills are an excellent predictor of how well they perform on false belief tests (Happe, 1995). The way that caregivers talk to children is also a good predictor of children's performance on these tests. Children whose caregivers frequently talk about thoughts and feelings tend to be good at understanding beliefs and belief-based emotions. Some psychologists speculate that children benefit from hearing psychological words such as *want, think, know,* and *sad;* others suggest that children benefit from the grammatically complex sentences that typically contain these psychological words; and some believe that caregivers who use psychological words are also more effective in getting children to reflect on mental states. Whatever the explanation, it is clear that language—and especially language about thoughts and feelings—is an important tool for helping children make sense of their own and others' minds (Harris, de Rosnay, & Pons, 2005).

Piaget Remixed. Cognitive development—from the sensorimotor stage to formal operations—is a complex journey, and Piaget's ideas about it were nothing less than groundbreaking. Although many of these ideas have held up quite well, in the last few decades, psychologists have discovered two important ways in which his claims must be qualified. First, Piaget thought that children graduated from one stage to another in the same way that they graduated from kindergarten to first grade: A child is in kindergarten *or* first grade, he is never in both, and there is a particular moment of transition to which everyone can point. Modern psychologists see development as a more continuous and less step-like progression than Piaget believed. Children who are transitioning between stages may perform more mature behaviors one day and less mature behaviors the next. Cognitive development is more like the change of seasons than it is like graduation.

A second qualification of Piaget's claims is that children acquire many of the abilities that Piaget described much *earlier* than he realized. For example, Piaget suggested that infants had no sense of object permanence because they did not actively search for objects that were moved out of their sight. But when researchers use experimental procedures that allow infants to "show what they know," even 4-month-olds display a sense of object permanence. Piaget suggested that it takes many years until children

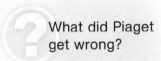

What did Piaget get wrong?

▲ Daniel Tammet has autism. He cannot drive a car or tell left from right. But he recently broke a European record by spending 5 hours, 9 minutes, and 24 seconds reciting the first 22,514 digits of pi from memory. "I just wanted to show people that disability needn't get in the way," he said (Johnson, 2005). Although only 10% of people with autism have extraordinary abilities such as this, they are 10 times more likely than other people to have such abilities. No one knows why.

theory of mind The idea that human behavior is guided by mental representations.

► As this 1635 painting by Van Dyke shows, children have typically been portrayed as little adults, with adult features, proportions, gestures, and dress. But modern research shows that children and adults think about the world in fundamentally different ways.

THE ROYAL COLLECTION © 2006 HER MAJESTY QUEEN ELIZABETH II

can overcome their egocentrism enough to realize that others do not know what they know, but new experimental procedures have detected some evidence of this understanding in 13-month-old infants (Baillargeon et al., 2010). Every year, it seems, research lowers the age at which babies can demonstrate their ability to perform sophisticated cognitive tasks.

Discovering Our Cultures

Piaget saw the child as a lone scientist who made observations, developed theories, and then revised those theories in light of new observations. And yet, most scientists don't start from scratch. Rather, they receive training from more experienced scientists and they inherit the theories and methods of their disciplines. According to Russian psychologist Lev Vygotsky, children do much the same thing. Vygotsky was born in 1896, the same year as Piaget, but unlike Piaget, he believed that cognitive development was largely the result of the child's interaction with members of his or her own culture rather than his or her interaction with concrete objects. Vygotsky noted that cultural tools, such as language and counting systems, exert a strong influence on cognitive development (Vygotsky, 1978).

For example, in English, the numbers beyond 20 are named by a decade (twenty) that is followed by a digit (one) and their names follow a logical pattern (twenty-one, twenty-two, twenty-three, etc.). In Chinese, the numbers from 11 to 19 are similarly constructed (ten-one, ten-two, ten-three . . .). But in English, the names of the numbers between 11 and 19 either reverse the order of the decade and the digit (sixteen, seventeen) or are entirely arbitrary (eleven, twelve). The difference in the regularity of these two systems makes a big difference to the children who must learn them. It is obvious to a Chinese child that 12—which is called "ten-two"—can be decomposed into 10 and 2, but it is not so obvious to an American child, who calls the number "twelve" (see **FIGURE 11.5**). In one study, children from many countries were asked to hand an experimenter a certain number of

How does culture affect cognitive development?

bricks. Some of the bricks were single, and some were glued together in strips of 10. When Asian children were asked to hand the experimenter 26 bricks, they tended to hand over two strips of 10 plus six singles. Non-Asian children tended to use the clumsier strategy of counting out 26 single bricks (Miura et al., 1994). Results such as these suggest that the regularity of the counting system that children inherit can promote or discourage their discovery of the fact that two-digit numbers can be decomposed (Gordon, 2004; Imbo & LeFevre, 2009).

Of course, if you've ever tried to train a pet snake, you already know that not all species are well prepared

DANIEL GILBERT

► Children are not lone explorers who discover the world for themselves but members of families, communities, and societies that teach them much of what they need to know.

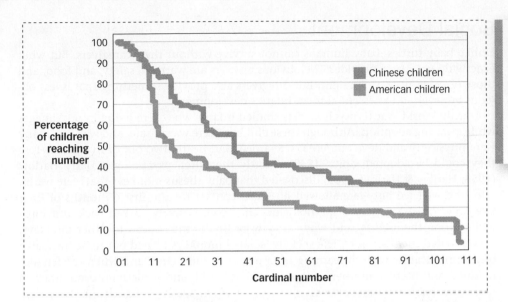

◄ FIGURE 11.5
Twelve or Two-Teen? As this graph shows, the percentage of American children who can count through the cardinal numbers drops off suddenly when they hit the number 11, whereas the percentage of Chinese children shows a more gradual decline (Miller, Smith, & Zhu, 1995).

to learn from others. But human beings are, and their ability to learn from others depends on three fundamental skills that they acquire early on (Meltzoff et al., 2009; Striano & Reid, 2006).

> If an adult turns her head to the left, both young infants (3 months) and older infants (9 months) will look to the left; but if the adult first closes her eyes and then looks to the left, the young infant will look to the left but the older infant will not (Brooks & Meltzoff, 2002). This suggests that older infants are not following the adult's head movements, but rather, they are following her gaze—trying to see what they think she is seeing. The ability to focus on what another person is focused on is known as *joint attention* (see **FIGURE 11.6**).

> An infant who approaches a new toy will often stop and look back at his or her mother, examining her face for cues about whether mom thinks the toy is or isn't dangerous. The ability to use another person's reactions as information about the world is known as *social referencing* (Kim, Walden, & Knieps, 2010; Walden & Ogan, 1988).

> Infants are natural mimics and will do what they see adults do (Jones, 2007). But very early on, infants learn to mimic adults' intentions rather than their actions. When an 18-month old infant sees an adult's hand slip as the adult tries to pull the lid off a jar, the infant won't copy the slip. Rather, the infant will perform the *intended* action by removing the lid (Meltzoff, 1995). The ability to do what another person does—or what another person meant to do—is known as *imitation*.

Joint attention, social referencing, and imitation are the three basic skills that allow infants to learn more sophisticated skills from other members of their species.

▼ FIGURE 11.6
Joint Attention Joint attention allows children to learn from others. When a 12-month-old infant interacts with an adult (a) who then looks at an object (b), the infant will typically look at the same object (c)—but only when the adult's eyes are open (Meltzoff et al., 2009).

Social Development

Unlike baby turtles, baby humans cannot survive without their caregivers. But what exactly do caregivers provide? The obvious answers are warmth, safety, and food, and those obvious answers are right. But caregivers also provide something that is less obvious but every bit as essential to an infant's development.

During World War II, psychologists studied infants who were living in orphanages while awaiting adoption. Although these children were warm, safe, and well fed, many were physically and developmentally retarded, and nearly two out of five died before they could be adopted (Spitz, 1949). Shortly thereafter, psychologist Harry Harlow (1958; Harlow & Harlow, 1965) discovered that baby rhesus monkeys that were warm, safe, and well fed but were allowed no social contact for the first 6 months of their lives developed a variety of pathologies. They compulsively rocked back and forth while biting themselves, and when they were finally introduced to other monkeys, they avoided them entirely. The socially isolated monkeys turned out to be incapable of communicating with or learning from others of their kind, and when the females matured and became mothers, they ignored, rejected, and sometimes even attacked their own babies. Harlow also discovered that when socially isolated monkeys were

HOT SCIENCE

Walk This Way

Parents often complain that their children won't take their advice. But recent research shows that even 18-month-old infants know when to listen to their parents—and when to ignore them.

Researchers (Tamis-LeMonda et al., 2008) built an inclined plane whose steepness could be adjusted (as shown in the photo below), put some infants at the top and their moms at the bottom, and then watched to see whether the infants would attempt to walk down the plane and toward their mothers. Sometimes the plane was adjusted so that it was clearly flat and safe, sometimes it was adjusted so that it was clearly steep and risky, and sometimes it was adjusted somewhere between these two extremes. Mothers were instructed either to encourage their infants to walk down the plane or to discourage them from doing so.

So what did the babies do? Did they trust their mothers or did they trust their eyes? As you can see in the figure below, when the inclined plane was clearly safe or clearly risky, infants ignored their mothers. They typically trotted down the flat plane even when mom advised against it and refused to try the risky plane even when mom said it was okay. But when the plane was somewhere between safe and risky, the infants tended to follow mom's advice.

These data show that infants use social information in a very sophisticated way. When their senses provide unambiguous information about the world, they ignore what people tell them. But when their senses leave them unsure about what to do, they readily accept parental advice. It appears that from the moment children start to walk, they know when to listen to their parents and when to shake their heads, roll their eyes, and do what they darn well please.

COURTESY OF KAREN ADOLPH

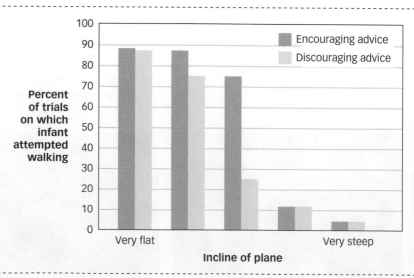

Percent of trials on which infant attempted walking

Incline of plane

Encouraging advice
Discouraging advice

put in a cage with two "artificial mothers"—one that was made of wire and dispensed food and one that was made of cloth and dispensed no food—they spent most of their time clinging to the soft cloth mother despite the fact that the wire mother was the source of their nourishment. Clearly, infants of all these species require something more from their caregivers than mere sustenance. But what?

Becoming Attached

When Konrad Lorenz was a child, he wanted to be a goose. As he explained in his Nobel Prize acceptance speech, "I yearned to become a wild goose and, on realizing that this was impossible, I desperately wanted to *have* one and, when this also proved impossible, I settled for having domestic ducks. . . . From a neighbour, I got a one day old duckling and found, to my intense joy, that it transferred its following response to my person." Every farmer knows that a baby duck or goose will normally follow its mother everywhere she goes, but what Lorenz discovered as a child (and proved scientifically as an adult) is that a newly hatched gosling will faithfully follow the first moving object to which it is exposed. If that object is a human being or a tennis ball, then the hatchling will ignore its mother and follow the object instead. Lorenz theorized that the first moving object a hatchling saw was somehow *imprinted* on its bird brain as "the thing I must always stay near" (Lorenz, 1952).

Psychiatrist John Bowlby was fascinated by this work as well as by the studies of rhesus monkeys reared in isolation and children reared in orphanages, and he sought

What is attachment?

to understand how human infants form attachments to their caregivers (Bowlby, 1969, 1973, 1980). Bowlby began by noting that from the moment they are born, goslings waddle after their mothers and monkeys cling to their mothers' furry chests because the newborns of both species must stay close to their caregivers to survive. Human babies, he suggested, have a similar need, but they are much less physically developed than goslings or monkeys and hence cannot waddle or cling. Because they cannot stay close to their caregivers, human babies pursue a different strategy: They do things that cause their caregivers to stay close to them. When a baby cries, gurgles, coos, makes eye contact, or smiles, most adults reflexively move toward the baby, and Bowlby claimed that this is *why* the baby emits these "come hither" signals.

Bowlby claimed that babies begin their lives by sending these signals to anyone within range to receive them, but during their first 6 months, they begin to keep a mental tally of who responds most often and most promptly, and they soon begin to target their signals to the best responder or *primary caregiver*. This person quickly becomes the emotional center of the infant's universe. Infants feel secure in the primary caregiver's presence and will happily crawl around, exploring their environments with their eyes, ears, fingers, and mouths. But if their primary caregiver gets too far away, infants begin to feel insecure, and like the imprinted gosling, they take action to decrease the distance between themselves and their primary caregiver, perhaps by crawling toward their caregiver or by crying until

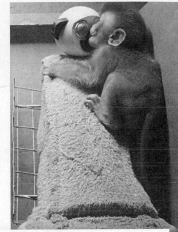

▲ Harlow's monkeys preferred the comfort and warmth of a soft cloth mother (right) to the wire mother (left) even when the wire mother was associated with food.

▼ Like goslings, human babies need to stay close to their mothers to survive. Unlike goslings, human babies know how to get their mothers to come to them rather than the other way around.

▲ Children are naturally social creatures who readily develop relationships with caregivers and peers. A recent study shows that toddlers who spend time with a responsive robot will begin to treat it like a classmate instead of like a toy (Tanaka, Cicourel, & Movellan, 2007).

attachment The emotional bond that forms between newborns and their primary caregivers.

strange situation A behavioral test developed by Mary Ainsworth that is used to determine a child's attachment style.

their caregiver moves toward them. Bowlby believed that all of this happens because evolution has equipped human infants with a social reflex that is every bit as basic as the physical reflexes that cause them to suck and to grasp. Human infants, Bowlby suggested, are predisposed to form an **attachment**—that is, *an emotional bond*—with a primary caregiver.

Given the fundamental importance of attachment, it is not surprising that infants who are deprived of the opportunity to become attached suffer a variety of social and emotional deficits (Gillespie & Nemeroff, 2007; O'Connor & Rutter, 2000; Rutter, O'Connor, & the English and Romanian Adoptees Study Team, 2004). And even when attachment does happen, it can happen in ways that are more or less successful (Ainsworth et al., 1978). Psychologist Mary Ainsworth developed what has come to be known as the **strange situation**, which is *a behavioral test used to determine a child's attachment style*. The test involves bringing a child and his or her primary caregiver (usually the child's mother) to a laboratory room and then staging a series of episodes, including ones in which the primary caregiver briefly leaves the room and then returns. Research shows that infants' reactions tend to fit one of four attachment styles.

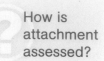

How is attachment assessed?

> Among American infants, the majority (about 60%) show a *secure* attachment style, meaning that, when the caregiver returns, infants who had been distressed by the caregiver's absence go to her and are calmed by her proximity, while those who had not been distressed acknowledge her return with a glance or greeting.

> Another 20% of American infants display an *avoidant* attachment style, meaning that they are generally not distressed when their caregiver leaves the room, and they generally do not acknowledge her when she returns.

> About 15% of American infants display an *ambivalent* attachment style, meaning that they are almost always distressed when their caregiver leaves the room, but then they rebuff their caregiver's attempt to calm them when she returns, arching their backs and squirming to get away.

> A very few American infants (5% or fewer) display a *disorganized* attachment style, with no consistent pattern of responses when their caregiver leaves or returns.

▶ It doesn't take a psychologist to see that this child is securely attached.

Research has shown that a child's behavior in the strange situation in the laboratory correlates fairly well with his or her behavior at home (Solomon & George, 1999) (see **FIGURE 11.7**). Nonetheless, it is not unusual for a child's attachment style to change over time (Lamb, Sternberg, & Prodromidis, 1992). And while some aspects of attachment styles appear to be stable across cultures—secure attachment is the most common style all over the world (van Ijzendoorn & Kroonenberg, 1988)—other aspects of attachment styles vary across cultures. For example, German children (whose parents tend to foster independence) are more likely to have avoidant than ambivalent attachment styles, whereas Japanese children (whose mothers typically stay home and do not leave them in the care of others) are more likely to have ambivalent than avoidant attachment styles (Takahashi, 1986).

Working Models

The capacity for attachment may be innate, but the quality of that attachment is influenced by the child, the primary caregiver, and their interaction. Infants seem to keep track of the responsiveness of their primary caregiver and use this information to create an **internal working model of relationships**, which is *a set of beliefs about the self, the primary caregiver, and the relationship between them* (Bretherton & Munholland, 1999). Infants with different attachment styles appear to have different working models of relationships (see **FIGURE 11.8** on the next page). Specifically, infants with a secure attachment style act as though they are certain that their primary caregiver will respond when they feel insecure, infants with an avoidant attachment style act as though they are certain that their primary caregiver will not respond, and infants with

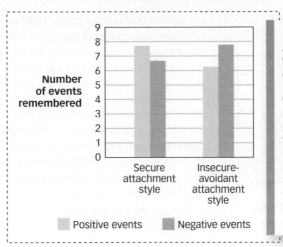

◀ **FIGURE 11.7**

Attachment Style and Memory We often remember best those events that fit with our view of the world. Researchers assessed 1-year-old children's attachment styles with the strange situation test. Two years later, the same group of children were shown a puppet show in which some happy events (e.g., the puppet got a present) or unhappy events (e.g., the puppet spilled his juice) occurred. Securely attached children later remembered more of the happy events than the unhappy ones, but insecurely attached children showed the opposite pattern (Belsky, Spritz, & Crnic, 1996).

internal working model of relationships A set of beliefs about the self, the primary caregiver, and the relationship between them.

THE REAL WORLD

When Mom's Away...

In 1947, about 30% of married American women worked outside the home. Fifty years later, that figure had doubled (Blau & Kahn, 2007). So what are all those working mothers doing with their children? The vast majority of working mothers entrust their children's care to someone else for some part of the day (see the art to the right). Some mothers worry that spending so much time away from their kids will impair the attachment process. Indeed, when asked what advice he had for working mothers, John Bowlby—the father of attachment theory—remarked, "I would remind them, if you want a job done properly, do it yourself" (Steele, 2008).

Was Bowlby right? To find out, the National Institute for Child Health and Human Development conducted a massive, long-term study of the effects of non-maternal day care on approximately 1,300 children living in a wide variety of settings in North America, who were tracked from birth to age 15. The study took millions of dollars and several decades to conduct, and its results surprised everyone: Non-maternal day care, it seems, has little effect on the quality of the attachment that children establish with their mothers (Friedman & Boyle, 2008). Although the attachment styles of infants and toddlers are strongly influenced by their mother's sensitivity and responsiveness, they are generally not influenced by the quality, amount, age of entry, stability, or type of day care they receive. As the scientific coordinator of the study explained, "We're finding again and again that child care is not the source of worry that existed when we started the study" (Shapiro, 2005).

But the results were not all good news. Although non-maternal day care had no large, direct effects on children's attachments, there was evidence of a subtle interaction. Infants who had insensitive and unresponsive mothers *and* who were left in poor-quality day care for more than 10 hours a week were especially likely to be insecurely attached. The bottom line? Most day care is just fine for most children. But if a child gets a double whammy—bad day care combined with a mother who is unresponsive and insensitive—the attachment process may well be impaired.

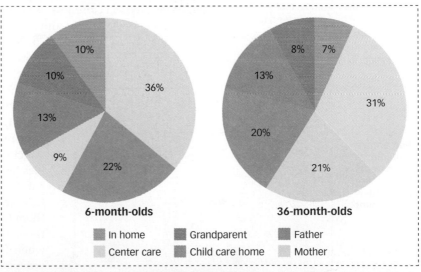

6-month-olds — 36-month-olds

■ In home ■ Grandparent ■ Father
■ Center care ■ Child care home ■ Mother

▲ **Time in Child Care** Who is watching the baby? Although "Mom" is a popular answer, children are watched more often by others than by mothers.

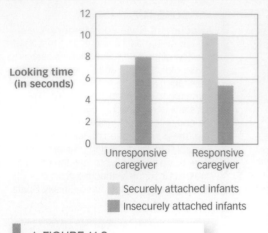

▲ FIGURE 11.8
Working Models Do infants really have internal working models? It appears they do. Psychologists know that infants stare longer when they see something they don't expect, and securely attached infants stare longer at a cartoon of a mother ignoring rather than comforting her child, whereas insecurely attached infants do just the opposite (Johnson, Dweck, & Chen, 2007).

▼ FIGURE 11.9
Parents' Attachment Styles Studies suggest that securely attached infants tend to have parents who have secure working models of attachment (van Ijzendoorn, 1995).

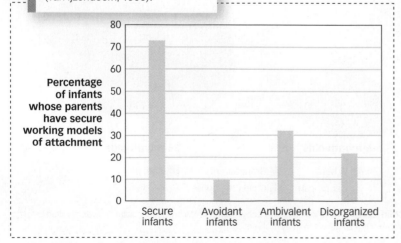

an ambivalent attachment style act as though they are uncertain about whether their primary caregiver will respond or not. Infants with a disorganized attachment style seem to be confused about their caregivers, which has led some psychologists to speculate that this style primarily characterizes children who have been abused (Carolson, 1998; Cicchetti & Toth, 1998).

Attachment is an interaction between two people; thus both of them—the primary caregiver and the child—play a role in determining the nature of the child's working model (see **FIGURE 11.9**). Different children are born with different **temperaments**, or *characteristic patterns of emotional reactivity* (Thomas & Chess, 1977). Whether measured by parents' reports or by physiological indices such as heart rate or cerebral blood flow, very young children vary in their tendency toward fearfulness, irritability, activity, positive affect, and other emotional traits (Rothbart & Bates, 1998). These differences are usually stable over time. For example, infants who react fearfully to novel stimuli—such as sudden movements, loud sounds, or unfamiliar people—tend to be more subdued, less social, and less positive at 4 years old (Kagan, 1997). Children who are negative and impulsive as youngsters tend to have behavioral and adjustment problems in adolescence and poorer relationships in adulthood (Caspi et al., 1995). These differences in temperament seem to emerge from stable differences in biology. For example, 10% to 15% of infants have highly reactive limbic systems that produce an "inhibited" temperament. These infants thrash and cry when shown a new toy or a new person; they grow into children who tend to avoid novel people, objects, and situations; and they ultimately become quiet, cautious, and sometimes shy adults (Schwartz et al., 2003). These studies suggest that from the earliest moments of life, some infants are prone to feel insecure when their primary caregiver leaves a room and to be inconsolable when she returns.

A caregiver's behavior also has an important influence on the infant's working model and attachment style. Studies have shown that mothers of securely attached infants tend to be especially sensitive to signs of their child's emotional state, especially good at detecting their infant's "request" for reassurance, and especially responsive to that request (Ainsworth et al., 1978; De Wolff & van Ijzendoorn, 1997). Mothers of infants with an ambivalent attachment style tend to respond inconsistently, only sometimes attending to their infants when they show signs of distress. Mothers of infants with an avoidant attachment style are typically indifferent to their child's need for reassurance and may even reject their attempts at physical closeness (Isabelle, 1993).

How do caregivers influence an infant's attachment style?

Research suggests that differences in how mothers respond are probably due in large measure to differences in their ability to read their infant's emotional state. Mothers who are highly sensitive to these signs are almost twice as likely to have a securely attached child as are mothers who are less sensitive (van Ijzendoorn & Sagi, 1999). Although such data are merely correlational, there is reason to suspect that a mother's sensitivity and responsiveness *cause* the infant's attachment style. Researchers studied a group of young mothers whose babies were particularly irritable or difficult. When the babies were about 6 months old, half the mothers participated in a training program designed to sensitize them to their babies' emotional signals and to encourage them to be more responsive. The results showed that when the children were 18 months, 24 months, and 3 years old, those whose mothers had received the training were more likely to have a secure attachment style than were those whose mothers did not (van den Boon, 1994,

1995). Another study found that when mothers think of their babies as unique individuals with emotional lives and not just as creatures with urgent physical needs, their infants end up more securely attached (Meins, 2003; Meins et al., 2001).

Does a baby's attachment style have any influence on his or her subsequent development? The jury is still out on that question. Children who were securely attached as infants do better than children who were not securely attached on a wide variety of measures, from the quality of their social relationships (Schneider, Atkinson, & Tardif, 2001; Steele et al., 1999; Vondra et al., 2001) to their academic achievement (Jacobson & Hoffman, 1997). Some psychologists have suggested that this is because children apply the working models they developed as infants to their later relationships with teachers and friends, which is to say that attachment style causes securely attached infants to become more successful children and adults (Sroufe, Egeland, & Kruetzer, 1990). But other psychologists argue that attachment style is correlated with later success only because both of these are caused by the same environment, which is to say that sensitive and responsive caregivers are causes of both the infant's attachment style and the child's subsequent success (Lamb et al., 1985). Because the data on the long-term consequences of attachment style are necessarily correlational, this debate will not be easily resolved. But it is not unreasonable to suspect that both of these arguments are right to some extent. (See the Where Do You Stand? box at the end of this chapter.)

temperaments Characteristic patterns of emotional reactivity.

Moral Development

From the moment of birth, human beings can make one distinction quickly and well, and that's the distinction between pleasure and pain. Before babies hit their very first diapers, they can tell when something feels good, they can tell when something feels bad, and they strongly prefer the former to the latter. But as they mature, they begin to notice that their pleasures ("Throwing food is fun") are often someone else's pains ("Throwing food makes Mom mad"). This is a problem. Human beings need each other to survive and thrive, and when people make others feel bad, then others tend to avoid them, exclude them, or retaliate against them. We are social animals, and it is in our own selfish interests to learn how to balance our needs and the needs of others. We do this by developing a new distinction—the distinction between right and wrong. "Bad behavior" usually involves the gratification of our own desires at the expense of someone else's, and most moral systems are a set of recommendations for balancing different people's competing needs (cf. Haidt, 2008; Turiel, 2006).

Knowing What's Right

How do children think about right and wrong? Piaget spent time playing marbles with children and quizzing them about how they came to know the rules of the game and what they thought should happen to children who broke them. By listening carefully to what children said, Piaget noticed that their moral thinking changed systematically over time in three important ways (Piaget, 1932/1965).

> **According to Piaget, what three shifts characterize moral development?**

> First, Piaget noticed that children's moral thinking tends to shift *from realism to relativism*. Very young children regard moral rules as real, inviolable truths about the world. For the young child, right and wrong are like day and night—they exist in the world and do not depend on what people think or say. That's why young children generally don't believe that a bad action, such as hitting someone, can be good even if everyone agreed to allow it. As they mature, children begin to realize that some moral rules (e.g., wives should obey their husbands) are inventions and not discoveries and that groups of people can therefore agree to adopt them, change them, or abandon them entirely.

▼ How do children learn to decide what is right and what is wrong?

"Well... could you wait?"

For feeding a family you can't beat **Bisquick**

> Second, Piaget noticed that children's moral thinking tends to shift *from prescriptions to principles*. Young children think of moral rules as guidelines for specific actions in specific situations ("Children should take turns playing marbles"). As they mature, children come to see that rules are expressions of more general principles, such as fairness and equity, which means that specific rules can be abandoned or modified when they fail to uphold the general principle ("If a child missed his turn, then it would be fair to give him two turns").

> Third and finally, Piaget noticed that children's moral thinking tends to shift from *outcomes* to *intentions*. For the young child, an unintentional action that causes great harm seems "more wrong" than an intentional action that causes slight harm because young children tend to judge the morality of an action by its outcome rather than by what the actor intended. As they mature, children begin to see that the morality of an action is critically dependent on the actor's state of mind.

Piaget's observations have generally held up quite well, though he once again seemed to overestimate the ages at which some of these transitions take place. For example, research shows that children as young as 3 years old do consider people's intentions when judging the morality of their actions (Yuill & Perner, 1988). Psychologist Lawrence Kohlberg picked up where Piaget left off and offered a more detailed theory of the development of moral reasoning (Kohlberg, 1963, 1986). According to Kohlberg, moral reasoning proceeds through three stages (each of which has two substages that we won't discuss here). Kohlberg based his theory on people's responses to a series of moral dilemmas such as this one:

> A woman was near death from a special kind of cancer. There was one drug that the doctors thought might save her. It was a form of radium that a druggist in the same town had recently discovered. The drug was expensive to make, but the druggist was charging ten times what the drug cost him to make. He paid $200 for the radium and charged $2,000 for a small dose of the drug. The sick woman's husband, Heinz, went to everyone he knew to borrow the money, but he could only get together about $1,000, which is half of what it cost. He told the druggist that his wife was dying and asked him to sell it cheaper or let him pay later. But the druggist said: "No, I discovered the drug and I'm going to make money from it." So Heinz got desperate and broke into the man's store to steal the drug for his wife. Should the husband have done that?

On the basis of their responses, Kohlberg concluded that most children are at the **preconventional stage**, *a stage of moral development in which the morality of an action is primarily determined by its consequences for the actor.* Immoral actions are those for which one is punished, and the appropriate resolution to any moral dilemma is to choose the behavior with the least likelihood of punishment. For example, children at this stage often base their moral judgment of Heinz on the relative costs of one decision ("It would be bad if he got blamed for his wife's death") and another ("It would be bad if he went to jail for stealing").

What are Kohlberg's three stages of moral development?

Kohlberg argued that at about the time of adolescence, children move to the **conventional stage**, which is *a stage of moral development in which the morality of an action is primarily determined by the extent to which it conforms to social rules.* Children at this stage believe that everyone should uphold the generally accepted norms of their cultures, obey the laws of society, and fulfill their civic duties and familial obligations. They believe that Heinz must weigh the dishonor he will bring upon himself and his family by stealing (i.e., breaking a law) against the guilt he will feel if he allows his wife to die (i.e., failing to fulfill a duty). Children at this stage are concerned not just about spankings and prison sentences but also about the approval of others. Immoral actions are those for which one is condemned.

© NORMAN GERSHMAN

▲ During WWII, Albanian Muslims shielded their Jewish neighbors from the Nazis because of a moral code they called *besa*, which means *oath of faith*. "There was no government conspiracy; no underground railroad; no organized resistance of any kind. Only individual Albanians, acting alone, to save the lives of people whose lives were in immediate danger," wrote Norman Gershman, who photographed Muslims such as Baba Haxhi Dede Reshatbardhi (pictured) who saved so many Jewish lives.

Finally, Kohlberg believed that some adults move to the **postconventional stage**, which is *a stage of moral development at which the morality of an action is determined by a set of general principles that reflect core values,* such as the right to life, liberty, and the pursuit of happiness. When a behavior violates these principles, it is immoral, and if a law requires these principles to be violated, then it should be disobeyed. For a person who has reached the postconventional stage, a woman's life is always more important than a shopkeeper's profits and so stealing the drug is not only a moral behavior, it is a moral obligation.

Research supports Kohlberg's general claim that moral reasoning shifts from an emphasis on punishment to an emphasis on social rules and finally to an emphasis on ethical principles (Walker, 1988). But research also suggests that these stages are not quite as discrete as Kohlberg thought. For instance, a single person may use preconventional, conventional, and postconventional thinking in different circumstances, which suggests that the developing person does not "reach a stage" so much as he "acquires a skill" that he may or may not use on a particular occasion.

The use of the male pronoun here is intentional. Because Kohlberg developed his theory by studying a sample of American boys, some critics have suggested that it does not describe the development of moral thinking in girls (Gilligan, 1982) or in non-Westerners (Simpson, 1974). The first of these criticisms has received little scientific support (Jaffee & Hyde, 2000; Turiel, 1998), but the second is well taken. For example, some non-Western societies value obedience and community over liberty and individuality; thus the moral reasoning of people in those societies may appear to reflect a conventional devotion to social norms when it actually reflects a postconventional consideration of ethical principles. Other critics have noted that while a child's level of moral reasoning is generally correlated with his or her own moral behavior (Blasi, 1980), that correlation is not particularly strong. This is particularly true when the moral behavior involves doing a good deed rather than refraining from doing a bad deed (Haidt, 2001; Thoma et al., 1999). These critics suggest that how people reason about morality may be interesting in the abstract, but it has little to do with how people actually behave in their everyday lives. So if moral reasoning doesn't determine moral behavior, then what does?

▲ Frank DiPascali helped Bernie Madoff bilk clients out of hundreds of millions of dollars. At his trial, he told the judge, "It was wrong, and I knew it was wrong at the time." Some scientists would take this as evidence that moral behavior is not driven by moral reasoning.

Feeling What's Right

Research on moral reasoning portrays children as little jurists who use rational analysis—sometimes simple and sometimes sophisticated—to distinguish between right and wrong. But moral dilemmas don't just make us think. They also make us *feel*. Consider the following scenario:

> You are standing on a bridge. Below you can see a runaway trolley hurtling down the track toward five people who will be killed if it remains on its present course. You are sure that you can save these people by flipping a lever that will switch the trolley onto a different track, where it will kill just one person instead of five. Is it morally permissible to divert the trolley and prevent five deaths at the cost of one?

Now consider a slightly different version of this problem:

> You and a large man are standing on a bridge. Below you can see a runaway trolley hurtling down the track toward five people who will be killed if it remains on its present course. You are sure that you can save these people by pushing the large man onto the track, where his body will be caught up in the trolley's wheels and stop it before it kills the five people. Is it morally permissible to push the large man and prevent five deaths at the cost of one?

These scenarios are illustrated in **FIGURE 11.10** on the next page. If you are like most people, you believe that it is morally permissible to sacrifice one person for the sake of five in the first case but not in the second case. And if you are like most people, you can't say why. Indeed, you probably didn't reach this conclusion by moral reasoning at all. Rather, you had a negative emotional reaction to the mere thought of pushing another human being into the path of an oncoming trolley, and that reaction was sufficient to

preconventional stage A stage of moral development in which the morality of an action is primarily determined by its consequences for the actor.

conventional stage A stage of moral development in which the morality of an action is primarily determined by the extent to which it conforms to social rules.

postconventional stage A stage of moral development at which the morality of an action is determined by a set of general principles that reflect core values.

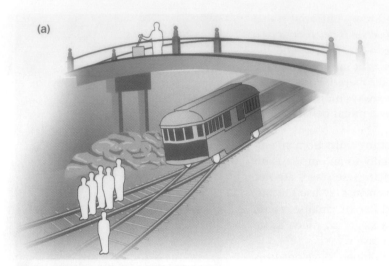

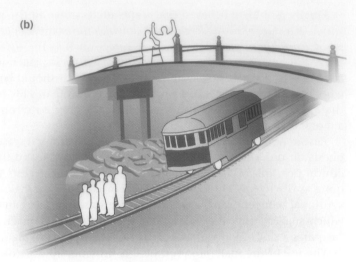

▲ FIGURE 11.10
The Trolley Problem Why does it seem permisssible to trade one life for five lives by pulling a switch but not by pushing a man from a bridge? Research suggests that the scenario shown in (b) elicits a more negative emotional response than does the scenario shown in (a), and this emotional response may be the basis for our moral intuitions.

convince you that pushing him would be wrong. You may have come up with a few good arguments to support this position, but those arguments probably followed rather than preceded your conclusion (Greene et al., 2001).

The way people respond to cases such as these has convinced some psychologists that moral judgments are the consequences—and not the causes—of emotional reactions (Haidt, 2001). According to this *moral intuitionist* perspective, we have evolved to react emotionally to a small family of events that are particularly relevant to reproduction and survival, and we have developed the distinction between right and wrong as a way of labeling and explaining these emotional reactions (Hamlin, Wynn, & Bloom, 2007). For instance, most of us think that incest disgusts us because it is wrong. But another possibility is that we consider it wrong because it disgusts us. Incest is a poor method for producing genetically viable offspring; thus nature may have selected for people who are disgusted by it. Our reasoning about the immorality of incest may follow from that disgust rather than cause it.

Do moral judgments come before or after emotional reactions?

Some research supports the moral intuitionist perspective. For example, people who have brain damage that prevents them from experiencing normal emotions tend to treat the two situations shown in Figure 11.10 as though they were identical, choosing in both cases to save more lives rather than fewer (Koenigs et al., 2007). In another study (Wheatley & Haidt, 2005), participants were hypnotized and told that whenever they heard the word *take,* they would experience "a brief pang of disgust . . . a sickening feeling in your stomach." After they came out of the hypnotic state, the participants were asked to rate the morality of several actions, ranging from incest to bribery. When the description of the action contained the word *take,* participants rated the action as less moral, suggesting that their feelings were guiding—rather than being guided by—their moral reasoning.

According to the moral intuitionist perspective, the reason most people consider it permissible to stop a trolley by pulling a switch but not by pushing someone onto the tracks is that people have negative emotional reactions to other people's physical pain (Greene et al., 2001). This aversion to others' suffering begins early in childhood (Warneken & Tomasello, 2009). When adults in one study pretended to hit their thumbs with a hammer, even very young children seemed alarmed and attempted to comfort them (Zahn-Waxler et al., 1992). These efforts are occasionally clumsy or inappropriate—for example, a toddler may offer a distressed adult a teddy bear—but they suggest that children are moved by other people's pain. Indeed, even very young children distinguish between actions that are wrong because they violate a social rule and actions that are wrong because they cause suffering. When asked whether it would be okay to leave toys on the floor in a school that allowed such behavior, young children tend to say it would. But when asked whether it would be okay to hit another child in a school that allowed such behavior, young children tend to say it would not (Smetana, 1981; Smetana & Braeges, 1990). Indeed, young children say that hitting is wrong even if an adult instructs someone to do it (Laupa & Turiel, 1986).

Children clearly think about transgressions that cause others to be observably distressed (e.g., hitting) differently from transgressions that do not (e.g., eating with one's fingers). Why might that be? One possibility is that observing distress automatically triggers an empathic reaction in the brain of the observer. Recent research has shown that some of the brain regions that are activated when people experience an unpleasant emotion are also activated when people see someone else experience that emotion (Carr et al., 2003). (See the discussion of mirror neurons in Chapter 3.) In one study, women received a shock or watched their romantic partners receive a shock on different parts of their bodies. The regions of the women's brains that processed information about the location of the shock were activated only when the women experienced the shock themselves, but the regions that processed emotional information were activated whether the women received the shock or observed it (Singer et al., 2004). Similarly, the emotion-relevant brain regions that are activated when a person smells a foul odor are also activated when the person sees someone else smelling the foul odor (Wicker et al., 2003). Studies such as these suggest that our brains respond to other people's *expressions* of distress by creating within us the *experience* of distress, and this mechanism may have evolved because it allows us to know instantly what others are feeling. The fact that we can actually *feel* another person's distress may explain why even a small child who is incapable of sophisticated moral reasoning still considers it wrong to inflict distress on others.

What are the two kinds of transgressions between which children clearly distinguish?

▼ Most people are upset by the suffering of others, and research suggests that even young children have this response, which may be the basis of their emerging morality.

© CREASOURCE/CORBIS

IN SUMMARY

○ Infants have a limited range of vision, but they can see and remember objects that appear within it. They learn to control their bodies from the top down and from the center out.

○ Infants slowly develop theories about how the world works. Piaget believed that these theories developed through four stages, in which children learn basic facts about the world, such as the fact that objects continue to exist even when they are out of sight, and the fact that objects have enduring properties that are not changed by superficial transformations. Children also learn that their minds represent objects; hence objects may not be as they appear, and others may not see them as the child does.

○ Cognitive development also comes about through social interactions in which children are given tools for understanding that have been developed over millennia by members of their cultures.

○ At a very early age, human beings develop strong emotional ties to their primary caregivers. The quality of these ties is determined both by the caregiver's behavior and the child's temperament.

○ People get along with each other by learning and obeying moral principles.

○ Children's reasoning about right and wrong is initially based on an action's consequences, but as they mature, children begin to consider the actor's intentions as well as the extent to which the action obeys abstract moral principles.

○ Moral intuitions may also be derived from one's emotional reactions to events, such as the suffering of others.

adolescence The period of development that begins with the onset of sexual maturity (about 11 to 14 years of age) and lasts until the beginning of adulthood (about 18 to 21 years of age).

puberty The bodily changes associated with sexual maturity.

primary sex characteristics Bodily structures that are directly involved in reproduction.

secondary sex characteristics Bodily structures that change dramatically with sexual maturity but that are not directly involved in reproduction.

Adolescence: Minding the Gap

Between childhood and adulthood is an extended developmental stage that may not qualify for a "hood" of its own but that is clearly distinct from the stages that come before and after. **Adolescence** is *the period of development that begins with the onset of sexual maturity (about 11 to 14 years of age) and lasts until the beginning of adulthood (about 18 to 21 years of age).* Unlike the transition from embryo to fetus or from infant to child, this transition is both sudden and clearly marked. In just 3 or 4 years, the average adolescent gains about 40 pounds and grows about 10 inches. Girls' growth rates begin to accelerate around the age of 10, and they reach their full heights at around 15½ years. Boys experience an equivalent growth spurt about 2 years later and reach their full heights at around 17½ years.

The growth spurt signals the onset of **puberty**, which refers to *the bodily changes associated with sexual maturity.* These changes involve **primary sex characteristics**, which are *bodily structures that are directly involved in reproduction,* for example, the onset of menstruation in girls and the enlargement of the testes, scrotum, and penis and the emergence of the capacity for ejaculation in boys. They also involve **secondary sex characteristics**, which are *bodily structures that change dramatically with sexual maturity but that are not directly involved in reproduction,* for example, the enlargement of the breasts and the widening of the hips in girls and the appearance of facial hair, pubic hair, underarm hair, and the lowering of the voice in both genders. This pattern of changes is caused by increased production of sex-specific hormones: estrogen in girls and testosterone in boys.

Just as the body changes during adolescence, so, too, does the brain. For example, there is a marked increase in the growth rate of tissue connecting different regions of the brain just before puberty (Thompson et al., 2000). Between the ages of 6 and 13, the connections between the temporal lobe (the brain region specialized for language) and the parietal lobe (the brain region specialized for understanding spatial relations) multiply rapidly and then stop—just about the time that the critical period for learning a language ends (see **FIGURE 11.11**).

How does the brain change at puberty?

But the most intriguing set of neural changes associated with adolescence occurs in the prefrontal cortex. An infant's brain forms many more new synapses than it actually needs, and by the time a child is 2 years old, she has about 15,000 synapses per neuron—which is twice as many as the average adult (Huttenlocher, 1979). This early period of synaptic proliferation is followed by a period of synaptic pruning in which those connections that

▶ Adolescents are often described as gawky because different parts of their faces and bodies mature at different rates. But as musician Justin Timberlake can attest, the gawkiness generally clears up.

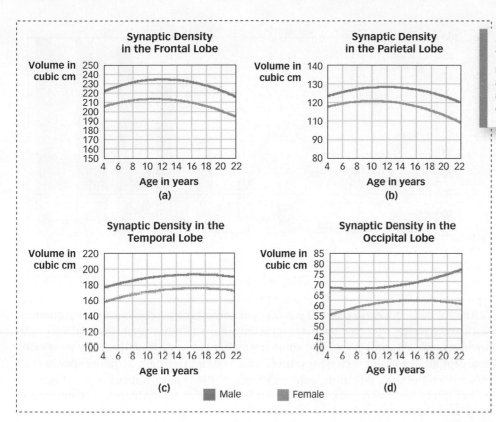

Your Brain on Puberty The development of neurons peaks in the frontal and parietal lobes at about age 12 (a, b), in the temporal lobe at about age 16 (c), and continues to increase in the occipital lobe through age 20 (d).

are not frequently used are eliminated. This is a clever system that allows our brain's wiring to be determined by both our genes and our experiences: Our genes "offer" a very large set of synaptic connections to the environment, which then "chooses" which ones to keep. Scientists used to think that this process ended early in life, but recent evidence suggests that the prefrontal cortex undergoes a second wave of synaptic proliferation just before puberty and a second round of synaptic pruning during adolescence (Giedd et al., 1999). Clearly, the adolescent brain is a work in progress.

The Protraction of Adolescence

Although the onset of puberty is largely determined by a genetic program (no one reaches puberty at 2 or 72), there is considerable variation across individuals (e.g., people tend to reach puberty at about the same age as their same-sexed parent did)

How has the onset of puberty changed over the last century?

and across cultures (e.g., African American girls tend to reach puberty before European American girls do; see **FIGURE 11.12** on the next page). There is also considerable variation across generations (Malina, Bouchard, & Beunen, 1988). For example, in Scandinavia, the United Kingdom, and the United States, the age of first menstruation was between 16 and 17 years in the 19th century but was approximately 13 years in 1960. Currently, about a third of all boys in the United States show some signs of genital maturity by the age of 9 (Reiter & Lee, 2001). A recent study (Aksglaede et al., 2009) found that the average age of breast development for Danish girls has decreased by an entire year since 1992! Puberty is accelerated by body fat (Kim & Smith, 1998), and the decrease in the age of the onset of puberty is due at least in part to improved diet and health (Ellis & Garber, 2000). But some scientists worry that physical maturity in women is being hastened by exposure to endocrine-disrupting chemicals that mimic estrogen in the body.

▲ Early puberty is big news.

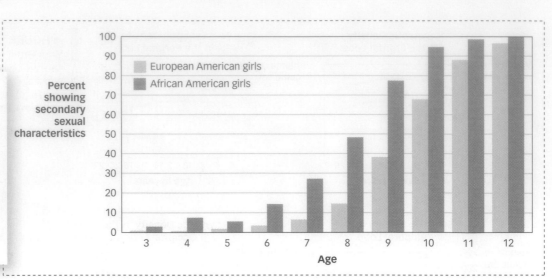

► FIGURE 11.12
Secondary Sexual Characteristics The graph shows the percentage of girls in each age group who show breast and/or pubic hair development. These characteristics appear earlier in African American than European American girls. There is no evidence that African American boys mature earlier than European American boys (Herman-Giddens et al., 1997).

BOB BURCH /INDEX STOCK

▲ About 60% of preindustrial societies don't even have a word for adolescence (Schlegel & Barry, 1991). When a Krobo female menstruates for the first time, older women take her into seclusion for 2 weeks and teach her about sex, birth control, and marriage. Afterward, a public ceremony called the durbar is held, and the young female who that morning was regarded as a child is thereafter regarded as an adult.

The increasingly early onset of puberty has important psychological consequences. Just two centuries ago, the gap between childhood and adulthood was relatively brief because people became physically adult at roughly the same time that they were ready to accept adult roles in society, and these roles did not normally require them to have extensive schooling. But in modern societies, people typically spend 3 to 10 years in school after they reach puberty. Thus, while the age at which people become physically adult has decreased, the age at which they are prepared or allowed take on adult responsibilities has increased, and so the period between childhood and adulthood has become *protracted*. What are the consequences of a protracted adolescence?

Adolescence is often characterized as a time of internal turmoil and external recklessness, and some psychologists have speculated that the protraction of adolescence is in part to blame for its bad reputation (Moffitt, 1993). According to these theorists, adolescents are adults who have temporarily been denied a place in adult society. American teenagers are subjected to 10 times as many restrictions as older adults, and twice as many restrictions as active-duty U.S. Marines or incarcerated felons (Epstein, 2007a). As such, they feel especially compelled to do things to demonstrate their adulthood, such as smoking, drinking, using drugs, having sex, and committing crimes. In a sense, adolescents are people who are forced to live in the gap between two worlds, and the so-called storm and stress of adolescence may be understood in part as a consequence of this dilemma. As one researcher noted, "Trapped in the frivolous world of peer culture, they learn virtually everything they know from one another rather than from the people they are about to become. Isolated from adults and wrongly treated like children, it is no wonder that some teens behave, by adult standards, recklessly or irresponsibly" (Epstein, 2007b).

But the storm and stress of adolescence is by no means inevitable (Steinberg & Morris, 2001). Teenagers in many cultures show few signs of adolescent turmoil and seem more intent on learning to become adults than on rebelling against them (Epstein, 2007b). Indeed, research suggests that even in American society, the "moody adolescent" who is a victim of "raging hormones" is largely a myth. Adolescents are no moodier than children (Buchanan, Eccles, & Becker, 1992), and fluctuations in their hormone levels have only a tiny impact on their moods (Brooks-Gunn, Graber, & Paikoff, 1994). And although the vast majority of adolescents do dabble in misbehavior, they don't actually major in it. For example, most adolescents in the United States get drunk at least once before they graduate from high school, but few develop drinking problems or allow alcohol to impair their academic success or personal relationships (Hughs, Power, & Francis, 1992; Johnston, Bachman, & O'Malley, 1997). Adolescents tend to

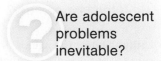

Are adolescent problems inevitable?

▲ These students at the University of Missouri (left) may be experimenting with reckless behavior, but they are unlikely to become reckless adults. Of course, the Vermont State Trooper (right) who is inspecting the car in which four teens died after a night of drinking would probably remind us that this only applies to those who live.

experiment, but their experiments appear to have few long-term consequences, and most adolescents who try drugs or break the law end up becoming sober, law-abiding adults (Steinberg, 1999). In short, adolescence is not a terribly troubled time for most people, and adolescents typically "age out" of the troubles they get themselves into (Sampson & Laub, 1995).

Sexuality

Adolescence is not an easy time for anyone, but it is especially difficult for some. Boys who reach puberty later than their peers often find this period especially stressful because immature boys may be less athletic and may feel less "manly"

What makes adolescence especially difficult?

than their peers (Petersen, 1985). Among girls, it is those who reach puberty earlier than their peers who are most likely to experience negative consequences ranging from distress to delinquency (Caspi, 1991; Mendle, Turkheimer, & Emery, 2007) (see **FIGURE 11.13**). There are many different reasons for this (Ge & Natsuaki, 2009). For example, early-maturing girls don't have as much time as their peers do to develop the skills necessary to cope with adolescence (Petersen & Grockett, 1985), but because they appear to be mature, others expect them to act like adults. Early-maturing girls also tend to receive attention from older males, who may lead them into a variety of unhealthy activities (Ge, Conger, & Elder, 1996). Some research suggests that the *timing* of puberty has a greater influence on emotional and behavioral problems than does the occurrence of puberty itself (Buchanan et al., 1992).

For some adolescents, puberty is additionally complicated by the fact that they are attracted to members of the same sex. Not only does this make them different from the majority of their peers, but with few exceptions, human cultures tend to disapprove of homosexual behavior and react to it with responses that range from snickering to beheading. In a recent survey (Pew Research Center for People & the Press, 2009b), about half of all Americans said that homosexuality is morally wrong—and America is more accepting of homosexuality than are many other nations (see **FIGURE 11.14** on the next page).

▼ FIGURE 11.13
Early Puberty Early puberty is a source of psychological distress for women (Ge, Conger, & Elder, 1996).

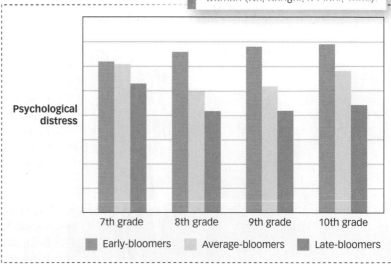

Psychological distress

7th grade 8th grade 9th grade 10th grade

■ Early-bloomers ■ Average-bloomers ■ Late-bloomers

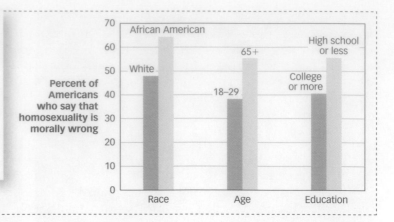

► FIGURE 11.14
Attitudes Toward Homosexuality
It isn't surprising that homosexual adolescents are reluctant to reveal their sexual orientations. A 2009 public opinion survey shows that about half of all Americans disapprove of homosexuality, though this attitude varies significantly by race, age, and level of education (Pew Research Center for People & the Press, 2009b).

For example, 98% of Nigerians and Kenyans believe that "homosexuality can never be morally justified" (Pew Research Center for People & the Press, 2006), and Uganda recently considered instituting the death penalty as punishment for homosexual behavior. Given so much social disapproval, it is little wonder that between 2% and 10% of adults classify themselves as homosexual but only .5% of young teenagers are willing to do the same (Garofalo et al., 1999).

What determines whether a person is sexually oriented toward the same or the opposite sex? Psychologists used to believe that a person's sexual orientation depended primarily on his or her upbringing. For example, psychoanalytic theorists suggested that boys who grow up with a domineering mother and a submissive father are less likely to identify with their father and are thereby more likely to become homosexual. But the fact is that scientific research has failed to identify *any* aspect of parenting that has a significant impact on sexual orientation (Bell, Weinberg, & Hammersmith, 1981). Indeed, children raised by homosexual couples and heterosexual couples are equally likely to become heterosexual adults (Patterson, 1995). There is also little support for the idea that a person's early sexual encounters have a lasting impact on his or her sexual orientation (Bohan, 1996).

Is sexual orientation a matter of nature or nurture?

On the other hand, there is mounting evidence that genes and biology play an important role in determining sexual orientation. Gay men and lesbians tend to have a larger proportion of gay and lesbian siblings than do heterosexuals (Bailey et al., 1999). Furthermore, the identical twin of a gay man (with whom he shares 100% of his genes) has a 50% chance of being gay, whereas the fraternal twin or nontwin brother of a gay man (with whom he shares 50% of his genes) has only a 15% chance (Bailey & Pillard, 1991; Gladue, 1994). A similar pattern has emerged in studies of women (Bailey et al., 1993). Some studies have found that the brains of gay people look like the brains of straight people of the opposite gender (Savic & Lindstrom, 2008). For example, the right and left hemispheres tend to be of different sizes among straight men and gay women, but tend to be of equal sizes among straight women and gay men. Some evidence suggests that the fetal environment may play a role in determining sexual orientation and that high levels of androgens in the womb may predispose a person—whether male or female—later to develop a sexual preference for women (Ellis & Ames, 1987; Meyer-Bahlberg et al., 1995).

Of course, biology cannot be the sole determinant of a person's sexual orientation because, as the foregoing studies indicate, homosexual men and women often have twins who are genetically identical, who shared their fetal environment, and who are nonetheless heterosexual. Although gay or bisexual males who acknowledge

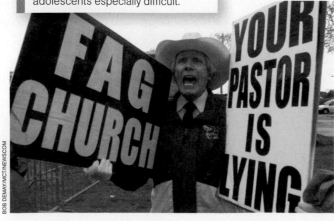

▼ The Reverend Fred Phelps, leader of the Westboro Baptist Church in Topeka, Kansas, makes no attempt to hide his hatred of gay people. Social disapproval makes the life of gay adolescents especially difficult.

their sexual orientations claim to have become aware of feelings of attraction toward other males at around the age of 8 and typically claim that they have "always been gay" (Savin-Williams, 1998), a sizable minority of lesbian women report that they were initially heterosexual and became lesbian only in midlife after experiencing an attraction to another woman (Kinnish, Strassberg, & Turner, 2005; Schneider, 2001). This fact fits with the general observation that women's sexuality is more plastic—that is, it can be oriented and reoriented more easily—than men's (Baumeister, 2004; Spitzer, 2003). Whether people's experiences do or do not influence their sexual orientation, there is no evidence that this orientation can be changed by so-called "conversion therapy" (American Psychological Association, 2009). It is also worth noting that about 1% of people claim to have no sexual orientation of any kind and have never experienced sexual attraction to either gender (Bogaert, 2004). Although the science of sexual orientation is still young and fraught with conflicting findings, it seems quite clear that sexual orientation is *not* simply a matter of choice.

But sexual behavior *is*—and American teenagers typically choose it. More than 65% of American women report having had sexual intercourse by age 18 and 90% by age 21

Why do many adolescents make unwise choices about sex?

(Hogan, Sun, & Cornwell, 2000). Unfortunately, teenagers' interest in sex often surpasses their knowledge about it. A quarter of American teenagers have had four or more sexual partners by their senior year in high school, but only about half report using a condom during their last intercourse (CDC, 2002). The United States has the highest rate of teen pregnancy in the developed world and the highest abortion rate in the Western world, not because American teens have more sex than others but because they are less knowledgeable about it. Most American parents do not talk to their children extensively about sex (Ansuini, Fiddler Woite, & Woite, 1996), and those who do start too late because they overestimate the age at which their children start having sex (Jaccard, Dittus, & Gordon, 1998) (see **FIGURE 11.15**).

Despite what some people believe, evidence suggests that sex education lowers the likelihood that teenagers will get pregnant or catch a sexually transmitted disease and does not increase the likelihood that they will have sex in the first place (Satcher, 2001). In fact, it seems to cause teenagers to delay having sex and to increase the likelihood that they will use birth control when they do (Mueller, Gavin, & Kulkarni, 2008). Nonetheless, sex education in American schools is often absent, sketchy, or based on the goal of abstinence rather than harm prevention. There is little evidence to suggest that

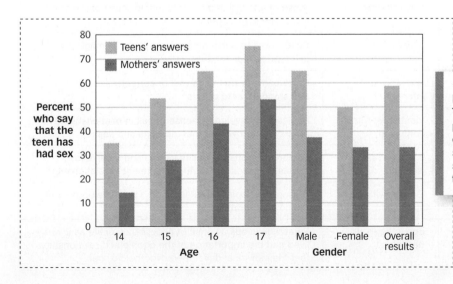

◄ FIGURE 11.15
Parental Misconceptions about Teenage Sex When American parents talk to teens about sex, it is often too little and too late. Research shows that American teens have sex earlier than their parents think they do (Jaccard et al., 1998).

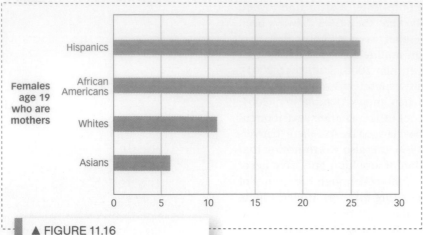

▲ **FIGURE 11.16**
Teen Pregnancy The likelihood of an American teenager becoming pregnant differs dramatically across sub-cultures (Pew Hispanic Center, 2009).

abstinence-only programs are effective (Kohler, Manhart, & Lafferty, 2008), and some studies suggest that teens who take "abstinence pledges" are just as likely to have sex as those who don't but are less likely to use birth control (Rosenbaum, 2009). Abortion, AIDS, and other sexually transmitted diseases are just some of the unfortunate consequences of sexual ignorance. Teenage pregnancy is another (see **FIGURE 11.16**). Teenage mothers fare more poorly than teenage women without children on almost every measure of academic and economic achievement, and their children fare more poorly on most measures of educational success and emotional well-being than do the children of older mothers (Olausson et al., 2001).

Parents and Peers

"Who am I?" is a question asked by both amnesiacs and adolescents, but they ask it for different reasons. The child's view of herself and her world is tightly tied to the views of her parents, but puberty creates a new set of needs that begins to snip away at these bonds by orienting the adolescent toward peers rather than parents. The psychologist Erik Erikson characterized each stage of life by the major task confronting the individual at that stage, and he suggested that the major task of adolescence was the development of an adult identity (see **TABLE 11.2**). Whereas children define themselves almost entirely in terms of their relationships with parents and siblings, adolescence marks a shift in emphasis from family relations to peer relations.

Two things can make this shift difficult. First, children cannot choose their parents, but adolescents can choose their peers. As such, adolescents have the

▼ According to Erikson, at each "stage" of development a "key event" creates a challenge or "crisis" that a person can resolve positively or negatively.

TABLE 11.2

Erikson's Stages of Human Development

Ages	Stage	Key Event	Crisis	Positive Resolution
1. Birth to 12 to 18 months	Oral-sensory	Feeding	Trust vs. mistrust	Child develops a belief that the environment can be counted on to meet his or her basic physiological and social needs.
2. 18 months to 3 years	Muscular-anal	Toilet training	Autonomy vs. shame/doubt	Child learns what he or she can control and develops a sense of free will and corresponding sense of regret and sorrow for inappropriate use of self-control.
3. to 6 years	Locomotor	Independence	Initiative vs. guilt	Child learns to begin action, to explore, to imagine, and to feel remorse for actions.
4. 6 to 12 years	Latency	School	Industry vs. inferiority	Child learns to do things well or correctly in comparison to a standard or to others.
5. 12 to 18 years	Adolescence	Peer relationships	Identity vs. role confusion	Adolescent develops a sense of self in relationship to others and to own internal thoughts and desires.
6. 19 to 40 years	Young adulthood	Love relationships	Intimacy vs. isolation	Person develops the ability to give and receive love; begins to make long-term commitment to relationships.
7. 40 to 65 years	Middle adulthood	Parenting	Generativity vs. stagnation	Person develops interest in guiding the development of the next generation.
8. 65 to death	Maturity	Reflection on and acceptance of one's life	Ego integrity vs. despair	Person develops a sense of acceptance of life as it was lived and the importance of the people and relationships that the individual developed over the life span.

power to shape themselves by joining groups that will lead them to develop new values, attitudes, beliefs, and perspectives. In a sense, the adolescent has the opportunity to invent the adult he or she will soon become, and the responsibility this opportunity entails can be overwhelming. Second, as adolescents strive for greater autonomy, their parents naturally rebel. For instance, parents and adolescents tend to disagree about the age at which certain adult behaviors, such as staying out late or having sex, become permissible, and you don't need a psychologist to tell you which position each party tends to hold (Holmbeck & O'Donnell, 1991). Because adolescents and parents often have different ideas about who should control the adolescent's behavior, their relationships may become more conflictive and less close and their interactions briefer and less frequent (Larson & Richards, 1991).

How do family and peer relationships change during adolescence?

"So I blame you for everything—whose fault is that?"

But these conflicts and tensions are not as dramatic, pervasive, and inevitable as many seem to believe (Chung, Flook, & Fuligni, 2009). For example, adolescents tend to have aspirations and values that are quite similar to those of their parents (Elder & Conger, 2000), and familial bickering tends to be about much smaller issues, such as dress and language, which explains why teenagers argue more with their mothers (who are typically in charge of such issues) than with their fathers (Caspi et al., 1993). Furthermore, in cultures that emphasize the importance of duty and obligation, parents and adolescents may show few if any signs of tension and conflict (Greenfield et al., 2003).

As adolescents pull away from their parents, they move toward their peers. Studies show that across a wide variety of cultures, historical epochs, and even species, peer relations evolve in a similar way (Dunphy, 1963; Weisfeld, 1999). Young adolescents initially form groups or "cliques" (Brown, Mory, & Kinney, 1994) with others of their gender, many of whom were friends during childhood. Next, male cliques and female cliques begin to meet in public places, such as town squares or shopping malls, and they begin to interact—but only in groups and only in public. After a few years, the older members of these single-sex cliques "peel off" and form smaller, mixed-sex cliques, which may assemble in private as well as in public but usually assemble as a group. Finally, couples (typically a male and a female) "peel off" from the small, mixed-sex clique and begin romantic relationships.

Studies show that throughout adolescence, people spend increasing amounts of time with opposite-sex peers while maintaining the amount of time they spend with same-sex peers (Richards et al., 1998), and they accomplish this by spending less time with their parents (Larson & Richards, 1991). Although peers exert considerable influence on the adolescent's beliefs and behaviors—both for better and for worse—this influence generally occurs because adolescents respect, admire, and like their peers and not because their peers pressure them (Susman et al., 1994). In fact, as they age, adolescents show an increasing tendency to resist peer pressure (Steinberg & Monahan, 2007). Acceptance by peers is of tremendous importance to adolescents, and those who are rejected by their peers tend to be withdrawn, lonely, and depressed (Pope & Bierman, 1999). Fortunately for those of us who were seventh-grade nerds, individuals who are unpopular in early adolescence can become popular in later adolescence as their peers become less rigid and more tolerant (Kinney, 1993).

▼ Adolescents form same-sex cliques that meet opposite-sex cliques in public places. Eventually, these people will form mixed-sex cliques, pair off into romantic relationships, get married, and have children who will take their places at the mall.

IN SUMMARY

○ Adolescence is a stage of development that is distinct from those stages that come before and after it. It begins with a growth spurt and with puberty, the onset of sexual maturity of the human body. Puberty is occurring earlier than ever before, and the entrance of young people into adult society is occurring later.

○ During this "in-between stage," adolescents are somewhat more prone to do things that are risky or illegal, but they rarely inflict serious or enduring harm on themselves or others.

○ During adolescence, sexual interest intensifies, and in some cultures, sexual activity begins. Sexual activity typically follows a script, many aspects of which are standard across cultures. Although most people are attracted to members of the opposite sex, some are not, and research suggests that biology plays a key role in determining a person's sexual orientation.

○ As adolescents seek to develop their adult identities, they seek increasing autonomy from their parents and become more peer-oriented, forming single-sex cliques, followed by mixed-sex cliques, and finally pairing off as couples.

▼ FIGURE 11.17

Changing Personality Personality is just one of the many things that continue to change throughout adulthood. Research shows that, as adults age, they become more emotionally stable and conscientious but less socially vital and less open to experience (Roberts & Mroczek, 2008).

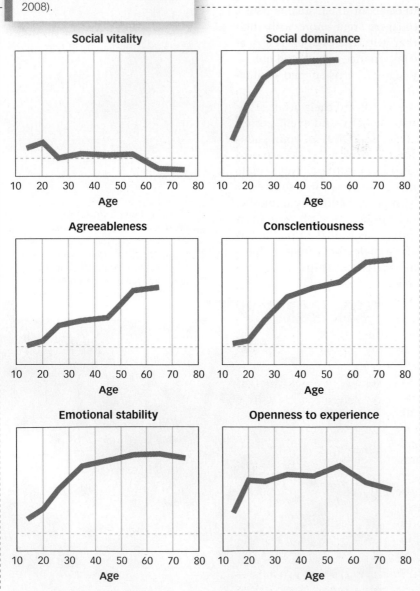

Adulthood: Going Happily Downhill

It takes fewer than 7,000 days for a single-celled zygote to become a registered voter. The speed of our physical development is initially quite rapid and then slows in **adulthood**, which is *the stage of development that begins around 18 to 21 years and ends at death*. Because physical change slows from a gallop to a crawl, we sometimes have the sense that adulthood is a destination to which development delivers us and that once we've arrived, our journey is complete. But that's not true. Although they are less noticeable, many physical, cognitive, and emotional changes take place between our first legal beer and our last legal breath (see **FIGURE 11.17**).

Changing Abilities

The early 20s are the peak years for health, stamina, vigor, and prowess, and because our psychology is so closely tied to our biology, these are also the years during which most of our cognitive abilities are at their sharpest. At this very moment you see farther, hear better, remember more, and weigh less than you ever will again. Enjoy it. This glorious moment at life's summit will last for a few dozen more months—and then, somewhere between the ages of 26 and 30, you will begin the slow and steady decline that does not end until you do. A mere 10 or 15 years after puberty, your body will begin to deteriorate in almost every way: Your muscles will be replaced by fat, your skin will become less elastic, your hair will thin and your bones will weaken, your sensory abilities will become less acute, and your brain cells will die at an

adulthood The stage of development that begins around 18 to 21 years and ends at death.

accelerated rate. Eventually, if you are a woman, your ovaries will stop producing eggs and you will become infertile. Eventually, if you are a man, your erections will be fewer and farther between. Indeed, other than being more resistant to colds and less sensitive to pain, older bodies just don't work as well as younger ones do.

As these physical changes accumulate, they will begin to have measurable psychological consequences (Salthouse, 2006) (see **FIGURE 11.18** on the next page). For instance, as your brain ages, your prefrontal cortex and its associated subcortical connections will deteriorate more quickly than will the other areas of your brain (Raz, 2000); thus you will experience the most noticeable cognitive decline on tasks that require effort, initiative, or strategy. Everyone knows that memory gets worse with age, but not all kinds of memory worsen at the same rate. Older adults show a much more pronounced decline

What physical and psychological changes are associated with adulthood?

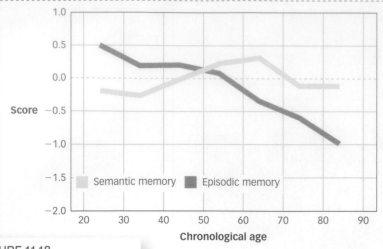

▲ FIGURE 11.18
Cognitive Decline Knowledge lasts a lifetime, but the ability to use it does not. After the age of 20, people show dramatic declines on most measures of cognitive performance even though their level of knowledge remains stable (Salthouse, 2006).

on tests of working memory (the ability to hold information "in mind") than on tests of long-term memory (the ability to retrieve information), a much more pronounced decline on tests of episodic memory (the ability to remember particular past events) than on tests of semantic memory (the ability to remember general information such as the meanings of words), and a much more pronounced decline on tests of retrieval (the ability to "go find" information in memory) than on tests of recognition (the ability to decide whether information was encountered before).

And yet, while the cognitive machinery gets rustier with age, research suggests that the operators of that machinery often compensate by using it more skillfully (Bäckman & Dixon, 1992; Salthouse, 1987). Although older chess players *remember* chess positions more poorly than younger players do, they *play* as well as younger players because they search the board more efficiently (Charness, 1981). Although older typists *react* more slowly than younger typists do, they *type* as quickly and accurately as younger typists because they are better at anticipating the next word (Salthouse, 1984). Older airline pilots are considerably worse than younger pilots when it comes to keeping a list

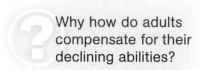

Why how do adults compensate for their declining abilities?

of words in short-term memory, but this age difference disappears when those words are the "heading commands" that pilots receive from the control tower every day (Morrow et al., 1994). This pattern of errors suggests that older adults are somehow compensating for age-related declines in memory and attention.

How do they do it? When young adults try to keep verbal information in working memory, the left prefrontal cortex is more strongly activated than the right, and when young adults try to keep spatial information in working memory, the right prefrontal cortex is more strongly activated than the left (Smith & Jonides, 1997). But this *bilateral asymmetry* is not seen among older adults, and some scientists take this to mean that older brains compensate for the declining abilities of one neural structure by calling on other neural structures to help out (Cabeza, 2002; see **FIGURE 11.19**). The young brain can be characterized as a group of specialists, but as these specialists becomes older and less able, they begin to work together on tasks that each once handled independently. In short, the machinery of body and brain do break down with age, but a seasoned driver in an old jalopy can often hold his own against a rookie in a hot rod.

▼ One week before his 58th birthday, US Airways pilot Chesley Sullenberger made a perfect emergency landing in the Hudson River and saved the lives of everyone on board. None of the passengers wish they'd had a younger pilot.

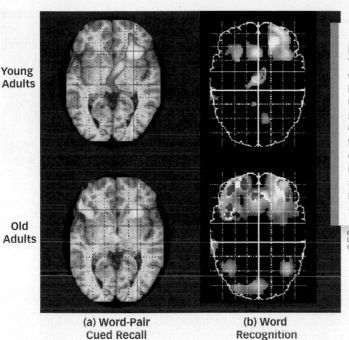

◀ FIGURE 11.19
Bilaterality in Older and Younger Brains Across a variety of tasks, older adult brains show bilateral activation and young adult brains show unilateral activation. One possible explanation for this is that older brains compensate for the declining abilities of one neural structure by calling on other neural structures for help (Cabeza, 2002).

ROBERTO CABEZA, CENTER FOR COGNITIVE NEUROSCIENCE, DUKE UNIVERSITY. (A) CABEZA ET AL. (1997A); (B) BACKMAN ET AL. (1997).

(a) Word-Pair Cued Recall

(b) Word Recognition

Changing Goals

One reason why Grandpa can't find his car keys is that his prefrontal cortex doesn't function like it used to. But another reason is that the location of car keys just isn't the sort of thing that grandpas spend their precious time memorizing. According to *socioemotional selectivity theory* (Carstensen & Turk-Charles, 1994), younger adults are generally oriented toward the acquisition of information that will be useful to them in the future (e.g., reading news), whereas older adults are generally oriented toward information that brings emotional satisfaction in the present (e.g., reading novels). Because

How do informational goals change in adulthood?

young people have such long futures, they *invest* their time attending to, thinking about, and remembering potentially *useful information* that may serve them well in the many days to come. But older people have shorter futures and so they *spend* their time attending to, thinking about, and remembering *positive information* that serves them well in the moment (see **FIGURE 11.20**).

Older people perform much more poorly than younger people when they are asked to remember a series of unpleasant faces, but perform only slightly more poorly when they are asked to remember a series of pleasant faces (Mather & Carstensen, 2003). Whereas younger adults show activation of the amygdala when they see both pleasant and unpleasant pictures, older adults show greater activation when they see pleasant pictures than when they see unpleasant pictures (Mather et al., 2004). Apparently, older adults just don't attend to information that doesn't make them happy. As people age, they tend to experience far fewer negative emotions and many more complex emotions (Carstensen et al., 2000; Charles, Reynolds, & Gatz, 2001; Mroczek & Spiro, 2005). What's more, older people seem better able than younger people to sustain their positive emotional experiences and to curtail their negative ones (Lawton et al., 1992; Mather & Carstensen, 2005).

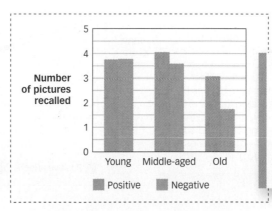

Number of pictures recalled

Young Middle-aged Old

■ Positive ■ Negative

◀ FIGURE 11.20
Memory for Pictures Memory declines with age in general, but the ability to remember negative information—such as unpleasant pictures—declines much more quickly than the ability to remember positive information (Carstensen et al., 2000).

► As people age, they prefer to spend time with family and a few close friends rather than large circles of acquaintances.

"Two Stones tickets, please, senior discount."

Many of these same changes occur among younger people whose futures are shortened by terminal illness (Carstensen & Fredrickson, 1998).

These cognitive and emotional changes influence the activities in which older people engage. Because a shortened future orients people toward emotionally satisfying rather than intellectually profitable information, older adults become more selective about their interaction partners, choosing to spend time with family and a few close friends rather than with a large circle of acquaintances. One study followed a group of people from the 1930s to the 1990s and found that their rate of interaction with acquaintances declined from early to middle adulthood, but their rate of interaction with spouses, parents, and siblings remained stable or increased (Carstensen, 1992). A study of older adults who ranged in age from 69 to 104 found that the oldest adults had fewer peripheral social partners than the younger adults did, but they had just as many emotionally close partners whom they identified as member of their "inner circle" (Lang & Carstensen, 1994). Apparently, "Let's go meet some new people" just isn't something that most 60-year-olds tend to say.

Is late adulthood a happy or unhappy time for most people?

Together, these cognitive, emotional, and behavioral changes tend to make later adulthood one of the most satisfying periods of a human life (see **FIGURE 11.21**). In a recent survey, 38% of people over 65 described themselves as very happy, but only 28% of 18- to 29-year-olds said the same (Pew Research Center for the People & the Press, 1997). One reason

► FIGURE 11.21

Happiness and Age Despite what our youth-oriented culture would have you believe, people's overall happiness generally increases with age. As this graph shows, people experience a small decrease in positive affect beginning around age 55, but this is more than compensated for by the large decrease in negative affect that begins around the age of 15 and continues through middle age (Charles, Reynolds, & Gatz, 2001).

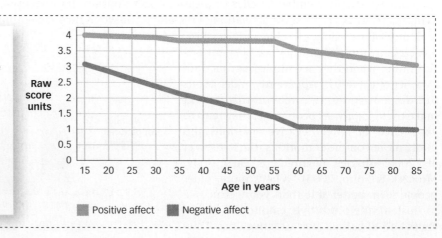

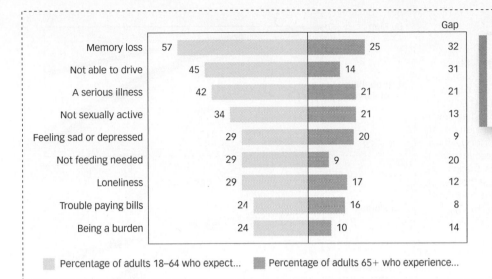

		Gap
Memory loss	57 ... 25	32
Not able to drive	45 ... 14	31
A serious illness	42 ... 21	21
Not sexually active	34 ... 21	13
Feeling sad or depressed	29 ... 20	9
Not feeding needed	29 ... 9	20
Loneliness	29 ... 17	12
Trouble paying bills	24 ... 16	8
Being a burden	24 ... 10	14

▢ Percentage of adults 18–64 who expect...   ▮ Percentage of adults 65+ who experience...

◀ FIGURE 11.22
Not So Bad Research shows that young adults overestimate the problems of old age (Pew Research Center for People & the Press, 2009a).

why Western culture is so obsessed with youth is that young adults vastly overestimate the problems of aging (Pew Research Center for People & the Press, 2009a) (see **FIGURE 11.22**). Research suggests that aging doesn't have to be bad at all, and that it is one of the best ways to increase one's share of happiness.

Changing Roles

The psychological separation from parents that begins in adolescence usually becomes a physical separation in adulthood. In virtually all human societies, young adults leave home, get married, and have children of their own. Marriage and parenthood are two of the most significant aspects of adult life, and you will probably experience both of them. Census statistics suggest that if you are a college-age American, you are likely to get married at around the age of 27, have approximately 1.8 children, and consider both your partner and your children to be your greatest sources of joy. Indeed, in a recent survey, a whopping 93% of American mothers said that their children were a source of happiness all or most of the time (Pew Research Center, 1997).

But do marriage and children really make us happy? Research has consistently shown that married people live longer (see **FIGURE 11.23** on the next page), have more frequent sex (and enjoy that sex more), and earn several times as much money as un-married people do (Waite, 1995). Given these differ-ences, it is no surprise that married people consistently report being happier than unmarried people—whether those unmarried people are single, widowed, divorced, or cohabiting (Johnson & Wu, 2002). That's why many researchers consider mar-riage one of the best investments individuals can make in their own happiness. But other researchers suggest that married people may be happier because happy people may be more likely to get married and that marriage may be the consequence—and not the cause—of happiness (Lucas et al., 2003). The general consensus among scien-tists seems to be that both of these positions have merit: even before marriage, people who end up married tend to be happier than those who never marry, but marriage does seem to confer further benefits.

What does research say about marriage, children, and happiness?

Children are another story. In general, research suggests that children decrease rather than increase their parents' happiness (DiTella, MacCulloch, & Oswald, 2003). For ex-ample, parents typically report lower marital satisfaction than do nonparents—and the

▲ In 2008, Min Bahadur Sherchan, 76, became the oldest person to scale Mount Everest. Data suggest that the last decades of life are for many people the most satisfying.

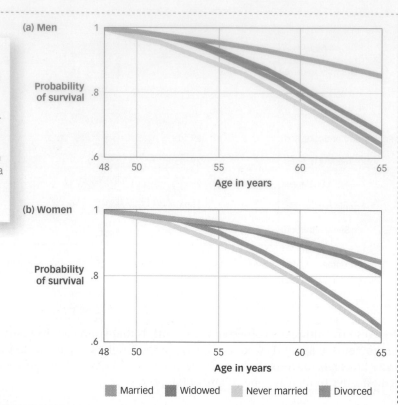

▶ FIGURE 11.23
Til Death Do Us Part Married people live longer than unmarried people, and this is true of both men and women. But while widowed men die as young as never-married and divorced men do (a), widowed women live longer than never-married or divorced women do (b). In other words, the loss of a wife is always bad, but the loss of a husband is only bad if he's still alive! (Lillard & Waite, 1995)

▲ Does marriage make people happy or do happy people tend to get married?

more children they have, the less satisfaction they report (Twenge, Campbell, & Foster, 2003). Studies of marital satisfaction at different points in the life span reveal an interesting pattern of peaks and valleys: Marital satisfaction starts out high, plummets at about the time that the children are in diapers, begins to recover, plummets again when the children are in adolescence, and returns to its premarital levels only when children leave home (see **FIGURE 11.24**). Given that mothers typically do much more child care than fathers, it is not surprising that the negative impact of parenthood is stronger for women than for men. Women with young children are especially likely to experience role conflicts ("How am I supposed to manage being a full-time lawyer and a full-time mother?") and restrictions of freedom ("I never get to play tennis anymore"). A study that measured the moment-to-moment happiness of American women as they went about their daily activities found that women were less happy when taking care of their children

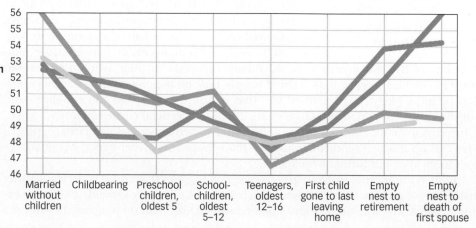

▶ FIGURE 11.24
Marital Satisfaction over the Life Span This graph shows the results of four independent studies of marital satisfaction among men and women. All four studies suggest that marital satisfaction is highest before children are born and after they leave home (Walker, 1977).

than when eating, exercising, shopping, napping, or watching television—and only slightly happier than when they were doing housework (Kahneman et al., 2004). *Thinking* about children is a delight, but *raising* children is hard work. Perhaps that's why when women in a national survey were asked to name a mother's most important quality, mothers of grown children were most likely to name "love," whereas mothers of young children were most likely to name "patience" (Pew Research Center, 1997).

Does all of this mean that people would be happier if they didn't have children? Not necessarily. Because researchers cannot randomly assign people to be parents or nonparents, studies of the effects of parenthood are necessarily correlational. People who want children and have children may be somewhat less happy than people who neither want them nor have them, but it is possible that people who want children would be even less happy if they didn't have them. What seems clear is that raising children is a challenging job that most people find to be meaningful and rewarding—especially when it's over.

IN SUMMARY

○ Older adults show declines in working memory, episodic memory, and retrieval tasks, but they often develop strategies to compensate.

○ Gradual physical decline begins early in adulthood and has clear psychological consequences, some of which are offset by increases in skill and expertise.

○ Older people are more oriented toward emotionally satisfying information, which influences their basic cognitive performance, the size and structure of their social networks, and their general happiness.

○ For most people, adulthood means leaving home, getting married, and having children. People who get married are typically happier, but children and the responsibilities that parenthood entails present a significant challenge, especially for women.

WhereDoYouStand?

A License to Rear

Common law states that "when practice of a profession or calling requires special knowledge or skill and intimately affects public health, morals, order or safety, or general welfare, legislature may prescribe reasonable qualifications for persons desiring to pursue such professions or calling and require them to demonstrate possession of such qualifications by examination." Most of us would probably agree that this is reasonable and that people who want to operate automobiles, use firearms, pilot airplanes, or perform surgeries should be required to demonstrate their proficiency and obtain a license. After all, if people were allowed to practice law or build bridges without first demonstrating their knowledge and skill, the public welfare would be gravely compromised.

So why not apply this logic to parenting? Why not outlaw reproduction by citizens who can't qualify for a parenting license? This suggestion may sound outrageous, but it has actually become the subject of serious debate among ethicists who are trying to decide how best to balance the interests of parents against the damage that bad parenting does to children and society (Tittle, 2004; Warnock, 2003). The arguments *against* parental licensing are obvious: People have a fundamental right to reproduce; people have different definitions of "good parenting"; a licensing system would invite abuse by governments that want to limit the reproduction of citizens who have the wrong genes, the wrong skin color, or the wrong political beliefs. Americans are naturally suspicious of governmental intrusion into private affairs, and what could be more private than the decision to have a child?

But the arguments in favor of licensing are also quite compelling. Consider just a few:

- Bad flossing is a private affair. Bad parenting is not. Every one of us pays the price when parents abuse, neglect, or fail to educate their children. Bad parents impose significant social and economic burdens on the rest of society—not to mention on their own children. Society has a clear interest in *preventing* (and not just punishing) abusive and negligent parenting.

- Licensing is not meant to stop people from having children—it is meant to make bad parents into good ones. Driver's education turns bad drivers into good drivers, but most people wouldn't sign up for such training if they didn't have to in order to qualify for a driver's license. Licensing would motivate people to learn the things that every parent should know.

- If we demand that people meet certain standards before they are allowed to *adopt* children, then why should we not demand that they meet the same standards before being allowed to *bear* children? Are our biological children worth less than our adopted ones?

- All licensing systems are open to abuse. But is there any reason to believe that this one would be more open to abuse than others? And are the costs of abuse clearly greater than the costs of having no licensing system at all?

Anyone who has read George Orwell's *1984* or Aldous Huxley's *Brave New World* will find the notion of parental licensing more than a little frightening. And yet the arguments in its favor are not absurd. Bad parenting is a real problem. Is parental licensing the right solution, or is it a cure that's worse than the illness? Where do you stand?

Chapter Review

KEY CONCEPT QUIZ

1. The sequence of prenatal development is
   a. fetus, embryo, zygote.
   b. zygote, embryo, fetus.
   c. embryo, zygote, fetus.
   d. zygote, fetus, embryo.

2. Learning begins
   a. in the womb.
   b. at birth.
   c. in the newborn stage.
   d. in infancy.

3. The proximodistal rule states that
   a. motor skills emerge in sequence from the center to the periphery.
   b. motor skills emerge in sequence from the top to the bottom.
   c. motor skills such as rooting are hardwired by nature.
   d. simple motor skills disappear as more sophisticated motor skills emerge.

4. Motor skills, such as reaching, are
   a. acquired in an orderly sequence and on a strict timetable.
   b. acquired on a strict timetable, but not in an orderly sequence.
   c. influenced by the baby's incentive.
   d. acquired by the same method by all babies.

5. Piaget believed that infants construct _____ , which are theories about the way the world works.
   a. assimilations
   b. accommodations
   c. schemas
   d. habituations

6. Once children understand that human behavior is guided by mental representations, they are said to have acquired
   a. joint attention.
   b. a theory of mind.
   c. formal operational ability.
   d. egocentrism.

7. When infants in a new situation examine their mother's face for cues about what to do, they are demonstrating an ability known as
   a. joint attention.
   b. social referencing.
   c. imitation.
   d. all of the above

8. The capacity for attachment may be innate, but the quality of attachment is influenced by
   a. the child's temperament.
   b. the primary caregiver's ability to read their child's emotional state.
   c. the interaction between the child and the primary caregiver.
   d. all of the above

9. A child's attachment style is
   a. assessed by a behavioral test known as the strange situation.
   b. most commonly a secure attachment style, except across cultures.
   c. generally different in the home than it appears in the laboratory.
   d. unchangeable over time.

10. According to Kohlberg, each stage in the development of moral reasoning is characterized by a specific focus. What is the correct sequence of these stages?
    a. focus on consequences, focus on ethical principles, focus on social rules
    b. focus on ethical principles, focus on social rules, focus on consequences
    c. focus on consequences, focus on social rules, focus on ethical principles
    d. focus on social rules, focus on consequences, focus on ethical principles

11. Evidence indicates that American adolescents are
    a. moodier than children.
    b. victims of raging hormones.
    c. likely to develop drinking problems.
    d. living in a protracted gap between childhood and adulthood.

12. Scientific evidence suggests that _____ play a key role in determining a person's sexual orientation.
    a. personal choices
    b. parenting styles
    c. sibling relationships
    d. genes and biology

13. Adolescents place the greatest emphasis on relationships with
    a. peers.
    b. parents.
    c. siblings.
    d. non-parental authority figures.

14. The peak years for health, stamina, vigor, and prowess are
    a. childhood.
    b. the early teens.
    c. the early 20s.
    d. the early 30s.

15. Data suggest that, for most people, the last decades of life are
    a. characterized by an increase in negative emotions.
    b. spent attending to the most useful information.
    c. extremely satisfying.
    d. a time during which they begin to interact with a much wider circle of people.

KEY TERMS

developmental psychology (p. 424)
zygote (p. 425)
germinal stage (p. 425)
embryonic stage (p. 425)
fetal stage (p. 426)

myelination (p. 426)
teratogens (p. 426)
fetal alcohol syndrome (p. 426)
infancy (p. 427)
motor development (p. 428)

reflexes (p. 428)
cephalocaudal rule (p. 428)
proximodistal rule (p. 428)
cognitive development (p. 429)
sensorimotor stage (p. 430)

schemas (p. 430)
assimilation (p. 430)
accommodation (p. 430)
object permanence (p. 431)
childhood (p. 432)
preoperational stage (p. 432)

concrete operational stage (p. 432)

conservation (p. 432)

formal operational stage (p. 433)

egocentrism (p. 433)

theory of mind (p. 434)

attachment (p. 440)

strange situation (p. 440)

internal working model of relationships (p. 441)

temperaments (p. 442)

preconventional stage (p. 444)

conventional stage (p. 444)

postconventional stage (p. 445)

adolescence (p. 448)

puberty (p. 448)

primary sex characteristics (p. 448)

secondary sex characteristics (p. 448)

adulthood (p. 456)

CRITICAL THINKING QUESTIONS

1. Young children don't realize that other people can see the world differently than they do. That statement describes most little kids, but it also describes most adults from time to time. What are some examples of adult egocentrism, and why doesn't it ever completely go away?

2. Some parents believe that teaching adolescents about birth control and then expecting them to abstain is like giving them the keys to a car and then expecting them not to drive.

Other parents believe that adolescents make their own decisions about sex, and that it is better for those decisions to be made on the basis of knowledge rather than ignorance. How would you design a study to help settle this argument?

3. Data suggest that later adulthood is an especially rewarding time of life for most people. So why do so many of us think that being young is better than being old? Is this just a matter of ignorance, or does our society actively perpetrate this myth?

RECOMMENDED READINGS

Bloom, P. (2004). *Descartes' baby: How the science of child development explains what makes us human.* New York: Basic Books.

Most of us feel that we are a mind that inhabits a body. But why? Why have people traditionally thought of their bodies as mere vehicles for something immaterial—a mind, a psyche, or a soul? In this fascinating book full of great insights and startling examples, Paul Bloom suggests that infants naturally divide the world into the physical and the mental and that this early distinction gives rise to our dualist intuitions.

DeLoache, J. S., & Gottlieb, A. (2000). *A world of babies: Imagined childcare guides for seven societies.* Cambridge, UK: Cambridge University Press.

Judy DeLoache and Alma Gottlieb explore cultural differences in child-rearing practices in seven cultures in this book. Written as a series of fictional child-care manuals in the style of *Dr. Spock's Baby and Child Care,* the authors use factual information from real sources as well as research by psychologists, anthropologists, and historians.

Gopnik, A., Meltzoff, A., & Kuhl, P. (1999). *The scientist in the crib: What early learning tells us about the mind.* New York: Harper-Collins.

Developmental scientists Alison Gopnik, Andrew Meltzoff, and Patricia Kuhl present decades of research on cognitive development that reveals what infants know and how they learn about people, objects, and language. The authors suggest that babies are born knowing a lot more than previously thought by psychologists such as Piaget, and they describe their own and other developmentalists' research in this accessible book.

The Up Series: *Seven up, 7 plus seven, 21 up, 28 up, 35 up, 42 up, 49 up.* (1964–2005).

A remarkable series of seven documentary films follows the lives of 14 British people from age 7 to (so far) age 49. (*Seven Up* was directed by Paul Almond, while the other films were directed by Michael Apted.) In 1964, specific participants were selected to represent the range of socioeconomic backgrounds in England. The filmmakers wanted to explore the idea that people's futures were predetermined by their place in British society and all that comes with it, such as attendance at elite universities and entry into the business and financial world. Over the course of four decades, this proved to be true for some of the participants, but others from both upper and middle classes diverged from the paths expected for their lives. *56 Up* will be filmed in 2011 or 2012.

ANSWERS TO KEY CONCEPT QUIZ

1. b; 2. a; 3. a; 4. c; 5. c; 6. b; 7. b; 8. d; 9. a; 10. c; 11. d; 12. d; 13. a; 14. c; 15. c.

Need more help? Additional resources are located at the book's free companion Web site at:
www.worthpublishers.com/schacter

12

Personality

Amy Winehouse is a singer known for her personality. Her music has personality, yes—a bluesy, boozy contralto that seems carefully composed to sound as though she doesn't care. The songs she chooses have personality, too, like the memorable "Rehab" ("They tried to make me go to rehab, I said 'No, no, no'"). Her life, at least as it's portrayed in gossip magazines and websites, is an expression of personality as well. If you believe all you read, she's had marriage troubles, drug troubles, drinking troubles, family troubles, international diplomacy troubles, and more. On top of all that, she's collected enough bad tattoos to rival the Sunday comics. How much of this is real and how much is a show we don't know. But she's one of a kind. Amy Winehouse has personality in an important sense—she has qualities that make her psychologically different from other people.

▶ Singer Amy Winehouse arrives at the MTV Movie Awards in Los Angeles, 2007.
AP PHOTO/KEVORK DJANSEZIAN

personality An individual's characteristic style of behaving, thinking, and feeling.

self-report A series of answers to a questionnaire that asks people to indicate the extent to which sets of statements or adjectives accurately describe their own behavior or mental state.

THE FORCES THAT CREATE ANY ONE PERSONALITY ARE ALWAYS something of a mystery. Your personality is different from anyone else's and expresses itself pretty consistently across settings—at home, in the classroom, and elsewhere. But how and why do people differ psychologically? By studying many unique individuals, psychologists seek to gather enough information to scientifically answer these, the central questions of personality psychology.

Personality *is an individual's characteristic style of behaving, thinking, and feeling.* Whether Amy Winehouse's quirks are real or merely for publicity, they are certainly hers and they show her distinct personality. In this chapter, we will explore personality, first by looking at what it is and how it is measured and then by focusing on each of four main approaches to understanding personality—trait-biological, psychodynamic, humanistic-existential, and social cognitive. (Psychologists have personalities, too, so their different approaches, even to the topic of personality, shouldn't be that surprising.) At the end of the chapter, we will discuss the psychology of self to see how our views of what we are like can shape and define our personality.

Personality: What It Is and How It Is Measured

If someone said, "You have no personality," how would you feel? Like a cookie-cutter person, a boring, grayish lump who should go out and get a personality as soon as possible? As a rule, people don't usually strive for a personality——one seems to develop naturally as we travel through life. As psychologists have tried to understand the process of personality development, they have pondered questions of description (How do people differ?), explanation (Why do people differ?), and the more quantitative question of measurement (How can personality be assessed?).

Describing and Explaining Personality

As the first biologists earnestly attempted to classify all plants and animals—whether lichens or ants or fossilized skunks—personality psychologists began by labeling and describing different personalities. And just as biology came of age with Darwin's theory of evolution, which *explained* how differences among species arose, the maturing study of personality has also developed explanations of the basis for psychological differences among people.

Most personality psychologists focus on specific, psychologically meaningful individual differences—characteristics such as honesty or anxiousness or moodiness. Still, personality is often in the eye of the beholder. When one person describes another as

▼ How would you describe each of these personalities?

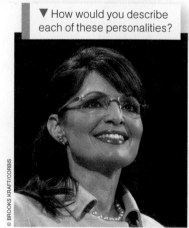

"a conceited jerk," for example, you may wonder whether you have just learned more about the describer or the person being described. Interestingly, studies that ask acquaintances to describe each other find a high degree of similarity among any one individual's descriptions of many different people ("Jason thinks that Bob is considerate, Renata is kind, and Gina is nice to others"). In contrast, resemblance is quite low when many people describe one person ("Bob thinks Jason is smart, Renata thinks he is competitive, and Gina thinks he has a good sense of humor") (Dornbusch et al., 1965).

What does it mean to say that personality is in the eye of the beholder?

What leads Amy Winehouse to all her entertaining extremes? In general, explanations of personality differences are concerned with (1) *prior events* that can shape an individual's personality or (2) *anticipated events* that might motivate the person to reveal particular personality characteristics. In a biological prior event, Amy received genes from her parents that may have led her to alcohol abuse and broken loves. Researchers interested in events that happen prior to our behavior delve into our subconscious and into our circumstances and interpersonal surroundings as well as studying our biology and brains.

Amy Winehouse seems to be looking for something—maybe love, maybe alcohol, maybe fame, maybe yet something else. The consideration of *anticipated events* emphasizes the person's own perspective and often seems intimate and personal in its reflection of the person's inner life—hopes, fears, and aspirations. Of course, our understanding of the puzzle of Amy's path to rehab—or the life of any woman or man—also depends on insights into the interaction between the past and future: We need to know how her history may have shaped her motivations. Personality psychologists study questions of how our personalities are determined by the forces in our minds and in our personal history of heredity and environment and by the choices we make and the goals we seek.

"Do you mind if I say something helpful about your personality?"

Measuring Personality

Of all the things psychologists have set out to measure, personality must be one of the toughest. How do you capture the uniqueness of a person—like a moonbeam in a jar? The general personality measures can be classified broadly into personality inventories and projective techniques.

Personality Inventories

To learn about an individual's personality, you could follow the person around and, clipboard in hand, record every single thing the person does, says, thinks, and feels—including how long this goes on before the person calls the police. Some observations might involve your own impressions ("Day 5: seems to be getting irritable"); others would involve objectively observable events that anyone could verify ("Day 7: grabbed my pencil and broke it in half, then bit my hand").

Psychologists have figured out ways to obtain objective data on personality without driving their subjects to distraction. The most popular technique is the **self-report**—*a series of answers to a questionnaire that asks people to indicate the extent to which sets of statements or adjectives accurately describe their own behavior or mental state.* The respondent typically produces a self-description by circling a number on a scale or indicating whether an item is true or false. The researcher then combines the answers to get a general sense of the individual's personality with respect to a particular domain. **TABLE 12.1** shows several items from a self-report test of sensation seeking, the tendency to seek out new and exciting sensations (Zuckerman et al., 1964). In this case, the respondent is asked to indicate whether each statement is true or false. A person with high levels of sensation seeking would mark most of these statements "true."

TABLE 12.1

Sensation-Seeking Scale

Circle One		Sample Items
T	F	I enjoy getting into new situations where you can't predict how things will turn out.
T	F	I'll try anything once.
T	F	I sometimes do "crazy" things just for fun.
T	F	I like to explore a strange city or section of town by myself, even if it means getting lost.

Source: Zuckerman et al., 1964.

Minnesota Multiphasic Personality Inventory (MMPI-2) A well-researched, clinical questionnaire used to assess personality and psychological problems.

projective techniques A standard series of ambiguous stimuli designed to elicit unique responses that reveal inner aspects of an individual's personality.

Rorschach Inkblot Test A projective personality test in which individual interpretations of the meaning of a set of unstructured inkblots are analyzed to identify a respondent's inner feelings and interpret his or her personality structure.

Thematic Apperception Test (TAT) A projective personality test in which respondents reveal underlying motives, concerns, and the way they see the social world through the stories they make up about ambiguous pictures of people.

How is a self-report scale created? The usual strategy is to collect sets of self-descriptive statements that indicate different degrees of a personality characteristic. To measure friendliness, for example, you could ask people to rate their agreement with statements ranging from "I am somewhat friendly" to "I am very outgoing," and even to "I love being around people every minute of the day." Adding up the number of statements the person endorses that indicate friendliness (and subtracting endorsements of those that indicate unfriendliness) yields a measure of the person's self-reported friendliness. This kind of personality scale uses multiple answers to a variety of items that are related in content to gauge the underlying personality characteristic. Scales based on the content of self-reports have been devised to assess a whole range of personality characteristics, all the way from general tendencies such as overall happiness (Lyubomirsky, 2008; Lyubomirsky & Lepper, 1999) to specific ones such as responding rapidly to insults (Swann & Rentfrow, 2001) or complaining about poor service (Lerman, 2006).

Surprisingly, good self-report scales can also be constructed without much attention to the specific content of the items. If people in some identifiable group (for example, convicted criminals) answer *any* self-report item differently than do other people, answers on that item can be used to predict membership in that group. This *actuarial method* can be used to gauge personality even when the self-report items are not clearly related in content to the characteristic being measured. If convicted criminals happened to like turnips (even just a little), reports of a love for turnips could be used along with other reports to predict a tendency toward criminality! This is a subtle way to measure personality characteristics of which the person may not even be aware.

The actuarial method is the basis of the **Minnesota Multiphasic Personality Inventory (MMPI-2)**, *a well-researched, clinical questionnaire used to assess personality and psychological problems.* The MMPI-2 consists of more than 500 descriptive statements—for example, "I often feel like breaking things," "I think the world is a dangerous place," and "I'm good at socializing"—to which the respondent answers "true," "false," or "cannot say." Its 10 main subscales were generated by studying how specific groups of people as compared to the general population completed the items and then creating the scales from the items that these groups answered differently (Butcher & Williams, 2000). The MMPI-2 measures tendencies toward clinical problems—for example, depression, hypochondria, anxiety, paranoia, and unconventional ideas or bizarre thoughts and beliefs—as well as some general personality characteristics, such as degree of masculine and feminine gender role identification, sociability versus social inhibition, and impulsivity. The MMPI-2 also includes *validity scales* that assess a person's attitudes toward test taking and any tendency to try to distort the results by faking answers.

Personality inventories such as the MMPI-2 are easy to administer: Just give someone a pencil and away they go. The person's scores can be calculated by computer and compared with the average ratings of thousands of other test takers. Because no interpretation of the responses is needed, biases are minimized. Of course, an accurate reading of personality will only occur if people provide honest responses—especially about characteristics that might be unflattering—and if they don't always agree or always disagree—a phenomenon known as *response style*. The validity scales cannot take these problems away altogether, but they can detect them well enough to make personality inventories generally effective means of testing, classifying, and researching many personality characteristics.

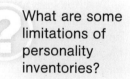

What are some limitations of personality inventories?

Projective Techniques

The second major class of tools for evaluating personality, the **projective techniques**, consist of *a standard series of ambiguous stimuli designed to elicit unique responses that reveal inner aspects of an individual's personality.* The developers of projective tests assumed that people will project personality factors that are out of awareness—wishes, concerns, impulses, and ways of seeing the world—onto ambiguous stimuli and will not censor these responses. If you and a friend were looking at the sky one day and she became upset because one cloud looked to her like a monster, her response might reveal more about her inner life than her answer to a direct question about her fears.

Probably the best-known technique is the **Rorschach Inkblot Test**, *a projective personality test in which individual interpretations of the meaning of a set of unstructured inkblots are analyzed to identify a respondent's inner feelings and interpret his or her personality structure.* An example inkblot is shown in **FIGURE 12.1**. Responses are scored according to complicated systems (derived in part from research with patients) that classify what people see (Exner, 1993; Rapaport, 1946). For example, most people who look at Figure 12.1 report seeing birds or people, so someone who is unable to see obvious items when he or she responds to a blot may be having difficulty perceiving the world as others do.

Can psychologists using the Rorschach test discover aspects of personality that are usually hidden, even from the person taking the test? Critics argue that although the Rorschach captures some of the more complex and private aspects of personality, the test is open to the subjective interpretation and theoretic biases of the examiner. In fact, to have value, a test of personality should permit prediction of a person's behavior, but evidence is sparse that Rorschach test scores have such predictive value (Dawes, 1994; Garb et al., 2005; Wood et al., 2003). Some psychologists still use the technique, but it is losing its popularity (Garb, 1999; Widiger, 2001).

The **Thematic Apperception Test (TAT)** *is a projective personality test in which respondents reveal underlying motives, concerns, and the way they see the social world through the stories they make up about ambiguous pictures of people.* To get a sense of the test, look at **FIGURE 12.2**. Who are those people, and what are they doing and thinking? What led them to this moment, and what will happen next? Different people tell very different stories about this image, as they do about the standard images in the TAT set. In creating the stories, the test taker is thought to identify with the main characters and to project his or her view of others and the world onto the other details in the drawing.

Many of the TAT drawings tend to elicit a consistent set of themes, such as successes and failures, competition and jealousy, conflict with parents and siblings, feelings about intimate relationships, aggression and sexuality. The sample card shown in Figure 12.2 tends to elicit themes regarding mother-daughter relationships, aging, and concerns regarding femininity and women's roles (Murray, 1943). Here is one young woman's response to the drawing—one that seems to reveal her own personal situation and a conflict between her wish for independence and fear that this is wrong and is punishable by a tragic loss: "The old lady in the background seems angry and thinks the younger one is making a big mistake. Maybe they're related. . . . Everything the young woman does is wrong in her mother's eyes. The daughter just wants to get away and live her own life but is too guilty to leave her mother's side, thinking it will hurt her. In the end, hmm? The girl does leave and the mother dies."

Projective tests remain controversial in psychology. Critics argue that such tests are open to the subjective interpretation and theoretic biases of the examiner. Although a TAT story like the above may *seem* revealing, the examiner must always add an interpretation (Was this about the client's actual mother, about her own conflicted desires for independence, about trying to be funny or creative or oddball?), and that interpretation could well be the scorer's *own* projection into the mind of the test taker. Thus, despite the rich picture of a personality and the insights into an individual's motives that these tests offer, projective tests should be understood primarily as a way in which a psychologist can get to know someone personally and intuitively (McClelland et al., 1953). When measured by rigorous scientific criteria, the TAT, like the Rorschach and other projective tests, has not been found to be reliable or valid in predicting behavior (Lilienfeld, Lynn, & Lohr, 2003).

Why might a projective test like the TAT story be less than reliable?

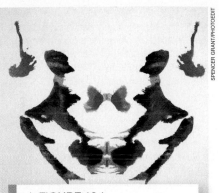

▲ FIGURE 12.1
Sample Rorschach Inkblot Test takers are shown a card such as this sample and asked, "What might this be?" What they perceive, where they see it, and why it looks that way are assumed to reflect unconscious aspects of their personality.

(Behn-Rorschach Test, Verlag Hans Huber, Bern, Switzerland, 1941.)

▼ FIGURE 12.2
Sample TAT Card Test takers are shown cards with ambiguous scenes such as this sample and are asked to tell a story about what is happening in the picture. The main themes of the story, the thoughts and feelings of the characters, and how the story develops and resolves are considered useful indices of unconscious aspects of an individual's personality (Murray, 1943).

► The electronically activated recorder sampled conversations of hundreds of participants and found that women and men are equally talkative (Mehl et al., 2009).

THANKS TO STEPHANIE LEVITT; ©MATTHIAS MEHL, UNIVERSITY OF ARIZONA

New personality measurement methods are moving beyond both personality inventories and projective tests (Robins, Fraley, & Krueger, 2007). High-tech methods such as wireless communication, real-time computer analysis, and automated behavior identification open the door to personality measurements that are leaps beyond "following the person around with a clipboard"—and can lead to surprising findings. The stereotype that women are more talkative than men, for example, was challenged by findings when 396 college students in the United States and Mexico each spent several days wearing an "EAR"—an electronically activated recorder—that captured random snippets of their talk (Mehl et al., 2009). The result? Women and men were *equally* talkative, each averaging about 16,000 words per day. The advanced measurement of how people differ (and how they do not) is a key step in understanding personality.

IN SUMMARY

○ In psychology, personality refers to a person's characteristic style of behaving, thinking, and feeling.

○ Personality psychologists attempt to find the best ways to describe personality, to explain how personalities come about, and to measure personality.

○ Two general classes of personality tests are personality inventories, such as the MMPI-2, and projective techniques, such as the Rorschach Inkblot Test and the TAT.

The Trait Approach: Identifying Patterns of Behavior

Imagine writing a story about the people you know. To capture their special qualities, you might describe their traits: Lulu is *friendly, aggressive,* and *domineering;* Seth is *flaky, humorous,* and *superficial.* With a dictionary and a free afternoon, you might even be able to describe Gino as *perspicacious, flagitious,* and *callipygian.* The trait approach to personality uses such trait terms to characterize differences among individuals. In attempting to create manageable and meaningful sets of descriptors, trait theorists face two significant challenges: narrowing down the almost infinite set of adjectives and answering the more basic question of why people have particular traits—whether they arise from biological or hereditary foundations.

Traits as Behavioral Dispositions and Motives

One way to think about personality is as a combination of traits. This was the approach of Gordon Allport (1937), one of the first trait theorists, who believed people could be described in terms of traits just as an object could be described in terms of its properties. He saw a **trait** as *a relatively stable disposition to behave in a particular and*

trait A relatively stable disposition to behave in a particular and consistent way.

consistent way. For example, a person who keeps his books organized alphabetically in bookshelves, hangs his clothing neatly in the closet, knows the schedule for the local bus, keeps a clear agenda in a daily planner, and lists birthdays of friends and family in his calendar can be said to have the trait of *orderliness.* This trait consistently manifests itself in a variety of settings.

The "orderliness" trait describes a person but doesn't explain his or her behavior. *Why* does the person behave in this way? There are two basic ways in which a trait might serve as an explanation—the trait may be a preexisting dis-

How might traits explain behavior?

position of the person that causes the person's behavior, or it may be a motivation that guides the person's behavior. Allport saw traits as preexisting dispositions, causes of behavior that reliably trigger the behavior. The person's orderliness, for example, is an inner property of the person that will cause the person to straighten things up and be tidy in a wide array of situations. Other personality theorists, such as Henry Murray (the originator of the TAT), suggested instead that traits reflect motives. Just as a hunger motive might explain someone's many trips to the snack bar, a need for orderliness might explain the neat closet, organized calendar, and familiarity with the bus schedule (Murray & Kluckhohn, 1953). As a rule, researchers examining traits as causes have used personality inventories to measure them, whereas those examining traits as motives have more often used projective tests.

What kinds of personality traits have been studied? Among the hundreds of traits that researchers have described and measured is right-wing *authoritarianism,* or the tendency toward political conservatism, obedience to authority, and conformity. In the 1940s, this characteristic drew the attention of researchers who, in the wake of World War II, were trying to understand what had made people support the rise of Nazi Germany and Fascism (Adorno et al., 1950). Although research on the personality traits that lead to political conservatism continues (Jost et al., 2003), the topic became less focal for researchers once World War II receded into history. Examples of other traits that have come into vogue over the years include cognitive complexity, defensiveness, hypnotizability, sensation seeking, and optimism. As with television shows and hairstyles, fashions in trait dimensions come and go over time.

▲ By most accounts, Kim Jong Il of North Korea is a despotic ruler who starves his people, insists on worshipful loyalty, and puts the world on edge by testing nuclear weapons. Why would anyone want to follow such a dictator? The study of the authoritarian personality was inspired by the idea that some people might follow most anyone because their personalities make them adhere to hierarchies of authority, submitting to those above them and dominating those below.

The Search for Core Traits

Picking a fashionable trait and studying it in depth doesn't get us very far in the search for the core of human character—for the basic set of traits that define how humans differ from one another. People may differ strongly in their choice of Coke versus Pepsi, but is this difference important? How have researchers tried to discover such core traits?

Classification Using Language

The study of core traits began with an exploration of how personality is represented in the store of wisdom we call language. Generation after generation, people have described people with words, so early psychologists proposed that core traits could be discerned by finding the main themes in all the adjectives used to describe personality. In one such analysis, a painstaking count of relevant words in a dictionary of English resulted in a list of over 18,000 potential traits (Allport & Odbert, 1936)! Attempts to narrow down the list to a more manageable set depend on the idea that traits might be related in a hierarchical pattern (see **FIGURE 12.3** on the next page), with more general or abstract traits at higher levels than more specific or concrete traits. Perhaps the more abstract traits represent the core of personality.

To identify this core, researchers have used the computational procedure called *factor analysis,* described in Chapter 10, which sorts trait terms or self-descriptions into a small number of underlying dimensions, or "factors," based on how people use the traits to rate themselves. In a typical study using factor analysis, hundreds of people rate themselves on hundreds of adjectives, indicating how accurately each one describes their

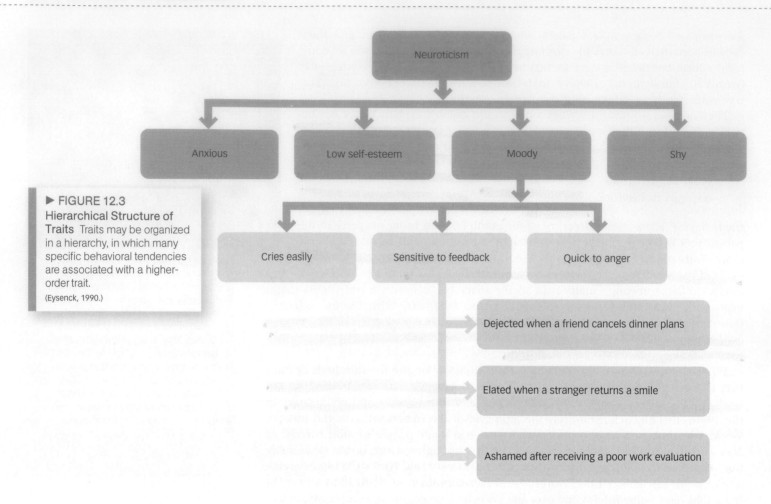

▶ **FIGURE 12.3**
Hierarchical Structure of Traits Traits may be organized in a hierarchy, in which many specific behavioral tendencies are associated with a higher-order trait.
(Eysenck, 1990.)

personality. The researcher then calculates the patterns to determine similarities in the raters' usage—whether, for example, people who describe themselves as *ambitious* also describe themselves as *active* but not *laid-back* or *contented*. Factor analysis can also reveal which adjectives are unrelated. For example, if people who describe themselves as *ambitious* are neither more nor less likely to describe themselves as *creative* or *innovative*, the factor analysis would reveal that *ambitiousness* and *creativity/innovativeness* represent different factors. Each factor is typically presented as a continuum, ranging from one extreme trait, such as *ambitious*, to its opposite, in this case, *laid-back*.

Different factor analysis techniques have yielded different views of personality structure. Cattell (1950) proposed a 16-factor theory of personality—way down from 18,000, but still a lot—whereas others have proposed theories with far fewer basic dimensions (John, Naumann, & Soto, 2008). Hans Eysenck (1967) simplified things nicely with a model of personality with only two major traits (although he later expanded that to three). Eysenck's two-factor analysis identified one dimension that distinguished people who are sociable and active (extraverts) from those who are more introspective and quiet (introverts). His analysis also identified a second dimension ranging from the tendency to be very neurotic or emotionally unstable to the tendency to be more emotionally stable. He believed that many behavioral tendencies could be understood in terms of their relation to these core traits.

How many personality factors are there?

The Big Five Dimensions of Personality

Today many factor analysis researchers agree that personality is best captured by 5 factors rather than 2, 3, 16, or 18,000 (John & Srivastava, 1999; McCrae & Costa, 1999). The **Big Five**, as they are affectionately called, are *the traits of the five-factor model: conscientiousness, agreeableness, neuroticism, openness to experience, and extraversion* (see

Big Five The traits of the five-factor model: conscientiousness, agreeableness, neuroticism, openness to experience, and extraversion.

TABLE 12.2). (Remember them by the initials C.A.N.O.E.) The five-factor model, which overlaps with the pioneering work of Cattell and Eysenck, is now widely preferred for several reasons. First, modern factor analysis techniques confirm that this set of five factors strikes the right balance between accounting for as much variation in personality as possible while avoiding overlapping traits. Second,

What are the strengths of the five-factor model?

in a large number of studies using different kinds of data—people's descriptions of their own personalities, other people's descriptions of their personalities, interviewer checklists, and behavioral observation—the same five factors have emerged. Third, and perhaps most important, the basic five-factor structure seems to show up across a wide range of participants, including children, adults in other cultures, and even among those who use other languages, suggesting that the Big Five may be universal (John & Srivastava, 1999).

In fact, the Big Five dimensions are so "universal" that they show up even when people are asked to evaluate the traits of complete strangers (Passini & Norman, 1966). This finding suggests that these dimensions of personality might reside "in the eye of the beholder"—categories that people use to evaluate others regardless of how well they know them. However, it's not all perception. The reality of these traits has been clearly established in research showing that self-reports on the Big Five are associated with predictable patterns of behavior and social outcomes (see the Hot Science box). People identified as high in extraversion, for example, tend to choose to spend time with lots of other people and are more likely than introverts to look people in the eye. People high in conscientiousness generally perform well at work and tend to live longer. People low on conscientiousness and low in agreeableness are more likely than average to be juvenile delinquents (John & Srivastava, 1999).

Research on the Big Five has shown that people's personalities tend to remain stable through their lifetime, scores at one time in life correlating strongly with scores at later dates, even later decades (Caspi, Roberts, & Shiner, 2005). William James offered the opinion that ". . . in most of us, by the age of thirty, the character has set like plaster, and will never soften again" (James, 1890, p. 121), but this turns out to be too strong a view. Some variability is typical in childhood, and though there is less in adolescence, some personality change can even occur in adulthood for some people (Srivistava et al., 2003).

Traits as Biological Building Blocks

Can we explain *why* a person has a stable set of personality traits? Many trait theorists have argued that immutable brain and biological processes produce the remarkable stability of traits over the life span. Allport viewed traits as characteristics of the brain that influence the way people respond to their environment. And as you will see, Eysenck searched for a connection between his trait dimensions and specific individual differences in the workings of the brain.

Brain damage certainly can produce personality change, as the classic case of Phineas Gage so vividly demonstrates (see Chapter 3). You may recall that after the blasting accident that blew a steel rod through his frontal lobes, Gage showed a dramatic loss of social appropriateness and conscientiousness (Damasio, 1994). In fact, when someone experiences a profound change in personality, testing often reveals the presence of such brain pathologies as Alzheimer's disease, stroke, or brain tumor (Feinberg, 2001). The administration of antidepressant medication and other pharmaceutical treatments that change brain chemistry can also trigger personality changes, making people, for example, somewhat more extraverted and less neurotic (Bagby et al., 1999; Knutson et al., 1998).

TABLE 12.2

The Big Five Factor Model

Conscientiousness	organized · · · · · · · · · · · · · disorganized
	careful · · · · · · · · · · · · · · · careless
	self-disciplined · · · · · · · · · · · weak-willed
Agreeableness	softhearted · · · · · · · · · · · · · · ruthless
	trusting · · · · · · · · · · · · · · · suspicious
	helpful · · · · · · · · · · · · · · uncooperative
Neuroticism	worried · · · · · · · · · · · · · · · · · · calm
	insecure · · · · · · · · · · · · · · · · · secure
	self-pitying · · · · · · · · · · · · · self-satisfied
Openness to experience	imaginative · · · · · · · · · · · · down-to-earth
	variety · · · · · · · · · · · · · · · · · routine
	independent · · · · · · · · · · · · · conforming
Extraversion	social · · · · · · · · · · · · · · · · · · retiring
	fun loving · · · · · · · · · · · · · · · · sober
	affectionate · · · · · · · · · · · · · · reserved

Source: McCrae & Costa, 1999, 1990.

Genes, Traits, and Personality

Some of the most compelling evidence for the importance of biological factors in personality comes from the domain of behavioral genetics. Like researchers studying genetic influences on intelligence (see Chapter 10), personality psychologists have looked at correlations between the traits in monozygotic, or identical, twins, who share the same genes, and dizygotic, or fraternal, twins, who on average share only half of their

HOT SCIENCE

Personality on the Surface

When you judge someone as friend or foe, interesting or boring, worth hiring or firing, how do you do it? It's nice to think that your impressions of personality are based on solid foundations—something deep. You wouldn't judge personality based on something as shallow as someone's looks, would you? Or what about the appearance of a person's room? The music the person prefers? The person's web page? These things may seem to be flimsy bases for understanding personality, but it turns out that some valid personality judgments can be made from exactly such superficial cues. And in certain cases, such judgments are remarkably accurate.

People in one study were asked to make personality judgments of the occupants of business offices and dormitory rooms (Gosling et al., 2002). The occupants were not present, though, and photos and identifying information were hidden. So, observers only had the rooms' contents and arrangement to go on. Even with just their offices and rooms as evidence, observ-

ers rating occupants on the Big Five trait dimensions were very accurate in judging openness to experience, and also good at assessing conscientiousness and extraversion. How could they do this? They reported using specific cues: Occupants high in openness had distinctive, unconventional rooms; those high in conscientiousness had spaces that were well organized and uncluttered; those high in extraversion had rooms that were warm, decorated, and inviting. Agreeableness and neuroticism, on the other hand, were not linked to specific room features. Not every personality trait reveals itself in your stuff.

Are music preferences also surface indicators of your personality? A study of the personalities and music picks of some 3,000 students in Texas found several clear links (Rentfrow & Gosling, 2003). People who like their music upbeat and conventional (pop, country) tend to be extraverted, agreeable, and conscientious. Those who prefer music that is energetic and rhythmic (hip-hop or dance) are likely to be extraverted. Those who want music more reflective and complex (jazz, classical) or intense

and rebellious (rock, alternative) are high in openness to experience. You may not think you're revealing your personality by playing your stereo, but you are.

Personality is related to yet other surface characteristics. Extraverts smile more than others and appear more stylish and healthy (Naumann et al., 2009), for example, and people high in openness to experience are more likely to have tattoos and other body modifications (Nathanson, Paulhus, & Williams, 2006). Findings like these suggest that people can manipulate their surface identities to try to make desired impressions on others—and that surface signs of personality might therefore be false or misleading. However, a study of Facebook pages—which are clearly surface expressions of personality intended for others to see—found that the personalities people project online are more highly related to their real personalities than to the personalities they describe as their ideals (Back et al., in press). The signs of personality that appear on the surface may be more than skin deep.

▲ A closet isn't just a place for clothes. In some cases, it's a personality test.

genes. The evidence has been generally consistent: In one review of studies involving over 24,000 twin pairs, for example, identical twins proved markedly more similar to each other in personality than did fraternal twins (Loehlin, 1992).

What do studies of twins tell us about personality?

Simply put, the more genes you have in common with someone, the more similar your personalities are likely to be. Genetics seems to influence most personality traits, and current estimates place the average genetic component of personality in the range of .40 to .60. These heritability coefficients, as you learned in Chapter 10, indicate that roughly half the variability among individuals results from genetic factors (Bouchard & Loehlin, 2001). Genetic factors do not account for everything, certainly—the remaining half of the variability in personality remains to be explained by differences in life experiences and other factors—but they appear to be remarkably influential (see also the Real World box on the next page). Studies of twins suggest that the extent to which the Big Five traits derive from genetic differences ranges from .35 to .49 (see **TABLE 12.3**).

As in the study of intelligence, potential confounding factors must be ruled out to ensure that effects are truly due to genetics and not to environmental experiences. Are identical twins treated more similarly, and do they have a greater *shared environment* than fraternal twins? As children, were they dressed in the same snappy outfits and placed on the same Little League teams, and could this somehow have produced similarities in their personalities? Studies of identical twins reared far apart in adoptive families—an experience that pretty much eliminates the potential effect of shared environmental factors—suggest that shared environments have little impact: Reared-apart identical twins end up at least as similar in personality as those who grow up together (McGue & Bouchard, 1998; Tellegen et al., 1988).

Indeed, one provocative, related finding is that such shared environmental factors as parental divorce or parenting style may have little direct impact on personality (Plomin & Caspi, 1999). According to these researchers, simply growing up in the same family does not make people very similar: In fact, when two siblings are similar, this is thought to be primarily due to genetic similarities.

Researchers have also assessed specific behavioral and attitude similarities in twins, and the evidence for heritability in these studies is often striking. When 3,000 pairs of identical and fraternal twins were asked their opinions on political and social issues, such as the death penalty, censorship, and nudist camps, significantly high heritability estimates were obtained for these and many other attitudes—for example, the score for views on the death penalty was approximately .50 (Martin et al., 1986). A specific gene directly responsible for attitudes on the death penalty or any other specific behavior or attitude is extremely unlikely. Rather, a set of genes—or, more likely, many sets of genes interacting—may produce a specific physiological characteristic such as a tendency to have a strong fear reaction in anticipation of punishment. This biological factor may then shape the person's belief about a range of social issues, perhaps including whether the fear of punishment is effective in deterring criminal behavior (Tesser, 1993).

Do Animals Have Personalities?

Another source of evidence for the biological basis of human personality comes from the study of nonhuman animals. Any dog owner, zookeeper, or cattle farmer can tell you that individual animals have characteristic patterns of behavior. One Missouri woman who reportedly enjoyed raising chickens in her suburban home said that "the best part" was "knowing them as individuals" (Tucker, 2003). As far as we know, this pet owner did not give her feathered companions a personality test, though researcher Sam Gosling (1998) used this approach in a study of a group of spotted hyenas. Well, not exactly. He recruited four human observers to use personality scales to rate the different hyenas in the group. When he examined ratings on the scales, he found five dimensions, of which three closely resembled the Big Five traits of neuroticism (i.e., fearfulness, emotional reactivity), openness to experience (i.e., curiosity), and agreeableness (i.e., absence of aggression).

TABLE 12.3

Heritability Estimates for the Big Five Personality Traits

Trait Dimension	Heritability
Conscientiousness	.38
Agreeableness	.35
Neuroticism	.41
Openness	.45
Extraversion	.49

Source: Loehlin, 1992.

▼ University of Texas graduate student Bryan McCann, member of the Campaign to End the Death Penalty, marches with fellow protestors down Congress Avenue in Austin to call for an end to capital punishment. Many of our opinions and attitudes, such as our view of capital punishment, appear to be shaped by our genes—so odds are that this protest is something his family would approve.

MONTY MARION/STAR PHOTO

Do Different Genders Lead to Different Personalities?

Do you think there is a typical "female" personality or a typical "male" personality? Researchers have found some reliable differences between men and women with respect to their self-reported traits, attitudes, and behaviors (Feingold, 1994). Some of these findings conform to North American stereotypes of "masculine" and "feminine." For example, researchers have found women to be more verbally expressive, more sensitive to nonverbal cues, and more nurturing than are men. Men are more physically aggressive than women, but women engage in more social relationship aggression (e.g., ignoring someone) than do men (Eagly & Steffen, 1986). Other gender differences include more assertiveness, slightly higher self-esteem, a more casual approach to sex, and greater sensation seeking in men compared with women. On the Big Five, women tend to be higher on agreeableness and neuroticism than men, but the genders do not differ in openness to experience. On a variety of other personality characteristics, including helpfulness and sexual desire, men and women on average show no reliable differences. Overall, men and women seem to be far more similar in personality than they are different (Hyde, 2005).

Sex differences in personality can be a hot button topic. For example, the former president of Harvard University, Lawrence Summers, was criticized widely for remarking that women might not have the "intrinsic aptitude" to pursue careers in science—criticism so fierce that it culminated in his resignation. Many people assume, as did Summers, that if men and women are found to differ on a given psychological characteristic, the reason must be biological. And although biology does play a significant role in shaping personality, there is certainly a lot more to being female or male than having a Y or a second X chromosome. Indeed, the evidence for the biological underpinnings of observed personality differences between men and women, such as a possible link between hormones and gender differences in aggression, is as yet inconclusive (Inoff-Germain et al., 1988).

The debate about the origins of gender differences in personality often involves contrasting an evolutionary biological perspective

GIFT OF JEAN AND FRANCIS MARSHALL/BERKELEY ART MUSEUM/PACIFIC FILM ARCHIVE

▲ Cultures differ in their appreciation of male and female characteristics, but the Hindu deity Ardhanarishwara represents the value of combining both parts of human nature. Male on one side and female on the other, this god is symbolic of the dual nature of the sacred. The only real problem with such side-by-side androgyny comes in finding clothes to fit.

with a social cognitive perspective known as *social role theory*. The evolutionary perspective holds that men and women have evolved different personality characteristics in part because their reproductive success depends on different behaviors. For instance, aggressiveness in men may have an adaptive value in intimidating sexual rivals; women who are agreeable and nurturing may have evolved to protect and ensure the survival of their offspring (Campbell, 1999) as well as to secure a reliable mate and provider (Buss, 1989).

According to social role theory, personality characteristics and behavioral differences between men and women result from cultural standards and expectations that assign them—socially permissible jobs, activities, and family positions (Eagly & Wood, 1999). Because of their physical size and their freedom from childbearing, men historically took roles of greater power—roles that in postindustrial society don't necessarily require physical strength. These differences then snowball, with men generally taking roles that require assertiveness and aggression (e.g., executive, school principal, surgeon) and women pursuing roles that emphasize greater supportiveness and nurturance (e.g., nurse, day-care worker, teacher).

Regardless of the source of gender differences in personality, the degree to which people identify personally with masculine and feminine stereotypes may tell us about important personality differences between individuals. Sandra Bem (1974) designed a scale, the Bem Sex Role Inventory, that assesses the degree of identification with stereotypically masculine and feminine traits. Bem suggested that psychologically *androgynous* people—those who adopt the "best of both worlds," identifying both with positive feminine traits (such as kindness) and positive masculine traits (such as assertiveness)—might be better adjusted than are people who identify strongly with only one sex role. Androgyny has benefits (Lefkowitz & Zeldow, 2006), but it is particularly beneficial for women—perhaps because many of the traits stereotypically associated with masculinity (such as assertiveness and achievement) are related to psychological health (Cook, 1985).

Bem Sex Role Inventory Sample Items

Respondents taking the Bem Sex Role Inventory rate themselves on each of the items without seeing the gender categorization. Then the scale is scored for masculinity (use of stereotypically masculine items), femininity (use of stereotypically feminine items), and androgyny (the tendency to use both the stereotypically masculine and feminine adjectives to describe oneself) (Bem, 1974).

Masculine items:	Feminine items:
Self-reliant	Yielding
Defends own beliefs	Affectionate
Independent	Flatterable
Assertive	Sympathetic
Forceful	Sensitive to the needs of others

In similar studies of guppies and octopi, individual differences in traits resembling extraversion and neuroticism were reliably observed (Gosling & John, 1999). In each study, researchers identified particular behaviors that they felt reflected each trait based on their observation of the animals' normal repertoire of activities. Octopi, for example, seldom get invited out to parties, and so they cannot be assessed for their socializing tendencies ("He was all hands!"), but they do vary in terms of whether they prefer to eat in the safety of their den or are willing to venture out at feeding time, and so a behavior that corresponds to extraversion can reasonably be assessed (Gosling & John, 1999). Because different observers seem to agree on where an animal falls on a given dimension, the findings do not simply reflect a particular observer's imagination or tendency to *anthropomorphize*, that is, to attribute human characteristics to nonhuman animals. Such findings of cross-species commonality in behavioral styles help support the idea that there are biological mechanisms that underlie personality traits shared by many species.

◄ How would you rate this duck? Is it antagonistic or agreeable? Neurotic or emotionally stable? Researchers have found that even animals appear to have personalities. Or should they be called animalities?

GK HART/VIKKI HART/PUNCHSTOCK/GETTY IMAGES

From an evolutionary perspective, differences in personality reflect alternative adaptations that species—human and nonhuman—have evolved to deal with the challenges of survival and reproduction. For example, if you were to hang around a bar for an evening or two, you would soon see that humans have evolved more than one way to attract and keep a mate. People who are extraverted would probably show off to attract attention, whereas you'd be likely to see people high in agreeableness displaying affection and nurturance (Buss, 1996). Both approaches might work well to attract mates and reproduce successfully—depending on the environment. Through this process of natural selection, those characteristics that have proved successful in our evolutionary struggle for survival have been passed on to future generations.

? Why study animal behavioral styles?

Traits in the Brain

But what neurophysiological mechanisms influence the development of personality traits? Much of the thinking on this topic has focused on the extraversion-introversion dimension. In his personality model, Eysenck (1967) speculated that extraversion and introversion might arise from individual differences in alertness. Extraverts may need to seek out social interaction, parties, and even mayhem in the attempt to achieve full mental stimulation, whereas introverts may avoid these situations because they are so sensitive that such stimulation is unpleasant.

Eysenck argued that differences in levels of cortical arousal underlie differences between extraverts and introverts. Extraverts pursue stimulation because their *reticular formation*—the part of the brain that regulates arousal, or alertness (as described in Chapter 3)—is not easily stimulated. To achieve greater cortical arousal and feel fully alert, Eysenck argued, extraverts are drawn to activities such as listening to loud music and having a lot of social contact. In contrast, introverts may prefer reading or quiet activities because their cortex is very easily stimulated to a point higher than optimal.

? What neurological differences explain why extraverts pursue more stimulation than introverts?

▼ Is Lady Gaga an extravert? Her publicity website notes that, as a child, she would innocently greet a new babysitter with nothing on but her birthday suit. Yes, probably an extravert.

KEVIN MAZUR/WIREIMAGE/GETTY IMAGES

Behavioral and physiological research generally supports Eysenck's view. When introverts and extraverts are presented with a range of intense stimuli, introverts respond more strongly, including salivating more when a drop of lemon juice is placed on their tongues and reacting more negatively to electric shocks or loud noises (Bartol & Costello, 1976; Stelmack, 1990). This reactivity has an impact on the ability to concentrate: Extraverts tend to perform well at tasks that are done in a noisy, arousing context—such as bartending or teaching—whereas introverts are better at tasks that require concentration in tranquil contexts—such as the work of a librarian or nighttime security guard (Geen, 1984; Lieberman & Rosenthal, 2001; Matthews & Gilliland, 1999).

In a refined version of Eysenck's ideas about arousability, Jeffrey Gray (1970) proposed that the dimensions of extraversion/introversion and neuroticism reflect two basic brain systems. The *behavioral activation system (BAS)*, essentially a "go" system, activates approach behavior in response to the anticipation of reward. The extravert has a highly reactive BAS and will actively engage the environment, seeking social reinforcement and on the "go." The *behavioral inhibition system (BIS)*, a "stop" system, inhibits behavior in response to stimuli signaling punishment. The emotionally unstable person, in turn, has a highly reactive BIS and will focus on negative outcomes and be on the lookout for "stop" signs. Because these two systems operate independently, it is possible for someone to be both a "go" and a "stop" person, simultaneously activated and inhibited—and caught in a constant conflict between these two traits. Studies of brain electrical activity (EEG) and functional brain imaging (fMRI) suggest that individual differences in activation and inhibition arise through the operation of distinct brain systems underlying these tendencies (DeYoung & Gray, 2009).

IN SUMMARY

○ The trait approach tries to identify personality dimensions that can be used to characterize an individual's behavior. Researchers have attempted to boil down the potentially huge array of things people do, think, and feel into some core personality dimensions.

○ Many personality psychologists currently focus on the Big Five personality factors: conscientiousness, agreeableness, neuroticism, openness to experience, and extraversion.

○ To address the question of why traits arise, trait theorists often adopt a biological perspective, seeing personality largely as the result of genetic influences on brain mechanisms.

▲ Sigmund Freud was the first psychology theorist to be honored with his own bobble-head doll. Let's hope he's not the last.

THE PHOTO WORKS

The Psychodynamic Approach: Forces That Lie beneath Awareness

Rather than trying to understand personality in terms of broad theories for describing individual differences, Freud looked for personality in the details—the meanings and insights revealed by careful analysis of the tiniest blemishes in a person's thought and behavior. Working with patients who came to him with disorders that did not seem to have any physical basis, he began by interpreting the origins of their everyday mistakes and memory lapses—errors that have come to be called "Freudian slips."

Freud used the term *psychoanalysis* to refer to both his theory of personality and his method of treating patients. Freud's ideas were the first of many theories building on his basic idea that personality is a mystery to the person who "owns" it because we can't know our own deepest motives. The theories of Freud and his followers (discussed in Chapter 15) are referred to as the **psychodynamic approach**. According to this approach, *personality is formed by needs, strivings, and desires largely operating outside of awareness—motives that can produce emotional disorders*. The real engines of personality, in this view, are forces of which we are largely unaware.

Psychologists call this construct the **dynamic unconscious**—*an active system encompassing a lifetime of hidden memories, the person's deepest instincts and desires, and the person's inner struggle to control these forces*. The power of the unconscious comes from its early origins—experiences that shaped the mind before a person could even put thoughts and feelings into words—and from its contents, which are embarrassing, unspeakable, and even frightening because they operate without any control by consciousness. Imagine having violent competitive feelings toward your father ("I wish I could beat the old man at something, or just beat him up") or a death wish toward a sibling ("It would be so great if my snotty sister just fell down a well"). Whew! Impulses like that are assumed to remain in the unconscious because such powerful forces would be too much for consciousness to bear. This battle goes on beneath the surface in an ongoing struggle among parts of the mind.

The Structure of the Mind: Id, Ego, and Superego

To explain the emotional difficulties that beset his patients, Freud proposed that the mind consists of three independent, interacting, and often conflicting systems: the id, the ego, and the superego.

The most basic system, the **id,** is *the part of the mind containing the drives present at birth; it is the source of our bodily needs, wants, desires, and impulses, particularly our sexual and aggressive drives.* The id operates according to the *pleasure principle,* the psychic force that motivates the tendency to seek immediate gratification of any impulse. If governed by the id alone, you would never be able to tolerate the buildup of hunger while waiting to be served at a restaurant but would simply grab food from tables nearby.

All that the id can do is wish. The **ego** is *the component of personality, developed through contact with the external world, that enables us to deal with life's practical demands.* The ego operates according to the *reality principle,* the regulating mechanism that enables the individual to delay gratifying immediate needs and function effectively in the real world. The ego helps you resist the impulse to snatch others' food and also finds the restaurant and pays the check.

The final system of the mind is the **superego,** *the mental system that reflects the internalization of cultural rules, mainly learned as parents exercise their authority.* The superego consists of a set of guidelines, internal standards, and other codes of conduct that regulate and control our behaviors, thoughts, and fantasies. It acts as a kind of conscience, punishing us when it finds we are doing or thinking something wrong (by producing guilt or other painful feelings) and rewarding us (with feelings of pride or self-congratulation) for living up to ideal standards.

▼ Cigar, pencil, skyscraper, hammer . . . zeppelin? Freud believed that the id represents its wishes in terms of symbols. He would probably have been delighted with the symbolic objects in this photo.

◀ The timeless illustration of the "bad side" and "good side" fighting for the person's mind resembles what Freud described as the inner struggle between id and superego for control of the ego.

psychodynamic approach An approach that regards personality as formed by needs, strivings, and desires largely operating outside of awareness—motives that can also produce emotional disorders.

dynamic unconscious An active system encompassing a lifetime of hidden memories, the person's deepest instincts and desires, and the person's inner struggle to control these forces.

id The part of the mind containing the drives present at birth; it is the source of our bodily needs, wants, desires, and impulses, particularly our sexual and aggressive drives.

ego The component of personality, developed through contact with the external world, that enables us to deal with life's practical demands.

superego The mental system that reflects the internalization of cultural rules, mainly learned as parents exercise their authority.

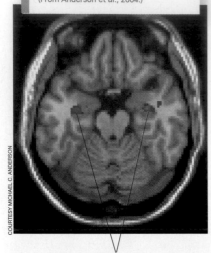

▼ FIGURE 12.4
Decreased Hippocampal Activity during Memory Suppression fMRI scans of people intentionally trying to forget a list of words reveal reduced activation (shown in blue) in the left and right hippocampal areas.
(From Anderson et al., 2004.)

Hippocampus

defense mechanisms Unconscious coping mechanisms that reduce anxiety generated by threats from unacceptable impulses.

rationalization A defense mechanism that involves supplying a reasonable-sounding explanation for unacceptable feelings and behavior to conceal (mostly from oneself) one's underlying motives or feelings.

reaction formation A defense mechanism that involves unconsciously replacing threatening inner wishes and fantasies with an exaggerated version of their opposite.

projection A defense mechanism that involves attributing one's own threatening feelings, motives, or impulses to another person or group.

According to Freud, the relative strength of the interactions among the three systems of mind—that is, which system is usually dominant—determines an individual's basic personality structure. The id force of personal needs, the superego force of social pressures to quell those needs, and the ego force of reality's demands together create constant controversy, almost like a puppet theater or a bad play.

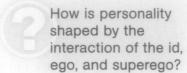 How is personality shaped by the interaction of the id, ego, and superego?

Dealing with Inner Conflict

According to Freud, the dynamics among the id, ego, and superego are largely governed by *anxiety,* an unpleasant feeling that arises when unwanted thoughts or feelings occur—such as when the id seeks a gratification that the ego thinks will lead to real-world dangers or the superego sees as eliciting punishment. When the ego receives an "alert signal" in the form of anxiety, it launches into a defensive position in an attempt to ward off the anxiety. According to Freud, it first tries *repression,* which, as you read in Chapter 5, is a mental process that removes painful experiences and unacceptable impulses from the conscious mind. Repression is sometimes referred to as "motivated forgetting." Indeed, functional imaging studies suggest the repression of memories may involve decreased activation of the hippocampus—a region (as discussed in Chapter 6) that is central to memory (Anderson et al., 2004) (see **FIGURE 12.4**).

Repression may not be adequate to keep unacceptable drives from entering consciousness. When such material begins to surface, the ego can employ other means of self-deception, called **defense mechanisms**, which are *unconscious coping mechanisms that reduce anxiety generated by threats from unacceptable impulses.* Anna Freud (1936), Freud's daughter and a psychodynamic theorist, identified a number of defense mechanisms and detailed how they operate. Let's look at a few of the most common.

> **Rationalization** is *a defense mechanism that involves supplying a reasonable-sounding explanation for unacceptable feelings and behavior to conceal (mostly from oneself) one's underlying motives or feelings.* For example, someone who drops a class after having failed an exam might tell herself that she is quitting because poor ventilation in the classroom made it impossible to concentrate.

> **Reaction formation** is *a defense mechanism that involves unconsciously replacing threatening inner wishes and fantasies with an exaggerated version of their opposite.* Examples include being excessively nice to someone you dislike, finding yourself very worried and protective about a person you have thoughts of hurting, or being cold and indifferent toward someone to whom you are strongly attracted. A revealing example of reaction formation was discovered in research on men who report *homophobia*—the dread of gay men and lesbians (Adams, Wright, & Lohr, 1996). Homophobic participants, heterosexual men who agreed with statements such as "I would feel nervous being with a group of homosexuals," and a comparison group of nonhomophobic men were shown videos of sexual activity, including heterosexual, gay male, and lesbian segments. Each man's sexual arousal was then assessed by means of a device that measures penile swelling. Curiously, the homophobic men showed greater arousal to the male homosexual images than did men in a control group. The psychoanalytic interpretation seems clear: Men troubled by their own homosexual arousal formed opposite reactions to this unacceptable feeling, turning their unwanted attraction into "dread."

> **Projection** is *a defense mechanism that involves attributing one's own threatening feelings, motives, or impulses to another person or group.* For example, people who think that they themselves are overly rigid or dishonest may have a tendency to judge other people as having the same qualities (Newman, Baumeister, & Duff, 1995).

> **Regression** is *a defense mechanism in which the ego deals with internal conflict and perceived threat by reverting to an immature behavior or earlier stage of development,* a time when things felt safer and more secure. Examples of regression include the use of baby talk or whining in a child (or adult) who has already mastered appropriate speech or a return to thumb sucking, teddy bear cuddling, or watching cartoons in response to something distressing.

The youngest daughter of Sigmund Freud, Anna Freud (1895–1982) was a psychodynamic theorist who made many contributions to psychoanalysis. She is particularly well known for advancing the understanding of psychological defense mechanisms. This photo was taken in 1914.

FREUD MUSEUM, LONDON

> **Displacement** is *a defense mechanism that involves shifting unacceptable wishes or drives to a neutral or less threatening alternative.* Displacement should be familiar to you if you've ever slammed a door, thrown a textbook across a room, or yelled at your roommate or your cat when you were really angry at your boss.

> **Identification** is *a defense mechanism that helps deal with feelings of threat and anxiety by enabling us unconsciously to take on the characteristics of another person who seems more powerful or better able to cope.* A child whose parent bullies or severely punishes her may later take on the characteristics of that parent and begin bullying others.

> **Sublimation** is *a defense mechanism that involves channeling unacceptable sexual or aggressive drives into socially acceptable and culturally enhancing activities.* Football, rugby, and other contact sports, for example, may be construed as culturally sanctioned and valued activities that channel our aggressive drives.

regression A defense mechanism in which the ego deals with internal conflict and perceived threat by reverting to an immature behavior or earlier stage of development.

displacement A defense mechanism that involves shifting unacceptable wishes or drives to a neutral or less-threatening alternative.

identification A defense mechanism that helps deal with feelings of threat and anxiety by enabling us unconsciously to take on the characteristics of another person who seems more powerful or better able to cope.

sublimation A defense mechanism that involves channeling unacceptable sexual or aggressive drives into socially acceptable and culturally enhancing activities.

Through reaction formation, a person defends against underlying feelings, such as covering hostility with an exaggerated display of affection. Maybe there's more to this sibling squeeze than love?

TODD WARNOCK/GETTY IMAGES

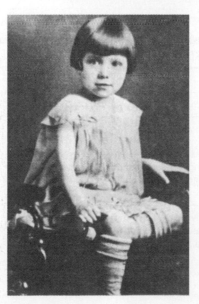

A photo of regression? The young woman shown in the photograph on the left grew up under harsh circumstances: family strife, instability, and substance abuse, among other horrors. At age 17, she discovered a photograph of herself taken when she was 5 years old (middle), after which she adopted the look and mannerisms of a 5-year-old child. The image on the right shows the same woman after regression. (Masserman, 1961.)

"I'm sorry, I'm not speaking to anyone tonight. My defense mechanisms seem to be out of order."

Defense mechanisms are useful (Cramer, 2008). They help us overcome anxiety and engage effectively with the outside world. The ego's capacity to use defense mechanisms in a healthy and flexible fashion may depend on the nature of early experiences with caregivers, the defense mechanisms they used, and possibly some biological and temperamental factors as well (McWilliams, 1994). Our characteristic style of defense becomes our signature in dealing with the world—and an essential aspect of our personality.

How can our defense mechanisms be useful?

Psychosexual Stages and the Development of Personality

Freud had a great talent for coming up with troubling, highly controversial ideas. People in Victorian society did not openly discuss how much fun it is to suck on things, or the frustrations of their own toilet training, or their childhood sexual desire for their mother. Many consider Freud's views on personality development to be fanciful or just plain rude, and they are no longer widely held because little research evidence supports them; nevertheless, people find this part of his legacy oddly fascinating.

Freud believed that a person's basic personality is formed before 6 years of age during a series of sensitive periods, or life stages, when experiences influence all that will follow. Freud called these periods **psychosexual stages**, defined as *distinct early life stages through which personality is formed as children experience sexual pleasures from specific body areas and caregivers redirect or interfere with those pleasures*. He argued that as a result of adult interference with pleasure-seeking energies, the child experiences conflict. At each stage, a different bodily region, or *erotogenic* zone, dominates the child's subjective experience—for example, during the oral stage, pleasure centers on the mouth. Each region represents a battleground between the child's id impulses and the adult external world. **TABLE 12.4** provides a summary of the psychosexual stages.

Problems and conflicts encountered at any psychosexual stage, Freud believed, will influence personality in adulthood. Conflict resulting from a person's being deprived or, paradoxically, overindulged at a given stage could result in **fixation**, meaning that the *person's pleasure-seeking drives become stuck, or arrested, at that psychosexual stage*. Freud described particular personality traits as being derived from fixations at the different psychosexual stages. Here's how he explained the effects of fixation.

psychosexual stages Distinct early life stages through which personality is formed as children experience sexual pleasures from specific body areas and caregivers redirect or interfere with those pleasures.

fixation A phenomenon in which a person's pleasure-seeking drives become psychologically stuck, or arrested, at a particular psychosexual stage.

oral stage The first psychosexual stage, in which experience centers on the pleasures and frustrations associated with the mouth, sucking, and being fed.

anal stage The second psychosexual stage, which is dominated by the pleasures and frustrations associated with the anus, retention and expulsion of feces and urine, and toilet training.

phallic stage The third psychosexual stage, during which experience is dominated by the pleasure, conflict, and frustration associated with the phallic-genital region as well as coping with powerful incestuous feelings of love, hate, jealousy, and conflict.

Oedipus conflict A developmental experience in which a child's conflicting feelings toward the opposite-sex parent are (usually) resolved by identifying with the same-sex parent.

latency stage The fourth psychosexual stage, in which the primary focus is on the further development of intellectual, creative, interpersonal, and athletic skills.

genital stage The final psychosexual stage, a time for the coming together of the mature adult personality with a capacity to love, work, and relate to others in a mutually satisfying and reciprocal manner.

TABLE 12.4					
The Psychosexual Stages					
Stage	**Oral**	**Anal**	**Phallic**	**Latency**	**Genital**
Age	0–18 months	2–3 years	3–5 years	5–13 years	Adulthood
Erotogenic zone	Mouth	Anus/urethra	Penis/clitoris	–	Penis/vagina
Areas of conflict with caregiver	Feeding, weaning	Toileting	Masturbation (Oedipus conflict)	–	Adult responsibilities
Associated personality features	Talkative, dependent, addictive, needy	Orderly, controlling, disorganized, sloppy	Flirtatious, vain, jealous, competitive	–	Authentic investments in love and work; capacity for healthy adult relationships

In the first year and a half of life, the infant is in the **oral stage**, *during which experience centers on the pleasures and frustrations associated with the mouth, sucking, and being fed.* Infants who are deprived of pleasurable feeding or indulgently overfed may develop an oral personality; that is, their lives will center on issues related to fullness and emptiness and what they can "take in" from others and the environment. When angry, such people may express themselves with "biting" sarcasm and "mouth off" at others—referred to as *oral aggression.* Personality traits associated with the oral stage include depression, lack of trust, envy, and demandingness.

Between 2 and 3 years of age, the child moves on to the **anal stage**, *during which experience is dominated by the pleasures and frustrations associated with the anus, retention and expulsion of feces and urine, and toilet training.* From the toddler's perspective, the soiling of one's diapers is a wonderful convenience that can feel pretty good. But sooner or later caregivers begin to disagree, and their opinions are voiced more strongly as the child gets older. Individuals who have had difficulty negotiating this conflict may develop a rigid personality and remain preoccupied with issues of control of others and of themselves and their emotions. They may be preoccupied with their possessions, money, issues of submission and rebellion, and concerns about cleanliness versus messiness.

Between the ages of 3 and 5 years, the child is in the **phallic stage**, *during which experience is dominated by the pleasure, conflict, and frustration associated with the phallic-genital region as well as coping with powerful incestuous feelings of love, hate, jealousy, and conflict.* In part, parental concerns about the child's developing awareness of the genital region set off the conflict: The child may touch his or her genitals in public or explore masturbation and may be curious about the parent's genitals.

According to Freud, boys in the phallic stage experience the **Oedipus conflict**, *a developmental experience in which a child's conflicting feelings toward the opposite-sex parent are (usually) resolved by identifying with the same-sex parent.* (In Greek myth, Oedipus was a young man who, unknowingly, killed his father and ended up marrying his mother.) Freud thought that, around age 4 or 5, boys wonder about their love affair with Mommy, noticing she has positive feelings for someone else (Daddy)—and experiencing jealousy. Freud believed individuals must give up their Oedipal desires if they are to be able to move on and build a life with a partner in the future. Males who are unable to resolve the Oedipus conflict and who get stuck in the phallic stage tend to be unusually preoccupied with issues of seduction, jealousy, competition, power, and authority. Females stuck in this phase, Freud thought, would display seductiveness, flirtatiousness, and jealousy.

A more relaxed period in which children are no longer struggling with the power of their sexual and aggressive drives occurs between the ages of 5 and 13, as children experience the **latency stage**, *in which the primary focus is on the further development of intellectual, creative, interpersonal, and athletic skills.* Because Freud believed that the most significant aspects of personality development occur during the first three psychosexual stages (before the age of 5 years), psychodynamic psychologists do not speak of fixation at the latency period. Simply making it to the latency period relatively undisturbed by conflicts of the earlier stages is a sign of healthy personality development.

At puberty and thereafter, the fifth and final stage of personality development occurs. This, the **genital stage,** is *the time for the coming together of the mature adult personality with a capacity to love, work, and relate to others in a mutually satisfying and reciprocal manner.* The degree to which the individual is encumbered by unresolved conflicts at the earlier stages will impact whether he or she will be able to achieve a genital level of development. Freud believed that people who are fixated in a prior stage fail in developing healthy adult sexuality and a well-adjusted adult personality.

What should we make of all this? On the one hand, the psychoanalytic theory of psychosexual stages offers an intriguing picture of early family relationships and the extent to which they allow the child to satisfy basic needs and wishes. The theory

▲ One of the id's desires is to make a fine mess—a desire that is often frustrated early in life, perhaps during the anal stage. Famous painter Jackson Pollack found a way to make extraordinarily fine messes—behavior that at some level all of us envy.

▼ *Oedipus Rex*, Classical Greek Play by Sophocles According to the psychodynamic approach, at 4 or 5 years of age children are in the throes of the Oedipus conflict. At this time, children experience intense feelings of love, hate, jealousy, and anxiety related to their longings toward their parents and the wish for an exclusive love relationship with their fathers or mothers.

"During the next stage of my development, Dad, I'll be drawing closer to my mother—I'll get back to you in my teens."

picks up on themes that seem to ring true in many cases—you may very well know people who seem to be "oral" or "anal," for example, or who have issues about sexuality that seem to have had a great influence on their personalities. On the other hand, critics argue that psychodynamic explanations are too complex and tend to focus on after-the-fact interpretation rather than testable prediction. Describing a person fixated at the oral stage as "biting," for example, seems just so much wordplay—not the basis of a scientific theory. And the control issues that preoccupy an adult with a so-called anal character might reflect an inborn headstrong and controlling temperament and have nothing to do with a parental style of toilet training. The psychosexual stage theory offers a compelling set of story plots for interpreting lives once they have unfolded but has not generated the kinds of clear-cut predictions that inspire research.

Why do critics say Freud's psychosexual stages are more interpretation than explanation?

IN SUMMARY

○ Freud believed that the personality results from forces that are largely unconscious, shaped by the interplay among id, ego, and superego.

○ Defense mechanisms are methods the mind may use to reduce anxiety generated from unacceptable impulses.

○ Freud also believed that the developing person passes through a series of psychosexual stages and that individuals who fail to progress beyond one of the stages have corresponding personality traits.

The Humanistic-Existential Approach: Personality as Choice

In the 1950s and 1960s, psychologists began to try to understand personality from a viewpoint quite different from trait theory's biological determinism and Freud's focus on unconscious drives from unresolved child experiences. These new humanistic and existential theorists turned attention to how humans make *healthy choices* that create their personalities. *Humanistic psychologists* emphasized a positive, optimistic view of human nature that highlights people's inherent goodness and their potential for personal growth. *Existentialist psychologists* focused on the individual as a responsible agent who is free to create and live his or her life while negotiating the issue of meaning and the reality of death. The *humanistic-existential approach* integrates these insights with a focus on how a personality can become optimal.

Human Needs and Self-Actualization

Humanists see the **self-actualizing tendency**, *the human motive toward realizing our inner potential*, as a major factor in personality. The pursuit of knowledge, the expression of one's creativity, the quest for spiritual enlightenment, and the desire to give to society are all examples of self-actualization. As you saw in Chapter 8, the noted humanistic theorist Abraham Maslow (1970) proposed a *hierarchy of needs*, a model of essential human needs arranged according to their priority, in which basic physiological and safety needs must be satisfied before a person can afford to focus on higher-level psychological needs. Only when these basic needs are satisfied can you pursue higher needs, culminating in *self-actualization*—the need to be good, to be fully alive, and to find meaning in life.

What is it to be self-actualized?

self-actualizing tendency The human motive toward realizing our inner potential.

◄ Being All You Can Be The area called "Garbage City" outside Cairo is becoming known as one of the "green" places on Earth. Recycling and repurposing salvages almost 80% of waste here. To self-actualize, you don't have to start with much.

Humanist psychologists explain individual personality differences as arising from the various ways that the environment facilitates—or blocks—attempts to satisfy psychological needs. Like a wilting plant deprived of water, sunshine, and nutrients, an individual growing up in an arid social environment can fail to develop his or her unique potential. For example, someone with the inherent potential to be a great scientist, artist, parent, or teacher might never realize these talents if his or her energies and resources are instead directed toward meeting basic needs of security, belongingness, and the like. Research indicates that when people shape their lives around goals that do not match their true nature and capabilities, they are less likely to be happy than those whose lives and goals do match (Ryan & Deci, 2000).

It feels great to be doing exactly what you are capable of doing. Mihaly Csikszentmihalyi (1990) found that engagement in tasks that exactly match one's abilities creates a mental state of energized focus that he called *flow* (see **FIGURE 12.5**). Tasks that are below our abilities cause boredom, those that are too challenging cause anxiety, and those that are "just right" lead to the experience of flow. If you know how to play the piano, for example, and are playing a Chopin prelude that you know well enough that it just matches your abilities, you are likely to experience this optimal state. People report being happier at these times than at any other times. Humanists believe that such peak experiences, or states of flow, reflect the realization of one's human potential and represent the height of personality development.

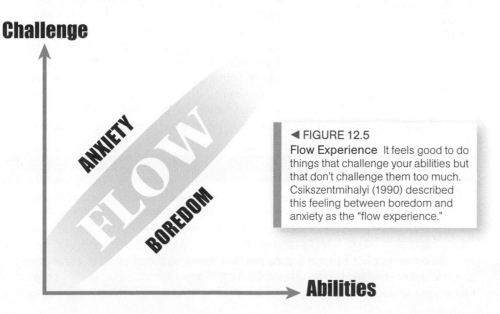

◄ FIGURE 12.5
Flow Experience It feels good to do things that challenge your abilities but that don't challenge them too much. Csikszentmihalyi (1990) described this feeling between boredom and anxiety as the "flow experience."

existential approach A school of thought that regards personality as governed by an individual's ongoing choices and decisions in the context of the realities of life and death.

social cognitive approach An approach that views personality in terms of how the person thinks about the situations encountered in daily life and behaves in response to them.

person-situation controversy The question of whether behavior is caused more by personality or by situational factors.

Personality as Existence

Existentialists agree with humanists about many of the features of personality but focus on challenges to the human condition that are more profound than the lack of a nurturing environment. Rollo May (1983) and Victor Frankl (2000), for example, argued that specific aspects of the human condition, such as awareness of our own existence and the ability to make choices about how to behave, have a double-edged quality: They bring an extraordinary richness and dignity to human life, but they also force us to confront realities that are difficult to face, such as the prospect of our own death. The **existential approach** *regards personality as governed by an individual's ongoing choices and decisions in the context of the realities of life and death.*

According to the existential perspective, the difficulties we face in finding meaning in life and in accepting the responsibility of making free choices provoke a type of anxiety existentialists call *angst* (the anxiety of fully being). The human ability to consider limitless numbers of goals and actions is exhilarating, but it can also open the door to profound questions such as "Why am I here?" and "What is the meaning of my life?"

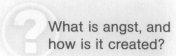
What is angst, and how is it created?

Thinking about the meaning of existence also can evoke an awareness of the inevitability of death. What, then, should we do with each moment? What is the purpose of living if life as we know it will end one day, perhaps even today? Alternatively, does life have more meaning given that it is so temporary? Existential theorists do not suggest that people consider these profound existential issues on a day-to-day and moment-to-moment basis. Rather than ruminate about death and meaning, people typically pursue superficial answers that help them deal with the angst and dread they experience, and the defenses they construct form the basis of their personalities (Binswanger, 1958; May, 1983).

Unfortunately, security-providing defense mechanisms can be self-defeating and stifle the potential for personal growth. The pursuit of superficial relationships can make possible the avoidance of real intimacy. A fortress of consumer goods can provide a false sense of security. Immersion in drugs or addictive behaviors such as compulsive web browsing, video gaming, or television watching can numb the mind to existential realities.

If defenses are so thin and pointless, how do you deal with existence? For existentialists, the solution is to face the issues square-on and learn to accept and tolerate the pain of existence. Indeed, being fully human means confronting existential realities rather than denying them or embracing comforting illusions. This requires the courage to accept the inherent anxiety and the dread of nonbeing that is part of being alive. Such courage may be bolstered by developing supportive relationships with others who can supply unconditional positive regard. There's something about being loved that helps take away the angst.

IN SUMMARY

○ The humanistic-existential approach to personality grew out of philosophical traditions that are at odds with most of the assumptions of the trait and psychoanalytic approaches.

○ Humanists see personality as directed by an inherent striving toward self-actualization and development of our unique human potentials.

○ Existentialists focus on angst and the defensive response people often have to questions about the meaning of life and the inevitability of death.

The Social Cognitive Approach: Personalities in Situations

What is it like to be a person? The social cognitive approach to personality explores what it is like to be the person who tries to understand what to do in life's many encounters with people, events, and situations. The **social cognitive approach** *views personality in terms of how the person thinks about the situations encountered in daily life and behaves in response to them.* Bringing together insights from social psychology, cognitive psychology, and learning theory, this approach emphasizes how the person experiences and construes situations (Bandura, 1986; Mischel & Shoda, 1999; Ross & Nisbett, 1991; Wegner & Gilbert, 2000).

The idea that situations cause behavior became clear in basic studies of learning. Consider how the late B. F. Skinner, the strict behaviorist and observer of rats and pigeons (see Chapter 7), would explain your behavior right now. If you have been reinforced in the past by getting good grades when studying only the night before an exam, he would have predicted that you are in fact reading these words for the first time the night before the test! If you have been reinforced for studying well in advance, he would have predicted that you are reading this chapter with plenty of time to spare. For a behaviorist, then, differences in behavior patterns reflect differences in how the behaviors have been rewarded in past situations.

Researchers in social cognition agree that the situation and learning history are key determinants of behavior, but they go much further than Skinner would have in looking inside the psychological "black box" of the mind to examine the thoughts and feelings that come between the situation and the person's response to it. Because human "situations" and "reinforcements" are radically open to interpretation, social cognitive psychologists focus on how people *perceive* their environments. People think about their goals, the consequences of their behavior, and how they might achieve certain things in different situations (Lewin, 1951). The social cognitive approach looks at how personality and situation interact to cause behavior, how personality contributes to the way people construct situations in their own minds, and how people's goals and expectancies influence their responses to situations.

> **How do researchers in social cognition agree with behaviorists and how do they disagree?**

▲ **The Situation** Mike "The Situation" Sorrentino is a character on the *Jersey Shore* reality TV show. Sometimes personalities think they're situations.

SCOTT GRIES/PICTURE GROUP

Consistency of Personality across Situations

Although social cognitive psychologists attribute behavior both to the individual's personality and to his or her situation, situation can often trump personality. For example, a person would have to be pretty strange to act exactly the same way at a memorial service and at a toga party. In their belief that the strong push and pull of situations can influence almost everyone, social cognitive psychologists are somewhat at odds with the basic assumptions of classic personality psychology—that is, that personality characteristics (such as traits, needs, unconscious drives) cause people to behave in the same way across situations and over time. At the core of the social cognitive approach is a natural puzzle, the **person-situation controversy**, which focuses on *the question of whether behavior is caused more by personality or by situational factors.*

This controversy began in earnest when Walter Mischel (1968) argued that measured personality traits often do a poor job of predicting individuals' behavior. Mischel reviewed decades of research that compared scores on standard personality tests with actual behavior, looking at evidence from studies asking questions such as, "Does a person with a high score on a test of introversion actually spend more time alone than someone with a low score?" Mischel's disturbing conclusion: The average correlation between trait and behavior is only about .30. This is certainly better than zero (i.e., chance) but not very good when you remember that a perfect prediction is represented by a correlation of 1.0.

▼ Is a student who cheats on a test more likely than others to steal candy or lie to her grandmother? Social cognitive research indicates that behavior in one situation does not necessarily predict behavior in a different situation.

DIGITAL VISION/GETTYIMAGES

CULTURE & COMMUNITY

Does your personality change according to which language you're speaking? The personalities of people in groups speaking different languages often can diverge. A study revealed that personality tests taken by English-speaking Americans and Spanish-speaking Mexicans differ reliably: The Americans were found to be more extraverted, more agreeable, and more conscientious than the Mexicans (Ramirez-Esparza et al., 2004). But why? To see if language might play a role in this difference, the researchers then sought out Spanish-English bilinguals in Texas, California, and Mexico and gave them the personality scale in each language. And in fact, language was a key: Scores of the bilingual participants were more extraverted, agreeable, and conscientious when they took the test in English than when they took it in Spanish. Personality may be influenced by the group you belong to because of the language you are speaking.

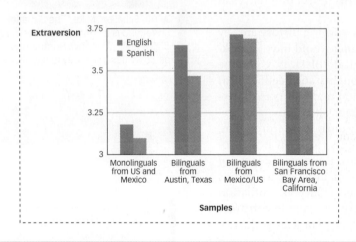

Mischel also noted that knowing how a person will behave in one situation is not particularly helpful in predicting the person's behavior in another situation. For example, in classic studies Hartshorne and May (1928) assessed children's honesty by examining their willingness to cheat on a test and found that such dishonesty was not consistent from one situation to another. The assessment of a child's trait of honesty in a cheating situation was of almost no use in predicting whether the child would act honestly in a different situation—such as when given the opportunity to steal money. Mischel proposed that measured traits do not predict behaviors very well because behaviors are determined more by situational factors than personality theorists were willing to acknowledge.

Is there no personality, then? Do we all just do what situations require? The person-situation controversy has inspired many studies in the years since Mischel's critique, and it turns out that information about both personality and situation are necessary to predict behavior (Fleeson, 2004; Mischel, 2004). Some situations are particularly powerful, leading most everyone to behave similarly regardless of personality (Cooper & Withey, 2009). At a funeral, after all, most everyone looks somber, and at an earthquake, most everyone shakes. But in situations that are weaker, personality can come forward to influence behavior (Funder, 2001). Among the children in Hartshorne and May's studies, cheating versus not cheating on a test was actually a fairly good predictor of cheating on a test later—as long as the situation was similar (Hartshorne & May, 1928). Personality consistency, then, appears to be a matter of when and where a certain kind of behavior tends to be shown (see the Culture & Community box). Social cognitive theorists believe these patterns of personality consistency in response to situations arise from the way different people construe situations and from the ways different people pursue goals within situations.

Personal Constructs

How can we understand differences in the way situations are interpreted? Recall our notion of personality often existing "in the eye of the beholder." Situations may exist "in the eye of the beholder" as well. One person's gold mine may be another person's hole in the dirt. George Kelly (1955) long ago realized that these differences in perspective could be used to understand the *perceiver's* personality. He suggested that people view the social world from differing perspectives and that these different views arise through the application of **personal constructs,** *dimensions people use in making sense of their experiences.* Consider, for example, different individuals' personal constructs of a clown: One person may see him as a source of fun, another as a tragic figure, and yet another as so frightening that the circus is off-limits.

Why doesn't everyone love clowns?

Here's how Kelly assessed personal constructs about social relationships: He'd ask people to (1) list the people in their life, (2) consider three of the people and state a way in which two of them were similar to each other and different from the third, and

personal constructs Dimensions people use in making sense of their experiences.

outcome expectancies A person's assumptions about the likely consequences of a future behavior.

locus of control A person's tendency to perceive the control of rewards as internal to the self or external in the environment.

(3) repeat this for other triads of people to produce a list of the dimensions used to classify friends and family. One respondent might focus on the degree to which people (self included) are lazy or hardworking, for example; someone else might attend to the degree to which people are sociable or unfriendly.

Kelly proposed that different personal constructs (*construals*) are the key to personality differences—that is, that different construals lead to disparate behaviors. Taking a long break from work for a leisurely lunch might seem lazy to you. To your friend, the break might seem an ideal opportunity for catching up with friends, so he will wonder why you always choose to eat at your desk. Social cognitive theory explains different responses to situations with the idea that people see things in different ways.

Personal Goals and Expectancies

Social cognitive theories also recognize that a person's unique perspective on situations is reflected in his or her personal goals, which are often conscious. In fact, people can usually tell you their goals, whether they are to "find a date for this weekend," "get a good grade in psych," "establish a fulfilling career," or just "get this darn bag of chips open." These goals often reflect the tasks that are appropriate to the person's situation and in a larger sense fit the person's role and stage of life (Cantor, 1990; Klinger, 1977; Little, 1983; Vallacher & Wegner, 1985). For instance, common goals for adolescents include being popular, achieving greater independence from parents and family, and getting into their first-choice college. Common goals for adults include developing a meaningful career, finding a mate, securing financial stability, and starting a family.

People translate goals into behavior in part through **outcome expectancies**, *a person's assumptions about the likely consequences of a future behavior.* Just as a laboratory rat learns that pressing a bar releases a food pellet, we learn that "if I am friendly toward people, they will be friendly in return" or "if I ask people to pull my finger, they will withdraw from me." So we learn to perform behaviors that we expect will have the outcome of moving us closer to our goals. Outcome expectancies are learned through direct experience, both bitter and sweet, and through merely observing other people's actions and their consequences.

Outcome expectancies combine with a person's goals to produce the person's characteristic style of behavior. An individual with the goal of making friends and the expectancy that being kind will produce warmth in return is likely to behave very differently from an individual whose goal is to achieve fame at any cost and who believes that shameless self-promotion is the route to fame. We do not all want the same things from life, clearly, and our personalities largely reflect the goals we pursue and the expectancies we have about the best ways to pursue them.

People differ in their generalized expectancy for achieving goals. Some people seem to feel that they are fully in control of what happens to them in life, whereas others feel that the world doles out rewards and punishments to them irrespective of their actions. Julian Rotter (1966) developed a questionnaire (see **TABLE 12.5** on the next page) to measure *a person's tendency to perceive the control of rewards as internal to the self or external in the environment,* a disposition he called **locus of control**. People whose answers suggest that they believe they control their own destiny are said to have an *internal* locus of control, whereas those who believe that outcomes are random, determined by luck, or controlled by other people are described as having an *external* locus of control. These beliefs translate into individual differences in emotion and behavior. For example, people with an internal locus of

What is the advantage of an internal locus of control?

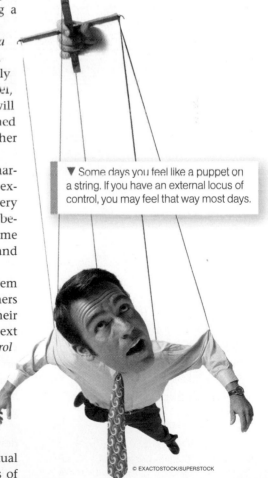

▲ Are two of these people taller and one shorter? Are two bare-headed while one wears a hood? Or are two the daughters and one the mom? George Kelly held that the personal constructs we use to distinguish among people in our lives are basic elements of our own personalities.

▼ Some days you feel like a puppet on a string. If you have an external locus of control, you may feel that way most days.

© EXACTOSTOCK/SUPERSTOCK

TABLE 12.5

Rotter's Locus-of-Control Scale

For each pair of items, choose the option that most closely reflects your personal belief. Then turn the book upside down to see if you have more of an internal or external locus of control.

1. a. Many of the unhappy things in people's lives are partly due to bad luck.
   b. People's misfortunes result from the mistakes they make.

2. a. I have often found that what is going to happen will happen.
   b. Trusting to fate has never turned out as well for me as making a decision to take a definite course of action.

3. a. Becoming a success is a matter of hard work; luck has little or nothing to do with it.
   b. Getting a good job depends mainly on being in the right place at the right time.

4. a. When I make plans, I am almost certain that I can make them work.
   b. It is not always wise to plan too far ahead because many things turn out to be a matter of good or bad fortune anyhow.

Source: Rotter, 1966.

Answer: A more internal locus of control would be reflected in choosing options 1b, 2b, 3a, and 4a.

control tend to be less anxious, achieve more, and cope better with stress than do people with an external orientation (Lefcourt, 1982). To get a sense of your standing on this trait dimension, choose one of the options for each of the sample items from the locus-of-control scale in Table 12.5.

IN SUMMARY

○ The social cognitive approach focuses on personality as arising from individuals' behavior in situations. Situations and persons mean different things to different people, as suggested by Kelly's personal construct theory.

○ According to social cognitive personality theorists, the same person may behave differently in different situations but should behave consistently in similar situations.

○ People translate their goals into behavior through outcome expectancies, their assumptions about the likely consequences of future behaviors.

The Self: Personality in the Mirror

Imagine that you wake up tomorrow morning, drag yourself into the bathroom, look into the mirror, and don't recognize the face looking back at you. This was the plight of a patient studied by neurologist Todd Feinberg (2001). The woman, married for 30 years and the mother of two grown children, one day began to respond to her mirror image as if it were a different person. She talked to and challenged the person in the mirror. When there was no response, she tried to attack it as if it were an intruder. Her husband, shaken by this bizarre behavior, brought her to the neurologist, who was gradually able to convince her that the image in the mirror was in fact herself.

Most of us are pretty familiar with the face that looks back at us from every mirror. We developed the ability to recognize ourselves in mirrors by 18 months of age (as discussed in Chapter 5), and we share this skill with chimpanzees and other apes who have been raised in the presence of mirrors. Self-recognition in mirrors signals our amazing capacity for reflexive thinking, for directing attention to our own thoughts, feelings, and actions—

◀ What do these self-portraits of Frida Kahlo, M. C. Escher, Norman Rockwell, Salvador Dalí, Wanda Wulz, and Jean-Michel Basquiat reveal about each artist's self-concept?

an ability that enables us to construct ideas about our own personality. Unlike a cow, which will never know that it has a poor sense of humor, or a cat, which will never know that it is awfully friendly (for a cat), humans have rich and detailed self-knowledge.

Admittedly, none of us know all there is to know about our own personality (or psychodynamic psychologists would be out of work). In fact, sometimes others may know us better than we know ourselves (Vazire & Mehl, 2008). But we do have enough self-knowledge to reliably respond to personality inventories and report on our traits and behaviors. These observations draw on what we think about ourselves—our *self-concept*—and on how we feel about ourselves—our *self-esteem*. Self-concept and self-esteem are critically important facets of personality, not just because they reveal how people see their own personalities, but because they also guide how people think others will see them.

Self-Concept

In his renowned psychology textbook, William James (1890) included a theory of self in which he pointed to the self's two facets, the *I* and the *Me*. The *I* is the self that thinks, experiences, and acts in the world; it is the self as a *knower*.
The *Me* is the self that is an object in the world; it is the self that is *known*. The *I* is much like consciousness, then, a perspective on all of experience (see Chapter 5), but the *Me* is less mysterious: It is just a concept of a person.

 Explain the difference between "I" and "Me."

If asked to describe your *Me,* you might mention your physical characteristics (male or female, tall or short, dark-skinned or light), your activities (listening to hip-hop, alternative rock, jazz, or classical music), your personality traits (extraverted or introverted, agreeable or independent), or your social roles (student, son or daughter, member of a hiking club, manager of a noodle factory). These features make up the **self-concept**, *a person's explicit knowledge of his or her own behaviors, traits, and other personal characteristics.* A person's self-concept is an organized body of knowledge that develops from social experiences and has a profound effect on a person's behavior throughout life.

self-concept A person's explicit knowledge of his or her own behaviors, traits, and other personal characteristics.

▲ A key element in personality involves the stories, myths, and fairy tales we tell ourselves about our lives. Are you living the story of the prince or princess in a castle—or are you the troll in the woods?

Self-Concept Organization

Almost everyone has a place for memorabilia, a drawer or box somewhere that holds all those sentimental keepsakes—photos, yearbooks, cards and letters, maybe that scrap of the old security blanket—all memories of "life as *Me.*" Perhaps you've wanted to organize these things sometime but have never gotten around to it. Fortunately, the knowledge of ourselves that we store in our *autobiographical memory* seems to be organized naturally in two ways—as narratives about episodes in our lives and in terms of traits (as would be suggested by the distinction between episodic and semantic memory discussed in Chapter 6).

The aspect of the self-concept that is a *self-narrative*—a story that we tell about ourselves—can be brief or very lengthy. Your life story could start with your birth and upbringing, describe a series of defining moments, and end where you are today. You could select specific events and experiences, goals and life tasks, and memories of places and people that have influenced you. Self-narrative organizes the highlights (and low blows) of your life into a story in which you are the leading character and binds them together into your self-concept (McAdams, 1993; McLean, 2008). Psychodynamic and humanistic-existential psychologists suggest that people's self-narratives reflect their fantasies and thoughts about core motives and approaches to existence.

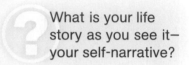

What is your life story as you see it—your self-narrative?

Self-concept is also organized in a more abstract way, in terms of personality traits. Just as you can judge an object on its attributes ("Is this apple green?"), you are able to judge yourself on any number of traits—whether you are considerate or smart or lazy or active or, for that matter, green—and do so quite reliably, making the same rating on multiple occasions. Hazel Markus (1977) observed that each person finds certain unique personality traits particularly important for conceptualizing the self. One person might define herself as independent, for example, whereas another might not care much about her level of independence but instead emphasize her sense of style. Markus called the traits people use to define themselves *self-schemas,* emphasizing that they draw information about the self into a coherent scheme. In one study, Markus (1977) asked people to indicate whether they had a trait by pressing response buttons marked "me" or "not me." She found that participants' judgment reaction times were faster for self-schemas than for other traits. It's as though some facets of the self-concept have almost a "knee-jerk" quality—letting us tell quickly who we are and who we are not.

Research also shows that the traits people use to judge the self tend to stick in memory. When people make judgments of themselves on traits, they later recall the traits better than when they judge other people on the same traits (Rogers, Kuiper, & Kirker, 1977). For example, answering a question such as, "Are you generous?"—no matter what your answer—is likely to enhance your memory for the trait generous. In studies of this effect of *self-relevance* on memory, researchers using imaging technologies have found that the simple activity of making judgments about the trait self-concept is accompanied by activation of the medial prefrontal cortex (MPFC)—a brain area involved in understanding people (Mitchell, Heatherton, & Macrae, 2002). This activation is stronger, however, when people are judging their own standing on traits (see **FIGURE 12.6**) than when they are judging the standing of someone else (Kelley et al., 2002). Such stronger activation, then, is linked with better memory for the traits being judged (Macrae et al., 2004). Studies have not been entirely conclusive about which brain areas are most involved in the processing of self-information (Morin, 2002), but they do show that memory for traits is strengthened when the MPFC is activated during self-judgments.

"I will not talk to myself, I will not talk to myself."

How do our behavior self-narratives and trait self-concepts compare? These two methods of self-conceptualization don't always match up. You may think of yourself as an honest person, for example, but also recall that time you nabbed a handful of change from your parents' dresser and conveniently forgot to replace it. The traits we

Why don't traits always reflect knowledge of behavior?

use to describe ourselves are generalizations, and not every episode in our life stories may fit. In fact, research suggests that the stores of knowledge about our behaviors and traits are not very well integrated (Kihlstrom, Beer, & Klein, 2002). In people who develop amnesia, for example, memory for behaviors can be lost even though the trait self-concept remains stable (Klein, 2004). People can have a pretty strong sense of who they are even though they may not remember a single example of when they acted that way.

Causes and Effects of Self-Concept

How do self-concepts arise, and how do they affect us? In some sense, you learn more about yourself every day. People tell you that you were a jerk last night, for instance, or that you're looking good today. Although we can gain self-knowledge in private moments of insight, we more often arrive at our self-concepts through interacting with others. Young children in particular receive plenty of feedback from their parents, teachers, siblings, and friends about their characteristics, and this helps them to form an idea of who they are. Even adults would find it difficult to hold a view of the self as "kind" or "smart" if no one else ever shared this impression. The sense of self, then, is largely developed and maintained in relationships with others.

Over the course of a lifetime, however, we become less and less impressed with what others have to say about us. Social theorist George Herbert Mead (1934) observed that all the things people have said about us accumulate after a while into what we see as a kind of consensus held by the "generalized other." We typically adopt this general view of ourselves that is as stable as our concept of anything at all and hold on to it stubbornly. As a result, the person who says you're a jerk may upset you momentarily—but you bounce back, secure in the knowledge that you're not truly a jerk. And just as we might argue vehemently with someone who tried to tell us a refrigerator is a pair of underpants or that up is actually down and to the left, we are likely to defend our self-concept against anyone whose view of us departs from our own.

Because it is so stable, a major effect of the self-concept is to promote consistency in behavior across situations (Lecky, 1945). As existential theorists emphasize, people derive a comforting sense of familiarity and stability from knowing

How does self-concept influence behavior?

who they are. We tend to engage in what William Swann (1983, 2010) has called **self-verification**, *the tendency to seek evidence to confirm the self-concept,* and we find it disconcerting if someone sees us quite differently from the way we see ourselves. In one study, Swann (1983) gave people who considered themselves submissive feedback that they seemed very dominant and forceful. Rather than accepting this discrepant information, they went out of their way to act in an extremely submissive manner. Our tendency to project into the world our concept of the self contributes to personality coherence. This talent for self-reflection enables the personality to become self-sustaining.

Self-Esteem

When you think about yourself, do you feel good and worthy? Do you like yourself, or do you feel bad and have negative, self-critical thoughts? **Self-esteem** is *the extent to which an individual likes, values, and accepts the self.* Thousands of studies have examined differences between people with high self-esteem (who generally like themselves) and those with relatively low self-esteem (who are less keen on, and may actively dislike, themselves).

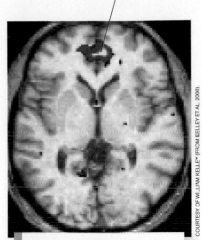

Medial prefrontal cortex

▲ FIGURE 12.6
Self-Concept in the Brain fMRI scans reveal that the medial prefrontal cortex (MPFC) is activated (shown here in red and yellow) when people make judgments of whether they possess certain personality traits compared to judging whether the traits apply to someone else.
(From Kelley et al., 2002.)

"I don't want to be defined by who I am."

self-verification The tendency to seek evidence to confirm the self-concept.

self-esteem The extent to which an individual likes, values, and accepts the self.

TABLE 12.6

Rosenberg Self-Esteem Scale

Consider each statement and circle SA for strongly agree, A for agree, D for disagree, and SD for strongly disagree.

1. On the whole, I am satisfied with myself.	SA	A	D	SD
2. At times, I think I am no good at all.	SA	A	D	SD
3. I feel that I have a number of good qualities.	SA	A	D	SD
4. I am able to do things as well as most other people.	SA	A	D	SD
5. I feel I do not have much to be proud of.	SA	A	D	SD
6. I certainly feel useless at times.	SA	A	D	SD
7. I feel that I'm a person of worth, at least on an equal plane with others.	SA	A	D	SD
8. I wish I could have more respect for myself.	SA	A	D	SD
9. All in all, I am inclined to feel that I am a failure.	SA	A	D	SD
10. I take a positive attitude toward myself.	SA	A	D	SD

Source: Rosenberg, 1965.

Scoring: For items 1, 3, 4, 7, and 10, SA = 3, A = 2, D = 1, SD = 0; for items 2, 5, 6, 8, and 9, the scoring is reversed, with SA = 0, A = 1, D = 2, SD = 3. The higher the total score, the higher one's self-esteem.

Researchers who study self-esteem typically ask participants to fill out a self-esteem questionnaire, such as one shown in **TABLE 12.6** (Rosenberg, 1965). This widely used measure of self-esteem asks people to evaluate themselves in terms of each statement. People who strongly agree with the positive statements about themselves and strongly disagree with the negative statements are considered to have high self-esteem.

Although some personality psychologists have argued that self-esteem determines virtually everything about a person's life—from the tendency to engage in criminal activity and violence to professional success—evidence has accumulated that the benefits of high self-esteem are less striking and all-encompassing but still significant. In general, compared with people with low self-esteem, those with high self-esteem tend to live happier and healthier lives, cope better with stress, and be more likely to persist at difficult tasks. In contrast, individuals with low self-esteem are more likely—for example—to perceive rejection in ambiguous feedback from others and develop eating disorders than those with high self-esteem (Baumeister et al., 2003). How does this aspect of personality develop, and why does everyone—whether high or low in self-esteem—seem to *want* high self-esteem?

Sources of Self-Esteem

Some psychologists contend that high self-esteem arises primarily from being accepted and valued by significant others (Brown, 1993). Other psychologists focus on the influence of specific self-evaluations, judgments about one's value or competence in specific domains such as appearance, athletics, or scholastics.

An important factor is whom people choose for comparison. For example, James (1890) noted that an accomplished athlete who is the second best in the world should feel pretty proud, but this athlete might not if the standard of comparison involves being best in the world. In fact, athletes in the 1992 Olympics who had won silver medals looked less happy during the medal ceremony than those who had won bronze (Medvec, Madey, & Gilovich, 1995). If the actual self is seen as falling short of the ideal

How do comparisons with others affect self-esteem?

◄ Silver medalist Duje Draganja of Croatia, gold medalist G. Hall Jr. of the United States, and bronze medalist Roland Schoeman of South Africa show off their medals following their 50-meter swimming final. Notice the expression on Draganja's face compared to those of the gold and bronze medalists.

self—the person that they would like to be—people tend to feel sad or dejected; when they become aware that the actual self is inconsistent with the self they have a duty to be, they are likely to feel anxious or agitated (Higgins, 1987).

Unconscious perspectives we take on feedback can also affect our sense of self-worth. In one study, researchers looked at the effect of an authority figure's disapproval on self-esteem. They examined the self-esteem of young, Catholic, female participants who had read an article from *Cosmopolitan* that described a woman's sexual dream (in PG-13 language) and who had either seen a photo of a disapproving-looking pope or a photo of an unfamiliar disapproving person. The photos were shown subliminally—that is, in such brief flashes that the women could not consciously recognize whom they had seen. In self-ratings made afterward, the women in the disapproving-pope group showed a marked reduction in self-esteem compared with the other women: They rated themselves as less competent, more anxious, and less moral. In the words of the researchers, self-esteem can be influenced when an important authority figure is "watching you from the back of your mind" (Baldwin, Carrell, & Lopez, 1989, p. 435).

Self-esteem is also affected by what kinds of domain we consider most important in our self-concept. One person's self-worth might be entirely contingent on, for example, how well she does in school, whereas another's self-worth might be based on his physical attractiveness (Crocker & Wolfe, 2001; Pelham, 1985). The first person's self-esteem might receive a big boost when she gets an "A" on an exam, but much less of a boost when she's complimented on her new hairstyle—and this effect might be exactly reversed in the second person.

▲ Fleeting thoughts of authorities can influence self-esteem. Catholic girls shown subliminal photos of Pope John Paul II experienced reduced self-esteem.

The Desire for Self-Esteem

What's so great about self-esteem? Why do people want to see themselves in a positive light and avoid seeing themselves negatively? The key theories on the benefits of self-esteem focus on status, belonging, and security.

Does self-esteem feel good because it reflects our degree of social dominance or status? People with high self-esteem seem to carry themselves in a way that is similar to high-status animals of other social species. Dominant male gorillas, for example, appear confident and comfortable and not anxious or withdrawn. Perhaps high self-esteem in humans reflects high social status or suggests that the person is worthy of respect, and this perception triggers natural affective responses (Barkow, 1980; Maslow, 1937).

How might self-esteem have played a role in evolution?

Could the desire for self-esteem come from a basic need to belong or be related to others? Evolutionary theory holds that early humans who managed to survive to pass

▶ Are you hot or not? Self-esteem is like an inner gauge of how much a person feels included by others at any given moment.

THE U.S. CONSUMER PRODUCT SAFETY COMMISSION

on their genes were those able to maintain good relations with others rather than being cast out to fend for themselves. Clearly, belonging to groups is adaptive, as is knowing whether you are accepted. Thus, self-esteem could be a kind of *sociometer,* an inner gauge of how much a person feels included by others at any given moment (Leary & Baumeister, 2000). According to evolutionary theory, then, we seek higher self-esteem because we have evolved to seek out belongingness in our families, work groups, and culture, and higher self-esteem indicates that we are being accepted.

The idea that self-esteem is a matter of security is consistent with the existential and psychodynamic approaches to personality. The studies of "mortality salience" discussed in Chapter 8 suggest that the source of distress underlying negative self-esteem is ultimately the fear of death (Solomon, Greenberg, & Pyszczynski, 1991). In this view, humans find it anxiety provoking, in fact terrifying, to contemplate their own mortality, and so they try to defend against this awareness by immersing themselves in activities (such as earning money or dressing up to appear attractive) that their culture defines as meaningful and valuable. The desire for self-esteem is a need to find value in ourselves as a way of escaping the anxiety associated with recognizing our mortality. The higher our self-esteem, the less anxious we feel with the knowledge that someday we will no longer exist.

Whatever the reason that low self-esteem feels so bad and high self-esteem feels so good, people are generally motivated to see themselves positively. In fact, we often process information in a biased manner in order to feel good about the self. Research on the **self-serving bias** shows that *people tend to take credit for their successes but downplay responsibility for their failures.* You may have noticed this tendency in yourself, particularly in terms of the attributions you make about exams when you get a good grade ("I studied really intensely, and I'm good at that subject") or a bad grade ("The test was ridiculously tricky and the professor is a nimnutz").

On the whole, most people satisfy the desire for high self-esteem and maintain a reasonably positive view of self by engaging in the self-serving bias (Miller & Ross, 1975; Shepperd, Malone, & Sweeny, 2008). In fact, if people are asked to rate themselves across a range of characteristics, they tend to see themselves as better than the average person in most domains (Alicke et al., 1995). For example, 90% of drivers de-

"I got into the stupidest thing with my reflection this morning."

BRUCE ERIC KAPLAN/THE NEW YORKER COLLECTION/ CARTOONBANK.COM

scribe their driving skills as better than average, and 86% of workers rate their performance on the job as above average. Even among university professors, 94% feel they are above average in teaching ability compared with other professors (Cross, 1977). These kinds of judgments simply cannot be accurate, statistically speaking, since the average of a group of people has to be the average, not better than average! This particular error may be adaptive, however. People who do not engage in this self-serving bias to boost their self-esteem tend to be more at risk for depression, anxiety, and related health problems (Taylor & Brown, 1988).

On the other hand, a few people take positive self-esteem to the extreme. Unfortunately, seeing yourself as way, way better than average—a trait called **narcissism**, *a grandiose view of the self combined with a tendency to seek admiration from and exploit others*—brings some costs. In fact, at its extreme, narcissism is considered a personality disorder (see Chapter 14). Research has documented disadvantages of an overinflated view of self, most of which arise from the need to defend that grandiose view at all costs. For example, when highly narcissistic adolescents were given reason to be ashamed of their performance on a task, their aggressiveness increased—in the form of willingness to deliver loud blasts of noise to punish their opponent in a laboratory game (Thomaes et al., 2008).

Implicit Egotism

What's your favorite letter of the alphabet? About 30% of people answer by picking what just happens to be the first letter of their first name. Could this choice indicate that some people think so highly of themselves that they base judgments of seemingly unrelated topics on how much it reminds them of themselves?

This *name-letter effect* was discovered some years ago (Nuttin, 1985), but only recently have researchers gone on to discover how broad the egotistic bias in preferences can be. Brett Pelham and his colleagues have found subtle yet systematic biases toward this effect when people choose their home cities, streets, and even occupations (Pelham, Mirenberg, & Jones, 2002). When the researchers examined the rolls of people moving into several southern states, for example, they found people named George were more likely than those with other names to move to Georgia. The same was true for Florences (Florida), Kenneths (Kentucky), and Louises (Louisiana). You can guess where the Virginias tended to relocate. People whose last name is Street seem biased toward addresses ending in *street*, whereas Lanes like lanes. The name effect seems to work for occupations as well: Slightly more people named Dennis and Denise chose dentistry and Lauras and Lawrences chose law compared with other occupations. Although the biases are small (if your name is Wally, you don't *have* to move to Walla Walla), they are consistent across many tests of the hypothesis.

Do people choose homes and occupations based in part on their own names?

These biases have been called expressions of *implicit egotism* because people are not typically aware that they are influenced by the wonderful sound of their own names (Pelham, Carvallo, & Jones, 2005). When Buffy moves to Buffalo, she is not likely to volunteer that she did so because it matched her name. Yet people who show this egotistic bias in one way also tend to show it in others: People who strongly prefer their own name letter also are likely to pick their birth date as their favorite number (Koole, Dijksterhuis, & van Knippenberg, 2001). And people who like their name letter were also found to evaluate themselves positively on self-ratings of personality traits. This was especially true when the self-ratings were made in response to instructions to work *quickly*. The people who preferred their name letter made snap judgments of themselves that leaned in a positive direction—suggesting that their special self-appreciation was an automatic response.

self-serving bias People's tendency to take credit for their successes but downplay responsibility for their failures.

narcissism A trait that reflects a grandiose view of the self combined with a tendency to seek admiration from and exploit others.

▶ If you were trying to light up a room with a letter, would your first choice also be your initial?

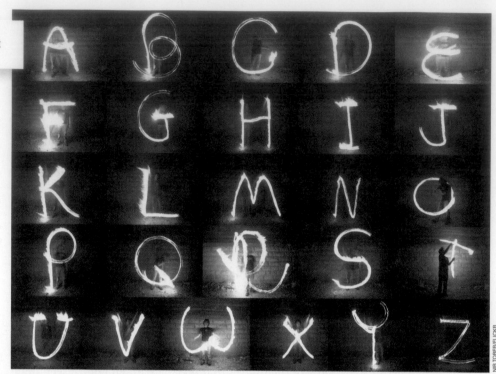

NIR TOBER/FLICKR

At some level, of course, a bit of egotism is probably good for us. It's sad to meet someone who hates her own name or whose snap judgment of self is, "I'm worthless." Yet in another sense, implicit egotism is a curiously subtle error—a tendency to make biased judgments of what we will do and where we will go in life just because we happen to have a certain name. Yes, the bias is only a small one. But your authors wonder: Could we have found better people to work with had we not fallen prey to this bias in our choice of colleagues?

The self is the part of personality that the person knows and can report about. Some of the personality measures we have seen in this chapter—such as personality inventories based on self-reports—are really no different from measures of self-concept. Both depend on the person's perceptions and memories of the self's behavior and traits. But personality runs deeper than this as well. The unconscious forces identified in psychodynamic approaches provide themes for behavior, and sources of mental disorder, that are not accessible for self-report. The humanistic and existential approaches remind us of the profound concerns we humans face and the difficulties we may have in understanding all the forces that shape our self-views. Finally, in emphasizing how personality shapes our perceptions of social life, the social cognitive approach brings the self back to center stage. The self, after all, is the hub of each person's social world.

IN SUMMARY

○ The self-concept is a person's knowledge of self, including both specific self-narratives and more abstract personality traits or self-schemas.

○ People's self-concept develops through social feedback, and people often act to try to confirm these views through a process of self-verification.

○ Self-esteem is a person's evaluation of self; it is derived from being accepted by others, as well as by how we evaluate ourselves by comparison to others. Theories proposed to explain why we seek positive self-esteem suggest that we do so to achieve perceptions of status, or belonging, or of being symbolically protected against mortality.

○ People strive for positive self-views through self-serving biases and implicit egotism.

Personality Testing for Fun and Profit

Many people enjoy filling out personality tests. In fact, dozens of websites, magazine articles, and popular books offer personality tests to complete as well as handy summaries of test scores. Google *personality test* and you'll see. Unfortunately, many personality tests are no more than a collection of questions someone has put together to offer entertainment to test takers. These tests yield a sense of self-insight that is no more valid than what you might get from the random "wisdom" of a fortune cookie or your daily horoscope.

The personality tests discussed in this chapter are more valid, of course: They have been developed and refined to offer reliable predictions of a person's tendencies. Still, the validity of many personality tests, particularly the projective tests, remains controversial, and critics question whether personality tests should be used for serious purposes.

Would one or more personality tests help you decide what career path to follow after college? Research findings have demonstrated correlations between personality dimensions and certain work-related indicators. In research on the Big Five, for example, people who are high in extraversion have been found to do well in sales and management positions. And as you might expect, people scoring high in conscientiousness tend to get better job performance ratings, while people high in agreeableness and low in neuroticism do well in jobs that require working in groups (John & Srivastava, 1999).

In fact, business, government, and the military often use personality tests in hiring. And vocational counselors use the Myers-Briggs Type Indicator personality test (which primarily assesses the individual's standing on the extraversion/introversion personality dimension) to direct people toward occupations that match their strengths. Although such tests have been criticized for their flimsy theoretical and research foundations (Paul, 2004), businesses have not abandoned them. The possibility also exists that such tests might someday be used to predict whether criminals behind bars have been rehabilitated or might return to crime if released. If tests could be developed that would predict with certainty whether a person would be likely to commit a violent crime or become a terrorist or a sexual predator, do you think such tests should be used to make decisions about people's lives?

Think of all you have learned about the different approaches to personality, the strengths and weaknesses of different kinds of tests, the person-situation controversy, and the fact that personality measures do correlate significantly (although not perfectly) with a person's behaviors. Are personality tests useful for making decisions about people now? If such tests were perfected, should they be used in the future? Where do you stand?

Chapter Review

KEY CONCEPT QUIZ

1. From a psychological perspective, personality refers to
   a. a person's characteristic style of behaving, thinking, and feeling.
   b. physiological predispositions that manifest themselves psychologically.
   c. past events that have shaped a person's current behavior.
   d. choices people make in response to cultural norms.

2. Projective techniques to assess personality involve
   a. personal inventories.
   b. self-reporting.
   c. responses to ambiguous stimuli.
   d. actuarial methodology.

3. A relatively stable disposition to behave in a particular and consistent way is a
   a. motive.
   b. goal.
   c. trait.
   d. reflex.

4. Which of the following is NOT one of the Big Five personality factors?
   a. conscientiousness
   b. agreeableness
   c. neuroticism
   d. orderliness

5. Compelling evidence for the importance of biological factors in personality is best seen in studies of
   a. parenting styles.
   b. identical twins reared apart.
   c. brain damage.
   d. factor analysis.

6. Which of Freud's systems of the mind would impel you to, if hungry, start grabbing food off people's plates upon entering a restaurant?
   a. the id
   b. the reality principle
   c. the ego
   d. the pleasure principle

7. After performing poorly on an exam, you drop a class, saying that you and the professor are just a poor match. According to Freud, what defense mechanism are you employing?
   a. regression
   b. rationalization
   c. projection
   d. reaction formation

8. According to Freud, a person who is preoccupied with his or her possessions, money, issues of submission and rebellion, and concerns about cleanliness versus messiness is fixated at which psychosexual stage?
   a. the oral stage
   b. the anal stage

   c. the latency stage
   d. the genital stage

9. Humanists see personality as directed toward the goal of
   a. existentialism.
   b. self-actualization.
   c. healthy adult sexuality.
   d. sublimation.

10. According to the existential perspective, the difficulties we face in finding meaning in life and in accepting the responsibility for making free choices provoke a type of anxiety called
    a. angst.
    b. flow.
    c. the self-actualizing tendency.
    d. mortality salience.

11. Which of the following is NOT an emphasis of the social cognitive approach?
    a. how personality and situation interact to cause behavior
    b. how personality contributes to the way people construct situations in their own minds
    c. how people's goals and expectancies influence their responses to situations
    d. how people confront realities rather than embrace comforting illusions

12. According to social cognitive theorists, _____ are the dimensions people use in making sense of their experiences.
    a. personal constructs
    b. outcome expectancies
    c. loci of control
    d. personal goals

13. What we think about ourselves is referred to as our _____ and how we feel about ourselves is referred to as our _____ .
    a. self-narrative; self-verification
    b. self-concept; self-esteem
    c. self-concept; self-verification
    d. self-esteem; self-concept

14. On what do the key theories on the benefits of self-esteem focus?
    a. status
    b. belonging
    c. security
    d. all of the above

15. When people take credit for their successes but downplay responsibility for their failures, they are exhibiting
    a. narcissism.
    b. implicit egoism.
    c. the self-serving bias.
    d. the name-letter effect.

KEY TERMS

personality (p. 468)

self-report (p. 469)

Minnesota Multiphasic Personality Inventory (MMPI-2) (p. 470)

projective techniques (p. 470)

Rorschach Inkblot Test (p. 471)

Thematic Apperception Test (TAT) (p. 471)

trait (p. 472)

Big Five (p. 474)

psychodynamic approach (p. 480)

dynamic unconscious (p. 480)

id (p. 481)

ego (p. 481)

superego (p. 481)

defense mechanisms (p. 482)

rationalization (p. 482)

reaction formation (p. 482)

projection (p. 482)

regression (p. 483)

displacement (p. 483)

identification (p. 483)

sublimation (p. 483)

psychosexual stages (p. 484)

fixation (p. 484)

oral stage (p. 485)

anal stage (p. 485)

phallic stage (p. 485)

Oedipus conflict (p. 485)

latency stage (p. 485)

genital stage (p. 485)

self-actualizing tendency (p. 486)

existential approach (p. 488)

social cognitive approach (p. 489)

person-situation controversy (p. 489)

personal constructs (p. 490)

outcome expectancies (p. 491)

locus of control (p. 491)

self-concept (p. 493)

self-verification (p. 495)

self-esteem (p. 495)

self-serving bias (p. 498)

narcissism (p. 499)

CRITICAL THINKING QUESTIONS

1. The text says that "there's something about being loved that helps take away the angst." According to a humanist or existentialist, what are some specific ways love could take away angst?

2. The text discusses how behavior self-narratives and trait self-concepts don't always match up. Think about your own self-narrative and self-concept. Are there areas that don't match up? How might you explain that?

3. Is it possible for someone to have too much self-esteem?

RECOMMENDED READINGS

Feinberg, T. E. (2001). *Altered egos: How the brain creates the self.* New York: Oxford University Press.

A fascinating review of the links between the brain and the experience of the self. This book covers issues of consciousness, identity, and the self and examines how people with various forms of brain injury develop changes in awareness of self, mind, and body.

Freud, S. (1952). *A general introduction to psychoanalysis.* New York: Pocket Books.

Sigmund Freud's own introduction to psychoanalytic theory. This version is among the most readable and concise, with a wide array of examples.

Gosling, S. (2008). *Snoop: What your stuff says about you.* New York: Basic Books.

Can you tell what people are like by snooping through their bedrooms and offices? This volume makes the case that personality is reflected in the objects we collect.

Paul, A. M. (2004). *The cult of personality testing.* New York: Free Press.

A critique of personality testing, this book examines how tests can be unreliable and invalid and asks whether employers, therapists, or courts should trust personality test results.

ANSWERS TO KEY CONCEPT QUIZ

1. a; 2. c; 3. c; 4. d; 5. b; 6. a; 7. b; 8. b; 9. b; 10. a; 11. d; 12. a; 13. b; 14. d; 15. c.

Need more help? Additional resources are located at the book's free companion Web site at: **www.worthpublishers.com/schacter**

13

Social Psychology

---O---

erry, Robert, and John have just one thing in common: They've all been tortured. Terry was an American journalist working in Lebanon when he was kidnapped by Hezbollah guerrillas; Robert was a semi-pro boxer living in Louisiana when he was arrested and sent to prison; and John was a naval aviator when he was shot down and captured by the North Vietnamese. All three men endured a variety of tortures, and all agree about which was the worst.

> "I'm afraid I'm beginning to lose my mind, to lose control completely," wrote the journalist. "I wish I could die. I ask God often to finish this, to end it any way that pleases Him."

> "It was a nightmare," wrote the prisoner. "I saw men so desperate that they ripped prison doors apart, starved and mutilated themselves . . . it takes every scrap of humanity to stay focused and sane."

> "It's an awful thing," wrote the soldier. "It crushes your spirit and weakens your resistance more effectively than any other form of mistreatment."

The technique these three men are describing has nothing to do with electric shock or water-boarding. It does not require wax, rope, or razor blades. It is a remarkably simple technique that has been used for thousands of years to break the body and destroy the mind. It is called solitary confinement. John McCain spent two years in a cell by himself, Terry Anderson spent seven, and Robert King spent twenty-nine.

When we think of torture, we usually think of techniques designed to cause pain by depriving people of something they desperately need, such as oxygen, water, food, or sleep. But the need for social interaction is every bit as vital. "Physical torture may have ended," wrote one American prisoner of war, "but there is still no torture worse than years of solitary confinement" (Howes, 1993, p. 55). Indeed, studies of prisoners show that extensive periods of isolation can induce symptoms typical of psychosis, such as "florid delirium, characterized by severe confusional, paranoid, and hallucinatory features, and also intense agitation and random, impulsive, often self-directed violence" (Grassian, 2006). Even in smaller doses, social isolation takes a toll. Ordinary people who are socially isolated are more likely to become depressed, to become ill, and to die prematurely. In fact, feeling isolated is as bad for your health as being obese or smoking (Cacioppo & Patrick, 2008; House, Landis, & Umberson, 1988).

◄ **Terry Anderson** (left), **Robert King** (middle), and **John McCain** (right) each spent years in isolation and described it as the worst form of torture.

R. WATSON/UPI/NEWSCOM   © ANN HARKNESS   © BROOKS KRAFT/CORBIS

WHAT KIND OF ANIMAL GETS SICK OR GOES CRAZY when left alone? Our kind. Human beings are the most social species on the planet and everything about us— from the structure of our brains to the structure of our societies—is influenced by that fact. **Social psychology** is *the study of the causes and consequences of sociality.* We'll start our tour of social psychology by examining *social behavior*—how people interact with each other—and we'll see how social behavior solves a problem that every living creature faces. Next we'll examine *social influence*—how people change each other—and we'll see that people have three basic motivations that make them susceptible to influence. Finally, we'll examine *social cognition*—how people understand each other—and we'll see how people use information about another person's affiliations and actions to make judgments and to make mistakes.

Social Behavior: Interacting with People

Centipedes aren't social. Neither are snails or brown bears. In fact, most animals are loners who prefer solitude to company. So why don't we?

All animals must survive and reproduce, and being social is one strategy for accomplishing these two important goals. When it comes to finding food or fending off enemies, herds and packs and flocks can often do what individuals can't, and that's why over millions of years many different species have found it useful to become social. But of the thousands and thousands of social species on our planet, only four have become *ultra-social,* which means that they form societies in which large numbers of individuals divide labor and cooperate for mutual benefit. Those four species are the hymenoptera (i.e., ants, bees, and wasps), the termites, the naked mole rats, and us (Haidt, 2006). Of these four, we are the only one whose societies consist of genetically *un*related individuals, and some scientists believe that the primary reason why we evolved such big brains is to deal with the complexities that these large-scale societies introduce (Dunbar & Shultz, 2007; Smith et al., 2010).

▲ According to Facebook, Lady Gaga has nearly 20 million friends, none of whom share her genes. Human beings are the only animal that builds large-scale social networks of unrelated individuals.

Being the most social of the ultra-social animals has allowed our species to out-survive and out-reproduce everyone else. If 10,000 years ago you had rounded up all the mammals on Earth and placed them on a gigantic bathroom scale, human beings would have accounted for about .01% of the total weight. Today we would account for 98%. We are world champions of survival and reproduction because we are so deeply social, and as you are about to see, much of our social behavior revolves around these two basic goals.

Survival: The Struggle for Resources

Some animals eat plants, some animals eat animals, and some animals eat everything. But regardless of what they eat, every living creature faces the same problem: survival. To survive, animals need resources such as food, water, and shelter. These resources are always scarce, because if they were plentiful, then the animal population would increase until they weren't. Scarce resources are a perpetual problem, and human beings solve this problem by hurting each other and by helping each other. *Hurting* and *helping* are antonyms and you might expect them to have little in common, but as you will see, these very different behaviors are merely two solutions to one problem (Hawley, 2002).

Aggression

The simplest way to solve the problem of scarce resources is to take the resources and kick the beans out of anyone who tries to stop you. **Aggression** is *behavior whose purpose is to harm another* (Anderson & Bushman, 2002; Bushman & Huesmann, 2010), and it is a strategy used by just about every animal on the planet. Aggression is not something that animals do for its own sake but, rather, as a way of getting the resources they want. This idea is captured by the **frustration-aggression hypothesis**, which suggests that *animals aggress when and only when their goals are frustrated* (Dollard et al., 1939). The chimp wants the banana (goal) but the pelican is about to take it (frustration), so the chimp threatens the pelican with his fist (aggression). The robber wants the money (goal) but the teller has it all locked up (frustration), so the robber threatens the teller with a gun (aggression).

The frustration-aggression hypothesis may be right, but some psychologists believe it is incomplete. They argue that the real cause of aggressive behavior is negative affect, and that the inability to reach a goal is just one of many things that brings about negative affect (Berkowitz, 1990). If animals aggress when they feel bad, then anything that makes them feel bad should increase aggression—and evidence suggests that this is just what happens. Laboratory rats that are given painful electric shocks will attack anything in their cage, including other animals, stuffed dolls, or even tennis balls (Kruk et al., 2004). People who are asked to put their hands in ice water, or to smell an unpleasant odor, or to sit in a very hot room are more likely to aggress against others (Anderson, 1989; Anderson, Bushman, & Groom, 1997). The idea that aggression is a response to negative affect may even explain why so many acts of aggression—from violent crime to athletic brawls—are more likely to occur on hot days when people are feeling irritated and uncomfortable (see **FIGURE 13.1**).

Of course, not everyone aggresses every time they feel bad. So who does—and why? Both biology and culture play a role in determining if and when people will aggress.

Biology and Aggression. The single best predictor of aggression is gender (Wrangham & Peterson, 1997). Crimes such as assault, battery, and murder are almost exclusively perpetrated by men—and especially by young men—who are responsible for about 90% of the murders and 80% of the violent crimes in the United States (Strueber, Lueck, & Roth, 2006). Although most societies encourage males to be more aggressive than females, male aggressiveness is not merely the product of socialization. Many studies show that aggression is strongly correlated with the presence of testosterone, which is typically higher in men than in women (see Chapter 11), in younger men than in older men, and in violent criminals than in nonviolent criminals (Dabbs et al., 1995).

> **Why are men more physically aggressive than women?**

social psychology The study of the causes and consequences of sociality.

aggression Behavior whose purpose is to harm another.

frustration-aggression hypothesis A principle stating that animals aggress only when their goals are thwarted.

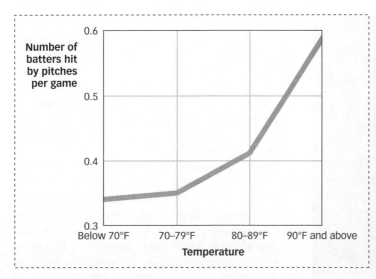

◀ FIGURE 13.1
Hot and Bothered In this 2009 baseball game, Boston Red Sox slugger Kevin Youkilis is about to tackle Detroit Tigers pitcher Rick Procello after being hit by a pitch. Professional pitchers have awfully good aim, so when they hit batters with the baseball, it's safe to assume that it wasn't an accident. This figure shows the average number of batters who were hit by pitches per game during the 1986–1988 major-league seasons. As you can see, the temperature on the field was highly correlated with the likelihood of being beaned.

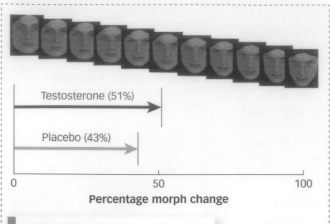

Testosterone (51%)

Placebo (43%)

0   50   100

Percentage morph change

▲ **FIGURE 13.2**
I Spy Threat Subjects who were given testosterone needed to see a more threatening expression before they were able to recognize it as such (van Honk & Schutter, 2007).

Testosterone doesn't just "turn aggression on" (Eisenegger et al., 2010); rather, it seems to promote aggression by making people feel concerned with their status, powerful, and confident in their ability to prevail. Male chimpanzees with high testosterone tend to stand tall and hold their chins high (Muller & Wrangham, 2004), and human beings with high testosterone walk more purposefully, focus more directly on the people they are talking to, and speak in a more forward and independent manner (Dabbs et al., 2001). Testosterone also lowers people's sensitivity to signs of threat. Subjects in one experiment watched a face as its expression changed from neutral to threatening and were asked to respond as soon as the expression became threatening (see **FIGURE 13.2**). Subjects who were given a small dose of testosterone before the experiment were slower to recognize the threatening expression (van Honk & Schutter, 2007). Failing to recognize that someone else is getting angry isn't a bad way to end up in a fight.

One of the most reliable ways to elicit aggression in males is to challenge their status or dominance. Indeed, three quarters of all murders can be classified as "status competitions" or "contests to save face" (Daly & Wilson, 1988). Contrary to popular wisdom, it isn't men with *low* self-esteem but men with unrealistically *high* self-esteem who are most prone to aggression, because such men are especially likely to perceive others' actions as a challenge to their inflated sense of their own status (Baumeister, Smart, & Boden, 1996). Although women can be just as aggressive as men, their aggression tends to be more premeditated than impulsive and more likely to be focused on attaining or protecting a resource than on attaining or protecting their status. Women are *much* less likely than men to aggress without provocation or to aggress in ways that cause physical injury, but they are only *slightly* less likely than men to aggress when provoked or to aggress in ways that cause psychological injury (Bettencourt & Miller, 1996; Eagly & Steffen, 1986). Indeed, women may even be *more* likely than men to aggress by causing social harm—for example, by ostracizing others or by spreading malicious rumors about them (Crick & Grotpeter, 1995).

Culture and Aggression. William James (1911, p. 272) wrote that "our ancestors have bred pugnacity into our bone and marrow and thousands of years of peace won't breed it out of us." Was he right? Although aggression is clearly part of our evolutionary heritage, it isn't inevitable. Indeed, the number of wars and the rate of murder have decreased by orders of magnitude in the last century alone. As psychologist Steven Pinker (2007) notes, "We have been getting kinder and gentler. Cruelty as entertainment, human sacrifice to indulge superstition, slavery as a labor-saving device, conquest as the mission statement of government, genocide as a means of acquiring real estate, torture and mutilation as routine punishment, the death penalty for misdemeanors and differences of opinion, assassination as the mechanism of political succession, rape as the spoils of war, pogroms as outlets for frustration, homicide as the major form of conflict resolution—all were unexceptionable features of life for most of human history. But, today, they are rare to nonexistent in the West, far less common elsewhere than they used to be, concealed when they do occur, and widely condemned when they are brought to light."

Just as aggression varies with time, so does it vary with geography—even within the geography of a single nation (see **FIGURE 13.3**). For example, violent crime in the United States is much more prevalent in the South, where men are taught to react aggressively when they feel their status has been challenged (Brown, Osterman, & Barnes, 2009; Nisbett & Cohen, 1996). In one set

▲ Men often aggress in response to status threats. In 2005, John Anderson (right) called Russell Tavares (above) a "nerd" on a social networking site. So Tavares got in his car, drove 1,300 miles, and burned down Anderson's trailer. "I didn't think anybody was stupid enough to try to kill anybody over an Internet fight," said Anderson. Tavares was later sentenced to seven years in prison.

AP PHOTO/MCLENNAN COUNTY SHERIFF'S DEPARTMENT

AP PHOTO/ JERRY LARSON

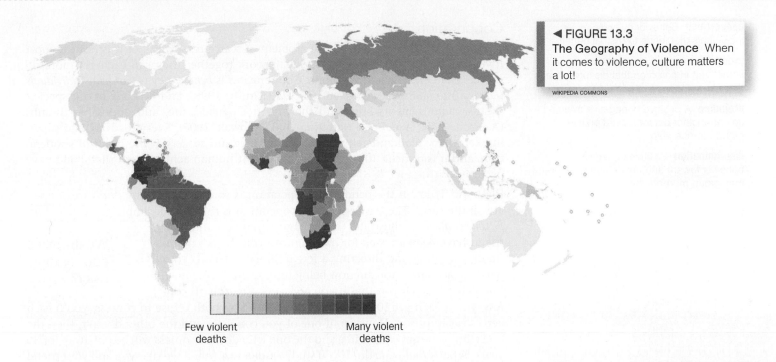

Few violent deaths   Many violent deaths

of experiments, researchers insulted volunteers from northern and southern states and found that the southerners were more likely to feel that their status had been diminished by the insult (Cohen et al., 1996). The southerners also experienced a greater increase in testosterone than did the northerners, and they were physically more assertive when a 6-foot 3-inch, 250-pound man got in their way as they left the experimental room.

What evidence suggests that culture can influence aggression?

Variation over time and geography shows that culture can play an important role in determining whether our innate capacity for aggression will result in aggressive behavior. People learn by example—which is why watching violent television shows and playing violent video games makes people more aggressive (Anderson & Bushman, 2001) and less cooperative (Sheese & Graziano, 2005)—but cultures can provide good examples as well as bad ones. In the mid-1980s, an unusual disease killed the most aggressive males in a particular troop of wild baboons in Kenya, leaving only the least aggressive males. A decade later, researchers discovered that a new "pacifist culture" had emerged among the descendants of the peaceful males. This new generation of male baboons were less aggressive, they groomed and affiliated with females, they were more tolerant of low-ranking males, and they showed fewer signs of physiological stress (Sapolsky & Share, 2004). If baboons can learn to get along, then surely people can too.

▲ Pitchers born in southern states are 40% more likely than those born in northern states to hit batters with their pitches (Timmerman, 2007).

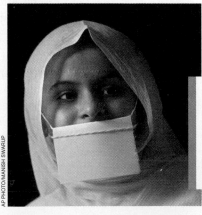

◄ Culture has a strong influence on violence. In Iraq, where murder is a part of everyday life, young boys stage a mock execution. In India, a teenager who is a member of the Jain religion wears a mask at all times so that she will not harm insects or microbes by inhaling them.

cooperation Behavior by two or more individuals that leads to mutual benefit.

group A collection of people who have something in common that distinguishes them from others.

prejudice A positive or negative evaluation of another person based on their group membership.

discrimination Positive or negative behavior toward another person based on their group membership.

Cooperation

Aggression is one way to solve the problem of scarce resources, but it is not the most inventive way, because when individuals work together they can each get more resources than either could get alone. **Cooperation** is *behavior by two or more individuals that leads to mutual benefit* (Deutsch, 1949; Pruitt, 1998), and it is one of our species' greatest achievements—right up there with language, fire, and opposable thumbs (Axelrod, 1984; Axelrod & Hamilton, 1981; Nowak, 2006). Every roadway and supermarket, every iPod and cell phone, every ballet and surgery is the result of cooperation, and it is difficult to think of an important human achievement that could have occurred without it.

Risk and Trust. If the benefit of cooperation is so clear, then why don't we cooperate all the time? The answer is that cooperation is *risky,* and a simple game called *the prisoner's dilemma* illustrates why. Imagine that you and your friend have been arrested for hacking into your bank's mainframe computer and directing a few million dollars to your personal accounts. You are now being interrogated separately. The detectives tell you that if you and your friend both confess, you'll each get 10 years in prison, and if you both refuse to confess, you'll each get 1 year in prison. However, if one of you confesses and the other doesn't, then the one who confesses will go free and the one who doesn't confess will be put away for 30 years. What should you do? If you study **FIGURE 13.4**, you'll see that you and your friend would both be wise to cooperate with each other. If you trust your friend and refuse to confess, and if your friend trusts you and refuses to confess, then you will both get a light sentence. But look what happens if you trust your friend and then your friend double-crosses you: Your friend gets to go home and wash his car while you spend the next three decades making license plates!

> **What makes cooperation risky?**

The prisoner's dilemma is more than a game. It mirrors the risks and benefits of cooperation in everyday life. For example, if everyone pays his or her taxes, then the tax rate stays low and everyone enjoys the benefits of sturdy bridges and first-rate museums. If no one pays taxes, then the bridges fall down and the museums shut their doors. There is clearly a *moderate* benefit to everyone if everyone pays taxes, but there is a *huge* benefit to the few non-cooperators who don't pay taxes while everyone else does because they get to use the bridges and enjoy the museums for free. This dilemma makes it difficult for people to decide whether to pay taxes and risk being chumps or to cheat and risk having the bridges collapse and the museums shut down. If you are like most people, you would be perfectly willing to cooperate in this sort of dilemma but you worry that others won't do the same. It's no wonder that when people are asked what single trait they most want those around them to have, the answer is *trustworthiness* (Cottrell, Neuberg, & Li, 2007) (see the Hot Science box on p. 512).

So cooperation is a good way to solve the problem of scarce resources, but it is risky. Is there anything you can do to minimize the risks? Yes, two things:

	COOPERATION (B does not confess)	NONCOOPERATION (B confesses)
COOPERATION (A does not confess)	A gets 1 year B gets 1 year	A gets 30 years B gets 0 years
NONCOOPERATION (A confesses)	A gets 0 years B gets 30 years	A gets 10 years B gets 10 years

▲ **FIGURE 13.4**
The Prisoner's Dilemma Game The prisoner's dilemma game illustrates the benefits and costs of cooperation. Players A and B receive benefits whose size depends on whether they independently decide to cooperate. Mutual cooperation leads to a relatively moderate benefit to both players, but if only one player cooperates, then the cooperator gets no benefit and the noncooperator gets a large benefit.

> First, you can learn how to spot a cheater, and evidence suggests that people are able to spot cheaters quite well. In the Wason card-selection task (shown in **FIGURE 13.5**), participants are asked to turn over two cards to test for violations of an abstract rule of the form "If P, then Q." Logic dictates that the best way to test for violations in this case is to turn over the cards marked P and Not Q. But because people have a *hypothesis-confirming bias,* only about 25% of the participants turn over the correct cards, and most turn over the cards marked P and Q. People find this exercise in abstract logic quite difficult. But when participants are asked to determine whether a *cheater* is violating a social rule that has precisely the same form—for

◀ **FIGURE 13.5**
The Wason Card-Selection Task In the Wason card-selection task, participants are asked to turn over two cards to test a rule of the form "If P, then Q." Logic dictates that they should turn over the card that says P and the card that says Not Q (top row). Studies show that very few people pick the correct cards. For example, when asked to determine whether a card with a vowel on one side has an even number on the other side (middle row), most people turn over E and 4 rather than E and 7. However, when the rule is a social rule (bottom row), people do much better. For instance, when people are shown the set of cards in the bottom row and are asked to turn over two cards to determine whether it is true that "anyone at the bar who is drinking beer is over 21," people usually pick the correct cards—Beer and 16—because they realize that turning over Coke and 25 will provide no information about whether a minor is drinking. The problems are logically identical, so why does it seem so easy in one case and so hard in another?

example, "If the man is drinking beer (P), then he is over 21 (Q)"—the number of participants who turn over the correct cards nearly triples (Cosmides, 1989). There is some controversy about why this happens (Cheng & Holyoak, 1989; Fodor, 2000; Gigerenzer & Hug, 1992), but one explanation is that human beings have a uniquely powerful capacity to detect cheaters that surpasses their capacity for logical reasoning in general.

> Second, you can react strongly when you detect someone cheating, and evidence suggests that people do (Bolton & Ockenfels, 2000). The *ultimatum game* requires one player (the divider) to divide a monetary prize into two parts and offer one of the parts to a second player (the decider), who can either accept or reject the offer. If the decider rejects the offer, then both players get nothing and the game is over. Studies show that deciders typically reject offers that they consider unfair because they'd rather get nothing than get cheated (Fehr & Gaechter, 2002; Thaler, 1988). In other words, people will *pay* to punish someone who has treated them unfairly. Nonhumans also seem to dislike unfair treatment. In one study, monkeys were willing to work for a slice of cucumber until they saw the experimenter give another monkey a more delicious food for doing less work (Brosnan & DeWaal, 2003). At that point the monkeys went on strike.

Groups and Favoritism. Cooperation requires that we take a risk by benefiting those who have not yet benefited us and then *trusting* them to do the same. But other than Mom, who can we really trust?

A **group** is *a collection of people who have something in common that distinguishes them from others.* Every one of us is a member of many groups—from families and teams to religions and nations. Although these groups are quite different, they have one thing in common, which is that the people in them tend to be especially nice to each other. **Prejudice** is *a positive or negative evaluation of another person based on their group membership,* and **discrimination** is *a positive or negative behavior toward another person based on their group membership* (Dovidio & Gaertner, 2010). One of the defining characteristics of groups is that their members are positively prejudiced toward other members and tend to discriminate in their favor. It doesn't take much to create this kind of favoritism (Efferson, Lalive, & Fehr, 2008). In one set of studies, participants were shown abstract paintings by two artists and were then divided into two groups based on their preference for one artist or the other (Tajfel, 1970; Tajfel et al., 1971).

How do groups lessen the risks of cooperation?

▲ Kevin Hart owns the Gator Motel in Fargo, Georgia, which he runs on an honor system: Guests arrive, stay as long as they like, and leave their payment on the dresser. If just a few people cheated, it would not affect the room rates, but if too many cheated, then prices would have to rise. How would you decide whether to pay or to cheat? Before answering this question, please notice the large dog.

"Hey, we're sheep. Everything seems like a good idea."

When participants were subsequently asked to allocate money to other participants, they consistently allocated more money to those in their group (Brewer, 1979). Indeed, people show positive prejudice and discrimination even when they are randomly assigned to completely meaningless groups such as "Group X" and "Group Y" (Hodson & Sorrentino, 2001; Locksley, Ortiz, & Hepburn, 1980). It appears that simply knowing that "I'm one of *us* and not one of *them*" is sufficient to produce favoritism. Because group members favor other group members, cooperation within the group is less risky.

But if groups have benefits, they also have costs. For example, when groups try to make decisions they rarely do better than the best member would have done alone—and they often do worse. One reason is that groups don't fully capitalize on the expertise of their members (Hackman & Katz, 2010). For instance, groups (such as a school board) often give too little weight to the opinions of members who are experts (the professor) and too much weight to the opinions of members who happen to be high in status (the mayor) or especially talkative (the mayor). Groups also tend to spend most of their time discussing information that is unimportant but known to everyone (the size of the gymnasium) and little time discussing information that is important but known to just a few (how a school in a different district solved its budget crisis). Finally, members of groups like to maintain harmony and thus are reluctant to "rock the boat" even when it clearly needs a good rocking. For all of these reasons, groups underperform individuals in a wide variety of tasks.

HOT SCIENCE

The Eyes Have It

Psychologist Melissa Bateson noticed that the faculty, staff, and students in her department at the University of Newcastle didn't always pay for their coffee, even though everyone knew how the "honor system" was supposed to work. What might be done about this problem?

People are typically more honest when they think that others are watching them, so for the next 10 weeks Bateson and her colleagues posted pictures of flowers or pictures of watchful eyes above the coffee pot, and then counted how much money people paid and how much coffee they consumed. As the data in the accompanying figure show, people were more likely to pay when there were eyes on the walls (Bateson, Nettle, & Roberts, 2006). It appears that even the slightest hint that we are being observed is enough to put us on our best behavior.

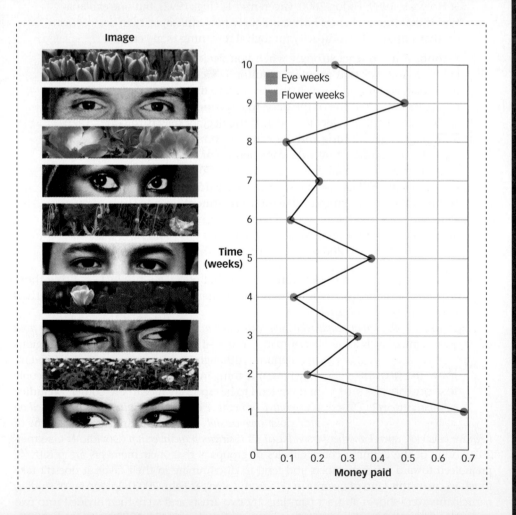

The costs of groups go beyond bad decisions because people in groups sometimes do terrible things that none of their members would do alone (Yzerbyt & Demoulin, 2010). Lynching, rioting, gang-raping—why do we behave so badly when we assemble in groups? One reason is **deindividuation**, which occurs *when immersion in a group causes people to become less concerned with their personal values*. We may want to grab the Rolex from the jeweler's window or plant a kiss on the attractive stranger in the library, but we don't do these things because they conflict with our personal values. Research shows that people are most likely to consider their personal values when their attention is focused on themselves (Wicklund, 1975), and being assembled in groups draws our attention to others and *away* from ourselves. As a result, we are less likely to consider our own personal values and to instead adopt the group's values (Postmes & Spears, 1998). A second reason why we behave badly in groups is **diffusion of responsibility**, which occurs when *individuals feel diminished responsibility for their actions because they are surrounded by others who are acting the same way*. When we're all alone, we know it is up to us to do the right thing; but when we see lots of other people around us, we may feel that it is somebody else's job (Darley & Latané, 1968). If you and one other student were taking an exam and you saw the other student cheating, you'd probably feel more responsible for reporting the incident than if you were taking that test in a room full of students (see **FIGURE 13.6**).

deindividuation A phenomenon that occurs when immersion in a group causes people to become less aware of their individual values.

diffusion of responsibility The tendency for individuals to feel diminished responsibility for their actions when they are surrounded by others who are acting the same way.

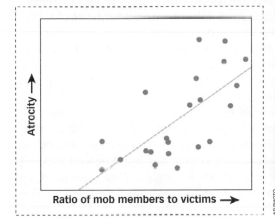

◄ FIGURE 13.6
Mob Size and Level of Atrocity Groups are capable of horrible things. These two men were rescued by police just as residents of their town prepared to lynch them for stealing a car. Because larger groups provide more opportunity for deindividuation and diffusion of responsibility, their atrocities become more horrible as the ratio of mob members to victims becomes larger (Leader, Mullen, & Abrams, 2007).

If groups make bad decisions and encourage bad behavior, then might we be better off without them? Probably not. One of the best predictors of a person's general well-being is the quality and extent of their social relationships and group memberships (Myers & Diener, 1995). People who are excluded from groups are typically anxious, lonely, depressed, and at increased risk for illness and premature death (Cacioppo & Patrick, 2008; Cohen, 1988; Leary, 1990). Indeed, being excluded from a group activates areas of the brain that are normally activated by physical pain (**FIGURE 13.7**; Eisenberger, Lieberman, & Williams, 2003). Belonging is not just a source of psychological and physical well-being but also a source of identity (Leary, 2010; Tajfel & Turner, 1986), which is why people typically describe themselves by listing the groups of which they are members ("I'm a Canadian architect"). Groups may cause us to misjudge and misbehave, but they seem to be key to our happiness and well-being.

◄ FIGURE 13.7
When people are excluded from a social group, (a) the anterior cingulate cortex (ACC) and (b) the right ventral prefrontal cortex (RVPC) become active. Interestingly, the ACC is commonly associated with the experience of physical pain and the RVPC is commonly associated with pain relief. Apparently, social exclusion causes people to feel pain and to make an effort to diminish it.

Eisenberger, N. I., Lieberman, M. D., & Williams, K. D. (2003). *Science*, 302, 290–292.

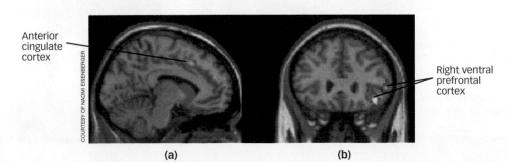

Anterior cingulate cortex

Right ventral prefrontal cortex

(a)   (b)

altruism Behavior that benefits another without benefiting oneself.

kin selection The process by which evolution selects for individuals who cooperate with their relatives.

reciprocal altruism Behavior that benefits another with the expectation that those benefits will be returned in the future.

Altruism

Cooperation is a way to solve the problem of scarce resources. But is this the only reason we cooperate with others? Aren't we ever just . . . well, *nice*? **Altruism** is *behavior that benefits another without benefiting oneself,* and for a very long time scientists and philosophers have debated whether people are ever truly altruistic.

Altruism appears to be common among animals—but appearances can be deceiving. For example, birds and squirrels give "alarm calls" when they see a predator, which puts them at increased risk of being eaten but allows their fellow birds and squirrels to escape. Ants and bees spend their lives caring for the offspring of the queen rather than bearing offspring of their own. But these behaviors are not really altruistic because the animals being helped are related to the animals

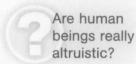
Are human beings really altruistic?

who are doing the helping. The squirrels most likely to give alarm calls are those most closely related to the other squirrels with whom they live (Maynard-Smith, 1965). Honeybees may raise the queen's offspring, but an odd genetic quirk makes honeybees more closely related to the queen's offspring than they would be to their own. Any animal that promotes the survival of its relatives is actually promoting the survival of its own genes (Hamilton, 1964). **Kin selection** is *the process by which evolution selects for individuals who cooperate with their relatives,* which means that cooperating with relatives is not really altruistic. Even cooperating with non-relatives isn't necessarily proof of altruism. Male baboons will risk injury to help an unrelated male baboon win a fight, and monkeys will spend time grooming unrelated monkeys when they could be doing something else. Is that altruism? Not necessarily. Careful studies of primates reveal that the individuals who perform such favors tend to receive favors in return. **Reciprocal altruism** is *behavior that benefits another with the expectation that those benefits will be returned in the future,* and despite the second word in this term, it isn't really very altruistic at all (Trivers, 1972b). Indeed, reciprocal altruism is merely cooperation extended over long periods of time.

The behavior of nonhuman animals provides little if any evidence of genuine altruism. But what about us? Are we any different? Like other animals, we tend to help our kin more than strangers (Burnstein, Crandall, & Kitayama, 1994; Komter, 2010) and we tend to expect those we help to help us in return (Burger et al., 2009). But unlike other animals, we do sometimes provide benefits to complete strangers who have no chance of repaying us (Batson, 2002; Warneken & Tomasello, 2009). We make anonymous donations to charity, tip waiters in restaurants to which we will never return, and hold the door for people who share precisely none of our genes. Our altruism is equally apparent in situations that really matter. As the World Trade Center burned on the morning of September 11, 2001, civilians in sailboats headed *toward* the destruction rather than away from it, initiating the largest waterborne evacuation in the history of the United States. As one observer remarked, "If you're out on the water in a pleasure craft and you see those buildings on fire, in a strictly rational sense you should head to New Jersey. Instead, people went into potential danger and rescued strangers. That's social" (Dreifus, 2003). Human beings can be heroes, and some studies even suggest that altruism is more common than we realize (Miller & Ratner, 1998).

▶ Ground squirrels put themselves in danger when they warn others about predators, but those they warn share their genes, so the behavior is not truly altruistic. In contrast, Christine Karg-Palerio donated her kidney anonymously to someone she'd never even met. "If I had a spare, I'd do it again," she said.

Reproduction: The Quest for Immortality

All animals have two goals: to survive and to reproduce. Social behavior facilitates the first of these goals, but it is an essential requirement for the second. Because we are a sexual species, we can't reproduce without getting very, very social. There are many steps on the road to reproduction, but the first one invariably involves finding someone of the opposite gender who wants to travel that road with us. How do we do that?

Selectivity

With the exception of a few well-known celebrities, people don't seem to mate randomly. Rather, they *select* their sexual partners, and the most obvious fact about this process is that women tend to be more selective than men (Feingold, 1992a; Fiore et al., 2010). In one study, an attractive person (who was working for the experimenters) approached an opposite-sex stranger on a college campus and asked one of two questions: "Would you go out tonight?" or "Would you go to bed with me?" About half of the men and women who were approached agreed to go out with the attractive person; but while *none* of the women agreed to go to bed with the person, *three quarters* of the men did (Clark & Hatfield, 1989).

Why are women choosier than men?

Why are women the choosier gender? One reason is that sex is potentially more costly for women than for men (Buss & Schmitt, 1993; Trivers, 1972a). Men produce billions of sperm in their lifetimes, their ability to conceive a child tomorrow is not inhibited by having conceived one today, and conception has no significant physical costs. On the other hand, women produce a small number of eggs in their lifetimes, conception eliminates their ability to conceive for at least 9 more months, and pregnancy produces physical changes that increase their nutritional requirements and put them at risk of illness and death. Therefore, if a man mates with a woman who does do not produce healthy offspring or who won't do her part to raise them, he's lost nothing but ten minutes and a teaspoon of semen. But if a woman makes the same mistake, she has lost a precious egg, borne the costs of pregnancy, risked her life in childbirth, and missed at least 9 months of other reproductive opportunities.

Basic biology may push women to be choosier then men, but culture can push just as hard. When cultures glorify promiscuous men as *playboys* and disparage promiscuous women as *sluts*, women may be more selective than men simply because the reputational costs of sex are much higher; but when cultures lower the costs of sex for women by providing access to effective birth control, by promoting the financial independence of women, or by adopting communal styles of child-rearing, women become less selective (Eagly & Wood, 1999; Kasser & Sharma, 1999). And when sex becomes expensive for men—for example, when they are choosing a long-term mate for a monogamous relationship rather than a short-term mate for a weekend—they turn out to be every bit as selective as women (Kenrick et al., 1990). Indeed, small changes in the courtship ritual can actually cause men to become *choosier* than women (see the Real World box on the next page). The point is that biology makes sex a riskier proposition for women than for men, but cultures can exaggerate, equalize, or even reverse those risks. The higher the risk, the more selective people tend to be.

DR. PAUL ZAHL/PHOTO RESEARCHERS

CREATAS IMAGES/PICTUREQUEST

▲ If men could become pregnant, how might their behavior change? Among sea horses, it is the male that carries the young, and not coincidentally, males are more selective than are females.

Attraction

For most of us, there are a very small number of people with whom we are willing to have sex, an even smaller number of people with whom we are willing to have children, and a staggeringly large number of people with whom we are unwilling to have either. So when we meet someone new, how do we decide which of these categories that person belongs in? Many things go into choosing a date, a lover, or a partner for life, but perhaps none is more important than the simple feeling we call *attraction* (Berscheid & Reiss, 1998). Research suggests that this feeling is caused by a range of factors that can be roughly divided into the situational, the physical, and the psychological.

Situational Factors. One of the best predictors of any kind of interpersonal relationship is the physical proximity of the people involved (Nahemow & Lawton, 1975). For example, in one study, students who had been randomly assigned to university housing were asked to name their three closest friends, and nearly half named their next-door neighbor (Festinger, Schachter, & Back, 1950). We tend to think that we select our romantic partners on the basis of their personalities, appearances, and so on—and we do—but we only get to select from the pool of people whom we have met, and the likelihood of meeting a potential partner naturally increases with proximity. Before you

THE REAL WORLD

Making the Move

When it comes to selecting romantic partners, women tend to be choosier than men, and most scientists think that has a lot to do with differences in their reproductive biology. But psychologists Eli Finkel and Paul Eastwick (2009) thought that it might also have something to do with the nature of the courtship dance itself.

When it comes to approaching a potential romantic partner, the person with the most interest should be most inclined to "make the first move." Of course, in most cultures, men are *expected* to make the first move. Could it be that making the first move *causes* men to think that they have more interest than women do and causes women to think they have less? In other words, could the rule about first moves be one of the *reasons* why women are choosier?

To find out, the researchers teamed up with a local speed dating service and created two kinds of speed dating events. In the "traditional event," the women stayed in their seats and the men moved around the room, stopping to spend a few minutes chatting with each woman. In the "nontraditional event," the men stayed in their seats and the women moved around the room, stopping to spend a few minutes chatting with each man. When the event was over, the researchers asked each man and woman privately to indicate whether they wanted to exchange phone numbers with any of the potential partners they'd met.

The results were striking (see the accompanying figure). When men made the move (as they traditionally do), women were the choosier gender. That is, men wanted to get a lot more phone numbers than women wanted to give. But when women made the move, men were the choosier gender, and women asked for more numbers than men were willing to hand over. Apparently, approaching someone makes us eager and being approached makes us cautious. One reason why women are so often the choosier gender may simply be that, in most cultures, men are expected to make the first move.

Rielle Hunter, the woman who had an affair with presidential candidate John Edwards, recently remarked,

"One thing I've learned about relationships and men is that you can never walk across the room for a man. If a man is attracted to you, he needs to take the first step" (Weiss, 2010). Science suggests she might just be right.

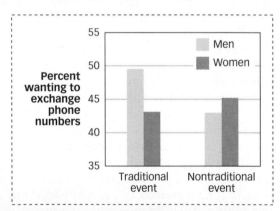

ever start auditioning and ruling out potential mates, geography has already ruled out 99.999% of the world's population for you. Proximity not only provides the opportunity for attraction but it also provides the motivation: People work especially hard to like those with whom they expect to have interaction (Darley & Berscheid, 1967). When you are assigned a roommate in college, you know that day-to-day existence will be a whole lot easier if you like them than if you don't, and so you go out of your way to notice their good qualities and ignore their bad ones.

Why does proximity influence attraction?

Proximity provides something else as well. Every time we encounter a person, that person becomes a bit more familiar to us, and people—like other animals—generally prefer familiar to novel stimuli. The **mere exposure effect** is *the tendency for the frequency of exposure to a stimulus to increase liking* (Bornstein, 1989; Zajonc, 1968). For instance, in some experiments, geometric shapes, faces, or alphabetical characters were flashed on a computer screen so quickly that participants were unaware of having seen them. These participants were then shown some of the "old" stimuli that had been flashed across the screen as well as some "new" stimuli that had not. Although they could not reliably tell which stimuli were old and which were new, participants tended to *like* the old stimuli better than the new ones (Monahan, Murphy, & Zajonc, 2000). The fact that mere exposure leads to liking may explain why college students who were randomly assigned to a seat during a brief psychology experiment were especially likely to be friends with the person they sat next to an entire year later (Back, Schmukle, & Egloff, 2008).

Although attraction can be the result of geographical accidents that put people in the same place at the same time, some places and times are better than others. In one study, experimenters observed men as they crossed a swaying suspension bridge. A young woman who was actually working for the experimenters approached the men either when they were in the middle of the bridge or after they had finished crossing it. The woman asked the men to complete a survey, and after they did so, she gave each man her telephone number and offered to explain her project in greater detail if he called. The men who had met the woman in the middle of the swaying bridge were much more likely to call than were the men who had met the woman only after they had crossed the bridge (Dutton & Aron, 1974). Why? You may recall from Chapter 8 that people can misinterpret physiological arousal as a sign of attraction (Byrne et al., 1975; Schachter & Singer, 1962). The men experienced more physiological arousal when they completed the questionnaire on the suspension bridge, and some of those men mistook that arousal for attraction. Apparently, a sheer blouse and a sheer drop have similar effects on men, who easily confuse the two.

mere exposure effect The tendency for liking to increase with the frequency of exposure.

◀ Michelle Obama probably prefers the picture on the right, but her husband probably prefers the picture on the left. Why? Because like most of us, she is used to seeing herself in the mirror. The mere exposure effect explains why people prefer mirror-reversed images of themselves and why their friends and families prefer normal images of them (Mita, Dermer, & Knight, 1977).

▶ When people are in arousing situations together, they may become attracted. Ben Bostic and Laura Zych were strangers when their US Air flight crash landed in the Hudson River in 2009. Now they are a couple.

Physical Factors. Once people are in the same place at the same time, they can begin to learn about each other's personal qualities, and in most cases, the first quality they learn about is the other person's appearance. You already know that appearance influences attraction, but research suggests that this influence may be stronger than you think. In one study, researchers arranged a dance for first-year university students and randomly assigned each student to an opposite-sex partner. Midway through the dance, the students confidentially reported how much they liked their partner, how attractive they thought their partner was, and how much they would like to see their partner again. The researchers measured many of the students' attributes—from their attitudes to their personalities—and they found that the partner's physical appearance was the *only* attribute that influenced the students' feelings of attraction (Walster et al., 1966). Field studies have revealed the same thing. For instance, one study found that a man's height and a woman's weight were among the best predictors of how many responses a personal ad received (Lynn & Shurgot, 1984), and another study found that physical attractiveness was the *only* factor that predicted the online dating choices of both women and men (Green, Buchanan, & Heuer, 1984).

Why is physical appearance so important?

Appearance is important in just about every context (Etcoff, 1999; Langlois et al., 2000). Beautiful people have more friends, more dates, more sex, and more fun than the rest of us do (Curran & Lippold, 1975), and they even earn about 10% more money over the courses of their lives (Hamermesh & Biddle, 1994; see **FIGURE 13.8**). We tend to think that beautiful people also have superior personal qualities (Dion, Berscheid, & Walster, 1972; Eagly et al., 1991), and in some cases they do. For instance, because beautiful people have more friends and more opportunities for social interaction, they tend to have better social skills than less beautiful people (Feingold, 1992b). Appearance is so powerful that it even influences how mothers treat their own children: Mothers are more affectionate and playful when their children are attractive than unattractive (Langlois et al., 1995). It is interesting to note that although men and women seem to be equally influenced by the appearance of their potential partners, men are more likely than women to acknowledge this fact (Feingold, 1990).

So yes, it pays to be beautiful. But what exactly constitutes beauty? There is no doubt that standards of beauty can vary across time and culture. In the United States, for example, most women want to be slender, but in Mauritania, young girls are forced to drink up to 5 gallons of high-fat milk every day so that they will someday be obese enough to attract a husband. As one Mauritanian woman noted, "Men want women to be fat, and so they are fat. Women want men to be skinny, and so they are skinny"

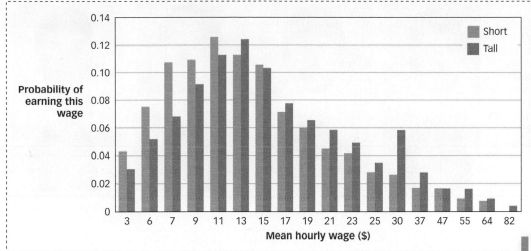

▲ FIGURE 13.8
Height Matters NFL quarterback Tom Brady is 6'4" and his wife, supermodel Gisele Bunchen, is 5'10". Research shows that tall people earn $789 more per inch per year. The graph shows the average hourly wage of adult White men in the United States classified by height (Mankiw & Weinzierl, 2010)

(LaFraniere, 2007). In the United States, most men want to be tall, but in Ghana, most men are short and consider height a curse. "To be a tall person can be quite embarrassing," said one particularly tall Ghanaian man. "When you are standing in a crowd, the short people start to jeer at you," said another (French, 1997).

But beauty is not entirely in the eye of the beholder. Different cultures may have some different standards of beauty, they also have a lot in common (Cunningham et al., 1995). For example:

> *Body shape.* Male bodies are considered most attractive when they approximate an inverted triangle (i.e., broad shoulders with a narrow waist and hips), and female bodies are considered most attractive when they approximate an hourglass (i.e., broad shoulders and hips with a narrow waist). In fact, the most attractive female body across many cultures seems to be the "perfect hourglass" in which the waist is precisely 70% the size of the hips (Singh, 1993).

> *Symmetry.* Human faces and bodies are generally considered more attractive when they are *bilaterally symmetrical*—that is, when the left half is a mirror image of the right (Perrett et al., 1999). In addition, faces are considered especially beautiful when their features approximate the average of the human population (Langlois & Roggman, 1990; Langlois, Roggman, & Musselman, 1994; see **FIGURE 13.9** on the next page).

◀ Standards of beauty differ across cultures. Mauritanian women long to be obese (left), and Ghanian men are grateful to be short (right).

COURTESY OF JUDITH LANGLOIS.

▶ FIGURE 13.9
The Attractive Norm When photos of human faces are "morphed" to create a composite, people tend to judge the composite as more attractive than its components because the composites are closer to the human average. The faces shown are (from left to right) composites of 4, 8, 16, and 22 faces, and most people think the faces on the right are more attractive than the faces on the left.

Langlois, J. H., & Roggman, L. A. (1990). *Psychological Science*, 1, 115–121.

> *Age.* Characteristics such as large eyes, high eyebrows, and a small chin make people look immature or "baby-faced" (Berry & McArthur, 1985). As a general rule, female faces are considered more attractive when they have immature features, but male faces are considered more attractive when they have mature features (Cunningham, Barbee, & Pike, 1990; Zebrowitz & Montepare, 1992).

Is there any rhyme or reason to this list of scenic attractions? Some psychologists think so. They argue that nature has designed us to be attracted to people who (a) have good genes and (b) will be good parents (Neuberg, Kenrick, & Schaller, 2010). The features we find attractive just so happen to be reliable indicators of these two things. For example:

What kind of information does physical appearance convey?

> *Body shape.* Testosterone causes male bodies to become "inverted triangles" just as estrogen causes female bodies to become "hourglasses." Men who are high in testosterone tend to be socially dominant and therefore have more resources to devote to their offspring, whereas women who are high in estrogen tend to be especially fertile and potentially have more offspring to make use of those resources. In other words, body shape is an indicator of male dominance and female fertility. In fact, women who have the "perfect hourglass" figure tend to bear healthier children than do women with other waist-to-hip ratios (Singh, 1993).

> *Symmetry.* Both symmetry and averageness are signs of genetic health (Jones et al., 2001; Thornhill & Gangestad, 1993), which may explain why people are so good at detecting them. Even newborn infants prefer composites (like those shown in Figure 13.9) to components (Langlois, Roggman, & Rieser-Danner, 1990; Rubenstein, Kalakanis, & Langlois, 1999). And women can discriminate symmetrical and asymmetrical men *by smell*—and their preference for symmetry is especially pronounced when they are ovulating (Thornhill & Gangestad, 1999).

> *Age.* Younger women are generally more fertile than older women, whereas older men generally have more resources than younger men. Thus, a youthful appearance is a signal of a woman's ability to bear children, just as a mature appearance is a signal of a man's ability to raise them. Studies have shown that women prefer older men and men prefer younger women across a wide variety of human cultures (Buss, 1989).

If the feeling we call *attraction* is simply nature's way of telling us that we are in the presence of a person who has good genes and a propensity to be a good parent, then it isn't any wonder that people in different epochs and different cultures appreciate so

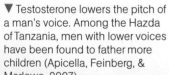

▼ Testosterone lowers the pitch of a man's voice. Among the Hazda of Tanzania, men with lower voices have been found to father more children (Apicella, Feinberg, & Marlowe, 2007).

© NIGEL PAVITT/JAI/CORBIS

many of the same features in the opposite sex. Of course, appreciation is one thing, and action is another. Studies show that while everyone may desire the most beautiful person in the room, most people tend to approach, date, and marry someone who is about as attractive as they are (Berscheid et al., 1971; Lee et al., 2008). (See the Where Do You Stand? box at the end of the chapter.)

Psychological Factors. If attraction is all about big biceps and high cheekbones, then why don't we just skip the small talk and pick our mates from photographs? Because for human beings, attraction is about much more than that. Physical appearance may determine who draws our attention and quickens our pulse, but once people begin interacting they quickly move beyond appearances (Cramer, Schaefer, & Reid, 1996; Regan, 1998). People's *inner* qualities—their personalities, points of view, attitudes, beliefs, values, ambitions, and abilities—play an important role in determining their sustained interest in each other, and there isn't much mystery about the kinds of inner qualities that most people find attractive. For example, intelligence, sense of humor, sensitivity, and ambition seem to be high on just about everybody's list (Daniel et al., 1985).

But just how much wit and wisdom do we want our mate to have? Research suggests that we are most attracted to people who are generally similar to us on most psychological dimensions (Byrne, Ervin, & Lamberth, 1970; Byrne & Nelson, 1965; Hatfield & Rapson, 1992; Neimeyer & Mitchell, 1988). We marry people with similar levels of education, religious backgrounds, ethnicities, socioeconomic statuses, and personalities (Botwin, Buss, & Shackelford, 1997; Buss, 1985; Caspi & Herbener, 1990). Indeed, of all the variables psychologists have ever studied, *gender* appears to be the only one for which the majority of people have a consistent preference for dissimilarity.

> Why is similarity such a powerful determinant of attraction?

Why is similarity so attractive? First, it's easy to interact with people who are similar to us because we can instantly agree on a wide range of issues, such as what to eat, where to live, how to raise children, and how to spend our money. Second, when someone shares our attitudes and beliefs, we feel a bit more confident that those attitudes and beliefs are correct (Byrne & Clore, 1970). Indeed, research shows that when the accuracy of a person's attitudes and beliefs is challenged, similarity becomes an even more important determinant of their attraction to others (Greenberg et al., 1990; Hirschberger, Florian, & Mikulincer, 2002). Third, if we like people who share our attitudes and beliefs, then we can reasonably expect them to like us for the same reason—and *being* liked is a powerful source of attraction (Aronson & Worchel, 1966; Backman & Secord, 1959; Condon & Crano, 1988). Although we tend to like people who like us, it is worth noting that we *especially* like people who like us and who *don't* like anyone else (Eastwick et al., 2007).

Our desire for similarity goes beyond attitudes and beliefs and extends to abilities as well. For example, we may admire extraordinary skill in athletes and actors, but when it comes to friends and lovers, extraordinary people can threaten our self-esteem and make us feel a bit nervous about our own competence (Tesser, 1991). As such, we are generally attracted to competent people who—like us—have small pockets of incompetence. Why? It seems that people who are annoyingly perfect are perfectly annoying. Having a flaw or two "humanizes" people and makes them seem more accessible—and more similar—to us (Aronson, Willerman, & Floyd, 1966).

Relationships

Selecting and attracting a mate is a prerequisite for reproduction. But the real work consists of bearing and raising the kids! For human beings, that work is ordinarily done in the context of committed, long-term, romantic relationships such as a marriage (Clark & Lemay, 2010). Only a few animals have relationships of this kind, so why are we among them?

One answer is that we're born half baked. Human beings have large heads to house their large brains; thus a fully developed human infant could not pass through its mother's birth canal. As such, human infants are *born before they are fully developed* and

▲ Similarity is a very strong source of attraction.

passionate love An experience involving feelings of euphoria, intimacy, and intense sexual attraction.

companionate love An experience involving affection, trust, and concern for a partner's well-being.

social exchange The hypothesis that people remain in relationships only as long as they perceive a favorable ratio of costs to benefits.

comparison level The cost-benefit ratio that people believe they deserve or could attain in another relationship.

thus need a great deal of care—often more than one parent can provide. If human infants were more like tadpoles—ready at birth to swim, find food, and escape predators—then their parents might not need to form and maintain relationships. But human infants are remarkably helpless creatures that require years of intense care before they can fend for themselves, so human adults do almost all of their reproducing in the context of committed, long-term relationships. (By the way, some baby birds also require more food than one adult caretaker can provide, and the adults of those species also tend to form long-term relationships.)

Why do people form long-term romantic relationships?

In most cultures, committed, long-term relationships are signified by marriage, and ours is no exception. The probability of marrying by age 40 is currently 81% for American men and 86% for American women (Goodwin, McGill, & Chandra, 2009). And most of those who marry will say they married for love. Indeed, about 85% of Americans say that they would not marry without love (Kephart, 1967; Simpson, Campbell, & Berscheid, 1986), the vast majority say they would sacrifice their other life goals to attain it (Hammersla & Frease-McMahan, 1990), and most list love as one of the two most important sources of happiness in life (Freedman, 1978). The fact that people marry for love seems so obvious that you may be surprised to learn that it became obvious only recently (Brehm, 1992; Fisher, 1993; Hunt, 1959). Throughout history, marriage has traditionally served a variety of economic (and decidedly unromantic) functions, ranging from cementing agreements between clans to paying back debts—and in many cultures, that's precisely how it is still regarded. Ancient Greeks and Romans married, but they considered love a form of madness (Heine, 2010). Twelfth-century Europeans married but thought of love as a game to be played by knights and ladies of the court (who happened to be married, but not to the knights). Indeed, it wasn't until the 17th century that Westerners began seriously considering the possibility that love might actually be a *reason* to get married.

But is it? People who get married usually think they will stay married, and a whole lot of them are wrong. For every two couples who got married in 2008, one couple got divorced (Tejada-Vera & Sutton, 2009). Although there are many reasons for divorce (Gottman, 1994; Karney & Bradbury, 1995), one is that couples don't always have a clear understanding of what love is. Indeed, a language that uses the same word to describe the deepest forms of intimacy ("I love Emily") and the most shallow forms of satisfaction ("I love ketchup") is bound to confuse the people who speak it (Reis & Aron, 2008), which is one of the reasons why people debate endlessly the question of whether they are really "in love." Psychologists try to sidestep this confusion by distinguishing between two basic kinds of love—**passionate love**, which is *an experience involving feelings of euphoria, intimacy, and intense sexual attraction,* and **companionate love**, which is *an experience involving affection, trust, and concern for a partner's well-being* (Acevedo & Aron, 2009; Hatfield, 1988; Rubin, 1973; Sternberg, 1986). The ideal romantic relationship gives rise to both types of love, but the speeds, trajectories, and durations of the two experiences are markedly different (**FIGURE 13.10**).

▼ Are people more like cattle or robins? In most ways, we are more like any mammal than we are like any bird, but songbirds and people do share one thing that cattle don't: Their young are helpless at birth and thus require significant parental care. Interestingly, adult robins and adult human beings (but not adult cattle) have enduring relationships. And sing.

Passionate love is what brings people together; it has a rapid onset, reaches its peak quickly, and begins to diminish within just a few months (Aron et al., 2005). Companionate love is what keeps people together; it takes some time to get started, grows slowly, and need never stop growing (Gonzaga et al., 2001). In other words, the love we feel early in a relationship is not the same love we feel later. When people marry for passionate love, they may not choose a partner with whom they can easily develop companionate love, and if they don't understand how quickly passionate love cools, they may blame their partners when it does. In many cultures, parents try to keep children from making these mistakes by choosing their marriage partners for them. Some studies suggest that these "arranged marriages" yield greater satisfaction over the long term than do "love matches" (Yelsma & Athappilly, 1988), but other studies suggest the opposite (Xiaohe & Whyte, 1990). If there *are* any benefits to arranged marriage, they may derive from the fact that parents are less likely to pick partners on the basis of passionate love and more likely to pick partners who have a high potential for companionate love (Haidt, 2006).

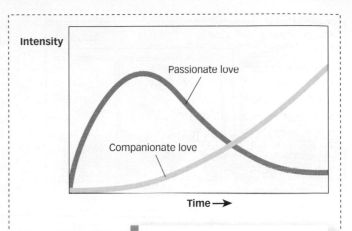

▲ FIGURE 13.10
Passionate and Companionate Love Companionate and passionate love have different time courses and trajectories. Passionate love begins to cool within just a few months, but companionate love can grow slowly but steadily over years.

We've examined some of the factors that draw people into intimate relationships, but what determines when people will be drawn out? Although feelings of love, happiness, and satisfaction may lead us to marriage, the lack of those feelings doesn't seem to lead us to divorce. Marital satisfaction is only weakly correlated with marital stability (Karney & Bradbury, 1995), suggesting that relationships break up or remain intact for reasons other than the satisfaction of those involved (Drigotas & Rusbult, 1992; Rusbult & Van Lange, 2003). Relationships offer benefits, such as love, sex, and financial security, but they also exact costs, such as increased responsibility, increased conflict, and loss of freedom. **Social exchange** is *the hypothesis that people remain in relationships only as long as they perceive a favorable ratio of costs to benefits* (Homans, 1961; Thibaut & Kelley, 1959). For example, a relationship that provides an acceptable level of benefits at a reasonable cost will probably be maintained, and one that doesn't won't. Research suggests that this hypothesis is generally true with three important caveats:

> **How do people weigh the costs and benefits of their relationships?**

> People compare their cost-benefit ratios to the alternatives. A person's **comparison level** refers to *the cost-benefit ratio that people believe they deserve or could attain in another relationship* (Rusbult et al., 1991; Thibaut & Kelley, 1959). A cost-benefit ratio that is acceptable to two people who are stranded on a desert island might not be acceptable to the same two people if they were living in a large city where each had access to other potential partners. A cost-benefit ratio seems favorable when we feel that it is the best we can or should do.

◀ In India, brides and grooms typically do not meet until their wedding day.

DINODIA IMAGES/ALAMY

"This next one goes out to all those who have ever been in love, then become engaged, gotten married, participated in the tragic deterioration of a relationship, suffered the pains and agonies of a bitter divorce, subjected themselves to the fruitless search for a new partner, and ultimately resigned themselves to remaining single in a world full of irresponsible jerks, noncommittal weirdos, and neurotic misfits."

> People may want their cost-benefit ratios to be high, but they also want them to be about the same as their partner's. Most people seem to prefer **equity**, which is *a state of affairs in which the cost-benefit ratios of two partners are roughly equal* (Bolton & Ockenfels, 2000; Messick & Cook, 1983; Walster, Walster, & Berscheid, 1978). For example, spouses are more distressed when their respective cost-benefit ratios are *different* than when their cost-benefit ratios are *unfavorable*—and this is true even when their cost-benefit ratio is *more* favorable than their partner's (Schafer & Keith, 1980).

> Relationships can be thought of as investments into which people pour resources such as time, money, and affection, and research suggests that after people have poured significant resources into their relationships, they are more willing to settle for less favorable cost-benefit ratios (Kelley, 1983; Rusbult, 1983). This is one of the reasons why people are much more likely to end new marriages than old ones (Bramlett & Mosher, 2002; Cherlin, 1992).

IN SUMMARY

○ Survival and reproduction require scarce resources, and aggression and cooperation are two ways to get them.

○ Aggression often results from negative affect, which can be caused by almost anything—from being insulted to being hot. The likelihood that a person will aggress when they feel negative affect is determined both by biological factors (such as testosterone level) and cultural factors (such as religion).

○ Cooperation is beneficial but risky, and one strategy for reducing its risks is to form groups whose members are biased in favor of each other. Unfortunately, groups often show prejudice and discrimination toward those who are not members, they sometimes make poor decisions, and they may even take extreme actions that no individual member would take alone.

○ Human beings can behave altruistically, though behaviors that appear to be altruistic sometimes have hidden benefits for the person who does them.

○ Biology and culture tend to make the costs of reproduction higher for women than for men, which is one reason why women tend to be choosier when selecting potential mates.

○ Attraction is determined by situational factors (such as proximity), physical factors (such as symmetry), and psychological factors (such as similarity).

○ Human reproduction usually occurs within the context of a long-term relationship. People weigh the costs and benefits of their relationships and tend to dissolve them when they think they can or should do better, when they and their partners have very different cost-benefit ratios, or when they have little invested in the relationship.

▲ According to *Time*, the world's most influential person in 2010 was Mir-Hossein Mousavi, the leader of a political movement that opposes the government of Iran.

Social Influence: Controlling People

Those of us who grew up watching cartoons on Saturday mornings have usually thought a bit about which of the standard superpowers we'd most like to have. Super-strength and super-speed have obvious benefits, invisibility and x-ray vision could be interesting as well as lucrative, and there's a lot to be said for flying. But when it comes right down to it, the ability to control other people would surely be most useful. After all, who needs to lift a tractor or catch a bad guy if they can get someone else to do it for them? The things we want from life—gourmet food, interesting jobs, big houses, fancy cars—can be given to us by others, and the things we want most—loving families, loyal friends, admiring children, appreciative employers—cannot be had in any other way.

Social influence is *the ability to control another person's behavior* (Cialdini & Trost, 1998). But how does it work? If you want someone to give you their time, money, allegiance, or affection, you'd be wise to consider first what it is *they* want. People have three basic motivations that make them susceptible to social influence (Bargh, Gollwitzer, & Oettingen, 2010). First, people are motivated to experience pleasure and to avoid experiencing pain (the *hedonic motive*). Second, people are motivated to be accepted and to avoid being rejected (the *approval motive*). Third, people are motivated to believe what is right and to avoid believing what is wrong (the *accuracy motive*). As you will see, most social influence attempts appeal to one or more of these motives.

The Hedonic Motive: Pleasure Is Better Than Pain

If there is an animal that prefers pain to pleasure it must be very good at hiding, because scientists have never seen it. Pleasure-seeking is the most basic of all motives, and social influence often involves creating situations in which others can achieve more pleasure by doing what we want them to do than by doing something else. Parents, teachers, governments, and businesses often try to influence our behavior by offering rewards and threatening punishments (see **FIGURE 13.11**). There's nothing mysterious about how these influence attempts work, and they are often quite effective. When the Republic of Singapore warned its citizens that anyone caught chewing gum in public would face a year in prison and a $5,500 fine, the rest of the world seemed either outraged or amused. When all the criticism and chuckling subsided, though, it was hard to ignore the fact that the incidence of felonious gum-chewing in Singapore had fallen to an all-time low.

How effective are rewards and punishments?

You'll recall from Chapter 6 that even a sea slug will repeat behaviors that are followed by rewards and avoid behaviors that are followed by punishments. Although the same is generally true of human beings, there are some instances in which rewards and punishments can backfire. For example, children in one study were allowed to play with colored markers and then some were given a "Good Player Award." When the children were given markers the next day, those who had received an award were less likely to play with them than were those who had not received an award (Lepper, Greene, & Nisbett, 1973). Why? Because children who had received an award the first day came to think of drawing as something one did to receive rewards, and if no one was going to give them an award, then why should they do it (Deci, Koestner, & Ryan, 1999)? Similarly, reward and punishment can backfire simply because people don't like to feel manipulated. Researchers placed signs in two restrooms on a college campus—one reading, "Please don't write on these walls" and another reading, "Do not

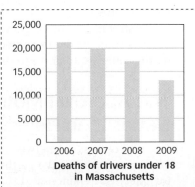

◄ FIGURE 13.11

The Cost of Speeding The penalty for speeding in Massachusetts used to be a modest fine. In 2006, the legislature changed the law so that drivers under 18 who are caught speeding now lose their licenses for 90 days—and to get them back they have to pay $500, attend 8 hours of training classes, and retake the state's driving exam. Guess what? Deaths among drivers under 18 fell by 38% in just 3 years. In other words, more than 8,000 young lives were saved by appealing to the hedonic motive.

http://www.boston.com/news/local/massachusetts/arti cles/2010/04/18/steep_drop_in_teen_driver_fatalities/

Deaths of drivers under 18 in Massachusetts

CULTURE & COMMUNITY

Free parking People don't like to be manipulated, and they get upset when someone threatens their freedom to do as they wish. Is this a uniquely Western reaction? To find out, psychologist Eva Jonas and her colleagues asked college students one of two favors and then measured how irritated they felt (Jonas et al., 2009). In one case, they asked students if they would give up their right to park on campus for a week ("Would you mind if I used your parking card so I can participate in a research project in this building?"). In the other case, they asked students if they would give up *everyone's* right to park on campus for a week ("Would you mind if we closed the entire parking lot for a tennis tournament?"). How did students react to these requests?

It depended on their culture. As the accompanying figure shows, European American students were more irritated by a request that limited their freedom than by a request that limited everyone's freedom ("If nobody can park, that's inconvenient. But if everybody except *me* can park, that's unfair!"). But Latino students and Asian American students had precisely the opposite reactions ("The needs of the requestor outweigh the needs of one student, but they don't outweigh the needs of all students"). It appears that people do indeed value freedom—but not necessarily their own.

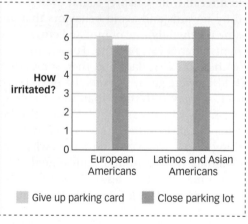

write on these walls under any circumstances." Two weeks later, the walls in the second restroom had more graffiti than the walls in the first restroom did, presumably because students didn't appreciate the threatening tone of the second sign and wrote on the walls just to prove to themselves that they could (Pennebaker & Sanders, 1976).

The Approval Motive: Acceptance Is Better Than Rejection

Other people stand between us and starvation, predation, loneliness, and all the other things that make getting shipwrecked such a bad idea. We depend on others for safety, sustenance, and solidarity, and thus we are powerfully motivated to have others like us, accept us, and approve of us (Baumeister & Leary, 1995; Leary, 2010). Like any motive, this one leaves us vulnerable to social influence.

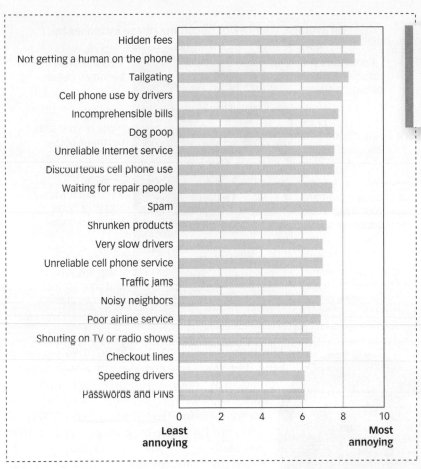

Hidden fees
Not getting a human on the phone
Tailgating
Cell phone use by drivers
Incomprehensible bills
Dog poop
Unreliable Internet service
Discourteous cell phone use
Waiting for repair people
Spam
Shrunken products
Very slow drivers
Unreliable cell phone service
Traffic jams
Noisy neighbors
Poor airline service
Shouting on TV or radio shows
Checkout lines
Speeding drivers
Passwords and PINs

0   2   4   6   8   10

Least annoying   **Most annoying**

◀ Other people are the source of most of our rewards—and, it appears, most of our punishments. In a 2010 survey that asked Americans to identify the things that annoyed them most, 19 of the top 20 annoyances were caused by other people, and one was caused by other people's dogs.

Normative Influence

When getting on an elevator you are supposed to face forward, and you shouldn't talk to the person next to you even if you were talking to that person before you got on the elevator unless you are the only two people on the elevator, in which case it's okay to talk and face sideways but still not backward. Although no one ever taught you this rule, you probably picked it up somewhere along the way. The unwritten rules that govern social behavior are called **norms**, which are *customary standards for behavior that are widely shared by members of a culture* (Miller & Prentice, 1996). We learn norms with exceptional ease and we obey them with exceptional fidelity because we know that if we don't, others won't approve of us. **Normative influence** occurs when *another person's behavior provides information about what is appropriate* (see **FIGURE 13.12** on the next page). For example, every human culture has a **norm of reciprocity**, which is *the unwritten rule that people should benefit those who have benefited them* (Gouldner, 1960). When a friend buys you lunch, you return the favor; and if you don't, your friend gets miffed. Indeed, the norm of reciprocity is so strong that when researchers randomly pulled the names of strangers from a telephone directory and sent them all Christmas cards, they received Christmas cards back from most (Kunz & Woolcott, 1976). Social influence techniques often trade on the norm of reciprocity. For example, waiters and waitresses get bigger tips when they give customers a piece of candy along with the bill because customers feel obligated to do "a little extra" for those who have done "a little extra" for them (Strohmetz et al., 2002).

How are we influenced by other people's behavior?

norm A customary standard for behavior that is widely shared by members of a culture.

normative influence A phenomenon that occurs when another person's behavior provides information about what is appropriate.

norm of reciprocity The unwritten rule that people should benefit those who have benefited them.

► FIGURE 13.12
The Perils of Connection Other people's behavior defines what's "normal," which is one of the reasons why obesity "spreads" through social networks (Christakis & Fowler, 2007).

Source: Analysis of 12,067 participants in the Framingham Heart Study from 1971 to 2003 James Abundis/Globe Staff

On average, your risk of becoming obese increases by ...

... 57% if someone you consider a friend becomes obese.

... 171% if a very close friend becomes obese.

... 100% if you are a man and your male friend becomes obese.

... 38% if you are a woman and your female friend becomes obese.

... 37% if your spouse becomes obese.

... 40% if one of your siblings becomes obese.

... 67% if you are a woman and your sister becomes obese.

... 44% if you are a man and your brother becomes obese.

©FRANCIS DEAN/DEAN PICTURES/THE IMAGE WORKS

▲ Have you ever wondered which big spender left the bill as a tip? In fact, the bills are often put there by the very people you are tipping because they know that the presence of paper money will suggest to you that others are leaving big tips and that it would be socially appropriate for you to do the same. By the way, the customary gratuity for someone who writes a textbook for you is 15%. But most students send more.

TED SZCZEPANSKI FOR WORTH PUBLISHERS

The norm of reciprocity always involves swapping, but the swapping doesn't always involve favors. The **door-in-the-face technique** is *a strategy that uses reciprocating concessions to influence behavior.* Here's how it works: You ask someone for something more valuable than you really want, you wait for that person to refuse (to "slam the door in your face"), and then you ask the person for what you really want. In one study, researchers asked college students to volunteer to supervise adolescents who were going on a field trip, and only 17% of the students agreed. But when the researchers first asked students to commit to spending 2 hours per week for 2 years working at a youth detention center (to which every one of the students said no) and *then* asked them if they'd be willing to supervise the field trip, 50% of the students agreed (Cialdini et al., 1975). Why? The norm of reciprocity. The researchers began by asking for a large favor, which the student refused. Then the researchers made a concession by asking for a smaller favor. Because the researchers made a concession, the norm of reciprocity demanded that the student make one too—and half of them did!

Conformity

People can influence us by invoking familiar norms. But if you've ever found yourself sneaking a peek at the diner next to you, hoping to discover whether the little fork is supposed to be used for the shrimp or the salad, then you know that other people can also influence us by defining *new* norms in ambiguous, confusing, or novel situations. **Conformity** is *the tendency to do what others do simply because others are doing it,* and it results in part from normative influence.

Why do we do what we see other people doing?

In a classic study, psychologist Solomon Asch had participants sit in a room with seven other people who appeared to be
ordinary participants but who were actually actors (Asch, 1951,
1956). An experimenter explained that the participants would
be shown cards with three printed lines and that their job was
simply to say which of the three lines matched a "standard line"
that was printed on another card (**FIGURE 13.13**). The experimenter held up a card and then asked each person to answer in
turn. The real participant was among the last to be called on.
Everything was normal on the first two trials, but on the third
trial, something odd happened: The actors all began giving the
same wrong answer! What did the real participants do? Seventy-
five percent of them conformed and announced the wrong answer on at least one trial. Subsequent research has shown that
these participants didn't actually misperceive the length of the lines but were instead
succumbing to normative influence (Asch, 1955; Nemeth & Chiles, 1988). Giving the
wrong answer was apparently the right thing to do, and so participants did it.

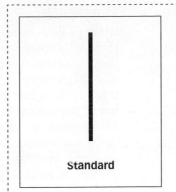
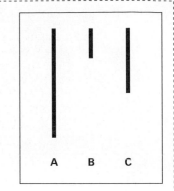

▲ FIGURE 13.13
Asch's Conformity Study If you
were asked which of the lines on the
right—A, B, or C—matches the standard
line on the left, what would you say?
Research on conformity suggests
that your answer would depend, in
part, on how other people in the room
answered the same question.

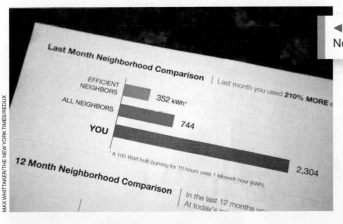

◄ The perplexed research participant
(center), flanked by confederates (who
are "in" on the experiment), is on the
verge of conformity in one of Solomon
Asch's line-judging experiments.

The behavior of others can tell us what is proper, appropriate, expected, and accepted—
in other words, it can define a norm—and once a norm is defined, we feel obliged to
honor it. When a Holiday Inn in Tempe, Arizona, left a variety of different "message
cards" in guests' bathrooms in the hopes of convincing those guests to reuse their towels
rather than laundering them every day, it discovered that the single most effective message was the one that simply read: "Seventy five percent of our guests use their towels
more than once" (Cialdini, 2005). When the Sacramento Municipal Utility District randomly selected 35,000 customers and sent them electric bills showing how their energy
consumption compared to that of their neighbors (see **FIGURE 13.14**), consumption fell by
2% (Kaufman, 2009). Clearly, normative influence can be a force for good.

◄ FIGURE 13.14
Normative Influence at Work

door-in-the-face technique A strategy that
uses reciprocating concessions to
influence behavior.

conformity The tendency to do what others
do simply because others are doing it.

Obedience

Other people's behavior can provide information about norms, but in most situations there are a few people whom we all recognize as having special authority both to define the norms and to enforce them. The usher at a movie theater may be an underpaid high school student who isn't allowed to drink, drive, vote, or stay up past 10:00 p.m. on a school night, but in the context of the theater, the usher is the authority. So when the usher asks you to take your feet off the seat in front of you, you obey. **Obedience** is *the tendency to do what powerful people tell us to do.*

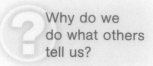

Why do we do what others tell us?

Why do we obey powerful people? Well, yes, sometimes they have guns. But while powerful people are often capable of rewarding and punishing us, research shows that much of their influence is *normative* (Tyler, 1990). Psychologist Stanley Milgram (1963) demonstrated this in one of psychology's most infamous experiments. The participants in this experiment met a middle-aged man who was introduced as another participant but who was actually a trained actor. An experimenter in a lab coat explained that the participant would play the role of *teacher* and the actor would play the role of *learner*. The teacher and learner would sit in different rooms, the teacher would read words to the learner over a microphone, and the learner would then repeat the words back to the teacher. If the learner made a mistake, the teacher would press a button that delivered an electric shock to the learner (**FIGURE 13.15**). The shock-generating machine (which wasn't actually hooked up, of course) offered 30 levels of shock, ranging from 15 volts (labeled "slight shock") to 450 volts (labeled "Danger: severe shock").

After the learner was strapped into his chair, the experiment began. When the learner made his first mistake, the participant dutifully delivered a 15-volt shock. As the learner made more mistakes, he received more shocks. When the participant delivered the 75-volt shock, the learner cried out in pain. At 150 volts, the learner screamed, "Get me out of here. I told you I have heart trouble . . . I refuse to go on. Let me out!" With every shock, the learner's screams became more agonized as he pleaded pitifully for his freedom. Then, after receiving the 330-volt shock, the learner stopped responding altogether. Participants were naturally upset by all of this, and they typically asked the experimenter to stop the experiment. But the experimenter simply replied, "You have no choice; you must go on." The experimenter never threatened the participant with punishment of any kind. Rather, he just stood there with his clipboard in hand and calmly instructed the participant to continue. What did the participants do? Eighty percent of the participants continued to shock the learner even after he screamed, complained, pleaded, and then fell silent. And 62% went all the way, delivering the highest possible voltage. Although Milgram's study was conducted nearly half a century ago, a recent replication revealed about the same rate of obedience (Burger, 2009).

► Is this the face of a monster? In this photo, Nazi war criminal Adolph Eichmann sits before the District Court of Jerusalem. Eichmann acknowledged that he sent millions of Jews to their deaths but argued that he was merely obeying authority. He was sentenced to death and hanged in 1962.

► **FIGURE 13.15**
Milgram's Obedience Studies The learner (left) being hooked up to the shock generator (right) that was used in Stanley Milgram's obedience studies.

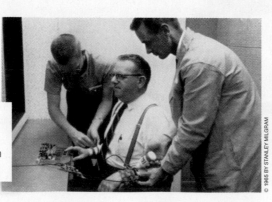

Were these people psychopathic sadists? Would normal people electrocute a stranger just because some guy in a lab coat told them to? The answer, it seems, is *yes*—as long as *normal* means being sensitive to social norms. The participants in this experiment knew that hurting others is *often* wrong but not *always* wrong: Doctors give painful injections, and teachers give painful exams. There are many situations in which it is permissible—and even desirable—to cause someone to suffer in the service of a higher goal. The experimenter's calm demeanor and persistent instruction suggested that he, and not the participant, knew what was appropriate in this particular situation, and so the participant did as ordered. Subsequent research confirmed that participants' obedience was due to normative pressure. When the experimenter's authority to define the norm was undermined—for example, when a second experimenter appeared to disagree with the first or when the instructions were given by a person who wasn't wearing a lab coat—participants rarely obeyed the instructions (Milgram, 1974; Miller, 1986).

obedience The tendency to do what powerful people tell us to do.

attitude An enduring positive or negative evaluation of an object or event.

belief An enduring piece of knowledge about an object or event.

informational influence A phenomenon that occurs when a person's behavior provides information about what is good or right.

The Accuracy Motive: Right Is Better Than Wrong

When you are hungry, you open the refrigerator and grab an apple because you know that apples (a) taste good and (b) are in the refrigerator. This action, like most actions, relies on both an **attitude**, which is *an enduring positive or negative evaluation of an object or event,* and a **belief**, which is *an enduring piece of knowledge about an object or event.* In a sense, our attitudes tell us what we should do ("Eat an apple") and our beliefs tell us how to do it ("Start by opening the fridge"). If our attitudes or beliefs are inaccurate—that is, if we can't tell good from bad or right from wrong—then our actions are likely to be fruitless. Because we rely so much on our attitudes and beliefs, it isn't surprising that we are motivated to have the right ones. And that motivation leaves us vulnerable to social influence.

Informational Influence

If everyone in the shopping mall suddenly ran screaming for the exit, you'd probably join them—not because you were afraid that they would otherwise disapprove of you, but because their behavior would suggest to you that there was something worth running from. **Informational influence** occurs when *another person's behavior provides information about what is good or right.* You can observe the power of informational influence yourself just by standing in the middle of the sidewalk, tilting back your head, and staring at the top of a tall building. Research shows that within just a few minutes, other people will stop and stare too (Milgram, Bickman, & Berkowitz, 1969). Why? They will assume that if you are looking, then there must be something worth looking at.

How do informational and normative influence differ?

You are the constant target of informational influence. When a salesperson tells you that "most people buy the deluxe model," she is artfully suggesting that you should take other people's behavior as information about the quality of the product. Advertisements that refer to soft drinks as "popular" or books as "best sellers" are reminding you that other people are buying these particular sodas and novels, which suggests that they know something you don't and that you'd be wise to follow their example. Situation comedies provide "laugh tracks" because the producers know that when you hear other people laughing, you will mindlessly assume that something must be funny (Nosanchuk & Lightstone, 1974). Bars and nightclubs make people stand in line to get in

◀ Is McDonald's trying to keep track of sales from the parking lot? Probably not. Rather, they want you to know that other people are buying their hamburgers, which suggests that they are worth buying, which, in turn, suggests that you just might want to stop and have one yourself right about now.

RICHARD CUMMINS/CORBIS

► In 1953, Charlie Douglass (1910–2003) invented the Laff Box because he suspected that television viewers would think a show was funny if they heard other people laughing. Research has since shown that Douglass's intuition was right.

STEVE KELLEY, COURTESY OF BOB DOUGLASS

even when there is plenty of room because they know that passersby will see the line and assume that there must be something worth waiting for. In short, the world is full of objects and events that we know little about, and we can often cure our ignorance by paying attention to the way in which others are acting toward them. Alas, the very thing that makes us open to information leaves us open to manipulation as well.

Persuasion

When the next presidential election rolls around, two things will happen. First, the candidates will say that they intend to win your vote by making arguments that focus on the issues. Second, the candidates will then avoid arguments, ignore issues, and attempt to win your vote with a variety of cheap tricks. What the candidates promise to do and what they actually do reflect two basic forms of **persuasion**, which occurs when *a person's attitudes or beliefs are influenced by a communication from another person* (Albarracín & Vargas, 2010; Petty & Wegener, 1998). The candidates will promise to persuade you by demonstrating that their positions on the issues are the most practical, intelligent, fair, and beneficial. Having made that promise, they will then devote most of their financial resources to persuading you by other means—for example, by dressing nicely and smiling a lot, by surrounding themselves with famous athletes and movie stars, by repeatedly pairing their opponent's picture with one of Adolf Hitler or Osama bin Laden, and so on. In other words, the candidates will promise to engage in **systematic persuasion**, which refers to *the process by which attitudes or beliefs are changed by appeals to reason*, but they will spend most of their time and money engaged in **heuristic persuasion**, which refers to *the process by which attitudes or beliefs are changed by appeals to habit or emotion* (Chaiken, 1980; Petty & Cacioppo, 1986).

How do these two forms of persuasion work? *Systematic persuasion* appeals to logic and reason, and assumes that people will be more persuaded when evidence and arguments are strong rather than weak. *Heuristic persuasion* appeals to

When is it more effective to appeal to reason or to emotion?

▼ Because cars are relatively expensive, people are motivated to process information about them and are therefore persuaded by facts. Because shoes are relatively inexpensive, people are not motivated to process information about them and are therefore persuaded by celebrity endorsements.

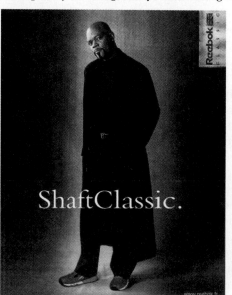

To crash with a Volvo is extremely safe.

If you're sitting in a Saab.

Saab 9-5. Sweden's safest car. In real life.

GENERAL MOTORS LLC. USED WITH PERMISSION, GM MEDIA ARCHIVES

ShaftClassic.

THE ADVERTISING ARCHIVES

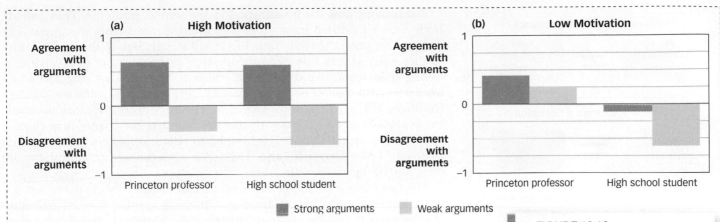

▲ FIGURE 13.16
Systematic and Heuristic Persuasion (a) *Systematic persuasion.* When students were motivated to analyze arguments because they would be personally affected by them, their attitudes were influenced by the strength of the arguments (strong arguments were more persuasive than weak arguments) but not by the status of the communicator (the Princeton professor was not more persuasive than the high school student). (b) *Heuristic persuasion.* When students were not motivated to analyze arguments because they would not be personally affected by them, their attitudes were influenced by the status of the communicator (the Princeton professor was more persuasive than the high school student) but not by the strength of the arguments (strong arguments were no more persuasive than weak arguments) (Petty, Cacioppo, & Goldman, 1981).

habit and emotion, and assumes that rather than weighing evidence and analyzing arguments, people will often use *heuristics* (simple shortcuts or "rules of thumb") to help them decide whether to believe a communication (see Chapter 9). Which form of persuasion will be more effective depends on whether the person is willing and able to weigh evidence and analyze arguments.

For example, in one study, university students heard a speech that contained either strong or weak arguments in favor of instituting comprehensive exams at their school (Petty, Cacioppo, & Goldman, 1981). Some students were told that the speaker was a Princeton University professor, and others were told that the speaker was a high school student—a bit of information that could be used as a shortcut to decide whether to believe the speech. Some students were told that their university was considering implementing these exams right away, whereas others were told that their university was considering implementing these exams in 10 years—a bit of information that made only some students feel motivated to analyze the evidence. As **FIGURE 13.16** shows, when students were motivated to analyze the evidence, they were systematically persuaded—that is, their attitudes and beliefs were influenced by the strength of the arguments but not by the status of the speaker. But when students were not motivated to analyze the evidence, they were heuristically persuaded—that is, their attitudes and beliefs were influenced by the status of the speaker but not by the strength of the arguments.

Consistency

If a friend told you that rabbits had just staged a coup in Antarctica and were halting all carrot exports, you probably wouldn't Google it to see if it was true. You'd know right away that your friend was joking (or at least seriously misinformed) because the statement is logically inconsistent with other things that you know are true—for example, that rabbits do not foment revolution and that Antarctica does not export carrots. People evaluate the accuracy of new beliefs by assessing their *consistency* with old beliefs, and although this is not a foolproof method for determining whether something is true, it provides a pretty good approximation. We are motivated to be accurate, and because consistency is a rough measure of accuracy, we are motivated to be consistent as well (Cialdini, Trost, & Newsom, 1995).

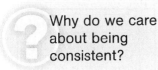

Why do we care about being consistent?

That motivation leaves us vulnerable to social influence. For example, the **foot-in-the-door** technique is *a technique that involves a small request followed by a larger request* (Burger, 1999). In one study (Freedman & Fraser, 1966), experimenters went to a neighborhood and knocked on doors to see if they could convince homeowners to agree to have a big ugly "Drive Carefully" sign installed in their front yards. One group of homeowners was simply asked to install the sign, and only 17% said yes. A second group of homeowners was first asked to sign a petition urging the state legislature to promote safe driving (which almost all agreed to do) and was *then* asked to install the ugly sign. And 55% said yes! Why would homeowners be more likely to grant two requests than one?

persuasion A phenomenon that occurs when a person's attitudes or beliefs are influenced by a communication from another person.

systematic persuasion The process by which attitudes or beliefs are changed by appeals to reason.

heuristic persuasion The process by which attitudes or beliefs are changed by appeals to habit or emotion.

foot-in-the-door technique A technique that involves a small request followed by a larger request.

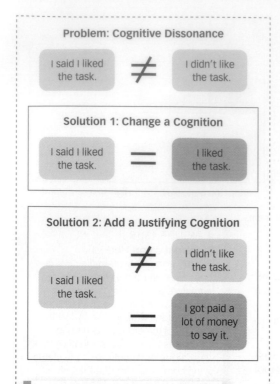

▲ FIGURE 13.17
Alleviating Cognitive Dissonance Suffering for something of little value can cause cognitive dissonance. One way to alleviate that dissonance is to change your belief about the value of the thing you suffered for.

Just imagine how the homeowners in the second group felt. They had already signed a petition stating that they thought safe driving was important, and yet they knew they didn't want to install an ugly sign in their front yards. As they wrestled with this inconsistency, they probably began to experience a feeling called **cognitive dissonance**, which is *an unpleasant state that arises when a person recognizes the inconsistency of his or her actions, attitudes, or beliefs* (Festinger, 1957). When people experience cognitive dissonance they naturally try to alleviate it, and one way to alleviate cognitive dissonance is to change one's actions, attitudes, or beliefs in order to restore consistency among them (Aronson, 1969; Cooper & Fazio, 1984). Allowing the sign to be installed in their yards did precisely that.

The fact that we often alleviate cognitive dissonance by changing our actions, attitudes, or beliefs can leave us vulnerable to other people's efforts to change them for us. In one study, female college students applied to join a weekly discussion on "the psychology of sex." Women in the control group were allowed to join the discussion, but women in the experimental group were allowed to join the discussion only after first passing an embarrassing test that involved reading pornographic fiction to a strange man. Although the carefully staged discussion was as dull as possible, women in the experimental group found it more interesting than did women in the control group (Aronson & Mills, 1958). Why? Women in the experimental group knew that they had paid a steep price to join the group ("I read all that porn out loud!"), but that belief was inconsistent with the belief that the discussion was worthless. As such, the women experienced cognitive dissonance, which they alleviated by changing their beliefs about the value of the discussion. (See the top half of **FIGURE 13.17**.) We normally think that people pay for things because they value them, but as this study shows, people sometimes value things because they've paid for them. It is little wonder that some fraternities use hazing to breed loyalty, that some religions require their adherents to make large personal or monetary sacrifices, that some gourmet restaurants charge outrageous amounts to keep their patrons coming back, or that some men and women play hard to get to maintain their suitors' interest.

? What happens when we are inconsistent?

We are motivated to be consistent, but there are inevitably times when we just can't—for example, when we tell a friend that her new hairstyle is "daring" when it actually resembles a wet skunk after an unfortunate encounter with a snowblower. Why don't we experience cognitive dissonance under such circumstances and come to believe our own lies? Because while telling a friend that her hairstyle is daring is inconsistent with the

◄ Members of the Virginia Military Institute freshman class scramble up a muddy hill while upper-classmen hold their feet (left), and members of Michigan Tech University's Sigma Tau Gamma fraternity brave subzero wind chill to participate in the group's annual "Grundy Run" through the campus (right). Why do social groups "haze" their initiates?

belief that her hairstyle is hideous, it is perfectly consistent with the belief that one should be nice to one's friends. When small inconsistencies are *justified* by large consistencies, cognitive dissonance is reduced.

For example, participants in one study were asked to perform a dull task that involved turning knobs one way, then the other, and then back again. After the participants were sufficiently bored, the experimenter explained that he desperately needed a few more people to volunteer for the study, and he asked the participants to go into the hallway, find another person, and tell that person that the knob-turning task was great fun. The experimenter offered some participants $1 to tell this lie, and he offered other participants $20. All participants agreed to tell the lie, and after they did so, they were asked to report their true enjoyment of the knob-turning task. The results showed that participants liked the task *more* when they were paid $1 than $20 to lie about it (Festinger & Carlsmith, 1959). Why? Because the belief *this knob-turning task is dull* was inconsistent with the belief *I recommended the task to that person in the hallway,* but the latter belief was perfectly consistent with the belief that *$20 is a lot of money.* For some participants, the large payment justified the lie, so only those people who received the small payment experienced cognitive dissonance. As such, only the participants who received $1 felt the need to restore consistency by changing their beliefs about the enjoyableness of the task (see the bottom half of Figure 13.17).

▲ People aren't the only ones who value what they work for. Recent research shows that male rats prefer female rats who make them work hard for sex (Ismail et al., 2009).

IN SUMMARY

○ People are motivated to experience pleasure and avoid pain (the hedonic motive), and thus can be influenced by rewards and punishments, though these can sometimes backfire.

○ People are motivated to attain the approval of others (the approval motive), and thus can be influenced by social norms, such as the norm of reciprocity. People often look to the behavior of others to determine what's normative, and they often end up conforming or obeying, sometimes with disastrous results.

○ People are motivated to know what is true (the accuracy motive), and thus can be influenced by other people's behaviors and communications. This motivation also causes them to seek consistency among their attitudes, beliefs, and actions.

Social Cognition: Understanding People

Justin Bieber is a musical genius. That sentence may or may not be true (probably not), but it almost certainly activated your medial prefrontal cortex, which is an area of your brain that is activated when you think about the attributes of other people but not about the attributes of inanimate objects such as houses or tools (Mitchell, Heatherton, & Macrae, 2002). Although most of your brain shows diminished activity when you are at rest, this area remains active all the time (Buckner, Andrews-Hanna, &

cognitive dissonance An unpleasant state that arises when a person recognizes the inconsistency of his or her actions, attitudes, or beliefs.

social cognition The processes by which people come to understand others.

stereotyping The process by which people draw inferences about others based on their knowledge of the categories to which others belong.

▶ Thinking about Justin Bieber activates your medial prefrontal cortex, and thinking about you activates his. Lately, he's been thinking about you a lot.

Schacter, 2008). Why does your brain have a specific area that is dedicated to processing information about just *one* of the millions of objects you might encounter, and why is this area constantly working?

Of the millions of objects you might encounter, other human beings are the most important. **Social cognition** is *the processes by which people come to understand others,* and you do it all day long. Whether you know it or not, your brain is constantly making inferences about others people's thoughts and feelings, beliefs and desires, abilities and aspirations, intentions, needs, and characters. It bases these inferences on two kinds of information: the categories to which people belong, and the things they do and say.

Stereotyping: Drawing Inferences from Categories

You'll recall from Chapter 9 that categorization is the process by which people identify a stimulus as a member of a class of related stimuli. Once we have identified a novel stimulus as a member of a category ("That's a textbook"), we can then use our knowledge of the category to make educated guesses about the properties of the novel stimulus ("It's probably expensive") and act accordingly ("I think I'll download it illegally").

What we do with textbooks we also do with people. No, not the illegal downloading part. The educated guessing part. **Stereotyping** is *the process by which we draw inferences about others based on knowledge of the categories to which they belong.* The moment we categorize a person as an adult, a male, a baseball player, and a Russian, we can use our knowledge of those categories to make some educated guesses about him—for example, that he shaves his face but not his legs, that he understands the infield fly rule, and that he knows more about vodka than we do. When we offer children candy instead of cigarettes or ask gas station attendants for directions instead of dating advice, we are making inferences about people whom we have never met before based solely on their category membership. As these examples suggest, stereotyping is a very useful process (Allport, 1954). And yet, ever since the word was coined by the journalist Walter Lippmann in 1936, it has had a distasteful connotation. Why? Because stereotyping is a useful process that can often produce harmful results, and it does so because stereotypes tend to have four properties: They are inaccurate, overused, self-perpetuating, and automatic.

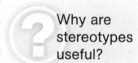

Why are stereotypes useful?

▲ Stereotypes can be inaccurate. Shlomo Koenig does not fit most people's stereotype of a police officer or a rabbi, but he is both.

Stereotypes Can Be Inaccurate

The inferences we draw about individuals are only as accurate as our stereotypes about the categories to which they belong. Although there was no evidence to indicate that Jews were especially materialistic or that African Americans were especially lazy, American college students held such beliefs for most of the last century (G. M. Gilbert, 1951; Karlins, Coffman, & Walters, 1969; Katz & Braly, 1933). They weren't born holding these beliefs, so how did they acquire them? There are only two ways to acquire a belief about anything: to see for yourself or to take somebody else's word for it. In fact, most of what we know about the members of human categories is hearsay—stuff we picked up from friends and uncles, from novels and newspapers, from jokes and movies and late-night television. Many of the people who believe stereotypes about Jews or African Americans have never actually met someone who is Jewish or African American, and their beliefs are a result of listening too closely to what others told them. In the process of inheriting the wisdom of our culture, it is inevitable that we also will inherit its ignorance too.

But even direct observation can produce inaccurate stereotypes. For example, research participants in one study were shown a long series of positive and negative behaviors and were told that each behavior had been performed by a member of one of two groups: Group A or Group B (**FIGURE 13.18**). There were more positive than negative behaviors in the series, and there were more members of Group A than of Group B. In other words, negative behaviors were rarer than positive behaviors, and Group B members were rarer than Group A members. The series of behaviors was carefully arranged so that each group behaved negatively exactly one third of the time. After seeing the series, participants correctly remembered that Group A had behaved negatively one third of the time. However, they incorrectly remembered that Group B had behaved negatively more than *half* the time (Hamilton & Gifford, 1976).

Why aren't stereotypes changed by experience?

Why did this happen? Bad behavior was rare and being a member of Group B was rare; thus participants were especially likely to notice when the two co-occurred ("Aha! There's one of those unusual Group B people doing an unusually awful thing again"). These findings help explain why members of majority groups tend to overestimate the number of crimes (which are relatively rare events) committed by members of minority groups (who are relatively rare people; that's why they're in the minority). Even when we directly observe people, we can end up with inaccurate beliefs about the groups to which they belong.

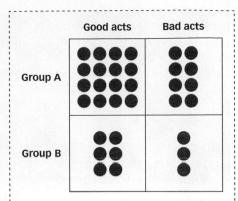

▲ FIGURE 13.18
Seeing Correlations That Aren't Really There Both Group A and Group B each perform two thirds good acts and one third bad acts. However, "Group B" and "bad acts" are both rare, leading people to notice and remember their co-occurrence, which leads them to perceive a correlation between group membership and behavior that isn't really there.

Stereotypes Can Be Overused

Because all thumbtacks are pretty much alike, our beliefs about thumbtacks ("small, cheap, painful when chewed") are quite useful, and we will rarely be mistaken if we generalize from one thumbtack to another. Human categories, however, are so variable that our stereotypes may offer only the vaguest of clues about the individuals who populate those categories. You probably believe that men have greater upper body strength than women do, and this belief is right *on average*. But the upper body strength of individuals *within* each of these categories is so varied that you cannot easily predict how much weight a particular person can lift simply by knowing that person's gender. The inherent variability of human categories makes stereotypes much less useful than they might otherwise be.

How does categorization warp perception?

Alas, we don't always recognize this because the mere act of categorizing a stimulus tends to warp our perceptions of that category's variability. For instance, participants in some studies were shown a series of lines of different lengths (**FIGURE 13.19**) (McGarty & Turner, 1992; Tajfel & Wilkes, 1963). For one group of participants, the longest lines were labeled *A* and the shortest lines were labeled *B,* as they are on the right side of Figure 13.19. For the second group of participants, the lines were shown without these

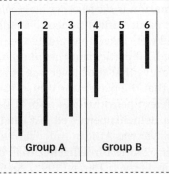

◀ FIGURE 13.19
How Categorization Warps Perception People who see the lines on the right tend to *overestimate the similarity* of lines 1 and 3 and *underestimate the similarity* of lines 3 and 4. Simply labeling lines 1 through 3 "Group A" and lines 4 through 6 "Group B" causes the lines within a group to seem more similar to each other than they really are and the lines in different groups to seem more different from each other than they really are.

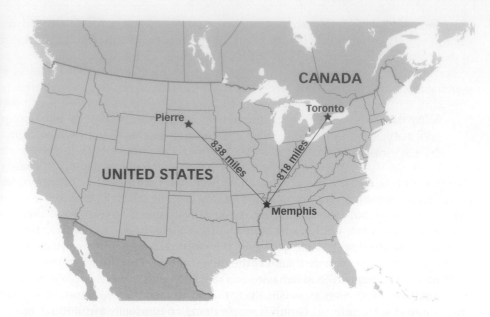

▲ FIGURE 13.20
Perceiving Categories Categorization can influence how we see colors and how we estimate distances.

category labels, as they are on the left side of Figure 13.19. Interestingly, those participants who saw the category labels *overestimated* the similarity of the lines that shared a label and *underestimated* the similarity of lines that did not.

You've probably experienced this phenomenon yourself. For instance, we all identify colors as members of categories such as *blue* or *green,* and this leads us to overestimate the similarity of colors that share a category label and to underestimate the similarity of colors that do not. That's why we see discrete *bands* of color when we look at rainbows, which are actually a smooth continuum of colors (see **FIGURE 13.20**). That's also why we tend to underestimate the distance between cities that are in the same country, such as Memphis and Pierre, and overestimate the distance between cities that are in different countries, such as Memphis and Toronto (Burris & Branscombe, 2005). What's true of colors and distances is true of people as well. The mere act of categorizing people as Blacks or Whites, Jews or Gentiles, artists or accountants, can cause us to underestimate the variability within those categories ("All artists are wacky") and to overestimate the variability between them ("Artists are much wackier than accountants"). When we underestimate the variability of a human category, we overestimate how useful our stereotypes can be.

Stereotypes Can Be Self-Perpetuating

When we meet a man who likes ballet more than football or a senior citizen who likes hip-hop more than easy-listening, why don't we recognize that our stereotypes are inaccurate? Stereotypes are a bit like viruses, and once they take up residence inside us, they perpetuate themselves and resist even our most concerted efforts to eradicate them. Stereotypes are self-perpetuating for three reasons:

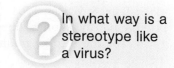

In what way is a stereotype like a virus?

> **Perceptual confirmation** is *the tendency for people to see what they expect to see.* In one study, participants listened to a radio broadcast of a college basketball game and were asked to evaluate the performance of one of the players. Although all participants heard the same prerecorded game, some were led to believe that the player was African American and others were led to believe that the player was White. Participants' stereotypes led them to expect different performances from athletes of different ethnic origins—and the participants perceived just what they expected. Those who believed the player was African American thought he had exhibited greater athletic ability but less intelligence than did those who thought he was White (Stone, Perry, & Darley, 1997). Stereotypes perpetuate

perceptual confirmation A phenomenon that occurs when observers perceive what they expect to perceive.

self-fulfilling prophecy The tendency for people to cause what they expect to see.

subtyping The tendency for people who are faced with disconfirming evidence to modify their stereotypes rather than abandon them.

themselves in part by biasing our perception of individuals, leading us to believe that those individuals have confirmed our stereotypes even when they have not (Fiske, 1998) (see the Hot Science box).

> **Self-fulfilling prophecy** is *the tendency for people to cause what they expect to see*. When people know that observers have a negative stereotype about them, they may experience *stereotype threat,* or fear of confirming an observer's stereotype (Aronson & Steele, 2004; Schmader, Johns, & Forbes, 2008; Walton & Spencer, 2009). Ironically, this fear can cause people to behave in precisely the way that the stereotype predicts. In one study (Steele & Aronson, 1995), African American and White students were given a test, and half the students in each group were asked to list their race at the top of the exam. Students who were not asked to list their race performed well; but when students were asked to list their races, African American students became anxious and performed poorly (**FIGURE 13.21**). Stereotypes perpetuate themselves in part by causing the stereotyped individual to behave in ways that confirm the stereotype.

> **Subtyping** is *the tendency for people who are faced with disconfirming evidence to modify their stereotypes rather than abandon them* (Weber & Crocker, 1983). For example, people tend to believe that public relations agents are sociable. In one study, participants learned about a PR agent who was *slightly* unsociable, and the results showed that their stereotypes about PR agents shifted a bit to accommodate this new information. But when participants learned about a PR agent who was *extremely* unsociable, their stereotypes did not change at all (Kunda & Oleson, 1997). Instead, they tended to think of the extremely unsociable PR agent as "an exception to the rule" and thereby preserve their stereotypes about PR agents in general. Subtyping is a powerful method for preserving our stereotypes in the face of contradictory evidence.

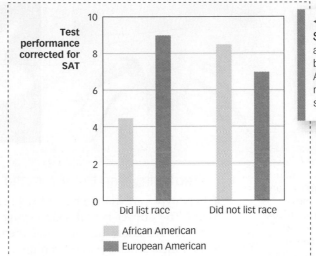

◄ FIGURE 13.21
Stereotype Threat When asked to indicate their race before starting a test, African American students perform more poorly than their SAT scores suggest they should.

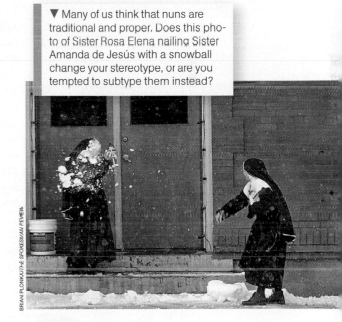

▼ Many of us think that nuns are traditional and proper. Does this photo of Sister Rosa Elena nailing Sister Amanda de Jesús with a snowball change your stereotype, or are you tempted to subtype them instead?

BRIAN PLONKA/THE SPOKESMAN-REVIEW

HOT SCIENCE

The Color of Expectations

Psychologists often say that people see what they expect to see, and new research shows that this is true in the most literal sense (Hansen et al., 2006). Subjects were shown pictures of different-colored objects on a computer display and were asked to adjust the color on the display until the object appeared gray. When the object was a yellow blob, subjects did this quite well; but when the object was a yellow banana, they went beyond gray and made it slightly blue (see the accompanying figure). Why? Because even after the banana had objectively become gray, subjects continued to see it as slightly yellow because they expected a banana to be yellow; thus they kept adjusting the knob toward blue. Psychologists have long known that expectations can color our perceptions of people, but apparently they can color our perceptions of color as well.

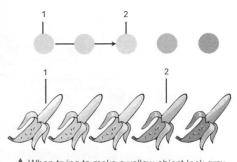

▲ When trying to make a yellow object look gray, subjects adjusted from 1 to 2.

▲ Research on unconscious stereotyping shows that Americans find it easier to associate Black faces with negative stimuli (such as spiders) and White faces with positive stimuli (such as flowers) than the other way around. Interestingly, both Black and White Americans show this pattern of responses, suggesting that these associations are learned through exposure to mass media.

Stereotyping Can Be Automatic

If stereotypes are inaccurate and self-perpetuating, then why don't we just stop using them? The answer is that stereotyping happens *unconsciously* (which means that we don't always know we are using them) and *automatically* (which means that we often cannot avoid using them even when we try) (Banaji & Heiphetz, 2010; Greenwald, McGhee, & Schwartz, 1998; Greenwald & Nosek, 2001).

? Can we decide not to stereotype?

For example, in one study, photos of Black or White men holding guns or cameras were flashed on a computer screen for less than 1 second each. Participants earned money by pressing a button labeled "shoot" whenever the man on the screen was holding a gun but lost money if they shot a man holding a camera. The participants made some mistakes, of course, but the kinds of mistakes they made were quite disturbing: Participants were more likely to shoot a man holding a camera when that man was Black and less likely to shoot a man holding a gun when that man was White (Correll et al., 2002). Although the photos appeared on the screen so quickly that participants did not have enough time to consciously consult their stereotypes, those stereotypes worked unconsciously, causing them to mistake a camera for a gun when it was in the hands of a Black man and a gun for a camera when it was in the hands of a White man. Interestingly, Black participants were just as likely to make this pattern of errors as were White participants.

Stereotypes comprise all the information that we have absorbed over the years about members of different human categories, for better or for worse, and we can't *decide* not to use that information any more than we can *decide* not to see the color green, not to remember our high school graduation, or not to smell French fries. In

▲ In 2007, Reuters news photographer Namir Noor-Eldeen was shot to death in Iraq by American soldiers in a helicopter who mistook his camera for a weapon. Would they have made the same mistake if Noor-Eldeen had been blonde or female?

↑ Namir w/camera

Thats a weapon.
Yeah.

fact, trying not to use stereotypes can make matters worse instead of better. Participants in one study were shown a photograph of a tough-looking male "skinhead" and were asked to write an essay describing a typical day in his life. Some of the participants were told that they should not allow their stereotypes about skinheads to influence their essays, and others were given no such instructions. Next, the experimenter brought each participant to a room with eight empty chairs. The first chair had a jacket draped over it, and the experimenter explained that it belonged to a skinhead, who had gone to use the restroom. Where did participants choose to sit? Participants who had been told not to use their stereotypes sat farther away from the skinhead's jacket than did participants who had been given no instructions (Macrae et al., 1994). Apparently, trying hard not to do something can make us more inclined to do it (Wegner et al., 1987).

Stereotypes are difficult to set aside. As the Reverend Jesse Jackson said, "There is nothing more painful to me at this stage in my life than to walk down the street and hear footsteps and start thinking about robbery—then look around and see somebody white and feel relieved" (Goldberg, 1999).

DANIEL ACKER/BLOOMBERG VIA GETTY IMAGES

Although stereotyping is unconscious and automatic, it is not inevitable (Blair, 2002; Kawakami et al., 2000; Milne & Grafman, 2001; Rudman, Ashmore, & Gary, 2001). For instance, police officers who receive special training before participating in the "camera or gun" experiment described earlier do not show the same biases that ordinary people do (Correll et al., 2007). Like ordinary people, they take a few milliseconds longer to decide not to shoot a Black man than a White man, indicating that stereotypes influenced their thinking. But unlike ordinary people, they don't actually *shoot* Black men more often than White men, indicating that they have learned how to keep their stereotypes from influencing their behavior.

Attribution: Drawing Inferences from Actions

In 1963, Dr. Martin Luther King Jr. gave a speech in which he described his vision for America: "I have a dream that my four children will one day live in a nation where they will not be judged by the color of their skin but by the content of their character." Research on stereotyping demonstrates that Dr. King's concerns were well justified. We do indeed judge others by the color of their skin—as well as by their gender, nationality, religion, age, and occupation—and in so doing, we sometimes make tragic errors. But are we any better at judging people by the content of their character? If we could "turn off" our stereotypes and treat each person as an individual, would we judge these individuals accurately?

Not necessarily. Treating a person as an individual means judging them by their own words and deeds. This is more difficult than it sounds because the relationship

Why don't people's behavior always tell us something about them?

between what a person *is* and what a person *says or does* is not always straightforward. An honest person may lie to save a friend from embarrassment, and a dishonest person may tell the truth to bolster her credibility. Happy people have some rotten days, polite people can be rude in traffic, and people who despise us can be flattering when they need a favor. In short, people's behavior sometimes tells us about the kind of people they are, but sometimes it simply tells us about the kind of situation they happen to be in.

To understand people, we need to know not only what they did but also why they did it. Is the batter who hit the home run a talented slugger, or was the wind blowing in just the right direction? Is the politician who gave the pro-life speech really opposed to abortion, or was she just trying to win the conservative vote?

In this photo, Congressman Tom Delay has just given a speech to the National Rifle Association. How do we decide whether to attribute his behavior to a disposition (he really opposes gun control) or a situation (he is just trying to get votes)?

MICHAEL STRAVATO/GETTY IMAGES

"For God's sake, think! Why is he being so nice to you?"

When we answer questions such as these, we are making **attributions**, which are *inferences about the causes of people's behaviors* (Epley & Waytz, 2010; Gilbert, 1998). We make *situational attributions* when we decide that a person's behavior was caused by some temporary aspect of the situation in which it happened ("He was lucky that the wind carried the ball into the stands"), and we make *dispositional attributions* when we decide that a person's behavior was caused by his or her relatively enduring tendency to think, feel, or act in a particular way ("He's got a great eye and a powerful swing").

How do we know whether to make a dispositional or a situational attribution? According to the *covariation model* (Kelley, 1967), we use three kinds of information: consistency, distinctiveness, and consensus. For example, imagine that you wanted to know why your neighbor didn't mow his lawn last weekend: Is he lazy (dispositional attribution) or did bad weather keep him indoors (situational attribution)? According to the covariation model, you should consider information about the *regularity* of your neighbor's action (consistency information), information about the *generality* of his action (distinctiveness information), and information about the *typicality* of his action (consensus information). If your neighbor rarely mows his lawn ("not mowing" is consistent over time), if he avoided every other form of work last weekend (lawn mowing is not distinctive), and if everyone else on the block mowed their lawns last weekend (his action is not consensual with the actions of others), then you should probably make a dispositional attribution. On the other hand, if your neighbor usually mows his lawn on the weekend (his current action of "not mowing" is inconsistent over time), if he fixed the screen door and painted the kitchen last weekend (his action is distinctive), and if no one else on the block mowed their lawns last weekend (his action is consensual with the actions of others), then you should probably make a situational attribution. As **FIGURE 13.22** shows, patterns of consistency, distinctiveness, and consensus provide useful information about the cause of a person's behavior.

▶ FIGURE 13.22

The Covariation Model of Attribution Harold Kelley's covariation model tells us how to use information to make an attribution for another person's action, such as his failure to mow the lawn last week. If the person's action is consistent (he often fails to mow the lawn) but not distinctive (he avoids other kinds of work) and not consensual (other people did mow their lawns last week), then the model tells us to make a dispositional attribution. If the person's action is not consistent (he usually mows his lawn) but is distinctive (he doesn't avoid other kinds of work) and consensual (other people didn't mow their lawns last week), the model tells us to make a situational attribution

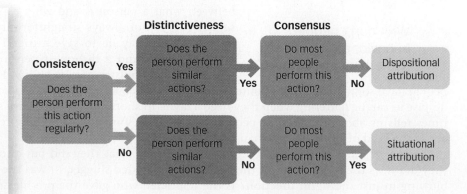

◀ Gustav Ichheiser was the first psychologist to describe the correspondence bias. In 1949, he wrote: "We all have in everyday life the tendency to interpret and evaluate the behavior of other people in terms of specific personality characteristics rather than in terms of specific social situations in which those people are placed. . . . Many things which happened between the two world wars would not have happened if social blindness had not prevented the privileged from understanding the predicament of those who were living in an invisible jail."

As sensible as this seems, research suggests that people don't always use this information as they should. The **correspondence bias** is *the tendency to make a dispositional attribution even when a person's behavior was caused by the situation* (Gilbert & Malone, 1995; Jones & Harris, 1967; Ross, 1977). This bias is so common that it is sometimes called the *fundamental attribution error*. For example, volunteers in one experiment

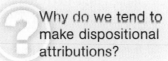 **Why do we tend to make dispositional attributions?**

played a trivia game in which one participant acted as the "quizmaster" and made up a list of unusual questions, another participant acted as the "contestant" and tried to answer those questions, and a third participant acted as the "observer" and simply watched the game. The quizmasters tended to ask tricky questions based on their own idiosyncratic knowledge, and contestants were generally unable to answer them. After watching the game, the observers were asked to decide how knowledgeable the quizmaster and the contestant were. Although the quizmasters had asked good questions and the contestants had given bad answers, it should have been clear to the observers that all this asking and answering was a product of the roles they had been assigned to play and that the contestant would have asked equally good questions and the quizmaster would have given equally bad answers had their roles been reversed. And yet observers tended to rate the quizmaster as more knowledgeable than the contestant (Ross, Amabile, & Steinmetz, 1977) and were more likely to choose the quizmaster as their own partner in an upcoming game (Quattrone, 1982). Even when we know that a successful athlete had a home field advantage or that a successful entrepreneur had family connections, we tend to attribute their success to talent and tenacity.

What causes the correspondence bias? First, the situational causes of behavior are often invisible (Ichheiser, 1949). For example, professors tend to assume that fawning students really do admire them in spite of the strong incentive for students to suck up to those who control their grades. The problem is that professors can literally *see* the student laughing at witless jokes and applauding after boring lectures, but they cannot *see* "control over grades." Situations are not as tangible or visible as behaviors, so it is all too easy to ignore them (Taylor & Fiske, 1978). Second, situational attributions tend to be more complex than dispositional attributions and require more time and attention. When participants in one study were asked to perform a mentally taxing task (namely, keeping a seven-digit number in mind) while making attributions, they had no difficulty making dispositional attributions, but they found it quite difficult to make situational attributions (Gilbert, Pelham, & Krull, 1988; Winter & Uleman, 1984). In short, information about situations is hard to get and hard to use; thus we are prone to believe that others' actions are caused by their dispositions.

attribution An inference about the cause of a person's behavior.

correspondence bias The tendency to make a dispositional attribution even when a person's behavior was caused by the situation.

► The Kennedy brothers (Senator Robert, Senator Ted, and President John) and the Bush brothers (Governor Jeb and President George) were all very successful men with very successful fathers. Was their success due to the content of their characters or to the money and fame that came with their family names?

Although the correspondence bias is quite robust, it is more likely to occur under some circumstances than others (Choi, Nisbett, & Norenzayan, 1999; D'Agostino & Fincher-Kiefer, 1992; Fein, Hilton, & Miller, 1990). For example, we are more prone to correspondence bias when judging other people's behavior than when judging our own. The **actor-observer effect** is *the tendency to make situational attributions for our own behaviors while making dispositional attributions for the identical behavior of others* (Jones & Nisbett, 1972). When college students are asked to explain why they and their friends chose their majors, they tend to explain their own choices in terms of situations ("I chose economics because my parents told me I have to support myself as soon as I'm done with college") and their friends' choices in terms of dispositions ("Norma chose economics because she's materialistic") (Nisbett et al., 1973). The actor-observer effect occurs because people typically have more information about the situations that caused their own behavior than about the situations that caused other people's behavior. We can remember getting the please-major-in-something-practical lecture from our parents, but we weren't at Norma's house to see her get the same lecture. As observers, we are naturally focused on another person's behavior, but as actors, we are quite literally focused on the situations in which our behavior occurs. Indeed, when people are shown videotapes of their conversations that allow them to see themselves from their partner's point of view, they tend to make dispositional attributions for their own behavior and situational attributions for their partner's (Storms, 1973; Taylor & Fiske, 1975).

IN SUMMARY

○ People make inferences about others based on the categories to which they belong (stereotyping). This method can lead them to misjudge others because stereotypes can be inaccurate, overused, self-perpetuating, unconscious, and automatic.

○ People make inferences about others based on their behaviors. This method can lead them to misjudge others because people tend to attribute actions to dispositions even when they should attribute them to situations.

actor-observer effect The tendency to make situational attributions for our own behaviors while making dispositional attributions for the identical behavior of others.

WhereDoYouStand?

The Model Employee

When Elizabeth Nill walks into an Abercrombie & Fitch store, they usually offer her a job. "Every time this happens my little sister says 'Not again'" (Greenhouse, 2003). Is it her years of retail experience or her keen eye for fashion? Nope. Elizabeth is tall, slender, young, and gorgeous—and according to a former assistant store manager, it is the company's policy to recruit such people to the sales force. "We were supposed to approach someone in the mall who we think will look attractive in our store. If that person said, 'I never worked in retailing before,' we said: 'Who cares? We'll hire you.' But if someone came in who had lots of retail experience and not a pretty face, we were told not to hire them at all."

Recruiting people on the basis of their looks seems more than a little unfair (Rhode, 2010). After all, not everyone is blessed with flawless skin and shiny hair. Retailers can't discriminate against people on the basis of race or religion, so why should they be allowed to discriminate on the basis of physical attractiveness? Retailers respond by noting that they didn't invent human nature and that customers simply prefer to shop at stores staffed by attractive people. As one shopper admitted, "If you see an attractive person working in the store wearing Abercrombie clothes, it makes you want to wear it too." Most people think that businesses have the right to hire the person for the job, and if a salesperson's job is to sell clothing, then attractive people may do the job best.

Should businesses be required to disregard a person's physical attractiveness when making hiring decisions, or do they have a right to give customers what they want? Where do you stand?

Chapter Review

KEY CONCEPT QUIZ

1. _____ describes the use of force to acquire scarce resources.
   a. Aggression
   b. Frustration
   c. Goal-setting
   d. Sociality

2. Someone who hacks into your computer, steals your personal information, and uses it to purchase goods and services in your name is acting on the principle of
   a. aggression.
   b. social cognition.
   c. negative affect.
   d. frustration-aggression.

3. Why are acts of aggression—from violent crime to athletic brawls—more likely to occur on hot days when people are feeling irritated and uncomfortable?
   a. frustration
   b. negative affect
   c. resource scarcity
   d. biology and culture interaction

4. What is the single best predictor of aggression?
   a. temperament
   b. age
   c. gender
   d. status

5. The prisoner's dilemma game illustrates
   a. the hypothesis-confirming bias.
   b. the diffusion of responsibility.
   c. group polarization.
   d. the benefits and costs of cooperation.

6. Which of the following is NOT a downside of being in a group?
   a. Groups are positively prejudiced toward other members and tend to discriminate in their favor.
   b. Groups often show prejudice and discrimination toward nonmembers.
   c. Groups sometimes make poor decisions.
   d. Groups may take extreme actions an individual member would not take alone.

7. Which of the following BEST describes reciprocal altruism?
   a. people becoming less concerned with personal values through immersion in a group
   b. anxiety, loneliness, and depression being caused by exclusion from a group
   c. cooperation extended over long periods of time
   d. the evolutionary process by which individuals cooperate with their relatives

8. Which of the following is NOT an explanation for increased selectivity by women in choosing a mate?
   a. Sex is potentially more costly for women than for men.
   b. Communal styles of child-rearing argue for increased selectivity.

c. The reputational costs of sex are historically much higher for women than for men.

d. Pregnancy increases women's nutritional requirements and puts them at risk of illness and death

9. In terms of attraction, which of the following is a situational factor?
   a. proximity
   b. similarity
   c. appearance
   d. personality

10. Currently, the probability of marrying by age 40 is approximately _____ for American men and _____ for American women.
    a. 50%; 50%
    b. 80%; 8%
    c. 25%; 75%
    d. 65%; 5%

11. The hypothesis that people remain in relationships only as long as they perceive a favorable ratio of costs to benefits is referred to as
    a. companionate love.
    b. the exposure effect.
    c. social exchange.
    d. equity.

12. The _____ motive describes how people are motivated to experience pleasure and to avoid experiencing pain.
    a. emotional
    b. accuracy

c. approval
d. hedonic

13. The tendency to do what authorities tell us to do simply because they do so is known as
    a. persuasion.
    b. obedience.
    c. conformity.
    d. the self-fulfilling prophecy.

14. What is the process by which people come to understand others?
    a. dispositional attribution
    b. the accuracy motive
    c. social cognition
    d. cognitive dissonance

15. The tendency to make a dispositional attribution even when a person's behavior was caused by the situation is referred to as
    a. comparison leveling.
    b. stereotyping.
    c. covariation.
    d. correspondence bias.

KEY TERMS

social psychology (p. 506)

aggression (p. 507)

frustration-aggression hypothesis (p. 507)

cooperation (p. 510)

group (p. 511)

prejudice (p. 511)

discrimination (p. 511)

deindividuation (p. 513)

diffusion of responsibility (p. 513)

altruism (p. 514)

kin selection (p. 514)

reciprocal altruism (p. 514)

mere exposure effect (p. 517)

passionate love (p. 522)

companionate love (p. 522)

social exchange (p. 523)

comparison level (p. 523)

equity (p. 524)

social influence (p. 525)

norms (p. 527)

normative influence (p. 527)

norm of reciprocity (p. 527)

door-in-the-face technique (p. 528)

conformity (p. 528)

obedience (p. 530)

attitude (p. 531)

belief (p. 531)

informational influence (p. 531)

persuasion (p. 532)

systematic persuasion (p. 532)

heuristic persuasion (p. 532)

foot-in-the-door technique (p. 533)

cognitive dissonance (p. 534)

social cognition (p. 536)

stereotyping (p. 536)

perceptual confirmation (p. 538)

self-fulfilling prophecy (p. 539)

subtyping (p. 539)

attributions (p. 542)

correspondence bias (p. 543)

actor-observer effect (p. 544)

CRITICAL THINKING QUESTIONS

1. Both culture and biology can make people more or less likely to respond to negative affect by aggressing. If the president of the United States asked you to come up with three ways to reduce aggression in America, what would you suggest?

2. If you could take a pill that made you completely immune to social influence, would you do it? Would you want others to do it? What would be the benefits and what would be the costs?

3. Stereotypes are natural, essential, and harmful. Even though we can't eliminate them, we might be able to eliminate some of their most harmful effects. How could that be accomplished?

RECOMMENDED READINGS

Buss, D. M. (2003). *The evolution of desire: Strategies of human mating* (rev. 4th ed.). New York: Basic Books.

David Buss surveys research on intimate relationships from the evolutionary perspective. *Kirkus Reviews* called it "scientifically rigorous," and the *Philadelphia Inquirer* called it "clear, coherent, and convincing."

Cacioppo, J. T., & Patrick, W. (2009). *Loneliness. Human nature and the need for social connection.* New York: Norton.

The authors show just how deep our need for social interaction goes, and just how badly we do when that need is unmet. *Library Journal* called it "superb" and *Publishers Weekly* described it as "a solid scientific look at the physical and emotional impact of loneliness."

Christakis, N. A., & Fowler, J. H. (2010). *Connected: The surprising power of our social networks and how they shape our lives.* New York: Little, Brown, & Co.

The authors explain how everything from altruism to obesity to happiness spreads through social networks. According to the *New York Times*, this book is "in a category of works of brilliant originality that can stimulate and enlighten and can sometimes even change the way we understand the world."

Cialdini, R. B. (2006). *Influence: The psychology of persuasion* (rev. ed.). New York: Harper.

The revised edition of this classic is an engaging discussion of techniques for wielding and escaping social influence. *Amazon* called it "the best book ever on what is increasingly becoming the science of persuasion."

ANSWERS TO KEY CONCEPT QUIZ

1. a; 2. d; 3. b; 4. c; 5. d; 6. a; 7. c; 8. b; 9. a; 10. b; 11. c; 12. d; 13. b; 14. c; 15. d.

Need more help? Additional resources are located at the book's free companion Web site at:
www.worthpublishers.com/schacter

14

Psychological Disorders

Virginia Woolf left her walking stick on the bank of the river, put a large stone in the pocket of her coat, and made her way into the water. Her body was found 3 weeks later. She had written to her husband: "Dearest, I feel certain I am going mad again. . . . And I shan't recover this time. I begin to hear voices, and I can't concentrate. So I am doing what seems the best thing to do" (Dally, 1999, p. 182). Thus, near Rodmell, Sussex, England, on March 28, 1941, life ended for the prolific novelist and essayist, central figure of the avant-garde literary salon known as the Bloomsbury Group, influential feminist—and unfortunate victim of lifelong "breakdowns," with swings in mood between wretched depression and manic excitement.

The madness afflicting Woolf is now known as bipolar disorder. At one extreme were her episodes of depression—sullen, despondent, her creativity at a halt, she was sometimes bedridden for months by her illness. These periods alternated with mania, when, as her husband, Leonard, recounted, "She talked almost without stopping for 2 or 3 days, paying no attention to anyone in the room or anything said to her." Her language "became completely incoherent, a mere jumble of dissociated words." At the height of her spells, birds spoke to her in Greek, her dead mother reappeared and scolded her, and voices commanded her to "do wild things." She refused to eat, wrote pages of nonsense, and launched tirades of abuse at her husband and her companions (Dally, 1999, p. 240).

Between these phases, Woolf somehow managed a brilliant literary life. Her Victorian family had seen no reason for a woman to attend university, but the absence of schooling did not prevent her from becoming the extraordinary intellectual figure celebrated in the title of Edward Albee's play *Who's Afraid of Virginia Woolf?* (1962). All told, she produced nine novels, a play, five volumes of essays, and more than 14 volumes of diaries and letters. Her novels broke away from traditions of strict plot and setting to explore the inner lives and musings of her characters, and her observations revealed a keen appreciation of her own experience of psychological disorder. In a letter to a friend, she remarked, "As an experience, madness is terrific . . . and not to be sniffed at, and in its lava I still find most of the things I write about" (Dally, 1999, p. 240). The price that Woolf paid for her genius, of course, was a dear one, and her husband and companions shared the burden of dealing with her disorder. Disorders of the mind can create immense pain.

▶ English novelist and critic Virginia Woolf (1882–1941), 1937. Her lifelong affliction with bipolar disorder ended in suicide, but the manic phases of her illness helped to fuel her prolific writing.
THE PRINT COLLECTOR/ALAMY

SYMPTOMS REFLECTING ABNORMALITIES OF THE MIND, CALLED *psychological*, or *mental*, *disorders*, are hard to define and explain. Psychiatrists and psychologists agree that a psychological disorder is not, say, extreme anxiety before a chemistry test or deep sadness at the death of a beloved pet. To qualify as a mental disorder, thoughts, feelings, and emotions must be persistent, harmful to the person experiencing them, and uncontrollable. About half of Americans will develop some type of mental disorder during the course of their lives (Kessler et al., 2005)—at a substantial cost in health, productivity, and happiness. Data compiled by the Global Burden of Disease study reveal that, after cardiovascular disease, mental disorders are the second-greatest contributor to a loss of years of healthy life (Rodgers et al., 2004). Problems of the head are nearly as great a plague on humanity as problems of the heart.

Psychologists who study mental disorders seek to uncover ways to understand, treat, and prevent such human misery. The study of psychological disorders can be unsettling because you may well see yourself mirrored in the various conditions. Like medical students who come to worry about their own symptoms with each new disease they examine, students of abnormal psychology can catch their own version of "medical students' disease," noticing personal oddities as they read about the peculiarities of others (Woods, Natterson, & Silverman, 1966). Is your late-night frenzy to finish an assignment a kind of mania? Is your fear of snakes a phobia? Does forgetting where you left your keys qualify you for diagnosis with a dissociative disorder? Please relax. You may not always avoid self-diagnosis, but you're not alone. Studying mental disorders heightens everyone's sensitivity to his or her own eccentricities. In fact, you would be "abnormal" if studying mental disorders *didn't* make you reflect on yourself.

In this chapter, we first consider the question: What is abnormal? Virginia Woolf's bouts of depression and mania and her eventual suicide certainly seem abnormal, but at times, she was fine. The enormously complicated human mind can produce behaviors, thoughts, and emotions that change radically from moment to moment. How do psychologists decide that a particular mind is disordered? We will examine the key factors that must be weighed in making such a decision. Our exploration of psychological disorders will then focus on each of several major forms of mental disorder, including anxiety disorders, mood disorders, dissociative disorders, schizophrenia, and personality disorders. As we view each of these problems, we will look at how they can influence the person's thought and behavior and at what is known about their prevalence and their causes.

Identifying Psychological Disorders: What Is Abnormal?

The idea of a *psychological disorder* is a relatively recent invention, historically speaking. People who act strangely or report bizarre thoughts or emotions have been known since ancient times, but their difficulties were often understood in the context of religion or the supernatural. In some cultures and religious traditions, madness is still interpreted as possession by animal spirits or demons, as enchantment by a witch or shaman, or as God's punishment for wrongdoing. In many societies, including our own, people with psychological disorders have been feared and ridiculed, and often treated as criminals—punished, imprisoned, or put to death for their "crime" of deviating from the normal.

medical model The conceptualization of psychological disorders as diseases that, like physical diseases, have biological causes, defined symptoms, and possible cures.

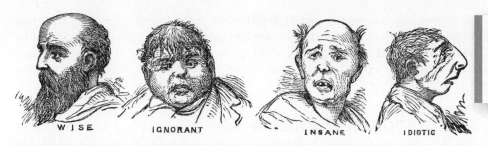

WISE   IGNORANT   INSANE   IDIOTIC

◄ According to the theory of "physiognomy," mental disorders could be diagnosed from facial features. This fanciful theory is now considered superstition but was popular from antiquity until the early 20th century.

SPENCER 1929

Over the past 200 years, these ways of looking at psychological abnormalities have largely been replaced in industrialized areas of the world by a **medical model**, *the conceptualization of psychological disorders as diseases that, like physical diseases, have biological causes, defined symptoms, and possible cures.* Treating abnormal behavior in the way we treat illness suggests that a first step is to determine the nature of the problem through *diagnosis.* In diagnosis, clinicians seek to determine the nature of the patient's mental disease by assessing *symptoms*—behaviors, thoughts, and emotions suggestive of an underlying abnormal *syndrome,* a coherent cluster of symptoms usually due to a single cause. So, for example, just as a fever, sniffles, and cough are symptoms of a cold, Virginia Woolf's extreme moods, alternating between despondency and wild enthusiasm, can be seen as symptoms of her bipolar disorder.

? What's the first step in helping someone with a psychological disorder?

As useful as the medical model can be, it should nonetheless be viewed with some skepticism. Every action or thought suggestive of abnormality cannot be traced to an underlying disease (American Psychiatric Association, 2000; Keisler, 1999; Persons, 1986). And, as you will discover in Chapter 15, some of the most successful treatments for abnormal behavior or thought focus on simply eliminating the behavior or thought; no effort is made to treat the root "syndrome." Nevertheless, the medical model is still a vast improvement over older alternatives—such as viewing psychological disorders as the work of witchcraft or as punishment for sin. Viewing psychological disorders as medical problems reminds us that people who are suffering deserve care and treatment, not condemnation.

© HULTON-DEUTSCH COLLECTION/CORBIS

◄ According to the theory of "phrenology," mental disorders could be diagnosed from bumps on the head. In 1905, Henry C. Lavery patented this automatic device with adjustable probes for gauging disorders by measuring the shape of the skull. It was useful mainly as a way of making money change hands at county fairs.

To understand how psychological disorders are defined and diagnosed, we'll first consider definitions of normal and abnormal behavior. Then we'll look at how mental disorders are categorized into groups, how the causes and cures of disorders are viewed in the medical model, and what consequences can occur—for better or for worse—when such disorders are diagnosed.

Classification of Disorders

To facilitate diagnosis, psychologists have generally adopted an approach developed by psychiatrists—physicians concerned with treatment of mental disorders—who use a system for classifying mental disorders. In 1952, in recognition of the need to have a consensual diagnostic system for therapists and researchers, the first version of the *Diagnostic and Statistical Manual of Mental Disorders* (*DSM*) was published, followed by a revision in 1968 (*DSM-II*). These early versions provided a common language for talking about disorders, but the diagnostic criteria were still often vague and based on tenuous theoretical assumptions.

The current version of this manual is the *Diagnostic and Statistical Manual of Mental Disorders* (Fourth Edition, Text Revision), or *DSM-IV-TR* (American Psychiatric Association, 2000). The **DSM-IV-TR** is *a classification system that describes the features used to diagnose each recognized mental disorder and indicates how the disorder can be distinguished from other, similar problems.* Each disorder is named and classified as though it were a distinct illness. The major mental disorders distinguished in the *DSM-IV-TR* are shown in **TABLE 14.1**.

A major misconception is the idea that a mental disorder can be defined entirely in terms of deviation from the average, the typical, or "healthy." Yes, people who have mental disorders may behave, think, or experience emotions in unusual ways, but simple departure from the norm can't be the whole picture, or we'd rapidly be diagnosing mental disorders in the most creative and visionary people—anyone whose ideas deviate from those around them. And unfortunately, diagnosing people with mental disorders when they do things you don't like is not all that uncommon. Physicians before the Civil War diagnosed escaped slaves with "drapetomania" (Szasz, 1987), and it was only in 1974 that homosexuality was dropped from the list of psychological disorders (Kutchins & Kirk, 1997). The definition of psychological disorder shouldn't be a popularity contest.

Why is mental disorder more than simply a departure from the norm?

▶ Social disorder isn't mental disorder. Violence erupted in Athens in March 2010 as protesters were outraged by government cutbacks made in response to huge budget deficits. Rioting might seem disordered on the surface, but the *DSM-IV-TR* definition of mental disorders rules out political dissidence and social deviance.

ARIS MESSINIS/AFP/GETTY IMAGES

TABLE 14.1

Main *DSM-IV-TR* Categories of Mental Disorders

1. **Disorders usually first diagnosed in infancy, childhood, or early adolescence:** These include mental retardation, bed-wetting, etc.

2. **Delirium, dementia, amnestic, and other cognitive disorders:** These are disorders of thinking caused by Alzheimer's, human immunodeficiency virus (HIV) and acquired immunodeficiency syndrome (AIDS), Parkinson's disease, etc.

3. **Mental disorders due to a general medical condition not elsewhere classified:** These include problems caused by physical deterioration of the brain due to disease, drug use, etc.

4. **Substance-related disorders:** These problems are caused by dependence on alcohol, cocaine, tobacco, and so forth (see Chapter 8).

5. **Schizophrenia and other psychotic disorders:** This is a group of disorders characterized by major disturbances in perception, language and thought, emotion, and behavior (this chapter).

6. **Mood disorders:** These are problems associated with severe disturbances of mood, such as depression, mania, or alternating episodes of both (this chapter).

7. **Anxiety disorders:** These include problems associated with severe anxiety, such as phobias and obsessive-compulsive disorder (this chapter), and posttraumatic stress disorder (see Chapter 15).

8. **Somatoform disorders:** These are problems related to unusual preoccupation with physical health or physical symptoms with no physical cause (see Chapter 15).

9. **Factitious disorders.** These are disorders that the individual adopts to satisfy some economic or psychological need (see Chapter 15).

10. **Dissociative disorders:** In these types of disorders, the normal integration of consciousness, memory, or identity is suddenly and temporarily altered, such as amnesia and dissociative identity disorder (this chapter).

11. **Sexual and gender identity disorders:** These include problems related to unsatisfactory sexual activity, finding unusual objects or situations arousing, gender identity problems, and so forth.

12. **Eating disorders:** These are problems related to food, such as anorexia nervosa and bulimia nervosa (see Chapter 10).

13. **Sleep disorders:** These include serious disturbances of sleep, such as insomnia, sleep terrors, or hypersomnia (see Chapter 8).

14. **Impulse control disorder not elsewhere classified:** These problems include kleptomania, pathological gambling, and pyromania.

15. **Adjustment disorders:** These problems are related to specific stressors such as divorce, family discord, and economic concern.

16. **Personality disorders:** These problems are related to lifelong behavior patterns such as self-centeredness, overdependency, and antisocial behaviors (this chapter).

17. **Other conditions that may be a focus of clinical attention:** These include problems related to physical or sexual abuse, relational problems, and occupational problems.

Source: From the *DSM-IV-TR* (American Psychiatric Association, 2000).

The *DSM-IV-TR* definition takes these concerns into account by focusing on three key elements that must be present for a cluster of symptoms to qualify as a potential mental disorder:

> A disorder is manifested in symptoms that involve *disturbances in behavior, thoughts, or emotions.*

> The symptoms are associated with significant *personal distress or impairment.*

> The symptoms stem from an *internal dysfunction* (biological, psychological, or both).

DSM-IV-TR (Diagnostic and Statistical Manual of Mental Disorders [Fourth Edition, Text Revision]) A classification system that describes the features used to diagnose each recognized mental disorder and indicates how the disorder can be distinguished from other, similar problems.

So, on the one hand, if someone experiences extreme sadness and distress after the death of a loved one, for example, this would not be indicative of a mental disorder because bereavement is a normal, expected response that does not originate from internal dysfunction. On the other hand, a prolonged period of unremitting sadness that interferes with a person's ability to perform the activities of everyday life might indeed indicate depression, which is an example of a mood disorder.

As these examples suggest, determining the degree to which a person has a psychological disorder is always difficult. Psychological disorder exists along a continuum from normal to abnormal without a bright line of separation. The *DSM-IV-TR* recognizes this explicitly by recommending that diagnoses include a *global assessment of functioning,* a 0 to 100 rating of the person, with more severe disorders indicated by lower numbers and more effective functioning by higher numbers (see **TABLE 14.2**).

Why is it difficult to make reliable diagnoses?

Even so, the path to reliable diagnosis remains thorny. In general, the *DSM-IV-TR* produces better diagnostic reliability than did earlier *DSM* versions, but critics argue that much room for improvement remains. Work on *DSM-V* is under way (e.g., Stein et al., 2010), but in the meantime, many diagnostic categories continue to depend on interpretation-based criteria rather than on observable behavior, and diagnosis continues to focus on patient self-reports (which are susceptible to censorship and distortion). Levels of agreement among different diagnosticians can vary depending on the diagnostic category (Bertelsen, 1999; Nathan & Langenbucher, 1999). Agreement among diagnosticians on, say, whether a patient has schizophrenia may even depend on the clinic setting. Such disagreement may not reflect differences in the prevalence of schizophrenia in various localities but rather in the array of symptoms that the clinicians were trained to expect in people with the disease (Keller et al., 1995).

Diagnostic difficulty is further increased when a person suffers from more than one disorder. As shown in **FIGURE 14.1,** for example, people with depression (a mood disorder) often have secondary diagnoses of anxiety disorders. *The co-occurrence of two or more disorders in a single individual* is referred to as **comorbidity** and is relatively common in patients seen within the *DSM* diagnostic system (Kessler et al., 1994). Comorbidity raises a host of confusing possibilities: A person could be depressed because a phobia makes social situations impossible, or the person could be phobic about showing a despairing mood in public, or the disorders could be unrelated but co-occurring. Diagnosticians try hard to solve the problem of comorbidity because understanding the underlying basis for a person's disorder may suggest methods of treatment.

ARNIE LEVIN/THE NEW YORKER COLLECTION/ CARTOONBANK.COM

"First off, you're not a nut. You're a legume."

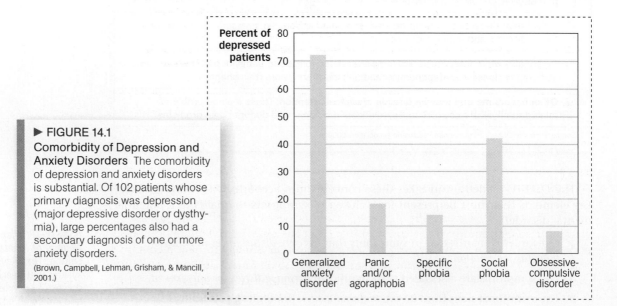

▶ FIGURE 14.1

Comorbidity of Depression and Anxiety Disorders The comorbidity of depression and anxiety disorders is substantial. Of 102 patients whose primary diagnosis was depression (major depressive disorder or dysthymia), large percentages also had a secondary diagnosis of one or more anxiety disorders.

(Brown, Campbell, Lehman, Grisham, & Mancill, 2001.)

TABLE 14.2

Global Assessment of Functioning (GAF) Scale

Code	Description
100 | 91	**Superior functioning in a wide range of activities; life's problems never seem to get out of hand; the individual is sought out by others because of his or her many positive qualities. No symptoms.**
90 | 81	**Absent or minimal symptoms** (e.g., mild anxiety before an exam), **good functioning in all areas, interested and involved in a wide range of activities, socially effective, generally satisfied with life, no more than everyday problems or concerns** (e.g., an occasional argument with family members).
80 | 71	**If symptoms are present, they are transient and expectable reactions to psychosocial stressors** (e.g., difficulty concentrating after family argument); **the individual experiences no more than slight impairment in social, occupational, or school functioning** (e.g., temporarily falling behind in schoolwork).
70 | 61	**Some mild symptoms** (e.g., depressed mood and mild insomnia) **OR some difficulty in social, occupational, or school functioning** (e.g., occasional truancy or theft within the household), **but the individual generally functions pretty well and is able to have some meaningful interpersonal relationships.**
60 | 51	**Moderate symptoms** (e.g., flat affect and circumstantial speech, occasional panic attacks) **OR moderate difficulty in social, occupational, or school functioning** (e.g., few friends, conflicts with peers or co-workers).
50 | 41	**Serious symptoms** (e.g., suicidal ideation, severe obsessional rituals, frequent shoplifting) **OR any serious impairment in social, occupational, or school functioning** (e.g., no friends, unable to keep a job).
40 | 31	**Some impairment in reality testing or communication** (e.g., speech is at times illogical, obscure, or irrelevant) **OR major impairment in several areas, such as work or school, family relations, judgment, thinking, or mood** (e.g., depressed adult avoids friends, neglects family, and is unable to work; child frequently beats up younger children, is defiant at home, and is failing at school).
30 | 21	**Behavior is considerably influenced by delusions or hallucinations OR serious impairment in communication or judgment** (e.g., sometimes incoherent, acts grossly inappropriately, suicidal preoccupation) **OR inability to function in almost all areas** (e.g., stays in bed all day; no job, home, or friends).
20 | 11	**Some danger of hurting self or others** (e.g., suicide attempts without clear expectation of death; frequently violent; manic excitement) **OR occasionally fails to maintain minimal personal hygiene** (e.g., smears feces) **OR gross impairment in communication** (e.g., largely incoherent or mute).
10 | 1	**Persistent danger of severely hurting self or others** (e.g., recurrent violence) **OR persistent inability to maintain minimal personal hygiene OR serious suicidal act with clear expectation of death.**

Source: From the *DSM-IV-TR* (American Psychiatric Association, 2000).

Causation of Disorders

The medical model of psychological disorder suggests that knowing a person's diagnosis is useful because any given category of mental illness is likely to have a distinctive cause. In other words, just as different viruses, or bacteria, or types of trauma, or genetic abnormalities cause different physical illnesses, so a specifiable pattern of causes (or *etiology*) may exist for different psychological disorders. The medical model also suggests that each category of psychological disorder is likely to have a common *prognosis,* a typical course over time and susceptibility to treatment and cure. Unfortunately, this basic medical model is usually an oversimplification; it is rarely useful to focus on a *single cause* that is *internal* to the person and that suggests a *single cure*.

comorbidity The co-occurrence of two or more disorders in a single individual.

▲ The Mad Hatter in *Alice in Wonderland* was Lewis Carroll's portrayal of a mental disorder common among hatmakers in the 1800s. Hatters could become "mad as a hatter" because they unwittingly exposed themselves to a mercury compound with serious side effects when they processed fur into felt for hats.

"Mad Hatter syndrome," first described in the 1800s in workers who used a mercury compound in making felt hats, was one of those rare single-cause disorders. The symptoms: trembling, loss of memory and coordination, slurred speech, depression, and anxiety. The cause: mercury poisoning. The cure: getting out of the hat business. Things are seldom so simple, however, and a full explanation of all the different ways in which the mind can become disordered needs to take into account multiple levels of causation.

An integrated perspective that incorporates biological, psychological, and environmental factors offers the most comprehensive and useful framework for understanding most psychological disorders. On the biological side, the focus is on genetic influences, biochemical imbalances, and structural abnormalities of the brain. The psychological perspective focuses on maladaptive learning and coping, cognitive biases, dysfunctional attitudes, and interpersonal problems. Environmental factors include poor socialization, stressful life circumstances, and cultural and social inequities. The complexity of causation suggests that different individuals can experience a similar psychological disorder (e.g., depression) for different reasons. A person might fall into depression as a result of biological causes (e.g., genetics, hormones), psychological causes (e.g., faulty beliefs, hopelessness, poor strategies for coping with loss), environmental causes (e.g., stress or loneliness), or (more likely) as a result of some combination of these factors. And, of course, multiple causes mean there may not be single cures.

? Why does assessment require looking at a number of factors?

The observation that most disorders have both internal (biological and psychological) *and* external (environmental) causes has given rise to a theory known as the **diathesis-stress model**, which suggests that *a person may be predisposed for a psychological disorder that*

CULTURE & COMMUNITY

Can people in different parts of the world have different mental disorders? Many of the major forms of psychological disorders, such as schizophrenia, are stable across cultures, but some psychological problems appear in some cultures and not others. Stress is more likely to be exhibited as depression or anxiety in Western societies, for example, but more likely to be manifested in physical problems, such as fatigue or weakness, in China (Kleinman, 1986, 1988).

To aid researchers and therapists in their quest to understand the relevance of cultural factors to mental health, the *DSM-IV-TR* includes a description of various "culture-bound syndromes," disorders that appear only in some cultures. Here's a sample.

- *Ataque de nervios.* A type of distress principally reported among Latinos with symptoms including uncontrollable shouting, attacks of crying, trembling, heat in the chest rising into the head, and verbal or physical aggression.

- *Ghost sickness.* A preoccupation with death and the dead observed among members of some Native American tribes. Symptoms can include bad dreams, weakness, feelings of danger, loss of appetite, fainting, dizziness, fear, anxiety, hallucinations, loss of consciousness, confusion, feelings of futility, and a sense of suffocation.

- *Koro.* A sudden and intense anxiety that the penis (or in females, the vulva or nipples) will recede into the body and possibly cause death. The syndrome is reported in South and East Asia and at times occurs as local epidemics.

- *Mal de ojo.* A concept widely found in Mediterranean cultures, *mal de ojo* is a Spanish phrase translated into English as "evil eye" and is believed to result from looking at someone, usually a child, with envy. The target of the envy can develop a variety of symptoms, including fitful sleep, crying without apparent cause, diarrhea, vomiting, and fever.

diathesis-stress model Suggests that a person may be predisposed for a mental disorder that remains unexpressed until triggered by stress.

remains unexpressed until triggered by stress. The diathesis is the internal predisposition, which could be genetic, and the stress is the external trigger. For example, most people were able to cope with their strong emotional reactions to the terrorist attack of September 11, 2001. However, for some who had a predisposition to negative emotions or were already contending with major life stressors, the horror of the events may have overwhelmed their ability to cope, thereby precipitating a psychological disorder. Although diatheses can be inherited, it's important to remember that heritability is not destiny. A person who inherits a diathesis may never encounter the precipitating stress, whereas someone with little genetic propensity to a disorder may come to suffer from it given the right pattern of stress. The tendency to oversimplify mental disorders by attributing them to single, internal causes is nowhere more evident than in the interpretation of the role of the brain in psychological disorders. Brain scans of people with and without disorders can give rise to an unusually strong impression that psychological problems are internal—after all, there it is!—and perhaps also permanent, inevitable, and even untreatable. Brain influences and processes are fundamentally important for knowing the full story of psychological disorders but are not the only chapter in that story.

What are the limitations of using brain scans for diagnosing?

Searching for the biological causes of psychological disorders in the brain and body also tends to invite a particular error in explanation—the *intervention-causation fallacy.* This fallacy involves the assumption that if a treatment is effective, it must address the cause of the problem. This may sometimes be true, but it is certainly not a general rule. To get a sense of the error in this logic, imagine that you've spent sleepless night after sleepless night worrying about a loved one who was recently hospitalized with a serious illness. You discover that taking a sleeping medicine before bed helps you sleep. On the basis of your favorable response, should we conclude that your insomnia was caused by a deficiency of sleeping pills—that a part of your brain needed the chemicals in the pills? Of course not. Your anxiety and sleeplessness were due to your loved one's illness, not to the absence of a pill. Be cautious about drawing inferences about causality based on responsiveness to treatment; the cure does not necessarily point to the cause.

The diagnosis and classification of mental disorders is a useful basis for exploring causes and cures of psychological problems. At the same time, these tools make it all too easy to assume that the problems arise from single, internal causes that are inherited and involve brain dysfunction—and that therefore can be dispelled with an intervention that simply eliminates the cause. Psychological problems are usually more challenging and complicated than this ideal model would suggest.

Dangers of Labeling

An important complication in the diagnosis and classification of psychological disorders is the effect of labeling. Psychiatric labels can have negative consequences, since many of these labels carry the baggage of negative stereotypes and stigma, such as the idea that mental disorder is a sign of personal weakness or the idea that psychiatric patients are dangerous. The stigma associated with mental disorders may explain why nearly 70% of people with diagnosable psychological disorders do not seek treatment (Kessler et al., 1996; Regier et al., 1993; Sussman, Robins, & Earls, 1987).

Unfortunately, educating people about mental disorders does not dispel the stigma borne by those with these diseases (Phelan et al., 1997). In fact, expectations created by psychiatric labels can sometimes even compromise the judgment of mental health professionals (Garb, 1998; Langer & Abelson, 1974; Temerlin & Trousdale, 1969). In a classic demonstration of this phenomenon, psychologist David Rosenhan and six associates reported to different mental hospitals complaining of "hearing voices"—a symptom sometimes found in people with schizophrenia. Each was admitted to a hospital, and each promptly reported that the symptom had ceased. Even so, hospital staff were reluctant to identify these "patients" as normal: It took an average of 19 days for these "patients" to secure

Why might someone avoid seeking help?

▼ Feeling lonely and depressed? Join the society of loners!

their release, and even then they were released with the diagnosis of "schizophrenia in remission" (Rosenhan, 1973). Apparently, once hospital staff had labeled these "patients" as having a psychological disease, the label stuck.

These effects of labeling are particularly disturbing in light of evidence that the incarceration of mental patients is seldom necessary. One set of studies in Vermont followed the lives of mental patients who were thought to be too dangerous to release and therefore had been kept in the back wards of institutions for years. Their release resulted in no harm to the community (Harding et al., 1987), and further studies have shown that mental patients are typically no more likely to be violent than anyone else (Elbogen & Johnson, 2009; Monahan, 1992). Yet once a person has been labeled as having a psychological disorder, the label becomes a kind of prison that makes it difficult to return to life as a nonpatient (Seitler, 2008).

Labeling may even affect how the labeled person views him- or herself; persons given such a label may come to view themselves not just as mentally disordered, but as hopeless or worthless. Such a view may cause these persons to develop an attitude of defeat and, as a result, to fail to work toward their own recovery. As one small step toward counteracting such consequences, clinicians have adopted the important practice of applying labels to the disorder and not to the person with the disorder. For example, a patient might be described as "a person with schizophrenia," not as "a schizophrenic." You'll notice that we follow this model in the text.

IN SUMMARY

○ The study of psychological disorders follows a medical model in which symptoms are understood to indicate an underlying disorder.

○ The *DSM-IV-TR* is a classification system that defines a psychological disorder as occurring when the person experiences disturbances of thought, emotion, or behavior that produce distress or impairment and that arise from internal sources.

○ The classification system includes a global assessment of functioning and a set of categories of disorder, but comorbidity of disorders is common.

○ Many psychological disorders arise from multiple causes or as a result of the interaction of diathesis (internal predisposition) and stress. It is a common error to assume that an intervention that cures a disorder reflects the cause of the disorder.

Anxiety Disorders: When Fears Take Over

"Okay, time for a pop quiz that will be half your grade for this class!" If your instructor had actually said that, you would probably have experienced a wave of anxiety and dread. Your reaction would be appropriate and—no matter how intense the feeling—not be a sign that you have a mental disorder. In fact, situation-related anxiety is normal and can be adaptive—in this case, perhaps by reminding you to keep up with your textbook assignments so you are prepared for pop quizzes. When anxiety arises that is out of proportion to real threats and challenges, however, it is maladaptive: It can take hold of people's lives, stealing their peace of mind and undermining their ability to function normally. Pathological anxiety is expressed as an **anxiety disorder**, *the class of mental disorder in which anxiety is the predominant feature*. People commonly experience more than one type of anxiety disorder at a given time, and there is significant comorbidity between anxiety and depression (Brown & Barlow, 2002). Among the anxiety disorders recognized in the *DSM-IV-TR* are *generalized anxiety disorder*, *phobic disorders*, *panic disorder*, and *obsessive-compulsive disorder*.

When is anxiety harmful, and when is it helpful?

anxiety disorder The class of mental disorder in which anxiety is the predominant feature.

Generalized Anxiety Disorder

Terry, a 31-year-old man, began to experience debilitating anxiety during his first year as an internal medicine resident. The 36-hour on-call periods were grueling, and he became concerned that he and other interns were making too many errors and oversights. He worried incessantly for a year and finally resigned his position. However, he continued to be plagued with anxiety about making mistakes—self-doubt that extended to his personal relationships. When he eventually sought treatment, he described himself as "worthless" and unable to control his debilitating anxiety, and he complained of headaches and constant fatigue (Vitkus, 1996).

Terry's symptoms are typical of **generalized anxiety disorder (GAD)**—called *generalized* because the unrelenting worries are not focused on any particular threat; they are, in fact, often exaggerated and irrational. In people suffering from GAD, *chronic excessive worry is accompanied by three or more of the following symptoms: restlessness, fatigue, concentration problems, irritability, muscle tension, and sleep disturbance.* The uncontrollable worrying produces a sense of loss of control that can so erode self-confidence that simple decisions seem fraught with dire consequences. For example, Terry needed to buy a new suit for a special occasion but began shaking and sweating when he approached a clothing store because he was afraid of choosing the "wrong" suit. He became so anxious that he could not even enter the store.

About 5% of North Americans are estimated to suffer from GAD at some time in their lives (Kessler et al., 1994). GAD occurs more frequently in lower socioeconomic groups than in middle- and upper-income groups (Blazer et al., 1991) and is approximately twice as common in women as in men (Eaton et al., 1994). Research suggests that both biological and psychological factors contribute to the risk of GAD. Family studies indicate a mild to modest level of heritability (Norrholm & Ressler, 2009). Although identical twin studies of GAD are rare, some evidence suggests that compared with fraternal twins, identical twins have modestly higher *concordance rates* (the percentage of pairs that share the characteristic) (Hettema, Neale, & Kendler, 2001). Moreover, teasing out environmental versus personality influences on concordance rates is quite difficult.

What factors contribute to GAD?

Some patients with GAD respond to certain prescription drugs, which suggests that neurotransmitter imbalances may play a role in the disorder. The precise nature of this imbalance is not clear, but *benzodiazepines*—a class of sedative drugs discussed in Chapter 15 (e.g., Valium, Librium) that appear to stimulate the neurotransmitter *gamma-aminobutyric acid (GABA)*—can sometimes reduce the symptoms of GAD. However, other drugs that do not directly affect GABA levels (e.g., buspirone and antidepressants such as Prozac) can also be helpful in the treatment of GAD (Gobert et al., 1999; Michelson et al., 1999; Roy-Byrne & Cowley, 1998). To complicate matters, these different prescription drugs do not help all patients and, in some cases, can produce serious side effects and dependency.

Psychological explanations focus on anxiety-provoking situations in explaining high levels of GAD. The condition is especially prevalent among people who have low incomes, are living in large cities, or are trapped in environments rendered unpredictable by political and economic strife. The relatively high rates of GAD among women may also be related to stress because women are more likely than men to live in poverty, experience discrimination, or be subjected to sexual or physical abuse (Koss, 1990; Strickland, 1991). Research shows that unpredictable traumatic experiences in childhood increase the risk of developing GAD, and this evidence also supports the idea

▼ Potential anxiety victims? Generalized anxiety disorder is more common for women and children living below the poverty line than for others.

MICHAEL NEWMAN/PHOTOEDIT

phobic disorders Disorders characterized by marked, persistent, and excessive fear and avoidance of specific objects, activities, or situations.

specific phobia A disorder that involves an irrational fear of a particular object or situation that markedly interferes with an individual's ability to function.

social phobia A disorder that involves an irrational fear of being publicly humiliated or embarrassed.

preparedness theory The idea that people are instinctively predisposed toward certain fears.

that stressful experiences play a role (Torgensen, 1986). Moreover, major life changes (new job, new baby, personal loss, physical illness, and so forth) often immediately precede the development of GAD (Blazer, Hughes, & George, 1987). Still, many people who might be expected to develop GAD don't, supporting the diathesis-stress notion that personal vulnerability must also be a key factor in this disorder.

Phobic Disorders

Consider Mary, a 47-year-old mother of three, who sought treatment for *claustrophobia*—an intense fear of enclosed spaces. She traced her fear to childhood, when her older siblings would scare her by locking her in closets and confining her under blankets. Her own children grown, she wanted to find a job but could not because of a terror of elevators and other confined places that, she felt, shackled her to her home (Carson, Butcher, & Mineka, 2000). Many people feel anxious in enclosed spaces, but Mary's fears were abnormal and dysfunctional because they were wildly disproportional to any actual risk and because they imposed unwanted restrictions on her life.

Unlike the generalized anxiety of GAD, anxiety in a phobic disorder is more specific. The *DSM* describes **phobic disorders** as characterized by *marked, persistent, and excessive fear and avoidance of specific objects, activities, or situations*. An individual with a phobic disorder recognizes that the fear is irrational but cannot prevent it from interfering with everyday functioning.

A **specific phobia** is *an irrational fear of a particular object or situation that markedly interferes with an individual's ability to function*. Specific phobias fall into five categories: (1) animals (e.g., dogs, cats, rats, snakes, spiders); (2) natural environments (e.g., heights, darkness, water, storms); (3) situations (e.g., bridges, elevators, tunnels, enclosed places); (4) blood, injections, and injury; and (5) other phobias, including illness and death. Most people expect many more categories because they've heard some of the fanciful Greek or Latin terms invented for very specific phobias. One website lists phobias (www.phobialist.com) that include, among others, "kathisophobia" (a fear of sitting down), "homichlophobia" (fear of fog), and "ephebiphobia" (fear of teenagers). The terms sound technical enough to be included in the *DSM*, but you won't find them there. These curious pseudo-medical terms obscure the fact that specific phobias share common symptoms and are merely aimed at different objects. Approximately 11% of people in the United States will develop a specific phobia during their lives and—for unknown reasons—the risk seems to be increasing in younger generations (Magee et al., 1996). With few exceptions (e.g., fear of heights), specific phobias are much more common among women than among men, with a ratio of about 4 to 1 (Kessler et al., 1994; Kessler et al., 1996).

▼ No fear of heights here. Construction workers eat their lunches atop a steel beam 800 feet above ground during the 1932 construction of the RCA Building (now the GE Building) in Rockefeller Center in Manhattan.

BETTMANN/CORBIS

Social phobia involves *an irrational fear of being publicly humiliated or embarrassed*. Social phobia can be restricted to situations such as public speaking, eating in public, or urinating in a public bathroom or generalized to a variety of social situations that involve being observed or interacting with unfamiliar people. Individuals with social phobia try to avoid situations where unfamiliar people might evaluate them, and they experience intense anxiety and distress when public exposure is unavoidable. Social phobia can develop in childhood, but it typically emerges between early adolescence and the age of 25 (Schneier et al., 1992). Many people experience social phobia—about 11% of men and 15% of women qualify for diagnosis at some time in their lives (Kessler et al., 1994). Even higher rates are found among people who are undereducated, have low incomes, or both (Magee et al., 1996).

Why are phobias so common? The high rates of both specific and social phobias suggest a predisposition to be fearful of certain objects and situations. Indeed, most of the situations and objects of people's phobias could pose a real threat—for example, falling from a high place or being attacked by a vicious dog or poisonous snake or spider. Social situations have their own dangers. A roomful of strangers may not attack or bite, but they could form impressions that affect your prospects for friends, jobs, or marriage. And of course, in some very rare cases, they could attack or bite.

Why might we be predisposed to certain phobias?

Observations such as these are the basis for the **preparedness theory** of phobias, which maintains that *people are instinctively predisposed toward certain fears*. The preparedness theory, proposed by Martin E. P. Seligman (1971), is supported by research showing that both humans and monkeys can quickly be conditioned to have a fear response for stimuli such as snakes and spiders but not for neutral stimuli such as flowers or toy rabbits (Cook & Mineka, 1989; Öhman, Dimberg, & Ost, 1985). Similarly, research on facial expressions has shown that people are more easily conditioned to fear angry facial expressions than other types of expressions (Öhman, 1996; Öhman, Dimburg, & Öst, 1985; Woody & Nosen, 2008). Phobias are particularly likely to form for objects that evolution has predisposed us to avoid. This idea is also supported by studies of the heritability of phobias. Family studies of specific phobias indicate greater concordance rates for identical than for fraternal twins (Kendler, Myers, & Prescott, 2002; Kendler et al., 1992; O'Laughlin & Malle, 2002). Other studies have found that over 30% of first-degree relatives (parents, siblings, or children) of patients with specific phobias also have a phobia (Fryer et al., 1990).

Temperament may also play a role in vulnerability to phobias. Researchers have found that infants who display excessive shyness and inhibition are at an increased risk for developing a phobic behavior later in life (Hirschfeld et al., 1992; Morris, 2001; Stein, Chavira, & Jang, 2001). Neurobiological factors may also play a role. Abnormalities in the neurotransmitters serotonin and dopamine are more common in individuals who report phobias than they are among people who don't (Stein, 1998). In addition, individuals with phobias sometimes show abnormally high levels of activity in the amygdala, an area of the brain linked with the development of emotional associations (discussed in Chapter 8 and in Hirschfeld et al., 1992; Stein et al., 2001).

This evidence does not rule out the influence of environments and upbringing on the development of phobic overreactions. As learning theorist John Watson (1924) demonstrated many years ago, phobias can be classically conditioned (see our Chapter 7 discussion of Little Albert and the white rat). Similarly, the discomfort of a dog bite could create a conditioned association between dogs and pain, resulting in an irrational fear of all dogs. The idea that phobias are learned from emotional experiences with feared objects, however, is not a complete explanation for the occurrence of phobias. Most studies find that people with phobias are no more likely than people without phobias to recall personal experiences with the feared object that could have provided the basis for classical conditioning (Craske, 1999; McNally & Steketee, 1985). Moreover, many people are bitten by dogs, but few develop phobias. Despite its shortcomings, however, the idea that this is a matter of learning provides a useful model for therapy (see Chapter 15).

▼ The preparedness theory explains why most merry-go-rounds carry children on beautiful horses. This mom might have some trouble getting her daughter to ride on a big spider or snake.

COURTESY OF DANIEL WEGNER

panic disorder A disorder characterized by the sudden occurrence of multiple psychological and physiological symptoms that contribute to a feeling of stark terror.

agoraphobia An extreme fear of venturing into public places.

Panic Disorder

If you suddenly found yourself in danger of death, a wave of panic might wash over you. People who suffer panic attacks are frequently overwhelmed by such intense fears and by powerful physical symptoms of anxiety—in the absence of actual danger. Mindy, a 25-year-old art director, had been having panic attacks with increasing frequency, often two or three times a day, when she finally sought help at a clinic. The attacks began with a sudden wave of "horrible fear" that seemed to come out of nowhere, often accompanied by trembling, nausea, and a tightening of the chest. The attacks began when she was in high school and had continued intermittently ever since. During an episode, Mindy feared that she would do something crazy (Spitzer et al., 1994).

Mindy's condition, called **panic disorder,** is characterized by *the sudden occurrence of multiple psychological and physiological symptoms that contribute to a feeling of stark terror.* The acute symptoms of a panic attack typically last only a few minutes and include shortness of breath, heart palpitations, sweating, dizziness, depersonalization (a feeling of being detached from one's body) or derealization (a feeling that the external world is strange or unreal), and a fear that one is going crazy or about to die. Not surprisingly, panic attacks often send people rushing to emergency rooms or their physicians' offices for what they believe is either an acute cardiac, respiratory, or neurological episode (Hirschfeld, 1996). Unfortunately, because many of the symptoms mimic various medical disorders, a correct diagnosis may take years in spite of costly medical tests that produce normal results (Katon, 1994). According to the *DSM-IV-TR* diagnostic criteria, a person has panic disorder only on experiencing recurrent unexpected attacks and reporting significant anxiety about having another attack.

A common complication of panic disorder is **agoraphobia,** *a specific phobia involving a fear of venturing into public places.* Many individuals with agoraphobia are not frightened of public places in themselves; instead, they are afraid of having a panic attack in a public place or around strangers who might view them with disdain or fail to help them. In severe cases, people who have panic disorder with agoraphobia are unable to leave home, sometimes for years on end.

What is it about public places that many agoraphobics fear?

Approximately 22% of the U.S. population reports having had at least one panic attack (Kessler et al., 2006), typically during a period of intense stress (Telch, Lucas, & Nelson, 1989). An occasional episode is not sufficient for a diagnosis of panic disorder—the individual also has to experience significant dread and anxiety about having another attack. When this criterion is applied, approximately 3.5% of people will have diagnosable panic disorder sometime in their lives, and of those, about three out of seven will also develop agoraphobia (Kessler et al., 1994). Panic disorder is especially prevalent among women, who are twice as likely to be diagnosed with it as are men (Weissman et al., 1997). Family studies suggest a modest hereditary component to panic disorder. If one identical twin has the disorder, the likelihood of the other twin having it is about 30% (Crowe, 1990; Kendler et al., 1995; Torgensen, 1983).

In an effort to understand the role that physiological arousal plays in panic attacks, researchers have compared the responses of experimental participants with and without panic disorder to *sodium lactate,* a chemical that produces rapid, shallow breathing and heart palpitations. Those with panic disorder were found to be acutely sensitive to the drug; within a few minutes after administration, 60% to 90% experienced a panic attack. Participants without the disorder rarely responded to the drug with a panic attack (Liebowitz et al., 1985).

The difference in responses to the chemical may be due to differing interpretations of physiological signs of anxiety—that is, people who experience panic attacks may be hypersensitive to physiological signs of anxiety, which they interpret as having disastrous consequences for their well-being. Supporting this cognitive explanation is research showing that people who are high in anxiety sensitivity (i.e., they believe that bodily arousal and other symptoms of anxiety can have dire consequences) have an elevated risk for experiencing panic attacks (Li & Zinbarg, 2007). Thus, panic attacks may be traceable to the fear of fear itself.

▼ In panic disorder with agoraphobia, the fear of having a panic attack in public may prevent the person from going outside.

BOB DAEMMRICH/THE IMAGE WORKS

Obsessive-Compulsive Disorder

Although anxiety plays a role in obsessive-compulsive disorder, the primary symptoms are unwanted, recurrent thoughts and actions. You've probably had the experience of having something—say, a silly song—pop into your head and "play" over and over, or you've started to do something pointless—like counting ceiling tiles during a boring lecture—and found it hard to stop. In some people, such repetitive thoughts and actions become a serious problem.

Karen, a 34-year-old with four children, sought treatment after several months of experiencing intrusive, repetitive thoughts in which she imagined that one or more of her children was having a serious accident. In addition, an extensive series of protective counting rituals hampered her daily routine. For example, when grocery shopping, Karen had the feeling that if she selected the first item (say, a box of cereal) on a shelf, something terrible would happen to her oldest child. If she selected the second item, some unknown disaster would befall her second child, and so on for the four children. The children's ages were also important. The sixth item in a row, for example, was associated with her youngest child, who was 6 years old.

Karen's preoccupation with numbers extended to other activities, most notably the pattern in which she smoked cigarettes and drank coffee. If she had one cigarette, she felt that she had to smoke at least four in a row or one of her children would be harmed in some way. If she drank one cup of coffee, she felt compelled to drink four more to protect her children from harm. She acknowledged that her counting rituals were irrational, but she found that she became extremely anxious when she tried to stop (Oltmanns, Neale, & Davison, 1991).

Karen's symptoms are typical of **obsessive-compulsive disorder (OCD)**, in which *repetitive, intrusive thoughts (obsessions) and ritualistic behaviors (compulsions) designed to fend off those thoughts interfere significantly with an individual's functioning*. Anxiety plays a role in this disorder because the obsessive thoughts typically produce anxiety, and the compulsive behaviors are performed to reduce it. It is not uncommon for people to have occasional intrusive thoughts that prompt ritualistic behavior (e.g., double or triple checking to be sure the garage door is closed or the oven is off), but the obsessions and compulsions of OCD are intense, frequent, and experienced as irrational and excessive. Attempts to cope with the obsessive thoughts by trying to suppress or ignore them are of little or no benefit. In fact (as discussed in Chapter 5), thought suppression can backfire, increasing the frequency and intensity of the obsessive thoughts (Wegner, 1989; Wenzlaff & Wegner, 2000).

How effective is willful effort at curing OCD?

Approximately 1.3% of people will develop OCD sometime in their lives, with somewhat lower rates in Asian cultures (Somers et al., 2006). Women tend to be more susceptible than men, but the difference is not large (Karno & Golding, 1991). The most common obsessions involve contamination, aggression, death, sex, disease, orderliness, and disfigurement (Jenike, Baer, & Minichiello, 1986; Rachman & DeSilva, 1978). Compulsions typically take the form of cleaning, checking, repeating, ordering/arranging, and counting (Antony, Downie, & Swinson, 1998a). Although compulsive behavior is always excessive, it can vary considerably in intensity and frequency. For example, fear of contamination may lead to 15 minutes of hand washing in some individuals, while others may need to spend hours with disinfectants and extremely hot water, scrubbing their hands until they bleed.

The obsessions that plague individuals with OCD typically derive from concerns that could pose a real threat (such as contamination, aggression, disease), which supports preparedness theory. Thinking repeatedly about whether we've left a stove burner on when we leave the house makes sense, after all, if we want to return to a house that is not "well done." The concept of preparedness places OCD in the same evolutionary context as phobias (Szechtman & Woody, 2006). However, as with phobias, we need to consider other factors to explain why fears that may have served an evolutionary purpose can become so distorted and maladaptive.

▼ Have you ever counted the tiles in the ceiling just out of boredom in a class? What if you were obsessed with counting tiles and came upon the Nasr ol Molk mosque In Shiraz, Iran? There goes the weekend.

DYNAMOSQUITO/FLICKR

Family studies indicate a moderate genetic heritability for OCD: Identical twins show a higher concordance than do fraternal twins. Relatives of individuals with OCD may not have the disorder themselves, but they are at greater risk for other types of anxiety disorders than are members of the general public (Billet, Richter, & Kennedy, 1998). Researchers have not determined the biological mechanisms that may contribute to OCD (Friedlander & Desrocher, 2006), but one hypothesis implicates heightened neural activity in the caudate nucleus of the brain, a portion of the basal ganglia (discussed in Chapter 3) known to be involved in the initiation of intentional actions (Rappoport, 1990). Drugs that increase the activity of the neurotransmitter serotonin in the brain can inhibit the activity of the caudate nucleus and relieve some of the symptoms of obsessive-compulsive disorder (Hansen et al., 2002). However, this finding does not indicate that overactivity of the caudate nucleus is the cause of OCD. It could also be an effect of the disorder: Patients with OCD often respond favorably to psychotherapy and show a corresponding reduction in activity in the caudate nucleus (Baxter et al., 1992).

IN SUMMARY

○ People with anxiety disorders have irrational worries and fears that undermine their ability to function normally.

○ Generalized anxiety disorder (GAD) involves a chronic state of anxiety, whereas phobic disorders involve anxiety tied to a specific object or situation.

○ People who suffer from panic disorder experience a sudden and intense attack of anxiety that is terrifying and can lead them to become agoraphobic and housebound for fear of public humiliation.

○ People with obsessive-compulsive disorder experience recurring, anxiety-provoking thoughts that compel them to engage in ritualistic, irrational behavior.

Mood Disorders: At the Mercy of Emotions

You're probably in a mood right now. Maybe you're happy that it's almost time to get a snack or saddened by something you heard on the radio—or you may feel good or bad without having a clue why. As you learned in Chapter 8, moods are relatively long-lasting, nonspecific emotional states—and *nonspecific* means we often may have no idea what has caused a mood. Changing moods lend variety to our experiences, like different-colored lights shining on the stage as we play out our lives. However, for people like Virginia Woolf and others with mood disorders, moods can become so intense that they are pulled or pushed into life-threatening actions. **Mood disorders—** *mental disorders that have mood disturbance as their predominant feature*—take two main forms: depression and bipolar disorder.

Depressive Disorders

Most people occasionally feel depressed, pessimistic, and unmotivated. But these periods are relatively short-lived and mild. Depression is much more than such sadness. The experience of R. A., a 58-year-old man who visited his primary care physician for treatment of his diabetes, is fairly typical. During the visit, he mentioned difficulties falling asleep and staying asleep that left him chronically fatigued. He complained that over the past 6 months, he'd stopped exercising and gained 12 pounds and had

mood disorders Mental disorders that have mood disturbance as their predominant feature.

major depressive disorder A disorder characterized by a severely depressed mood that lasts 2 weeks or more and is accompanied by feelings of worthlessness and lack of pleasure, lethargy, and sleep and appetite disturbances.

dysthymia A disorder that involves the same symptoms as in depression only less severe, but the symptoms last longer, persisting for at least 2 years.

double depression A moderately depressed mood that persists for at least 2 years and is punctuated by periods of major depression.

seasonal affective disorder (SAD) Depression that involves recurrent depressive episodes in a seasonal pattern.

BRIDGEMAN ART LIBRARY

◀ *The Blue Devils.* George Cruikshank (1806–77) portrays a depressed man tormented by demons offering him methods of suicide, appearing as bill collectors, and making a funeral procession.

lost interest in socializing. Nothing he normally enjoyed, including sexual activity, could give him pleasure anymore; he had trouble concentrating and was forgetful, irritable, impatient, and frustrated (Lustman, Caudle, & Clouse, 2002). R. A.'s sense of hopelessness and weariness and his lack of normal pleasures goes far beyond normal sadness; it is also different from the normal responses of sorrow and grief that accompany a tragic situation such as the death of a loved one (Bowlby, 1980). Instead, depressive mood disorders are dysfunctional, chronic, and fall outside the range of socially or culturally expected responses.

? **What is the difference between depression and sadness?**

BRUCE ERIC KAPLAN/THE NEW YORKER COLLECTION/CARTOONBANK.COM

Major depressive disorder, also known as unipolar depression, is characterized by *a severely depressed mood that lasts 2 or more weeks and is accompanied by feelings of worthlessness and lack of pleasure, lethargy, and sleep and appetite disturbances.* The bodily symptoms in major depression may seem contrary—sleeping too much or sleeping very little, for example, or overeating or failing to eat. Great sadness or despair is not always present, although intrusive thoughts of failure or ending one's life are not uncommon. In a related condition called **dysthymia**, *the same cognitive and bodily problems as in depression are present, but they are less severe and last longer, persisting for at least 2 years.* When both types co-occur, the resulting condition is called **double depression** and is defined as *a moderately depressed mood that persists for at least 2 years and is punctuated by periods of major depression.*

Some people experience *recurrent depressive episodes in a seasonal pattern,* commonly known as **seasonal affective disorder (SAD).** In most cases, the episodes begin in fall or winter and remit in spring, and this pattern is due to reduced levels of light over the colder seasons (Westrin & Lam, 2007). Recurrent summer depressive episodes are not unknown. A winter-related pattern of depression appears to be more prevalent in higher latitudes.

ARCTIC IMAGES/ALAMY

◀ A time for seasonal affective disorder. When the sun goes away, sadness can play.

DESIREE NAVARRO/GETTY IMAGES

▲ Actress Brooke Shields experienced severe postpartum depression and wrote a book about it.

helplessness theory The idea that individuals who are prone to depression automatically attribute negative experiences to causes that are internal (i.e., their own fault), stable (i.e., unlikely to change), and global (i.e., widespread).

On average, major depression lasts about 12 weeks (Eaton et al., 2008). However, without treatment, approximately 80% of individuals will experience at least one recurrence of the disorder (Judd, 1997; Mueller et al., 1999). Compared with people who have a single episode, individuals with recurrent depression have more severe symptoms, higher rates of depression in their families, more suicide attempts, and higher rates of divorce (Merikangas, Wicki, & Angst, 1994). The median lifetime risk for depression of about 16% seems to be increasing in younger generations (Lavori et al., 1987; Wittchen, Knauper, & Kessler, 1994). For example, a large international study found evidence of a substantial global increase in the risk for depression across the past century (Cross-National Collaborative Research Group, 1992).

This situation is especially dire for women because they are diagnosed with depression at a rate twice that of men (Grigoriadis & Robinson, 2007). Socioeconomic standing has been invoked as an explanation for women's heightened risk: Their incomes are lower than those of men, and poverty could cause depression. Sex differences in hormones are another possibility: Estrogen, androgen, and progesterone influence depression; some women experience *postpartum depression* (depression following childbirth) due to changing hormone balances. It is also possible that the higher rate of depression in women reflects greater willingness by women to face their depression and seek out help, leading to higher rates of diagnosis.

? Why do more women than men experience depression?

Susan Nolen-Hoeksema (2008) has examined the evidence and argues that these causes are not sufficient to explain the size of the sex difference in depression. She believes that the culprit is response style—women's tendency to accept, disclose, and ruminate on their negative emotions in contrast with men's tendency to deny negative emotions and engage in self-distraction such as work and drinking alcohol. Perhaps women's higher rates reflect willingness to face their depression. The search for causes of this disorder in women and men continues and extends to biological and psychological factors.

Biological Factors

Heritability estimates for major depression typically range from 33% to 45% (Plomin et al., 1997; Wallace, Schnieder, & McGuffin, 2002). However, as with most types of mental disorders, heritability rates vary as a function of severity. For example, a relatively large study of twins found that the concordance rates for severe major depression (defined as three or more episodes) were quite high, with a rate of 59% for identical twins and 30% for fraternal twins (Bertelsen, Harvald, & Hauge, 1977). In contrast, concordance rates for less severe major depression (defined as fewer than three episodes) fell to 33% for identical twins and 14% for fraternal twins. Heritability rates for dysthymia are low and inconsistent (Plomin et al., 1997).

Beginning in the 1950s, researchers noticed that drugs that increased levels of the neurotransmitters norepinephrine and serotonin could sometimes reduce depression. This observation suggested that depression might be caused by an absolute or relative depletion of these neurotransmitters and sparked a revolution in the pharmacological treatment of depression (Schildkraut, 1965), leading to the development and widespread use of such popular prescription drugs as Prozac and Zoloft (see Chapter 15). Further research has shown, however, that reduced levels of these neurotransmitters cannot be the whole story. For example, some studies have found *increases* in norepinephrine activity among depressed patients (Thase & Howland, 1995). Moreover, even though the antidepressant medications change neurochemical transmission in less than a day, they typically take at least 2 weeks to relieve depressive symptoms. A biochemical model of depression has yet to be developed that accounts for all the evidence.

Depression may involve diminished activity in the left prefrontal cortex and increased activity in the right prefrontal cortex (see **FIGURE 14.2**)—areas of the brain involved in the processing of emotions (Davidson, 2004; Davidson et al., 2002).

For example, stroke patients with damage to the left prefrontal cortex often experience higher levels of depression than would otherwise be expected (Robinson & Downhill, 1995). Severely depressed individuals who do not have brain damage often show diminished activity in the anterior (prefrontal) regions of the cerebral hemispheres—especially on the left side (Thase & Howland, 1995). These abnormal activity patterns may be effects of the mood disturbance, or they may cause people to be more susceptible to depression. The possibility that activity in this brain area does cause depression is supported by the findings that similar types of brain abnormalities occur in patients in remission (Henriques & Davidson, 1990) and in children who are at risk for depression (Tomarken, Simien, & Garber, 1994). Despite these clues, the role of distinct brain regions in vulnerability to depression is still not well understood (Koenigs et al., 2008).

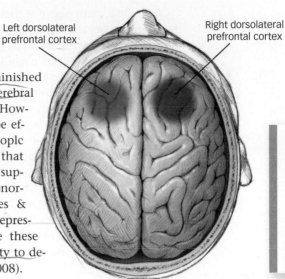

Left dorsolateral prefrontal cortex

Right dorsolateral prefrontal cortex

◀ FIGURE 14.2
Brain and Depression
Reduced activation in the left dorsolateral prefrontal cortex (blue) and increased activation in the right dorsolateral prefrontal cortex (red) have been found to be linked with depression in several studies.

Psychological Factors

If optimists see the world through rose-colored glasses, depressed individuals seem to view it through lenses that are smudged dark gray. Their negative cognitive style is remarkably consistent and, some argue, begins in childhood with experiences that foster pessimism and low self-worth (Blatt & Homann, 1992; Gibb, Alloy, & Tierney, 2001). One of the first theorists to emphasize the role of thought in depression, Aaron Beck (1967), noted that his depressed patients distorted perceptions of their experiences and embraced dysfunctional attitudes that promoted and maintained negative mood states.

Elaborating on this idea, researchers have proposed a theory of depression that emphasizes the role of people's negative inferences about the causes of their experiences (Abramson, Seligman, & Teasdale, 1978). **Helplessness theory** maintains that *individuals who are prone to depression automatically attribute negative experiences to causes that are internal (i.e., their own fault), stable (i.e., unlikely to change), and global (i.e., widespread).* For example, a student at risk for depression might view a bad grade on a math test as a sign of low intelligence (internal) that will never change (stable) and that will lead to failure in all his or her future endeavors (global). In contrast, a student without this tendency might have the opposite response, attributing the grade to something external (poor teaching), unstable (a missed study session), and/or specific (boring subject).

What is helplessness theory?

Supporting the role of thought in depression is a large body of evidence that depressed individuals' judgments, memories, and attributions are negatively biased (Abramson et al., 2002; Blatt & Zuroff, 1992; Coyne & Whiffen, 1995; Wenzlaff & Grozier, 1988). However, in these studies thoughts and judgments were assessed *during* depression, raising the possibility that the biases may be a consequence rather than a cause of the mood disturbance. To demonstrate that negative thoughts contribute to depression, the thoughts must *precede* the development of the disorder. With a few exceptions (Alloy, Jacobson, & Acocella, 1999), research has not detected obvious signs of maladaptive thinking prior to the onset of the depressive mood disturbance (Ingram, Miranda, & Segal, 1998).

◀ Man Ray (1890–1976) offered a caricature of sadness as art in *Tears*, 1930–32.

Of course, prior negative thoughts may exist in disguised forms as subtle tendencies to attend to negative information or interpret feedback in a negative way. Indeed, numerous studies suggest that people at risk for depression have latent depressive biases that can be activated by negative moods (Ingram et al., 1998). Thus, a gloomy, rainy afternoon could evoke a mood of sadness and isolation, and instead of taking the initiative and calling someone to chat, the person at risk would become dejected. Once activated, these latent biases may contribute to a progressive worsening of mood that can result in depression (see the Real World box).

Negative thinking can be hard to detect in individuals at risk for depression because they are struggling to suppress the thoughts that threaten their emotional well-being. Thought suppression is an effortful process that can be disrupted when cognitive resources are depleted (see Chapter 5). Not surprisingly, then, when cognitive demands arise (time pressures, distraction, stress, and so forth), individuals who are at risk for depression often display heightened levels of negative thinking (Wenzlaff & Bates, 1998; Wenzlaff & Eisenberg, 2001). They may worry about failures, think that people are avoiding them, or wonder whether anything is worthwhile. This breakdown in

THE REAL WORLD

Suicide Risk and Prevention

Overall, suicide is the 11th leading cause of death in the United States and the third most common form of death among high school and college students (King, 1997). In 2006, 11 out of 100,000 Americans died by suicide—a total of 33,300 in the nation that year (Centers for Disease Control and Prevention, 2010). Although people have various reasons for taking their own lives, approximately 50% of those who kill themselves do so during a depressive episode (Isacsson & Rich, 1997). The lifetime risk of suicide in people with mood disorders is about 4%, compared to a risk of only .5% in the general population (Bostwick & Pankratz, 2000). In the United States, women attempt suicide about two to three times more often than men. However, because men typically use more lethal methods than do women (such as guns versus pills), men are three to four times more likely to actually kill themselves than are women (Canetto & Lester, 1995). The tragic effects of suicide extend beyond the loss of life, compounding the grief of families and loved ones who must contend with feelings of abandonment, guilt, shame, and futility.

Researchers have identified a variety of motives for suicide, including a profound sense of alienation, intolerable psychological or physical suffering or both, hopelessness, an escape from feelings of worthlessness, and a desperate cry for help (Durkheim, 1951; Joiner, 2006). Suicide rates increase with age, and aging White men are especially at risk (Joiner, 2006; National Institute of Mental Health, 2010). Studies also show an increased risk of suicide among family members with a relative who committed suicide (Kety, 1990; Mann et al., 1999). This elevated risk may be a function of biological factors in depression, or suicide could be contagious, with exposure making it a more salient option during desperate times. Contagious effects are suggested by the occasional "clusters" of suicides in which several people—usually teenagers—attempt to kill themselves following a highly publicized case (Gould, 1990).

The contagion of suicide has been called the "Werther effect" after the rash of suicides that followed the 1774 publication of Goethe's tale of a young romantic who shot himself over a lost love. Werther was wearing a blue coat and yellow vest when he took his life, and so many young men

◀ A rash of suicides by young men in blue coats and yellow vests followed when Goethe described the suicide of a young man so dressed in *The Sorrows of Young Werther* (1774).

were found dead in similar garb that the book was banned in several countries. In fact, suicide in the United States has been found to increase after nationally televised news or feature stories about suicide (Phillips & Carstensen, 1986), but imitation is not inevitable and the effect is not always found (Hittner, 2005). When rock musician Kurt Cobain shot himself in 1994, the Werther effect was not found in his home town of Seattle (Jobes et al., 1996) or in another study done in Australia (Martin & Koo, 1997).

How can you tell if someone is at risk for suicide? Unfortunately, definitive prediction is impossible, but a variety of warning signs can suggest an increased risk (Substance Abuse and Mental Health Services Administration, 2005). Any one sign is a cause for concern, and the risk is especially serious when several occur together. Some signs:

mental control may explain why stressful life events such as a prolonged illness or the loss of a loved one often precede a descent into depression (Monroe & Reid, 2009). Ironically, thought suppression itself may intensify depressive thoughts and ultimately contribute to relapse (Beevers & Meyer, 2008; Wenzlaff, 2005).

Bipolar Disorder

If depression is bad, would the opposite be better? Not for Virginia Woolf or for Julie, a 20-year-old college sophomore. When first seen by a clinician, Julie had gone 5 days without sleep and, like Woolf, was extremely active and expressing bizarre thoughts and ideas. She proclaimed to friends that she did not menstruate because she was "of a third sex, a gender above the two human sexes." She claimed to be a "superwoman," capable of avoiding human sexuality and yet still able to give birth. Preoccupied with the politics of global disarmament, she felt that she had switched souls with the senior senator from her state, had tapped into his thoughts and memories, and could save the world from nuclear destruction. She began to campaign for an elected position in

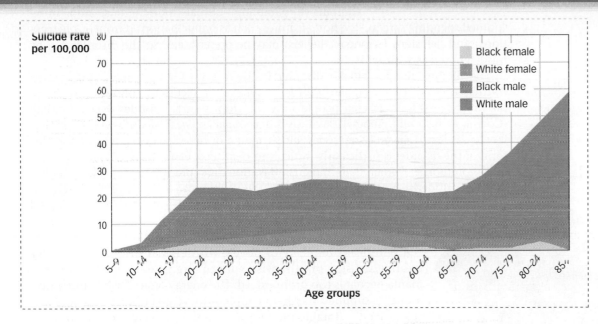

◄ Suicide rates in the United States reveal that men are more likely to commit suicide than women at all ages, that men's likelihood of suicide grows in early adulthood, and that White men remain most suicide prone throughout life—with a spike in the later years.
(From National Institute of Mental Health, 2003.)

- Talk about suicide. About 90% of people who are suicidal discuss their intentions, so this obvious warning sign should not be dismissed as simply a means of getting attention. Although most people who threaten suicide do not actually attempt it, they are at greater risk than those who do not talk about it.
- An upturn in mood following a prolonged depressive episode. Surprisingly, suicide risk increases at this point. In fact, a sudden lifting of mood may reflect relief at the prospect that suicide will end the emotional suffering.
- A failed love interest, romantic breakup, or loss of a loved one through separation or death.

- A severe, stressful event that is especially shameful or humiliating.
- A family history of suicide, especially of a parent.
- Unusual reckless or risky behavior, seemingly carried out without thinking.
- An unexplained decline in school or workplace performance.
- Withdrawal from friends, family, and regular activities.
- Expressing feelings of being trapped, as though there's "no way out."
- "Cleaning house" by giving away prized possessions.
- Increased alcohol or drug use. Substance abuse is associated with

approximately 25% to 50% of suicides and is especially associated with adolescent suicides (Conwell et al., 1996; Woods et al., 1997).

Although discussing suicide with someone possibly at risk might seem to increase actual risk, a caring listener can help put issues in better perspective and reduce feelings of isolation. Anyone who is potentially suicidal should be encouraged to seek professional help. Colleges and universities have student counseling centers, and most cities have suicide prevention centers with 24-hour hotlines and walk-in emergency counseling. The U.S. National Suicide Prevention Lifeline is 1-800-273-TALK.

"Those? Oh, just a few souvenirs from my bipolar-disorder days."

the U.S. government (even though no elections were scheduled at that time). Worried that she would forget some of her thoughts, she had been leaving hundreds of notes about her ideas and activities everywhere, including on the walls and furniture of her dormitory room (Vitkus, 1999).

In addition to her manic episodes, Julie—like Woolf—had a history of depression. The diagnostic label for their constellation of symptoms is **bipolar disorder**—*an unstable emotional condition characterized by cycles of abnormal, persistent high mood (mania) and low mood (depression).* In about two thirds of patients, manic episodes immediately precede or immediately follow depressive episodes (Whybrow, 1997). The depressive phase of bipolar disorder is often clinically indistinguishable from major depression (Johnson et al., 2009). In the manic phase, which must last at least a week to meet *DSM* requirements, mood can be elevated, expansive, or irritable. Other prominent symptoms include grandiosity, decreased need for sleep, talkativeness, racing thoughts, distractibility, and reckless behavior (such as compulsive gambling, sexual indiscretions, and unrestrained spending sprees). Psychotic features such as hallucinations (erroneous perceptions) and delusions (erroneous beliefs) may be present, and so the disorder can be misdiagnosed as schizophrenia.

The lifetime risk for bipolar disorder is about 1.3% for both men and women (Wittchen et al., 1994). Bipolar disorder is typically a recurrent condition, with approximately 90% of afflicted people suffering from several episodes over a lifetime (Coryell et al., 1995). About 10% of cases have *rapid cycling bipolar disorder,* characterized by at least four mood episodes (either manic or depressive) every year, and this form of the disorder is particularly difficult to treat (Post et al., 2008). Rapid cycling is more common in women than in men and is sometimes precipitated by taking certain kinds of antidepressant drugs (Liebenluft, 1996; Whybrow, 1997). Unfortunately, bipolar disorder tends to be persistent. In one study, 24% of patients had relapsed within 6 months of recovery from an episode, and 77% had at least one new episode within 4 years of recovery (Coryell et al., 1995).

A significant minority of people with bipolar disorder are highly creative, artistic, or otherwise outstanding in some way. Before the mania becomes too pronounced, the energy, grandiosity, and ambition that it supplies may help people achieve great things. In addition to Virginia Woolf, notable individuals thought to have had the disorder include Abraham Lincoln, Ernest Hemingway, Winston Churchill, and Theodore Roosevelt.

Biological Factors

Among the various mental disorders, bipolar disorder has the highest rate of heritability, with concordance from 40% to 70% for identical twins and 10% for fraternal twins (Craddock & Jones, 1999). Occasional families are found in which a single gene gives rise to the disorder, but most often the disorder is *polygenic,* arising from the interaction of multiple genes, and these have been difficult to identify (Goodwin & Ghaemi, 1998; Plomin et al., 1997). Biochemical imbalances may be involved in bipolar disorder, but specific neurotransmitters have not been identified. Some researchers have suggested that low levels of serotonin and norepinephrine may contribute to the emotional roller coaster that characterizes bipolar disorder (Whybrow, 1997). This notion is not well substantiated and doesn't explain why lithium, a chemical unrelated to these neurotransmitters, often helps stabilize both the depressive and manic symptoms associated with bipolar disorder.

▲ Winston Churchill made a pet of his bipolar illness, calling his depression the "black dog" that followed him around.

Psychological Factors

Stressful life experiences often precede manic and depressive episodes (Johnson et al., 2008). One study found that severely stressed patients took an average of three times longer to recover from an episode than did patients not affected by stress (Johnson & Miller, 1997). The stress-disorder relationship is not simple, however: High levels of stress have less impact on patients with extraverted personalities than on those who are more introverted (Swednsen et al., 1995). Personality characteristics such as neuroticism and conscientiousness have also been found to predict increases in bipolar symptoms over time (Lozano & Johnson, 2001). Finally, patients living with family members who are hostile toward or critical of the patient are more likely to relapse than patients with supportive families (Miklowitz et al., 1988).

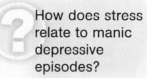 **How does stress relate to manic depressive episodes?**

IN SUMMARY

○ Mood disorders are mental disorders in which a disturbance in mood is the predominant feature.

○ Major depression (or unipolar depression) is characterized by a severely depressed mood lasting at least 2 weeks; symptoms include excessive self-criticism, guilt, difficulty concentrating, suicidal thoughts, sleep and appetite disturbances, and lethargy. Dysthymia, a related disorder, involves less severe symptoms that persist for at least 2 years.

○ Bipolar disorder is an unstable emotional condition involving extreme mood swings of depression and mania. The manic phase is characterized by periods of abnormally and persistently elevated, expansive, or irritable mood, lasting at least 1 week.

Dissociative Disorders: Going to Pieces

Can the human mind come apart? Could a person forget who she is one day but remember the next? Mary, a 35-year-old social worker being treated with hypnosis for chronic pain in her forearm, mentioned to her doctor that she often found her car low on fuel in the morning despite her having filled it with gas the day before. Overnight the odometer would gain 50 to 100 miles, even though she had no memory of driving the car.

During one hypnotic session, Mary suddenly blurted out in a strange voice, "It's about time you knew about me." In the new voice, she identified herself as "Marian" and described the drives that she took at night, which were retreats to the nearby hills to "work out problems." Mary knew nothing of "Marian" and her nighttime adventures. Marian was as abrupt and hostile as Mary was compliant and caring. In the course of therapy, six other personalities emerged (including one who claimed to be a 6-year-old child), and considerable tension and disagreement developed among the personalities. On one occasion, one of the personalities threatened suicide and forbade the therapist from discussing it with the other personalities, noting that it would be "a violation of doctor-patient confidentiality" (Spitzer et al., 1994).

Mary suffers from a type of **dissociative disorder**, *a condition in which normal cognitive processes are severely disjointed and fragmented, creating significant disruptions in memory, awareness, or personality that can vary in length from a matter of minutes to many years.* To some extent, a bit of dissociation, or "splitting," of cognitive processes is normal. For example, research on implicit memory shows that we often retain and are influenced by information that we do not consciously remember (discussed in Chapter 6). Moreover, we can engage in more than one activity or mental process while maintaining only dim awareness of the perceptions and decisions that guide other behaviors (such as talking while driving a car). Our ordinary continuity of memory and awareness of our personal identity contrasts with Mary's profound cognitive fragmentation and blindness to her own mental processes and states.

bipolar disorder An unstable emotional condition characterized by cycles of abnormal, persistent high mood (mania) and low mood (depression).

dissociative disorder A condition in which normal cognitive processes are severely disjointed and fragmented, creating significant disruptions in memory, awareness, or personality that can vary in length from a matter of minutes to many years.

A moment ago she was the nicest girl in town . . .
A moment from now she will be anybody's pick-up!

The Three Faces of Eve.

JOANNE WOODWARD · DAVID WAYNE · LEE J. COBB · NUNNALLY JOHNSON

© 20TH CENTURY FOX/THE KOBAL COLLECTION

▲ Joanne Woodward played Eve White, a woman with dissociative identity disorder, in the 1957 film *The Three Faces of Eve.* This film and others dramatized the disorder and by increasing public awareness stimulated more frequent diagnosis of this problem. It is not clear, though, whether the increased awareness led to greater accuracy in finding cases of the disorder that were already present or if it shaped how people behave (and what therapists tried to find) and so *created* more cases of the disorder.

dissociative identity disorder (DID) The presence within an individual of two or more distinct identities that at different times take control of the individual's behavior.

dissociative amnesia The sudden loss of memory for significant personal information.

dissociative fugue The sudden loss of memory for one's personal history, accompanied by an abrupt departure from home and the assumption of a new identity.

Dissociative Identity Disorder

Dissociative identity disorder (DID) is characterized by *the presence within an individual of two or more distinct identities that at different times take control of the individual's behavior.* The most dramatic form of dissociative disorder, DID has attracted considerable popular attention. When the original personality, or *host personality*, is dominant, the individual often is unaware of the alternate personalities, or *alters* (as in Mary's case). However, the alters typically know about the host personality and about each other. The number of distinct identities can range considerably, with some cases numbering more than a hundred. Sometimes alters share certain characteristics; sometimes they are dissimilar—assuming different vocal patterns, dialects, ages, morals, and even gender identities. No longer called "multiple personality disorder" because the term implies that more than one person is in "residence," the disorder is now conceptualized as involving multiple patterns of thought and behavior, each of which is associated with a different identity.

Prior to 1970, DID was considered rare, with only about 100 cases reported in the professional literature worldwide. However, since that time, the number of reported cases grew enormously until the late 1990s—and then oddly shrank again (Piper & Merskey, 2004). Recent estimates are that between .5% and 1% of the general population suffers from the disorder, with a female to male prevalence of about 9 to 1 (Maldonado & Butler, 1998). Most patients are diagnosed when they are in their 20s or 30s, although the actual age of onset is probably during childhood (Maldonado & Butler, 1998; Putnam et al., 1986).

The strange transition of DID—from a rare disorder to a minor epidemic and back again—has raised concerns that the disorder is a matter of faking or fashion (Piper & Merskey, 2004; Spanos, 1994). The most common explanation targets psychotherapists who, though often well meaning, are said to have created the disorder in patients who are vulnerable to their suggestive procedures. Accounts of how therapists treat DID, often using hypnosis, have revealed some cajoling and coaxing of clients into reporting evidence of alternate personalities (Acocella, 1999).

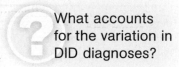

What accounts for the variation in DID diagnoses?

Many patients with DID report a history of severe childhood abuse and trauma (Coons, 1994; Putnam et al., 1986), and such evidence supports a popular explanation rooted in psychodynamic theory. From this viewpoint, the helpless child, confronted with intolerable abuse and trauma, responds with the primitive psychological defense of splitting or dissociating to escape the pain and horror. But the theory linking trauma and dissociation has some problems. Curiously, early abuse and trauma are especially prevalent in low-income households, while cases of multiple personality occur almost exclusively among people of middle income (Acocella, 1999). Also suspicious is the finding that the evidence of abuse in DID patients is seldom corroborated by anyone other than the patient (Piper & Merskey, 2004). These unusual facts suggest that trauma may not cause DID—and rather that a common error of memory is suffered by DID patients.

Where would this memory error come from? Critics of the psychodynamic explanation of DID have raised the possibility that individuals who exhibit both trauma and DID may be responding to their therapists' expectations that the two are linked (Humphreys & Dennett, 1989; Kluft, 1991; Lalonde et al., 2001). The widespread popularity of the theory that trauma leads to dissociation may have led therapists to seek evidence of this link in their clients (Loewenstein, 2007). Although there remain some commentators who hold that traumatic events cause DID (Gleaves et al., 2000), it seems more likely that such causation is an illusion of patients' memories. What we know for sure is that dissociative identity disorder is poorly understood and that deep questions exist about what it is, how it arises, and how it can be treated.

Dissociative Amnesia and Dissociative Fugue

Amnesia, The Bourne Identity, Eternal Sunshine of the Spotless Mind, 50 First Dates, Memento, The Forgotten, and *The Man without a Past*—these movies reveal Hollywood's fascination with forms of dissociative disorder involving memory. The memory oddities invented for film don't always correspond to the real disorders, dissociative amnesia and dissociative fugue. These conditions (by *DSM* definition) cannot result from normal forgetting or brain injury, drugs, or another mental disorder (e.g., post-traumatic stress disorder).

◄ Call me "Al." A man identified only by the name "Al" gave a news conference in Denver in 2006 in hopes that someone might be able to tell him more about himself. A victim of a dissociative fugue state, he had no memory of his identity or his life. His fiancée recognized him on TV and confirmed his identity as Jeffrey Alan Ingram, an unemployed machinist from Olympia, Washington.

AP PHOTO/*THE DENVER POST*, KARL GEHRING

> **Dissociative amnesia** is *the sudden loss of memory for significant personal information.* The memory loss is typically for a traumatic specific event or period of time but can involve extended periods (months or years) of a person's life (Kihlstrom, 2005).

> **Dissociative fugue** involves *the sudden loss of memory for one's personal history, accompanied by an abrupt departure from home and the assumption of a new identity.* The fugue state is usually associated with stressful life circumstances and can be brief or lengthy.

"Burt," a 42-year-old short-order cook in a small town, came to the attention of police when he got into a heated altercation with another man in a diner. When the police took "Burt" to the hospital, they discovered that he had no identification documents and was clueless about his past. While he was in the hospital, the police matched his description to that of Gene Saunders, a resident of a city 200 miles away who had disappeared a month earlier. When Gene Saunders's wife came to identify him, he denied knowing her and his real identity. Before he disappeared, Gene Saunders had been experiencing considerable difficulties at home and at work and had become withdrawn and irritable. Two days before he left, he had a violent argument with his 18-year-old son, who accused him of being a failure (Spitzer et al., 1994).

How do dissociative fugue and dissociative amnesia differ from other kinds of memory impairments?

Both dissociative amnesia and dissociative fugue usually emerge in adulthood and rarely occur after the age of 50 (Sackeim & Devanand, 1991). Dissociative fugue states usually end rather abruptly, and victims typically recover their memories and personal identities. Dissociative amnesia may also be temporary: People have lost significant personal memories and then recovered them later (Brenneis, 2000; Schooler, Bendiksen, & Ambadar, 1997).

IN SUMMARY

○ Dissociative disorders involve severely disjointed and fragmented cognitive processes reflected in significant disruptions in memory, awareness, or personality.

○ People with dissociative identity disorder (DID) shift between two or more identities that are distinctive from each other in terms of personal memories, behavioral characteristics, and attitudes.

○ Previously rare, reported cases of DID increase and decrease over time, leading some researchers to believe that it may be overdiagnosed or even created in therapy.

○ Dissociative amnesia and dissociative fugue involve significant memory loss that is too extensive to be the result of normal forgetting and cannot be attributed to brain injury, drugs, or another mental disorder.

schizophrenia A disorder characterized by the profound disruption of basic psychological processes; a distorted perception of reality; altered or blunted emotion; and disturbances in thought, motivation, and behavior.

delusion A patently false belief system, often bizarre and grandiose, that is maintained in spite of its irrationality.

hallucination A false perceptual experience that has a compelling sense of being real despite the absence of external stimulation.

disorganized speech A severe disruption of verbal communication in which ideas shift rapidly and incoherently from one to another unrelated topic.

grossly disorganized behavior Behavior that is inappropriate for the situation or ineffective in attaining goals, often with specific motor disturbances.

catatonic behavior A marked decrease in all movement or an increase in muscular rigidity and overactivity.

negative symptoms Emotional and social withdrawal; apathy; poverty of speech; and other indications of the absence or insufficiency of normal behavior, motivation, and emotion.

Schizophrenia: Losing the Grasp on Reality

Margaret, a 39-year-old mother, believed that God was punishing her for marrying a man she did not love and bringing two children into the world. As her punishment, God had made her and her children immortal so that they would have to suffer in their unhappy home life forever—a realization that came to her one evening when she was washing dishes and saw a fork lying across a knife in the shape of a cross. Margaret found further support for her belief in two pieces of evidence: First, a local television station was rerunning old episodes of *The Honeymooners,* a 1950s situation comedy in which the main characters often argue and shout at each other. She saw this as a sign from God that her own marital conflict would go on forever. Second, she believed (falsely) that the pupils of her children's eyes were fixed in size and would neither dilate nor constrict—a sign of their immortality. At home, she would lock herself in her room for hours and sometimes days. The week before her diagnosis, she kept her 7-year-old son home from school so that he could join her and his 4-year-old sister in reading aloud from the Bible (Oltmanns et al., 1991). Margaret was suffering from schizophrenia, one of the most devastating and mystifying of the mental disorders.

Symptoms and Types of Schizophrenia

Schizophrenia is characterized by *the profound disruption of basic psychological processes; a distorted perception of reality; altered or blunted emotion; and disturbances in thought, motivation, and behavior.* Traditionally, schizophrenia was regarded primarily as a disturbance of thought and perception, in which the sense of reality becomes severely distorted and confused. However, this condition is now understood to take different forms affecting a wide range of functions. According to the *DSM-IV-TR,* schizophrenia is diagnosed when two or more of the following symptoms emerge during a continuous period of at least 1 month with signs of the disorder persisting for at least 6 months: *delusion, hallucination, disorganized speech, grossly disorganized behavior* or *catatonic behavior,* and *negative symptoms.* Let's consider each symptom in detail.

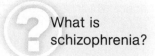

What is schizophrenia?

> **Delusion** is *a patently false belief system, often bizarre and grandiose, that is maintained in spite of its irrationality.* For example, an individual with schizophrenia may believe that he or she is Jesus Christ, Napoleon, Joan of Arc, or some other famous person. Such delusions of identity have helped foster the misconception that schizophrenia involves multiple personalities. Unlike dissociative identity disorder, however, adopted identities in schizophrenia do not alternate, exhibit amnesia for one another, or otherwise "split." Delusions of persecution are also common. The patient's belief that the CIA, demons, extraterrestrials, or other malevolent forces are conspiring to harm the patient or control his or her mind may represent an attempt to make sense of the tormenting delusions (Roberts, 1991). People with schizophrenia have little or no insight into their disordered perceptual and thought processes (Karow et al., 2007). Without understanding that they have lost control of their own minds, they may develop unusual beliefs and theories that attribute control to external agents.

> **Hallucination** is *a false perceptual experience that has a compelling sense of being real despite the absence of external stimulation.* The perceptual disturbances associated with schizophrenia can include hearing, seeing, or smelling things that are not there or having tactile sensations in the absence of relevant sensory stimulation. Schizophrenic hallucinations are often auditory—for example, hearing voices that no one else can hear. Among people with schizophrenia, some 65% report hearing voices repeatedly (Frith &

"I want to see other hallucinations."

Fletcher, 1995). British psychiatrist Henry Maudsley (1886) long ago proposed that these voices are in fact produced in the mind of the schizophrenic individual, and recent research substantiates his idea. In one PET imaging study, auditory hallucinations were accompanied by activation in Broca's area—the part of the brain (as discussed in Chapter 3) associated with the production of language (McGuire, Shah, & Murray, 1993). Unfortunately, the voices heard in schizophrenia seldom sound like the self or like a kindly uncle offering advice. They command, scold, suggest bizarre actions, or offer snide comments. One patient reported a voice saying, "He's getting up now. He's going to wash. It's about time" (Frith & Fletcher, 1995).

> **Disorganized speech** is *a severe disruption of verbal communication in which ideas shift rapidly and incoherently from one to another unrelated topic.* The abnormal speech patterns in schizophrenia reflect difficulties in organizing thoughts and focusing attention. Responses to questions are often irrelevant, ideas are loosely associated, and words are used in peculiar ways. For example, asked by her doctor, "Can you tell me the name of this place?" one patient with schizophrenia responded, "I have not been a drinker for 16 years. I am taking a mental rest after a 'carter' assignment of 'quill.' You know, a 'penwrap.' I had contracts with Warner Brothers Studios and Eugene broke phonograph records but Mike protested. I have been with the police department for 35 years. I am made of flesh and blood—see, Doctor" [pulling up her dress] (Carson et al., 2000, p. 474).

> **Grossly disorganized behavior** is *behavior that is inappropriate for the situation or ineffective in attaining goals, often with specific motor disturbances.* A patient might exhibit constant childlike silliness, improper sexual behavior (such as masturbating in public), disheveled appearance, or loud shouting or swearing. Specific motor disturbances might include strange movements, rigid posturing, odd mannerisms, bizarre grimacing, or hyperactivity. **Catatonic behavior** is *a marked decrease in all movement or an increase in muscular rigidity and overactivity.* Patients with *catatonia* may actively resist movement (when someone is trying to move them) or become completely unresponsive and unaware of their surroundings in a *catatonic stupor.* In addition, patients receiving drug therapy may exhibit motor symptoms (such as rigidity or spasm) as a side effect of the medication. Indeed, the *DSM-IV-TR* has proposed a diagnostic category labeled "medication-induced movement disorders" that identifies motor disturbances arising from the use of medications of the sort commonly used to treat schizophrenia.

> **Negative symptoms** include *emotional and social withdrawal; apathy; poverty of speech; and other indications of the absence or insufficiency of normal behavior, motivation, and emotion.* These symptoms refer to things missing in people with schizophrenia, in contrast to the positive symptoms (such as hallucinations) that appear more in people with schizophrenia than in other people. Negative symptoms may rob people of emotion, for example, leaving them with flat, deadpan responses. Or their ability to act willfully may be reduced, their interest in people or events undermined, or their capacity to focus attention impaired.

▲ *The Clown Voice*, 2003. Artist Elizabeth Autumn Daniels writes, "When I was about 17, I started hallucinating and thinking people were out to get me. . . . I thought that people were going to bomb my house. I was hearing 10 voices in my head nonstop. . . . Turns out I am paranoid schizophrenic. . . . But finally the past couple of months I have found the right medication. . . . I have been drawing and painting since I was 5 years old. . . . And now it is helping me heal. I drew this because the clown is what I saw when I heard one of the voices in my head. . . ."

◄ A patient suffering from catatonic schizophrenia may assume an unusual posture and fail to move for hours.

The various symptoms of schizophrenia do not all occur in every case. Instead, the disorder can take quite different forms. Recent editions of the *DSM* have identified five subtypes of schizophrenia (see **TABLE 14.3**). Three of these types—*paranoid, catatonic,* and *disorganized*—depend primarily on the relative prominence of various symptoms. The paranoid type involves preoccupation with delusions and hallucinations; the catatonic type involves immobility and stupor or agitated, purposeless motor activity; the disorganized type is often the most severe, featuring disorganized speech and behavior and flat or inappropriate emotion. The *DSM-IV-TR* reserves the *undifferentiated type* for cases that do not neatly fall into these three categories and the *residual type* for individuals who have substantially recovered from at least one schizophrenic episode but still have lingering symptoms.

What are the subtypes of schizophrenia?

Schizophrenia occurs in about 1% of the population (Jablensky, 1997) and is slightly more common in men than in women (McGrath et al., 2008). Early versions of the *DSM* suggested that schizophrenia might have a very early onset—in the form of infantile autism (see the Hot Science box)—but more recent studies suggest that the disorders are distinct and that schizophrenia rarely develops before early adolescence (Rapoport et al., 2009). The first episode typically occurs in late adolescence or early adulthood (Gottesman, 1991). Despite its relatively low frequency, schizophrenia is the primary diagnosis for nearly 40% of all admissions to state and county mental hospitals; it is the second most

TABLE 14.3

Types of Schizophrenia

Types	Characteristics
Paranoid type	Symptoms dominated by absurd, illogical, and changeable delusions, frequently accompanied by vivid hallucinations, with a resulting impairment of critical judgment and erratic, unpredictable, and occasionally dangerous behaviors. In chronic cases, there is usually less disorganization of behavior than in other types of schizophrenia and less extreme withdrawal from social interaction.
Catatonic type	Often characterized by alternating periods of extreme withdrawal and extreme excitement, although in some cases one or the other reaction predominates. In the withdrawal reaction, there is a sudden loss of all animation and a tendency to remain motionless for hours or even days in a single position. The person may undergo an abrupt change, with excitement coming on suddenly; the person may talk or shout incoherently, pace rapidly, and engage in uninhibited, impulsive, and frenzied behavior. In this state, an individual may be dangerous.
Disorganized type	Usually occurs at an earlier age than most other types of schizophrenia and represents a more severe disintegration of the personality. Emotional distortion and blunting typically are manifested in inappropriate laughter and silliness, peculiar mannerisms, and bizarre, often obscene behavior.
Undifferentiated type	A pattern of symptoms in which there is a rapidly changing mixture of all or most of the primary indicators of schizophrenia. Commonly observed are indications of perplexity, confusion, emotional turmoil, delusions, excitement, dreamlike withdrawal, depression, and fear. Most often this picture is seen in patients who are in the process of breaking down and developing schizophrenia. It is also seen, however, when major adjustment demands impinge on a person with an already-established schizophrenic psychosis. In such cases, it frequently foreshadows an impending change to another primary schizophrenic subtype.
Residual type	Mild indication of schizophrenia shown by individuals in remission following a schizophrenic episode.

frequent diagnosis for inpatient psychiatric admission at other institutions (Rosenstein, Milazzo-Sayre, & Manderscheid, 1990). The disproportionate rate of hospitalization for schizophrenia is a testament to the devastation it causes in people's lives.

Some of the symptoms found in schizophrenia appear in people without the disorder. In one study of 375 college students, 71% of participants reported hearing brief, occasional hallucinated voices during periods of wakefulness, and 39% had heard their own thoughts spoken aloud (Linszen et al., 1997; Posey & Losch, 1983). Delusional thoughts can occur outside schizophrenia as well. If beliefs about scientifically unverified, paranormal experiences are any gauge, many people appear to hold some pretty odd notions. For example, in a survey of 60,000 adults, 50% expressed a belief in thought transference between two people, 25% said they believe in ghosts, and 25% in reincarnation (Cox & Cowling, 1989). These observations don't mean that schizophrenia is widespread—they remind us instead that diagnosing psychological disorders must take into account the complexity of the mind and the glimmerings of madness in us all.

HOT SCIENCE

Autism and Childhood Disorders

Are the categories of psychological disorder in children just junior versions of the adult DSM? Or are childhood disorders unique? There are many parallels between childhood and adult mental problems—anxiety disorders and mood disorders, for example, appear with similar symptoms no matter when they occur in the life span. But there are also *early-onset disorders* recognized in the DSM as problems in children: mental retardation, learning disorders, communication disorders, motor skill disorders, eating and elimination disorders, conduct disorders, attention-deficit hyperactivity disorder, and autistic disorder. Some of these problems resolve as the person develops, but others do not.

One childhood disorder is the focus of new research attention because it has become increasingly prevalent in recent years (Fombonne, 2009). *Autistic disorder* involves abnormal or impaired development of communication and social interaction and a markedly restricted repertoire of activities or interests. Signs of autism can arise in early infancy. Most infants respond to facial expressions in the first few months, sometimes even rewarding a smile with a smile in return— whereas a baby with profound autism may not do this even at 6 months of age. Some children who become autistic progress normally for the first years, only to develop the disorder at age 2 or 3 or even later.

Whenever it emerges, autism can be profoundly debilitating. The disorder often

▲ It's a good sign when a baby smiles for you. Even better if the baby can fly. COURTESY OF DANIEL WEGNER

involves an inability to interact socially, with little eye contact or social responsiveness, and it can lead to restricted, repetitive behaviors, and even recurring self-harm. Early theories of autism sometimes described it as "childhood schizophrenia," but it is now understood as a distinct disorder. In fact, schizophrenia is rarely diagnosed in children, emerging mainly in adolescence or young adulthood (Kessler & Wang, 2008). Autism is not always severe, with various degrees of disorder along a spectrum that includes milder forms such as Asperger's syndrome (Goldstein et al., 2008). Sometimes the disorder can even bring unique talents. People with autism may show remarkable abilities—for example, the ability to perceive or remember details, or to master symbol systems such as mathematics or music (Happé & Vital, 2009). These gifts come with the cost, however, of

poor social perception—a limited ability to perceive others' minds and desires.

The renowned behavioral scientist and author Temple Grandin has written of her personal experience with autistic disorder (e.g., Grandin, 2006). She was diagnosed with autism at age 3, started learning to talk late, and then suffered teasing for odd habits and "nerdy" behavior. She developed ways to cope, though, and found a niche through her special talent—the ability to understand animal behavior (Sacks, 1996). She is now Doctor of Animal Science and professor at Colorado State University; celebrated author of books such as *Animals in Translation*; designer of animal handling systems used widely in ranching, farming, and zoos; and the central character in an HBO movie based on her life. Not every person with autism has such abilities, and portrayals of autism in movies (such as *Rain Man, Snow Cake, Mozart and the Whale*) often exaggerate the realities of the disorder (Draaisma, 2009). Still, it is good to know that some burdens in life may not only be lifted over time, but can be uplifting.

So, what happens to people with autism when they are no longer children? Temple Grandin's story lets us know that there are happy endings. But people diagnosed with autism as children have highly variable trajectories, with some achieving normal or better-than-normal functioning and others remaining the victims of profound disorder. Autism is a childhood disorder that in adulthood can turn out many ways.

Biological Factors

In 1899, when German psychiatrist Emil Kraepelin first described the syndrome we now know as schizophrenia, he remarked that the disorder was so severe that it suggested "organic," or biological, origins (Kraepelin, 1899). Over the years, accumulating evidence for the role of biology in schizophrenia has come from studies of genetic factors, biochemical factors, and neuroanatomy.

Genetic Factors

Family studies indicate that the closer a person's genetic relatedness to a person with schizophrenia, the greater the likelihood of developing the disorder (Gottesman, 1991). As shown in **FIGURE 14.3,** concordance rates increase dramatically with biological relatedness. The rates are estimates and vary considerably from study to study, but almost every study finds the average concordance rates higher for identical twins (48%) than for fraternal twins (17%), which suggests a genetic component for the disorder (Torrey et al., 1994).

Although genetics clearly has a strong predisposing role in schizophrenia, considerable evidence suggests that the prenatal and perinatal environments may also affect concordance rates in identical twins (Jurewicz, Owen, & O'Donovan, 2001; Thaker, 2002; Torrey et al., 1994). For example, because approximately 70% of identical twins share the same prenatal blood supply, toxins in the mother's blood could contribute to the high concordance rate. When one twin develops schizophrenia and the other twin does not, birth records often show that the afflicted twin is second born and had a lower birth weight (Wahl, 1976).

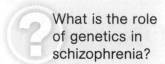 **What is the role of genetics in schizophrenia?**

Biochemical Factors

During the 1950s, major tranquilizers were discovered that could reduce the symptoms of schizophrenia by lowering levels of the neurotransmitter dopamine. The effectiveness of many drugs in alleviating schizophrenic symptoms is related to the drugs' capacity to reduce dopamine's role in neurotransmission in certain brain tracts.

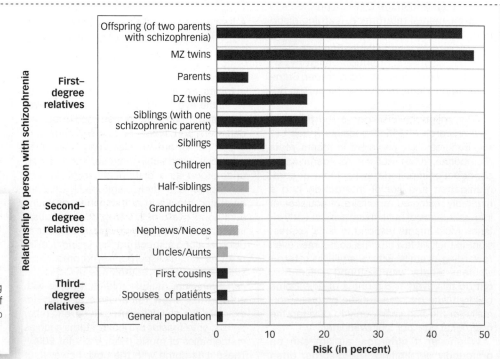

▶ FIGURE 14.3
Average Risk of Developing Schizophrenia The risk of schizophrenia among biological relatives is greater for those with greater degrees of relatedness. An identical (MZ) twin of a twin with schizophrenia has a 48% risk of developing schizophrenia, for example, and offspring of two parents with schizophrenia have a 46% risk of developing the disorder.
(Adapted from Gottesman, 1991.)

This finding suggested the **dopamine hypothesis**, the *idea that schizophrenia involves an excess of dopamine activity*. The hypothesis has been invoked to explain why amphetamines, which increase dopamine levels, often aggravate the symptoms of schizophrenia (Iverson, 2006).

If only things were so simple. Considerable evidence suggests that this hypothesis is inadequate (Moncrieff, 2009). For example, many individuals with schizophrenia do not respond favorably to dopamine-blocking drugs (e.g., major tranquilizers), and those who do seldom show a complete remission of symptoms. Moreover, the drugs block dopamine receptors very rapidly, yet individuals with schizophrenia typically do not show a beneficial response for weeks. Finally, research has implicated other neurotransmitters in schizophrenia, suggesting that the disorder may involve a complex interaction among a host of different biochemicals (Risman et al., 2008; Sawa & Snyder, 2002). In sum, the precise role of neurotransmitters in schizophrenia has yet to be determined.

Neuroanatomy

When neuroimaging techniques became available, researchers immediately started looking for distinctive anatomical features of the brain in individuals with schizophrenia. The earliest observations revealed enlargement of the *ventricles,* hollow areas filled with cerebrospinal fluid, lying deep within the core of the brain (see **FIGURE 14.4**) (Johnstone et al., 1976). In some patients—primarily those with chronic, negative symptoms—the ventricles were abnormally enlarged, suggesting a loss of brain tissue mass that could arise from an anomaly in prenatal development (Arnold et al., 1998; Heaton et al., 1994).

Understanding the significance of this brain abnormality for schizophrenia is complicated by several factors, however. First, such enlarged ventricles are found in only a minority of cases of schizophrenia. Second, some individuals who do not have schizophrenia also show evidence of enlarged ventricles. Finally, this type of brain abnormality can be caused by the long-term use of some types of antipsychotic medications commonly prescribed in schizophrenia (Breggin, 1990; Gur et al., 1998).

Neuroimaging studies provide evidence of a variety of brain abnormalities in schizophrenia. Paul Thompson and his colleagues (2001) examined changes in the brains of adolescents whose MRI scans could be traced sequentially from the onset of schizophrenia. By morphing the images onto a standardized brain, the researchers were able to detect progressive tissue loss beginning in the parietal lobe and eventually encompassing much of the brain (see **FIGURE 14.5** on the next page). All adolescents lose some gray matter over time in a kind of normal "pruning" of the brain, but in the case of those developing schizophrenia, the loss was dramatic enough to seem pathological. A variety of specific brain changes found in other studies suggest a clear relationship between biological changes in the brain and the progression of schizophrenia (Shenton et al., 2001).

dopamine hypothesis The idea that schizophrenia involves an excess of dopamine activity.

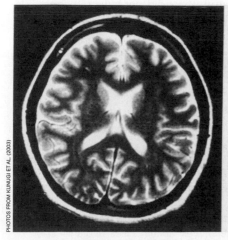

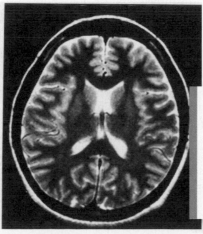

PHOTOS FROM KUNUGI ET AL. (2003)

(a) Twin with schizophrenia   **(b)** Twin without schizophrenia

◀ FIGURE 14.4

Enlarged Ventricles in Schizophrenia These MRI scans of monozygotic twins reveal that the twin affected by schizophrenia (a) shows enlarged ventricles (all the central white space) as compared to the unaffected twin (b).

(From Kunugi et al., 2003.)

Side views   Top view

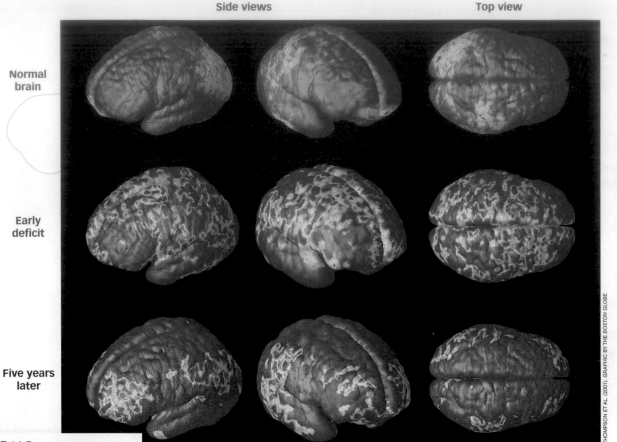

Normal brain

Early deficit

Five years later

No tissue loss

Most tissue loss

THOMPSON ET AL. (2001). GRAPHIC BY THE BOSTON GLOBE.

▲ FIGURE 14.5
Brain Tissue Loss in Adolescent Schizophrenia MRI scan composites reveal brain tissue loss in adolescents diagnosed with schizophrenia. Normal brains (top) show minimal loss due to "pruning." Early deficit scans (middle) reveal loss in the parietal areas. Patients at this stage may experience symptoms such as hallucinations or bizarre thoughts. Scans 5 years later (bottom) reveal extensive tissue loss over much of the cortex. Patients at this stage are likely to suffer from delusions, disorganized speech and behavior, and negative symptoms such as social withdrawal.

(From Thompson et al., 2001)

Psychological Factors

With all these potential biological contributors to schizophrenia, you might think there would be few psychological or social causes of the disorder. However, several studies do suggest that the family environment plays a role in the development of and recovery from the condition. One large-scale study compared the risk of schizophrenia in children adopted into healthy families and those adopted into severely disturbed families (Tienari et al., 2004). (Disturbed families were defined as those with extreme conflict, lack of communication, or chaotic relationships.) Among children whose biological mothers had schizophrenia, the disturbed environment increased the likelihood of developing schizophrenia—an outcome that was not found among children who were also reared in disturbed families but whose biological mothers did *not* have schizophrenia. This finding provides support for the diathesis-stress model described earlier.

IN SUMMARY

○ Schizophrenia is a severe psychological disorder involving hallucinations, disorganized thoughts and behavior, and emotional and social withdrawal.

○ Schizophrenia affects only 1% of the population, but it accounts for a disproportionate share of psychiatric hospitalizations.

○ The first drugs that reduced the availability of dopamine sometimes reduced the symptoms of schizophrenia, suggesting that the disorder involved an excess of dopamine activity, but recent research suggests that schizophrenia may involve a complex interaction among a variety of neurotransmitters.

○ Risks for developing schizophrenia include genetic factors, biochemical factors (perhaps a complex interaction among many neurotransmitters), brain abnormalities, and a stressful home environment.

Personality Disorders: Going to Extremes

Think for a minute about high school acquaintances whose personalities made them stand out—not necessarily in a good way. Was there a space ball, for example, a person who didn't seem to make sense, wore strange outfits, sometimes wouldn't respond in conversation—or would respond by bringing up weird things like astrology or mind reading? Or perhaps a drama queen, someone whose theatrics and exaggerated emotions turned everything into a big deal? And don't forget the neat freak, the perfectionist obsessed with control, who had the perfectly organized locker, precisely arranged hair, and sweater with zero lint balls. One way to describe such people is to say they simply have *personalities,* the unique patterns of traits we explored in Chapter 12. But sometimes personality traits can become so rigid and confining that they blend over into mental disorders. **Personality disorders** are *disorders characterized by deeply ingrained, inflexible patterns of thinking, feeling, or relating to others or controlling impulses that cause distress or impaired functioning.* Let's look at the types of personality disorders and then take a closer look at one that sometimes lands people in jail—*antisocial personality disorder.*

Types of Personality Disorders

The *DSM-IV-TR* lists 10 personality disorders (see **TABLE 14.4** on the next page). They fall into three clusters—*odd/eccentric, dramatic/erratic,* and *anxious/inhibited.* The high school space ball, for example, could have *schizotypal personality disorder* (odd/eccentric cluster); the drama queen could have *histrionic personality disorder* (dramatic/erratic cluster); the neat freak could have *obsessive-compulsive personality disorder* (anxious/inhibited cluster). In fact, browsing through the list may awaken other high school memories. Don't rush to judgment, however. Most of those kids are probably quite healthy and fall far short of qualifying for a diagnosis—after all, high school can be a rocky time for everyone. The *DSM-IV-TR* even notes that early personality problems often do not persist into adulthood. Still, the array of personality disorders suggests that there are multiple ways an individual's gift of a unique personality could become a burden.

Personality disorders are the most controversial classifications in the *DSM-IV-TR* for several reasons. First, critics question whether having a problem personality is really a disorder. Given that 14.8% of the U.S. population has a personality disorder that fits a *DSM* description (Grant et al., 2004), perhaps it might be better just to admit that a lot of people are difficult and leave it at that. Another question is whether personality problems correspond to "disorders" in that there are distinct *types* or whether such problems might be better understood as extreme values on trait *dimensions* such as the Big Five traits discussed in Chapter 12 (Trull & Durrett, 2005). Finally, definitions of many personality problems share characteristics with the major disorders and may be mild versions of these conditions. Overall, for example, roughly half of people with an anxiety or mood disorder have a comorbid personality disorder (Van Velzen & Emmelkamp, 1996). Research is ongoing on these various questions (Oldham, Skodol, & Bender, 2005).

Many people with personality disorders won't admit to them, and this adds a further diagnostic complication. Personality measurement depends largely on self-reports—a pointless undertaking when self-insight is the exception rather than the rule. Not incidentally, people with exaggerated personalities create problems for themselves, disturb those around them, and often seem unaware of the high impact their personalities can have. It's as if their disorder blinds them to their disorder. People

Why is self-reporting a problem in diagnosing personality disorders?

suffering from paranoid personality disorder, for example, are suspicious of anyone who accuses them of paranoia; similarly, people with narcissistic personality disorder are likely to see comments on their personality as mere jealousy. It's difficult to see a troubled personality from the inside.

▼ **The Perfect Home** Ever browse a copy of *Architectural Digest* and wonder who would live in one of those perfect homes? A person with obsessive-compulsive personality disorder might fit right in. This personality disorder (characterized by excessive perfectionism) should not be mistaken, by the way, for obsessive-compulsive disorder—the anxiety disorder in which the person suffers from repeated unwanted thoughts or actions.

GETTY IMAGES/IMAGE SOURCE

TABLE 14.4

Clusters of Personality Disorders

Cluster	Personality Disorder	Characteristics
A. Odd/ Eccentric	Schizotypal	Peculiar or eccentric manners of speaking or dressing. Strange beliefs. "Magical thinking" such as belief in ESP or telepathy. Difficulty forming relationships. May react oddly in conversation, not respond, or talk to self. Speech elaborate or difficult to follow. (Possibly a mild form of schizophrenia.)
	Paranoid	Distrust in others, suspicion that people have sinister motives. Apt to challenge the loyalties of friends and read hostile intentions into others' actions. Prone to anger and aggressive outbursts but otherwise emotionally cold. Often jealous, guarded, secretive, overly serious.
	Schizoid	Extreme introversion and withdrawal from relationships. Prefers to be alone, little interest in others. Humorless, distant, often absorbed with own thoughts and feelings, a daydreamer. Fearful of closeness, with poor social skills, often seen as a "loner."
B. Dramatic/ Erratic	Antisocial	Impoverished moral sense or "conscience." History of deception, crime, legal problems, impulsive and aggressive or violent behavior. Little emotional empathy or remorse for hurting others. Manipulative, careless, callous. At high risk for substance abuse and alcoholism.
	Borderline	Unstable moods and intense, stormy personal relationships. Frequent mood changes and anger, unpredictable impulses. Self-mutilation or suicidal threats or gestures to get attention or manipulate others. Self-image fluctuation and a tendency to see others as "all good" or "all bad."
	Histrionic	Constant attention seeking. Grandiose language, provocative dress, exaggerated illnesses, all to gain attention. Believes that everyone loves them. Emotional, lively, overly dramatic, enthusiastic, and excessively flirtatious. Shallow and labile true emotions. "Onstage."
	Narcissistic	Inflated sense of self-importance, absorbed by fantasies of self and success. Exaggerates own achievement, assumes others will recognize they are superior. Good first impressions but poor longer-term relationships. Exploitative of others.
C. Anxious/ Inhibited	Avoidant	Socially anxious and uncomfortable unless they are confident of being liked. In contrast with schizoid person, yearns for social contact. Fears criticism and worries about being embarrassed in front of others. Avoids social situations due to fear of rejection.
	Dependent	Submissive, dependent, requiring excessive approval, reassurance, and advice. Clings to people and fears losing them. Lacking self-confidence. Uncomfortable when alone. May be devastated by end of close relationship or suicidal if breakup is threatened.
	Obsessive-compulsive	Conscientious, orderly, perfectionist. Excessive need to do everything "right." Inflexibly high standards and caution can interfere with their productivity. Fear of errors can make them strict and controlling. Poor expression of emotions. (*Not* the same as obsessive-compulsive disorder.)

Source: From *DSM-IV-TR* (American Psychiatric Association, 2000).

Although some self-report surveys designed to assess personality disorders have proved useful (Clark, 2007), the lack of insight typical of personality disorders renders most instruments untrustworthy. To solve this problem, researchers have turned to *peer nomination* measures, reports by others who know the person. Just like your high school classmates who gossiped about the personality problems of their peers, people in any group seem to develop common conceptions of which members are most troubled or troubling. Research on peer nominations in college sororities and fraternities and in groups of military recruits reveals that groups arrive at remarkably homogeneous assessments of their personality-disordered members (Oltmanns & Turkheimer, 2006). Through gossip or through personal experience with the "square pegs in round holes," everybody seems to know who is paranoid, dependent, avoidant, or unusual in some other way. Peer nominations using basic reports of the behavior of people in a group can predict which members will have further problems—such as dropping out of college or being discharged early from the military (Fiedler, Oltmanns, & Turkheimer, 2004).

The common feature of personality disorders is a failure to take other people's perspectives, particularly on the self. People with personality disorders often blame others, society, or the universe for their difficulties, distorting their perceptions of the world in a way that makes the personality disorder seem perfectly normal—at least to them. In many of the personality disorders, this blindness perpetuates the disorder and so hurts the person who suffers from it: People with personality disorders are often unhappy or depressed. Antisocial personality disorder, however, is particularly likely to go beyond harm to self and to exact a cost on anyone who knows the person—because the individual with antisocial personality disorder also lacks insight into what it means to hurt others.

▲ Military recruits going through basic training develop knowledge of one another's personalities. Their judgments of one another at the end of training—peer nominations—produce valid predictions of who will later receive early discharge from the military.

Antisocial Personality Disorder

Henri Désiré Landru began using the personal columns to attract a woman "interested in matrimony" in Paris in 1914, and he succeeded in seducing 10 of them. He bilked them of their savings, poisoned them, and cremated them in his stove, also disposing of a boy and two dogs along the way. He recorded his murders in a notebook and maintained a marriage and a mistress all the while. The gruesome actions of serial killers such as Landru leave us frightened and wondering; however, bullies, compulsive liars, and even drivers who regularly speed through a school zone share the same shocking blindness to human pain. The *DSM-IV-TR* suggests that any pattern of extreme disregard for other people should be considered a personality disorder and offers the category **antisocial personality disorder (APD)**, defined as *a pervasive pattern of disregard for and violation of the rights of others that begins in childhood or early adolescence and continues into adulthood.*

Adults with an antisocial personality diagnosis typically have a history of *conduct disorder* before the age of 15—problems such as aggression, destruction of property, rule violations, and deceitfulness, lying, or stealing. Early fire setting and cruelty to animals often predict antisocial tendencies. In adulthood, then, the diagnosis of APD is given to individuals who show three or more of a set of seven diagnostic signs: illegal behavior, deception, impulsivity, physical aggression, recklessness, irresponsibility, and a lack of remorse for wrongdoing. About 3.6% of the general population has antisocial personality disorder, and the rate of occurrence in men is three times the rate in women (Grant et al., 2004).

? What are some of the factors that contribute to APD?

The terms *sociopath* and *psychopath* describe people with APD who are especially coldhearted, manipulative, and ruthless—yet may be glib and charming (Cleckley, 1976; Hare, 1998). Although psychologists usually try to explain the development of abnormal behavior as a product of childhood experiences or difficult life circumstances, those who work with APD seem less forgiving, often noting the sheer dangerousness of people with this disorder. Many people with APD do commit crimes, and

antisocial personality disorder (APD)
A pervasive pattern of disregard for and violation of the rights of others that begins in childhood or early adolescence and continues into adulthood.

HOT SCIENCE

Positive Psychology

You are now familiar with some of the most difficult challenges we face—profound, painful mental problems that can cause great unhappiness. However, psychologists' interests go beyond the negative aspects of life. Early on, for example, William James (1902) recommended a focus on "healthy mindedness" in contrast to looking only at "sick souls." The desire to look on the sunny side of the mind has popped up often in the history of psychology, and others who have shared this vision include humanistic psychologists such as Abraham Maslow (see Chapter 8) and Carl Rogers (see Chapter 15).

Most recently, the desire to emphasize the positive has surfaced in a flourishing movement known as *positive psychology*—an approach that seeks to understand what makes our lives pleasant, good, and meaningful. Martin E. P. Seligman has championed this movement, suggesting that human happiness and virtue deserve the same careful study usually devoted to mental disorders. In contrast to the *DSM*, for example, Seligman and his colleagues (Peterson & Seligman, 2004) introduced a complementary system for classifying, *Character Strengths and Virtues,* the *CSV* (see the accompanying table). These positive qualities are seldom mentioned in the *DSM,* of course, as they show the mind in good order rather than in disorder.

In line with the *CSV* system's positive approach, no individual is expected to have every strength or virtue, and individuals are not supposed to "keep score" by measuring themselves with this list. Rather, the list illustrates our potential to build personal strengths that help to make us happy and human. Listing positive characteristics of people makes for a kind of celebration, an appreciation of what being a person can be.

The positive psychology movement has been particularly effective in stimulating research on happiness (Snyder & Lopez, 2009). Each of us claims to be something of an expert on what will make us happy (Chocolate, please, lots of it, and on the double! Or should I request world peace? No, no, a speedboat . . .), but it is often surprising just how mistaken we can be about what will bring us the joy we desire (Gilbert, 2006). Research supplies some happy facts:

- Money can buy happiness, but only a little. Wealthy people are only the tiniest bit happier than the average person (Diener, Horwitz, & Emmons, 1985), but extreme poverty is associated with less happiness—particularly in cultures where such poverty is rare (Diener & Biswas-Diener, 2002).
- Friends make you happy. People report that the main source of their happiness is relationships—with their friends, spouses, and children (*Time* poll, 2005). As the old saying goes, people on their deathbed never say, "I should have spent more time at work."
- Some people do "live happily ever after." Married people are happier than singles, especially right after getting married and then again when their children are grown (Coombs, 1991). Their greater happiness may be, however, because they were happier to begin with (Lucas et al., 2003).
- Happiness is born, not made. Twin studies reveal that as much as 50% of variability in happiness is due to genetic factors (Lykken & Tellegen, 1996). Ideally, try to be born happy.
- Happy times may not last. People regularly overestimate the degree to which positive events (such as winning the lottery) will make them happy. They fail to appreciate their own tendency to adjust

psychologically to emotional experiences and "get over it," no matter what "it" is (Gilbert & Wilson, 2009).
- Happy days may be here again. Although happiness decreases gradually until about age 50, it then rises steadily for the next 25 years (Stone et al., 2010).
- Happiness comes from goodness. Doing good deeds or seeing them done can lead to feelings of elevation and happiness (Haidt, 2006).

More happy facts are surfacing every day, as many researchers have joined the movement toward positive psychology (Gable & Haidt, 2005). This movement provides a balance to the common focus of the field on the negative side, the psychological disorders. Knowing about these disorders does aid in understanding how the mind works. All too often, though, the focus in studying psychological disorders can be too gloomy, a reminder of the perils of being "only human." Like the good physician who brings to a patient's bedside both an analytical appreciation of the patient's disorder and a warm smile to help the patient through the rough times, the field of psychology must temper the bitter with the sweet. Psychological science can be most effective when it unites the problem-solving approach of studying disorders with the ideals and optimism of studying wellness.

Virtue	Definition	Specific Strengths
Wisdom and knowledge	Cognitive strengths that entail the acquisition and use of knowledge	Creativity, open-mindedness, curiosity, love of learning, perspective
Courage	Emotional strengths that involve the exercise of will to accomplish goals in the face of opposition, external or internal	Authenticity, bravery, persistence, zest
Humanity	Interpersonal strengths that involve tending and befriending others	Kindness, love, social intelligence
Justice	Civic strengths that underlie healthy community life	Fairness, leadership, teamwork
Temperance	Strengths that protect against excess	Forgiveness, modesty, prudence, self-regulation
Transcendence	Strengths that forge connections to the larger universe and provide meaning	Appreciation of beauty and excellence, gratitude, hope, humor, religiousness

Source: From Peterson and Seligman (2004), *Character Strengths and Virtues.*

many are caught because of the frequency and flagrancy of their infractions. Among 22,790 prisoners in one study, 47% of the men and 21% of the women were diagnosed with antisocial personality disorder (Fazel & Danesh, 2002). Statistics such as these support the notion of a "criminal personality."

Both the early onset of conduct problems and the lack of success in treatment suggest that career criminality has an internal cause (Lykken, 1995). Evidence of brain abnormalities in people with APD is also accumulating (Blair, Peschardt, & Mitchell, 2005). One line of investigation has looked at sensitivity to fear in psychopaths and individuals who show no such psychopathology. For example, criminal psychopaths who are shown negative emotional words such as *hate* or *corpse* exhibit less activity in the amygdala and hippocampus than do noncriminals (Kiehl et al., 2001). The two brain areas are involved in the process of fear conditioning (Patrick, Cuthbert, & Lang, 1994), so their relative inactivity in such studies suggests that psychopaths are less sensitive to fear than are other people. Violent psychopaths can target their aggression toward the self as well as others, often behaving in reckless ways that lead to violent ends. It might seem peaceful to go through life "without fear," but perhaps fear is useful in keeping people from the extremes of antisocial behavior.

The psychological disorders we have examined in this chapter represent a tragic loss of human potential. The contentment, peace, and love that people could be enjoying are crowded out by pain and suffering when the mind goes awry to create disorders (see the Hot Science box). A scientific approach to mental disorders that views them through a medical model is beginning to sort out their symptoms and causes. As we will see in the next chapter, this approach already offers treatments for some disorders that are remarkably effective and for other disorders offers hope that pain and suffering can be alleviated in the future.

▲ Henri Desiré Landru (1869–1922), a serial killer who met widows through ads he placed in newspapers' lonely hearts columns. After obtaining enough information to embezzle money from them, he murdered 10 women and the son of one of the women. He was executed for serial murder in 1922.

IN SUMMARY

○ Personality disorders are deeply ingrained, inflexible patterns of thinking, feeling, relating to others, or controlling impulses that cause distress or impaired functioning.

○ They include three clusters—odd/eccentric, dramatic/erratic, and anxious/inhibited.

○ The classification of these disorders is controversial because they may be no more than extreme examples of normal personality, may represent personality dimensions rather than types of disorder, and are often comorbid with other disorders.

○ Antisocial personality disorder is associated with a lack of moral emotions and behavior; people with antisocial personality disorder can be manipulative, dangerous, and reckless, often hurting others and sometimes hurting themselves.

│ WhereDoYouStand? │

Genetic Tests for Risk of Psychological Disorders

Today, you don't have to worry about it. Genetic testing for psychological disorders is not advanced enough that you could learn if you're genetically prone toward a disorder. But in the not-too-distant future, you may be able to find out if your genes show an elevated risk for a problem—merely by providing a saliva specimen. Genetic patterns underlying certain forms of bipolar mood disorder, for example, may be clear enough that genetic testing for risk of the disorder is possible (Couzin, 2008; Joo et al., 2009).

A genetic diagnosis could be very helpful. If your life is miserable and you're overwhelmed with problems, it might be nice to put a label on what's wrong, even if that diagnosis is not good news. In the case of bipolar disorder, years may elapse between the onset of symptoms and a diagnosis, and the end of the uncertainty that comes with knowing the problem may bring a kind of relief. Having a name for the disorder doesn't guarantee effective treatment, of course, but it is a key first step.

But what if you have a genetic tendency toward the disorder but don't have any symptoms? Then would you want to know about your genes? For that matter, you might have a genetic tendency that will never be expressed—suspicious saliva with no actual disorder. Suspecting that you might become bipolar could create problems all by itself. Every little symptom could be meaningful. Was I being manic just now? Was I acting depressed? Any mood shift might be an alarm bell, and worrying about your genes could be a constant source of stress. So, would you want to know your genetic risk for a psychological disorder, or would you rather not? Where do you stand?

Chapter Review

KEY CONCEPT QUIZ

1. The conception of psychological disorders as diseases that have symptoms and possible cures is referred to as
   a. the medical model.
   b. physiognomy.
   c. the root syndrome framework.
   d. a diagnostic system.

2. The *DSM-IV-TR* is best described as a
   a. medical model.
   b. classification system.
   c. set of theoretical assumptions.
   d. collection of psychological definitions.

3. Comorbidity of disorders refers to
   a. symptoms stemming from internal dysfunction.
   b. the relative risk of death arising from a disorder.
   c. the co-occurrence of two or more disorders in a single individual.
   d. the existence of disorders on a continuum from normal to abnormal.

4. Irrational worries and fears that undermine one's ability to function normally are an indication of
   a. genetic abnormality.   c. diathesis.
   b. dysthymia.   d. anxiety disorder.

5. A(n) _____ disorder involves anxiety tied to a specific object or situation.
   a. generalized anxiety   c. panic
   b. environmental   d. phobic

6. Agoraphobia often develops as a result of
   a. preparedness theory.   c. panic disorder.
   b. obsessive-compulsive disorder. d. social phobia.

7. Kelly's fear of germs leads her to wash her hands repeatedly throughout the day, often for a half hour or more, under extremely hot water. From which disorder does Kelly suffer?
   a. panic attacks
   b. obsessive-compulsive disorder
   c. phobia
   d. generalized anxiety disorder

8. Major depression is characterized by a severely depressed mood that lasts at least
   a. 2 weeks.   c. 1 month.
   b. 1 week.   d. 6 months.

9. Extreme moods swings between _____ characterize bipolar disorder.
   a. depression and mania   c. anxiety and arousal
   b. stress and lethargy   d. obsessions and compulsions

10. A dissociative disorder is characterized by significant disruptions in which of the following?
    a. memory   c. personality
    b. awareness   d. all of the above

11. Which of the following is an accurate statement regarding dissociative identity disorder?
    a. The disorder is also called "multiple personality disorder."
    b. The "host" individual is aware of the alternate personalities.
    c. Some researchers believe the disorder is created in therapy.
    d. Recent estimates are that approximately 5% of the population suffers from the disorder.

12. Schizophrenia is characterized by which of the following?
    a. hallucinations
    b. disorganized thoughts and behavior
    c. emotional and social withdrawal
    d. all of the above

13. Schizophrenia affects approximately _____ % of the population and accounts for approximately _____ % of admissions to state and county mental hospitals.
    a. 5; 20   c. 1; 1
    b. 5; 5   d. 1; 40

14. Which of the following is a common feature of personality disorders?
    a. failure to take other people's perspectives
    b. excessive fear of rejection
    c. unstable moods
    d. overly dramatic attempts at attention seeking

15. Which of the following is NOT one of the identified personality disorder clusters?
    a. odd/eccentric   c. anxious/inhibited
    b. dramatic/erratic   d. impulsivity/aggression

KEY TERMS

medical model (p. 551)
DSM-IV-TR (p. 552)
comorbidity (p. 554)
diathesis-stress model (p. 556)
anxiety disorder (p. 558)

generalized anxiety disorder (GAD) (p. 559)
phobic disorders (p. 560)
specific phobia (p. 560)
social phobia (p. 560)

preparedness theory (p. 561)
panic disorder (p. 562)
agoraphobia (p. 562)
obsessive-compulsive disorder (OCD) (p. 563)

mood disorders (p. 564)
major depressive disorder (p. 565)
dysthymia (p. 565)
double depression (p. 565)

CRITICAL THINKING QUESTIONS

1. Psychological disorders can be caused by biological, psychological, and environmental factors. The diathesis-stress model suggests that a person may be predisposed for a psychological disorder that remains unexpressed until triggered by stress.

   Suppose that two identical twins (with the same genetic profile) grow up in the same household (sharing the same parents, the same basic diet, the same access to television, and so on). As a teenager, one twin but not the other develops a mental disorder such as schizophrenia. How could this be?

2. Phobias are anxiety disorders that involve excessive and persistent fear of a specific object, activity, or situation. Some phobias may be learned through classical conditioning, in which a conditioned stimulus (CS) that is paired with an anxiety-evoking stimulus (US) itself comes to elicit a fear response (CR).

   Suppose your friend has a phobia of dogs that is so intense that he is afraid to go outside in case one of his neighbors' dogs barks at him. Using the principles of classical conditioning you learned in Chapter 7, how might you help him overcome his fear?

3. Major depression (also known as unipolar depression) is characterized by a severely depressed mood, accompanied by feelings of worthlessness and lack of pleasure, and by sleep and appetite disturbances. To be characterized as major depression, the episode must last at least 2 weeks, but on average episodes last about 6 months.

   Both seasonal affective disorder (SAD) and bipolar disorder involve shorter, but cyclically recurring, depressive episodes. If you have a friend who experiences recurring periods of severe depression, how would you determine whether she is suffering from SAD or bipolar disorder?

RECOMMENDED READINGS

Jamison, K. R. (2001). *Night falls fast: Understanding suicide.* New York: Picador USA.

Kay Jamison, author of the national best seller *An Unquiet Mind* and a researcher on mood disorders, examines the phenomenon of suicide using data and powerful examples. She discusses factors—biological, psychological, and sociocultural—that contribute to suicide and points out the remarkable lack of attention given to this common killer that claims thousands of lives each year.

Rapoport, J. (1989). *The boy who couldn't stop washing: The experience and treatment of obsessive-compulsive disorder.* New York: Penguin.

This brief book focuses on obsessive-compulsive disorder, offering both individual stories and general information about the symptoms, causes, and treatment of the disorder. In suggesting

drug treatments of the disorder, it focuses on the brain rather than the mind as a cause.

Saks, E. R. (2007). *The center cannot hold: My journey through madness.* New York: Hyperion Books.

This is not light reading. The memoir of a law professor who developed schizophrenia, this book describes how "Consciousness gradually loses its coherence. One's center gives way. . . . The 'me' becomes a haze, and the solid center from which one experiences reality breaks up like a bad radio signal."

Torrey, E. F. (2006). *Surviving schizophrenia: A manual for families, patients, and providers.* New York: Harper.

What can be done if you or someone you know is stricken with this destructive disorder? In a thorough and readable guide, Torrey explains what schizophrenia means and how people can try to cope.

ANSWERS TO KEY CONCEPT QUIZ

1. a; 2. b; 3. c; 4. d; 5. d; 6. c; 7. b; 8. a; 9. a; 10. d; 11. c; 12. d; 13. d; 14. a; 15. d.

Need more help? Additional resources are located at the book's free companion Web site at: **www.worthpublishers.com/schacter**

15

Treatment of Psychological Disorders

----------○----------

The plane was still at the gate, but Lisa was buckled in her seat with her hands tightly squeezing the armrests, her knuckles white. She glanced out the window, swallowed hard, and then stole a look at the people across the aisle. They seemed calm, but she didn't feel calm at all. Her heart was pounding, and then she noticed that the plane was starting to move. She was deathly afraid of flying, but she hoped that this flight might be easier. After all, she wasn't really in a plane. Instead, she was seated in a psychologist's office, wearing virtual reality goggles that projected the sights and sounds of the flight all around her. She was in therapy.

Psychological therapy takes many forms. In this case, Lisa's fear was being treated with a relatively new technique called *virtual reality therapy*. The therapist sat nearby during the virtual flight and encouraged Lisa to progress at her own pace through the stages of air travel that made her anxious—sitting on a plane with the engines off, sitting on a plane with the engines on, taxiing on the runway, a smooth takeoff and a smooth flight, a smooth landing, a close pass similar to a missed landing, a rough landing, a turbulent flight, and a rough takeoff. Lisa came back for six sessions over several weeks, and at the end of her virtual travels she reported feeling no anxiety about any of these virtual events. With the therapist's encouragement, she soon took the step of flying in a real plane (Rothbaum et al., 1996). For many people who might otherwise have debilitating fears or phobias, virtual reality therapy offers a treatment option that can be remarkably effective (Powers & Emmelkamp, 2008).

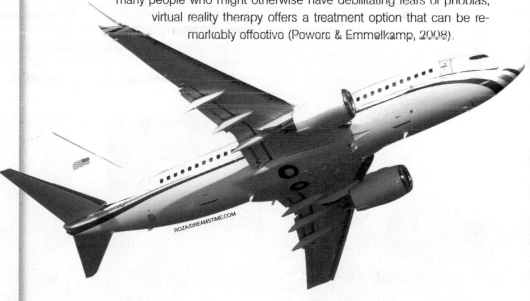

ROZA/DREAMSTIME.COM

THERE ARE A NUMBER OF WAYS TO TREAT MOST psychological disorders, with the goal of changing a person's thoughts, behaviors, emotions, or coping skills. Treatments requiring a person to wear wraparound video goggles are not yet commonplace, but the variety and ingenuity of goggle-free treatment techniques are remarkable. In this chapter, we will explore the most common approaches to psychological treatment. We will examine why people need to seek psychological help in the first place, and then explore how psychotherapy for individuals is built on the major theories of the causes and cures of disorders—including psychoanalytic, behavioral, cognitive, and humanistic/existential theories—and explore how psychotherapy can be conducted for people in groups as well. We'll look into medical and biological approaches to treatment that focus on understanding the brain's role in disorders. Finally, we will discuss whether treatment works, as well as how we know that treatment works.

Treatment: Getting Help to Those Who Need It

Estimates suggest that almost one in five people suffers from some type of mental disorder (Narrow et al., 2002). The personal costs of these disorders involve anguish to the sufferers as well as interference in their ability to carry on the activities of daily life. Think about Lisa, our fearful flyer. If she did not (or could not) seek treatment, she would be unable to take advantage of air travel—but there's more. Some people with fear of airplanes develop difficulty with simple day-to-day tasks due to a disabling fear of encountering anything that could even remind them of airplanes. Watching an airplane trip on television might be too much to bear, and even the sound of airplanes flying overhead could be so frightening as to keep the person at home all the time.

? What are some of the personal, social, and financial costs of mental illness?

Beyond the personal costs, the social burdens associated with mental disorders are also enormous. For example, people with anxiety disorders report levels of impairment in their daily lives that are comparable to or higher than those of people with chronic medical illnesses, such as multiple sclerosis or end-stage renal disease (Antony et al., 1998b). Impairment is widespread, affecting family life, the ability to work, maintenance

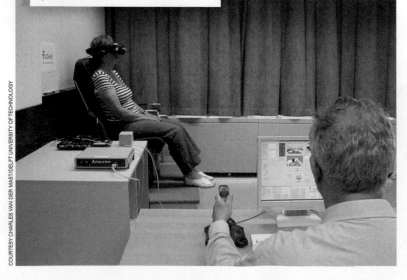

▼ Virtual reality therapy offers new possibilities for treating people with psychological disorders, especially phobias. Clients can practice engaging in "virtual experiences" before tackling the real-life experiences they fear. On the left is a therapist conducting a virtual flight, on the right, the client's virtual "view" out the "plane" window.

of friendships, and more. A person with schizophrenia or severe depression may be unable to hold down a job or even get organized enough to collect a welfare check, and people with many disorders stop getting along with family or people who are trying to help. At the extreme, victims of some disorders can become violent and dangerous to themselves or others.

There are financial costs too. One set of calculations found that the annual financial burden of anxiety disorders alone in the United States was $42.3 billion, or $1,542 per sufferer, including costs of treatment, diminished productivity, and absenteeism in the workplace (Greenberg et al., 1999). If we add in similar figures for schizophrenia, mood disorders, substance abuse, and all the other psychological problems, the overall costs are astronomical. In addition to the personal benefits of treatment, then, society also stands to benefit from the effective treatment of psychological disorders.

Why People Cannot or Will Not Seek Treatment

A physical symptom such as a toothache would send most people to the dentist—a trip that usually results in a successful treatment. The clear source of pain and the obvious solution make for a quick and effective response. In contrast, the path from a mental disorder to a successful treatment is often far less clear. Despite the high prevalence of psychological problems in the general population, most people who suffer from such problems do not receive help. One national survey of more than 1,600 adults diagnosed with depression or an anxiety disorder found that only 30% received appropriate treatment for the problem—despite the fact that 83% had seen a health care provider in the previous year (in most cases, a family doctor) (Young et al., 2001). People may fail to get treatment because of three major problems:

What are the obstacles to help/treatment for the mentally ill?

1. *People may not realize that their disorder needs to be treated.* Mental illness is often not taken nearly as seriously as physical illness, perhaps because the origin of mental illness is "hidden" and usually cannot be diagnosed by a blood test or x-ray. The stigma of mental illness often includes beliefs that mental problems can be solved by "mind over matter." In other words, some people believe that mental illness is a sign of personal weakness or that people suffering from mental illness are not trying hard enough to help themselves.

2. *There may be barriers to treatment, such as beliefs and circumstances that keep people from getting help.* Individuals may believe that they should be able to handle things themselves. In some cases, families discourage their loved ones from seeking help because the public acknowledgment of a psychological disorder may be seen as an embarrassment to the family. In other cases, there may be financial obstacles to getting treatment, such as lack of medical insurance that covers treatment for mental health disorders. Barriers may even arise from treatment providers or facilities themselves, including such factors as long waiting lists, lack of funding for adequate staffing, or lack of staff education about the most up-to-date treatments. Cultural and gender factors may also affect who seeks treatment and who does not. For example, one study of college students found that being male predicted negative attitudes toward seeking psychological help, suggesting that men may be less likely than women to seek psychological services (Komiya, Good, & Sherrod, 2000).

3. *Even people who acknowledge they have a problem may not know where to look for services.* Like finding a good lawyer or plumber, finding the right psychologist can be more difficult than simply flipping through the yellow pages or searching online. This confusion is understandable given the plethora of different types of treatments available (see the Real World box on the next page).

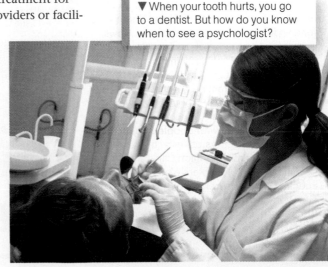

▼ When your tooth hurts, you go to a dentist. But how do you know when to see a psychologist?

AP PHOTO/PHOTO RESEARCHERS

THE REAL WORLD

Types of Psychotherapists

What do you do if you're ready to seek the help of a mental health professional? To whom do you turn? Therapists have widely varying backgrounds and training, and this affects the kinds of services they offer. Before you choose a therapist, it is useful to have an understanding of a therapist's background, training, and areas of expertise. There are several major "flavors":

- **Psychologist** A psychologist who practices psychotherapy holds a doctorate with specialization in clinical psychology (a PhD or PsyD). This degree takes about 5 years to complete, and the psychologist will have extensive training in therapy, the assessment of psychological disorders, and research. The psychologist will sometimes have a specialty, such as working with adolescents or helping people overcome sleep disorders, and will usually conduct therapy that involves talking. Psychologists must be licensed by the state, and most states require candidates to complete about 2 years of supervised practical training and a competency exam. If you look for a *psychologist* in the Yellow Pages or through a clinic, you will usually find someone with this background.

- **Psychiatrist** A psychiatrist is a medical doctor who has completed an M.D. with specialized training in assessing and treating mental disorders. Psychiatrists can prescribe medications, and some also practice psychotherapy. General practice physicians can also prescribe medications for mental disorders and often are the first to see people with such disorders because people consult them for a wide range of health problems. However, general practice physicians do not typically receive much training in the diagnosis or treatment of mental disorders, and they do not practice psychotherapy.

- **Social worker** Social workers have a master's degree in social work and have training in working with people in dire life situations such as poverty, homelessness, or family conflict. Clinical or psychiatric social workers also receive special training to help people in these situations who have mental disorders. Social workers often work in government or private social service agencies, and they also may work in hospitals or have a private practice.

- **Counselor** Counselors have a wide range of training. To be a counseling psychologist, for example, requires a doctorate and practical training—the title uses that key term *psychologist* and is regulated by state laws. But states vary in how they define *counselor*. In some cases, a counselor must have a master's degree and extensive training in therapy, whereas in others, this person may have minimal training or relevant education. Counselors who work in schools usually have a master's degree and specific training in counseling in educational settings.

Some people offer therapy under made-up terms that sound professional—"mind/body healing therapist," for example, or "marital adjustment adviser." Often these terms are simply invented to mislead clients and avoid licensing boards, and the "therapist" may have no training or expertise at all. And, of course, there are a few people who claim to be licensed practitioners who are not: Louise Wightman, who had once worked as stripper "Princess Cheyenne," was convicted of fraud in 2007 after conducting psychotherapy as a psychologist with dozens of clients. She claimed she didn't know the PhD degree she had purchased over the Internet was bogus (Associated Press, 2007). People who offer therapy may be well-meaning and even helpful, but they could do harm too. To be safe, it is important to shop wisely for a therapist whose training and credentials reflect expertise and inspire confidence.

How should you shop? One way is to start with people you know—your general practice physician, a school counselor, or a trusted friend or family member who might know of a good therapist. Or you can visit your college clinic or hospital or contact an Internet site of an organization such as the American Psychological Association that offers referrals to licensed mental health care providers. When you do contact someone, they will often be able to provide you with further advice about who would be just the right kind of therapist to consult.

Before you agree to see a therapist for treatment, you should ask questions such as those below to evaluate whether the therapist's style or background is a good match for your problem:

- What type of therapy do you practice?
- What types of problems do you usually treat?
- For how long do you usually see people in therapy?
- Will our work involve "talking" therapy, medications, or both?
- How effective is this type of therapy for the type of problem I'm having?
- What are your fees for therapy, and will health insurance cover them?

Not only will the therapist's answers to these questions tell you about his or her background and experience, but they will also tell you about his or her approach to treating clients. You can then make an informed decision about the type of service you need.

Although you should consider what type of therapist would best fit your needs, the therapist's personality and approach can sometimes be as important as his or her background or training. You should seek out someone who is willing and open to answer questions, who has a clear understanding about the type of problem leading you to seek therapy, and who shows general respect and empathy for you. A therapist is someone you are entrusting with your mental health, and you should only enter into such a relationship when you and the therapist have good rapport.

▼ Which one? Finding the right psychotherapist can seem like finding the best watermelon: You won't really know until you've had a taste. Shoppers sometimes thump melons on the theory that the sweetest ones sound different, but no one quite knows how a good one will sound. In the case of psychotherapists, fortunately, no thumping is required. You can find out about their qualifications in advance and even talk to several to see which one seems right.

STUART DEE/GETTY IMAGES

Even when people seek and find help, they sometimes do not receive the most effective treatments, which further complicates things. For example, although cognitive and behavioral therapies yield the best results for treating anxiety disorders, most people do not receive these treatments. In one study, most individuals seeking help in a clinic specializing in anxiety disorders reported having previously received treatments other than cognitive or behavioral therapy for their anxiety problems even though there is little evidence for the effectiveness of these other approaches for anxiety disorders. Only about one third of people reported previously receiving the treatment approaches most strongly supported by prior research (Rowa et al., 2000). Clearly, before choosing or prescribing a therapy, we need to know what kinds of treatments are available and understand which treatments are best for particular disorders.

Approaches to Treatment

Treatments can be divided broadly into two kinds: psychotherapy, in which a person interacts with a psychotherapist, and medical or biological treatments, in which the mental disorder is treated with drugs or surgery. In some cases, both psychotherapy *and* biological treatments are used. Lisa's fear of flying, for example, might be treated not only with the virtual reality therapy you read about (a form of psychotherapy) in preparation for the real flight but also with antianxiety medications in the hours before the actual takeoff. For many years, psychotherapy was the main form of treatment for psychological disorders because few medical or biological options were available. But alongside psychotherapy, there have always been folk remedies that depend on biology. As we learn more about the biology and chemistry of the brain, approaches to mental health that begin with the brain are becoming increasingly widespread. As you'll see later in the chapter, often the most effective treatments combine both psychotherapy and medications.

▲ Early mental health workers used water dowsing, or "hydrotherapy," for psychological disorders. Here a patient at the Pennsylvania Hospital for the Insane gets a cold "Douche Bath" (Haskell, 1869). Such treatments were given in the forlorn hope that something might work, but often they were simply torture—not unlike the "waterboarding" used in CIA interrogations during the George W. Bush administration.

CULTURE & COMMUNITY

Is psychotherapy the same around the world? Not at all. Some psychotherapies are indigenous to particular cultures. For example, two well-known therapies influenced by Buddhism originated in Japan: Morita therapy and Naikan therapy (Sato, 2001).

Morita therapy instructs patients that feelings cannot be changed and are to be accepted. Actions can be taken to achieve goals, in spite of feelings, and these actions may in turn increase positive feelings. In Naikan, patients are asked to think about what they can do for others. They examine instances of care and benevolence they received from another person, recollect memories of what they returned to that person, and recall any trouble or worries they have given to that person. The goal of Naikan therapy is to have patients realize their indebtedness to their significant others, their mothers in particular.

psychotherapy An interaction between a therapist and someone suffering from a psychological problem, with the goal of providing support or relief from the problem.

eclectic psychotherapy Treatment that draws on techniques from different forms of therapy, depending on the client and the problem.

psychodynamic psychotherapies A general approach to treatment that explores childhood events and encourages individuals to develop insight into their psychological problems.

resistance A reluctance to cooperate with treatment for fear of confronting unpleasant unconscious material.

IN SUMMARY

○ Mental illness is often misunderstood, and because of this, it too often goes untreated.

○ Untreated mental illness can be extremely costly, affecting an individual's ability to function and also causing social and financial burdens.

○ Many people who suffer from mental illness do not get the help they need; they may be unaware that they have a problem, they may face obstacles to getting treatment, or they simply may not know where to turn.

○ Treatments include psychotherapy, which focuses on the mind, and medical and biological methods, which focus on the brain and body.

Psychological Therapies: Healing the Mind through Interaction

Psychological therapy, or **psychotherapy**, *is an interaction between a therapist and someone suffering from a psychological problem, with the goal of providing support or relief from the problem.* Currently over 400 different systems of psychotherapy exist. Although there are similarities among all the psychotherapies, each approach is unique in its goals, aims, and methods. A survey of 1,000 psychotherapists asked them to describe their main theoretical orientation (Norcross, Hedges, & Castle, 2002; see **FIGURE 15.1**). Over a third reported using **eclectic psychotherapy**, *a form of psychotherapy that involves drawing on techniques from different forms of therapy, depending on the client and the problem.* This allows the therapists to apply an appropriate theoretical perspective that is suited to the problem at hand rather than adhering to a single theoretical perspective for all clients and all types of problems. Nevertheless, as Figure 15.1 shows, the majority of psychotherapists use a single approach, such as psychodynamic therapy, behavioral and cognitive therapies, humanistic and existential therapies, or group therapy. We'll examine each of those four major branches of psychotherapy in turn.

Psychodynamic Therapy

Psychodynamic psychotherapy has its roots in Freud's psychoanalytically oriented theory of personality (see Chapter 12). **Psychodynamic psychotherapies** *explore childhood events and encourage individuals to use this understanding to develop insight into their psychological problems.* There are a number of different psychodynamic therapies that can vary substantially, but they all share the belief that the path to overcoming psychological problems is to develop insight into the unconscious memories, impulses, wishes, and conflicts that are assumed to underlie these problems. Psychodynamic therapies include psychoanalysis and modern psychodynamic therapy, such as interpersonal psychotherapy.

What is the commonly held belief behind all psychodynamic therapies?

Psychoanalysis

As you saw in Chapter 12, *psychoanalysis* assumes that humans are born with aggressive and sexual urges that are repressed during childhood development through the use of defense mechanisms. Psychoanalysts encourage their clients to bring these repressed conflicts into consciousness so that the clients can understand them and reduce their unwanted influences. Psychoanalysts focus a great deal on early childhood events because they believe that urges and conflicts were likely to be repressed during this time.

▼ FIGURE 15.1
Approaches to Psychotherapy in the 21st Century This chart shows the percentage of psychologists (from among 1,000 members of the American Psychological Association's Division of Psychotherapy) who have various primary psychotherapy orientations (adapted from Norcross et al., 2002).

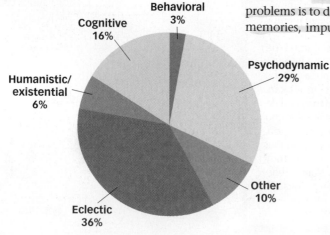

Traditional psychoanalysis takes place over an average of 3 to 6 years, with four or five sessions per week (Ursano & Silberman, 2003). During a session, the client reclines on a couch, facing away from the analyst, and is asked to express whatever thoughts and feelings come to mind. Occasionally, the analyst may comment on some of the information presented by the client, but the analyst does not express his or her values and judgments. The stereotypic image you might have of psychological therapy—a person lying on a couch talking to a person sitting in a chair—springs from this approach.

How to Develop Insight

The goal of psychoanalysis is for the client to understand the unconscious in a process Freud called developing insight. A psychoanalyst can use several key techniques to help the client develop insight, including these:

Free Association. In free association, the client reports every thought that enters the mind, without censorship or filtering. This strategy allows the stream of consciousness to flow unimpeded. If the client stops, the therapist prompts further associations ("And what does that make you think of?"). The therapist may then look for themes that recur during therapy sessions.

▲ In traditional psychoanalysis, the patient lies on a couch, with the therapist sitting behind, out of the patient's view. This also happens in the comics.

Dream Analysis. Psychoanalysis treats dreams as metaphors that symbolize unconscious conflicts or wishes and that contain disguised clues that the therapist can help the client understand. A psychoanalytic therapy session might begin with an invitation for the client to recount a dream, after which the client might be asked to participate in the interpretation by freely associating to the dream.

Interpretation. This is the process by which the therapist deciphers the meaning (e.g., unconscious impulses or fantasies) underlying what the client says and does. Interpretation is used throughout therapy, during free association and dream analysis, as well as in other aspects of the treatment. During the process of interpretation, the analyst suggests possible meanings to the client, looking for signs that the correct meaning has been discovered. Unfortunately, a correct interpretation is usually not accompanied by giant flashing neon lights. The analyst could overinterpret the client's thoughts and emotions and sometimes even contribute interpretations that are far from the truth. For example, the discovery that a client had a traumatic sexual experience with a visiting relative as a child might seem so important to the analyst that it could suggest a way of understanding many of the client's dreams and associations. But this particular event actually might *not* be the basis of the client's unconscious conflicts, in which case the therapist would be directing the client to an insight that is really no insight at all.

Analysis of Resistance. In the process of "trying on" different interpretations of the client's thoughts and actions, the analyst may suggest an interpretation that the client finds particularly unacceptable. **Resistance** is *a reluctance to cooperate with treatment for fear of confronting unpleasant unconscious material.* For example, the therapist might suggest that the client's problem with obsessive health worries could be traced to a childhood rivalry with her mother for her father's love and attention. The client could find the suggestion insulting and fervently resist the interpretation. Curiously, the analyst might interpret this resistance as a signal not that the interpretation is wrong but instead that the interpretation is on the right track. If a client always shifts the topic of discussion away from a particular idea, that might signal to the therapist that this is indeed an issue the client could be directed to confront in order to develop insight.

? What might a client's resistance signal to a therapist?

"I'll say a normal word, then you say the first sick thing that pops into your head."

"Not so fast, Mr. Hodges."

The Process of Transference

These psychoanalytic techniques may be used over the course of an intensive and lengthy process of analysis. During this process, the client and psychoanalyst often develop a close relationship. Freud noticed this relationship developing in his analyses and was at first troubled by it: Clients would develop an unusually strong attachment to him, almost as though they were viewing him as a parent or a lover, and he worried that this could interfere with achieving the goal of insight. Over time, however, he came to believe that the development and resolution of this relationship was a key process of psychoanalysis.

Transference occurs *when the analyst begins to assume a major significance in the client's life and the client reacts to the analyst based on unconscious childhood fantasies.* Successful psychoanalysis involves analyzing the transference so that the client understands this reaction and why it occurs. In fact, insight, the ultimate goal of psychoanalysis, may be enhanced because interpretations of the client's interaction with the therapist also have implications for the client's past and future relationships (Andersen & Berk, 1998).

Beyond Psychoanalysis

Although Freud's insights and techniques are fundamental, modern psychodynamic theory reflects the contributions of many who followed, including several of Freud's students who broke away from him and developed their own approaches to psychotherapy. Carl Jung (1875–1961) and Alfred Adler (1870–1937) agreed with Freud that insight was a key therapeutic goal but disagreed that insight usually involves unconscious conflicts about sex and aggression (Arlow, 2000). Instead, Jung emphasized what he called the *collective unconscious,* the culturally determined symbols and myths that are shared among all people that, he argued, could serve as a basis for interpretation beyond sex or aggression. Adler believed that emotional conflicts are the result of perceptions of inferiority and that psychotherapy should help people overcome problems resulting from inferior social status, sex roles, and discrimination.

> **In what common ways do other psychodynamic theories differ from Freudian analysis?**

Other analysts to break with Freud were Melanie Klein (1882–1960), who believed that primitive fantasies of loss and persecution (e.g., worrying about a parent dying or about being bullied) were important factors underlying mental illness, and Karen Horney (1885–1952), who disagreed with Freud about inherent differences in the psychology of men and women and traced such differences to society and culture rather than biology. All of these approaches to psychotherapy stress that the individual is part of a larger society and that conflicts can reflect the individual's role in that society.

These social themes have been developed most explicitly in **interpersonal psychotherapy (IPT),** *a form of psychotherapy that focuses on helping clients improve current relationships* (Weissman, Markowitz, & Klerman, 2000). Therapists using IPT try to focus treatment on the person's interpersonal behaviors and feelings. They pay particular attention to the client's grief (an exaggerated reaction to the loss of a loved one), role disputes (conflicts with a significant other), role transitions (changes in life status, such as starting a new job, getting married, or retiring), or interpersonal deficits (lack of the necessary skills to start or maintain a relationship). The treatment focuses on interpersonal functioning with the assumption that, as interpersonal relations improve, symptoms will subside.

Modern psychodynamic psychotherapies such as IPT differ from classical psychoanalysis in many ways. For starters, the therapist and client typically sit face-to-face. In addition, therapy is less intensive, with meetings often occurring only once a week and therapy lasting months rather than years. In contrast to classical psychoanalysis, modern psychodynamic therapists are more likely to see relief from symptoms as a reasonable goal for therapy (in addition to the goal of facilitating insight), and they

▲ Sigmund Freud, with his mother, Amalia, on her 90th birthday.

▲ Psychodynamic therapists Carl Jung (1875–1961), Alfred Adler (1870–1937), Melanie Klein (1882–1960), and Karen Horney (1885–1952).

are more likely to offer support or advice in addition to interpretation (Henry et al., 1994). Therapists are also now less likely to interpret a client's statements as a sign of unconscious sexual or aggressive impulses. However, other concepts, such as transference and fostering insight into unconscious processes, remain features of most psychodynamic therapies. Psychodynamic psychotherapy has had an enormous impact on how emotional problems are treated, influencing most subsequent schools of therapy in some form. Freud's couch cast a long shadow.

Behavioral and Cognitive Therapies

Unlike psychodynamic psychotherapy, which emphasizes early developmental processes as the source of psychological dysfunction, behavioral and cognitive treatments emphasize the current factors that contribute to the problem—maladaptive behaviors and dysfunctional thoughts.

Behavior Therapy

The idea of focusing treatment on the client's behavior rather than the client's unconscious was inspired by behaviorism. As you read in Chapter 1, behaviorists rejected theories that were based on "invisible" mental properties that were difficult to test and impossible to observe directly. Behaviorists found psychoanalytic ideas particularly hard to test: How do you know whether a person has an unconscious conflict or whether insight has occurred? Behavioral principles, in contrast, focused solely on behaviors that could be observed (e.g., avoidance of a feared object, such as refusing to get on an airplane). **Behavior therapy** assumes that *disordered behavior is learned and that symptom relief is achieved through changing overt maladaptive behaviors into more constructive behaviors.* A variety of behavior therapy techniques have been developed for many disorders, based on the learning principles you encountered in Chapter 7—including operant conditioning procedures (which focus on reinforcement and punishment) and classical conditioning procedures (which focus on extinction). Here are three examples of behavior therapy techniques in action:

 What primary problem did behaviorists have with psychoanalytic ideas?

Eliminating Unwanted Behaviors. How would you change a 3-year-old boy's habit of throwing tantrums at the grocery store? A behavior therapist might investigate what happens after the tantrum: Did the child get candy to "shut him up"? Did the mortified parent provide a lot of attention, begging the child to be quiet? The study of operant conditioning shows that behavior can be predicted by its *consequences* (the reinforcing or punishing events that follow). Adjusting these might help change the behavior. Making the consequences less reinforcing (no candy) and more punishing (a period of time-out in the car while the parent watches from nearby rather than providing a rush of attention) could eliminate the problem behavior.

transference An event that occurs in psychoanalysis when the analyst begins to assume a major significance in the client's life and the client reacts to the analyst based on unconscious childhood fantasies.

interpersonal psychotherapy (IPT) A form of psychotherapy that focuses on helping clients improve current relationships.

behavior therapy A type of therapy that assumes that disordered behavior is learned and that symptom relief is achieved through changing overt maladaptive behaviors into more constructive behaviors.

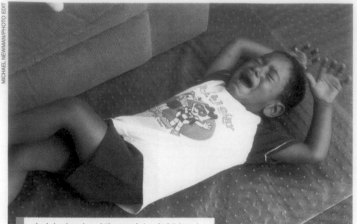

▲ A behavioral therapist might treat this temper tantrum with an analysis of the antecedents, behavior, and consequences of the act.

Promoting Desired Behaviors. In a psychiatric hospital, patients may sometimes become unresponsive and apathetic, withdrawing from social interaction and failing to participate in treatment programs. A behavior therapy technique sometimes used in such cases is the **token economy,** which involves giving clients *"tokens" for desired behaviors, which they can later trade for rewards.* Tokens for behaviors such as cleaning their rooms, getting exercise, or helping other patients signal positive reinforcement because they can be exchanged for rewards such as time away from the hospital, television privileges, and special foods. Token economies have proven to be effective while the system of rewards is in place, but the learned behaviors are not usually maintained when the reinforcements are discontinued (Glynn, 1990). Similar systems used in classrooms to encourage positive behaviors may work temporarily but can undermine students' interest in these behaviors when the reinforcements are no longer available (Lepper & Greene, 1976). A child who is rewarded for controlling his temper in class may become an ogre on the playground when no teacher is present to offer rewards for good behavior.

Reducing Unwanted Emotional Responses. One of the most powerful ways to reduce fear is by gradual *exposure* to the feared object or situation, a behavioral method originated by psychiatrist Joseph Wolpe (1958). **Exposure therapy** involves *confronting an emotion-arousing stimulus directly and repeatedly, ultimately leading to a decrease in the emotional response.* This technique depends on the processes of habituation and response extinction that were originally discovered in the study of classical conditioning (see Chapter 7). Wolpe called this form of treatment **systematic desensitization,** *a procedure in which a client relaxes all the muscles of his or her body while imagining being in increasingly frightening situations.* For example, a client who fears going to the dentist might first imagine seeing a photo of a dentist,

How might exposure therapy help treat a phobia or fear of a specific object?

▼ An exposure therapy client with obsessive-compulsive disorder who fears contamination in public restrooms might be given "homework" to visit three such restrooms in a week, turn the water in the sink on and off, and then *not* wash up. This particular restroom could take days.

followed by imagining seeing a dentist in the office, followed eventually by imagining sitting in the dentist's chair and opening wide for a dental procedure—all while engaging in exercises that relax the muscles of the body. It's now known that *in vivo exposure*, or live exposure, is more effective than imaginary exposure (Choy, Fyer, & Lipsitz, 2007). In other words, if a person fears social situations, it is better for that person to practice social interaction than to merely imagine it. Behavioral therapists use an exposure hierarchy to expose the client gradually to the feared object or situation. Easier situations are practiced first, and as fear decreases, the client progresses to more difficult or frightening situations (see **TABLE 15.1**).

Exposure therapy can also help people overcome unwanted emotional and behavioral responses through *exposure with response prevention*. A patient with obsessive-compulsive disorder, for example, might have recurrent thoughts that his hands are dirty and need washing. Washing stops the uncomfortable feelings of contamination only briefly, though, and the patient washes again and again in search of relief. In exposure with response prevention, the patient might be asked in therapy to get his hands dirty on purpose and leave them dirty for hours. He may need to do this only a few times to break the cycle and be freed from the obsessive ritual (Foa et al., 2007).

TABLE 15.1

Exposure Hierarchy for Social Phobia

Item	Fear (0–100)
1. Have a party and invite everyone from work	99
2. Go to a holiday party for 1 hour without drinking	90
3. Invite Cindy to have dinner and see a movie	85
4. Go for a job interview	80
5. Ask boss for a day off work	65
6. Ask questions in a meeting at work	65
7. Eat lunch with coworkers	60
8. Talk to a stranger on the bus	50
9. Talk to cousin on the telephone for 10 minutes	40
10. Ask for directions at the gas station	35

token economy A form of behavior therapy in which clients are given "tokens" for desired behaviors, which they can later trade for rewards.

exposure therapy An approach to treatment that involves confronting an emotion-arousing stimulus directly and repeatedly, ultimately leading to a decrease in the emotional response.

systematic desensitization A procedure in which a client relaxes all the muscles of his or her body while imagining being in increasingly frightening situations.

cognitive therapy A form of psychotherapy that involves helping a client identify and correct any distorted thinking about self, others, or the world.

cognitive restructuring A therapeutic approach that teaches clients to question the automatic beliefs, assumptions, and predictions that often lead to negative emotions and to replace negative thinking with more realistic and positive beliefs.

Cognitive Therapy

Whereas behavior therapy doesn't take into account a person's thoughts and feelings, and instead focuses on an individual's behavior, **cognitive therapy** focuses on *helping a client identify and correct any distorted thinking about self, others, or the world* (e.g., Beck & Weishaar, 2000). For example, behaviorists might explain a phobia as the outcome of a classical conditioning experience such as being bitten by a dog, where the dog bite leads to the development of a dog phobia through the simple association of the dog with the experience of pain. Cognitive theorists might instead emphasize the *meaning* of the event. It might not be the event itself that caused the fear, but rather the individual's beliefs and assumptions about the event and the feared stimulus. In the case of a dog bite, cognitive theorists might focus on a person's new or strengthened belief that dogs are dangerous to explain the fear.

Cognitive therapies use a principal technique called **cognitive restructuring**, which *involves teaching clients to question the automatic beliefs, assumptions, and predictions that often lead to negative emotions and to replace negative thinking with more realistic and positive beliefs.* Specifically, clients are taught to examine the evidence for and against a particular belief or to be more accepting of outcomes that may be undesirable yet still manageable. For example, a depressed client may

? How might a client restructure a negative self-image into a positive one?

believe that she is stupid and will never pass her college courses—all on the basis of one poor grade. In this situation, the therapist would work with the client to examine the validity of this belief. The therapist would consider relevant evidence such as grades on previous exams, performance on other coursework, and examples of intelligence outside school. It may be that the client has never failed a course before and has achieved good grades in this particular course in the past. In this case, the therapist would encourage the client to consider all this information in determining whether she is truly "stupid." **TABLE 15.2** on the next page shows a variety of potentially irrational ideas—beliefs and convictions that could be true or that could be false—and so serve to unleash unwanted emotions such as anger, depression, or anxiety. Any of these irrational beliefs might bedevil a person with serious emotional problems if left unchallenged and so are potential targets for cognitive restructuring.

Some forms of cognitive therapy include techniques for coping with unwanted thoughts and feelings, techniques that resemble meditation (see Chapter 5). Clients may be encouraged to attend to their troubling thoughts or emotions or be given

▲ Western cognitive therapy meets the Eastern Buddhist meditation tradition as Aaron Beck greets his holiness the Dalai Lama at the International Congress for Cognitive Psychotherapy in 2005. Beck's approach to psychotherapy helps people change maladaptive thinking patterns in a direct and rational approach, whereas the practice of Buddhism expressed by the Dalai Lama aims to create mental peace through meditation. Here they seem to be amused by each other's choice of clothing.

TABLE 15.2

Common Irrational Beliefs and the Emotional Responses They Can Cause

Belief	Emotional Response
I have to get this done immediately. I must be perfect. Something terrible will happen.	Anxiety, stress
Everyone is watching me. I won't be able to make friends. People know something is wrong with me.	Embarrassment, social anxiety
I'm a loser and will always be a loser. Nobody will ever love me.	Sadness, depression
She did that to me on purpose. He is evil and should be punished. Things ought to be different.	Anger, irritability

meditative techniques that allow them to gain a new focus (Hofmann & Asmundson, 2008). One such technique, called **mindfulness meditation,** *teaches an individual to be fully present in each moment; to be aware of his or her thoughts, feelings, and sensations; and to detect symptoms before they become a problem.* Researchers have found mindfulness meditation to be helpful for preventing relapse in depression. In one study, people recovering from depression were about half as likely to relapse during a 60-week assessment period if they received mindfulness meditation–based cognitive therapy than if they received treatment as usual (Teasdale, Segal, & Williams, 2000).

Cognitive Behavioral Therapy

Historically, cognitive and behavioral therapies were considered distinct systems of therapy, and some people continue to follow this distinction, using solely behavioral *or* cognitive techniques. Today, the extent to which therapists use cognitive versus behavioral techniques depends on the individual therapist as well as the type of problem being treated. Most therapists working with anxiety and depression use *a blend of cognitive and behavioral therapeutic strategies,* often referred to as **cognitive behavioral therapy,** or CBT. In a way, this technique acknowledges that there may be behaviors that people cannot control through rational thought but also that there are ways of helping people think more rationally when thought does play a role. In contrast to traditional behavior therapy and cognitive therapy, CBT is "problem focused," meaning that it is undertaken for specific problems (e.g., reducing the frequency of panic attacks or returning to work after a bout of depression), and "action oriented," meaning that the therapist tries to assist the client in selecting specific strategies to help address those problems. The client is expected to *do* things, such as practice relaxation exercises or use a diary to monitor relevant symptoms (e.g., the severity of depressed mood, panic attack symptoms). This is in contrast to psychodynamic or other therapies where goals may not be explicitly discussed or agreed on and the client's only necessary action is to attend the therapy session.

CBT also contrasts with psychodynamic approaches in its assumptions about what the client can know. CBT is *transparent* in that nothing is withheld from the client. By the end of the course of therapy, most clients have a very good understanding of the treatment they have received as well as the specific techniques that are used to make the desired changes. For example, clients with obsessive-compulsive disorder who fear contamination would feel confident in knowing how to confront feared situations

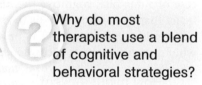

Why do most therapists use a blend of cognitive and behavioral strategies?

▲ There's nothing funny about depression.

ADRI BERGER/GETTY IMAGES

such as public washrooms and why confronting this situation is helpful. In this way, the CBT model of therapy differs from the more mystical relationship between the therapist and client in psychodynamic psychotherapy, in which the therapist serves almost as a kind of spiritual guide urging the client toward insight.

Cognitive behavioral therapies have been found to be effective for a number of disorders (Butler et al., 2006). Substantial effects of CBT have been found for unipolar depression, generalized anxiety disorder, panic disorder, social phobia, post-traumatic stress disorder, and childhood depressive and anxiety disorders. CBT has moderate but less substantial effects for marital distress, anger, somatic disorders, and chronic pain. Just as a student doing well in school seems to enjoy taking exams, practitioners of CBT have had enough success that they often seem to enjoy talking about the importance of assessing the effectiveness of psychological treatments (Shafran et al., 2009).

Humanistic and Existential Therapies

Humanistic and existential therapies emerged in the middle of the 20th century, in part as a reaction to the negative views that psychodynamic psychotherapies hold about human nature. Psychodynamic approaches emphasize unconscious drives toward sex and aggression, as we noted earlier. Humanistic and existential therapies assume that human nature is generally positive, and they emphasize the natural tendency of each individual to strive for personal improvement. Humanistic and existential therapies share the assumption that psychological problems stem from feelings of alienation and loneliness—and that these feelings can be traced to failures to reach one's potential (in the humanistic approach) or from failures to find meaning in life (in the existential approach). Although interest in these approaches peaked in the 1960s and 1970s, some therapists continue to use these approaches today. Two well-known types are person-centered therapy (a humanistic approach) and Gestalt therapy (an existential approach).

How does a humanistic view of human nature differ from a psychodynamic view?

Person-Centered Therapy

Person-centered therapy (also known as client-centered therapy) *assumes that all individuals have a tendency toward growth and that this growth can be facilitated by acceptance and genuine reactions from the therapist.* Psychologist Carl Rogers (1902–87) developed person-centered therapy in the 1940s and 1950s (Rogers, 1951). Person-centered therapy assumes that each individual is qualified to determine his or her own goals for therapy, such as feeling more confident or making a career decision, and even the frequency and length of therapy. In this type of nondirective treatment, the therapist tends not to provide advice or suggestions about what the client should be doing. Instead, the therapist paraphrases the client's words, mirroring the client's thoughts and sentiments (e.g., "I think I hear you saying . . ."). Person-centered therapists believe that with adequate support, the client will recognize the right things to do.

Rogers encouraged person-centered therapists to demonstrate three basic qualities: congruence, empathy, and unconditional positive regard. Congruence refers to openness and honesty in the therapeutic relationship and ensuring that the therapist communicates the same message at all levels. For example, the same message must be communicated in the therapist's words, the therapist's facial expression, and the therapist's body language. Saying "I think your concerns are valid" while smirking would simply not do. Empathy refers to the continuous process of trying to understand the client by getting inside his or her way of thinking, feeling, and understanding the world. Seeing the world from the client's perspective enables the therapist to better appreciate the client's apprehensions, worries, or fears. Finally, the therapist must treat the client with unconditional positive regard by providing a nonjudgmental, warm, and accepting environment in which the client can feel safe expressing his or her thoughts and feelings.

mindfulness meditation A form of cognitive therapy that teaches an individual to be fully present in each moment; to be aware of his or her thoughts, feelings, and sensations; and to detect symptoms before they become a problem.

cognitive behavioral therapy (CBT) A blend of cognitive and behavioral therapeutic strategies.

person-centered therapy An approach to therapy that assumes all individuals have a tendency toward growth and that this growth can be facilitated by acceptance and genuine reactions from the therapist.

Gestalt therapy An existentialist approach to treatment with the goal of helping the client become aware of his or her thoughts, behaviors, experiences, and feelings and to "own" or take responsibility for them.

Here is an example of what person-centered therapy might sound like for a client who is dealing with conflicted feelings about her daughter being away at college (Raskin & Rogers, 2000).

Client: I'm having a lot of problems dealing with my daughter. She's 20 years old; she's in college; I'm having a lot of trouble letting her go . . . And I have a lot of guilt feelings about her; I have a real need to hang on to her.

Therapist: A need to hang on so you can kind of make up for the things you feel guilty about—is that part of it?

Client: There's a lot of that . . . Also, she's been a real friend to me and filled my life . . . And it's very hard . . . a lot of empty places now that she's not with me.

Therapist: The old vacuum, sort of, when she's not there.

Client: Yes. Yes. I would also like to be the kind of mother that could be strong and say, you know, "Go and have a good life," and this is really hard for me to do.

Therapist: It's very hard to give up something that's been so precious in your life but also something that has caused you pain when you mentioned guilt.

Client: Yeah, and I'm aware that I have some anger toward her that I don't always get what I want. I have needs that are not met. And, uh, I don't feel I have a right to those needs. You know. . . . She's a daughter; she's not my mother—though sometimes I feel as if I'd like her to mother me. . . . It's very difficult for me to ask for that and have a right to it.

Therapist: So it may be unreasonable, but still, when she doesn't meet your needs, it makes you mad.

Client: Yeah, I get very, very angry with her.

From this example you can see that the goal of the exchange was not to uncover repressed conflicts, as in psychodynamic therapy, or to challenge unrealistic thoughts, as in cognitive behavior therapy. Instead, the person-centered therapist tried to understand the client's experience and reflect that experience back to her in a supportive way, encouraging the client's natural tendency toward growth. This style of therapy is reminiscent of psychoanalysis in its way of encouraging the client toward the free expression of thoughts and feelings, but humanistic therapies clearly start from a set of assumptions about human nature that differ diametrically from those of psychodynamic theories.

Gestalt Therapy

Gestalt therapy was founded by Frederick "Fritz" Perls (1893–1970) and colleagues in the 1940s and 1950s (Perls, Hefferkine, & Goodman, 1951). **Gestalt therapy** *has the goal of helping the client become aware of his or her thoughts, behaviors, experiences, and feelings and to "own" or take responsibility for them.* Gestalt therapists are encouraged to be enthusiastic and warm toward their clients, an approach they share with person-centered therapists. To help facilitate the client's awareness, Gestalt therapists also reflect back to the client their impressions of the client.

Gestalt therapy emphasizes the experiences and behaviors that are occurring at that particular moment in the therapy session. For example, if a client is talking about something stressful that occurred during the previous week, the therapist might shift the attention to the client's current experience by asking, "How do you feel as you describe what happened to you?" This technique is known as focusing. Clients are also encouraged to put their feelings into action. One way to do this is the empty

▼ As part of Gestalt therapy, clients may be encouraged to imagine that another person is sitting across from them in a chair. The client then moves from chair to chair, role-playing what he or she would say to the imagined person and what that person would answer.

PHOTOALTO/ALAMY

chair technique, in which the client imagines that another person (e.g., a spouse, a parent, a coworker) is in an empty chair, sitting directly across from the client. The client then moves from chair to chair, alternating from role-playing what he or she would say to the other person and what he or she imagines the other person would respond. Gestalt techniques originated as a form of psychotherapy but are now often used in counseling or "life coaching" to help people prepare for new job or family situations (Grant, 2008).

"Don't make me come over there!"

Groups in Therapy

It is natural to think of psychopathology as an illness that affects only the individual. A particular person "is depressed," for example, or "has anxi-

> **When is group therapy the best option?**

ety." Yet each person lives in a world of other people, and interactions with others may intensify and even create disorders. A depressed person may be lonely after moving away from friends and loved ones, or an anxious person could be worried about pressures from parents. These ideas suggest that people might be able to recover from disorders in the same way they got into them—not just as an individual effort, but through social processes.

Couples and Family Therapy

When a couple is "having problems," neither individual may be suffering from any psychopathology. Rather, it may be the relationship itself that is disordered. *Couples therapy* is when a married, cohabitating, or dating couple is seen together in therapy to work on problems usually arising within the relationship. A traditional use of couples therapy might involve a couple seeking help because they are unhappy with their relationship. In this scenario, both members of the couple are expected to attend therapy sessions and the problem is seen as arising from their interaction rather than from the problems of one half of the couple. Treatment strategies would target changes in *both* parties, focusing on ways to break their repetitive dysfunctional pattern (Watzlawick, Beavin, & Jackson, 1967).

There are cases when therapy with even larger groups is warranted. An individual may be having a problem—say, an adolescent is abusing alcohol—but the source of the problem is the individual's relationships with family members; perhaps the mother is herself an alcoholic who subtly encourages the adolescent to drink and the father travels and neglects the family. In this case, it could be useful for the therapist to work with the whole group at once in *family therapy*—psychotherapy involving members of a family. Family therapy can be particularly effective when adolescent children are having problems (Masten, 2004).

In family therapy, the "client" is the entire family. Family therapists believe that problem behaviors exhibited by a particular family member are the result of a dysfunctional family. For example, an adolescent girl suffering from bulimia might be treated in therapy with her mother, father, and older brother. The therapist would work to understand how the family members relate to one another, how the family is organized, and how it changes over time. In discussions with the family, the therapist might discover

▼ What to do when your marriage is in a rut? One option is to enter couples therapy. Another option is to go out on a screwball comedy "date night" and fall into a wacky mistaken-identity misadventure with several unsavory characters on the way to rediscovering the magic in your marriage. Your choice.

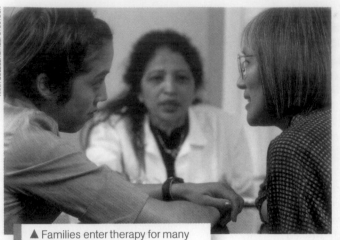

▲ Families enter therapy for many reasons, sometimes to help particular members and other times because there are problems in one or more of the relationships in the family.

that the parents' excessive enthusiasm about her brother's athletic career led the girl to try to gain their approval by controlling her weight to become "beautiful." Both couples and family therapy involve more than one person attending therapy together, and the problems and solutions are seen as arising from the *interaction* of these individuals rather than simply from any one individual.

Group Therapy

Taking these ideas one step further, if individuals (or families) can benefit from talking with a psychotherapist, perhaps they can also benefit from talking with other clients who are talking with the therapist. This is **group therapy**, *a technique in which multiple participants (who often do not know one another at the outset) work on their individual problems in a group atmosphere.* The therapist in group therapy serves more as a discussion leader than as a personal therapist, conducting the sessions both by talking with individuals and by encouraging them to talk with one another. Group therapy is often used for people who have a common problem, such as substance abuse, but it can also be used for those with differing problems.

Why do people choose group therapy? One advantage is that groups provide a context in which clients can practice relating to others. People in group therapy have a "built-in" set of peers whom they have to talk to and get along with on a regular basis. This can be especially helpful for clients who are otherwise socially isolated. Second, attending a group with others who have similar problems shows clients that they are not alone in their suffering. Third, group members model appropriate behaviors for one another and share their insights about how to deal with their problems. Fourth, group therapy is often just as effective as individual therapy (e.g., Jonsson & Hougaard, 2008), so, on average, whoever is paying for group therapy gets a bargain.

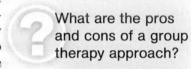

What are the pros and cons of a group therapy approach?

Group therapy also has disadvantages. It may be difficult to assemble a group of individuals who have similar needs. This is particularly an issue with CBT, which tends to focus on specific problems such as depression or panic disorder. Group therapy may become a problem if one or more members undermine the treatment of other group members. This can occur if some group members dominate the discussions, threaten other group members, or make others in the group uncomfortable (e.g., attempting to date other members). Finally, clients in group therapy get less attention than they might in individual psychotherapy. As a result, those who tend to participate less in the group may not benefit as much as those who participate more.

Self-Help and Support Groups

An important offshoot of group therapy is the concept of *self-help groups* and *support groups,* which are discussion or Internet chat groups that focus on a particular disorder or difficult life experience and are often run by peers who have themselves struggled with the same issues. The most famous self-help and support groups are Alcoholics Anonymous (AA), Gamblers Anonymous, and Al-Anon (a program for the family and friends of those with alcohol problems). Other self-help groups offer support to cancer survivors or to parents of children with autism or to people with mood disorders, eating disorders, substance abuse problems, and self-harming disorders—in fact, self-help and support groups exist for just about every psychological disorder. In addition to being cost-effective, self-help and support groups allow people to realize that they are not the only ones with a particular problem and give them the opportunity to offer guidance and support to each other based on personal experiences of success.

What are the pros and cons of self-help support groups?

group therapy Therapy in which multiple participants (who often do not know one another at the outset) work on their individual problems in a group atmosphere.

◀ Self-help groups are a cost-effective, time-effective, and treatment-effective solution for dealing with some types of psychological problems.

In some cases, though, self-help and support groups can do more harm than good. Some members may be disruptive or aggressive or encourage one another to engage in behaviors that are countertherapeutic (e.g., avoiding feared situations or using alcohol to cope). People with moderate problems may be exposed to others with severe problems and may become oversensitized to symptoms they might otherwise have not found disturbing. Because self-help and support groups are usually not led by trained therapists, mechanisms to evaluate these groups or to ensure their quality are rarely in place.

Today, AA has more than 2 million members in the United States, with 185,000 group meetings that occur around the world (Mack, Franklin, & Frances, 2003). Members are encouraged to follow "12 steps" to reach the goal of lifelong abstinence from all drinking, and the steps include believing in a higher power, practicing prayer and meditation, and making amends for harm to others. Most members attend group meetings several times per week, and between meetings they receive additional support from their "sponsor." A few studies examining the effectiveness of AA have been conducted, and it appears that individuals who participate tend to overcome problem drinking with greater success than those who do not participate in AA (Fiorentine, 1999; Morgenstern et al., 1997). However, several tenets of the AA philosophy are not supported by the research. We know that the general AA program is useful, but questions about which parts of this program are most helpful have yet to be studied.

Considered together, the many social approaches to psychotherapy reveal how important interpersonal relationships are for each of us. It may not always be clear how psychotherapy works, whether one approach is better than another, or what particular theory should be used to understand how problems have developed. What is clear, however, is that social interactions between people—both in individual therapy and in all the different forms of therapy in groups—can be useful in treating psychological disorders.

"So, you're being attacked by an angry badger…".

IN SUMMARY

- ○ Psychodynamic therapies, including psychoanalysis, emphasize helping clients gain insight into their unconscious conflicts.

- ○ Behavior therapy applies learning principles to specific behavior problems; cognitive therapy aims at challenging irrational thoughts. Cognitive behavior therapy (CBT) merges these approaches.

- ○ Humanistic approaches (e.g., person-centered therapy) and existential approaches (e.g., Gestalt therapy) focus on helping people to develop a sense of personal worth.

- ○ Group therapies target couples, families, or groups of clients brought together for the purpose of therapy.

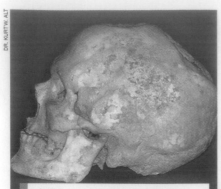

▲ This is a trepanned skull from a Stone Age burial site (about 5900–6200 BCE) in the Alsace region of France. Two holes were drilled in the skull, and the patient lived afterward, as shown by the regrowth of bone covering the holes (from Alt et al., 1997). Don't try this at home.

Medical and Biological Treatments: Healing the Mind through the Brain

Ever since someone discovered that a whack to the head can affect the mind, people have suspected that direct brain interventions might hold the keys to a cure for psychological disorders. Archaeological evidence, for example, indicates that the occasional human thousands of years ago was "treated" for some malady by the practice of trepanning—drilling a hole in the skull, perhaps in the belief that this would release evil spirits that were affecting the mind (Alt et al., 1997). Surgery for psychological disorders is a last resort nowadays, and treatments that focus on the brain usually involve interventions that are less dramatic. The use of drugs to influence the brain was also discovered in prehistory (alcohol, for example, has been around for a long time). Since then, drug treatments have grown in variety and effectiveness to become what is now the most common medical approach in treating psychological disorders.

Antipsychotic Medications

The story of drug treatments for severe psychological disorders starts in the 1950s, with chlorpromazine (brand name Thorazine), which was originally developed as a sedative but which, when administered to people with schizophrenia, often left them euphoric and docile when they had formerly been agitated and incorrigible (Barondes, 2003). Chlorpromazine was the first in a series of **antipsychotic drugs**, which *treat schizophrenia and related psychotic disorders,* and which completely changed the way schizophrenia was managed. Other related medications, such as thioridazine (Mellaril) and haloperidol (Haldol), followed. Before the introduction of antipsychotic drugs, people with schizophrenia often exhibited bizarre symptoms and were sometimes so disruptive and difficult to manage that the only way to protect them (and other people) was to keep them in asylums (see the Real World box). In the period following the introduction of these drugs, the number of people in psychiatric hospitals decreased by more than two thirds. Antipsychotic drugs made possible the deinstitutionalization of hundreds of thousands of people and gave a major boost to the field of **psychopharmacology**, *the study of drug effects on psychological states and symptoms.*

? What do antipsychotic drugs do?

Antipsychotic medications are believed to block dopamine receptors in parts of the brain such as the mesolimbic area, an area between the tegmentum (in the midbrain) and various subcortical structures (see Chapter 3). The medication reduces dopamine activity in these areas. As you read in Chapter 14, the effectiveness of schizophrenia medications led to the "dopamine hypothesis," suggesting that schizophrenia may be caused by excess dopamine in the synapse. Research has indeed found that dopamine overactivity in the mesolimbic area of the brain is related to the more bizarre positive symptoms of schizophrenia, such as hallucinations and delusions (Marangell et al., 2003).

Although antipsychotic drugs work well for positive symptoms, it turns out that negative symptoms of schizophrenia, such as emotional numbing and social withdrawal, may be related to dopamine *under*activity in the mesocortical areas of the brain (connections between parts of the tegmentum and the cortex). This may help explain why antipsychotic medications do not relieve negative symptoms well. Instead of a medication that blocks dopamine receptors, negative symptoms require a medication that *increases* the amount of dopamine available at the synapse. This is a good example of how medical treatments can have broad psychological effects but not target specific psychological symptoms.

After the introduction of antipsychotic medications, there was little change in the available treatments for schizophrenia for more than a quarter of a century. However, in the 1990s, a new class of antipsychotic drugs was introduced. These newer drugs,

antipsychotic drugs Medications that are used to treat schizophrenia and related psychotic disorders.

psychopharmacology The study of drug effects on psychological states and symptoms.

"The drug has, however, proved more effective than traditional psychoanalysis."

THE REAL WORLD

Tales from the Madhouse

Society has never quite known what to do with people who have severe mental disorders. For much of recorded history, mentally ill people have been victims of maltreatment, languishing as paupers in the streets or, worse, suffering inhumane conditions in prisons. It was something of a reform, then, when in the 18th century, the few private "madhouses" for the rich became models for the establishment of public asylums in England and France. At the time, no one cared much about any harmful effects of using derogatory terms for the patients of these institutions, so asylums were unashamedly named for their services to "lunatics," "idiots," and "the insane."

In North America, the asylum movement for humane treatment of the mentally ill was fostered initially by Dr. Benjamin Rush (a signer of the Constitution) and later by mental health crusader Dorothea Dix. Dix visited jails and almshouses in Massachusetts and in 1843 reported to the legislature widespread cruelty toward the insane. She witnessed inmates who were in chains, unclothed even in winter, and abused physically and sexually by their keepers. At the Shelburne jail, she recounted finding "a human being, partially extended, cast upon his back amidst a mass of filth. The mistress says 'He's cleaned out now and then; but what's the use for such a creature?'" (Gollaher, 1995). Dix developed a remarkably effective personal campaign across North America and Europe that eventually resulted in the building of hundreds of asylums for the mentally ill.

The creation of asylums encouraged humane treatment but did not guarantee it. London's St. Mary's of Bethlehem Hospital, known for inspiring the term *bedlam*, was typical—even charging visitors to view the inmates as a way of financing the institution. One visitor to this human zoo in 1753 remarked, "To my great surprise, I found at least a hundred people, who, having paid their two pence apiece, were suffered, unattended, to run rioting up and down the wards, making sport and diversion of the miserable inhabitants" (Hitchcock, 2005). To some degree, the abuse of insane inmates by jailers simply was transformed into the abuse of mental patients by asylum workers. For severe disorders, there often was no "treatment" at all, and the focus of the asylum instead was merely on custody (Jones, 1972). More recent exposés of mental hospital life, films such as *Titicut Follies* and *One Flew over the Cuckoo's Nest*, reveal that asylums can be bedlams even in our ostensibly enlightened times.

These weaknesses of the asylum movement eventually led to another revolution in mental health treatment—the deinstitutionalization movement of the 1960s. Drugs were being discovered that helped people to manage their disorders and live outside hospitals. With the funding of a "community mental health" initiative by the Kennedy administration, dozens of mental hospitals across the United States were closed, and meanwhile, thousands of patients were trained to shop, cook, take public transportation, and otherwise deal with living outside the hospital. Former asylum patients were returned to their families or placed in foster homes or group apartments, but in too many cases they were simply released with nowhere to go. Treatment of all but the most untreatable patients was managed through community mental health centers—support units to provide emergency inpatient care as needed but mainly supplying outpatient treatment and assistance in community living (Levine, 1981).

Has this experiment worked? The jury is still out because many problems remain. Treatment for some severe disorders has improved since deinstitutionalization began. The basic drugs that helped people to manage their lives outside mental hospitals have been refined and improved. But federal

▲ Dorothea Dix (1802–77) was a pioneer in the reform of treatment for the mentally ill.

funding of the network of community mental health centers was abandoned by the Reagan administration in the 1980s, and state-funded programs and private managed care providers have not made up the difference (Cutler, Bevilacqua, & McFarland, 2003). So, on the one hand, the current approach of deinstitutionalization has increased the autonomy of people with severe mental illnesses, allowing them greater freedom from asylums. But on the other hand, this approach puts many of these people on the streets, where they remain homeless, poor, vulnerable, and sometimes dangerous. In fact, some 1.7 million Americans used homeless shelters or transitional housing in 2007 (*The State of the Nation's Housing*, 2009). It is not clear that in several hundred years real progress has been made.

▲ **Missouri State Lunatic Asylum (1884)** This asylum represents a somewhat idyllic image of treatment for psychological disorders. Life inside the asylum often presented quite a different reality.

which include clozapine (Clozaril), risperidone (Risperidal), and olanzepine (Zyprexa), have become known *as atypical antipsychotics* (the older drugs are now often referred to as *conventional* or *typical* antipsychotics). Unlike the older antipsychotic medications, these newer drugs appear to affect both the dopamine and serotonin systems, blocking both types of receptors. The ability to block serotonin receptors appears to be a useful addition since enhanced serotonin activity in the brain has been implicated in some of the core difficulties in schizophrenia, such as cognitive and perceptual disruptions, as well as mood disturbances. This may explain why atypical antipsychotics work at least as well as older drugs for the positive symptoms of schizophrenia but also work fairly well for negative symptoms (Bradford, Stroup, & Lieberman, 2002).

What are the advantages of the newer, atypical antipsychotic medications?

Like most medications, antipsychotic drugs have side effects. The side effects can be sufficiently unpleasant that some people "go off their meds," preferring their symptoms to the drug. One side effect that often occurs with long-term use is *tardive dyskinesia,* a condition of involuntary movements of the face, mouth, and extremities. In fact, patients often need to take another medication to treat the unwanted side effects of the conventional antipsychotic drugs. Side effects of the newer medications tend to be different and sometimes milder than those of the older antipsychotics. For that reason, the atypical antipsychotics are now usually the front-line treatments for schizophrenia (Marangell et al., 2003).

Antianxiety Medications

Antianxiety medications are *drugs that help reduce a person's experience of fear or anxiety.* The most commonly used antianxiety medications are the benzodiazepines, a type of tranquilizer that works by facilitating the action of the neurotransmitter gamma-aminobutyric acid (GABA). As you read in Chapter 3, GABA inhibits certain neurons in the brain, producing a calming effect for the person. Commonly prescribed benzodiazepines include diazepam (Valium), lorazepam (Ativan), and alprazolam (Xanax). The benzodiazepines typically take effect in a matter of minutes and are effective for reducing symptoms of anxiety disorders (Roy-Byrne & Cowley, 2002).

What are some reasons for caution when prescribing antianxiety medications?

Nonetheless, these days doctors are relatively cautious when prescribing benzodiazepines. One concern is that these drugs have the potential for abuse. They are often associated with the development of *tolerance,* which is the need for higher dosages over time to achieve the same effects following long-term use (see Chapter 5). Furthermore, after people become tolerant of the drug, they risk significant withdrawal symptoms following discontinuation. Some withdrawal symptoms include increased heart rate, shakiness, insomnia, agitation, and anxiety—the very symptoms the drug was taken to eliminate! Therefore, patients who take benzodiazepines for extended periods may have difficulty coming off these drugs and should discontinue their medications gradually to minimize withdrawal symptoms (Schatzberg, Cole, & DeBattista, 2003). Another consideration when prescribing benzodiazepines is their side effects. The most common side effect is drowsiness, although benzodiazepines can also have negative effects on coordination and memory. And benzodiazepines combined with alcohol can depress respiration, potentially causing accidental death.

▲ People with schizophrenia are two to three times more likely to smoke tobacco than the average person (Kelly & McCreadie, 2000). Several explanations are being tested for this, including the possibility that people with schizophrenia seek out nicotine to reduce their symptoms. If this is true, their "self-medication" may point the way toward new drug treatments for the disorder that might be more helpful and less harmful than smoking.

WHAT'S NEW IN PHARMACOLOGY
by Maira Kalman and Rick Meyerowitz

ASK YOUR DOCTOR

Dysplosives	Nostalgics	Antipepsodines	Pandemonics
Preventidrool	Nothin	Theatrical (overactin)	Hypochondriax
Revoltin	Miketycin	Monrodoctrin	Credenza
Cucumberdil	Neo-sufferin	Espresso bismol	Hydrocortidrek
Dixichixil	Pseudointellectuol	Ibuproblem	Relapsin
Preventafit	Benumbitussin	Phenaminafenafinaphen	Schwarzeneggra
Krazyglucosamine	Trafficort	Globbinlarynx	Thatsol

When anxiety leads to insomnia, drugs known as hypnotics may be useful as sleep aids. One such drug, zolpidem (Ambien), is in wide use and is often effective, but with some reports of sleep-walking, sleep-eating, and even sleep-driving (Hughes, 2007). Another alternative for anxiety is buspirone (Buspar), which has been shown to reduce anxiety among individuals who suffer from generalized anxiety disorder (Roy-Byrne & Cowley, 2002).

Antidepressants and Mood Stabilizers

Antidepressants are *a class of drugs that help lift people's moods.* They were first introduced in the 1950s, when iproniazid, a drug that was used to treat tuberculosis, was found to elevate mood (Selikoff, Robitzek, & Ornstein, 1952). Iproniazid is a *monoamine oxidase inhibitor (MAOI),* a medication that prevents the enzyme monoamine oxidase from breaking down neurotransmitters such as norepinephrine, serotonin, and dopamine. However, despite their effectiveness, MAOIs are rarely prescribed anymore. MAOI side effects such as dizziness and loss of sexual interest are often difficult to tolerate, and these drugs interact with many different medications, including over-the-counter cold medicines. They also can cause dangerous increases in blood pressure when taken with foods that contain tyramine, a natural substance formed from the breakdown of protein in certain cheeses, beans, aged meats, soy products, and draft beer.

"Your therapy will be a combination of drugs and clowns."

A second category of antidepressants is the tricyclic antidepressants, which were also introduced in the 1950s. These include drugs such as imipramine (Tofranil) and amitriptyline (Elavil). These medications block the reuptake of norepinephrine and serotonin, thereby increasing the amount of neurotransmitter in the synaptic space between neurons. The most common side effects of tricyclic antidepressants include dry mouth, constipation, difficulty urinating, blurred vision, and racing heart (Marangell et al., 2003). Although these drugs are still prescribed, they are used much less frequently than they were in the past because of these side effects.

What are the most common antidepressants used today? How do they work?

Among the most commonly used antidepressants today are the *selective serotonin reuptake inhibitors,* or SSRIs, which include drugs such as fluoxetine (Prozac), citalopram (Celexa), and paroxetine (Paxil). The SSRIs work by blocking the reuptake of serotonin in the brain, which makes more serotonin available in the synaptic space between neurons. The greater availability of serotonin in the synapse gives the neuron a better chance of "recognizing" and using this neurotransmitter in sending the desired signal. The SSRIs were developed based on hypotheses that low levels of serotonin are a causal factor in depression (see Chapter 12). Supporting this hypothesis, SSRIs are effective for depression, as well as for a wide range of other problems. SSRIs are called "selective" because, unlike the tricyclic antidepressants, which work on the serotonin and norepinephrine systems, SSRIs work more specifically on the serotonin system (see **FIGURE 15.2** on the next page).

Finally, antidepressants such as Effexor (venlafaxine) and Wellbutrin (ibupropion) offer other alternatives. Effexor is an example of a serotonin and norepinephrine reuptake inhibitor (SNRI); whereas SSRIs act only upon serotonin, SNRIs act on both serotonin and norepinephrine. Wellbutrin, in contrast, is a norepinephrine and dopamine reuptake inhibitor. These and other newly developed antidepressants appear to have fewer (or at least different) side effects than the tricyclic antidepressants and MAOIs.

Most antidepressants can take up to a month before they start to have an effect on mood. Besides relieving symptoms of depression, almost all of the antidepressants effectively treat anxiety disorders, and many of them can resolve other problems, such as eating disorders. In fact, several companies that manufacture SSRIs

antianxiety medications Drugs that help reduce a person's experience of fear or anxiety.

antidepressants A class of drugs that help lift people's mood.

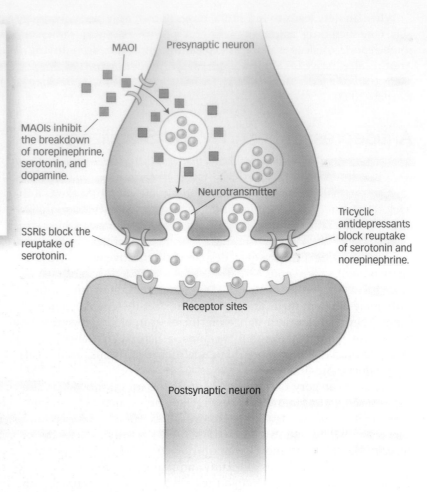

▶ **FIGURE 15.2**
Antidepressant Drug Actions Antidepressant drugs, such as MAOIs, SSRIs, and tricyclic antidepressants, act on neurotransmitters such as serotonin, dopamine, and norepinephrine by inhibiting their breakdown and blocking reuptake. These actions make more of the neurotransmitter available for release and leave more of the neurotransmitter in the synaptic gap to activate the receptor sites on the postsynaptic neuron. These drugs relieve depression and often alleviate anxiety and other disorders.

have marketed their drugs as treatments for anxiety disorders rather than for their antidepressant effects. Although antidepressants can be effective in treating major depression (see the Hot Science box), they are not recommended for treating bipolar disorder, which is characterized by manic or hypomanic episodes (see Chapter 14). Antidepressants are not prescribed because they might actually trigger a manic episode in a person with bipolar disorder. Instead, bipolar disorder is treated with *mood stabilizers*, which are medications used to suppress swings between mania and depression. Commonly used mood stabilizers include lithium and valproate. Even in unipolar depression, lithium is sometimes effective when combined with traditional antidepressants in people who do not respond to antidepressants alone.

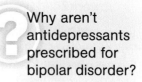 Why aren't antidepressants prescribed for bipolar disorder?

Lithium has been associated with possible long-term kidney and thyroid problems, so people taking lithium must monitor their blood levels of lithium on a regular basis. Furthermore, lithium has a precise range in which it is useful for each person, another reason it should be closely monitored with blood tests. Valproate, in contrast, does not require such careful blood monitoring. Although valproate may have side effects, it is currently the most commonly prescribed drug in the United States for bipolar disorder (Schatzberg, Cole, & DeBattista, 2003). In sum, although the antidepressants are effective for a wide variety of problems, mood stabilizers may be required when a person's symptoms include extreme swings between highs and lows, such as experienced with bipolar disorder.

Herbal and Natural Products

In a survey of more than 2,000 Americans, 7% of those suffering from anxiety disorders and 9% of those suffering from severe depression reported using alternative "medications" such as herbal medicines, megavitamins, homeopathic remedies, or naturopathic remedies to treat these problems (Kessler et al., 2001). Major reasons people use these products are that they are easily available over the counter, are less expensive, and are perceived as "natural" alternatives to "drugs." Are herbal and natural products effective in treating mental health problems, or are they just so much "snake oil"?

Why are herbal remedies used? Are they actually effective?

The answer to this question isn't simple. Herbal products are not considered medications by regulatory agencies (e.g., the U.S. Food and Drug Administration) and are exempt from rigorous research to establish their safety and effectiveness. Instead, herbal products are classified as nutritional supplements and regulated in the same way as foods. There is little scientific information

---

HOT SCIENCE

Happy Pills? Antidepressants for Ordinary Sadness

Imagine a world in which no one ever needs to be sad. Happiness, joy, and contentment are everywhere because sadness can be erased with a drug. This was the utopian vision of novelist Aldous Huxley's *Brave New World* (1932), where people of the future use *soma*, a happiness drug. After the pills were taken, "Eyes shone, cheeks were flushed, the inner light of universal benevolence broke out on every face in happy, friendly smiles." In Huxley's fictional world, soma for everyone didn't turn out so well because of unexpected side effects—the loss of anger, passion, and ambition. Could antidepressants have a similar downside in our world?

Antidepressant drugs indeed come with side effects. In the case of the tricyclics and MAOIs, these can be unpleasant and dangerous enough that people risk them only to escape debilitating depression. The SSRIs, however, have milder side effects, at least at first, and so start to seem attractive for those who are not seriously depressed and are simply hoping to feel happier. Books like *Listening to Prozac* (Kramer, 1993) suggest that these drugs can fine-tune happiness and increase the quality of life for anyone. People taking Prozac do report increased extraversion and decreased neuroticism, improvements in personality that most anyone would desire (Tang et al., 2009). Commentators are increasingly wondering if ordinary sadness should be treated

FOREWORD BY CHRISTOPHER HITCHENS

BRAVE NEW WORLD

ALDOUS HUXLEY

INCLUDING BRAVE NEW WORLD REVISITED

▲ In Huxley's novel, a drug to make people happy had unintended side effects.

BRAVE NEW WORLD © 1932, 1946 BY ALDOUS HUXLEY. BRAVE NEW WORLD REVISITED © 1958 BY ALDOUS HUXLEY. FORWARD TO THIS COMBINED EDITION BY CHRISTOPHER HITCHENS. REPRINTED BY PERMISSION OF HARPERCOLLINS PUBLISHERS.

as a psychological disorder (Horwitz & Wakefield, 2007). Should we be popping antidepressants like vitamins?

The answer is clearly *No*. It turns out that antidepressants have not just one

catch but several. The main problem is that SSRIs only increase happiness above the level that can be achieved with placebo treatment for people who are clinically depressed. You might as well be popping M&Ms from an SSRI bottle. A statistical summary of the findings of multiple studies (known as a *meta-analysis*) found that SSRIs are no better than placebo treatments for people suffering only from ordinary sadness (Fournier et al., 2010). People who are not seriously depressed, but who claim to have found new happiness with SSRI treatment, may well be responding to the improvement in hopefulness for a cure that accompanies any nonspecific treatment.

And unfortunately, side effects of SSRIs are very real (Masand & Gupta, 2002). Common initial complaints include nausea, dry mouth, and headache, which can be followed by later problems of weight gain and loss of sexual interest or ability. Interactions of SSRIs with other drugs can be serious and must be monitored—and unpleasant symptoms following discontinuation of treatment can be severe. Suicide rates do not seem to increase among SSRI users (Khan et al., 2003), which is one good thing, but risking these other side effects in return for nothing more than a placebo seems a steep price. No wonder SSRIs are called antidepressants rather than happy pills—they're only really useful if you are depressed.

► Many of the "natural" remedies and treatments available at health food and supplement stores come with little or no evidence of effectiveness and no claims for any specific benefit on the label, but the price tag is usually quite clear.

about herbal products, including possible interactions with other medications, possible tolerance and withdrawal symptoms, side effects, appropriate dosages, how they work, or even *whether* they work—and the purity of these products often varies from brand to brand (Jordan, Cunningham, & Marles, 2010).

There is some research support for the effectiveness of some herbal and natural products, but the evidence is not overwhelming (Lake, 2009). Products such as inositol (a bran derivative), kava (an herb related to black pepper), omega-3 fish oil (a fish oil), and SAM-e (an amino acid derivative) are sold as health foods and are described as having positive psychological effects of various kinds, but the evidence is mixed. For example, in the case of St. John's wort (a wort, it turns out, is an herb), some studies have shown it has an advantage over a placebo condition (e.g., Lecrubier et al., 2002), whereas others show no advantage (e.g., Hypericum Depression Trial Study Group, 2002). Although herbal medications and treatments are worthy of continued research, these products should be closely monitored and used judiciously until more is known about their safety and effectiveness. After all, a drug with no documented main effects could still have very serious side effects.

Combining Medication and Psychotherapy

Psychologists looking for effective ways to treat psychological disorders get pretty excited about the progress of drug therapy. New drugs appear with some regularity, improving on prior medications and suggesting even greater improvements to come. At the same time, as we have seen, drugs can be blunt instruments as treatment devices, producing general changes in mood or relieving unpleasant symptoms—but leaving specific problems untreated. How can we bring medication and psychotherapy together to produce comprehensive treatments?

Many studies have compared psychological treatments, medication, and combinations of these approaches for addressing psychological disorders. The results of these studies often depend on the particular problem being considered. For example, in the cases of schizophrenia and bipolar disorder, researchers have found that medication is a necessary part of treatment, and studies have tended to examine whether adding psychotherapeutic treatments such as social skills training or cognitive behavioral treatment can be helpful. In the case of anxiety disorders, medication and psychotherapy may be about equally effective. One study compared cognitive behavior therapy, imipramine (the antidepressant also known as Tofranil), and the combination of these treatments (CBT plus imipramine) with a placebo (administration of an inert medication) for the treatment of panic disorder (Barlow et al., 2000). After 12 weeks of treatment, either CBT alone or imipramine alone was found to be superior to a placebo. For the CBT-plus-imipramine condition, the response rate also exceeded the placebo one but was not significantly better than that for either CBT or imipramine alone. In other words, either treatment was better than nothing, but the combination of treatments was not significantly more effective than one or the other (see **FIGURE 15.3**).

Given that both therapy and medications are effective, one question is whether they work through similar mechanisms. A study of people with social phobia examined patterns of cerebral blood flow following treatment using either citalopram (an SSRI) or CBT (Furmark et al., 2002). Patients in both groups were alerted to the possibility that they would soon have to speak in public. In both groups, those who responded to treatment showed similar reductions in activation in the amygdala,

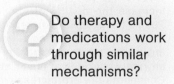

Do therapy and medications work through similar mechanisms?

"These medicines all taste pretty good—let's approve them."

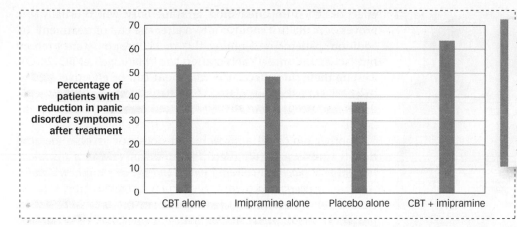

The Effectiveness of Medication and Psychotherapy for Panic Disorder One study of CBT and medication (imipramine) for panic disorder found that the effects of CBT, medication, and treatment that combined CBT and medication were not significantly different over the short term, though all three were superior to the placebo condition (Barlow et al., 2000).

hippocampus, and neighboring cortical areas during this challenge (see **FIGURE 15.4**). As you'll recall from Chapter 6, the amygdala and hippocampus play significant roles in memory for emotional information. These findings suggest that both therapy and medication affect the brain in regions associated with a reaction to threat. Although it might seem that events that influence the brain should be physical—after all, the brain is a physical object—both the physical administration of a drug and the psychological application of psychotherapy produce similar influences on the brain.

One complication in combining medication and psychotherapy is that these treatments are often provided by different people. Psychiatrists are trained in the administration of medication in medical school (and they may also provide psychotherapy), whereas psychologists provide psychotherapy but not medication. This means that the coordination of treatment often requires cooperation between psychologists and psychiatrists.

The question of whether psychologists should be licensed to prescribe medications has been a source of debate among physicians as well as among psychologists (Fox et al., 2009). Only Louisiana and New Mexico currently allow licensed and specially trained psychologists prescription privileges, but nine more states are currently considering it (Munsey, 2008). Opponents argue that psychologists do not have the medical training to understand how medications interact with other drugs. On the other hand, proponents of prescription privileges argue that patient safety would not be compromised as long as rigorous training procedures were established. This issue remains a focus of debate, so at present, the coordination of medication and psychotherapy usually involves a team effort of psychiatry and psychology.

▼ FIGURE 15.4
The Effects of Medication and Therapy in the Brain PET scans of patients with social phobia showed similar reductions in activations of the amygdala/hippocampus region after they had received treatment with CBT (shown on the left) and citalopram, an SSRI (shown on the right) (from Furmark et al., 2002).

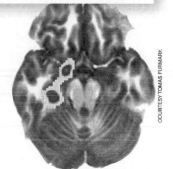

CBT   Medication

Biological Treatments beyond Medication

Medication can be an effective biological treatment, but for some people medications do not work or side effects are intolerable. If this group of people doesn't respond to psychotherapy either, what other options do they have to achieve symptom relief? Some additional avenues of help are available, but some are risky or poorly understood.

Where do people turn if medication and therapy are unsuccessful?

One example is **electroconvulsive therapy (ECT)**, more commonly known as "shock therapy," which is *a treatment that involves inducing a mild seizure by delivering an electrical shock to the brain.* The shock is applied to the person's scalp for less than a second. ECT is primarily used to treat severe depression, although it may also be useful for treating mania (Mukherjee, Sackeim, & Schnur, 1994). Patients are pretreated with muscle relaxants and are under general anesthetic, so they are not conscious of the procedure. The main side

electroconvulsive therapy (ECT) A treatment that involves inducing a mild seizure by delivering an electrical shock to the brain.

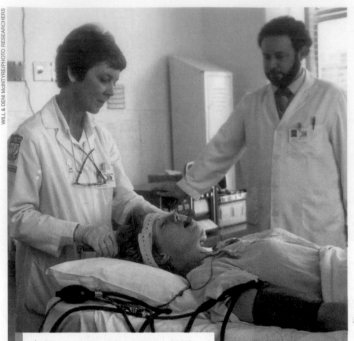

WILL & DENI McINTYRE/PHOTO RESEARCHERS

▲ Electroconvulsive therapy (ECT) can be an effective treatment for severe depression. To reduce the side effects, it is administered under general anesthesia.

effect of ECT is impaired short-term memory, which usually improves over the first month or two after the end of treatment. In addition, patients undergoing this procedure sometimes report headaches and muscle aches afterward (Marangell et al., 2003). Despite these side effects, the treatment can be effective: ECT is more effective than simulated ECT, than placebo, and than antidepressant drugs such as tricyclics and MAOIs (Pagnin et al., 2008).

Another biological approach that does not involve medication is **transcranial magnetic stimulation (TMS),** *a treatment that involves placing a powerful pulsed magnet over a person's scalp, which alters neuronal activity in the brain* (George, Lisanby, & Sackeim, 1999). As a treatment for depression, the magnet is placed just above the right or left eyebrow in an effort to stimulate the right or left prefrontal cortex—areas of the brain implicated in depression. TMS is an exciting development because it is noninvasive and has fewer side effects than ECT (see Chapter 3). Side effects are minimal; they include mild headache and small risk of seizure, but TMS has no impact on memory or concentration. TMS may be particularly useful in treating depression that is unresponsive to medication (Avery et al., 2009). In fact, a study comparing TMS to ECT found that both procedures were effective, with no significant differences between them (Janicak et al., 2002). Other studies have found that TMS can also be used to treat auditory hallucinations in schizophrenia (Aleman, Sommer, & Kahn, 2007).

Phototherapy, *a therapy that involves repeated exposure to bright light,* may be helpful to people who have a seasonal pattern to their depression. This could include people suffering with seasonal affective disorder (SAD; see Chapter 14), or those who experience depression only in the winter months due to the lack of light. Typically, the patient is exposed to bright light in the mornings, using a lamp designed for this purpose. Treatments lasting 2 hours each day for a week seem to be effective, at least in the short term (Terman et al., 1989).

In very rare cases, **psychosurgery,** *the surgical destruction of specific brain areas,* is used to treat certain psychological disorders, such as obsessive-compulsive disorder (OCD). Psychosurgery has a controversial history, beginning in the 1930s with the invention of the lobotomy by Portuguese physician Egas Moniz (1874–1955). After discovering that certain surgical procedures on animal brains calmed behavior, Moniz began to use similar techniques on violent or agitated human patients. Lobotomies involved inserting an instrument into the brain through the patient's eye socket or through holes drilled in the side of the head. The objective was to sever connections between the frontal lobes and inner brain structures such as the thalamus, known to be involved in emotion. Although some lobotomies produced highly successful results and Moniz received the 1949 Nobel Prize for his work, significant side effects such as extreme lethargy or childlike impulsivity detracted from these benefits. Lobotomy was used too widely for years, leaving many people devastated by these permanent side effects, and there is an ongoing movement challenging the award of the Nobel to Moniz. The development of antipsychotic drugs in the 1950s provided a safer way to treat violent patients and brought the practice of lobotomy to an end (Swayze II, 1995).

Today, psychosurgeries are far more precise than lobotomies of the 1930s and 1940s in targeting particular brain areas to lesion. This increased precision has produced better results. For example, patients suffering from obsessive-compulsive disorder who fail to respond to treatment (including several trials

▼ Repeated exposure to bright light has been proven to be useful for treating seasonal affective disorder, a form of depression that occurs only in the winter months, probably in reaction to reduced sunlight.

COURTESY NORTHERN LIGHT TECHNOLOGIES

of medications and cognitive behavioral treatment) may benefit from specific surgical procedures called *cingulotomy* and *anterior capsulotomy*. Cingulotomy involves destroying part of the cingulate gyrus and corpus callosum (see Chapter 3). Anterior capsulotomy involves creating small lesions to disrupt the pathway between the caudate nucleus and putamen. Long-term follow-up studies suggest that more than a quarter of patients with OCD who do not respond to standard treatments report significant benefit following psychosurgery, with relatively few side effects (Baer et al., 1995; Cumming et al., 1995; Hay et al., 1993). However, due to the intrusive nature of psychosurgery and a lack of controlled studies, these procedures are currently reserved for the most severe cases.

◄ Rosemary Kennedy, sister of President John F. Kennedy, was intellectually challenged from childhood and had violent tantrums and rages that began in her early 20s. Her family agreed to her treatment with a lobotomy at St. Elizabeth's Hospital in Washington, DC, in 1942, but it went very wrong. She became permanently paralyzed on one side, incontinent, and unable to speak coherently, and she spent the rest of her life in institutions.

UNDERWOOD & UNDERWOOD/CORBIS

Psychosurgery can also be used nondestructively. In a treatment pioneered only recently, a small, battery-powered device is implanted in the brain to deliver *deep brain stimulation*. This technique has been successful for OCD treatment (Abelson et al., 2009) and can provide benefits for people with a variety of neurologic conditions. The tremor that accompanies Parkinson's disease has proven to be treatable in this way (Perlmutter & Mink, 2006), as have some cases of severe depression that are otherwise untreatable (Mayberg et al., 2005). The early view of psychosurgery as a treatment of last resort is being replaced by a cautious hope that certain direct interventions in the brain can have beneficial effects.

IN SUMMARY

- ○ Medications have been developed to treat many psychological disorders, including antipsychotic medications (used to treat schizophrenia and psychotic disorders), antianxiety medications (used to treat anxiety disorders), and antidepressants (used to treat depression and related disorders).

- ○ Medications are often combined with psychotherapy.

- ○ Other biomedical treatments include electroconvulsive therapy (ECT), transcranial magnetic stimulation (TMS), and psychosurgery—this last used in extreme cases, when other methods of treatment have been exhausted.

Treatment Effectiveness: For Better or for Worse

Think back to our fearful flyer Lisa at the beginning of the chapter. What if, instead of virtual reality therapy, Lisa had been assigned by her therapist to a drug treatment or to psychosurgery? For that matter, what if her therapy was to walk around for a week wearing a large false nose? Could these alternatives have been just as effective for treating her phobia? Through this chapter, we have explored various psychological and biomedical treatments that may help people with psychological disorders. But do these treatments actually work, and which ones work better than the others?

As you learned in Chapter 2, pinning down a specific cause for an effect can be a difficult detective exercise. The detection is made even more difficult because people may approach treatment evaluation very unscientifically, often by simply noticing an improvement (or no improvement or that dreaded decline) and reaching a conclusion based on that sole observation. Treatment evaluation can be susceptible to illusions that can only be overcome by scientific evaluation of the effectiveness of treatments.

transcranial magnetic stimulation (TMS) A treatment that involves placing a powerful pulsed magnet over a person's scalp, which alters neuronal activity in the brain.

phototherapy A therapy that involves repeated exposure to bright light.

psychosurgery Surgical destruction of specific brain areas.

Treatment Illusions

Imagine you're sick and the doctor says, "Take a pill." You follow the doctor's orders, and you get better. To what do you attribute your improvement? If you're like most people, you reach the conclusion that the pill cured you. How could this be an illusion? There are at least three ways: Maybe you would have gotten better any-

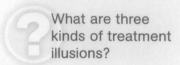 **What are three kinds of treatment illusions?**

way; maybe the pill wasn't the active ingredient in your cure; or maybe after you're better, you mistakenly remember having been more ill than you really were. These possibilities point to three potential illusions of treatment—illusions produced by natural improvement, by nonspecific treatment effects, and by reconstructive memory.

Natural improvement is the tendency of symptoms to return to their mean or average level. The illusion in this case happens when you conclude mistakenly that a treatment has made you better when you would have gotten better anyway. People typically turn to therapy or medication when their symptoms are at their worst, so they start their personal "experiment" to see if treatment makes them improve at a time when things couldn't get much worse. When this is the case, the client's symptoms will often improve regardless of whether there was any treatment at all; when you're at rock bottom, there's nowhere to move but up. In most cases, for example, depression that becomes severe enough to make a person a candidate for treatment will tend to lift in several months. A person who enters therapy for depression may develop an illusion that the therapy works because the therapy coincides with the typical course of the illness and the person's natural return to health.

Another treatment illusion occurs when a client or therapist attributes the client's improvement to a feature of treatment, although that feature wasn't really the active element that caused improvement. Recovery could be produced by *nonspecific treatment effects* that are not related to the specific mechanisms by which treatment is supposed to be working. For example, the doctor prescribing the medication might simply be a pleasant and hopeful individual who gives the client a sense that things will improve. Client and doctor alike might attribute the client's improvement to the effects of medication on the brain, whereas the true active ingredient was the warm relationship with the good doctor.

Simply knowing that you are getting a treatment can be a nonspecific treatment effect. These instances include the positive influences that can be produced by a **placebo**, *an inert substance or procedure that has been applied with the expectation that a healing response will be produced.* For example, if you take a sugar pill that does not contain any painkiller for a headache thinking it is Tylenol or aspirin, this pill is a placebo. Placebos can have profound effects in the case of psychological treatments. Research shows that a large percentage of individu-

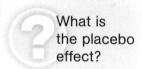 **What is the placebo effect?**

als with anxiety, depression, and other emotional problems experience significant improvement after a placebo treatment. Chapter 16 further discusses how placebo effects may occur as well as their influence on the brain.

One study compared the decrease in symptoms of obsessive-compulsive disorder between adolescents taking Prozac (fluoxetine) and those taking a placebo (Geller et al., 2001). Participants receiving medication showed a dramatic decrease in symptoms over the course of the 13-week study. Those taking a placebo also showed a reduction in symptoms, and the difference between the Prozac and placebo groups only became significant in the seventh week of treatment (see **FIGURE 15.5**). In fact, some psychologists estimate that up to 75% of the effects shown by antidepressant medications are due to the placebo effect (Kirsch & Sapirstein, 1998).

A third treatment illusion can come about when the client's motivation to get well causes errors in *reconstructive memory* for the original symptoms. You might think that you've improved because of a treatment when in fact you're simply misremembering—mistakenly believing that your symptoms before treatment were worse than they actually were. This tendency was first observed in research examining the effectiveness

"If this doesn't help you don't worry, it's a placebo."

P. C. VEY/THE NEW YORKER COLLECTION/CARTOONBANK.COM

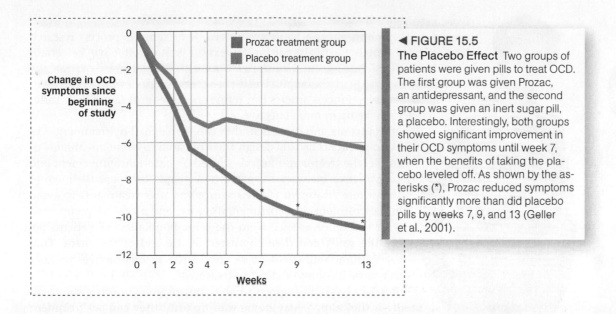

◄ **FIGURE 15.5**
The Placebo Effect Two groups of patients were given pills to treat OCD. The first group was given Prozac, an antidepressant, and the second group was given an inert sugar pill, a placebo. Interestingly, both groups showed significant improvement in their OCD symptoms until week 7, when the benefits of taking the placebo leveled off. As shown by the asterisks (*), Prozac reduced symptoms significantly more than did placebo pills by weeks 7, 9, and 13 (Geller et al., 2001).

of a study skills class (Conway & Ross, 1984). Some students who wanted to take the class were enrolled, while others were randomly assigned to a waiting list until the class could be offered again. When their study abilities were measured afterward, those students who took the class were no better at studying than their wait-listed counterparts. However, those who took the class *said* that they had improved. How could this be? Those participants recalled their study skills before the class as being worse than they actually had been. This motivated reconstruction of the past was dubbed by the researchers "getting what you want by revising what you had" (Conway & Ross, 1984). A client who forms a strong expectation of success in therapy might conclude later that even a useless treatment had worked wonders—by recalling past symptoms and troubles as worse than they were and thereby making the treatment seem effective.

A person who enters treatment is often anxious to get well and so may be especially likely to succumb to errors and illusions in assessing the effectiveness of the treatment. Treatments can look as if they worked when illusions lead us to ignore natural improvement, to overlook nonspecific treatment effects (e.g., the placebo effect), and to reconstruct our pretreatment history as worse than it was. Such treatment illusions can be overcome by using scientific methods to evaluate treatments—rather than trusting only our potentially faulty personal skills of observation.

Treatment Studies

How can treatment be evaluated in a way that allows us to choose treatments that work and not waste time with procedures that may be useless or even harmful? Treatment studies depend generally on the research design concepts covered in Chapter 2 but also depend on some ideas that are unique to the evaluation of psychological treatments.

There are two main types of treatment studies: outcome studies and process studies. *Outcome studies* are designed to evaluate *whether* a particular treatment works, often in relation to some other treatment or a control condition. For example, to study the outcome of treatment for depression, researchers might compare the self-reported moods and symptoms of two groups of people who were initially depressed—those who had received a treatment for 6 weeks and a control group who had also been selected for the study but had been assigned to a waiting list for later treatment and were simply tested 6 weeks after their selection. The outcome study could determine whether this treatment had any benefit.

placebo An inert substance or procedure that has been applied with the expectation that a healing response will be produced.

Process studies are designed to answer questions regarding *why* a treatment works or under what circumstances a treatment works. For example, process research might examine whether a treatment for depression is more effective for certain clients than others. Process studies also can examine whether some parts of the treatment are particularly helpful, whereas others are irrelevant to the treatment's success. Process studies can refine therapies and target their influence to make them more effective.

Both outcome and process studies can be plagued by treatment illusions, so scientists usually design their research to overcome them. For example, the treatment illusions caused by natural improvement and reconstructive memory happen when people compare their symptoms before treatment to their symptoms after treatment. To avoid this, a treatment (or experimental) group and a control group need to be randomly selected from the same population of patients before the study and then compared at the end of treatment. That way, natural improvement or motivated reconstructive memory can't cause illusions of effective treatment.

But what should happen to the control group during the treatment? If they simply stay home waiting until they can get treatment later (a wait-list control group), they won't receive the nonspecific effects of the treatment that the treatment group enjoys (such as visiting the comforting therapist or taking a medication). So, ideally, a treatment should be assessed in a *double blind experiment*—a study in which both the patient and the researcher/therapist are uninformed about which treatment the patient is receiving (see Chapter 2). In the case of drug studies, this isn't hard to arrange because active drugs and placebos can be made to look alike to both the patients and the researchers during the study. Keeping both patients and researchers "in the dark" is much harder in the study of psychotherapy; in fact, it may even be impossible. Both the patient and the therapist can easily notice the differences in treatments such as psychoanalysis and behavior therapy, for example, so there's no way to keep the beliefs and expectations of both patient and therapist out of the picture in evaluating psychotherapy effectiveness.

? Why is a double blind experiment so important in assessing treatment effectiveness?

▲ Many psychological disorders don't play favorites with one gender or the other, but anxiety and depression are more common for women than for men.

COLLEEN CAHILL/AGEFOTOSTOCK

Which Treatments Work?

The distinguished psychologist Hans Eysenck (1916–97) reviewed the relatively few studies of psychotherapy effectiveness available in 1957 and raised a furor among therapists by concluding that psychotherapy—particularly psychoanalysis—not only was ineffective but seemed to *impede* recovery (Eysenck, 1957). Much larger numbers of

TABLE 15.3

Some Well-Established Psychological Treatments

Type of Treatment	Patient's Problem
Cognitive behavior therapy	Panic disorder with and without agoraphobia
Cognitive therapy	Depression
Cognitive therapy	Bulimia
Interpersonal therapy	Depression
Behavior therapy (exposure and response prevention)	Obsessive-compulsive disorder
Behavior therapy	Childhood enuresis (bed wetting)
Behavior therapy	Marital difficulties

studies have been examined statistically since then, and they support a more optimistic conclusion: The typical psychotherapy client is better off than three quarters of untreated individuals (Seligman, 1995; Smith, Glass, & Miller, 1980). Although critiques of psychotherapy continue to point out weaknesses in how patients are tested, diagnosed, and treated (Baker, McFall, & Shoham, 2009; Dawes, 1994), strong evidence generally supports the effectiveness of many treatments (Nathan & Gorman, 2007), including psychodynamic therapy (Shedler, 2010). The key question then becomes, Which treatments are effective for which problems (Hunsley & Di Giulio, 2002)?

? What is the current thinking about the effectiveness of psychotherapy?

One of the most enduring debates in clinical psychology concerns how the various psychotherapies compare to one another. Some psychologists have argued for years that evidence supports the conclusion that most psychotherapies work about equally well. In this view, it is the nonspecific factors shared by all forms of psychotherapy, such as contact with and empathy from a professional, that contribute to change (Luborsky et al., 2002; Luborsky & Singer, 1975). In contrast, others have argued that there are important differences among therapies and that certain treatments are more effective than others, especially for treating particular types of problems (Beutler, 2002; Hunsley & Di Giulio, 2002). Yet others have noted that some treatments such as long-term psychodynamic therapy are not easily studied, because of the difficulty of establishing a control group and because the therapy typically takes a long time—but this doesn't mean that psychotherapy may not be effective nonetheless.

In 1995, the American Psychological Association (APA) published one of the first attempts to define criteria for determining whether a particular type of psychotherapy is effective for a particular problem (Task Force on Promotion and Dissemination of Psychological Procedures, 1995). The official criteria for empirically validated treatments defined two levels of empirical support: *well-established treatments,* those with a high level of support, and *probably efficacious treatments,* those with preliminary support. After these criteria were established, a list of empirically supported treatments was published by the APA (Chambless et al., 1998; Woody & Sanderson, 1998). **TABLES 15.3** and **15.4** show examples of each kind of treatment.

Even trickier than the question of establishing whether a treatment works is whether a psychotherapy or medication might actually do damage. The dangers of drug treatment should be clear to anyone who has read a magazine ad for a drug—and studied the fine print with its list of side effects, potential drug interactions, and complications.

TABLE 15.4

Some Probably Efficacious Psychological Treatments

Type of Treatment	Patient's Problem
Behavior therapy	Cocaine abuse
Brief psychodynamic therapy	Opiate dependence
Cognitive behavior therapy	Opiate dependence
Brief psychodynamic therapy	Depression
Interpersonal therapy	Bulimia
Behavior therapy	Offensive sexual behavior

iatrogenic illness A disorder or symptom that occurs as a result of a medical or psychotherapeutic treatment.

Many drugs used for psychological treatment may be addictive, creating long-term dependency with serious withdrawal symptoms. The strongest critics of drug treatment claim that drugs do no more than trade one unwanted symptom for another—trading depression for sexual disinterest, anxiety for intoxication, or agitation for lethargy and dulled emotion (see, e.g., Breggin, 2000).

The dangers of psychotherapy are more subtle, but one is clear enough in some cases that there is actually a name for it: **Iatrogenic illness** is *a disorder or symptom that occurs as a result of a medical or psychotherapeutic treatment itself* (e.g., Boisvert & Faust, 2002). Such an illness might arise, for example, when a psychotherapist becomes convinced that a client has a disorder that in fact the client does not have. As a result, the therapist works to help the client accept that diagnosis and participate in psychotherapy to treat that disorder. Being treated for a disorder can, under certain conditions, make a person show signs of that very disorder—and so an iatrogenic illness is born.

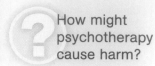

How might psychotherapy cause harm?

There are cases of patients who have been influenced through hypnosis and repeated suggestions in therapy to believe that they have dissociative identity disorder (even coming to express multiple personalities) or to believe that they were subjected to traumatic events as a child and "recover" memories of such events when investigation reveals no evidence for these problems prior to therapy (Acocella, 1999; McNally, 2003; Ofshe & Watters, 1994). There are people who have entered therapy with a vague sense that something odd has happened to them and who emerge after hypnosis or other imagination-enhancing techniques with the conviction that their therapist's theory was right: They were abducted by space aliens (Clancy, 2005). Needless to say, a therapy that leads patients to develop such bizarre beliefs is doing more harm than good.

To regulate the potentially powerful influence of therapies, psychologists hold themselves to a set of ethical standards for the treatment of people with mental disorders (American Psychological Association, 2002). Adherence to these standards is required for membership in the American Psychological Association, and state licensing boards also monitor adherence to ethical principles in therapy. These ethical standards include (1) striving to benefit clients and taking care to do no harm; (2) establishing relationships of trust with clients; (3) promoting accuracy, honesty, and truthfulness; (4) seeking fairness in treatment and taking precautions to avoid biases; and (5) respecting the dignity and worth of all people. When people suffering from mental disorders come to psychologists for help, adhering to these guidelines is the least that psychologists can do. Ideally, in the hope of relieving this suffering, they can do much more.

IN SUMMARY

○ Observing improvement during treatment does not necessarily mean that the treatment was effective; it might instead reflect natural improvement, nonspecific treatment effects (e.g., the placebo effect), and reconstructive memory processes.

○ Treatment studies focus on both treatment outcomes and processes, using scientific research methods such as double blind techniques and placebo controls.

○ Treatments for psychological disorders are generally more effective than no treatment at all, but some are more effective than others for certain disorders, and both medication and psychotherapy have dangers that ethical practitioners must consider carefully.

WhereDoYouStand?

Is Online Psychotherapy a Good Idea?

If you're on the Internet and have an hour and a credit card, you can get psychotherapy right now. Online psychotherapy, or e-therapy, is offered by dozens of web services—therapy by e-mail, live chat, message posting, interactive blogging, and more. Yes, you can be old fashioned and get therapy by phone—but better yet, switch on your laptop camera for a *Skype* videoconference with a therapist, or create an avatar for yourself and get therapy in the *Second Life* virtual world.

An avatar might be a bit much, but some of this sounds like a great idea. E-therapy is as convenient as the nearest online computer, and there's something enticing about therapy you get at your own pace and in your own space. In addition, e-therapy can be less expensive than standard therapy and offers greater anonymity. For those who live far from a therapist, e-therapy may be the only way to get the help you want.

So what's the downside? There are several. In fact, the rapid growth of e-therapy has led to rapid growth in debate about its ethics and effectiveness (Abbott, Klein, & Ciechomski, 2008; Childress, 2000; Humphreys, Winzelberg, & Klaw, 2000). It's not easy to judge the trustworthiness of a website selling hubcaps, after all, let alone one offering psychological services that could change your life. You should be careful to learn the therapist's credentials and find out what the therapist

is likely to do, just as you would offline (see the Real World box on types of psychotherapists, p. 592). When you find the right therapist, e-therapy can be effective (e.g., Germain et al., 2009)—but you should be aware that it has some shortcomings.

Electronic communication usually requires skills at reading and keyboarding, and also means you must bridge the gap from onscreen messages to understanding a real, live human. With e-therapy (unless you're on video), you lose the nonverbal communication that usually helps you understand a person's meaning and genuineness—tone of voice, gestures, facial expressions, and those hard-to-describe nuances that really let people know each other. E-therapy can also be awkward as client and therapist take turns without immediate feedback, and it can be hard for a therapist to recognize and intervene in crisis situations (Rochlen, Zack, & Speyer, 2004). On top of all this, there is also the *online disinhibition effect* (Suler, 2004): People online seem to self-disclose more deeply and act on impulse more frequently than they would in person. For a therapist trying to discern a client's true feelings and offer help, such online "flaming" can tangle communication.

So is psychotherapy online a good way to get people convenient help? Or is it a poor substitute for real therapy that may cause miscommunication and undermine psychological health? Where do you stand?

Chapter Review

KEY CONCEPT QUIZ

1. Which of the following is NOT a reason why people fail to get treatment for mental illness?
   a. People may not realize that their disorder needs to be treated.
   b. Levels of impairment for people with mental illness are comparable to or higher than those of people with chronic medical illnesses.
   c. There may be barriers to treatment, such as beliefs and circumstances that keep people from getting help.
   d. Even people who acknowledge they have a problem may not know where to look for services.

2. Eclectic psychotherapy involves
   a. a concentration on the interpretation of dreams.
   b. introducing patients to strange situations.
   c. drawing on techniques from different forms of therapy.
   d. the analysis of resistance.

3. The different psychodynamic therapies all share an emphasis on
   a. the influence of the collective unconscious.
   b. the importance of taking responsibility for psychological problems.
   c. combining behavioral and cognitive approaches.
   d. developing insight into the unconscious sources of psychological disorders.

4. Which psychoanalytic technique involves the client reporting every thought that enters his or her mind, without censorship or filtering?
   a. transference
   b. free association
   c. interpretation
   d. resistance analysis

5. Which type of therapy would likely work best for someone with an irrational fear of heights?
   a. psychodynamic
   b. cognitive
   c. behavioral
   d. humanistic

6. Mindfulness meditation is part of which kind of therapy?
   a. interpersonal
   b. humanistic
   c. behavioral
   d. cognitive

7. Which type of therapy emphasizes action on the part of the patient, as well as complete transparency as to the specifics of the treatment?
   a. cognitive behavioral
   b. humanistic
   c. existential
   d. group

8. Examining the failure to reach one's potential reflects the _____ approach while examining one's failure to find meaning in life reflects the _____ approach.
   a. cognitive; behavioral
   b. humanistic; existential
   c. psychodynamic; cognitive behavioral
   d. existential; humanistic

9. Self-help groups are an important offshoot of
   a. cognitive behavioral therapy.
   b. support groups.
   c. person-centered therapy.
   d. group therapy.

10. Antipsychotic drugs were developed to treat
    a. depression.
    b. schizophrenia.
    c. anxiety.
    d. mood disorders.

11. Atypical antipsychotic drugs
    a. act on different neurotransmitters depending on the patient.
    b. affect only the dopamine system.

c. affect only the serotonin system.
d. act on both the dopamine and serotonin systems.

12. Which of the following statements is NOT accurate regarding antidepressants?
    a. Current antidepressants act on combinations of different neurotransmitter systems.
    b. Antidepressants have had significantly positive results in the treatment of bipolar disorder.
    c. Antidepressants are also prescribed to treat anxiety.
    d. Most antidepressants can take up to a month before they start to have an effect on mood.

13. What do electroconvulsive therapy, transcranial magnetic stimulation, and phototherapy all have in common?
    a. They incorporate herbal remedies in their treatment regimens.
    b. They may result in the surgical destruction of certain brain areas.
    c. They are considered biological treatments beyond medication.
    d. They are typically used in conjunction with psychotherapy.

14. Which treatment illusion occurs when a client or therapist attributes the client's improvement to a feature of treatment, although that feature wasn't really the active element that caused improvement?
    a. nonspecific treatment effects
    b. natural improvement
    c. error in reconstructive memory
    d. regression to the mean

15. Current studies indicate that the typical psychotherapy client is better off than _____ of untreated individuals.
    a. one half
    b. the same number
    c. one fourth
    d. three fourths

KEY TERMS

psychotherapy (p. 594)

eclectic psychotherapy (p. 594)

psychodynamic psychotherapies (p. 594)

resistance (p. 595)

transference (p. 596)

interpersonal psychotherapy (IPT) (p. 596)

behavior therapy (p. 597)

token economy (p. 598)

exposure therapy (p. 598)

systematic desensitization (p. 598)

cognitive therapy (p. 599)

cognitive restructuring (p. 599)

mindfulness mediation (p. 600)

cognitive behavioral therapy (CBT) (p. 600)

person-centered therapy (p. 601)

Gestalt therapy (p. 602)

group therapy (p. 604)

antipsychotic drugs (p. 606)

psychopharmacology (p. 606)

antianxiety medications (p. 608)

antidepressants (p. 609)

electroconvulsive therapy (ECT) (p. 613)

transcranial magnetic stimulation (TMS) (p. 614)

phototherapy (p. 614)

psychosurgery (p. 614)

placebo (p. 616)

iatrogenic illness (p. 620)

CRITICAL THINKING QUESTIONS

1. Psychodynamic psychotherapies focus on exploring childhood events to understand current psychological problems. In contrast, behavioral therapy assumes that disordered behavior is learned and that symptom relief is achieved through changing behaviors, sometimes through conditioning principles, while cognitive therapies use cognitive restructuring to teach clients to replace negative thinking with more realistic and positive beliefs.

   Suppose a young man comes to visit a therapist, reporting that he's been extremely depressed since the death of his mother, who raised him single-handedly after his father died; it's been over a year since her death, but the man is still experiencing extreme sadness and hopelessness, as well as loss of appetite and trouble sleeping.

   How might a psychologist who follows each of the above systems begin therapy?

2. Some antidepressant medications, called benzodiazepines, work by facilitating the action of the neurotransmitter GABA, which inhibits certain types of neurons in the brain.

   Back in Chapter 5, you read about a widely used, legally available psychoactive drug that also increases GABA. What was it? How are the effects of this drug similar to those of the benzodiazepines?

3. Treatment illusions occur when an individual's improvement is mistakenly attributed to a treatment for a mental disorder.

   Suppose you experience a severe panic attack every time you walk into your organic chemistry class; the symptoms are so bad that you can't concentrate on the lesson, and you're sure you'll fail the class. You visit a psychiatrist, who prescribes an antianxiety medication. The next time you attend the class, you feel much calmer and more confident. Possibly, the medication is causing chemical changes in your brain that are resulting in a reduction of anxiety. But name three other ways in which treatment illusions could be responsible for your reduction in symptoms.

RECOMMENDED READINGS

Drummond, E. H. (2006). *The complete guide to psychiatric drugs: Straight talk for best results* (rev. and exp. ed.). Hoboken, NJ: Wiley.

This book is aimed at the consumer who is taking medication to deal with a psychological problem. It provides information to help make the decision, reviews which medications work for which problems, and offers practical advice about medication use.

El-Hai, J. (2005). *The lobotomist: A maverick medical genius and his tragic quest to rid the world of mental illness.* New York: Wiley.

This biography of Dr. Walter Freeman, an American physician who promoted the use of lobotomies as a treatment for all kinds of mental illness, sheds light on the darker history of psychiatry and medical approaches to treating psychological disorders.

Gurman, A. S., & Messer, S. B. (Eds.). (2003). *Essential psychotherapies* (2nd ed.). New York: Guilford Press.

This is a great book for those interested in learning more about different types of psychotherapy.

Lilienfeld, S. O., Lynn, S. J., & Lohr, J. M. (Eds.). (2003). *Science and pseudoscience in clinical psychology.* New York: Guilford Press.

A rigorous examination of techniques used in psychological assessment and therapy that are popular and influential but are also somewhat controversial, often lacking strong research to back them up.

ANSWERS TO KEY CONCEPT QUIZ

1. b; 2. c; 3. d; 4. b; 5. c; 6. d; 7. a; 8. b; 9. d; 10. b; 11. d; 12. b; 13. c; 14. a; 15. d.

Need more help? Additional resources are located at the book's free companion Web site at: **www.worthpublishers.com/schacter**

16

Stress and Health

---○---

The 53-year-old patient was semi-comatose with severe bronchial asthma when he was admitted to a hospital on July 13, 1960. Mr. X (fortunately, not his real name) was treated and discharged symptom-free after a few days and went directly to his mother's home—where, in a matter of hours, he was wheezing so badly that he arrived back at the hospital in near-terminal condition. After two more severe attacks at his mother's house, a psychotherapist recommended that he not visit his mother again. A month later, Mr. X phoned his mother. He was found an hour later blue and gasping for breath and was pronounced dead shortly thereafter.

How did Mr. X die? The autopsy report cited heart damage from lack of oxygen as the cause of death, but interviews with his family and doctors revealed a more complicated story (Mathis, 1964). His first asthma attack had occurred shortly after he received a profitable offer for the family business and told his mother he wanted to sell. His mother was upset, but, urged on by his wife, he decided to take the offer. In an angry confrontation, his mother said, "Do this and something dire will happen to you." Two days later he had his first incident of mild wheezing. His asthma became much worse after the business was sold, and during his many hospitalizations, Mr. X came to recognize that his troubles might be due to fear of his mother's curse. On the day of his death, he expressed the belief that he was "allergic" to his mother and worried that her past predictions had been infallible. In the telephone conversation that preceded his death, he told his mother that he thought he was getting better. She replied by repeating her warning of "dire results."

▶ Imagine that someone ordered an authentic voodoo doll from New Orleans, named it after you, and started sticking it with pins in your presence. Even if you didn't believe in curses at all, might this be stressful?

iSTOCKPHOTO

CAN A PERSON LITERALLY BE FRIGHTENED TO DEATH? Perhaps. The case of Mr. X resembles the phenomenon of "voodoo death" examined by physiologist Walter B. Cannon (1942). Cannon reviewed reports from around the world—often from traditional cultures in which death curses are taken very seriously—and found evidence for a profound connection between mind and body. Just as physical trauma can cause reduced blood pressure, rapid shallow pulse, and the deprivation of oxygen to the body's vital organs, so great fear can evoke physiological reactions that eventually result in death. Although such deaths are rare and their causes are always open to interpretation, the case of Mr. X shows how harm to the mind may provoke illness of the body.

Now, on an average day, you probably don't get a death curse from your mom. But modern life can present a welter of frights, bothers, and looming disasters that might make a nasty call from a loved one almost a relief. A wild driver may challenge your rights as a pedestrian, a band of evil professors may impose impossible project deadlines, or a fire may leave you out on the street. Perhaps it's just the really, really awful weather. Life has its **stressors**, *specific events or chronic pressures that place demands on a person or threaten the person's well-being.* Although such stressors rarely result in sudden death, they do have both immediate and cumulative effects that can influence health.

In this chapter, we'll look at what psychologists and physicians have learned about the kinds of life events that produce **stress**, *the physical and psychological response to internal or external stressors;* typical responses to such stressors; and ways to manage stress. Stress has such a profound influence on health that we consider stress and health together in this chapter. And because sickness and health are not merely features of the physical body, we then consider the more general topic of **health psychology**, *the subfield of psychology concerned with ways psychological factors influence the causes and treatment of physical illness and the maintenance of health.* You will see how perceptions of illness can affect its course and how health-promoting behaviors can improve the quality of people's lives.

Sources of Stress: What Gets to You

First of all, what are the sources of stress? A natural catastrophe, such as a hurricane, earthquake, or volcanic eruption, is an obvious source. But, for most of us, stressors are personal events that affect the comfortable pattern of our lives and little annoyances that bug us day after day. Let's look at the life events that can cause stress, chronic sources of stress, and the relationship between lack of perceived control and the impact of stressors.

Stressful Events

People often seem to get sick after major life events. In pioneering work, Thomas Holmes and Richard Rahe (1967) followed up on this observation, proposing that major life changes cause stress and that increased stress causes illness. To test their idea, they asked people to rate the magnitude of readjustment required by each of many events found to be associated with the onset of illness (Rahe et al., 1964). The resulting list of life events is remarkably predictive: Simply adding up the degree of life change for a person is a significant indicator of the person's future illness (Miller, 1996). A person who is divorced and loses a job and has a friend die all in a year, for example, is more likely to get sick than one who escapes the year with only a divorce.

A version of this list adapted for the life events of college students (and sporting the snappy acronym CUSS, for College Undergraduate Stress Scale) is shown in **TABLE 16.1**.

stressors Specific events or chronic pressures that place demands on a person or threaten the person's well-being.

stress The physical and psychological response to internal or external stressors.

health psychology The subfield of psychology concerned with ways psychological factors influence the causes and treatment of physical illness and the maintenance of health.

TABLE 16.1

College Undergraduate Stress Scale

Event	Stress Rating	Event	Stress Rating
Being raped	100	Talking in front of class	72
Finding out that you are HIV positive	100	Lack of sleep	69
Being accused of rape	98	Change in housing situation (hassles, moves)	69
Death of a close friend	97	Competing or performing in public	69
Death of a close family member	96	Getting in a physical fight	66
Contracting a sexually transmitted disease (other than AIDS)	94	Difficulties with a roommate	66
		Job changes (applying, new job, work hassles)	65
Concerns about being pregnant	91	Declaring a major or concerns about future plans	65
Finals week	90	A class you hate	62
Concerns about your partner being pregnant	90	Drinking or use of drugs	61
Oversleeping for an exam	89	Confrontations with professors	60
Flunking a class	89	Starting a new semester	58
Having a boyfriend or girlfriend cheat on you	85	Going on a first date	57
Ending a steady dating relationship	85	Registration	55
Serious illness in a close friend or family member	85	Maintaining a steady dating relationship	55
Financial difficulties	84	Commuting to campus or work or both	54
Writing a major term paper	83	Peer pressures	53
Being caught cheating on a test	83	Being away from home for the first time	53
Drunk driving	82	Getting sick	52
Sense of overload in school or work	82	Concerns about your appearance	52
Two exams in one day	80	Getting straight A's	51
Cheating on your boyfriend or girlfriend	77	A difficult class that you love	48
Getting married	76	Making new friends; getting along with friends	47
Negative consequences of drinking or drug use	75	Fraternity or sorority rush	47
Depression or crisis in your best friend	73	Falling asleep in class	40
Difficulties with parents	73	Attending an athletic event	20

Source: Renner & Mackin (1998). *Note:* To compute your personal life change score, sum the stress ratings for all events that have happened to you in the last year.

To assess your stressful events, check off any events that have happened to you in the past year and sum your point total. In a large sample of students in an introductory psychology class, the average was 1,247 points, ranging from 182 to 2,571 (Renner & Mackin, 1998).

Where are you on the stress scale?

Looking at the list, you may wonder why positive events are included. Stressful life events are unpleasant, right? Why would getting married be stressful? Isn't a wedding supposed to be fun? Research has shown that compared with negative events, positive events produce less

► Students under stress. When you signed up for college, did they mention walking to early morning exams in the cold? Probably not.

psychological distress and fewer physical symptoms (McFarlane et al., 1980), and the happiness can sometimes even counteract the effects of negative events (Fredrickson, 2000). However, positive events often require readjustment and preparedness that many people find extremely stressful (e.g., Brown & McGill, 1989), so these events are included in computing life-change scores.

Chronic Stressors

Life would be simpler if an occasional stressful event such as a wedding or a lost job were the only pressure we faced. At least each event would be limited in scope, with a beginning, a middle, and, ideally, an end. But unfortunately, life brings with it continued exposure to **chronic stressors,** *sources of stress that occur continuously or repeatedly.* Strained relationships, long lines at the supermarket, nagging relatives, overwork, money troubles—small stressors that may be easy to ignore if they happen only occasionally can accumulate to produce distress and illness. People who report having a lot of daily hassles also report more psychological symptoms (Kanner et al., 1981) and physical symptoms (Delongis et al., 1982), and these effects often have a greater and longer-lasting impact than major life events.

Many chronic stressors are linked to particular environments. For example, features of city life—noise, traffic, crowding, pollution, and even the threat of violence—provide particularly insistent sources of chronic stress. Rural areas have their own chronic stressors, of course, especially isolation and lack of access to amenities such as health care. The realization that chronic stressors are linked to environments has spawned the subfield *environmental psychology,* the scientific study of environmental effects on behavior and health.

What are some examples of environmental factors that cause chronic stress?

"I can't find that much hair in a drain and not see stress issues."

In one study of the influence of noise on children, environmental psychologists looked at the impact of attending schools under the flight path to Los Angeles International Airport. Did the noise of more than 300 jets flying overhead each day have an influence beyond making kids yell to be heard? Compared with children matched for race, economic background, and ethnicity who attended nearby schools away from the noise, children going to school in the flight path had higher blood pressure and gave up more easily when working on difficult problems and puzzles (Cohen et al., 1980). Next time you fly into LA, please try to do so more quietly for the children.

chronic stressor A source of stress that occurs continuously or repeatedly.

CULTURE & COMMUNITY

Can being the target of discrimination cause stress and illness?

It is difficult to be a stranger in a strange land. It's even worse if the people in this land discriminate against you. In a study by Suarez-Morales and Lopez (2009), preadolescents in Miami–Dade County, Florida, who had immigrated from Cuba and other Hispanic cultures were asked to report whether they had experienced discrimination in the United States (agreeing, e.g., that "Because of the group I am in, I don't get the grades I deserve"). Those who reported discrimination also reported higher levels of worrying, anxiety, and bodily symptoms of stress.

You might wonder whether the discrimination caused the stress symptoms or whether there is some other causal connection. For example, maybe people who complain about problems in one area tend to complain about other problems as well. Studies looking at which comes first—suffering discrimination or experiencing health problems—show that discrimination is indeed the culprit (Pascoe & Richman, 2009). Being a stranger in a strange land can make you sick.

CUBAN ~ AMERICAN

TONY MENDOZA

Perceived Control over Stressful Events

What do death curses, catastrophes, stressful life changes, and daily hassles have in common? Right off the bat, of course, their threat to the person or the status quo is easy to see. Stressors challenge you to *do something*—to take some action to eliminate or overcome the stressor.

Paradoxically, events are most stressful when there is *nothing to do*—no way to deal with the challenge. Expecting that you will have control over what happens to you is associated with effectiveness in dealing with stress. Researchers David Glass and Jerome Singer (1972), in classic studies of *perceived control,* looked

? What makes events stressful?

at the aftereffects of loud noise on people who could or could not control it. Participants were asked to solve puzzles and proofread in a quiet room or in a room filled with noise as loud as that in classrooms under the LA flight path. Glass and Singer found that bursts of such noise hurt people's performance on the tasks after the noise was over. However, this dramatic decline in performance was prevented among participants who were told during the noise period that they could stop the noise just by pushing a button. They didn't actually take this option, but access to the "panic button" shielded them from the detrimental effects of the noise.

Subsequent studies have found that a lack of perceived control underlies other stressors too. The stressful effects of crowding, for example, appear to stem from the feeling that you can't control getting away from the crowded conditions (Sherrod, 1974). Being jammed into a crowded dormitory room may be easier to handle, after all, the moment you realize you could take a walk and get away from it all.

▼ When the cabin attendant announces that "we have a full cabin on this flight," conditions can be stressful not so much because of the crowding, but because there is no obvious control over the crowding. Taking control, for example, by keeping busy or wearing headphones to decrease contact with others or even by talking with people and getting to know them may help decrease the stress.

MEDIACOLOR/ALAMY

fight-or-flight response An emotional and physiological reaction to an emergency that increases readiness for action.

general adaptation syndrome (GAS) A three-stage physiological response that appears regardless of the stressor that is encountered.

IN SUMMARY

○ Stressors are events and threats that place specific demands on a person or threaten well-being.

○ Sources of stress include major life events (even the happy ones), catastrophic events, and chronic hassles—some of which can be traced to an environment.

○ Events are most stressful when we perceive that there is no way to control or deal with the challenge.

Stress Reactions: All Shook Up

An accident at the Three Mile Island nuclear plant near Harrisburg, Pennsylvania, on March 28, 1979, created a near meltdown in the reactor and released radioactivity into the air and into the Susquehanna River. The situation was out of control for 2 days, on the brink of a major disaster that was averted only when plant operators luckily made the right decision to repressurize the coolant system. Local residents fled the area. Most eventually returned when the danger had subsided, but they suffered lasting effects of the stress associated with this potentially deadly event.

A study conducted a year and a half later compared area residents with people from unaffected areas (Fleming et al., 1985). The local group showed physical signs of stress: They had relatively high levels of *catecholamines* (biochemicals indicating the activation of emotional systems), and they had fewer white blood cells available to fight infection (Schaeffer et al., 1985). The residents also suffered psychological effects, including higher levels of anxiety, depression, and alienation compared with people elsewhere. Even on a simple proofreading task, residents performed more poorly than did people from unaffected areas. Because the radiation released was not sufficient to account for any of these effects, they were attributed to the aftermath of stress. Stress can produce changes in every system of the body and mind, stimulating both physical reactions and psychological reactions. Let's consider each in turn.

Physical Reactions

Before he became interested in voodoo death, Walter Cannon (1929) coined a phrase to describe the body's response to any threatening stimulus: the **fight-or-flight response**, *an emotional and physiological reaction to an emergency that increases readiness*

▶ A near meltdown occurred at the Three Mile Island nuclear plant near Harrisburg, Pennsylvania, on March 28, 1979. Residents of the area showed both physical and psychological stress responses—just from knowing they were in danger.

JOHN S. ZEEDICK/GETTY IMAGES

for action. The mind asks, "Should I stay and battle this somehow, or should I run like mad?" And the body prepares to react. If you're a cat at this time, your hair stands on end. If you're a human, your hair stands on end, too, but not as visibly. Cannon recognized this common response across species and suspected that it might be the body's first mobilization to any threat. Research conducted since Cannon's discovery has revealed what is happening in the brain and body during this reaction.

How does the body react to a flight-or-flight situation?

Brain activation in response to threat occurs in the hypothalamus, stimulating the nearby pituitary gland, which in turn releases a hormone known as ACTH (short for adrenocorticotropic hormone). ACTH travels through the bloodstream and stimulates the adrenal glands atop the kidneys (see **FIGURE 16.1**). In this cascading response of the *HPA axis* (for *h*ypothalamus, *p*ituitary, *a*drenal), the adrenal glands are then stimulated to release hormones, including the *catecholamines* mentioned earlier (epinephrine and norepinephrine), which increase sympathetic nervous system activation (and therefore increase heart rate, blood pressure, and respiration rate) and decrease parasympathetic activation (see Chapter 3). The increased respiration and blood pressure make more oxygen available to the muscles to energize attack or to initiate escape. The adrenal glands also release *cortisol,* a hormone that increases the concentration of glucose in the blood to make fuel available to the muscles. Everything is prepared for a full-tilt response to the threat.

General Adaptation Syndrome

What might have happened to Three Mile Island's neighbors if the sirens had wailed again and again for days or weeks at a time? Starting in the 1930s, Hans Selye, a Canadian physician, undertook a variety of experiments that looked at the physiological consequences of severe threats to well-being. He subjected rats to heat, cold, infection, trauma, hemorrhage, and other prolonged stressors, making few friends among the rats or their sympathizers but learning a lot about stress. His stressed-out rats developed physiological responses that included an enlarged adrenal cortex, shrinking of the lymph glands, and ulceration of the stomach. Noting that many different kinds of stressors caused similar patterns of physiological change, he called the reaction **general adaptation syndrome (GAS),** which he defined as *a three-stage physiological stress response that appears regardless of the stressor that is encountered.* The GAS is *nonspecific;* that is, the response doesn't vary, no matter what the source of the repeated stress.

What are the three phases of GAS?

None of this is very good news. Although Friedrich Nietzsche once said, "What does not kill me makes me stronger," Selye found that severe stress takes a toll on the body. He saw the GAS as occurring in three phases (see **FIGURE 16.2** on the next page):

> First comes the *alarm phase,* in which the body rapidly mobilizes its resources to respond to the threat. Energy is required, and the body calls on its stored fat and muscle. The alarm phase is equivalent to Cannon's fight-or-flight response.

> Next, in the *resistance phase,* the body adapts to its high state of arousal as it tries to cope with the stressor. Continuing to draw on resources of fat and muscle, it shuts down unnecessary processes: digestion, growth, and sex drive stall; menstruation stops; production of testosterone and sperm decreases. The body is being taxed to generate resistance, and all the fun stuff is put on hold.

> If the GAS goes on for long enough, the *exhaustion phase* sets in. The body's resistance collapses. Many of the resistance-phase defenses create gradual damage as they operate, leading to costs for the body that can include susceptibility to infection, tumor growth, aging, irreversible organ damage, or death.

▲ FIGURE 16.1
HPA Axis Just a few seconds after a fearful stimulus is perceived, the hypothalamus activates the pituitary gland to release adrenocorticotropic hormone (ACTH). The ACTH then travels through the bloodstream to activate the adrenal glands to release catecholamines and cortisol, which energize the fight-or-flight response.

▲ Hans Selye with rat. Given all the stress Selye put rats under, this one looks surprisingly calm.

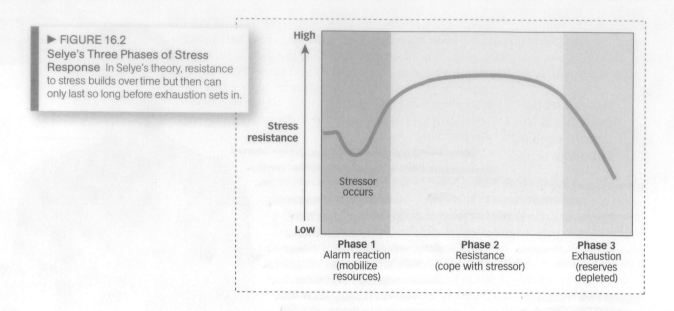

► FIGURE 16.2
Selye's Three Phases of Stress Response In Selye's theory, resistance to stress builds over time but then can only last so long before exhaustion sets in.

Stress Effects on the Immune Response

The **immune system** is *a complex response system that protects the body from bacteria, viruses, and other foreign substances*. The system includes white blood cells such as **lymphocytes** (including T cells and B cells), *cells that produce antibodies that fight infection.* The immune system is remarkably responsive to psychological influences. *Psychoneuroimmunology* is the study of how the immune system responds to psychological variables, such as the presence of stressors. Stressors can cause hormones known as glucocorticoids to flood the brain, wearing down the immune system and making it less able to fight invaders (Webster Marketon & Glaser, 2008).

How does stress affect the immune system?

For example, in one study, medical student volunteers agreed to receive small wounds to the roof of the mouth. Researchers observed that these wounds healed more slowly during exam periods than during summer vacation (Marucha, Kiecolt-Glaser, & Favagehi, 1998). In another study, a set of selfless, healthy volunteers permitted researchers to swab common cold virus in their noses (Cohen et al., 1998). You might think that a direct application of the virus would be like exposure to a massive full-facial sneeze and that all the participants would catch colds. The researchers observed, though, that some people got colds and others didn't—and stress helped account for the difference. Volunteers who had experienced chronic stressors (lasting a month or longer) were especially likely to suffer colds. In particular, participants who had lost a job or who were going through extended interpersonal problems with family or friends were most susceptible to the virus. Brief stressful life events (those lasting less than a month) had no impact.

The effect of stress on immune response may help to explain why social status is related to health. Studies of British civil servants beginning in the 1960s found that mortality varied precisely with civil service grade: the higher the classification, the lower the rates of death, regardless of cause (Marmot et al., 1991). One explanation is that people in lower-status jobs more often engage in unhealthy behavior such as smoking and drinking alcohol, and there is evidence of this. But there is also evidence that the stress of living life at the bottom levels of society increases risk of infections by weakening the immune system. People who perceive themselves as low in social status are more prone to suffer from respiratory infections, for example, than those who do not bear this social burden—and the same holds true for low-status male monkeys (Cohen, 1999).

immune system A complex response system that protects the body from bacteria, viruses, and other foreign substances.

lymphocytes White blood cells that produce antibodies that fight infection.

Stress and Cardiovascular Health

The heart and circulatory system are also sensitive to stress. For example, for several days after Iraq's 1991 missile attack on Israel, heart attack rates went up markedly among citizens in Tel Aviv (Meisel et al., 1991). The full story of how stress affects the cardiovascular system starts earlier than the occurrence of a heart attack, however: Chronic stress creates changes in the body that increase later vulnerability to this condition.

The main cause of coronary heart disease is *atherosclerosis*, a gradual narrowing of the arteries that occurs as fatty deposits, or plaque, build up on the inner walls of the arteries. Narrowed arteries result in a reduced blood supply and, eventually, when an artery is blocked by a blood clot or by detached plaque, in a heart attack. Although smoking, a sedentary lifestyle, and a diet high in fat and cholesterol can cause coronary heart disease, chronic stress is a major contributor (Krantz & McCeney, 2002). As a result of stress-activated arousal of the sympathetic nervous system, blood pressure goes up and stays up, and this gradually damages the blood vessels. The damaged vessels accumulate plaque,

THE REAL WORLD

Why Sickness Feels Bad: Psychological Effects of Immune Response

Why does it feel so bad to be sick? You notice scratchiness in your throat or the start of sniffles, and you think you might be coming down with something. And in just a few short hours, you're achy all over, energy gone, no appetite, feverish, feeling dull and listless. You're sick. The question is, why does it have to be like this? Why couldn't it feel good? As long as you're going to have to stay at home and miss out on things anyway, couldn't sickness be less of a pain?

Sickness makes you miserable for good reason. Misery is part of the *sickness response*, a coordinated, adaptive set of reactions to illness organized by the brain (Hart, 1988; Watkins & Maier, 2005). Feeling sick keeps you home, where you'll spread germs to fewer people. More importantly, the sickness response makes you withdraw from activity and lie still, conserving the energy for fighting illness that you'd normally expend on other behavior. Appetite loss is similarly helpful: The energy spent on digestion is conserved. Thus, the behavioral changes that accompany illness are not random side effects; they help the body fight disease. These responses become prolonged and exaggerated with aging—subtle signs that we are losing the fight (Barrientos et al., 2009).

How does the brain know it should do this? The immune response to an infection begins with one of the components of the immune response, the activation of

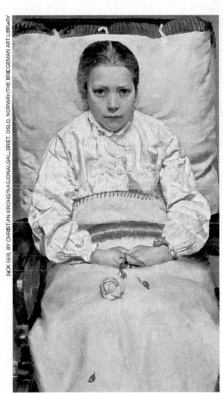

SICK GIRL BY CHRISTIAN KROHG/NASJONALGALLERIET, OSLO, NORWAY/THE BRIDGEMAN ART LIBRARY

▲ Sickness not only feels bad but it also shows. The pain of being ill has an emotional wallop like mild depression.

white blood cells that "eat" microbes and also release *cytokines*, proteins that circulate through the body and communicate among the other white blood cells—and also communicate the sickness response to the brain (Maier & Watkins, 1998). Administration of cytokines to an animal can artificially create the sickness response, and administration of drugs that oppose the action of cytokines can block the sickness response even during an ongoing infection. Cytokines do not enter the brain, but they activate the vagus nerve that runs from the intestines, stomach, and chest to the brain and induce the "I am infected" message (Goehler et al., 2000). Perhaps this is why we often feel sickness in the "gut," a gnawing discomfort in the very center of the body.

Interestingly, the sickness response can be prompted without any infection at all—merely by the introduction of stress. The stressful presence of a predator's odor, for instance, can produce the sickness response of lethargy in an animal—along with symptoms of infection such as fever and increased white blood cell count (Maier & Watkins, 2000). In humans, the connection between sickness response, immune reaction, and stress is illustrated in depression, a condition in which all the sickness machinery runs at full speed. So in addition to fatigue and malaise, depressed people show signs characteristic of infection, including high levels of cytokines circulating in the blood (Maes, 1995). Just as illness can make you feel a bit depressed, severe depression seems to recruit the brain's sickness response and make you feel ill (Watkins & Maier, 2005).

and the more plaque, the greater the likelihood of coronary heart disease. For example, a large study of Finnish men age 42 to 60 found that those who exhibited elevated blood pressure in response to stress and who reported that their work environment was especially stressful showed progressive atherosclerosis of a major artery in the neck during the 4-year study (Everson et al., 1997).

How does chronic stress increase the chance of a heart attack?

In the 1950s, cardiologists Meyer Friedman and Ray Rosenman (1974) conducted a revolutionary study that demonstrated a link between work-related stress and coronary heart disease. They interviewed and tested 3,000 healthy middle-age men and then tracked their subsequent cardiovascular health. Based on their research, Friedman and Rosenman developed the concept of the **Type A behavior pattern**, which is characterized by *a tendency toward easily aroused hostility, impatience, a sense of time urgency, and competitive achievement strivings,* and they compared Type A individuals to those with a less driven behavior pattern (sometimes called *Type B*). The Type A men were identified not only by their answers to questions in the interview (agreeing that they walk and talk fast, work late, set goals for themselves, work hard to win, and easily get frustrated and angry at others) but also by the pushy and impatient way in which they answered the questions. They watched the clock, barked back answers, and interrupted the interviewer, at some points even slapping him with a fish. Okay, the part about the fish is wrong, but you get the idea: These people were intense. The researchers found that of the 258 men who had heart attacks in the 9 years following the interview, over two thirds had been classified as Type A and only one third had been classified as Type B.

▲ Road rage starts to make sense when you believe that all the other drivers on the road are trying to kill you.

ROY MORSCH/AGE FOTOSTOCK

A later study of stress and anger tracked medical students for up to 48 years to see how their behavior while they were young related to their later susceptibility to coronary problems (Chang et al., 2002). Students who responded to stress with anger and hostility were found to be three times more likely later to develop premature heart disease and six times more likely to have an early heart attack than were students who did not respond with anger. Hostility, particularly in men, predicts heart disease better than any other major causal factor, such as smoking, high caloric intake, or even high levels of LDL cholesterol (Niaura et al., 2002; see also **FIGURE 16.3**). Stress affects the cardiovascular system to some degree in everyone but is particularly harmful in those people who respond to stressful events with hostility.

What causal factor most predicts heart attacks?

▶ FIGURE 16.3
Hostility and Coronary Heart Disease Of 2,280 men studied over the course of 3 years, 45 suffered coronary heart disease (CHD) incidents, such as heart attack. Many more of these incidents occurred in the group who had initially scored above the 80th percentile in hostility (Niaura et al., 2002).

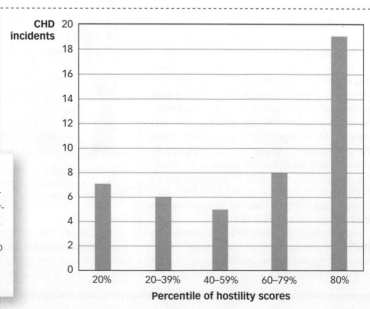

Psychological Reactions

The body's response to stress is intertwined with responses of the mind. Perhaps the first thing the mind does is try to sort things out—to interpret whether an event is threatening or not and, if it is, whether something can be done about it.

Stress Interpretation

The interpretation of a stimulus as stressful or not is called *primary appraisal* (Lazarus & Folkman, 1984). Primary appraisal allows you to realize that a small dark spot on your shirt is a stressor ("Spider!") or that a 70-mile-per-hour drop from a great height in a small car full of screaming people may not be ("Roller coaster!").

In a demonstration of the importance of interpretation, researchers used a gruesome film of a subincision—a kind of genital surgery that is part of some tribal initiation rites—to severely stress volunteer participants (Speisman et al., 1964). Self-reports and participants' autonomic arousal (heart rate and skin conductance level) were the measures of stress. Before viewing the film, one group heard an introduction that downplayed the pain and emphasized the coming-of-age aspect of the initiation. This interpretation markedly reduced the film viewers' stress compared with another group whose viewing was preceded by a lecture accentuating the pain and trauma.

The next step in interpretation is *secondary appraisal*—determining whether the stressor is something you can handle or not—that is, whether you have control over the event (Lazarus & Folkman, 1984). Interestingly, the body responds differently depending on whether the stressor is perceived as a *threat* (a stressor you believe you might *not* be able to overcome) or a *challenge* (a stressor you feel fairly confident you can control) (Blascovich & Tomaka, 1996). The same midterm exam could be a challenge if you were well prepared and a threat if you had neglected to study.

What is the difference between a threat and a challenge?

Although both threats and challenges raise heart rate, threats increase vascular reactivity (such as constriction of the blood vessels, which can lead to high blood pressure). In one study, researchers found that an interaction as innocuous as a conversation can produce threat or challenge responses depending on the race of the conversation partner. Asked to talk with another, unfamiliar student, White students showed a challenge reaction when the student was White and a threat reaction when the student was African American (Mendes et al., 2002). Similar threat responses were found when White students interacted with an unexpected parter—such as an Asian student with a southern U. S. accent (Mendes et al., 2007). It's as if social unfamiliarity creates the same kind of stress as lack of preparedness for an exam. In fact, doing "homework" (having previously interacted with members of an unfamiliar group) tempers the threat reaction (Blascovich et al., 2001).

Stress Disorders

Psychological reactions to stress can lead to stress disorders. For example, a person who lives through a terrifying and uncontrollable experience may develop **post-traumatic stress disorder (PTSD)**, a disorder characterized by *chronic physiological arousal, recurrent unwanted thoughts or images of the trauma, and avoidance of things that call the traumatic event to mind.*

Psychological scars left by traumatic events are nowhere more apparent than in war. Many soldiers returning from combat have PTSD symptoms, including flashbacks of battle, exaggerated anxiety and startle reactions, and even medical conditions that do not arise from physical damage (e.g., paralysis or chronic fatigue). Most of these symptoms are normal, appropriate responses to horrifying events;

Type A behavior pattern The tendency toward easily aroused hostility, impatience, a sense of time urgency, and competitive achievement strivings.

post-traumatic stress disorder (PTSD) A disorder characterized by chronic physiological arousal, recurrent unwanted thoughts or images of the trauma, and avoidance of things that call the traumatic event to mind.

◀ The traumatic events of war leave many debilitated by PTSD. But because PTSD is an invisible wound that is difficult to diagnose with certainty, the Pentagon has decided that psychological casualties of war are not eligible for the Purple Heart—the hallowed medal given to those wounded or killed by enemy action (Alvarez & Eckholm, 2009).

FACESOFWAR.NL

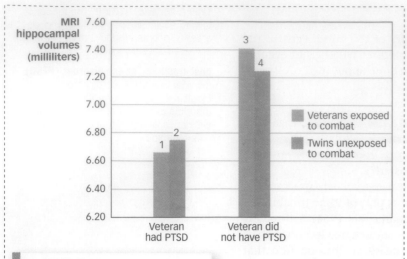

▲ FIGURE 16.4
Hippocampal Volumes of Vietnam Veterans and Their Identical Twins Average hippocampal volumes for four groups of participants: (1) combat-exposed veterans who developed PTSD; (2) their combat-unexposed twins with no PTSD themselves; (3) combat-exposed veterans who never developed PTSD; and (4) their unexposed twins, also with no PTSD. Smaller hippocampal volumes were found both for the combat-exposed veterans with PTSD (group 1) and their twins who had not been exposed to combat (group 2) in comparison to veterans without PTSD (group 3) and their twins (group 4). This pattern of findings suggests that an inherited smaller hippocampus may make some people sensitive to conditions that cause PTSD (Gilbertson et al., 2002).

for most people, the symptoms subside with time. In PTSD, the symptoms can last much longer. For example, the Centers for Disease Control (1988) found that even 20 years after the Vietnam War, 15% of veterans who had seen combat continued to report lingering symptoms. This long-term psychological response is now recognized not only among the victims, witnesses, and perpetrators of war but also among ordinary people who are traumatized by any of life's terrible events. At some time over the course of their lives, about 8% of Americans are estimated to suffer from PTSD (Kessler et al., 1995).

Not everyone who is exposed to a traumatic event develops PTSD, suggesting that people differ in their degree of sensitivity to trauma. Research using magnetic resonance imaging (MRI) to examine brain structures has found one possible indication of such sensitivity. In some studies comparing people without and with PTSD, the hippocampus was found to be smaller in volume among individuals with PTSD (Stein et al., 1997). This raises an important question: Does the reduced hippocampal volume reflect a preexisting condition that makes the brain sensitive to stress, or does the traumatic stress itself somehow kill nerve cells? One study suggests that although a group of combat veterans with PTSD showed reduced hippocampal volume, so do the identical (monozygotic) twins of those men (see **FIGURE 16.4**)—even though those twins had never had any combat exposure or developed PTSD (Gilbertson et al., 2002). This suggests that the veterans' reduced hippocampal volumes weren't caused by the combat exposure; instead, both these veterans and their twin brothers might have had a smaller hippocampus to begin with, a preexisting condition that made them susceptible to developing PTSD when they were later exposed to trauma.

What structure in the brain might be an indicator for susceptibility to PTSD?

Burnout

Did you ever take a class from an instructor who had lost interest in the job? The syndrome is easy to spot: The teacher looks distant and blank, almost robotic, giving predictable and humdrum lessons each day—as if it doesn't matter whether anyone is listening. Now imagine *being* this instructor. You decided to teach because you wanted to shape young minds. You worked hard, and for a while things were great. But one day, you look up to see a roomful of miserable students who are bored and don't care about anything you have to say. They text-message while you talk and start shuffling papers and putting things away long before the end of class. You're happy at work only when you're not in class. When people feel this way, especially about their jobs or careers, they are suffering from **burnout**, *a state of physical, emotional, and mental exhaustion created by long-term involvement in an emotionally demanding situation and accompanied by lowered performance and motivation.*

Burnout is a particular problem in the helping professions (Freudenberger, 1974; Pines & Aronson, 1988). Teachers, nurses, clergy, doctors, dentists, psychologists, social workers, police officers, and others who repeatedly encounter emotional turmoil on the job may only be able to work productively for a limited time. Eventually, many succumb to symptoms of burnout: overwhelming exhaustion, a deep cynicism and detachment from the job, and a sense of ineffectiveness and lack of accomplishment (Maslach, 2003). Their unhappiness can even spread to others; people with burnout tend to become disgruntled employees who revel in their coworkers' failures and ignore their coworkers' successes (Brenninkmeijer, Vanyperen, & Buunk, 2001).

Why is burnout a problem especially in the helping professions?

What causes burnout? One theory suggests that the culprit is using your job to give meaning to your life (Pines, 1993). If you define yourself only by your career and gauge your self-worth by success at work, you risk having nothing left when work fails. For example, a teacher in danger of burnout might do well to invest time in family, hobbies, or other self-expressions. Others argue that some emotionally stressful jobs lead to burnout no matter how they are approached and active efforts to overcome the stress before burnout occurs are important. The stress management techniques discussed in the next section may be lifesavers for people in such jobs.

◀ Is there anything worse than taking a horribly boring class? How about being the teacher of that class?

IN SUMMARY

○ The body responds to stress with an initial fight-or-flight reaction, which activates the hypothalamus-pituitary-adrenal (HPA) axis and prepares the body to face the threat or run away from it. Chronic stress can overtax the body, causing susceptibility to infection, aging, tumors and organ damage, and death.

○ The psychological response to stress can, if prolonged, lead to anxiety disorders such as PTSD or to burnout.

Stress Management: Dealing with It

Most college students (92%) say they occasionally feel overwhelmed by the tasks they face, and over a third say they have dropped courses or received low grades in response to severe stress (Deuenwald, 2003). No doubt you are among the lucky 8% who are entirely cool and report no stress. But just in case you're not, you may appreciate our exploration of stress management techniques—ways to counteract psychological and physical stress reactions directly by managing your mind and body, and ways to side-step stress by managing your situation. These techniques resemble some of the forms of cognitive behavior therapy we explored in Chapter 15, but they are strategies people often exercise on their own, without the help of a therapist.

Mind Management

Stressful events are magnified in the mind. If you fear public speaking, for example, just the thought of an upcoming presentation to a group can create anxiety. And if you do break down during a presentation—going blank, for example, or blurting out something embarrassing—intrusive memories of this stressful event could echo in your mind afterward. A significant part of stress management, then, is control of the mind.

Repressive Coping

Controlling your thoughts isn't easy, but some people do seem to be able to banish unpleasant thoughts from mind. This style of dealing with stress, called **repressive coping**, is *characterized by avoiding situations or thoughts that are reminders of a stressor and maintaining an artificially positive viewpoint*. Everyone has *some* problems, of course, but repressors are good at deliberately ignoring them (Barnier, Levin, & Maher, 2004). So, for example, when repressors suffer a heart attack, they are less likely than other people to report intrusive thoughts of their heart problems in the days and weeks that follow (Ginzburg, Solomon, & Bleich, 2002).

burnout A state of physical, emotional, and mental exhaustion created by long-term involvement in an emotionally demanding situation and accompanied by lowered performance and motivation.

repressive coping Avoiding situations or thoughts that are reminders of a stressor and maintaining an artificially positive viewpoint.

▲ Actress Brittany Murphy's death in 2009 was ruled cardiac arrest due to illness and multiple drug intoxication. It is impossible to know just what happened, but her excessive self-medication and failure to seek medical help for pneumonia sounds like repressive coping.

Like Mr. X, who was persuaded to avoid his mother's home as a way of keeping her frightening threats out of mind, people often rearrange their lives in order to avoid stressful situations. Many victims of rape, for example, not only avoid the place where the rape occurred, but may move away from their home or neighborhood (Ellis, 1983). Anticipating and attempting to avoid reminders of the traumatic experience, they become wary of strangers, especially men who resemble the assailant, and they check doors, locks, and windows more frequently than before. It may make sense to try to avoid stressful thoughts and situations if you're the kind of person who is good at putting unpleasant thoughts and emotions out of mind (Coifman et al., 2007). For some people, however, the avoidance of unpleasant thoughts and situations is so difficult it can turn into a grim preoccupation (Parker & McNally, 2008; Wegner & Zanakos, 1994). For those who can't avoid negative emotions effectively, it may be better to come to grips with them. This is the basic idea of rational coping.

When is it useful to avoid stressful thoughts and when is avoidance a problem?

Rational Coping

Rational coping involves *facing the stressor and working to overcome it.* This strategy is the opposite of repressive coping and so may seem to be the most unpleasant and unnerving thing you could do when faced with stress. It requires approaching rather than avoiding a stressor in order to lessen its longer-term negative impact (Hayes, Strosahl, & Wilson, 1999). Rational coping is a three-step process: *acceptance,* coming to realize that the stressor exists and cannot be wished away; *exposure,* attending to the stressor, thinking about it, and even seeking it out; and *understanding,* working to find the meaning of the stressor in your life.

What are the three steps in rational coping?

When the trauma is particularly intense, rational coping may be difficult to undertake. In rape trauma, for example, even accepting that the rape happened takes time and effort; the initial impulse is to deny the event and try to live as though it had never occurred. Psychotherapy may help during the exposure step by helping victims to confront and think about what happened. Using a technique called "prolonged exposure," rape survivors relive the traumatic event in their imagination by recording a verbal account of the event and then listening to the recording daily. In one study, rape survivors were instructed to seek out objectively safe situations that caused them anxiety or that they had avoided. This sounds like bitter medicine indeed, but it is remarkably effective, producing significant reductions in anxiety and PTSD symptoms compared to no therapy and compared to other therapies that promote more gradual and subtle forms of exposure (Foa et al., 1999).

► How do you cope rationally with an earthquake? This survivor of the devastating January 2010 Haitian earthquake looks for belongings in the wreckage.

The third element of rational coping involves coming to an understanding of the meaning of the stressful events. A trauma victim may wonder again and again, "Why me?" or "How did it happen?" or "Why?" Survivors of incest frequently voice the desire to make sense of their trauma (Silver, Boon, & Stones, 1983)—a process that is difficult, even impossible, during bouts of suppression and avoidance.

Reframing

Changing the way you think is another way to cope with stressful thoughts. **Reframing** involves *finding a new or creative way to think about a stressor that reduces its threat.* If you experience anxiety at the thought of public speaking, for example, you might reframe by shifting from thinking of an audience as evaluating you to thinking of yourself as evaluating them, and this might make speech-giving easier.

Reframing can be an effective way to prepare for a moderately stressful situation, but if something like public speaking is so stressful that you can't bear to think about it until you absolutely must, the technique may be not be usable. **Stress inoculation training (SIT)** is *a reframing technique that helps people to cope with stressful situations by developing positive ways to think about the situation.* For example, in one study, people who had difficulty controlling their anger were trained to rehearse thoughts such as "Just roll with the punches; don't get bent out of shape," "You don't need to prove yourself," "I'm not going to let him get to me," "It's really a shame he has to act like this," and "I'll just let him make a fool of himself." Anger-prone people who practiced these thoughts were less likely to become physiologically aroused in response to laboratory-based provocations, both imaginary and real. Subsequent research on SIT has revealed that it can be useful, too, for helping people who have suffered prior traumatic events to become more comfortable living with those events (Foa & Meadows, 1997).

▲ Stressed about giving a speech? One way to reframe is to appreciate that at least your audience probably doesn't look like this.

How has writing about stressful events been shown to be helpful?

Reframing apparently can take place spontaneously if people are given the opportunity to spend time thinking and writing about stressful events. In an important series of studies, Jamie Pennebaker (1989) found that the physical health of a group of college students improved after they spent a few hours writing about their deepest thoughts and feelings. Compared with students who had written about something else, members of the self-disclosure group were less likely in subsequent months to visit the student health center; they also used less aspirin and achieved better grades (Pennebaker & Chung, 2007). In fact, engaging in such expressive writing was found to improve immune function (Pennebaker, Kiecolt-Glaser, & Glaser, 1988), while suppressing emotional topics weakened it (Petrie, Booth, & Pennebaker, 1998). The positive effect of self-disclosing writing may reflect its usefulness in reframing trauma and reducing stress.

Body Management

Stress can express itself as tension in your neck muscles, back pain, a knot in your stomach, sweaty hands, or the harried face you glimpse in the mirror. Because stress so often manifests itself through bodily symptoms, bodily techniques such as relaxation, biofeedback, and aerobic exercise are useful in its management.

Relaxation

Imagine for a moment that you are scratching your chin. Don't actually do it; just think about it and notice that your body participates by moving ever so slightly, tensing and relaxing in the sequence of the imagined action. Edmund Jacobson (1932)

rational coping Facing a stressor and working to overcome it.

reframing Finding a new or creative way to think about a stressor that reduces its threat.

stress inoculation training (SIT) A therapy that helps people to cope with stressful situations by developing positive ways to think about the situation.

relaxation therapy A technique for reducing tension by consciously relaxing muscles of the body.

relaxation response A condition of reduced muscle tension, cortical activity, heart rate, breathing rate, and blood pressure.

biofeedback The use of an external monitoring device to obtain information about a bodily function and possibly gain control over that function.

social support The aid gained through interacting with others.

discovered these effects with *electromyography* (EMG), a technique used to measure the subtle activity of muscles. A person asked to imagine rowing a boat or plucking a flower from a bush would produce slight levels of tension in the muscles involved in performing the act. Jacobson also found that thoughts of relaxing the muscles sometimes reduced EMG readings when the people didn't even report feeling tense. Our bodies respond to all the things we think about doing every day. These thoughts create muscle tension even when we think we're doing nothing at all.

These observations led Jacobson to develop **relaxation therapy**—*a technique for reducing tension by consciously relaxing muscles of the body.* A person in relaxation therapy may be asked to relax specific muscle groups one at a time or to imagine warmth flowing through the body or to think about a relaxing situation. Meditation, hypnosis, yoga, and prayer have some elements in common with relaxation therapy (see Chapter 5). These activities all draw on a **relaxation response**, *a condition of reduced muscle tension, cortical activity, heart rate, breathing rate, and blood pressure* (Benson, 1990). Basically, as soon as you get in a comfortable position, quiet down, and focus on something repetitive or soothing that holds your attention, you relax.

What do meditation, hypnosis, yoga, and prayer have in common?

Relaxing on a regular basis can reduce symptoms of stress (Carlson & Hoyle, 1993) and even reduce blood levels of cortisol, the biochemical marker of the stress response (McKinney et al., 1997). For example, in patients who are suffering from tension headache, relaxation reduces the tension that causes the headache; in people with cancer, relaxation makes it easier to cope with stressful treatments; in people with stress-related cardiovascular problems, relaxation can reduce the high blood pressure that puts the heart at risk (Mandle et al., 1996).

Biofeedback

Wouldn't it be nice if, instead of having to learn to relax, you could just flip a switch and relax as fast as possible? **Biofeedback**, *the use of an external monitoring device to obtain information about a bodily function and possibly gain control over that function,* was developed with this goal of high-tech relaxation in mind. You might not be aware right now of whether your fingers are warm or cold, for example, but with an electronic thermometer displayed before you, the ability to sense your temperature might allow you (with a bit of practice) to make your hands warmer or cooler at will (e.g., Roberts & McGrady, 1996).

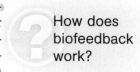

Biofeedback can help people control physiological functions they are not likely to become aware of in other ways. For example, you probably have no idea right now what brainwave patterns you are producing. In the late 1950s, Joe Kamiya (1969), a psychologist using the electroencephalograph

How does biofeedback work?

▼ Biofeedback gives people access to visual or audio feedback showing levels of psychophysiological functions such as heart rate, breathing, brain electrical activity, or skin temperature that they would otherwise be unable to sense directly.

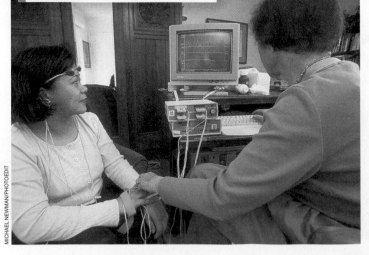

MICHAEL NEWMAN/PHOTOEDIT

(also called the EEG and discussed in Chapter 3), initiated a brain-wave biofeedback revolution when he found that people could change their brain waves from alert beta patterns to relaxed alpha patterns and back again when they were permitted to monitor their own EEG readings.

Recent studies suggest that EEG biofeedback (or neurofeedback) is moderately successful in treating brain-wave abnormalities in disorders such as epilepsy (Yucha & Gilbert, 2004). Often, however, the use of biofeedback to produce relaxation in the brain turns out to be a bit of technological overkill and may not be much more effective than simply having the person stretch out in a hammock and hum a happy tune. Unfortunately, biofeedback is not a magic bullet that gives people control over stress-induced health troubles, but it has proven useful as a technique for pursuing the benefits of relaxation (Moss et al., 2002). People who find that they cannot relax successfully through relaxation therapy may find that biofeedback provides a useful alternative.

Aerobic Exercise

A jogger nicely decked out in a neon running suit bounces in place at the crosswalk and then springs away when the signal changes. It is tempting to assume this jogger is the picture of psychological health—happy, unstressed, and even downright exuberant. As it turns out, the stereotype is true: Studies indicate that *aerobic exercise* (exercise that increases heart rate and oxygen intake for a sustained period) is associated with psychological well-being (Hassmen, Koivula, & Uutela, 2000). But does exercise *cause* psychological well-being, or does psychological well-being cause people to exercise? Perhaps general happiness is what inspires the jogger's bounce. Or could some unknown third factor (neon pants?) cause both the need to exercise and the sense of well-being? As we've mentioned many times, correlation does not always imply causation.

To try to tease apart causal factors, researchers have randomly assigned people to aerobic exercise activities and no-exercise comparison groups and have found that exercise actually does promote stress relief and happiness. In one experiment, mildly depressed college women were randomly placed in a 10-week program of aerobic exercise (1 hour, twice each week), a program of relaxation, or no treatment. The exercise group became less depressed over the course of the program, improving more than the relaxation group and the control group (McCann & Holmes, 1984). Subsequent studies have found that as little as 10 minutes of exercise at a time can yield a positive mood boost (Hanson, Stevens, & Coast, 2001).

The reasons for this positive effect are unclear. Researchers have suggested that the effect results from increases in the body's production of neurotransmitters such as serotonin, which can have a positive effect on mood (as discussed in Chapter 3) or from increases in the production of endorphins—the endogenous opioids discussed in Chapters 3 and 5 (Jacobs, 1994).

Beyond boosting positive mood, exercise also stands to keep you healthy into the future. Current U.S. government recommendations suggest that 30 minutes of moderately vigorous exercise per day will reduce the risk of chronic illness (Dietary Guidelines Advisory Committee, 2005). Perhaps the simplest thing you can do to improve your happiness and health, then, is to regularly participate in an aerobic activity. Pick something you find fun: Sign up for a dance class, get into a regular basketball game, or start paddling a canoe—just not all at once.

? What are the benefits of exercise?

▲ Exercise is helpful for the reduction of stress, unless, like John Stibbard, your exercise involves carrying the Olympic torch on a wobbly suspension bridge over a 70-meter gorge.

Situation Management

After you have tried to manage stress by managing your mind and managing your body, what's left to manage? Look around and you'll notice a whole world out there. Perhaps that could be managed as well. Situation management involves changing your life situation as a way of reducing the impact of stress on your mind and body. Ways to manage your situation can include seeking out social support and finding a place for humor in your life.

Social Support

The wisdom of the National Safety Council's first rule—"Always swim with a buddy"—is obvious when you're in water over your head, but people often don't realize that the same principle applies whenever danger threatens. Other people can offer help in times of stress. **Social support** is *aid gained through interacting with others*. One of the more self-defeating things you can do in life is to fail to connect to people in this way. Just failing to get married, for example, is bad for your health. Unmarried individuals have an elevated risk of mortality from cardiovascular disease, cancer, pneumonia and influenza, chronic obstructive pulmonary disease, and liver disease and cirrhosis (Johnson et al., 2000). More generally, good ongoing relationships with friends and family and participation in social activities and religious groups can be as healthy for you as exercising and avoiding smoking (House, Landis, & Umberson, 1988; Umberson et al., 2006).

Social support is helpful on many levels:

> An intimate partner can help you remember to get your exercise and follow your doctor's orders, and together you'll probably follow a more healthy diet than you would all alone with your snacks.

> Talking about problems with friends and family can offer many of the benefits of professional psychotherapy, usually without the hourly fees.

> Sharing tasks and helping each other when times get tough can reduce the amount of work and worry in each other's lives.

The helpfulness of strong social bonds, though, transcends mere convenience. Lonely people are more likely than others to be stressed and depressed (Baumeister & Leary, 1995), and they can be more susceptible to illness because of lower-than-normal levels of immune functioning (Kiecolt-Glaser et al., 1984).

Many first-year college students experience something of a crisis of social support. No matter how outgoing and popular they were in high school, newcomers typically find the task of developing satisfying new social relationships quite daunting. New friendships can seem shallow, connections with teachers may be perfunctory and even threatening, and social groups that are encountered can seem like islands of lost souls ("Hey, we're forming a club to investigate the lack of clubs on campus—want to join?"). Not surprisingly, research shows that students reporting the greatest feelings of isolation also show reduced immune responses to flu vaccinations (Pressman et al., 2005). Time spent getting to know people in new social situations can be an investment in your own health.

The value of social support in protecting against stress may be very different for women and men: Whereas women seek support under stress, men do not. The fight-or-flight response to stress may be largely a male reaction, according to research on sex differences by Shelley Taylor (2002). Taylor suggests that the female response to stress is to *tend-and-befriend* by taking care of people and bringing them together. Like males, human females respond to stressors with sympathetic nervous system arousal and the release of epinephrine and norepinephrine; but unlike males, they also release the hormone *oxytocin,* a hormone secreted by the pituitary gland in pregnant and nursing mothers. In the presence of estrogen, oxytocin triggers social responses—a tendency to seek out social contacts, nurture others, and create and maintain cooperative groups. After a hard day at work, a man may come home frustrated and worried about his job and end up drinking a beer and fuming alone. A woman under the same type of stress may instead play with her kids or talk to friends on the phone. The tend-and-befriend response to stress may help to explain why women are healthier and have a longer life span than do men. The typical male response amplifies the unhealthy effects of stress, whereas the female response takes a lesser toll on her mind and body—and provides social support for the people around her as well.

▲ There's really no need for escape; getting married can often be good for your health.

BURKE/TRIOLO PRODUCTIONS/GETTY IMAGES

? Why is the hormone oxytocin a health advantage for women?

Humor

Wouldn't it be nice to laugh at your troubles and move on? Most of us recognize that humor can diffuse unpleasant situations and bad feelings, and it makes sense that bringing some fun into your life could help to reduce stress. The extreme point of view on this topic is staked out in self-help books with titles such as *Health, Healing, and the Amuse System* and *How Serious Is This? Seeing Humor in Daily Stress.* Is laughter truly the best medicine? Should we close down the hospitals and send in the clowns?

There is a kernel of truth to the theory that humor can help us cope with stress. For example, humor can reduce sensitivity to pain and distress, as researchers found when they subjected volunteers to an overinflated blood pressure cuff. Participants were more tolerant of the pain during a laughter-inducing comedy audiotape than during a neutral tape or instructed relaxation (Cogan et al., 1987).

How does humor mitigate stress?

Humor can also reduce the time needed to calm down after a stressful event. For example, men viewing a highly stressful film about three industrial accidents were asked to narrate the film aloud either by describing the events seriously or by making their commentary as funny as possible. Although men in both groups reported feeling tense while watching the film and showed increased levels of sympathetic nervous arousal (increased heart rate and skin conductance, decreased skin temperature), those looking for humor in the experience bounced back to normal arousal levels more quickly than did those in the serious-story group (Newman & Stone, 1996).

If laughter and fun can alleviate stress quickly in the short term, do the effects accumulate to improve health and longevity? Sadly, the evidence suggests not (Provine, 2000). A study titled "Do Comics Have the Last Laugh?" tracked the longevity of comedians in comparison to other entertainers and nonentertainers (Rotton, 1992). It was found that the comedians died younger—perhaps after too many nights on stage thinking, *I'm dying out here.*

"I don't think it's anything serious."

IN SUMMARY

○ The management of stress involves strategies for influencing the mind, the body, and the situation.

○ People try to manage their minds by trying to suppress stressful thoughts or avoid the situations that produce them, by rationally coping with the stressor, and by reframing.

○ Body management strategies involve attempting to reduce stress symptoms through relaxation, biofeedback, and aerobic exercise.

○ Overcoming stress by managing your situation can involve seeking out social support or attempting to find humor in stressful events.

The Psychology of Illness: When It's in Your Head

One of the mind's main influences on the body's health and illness is the mind's sensitivity to bodily symptoms. No doubt Mr. X, the poor victim of "voodoo death" discussed at the beginning of this chapter, had his attention radically reoriented toward his body by his mother's repeated warning that something bad would happen. This sensitivity may have then amplified his fear of dying and so aggravated his asthma. Noticing what is wrong with the body can be helpful when it motivates a search for treatment, but sensitivity can also lead to further problems when it snowballs into a preoccupation with illness that itself can cause harm.

Recognizing Illness and Seeking Treatment

You probably weren't thinking about your breathing a minute ago, but now that you're reading this sentence, you notice it. Sometimes we are very attentive to our bodies. At other times, the body seems to be on "automatic," running along unnoticed until specific symptoms announce themselves or are pointed out by an annoying textbook writer.

▼ Headache, as envisioned by caricaturist George Cruikshank (1792–1878).

NATIONAL LIBRARY OF MEDICINE, NATIONAL INSTITUTE OF HEALTH

Directing attention toward the body or away from it can influence the symptoms we perceive. When people are bored, for example, they have more attention available to direct toward their bodies and so focus more on physical symptoms. Pennebaker (1980) audiotaped classrooms and found that people are more likely to cough when someone else has just coughed—but that such psychological contagion is much more likely at boring points in a lecture. Interestingly, coughing is not something people do on purpose (as Pennebaker found when he recorded clusters of coughs among sleeping firefighters). Thus, awareness and occurrence of physical symptoms can be influenced by psychological factors beyond our control.

People differ substantially in the degree to which they attend to and report bodily symptoms. People who report many physical symptoms tend to be negative in other ways as well—describing themselves as anxious, depressed, and under stress (Watson & Pennebaker, 1989). Do people with many symptom complaints truly have a lot of problems or are they just high-volume complainers? To answer this question, researchers used fMRI brain scans to compare severity

What is the relationship between pain and activity in the brain?

of reported symptoms with degree of activation in brain areas usually associated with pain experience. Volunteers underwent several applications of a thermal stimulus (of 110° to 120° F) to the leg, and, as you might expect, some of the participants found it more painful than did others. Scans during the painful events revealed that the anterior cingulate cortex, somatosensory cortex, and prefrontal cortex (areas known to respond to painful body stimulation) were particularly active in those participants who reported higher levels of pain experience. Because other brain areas sensitive to pain such as the thalamus were not particularly active (see **FIGURE 16.5**), the researchers concluded that more reporting of pain is suggestive of greater activation but only of some of the brain areas linked with pain (Coghill, McHaffie, & Yen, 2003; see the Hot Science box).

In contrast to complainers are those who underreport symptoms and pain or ignore or deny the possibility that they are sick. Insensitivity to symptoms comes with costs: It can delay the search for treatment, sometimes with serious repercussions. Of 2,404 patients in one study who had been treated for a heart attack, 40% had delayed going to the hospital for over 6 hours from the time they first noticed suspicious symptoms (Gurwitz et al., 1997). Severe chest pain or a history of prior heart surgery did send people to the hospital in a hurry. Those with more subtle symptoms often waited around for hours, however, not calling an ambulance or their doctor, just hoping the

▼ How much does it hurt? Pain is a psychological state that can be difficult to measure. One way to put a number on a pain is to have people judge with reference to the external expression of the internal state.

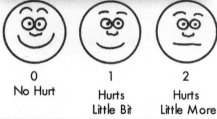

0	1	2	3	4	5
No Hurt	Hurts Little Bit	Hurts Little More	Hurts Even More	Hurts Whole Lot	Hurts Worst

FACES FROM HOCKENBURY, M. J., AND WILSON, D., *WONG'S ESSENTIALS OF PEDIATRIC NURSING*, ED. 8. ST. LOUIS, 2009, MOSBY. USED WITH PERMISSION. COPYRIGHT MOSBY.

▶ FIGURE 16.5
The Brain in Pain fMRI scans of brain activation in high- (left) and low-pain-sensitive (right) individuals during painful stimulation. The anterior cingulate cortex and primary somatosensory areas show greater activation in high-pain-sensitive individuals. Levels of activation are highest in yellow and red, then light blue and dark blue (Coghill, McHaffie, & Yen, 2003).

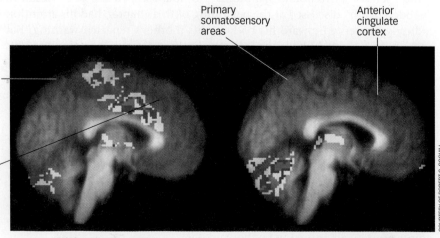

High Pain Sensitivity   Low Pain Sensitivity

COURTESY OF ROBERT C. COGHILL

problem would go away—which was not a good idea because many of the treatments that can reduce the damage of a heart attack are most useful when provided early. When it comes to your own health, protecting your mind from distress through the denial of illness can result in exposing your body to great danger.

HOT SCIENCE

This Is Your Brain on Placebos

There is something miraculous about Band-Aids. Your standard household toddler typically *requires* one for any injury at all, expecting and often achieving immediate relief. It is not unusual to find the child who reports a stomachache "cured" if a Band-Aid has been applied to the tummy by a helpful adult. Of course, the Band-Aid is not *really* helping the pain—or is it?

Physicians and psychologists have long puzzled over the placebo effect, *a clinically significant psychological or physiological response to a therapeutically inert substance or procedure.* The classic placebo is the sugar pill, but Band-Aids, injections, heating pads, neck rubs, homeopathic remedies, and kind words can have placebo effects (Diederich & Goetz, 2008). Even sham brain surgery can be more effective than no treatment at all (McRae et al., 2004). The effect is most marked, however, when the patient knows that a treatment is taking place (Stewart-Williams, 2004). This is also true of active treatments—a morphine injection works much better if you know you're getting it (Benedetti, Maggi, & Lopiano, 2003a). Knowledge effects can be remarkably specific, mirroring in detail what patients believe about the nature of medicine—for example, that two pills work better than one and an injection works better than just a pill (de Craen et al., 1999).

How do placebos operate? Do people being treated for pain really feel the pain but distort their report of the experience to make it fit their beliefs about treatment? Or does the placebo actually reduce the pain a patient experiences? Howard Fields and Jon Levine (1984) discovered that placebos trigger the release of endorphins (or *endogenous opioids*), painkilling chemicals similar to morphine that are produced by the brain (see Chapter 5). In their experiments, they found that an injection of naloxone, an opioid-blocking drug, typically reduces the benefit both of an opioid such as morphine and a placebo injection, suggesting that the placebo has its painkilling effects because it triggers the release of endorphins.

In another advance in the study of these effects, placebos were found to lower the activation of specific brain areas associated with pain. One set of fMRI studies examined brain activation as volunteers were exposed to electric shock or heat (Wager et al., 2004). In preparation for some exposures to these painful stimuli, a placebo cream was applied to the skin, and the participant was told it was an analgesic that would reduce the pain. Other participants merely experienced the pain. As you can see in the accompanying figure, the fMRI scans showed decreased activation during placebo analgesia in the *thalamus, anterior cingulate cortex,* and *insula,* pain-sensitive brain regions that were activated during untreated pain. These findings suggest that placebos are not leading people to misreport their pain experience, but rather are reducing brain activity in areas that normally are active during pain experience.

Such findings don't mean that next time your stomach aches, you can break out a Band-Aid and heal yourself. Part of the placebo effect is dependent on the conscious expectation that the placebo will work, and it could be a challenge to make yourself believe you will feel better when you don't. Part of the placebo effect is unconscious, though—a tendency to feel better that is learned through classical conditioning. When you've been healed in the past by a particular doctor or form of treatment, or in a certain setting, unconscious learning mechanisms may lead to improvement if you simply encounter a similar doctor, treatment, or setting again—even if you don't consciously expect to improve (Benedetti et al., 2003b). There's something comforting about returning to things that have given you comfort in the past.

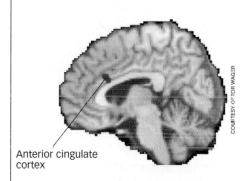

Anterior cingulate cortex

Insula

Thalamus

▲ **The Brain's Response to Placebo** fMRI scans reveal that some brain regions normally activated when people report pain in response to shocks are deactivated when these individuals are given a placebo analgesic during the shock. These regions include the anterior cingulate cortex (shown in the top image, a right medial view of the brain) and the insula and thalamus (both shown in the bottom image, a ventral view of the brain) (Wager et al., 2004).

▲ Can a Band-Aid cure a stomachache? Looks like someone here is feeling no pain.

Somatoform Disorders

The flip side of denial is excessive sensitivity to illness, and it turns out that sensitivity also has its perils. Indeed, hypersensitivity to symptoms or to the possibility of illness underlies a variety of psychological problems and can also undermine physical health. Psychologists studying **psychosomatic illness**, *an interaction between mind and body that can produce illness*, explore ways in which mind (psyche) can influence body (soma) and vice versa. The study of mind-body interactions focuses on psychological disorders called **somatoform disorders**, in which *the patient displays physical symptoms not fully explained by a general medical condition*. These are psychological disorders like those discussed in Chapter 14, but their association with symptoms in the body makes them relevant to this chapter's concern with health. Hypochondriasis is the best known of these disorders, but other somatoform disorders include somatization disorder and conversion disorder.

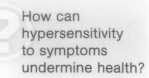

How can hypersensitivity to symptoms undermine health?

> **Hypochondriasis** is *a psychological disorder in which a person is preoccupied with minor symptoms and develops an exaggerated belief that the symptoms signify a life-threatening illness*. You may know people who constantly worry about their health, and these poor souls can mentally turn every cough into tuberculosis and every headache into a brain tumor. It is said that fairy-tale author Hans Christian Andersen (1805–75) was a hypochondriac, talking about his ailments and their possible meaning with anyone who would listen. It is also said that he had a morbid fear of being buried alive and placed a note by his bed each night as he slept explaining, "I only *appear* to be dead." For a hypochondriac, the tendency to catastrophize symptoms by imagining their worst possible interpretation can become a chronic source of anxiety.

> **Somatization disorder** involves *combinations of multiple physical complaints that have no medical explanation*. Chronic symptoms often lead the person to seek medical attention, sometimes from more than one physician at the same time. Unlike hypochondriasis, with its anxiety about an underlying disease, somatization disorder involves a greater focus on symptoms. The patient will usually complain of many symptoms—multiple pains in different parts of the body, gastrointestinal symptoms such as nausea or food intolerance, sexual symptoms such as irregular menstrual periods, and physical problems such as weakness or difficulty swallowing (Noyes, Stuart, & Watson, 2008). Such patients seem to be searching for someone to sympathize with their many physical problems, but often they only succeed in alienating their loved ones and doctors with their persistent complaints.

> Another somatoform disorder is **conversion disorder**, *a disorder characterized by apparently debilitating physical symptoms that appear to be voluntary—but that the person experiences as involuntary*. The patient might experience seizures, blindness, deafness, paralysis, or insensitivity to touch or pain in some body part, symptoms usually traced to neurological causes. On examination, however, the conversion disorder patient shows no neural basis for the symptom. The symptom may come or go over time and can sometimes be overcome when the patient's attention is diverted from it. A patient lying in bed with a "paralysis" of the leg, for example, might inadvertently move it to retain balance when the other leg is lifted by the physician. Yet such patients are not consciously feigning the symptoms and may be incapacitated for years with their "pseudoneurological" problems. Conversion symptoms may spontaneously resolve, but the disorder is difficult to treat and in some patients the absent symptoms are later replaced by others (Kroenke, 2007).

psychosomatic illness An interaction between mind and body that can produce illness.

somatoform disorders The set of psychological disorders in which the person displays physical symptoms not fully explained by a general medical condition.

hypochondriasis A psychological disorder in which a person is preoccupied with minor symptoms and develops an exaggerated belief that the symptoms signify a life-threatening illness.

somatization disorder A psychological disorder involving combinations of multiple physical complaints with no medical explanation.

conversion disorder A disorder characterized by apparently debilitating physical symptoms that appear to be voluntary—but that the person experiences as involuntary.

sick role A socially recognized set of rights and obligations linked with illness.

Such cases fascinated Sigmund Freud and other physicians early in the history of psychology because they demonstrated that the mind could produce physical illnesses without any physiological cause. More women than men develop conversion and somatization disorders, and early investigators called these disorders "hysteria" in the mistaken belief that these strange symptoms originated from the womb. Current theories focus on the idea that such symptoms occur as a result of breakdowns in the psychological processes underlying voluntary movement and attention (Hallett et al., 2005).

On Being a Patient

Getting sick is more than a change in physical state; it can involve a transformation of identity. This change can be particularly profound with a serious illness: A kind of cloud settles over you, a feeling that you are now different, and this transformation can influence everything you feel and do in this new world of illness. You even take on a new role in life: a **sick role**—*a socially recognized set of rights and obligations linked with illness* (Parsons, 1975). The sick person is absolved of responsibility for many everyday obligations and enjoys exemption from normal activities. For example, in addition to skipping school and homework and staying on the couch all day, a sick child can watch TV and avoid eating anything unpleasant at dinner. At the extreme, the sick person can get away with being rude, lazy, demanding, and picky. In return for these exemptions, the sick role also incurs obligations. The properly "sick" individual cannot appear to enjoy the illness or reveal signs of wanting to be sick and must also take care to pursue treatment to end this "undesirable" condition. Parsons observed that illness has psychological, social, and even moral components. You may recall times when you have felt the conflict between sickness and health as though it were a moral decision: Should you drag yourself out of bed and try to make it to the chemistry exam or just slump back under the covers and wallow in your "pain"?

"There are many questions, of course, that won't be answered till the autopsy."

Some people feign medical or psychological symptoms to achieve something they want, a type of behavior called *malingering*. Because many symptoms of illness cannot be faked—even facial expressions of pain are difficult to simulate (Williams, 2002)—malingering is possible only with a restricted number of illnesses. Faking illness is suspected when the secondary gains of illness—such as the ability to rest, to be freed from performing unpleasant tasks, or to be helped by others—outweigh the costs. Such gains can be very subtle, as when a child stays in bed because of the comfort provided by an otherwise distant parent, or they can be obvious, as when insurance benefits turn out to be a cash award for Best Actor. Some behaviors that may lead to illness may not be under the patient's control; for example, self-starvation may be part of an uncontrollable eating disorder (see Chapter 8). For this reason, malingering can be difficult to diagnose and treat (Feldman, 2004).

? What benefits might come from being ill?

Patient-Practitioner Interaction

Medical care usually occurs through a strange interaction. On one side is a patient, often miserable, who expects to be questioned and examined and possibly prodded, pained, or given bad news. On the other side is a health care provider, who hopes to obtain useful information from the patient, help in some way, cope with the emotional part of the interaction, and achieve all of this as efficiently as possible because more patients are waiting. Seems less like a time for healing than an occasion for major awkwardness.

One of the keys to an effective medical care interaction is physician empathy (Spiro et al., 1994).

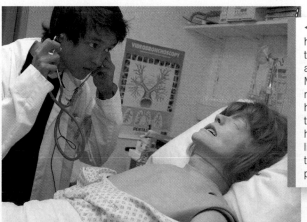

◀ Doctor and patient have two modes of interaction, the technical and the interpersonal. Medical training with robot patients may help doctors learn the technical side of health care, but it is likely to do little to improve the interpersonal side.

DAN ATKIN/ALAMY

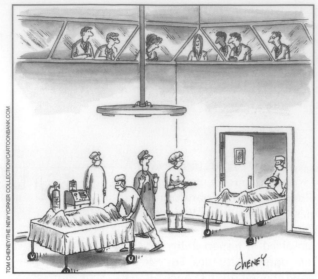

"Next, an example of the very same procedure when done correctly"

To offer successful treatment, the physician must simultaneously understand the patient's physical state and psychological state. Physicians often err on the side of failing to acknowledge patients' emotions, focusing instead on technical issues of the case (Suchman et al., 1997). This is particularly unfortunate because a substantial percentage of patients who seek medical care do so for treatment of psychological and emotional problems (Taylor, 1986). As the Greek physician Hippocrates wrote in the 4th century BC, "Some patients, though conscious that their condition is perilous, recover their health simply through their contentment with the goodness of the physician." The best physician treats the patient's mind as well as the patient's body.

Another important part of the medical care interaction is motivating the patient to follow the prescribed regimen of care (Cohen, 1979).

When researchers check compliance by counting the pills remaining in a patient's bottle after a prescription has been under way, they find that patients often do an astonishingly poor job of following doctors' orders (see **FIGURE 16.6**). Compliance deteriorates when the treatment must be *frequent*, as when eyedrops for glaucoma are required every few hours, or *inconvenient* or *painful*, such as drawing blood or performing injections in managing diabetes. Finally, compliance decreases *as the number of treatments increases*. This is a worrisome problem especially for older patients, who may have difficulty remembering when to take which pill. Failures in medical care may stem from the failure of health care providers to recognize the psychological challenges that are involved in self-care. Helping people to follow doctors' orders involves psychology, not medicine, and is an essential part of promoting health.

Why is it important that a physician be empathic?

▶ FIGURE 16.6

Antacid Intake A scatter plot of antacid intake measured by bottle count plotted against patient's stated intake for 116 patients. When the actual and stated intakes are the same, the point lies on the diagonal line; when stated intake is greater than actual, the point lies above the line. Most patients exaggerated their intake (Roth & Caron, 1978).

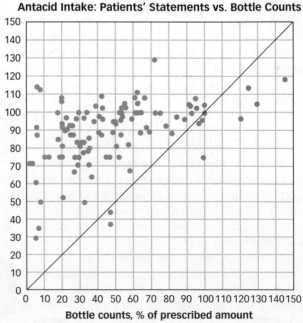

IN SUMMARY

○ The psychology of illness concerns how sensitivity to the body leads people to recognize illness and seek treatment.

○ Somatoform disorders, such as hypochondriasis, can stem from too much sensitivity.

○ The sick role is a set of rights and obligations linked with illness; some people fake illness in order to accrue those rights.

○ Successful health care providers interact with their patients to understand both the physical state and the psychological state.

The Psychology of Health: Feeling Good

Two kinds of psychological factors influence personal health: health-relevant personality traits and health behavior. Personality can influence health through relatively enduring traits that make some people particularly susceptible to health problems or stress while sparing or protecting others. The Type A behavior pattern is an example. Because personality is not typically something we choose ("I'd like a bit of that sense of humor and extraversion over there, please, but hold the whininess"), this source of health can be outside personal control. In contrast, engaging in positive health behaviors is something anyone can do, at least in principle.

Personality and Health

Different health problems seem to plague different social groups. For example, men are more susceptible to heart disease than are women, and African Americans are more susceptible to asthma than are Asian or European Americans. Beyond these general social categories, personality turns out to be a factor in wellness, with individual differences in optimism and hardiness important influences.

Optimism

Pollyanna is one of literature's most famous optimists. Eleanor H. Porter's 1913 novel portrayed Pollyanna as a girl who greeted life with boundless good cheer even when she was orphaned and sent to live with her cruel aunt. Her response to a sunny day was to remark on the good weather, of course—but her response to a gloomy day was to point out how lucky it is that not every day is gloomy! Her crotchety Aunt Polly had exactly the opposite attitude, somehow managing to turn every happy moment into an opportunity for strict correction. A person's level of optimism or pessimism tends to be fairly stable over time, and research comparing the personalities of twins reared together versus those reared apart suggests that this stability arises because these traits are moderately heritable (Plomin et al., 1992). Perhaps Pollyanna and Aunt Polly were each "born that way."

An optimist who believes that "in uncertain times, I usually expect the best" is likely to be healthier than a pessimist who believes that "if something can go wrong for me, it will." In a study of 309 patients who had undergone coronary artery bypass surgery, for example, researchers found that initial levels of optimism were related to patients' postoperative health (Scheier et al., 1999). Patients with higher levels of overall optimism (not merely optimism about the particular surgery) were less likely than other patients after their surgery to need rehospitalization for complications such as infection, heart attacks, or further surgery.

Such findings are encouraging for optimists (what wouldn't be?), but studies like this one showing that optimism directly improves physical health are relatively rare (Segerstrom, 2005). Rather than improving physical health directly, optimism seems to aid in the maintenance of *psychological* health in the face of physical health problems. When sick, optimists

▲ In the 1960 film version, Hayley Mills as Pollyanna even manages to find the sunny side of her own accidental fall and paralysis.

are more likely than pessimists to maintain positive emotions, avoid negative emotions such as anxiety and depression, stick to medical regimens their caregivers have prescribed, and keep up their relationships with others. Among women who have surgery for breast cancer, for example, optimists are less likely to experience distress and fatigue after treatment than are pessimists, largely because they keep up social contacts and recreational activities during their treatment (Carver, Lehman, & Antoni, 2003).

? Who's healthier, the optimist or the pessimist? Why?

The benefits of optimism raise an important question: If the traits of optimism and pessimism are stable over time—even resistant to change—can pessimists ever hope to gain any of the advantages of optimism (Heatherton & Weinberger, 1994)? Research has shown that even die-hard pessimists can be trained to become significantly more optimistic and that this training can improve their psychosocial health outcomes. For example, pessimistic breast cancer patients who received 10 weeks of training in stress management techniques became more optimistic and were less likely than those who received only relaxation exercises to suffer distress and fatigue during their cancer treatments (Antoni et al., 2001).

Hardiness

Some people seem to be thick-skinned, somehow able to take stress or abuse that could be devastating to others. Are there personality traits that contribute to such resilience and offer protection from stress-induced illness? To identify such traits, Suzanne Kobasa (1979) studied a group of stress-resistant business executives. These individuals reported high levels of stressful life events but had histories of relatively few illnesses compared with a similar group who succumbed to stress by getting sick. The stress-resistant group (Kobasa called them *hardy*) shared several traits, all conveniently beginning with the letter *C*. They showed a sense of *commitment*, an ability to become involved in life's tasks and encounters rather than just dabbling. They exhibited a belief in *control*, the expectation that their actions and words have a causal influence over their lives and environment. And they were willing to accept *challenge*, undertaking change and accepting opportunities for growth.

▲ Sometimes hardiness tips over the edge into foolhardiness. Members of the Coney Island Polar Bear Club take that plunge every Sunday of winter.

Can just anyone develop hardiness? Researchers have attempted to teach hardiness with some success. In one such attempt, participants attended 10 weekly "hardiness training" sessions, in which they were encouraged to examine their stresses, develop action plans for dealing with them, explore their bodily reactions to stress, and find ways to compensate for unchangeable situations without falling into self-pity. Compared with control groups (who engaged in relaxation and meditation training or in group discussions about stress), the hardiness-training group reported greater reductions in their perceived personal stress as well as fewer symptoms of illness (Maddi, Kahn, & Maddi, 1998). Hardiness training can have similar positive effects in college students, for some even boosting their GPA (Maddi et al., 2009).

Health-Promoting Behaviors and Self-Regulation

Even without changing our personalities at all, we can do certain things to be healthy. The importance of healthy eating, safe sex, and giving up smoking are common knowledge. But we don't seem to be acting on the basis of this knowledge. At the turn of the 21st century, 67% of Americans over 20 are overweight or obese (National Center for Health Statistics, 2008). The prevalence of unsafe sex is difficult to estimate, but 65 million Americans currently suffer from an incurable sexually transmitted disease (STD), while 15 million contract one or more new STDs each year (Weinstock, Berman, & Cates, 2004)—and another million live with human immunodeficiency virus/acquired immune deficiency syndrome (HIV/AIDS), which is usually contracted through unprotected sex with an infected partner (Centers for Disease Control, 2006). And despite endless warnings, 21% of Americans still smoke cigarettes (Pleis et al., 2009). What's going on?

self-regulation The exercise of voluntary control over the self to bring the self into line with preferred standards.

Self-Regulation

Doing what is good for you is not necessarily easy. Mark Twain once remarked, "The only way to keep your health is to eat what you don't want, drink what you don't like, and do what you'd druther not." Engaging in health-promoting behaviors involves **self-regulation**, *the exercise of voluntary control over the self to bring the self into line with preferred standards.* When you decide on a salad rather than a cheeseburger, for instance, you control your impulse and behave in a way that will help to make you the kind of person you would prefer to be—a healthy one. Self-regulation often involves putting off immediate gratification for longer-term gains (see Chapter 5).

Self-regulation requires a kind of inner strength or willpower. One theory suggests that self-control is a kind of strength that can be fatigued (Baumeister, Heatherton, & Tice, 1995; Baumeister, Vohs, & Tice, 2007). In other words, trying to exercise control in one area may exhaust self-control, leaving behavior in other areas unregulated. To test this theory, researchers seated hungry volunteers near a batch of fresh, hot, chocolate chip cookies. They asked some participants to leave the cookies alone but help themselves to a healthy snack of radishes, whereas others were allowed to indulge. When later challenged with an impossibly difficult figure-tracing task, the self-control group was more likely than the self-indulgent group to abandon the difficult task—behavior interpreted as evidence that they had depleted their pool of self-control

▲ Nobody ever said self-control was easy. Probably the only reason you're able to keep yourself from eating this cookie is that it's just a picture of a cookie. Really. Don't eat it.

(Baumeister et al., 1998). The take-home message from this experiment is that to control behavior successfully, we need to choose our battles, exercising self-control mainly on the personal weaknesses that are most harmful to health.

? Why is it difficult to achieve and maintain self-control?

Sometimes, though, self-regulation is less a matter of brute force than of strategy. Martial artists claim that anyone can easily overcome a large attacker with the use of the right moves, and overcoming our own unhealthy impulses may also be a matter of finesse. Let's look carefully at healthy approaches to some key challenges for self-regulation—eating, safe sex, and smoking—to learn what "smart moves" can aid us in our struggles.

Eating Wisely

In many Western cultures, the weight of the average citizen is increasing alarmingly. One explanation is based on our evolutionary history: In order to ensure their survival, our ancestors found it useful to eat well in times of plenty to store calories for leaner times. In postindustrial societies in the 21st century, however, there are no leaner times, and people can't burn all of the calories they consume (Pinel, Assanand, & Lehman, 2000). But why, then, isn't obesity endemic throughout the Western world? Why are people in France leaner on average than Americans even though their foods are high in fat? One reason has to do with average portion, which is far smaller in France than in the United States. Activity level in France is also greater. Research by Paul Rozin and his colleagues finds that the time people spend eating differs between cultures as well. At a McDonald's in France, meals take an average of 22 minutes, whereas in the United States, they take under 15 minutes (Rozin, Bauer, & Cantanese, 2003). Right now Americans seem to be involved in some kind of national eating contest.

▼ Is eating a contest? North American culture makes excessive eating almost a competition, but it's hard to find winners.

Short of moving to France, what can you do? Studies indicate that dieting doesn't always work because the process of conscious self-regulation can be easily undermined by stress, leading people who are trying to control themselves to lose control by overindulging in the very behavior they had been trying to overcome. This may remind you of a general principle discussed in Chapter 5: Trying hard not to do something can often directly produce the unwanted behavior (Wegner, 1994a, 1994b).

The restraint problem may be inherent in the very act of self-control (Polivy & Herman, 1992). Rather than dieting, then, heading toward normal weight should involve a new emphasis on

"And, on the lowest end of the caloric spectrum, we offer a leather chew toy."

exercise and nutrition (Prochaska & Sallis, 2004). In emphasizing what is good to eat, the person can freely think about food rather than trying to suppress thoughts about it. A focus on increasing activity rather than reducing food intake, in turn, gives people another positive and active goal to pursue. Self-regulation is more effective when it focuses on what to do rather than on what not to do (Molden, Lee, & Higgins, 2009; Wegner & Wenzlaff, 1996).

Why is exercise a more effective weight-loss choice than dieting?

Avoiding Sexual Risks

People put themselves at risk when they have unprotected vaginal, oral, or anal intercourse with many sexual partners or with partners who themselves have many sexual partners, exhibit symptoms of STDs, are HIV positive, or are intravenous drug users. Sexually active adolescents and adults are usually aware of such risks, not to mention the risk of unwanted pregnancy, and yet many behave in risky ways nonetheless.

Why doesn't awareness translate into avoidance? Risk-takers harbor an *illusion of unique invulnerability,* a systematic bias toward believing that they are less likely to fall victim to the problem than are others (Perloff & Fetzer, 1986). For example, a study of sexually active female college students found that respondents judged their own likelihood of getting pregnant in the next year as under 10% but estimated the average for other females at the university to be 27% (Burger & Burns, 1988). Paradoxically, this illusion was even stronger among women in the sample who reported using inadequate or no contraceptive techniques. The tendency to think *It won't happen to me* may be most pronounced when it probably will.

Risky sex is often the impulsive result of last-minute emotions. When thought is further blurred by alcohol or recreational drugs, people often fail to use the latex condoms that can reduce their exposure to the risks of pregnancy, HIV, and many other STDs. Like other forms of self-regulation, the avoidance of

Why does planning ahead reduce sexual risk-taking?

sexual risk requires the kind of planning that can be easily undone by circumstances that hamper the ability to think ahead. One approach to reducing sexual risk-taking, then, is simply finding ways to help people plan ahead. Sex education programs offer adolescents just such a chance by encouraging them at a time when they have not had much sex experience to think about what they might do when they will need to make decisions. Although sex education is sometimes criticized as increasing adolescents' awareness of and interest in sex, the research evidence is clear: Sex education reduces the likelihood that adolescents will engage in unprotected sexual activity and benefits their health (American Psychological Association, 2005). The same holds true for adults.

Not Smoking

One in two smokers dies prematurely from smoking-related diseases such as lung cancer, heart disease, emphysema, and cancer of the mouth and throat. Lung cancer itself kills more people than any other form of cancer, and smoking causes 80% of lung cancers. Although the overall rate of smoking in the United States is declining, new smokers abound, and many can't seem to stop. College students are puffing away along with everyone else, with 20% of college students currently smoking (Thompson et al., 2007). In the face of all the devastating health consequences, why don't people quit?

Nicotine, the active ingredient in cigarettes, is addictive, and so smoking is difficult to stop once the habit is established (discussed in Chapter 5). As in other forms of self-regulation, the resolve to quit smoking is fragile and seems to break down under stress. In the months following 9/11, for example, cigarette sales jumped 13% in Massachusetts (Phillips, 2002). And for some time after quitting, ex-smokers remain sensitive to cues in the environment: Eating or drinking, a bad mood, anxiety, or just seeing someone else smoking is enough to make them want a cigarette (Shiffman et al., 1996). The good news is that the urge decreases and people become less likely to relapse the longer they've been away from nicotine.

Psychological programs and techniques to help people kick the habit include nicotine replacement systems such as gum and skin patches, counseling programs, and hypnosis—but these programs are not always successful. Trying again and again in different ways is apparently the best approach (Schachter, 1982). After all, to quit smoking forever, you only need to quit one more time than you start up. But like the self-regulation of eating and sexuality, the self-regulation of smoking can require effort and thought. The ancient Greeks blamed self-control problems on *akrasia*, or "weakness of will." Modern psychology focuses less on blaming a person's character for poor self-regulation and points instead toward the difficulty of the task. Keeping healthy by behaving in healthy ways is one of the great challenges of life.

To quit smoking forever, how many times do you need to quit?

IN SUMMARY

○ The connection between mind and body can be revealed through the influences of personality and self-regulation of behavior on health.

○ The personality traits of optimism and hardiness are associated with reduced risk for illnesses, perhaps because people with these traits can fend off stress.

○ The self-regulation of behaviors such as eating, sexuality, and smoking is difficult for many people because self-regulation is easily disrupted by stress; strategies for maintaining self-control can pay off with significant improvements in health and quality of life.

WhereDoYouStand?

Should Smoking Appear On the Silver Screen?

When Sigourney Weaver's character smoked onscreen in the film *Avatar*, public health watchdogs complained. A spokesman for the Center for Tobacco Control Research and Education at the University of California, San Francisco, suggested that the smoking in the movie created millions of dollars in free advertising for tobacco companies. Director of *Avatar* James Cameron defended the movie, claiming that Weaver's character was rude and obnoxious—not likely to be an inspirational role model to teenagers (Cieply, 2010). But the question remains: Does smoking in movies cause adolescents to take up the habit?

This is a difficult question for research. How could you in good conscience do an experiment in which adolescents are randomly assigned to watch movies featuring smoking? Even if those in the control group are not shown such films, if just one in the experimental group takes up smoking as a result, that seems like too many. Researchers have resorted, then, to tracking the movies that teenagers freely choose to watch in daily life to see whether there is any association between exposure to smoking in movies and the tendency to take up smoking. There is, and the association is strong across many studies (Charlesworth & Glantz, 2005).

As we've noted before, such an association does not establish causation. But studies of adolescent smoking reveal interesting details that help to fill out the causal theory. For example, adolescents whose favorite stars smoke onscreen are more inclined to be smokers than are adolescents whose favorite stars don't smoke. Those whose favorite star smoked in several films (for example, Leonardo DiCaprio, Sharon Stone, or John Travolta) were three times more likely themselves to smoke than those whose favorite star did not smoke onscreen (Tickle et al., 2001). There are clear hints, then, that smoking in movies may cause nonsmokers to take it up—but without experimental research, we can't know this for certain. The question then becomes: Should smoking be shown onscreen or not? Where do you stand?

Chapter Review

KEY CONCEPT QUIZ

1. If you live in a dense urban area in which there are considerable traffic, noise, and pollution, to what kinds of stressors are you likely exposed?
   a. cultural stressors
   b. intermittent stressors
   c. chronic stressors
   d. positive stressors

2. In an experiment, two groups are subject to distractions while attempting to complete a task. Group A is told they can quiet the distractions by pushing a button. This information is withheld from Group B. Why will Group A's performance at the task likely be better than Group B's?
   a. Group B is working in a different environment.
   b. Group A has perceived control over a source of performance-impeding stress.
   c. Group B is less distracted than Group A.
   d. The distractions affecting Group B are now chronic.

3. The brain activation that occurs in response to a threat begins in the
   a. pituitary gland.
   b. hypothalamus.
   c. adrenal gland.
   d. corpus callosum.

4. According to the general adaptation syndrome, during the _____ phase, the body adapts to its high state of arousal as it tries to cope with a stressor.
   a. exhaustion
   b. alarm
   c. resistance
   d. energy

5. Which of the following statements is most accurate regarding the physiological response to stress?
   a. Type A behavior patterns have psychological but not physiological ramifications.
   b. The link between work-related stress and coronary heart disease is unfounded.
   c. Stressors can cause hormones to flood the brain, strengthening the immune system.
   d. The immune system is remarkably responsive to psychological influences.

6. Which of the following is NOT an accurate statement regarding the psychological reaction to stress?
   a. Stress disorders do not have a psychological basis.
   b. The body's response to stress is intertwined with responses of the mind.
   c. Stress levels depend on the psychological interpretation of a stimulus.
   d. Emotionally stressful jobs can lead to psychological disorders.

7. Engaging in aerobic exercise is a way of managing stress by managing the
   a. mind.
   b. body.
   c. situation.
   d. intake of air.

8. Finding a new or creative way to think about a stressor that reduces its threat is called
   a. stress inoculation.
   b. repressive coping.
   c. reframing.
   d. rational coping.

9. Which somatoform disorder is characterized by apparently debilitating physical symptoms that appear to be voluntary?
   a. pseudoneurological syndrome
   b. conversion disorder
   c. hypochondriasis
   d. somatization disorder

10. Faking an illness is a violation of
    a. malingering.
    b. somatoform disorder.
    c. the sick role.
    d. the Type B pattern of behavior.

11. Which of the following describes a successful health care provider?
    a. displays empathy
    b. pays attention to both the physical and psychological state of the patient
    c. uses psychology to promote patient compliance
    d. all of the above.

12. When sick, optimists are more likely than pessimists to
    a. maintain positive emotions.
    b. become depressed.
    c. ignore their caregiver's advice.
    d. avoid contact with others.

13. Which of the following is NOT a trait associated with hardiness?
    a. a sense of commitment
    b. an aversion to criticism
    c. a belief in control
    d. a willingness to accept challenge

14. Stress _____ the self-regulation of behaviors such as eating and smoking.
    a. strengthens
    b. has no effect on
    c. disrupts
    d. normalizes

KEY TERMS

CRITICAL THINKING QUESTIONS

1. Review the events in the stress scale (Table 16.1 on p. 627), and evaluate which of them are something a person has control over and which are not. How does the potential for control of an event relate to the stress rating?

2. Have you ever experienced burnout? If so, what coping techniques worked for you? What techniques could be used to help people in helping professions—such as teachers, doctors, or nurses—to prevent burnout from stress?

3. Have you ever ridden on public transportation sitting next to a person with a hacking cough? We are bombarded by advertisements for medicines designed to suppress symptoms of illness so we can keep going. Is staying home with a cold socially acceptable or considered malingering? How does this jibe with the concept of the "sick role," *a socially recognized set of rights and obligations linked with illness*?

4. One of the reasons given in the text for the fact that people in France are leaner than people in the United States is that the average fast-food meal in France is 22 minutes, while in the United States it's 15 minutes. How could the length of the average meal influence an individual's body weight?

RECOMMENDED READINGS

Evans, D. (2004). *Placebo: Mind over matter in modern medicine.* New York: Oxford University Press.

Can we think ourselves well? One of the tempting puzzles of health psychology is how some treatments can be effective simply because people believe they will work.

Pennebaker, J. W. (1990). *Opening up: The healing power of confiding in others.* New York: Morrow.

This engaging book explains why self-disclosure is useful, recounting Pennebaker's experiments, which found that people who are encouraged to express their thoughts and feelings about their stresses and traumas showed health improvements.

Sapolsky, R. M. (2004). *Why zebras don't get ulcers* (3rd ed.). New York: Holt.

This book covers the technical side of stress in a way that is accessible to the layperson. Sapolsky masterfully presents a wide range of facts, discoveries, and anecdotes on the biology and psychology of stress in humans and other species.

Taylor, S. E. (2003). *The tending instinct: Women, men, and the biology of relationships.* New York: Owl Books.

Women and men react to stress differently, a point beautifully made in a book that fosters in the reader a new appreciation of the importance of nurturance and communication in health and relationships.

ANSWERS TO KEY CONCEPT QUIZ

1. c; 2. b; 3. b; 4. c; 5. d; 6. a; 7. b; 8. c; 9. b; 10. c; 11. d; 12. a; 13. b; 14. c.

Need more help? Additional resources are located at the book's free companion Web site at:
www.worthpublishers.com/schacter

Glossary

absentmindedness A lapse in attention that results in memory failure. (p. 244)

absolute threshold The minimal intensity needed to just barely detect a stimulus. (p. 129)

accommodation The process by which the eye maintains a clear image on the retina. (p. 135)

accommodation The process by which infants revise their schemas in light of new information. (p. 430)

acetylcholine (ACH) A neurotransmitter involved in a number of functions, including voluntary motor control. (p. 87)

acquisition The phase of classical conditioning when the CS and the US are presented together. (p. 266)

action potential An electric signal that is conducted along a neuron's axon to a synapse. (p. 84)

activation-synthesis model The theory that dreams are produced when the brain attempts to make sense of activations that occur randomly during sleep. (p. 198)

actor-observer effect The tendency to make situational attributions for our own behaviors while making dispositional attributions for the identical behavior of others. (p. 544)

adolescence The period of development that begins with the onset of sexual maturity (about 11 to 14 years of age) and lasts until the beginning of adulthood (about 18 to 21 years of age). (p. 448)

adulthood The stage of development that begins around 18 to 21 years and ends at death. (p. 456)

aggression Behavior whose purpose is to harm another. (p. 507)

agonists Drugs that increase the action of a neurotransmitter. (p. 88)

agoraphobia An extreme fear of venturing into public places. (p. 562)

alcohol myopia A condition that results when alcohol hampers attention, leading people to respond in simple ways to complex situations. (p. 204)

algorithm A well-defined sequence of procedures or rules that guarantees a solution to a problem. (p. 370)

altered states of consciousness Forms of experience that depart from the normal subjective experience of the world and the mind. (p. 190)

altruism Behavior that benefits another without benefiting oneself. (p. 514)

amygdala A part of the limbic system that plays a central role in many emotional processes, particularly the formation of emotional memories. (p. 99)

anal stage The second psychosexual stage, which is dominated by the pleasures and frustrations associated with the anus, retention and expulsion of feces and urine, and toilet training. (p. 485)

analogical problem solving Solving a problem by finding a similar problem with a known solution and applying that solution to the current problem. (p. 377)

anorexia nervosa An eating disorder characterized by an intense fear of being fat and severe restriction of food intake. (p. 330)

antagonists Drugs that block the function of a neurotransmitter. (p. 88)

anterograde amnesia The inability to transfer new information from the short-term store into the long-term store. (p. 228)

antianxiety medications Drugs that help reduce a person's experience of fear or anxiety. (p. 608)

antidepressants A class of drugs that help lift people's mood. (p. 609)

antipsychotic drugs Medications that are used to treat schizophrenia and related psychotic disorders. (p. 606)

antisocial personality disorder (APD) A pervasive pattern of disregard for and violation of the rights of others that begins in childhood or early adolescence and continues into adulthood. (p. 583)

anxiety disorder The class of mental disorder in which anxiety is the predominant feature. (p. 558)

aphasia Difficulty in producing or comprehending language. (p. 357)

apparent motion The perception of movement as a result of alternating signals appearing in rapid succession in different locations. (p. 154)

appraisal An evaluation of the emotion-relevant aspects of a stimulus. (p. 313)

approach motivation A motivation to experience positive outcomes. (p. 341)

area A1 A portion of the temporal lobe that contains the primary auditory cortex. (p. 159)

area V1 The part of the occipital lobe that contains the primary visual cortex. (p. 141)

assimilation The process by which infants apply their schemas in novel situations. (p. 430)

association areas Areas of the cerebral cortex that are composed of neurons that help provide sense and meaning to information registered in the cortex. (p. 102)

attachment The emotional bond that forms between newborns and their primary caregivers. (p. 440)

attitude An enduring positive or negative evaluation of an object or event. (p. 531)

attribution An inference about the cause of a person's behavior. (p. 542)

autonomic nervous system (ANS) A set of nerves that carries involuntary and automatic commands that control blood vessels, body organs, and glands. (p. 92)

availability bias Items that are more readily available in memory are judged as having occurred more frequently. (p. 369)

avoidance motivation A motivation not to experience negative outcomes. (p. 341)

axon The part of a neuron that transmits information to other neurons, muscles, or glands. (p. 79)

balanced placebo design A study design in which behavior is observed following the presence or absence of an actual stimulus and also following the presence or absence of a placebo stimulus. (p. 204)

basal ganglia A set of subcortical structures that directs intentional movements. (p. 99)

basilar membrane A structure in the inner ear that undulates when vibrations from the ossicles reach the cochlear fluid. (p. 159)

behavior Observable actions of human beings and nonhuman animals. (p. 2)

behavior therapy A type of therapy that assumes that disordered behavior is learned and that symptom relief is achieved through changing overt maladaptive behaviors into more constructive behaviors. (p. 597)

behavioral neuroscience An approach to psychology that links psychological processes to activities in the nervous system and other bodily processes. (p. 24)

behaviorism An approach that advocates that psychologists restrict themselves to the scientific study of objectively observable behavior. (p. 16)

belief An enduring piece of knowledge about an object or event. (p. 531)

belief bias People's judgments about whether to accept conclusions depend more on how believable the conclusions are than on whether the arguments are logically valid. (p. 383)

bias The distorting influences of present knowledge, beliefs, and feelings on recollection of previous experiences. (p. 253)

Big Five The traits of the five-factor model: conscientiousness, agreeableness, neuroticism, openness to experience, and extraversion. (p. 474)

binding problem How features are linked together so that we see unified objects in our visual world rather than free-floating or miscombined features. (p. 145)

binocular disparity The difference in the retinal images of the two eyes that provides information about depth. (p. 152)

biofeedback The use of an external monitoring device to obtain information about a bodily function and possibly gain control over that function. (p. 640)

biological preparedness A propensity for learning particular kinds of associations over others. (p. 275)

bipolar disorder An unstable emotional condition characterized by cycles of abnormal, persistent high mood (mania) and low mood (depression). (p. 570)

blind spot A location in the visual field that produces no sensation on the retina because the corresponding area of the retina contains neither rods nor cones and therefore has no mechanism to sense light. (p. 137)

blocking A failure to retrieve information that is available in memory even though you are trying to produce it. (p. 246)

bulimia nervosa An eating disorder characterized by binge eating followed by purging. (p. 330)

burnout A state of physical, emotional, and mental exhaustion created by long-term involvement in an emotionally demanding situation and accompanied by lowered performance and motivation. (p. 636)

Cannon-Bard theory A theory which asserts that a stimulus simultaneously triggers activity in the autonomic nervous system and emotional experience in the brain. (p. 311)

case method A method of gathering scientific knowledge by studying a single individual. (p. 65)

catatonic behavior A marked decrease in all movement or an increase in muscular rigidity and overactivity. (p. 575)

category-specific deficit A neurological syndrome that is characterized by an inability to recognize objects that belong to a particular category though the ability to recognize objects outside the category is undisturbed. (p. 367)

cell body The part of a neuron that coordinates information-processing tasks and keeps the cell alive. (p. 79)

central nervous system (CNS) The part of the nervous system that is composed of the brain and spinal cord. (p. 91)

cephalocaudal rule The "top-to-bottom" rule that describes the tendency for motor skills to emerge in sequence from the head to the feet. (p. 428)

cerebellum A large structure of the hindbrain that controls fine motor skills. (p. 96)

cerebral cortex The outermost layer of the brain, visible to the naked eye and divided into two hemispheres. (p. 97)

change blindness When people fail to detect changes to the visual details of a scene. (p. 155)

childhood The stage of development that begins at about 18 to 24 months and lasts until adolescence. (p. 432)

chromosomes Strands of DNA wound around each other in a double-helix configuration. (p. 108)

chronic stressor A source of stress that occurs continuously or repeatedly. (p. 628)

chunking Combining small pieces of information into larger clusters or chunks that are more easily held in short-term memory. (p. 226)

circadian rhythm A naturally occurring 24-hour cycle. (p. 191)

classical conditioning When a neutral stimulus produces a response after being paired with a stimulus that naturally produces a response. (p. 265)

cochlea A fluid-filled tube that is the organ of auditory transduction. (p. 159)

cocktail party phenomenon A phenomenon in which people tune in one message even while they filter out others nearby. (p. 180)

cognitive behavioral therapy (CBT) A blend of cognitive and behavioral therapeutic strategies. (p. 600)

cognitive development The emergence of the ability to think and understand. (p. 429)

cognitive dissonance An unpleasant state that arises when a person recognizes the inconsistency of his or her actions, attitudes, or beliefs. (p. 534)

cognitive map A mental representation of the physical features of the environment. (p. 288)

cognitive neuroscience A field that attempts to understand the links between cognitive processes and brain activity. (p. 25)

cognitive psychology The scientific study of mental processes, including perception, thought, memory, and reasoning. (p. 22)

cognitive restructuring A therapeutic approach that teaches clients to question the automatic beliefs, assumptions, and predictions that often lead to negative emotions and to replace negative thinking with more realistic and positive beliefs. (p. 599)

cognitive therapy A form of psychotherapy that involves helping a client identify and correct any distorted thinking about self, others, or the world. (p. 599)

cognitive unconscious The mental processes that give rise to the person's thoughts, choices, emotions, and behavior even though they are not experienced by the person. (p. 188)

color-opponent system Pairs of visual neurons that work in opposition. (p. 141)

comorbidity The co-occurrence of two or more disorders in a single individual. (p. 554)

companionate love An experience involving affection, trust, and concern for a partner's well-being. (p. 522)

comparison level The cost-benefit ratio that people believe they deserve or could attain in another relationship. (p. 523)

concept A mental representation that groups or categorizes shared features of related objects, events, or other stimuli. (p. 363)

concrete operational stage The stage of development that begins at about 6 years and ends at about 11 years, in which children learn how various actions or "operations" can affect or transform "concrete" objects. (p. 432)

conditioned response (CR) A reaction that resembles an unconditioned response but is produced by a conditioned stimulus. (p. 265)

conditioned stimulus (CS) A stimulus that is initially neutral and produces no reliable response in an organism. (p. 265)

cones Photoreceptors that detect color, operate under normal daylight conditions, and allow us to focus on fine detail. (p. 136)

conformity The tendency to do what others do simply because others are doing it. (p. 528)

conjunction fallacy When people think that two events are more likely to occur together than either individual event. (p. 370)

conscious motivation A motivation of which one is aware. (p. 340)

consciousness A person's subjective experience of the world and the mind. (pp. 8, 176)

conservation The notion that the quantitative properties of an object are invariant despite changes in the object's appearance. (p. 432)

consolidation The process by which memories become stable in the brain. (p. 229)

control group The group of people who are not treated in the particular way that the experimental group is treated in an experiment. (p. 60)

conventional stage A stage of moral development in which the morality of an action is primarily determined by the extent to which it conforms to social rules. (p. 444)

conversion disorder A disorder characterized by apparently debilitating physical symptoms that appear to be voluntary—but that the person experiences as involuntary. (p. 24)

cooperation Behavior by two or more individuals that leads to mutual benefit. (p. 510)

corpus callosum A thick band of nerve fibers that connects large areas of the cerebral cortex on each side of the brain and supports communication of information across the hemispheres. (p. 100)

correlation Two variables are said to "be correlated" when variations in the value of one variable are synchronized with variations in the value of the other. (p. 53)

correlation coefficient A measure of the direction and strength of a correlation, which is signified by the letter *r*. (p. 54)

correspondence bias The tendency to make a dispositional attribution even when a person's behavior was caused by the situation. (p. 543)

crystallized intelligence The ability to retain and use knowledge that was acquired through experience. (p. 401)

cultural psychology The study of how cultures reflect and shape the psychological processes of their members. (p. 28)

debriefing A verbal description of the true nature and purpose of a study. (p. 70)

deep structure The meaning of a sentence. (p. 351)

defense mechanisms Unconscious coping mechanisms that reduce anxiety generated by threats from unacceptable impulses. (p. 482)

deindividuation A phenomenon that occurs when immersion in a group causes people to become less aware of their individual values. (p. 513)

delusion A patently false belief system, often bizarre and grandiose, that is maintained in spite of its irrationality. (p. 574)

demand characteristics Those aspects of an observational setting that cause people to behave as they think they should. (p. 45)

dendrites The part of a neuron that receives information from other neurons and relays it to the cell body. (p. 79)

dependent variable The variable that is measured in a study. (p. 60)

depressants Substances that reduce the activity of the central nervous system. (p. 203)

developmental psychology The study of continuity and change across the life span. (p. 424)

deviation IQ A statistic obtained by dividing a person's test score by the average test score of people in the same age group and then multiplying the quotient by 100 (see *ratio IQ*). (p. 393)

diathesis-stress model Suggests that a person may be predisposed for a mental disorder that remains unexpressed until triggered by stress. (p. 556)

dichotic listening A task in which people wearing headphones hear different messages presented to each ear. (p. 180)

diffusion chain A process in which individuals initially learn a behavior by observing another individual perform that behavior, and then serve as a model from which other individuals learn the behavior. (p. 295)

diffusion of responsibility The tendency for individuals to feel diminished responsibility for their actions when they are surrounded by others who are acting the same way. (p. 513)

discrimination The capacity to distinguish between similar but distinct stimuli. (p. 269)

discrimination Positive or negative behavior toward another person based on their group membership. (p. 510)

disorganized speech A severe disruption of verbal communication in which ideas shift rapidly and incoherently from one to another unrelated topic. (p. 575)

displacement A defense mechanism that involves shifting unacceptable wishes or drives to a neutral or less-threatening alternative. (p. 483)

display rules Norms for the control of emotional expression. (p. 321)

dissociative amnesia The sudden loss of memory for significant personal information. (p. 573)

dissociative disorder A condition in which normal cognitive processes are severely disjointed and fragmented, creating significant disruptions in memory, awareness, or personality that can vary in length from a matter of minutes to many years. (p. 571)

dissociative fugue The sudden loss of memory for one's personal history, accompanied by an abrupt departure from home and the assumption of a new identity. (p. 573)

dissociative identity disorder (DID) The presence within an individual of two or more distinct identities that at different times take control of the individual's behavior. (p. 572)

door-in-the-face technique A strategy that uses reciprocating concessions to influence behavior. (p. 528)

dopamine A neurotransmitter that regulates motor behavior, motivation, pleasure, and emotional arousal. (p. 87)

dopamine hypothesis The idea that schizophrenia involves an excess of dopamine activity. (p. 578)

double depression A moderately depressed mood that persists for at least 2 years and is punctuated by periods of major depression. (p. 565)

double-blind An observation whose true purpose is hidden from both the observer and the person being observed. (p. 48)

drive An internal state generated by departures from physiological optimality. (p. 328)

drug tolerance The tendency for larger doses of a drug to be required over time to achieve the same effect. (p. 201)

DSM-IV-TR (*Diagnostic and Statistical Manual of Mental Disorders [Fourth Edition, Text Revision]*) A classification system that describes the features used to diagnose each recognized mental disorder and indicates how the disorder can be distinguished from other, similar problems. (p. 552)

dynamic unconscious An active system encompassing a lifetime of hidden memories, the person's deepest instincts and desires, and the person's inner struggle to control these forces. (pp. 187, 480)

dysthymia A disorder that involves the same symptoms as in depression, only less severe, but the symptoms last longer, persisting for at least 2 years. (p. 565)

echoic memory A fast-decaying store of auditory information. (p. 226)

eclectic psychotherapy Treatment that draws on techniques from different forms of therapy, depending on the client and the problem. (p. 594)

ego The component of personality, developed through contact with the external world, that enables us to deal with life's practical demands. (p. 481)

egocentrism The failure to understand that the world appears differently to different observers. (p. 433)

elaborative encoding The process of actively relating new information to knowledge that is already in memory. (p. 221)

electroconvulsive therapy (ECT) A treatment that involves inducing a mild seizure by delivering an electrical shock to the brain. (p. 613)

electroencephalograph (EEG) A device used to record electrical activity in the brain. (p. 114)

electromyograph (EMG) A device that measures muscle contractions under the surface of a person's skin. (p. 44)

electrooculograph (EOG) An instrument that measures eye movements. (p. 191)

embryonic stage The period of prenatal development that lasts from the second week until about the eighth week. (p. 425)

emotion A positive or negative experience that is associated with a particular pattern of physiological activity. (p. 310)

emotion regulation The use of cognitive and behavioral strategies to influence one's emotional experience. (p. 316)

emotional expression Any observable sign of an emotional state. (p. 317)

emotional intelligence The ability to reason about emotions and to use emotions to enhance reasoning. (p. 403)

empirical method A set of rules and techniques for observation. (p. 42)

empiricism The belief that accurate knowledge can be acquired through observation. (p. 40)

encoding The process by which we transform what we perceive, think, or feel into an enduring memory. (p. 220)

encoding specificity principle The idea that a retrieval cue can serve as an effective reminder when it helps re-create the specific way in which information was initially encoded. (p. 233)

endorphins Chemicals that act within the pain pathways and emotion centers of the brain. (p. 87)

episodic memory The collection of past personal experiences that occurred at a particular time and place. (p. 240)

equity A state of affairs in which the cost-benefit ratios of two partners are roughly equal. (p. 524)

evolutionary psychology A psychological approach that explains mind and behavior in terms of the adaptive value of abilities that are preserved over time by natural selection. (p. 26)

exemplar theory A theory of categorization that argues that we make category judgments by comparing a new instance with stored memories for other instances of the category. (p. 365)

existential approach A school of thought that regards personality as governed by an individual's ongoing choices and decisions in the context of the realities of life and death. (p. 488)

expectancy theory The idea that alcohol effects can be produced by people's expectations of how alcohol will influence them in particular situations. (p. 204)

experiment A technique for establishing the causal relationship between variables. (p. 59)

experimental group The group of people who are treated in a particular way, as compared to the control group, in an experiment. (p. 60)

explicit memory The act of consciously or intentionally retrieving past experiences. (p. 238)

exposure therapy An approach to treatment that involves confronting an emotion-arousing stimulus directly and repeatedly, ultimately leading to a decrease in the emotional response. (p. 598)

external validity A property of an experiment in which the variables have been operationally defined in a normal, typical, or realistic way. (p. 64)

extinction The gradual elimination of a learned response that occurs when the US is no longer presented. (p. 268)

extrinsic motivation A motivation to take actions that are not themselves rewarding but that lead to reward. (p. 338)

facial feedback hypothesis The hypothesis that emotional expressions can cause the emotional experiences they signify. (p. 320)

factor analysis A statistical technique that explains a large number of correlations in terms of a small number of underlying factors. (p. 398)

false recognition A feeling of familiarity about something that hasn't been encountered before. (p. 249)

family resemblance theory Members of a category have features that appear to be characteristic of category members but may not be possessed by every member. (p. 364)

fast mapping The fact that children can map a word onto an underlying concept after only a single exposure. (p. 352)

feature integration theory The idea that focused attention is not required to detect the individual features that comprise a stimulus, but is required to bind those individual features together. (p. 145)

fetal alcohol syndrome A developmental disorder that stems from heavy alcohol use by the mother during pregnancy. (p. 426)

fetal stage The period of prenatal development that lasts from the ninth week until birth. (p. 426)

fight-or-flight response An emotional and physiological reaction to an emergency that increases readiness for action. (p. 630)

fixation A phenomenon in which a person's pleasure-seeking drives become psychologically stuck, or arrested, at a particular psychosexual stage. (p. 484)

fixed interval schedule (FI) An operant conditioning principle in which reinforcements are presented at fixed time periods, provided that the appropriate response is made. (p. 282)

fixed ratio schedule (FR) An operant conditioning principle in which reinforcement is delivered after a specific number of responses have been made. (p. 283)

flashbulb memories Detailed recollections of when and where we heard about shocking events. (p. 254)

fluid intelligence The ability to see abstract relationships and draw logical inferences. (p. 401)

foot-in-the-door technique A technique that involves a small request followed by a larger request. (p. 533)

formal operational stage The stage of development that begins around the age of 11 and lasts through adulthood, in which children can solve nonphysical problems. (p. 433)

fovea An area of the retina where vision is the clearest and there are no rods at all. (p. 136)

framing effects When people give different answers to the same problem depending on how the problem is phrased (or framed). (p. 371)

fraternal twins (also called **dizygotic twins**) Twins who develop from two different eggs that were fertilized by two different sperm (see *identical twins*). (p. 405)

frequency distribution A graphical representation of the measurements arranged by the number of times each measurement was made. (p. 48)

frequency format hypothesis The proposal that our minds evolved to notice how frequently things occur, not how likely they are to occur. (p. 373)

frontal lobe A region of the cerebral cortex that has specialized areas for movement, abstract thinking, planning, memory, and judgment. (p. 102)

frustration-aggression hypothesis A principle stating that animals aggress only when their goals are thwarted. (p. 507)

full consciousness Consciousness in which you know and are able to report your mental state. (p. 181)

functional fixedness The tendency to perceive the functions of objects as fixed. (p. 380)

functionalism The study of the purpose mental processes serve in enabling people to adapt to their environment. (p. 10)

GABA (gamma-aminobutyric acid) The primary inhibitory neurotransmitter in the brain. (p. 87)

gate-control theory A theory of pain perception based on the idea that signals arriving from pain receptors in the body can be stopped, or *gated*, by interneurons in the spinal cord via feedback from two directions. (p. 164)

gene The unit of hereditary transmission. (p. 108)

general adaptation syndrome (GAS) A three-stage physiological response that appears regardless of the stressor that is encountered. (p. 631)

generalization A process in which the CR is observed even though the CS is slightly different from the original one used during acquisition. (p. 269)

generalized anxiety disorder (GAD) A disorder characterized by chronic excessive worry accompanied by three or more of the following symptoms: restlessness, fatigue, concentration problems, irritability, muscle tension, and sleep disturbance. (p. 559)

genetic dysphasia A syndrome characterized by an inability to learn the grammatical structure of language despite having otherwise normal intelligence. (p. 355)

genital stage The final psychosexual stage, a time for the coming together of the mature adult personality with a capacity to love, work, and relate to others in a mutually satisfying and reciprocal manner. (p. 485)

germinal stage The 2-week period of prenatal development that begins at conception. (p. 425)

Gestalt psychology A psychological approach that emphasizes that we often perceive the whole rather than the sum of the parts. (p. 20)

Gestalt therapy An existentialist approach to treatment with the goal of helping the client become aware of his or her thoughts, behaviors, experiences, and feelings and to "own" or take responsibility for them. (p. 602)

glial cells Support cells found in the nervous system. (p. 79)

glutamate A major excitatory neurotransmitter involved in information transmission throughout the brain. (p. 87)

grammar A set of rules that specify how the units of language can be combined to produce meaningful messages. (p. 348)

grossly disorganized behavior Behavior that is inappropriate for the situation or ineffective in attaining goals, often with specific motor disturbances. (p. 575)

group A collection of people who have something in common that distinguishes them from others. (p. 511)

group therapy Therapy in which multiple participants (who often do not know one another at the outset) work on their individual problems in a group atmosphere. (p. 604)

habituation A general process in which repeated or prolonged exposure to a stimulus results in a gradual reduction in response. (p. 299)

hair cells Specialized auditory receptor neurons embedded in the basilar membrane. (p. 159)

hallucination A false perceptual experience that has a compelling sense of being real despite the absence of external stimulation. (p. 574)

hallucinogens Drugs that alter sensation and perception and often cause visual and auditory hallucinations. (p. 207)

haptic perception The active exploration of the environment by touching and grasping objects with our hands. (p. 162)

harm reduction approach A response to high-risk behaviors that focuses on reducing the harm such behaviors have on people's lives. (p. 208)

health psychology The subfield of psychology concerned with ways psychological factors influence the causes and treatment of physical illness and the maintenance of health. (p. 626)

hedonic principle The notion that all people are motivated to experience pleasure and avoid pain. (p. 326)

helplessness theory The idea that individuals who are prone to depression automatically attribute negative experiences to causes that are internal (i.e., their own fault), stable (i.e., unlikely to change), and global (i.e., widespread). (p. 567)

heritability A measure of the variability of behavioral traits among individuals that can be accounted for by genetic factors. (p. 109)

heritability coefficient A statistic (commonly denoted as h^2) that describes the proportion of the difference between people's scores that can be explained by differences in their genes. (p. 406)

heuristic A fast and efficient strategy that may facilitate decision making but does not guarantee that a solution will be reached. (p. 370)

heuristic persuasion The process by which attitudes or beliefs are changed by appeals to habit or emotion. (p. 532)

hindbrain An area of the brain that coordinates information coming into and out of the spinal cord. (p. 96)

hippocampus A structure critical for creating new memories and integrating them into a network of knowledge so that they can be stored indefinitely in other parts of the cerebral cortex. (p. 99)

homeostasis The tendency for a system to take action to keep itself in a particular state. (p. 328)

human sexual response cycle The stages of physiological arousal during sexual activity. (p. 335)

humanistic psychology An approach to understanding human nature that emphasizes the positive potential of human beings. (p. 15)

hypnosis An altered state of consciousness characterized by suggestibility and the feeling that one's actions are occurring involuntarily. (p. 209)

hypnotic analgesia The reduction of pain through hypnosis in people who are susceptible to hypnosis. (p. 211)

hypochondriasis A psychological disorder in which a person is preoccupied with minor symptoms and develops an exaggerated belief that the symptoms signify a life-threatening illness. (p. 646)

hypothalamus A subcortical structure that regulates body temperature, hunger, thirst, and sexual behavior. (p. 98)

hypothesis A falsifiable prediction made by a theory. (p. 41)

hysteria A temporary loss of cognitive or motor functions, usually as a result of emotionally upsetting experiences. (p. 13)

iatrogenic illness A disorder or symptom that occurs as a result of a medical or psychotherapeutic treatment. (p. 620)

iconic memory A fast-decaying store of visual information. (p. 225)

id The part of the mind containing the drives present at birth; it is the source of our bodily needs, wants, desires, and impulses, particularly our sexual and aggressive drives. (p. 480)

identical twins (also called **monozygotic twins**) Twins who develop from the splitting of a single egg that was fertilized by a single sperm (see *fraternal twins*). (p. 405)

identification A defense mechanism that helps deal with feelings of threat and anxiety by enabling us unconsciously to take on the characteristics of another person who seems more powerful or better able to cope. (p. 483)

illusions Errors of perception, memory, or judgment in which subjective experience differs from objective reality. (p. 19)

illusory conjunction A perceptual mistake where features from multiple objects are incorrectly combined. (p. 145)

immune system A complex response system that protects the body from bacteria, viruses, and other foreign substances. (p. 632)

implicit learning Learning that takes place largely without awareness of the process or the products of information acquisition. (p. 298)

implicit memory The influence of past experiences on later behavior, even without an effort to remember them or an awareness of the recollection. (p. 238)

inattentional blindness A failure to perceive objects that are not the focus of attention. (p. 156)

independent variable The variable that is manipulated in an experiment. (p. 60)

infancy The stage of development that begins at birth and lasts between 18 and 24 months. (p. 427)

informational influence A phenomenon that occurs when a person's behavior provides information about what is good or right. (p. 531)

informed consent A written agreement to participate in a study made by an adult who has been informed of all the risks that participation may entail. (p. 69)

insomnia Difficulty in falling asleep or staying asleep. (p. 194)

intelligence The ability to direct one's thinking, adapt to one's circumstances, and learn from one's experiences. (p. 390)

intermittent reinforcement An operant conditioning principle in which only some of the responses made are followed by reinforcement. (p. 283)

intermittent-reinforcement effect The fact that operant behaviors that are maintained under intermittent-reinforcement schedules resist extinction better than those maintained under continuous reinforcement. (p. 284)

internal validity The characteristic of an experiment that establishes the causal relationship between variables. (p. 64)

internal working model of relationships A set of beliefs about the self, the primary caregiver, and the relationship between them. (p. 441)

interneurons Neurons that connect sensory neurons, motor neurons, or other interneurons. (p. 81)

interpersonal psychotherapy (IPT) A form of psychotherapy that focuses on helping clients improve current relationships. (p. 596)

intrinsic motivation A motivation to take actions that are themselves rewarding. (p. 338)

introspection The subjective observation of one's own experience. (p. 9)

ironic processes of mental control Mental processes that can produce ironic errors because monitoring for errors can itself produce them. (p. 186)

James-Lange theory A theory which asserts that stimuli trigger activity in the autonomic nervous system, which in turn produces an emotional experience in the brain. (p. 311)

just noticeable difference (JND) The minimal change in a stimulus that can just barely be detected. (p. 130)

kin selection The process by which evolution selects for individuals who cooperate with their relatives. (p. 514)

language A system for communicating with others using signals that are combined according to rules of grammar and to convey meaning. (p. 348)

language acquisition device (LAD) A collection of processes that facilitate language learning. (p. 355)

latency stage The fourth psychosexual stage, in which the primary focus is on the further development of intellectual, creative, interpersonal, and athletic skills. (p. 485)

latent content A dream's true underlying meaning. (p. 197)

latent learning A condition in which something is learned but it is not manifested as a behavioral change until sometime in the future. (p. 287)

law of effect The principle that behaviors that are followed by a "satisfying state of affairs" tend to be repeated and those that produce an "unpleasant state of affairs" are less likely to be repeated. (p. 277)

learning Experience that results in a relatively permanent change in the state of the learner. (p. 264)

limbic system A group of forebrain structures including the hypothalamus, the amygdala, and the hippocampus, which are involved in motivation, emotion, learning, and memory. (p. 99)

linguistic relativity hypothesis The proposal that language shapes the nature of thought. (p. 360)

locus of control A person's tendency to perceive the control of rewards as internal to the self or external in the environment. (p. 491)

long-term memory A type of storage that holds information for hours, days, weeks, or years. (p. 227)

long-term potentiation (LTP) A process where communication across the synapse between neurons strengthens the connection, making further communication easier. (p. 231)

loudness A sound's intensity. (p. 157)

lymphocytes White blood cells that produce antibodies that fight infection. (p. 632)

major depressive disorder A disorder characterized by a severely depressed mood that lasts 2 weeks or more and is accompanied by feelings of worthlessness and lack of pleasure, lethargy, and sleep and appetite disturbances. (p. 565)

manifest content A dream's apparent topic or superficial meaning. (p. 197)

manipulation The creation of an artificial pattern of variation in a variable in order to determine its causal powers. (p. 60)

marijuana The leaves and buds of the hemp plant. (p. 207)

matched pairs A technique whereby each participant is identical to one other participant in terms of a third variable. (p. 58)

matched samples A technique whereby the participants in two groups are identical in terms of a third variable. (p. 57)

mean The average value of all the measurements. (p. 49)

means-ends analysis A process of searching for the means or steps to reduce differences between the current situation and the desired goal. (p. 376)

measure A device that can detect the condition to which an operational definition refers. (p. 44)

median The value that is "in the middle"– i.e., greater than or equal to half the measurements and less than or equal to half the measurements. (p. 49)

medical model The conceptualization of psychological disorders as diseases that, like physical diseases, have biological causes, defined symptoms, and possible cures. (p. 551)

meditation The practice of intentional contemplation. (p. 213)

medulla An extension of the spinal cord into the skull that coordinates heart rate, circulation, and respiration. (p. 96)

memory The ability to store and retrieve information over time. (p. 220)

memory misattribution Assigning a recollection or an idea to the wrong source. (p. 247)

memory storage The process of maintaining information in memory over time. (p. 225)

mental control The attempt to change conscious states of mind. (p. 185)

mere exposure effect The tendency for liking to increase with the frequency of exposure. (p. 517)

metabolism The rate at which energy is used by the body. (p. 333)

mind Our private inner experience of perceptions, thoughts, memories, and feelings. (p. 2)

mind/body problem The issue of how the mind is related to the brain and the body. (p. 178)

mindfulness meditation A form of cognitive therapy that teaches an individual to be fully present in each moment; to be aware of his or her thoughts, feelings, and sensations; and to detect symptoms before they become a problem. (p. 600)

minimal consciousness A low-level kind of sensory awareness and responsiveness that occurs when the mind inputs sensations and may output behavior. (p. 181)

Minnesota Multiphasic Personality Inventory (MMPI) A well-researched, clinical questionnaire used to assess personality and psychological problems. (p. 470)

mode The value of the most frequently observed measurement. (p. 49)

monocular depth cues Aspects of a scene that yield information about depth when viewed with only one eye. (p. 151)

mood disorders Mental disorders that have mood disturbance as their predominant feature. (p. 564)

morphemes The smallest meaningful units of language. (p. 349)

morphological rules A set of rules that indicate how morphemes can be combined to form words. (p. 350)

mortality-salience hypothesis The prediction that people who are reminded of their own mortality will work to reinforce their cultural worldviews. (p. 337)

motivation The purpose for or psychological cause of an action. (p. 325)

motor development The emergence of the ability to execute physical action. (p. 428)

motor neurons Neurons that carry signals from the spinal cord to the muscles to produce movement. (p. 81)

myelin sheath An insulating layer of fatty material. (p. 79)

myelination The formation of a fatty sheath around the axons of a neuron. (p. 426)

narcissism A trait that reflects a grandiose view of the self combined with a tendency to seek admiration from and exploit others. (p. 499)

narcolepsy A disorder in which sudden sleep attacks occur in the middle of waking activities. (p. 195)

narcotics or opiates Highly addictive drugs derived from opium that relieve pain. (p. 206)

nativism The philosophical view that certain kinds of knowledge are innate or inborn. (p. 5)

nativist theory The view that language development is best explained as an innate, biological capacity. (p. 355)

natural correlation A correlation observed in the world around us. (p. 56)

natural selection Charles Darwin's theory that the features of an organism that help it survive and reproduce are more likely than other features to be passed on to subsequent generations. (p. 10)

naturalistic observation A technique for gathering scientific information by unobtrusively observing people in their natural environments. (p. 45)

need for achievement The motivation to solve worthwhile problems. (p. 340)

negative symptoms Emotional and social withdrawal; apathy; poverty of speech; and other indications of the absence or insufficiency of normal behavior, motivation, and emotion. (p. 575)

nervous system An interacting network of neurons that conveys electrochemical information throughout the body. (p. 91)

neurons Cells in the nervous system that communicate with one another to perform information-processing tasks. (p. 78)

neurotransmitters Chemicals that transmit information across the synapse to a receiving neuron's dendrites. (p. 86)

night terrors (or sleep terrors) Abrupt awakenings with panic and intense emotional arousal. (p. 196)

NMDA receptor A receptor site on the hippocampus that influences the flow of information between neurons by controlling the initiation of long-term potentiation. (p. 232)

nonshared environment Those environmental factors that are not experienced by all relevant members of a household (see *shared environment*). (p. 408)

norepinephrine A neurotransmitter that influences mood and arousal. (p. 87)

norm A customary standard for behavior that is widely shared by members of a culture. (p. 527)

norm of reciprocity The unwritten rule that people should benefit those who have benefited them. (p. 527)

normal distribution A mathematically defined frequency distribution in which most measurements are concentrated around the middle. (p. 48)

normative influence A phenomenon that occurs when another person's behavior provides information about what is appropriate. (p. 527)

obedience The tendency to do what powerful people tell us to do. (p. 530)

object permanence The idea that objects continue to exist even when they are not visible. (p. 431)

observational learning A condition in which learning takes place by watching the actions of others. (p. 293)

obsessive-compulsive disorder (OCD) A disorder in which repetitive, intrusive thoughts (obsessions) and ritualistic behaviors (compulsions) designed to fend off those thoughts interfere significantly with an individual's functioning. (p. 563)

occipital lobe A region of the cerebral cortex that processes visual information. (p. 101)

Oedipus conflict A developmental experience in which a child's conflicting feelings toward the opposite-sex parent are (usually) resolved by identifying with the same-sex parent. (p. 485)

olfactory bulb A brain structure located above the nasal cavity beneath the frontal lobes. (p. 167)

olfactory receptor neurons (ORNS) Receptor cells that initiate the sense of smell. (p. 166)

operant behavior Behavior that an organism produces that has some impact on the environment. (p. 278)

operant conditioning A type of learning in which the consequences of an organism's behavior determine whether it will be repeated in the future. (p. 277)

operational definition A description of a property in concrete, measurable terms. (p. 43)

oral stage The first psychosexual stage, in which experience centers on the pleasures and frustrations associated with the mouth, sucking, and being fed. (p. 485)

organizational encoding The process of categorizing information according to the relationships among a series of items. (p. 223)

outcome expectancies A person's assumptions about the likely consequences of a future behavior. (p. 491)

overjustification effect Circumstances when external rewards can undermine the intrinsic satisfaction of performing a behavior. (p. 280)

panic disorder A disorder characterized by the sudden occurrence of multiple psychological and physiological symptoms that contribute to a feeling of stark terror. (p. 562)

parasympathetic nervous system A set of nerves that helps the body return to a normal resting state. (p. 92)

parietal lobe A region of the cerebral cortex whose functions include processing information about touch. (p. 101)

passionate love An experience involving feelings of euphoria, intimacy, and intense sexual attraction. (p. 522)

perception The organization, identification, and interpretation of a sensation in order to form a mental representation. (p. 127)

perceptual confirmation A phenomenon that occurs when observers perceive what they expect to perceive. (p. 538)

perceptual constancy A perceptual principle stating that even as aspects of sensory signals change, perception remains consistent. (p. 148)

peripheral nervous system (PNS) The part of the nervous system that connects the central nervous system to the body's organs and muscles. (p. 91)

persistence The intrusive recollection of events that we wish we could forget. (p. 254)

personal constructs Dimensions people use in making sense of their experiences. (p. 490)

personality An individual's characteristic style of behaving, thinking, and feeling. (p. 468)

personality disorder Disorder characterized by deeply ingrained, inflexible patterns of thinking, feeling, or relating to others or controlling impulses that cause distress or impaired functioning. (p. 581)

person-centered therapy An approach to therapy that assumes all individuals have a tendency toward growth and that this growth can be facilitated by acceptance and genuine reactions from the therapist. (p. 601)

person-situation controversy The question of whether behavior is caused more by personality or by situational factors. (p. 489)

persuasion A phenomenon that occurs when a person's attitudes or beliefs are influenced by a communication from another person. (p. 532)

phallic stage The third psychosexual stage, during which experience is dominated by the pleasure, conflict, and frustration associated with the phallic-genital region as well as powerful incestuous feelings of love, hate, jealousy, and conflict. (p. 485)

phenomenology How things seem to the conscious person. (p. 176)

pheromones Biochemical odorants emitted by other members of its species that can affect an animal's behavior or physiology. (p. 167)

philosophical empiricism The philosophical view that all knowledge is acquired through experience. (p. 6)

phobic disorders Disorders characterized by marked, persistent, and excessive fear and avoidance of specific objects, activities, or situations. (p. 560)

phoneme The smallest unit of sound that is recognizable as speech rather than as random noise. (p. 349)

phonological rules A set of rules that indicate how phonemes can be combined to produce speech sounds. (p. 349)

phototherapy A therapy that involves repeated exposure to bright light. (p. 614)

phrenology A now defunct theory that specific mental abilities and characteristics, ranging from memory to the capacity for happiness, are localized in specific regions of the brain. (p. 6)

physiology The study of biological processes, especially in the human body. (p. 7)

pitch How high or low a sound is. (p. 157)

pituitary gland The "master gland" of the body's hormone-producing system, which releases hormones that direct the functions of many other glands in the body. (p. 98)

place code The cochlea encodes different frequencies at different locations along the basilar membrane. (p. 160)

placebo An inert substance or procedure that has been applied with the expectation that a healing response will be produced. (p. 616)

pons A brain structure that relays information from the cerebellum to the rest of the brain. (p. 96)

population The complete collection of participants who might possibly be measured. (p. 65)

postconventional stage A stage of moral development at which the morality of an action is determined by a set of general principles that reflect core values. (p. 445)

posthypnotic amnesia The failure to retrieve memories following hypnotic suggestions to forget. (p. 211)

post-traumatic stress disorder (PTSD) A disorder characterized by chronic physiological arousal, recurrent unwanted thoughts or images of the trauma, and avoidance of things that call the traumatic event to mind. (p. 635)

power The ability of a measure to detect the concrete conditions specified in the operational definition. (p. 45)

practical reasoning Figuring out what to do, or reasoning directed toward action. (p. 381)

preconventional stage A stage of moral development in which the morality of an action is primarily determined by its consequences for the actor. (p. 444)

prejudice A positive or negative evaluation of another person based on their group membership. (p. 511)

preoperational stage The stage of development that begins at about 2 years and ends at about 6 years, in which children have a preliminary understanding of the physical world. (p. 432)

preparedness theory The idea that people are instinctively predisposed toward certain fears. (p. 561)

primary sex characteristics Bodily structures that are directly involved in reproduction. (p. 448)

priming An enhanced ability to think of a stimulus, such as a word or object, as a result of a recent exposure to the stimulus. (p. 239)

proactive interference Situations in which information learned earlier impairs memory for information acquired later. (p. 244)

problem of other minds The fundamental difficulty we have in perceiving the consciousness of others. (p. 177)

procedural memory The gradual acquisition of skills as a result of practice or "knowing how" to do things. (p. 238)

prodigy A person of normal intelligence who has an extraordinary ability. (p. 402)

projection A defense mechanism that involves attributing one's own threatening feelings, motives, or impulses to another person or group. (p. 482)

projective techniques A standard series of ambiguous stimuli designed to elicit unique responses that reveal inner aspects of an individual's personality. (p. 470)

prospect theory Proposes that people choose to take on risk when evaluating potential losses and avoid risks when evaluating potential gains. (p. 373)

prospective memory Remembering to do things in the future. (p. 245)

prototype The "best" or "most typical" member of a category. (p. 364)

proximodistal rule The "inside-to-outside" rule that describes the tendency for motor skills to emerge in sequence from the center to the periphery. (p. 428)

psychoactive drug A chemical that influences consciousness or behavior by altering the brain's chemical message system. (p. 200)

psychoanalysis A therapeutic approach that focuses on bringing unconscious material into conscious awareness to better understand psychological disorders. (p. 14)

psychoanalytic theory Sigmund Freud's approach to understanding human behavior that emphasizes the importance of unconscious mental processes in shaping feelings, thoughts, and behaviors. (p. 13)

psychodynamic approach An approach that regards personality as formed by needs, strivings, and desires, largely operating outside of awareness—motives that can also produce emotional disorders. (p. 480)

psychodynamic psychotherapies A general approach to treatment that explores childhood events and encourages individuals to develop insight into their psychological problems. (p. 594)

psychology The scientific study of mind and behavior. (p. 2)

psychopharmacology The study of drug effects on psychological states and symptoms. (p. 606)

psychophysics Methods that measure the strength of a stimulus and the observer's sensitivity to that stimulus. (p. 129)

psychosexual stages Distinct early life stages through which personality is formed as children experience sexual pleasures from specific body areas and caregivers redirect or interfere with those pleasures. (p. 484)

psychosomatic illness An interaction between mind and body that can produce illness. (p. 646)

psychosurgery Surgical destruction of specific brain areas. (p. 614)

psychotherapy An interaction between a therapist and someone suffering from a psychological problem, with the goal of providing support or relief from the problem. (p. 594)

puberty The bodily changes associated with sexual maturity. (p. 448)

punisher Any stimulus or event that functions to decrease the likelihood of the behavior that led to it. (p. 278)

random assignment A procedure that uses a random event to assign people to the experimental or control group. (p. 62)

random sampling A technique for choosing participants that ensures that every member of a population has an equal chance of being included in the sample. (p. 66)

range The value of the largest measurement in a frequency distribution minus the value of the smallest measurement. (p. 51)

ratio IQ A statistic obtained by dividing a person's mental age by the person's physical age and then multiplying the quotient by 100 (see *deviation IQ*). (p. 391)

rational choice theory The classical view that we make decisions by determining how likely something is to happen, judging the value of the outcome, and then multiplying the two. (p. 369)

rational coping Facing a stressor and working to overcome it. (p. 638)

rationalization A defense mechanism that involves supplying a reasonable-sounding explanation for unacceptable feelings and behavior to conceal (mostly from oneself) one's underlying motives or feelings. (p. 482)

reaction formation A defense mechanism that involves unconsciously replacing threatening inner wishes and fantasies with an exaggerated version of their opposite. (p. 482)

reaction time The amount of time taken to respond to a specific stimulus. (p. 8)

reappraisal Changing one's emotional experience by changing the meaning of the emotion-eliciting stimulus. (p. 316)

reasoning A mental activity that consists of organizing information or beliefs into a series of steps to reach conclusions. (p. 381)

rebound effect of thought suppression The tendency of a thought to return to consciousness with greater frequency following suppression. (p. 185)

receptive field The region of the sensory surface that, when stimulated, causes a change in the firing rate of that neuron. (p. 138)

receptors Parts of the cell membrane that receive the neurotransmitter and initiate or prevent a new electric signal. (p. 86)

reciprocal altruism Behavior that benefits another with the expectation that those benefits will be returned in the future. (p. 514)

reconsolidation Memories can become vulnerable to disruption when they are recalled, requiring them to become consolidated again. (p. 229)

referred pain Feeling of pain when sensory information from internal and external areas converges on the same nerve cells in the spinal cord. (p. 164)

reflexes Specific patterns of motor response that are triggered by specific patterns of sensory stimulation. (p. 428)

refractory period The time following an action potential during which a new action potential cannot be initiated. (p. 85)

reframing Finding a new or creative way to think about a stressor that reduces its threat. (p. 639)

regression A defense mechanism in which the ego deals with internal conflict and perceived threat by reverting to an immature behavior or earlier stage of development. (p. 483)

rehearsal The process of keeping information in short-term memory by mentally repeating it. (p. 226)

reinforcement The consequences of a behavior that determine whether it will be more likely that the behavior will occur again. (p. 17)

reinforcer Any stimulus or event that functions to increase the likelihood of the behavior that led to it. (p. 278)

relaxation response A condition of reduced muscle tension, cortical activity, heart rate, breathing rate, and blood pressure. (p. 640)

relaxation therapy A technique for reducing tension by consciously relaxing muscles of the body. (p. 640)

reliability The tendency for a measure to produce the same measurement whenever it is used to measure the same thing. (p. 44)

REM sleep A stage of sleep characterized by rapid eye movements and a high level of brain activity. (p. 191)

representativeness heuristic A mental shortcut that involves making a probability judgment by comparing an object or event to a prototype of the object or event. (p. 371)

repression A mental process that removes unacceptable thoughts and memories from consciousness. (p. 187)

repressive coping Avoiding situations or thoughts that are reminders of a stressor and maintaining an artificially positive viewpoint. (p. 637)

resistance A reluctance to cooperate with treatment for fear of confronting unpleasant unconscious material. (p. 595)

response An action or physiological change elicited by a stimulus. (p. 17)

resting potential The difference in electric charge between the inside and outside of a neuron's cell membrane. (p. 83)

reticular formation A brain structure that regulates sleep, wakefulness, and levels of arousal. (p. 96)

retina Light-sensitive tissue lining the back of the eyeball. (p. 135)

retrieval The process of bringing to mind information that has been previously encoded and stored. (p. 220)

retrieval cue External information that helps bring stored information to mind. (p. 233)

retrieval-induced forgetting A process by which retrieving an item from long-term memory impairs subsequent recall of related items. (p. 235)

retroactive interference Situations in which information learned later impairs memory for information acquired earlier. (p. 244)

retrograde amnesia The inability to retrieve information that was acquired before a particular date, usually the date of an injury or operation. (p. 228)

rods Photoreceptors that become active under low-light conditions for night vision. (p. 136)

Rorschach Inkblot Test A projective personality test in which individual interpretations of the meaning of a set of unstructured inkblots are analyzed to identify a respondent's inner feelings and interpret his or her personality structure. (p. 471)

sample The partial collection of people drawn from a population. (p. 65)

savant A person of low intelligence who has an extraordinary ability. (p. 402)

schemas Theories about or models of the way the world works. (p. 430)

schizophrenia A disorder characterized by the profound disruption of basic psychological processes; a distorted perception of reality; altered or blunted emotion; and disturbances in thought, motivation, and behavior. (p. 574)

scientific method A set of principles about the appropriate relationship between ideas and evidence. (p. 40)

seasonal affective disorder (SAD) Depression that involves recurrent depressive episodes in a seasonal pattern. (p. 565)

secondary sex characteristics Bodily structures that change dramatically with sexual maturity but that are not directly involved in reproduction. (p. 448)

second-order conditioning Conditioning where the US is a stimulus that acquired its ability to produce learning from an earlier procedure in which it was used as a CS. (p. 268)

self-actualizing tendency The human motive toward realizing our inner potential. (p. 486)

self-concept A person's explicit knowledge of his or her own behaviors, traits, and other personal characteristics. (p. 493)

self-consciousness A distinct level of consciousness in which the person's attention is drawn to the self as an object. (p. 182)

self-esteem The extent to which an individual likes, values, and accepts the self. (p. 495)

self-fulfilling prophecy The tendency for people to cause what they expect to see. (p. 539)

self-regulation The exercise of voluntary control over the self to bring the self into line with preferred standards. (p. 651)

self-report A series of answers to a questionnaire that asks people to indicate the extent to which sets of statements or adjectives accurately describe their own behavior or mental state. (p. 469)

self-selection A problem that occurs when anything about a person determines whether he or she will be included in the experimental or control group. (p. 61)

self-serving bias People's tendency to take credit for their successes but downplay responsibility for their failures. (p. 498)

self-verification The tendency to seek evidence to confirm the self-concept. (p. 495)

semantic memory A network of associated facts and concepts that make up our general knowledge of the world. (p. 240)

sensation Simple stimulation of a sense organ. (p. 127)

sensorimotor stage A stage of development that begins at birth and lasts through infancy in which infants acquire information about the world by sensing it and moving around within it. (p. 430)

sensory adaptation Sensitivity to prolonged stimulation tends to decline over time as an organism adapts to current conditions. (p. 133)

sensory memory A type of storage that holds sensory information for a few seconds or less. (p. 225)

sensory neurons Neurons that receive information from the external world and convey this information to the brain via the spinal cord. (p. 81)

serotonin A neurotransmitter that is involved in the regulation of sleep and wakefulness, eating, and aggressive behavior. (p. 87)

shaping Learning that results from the reinforcement of successive steps to a final desired behavior. (p. 284)

shared environment Those environmental factors that are experienced by all relevant members of a household (see *nonshared environment*). (p. 407)

short-term memory A type of storage that holds nonsensory information for more than a few seconds but less than a minute. (p. 226)

sick role A socially recognized set of rights and obligations linked with illness. (p. 647)

signal detection theory An observation that the response to a stimulus depends both on a person's sensitivity to the stimulus in the presence of noise and on a person's response criterion. (p. 131)

sleep apnea A disorder in which the person stops breathing for brief periods while asleep. (p. 195)

sleep paralysis The experience of waking up unable to move. (p. 196)

social cognition The processes by which people come to understand others. (p. 536)

social cognitive approach An approach that views personality in terms of how the person thinks about the situations encountered in daily life and behaves in response to them. (p. 489)

social exchange The hypothesis that people remain in relationships only as long as they perceive a favorable ratio of costs to benefits. (p. 523)

social influence The ability to control another person's behavior. (p. 525)

social phobia A disorder that involves an irrational fear of being publicly humiliated or embarrassed. (p. 560)

social psychology A subfield of psychology that studies the causes and consequences of interpersonal behavior. (p. 27)

social psychology The study of the causes and consequences of sociality. (p. 507)

social support The aid gained through interacting with others. (p. 641)

somatic nervous system A set of nerves that conveys information into and out of the central nervous system. (p. 92)

somatization disorder A psychological disorder involving combinations of multiple physical complaints with no medical explanation. (p. 646)

somatoform disorders The set of psychological disorders in which the person displays physical symptoms not fully explained by a general medical condition. (p. 646)

somnambulism (sleepwalking) Occurs when the person arises and walks around while asleep. (p. 195)

source memory Recall of when, where, and how information was acquired. (p. 248)

specific phobia A disorder that involves an irrational fear of a particular object or situation that markedly interferes with an individual's ability to function. (p. 560)

spinal reflexes Simple pathways in the nervous system that rapidly generate muscle contractions. (p. 94)

spontaneous recovery The tendency of a learned behavior to recover from extinction after a rest period. (p. 269)

standard deviation A statistic that describes the average difference between the measurements in a frequency distribution and the mean of that distribution. (p. 51)

state-dependent retrieval The tendency for information to be better recalled when the person is in the same state during encoding and retrieval. (p. 234)

stereotyping The process by which people draw inferences about others based on their knowledge of the categories to which others belong. (p. 536)

stimulants Substances that excite the central nervous system, heightening arousal and activity levels. (p. 205)

stimulus Sensory input from the environment. (p. 8)

storage The process of maintaining information in memory over time. (p. 220)

strange situation A behavioral test developed by Mary Ainsworth that is used to determine a child's attachment style. (p. 440)

stress The physical and psychological response to internal or external stressors. (p. 626)

stress inoculation training (SIT) A therapy that helps people to cope with stressful situations by developing positive ways to think about the situation. (p. 639)

stressors Specific events or chronic pressures that place demands on a person or threaten the person's well-being. (p. 626)

structuralism The analysis of the basic elements that constitute the mind. (p. 9)

subcortical structures Areas of the forebrain housed under the cerebral cortex near the very center of the brain. (p. 97)

sublimation A defense mechanism that involves channeling unacceptable sexual or aggressive drives into socially acceptable and culturally enhancing activities. (p. 483)

subliminal perception A thought or behavior that is influenced by stimuli that a person cannot consciously report perceiving. (p. 188)

subtyping The tendency for people who are faced with disconfirming evidence to modify their stereotypes rather than abandon them. (p. 539)

suggestibility The tendency to incorporate misleading information from external sources into personal recollections. (p. 251)

sunk-cost fallacy A framing effect in which people make decisions about a current situation based on what they have previously invested in the situation. (p. 372)

superego The mental system that reflects the internalization of cultural rules, mainly learned as parents exercise their authority. (p. 481)

surface structure How a sentence is worded. (p. 351)

syllogistic reasoning Determining whether a conclusion follows from two statements that are assumed to be true. (p. 383)

sympathetic nervous system A set of nerves that prepares the body for action in threatening situations. (p. 92)

synapse The junction or region between the axon of one neuron and the dendrites or cell body of another. (p. 80)

synesthesia The perceptual experience of one sense that is evoked by another sense. (p. 126)

syntactical rules A set of rules that indicate how words can be combined to form phrases and sentences. (p. 350)

systematic desensitization A procedure in which a client relaxes all the muscles of his or her body while imagining being in increasingly frightening situations. (p. 598)

systematic persuasion The process by which attitudes or beliefs are changed by appeals to reason. (p. 532)

taste buds The organ of taste transduction. (p. 169)

tectum A part of the midbrain that orients an organism in the environment. (p. 96)

tegmentum A part of the midbrain that is involved in movement and arousal. (p. 97)

telegraphic speech Speech that is devoid of function morphemes and consists mostly of content words. (p. 352)

temperaments Characteristic patterns of emotional reactivity. (p. 442)

template A mental representation that can be directly compared to a viewed shape in the retinal image. (p. 150)

temporal code The cochlea registers low frequencies via the firing rate of action potentials entering the auditory nerve. (p. 161)

temporal lobe A region of the cerebral cortex responsible for hearing and language. (p. 102)

teratogens Agents that damage the process of development, such as drugs and viruses. (p. 426)

terminal buttons Knoblike structures that branch out from an axon. (p. 86)

thalamus A subcortical structure that relays and filters information from the senses and transmits the information to the cerebral cortex. (p. 98)

Thematic Apperception Test (TAT) A projective personality test in which respondents reveal underlying motives, concerns, and the way they see the social world through the stories they make up about ambiguous pictures of people. (p. 471)

theoretical reasoning Reasoning directed toward arriving at a belief. (p. 381)

theory A hypothetical explanation of a natural phenomenon. (p. 40)

theory of mind The idea that human behavior is guided by mental representations. (p. 434)

third-variable correlation The fact that two variables are correlated only because each is causally related to a third variable. (p. 57)

third-variable problem The fact that a causal relationship between two variables cannot be inferred from the naturally occurring correlation between them because of the ever-present possibility of third-variable correlation. (p. 59)

thought suppression The conscious avoidance of a thought. (p. 185)

timbre A listener's experience of sound quality or resonance. (p. 158)

token economy A form of behavior therapy in which clients are given "tokens" for desired behaviors, which they can later trade for rewards. (p. 598)

trait A relatively stable disposition to behave in a particular and consistent way. (p. 472)

transcranial magnetic stimulation (TMS) A treatment that involves placing a powerful pulsed magnet over a person's scalp, which alters neuronal activity in the brain. (p. 614)

transduction What takes place when many sensors in the body convert physical signals from the environment into encoded neural signals sent to the central nervous system. (p. 127)

transfer-appropriate processing The idea that memory is likely to transfer from one situation to another when the encoding context of the situations match. (p. 234)

transference An event that occurs in psychoanalysis when the analyst begins to assume a major significance in the client's life and the client reacts to the analyst based on unconscious childhood fantasies. (p. 596)

transience Forgetting what occurs with the passage of time. (p. 243)

trichromatic color representation The pattern of responding across the three types of cones that provides a unique code for each color. (p. 140)

two-factor theory A theory which asserts that emotions are inferences about the causes of physiological arousal. (p. 311)

two-factor theory of intelligence Spearman's theory suggesting that every task requires a combination of a general ability (which he called *g*) and skills that are specific to the task (which he called *s*). (p. 398)

Type A behavior pattern The tendency toward easily aroused hostility, impatience, a sense of time urgency, and competitive achievement strivings. (p. 634)

unconditioned response (UR) A reflexive reaction that is reliably produced by an unconditioned stimulus. (p. 265)

unconditioned stimulus (US) Something that reliably produces a naturally occurring reaction in an organism. (p. 265)

unconscious The part of the mind that operates outside of conscious awareness but influences conscious thoughts, feelings, and actions. (p. 13)

unconscious motivation A motivation of which one is not aware. (p. 340)

universality hypothesis The hypothesis that emotional expressions have the same meaning for everyone. (p. 318)

validity The extent to which a measurement and a property are conceptually related. (p. 44)

variable A property whose value can vary across individuals or over time. (p. 52)

variable interval schedule (VI) An operant conditioning principle in which behavior is reinforced based on an average time that has expired since the last reinforcement. (p. 282)

variable ratio schedule (VR) An operant conditioning principle in which the delivery of reinforcement is based on a particular average number of responses. (p. 283)

vestibular system The three fluid-filled semi-circular canals and adjacent organs located next to the cochlea in each inner ear. (p. 165)

visual acuity The ability to see fine detail. (p. 134)

visual imagery encoding The process of storing new information by converting it into mental pictures. (p. 222)

visual-form agnosia The inability to recognize objects by sight. (p. 143)

Weber's law The just noticeable difference of a stimulus is a constant proportion despite variations in intensity. (p. 130)

working memory Active maintenance of information in short-term storage. (p. 226)

zygote A fertilized egg that contains chromosomes from both a sperm and an egg. (p. 425)

References

Aarts, H., Custers, R., & Marien, H. (2008). Preparing and motivating behavior outside of awareness. *Science, 319*, 1639.

Abbott, J. M., Klein, B., & Ciechomski, L. (2008). Best practices in online therapy. *Journal of Technology in Human Services, 26*, 360–375.

Abel, T., Alberini, C., Ghirardi, M., Huang, Y.-Y., Nguyen, P., & Kandel, E. R. (1995). Steps toward a molecular definition of memory consolidation. In D. L. Schacter (Ed.), *Memory distortion: How minds, brains and societies reconstruct the past* (pp. 298–328). Cambridge, MA: Harvard University Press.

Abelson, J., Curtis, G., Sagher, O., Albucher, R., Harrigan, M., Taylor, S., et al. (2009). Deep brain stimulation for refractory obsessive-compulsive disorder. *Biological Psychiatry, 57*, 510–516.

Abrams, M., & Reber, A. S. (1988). Implicit learning: Robustness in the face of psychiatric disorders. *Journal of Psycholinguistic Research, 17*, 425–439.

Abramson, L. Y., Alloy, L. B., Hankin, B. L., Haeffel, G. J., MacCoon, D. G., & Gibb, B. E. (2002). Cognitive vulnerability-stress models of depression in a self-regulatory and psychobiological context. In I. H. Gotlib & C. L. Hammen (Eds.), *Handbook of depression* (pp. 268–294). New York: Guilford Press.

Abramson, L. Y., Seligman, M. E. P., & Teasdale, J. D. (1978). Learned helplessness in humans: Critique and reformulation. *Journal of Abnormal Psychology, 87*, 49–74.

Abromov, I., & Gordon, J. (1994). Color appearance: On seeing red—or yellow, or green, or blue. *Annual Review of Psychology, 45*, 451–485.

Acevedo, B. P., & Aron, A. (2009). Does a long-term relationship kill romantic love? *Review of General Psychology, 13*, 59–65.

Acevedo-Garcia, D., McArdle, N., Osypuk, T. L., Lefkowitz, B., & Krimgold, B. K. (2007). *Children left behind: How metropolitan areas are failing America's children.* Boston: Harvard School of Public Health.

Achter, J. A., Lubinski, D., & Benbow, C. P. (1996). Multipotentiality among the intellectually gifted: "It was never there and already it's vanishing." *Journal of Counseling Psychology, 43*, 65–76.

Acocella, J. (1999). *Creating hysteria: Women and multiple personality disorder.* San Francisco: Jossey-Bass.

Acton, G. S., & Schroeder, D. H. (2001). Sensory discrimination as related to general intelligence. *Intelligence, 29*, 263–271.

Adams, H. E., Wright, L. W., Jr., & Lohr, B. A. (1996). Is homophobia associated with homosexual arousal? *Journal of Abnormal Psychology, 105*, 440–445.

Addis, D. R., Wong, A. T., & Schacter, D. L. (2007). Remembering the past and imagining the future: Common and distinct neural substrates during event construction and elaboration. *Neuropsychologia, 45*, 1363–1377.

Addis, D. R., Wong, A. T., & Schacter, D. L. (2008). Age-related changes in the episodic simulation of future events. *Psychological Science, 19*, 33–41.

Adelmann, P. K., & Zajonc, R. B. (1989). Facial efference and the experience of emotion. *Annual Review of Psychology, 40*, 249–280.

Adolph, K. E., & Avoilio, A. M. (2000). Walking infants adapt locomotion to changing body dimensions. *Journal of Experimental Psychology: Human Perception and Performance, 26*, 1148–1166.

Adolphs, R., Russell, J. A., & Tranel, D. (1999). A role for the human amygdala in recognizing emotional arousal from unpleasant stimuli. *Psychological Science, 10*, 167–171.

Adolphs, R., Tranel, D., Damasio, H., & Damasio, A. R. (1995). Fear and the human amygdala. *The Journal of Neuroscience, 15*, 5879–5891.

Adorno, T. W., Frenkel-Brunswik, E., Levinson, D. J., & Sanford, R. N. (1950). *The authoritarian personality.* New York: Harper & Row.

Aggleton, J. (Ed.). (1992). *The amygdala: Neurobiological aspects of emotion, memory and mental dysfunction.* New York: Wiley-Liss.

Agin, D. (2007). *Junk science: An overdue indictment of government, industry, and faith groups that twist science for their own gain.* New York: Macmillan.

Aharon, I., Etcoff, N., Ariely, D., Chabris, C. F., O'Conner, E., & Breiter, H. C. (2001). Beautiful faces have variable reward value: fMRI and behavioral evidence. *Neuron, 32*, 537–551.

Ainslie, G. (2001). *Breakdown of will.* New York: Cambridge University Press.

Ainsworth, M. D. S., Blehar, M. C., Waters, E., & Wall, S. (1978). *Patterns of attachment: A psychological study of the strange situation.* Hillsdale, NJ: Lawrence Erlbaum.

Aksglaede, L., Sorensen, K., Petersen, J. H., Skakkebaek, N. E., & Juul, A. (2009). Recent decline in age at breast development: The Copenhagen puberty study. *Pediatrics, 123*(5), e932–e939.

Albarracín, D., & Vargas, P. (2010). Attitudes and persuasion: From biology to social responses to persuasive intent. In S. T. Fiske, D. T. Gilbert, & G. Lindzey (Eds.), *The handbook of social psychology* (5th ed., Vol. 1, pp. 389–422). New York: Wiley.

Albee, E. (1962). *Who's afraid of Virginia Woolf?* New York: Atheneum.

Aleman, A., Sommer, I. E., & Kahn, R. S. (2007). Efficacy of slow repetitive transcranial magnetic stimulation in the treatment of resistant auditory hallucinations in schizophrenia: A meta-analysis. *Journal of Clinical Psychiatry, 68*, 416–421.

Alicke, M. D., Klotz, M. L., Breitenbecher, D. L., Yurak, T. J., & Vredenburg, D. S. (1995). Personal contact, individuation, and the better-than-average effect. *Journal of Personality and Social Psychology, 68*, 804–824.

Allison, D. B., Fontaine, K. R., Manson, J. E., Stevens, J., & VanItallie, T. B. (1999). Annual deaths attributable to obesity in the United States. *Journal of the American Medical Association, 282*, 1530–1538.

Allison, D. B., Kaprio, J., Korkeila, M., Koskenvuo, M., Neale, M. C., & Hayakawa, K. (1996). The heritability of body mass index among an international sample of monozygotic twins reared apart. *International Journal of Obesity, 20*(6), 501–506.

Alloway, T. P., Gathercole, S. E., Kirkwood, H., & Elliott, J. (2009). The cognitive and behavioral characteristics of children with low working memory. *Child Development, 80*, 606–621.

Alloy, L. B., Jacobson, N. H., & Acocella, J. (1999). *Casebook in abnormal psychology* (4th ed.). New York: McGraw-Hill.

Allport, G. W. (1937). *Personality: A psychological interpretation.* New York: Holt.

Allport, G. W. (1954). *The nature of prejudice.* Cambridge, MA: Addison-Wesley.

Allport, G. W., & Odbert, H. S. (1936). Trait-names: A psycholexical study. *Psychological Monographs, 47*, 592.

Alt, K. W., Jeunesse, C., Buitrago-Téllez, C. H., Wächter, R., Boës, E., & Pichler, S. L. (1997). Evidence for stone age cranial surgery. *Nature, 387*, 360.

Alvarez, L. W. (1965). A pseudo experience in parapsychology. *Science, 148*, 1541.

Alvarez, L., & Eckholm, E. (2009, January 8). Pentagon: No Purple Hearts for PTSD. *The Boston Globe*, p. A4.

Amabile, T. M. (1996). *Creativity in context.* Boulder, CO: Westview Press.

American Psychiatric Association. (2000). *Diagnostic and statistical manual of mental disorders* (*DSM-IV-TR*) (4th ed.). Washington, DC: American Psychiatric Press.

American Psychological Association. (2002). *Ethical principles of psychologists and code of conduct.* Washington, DC: Author.

American Psychological Association. (2005). *Resolution in favor of empirically supported sex education and HIV prevention programs for adolescents.* Washington, DC: Author.

American Psychological Association. (2009). *Report of the American psychological association task force on appropriate therapeutic responses to sexual orientation.* Washington, DC: Author.

Anand, S., & Hotson, J. (2002). Transcranial magnetic stimulation: Neurophysiological applications and safety. *Brain and Cognition, 50*, 366–386.

Andersen, S. M., & Berk, J. S. (1998). Transference in everyday experience: Implications of experimental research for relevant clinical phenomena. *Review of General Psychology, 2*, 81–120.

Anderson, C. A. (1989). Temperature and aggression: Ubiquitous effects of heat on occurrence of human violence. *Psychological Bulletin, 106*, 74–96.

Anderson, C. A., Berkowitz, L., Donnerstein, E., Huesmann, L. R., Johnson, J. D., Linz, D., et al. (2003). The influence of media violence on youth. *Psychological Science in the Public Interest, 4*, 81–110.

Anderson, C. A., & Bushman, B. J. (2001). Effects of violent video games on aggressive behavior, aggressive cognition, aggressive affect, physiological arousal, and prosocial behavior: A meta-analytic review of the scientific literature. *Psychological Science, 12*(5), 353–359.

Anderson, C. A., & Bushman, B. J. (2002). Human aggression. *Annual Review of Psychology, 53*, 27–51.

Anderson, C. A., Bushman, B. J., & Groom, R. W. (1997). Hot years and serious and deadly assault: Empirical tests of the heat hypothesis. *Journal of Personality and Social Psychology, 73*, 1213–1223.

Anderson, J. R., & Schooler, L. J. (1991). Reflections of the environment in memory. *Psychological Science, 2*, 396–408.

Anderson, J. W., Johnstone, B. M., & Remley, D. T. (1999). Breastfeeding and cognitive development: A meta-analysis. *American Journal of Clinical Nutrition, 70*, 525–535.

Anderson, M. C. (2003). Rethinking interference theory: Executive control and the mechanisms of forgetting. *Journal of Memory and Language, 49*, 415–445.

Anderson, M. C., Bjork, R. A., & Bjork, E. L. (1994). Remembering can cause forgetting: Retrieval dynamics in long-term memory. *Journal of Experimental Psychology: Learning, Memory, & Cognition, 20*, 1063–1087.

Anderson, M. C., Ochsner, K. N., Kuhl, B., Cooper, J., Robertson, E., Gabrieli, S. W., et al. (2004). Neural systems underlying the suppression of unwanted memories. *Science, 303*, 232–235.

Anderson, R. C., Pichert, J. W., Goetz, E. T., Schallert, D. L., Stevens, K. V., & Trollip, S. R. (1976). Instantiation of general terms. *Journal of Verbal Learning and Verbal Behavior, 15*, 667–679.

Andrewes, D. (2001). *Neuropsychology: From theory to practice.* Hove, England: Psychology Press.

Andrews, I. (1982). Bilinguals out of focus: A critical discussion. *IRAL: International Review of Applied Linguistics in Language Teaching, 20*, 297–305.

Ansfield, M., Wegner, D. M., & Bowser, R. (1996). Ironic effects of sleep urgency. *Behavior Research and Therapy, 34*, 523–531.

Ansuini, C. G., Fiddler-Woite, J., & Woite, R. S. (1996). The source, accuracy, and impact of initial sexuality information on lifetime wellness. *Adolescence, 31*, 283–289.

Antoni, M. H., Lehman, J. M., Klibourn, K. M., Boyers, A. E., Culver, J. L., Alferi, S. M., et al. (2001). Cognitive-behavioral stress management intervention decreases the prevalence of depression and enhances benefit finding among women under treatment for early-stage breast cancer. *Health Psychology, 20*, 20–32.

Antony, M. M., Downie, F., & Swinson, R. (1998a). Diagnostic issues and epidemiology in obsessive-compulsive disorder. In R. Swinson, M. Antony, S. Rachman, &` M. Richter (Eds.), *Obsessive-compulsive disorder: Theory, research, and treatment* (pp. 3–32). New York: Guilford Press.

Antony, M. M., Roth, D., Swinson, R. P., Huta, V., & Devins, G. M. (1998b). Illness intrusiveness in individuals with panic disorder, obsessive compulsive disorder, or social phobia. *Journal of Nervous and Mental Disease, 186*, 311–315.

Apicella, C. L., Feinberg, D. R., & Marlowe, F. W. (2007). Voice pitch predicts reproductive success in male hunter-gatherers. *Biology Letters, 3*(6), 682–684.

Apperly, I. A., & Butterfill, S. A. (2009). Do humans have two systems to track beliefs and belief-like states? *Psychological Review, 116*, 953–970.

Archibold, R. C. (2006, July 17). Arizona ballot could become lottery ticket. *New York Times*, pp. A1, A15.

Arellano, D., Varona, J., & Perales, F. (2008). Generation and visualization of emotional states in virtual characters. *Computer Animation and Virtual Worlds, 19*(3–4), 259–270.

Aristotle. (trans. 1998). *The Nichomachean ethics* (D. W. Ross, Trans.). Oxford, England: Oxford University Press. (Original work from 350 BC)

Ariyasu, H., Takaya, K., Tagami, T., Ogawa, Y., Hosoda, K., Akamizu, T., et al. (2001). Stomach is a major source of circulating ghrelin, and feeding state determines plasma ghrelin-like immunoreactivity levels in humans. *Journal of Clinical Endocrinology and Metabolism, 86*, 4753–4758.

Arlow, J. A. (2000). Psychoanalysis. In R. J. Corsini & D. Wedding (Eds.), *Current psychotherapies* (6th ed., pp. 16–53). Itasca, IL: Peacock.

Armstrong, D. M. (1980). *The nature of mind.* Ithaca, NY: Cornell University Press.

Arnold, M. B. (Ed.). (1960). *Emotion and personality: Psychological aspects* (Vol. 1). New York: Columbia University Press.

Arnold, S. E., Trojanowski, J. Q., Gur, R. E., Blackwell, P., Han, L., & Choi, C. (1998). Absence of neurodegeneration and neural injury in the cerebral cortex in a sample of elderly patients with schizophrenia. *Archives of General Psychiatry, 55,* 225–232.

Aron, A., Fisher, H., Mashek, D., Strong, G., Li, H., & Brown, L. (2005). Reward, motivation, and emotion systems associated with early-stage intense romantic love. *Journal of Neurophysiology, 93,* 327–337.

Aronson, E. (1963). Effect of the severity of threat on the devaluation of forbidden behavior. *Journal of Abnormal and Social Psychology, 66,* 584–588.

Aronson, E. (1969). The theory of cognitive dissonance: A current perspective. In L. Berkowitz (Ed.), *Advances in experimental social psychology* (Vol. 4, pp. 1–34): Academic Press.

Aronson, E., & Mills, J. (1958). The effect of severity of initiation on liking for a group. *Journal of Abnormal and Social Psychology, 59,* 177–181.

Aronson, E., Willerman, B., & Floyd, J. (1966). The effect of a pratfall on increasing interpersonal attractiveness. *Psychonomic Science, 4,* 227–228.

Aronson, E., & Worchel, P. (1966). Similarity versus liking as determinants of interpersonal attractiveness. *Psychonomic Science, 5,* 157–158.

Aronson, J., & Steele, C. M. (2004). Stereotypes and the fragility of academic competence, motivation, and self-concept. In A. J. Elliot & C. S. Dweck (Eds.), *Handbook of competence and motivation* (pp. 436–456). New York: Guilford Press.

Asch, S. E. (1946). Forming impressions of personality. *Journal of Abnormal and Social Psychology, 41,* 258–290.

Asch, S. E. (1951). Effects of group pressure on the modification and distortion of judgments. In H. Guetzkow (Ed.), *Groups, leadership, and men* (pp. 177–190). Pittsburgh: Carnegie Press.

Asch, S. E. (1955). Opinions and social pressure. *Scientific American, 193,* 31–35.

Asch, S. E. (1956). Studies of independence and conformity: 1. A minority of one against a unanimous majority. *Psychological Monographs: General and Applied, 70,* 1–70.

Aschoff, J. (1965). Circadian rhythms in man. *Science, 148,* 1427–1432.

Aserinsky, E., & Kleitman, N. (1953). Regularly occurring periods of eye motility, and concomitant phenomena, during sleep. *Science, 118,* 273–274.

Ashby, F. G., & Ell, S. W. (2001). The neurobiology of human category learning. *Trends in Cognitive Sciences, 5,* 204–210.

Ashby, F. G., & O'Brien, J. B. (2005). Category learning and multiple memory systems. *Trends in Cognitive Sciences, 9,* 83–89.

Ashcraft, M. H. (1998). *Fundamentals of cognition.* New York: Longman.

Associated Press. (2007). Former stripper guilty of posing as psychologist. Boston: BostonHerald.com.

Astington, J. W., & Baird, J. (2005). *Why language matters for theory of mind.* Oxford, England: Oxford University Press.

Avery, D., Holtzheimer, P., III, Fawaz, W., Russo, J., Naumeier, J., Dunner, D., et al. (2009). A controlled study of repetitive transcranial magnetic stimulation in medication-resistant major depression. *Biological Psychiatry, 59,* 187–194.

Aviezer, H., Hassin, R. R., Ryan, J., Grady, C., Susskind, J., Anderson, A., et al. (2008). Angry, disgusted, or afraid? Studies on the malleability of emotion perception. *Psychological Science, 19,* 724–732.

Avolio, B. J., & Waldman, D. A. (1994). Variations in cognitive, perceptual, and psychomotor abilities across the working life span: Examining the effects of race, sex, experience, education, and occupational type. *Psychology and Aging, 9,* 430–442.

Axelrod, R. (1984). *The evolution of cooperation.* New York: Basic Books.

Axelrod, R., & Hamilton, W. D. (1981). The evolution of cooperation. *Science, 211,* 1390–1396.

Ayduk, O., Shoda, Y., Cervone, D., & Downey, G. (2007). Delay of gratification in children: Contributions to social-personality psychology. In *Persons in context: Building a science of the individual* (pp. 97–109). New York: Guilford Press.

Ayres, C. E. (1921). Instinct and capacity. 1. The instinct of belief-in-instincts. *Journal of Philosophy, 18,* 561–565.

Azuma, H., & Kashiwagi, K. (1987). Descriptors for an intelligent person: A Japanese study. *Japanese Psychological Research, 29,* 17–26.

Baars, B. J. (1986). *The cognitive revolution in psychology.* New York: Guilford Press.

Back, M. D., Schmukle, S. C., & Egloff, B. (2008). Becoming friends by chance. *Psychological Science, 19,* 439–440.

Back, M. D., Stropfer, J. M., Vazire, S., Gaddis, S., Schmukle, S. C., Egloff, B., & Gosling, S. (2010). Facebook profiles reflect actual personality not self-idealization. *Psychological Science, 21,* 372–374.

Backman, C. W., & Secord, P. F. (1959). The effect of perceived liking on interpersonal attraction. *Human Relations, 12,* 379–384.

Bäckman, L., Almkvist, O., Andersson, J., Nordberg, A., Winblad, B., Reineck, R., & Långström, B. (1997). Brain activation in young and older adults during implicit and explicit retrieval. *Journal of Cognitive Neuroscience, 9,* 378–391.

Bäckman, L., & Dixon, R. A. (1992). Psychological compensation: A theoretical framework. *Psychological Bulletin, 112,* 259–283.

Baddeley, A. D. (2001). Is working memory still working? *American Psychologist, 56,* 851–864.

Baddeley, A. D., & Hitch, G. J. (1974). Working memory. In S. Dornic (Ed.), *Attention and performance, 6,* 647–667. Hillsdale, NJ: Lawrence Erlbaum.

Baer, L., Rauch, S. L., Ballantine, H. T., Jr., Martuza, R., Cosgrove, R., Cassem, E., et al. (1995). Cingulotomy for intractable obsessive-compulsive disorder: Prospective long-term follow-up of 18 patients. *Archives of General Psychiatry, 52,* 384–392.

Bagby, R. M., Levitan, R. D., Kennedy, S. H., Levitt, A. J., & Joffe, R. T. (1999). Selective alteration of personality in response to noradrenergic and serotonergic antidepressant medication in depressed sample: Evidence of non-specificity. *Psychiatry Research, 86,* 211–216.

Bahrick, H. P. (1984). Semantic memory content in permastore: 50 years of memory for Spanish learned in school. *Journal of Experimental Psychology: General, 113,* 1–29.

Bahrick, H. P. (2000). Long-term maintenance of knowledge. In E. Tulving & F. I. M. Craik (Eds.), *The Oxford handbook of memory* (pp. 347–362). New York: Oxford University Press.

Bahrick, H. P., Hall, L. K., & Berger, S. A. (1996). Accuracy and distortion in memory for high school grades. *Psychological Science, 7,* 265–271.

Bahrick, H. P., Hall, L. K., & DaCosta, L. A. (2008). Fifty years of college grades: Accuracy and distortions. *Emotion, 8,* 13–22.

Bailey, J. M., & Pillard, R. C. (1991). A genetic study of male sexual orientation. *Archives of General Psychiatry, 48,* 1089–1096.

Bailey, J. M., Pillard, R. C., Dawood, K., Miller, M. B., Farrer, L. A., Trivedi, S., et al. (1999). A family history study of male sexual orientation using three independent samples. *Behavior Genetics, 29,* 79–86.

Bailey, J. M., Pillard, R. C., Neale, M. C., & Agyes, Y. (1993). Heritable factors influence sexual orientation in women. *Archives of General Psychiatry, 50,* 217–223.

Bailey, R. (2002, March 6). Hooray for designer babies! *Reason.com.* Retrieved September 30, 2007, from http://www.reason.com/news/show/34776.html

Baillargeon, R., Scott, R. M., & He, Z. (2010). False-belief understanding in infants. *Trends in Cognitive Sciences, 14*(3), 110–118.

Baillargeon, R., Spelke, E. S., & Wasserman, S. (1985). Object permanence in 5-month-old infants. *Cognition, 20,* 191–208.

Baker, T. B., Brandon, T. H., & Chassin, L. (2004). Motivational influences on cigarette smoking. *Annual Review of Psychology, 55,* 463–491.

Baker, T. B., McFall, R. M., & Shoham, V. (2009). Current status and future prospects of clinical psychology: Toward a scientifically principled approach to mental and behavioral health care. *Psychological Science in the Public Interest, 9,* 67–103.

Baldwin, M. W., Carrell, S. E., & Lopez, D. F. (1989). Priming relationship schemas: My advisor and the pope are watching me from the back of my mind. *Journal of Experimental Social Psychology, 26,* 435–454.

Baler, R. D., & Volkow, N. D. (2006). Drug addiction: The neurobiology of disrupted self-control. *Trends in Molecular Medicine, 12,* 559–566.

Baltes, P. B., & Reinert, G. (1969). Cohort effects in cognitive development of children as revealed by cross-sectional sequences. *Developmental Psychology, 1,* 169–177.

Banaji, M. R., & Heiphetz, L. (2010). Attitudes. In S. T. Fiske, D. T. Gilbert, & G. Lindzey (Eds.), *The handbook of social psychology* (5th ed., Vol. 1, pp. 348–388). New York: Wiley.

Bandura, A. (1965). Influence of models' reinforcement contingencies on the acquisition of imitative responses. *Journal of Social and Personality Psychology, 1,* 589–595.

Bandura, A. (1977). *Social learning theory.* Englewood Cliffs, NJ: Prentice Hall.

Bandura, A. (1986). *Social foundations of thought and action: A social cognitive theory.* Englewood Cliffs, NJ: Prentice Hall.

Bandura, A. (1994). Social cognitive theory of mass communication. In J. Bryant & D. Zillmann (Eds.), *Media effects: Advances in theory and research* (pp. 61–90). Hillsdale, NJ: Lawrence Erlbaum.

Bandura, A., Ross, D., & Ross, S. (1961). Transmission of aggression through imitation of adult models. *Journal of Abnormal and Social Psychology, 63,* 575–582.

Bandura, A., Ross, D., & Ross, S. (1963). Vicarious reinforcement and imitative learning. *Journal of Abnormal and Social Psychology, 67,* 601–607.

Banks, M. S., & Salapatek, P. (1983). Infant visual perception. In M. Haith & J. Campos (Eds.), *Handbook of child psychology: Biology and infancy.* New York: Wiley.

Banse, R., & Scherer, K. R. (1996). Acoustic profiles in vocal emotion expression. *Journal of Personality and Social Psychology, 70,* 614–636.

Bard, P. (1934). On emotional experience after decortication with some remarks on theoretical views. *Psychological Review, 41,* 309–329.

Bargh, J. A., & Chartrand, T. L. (1999). The unbearable automaticity of being. *American Psychologist, 54,* 462–479.

Bargh, J. A., Chen, M., & Burrows, L. (1996). The automaticity of social behavior: Direct effects of trait concept and stereotype activation on action. *Journal of Personality and Social Psychology, 71,* 230–244.

Bargh, J. A., Gollwitzer, P. M., Lee-Chai, A., Barndollar, K., & Trötschel, R. (2001). The automated will: Nonconscious activation and pursuit of behavioral goals. *Journal of Personality and Social Psychology, 81,* 1014–1027.

Bargh, J. A., Gollwitzer, P. M., & Oettingen, G. (2010). Motivation. In S. T. Fiske, D. T. Gilbert, & G. Lindzey (Eds.), *The handbook of social psychology* (5th ed., Vol. 1, pp. 263–311). New York: Wiley.

Bargh, J. A., & Morsella, E. (2008). The unconscious mind. *Perspectives on Psychological Science, 3,* 73–89.

Barker, A. T., Jalinous, R., & Freeston, I. L. (1985). Noninvasive magnetic stimulation of the human motor cortex. *Lancet, 2,* 1106–1107.

Barkow, J. (1980). Prestige and self-esteem: A biosocial interpretation. In D. R. Omark, F. F. Stayer, & D. G. Freedman (Eds.), *Dominance relations* (pp. 319–322). New York: Garland.

Barlow, D. H., Gorman, J. M., Shear, M. K., & Woods, S. W. (2000). Cognitive-behavioral therapy, imipramine, or their combination for panic disorder: A randomized controlled trial. *Journal of the American Medical Association, 283*(19), 2529–2536.

Barnier, A. J., Levin, K., & Maher, A. (2004). Suppressing thoughts of past events: Are repressive copers good suppressors? *Cognition and Emotion, 18,* 457–477.

Baron-Cohen, S. (1991). Do people with autism understand what causes emotion? *Child Development, 62,* 385–395.

Baron-Cohen, S., Leslie, A., & Frith, U. (1985). Does the autistic child have a "theory of mind"? *Cognition, 21,* 37–46.

Barondes, S. (2003). *Better than Prozac.* New York: Oxford University Press.

Barrientos, R. M., Watkins, L. R., Rudy, J. W., & Maier, S. F. (2009). Characterization of the sickness response in young and aging rats following *E. coli* infection. *Brain, Behavior, and Immunity, 23,* 450–454.

Bartlett, F. C. (1932). *Remembering: A study in experimental and social psychology.* Cambridge, England: Cambridge University Press.

Bartol, C. R., & Costello, N. (1976). Extraversion as a function of temporal duration of electric shock: An exploratory study. *Perceptual and Motor Skills, 42,* 1174.

Bartoshuk, L. M. (2000). Comparing sensory experiences across individuals: Recent psychophysical advances illuminate genetic variation in taste perception. *Chemical Senses, 25,* 447–460.

Bartoshuk, L. M., & Beauchamp, G. K. (1994). Chemical senses. *Annual Review of Psychology, 45,* 419–445.

Bates, E., & Goodman, J. C. (1997). On the inseparability of grammar and the lexicon: Evidence from acquisition, aphasia, and real-time processing. *Language and Cognitive Processes, 12,* 507–584.

Bateson, M., Nettle, D., & Roberts, G. (2006). Cues of being watched enhance cooperation in a real-world setting. *Biology Letters, 2*(3), 412–414.

Batson, C. D. (2002). Addressing the altruism question experimentally. In S. G. Post & L. G. Underwood (Eds.), *Altruism & altruistic love: Science, philosophy, & religion in dialogue* (pp. 89–105). London: Oxford University Press.

Baumeister, R. F. (2004). Gender and erotic plasticity: Sociocultural influences on the sex drive. *Sexual & Relationship Therapy, 19,* 133–139.

Baumeister, R. F., Bratslavsky, E., Muraven, M., & Tice, D. M. (1998). Ego depletion: Is the active self a limited resource? *Journal of Personality and Social Psychology, 74,* 1252–1265.

Baumeister, R. F., Campbell, J. D., Krueger, J. I., & Vohs, K. D. (2003). Does high self-esteem cause better performance, interpersonal success, happiness, or healthier lifestyles? *Psychological Science in the Public Interest, 4,* 1–44.

Baumeister, R. F., Cantanese, K. R., & Vohs, K. D. (2001). Is there a gender difference in strength of sex drive? Theoretical views, conceptual distinctions, and a review of relevant evidence. *Personality and Social Psychology Review, 5,* 242–273.

Baumeister, R. F., Heatherton, T. F., & Tice, D. M. (1995). *Losing control.* San Diego, CA: Academic Press.

Baumeister, R. F., & Leary, M. R. (1995). The need to belong: Desire for interpersonal attachments as a fundamental human motivation. *Psychological Bulletin, 117,* 497–529.

Baumeister, R. F., Smart, L., & Boden, J. M. (1996). Relation of threatened egotism to violence and aggression: The dark side of high self-esteem. *Psychological Review, 103,* 5–33.

Baumeister, R. F., Vohs, K. D., & Tice, D. M. (2007). The strength model of self-control. *Current Directions in Psychological Science, 16,* 351–355.

Baxter, L. R., Schwartz, J. M., Bergman, K. S., Szuba, M. P., Guze, B. H., Mazziotta, J. C., Alazraki, A., et al. (1992). Caudate glucose metabolic rate changes with both drug behavior therapy for obsessive-compulsive disorder. *Archives of General Psychiatry, 49,* 681–689.

Bayley, P. J., Frascino, J. C., & Squire, L. R. (2005a). Robust habit learning in the absence of awareness and independent of the medial temporal lobe. *Nature, 436,* 550–553.

Bayley, P. J., Gold, J. J., Hopkins, R. O., & Squire, L. R. (2005b). The neuroanatomy of remote memory. *Neuron, 46,* 799–810.

Bechara, A., Damasio, A. R., Damasio, H., & Anderson, S. W. (1994). Insensitivity to future consequences following damage to human prefrontal cortex. *Cognition, 50,* 7–15.

Bechara, A., Damasio, H., Tranel, D., & Damasio, A. R. (1997). Deciding advantageously before knowing the advantageous strategy. *Science, 275,* 1293–1295.

Bechara, A., Dolan, S., Denburg, N., Hindes, A., & Anderson, S. W. (2001). Decision-making deficits, linked to a dysfunctional ventro-medial prefrontal cortex, revealed in alcohol and stimulant abusers. *Neuropsychologia, 39,* 376–389.

Bechara, A., Tranel, D., & Damasio, H. (2000). Characterization of the decision-making deficit of patients with ventromedial prefrontal cortex lesions. *Brain, 123,* 2189–2202.

Beck, A. T. (1967). *Depression: Causes and treatment.* Philadelphia: University of Pennsylvania Press.

Beck, A. T., & Weishaar, M. (2000). Cognitive therapy. In R. J. Corsini & D. Wedding (Eds.), *Current psychotherapies* (6th ed., pp. 241–272). Itasca, IL: Peacock.

Beckers, G., & Zeki, S. (1995). The consequences of inactivating areas V1 and V5 on visual motion perception. *Brain, 118,* 49–60.

Beek, M. R., Levin, D. T., & Angelone, B. (2007). Change blindness blindness: Beliefs about the roles of intention and scene complexity in change detection. *Consciousness and Cognition, 16,* 31–51.

Beevers, C. G., & Meyer, B. (2008). I feel fine but the glass is still half empty: Thought suppression biases information processing despite recovery from a dysphoric mood state. *Cognitive Therapy and Research, 32,* 323–332.

Békésy, G. von. (1960). *Experiments in hearing.* New York: McGraw-Hill.

Bekinschtein, T. A., Shalom, D. E., Forcato, C., Herrera, M., Coleman, M. R., Manes, F. F., & Sigman, M. (2009). Classical conditioning in the vegetative and minimally conscious state. *Nature Neuroscience, 12,* 1343–1350.

Bell, A. P., Weinberg, M. S., & Hammersmith, S. K. (1981). *Sexual preference: Its development in men and women.* Bloomington: Indiana University Press.

Belsky, J., Spritz, B., & Crnic, K. (1996). Infant attachment security and affective-cognitive information processing at age 3. *Psychological Science, 7,* 111–114.

Bem, S. L. (1974). The measure of psychological androgyny. *Journal of Consulting and Clinical Psychology, 42,* 155–162.

Benedetti, F., Maggi, G., & Lopiano, L. (2003a). Open versus hidden medical treatment: The patient's knowledge about a therapy affects the therapy outcome. *Prevention & Treatment, 6,* Article 1. Retrieved June 23, 2003, from http://content.apa.org/psycarticles/2003-07872-001

Benedetti, F., Pollo, A., Lopiano, L., Lanotte, M., Vighetti, S., & Rainero, I. (2003b). Conscious expectation and unconscious conditioning in analgesic, motor, and hormonal placebo/nocebo responses. *The Journal of Neuroscience, 23,* 4315–4323.

Bennett, I. J., Romano, J. C., Howard, J. H., & Howard, D. V. (2008). Two forms of implicit learning in young adults with dyslexia. *Annals of the New York Academy of Sciences, 1145,* 184–198.

Benoit, S. C., Kemp, C. J., Elias, C. F., Abplanalp, W., Herman, J. P., Migrenne, S., et al. (2009). Palmitic acid mediates hypothalamic insulin resistance by altering pkc-theta subcellular localization in rodents. *The Journal of Clinical Investigation, 119*(9), 2577–2589.

Benson, H. (Ed.). (1990). *The relaxation response.* New York: Harper Torch.

Bereczkei, T., Vorgos, S., Gal, A., & Bernath, L. (1997). Resources, attractiveness, family commitment; Reproductive decisions in human mate choice. *Journal of Ethology, 103,* 681–699.

Berger, H. (1929). Über das Elektroenkephalogram des Menschen. *Archiv fuer Psychiatrie, 87,* 527–570.

Berglund, H., Lindstrom, P., & Savic, I. (2006). Brain response to putative pheromones in lesbian women. *Proceedings of the National Academy of Sciences, USA, 103,* 8269–8274.

Bering, J. (2004). A critical review of the "enculturation hypothesis": The effects of human rearing on great ape social cognition. *Animal Cognition, 7,* 201–212.

Berkerian, D. A., & Bowers, J. M. (1983). Eyewitness testimony: Were we misled? *Journal of Experimental Psychology: Learning, Memory, and Cognition, 9,* 139–145.

Berkowitz, L. (1990). On the formation and regulation of anger and aggression: A cognitive-neoassociationistic analysis. *American Psychologist, 45,* 494–503.

Bernard, L. L. (1924). *Instinct: A study in social psychology.* New York: Holt.

Bernat, J. L. (2009). Ethical issues in the treatment of severe brain injury: The impact of new technologies. *Annals of the New York Academy of Sciences, 1157,* 117–130.

Berridge, K. C. (2007). The debate over dopamine's role in reward: The case for incentive salience. *Psychopharmacology, 191,* 391–431.

Berry, D. S., & McArthur, L. Z. (1985). Some components and consequences of a babyface. *Journal of Personality and Social Psychology, 48,* 312–323.

Berry, J. W., Poortinga, Y. H., Segall, M. H., & Dasen, P. R. (1992). *Cross-cultural psychology: Research and applications.* New York: Cambridge University Press.

Berscheid, E., Dion, K., Walster, E., & Walster, G. W. (1971). Physical attractiveness and dating choice: A test of the matching hypothesis. *Journal of Experimental Social Psychology, 7*(2), 173–189.

Berscheid, E., & Reiss, H. T. (1998). Interpersonal attraction and close relationships. In D. T. Gilbert, S. T. Fiske, & G. Lindzey (Eds.), *The handbook of social psychology* (4th ed., Vol. 2, pp. 193–281). New York: McGraw-Hill.

Bertelsen, A. (1999). Reflections on the clinical utility of the ICD-10 and DSM-IV classifications and their diagnostic criteria. *Australian and New Zealand Journal of Psychiatry, 33,* 166–173.

Bertelsen, B., Harvald, B., & Hauge, M. (1977). A Danish twin study of manic-depressive disorders. *British Journal of Psychiatry, 130,* 330–351.

Bertenthal, B. I., Rose, J. L., & Bai, D. L. (1997). Perception-action coupling in the development of visual control of posture. *Journal of Experimental Psychology: Human Perception & Performance, 23,* 1631–1643.

Berthoud, H.-R., & Morrison, C. (2008). The brain, appetite, and obesity. *Annual Review of Psychology, 59,* 55–92.

Best, J. B. (1992). *Cognitive psychology* (3rd ed.). New York: West Publishing.

Bettencourt, B., A., & Miller, N. (1996). Gender differences in aggression as a function of provocation: A meta-analysis. *Psychological Bulletin, 119,* 422–447.

Beutler, L. E. (2002). The dodo bird is extinct. *Clinical Psychology: Science and Practice, 9,* 30–34.

Bialystok, E. (1999). Cognitive complexity and attentional control in the bilingual mind. *Child Development, 70,* 636–644.

Bialystok, E. (2009). Bilingualism: The good, the bad, and the indifference. *Bilingualism: Language and Cognitive Processes, 12,* 3–11.

Bialystok, E., & Hakuta, K. (1994). *In other words: The science and psychology of second-language acquisition.* New York: Basic Books.

Bickerton, D. (1990). *Language and species.* Chicago: University of Chicago Press.

Biederman, I. (1987). Recognition-by-components: A theory of human image understanding. *Psychological Review, 94,* 115–147.

Billet, E., Richter, J., & Kennedy, J. (1998). Genetics of obsessive-compulsive disorder. In R. Swinson, M. Anthony, S. Rachman, & M. Richter (Eds.), *Obsessive-compulsive disorder: Theory, research, and treatment* (pp. 181–206). New York: Guilford Press.

Binet, A. (1905). New methods for the diagnosis of the intellectual level of subnormals. *L'Année Psychologique, 12,* 191–244.

Binet, A. (1909). *Les idées modernes sur les enfants.* Paris: Flammarion.

Binswanger, L. (1958). The existential analysis school of thought. In R. May (Ed.), *Existence: A new dimension in psychiatry and psychology.* New York: Basic Books.

Birch, S. A. J., & Bloom, P. (2007). The curse of knowledge in reasoning about false beliefs. *Psychological Science, 18*(5), 382–386.

Bjork, D. W. (1983). *The compromised scientist: William James in the development of American psychology.* New York: Columbia University Press.

Bjork, D. W. (1993). *B. F. Skinner: A life.* New York: Basic Books.

Bjork, E. L., & Bjork, R. A. (2011). Making things hard on yourself, but in a good way: Creating desirable difficulties to enhance learning. In M. A. Gernsbacher, R. W. Pewe, L. M. Hough, & J. R. Pomerantz (Eds.), *Psychology and the real world: Essays illustrating fundamental contributions to society* (pp. 56–64). New York: Worth Publishers.

Bjork, R. A. (1975). Retrieval as a memory modifier: An interpretation of negative recency and related phenomena. In R. L. Solso (Ed.), *Information processing and cognition: The Loyola symposium* (pp. 123–144). Hillsdale, NJ: Lawrence Erlbaum.

Bjork, R. A., & Bjork, E. L. (1988). On the adaptive aspects of retrieval failure in autobiographical memory. In M. M. Gruneberg, P. E. Morris, & R. N. Sykes (Eds.), *Practical aspects of memory: Current research and issues* (pp. 283–288). Chichester, England: Wiley.

Blair, I. V. (2002). The malleability of automatic stereotypes and prejudice. *Personality and Social Psychology Review, 6,* 242–261.

Blair, J., Peschardt, K., & Mitchell, D. R. (2005). *Psychopath: Emotion and the brain.* Oxford, England: Blackwell.

Blake, D. T., Heiser, M. A., Caywood, M., & Merzenich, M. M. (2006). Experience-dependent adult cortical plasticity requires cognitive association between sensation and reward. *Neuron, 52,* 371–381.

Blascovich, J., Mendes, W. B., Hunter, S. B., Lickel, B., & Kowai-Bell, N. (2001). Perceiver threat in social interactions with stigmatized others. *Journal of Personality and Social Psychology, 80,* 253–267.

Blascovich, J., & Tomaka, J. (1996). The biopsychosocial model of arousal regulation. In M. P. Zanna (Ed.), *Advances in experimental social psychology* (Vol. 28, pp. 1–51). San Diego, CA: Academic Press.

Blasi, A. (1980). Bridging moral cognition and moral action: A critical review of the literature. *Psychological Bulletin, 88,* 1–45.

Blatt, S. J., & Homann, E. (1992). Parent-child interaction in the etiology of dependent and self-critical depression. *Clinical Psychology Review, 12,* 47–91.

Blatt, S. J., & Zuroff, D. C. (1992). Interpersonal relatedness and self-definition: Two prototypes for depression. *Clinical Psychology Review, 12,* 527–562.

Blau, F. D., & Kahn, L. M. (2007). Changes in the labor supply behavior of married women: 1980–2000. *Journal of Labor Economics, 25*(3), 393–438.

Blazer, D. G., Hughes, D., & George, L. D. (1987). Stressful life events and the onset of a generalized anxiety syndrome. *American Journal of Psychiatry, 144,* 1178–1183.

Blazer, D. G., Hughes, D. J., George, L. K., Swartz, M., & Boyer, R. (1991). Generalized anxiety disorder. In L. N. Robins & D. A. Regier (Eds.), *Psychiatric disorders in America* (Vol. 180–203). New York: Free Press.

Blesch, A., & Tuszynski, M. H. (2009). Spinal cord injury: Plasticity, regeneration and the challenge of translational drug development. *Trends in Neurosciences, 32,* 41–47.

Bliss, T. V. P. (1999). Young receptors make smart mice. *Nature, 401,* 25–27.

Bliss, T. V. P., & Lømo, W. T. (1973). Long-lasting potentiation of synaptic transmission in the dentate area of the anesthetized rabbit following stimulation of the perforant path. *Journal of Physiology, 232,* 331–356.

Bloch, C., Kaiser, A., Kuenzli, E., Zappatore, D., Haller, S., Franceschini, R., Luedi, G., Radue, E. W., & Nitsch, C. (2009). The age of second language acquisition determines the variability in activation elicited by narration in three languages in Broca's and Wernicke's area. *Neuropsychologia, 47,* 625–633.

Bloom, C. M., Venard, J., Harden, M., & Seetharaman, S. (2007). Non-contingent positive and negative reinforcement schedules of supersitious behaviors. *Behavioural Process, 75,* 8–13.

Bocanegra, B. R., & Zeelenberg, R. (2009). Emotion improves and impairs early vision. *Psychological Science, 20*(6), 707–713.

Boecker, H., Sprenger, T., Spilker, M. E., Henriksen, G., Koppenhoefer, M., Wagner, K. J., et al. (2008). The runner's high: Opioidergic mechanisms in the human brain. *Cerebral Cortex, 18,* 2523–2531.

Bogaert, A. F. (2004). Asexuality: Its prevalence and associated factors in a national probability sample. *The Journal of Sex Research, 41,* 279–287.

Bohan, J. S. (1996). *Psychology and sexual orientation: Coming to terms.* New York: Routledge.

Boinski, S., Quatrone, R. P., & Swartz, H. (2000). Substrate and tool use by brown capuchins in Suriname: Ecological contexts and cognitive bases. *American Anthropologist, 102,* 741–761.

Boisvert, C. M., & Faust, D. (2002). Iatrogenic symptoms in psychotherapy: A theoretical exploration of the potential impact of labels, language, and belief systems. *American Journal of Psychotherapy, 56,* 244–259.

Bolton, G. E., & Ockenfels, A. (2000). Erc: A theory of equity, reciprocity, and competition. *American Economic Review, 90,* 166–193.

Bond, C. F., Jr., & DePaulo, B. M. (2008). Individual differences in judging deception: Accuracy and bias. *Psychological Bulletin, 134*(4), 477–492.

Boomsma, D., Busjahn, A., & Peltonen, L. (2002). Classical twin studies and beyond. *Nature Reviews Genetics, 3,* 872–882.

Bootzin, R. R., Manber, R., Perlis, M. L., Salvio, M. A., & Wyatt, J. K. (1993). Sleep disorders. In P. B. Sutker & H. E. Adams (Eds.), *Comprehensive handbook of psychopathology* (2nd ed.). New York: Plenum Press.

Borkenau, P., & Liebler, A. (1995). Observable attributes as manifestations and cues of personality and intelligence. *Journal of Personality, 63,* 1–25.

Borkevec, T. D. (1982). Insomnia. *Journal of Consulting and Clinical Psychology, 50,* 880–895.

Born, R. T., & Bradley, D. C. (2005). Structure and function of visual area MT. *Annual Review of Neuroscience, 28,* 157–189.

Bornstein, R. F. (1989). Exposure and affect: Overview and meta-analysis of research, 1968–1987. *Psychological Bulletin, 106,* 265–289.

Boroditsky, L. (2001). Does language shape thought? Mandarin and English speakers' conceptions of time. *Cognitive Psychology, 43,* 1–22.

Bostwick, J. M., & Pankratz, S. (2000). Affective disorders and suicide risk: A reexamination. *American Journal of Psychiatry, 157,* 1925–1932.

Botwin, M. D., Buss, D. M., & Shackelford, T. K. (1997). Personality and mate preferences: Five factors in mate selection and marital satisfaction. *Journal of Personality, 65,* 107–136.

Bouchard, T. J., & Loehlin, J. C. (2001). Genes, evolution, and personality. *Behavioral Genetics, 31,* 243–273.

Bouchard, T. J., & McGue, M. (2003). Genetic and environmental influences on human psychological differences. *Journal of Neurobiology, 54,* 4–45.

Bourguignon, E. (1968). World distribution and patterns of possession states. In R. Prince (Ed.), *Trance and possession states* (pp. 3–34). Montreal, Canada: R. M. Burke Memorial Society.

Bouton, M. E. (1988). Context and ambiguity in the extinction of emotional learning: Implications for exposure therapy. *Behaviour Research and Therapy, 26,* 137–149.

Bower, B. (1999, October 30). The mental butler did it—research suggests that subconscious affects behavior more than thought. *Science News 156,* 208–282.

Bower, G. H. (1981). Mood and memory. *American Psychologist, 36,* 129–148.

Bower, G. H., Clark, M. C., Lesgold, A. M., & Winzenz, D. (1969). Hierarchical retrieval schemes in recall of categorical word lists. *Journal of Verbal Learning and Verbal Behavior, 8,* 323–343.

Bowers, K. S., Regehr, G., Balthazard, C., & Parker, D. (1990). Intuition in the context of discovery. *Cognitive Psychology, 22,* 72–110.

Bowlby, J. (1969). *Attachment and loss: Vol. 1. Attachment.* New York: Basic Books.

Bowlby, J. (1973). *Attachment and loss: Vol. 2. Separation.* New York: Basic Books.

Bowlby, J. (1980). *Attachment and loss: Vol. 3. Loss: Sadness and depression.* New York: Basic Books.

Bozarth, M. A. (Ed.). (1987). *Methods of assessing the reinforcing properties of abused drugs.* New York: Springer-Verlag.

Bozarth, M. A., & Wise, R. A. (1985). Toxicity associated with long-term intravenous heroin and cocaine self-administration in the rat. *Journal of the American Medical Association, 254,* 81–83.

Brackett, M. A., & Mayer, J. D. (2003). Convergent, discriminant, and incremental validity of competing measures of emotional intelligence. *Personality and Social Psychology Bulletin, 29,* 1147.

Brackett, M. A., Rivers, S. E., Shiffman, S., Lerner, N., & Salovey, P. (2006). Relating emotional abilities to social functioning: A comparison of self-report and performance measures of emotional intelligence. *Journal of Personality and Social Psychology, 91,* 780.

Brackett, M. A., Warner, R. M., & Bosco, J. (2005). Emotional intelligence and relationship quality among couples. *Personal Relationships, 12*(2), 197–212.

Bradford, D., Stroup, S., & Lieberman, J. (2002). Pharmacological treatments for schizophrenia. In P. E. Nathan & J. M. Gorman (Eds.), *A guide to treatments that work* (2nd ed., pp. 169–199). New York: Oxford University Press.

Bradmetz, J., & Schneider, R. (2004). The role of the counterfactually satisfied desire in the lag between false-belief and false-emotion attributions in children aged 4–7. *British Journal of Developmental Psychology, 22,* 185–196.

Braet, W., & Humphreys, G. W. (2009). The role of reentrant processes in feature binding: Evidence from neuropsychology and TMS on late onset illusory conjunctions. *Visual Cognition, 17,* 25–47.

Bramlett, M. D., & Mosher, W. D. (2001). *First marriage dissolution, divorce, and remarriage: United States* (Advance data from Vital and Health Statistics, No. 323). Hyattsville, MD: National Center for Health Statistics.

Bramlett, M. D., & Mosher, W. D. (2002). *Cohabitation, marriage, divorce, and remarriage in the United States* (Vital and Health Statistics Series 23, No. 22). Hyattsville, MD: National Center for Health Statistics.

Brandt, K. R., Gardiner, J. M., Vargha-Khadem, F., Baddeley, A. D., & Mishkin, M. (2009). Impairment of recollection but not familiarity in a case of developmental amnesia. *Neurocase, 15,* 60–65.

Braun, A. R., Balkin, T. J., Wesensten, N. J., Gwadry, F., Carson, R. E., Varga, M., et al. (1998). Dissociated pattern of activity in visual cortices and their projections during rapid eye movement sleep. *Science, 279,* 91–95.

Breazeal, C. (2003). Emotion and sociable humanoid robots. *International Journal of Human-Computer Studies, 59,* 119–155.

Breazeal, C. (2009). Role of expressive behaviour for robots that learn from people. *Philosophical Transactions of the Royal Society B, 364,* 3527–3538.

Breckler, S. J. (1994). Memory for the experiment of donating blood: Just how bad was it? *Basic and Applied Social Psychology, 15,* 467–488.

Brédart, S., & Valentine, T. (1998). Descriptiveness and proper name retrieval. *Memory, 6,* 199–206.

Breggin, P. R. (1990). Brain damage, dementia, and persistent cognitive dysfunction associated with neuroleptic drugs: Evidence, etiology, implications. *Journal of Mind and Behavior, 11,* 425–463.

Breggin, P. R. (2000). *Reclaiming our children.* Cambridge, MA: Perseus Books.

Brehm, S. S. (1992). *Intimate relationships* (2nd ed.). New York: McGraw-Hill.

Breland, K., & Breland, M. (1961). The misbehavior of organisms. *American Psychologist, 16,* 681–684.

Brennan, P. A., & Zufall, F. (2006). Pheromonal communication in vertebrates. *Nature, 444,* 308–315.

Brenneis, C. B. (2000). Evaluating the evidence: Can we find authenticated recovered memory? *Journal of the American Psychoanalytic Association, 17,* 61–77.

Brenninkmeijer, V., Vanyperen, N. W., & Buunk, B. P. (2001). I am not a better teacher, but others are doing worse: Burnout and perceptions of superiority among teachers. *Social Psychology of Education, 4*(3–4), 259–274.

Bretherton, I., & Munholland, K. A. (1999). Internal working models in attachment relationships: A construct revisited. In J. Cassidy & P. R. Shaver (Eds.), *Handbook of attachment: Theory, research and clinical applications* (pp. 89–114). New York: Guilford Press.

Brewer, M. B. (1979). In-group bias in the minimal intergroup situation: A cognitive-motivational analysis. *Psychological Bulletin, 86,* 307–324.

Brewer, W. F. (1996). What is recollective memory? In D. C. Rubin (Ed.), *Remembering our past: Studies in autobiographical memory* (pp. 19–66). New York: Cambridge University Press.

Broadbent, D. E. (1958). *Perception and communication.* London: Pergamon Press.

Broberg, D. J., & Bernstein, I. L. (1987). Candy as a scapegoat in the prevention of food aversions in children receiving chemotherapy. *Cancer, 60,* 2344–2347.

Broca, P. (1861). Remarques sur le siège de la faculté du langage articulé; suivies d'une observation d'aphemie (perte de la parole). *Bulletin de la société anatomique de Paris, 36,* 330–357.

Broca, P. (1863). Localisation des fonction cerebrales: Siège du langage articulé. *Bulletin de la société d'anthropologie de Paris, 4,* 200–202.

Brock, A. (1993). Something old, something new: The "reappraisal" of Wilhelm Wundt in textbooks. *Theory & Psychology, 3*(2), 235–242.

Brody, N. (2003). Construct validation of the Sternberg Triarchic Abilities Test: Comment and reanalysis. *Intelligence, 31*(4), 319–329.

Brooks, R., & Meltzoff, A. N. (2002). The importance of eyes: How infants interpret adult looking behavior. *Developmental Psychology, 38,* 958–966.

Brooks-Gunn, J., Graber, J. A., & Paikoff, R. L. (1994). Studying links between hormones and negative affect: Models and measures. *Journal of Research on Adolescence, 4,* 469–486.

Brosnan, S. F., & DeWaal, F. B. M. (2003). Monkeys reject unequal pay. *Nature, 425,* 297–299.

Brown, A. S. (2004). *The déjà vu experience.* New York: Psychology Press.

Brown, B. B., Mory, M., & Kinney, D. (1994). Casting crowds in a relational perspective: Caricature, channel, and context. In G. A. R. Montemayor & T. Gullotta (Eds.), *Advances in adolescent development: Personal relationships during adolescence* (Vol. 5, pp. 123–167). Newbury Park, CA: Sage.

Brown, J. D. (1993). Self-esteem and self-evaluation: Feeling is believing. In J. M. Suls (Ed.), *The self in social perspective: Psychological perspectives on the self* (Vol. 4, pp. 27–58). Hillsdale, NJ: Lawrence Erlbaum.

Brown, J. D., & McGill, K. L. (1989). The cost of good fortune: When positive life events produce negative health consequences. *Journal of Personality and Social Psychology, 57,* 1103–1110.

Brown, L. E., Wilson, E. T., & Gribble, P. L. (2009). Repetitive transcranial magnetic stimulation to the primary cortex interferes with motor learning by observing. *Journal of Cognitive Neuroscience, 21,* 1013–1022.

Brown, R. (1958). *Words and things.* New York: Free Press.

Brown, R., & Hanlon, C. (1970). Derivational complexity and order of acquisition in child speech. In J. R. Hayes (Ed.), *Cognition and the development of language* (pp. 11–53). New York: Wiley.

Brown, R., & Kulik, J. (1977). Flashbulb memories. *Cognition, 5,* 73–99.

Brown, R., & McNeill, D. (1966). The "tip-of-the-tongue" phenomenon. *Journal of Verbal Learning and Verbal Behavior, 5,* 325–337.

Brown, R. P., Osterman, L. L., & Barnes, C. D. (2009). School violence and the culture of honor. *Psychological Science, 20*(11), 1400–1405.

Brown, S. C., & Craik, F. I. M. (2000). Encoding and retrieval of information. In E. Tulving & F. I. M. Craik (Eds.), *The Oxford handbook of memory* (pp. 93–107). New York: Oxford University Press.

Brown, T. A., & Barlow, D. H. (2002). Classification of anxiety and mood disorders. In D. H. Barlow (Ed.), *Anxiety and its disorders: The nature and treatment of anxiety and panic* (2nd ed.). New York: Guilford Press.

Brown, T. A., Campbell, L. A., Lehman, C. L., Grisham, J. R., & Mancill, R. B. (2001). Current and lifetime comorbidity of the *DSM-IV* anxiety and mood disorders in a large clinical sample. *Journal of Abnormal Psychology, 110,* 585–599.

Brownell, K. D., Greenwood, M. R. C., Stellar, E., & Shrager, E. E. (1986). The effects of repeated cycles of weight loss and regain in rats. *Physiology and Behavior, 38,* 459–464.

Brownlee, S. (2002, March). Designer babies. *The Washington Monthly.*

Bruner, J. S. (1983). Education as social invention. *Journal of Social Issues, 39,* 129–141.

Brunet, A., Orr, S. P., Tremblay, J., Robertson, K., Nader, K., & Pitman, R. K. (2008). Effects of post-retrieval propranolol on psychophysiologic responding during subsequent script-driven traumatic imagery in posttraumatic stress disorder. *Journal of Psychiatric Research, 42,* 503–506.

Brunner, D. P., Dijk, D. J., Tobler, I., & Borbely, A. A. (1990). Effect of partial sleep deprivation on sleep stages and EEG power spectra. *Electroencephalography and Clinical Neurophysiology, 75,* 492–499.

Buchanan, C. M., Eccles, J. S., & Becker, J. B. (1992). Are adolescents the victims of raging hormones? Evidence for activational effects of hormones on moods and behavior at adolescence. *Psychological Bulletin, 111,* 62–107.

Buchanan, T. W. (2007). Retrieval of emotional memories. *Psychological Bulletin, 133,* 761–779.

Buck, L., & Axel, R. (1991). A novel multigene family may encode odorant receptors: A molecular basis for odor recognition. *Cell, 65,* 175–187.

Buckner, R. L., Andrews-Hanna, J. R., & Schacter, D. L. (2008). The brain's default network: Anatomy, function, and relevance to disease. *Annals of the New York Academy of Sciences, 1124,* 1–38.

Buckner, R. L., Petersen, S. E., Ojemann, J. G., Miezin, F. M., Squire, L. R., & Raichle, M. E. (1995). Functional anatomical studies of explicit and implicit memory retrieval tasks. *The Journal of Neuroscience, 15,* 12–29.

Burdick, K. E., Lencz, T., Funke, B., Finn, C. T., Szeszko, P. R., Kane, J. M., et al. (2006). Genetic variation in dtnbp1 influences general cognitive ability. *Human Molecular Genetics, 15*(10), 1563–1568.

Bureau of Justice Statistics. (2008). *Prisoners in 2007* (No. NCJ224280 by H. C. West and W. J. Sabol). Washington, DC: U.S. Department of Justice.

Burger, J. M. (1999). The foot-in-the-door compliance procedure: A multiple-process analysis and review. *Personality and Social Psychology Review, 3,* 303–325.

Burger, J. M. (2009). Replicating Milgram: Would people still obey today? *American Psychologist, 64,* 1–11.

Burger, J. M., & Burns, L. (1988). The illusion of unique invulnerability and the use of effective contraception. *Personality and Social Psychology Bulletin, 14,* 264–270.

Burger, J. M., Sanchez, J., Imberi, J. E., & Grande, L. R. (2009). The norm of reciprocity as an internalized social norm: Returning favors even when no one finds out. *Social Influence, 4*(1), 11–17.

Burke, D., MacKay, D. G., Worthley, J. S., & Wade, E. (1991). On the tip of the tongue: What causes word failure in young and older adults? *Journal of Memory and Language, 30,* 237–246.

Burkham, D. T., Ready, D. D., Lee, V. E., & LoGerfo, L. F. (2004). Social-class differences in summer learning between kindergarten and first grade: Model specification and estimation. *Sociology of Education, 77,* 1–31.

Burnstein, E., Crandall, C., & Kitayama, S. (1994). Some neo-Darwinian decision rules for altruism: Weighing cues for inclusive fitness as a function of the biological importance of the decision. *Journal of Personality and Social Psychology, 67,* 773–789.

Burrelli, J. (2008). Thirty-three years of women in S&E faculty positions. *InfoBrief* (NSF 08-308). Arlington, VA: National Science Foundation.

Burris, C. T., & Branscombe, N. R. (2005). Distorted distance estimation induced by a self-relevant national boundary. *Journal of Experimental Social Psychology, 41,* 305–312.

Bus driver charged with interstate bus crash. (2009, September 28). WCAX.com. Retrieved October 14, 2009, from http://www.wcax.com/Global/story.asp?S=11211696

Bushman, B. J., & Huesmann, L. R. (2010). Aggression. In S. T. Fiske, D. T. Gilbert, & G. Lindzey (Eds.), *The handbook of social psychology* (5th ed., Vol. 2). New York: Wiley.

Buss, D. M. (1985). Human mate selection. *American Scientist, 73,* 47–51.

Buss, D. M. (1989). Sex differences in human mate preferences: Evolutionary hypotheses tested in 37 cultures. *Behavioral and Brain Sciences, 12,* 1–49.

Buss, D. M. (1994). *The evolution of desire: Strategies of human mating.* New York: Basic Books.

Buss, D. M. (1996). Social adaptation and five major factors of personality. In J. S. Wiggins (Ed.), *The five-factor model of personality: Theoretical perspectives* (pp. 180–208). New York: Guilford Press.

Buss, D. M. (1999). *Evolutionary psychology: The new science of the mind.* Boston: Allyn & Bacon.

Buss, D. M. (2000). *The dangerous passion: Why jealousy is as necessary as love and sex.* New York: Free Press.

Buss, D. M., Abbott, M., Angleitner, A., Asherian, A., Biaggio, A., Blanco-Villasenor, A., et al. (1990). International preferences in selecting mates: A study of 37 cultures. *Journal of Cross-Cultural Psychology, 21,* 5–47.

Buss, D. M., Haselton, M. G., Shackelford, T. K., Bleske, A. L., & Wakefield, J. C. (1998). Adaptations, exaptations, and spandrels. *American Psychologist, 53,* 533–548.

Buss, D. M., & Schmitt, D. P. (1993). Sexual strategies theory: An evolutionary perspective on human mating. *Psychological Review, 100,* 204–232.

Butcher, J. N., & Williams, C. L. (2000). *Essentials of MMPI-2 and MMPI-A interpretation* (2nd ed.). Minneapolis: University of Minnesota Press.

Butler, A. C., Chapman, J. E., Forman, E. M., & Beck, A. T. (2006). The empirical status of cognitive-behavioral therapy: A review of meta-analyses. *Clinical Psychology Review, 26,* 17–31.

Butler, M. A., Corboy, J. R., & Filley, C. M. (2009). How the conflict between American psychiatry and neurology delayed the appreciation of cognitive dysfunction in multiple sclerosis. *Neuropsychology Review, 19,* 399–410.

Byrne, D., Allgeier, A. R., Winslow, L., & Buckman, J. (1975). The situational facilitation of interpersonal attraction: A three-factor hypothesis. *Journal of Applied Social Psychology, 5,* 1–15.

Byrne, D., & Clore, G. L. (1970). A reinforcement model of evaluative responses. *Personality: An International Journal, 1,* 103–128.

Byrne, D., Ervin, C. R., & Lamberth, J. (1970). Continuity between the experimental study of attraction and real-life computer dating. *Journal of Personality and Social Psychology, 16,* 157–165.

Byrne, D., & Nelson, D. (1965). Attraction as a linear function of proportion of positive reinforcements. *Journal of Personality and Social Psychology, 1,* 659–663.

Cabeza, R. (2002). Hemispheric asymmetry reduction in older adults: The HAROLD model. *Psychology and Aging, 17,* 85–100.

Cabeza, R., Grady, C. L., Nyberg, L., McIntosh, A. R., Tulving, E., Kapur, S., et al. (1997). Age-related differences in neural activity during memory encoding and retrieval: A positron emission tomography study. *The Journal of Neuroscience, 17,* 391–400.

Cabeza, R., Rao, S., Wagner, A. D., Mayer, A., & Schacter, D. L. (2001). Can medial temporal lobe regions distinguish true from false? An event-related fMRI study of veridical and illusory recognition memory. *Proceedings of the National Academy of Sciences, USA, 98,* 4805–4810.

Cacioppo, J. T., & Patrick, B. (2008). *Loneliness: Human nature and the need for social connection.* New York: W. W. Norton & Company.

Cahill, L., Haier, R. J., Fallon, J., Alkire, M. T., Tang, C., Keator, D., et al. (1996). Amygdala activity at encoding correlated with long-term, free recall of emotional information. *Proceedings of the National Academy of Sciences, USA, 93,* 8016–8021.

Cahill, L., & McGaugh, J. L. (1998). Mechanisms of emotional arousal and lasting declarative memory. *Trends in Neurosciences, 21,* 294–299.

Cajal, S. R. (1937). *Recollections of my life.* Cambridge, MA: The MIT Press.

Calder, A. J., Young, A. W., Rowland, D., Perrett, D. I., Hodges, J. R., & Etcoff, N. L. (1996). Facial emotion recognition after bilateral amygdala damage: Differentially severe impairment of fear. *Cognitive Neuropsychology, 13,* 699–745.

Calkins, M. W. (Ed.). (1930). *Mary Whiton Calkins* (Vol. 1). Worcester, MA: Clark University Press.

Callaghan, T., Rochat, P., Lillard, A., Claux, M. L., Odden, H., Itakura, S., et al. (2005). Synchrony in the onset of mental-state reasoning: Evidence from five cultures. *Psychological Science, 16,* 378–384.

Campbell, A. (1999). Staying alive: Evolution, culture, and women's intra-sexual aggression. *Behavioral & Brain Sciences, 22,* 203–252.

Campbell, C. M., Edward, R. R., & Fillingim, R. B. (2005). Ethnic differences in responses to multiple experimental pain stimuli. *Pain, 113,* 20–26.

Campbell, R., & Sais, E. (1995). Accelerated metalinguistic (phonological) awareness in bilingual children. *British Journal of Developmental Psychology, 13,* 61–68.

Canetto, S., & Lester, D. (1995). Gender and the primary prevention of suicide mortality. *Suicide and Life Threatening Behavior, 25,* 85–89.

Cannon, W. B. (1927). The James-Lange theory of emotion: A critical examination and alternate theory. *American Journal of Psychology, 39,* 106–124.

Cannon, W. B. (1929). *Bodily changes in pain, hunger, fear, and rage: An account of recent research into the function of emotional excitement* (2nd ed.). New York: Appleton-Century-Crofts.

Cannon, W. B. (1942). "Voodoo" death. *American Anthropologist, 44,* 182–190.

Cantor, N. (1990). From thought to behavior: "Having" and "doing" in the study of personality and cognition. *American Psychologist, 45,* 735–750.

Caparelli, E. C. (2007). TMS & fMRI: A new neuroimaging combinational tool to study brain function. *Current Medical Imaging Review, 3,* 109–115.

Caplan, A. L. (Ed.). (1992). *When medicine went mad: Bioethics and the Holocaust.* Totowa, NJ: Humana Press.

Carlson, C., & Hoyle, R. (1993). Efficacy of abbreviated progressive muscle relaxation training: A quantitative review of behavioral medicine research. *Journal of Consulting and Clinical Psychology, 61,* 1059–1067.

Carmichael Olson, H., Streissguth, A. P., Sampson, P. D., Barr, H. M., Bookstein, F. L., & Thiede, K. (1997). Association of prenatal alcohol exposure with behavioral and learning problems in early adolescence. *Journal of the American Academy of Child & Adolescent Psychiatry, 36*(9), 1187–1194.

Carolson, E. A. (1998). A prospective longitudinal study of attachment disorganization/disorientation. *Child Development, 69,* 1107–1128.

Carr, L., Iacoboni, M., Dubeau, M., Mazziotta, J. C., & Lenzi, G. L. (2003). Neural mechanisms of empathy in humans: A relay from neural systems for imitation to limbic areas. *Proceedings of the National Academy of Sciences, USA, 100,* 5497–5502.

Carroll, J. B. (1993). *Human cognitive abilities.* Cambridge, England: Cambridge University Press.

Carson, R. C., Butcher, J. N., & Mineka, S. (2000). *Abnormal psychology and modern life* (11th ed.). Boston: Allyn & Bacon.

Carstensen, L. L. (1992). Social and emotional patterns in adulthood: Support for socioemotional selectivity theory. *Psychology and Aging, 7,* 331–338.

Carstensen, L. L., & Fredrickson, B. L. (1998). Influence of HIV status and age on cognitive representations of others. *Health Psychology, 17,* 1–10.

Carstensen, L. L., Pasupathi, M., Mayr, U., & Nesselroade, J. R. (2000). Emotional experience in everyday life across the adult life span. *Journal of Personality and Social Psychology, 79,* 644–655.

Carstensen, L. L., & Turk-Charles, S. (1994). The salience of emotion across the adult life span. *Psychology and Aging, 9,* 259–264.

Carter, J. (1977). Drug abuse message to the Congress [Electronic version]. The American Presidency Project. Retrieved March 5, 2009, from http://www.presidency.ucsb.edu/ws/index.php?pid=7908

Carver, C. S. (2006). Approach, avoidance, and the self-regulation of affect and action. *Motivation and Emotion, 30,* 105–110.

Carver, C. S., Lehman, J. M., & Antoni, M. H. (2003). Dispositional pessimism predicts illness-related disruption of social and recreational activities among breast cancer patients. *Journal of Personality and Social Psychology, 84,* 813–821.

Carver, C. S., & White, T. L. (1994). Behavioral inhibition, behavioral activation, and affective responses to impending reward and punishment: The bis/bas scales. *Journal of Personality and Social Psychology, 67*(2), 319–333.

Casasanto, D., & Boroditsky, L. (2008). Time in the mind: Using space to think about time. *Cognition, 106,* 579–593.

Caspi, A., Henry, B., McGee, R. O., Moffitt, T. E., & Silva, P. A. (1995). Temperamental origins of child and adolescent behavior problems: From age three to age fifteen. *Child Development, 66,* 55–68.

Caspi, A., & Herbener, E. S. (1990). Continuity and change: Assortative marriage and the consistency of personality in adulthood. *Journal of Personality and Social Psychology, 58,* 250–258.

Caspi, A., Lynam, D., Moffitt, T. E., & Silva, P. A. (1993). Unraveling girls' delinquency: Biological, dispositional, and contextual contributions to adolescent misbehavior. *Developmental Psychology, 29,* 19–30.

Caspi, A., & Moffitt, T. E. (1991). Individual differences are accentuated during periods of social change: The sample case of girls at puberty. *Journal of Personality and Social Psychology, 61,* 157–168.

Caspi, A., Roberts, B. W., & Shiner, R. L. (2005). Personality development: Stability and change. *Annual Review of Psychology, 56,* 453–484.

Catrambone, R. (2002). The effects of surface and structural feature matches on the access of story analogs. *Journal of Experimental Psychology: Learning, Memory, & Cognition, 28,* 318–334.

Cattell, R. B. (1950). *Personality: A systematic, theoretical, and factual study.* New York: McGraw-Hill.

Ceci, S. J. (1991). How much does schooling influence general intelligence and its cognitive components? A reassessment of the evidence. *Developmental Psychology, 27,* 703–722.

Ceci, S. J., DeSimone, M., & Johnson, S. (1992). Memory in context: A case study of "Bubbles P.," a gifted but uneven memorizer. In D. J. Herrmann, H. Weingartner, A. Searleman, & C. McEvoy (Eds.), *Memory improvement: Implications for memory theory* (pp. 169–186). New York: Springer-Verlag.

Ceci, S. J., & Williams, W. M. (1997). Schooling, intelligence, and income. *American Psychologist, 52,* 1051–1058.

Centers for Disease Control and Prevention (CDC). (2002, June 28). Youth risk behavior surveillance. *Surveillance Summary, 51*(SS-4), 1–64. Washington, DC: Author.

Centers for Disease Control and Prevention (CDC). (2006). Epidemiology of HIV/AIDS—United States, 1981–2005. *Morbidity and Mortality Weekly Report, 55,* 589–592.

Centers for Disease Control and Prevention, National Center for Injury Prevention and Control. (2010). Web-based injury statistics query and reporting system (WISQARS). Retrieved April 10, 2010, from www.cdc.gov/ncipc/wisqars

Centers for Disease Control Vietnam Experience Study (CDC). (1988). Health status of Vietnam veterans: I. Psychosocial characteristics. *Journal of the American Medical Association, 259*(18), 2701–2708.

Chaiken, S. (1980). Heuristic versus systematic information processing and the use of source versus message cues in persuasion. *Journal of Personality and Social Psychology, 39,* 752–766.

Chalmers, D. (1996). *The conscious mind: In search of a fundamental theory.* New York: Oxford University Press.

Chambless, D. L., Baker, M. J., Baucom, D. H., Beutler, L. E., Calhoun, K. S., Crits-Christoph, P., et al. (1998). Update on empirically validated therapies, II. *Clinical Psychologist, 51*(1), 3–14.

Chandler, J., & Schwarz, N. (2009). How extending your middle finger affects your perception of others: Learned movements influence concept accessibility. *Journal of Experimental Social Psychology, 45,* 123–128.

Chandrashekar, J., Hoon, M. A., Ryba, N. J., & Zuker, C. S. (2006). The receptors and cells for human tastes. *Nature, 444,* 288–294.

Chang, P. P., Ford, D. E., Meoni, L. A., Wang, N., & Klag, M. J. (2002). Anger in young men and subsequent premature cardiovascular disease. *Archives of Internal Medicine, 162,* 901–906.

Charles, S. T., Reynolds, C. A., & Gatz, M. (2001). Age-related differences and change in positive and negative affect over 23 years. *Journal of Personality and Social Psychology, 80,* 136–151.

Charlesworth, A., & Glantz, S. A. (2005). Smoking in the movies increases adolescent smoking: A review. *Pediatrics, 116,* 1516–1528.

Charness, N. (1981). Aging and skilled problem solving. *Journal of Experimental Psychology: General, 110,* 21–38.

Charpak, G., & Broch, H. (2004). *Debunked!: ESP, telekinesis, and other pseudoscience* (B. K. Holland, Trans.). Baltimore, MD: The Johns Hopkins University Press.

Chartrand, T. L., & Bargh, J. A. (1999). The chameleon effect: The perception-behavior link and social interaction. *Journal of Personality and Social Psychology, 76,* 893–910.

Chartrand, T. L., & Kay, A. (2006). *Mystery moods and perplexing performance: Consequences of succeeding and failing at a nonconscious goal.* Unpublished manuscript.

Chebium, R. (2000). Kirk Bloodsworth, twice convicted of rape and murder, exonerated by DNA evidence. *CNN.com.* Retrieved June 20, 2000, from http://www.cnn.com/2000/LAW/06/20/bloodsworth.profile

Chen, E., Cohen, S., & Miller, G. E. (2010). How low socioeconomic status affects 2-year hormonal trajectories in children. *Psychological Science, 21*(1), 31–37.

Cheney, D. L., & Seyfarth, R. M. (1990). *How monkeys see the world.* Chicago: University of Chicago Press.

Cheng, D. T., Disterhoft, J. F., Power, J. M., Ellis, D. A., & Desmond, J. E. (2008). Neural substrates underlying human delay and trace eyeblink conditioning. *Proceedings of the National Academy of Sciences, USA, 105,* 8108–8113.

Cheng, P. W., & Holyoak, K. J. (1989). On the natural selection of reasoning theories. *Cognition, 33,* 285–313.

Cherlin, A. J. (Ed.). (1992). *Marriage, divorce, remarriage* (2nd ed.). Cambridge, MA: Harvard University Press.

Cherry, A., Dillon, M. E., & Rugh, D. (Eds.). (2002). *Substance abuse: A global view.* Westport, CT: Greenwood.

Cherry, C. (1953). Some experiments on the recognition of speech with one and two ears. *Journal of the Acoustical Society of America, 25,* 275–279.

Childress, C. A. (2000). Ethical issues in providing online psychotherapeutic interventions. *Journal of Medical Internet Research, 2*(1), e5.

Choi, I., Nisbett, R. E., & Norenzayan, A. (1999). Causal attribution across cultures: Variation and universality. *Psychological Bulletin, 125,* 47–63.

Chomsky, N. (1957). *Syntactic structures.* The Hague: Mouton.

Chomsky, N. (1959). A review of *Verbal Behavior* by B. F. Skinner. *Language, 35,* 26–58.

Chomsky, N. (1986). *Knowledge of language: Its nature, origin, and use.* New York: Praeger.

Chorover, S. L. (1980). *From Genesis to genocide : The meaning of human nature and the power of behavior control.* Cambridge, MA: The MIT Press.

Choy, Y., Fyer, A. J., & Lipsitz, J. D. (2007). Treatment of specific phobia in adults. *Clinical Psychology Review, 27,* 266–286.

Christakis, N. A., & Fowler, J. H. (2007). The spread of obesity in a large social network over 32 years. *New England Journal of Medicine, 357*(4), 370–379.

Christianson, S.-Å., & Loftus, E. F. (1987). Memory for traumatic events. *Applied Cognitive Psychology, 1,* 225–239.

Chung, G. H., Flook, L., & Fuligni, A. J. (2009). Daily family conflict and emotional distress among adolescents from Latin American, Asian, and European backgrounds. *Developmental Psychology, 45,* 1406–1415.

Cialdini, R. B. (2005). Don't throw in the towel: Use social influence research. *American Psychological Society, 18,* 33–34.

Cialdini, R. B., & Trost, M. R. (1998). Social influence: Social norms, conformity, and compliance. In D. T. Gilbert, S. T. Fiske, & G. Lindzey (Eds.), *The handbook of social psychology* (4th ed., Vol. 2, pp. 151–192). New York: McGraw-Hill.

Cialdini, R. B., Trost, M. R., & Newsom, J. T. (1995). Preference for consistency: The development of a valid measure and the discovery of surprising behavioral implications. *Journal of Personality and Social Psychology, 69,* 318–328.

Cialdini, R. B., Vincent, J. E., Lewis, S. K., Catalan, J., Wheeler, D., & Darby, B. L. (1975). Reciprocal concessions procedure for inducing compliance: The door-in-the-face technique. *Journal of Personality and Social Psychology, 31,* 206–215.

Ciarrochi, J. V., Chan, A. Y., & Caputi, P. (2000). A critical evaluation of the emotional intelligence concept. *Personality & Individual Differences, 28,* 539.

Cicchetti, D., & Toth, S. L. (1998). Perspectives on research and practice in developmental psychopathology. In I. E. Sigel & K. A. Renninger (Eds.), *Handbook of child psychology: Vol. 4. Child psychology in practice* (5th ed., pp. 479–583). New York: Wiley.

Cieply, M. (2010, January 3). James Cameron responds to critics of smoking in *Avatar. New York Times.*

Clancy, S. A. (2005). *Abducted: How people come to believe they were kidnapped by aliens.* Cambridge, MA: Harvard University Press.

Clancy, S. A., McNally, R. J., Schacter, D. L., Lenzenweger, M. F., & Pitman, R. K. (2002). Memory distortion in people reporting abduction by aliens. *Journal of Abnormal Psychology, 111,* 455–461.

Clancy, S. A., Schacter, D. L., McNally, R. J., & Pitman, R. K. (2000). False recognition in women reporting recovered memories of sexual abuse. *Psychological Science, 11,* 26–31.

Clark, L. A. (2007). Assessment and diagnosis of personality disorder: Perennial issues and emerging conceptualization. *Annual Review of Psychology, 58,* 227–257.

Clark, M. S., & Lemay, E. P. (2010). Close relationships. In S. T. Fiske, D. T. Gilbert, & G. Lindzey (Eds.), *The handbook of social psychology* (5th ed., Vol. 2). New York: Wiley.

Clark, R. D., & Hatfield, E. (1989). Gender differences in receptivity to sexual offers. *Journal of Psychology and Human Sexuality, 2,* 39–55.

Clark, R. E., Manns, J. R., & Squire, L. R. (2002). Classical conditioning, awareness and brain systems. *Trends in Cognitive Sciences, 6,* 524–531.

Clark, R. E., & Squire, L. R. (1998). Classical conditioning and brain systems: The role of awareness. *Science, 280,* 77–81.

Clayton, N. S., & Dickinson, A. (1998). Episodic-like memory during cache recovery by scrub jays. *Nature, 395,* 272–274.

Clayton, N. S., & Russell, J. (2009). Looking for episodic memory in animals and young children: Prospects for a new minimalism. *Neuropsychologia, 47,* 2330–2340.

Cleckley, H. M. (1976). *The mask of sanity* (5th ed.). St. Louis: Mosby.

Coe, C. L., & Lubach, G. R. (2008). Fetal programming prenatal origins of health and illness. *Current Directions in Psychological Science, 17,* 36–41.

Cogan, R., Cogan, D., Waltz, W., & McCue, M. (1987). Effects of laughter and relaxation on discomfort thresholds. *Journal of Behavioral Medicine, 10,* 139–144.

Coghill, R. C., McHaffie, J. G., & Yen, Y. (2003). Neural correlates of individual differences in the subjective experience of pain. *Proceedings of the National Academy of Sciences, USA, 100,* 8538–8542.

Cohen, D., Nisbett, R. E., Bowdle, B. F., & Schwarz, N. (1996). Insult, aggression, and the southern culture of honor: An "experimental ethnography." *Journal of Personality and Social Psychology, 70,* 945–960.

Cohen, G. (1990). Why is it difficult to put names to faces? *British Journal of Psychology, 81,* 287–297.

Cohen, S. (1988). Psychosocial models of the role of social support in the etiology of physical disease. *Health Psychology, 7,* 269–297.

Cohen, S. (1999). Social status and susceptibility to respiratory infections. *New York Academy of Sciences, 896,* 246–253.

Cohen, S., Evans, G. W., Krantz, D. S., & Stokols, D. (1980). Physiological, motivational, and cognitive effects of aircraft noise on children. *American Psychologist, 35,* 231–243.

Cohen, S., Frank, E., Doyle, W. J., Skoner, D. P., Rabin, B. S., & Gwaltney, J. M., Jr. (1998). Types of stressors that increase susceptibility to the common cold in healthy adults. *Health Psychology, 17,* 214–223.

Cohen, S. J. (Ed.). (1979). *New directions in patient compliance.* Lexington, MA: Heath.

Coifman, K. G., Bonanno, G. A., Ray, R. D., & Gross, J. J. (2007). Does repressive coping promote resilience? Affective-autonomic response discrepancy during bereavement. *Journal of Personality and Social Psychology, 92,* 745–758.

Colcombe, S. J., Erickson, K. I., Scalf, P. E., Kim, J. S., Prakesh, R., McAuley, E., et al. (2006). Aerobic exercise training increases brain volume in aging humans. *Journals of Gerontology Series A: Biological Sciences and Medical Sciences, 61,* 1166–1170.

Colcombe, S. J., Kramer, A. F., Erickson, K. I., Scalf, P., McAuley, E., Cohen, N. J., et al. (2004). Cardiovascular fitness, cortical plasticity, and aging. *Proceedings of the National Academy of Sciences, USA, 101,* 3316–3321.

Cole, M. (1996). *Cultural psychology: A once and future discipline.* Cambridge, MA: Belknap Press of Harvard University Press.

Coman, A., Manier, D., & Hirst, W. (2009). Forgetting the unforgettable through conversation: Social shared retrieval-induced forgetting of September 11 memories. *Psychological Science, 20,* 627–633.

Condon, J. W., & Crano, W. D. (1988). Inferred evaluation and the relation between attitude similarity and interpersonal attraction. *Journal of Personality and Social Psychology, 54,* 789–797.

Connors, E., Lundregan, T., Miller, N., & McEwen, T. (1997). *Convicted by juries, exonerated by science: Case studies in the use of DNA evidence to establish innocence after trial.* Collingdale, PA: Diane Publishing.

Conroy, D. E., Elliot, A. J., Thrash, T. M., Leary, M. R., & Hoyle, R. H. (2009). Achievement motivation. In *Handbook of individual differences in social behavior* (pp. 382–399). New York: Guilford Press.

Conway, M., & Ross, M. (1984). Getting what you want by revising what you had. *Journal of Personality and Social Psychology, 47,* 738–748.

Conwell, Y., Duberstein, P. R., Cox, C., Hermmann, J. H., Forbes, N. T., & Caine, E. D. (1996). Relationships of age and axis I diagnoses in victims of completed suicide: A psychological autopsy study. *American Journal of Psychiatry, 153,* 1001–1008.

Cook, E. P. (1985). *Psychological androgyny.* New York: Pergamon Press.

Cook, M., & Mineka, S. (1989). Observational conditioning of fear to fear-relevant versus fear-irrelevant stimuli in rhesus monkeys. *Journal of Abnormal Psychology, 98,* 448–459.

Cook, M., & Mineka, S. (1990). Selective associations in the observational conditioning of fear in rhesus monkeys. *Journal of Experimental Psychology: Animal Behavior Process, 16,* 372–389.

Coombs, R. H. (1991). Marital status and personal well-being: A literature review. *Family Relations, 40,* 97–102.

Coons, P. M. (1994). Confirmation of childhood abuse in child and adolescent cases of multiple personality disorder and dissociative disorder not otherwise specified. *Journal of Nervous and Mental Disease, 182,* 461–464.

Coontz, P. (2008). The responsible conduct of social research. In K. Yang & G. J. Miller (Eds.), *Handbook of research methods in public administration* (pp. 129–139). Boca Raton, FL: Taylor & Francis.

Cooper, H., Nye, B., Charlton, K., Lindsay, J., & Greathouse, S. (1996). The effects of summer vacation on achievement test scores: A narrative and meta-analytic review. *Review of Educational Research, 66*(3), 227–268.

Cooper, J., & Fazio, R. H. (1984). A new look at dissonance theory. In L. Berkowitz (Ed.), *Advances in experimental social psychology* (Vol. 17, pp. 229–266). New York: Academic Press.

Cooper, J. C., Hollon, N. G., Wimmer, G. E., & Knutson, B. (2009). Available alternative incentives modulate anticipatory nucleus accumbens activation. *Social Cognitive and Affective Neuroscience, 4,* 409–416.

Cooper, J. M., & Strayer, D. L. (2008). Effects of simulator practice and real-world experience on cell-phone related driver distraction. *Human Factors, 50,* 893–902.

Cooper, J. R., Bloom, F. E., & Roth, R. H. (2003). *Biochemical basis of neuropharmacology.* New York: Oxford University Press.

Cooper, M. L. (2006). Does drinking promote risky sexual behavior? A complex answer to a simple question. *Current Directions in Psychological Science, 15,* 19–23.

Cooper, W. H., & Withey, W. J. (2009). The strong situation hypothesis. *Personality and Social Psychology Review, 13,* 62–72.

Corbetta, M., Shulman, G. L., Miezin, F. M., & Petersen, S. E. (1995). Superior parietal cortex activation during spatial attention shifts and visual feature conjunction. *Science, 270,* 802–805.

Coren, S. (1997). *Sleep thieves.* New York: Free Press.

Corkin, S. (1984). Lasting consequences of bilateral medial temporal lobectomy: Clinical course and experimental findings in H. M. *Seminars in Neurology, 4,* 249–259.

Corkin, S. (2002). What's new with the amnesic patient HM? *Nature Reviews Neuroscience, 3,* 153–160.

Correll, J., Park, B., Judd, C. M., & Wittenbrink, B. (2002). The police officer's dilemma: Using ethnicity to disambiguate potentially threatening individuals. *Journal of Personality and Social Psychology, 83,* 1314–1329.

Correll, J., Park, B., Judd, C. M., Wittenbrink, B., Sadler, M. S., & Keesee, T. (2007). Across the thin blue line: Police officers and racial bias in the decision to shoot. *Journal of Personality and Social Psychology, 92,* 1006–1023.

Corsi, P. (1991). *The enchanted loom: Chapters in the history of neuroscience.* New York: Oxford University Press.

Corti, E. (1931). *A history of smoking* (P. England, Trans.). London: Harrap.

Coryell, W., Endicott, J., Maser, J. D., Mueller, T., Lavori, P., & Keller, M. (1995). The likelihood of recurrence in bipolar affective disorder: The importance of episode recency. *Journal of Affective Disorders, 33,* 201–206.

Cosmides, L. (1989). The logic of social exchange: Has natural selection shaped how humans reason? Studies with the Wason selection task. *Cognition, 31*(3), 187–276.

Cottrell, C. A., Neuberg, S. L., & Li, N. P. (2007). What do people desire in others? A sociofunctional perspective on the importance of different valued characteristics. *Journal of Personality and Social Psychology, 92,* 208–231.

Couzin, J. (2008). Gene tests for psychiatric risk polarize researchers. *Science, 319,* 274–277.

Cox, D., & Cowling, P. (1989). *Are you normal?* London: Tower Press.

Coyne, J. A. (2000, April 3). Of vice and men: Review of R. Tornhill and C. Palmer, *A natural history of rape. The New Republic,* pp. 27–34.

Coyne, J. C., & Whiffen, V. E. (1995). Issues in personality as diathesis for depression: The case of sociotropy-dependency and autonomy self-criticism. *Psychological Bulletin, 118,* 358–378.

Craddock, N., & Jones, I. (1999). Genetics of bipolar disorder. *Journal of Medical Genetics, 36,* 585–594.

Craik, F. I. M., Govoni, R., Naveh-Benjamin, M., & Anderson, N. D. (1996). The effects of divided attention on encoding and retrieval processes in human memory. *Journal of Experimental Psychology: General, 125,* 159–180.

Craik, F. I. M., & Tulving, E. (1975). Depth of processing and the retention of words in episodic memory. *Journal of Experimental Psychology: General, 104,* 268–294.

Cramer, P. (2008). Seven pillars of defense mechanism theory. *Social and Personality Psychology Compass, 2*(5), 1963–1981.

Cramer, R. E., Schaefer, J. T., & Reid, S. (1996). Identifying the ideal mate: More evidence for male-female convergence. *Current Psychology, 15,* 157–166.

Cranefield, P. F. (1970). On the origin of the phrase *nihil est in intellectu quod non prius fuerit in sensu. Journal of the History of Medicine and Allied Sciences, 25*(1), 77–80.

Craske, M. G. (1999). *Anxiety disorders: Psychological approaches to theory and treatment.* Boulder, CO: Westview Press.

Crick, N. R., & Grotpeter, J. K. (1995). Relational aggression, gender, and social-psychological adjustment. *Child Development, 66,* 710–722.

Crocker, J., & Wolfe, C. T. (2001). Contingencies of self-worth. *Psychological Review, 108*(3), 593–623.

Crombag, H. F. M., Wagenaar, W. A., & Van Koppen, P. J. (1996). Crashing memories and the problem of "source monitoring." *Applied Cognitive Psychology, 10,* 95–104.

Cross, E. S., Kraemer, D. J. M., Hamilton, A. F. de C., Kelley, W. M., & Grafton, S. T. (2009). Sensitivity of the action observation network to physical and observational learning. *Cerebral Cortex, 19,* 315–326.

Cross, P. (1977). Not can but will college teachers be improved? *New Directions for Higher Education, 17,* 1–15.

Cross-National Collaborative Research Group. (1992). The changing rate of major depression: Cross-national comparison. *Journal of the American Medical Association, 268,* 3098–3105.

Crowe, R. (1990). Panic disorder: Genetic considerations. *Journal of Psychiatric Researchers, 24,* 129–134.

Csikszentmihalyi, M. (1990). *Flow: The psychology of optimal experience.* New York: Harper & Row.

Csikszentmihalyi, M., & Larson, R. (1987). Validity and reliability of the experience-sampling method. *Journal of Nervous & Mental Disease, 175,* 526–536.

Cue, A., Koppel, J., & Hirst, W. (2007). Silence is not golden: A case of socially shared retrieval-induced forgetting. *Psychological Science, 18,* 727–733.

Cumming, S., Hay, P., Lee, T., & Sachdev, P. (1995). Neuropsychological outcome from psychosurgery for obsessive-compulsive disorder. *Australian and New Zealand Journal of Psychiatry, 29,* 293–298.

Cunningham, M. R., Barbee, A. P., & Pike, C. L. (1990). What do women want? Facial metric assessment of multiple motives in the perception of male facial physical attractiveness. *Journal of Personality and Social Psychology, 59,* 61–72.

Cunningham, M. R., Roberts, A. R., Barbee, A. P., Druen, P. B., & Wu, C.-H. (1995). "Their ideas of beauty are, on the whole, the same as ours": Consistency and variability in the cross-cultural perception of female physical attractiveness. *Journal of Personality and Social Psychology, 68,* 261–279.

Curran, J. P., & Lippold, S. (1975). The effects of physical attraction and attitude similarity on attraction in dating dyads. *Journal of Personality, 43,* 528–539.

Curtiss, S. (1977). *Genie: A psycholinguistic study of a modern-day "wild-child."* New York: Academic Press.

Cutler, D. L., Bevilacqua, J., & McFarland, B. H. (2003). Four decades of community mental health: A symphony in four movements. *Community Mental Health Journal, 39,* 381–398.

D'Agostino, P. R., & Fincher-Kiefer, R. (1992). Need for cognition and correspondence bias. *Social Cognition, 10,* 151–163.

Dabbs, J. M., Bernieri, F. J., Strong, R. K., Campo, R., & Milun, R. (2001). Going on stage: Testosterone in greetings and meetings. *Journal of Research in Personality, 35,* 27–40.

Dabbs, J. M., Carr, T. S., Frady, R. L., & Riad, J. K. (1995). Testosterone, crime, and misbehavior among 692 male prison inmates. *Personality and Individual Differences, 18,* 627–633.

Dahl, G., & Della Vigna, S. (2009). Does movie violence increase violent crime? *The Quarterly Journal of Economics, 124,* 677–734.

Daily annoyances: Consumer reports survey. (2010, January). *ConsumerReports.org.* Retrieved September 17, 2010, from http://www.consumerreports.org/cro/magazine-archive/2010/january/shopping/what-bugs-america-most/overview/what-bugs-america-most-ov.htm

Dally, P. (1999). *The marriage of heaven and hell: Manic depression and the life of Virginia Woolf.* New York: St. Martin's Griffin.

Dalton, P. (2003). Olfaction. In H. Pashler & S. Yantis (Eds.), *Stevens' handbook of experimental psychology: Vol. 1. Sensation and perception* (3rd ed., pp. 691–746). New York: Wiley.

Daly, M., & Wilson, M. (1988). Evolutionary social psychology and family homicide. *Science, 242,* 519–524.

Damasio, A. R. (1989). Time-locked multiregional retroactivation: A systems-level proposal for the neural substrates of recall and recognition. *Cognition, 33,* 25–62.

Damasio, A. R. (1994). *Descartes' error: Emotion, reason, and the human brain.* New York: Putnam.

Damasio, A. R. (2005). *Descartes' error: Emotion, reason, and the human brain* (ppbk. ed.) New York: Penguin.

Damasio, A. R., Grabowski, T. J., Bechara, A., Damasio, H., Ponto, L. L. B., Parvisi, J., et al. (2000). Subcortical and cortical brain activity during the feeling of self-generated emotions. *Nature Neuroscience, 3,* 1049–1056.

Damasio, H., Grabowski, T., Frank, R., Galaburda, A. M., & Damasio, A. R. (1994). The return of Phineas Gage: Clues about the brain from the skull of a famous patient. *Science, 264,* 1102–1105.

Damasio, H., Grabowski, T. J., Tranel, D., Hichwa, R. D., & Damasio, A. R. (1996). A neural basis for lexical retrieval. *Nature, 380,* 499–505.

Damsma, G., Pfaus, J. G., Wenkstern, D., Phillips, A. G., & Fibiger, H. C. (1992). Sexual behavior increases dopamine transmission in the nucleus accumbens and striatum of male rats: Comparison with novelty and locomotion. *Behavioral Neurosciences, 106,* 181–191.

Daniel, H. J., O'Brien, K. F., McCabe, R. B., & Quinter, V. E. (1985). Values in mate selection: A 1984 campus survey. *College Student Journal, 19,* 44–50.

Darley, J. M., & Berscheid, E. (1967). Increased liking caused by the anticipation of interpersonal contact. *Human Relations, 10,* 29–40.

Darley, J. M., & Latané, B. (1968). Bystander intervention in emergencies: Diffusion of responsibility. *Journal of Personality and Social Psychology, 8,* 377–383.

Dar-Nimrod, I., & Heine, S. J. (2006). Exposure to scientific theories affects women's math performance. *Science, 314,* 435.

Darwin, C. (2007). *The expression of the emotions in man and animals.* New York: Bibliobazaar. (Original work published 1899)

Darwin, C. (1998). *The expression of the emotions in man and animals* (P. Ekman, Ed.). New York: Oxford University Press. (Original work published 1872)

Darwin, C. J., Turvey, M. T., & Crowder, R. G. (1972). An auditory analogue of the Sperling partial report procedure: Evidence for brief auditory storage. *Cognitive Psychology, 3,* 255–267.

Dauer, W., & Przedborski, S. (2003). Parkinson's disease: Mechanisms and models. *Neuron, 39,* 889–909.

Daum, I., Schugens, M. M., Ackermann, H., Lutzenberger, W., Dichgans, J., & Birbaumer, N. (1993). Classical conditioning after cerebellar lesions in humans. *Behavioral Neuroscience, 107,* 748–756.

Davidson, R. J. (2004). What does the prefrontal cortex "do" in affect: Perspectives on frontal EEG asymmetry research. *Biological Psychology, 67,* 219–233.

Davidson, R. J., Ekman, P., Saron, C., Senulis, J., & Friesen, W. V. (1990). Emotional expression and brain physiology I: Approach/withdrawal and cerebral asymmetry. *Journal of Personality and Social Psychology, 58,* 330–341.

Davidson, R. J., Pizzagalli, D., Nitschke, J. B., & Putnam, K. (2002). Depression: Perspectives from affective neuroscience. *Annual Review of Psychology, 53,* 545–574.

Davidson, R. J., Putnam, K. M., & Larson, C. L. (2000). Dysfunction in the neural circuitry of emotion regulation—a possible prelude to violence. *Science, 289,* 591–594.

Davies, G. (1988). Faces and places: Laboratory research on context and face recognition. In G. M. Davies & D. M. Thomson (Eds.), *Memory in context: Context in memory* (pp. 35–53). New York: Wiley.

Davila Ross, M., Menzler, S., & Zimmermann, E. (2008). Rapid facial mimicry in orangutan play. *Biology Letters, 4*(1), 27–30.

Dawes, R. M. (1994). *House of cards: Psychology and psychotherapy built on myth.* New York: Free Press.

Dawood, K., Kirk, K. M., Bailey, J. M., Andrews, P. W., & Martin, N. G. (2005). Genetic and environmental influences on the frequency of orgasm in women. *Twin Research, 8,* 27–33.

Dawson, M., Soulieres, I., Gernsbacher, M. A., & Mottron, L. (2007). The level and nature of autistic intelligence. *Psychological Science, 18,* 657–662.

Dayan, P., & Huys, Q. J. M. (2009). Serotonin in affective control. *Annual Review of Neuroscience, 32,* 95–126.

de Araujo, I. E., Rolls, E. T., Velazco, M. I., Margot, C., & Cayeux, I. (2005). Cognitive modulation of olfactory processing. *Neuron, 46,* 671–679.

de Craen, A. J. M., Moerman, D. E., Heisterkamp, S. H., Tytgat, G. N. J., Tijssen, J. G. P., & Kleijnen, J. (1999). Placebo effect in the treatment of duodenal ulcer. *British Journal of Clinical Pharmacology, 48,* 853–860.

De Vries, M. H., Barth, A. C. R., Maiworm, S., Knecht, S., Zwitserlood, P., & Flöel, A. (in press). Electrical stimulation of Broca's area enhances implicit learning of an artificial grammar. *Journal of Cognitive Neuroscience.*

De Witte, P. (1996). The role of neurotransmitters in alcohol dependency. *Alcohol & Alcoholism, 31*(Suppl. 1), 13–16.

De Wolff, M., & van Ijzendoorn, M. H. (1997). Sensitivity and attachment: A meta-analysis on parental antecedents of infant attachment. *Child Development, 68,* 571–591.

Deák, G. O. (2006). Do children really confuse appearance and reality? *Trends in Cognitive Sciences, 10*(12), 546–550.

Deary, I. J. (2000). *Looking down on human intelligence: From psychometrics to the brain.* New York: Oxford University Press.

Deary, I. J., Batty, G. D., & Gale, C. R. (2008). Bright children become enlightened adults. *Psychological Science, 19*(1), 1–6.

Deary, I. J., Batty, G. D., Pattie, A., & Gale, C. R. (2008). More intelligent, more dependable children live longer: A 55-year longitudinal study of a representative sample of the Scottish nation. *Psychological Science, 19,* 874.

Deary, I. J., Der, G., & Ford, G. (2001). Reaction time and intelligence differences: A population based cohort study. *Intelligence, 29,* 389–399.

Deary, I. J., & Stough, C. (1996). Intelligence and inspection time: Achievements, prospects, and problems. *American Psychologist, 51,* 599–608.

Deary, I. J., Whiteman, M. C., Starr, J. M., Whalley, L. J., & Fox, H. C. (2004). The impact of childhood intelligence on later life: Following up the Scottish mental surveys of 1932 and 1947. *Journal of Personality and Social Psychology, 86,* 130–147.

DeCasper, A. J., & Spence, M. J. (1986). Prenatal maternal speech influences newborns' perception of speech sounds. *Infant Behavior and Development, 9,* 133–150.

Deci, E. L. (1971). Effects of externally mediated rewards on intrinsic motivation. *Journal of Personality and Social Psychology, 18,* 105–115.

Deci, E. L., Koestner, R., & Ryan, R. M. (1999). A meta-analytic review of experiments examining the effects of extrinsic rewards on intrinsic motivation. *Psychological Bulletin, 125,* 627–668.

Deese, J. (1959). On the prediction of occurrence of particular verbal intrusions in immediate recall. *Journal of Experimental Psychology, 58,* 17–22.

DeFelipe, J., & Jones, E. G. (1988). *Cajal on the cerebral cortex: An annotated translation of the complete writings.* New York: Oxford University Press.

Dehaene, S., Izard, V., Pica, P., & Spelke, E. (2006). Core knowledge of geometry in an Amazonian Indigene group. *Science, 311,* 381–384.

Delgado, M. R., Frank, R. H., & Phelps, E. A. (2005). Perceptions of moral character modulate the neural systems of reward during the trust game. *Nature Neuroscience, 8,* 1611–1618.

Delongis, A., Coyne, J. C., Dakof, G., Folkman, S., & Lazarus, R. S. (1982). Relationship of daily hassles, uplifts, and major life events to health status. *Health Psychology, 1,* 119–136.

Demb, J. B., Desmond, J. E., Wagner, A. D., Vaidya, C. J., Glover, G. H., & Gabrieli, J. D. E. (1995). Semantic encoding and retrieval in the left inferior prefrontal cortex: A functional MRI study of task difficulty and process specificity. *The Journal of Neuroscience, 15,* 5870–5878.

Dement, W. C. (1959, November 30). Dreams. *Time.*

Dement, W. C. (1978). *Some must watch while some must sleep.* New York: Norton.

Dement, W. C. (1999). *The promise of sleep.* New York: Delacorte Press.

Dement, W. C., & Kleitman, N. (1957). The relation of eye movements during sleep to dream activity: An objective method for the study of dreaming. *Journal of Experimental Psychology, 53,* 339–346.

Dement, W. C., & Wolpert, E. (1958). Relation of eye movements, body motility, and external stimuli to dream content. *Journal of Experimental Psychology, 55,* 543–553.

Dennett, D. (1991). *Consciousness explained.* New York: Basic Books.

DePaulo, B. M., Charlton, K., Cooper, H., Lindsay, J. J., & Muhlenbruck, L. (1997). The accuracy-confidence correlation in the detection of deception. *Personality and Social Psychology Review, 1,* 346–357.

DePaulo, B. M., Lindsay, J. J., Malone, B. E., Muhlenbruck, L., Charlton, K., & Cooper, H. (2003). Cues to deception. *Psychological Bulletin, 129,* 74–118.

DePaulo, B. M., Stone, J. I., & Lassiter, G. D. (1985). Deceiving and detecting deceit. In B. R. Schlenker (Ed.), *The self and social life* (pp. 323–370). New York: McGraw-Hill.

Der, G., Batty, G. D., & Deary, I. J. (2009). The association between IQ in adolescence and a range of health outcomes at 40 in the 1979 U.S. national longitudinal study of youth. *Intelligence, 37*(6), 573–580.

DeRosnay, M., Pons, F., Harris, P. L., & Morrell, J. M. B. (2004). A lag between understanding false belief and emotion attribution in young children: Relationships with linguistic ability and mothers' mental-state language. *British Journal of Developmental Psychology, 24*(1), 197–218.

Des Jarlais, D. C., McKnight, C., Goldblatt, C., & Purchase, D. (2009). Doing harm reduction better: Syringe exchange in the United States. *Addiction, 104*(9), 1331–1446.

DesJardin, J. L., Eisenberg, L. S., & Hodapp, R. M. (2006). Sound beginnings: Supporting families of young deaf children with cochlear implants. *Infants and Young Children, 19,* 179–189.

Deuenwald, M. (2003, June 12). Students find another staple of campus life: Stress. *New York Times.*

Deutsch, M. (1949). A theory of cooperation and competition. *Human Relations, 2,* 129–152.

DeVilliers, P. (2005). The role of language in theory-of-mind development: What deaf children tell us. In J. W. Astington & J. A. Baird (Eds.), *Why language matters for theory of mind* (pp. 266–297). Oxford, England: Oxford University Press.

DeYoung, C. G., & Gray, J. R. (2009). Personality neuroscience: Explaining individual differences in affect, behavior, and cognition. In P. J. Corr & G. Matthews (Eds.), *The Cambridge handbook of personality psychology* (pp. 323–346). New York: Cambridge University Press.

Diaconis, P., & Mosteller, F. (1989). Methods for studying coincidences. *Journal of the American Statistical Association, 84,* 853–861.

Diano, S., Farr, S. A., Benoit, S. C., McNay, E. C., da Silva, I., Horvath, B., et al. (2006). Ghrelin controls hippocampal spine synapse density and memory performance. *Nature Neuroscience, 9*(3), 381–388.

Dickens, W. T., & Flynn, J. R. (2001). Heritability estimates versus large environmental effects: The IQ paradox resolved. *Psychological Review, 108,* 346–369.

Diederich, N. J., & Goetz, C. G. (2008). The placebo treatments in neurosciences: New insights from clinical and neuroimaging studies. *Neurology, 71,* 677–684.

Diekelmann, S., Wilhelm, I., & Born, J. (2009). The whats and whens of sleep-dependent memory consolidation. *Sleep Medicine Reviews, 13,* 309–321.

Diener, E., & Biswas-Diener, R. (2002). Will money increase subjective well-being? *Social Indicators Research, 57,* 119–169.

Diener, E., Horwitz, J., & Emmons, R. A. (1985). Happiness of the very wealthy. *Social Indicators Research, 16,* 263–274.

Dietary Guidelines Advisory Committee. (2005). *Dietary guidelines for Americans 2005.* Retrieved October 15, 2007, from http://www.health.gov/dietaryguidelines

Dijksterhuis, A. (2004). Think different: The merits of unconscious thought in preference development and decision making. *Journal of Personality and Social Psychology, 87,* 586–598.

Dijksterhuis, A., Aarts, H., & Smith, P. K. (2005). The power of the subliminal: On subliminal persuasion and other potential applications. In

J. S. U. R. Hassin & J. A. Bargh (Eds.), *The new unconscious* (pp. 77–106). New York: Oxford University Press.

Dillbeck, M. C., & Orme-Johnson, D. W. (1987). Physiological differences between Transcendental Meditation and rest. *American Psychologist, 42,* 879–881.

Dimberg, U. (1982). Facial reactions to facial expressions. *Psychophysiology, 19,* 643–647.

Dion, K., Berscheid, E., & Walster, E. (1972). What is beautiful is good. *Journal of Personality and Social Psychology, 24,* 285–290.

DiTella, R., MacCulloch, R. J., & Oswald, A. J. (2003). The macroeconomics of happiness. *Review of Economics and Statistics, 85,* 809–827.

Dittrich, W. H., Troscianko, T., Lea, S., & Morgan, D. (1996). Perception of emotion from dynamic point-light displays represented in dance. *Perception, 25,* 727–738.

Dollard, J., Doob, L. W., Miller, N. E., Mowrer, O. H., & Sears, R. R. (1939). *Frustration and aggression.* Oxford, England: Yale University Press.

Domhoff, G. W. (2007). Realistic simulation and bizarreness in dream content: Past findings and suggestions for future research. In D. B. P. McNamara (Ed.), *The new science of dreaming: Content, recall, and personality correlates* (Vol. 22, pp. 1–27). Westport, CT: Praeger.

Domjan, M. (2005). Pavlovian conditioning: A functional perspective. *Annual Review of Psychology, 56,* 179–206.

Donner, T. H., Kettermann, A., Diesch, E., Ostendorf, F., Villringer, A., & Brandt, S. A. (2002). Visual feature and conjunction searches of equal difficulty engage only partially overlapping frontoparietal networks. *Neuroimage, 15,* 16–25.

Dornbusch, S. M., Hastorf, A. H., Richardson, S. A., Muzzy, R. E., & Vreeland, R. S. (1965). The perceiver and perceived: Their relative influence on categories of interpersonal perception. *Journal of Personality and Social Psychology, 1,* 434–440.

Dorus, S., Vallender, E. J., Evans, P. D., Anderson, J. R., Gilbert, S. L., Mahowald, M., et al. (2004). Accelerated evolution of nervous system genes in the origin of *Homo sapiens. Cell, 119,* 1027–1040.

Dovidio, J. F., & Gaertner, S. L. (2010). Intergroup bias. In S. T. Fiske, D. T. Gilbert, & G. Lindzey (Eds.), *The handbook of social psychology* (5th ed., Vol. 2). New York: Wiley.

Dowling, J. E. (1992). *Neurons and networks: An introduction to neuroscience.* Cambridge, MA: Harvard University Press.

Downer, J. D. C. (1961). Changes in visual gnostic function and emotional behavior following unilateral temporal damage in the "split-brain" monkey. *Nature, 191,* 50–51.

Downing, P. E., Chan, A. W. Y., Peelen, M. V., Dodds, C. M., & Kanwisher, N. (2006). Domain specificity in visual cortex. *Cerebral Cortex, 16,* 1453–1461.

Draaisma, B. (2009). Stereotypes of autism. *Philosophical Transactions of the Royal Society B: Biological Science, 364,* 1475–1480.

Draguns, J. G. (1980). Psychological disorders of clinical severity. In H. C. Triandis & J. G. Draguns (Eds.), *Handbook of cross-cultural psychology* (Vol. 6, pp. 99–174). Boston: Allyn & Bacon.

Dreifus, C. (2003, May 20). Living one disaster after another, and then sharing the experience. *New York Times,* p. D2.

Drigotas, S. M., & Rusbult, C. E. (1992). Should I stay or should I go? A dependence model of breakups. *Journal of Personality and Social Psychology, 62,* 62–87.

Druckman, D., & Bjork, R. A. (1994). *Learning, remembering, believing: Enhancing human performance.* Washington, DC: National Academy Press.

Duchaine, B. C., Yovel, G., Butterworth, E. J., & Nakayama, K. (2006). Prosopagnosia as an impairment to face-specific mechanisms: Elimination of the alternative hypotheses in a developmental case. *Cognitive Neuropsychology, 23,* 714–747.

Duckworth, A. L., & Seligman, M. E. P. (2005). Self-discipline outdoes IQ in predicting academic performance of adolescents. *Psychological Science, 16,* 939–944.

Dudycha, G. J., & Dudycha, M. M. (1933). Some factors and characteristics of childhood memories. *Child Development, 4,* 265–278.

Dunbar, R. I. M., & Shultz, S. (2007). Evolution in the social brain. *Science, 317,* 1344–1347.

Duncan, G. J., Yeung, W. J., Brooks-Gunn, J., & Smith, J. R. (1998). How much does childhood poverty affect the life chances of children? *American Sociological Review, 63,* 406–423.

Duncker, K. (1945). On problem-solving. *Psychological Monographs, 58*(5).

Dunlap, K. (1919). Are there any instincts? *Journal of Abnormal Psychology, 14,* 307–311.

Dunlop, S. A. (2008). Activity-dependent plasticity: Implications for recovery after spinal cord injury. *Trends in Neurosciences, 31,* 410–418.

Dunphy, D. C. (1963). The social structure of urban adolescent peer groups. *Sociometry, 26,* 230–246.

Durkheim, E. (1951). *Suicide: A study in sociology* (G. Simpson, Trans.). New York: Free Press.

Dutton, D. G., & Aron, A. P. (1974). Some evidence for heightened sexual attraction under conditions of high anxiety. *Journal of Personality and Social Psychology, 30,* 510–517.

Duval, S., & Wicklund, R. A. (1972). *A theory of objective self awareness.* New York: Academic Press.

Eacott, M. J., & Crawley, R. A. (1998). The offset of childhood amnesia: Memory for events that occurred before age 3. *Journal of Experimental Psychology. General, 127,* 22–33.

Eagly, A. H., Ashmore, R. D., Makhijani, M. G., & Longo, L. C. (1991). What is beautiful is good, but . . . : A meta-analytic review of research on the physical attractiveness stereotype. *Psychological Bulletin, 110,* 109–128.

Eagly, A. H., & Steffen, V. J. (1986). Gender and aggressive behavior: A meta-analytic review of the social psychological literature. *Psychological Bulletin, 100,* 309–330.

Eagly, A. H., & Wood, W. (1999). The origins of sex differences in human behavior: Evolved dispositions versus social roles. *American Psychologist, 54,* 408–423.

Eastwick, P. W., Finkel, E. J., Mochon, D., & Ariely, D. (2007). Selective versus unselective romantic desire: Not all reciprocity is created equal. *Psychological Science, 18,* 317–319.

Eaton, W. W., Kessler, R. C., Wittchen, H. U., & McGee, W. J. (1994). Panic and panic disorder in the United States. *American Journal of Psychiatry, 151,* 413–420.

Eaton, W. W., Shao, H., Nestadt, G., Lee, B. H., Bienvenu, O. J., & Zandi, P. (2008). Population-based study of first onset and chronicity of major depressive disorder. *Archives of General Psychiatry, 65,* 513–520.

Ebbinghaus, H. (1964). *Memory: A contribution to experimental psychology.* New York: Dover. (Original work published 1885)

Eddy, D. M. (1982). Probabilistic reasoning in clinical medicine: Problems and opportunities. In D. Kahneman, P. Slovic, & A. Tversky (Eds.), *Judgments under uncertainty: Heuristics and biases* (pp. 249–267). New York: Cambridge University Press.

Edgerton, V. R., Tillakaratne, J. K. T., Bigbee, A. J., deLeon, R. D., & Roy, R. R. (2004). Plasticity of the spinal neural circuitry after injury. *Annual Review of Neuroscience, 27,* 145–167.

Editorial. (2006, May 31). Bribing people to vote will not benefit system. *Yuma Sun.* Retrieved May 31, 2006, from http://www.yumasun.com/articles/people-21362-vote-voting.html

Edwards, W. (1955). The theory of decision making. *Psychological Bulletin, 51,* 201–214.

Efferson, C., Lalive, R., & Fehr, E. (2008). The coevolution of cultural groups and ingroup favoritism. *Science, 321,* 1844–1849.

Eich, J. E. (1980). The cue-dependent nature of state-dependent retention. *Memory & Cognition, 8,* 157–173.

Eich, J. E. (1995). Searching for mood dependent memory. *Psychological Science, 6,* 67–75.

Eichenbaum, H. (2008). *Learning & memory.* New York: Norton.

Eichenbaum, H., & Cohen, N. J. (2001). *From conditioning to conscious recollection: Memory systems of the brain.* New York: Oxford University Press.

Eickhoff, S. B., Dafotakis, M., Grefkes, C., Stoecker, T., Shah, N. J., Schnitzler, A., et al. (2008). fMRI reveals cognitive and emotional processing in a long-term comatose patient. *Experimental Neurology, 214,* 240–246.

Eimas, P. D., Siqueland, E. R., Jusczyk, P., & Vigorito, J. (1971). Speech perception in infants. *Science, 171,* 303–306.

Einstein, G. O., & McDaniel, M. A. (1990). Normal aging and prospective memory. *Journal of Experimental Psychology: Learning, Memory, and Cognition, 16,* 717–726.

Einstein, G. O., & McDaniel, M. A. (2005). Prospective memory: Multiple retrieval processes. *Current Direction in Psychological Science, 14,* 286–290.

Eisenberg, N., Fabes, R. A., Guthrie, I. K., & Reiser, M. (2000). Dispositional emotionality and regulation: Their role in predicting quality of social functioning. *Journal of Personality & Social Psychology, 78,* 136.

Eisenberger, N. I., Lieberman, M. D., & Williams, K. D. (2003). Does rejection hurt? An fMRI study of social exclusion. *Science, 302,* 290–292.

Eisenegger, C., Naef, M., Snozzi, R., Heinrichs, M., & Fehr, E. (2010). Prejudice and truth about the effect of testosterone on human bargaining behaviour. *Nature, 463,* 356–359.

Ekman, P. (1965). Differential communication of affect by head and body cues. *Journal of Personality and Social Psychology, 2,* 726–735.

Ekman, P. (1972). Universals and cultural differences in facial expressions of emotion. In J. K. Cole (Ed.), *Nebraska Symposium on Motivation, 1971* (pp. 207–283). Lincoln: University of Nebraska Press.

Ekman, P. (1992). *Telling lies.* New York: Norton.

Ekman, P. (2003). Darwin, deception, and facial expression. *Annals of the New York Academy of Sciences, 1000,* 205–221.

Ekman, P., & Friesen, W. V. (1968). Nonverbal behavior in psychotherapy research. In J. M. Shlien (Ed.), *Research in psychotherapy* (Vol. 3, pp. 179–216). Washington, DC: American Psychological Association.

Ekman, P., & Friesen, W. V. (1971). Constants across cultures in the face and emotion. *Journal of Personality and Social Psychology, 17,* 124–129.

Ekman, P., & Friesen, W. V. (1982). Felt, false, and miserable smiles. *Journal of Nonverbal Behavior, 6,* 238–252.

Ekman, P., Levenson, R. W., & Friesen, W. V. (1983). Autonomic nervous system activity distinguishes among emotions. *Science, 221,* 1208–1210.

Ekman, P., & O'Sullivan, M. (1991). Who can catch a liar? *American Psychologist, 46*(9), 913–920.

Ekman, P., O'Sullivan, M., & Frank, M. G. (1999). A few can catch a liar. *Psychological Science, 10,* 263–266.

Elbogen, E. B., & Johnson, S. C. (2009). The intricate link between violence and mental disorder. *Archives of General Psychiatry, 66*(2), 152–161.

Elder, G. H., & Conger, R. D. (2000). *Children of the land: Adversity and success in rural America.* Chicago: University of Chicago Press.

Eldridge, L. L., Knowlton, B. J., Furmanski, C. S., Bookheimer, S. Y., & Engel, S. A. (2000). Remembering episodes: A selective role for the hippocampus during retrieval. *Nature Neuroscience, 3,* 1149–1152.

Eldridge, M. A., Barnard, P. J., & Bekerian, D. A. (1994). Autobiographical memory and daily schemas at work. *Memory, 2,* 51–74.

Elfenbein, H. A., & Ambady, N. (2002). On the universality and cultural specificity of emotion recognition: A meta-analysis. *Psychological Bulletin, 128,* 203–235.

Elfenbein, H. A., Der Foo, M. D., White, J., & Tan, H. H. (2007). Reading your counterpart: The benefit of emotion recognition accuracy for effectiveness in negotiation. *Journal of Nonverbal Behavior, 31,* 205–223.

Ellenbogen, J. M., Payne, J. D., & Stickgold, R. (2006). The role of sleep in declarative memory consolidation: Passive, permissive, or none? *Current Opinion in Neurobiology, 16,* 716–722.

Elliott, R., Sahakian, B. J., Matthews, K., Bannerjea, A., Rimmer, J., & Robbins, T. W. (1997). Effects of methylphenidate on spatial working memory and planning in healthy young adults. *Psychopharmacology, 131,* 196–206.

Ellis, B. J., & Garber, J. (2000). Psychosocial antecedents of variation in girls' pubertal timing: Maternal depression, stepfather presence, and marital and family stress. *Child Development, 71,* 485–501.

Ellis, E. M. (1983). A review of empirical rape research: Victim reactions and response to treatment. *Clinical Psychology Review, 3,* 473–490.

Ellis, L., & Ames, M. A. (1987). Neurohormonal functioning in sexual orientation: A theory of homosexuality-heterosexuality. *Psychological Bulletin, 101,* 233–258.

Ellman, S. J., Spielman, A. J., Luck, D., Steiner, S. S., & Halperin, R. (1991). REM deprivation: A review. In S. J. Ellman & J. S. Antrobus (Eds.), *The mind in sleep: Psychology and psychophysiology* (2nd ed., pp. 329–376). New York: Wiley.

Ellsworth, P. C., & Scherer, K. R. (2003). Appraisal processes in emotion. In R. J. Davidson, K. R. Scherer, & H. H. Goldsmith (Eds.), *The handbook of affective science* (pp. 572–595). New York: Oxford University Press.

Emerson, R. C., Bergen, J. R., & Adelson, E. H. (1992). Directionally selective complex cells and the computation of motion energy in cat visual cortex. *Vision Research, 32,* 203–218.

Empson, J. A. (1984). Sleep and its disorders. In R. Stevens (Ed.), *Aspects of consciousness.* New York: Academic Press.

Epley, N., Savitsky, K., & Kachelski, R. A. (1999). What every skeptic should know about subliminal persuasion. *Skeptical Inquirer, 23,* 40–45, 58.

Epley, N., & Waytz, A. (2010). Mind perception. In S. T. Fiske, D. T. Gilbert, & G. Lindzey (Eds.), *The handbook of social psychology* (5th ed., Vol. 1, pp. 498–541). New York: Wiley.

Epstein, R. (2007a). *The case against adolescence: Rediscovering the adult in every teen.* New York: Quill Driver.

Epstein, R. (2007b). The myth of the teen brain. *Scientific American Mind, 18,* 27–31.

Erber, R., Wegner, D. M., & Therriault, N. (1996). On being cool and collected: Mood regulation in anticipation of social interaction. *Journal of Personality and Social Psychology, 70,* 757–766.

Erffmeyer, E. S. (1984). Rule-violating behavior on the golf course. *Perceptual and Motor Skills, 59,* 591–596.

Ericsson, K. A., & Charness, N. (1999). Expert performance: Its structure and acquisition. In S. J. Ceci & W. M. Williams (Eds.), *The nature-nurture debate: The essential readings* (pp. 200–256). Oxford, England: Blackwell.

Esterman, M., Verstynen, T., Ivry, R. B., & Robertson, L. C. (2006). Coming unbound: Disrupting automatic integration of synesthetic color and graphemes by transcranial magnetic stimulation of the right parietal lobe. *Journal of Cognitive Neuroscience, 18,* 1570–1576.

Etcoff, N. (1999). *Survival of the prettiest: The science of beauty.* New York: Doubleday.

Evans, G. W. (2004). The environment of childhood poverty. *American Psychologist, 59*(2), 77–92.

Evans, J. St. B., Barston, J. L., & Pollard, P. (1983). On the conflict between logic and belief in syllogistic reasoning. *Memory & Cognition, 11*, 295–306.

Evans, P. D., Gilbert, S. L., Mekel-Bobrov, N., Vallender, E. J., Anderson, J. R., Vaez-Azizi, L. M., et al. (2005). Microcephalin, a gene regulating brain size, continues to evolve adaptively in humans. *Science, 309*, 1717–1720.

Everson, S. A., Lynch, J. W., Chesney, M. A., Kaplan, G. A., Goldberg, D. E., Shade, S. B., et al. (1997). Interaction of workplace demands and cardiovascular reactivity in progression of carotid atherosclerosis: Population based study. *British Medical Journal, 314*, 553–558.

Exner, J. E. (1993). *The Rorschach: A comprehensive system: Vol. 1. Basic foundations.* New York: Wiley.

Eysenck, H. J. (1957). The effects of psychotherapy: An evaluation. *Journal of Consulting Psychology, 16*, 319–324.

Eysenck, H. J. (1967). *The biological basis of personality.* Springfield, IL: Charles C. Thomas.

Eysenck, H. J. (1990). Biological dimensions of personality. In L. A. Pervin (Ed.), *Handbook of personality: Theory and research* (pp. 244–276). New York: Guilford Press.

Falk, R., & McGregor, D. (1983). The surprisingness of coincidences. In P. Humphreys, O. Svenson, & A. Vari (Eds.), *Analysing and aiding decision processes* (pp. 489–502). New York: North Holland.

Fancher, R. E. (1979). *Pioneers of psychology.* New York: Norton.

Fantz, R. L. (1964). Visual experience in infants. Decreased attention to familiar patterns relative to novel ones. *Science, 164*, 668–670.

Farah, M. J., Illes, J., Cook-Deegan, R., Gardner, H., Kandel, E., King, P., et al. (2004). Neurocognitive enhancement: What can we do and what should we do? *Nature Reviews Neuroscience, 5*, 421–426.

Farah, M. J., & Rabinowitz, C. (2003). Genetic and environmental influences on the organization of semantic memory in the brain: Is "living things" an innate category? *Cognitive Neuropsychology, 20*, 401–408.

Farivar, R. (2009). Dorsal-ventral integration in object recognition. *Brain Research Reviews, 61*, 144–153.

Farooqi, I. S., Bullmore, E., Keogh, J., Gillard, J., O'Rahilly, S., & Fletcher, P. C. (2007). Leptin regulates striatal regions and human eating behavior. *Science, 317*, 1355.

Farooqi, I. S., Matarese, G., Lord, G. M., Keogh, J. M., Lawrence, E., Agwu, C., et al. (2002). Beneficial effects of leptin on obesity, T cell hyporesponsiveness, and neuroendocrine/metabolic dysfunction of human congenital leptin deficiency. *The Journal of Clinical Investigation, 110*(8), 1093–1103.

Farrar, M. J. (1990). Discourse and the acquisition of grammatical morphemes. *Journal of Child Language, 17*, 607–624.

Fazel, S., & Danesh, J. (2002). Serious mental disorder in 23,000 prisoners: A review of 62 surveys. *Lancet, 359*, 545–550.

Fechner, G. T. (1966). *Elements of psychophysics* (H. E. Alder, Trans.). New York: Holt, Rinehart and Winston. (Original work published 1860)

Feczer, D., & Bjorklund, P. (2009). Forever changed: Posttraumatic stress disorder in female military veterans, a case report. *Perspectives in Psychiatric Care, 45*, 278–291.

Fehr, E., & Gaechter, S. (2002). Altruistic punishment in humans. *Nature, 415*, 137–140.

Fein, S., Hilton, J. L., & Miller, D. T. (1990). Suspicion of ulterior motivation and the correspondence bias. *Journal of Personality and Social Psychology, 58*, 753–764.

Feinberg, T. E. (2001). *Altered egos: How the brain creates the self.* New York: Oxford University Press.

Feingold, A. (1990). Gender differences in effects of physical attractiveness on romantic attraction: A comparison across five research paradigms. *Journal of Personality and Social Psychology, 59*, 981–993.

Feingold, A. (1992a). Gender differences in mate selection preferences: A test of the parental investment model. *Psychological Bulletin, 112*, 125–139.

Feingold, A. (1992b). Good-looking people are not what we think. *Psychological Bulletin, 111*, 304–341.

Feingold, A. (1994). Gender differences in personality: A meta-analysis. *Psychological Bulletin, 116*, 429–456.

Feldman, D. E. (2009). Synaptic mechanisms for plasticity in neocortex. *Annual Review of Neuroscience, 32*, 33–55.

Feldman, M. D. (2004). *Playing sick.* New York: Brunner-Routledge.

Fernandez-Espejo, D., Junque, C., Vendrell, P., Bernabeu, M., Roig, T., Bargallo, N., et al. (2008). Cerebral response to speech in vegetative and minimally conscious states after traumatic brain injury. *Brain Injury, 22*, 882–890.

Ferster, C. B., & Skinner, B. F. (1957). *Schedules of reinforcement.* New York: Appleton-Century-Crofts.

Festinger, L. (1957). *A theory of cognitive dissonance.* Stanford, CA: Stanford University Press.

Festinger, L., & Carlsmith, J. M. (1959). Cognitive consequences of forced compliance. *Journal of Abnormal and Social Psychology, 58*, 203–210.

Festinger, L., Schachter, S., & Back, K. (1950). *Social pressures in informal groups: A study of human factors in housing.* Oxford, England: Harper & Row.

Fiedler, E. R., Oltmanns, T. F., & Turkheimer, E. (2004). Traits associated with personality disorders and adjustment to military life: Predictive validity of self and peer reports. *Military Medicine, 169*, 32–40.

Field, G. C. (1921). Faculty psychology and instinct psychology. *Mind, 30*, 257–270.

Fields, G. (2009, May 14). White House czar calls for end to "War on Drugs." *The Wall Street Journal*, p. A3. Retrieved May 14, 2009, from http://onlinc.wsj.com/article/SB124225891527617397.html

Fields, G., & Scheck, J. (2009, October 20). U.S. mellows on medical marijuana. *The Wall Street Journal.* Retrieved October 20, 2009, from http://online.wsj.com/article/SB125595221988793895.html?mod=WSJ_hps_MIDDLEFifthNews

Fields, H. L., & Levine, J. D. (1984). Placebo analgesia: A role for endorphins? *Trends in Neurosciences, 7*, 271–273.

Finkel, E. J., & Eastwick, P. W. (2009). Arbitrary social norms influence sex differences in romantic selectivity. *Psychological Science, 20*, 1290–1295.

Finkelstein, E. A., Trogdon, J. G., Cohen, J. W., & Dietz, W. (2009). Annual medical spending attributable to obesity: Payer- and service-specific estimates. *Health Affairs, 28*(5), w822–w831.

Finkelstein, K. E. (1999, October 17). Yo-Yo Ma's lost Stradivarius is found after wild search. *New York Times*, p. 34.

Finn, R. (1991). Different minds. *Discover, 12*, 54–59.

Fiore, A. T., Taylor, L. S., Zhong, X., Mendelsohn, G. A., & Cheshire, C. (2010). Who's right and who writes: People, profiles, contacts, and replies in online dating. *Proceedings of Hawaii International Conferences on Systems Science, 43.*

Fiorentine, R. (1999). After drug treatment: Are 12-step programs effective in maintaining abstinence? *American Journal of Drug and Alcohol Abuse, 25*, 93–116.

Fiorillo, C. D., Newsome, W. T., & Schultz, W. (2008). The temporal precision of reward prediction in dopamine neurons. *Nature Neuroscience, 11*, 966–973.

Fisher, H. E. (1993). *Anatomy of love: The mysteries of mating, marriage, and why we stray*. New York: Fawcett.

Fisher, R. P., & Craik, F. I. M. (1977). The interaction between encoding and retrieval operations in cued recall. *Journal of Experimental Psychology: Human Learning and Perception, 3*, 153–171.

Fiske, S. T. (1998). Stereotyping, prejudice, and discrimination. In D. T. Gilbert, S. T. Fiske, & G. Lindzey (Eds.), *The handbook of social psychology* (4th ed., Vol. 2, pp. 357–411). New York: McGraw-Hill.

Fiske, S. T. (2009). *Social beings: A core motives approach to social psychology* (2nd ed.). New York: Wiley.

Fleeson, W. (2004). Moving personality beyond the person-situation debate: The challenge and opportunity of within-person variability. *Current Directions in Psychological Science, 13*, 83–87.

Flegal, K. M., & Troiano, R. P. (2000). Changes in the distribution of body mass index of adults and children in the U.S. population. *International Journal of Obesity, 24*, 807–818.

Fleming, R., Baum, A., Gisriel, M. M., & Gatchel, R. J. (1985). Mediating influences of social support on stress at Three Mile Island. In A. Monat & R. S. Lazarus (Eds.), *Stress and coping: An anthology* (2nd ed., pp. 95–106). New York: Columbia University Press.

Fletcher, P. C., Shallice, T., & Dolan, R. J. (1998). The functional roles of prefrontal cortex in episodic memory. I. Encoding. *Brain, 121*, 1239–1248.

Flor, H., Nikolajsen, L., & Jensen, T. S. (2006). Phantom limb pain: A case of maladaptive CNS plasticity? *Nature Reviews Neuroscience, 7*, 873–881.

Flynn, E. (2008). Investigating children as cultural magnets: Do young children transmit redundant information along diffusion chains? *Philosophical Transactions of the Royal Society of London Series B, 363*, 3541–3551.

Flynn, E., & Whiten, A. (2008). Cultural transmission of tool-use in young children: A diffusion chain study. *Social Development, 17*, 699–718.

Flynn, J. R. (1984). The mean IQ of Americans: Massive gains 1932 to 1978. *Psychological Bulletin, 95*, 29–51.

Flynn, J. R. (1987). Massive IQ gains in 14 nations: What IQ tests really measure. *Psychological Bulletin, 101*, 171–191.

Flynn, J. R. (2009). *What is intelligence? Beyond the Flynn effect*. Cambridge, England: Cambridge University Press.

Foa, E. B., Dancu, C. V., Hembree, E. A., Jaycox, L. H., Meadows, E. A., & Street, G. P. (1999). A comparison of exposure therapy, stress inoculation training, and their combination for reducing posttraumatic stress disorder in female assault victims. *Journal of Consulting and Clinical Psychology, 67*, 194–200.

Foa, E. B., Liebowitz, M. R., Kozak, M. J., Davies, S., Campeas, R., Franklin, M. E., et al. (2007). Randomized, placebo-controlled trial of exposure and ritual prevention, clomipramine, and their combination in the treatment of obsessive-compulsive disorder. *Focus, 5*, 368–380.

Foa, E. B., & Meadows, E. A. (1997). Psychosocial treatments for posttraumatic stress disorder: A critical review. *Annual Review of Psychology, 48*, 449–480.

Fodor, J. (2000). Why we are so good at catching cheaters. *Cognition, 75*, 2932.

Fogassi, L., Ferrari, P. F., Gesierich, B., Rozzi, S., Chersi, F., & Rizzolatti, G. (2005). Parietal lobe: From action organization to intention understanding. *Science, 308*, 662–667.

Folley, B. S., & Park, S. (2005). Verbal creativity and schizotypal personality in relation to prefrontal hemispheric laterality: A behavioral and near-infrared optical imaging study. *Schizophrenia Research, 80*, 271–282.

Fombonne, E. (2009). Epidemiology of pervasive developmental disorders. *Pediatric Research, 65*, 5991–5998.

Forkstam, C., Hagoort, P., Fernández, G., Ingvar, M., & Petersson, K. M. (2006). Neural correlates of artificial syntactic structure classification. *Neuroimage, 32*, 956–967.

Fornazzari, L., Wilkinson, D. A., Kapur, B. M., & Carter, P. L. (1983). Cerebellar, cortical and functional impairment in toluene abusers. *Acta Neurologica Scandinavica, 67*, 319–329.

Foroni, F., & Semin, G. R. (2009). Language that puts you in touch with your bodily feelings: The multimodal responsiveness of affective expressions. *Psychological Science, 20*(8), 974–980.

Fournier, J. C., DeRubeis, R., Hollon, S. D., Dimidjian, S., Amsterdam, J. D., Shelton, R. C., et al. (2010). Antidepressant drug effects and depression severity. *Journal of the American Medical Association, 303*, 47–53.

Fouts, R. S., & Bodamer, M. (1987). Preliminary report to the National Geographic Society on "Chimpanzee intrapersonal signing." *Friends of Washoe, 7*, 4–12.

Fox, M. J. (2009). *Always looking up*. New York: Hyperion.

Fox, P. T., Mintun, M. A., Raichle, M. E., Miezin, F. M., Allman, J. M., Van Essen, D. C., et al. (1986). Mapping human visual cortex with positron emission tomography. *Nature, 323*, 806–809.

Fox, R. E., DeLeon, P. H., Newman, R., Sammons, M. T., Dunivin, D. L., & Baker, D. C. (2009). Prescriptive authority and psychology: A status report. *American Psychologist, 64*, 257–268.

Fragaszy, D. M., Izar, P., Visalberghi, E., Ottoni, E. B., & de Oliveria, M. G. (2004). Wild capuchin monkeys (*Cebus libidinosus*) use anvils and stone pounding tools. *American Journal of Primatology, 64*, 359–366.

Frank, M. G., Ekman, P., & Friesen, W. V. (1993). Behavioral markers and recognizability of the smile of enjoyment. *Journal of Personality and Social Psychology, 64*, 83–93.

Frank, M. G., & Stennet, J. (2001). The forced-choice paradigm and the perception of facial expressions of emotion. *Journal of Personality and Social Psychology, 80*, 75–85.

Frankl, V. (2000). *Man's search for meaning*. New York: Beacon Press.

Fredman, T., & Whiten, A. (2008). Observational learning from tool using models by human-reared and mother-reared capuchin monkeys (*Cebus apella*). *Animal Cognition, 11*, 295–309.

Fredrickson, B. L. (2000). Cultivating positive emotions to optimize health and well-being. *Prevention and Treatment, 3*.

Freedman, J. (1978). *Happy people: What happiness is, who has it, and why*. New York: Harcourt Brace Jovanovich.

Freedman, J. L., & Fraser, S. C. (1966). Compliance without pressure: The foot-in-the-door technique. *Journal of Personality and Social Psychology, 4*, 195–202.

Freeman, S., Walker, M. R., Borden, R., & Latané, B. (1975). Diffusion of responsibility and restaurant tipping: Cheaper by the bunch. *Personality and Social Psychology Bulletin, 1*, 584–587.

Freeman, T. P., Morgan, C. J. A., Klaassen, E., Das, R. K., Stefanovic, A., Brandner, B., & Curran, H. V. (2009). Superstitious conditioning as a model of delusion formation following chronic but not acute ketamine in humans. *Psychopharmacology, 206*, 563–573.

French, H. W. (1997, February 26). In the land of the small it isn't easy being tall. *New York Times*.

Freud, A. (1936). *The ego and the mechanisms of defense*. New York: International Universities Press.

Freud, S. (1938). The psychopathology of everyday life. In A. A. Brill (Ed.), *The basic writings of Sigmund Freud*. New York: Basic Books. (Original work published 1901)

Freud, S. (1953). Three essays on the theory of sexuality. In J. Strachey (Ed.), *The standard edition of the complete psychological works of Sigmund Freud* (Vol. 7, pp. 135–243). London: Hogarth Press. (Original work published 1905)

Freud, S. (1965). *The interpretation of dreams* (J. Strachey, Trans.). New York: Avon. (Original work published 1900)

Freudenberger, H. J. (1974). Staff burnout. *Journal of Social Issues, 30,* 159–165.

Frick, R. W. (1985). Communicating emotion: The role of prosodic features. *Psychological Bulletin, 97,* 412–429.

Fried, P. A., & Watkinson, B. (2000). Visuoperceptual functioning differs in 9- to 12-year-olds prenatally exposed to cigarettes and marijuana. *Neurotoxicology and Teratology, 22,* 11–20.

Friedlander, L., & Desrocher, M. (2006). Neuroimaging studies of obsessive-compulsive disorder in adults and children. *Clinical Psychology Review, 26,* 32–49.

Friedman, J. M. (2003). A war on obesity, not the obese. *Science, 299*(5608), 856–858.

Friedman, J. M., & Halaas, J. L. (1998). Leptin and the regulation of body weight in mammals. *Nature, 395*(6704), 763–770.

Friedman, M., & Rosenman, R. H. (1974). *Type A behavior and your heart.* New York: Knopf.

Friedman, S. L., & Boyle, D. E. (2008). Attachment in U.S. children experiencing nonmaternal care in the early 1990s. *Attachment & Human Development, 10*(3), 225–261.

Friedman, W. J. (1993). Memory for the time of past events. *Psychological Bulletin, 113,* 44–66.

Friedman-Hill, S. R., Robertson, L. C., & Treisman, A. (1995). Parietal contributions to visual feature binding: Evidence from a patient with bilateral lesions. *Science, 269,* 853–855.

Friesen, W. V. (1972). *Cultural differences in facial expressions in a social situation: An experimental test of the concept of display rules.* Unpublished doctoral dissertation, University of California, San Francisco.

Frith, C. D., & Fletcher, P. (1995). Voices from nowhere. *Critical Quarterly, 37,* 71–83.

Frith, U. (2001). Mind blindness and the brain in autism. *Neuron, 32,* 969–979.

Frith, U. (2003). *Autism: Explaining the enigma.* Oxford, England: Blackwell.

Fryer, A. J., Mannuzza, S., Gallops, M. S., Martin, L. Y., Aaronson, C., Gorman, J. M., et al. (1990). Familial transmission of simple phobias and fears. A preliminary report. *Archives of General Psychiatry, 47,* 252–256.

Fukui, H., Murai, T., Fukuyama, H., Hayashi, T., & Hanakawa, T. (2005). Functional activity related to risk anticipation during performance of the Iowa gambling task. *Neuroimage, 24,* 253–259.

Funder, D. C. (2001). Personality. *Annual Review of Psychology, 52,* 197–221.

Furmark, T., Tillfors, M., Marteinsdottir, I., Fischer, H., Pissiota, A., Långström, B., et al. (2002). Common changes in cerebral blood flow in patients with social phobia treated with citalopram or cognitive-behavioral therapy. *Archives of General Psychiatry, 59*(5), 425–433.

Fuster, J. M. (2003). *Cortex and mind.* New York: Oxford University Press.

Gable, S. L., & Haidt, J. (2005). What (and why) is positive psychology? *Review of General Psychology, 9,* 102–110.

Gais, S., Albouy, G., Boly, M., Dang-Vu, T. T., Darsaud, A., Desseilles, M., et al. (2007). Sleep transforms the cerebral traces of declarative memories. *Proceedings of the National Academy of Sciences, USA, 104,* 18778–18783.

Gais, S., & Born, J. (2004). Low acetylcholine during slow-wave sleep is critical for declarative memory consolidation. *Proceedings of the National Academy of Sciences, USA, 101,* 2140–2144.

Galanter, E. (1962). Contemporary psychophysics. In R. Brown, E. Galanter, E. H. Hess, & G. Mandler (Eds.), *New directions in psychology* (pp. 87–156). New York: Holt, Rinehart & Winston.

Galati, D., Scherer, K. R., & Ricci-Bitt, P. E. (1997). Voluntary facial expression of emotion: Comparing congenitally blind with normally sighted encoders. *Journal of Personality and Social Psychology, 73,* 1363–1379.

Galef, B. (1998). Edward Thorndike: Revolutionary psychologist, ambiguous biologist. *American Psychologist, 53,* 1128–1134.

Gallistel, C. R. (2000). The replacement of general-purpose learning models with adaptively specialized learning modules. In M. S. Gazzaniga (Ed.), *The new cognitive neurosciences* (pp. 1179–1191). Cambridge, MA: The MIT Press.

Gallo, D. A. (2006). *Associative illusions of memory.* New York: Psychology Press.

Gallup, G. G. (1977). Self-recognition in primates: A comparative approach to the bidirectional properties of consciousness. *American Psychologist, 32,* 329–338.

Gallup, G. G. (1997). On the rise and fall of self-conception in primates. *Annals of the New York Academy of Sciences, 818,* 73–84.

Galton, F. (1869). *Hereditary genius: An inquiry into its laws and consequences.* London: Macmillan/Fontana.

Garb, H. N. (1998). *Studying the clinician: Judgment research and psychological assessment.* Washington, DC: American Psychological Association.

Garb, H. N. (1999). Call for a moratorium on the use of the Rorschach inkblot test in clinical and forensic settings. *Assessment, 6,* 313–315.

Garb, H. N., Wood, J. M., Lilienfeld, S. O., & Nezworski, M. T. (2005). Roots of the Rorschach controversy. *Clinical Psychology Review, 25,* 97–118.

Garcia, J. (1981). Tilting at the windmills of academe. *American Psychologist, 36,* 149–158.

Garcia, J., & Koelling, R. A. (1966). Relation of cue to consequence in avoidance learning. *Psychonomic Science, 4,* 123–124.

Gardner, R. A., & Gardner, B. T. (1969). Teaching sign language to a chimpanzee. *Science, 165,* 664–672.

Garland, A. F., & Zigler, E. (1999). Emotional and behavioral problems among highly intellectually gifted youth. *Roeper Review, 22*(1), 41.

Garofalo, R., Cameon, W., Wissow, L. S., Woods, E. R., & Goodman, E. (1999). Sexual orientation and risk of suicide. *Archives of Pediatrics and Adolescent Medicine, 513,* 487.

Garry, M., Manning, C., Loftus, E. F., & Sherman, S. J. (1996). Imagination inflation: Imagining a childhood event inflates confidence that it occurred. *Psychonomic Bulletin & Review, 3,* 208–214.

Gathercole, S. E. (2008). Nonword repetition and word learning: The nature of the relationship. *Applied Psycholinguistics, 27,* 513–543.

Gazzaniga, M. S. (Ed.). (2000). *The new cognitive neurosciences.* Cambridge, MA: The MIT Press.

Gazzaniga, M. S. (2006). Forty-five years of split brain research and still going strong. *Nature Reviews Neuroscience, 6,* 653–659.

Ge, D., Fellay, J., Thompson, A. J., Simon, J. S., Shianna, K. V., Urban, T. J., et al. (2009). Genetic variation in il28b predicts hepatitis C treatment-induced viral clearance. *Nature, 461,* 399–401.

Ge, X. J., Conger, R. D., & Elder, G. H. (1996). Coming of age too early: Pubertal influences on girls' vulnerability to psychological distress. *Child Development, 67,* 3386–3400.

Ge, X. J., & Natsuaki, M. N. (2009). In search of explanations for early pubertal timing effects on developmental psychopathology. *Current Directions in Psychological Science, 18,* 327–331.

Geen, R. G. (1984). Preferred stimulation levels in introverts and extraverts: Effects on arousal and performance. *Journal of Personality and Social Psychology, 46,* 1303–1312.

Gegenfurtner, K. R., & Kiper, D. C. (2003). Color vision. *Annual Review of Neuroscience, 26*, 181–206.

Geller, D. A., Hoog, S. L., Heiligenstein, J. H., Ricardi, R. K., Tamura, R., Kluszynski, S., Jacobson, J. G., et al. (2001). Fluoxetine treatment for obsessive-compulsive disorder in children and adolescents: A placebo-controlled clinical trial. *Journal of the American Academy of Child and Adolescent Psychiatry, 40*, 773–779.

George, D. (1981). *Sweet man: The real Duke Ellington.* New York: Putnam.

George, M. S., Lisanby, S. H., & Sackeim, H. A. (1999), Transcranial magnetic stimulation: Applications in neuropsychiatry. *Archives of General Psychiatry, 56*, 300–311.

Germain, V., Marchand, A., Bouchard, S., Drouin, M., & Guay, S. (2009). Effectiveness of cognitive behavioral therapy administered by videoconference for posttraumatic stress disorder. *Cognitive Behavior Therapy, 38*, 42–53.

Gershoff, E. T. (2002). Corporal punishment by parents and associated child behaviors and experiences: A meta-analytic and theoretical review. *Psychological Bulletin, 128*, 539–579.

Gibb, B. E., Alloy, L. B., & Tierney, S. (2001). History of childhood maltreatment, negative cognitive styles, and episodes of depression in adulthood. *Cognitive Therapy and Research, 25*, 425–446.

Gibbons, F. X. (1990). Self-attention and behavior: A review and theoretical update. In M. P. Zanna (Ed.), *Advances in experimental social psychology* (Vol. 23, pp. 249–303). San Diego, CA: Academic Press.

Gick, M. L., & Holyoak, K. J. (1980). Analogical problem solving. *Cognitive Psychology, 12*, 306–355.

Giedd, J. N., Blumenthal, J., Jeffries, N. O., Castellanos, F. X., Liu, H., Zijdenbos, A., et al. (1999). Brain development during childhood and adolescence: A longitudinal MRI study. *Nature Neuroscience, 2*, 861–863.

Gigerenzer, G. (1996). The psychology of good judgment: Frequency formats and simple algorithms. *Journal of Medical Decision Making, 16*, 273–280.

Gigerenzer, G., & Hoffrage, U. (1995). How to improve Bayesian reasoning without instruction: Frequency formats. *Psychological Review, 102*, 684–704.

Gigerenzer, G., & Hug, K. (1992). Domain-specific reasoning: Social contracts, cheating, and perspective change. *Cognition, 43*, 127–171.

Gilbert, D. T. (1991). How mental systems believe. *American Psychologist, 46*, 107–119.

Gilbert, D. T. (1998). Ordinary personology. In D. T. Gilbert, S. T. Fiske, & G. Lindzey (Eds.), *The handbook of social psychology* (4th ed., Vol. 2, pp. 89–150). New York: McGraw-Hill.

Gilbert, D. T. (2006). *Stumbling on happiness.* New York: Knopf.

Gilbert, D. T., Brown, R. P., Pinel, E. C., & Wilson, T. D. (2000). The illusion of external agency. *Journal of Personality and Social Psychology, 79*, 690–700.

Gilbert, D. T., Gill, M. J., & Wilson, T. D. (2002). The future is now: Temporal correction in affective forecasting. *Organizational Behavior and Human Decision Processes, 88*, 430–444.

Gilbert, D. T., & Malone, P. S. (1995). The correspondence bias. *Psychological Bulletin, 117*, 21–38.

Gilbert, D. T., Pelham, B. W., & Krull, D. S. (1988). On cognitive busyness: When persons perceive meet persons perceived. *Journal of Personality and Social Psychology, 54*, 733–740.

Gilbert, D. T., & Wilson, T. D. (2009). Why the brain talks to itself: Sources of error in emotional prediction. *Philosophical Transactions of the Royal Society B: Biological Sciences, 364*, 1335–1341.

Gilbert, G. M. (1951). Stereotype persistence and change among college students. *Journal of Abnormal and Social Psychology, 46*, 245–254.

Gilbertson, M. W., Shenton, M. E., Ciszewski, A., Kasai, K., Lasko, N. B., Orr, S. P., et al. (2002). Smaller hippocampal volume predicts pathological vulnerability to psychological trauma. *Nature Neuroscience, 5*, 1242–1247.

Gillespie, C. F., & Nemeroff, C. B. (2007). Corticotropin-releasing factor and the psychobiology of early-life stress. *Current Directions in Psychological Science, 16*, 85–89.

Gillette, J., Gleitman, H., Gleitman, L., & Lederer, A. (1999). Human simulation of vocabulary learning. *Cognition, 73*, 135–176.

Gilligan, C. (1982). *In a different voice: Psychological theory and women's development.* Cambridge, MA: Harvard University Press.

Ginzburg, K., Solomon, Z., & Bleich, A. (2002). Repressive coping style, acute stress disorder, and posttraumatic stress disorder after myocardial infarction. *Psychosomatic Medicine, 64*, 748–757.

Giovanello, K. S., Schnyer, D. M., & Verfaellie, M. (2004). A critical role for the anterior hippocampus in relational memory: Evidence from an fMRI study comparing associative and item recognition. *Hippocampus, 14*, 5–8.

Gladue, B. A. (1994). The biopsychology of sexual orientation. *Current Directions in Psychological Science, 3*, 150–154.

Glass, D. C., & Singer, J. E. (1972). *Urban stress.* New York: Academic Press.

Gleaves, D. H., May, M. C., & Cardeña, E. (2000). An examination of the diagnostic validity of dissociative identity disorder. *Clinical Psychology Review, 21*, 577–608.

Gleaves, D. H., Smith, S. M., Butler, L. D., & Spiegel, D. (2004). False and recovered memories in the laboratory and clinic: A review of experimental and clinical evidence. *Clinical Psychology: Science and Practice, 11*, 3–28.

Glenwick, D. S., Jason, L. A., & Elman, D. (1978). Physical attractiveness and social contact in the singles bar. *Journal of Social Psychology, 105*, 311–312.

Glynn, S. M. (1990). Token economy approaches for psychiatric patients: Progress and pitfalls over 25 years. *Behavior Modification, 14*, 383–407.

Gneezy, U., & Rustichini, A. (2000). A fine is a price. *Journal of Legal Studies, 29*, 1–17.

Gobert, A., Rivet, J. M., Cistarelli, L., Melon, C., & Millan, M. J. (1999). Buspirone modulates basal and fluoxetine-stimulated dialysate levels of dopamine, noradrenaline, and serotonin in the frontal cortex of freely moving rats: Activation of serotonin 1A receptors and blockade of alpha2-adrenergic receptors underlie its actions. *Neuroscience, 93*, 1251–1262.

Goddard, H. H. (1913). *The Kallikak family: A study in the heredity of feeble-mindedness.* New York: Macmillan.

Godden, D. R., & Baddeley, A. D. (1975). Context-dependent memory in two natural environments: On land and underwater. *British Journal of Psychology, 66*, 325–331.

Goehler, L. E., Gaykema, R. P. A., Hansen, M. K., Anderson, K., Maier, S. F., & Watkins, L. R. (2000). Vagal immune-to-brain communication: A visceral chemosensory pathway. *Autonomic Neuroscience: Basic and Clinical, 85*, 49–59.

Goel, V. (2007). Anatomy of deductive reasoning. *Trends in Cognitive Sciences, 11*, 435–441.

Goel, V., & Dolan, R. J. (2003). Explaining modulation of reasoning by belief. *Cognition, 87*, 11–22.

Goetzman, E. S., Hughes, T., & Klinger, E. (1994). *Current concerns of college students in a midwestern sample.* Unpublished report, University of Minnesota, Morris.

Goff, L. M., & Roediger, H. L., III. (1998). Imagination inflation for action events—repeated imaginings lead to illusory recollections. *Memory & Cognition, 26*, 20–33.

Goldberg, J. (1999, June 20). The color of suspicion. *New York Times Magazine.*

Goldman, M. S., Brown, S. A., & Christiansen, B. A. (1987). Expectancy theory: Thinking about drinking. In H. T. Blane & K. E. Leonard (Eds.), *Psychological theories of drinking and alcoholism* (pp. 181–266). New York: Guilford Press.

Goldstein, R., Almenberg, J., Dreber, A., Emerson, J. W., Herschkowitsch, A., & Katz, J. (2008). Do more expensive wines taste better? Evidence from a large sample of blind tastings. *Journal of Wine Economics, 3,* 1–9.

Goldstein, R., & Herschkowitsch, A. (2008). *The wine trials.* Austin, TX: Fearless Critic Media.

Goldstein, S., Naglieri, J. A., & Ozonoff, S. (Eds.). (2008). *Assessment of autism spectrum disorders.* New York: Guilford Press.

Gollaher, D. (1995). *Voice for the mad: The life of Dorothea Dix.* New York: Free Press.

Gomez, C., Argandota, E. D., Solier, R. G., Angulo, J. C., & Vazquez, M. (1995). Timing and competition in networks representing ambiguous figures. *Brain and Cognition, 29,* 103–114.

Gontier, N. (2008). Genes, brains, and language: An epistemological examination of how genes can underlie human cognitive behavior. *Review of General Psychology, 12,* 170–180.

Gonzaga, G. C., Keltner, D., Londahl, E. A., & Smith, M. D. (2001). Love and the commitment problem in romantic relations and friendship. *Journal of Personality and Social Psychology, 81,* 247–262.

Goodale, M. A., & Milner, A. D. (1992). Separate visual pathways for perception and action. *Trends in Neurosciences, 15,* 20–25.

Goodale, M. A., & Milner, A. D. (2004). *Sight unseen.* Oxford, England: Oxford University Press.

Goodale, M. A., Milner, A. D., Jakobson, L. S., & Carey, D. P. (1991). A neurological dissociation between perceiving objects and grasping them. *Nature, 349,* 154–156.

Goodwin, F. K., & Ghaemi, S. N. (1998). Understanding manic-depressive illness. *Archives of General Psychiatry, 55,* 23–25.

Goodwin, P., McGill, B., & Chandra, A. (2009). *Who marries and when? Age at first marriage in the United States, 2002.* National Center for Health Statistics Data Brief 19.

Gootman, E. (2003, March 3). Separated at birth in Mexico, united at campuses on Long Island. *New York Times,* p. A25.

Gopie, N., & MacLeod, C. M. (2009). Destination memory: Stop me if I've told you this before. *Psychological Science, 20,* 1492–1499.

Gopnik, A., & Astington, J. W. (1988). Children's understanding of representational change and its relation to the understanding of false belief and the appearance reality distinction. *Child Development, 59,* 26–37.

Gopnik, M. (1990a). Feature-blind grammar and dysphasia. *Nature, 344,* 715.

Gopnik, M. (1990b). Feature blindness: A case study. *Language Acquisition: A Journal of Developmental Linguistics, 1,* 139–164.

Gordon, P. (2004). Numerical cognition without words: Evidence from Amazonia. *Science, 306,* 496–499.

Gosling, S. D. (1998). Personality dimensions in spotted hyenas (*Crocuta crocuta*). *Journal of Comparative Psychology, 112,* 107–118.

Gosling, S. D., & John, O. P. (1999). Personality dimensions in nonhuman animals: A cross-species review. *Current Directions in Psychological Science, 8,* 69–75.

Gosling, S. D., Ko, S. J., Mannarelli, T., & Morris, M. E. (2002). A room with a cue: Personality judgments based on offices and bedrooms. *Journal of Personality and Social Psychology, 82,* 379–398.

Gottesman, I. I. (1991). *Schizophrenia genesis: The origins of madness.* New York: Freeman.

Gottesman, I. I., & Hanson, D. R. (2005). Human development: Biological and genetic processes. *Annual Review of Psychology, 56,* 263–286.

Gottfredson, L. S. (1997). Mainstream science on intelligence: An editorial with 52 signatories, history, and bibliography. *Intelligence, 24,* 13–23.

Gottfredson, L. S. (2003). Dissecting practical intelligence theory: Its claims and evidence. *Intelligence, 31*(4), 343–397.

Gottfredson, L. S., & Deary, I. J. (2004). Intelligence predicts health and longevity, but why? *Current Directions in Psychological Science, 13,* 1–4.

Gottfried, J. A. (2008). Perceptual and neural plasticity of odor quality coding in the human brain. *Chemosensory Perception, 1,* 127–135.

Gottman, J. M. (1994). *What predicts divorce? The relationship between marital processes and marital outcomes.* Hillsdale, NJ: Lawrence Erlbaum.

Gould, M. S. (1990). Suicide clusters and media exposure. In S. J. Blumenthal & D. J. Kupfer (Eds.), *Suicide over the life cycle: Risk factors, assessment, and treatment of suicidal patients* (pp. 517–532). Washington, DC: American Psychiatric Press.

Gouldner, A. W. (1960). The norm of reciprocity. *American Sociological Review, 25,* 161–178.

Grady, C. L., McIntosh, A. R., Horwitz, B., & Rapoport, S. I. (2000). Age-related changes in the neural correlates of degraded and nondegraded face processing. *Cognitive Neuropsychology, 217,* 165–186.

Graf, P., & Schacter, D. L. (1985). Implicit and explicit memory for new associations in normal subjects and amnesic patients. *Journal of Experimental Psychology: Learning, Memory, and Cognition, 11,* 501–518.

Grandin, T. (2006). *Thinking in pictures: My life with autism (expanded edition).* Visalia, CA: Vintage.

Grant, A. M. (2008). Personal life coaching for coaches-in-training enhances goal attainment, insight, and learning. *Coaching, 1*(1), 54–70.

Grant, B. F., Hasin, D. S., Stinson, F. S., Dawson, D. A., Chou, S. P., & Ruan, W. J. (2004). Prevalence, correlates, and disability of personality disorders in the U.S.: Results from the National Epidemiologic Survey on Alcohol and Related Conditions. *Journal of Clinical Psychiatry, 65,* 948–958.

Grassian, S. (2006). Psychiatric effects of solitary confinement. *Journal of Law & Policy, 22,* 326–383.

Gray, H. M., Gray, K., & Wegner, D. M. (2007). Dimensions of mind perception. *Science, 315,* 619.

Gray, J. A. (1970). The psychophysiological basis of introversion-extraversion. *Behavior Research and Therapy, 8,* 249–266.

Gray, J. A. (1990). Brain systems that mediate both emotion and cognition. *Cognition and Emotion, 4,* 269–288.

Greeley, A. M. (1975). *The sociology of the paranormal: A reconnaissance.* Beverly Hills, CA: Sage.

Greely, H., Sahakian, B., Harris, J., Kessler, R. C., Gazzaniga, M., Campbell, P., et al. (2008). Towards responsible use of cognitive-enhancing drugs by the healthy. *Nature, 456*(7223), 702–705.

Green, D. A., & Swets, J. A. (1966). *Signal detection theory and psychophysics.* New York: Wiley.

Green, S. K., Buchanan, D. R., & Heuer, S. K. (1984). Winners, losers, and choosers: A field investigation of dating initiation. *Personality & Social Psychology Bulletin, 10,* 502–511.

Greenberg, J., Pyszczynski, T., Solomon, S., Rosenblatt, A., Veeder, M., Kirkland, S., et al. (1990). Evidence for terror management theory II: The effects of mortality salience on reactions to those who threaten or bolster the cultural worldview. *Journal of Personality and Social Psychology, 58,* 308–318.

Greenberg, J., Solomon, S., & Arndt, J. (2008). A basic but uniquely human motivation: Terror management. In J. Y. Shah & W. L. Gardner (Eds.), *Handbook of motivation science* (pp. 114–134). New York: Guilford Press.

Greenberg, P. E., Sisitsky, T., Kessler, R. C., Finkelstein, S. N., Berndt, E. R., Davidson, J. R. T., et al. (1999). The economic burden of anxiety disorders in the 1990s. *Journal of Clinical Psychiatry, 60,* 427–435.

Greene, J. D., Sommerville, R. B., Nystrom, L. E., Darley, J. M., & Cohen, J. D. (2001). An fMRI investigation of emotional engagement in moral judgment. *Science, 293,* 2105–2108.

Greenfield, P. M., Keller, H., Fuligni, A., & Maynard, A. (2003). Cultural pathways through universal development. *Annual Review of Psychology, 54,* 461–490.

Greenhouse, S. (2003, July 13). Going for the look, but risking discrimination. *New York Times.*

Greenwald, A. G. (1992). New look 3: Unconscious cognition reclaimed. *American Psychologist, 47,* 766–779.

Greenwald, A. G., McGhee, D. E., & Schwartz, J. L. K. (1998). Measuring individual differences in implicit cognition: The implicit association test. *Journal of Personality and Social Psychology, 74,* 1464–1480.

Greenwald, A. G., & Nosek, B. A. (2001). Health of the Implicit Association Test at age 3. *Zeitschrift für Experimentelle Psychologie, 48,* 85–93.

Grigoriadis, S., & Robinson, G. E. (2007). Gender issues in depression. *Journal of Clinical Psychiatry, 19,* 247–255.

Gronlund, S. D., Carlson, C. A., Dailey, S. B., & Goodsell, C. A. (2009). Robustness of the sequential lineup advantage. *Journal of Experimental Psychology: Applied, 15*(2), 140–152.

Gropp, E., Shanabrough, M., Borok, E., Xu, A. W., Janoschek, R., Buch, T., et al. (2005). Agouti-related peptide-expressing neurons are mandatory for feeding. *Nature Neuroscience, 8,* 1289–1291.

Gross, J. J. (1998). Antecedent- and response-focused emotion regulation: Divergent consequences for experience, expression, and physiology. *Journal of Personality and Social Psychology, 74,* 224–237.

Gross, J. J., & Munoz, R. F. (1995). Emotion regulation and mental health. *Clinical Psychology: Science and Practice, 2,* 151–164.

Groves, B. (2004, August 2). Unwelcome awareness. *The San Diego Union-Tribune,* p. 24.

Grudnick, J. L., & Kranzler, J. H. (2001). Meta-analysis of the relationship between intelligence and inspection time. *Intelligence, 29,* 523–535.

Guillery, R. W., & Sherman, S. M. (2002). Thalamic relay functions and their role in corticocortical communication: Generalizations from the visual system. *Neuron, 33,* 163–175.

Gur, R. E., Cowell, P., Turetsky, B. I., Gallacher, F., Cannon, T., Bilker, W., et al. (1998). A follow-up magnetic resonance imaging study of schizophrenia: Relationship of neuroanatomical changes to clinical and neurobehavioral measures. *Archives of General Psychiatry, 55,* 145–152.

Gurwitz, J. H., McLaughlin, T. J., Willison, D. J., Guadagnoli, E., Hauptman, P. J., Gao, X., et al. (1997). Delayed hospital presentation in patients who have had acute myocardial infarction. *Annals of Internal Medicine, 126,* 593–599.

Gusnard, D. A., & Raichle, M. E. (2001). Searching for a baseline: Functional imaging and the resting human brain. *Nature Reviews: Neuroscience, 2,* 685–694.

Gustafsson, J.-E. (1984). A unifying model for the structure of intellectual abilities. *Intelligence, 8,* 179–203.

Guthrie, R. V. (2000). Kenneth Bancroft Clark (1914–). In A. E. Kazdin (Ed.), *Encyclopedia of Psychology* (Vol. 2, p. 91). Washington, DC: American Psychological Association.

Hacking, I. (1975). *The emergence of probability.* New York: Cambridge University Press.

Hackman, D. A., & Farah, M. J. (2008). Socioeconomic status and the developing brain. *Trends in Cognitive Sciences, 13,* 65–73.

Hackman, J. R., & Katz, N. (2010). Group behavior and performance. In S. T. Fiske, D. T. Gilbert, & G. Lindzey (Eds.), *The handbook of social psychology* (5th ed., Vol. 2). New York: Wiley.

Haggard, P., & Tsakiris, M. (2009). The experience of agency: Feelings, judgments, and responsibility. *Current Directions in Psychological Science, 18,* 242–246.

Haidt, J. (2001). The emotional dog and its rational tail: A social intuitionist approach to moral judgment. *Psychological Review, 108,* 814–834.

Haidt, J. (2006). *The happiness hypothesis: Finding modern truth in ancient wisdom.* New York: Basic Books.

Haidt, J. (2008). Morality. *Perspectives in Psychological Science, 3,* 65–72.

Haidt, J., & Keltner, D. (1999). Culture and facial expression: Open-ended methods find more expressions and a gradient of recognition. *Cognition and Emotion, 13,* 225–266.

Hakuta, K. (1986). *Cognitive development of bilingual children.* Center for Language Education and Research, University of California, Los Angeles.

Hakuta, K. (1999). The debate on bilingual education. *Journal of Developmental and Behavioral Pediatrics, 20,* 36–37.

Hallett, M. (2000). Transcranial magnetic stimulation and the human brain. *Nature, 406,* 147–150.

Hallett, M., Cloninger, C. R., Fahn, S., & Jankovic, J. J. (Eds.). (2005). *The psychogenic movement disorders: Neurology and neuropsychiatry.* Philadelphia: Lippincott, Williams & Wilkins.

Halliday, R., Naylor, H., Brandeis, D., Callaway, E., Yano, L., & Herzig, K. (1994). The effect of D-amphetamine, clonidine, and yohimbine on human information processing. *Psychophysiology, 31,* 331–337.

Halpern, B. (2002). Taste. In H. Pashler & S. Yantis (Eds.), *Stevens' handbook of experimental psychology: Vol. 1. Sensation and perception* (3rd ed., pp. 653–690). New York: Wiley.

Halpern, D. F. (1997). Sex differences in intelligence: Implications for education. *American Psychologist, 52,* 1091–1102.

Halpern, D. F., Benbow, C. P., Geary, D. C., Gur, R. C., Hyde, J. S., & Gernsbacher, M. A. (2007). The science of sex differences in science and mathematics. *Psychological Science in the Public Interest, 8,* 1–51.

Hamermesh, D. S., & Biddle, J. E. (1994). Beauty and the labor market. *American Economic Review, 84,* 1174–1195.

Hamilton, A. F., & Grafton, S. T. (2006). Goal representation in human anterior intraparietal sulcus. *The Journal of Neuroscience, 26,* 1133–1137.

Hamilton, A. F., & Grafton, S. T. (2008). Action outcomes are represented in human inferior frontoparietal cortex. *Cerebral Cortex, 18,* 1160–1168.

Hamilton, D. L., & Gifford, R. K. (1976). Illusory correlation in interpersonal perception: A cognitive basis of stereotypic judgements. *Journal of Experimental Social Psychology, 12,* 392–407.

Hamilton, W. D. (1964). The genetical evolution of social behaviour. *Journal of Theoretical Biology, 7,* 1–16.

Hamlin, J. K., Wynn, K., & Bloom, P. (2007). Social evaluation by preverbal infants. *Nature, 450*(7169), 557–559.

Hammersla, J. F., & Frease-McMahan, L. (1990). University students' priorities: Life goals vs. relationships. *Sex Roles, 23,* 1–14.

Hansen, E. S., Hasselbalch, S., Law, I., & Bolwig, T. G. (2002). The caudate nucleus in obsessive-compulsive disorder. Reduced metabolism following treatment with paroxetine: A PET study. *International Journal of Neuropsychopharmacology, 5,* 1–10.

Hansen, T., Olkkonen, M., Walter, S., & Gegenfurtner, K. R. (2006). Memory modulates color appearance. *Nature Neuroscience, 9,* 1367–1368.

Hanson, C. J., Stevens, L. C., & Coast, J. R. (2001). Exercise duration and mood state: How much is enough to feel better? *Health Psychology, 20*, 267–275.

Happé, F. G. E. (1995). The role of age and verbal ability in the theory-of-mind performance of subjects with autism. *Child Development, 66*, 843–855.

Happé, F. G. E., & Vital, P. (2009). What aspects of autism predispose to talent? *Philosophical Transactions of the Royal Society B: Biological Science, 364*, 1369–1375.

Harding, C. M., Brooks, G. W., Ashikaga, T., Strauss, J. S., & Brier, A. (1987). The Vermont longitudinal study of persons with severe mental illness, II: Long-term outcome of subjects who retrospectively met DSM-III criteria for schizophrenia. *American Journal of Psychiatry, 144*, 727–735.

Hare, R. D. (1998). *Without conscience: The disturbing world of the psychopaths among us.* New York: Guilford Press.

Harkness, S., Edwards, C. P., & Super, C. M. (1981). Social roles and moral reasoning: A case study in a rural African community. *Developmental Psychology, 17*, 595–603.

Harlow, H. F. (1958). The nature of love. *American Psychologist, 13*, 573–685.

Harlow, H. F., & Harlow, M. L. (1965). The affectional systems. In A. M. Schrier, H. F. Harlow, & F. Stollnitz (Eds.), *Behavior of nonhuman primates* (Vol. 2). New York: Academic Press.

Harlow, J. M. (1848). Passage of an iron rod through the head. *Boston Medical and Surgical Journal, 39*, 389–393.

Harris, B. (1979). Whatever happened to Little Albert? *American Psychologist, 34*, 151–160.

Harris, P. L., de Rosnay, M., & Pons, F. (2005). Language and children's understanding of mental states. *Current Directions in Psychological Science, 14*, 69–73.

Harris, P. L., Johnson, C. N., Hutton, D., Andrews, G., & Cooke, T. (1989). Young children's theory of mind and emotion. *Cognition and Emotion, 3*, 379–400.

Hart, B. L. (1988). Biological basis of the behavior of sick animals. *Neuroscience and Biobehavioral Reviews, 12*, 123–137.

Hart, B., & Risley, T. R. (1995). *Meaningful differences in the everyday experience of young American children.* Baltimore, MD: Brookes.

Hartshorne, H., & May, M. (1928). *Studies in deceit.* New York: Macmillan.

Hasher, L., & Zacks, R. T. (1984). Automatic processing of fundamental information: The case of frequency of occurrence. *American Psychologist, 39*, 1372–1388.

Haskell, E. (1869). *The trial of Ebenezer Haskell, in lunacy, and his acquittal before Judge Brewster, in November, 1868, together with a brief sketch of the mode of treatment of lunatics in different asylums in this country and in England: with illustrations, including a copy of Hogarth's celebrated painting of a scene in old Bedlam, in London, 1635.* Philadelphia, PA: Ebenezer Haskell.

Haslam, C., Wills, A. J., Haslam, S. A., Kay, J., Baron, R., & McNab, F. (2007). Does maintenance of colour categories rely on language? Evidence to the contrary from a case of semantic dementia. *Brain and Language, 103*, 251–263.

Hassabis, D., Kumaran, D., Vann, S. D., & Maguire, E. A. (2007). Patients with hippocampal amnesia cannot imagine new experiences. *Proceedings of the National Academy of Sciences, USA, 104*, 1726–1731.

Hasselmo, M. E. (2006). The role of acetylcholine in learning and memory. *Current Opinion in Neurobiology, 16*, 710–715.

Hassin, R. R., Bargh, J. A., & Zimerman, S. (2009). Automatic and flexible: The case of non-conscious goal pursuit. *Social Cognition, 27*, 20–36.

Hassmen, P., Koivula, N., & Uutela, A. (2000). Physical exercise and psychological well-being: A population study in Finland. *Preventive Medicine, 30*, 17–25.

Hasson, U., Hendler, T., Bashat, D. B., & Malach, R. (2001). Vase or face? A neural correlate of shape-selective grouping processes in the human brain. *Journal of Cognitive Neuroscience, 13*, 744–753.

Hatfield, E. (1988). Passionate and companionate love. In R. J. Sternberg & M. L. Barnes (Eds.), *The psychology of love* (pp. 191–217). New Haven, CT: Yale University Press.

Hatfield, E., & Rapson, R. L. (1992). Similarity and attraction in close relationships. *Communication Monographs, 59*, 209–212.

Hausser, M. (2000). The Hodgkin-Huxley theory of the action potential. *Nature Neuroscience, 3*, 1165.

Hawley, P. H. (2002). Social dominance and prosocial and coercive strategies of resource control in preschoolers. *International Journal of Behavioral Development, 26*, 167–176.

Haxby, J. V., Gobbini, M. I., Furey, M. L., Ishai, A., Schouten, J. L., & Pietrini, P. (2001). Distributed and overlapping representations of faces and objects in ventral temporal cortex. *Science, 293*, 2425–2430.

Hay, P., Sachdev, P., Cumming, S., Smith, J. S., Lee, T., Kitchener, P., et al. (1993). Treatment of obsessive-compulsive disorder by psychosurgery. *Acta Psychiatrica Scandinavica, 87*, 197–207.

Hayes, J. E., Bartoshuk, L. M., Kidd, J. R., & Duffy, V. B. (2008). Supertasting and PROP bitterness depends on more than the TAS2R38 gene. *Chemical Senses, 23*, 255–265.

Hayes, K., & Hayes, C. (1951). The intellectual development of a home-raised chimpanzee. *Proceedings of the American Philosophical Society, 95*, 105–109.

Hayes, S. C., Strosahl, K., & Wilson, K. G. (1999). *Acceptance and commitment therapy: An experiential approach to behavior change.* New York: Guilford Press.

Hay-McCutcheon, M. J., Kirk, K. I., Henning, S. C., Gao, S. J., & Qi, R. (2008). Using early outcomes to predict later language ability in children with cochlear implants. *Audiology and Neuro-Otology, 13*, 370–378.

Health, United States. (2008). Hyattsville, MD: National Center for Health Statistics.

Heath, S. B. (1983). *Way with words: Language, life and work in communities and classrooms.* Cambridge, England: Cambridge University Press.

Heatherton, T. F., & Weinberger, J. L. (Eds.). (1994). *Can personality change?* Washington, DC: American Psychological Association.

Heaton, R., Paulsen, J. S., McAdams, L. A., Kuck, J., Zisook, S., Bra, D., et al. (1994). Neuropsychological deficits in schizophrenia: Relationship to age, chronicity, and dementia. *Archives of General Psychiatry, 51*, 469–476.

Hebb, D. O. (1949). *The organization of behavior.* New York: Wiley.

Hebl, M. R., & Heatherton, T. F. (1997). The stigma of obesity in women: The difference is Black and White. *Personality and Social Psychology Bulletin, 24*, 417–426.

Hebl, M. R., & Mannix, L. M. (2003). The weight of obesity in evaluating others: A mere proximity effect. *Personality and Social Psychology Bulletin, 29*, 28–38.

Heerey, E. A., Keltner, D., & Capps, L. M. (2003). Making sense of self-conscious emotion: Linking theory of mind and emotion in children with autism. *Emotion, 3*, 394–400.

Heider, F., & Simmel, M. (1944). An experimental study of apparent behavior. *American Journal of Psychology, 57*, 243–259.

Heine, S. J. (2010). Cultural psychology. In S. T. Fiske, D. T. Gilbert, & G. Lindzey (Eds.), *The handbook of social psychology* (5th ed., Vol. 2). New York: Wiley.

Henderlong, J., & Lepper, M. R. (2002). The effects of praise on children's intrinsic motivation: A review and synthesis. *Psychological Bulletin, 128,* 774–795.

Henriques, J. B., & Davidson, R. J. (1990). Regional brain electrical asymmetries discriminate between previously depressed and healthy control subjects. *Journal of Abnormal Psychology, 99,* 22–31.

Henry, W. P., Strupp, H. H., Schacht, T. E., & Gaston, L. (1994). Psychodynamic approaches. In A. E. Bergin & S. L. Garfield (Eds.), *Handbook of psychotherapy and behavior change* (pp. 467–508). New York: Wiley.

Herman, C. P., Roth, D. A., & Polivy, J. (2003). Effects of the presence of others on food intake: A normative interpretation. *Psychological Bulletin, 129,* 873–886.

Herman-Giddens, M. E., Slora, E. J., Wasserman, R. C., Bourdony, C. J., Bhapkar, M. V., Koch, G. G., et al. (1997). Secondary sexual characteristics and menses in young girls seen in office practice: A study from the pediatric research in office settings network. *Pediatrics and Perinatal Epidemiology, 99,* 505–512.

Herrmann, D. J., Raybeck, D., & Gruneberg, M. (2002). *Improving memory and study skills: Advances in theory and practice.* Seattle: Hogrefe and Huber.

Herrnstein, R. J. (1977). The evolution of behaviorism. *American Psychologist, 32,* 593–603.

Hertenstein, M. J., Holmes, R., McCullough, M., & Keltner, D. (2009). The communication of emotion via touch. *Emotion, 9,* 566–573.

Hertwig, R., Davis, J. N., & Sulloway, F. J. (2002). Parental investment: How an equity motive can produce inequality. *Psychological Bulletin, 128,* 728–745.

Hertwig, R., & Gigerenzer, G. (1999). The "conjunction fallacy" revisited: How intelligent inferences look like reasoning errors. *Journal of Behavioral Decision Making, 12,* 275–305.

Herz, R. S., & von Clef, J. (2001). The influence of verbal labeling on the perception of odors. *Perception, 30,* 381–391.

Hettema, J. M., Neale, M. C., & Kendler, K. S. (2001). A review and meta-analysis of the genetic epidemiology of anxiety disorders. *American Journal of Psychiatry, 158,* 1568–1578.

Heyes, C. M., & Foster, C. L. (2002). Motor learning by observation: Evidence from a serial reaction time task. *Quarterly Journal of Experimental Psychology (A), 55,* 593–607.

Heymsfield, S. B., Greenberg, A. S., Fujioka, K., Dixon, R. M., Kushner, R., Hunt, T., et al. (1999). Recombinant leptin for weight loss in obese and lean adults: A randomized, controlled, dose-escalation trial. *Journal of the American Medical Association, 282*(16), 1568–1575.

Hickok, G. (2009). Eight problems for the mirror neuron theory of action understanding in monkeys and humans. *Journal of Cognitive Neuroscience, 21,* 1229–1243.

Higgins, E. T. (1987). Self-discrepancy theory: A theory relating self and affect. *Psychological Review, 94,* 319–340.

Higgs, S., Williamson, A. C., Rotshtein, P., & Humphreys, G. W. (2008). Sensory-specific satiety is intact in amnesics who eat multiple meals. *Psychological Science, 19,* 623–628.

Hilgard, E. R. (1965). *Hypnotic susceptibility.* New York: Harcourt, Brace and World.

Hilgard, E. R. (1986). *Divided consciousness: Multiple controls in human thought and action.* New York: Wiley-Interscience.

Hillman, C. H., Erickson, K. I., & Kramer, A. F. (2008). Be smart, exercise your heart: Exercise effects on brain and cognition. *Nature Reviews Neuroscience, 9,* 58–65.

Hilts, P. (1995). *Memory's ghost: The strange tale of Mr. M and the nature of memory.* New York: Simon & Schuster.

Hintzman, D. L., Asher, S. J., & Stern, L. D. (1978). Incidental retrieval and memory for coincidences. In M. M. Gruneberg, P. E. Morris, & R. N. Sykes (Eds.), *Practical aspects of memory* (pp. 61–68). New York: Academic Press.

Hirschberger, G., Florian, V., & Mikulincer, M. (2002). The anxiety buffering function of close relationships: Mortality salience effects on the readiness to compromise mate selection standards. *European Journal of Social Psychology, 32,* 609–625.

Hirschfeld, D. R., Rosenbaum, J. F., Biederman, J., Bolduc, E. A., Faraone, S. V., Snidman, N., et al. (1992). Stable behavioral inhibition and its association with anxiety disorder. *Journal of the American Academy of Child and Adolescent Psychiatry, 31,* 103–111.

Hirschfeld, R. M. A. (1996). Panic disorder: Diagnosis, epidemiology, and clinical course. *Journal of Clinical Psychiatry, 57,* 3–8.

Hirst, W., Phelps, E. A., Buckner, R. L., Budson, A. E., Cuc, A., Gabrieli, J. D. E., et al. (2009). Long-term memory for the terrorist attack of September 11: Flashbulb memories, event memories, and the factors that influence their retention. *Journal of Experimental Psychology: General, 138,* 161–176.

Hirstein, W., & Ramachandran, V. S. (1997). Capgras syndrome: A novel probe for understanding the neural representation of the identity and familiarity of persons. *Proceedings: Biological Sciences, 264,* 437–444.

Hishakawa, Y. (1976). Sleep paralysis. In C. Guilleminault, W. C. Dement, & P. Passouant (Eds.), *Narcolepsy: Advances in sleep research* (Vol. 3, pp. 97–124). New York: Spectrum.

Hitchcock, S. T. (2005). *Mad Mary Lamb: Lunacy and murder in literary London.* New York: Norton.

Hittner, J. B. (2005). How robust is the Werther effect? A re-examination of the suggestion-imitation model of suicide. *Mortality, 10,* 193–200.

Hobson, J. A. (1988). *The dreaming brain.* New York: Basic Books.

Hobson, J. A., & McCarley, R. W. (1977). The brain as a dream-state generator: An activation-synthesis hypothesis of the dream process. *American Journal of Psychiatry, 134,* 1335–1368.

Hockley, W. E. (2008). The effects of environmental context on recognition memory and claims of remembering. *Journal of Experimental Psychology: Learning, Memory, & Cognition, 34,* 1412–1429.

Hodgkin, A. L., & Huxley, A. F. (1939). Action potential recorded from inside a nerve fibre. *Nature, 144,* 710–712.

Hodson, G., & Sorrentino, R. M. (2001). Just who favors the in-group? Personality differences in reactions to uncertainty in the minimal group paradigm. *Group Dynamics, 5,* 92–101.

Hoek, H. W., & van Hoeken, D. (2003). Review of the prevalence and incidence of eating disorders. *International Journal of Eating Disorders, 34,* 383–396.

Hoffrage, U., & Gigerenzer, G. (1996). The impact of information representation on Bayesian reasoning. In G. Cottrell (Ed.), *Proceedings of the Eighteenth Annual Conference of the Cognitive Science Society* (pp. 126–130). Mahwah, NJ: Lawrence Erlbaum.

Hoffrage, U., & Gigerenzer, G. (1998). Using natural frequencies to improve diagnostic inferences. *Academic Medicine, 73,* 538–540.

Hofmann, S. G., & Asmundson, G. J. G. (2008). Acceptance and mindfulness-based therapy: New wave or old hat? *Clinical Psychology Review, 28,* 1–16.

Hogan, D. P., Sun, R., & Cornwell, G. T. (2000). Sexual and fertility behaviors of American females age 15–19 years: 1985, 1990 and 1995. *American Journal of Public Health, 90,* 1421–1425.

Holland, P. C. (1981). Acquisition of representation-mediated conditioned food aversions. *Learning and Motivation, 12,* 1–18.

Holland, P. C. (2005). Amount of training effects in representation-mediated food aversion learning: No evidence of a role for associability changes. *Learning & Behavior, 33,* 464–478.

Holloway, G. (2001). *The complete dream book: What your dreams tell about you and your life*. Naperville, IL: Sourcebooks.

Holmbeck, G. N., & O'Donnell, K. (1991). Discrepancies between perceptions of decision making and behavioral autonomy. In R. L. Paikoff (Ed.), *New directions for child development: No. 51. Shared views in the family during adolescence*. San Francisco: Jossey-Bass.

Holmes, T. H., & Rahe, R. H. (1967). The social readjustment rating scale. *Journal of Psychosomatic Research, 11*, 213–318.

Homans, G. C. (1961). *Social behavior*. New York: Harcourt, Brace and World.

Hopper, L. M., Flynn, E. G., Wood, L. A. N., & Whiten, A. (2010). Observational learning of tool use in children: Investigating cultural spread through diffusion chains and learning mechanisms through ghost displays. *Journal of Experimental Child Psychology,*

Horn, J. L., & Cattell, R. B. (1966). Refinement and test of the theory of fluid and crystallized general intelligences. *Journal of Educational Psychology, 5*, 253–270.

Horner, V., Whiten, A., Flynn, E., & de Waal, F. B. M. (2006). Faithful replication of foraging techniques along cultural transmission chains by chimpanzees and children. *Proceedings of the National Academy of Sciences, USA, 103*, 13878–13883.

Horrey, W. J., & Wickens, C. D. (2006). Examining the impact of cell phone conversation on driving using meta-analytic techniques. *Human Factors, 48*, 196–205.

Horta, B. L., Victoria, C. G., Menezes, A. M., Halpern, R., & Barros, F. C. (1997). Low birthweight, preterm births and intrauterine growth retardation in relation to maternal smoking. *Pediatrics and Perinatal Epidemiology, 11*, 140–151.

Horwitz, A. V., & Wakefield, J. C. (2007). *The loss of sadness: How psychiatry transformed normal sorrow into depressive disorder*. New York: Oxford University Press.

Hosking, S. G., Young, K. L., & Regan, M. A. (2009). The effects of text messaging on young drivers. *Human Factors, 51*, 582–592.

House, J. S., Landis, K. R., & Umberson, D. (1988). Social relationships and health. *Science, 241*, 540–545.

Howard, I. P. (2002). Depth perception. In S. Yantis & H. Pashler (Eds.), *Stevens' handbook of experimental psychology: Vol. 1. Sensation and perception* (3rd ed., pp. 77–120). New York: Wiley.

Howard, J. H., Jr., & Howard, D. V. (1997). Age differences in implicit learning of higher order dependencies in serial patterns. *Psychology and Aging, 12*, 634–656.

Howard-Jones, P. A., Blakemore, S.-J., Samuel, E. A., Summers, I. R., & Claxton, G. (2005). Semantic divergence and creative story generation: An fMRI investigation. *Cognitive Brain Research, 25*, 240–250.

Howes, C. (1993). *Voices of the Vietnam POWs: Witnesses to their fight*. Oxford, England: Oxford University Press.

Howes, M., Siegel, M., & Brown, F. (1993). Early childhood memories—accuracy and affect. *Cognition, 47*, 95–119.

Hubbard, E. M., & Ramachandran, V. S. (2003). Refining the experimental lever. *Journal of Consciousness Studies, 10*, 77–84.

Hubbard, E. M., & Ramachandran, V. S. (2005). Neurocognitive mechanisms of synesthesia. *Neuron, 48*, 509–520.

Hubel, D. H. (1988). *Eye, brain, and vision*. New York: Freeman.

Hubel, D. H., & Wiesel, T. N. (1962). Receptive fields, binocular interaction and functional architecture in the cat's visual cortex. *Journal of Physiology, 160*, 106–154.

Hubel, D. H., & Wiesel, T. N. (1998). Early exploration of the visual cortex. *Neuron, 20*, 401–412.

Huesmann, L. R., Moise-Titus, J., Podolski, C.-L., & Eron, L. D. (2003). Longitudinal relations between children's exposure to TV violence and their aggressive and violent behavior in young adulthood: 1977–1992. *Developmental Psychology, 39*, 201–221.

Hughes, J. R. (2007). A review of sleepwalking (somnambulism): The enigma of neurophysiology and polysomnography with differential diagnosis of complex partial seizures. *Epilepsy & Behavior, 11*, 483–491.

Hughs, S., Power, T., & Francis, D. (1992). Defining patterns of drinking in adolescence: A cluster analytic approach. *Journal of Studies on Alcohol, 53*, 40–47.

Humphreys, K., Winzelberg, A., & Klaw, E. (2000). Psychologists' ethical responsibilities in Internet-based groups: Issues, strategies, and a call for dialogue. *Professional Psychology: Research and Practice, 31*, 493–496.

Humphreys, N., & Dennett, D. C. (1989). Speaking for our selves. *Raritan: A Quarterly Review, 9*, 68–98.

Hunsley, J., & Di Giulio, G. (2002). Dodo bird, phoenix, or urban legend? The question of psychotherapy equivalence. *Scientific Review of Mental Health Practice, 1*, 13–24.

Hunt, M. (1959). *The natural history of love*. New York: Knopf.

Hunter, J. E., & Hunter, R. F. (1984). Validity and utility of alternative predictors of job performance. *Psychological Bulletin, 96*, 72–98.

Hurvich, L. M., & Jameson, D. (1957). An opponent process theory of color vision. *Psychological Review, 64*, 384–404.

Hussey, E., & Safford, A. (2009). Perception of facial expression in somatosensory cortex supports simulationist models. *The Journal of Neuroscience, 29*(2), 301–302.

Huttenlocher, P. R. (1979). Synaptic density in human frontal cortex—developmental changes and effects of aging. *Brain Research, 163*, 195–205.

Huxley, A. (1932). *Brave new world*. London: Chatto and Windus.

Huxley, A. (1954). *The doors of perception*. New York: Harper & Row.

Hwang, D. Y., Gallo, D. A., Ally, B. A., Black, P. M., Schacter, D. L., & Budson, A. E. (2007). Diagnostic retrieval monitoring in patients with frontal lobe lesions: Further exploration of the distinctiveness heuristic. *Neuropsychologia, 45*, 2543–2552.

Hyde, J. S. (2005). The gender similarities hypothesis. *American Psychologist, 60*, 581–592.

Hyman, I. E., Jr., & Billings, F. J. (1998). Individual differences and the creation of false childhood memories. *Memory, 6*, 1–20.

Hyman, I. E., Jr., Boss, S. M., Wise, B. M., McKenzie, K. E., & Caggiano, J. M. (2010). Did you see the unicycling clown? Inattentional blindness while walking and talking on a cell phone. *Applied Cognitive Psychology, 24*(5), 597–607.

Hyman, I. E., Jr., & Pentland, J. (1996). The role of mental imagery in the creation of false childhood memories. *Journal of Memory and Language, 35*, 101–117.

Hypericum Depression Trial Study Group. (2002). Effect of *Hypericum perforatum* (St. John's wort) in major depressive disorder: A randomized controlled trial. *Journal of the American Medical Association, 287*, 1807–1814.

Iacoboni, M. (2009). Imitation, empathy, and mirror neurons. *Annual Review of Psychology, 60*, 653–670.

Iacoboni, M., & Dapretto, M. (2006). The mirror neuron system and the consequences of its dysfunction. *Nature Reviews Neuroscience, 7*, 942–951.

Iacoboni, M., Molnar-Szakacs, I., Gallese, V., Buccino, G., Mazziotta, J. C., & Rizzolatti, G. (2005). Grasping the intentions of others with one's own mirror neuron system. *PLoS Biology, 3*, 529–535.

Ichheiser, G. (1949). Misunderstandings in human relations: A study in false social perceptions. *American Journal of Sociology, 55* (Part 2):1–70.

Imbo, I., & LeFevre, J.-A. (2009). Cultural differences in complex addition: Efficient Chinese versus adaptive Belgians and Canadians. *Journal of Experimental Psychology: Learning, Memory, and Cognition, 35*, 1465–1476.

Inciardi, J. A. (2001). *The war on drugs III.* New York: Allyn & Bacon.

Ingram, R. E., Miranda, J., & Segal, Z. V. (1998). *Cognitive vulnerability to depression.* New York: Guilford Press.

Ingvar, M., Ambros-Ingerson, J., Davis, M., Granger, R., Kessler, M., Rogers, G. A., et al. (1997). Enhancement by an ampakine of memory encoding in humans. *Experimental Neurology, 146,* 553–559.

Inoff-Germain, G., Arnold, G. S., Nottelmann, E. D., & Susman, E. J. (1988). Relations between hormone levels and observational measures of aggressive behavior of young adolescents in family interactions. *Developmental Psychology, 24,* 129–139.

Inui, A. (2001). Ghrelin: An orexigenic and somatotrophic signal from the stomach. *Nature Reviews Neuroscience, 2,* 551–560.

Irvine, J. T. (1978). Wolof magical thinking: Culture and conservation revisited. *Journal of Cross-Cultural Psychology, 9,* 300–310.

Isabelle, R. A. (1993). Origins of attachment: Maternal interactive behavior across the first year. *Child Development, 64,* 605–621.

Isacsson, G., & Rich, C. L. (1997). Depression and antidepressants, and suicide: Pharmacoepidemiological evidence for suicide prevention. In R. W. Maris, M. M. Silverman, & S. S. Canetton (Eds.), *Review of suicidology* (pp. 168–201). New York: Guilford Press.

Isen, A. M., & Patrick, R. (1983). The effect of positive feelings on risk-taking: When the chips are down. *Organizational Behavior and Human Performance, 31,* 194–202.

Ishii, K., Reyes, J. A., & Kitayama, S. (2003). Spontaneous attention to word content versus emotional tone. *Psychological Science, 14*(1), 39–46.

Ismail, N., Gelez, H., Lachapelle, I., & Pfaus, J. (2009). Pacing conditions contribute to the conditioned ejaculatory preference for a familiar female in the male rat. *Physiology & Behavior, 96,* 201–208.

Ittelson, W. H. (1952). *The Ames demonstrations in perception.* Princeton, NJ: Princeton University Press.

Iverson, L. L. (2006). *Speed, Ecstasy, Ritalin: The science of amphetamines.* New York: Oxford University Press.

Izard, C. E. (1971). *The face of emotion.* New York: Appleton-Century-Crofts.

Jablensky, A. (1997). The 100-year epidemiology of schizophrenia. *Schizophrenia Research, 28,* 111–125.

Jaccard, J., Dittus, P. J., & Gordon, V. V. (1998). Parent-adolescent congruency in reports of adolescent sexual behavior and in communications about sexual behavior. *Child Development, 69,* 247–261.

Jacobs, B. L. (1994). Serotonin, motor activity, and depression-related disorders. *American Scientist, 82,* 456–463.

Jacobson, E. (1932). The electrophysiology of mental activities. *American Journal of Psychology, 44,* 677–694.

Jacobson, T., & Hoffman, V. (1997). Children's attachment representations: Longitudinal relations to school behavior and academic competency in middle childhood and adolescence. *Developmental Psychology, 33,* 703–710.

Jaffee, S., & Hyde, J. S. (2000). Gender differences in moral orientation: A meta-analysis. *Psychological Bulletin, 126,* 703–726.

Jahoda, G. (1993). *Crossroads between culture and mind.* Cambridge, MA: Harvard University Press.

James, T. W., Culham, J., Humphrey, G. K., Milner, A. D., & Goodale, M. A. (2003). Ventral occipital lesions impair object recognition but not object-directed grasping: An fMRI study. *Brain, 126,* 2463–2475.

James, W. (1884). What is an emotion? *Mind, 9,* 188–205.

James, W. (1890). *The principles of psychology.* Cambridge, MA: Harvard University Press.

James, W. (1902). *The varieties of religious experience: A study in human nature.* New York: Longman.

James, W. (1911). *Memories and studies.* New York: Longman.

Janicak, P. G., Dowd, S. M., Martis, B., Alam, D., Beedle, D., Krasuski, J., et al. (2002). Repetitive transcranial magnetic stimulation versus electroconvulsive therapy for major depression: Preliminary results of a randomized trial. *Biological Psychiatry, 51,* 659–667.

Jarvella, R. J. (1970). Effects of syntax on running memory span for connected discourse. *Psychonomic Science, 19,* 235–236.

Jarvella, R. J. (1971). Syntactic processing of connected speech. *Journal of Verbal Learning & Verbal Behavior, 10,* 409–416.

Jausovec, N., & Jausovec, K. (2005). Differences in induced gamma and upper alpha oscillations in the human brain related to verbal/performance and emotional intelligence. *International Journal of Psychophysiology, 56,* 223.

Jausovec, N., Jausovec, K., & Gerlic, I. (2001). Differences in event-related and induced electroencephalography patterns in the theta and alpha frequency bands related to human emotional intelligence. *Neuroscience Letters, 311,* 93.

Jaynes, J. (1976). *The origin of consciousness in the breakdown of the bicameral mind.* London: Allen Lane.

Jencks, C. (1979). *Who gets ahead? The determinants of economic success in America.* New York: Wiley.

Jenike, M. A., Baer, L., & Minichiello, W. E. (1986). *Obsessive-compulsive disorders: Theory and management.* Littleton, MA: PSG Publishing.

Jenkins, H. M., Barrera, F. J., Ireland, C., & Woodside, B. (1978). Signal-centered action patterns of dogs in appetitive classical conditioning. *Learning and Motivation, 9,* 272–296.

Jenkins, J. G., & Dallenbach, K. M. (1924). Obliviscence during sleep and waking. *American Journal of Psychology, 35,* 605–612.

Jobes, D. A., Berman, A. L., O'Carroll, P. W., Eastgard, S., & Knickmeyer, S. (1996). The Kurt Cobain suicide crisis: Perspectives from research, public health, and the news media. *Suicide and Life-Threatening Behavior, 26,* 269–271.

John, O. P., Naumann, L. P., & Soto, C. J. (2008). Paradigm shift to the integrative Big-Five trait taxonomy: History, measurement, and conceptual issues. In O. P. John, R. W. Robins, & L. A. Pervin (Eds.), *Handbook of personality: Theory and research* (pp. 114–158). New York: Guilford Press.

John, O. P., & Srivastava, S. (1999). The Big Five trait taxonomy: History, measurement, and theoretical perspectives. In L. A. Pervin & O. P. John (Eds.), *Handbook of personality: Theory and research* (2nd ed., pp. 102–138). New York: Guilford Press.

Johnson, C. A., Xiao, L., Palmer, P., Sun, P., Wang, Q., Wei, Y. L., et al. (2008). Affective decision-making deficits, linked to dysfunctional ventromedial prefrontal cortex, revealed in 10th grade Chinese adolescent binge drinkers. *Neuropsychologia, 46,* 714–726.

Johnson, D. H. (1980). The relationship between spike rate and synchrony in responses of auditory-nerve fibers to single tones. *Journal of the Acoustical Society of America, 68,* 1115–1122.

Johnson, D. R., & Wu, J. (2002). An empirical test of crisis, social selection, and role explanations of the relationship between marital disruption and psychological distress: A pooled time-series analysis of four-wave panel data. *Journal of Marriage and the Family, 64,* 211–224.

Johnson, J. D., Noel, N. E., & Sutter-Hernandez, J. (2000). Alcohol and male sexual aggression: A cognitive disruption analysis. *Journal of Applied Social Psychology, 30,* 1186–1200.

Johnson, J. S., & Newport, E. L. (1989). Critical period effects in second language learning: The influence of maturational state on the acquisition of English as a second language. *Cognitive Psychology, 21,* 60–99.

Johnson, K. (2002). Neural basis of haptic perception. In H. Pashler & S. Yantis (Eds.), *Stevens' handbook of experimental psychology: Vol. 1. Sensation and perception* (3rd ed., pp. 537–583). New York: Wiley.

Johnson, M. H., Dziurawiec, S., Ellis, H. D., & Morton, J. (1991). Newborns' preferential tracking of face-like stimuli and its subsequent decline. *Cognition, 40,* 1–19.

Johnson, M. K., Hashtroudi, S., & Lindsay, D. S. (1993). Source monitoring. *Psychological Bulletin, 114,* 3–28.

Johnson, N. J., Backlund, E., Sorlie, P. D., & Loveless, C. A. (2000). Marital status and mortality: The National Longitudinal Mortality Study. *Annual Review of Epidemiology, 10,* 224–238.

Johnson, R. (2005, February 12). A genius explains. *The Guardian.*

Johnson, S. (2004). *Mind wide open: Your brain and the neuroscience of everyday life.* New York: Scribner.

Johnson, S. C., Dweck, C. S., & Chen, F. S. (2007). Evidence for infants' internal working models of attachment. *Psychological Science, 18*(6), 501–502.

Johnson, S. L., Cuellar, A. K., & Miller, C. (2009). Unipolar and bipolar depression: A comparison of clinical phenomenology, biological vulnerability, and psychosocial predictors. In I. H. Gottlib & C. L. Hammen (Eds.), *Handbook of depression* (2nd ed., pp. 142–162). New York: Guilford Press.

Johnson, S. L., Cuellar, A. K., Ruggiero, C., Winnett-Perman, C., Goodnick, P., White, R., et al. (2008). Life events as predictors of mania and depression in bipolar 1 disorder. *Journal of Abnormal Psychology, 117,* 268–277.

Johnson, S. L., & Miller, I. (1997). Negative life events and time to recover from episodes of bipolar disorder. *Journal of Abnormal Psychology, 106,* 449–457.

Johnston, L., Bachman, J., & O'Malley, P. (1997). *Monitoring the future.* Ann Arbor, MI: Institute for Social Research.

Johnstone, E. C., Crow, T. J., Frith, C., Husband, J., & Kreel, L. (1976). Cerebral ventricular size and cognitive impairment in chronic schizophrenia. *Lancet, 2,* 924–926.

Joiner, T. E., Jr. (2006). *Why people die by suicide.* Cambridge, MA: Harvard University Press.

Jonas, E., Graupmann, V., Kayser, D. N., Zanna, M., Traut-Mattausch, E., & Frey, D. (2009). Culture, self, and the emergence of reactance: Is there a "universal" freedom? *Journal of Experimental Social Psychology, 45,* 1068–1080.

Jones, B. C., Little, A. C., Penton-Voak, I. S., Tiddeman, B. P., Burt, D. M., & Perrett, D. I. (2001). Facial symmetry and judgements of apparent health. Support for a "good genes" explanation of the attractiveness-symmetry relationship. *Evolution and Human Behavior, 22,* 417–429.

Jones, E. E., & Harris, V. A. (1967). The attribution of attitudes. *Journal of Experimental Social Psychology, 3,* 1–24.

Jones, E. E., & Nisbett, R. E. (1972). The actor and the observer: Divergent perceptions of the causes of behavior. In E. E. Jones, D. E. Kanouse, H. H. Kelley, R. E. Nisbett, S. Valins, & B. Weiner (Eds.), *Attribution: Perceiving the causes of behavior* (pp. 79–94). Morristown, NJ: General Learning Press.

Jones, K. (1972). *A history of mental health services.* London: Routledge and Kegan Paul.

Jones, S. S. (2007). Imitation in infancy. *Psychological Science, 18*(7), 593–599.

Jonsson, H., & Hougaard, E. (2008). Group cognitive behavioural therapy for obsessive-compulsive disorder: A systematic review and meta-analysis. *Acta Psychiatrica Scandinavica, 117,* 1–9.

Joo, E., Greenwood, T. A., Schork, N., McKinney, R. A., Satdovnick, D., Remick, D. A., et al. (2009). Suggestive evidence for linkage of SDHD features in bipolar disorder to chromosome 10p14. *American Journal of Medical Genetics Part B: Neuropsychiatric Genetics, 153B,* 260–268.

Jordan, S. A., Cunningham, D. G., & Marles, R. J. (2010). Assessment of herbal medicinal products: Challenges and opportunities to increase the knowledge base for safety assessment. *Toxicology and Applied Pharmacology, 243,* 198–216.

Jost, J. T., Glaser, J., Kruglanski, A. W., & Sullaway, F. J. (2003). Political conservatism as motivated social cognition. *Psychological Bulletin, 129,* 339–375.

Joyce, J. (1994). *Ulysses: The 1922 text.* Introduction and notes by Jeri Johnson. New York: Oxford University Press.

Judd, L. L. (1997). The clinical course of unipolar major depressive disorders. *Archives of General Psychiatry, 54,* 989–991.

Jung-Beeman, M. (2005). Bilateral brain processes for comprehending natural language. *Trends in Cognitive Sciences, 9,* 512–518.

Jung-Beeman, M., Bowden, E. M., Haberman, J., Frymiare, J. L., Arambel-Liu, S., Greenblatt, R., et al. (2004). Neural activity when people solve verbal problems with insight. *PLoS Biology, 2,* 500–510.

Jurewicz, I., Owen, R. J., & O'Donovan, M. C. (2001). Searching for susceptibility genes in schizophrenia. *European Neuropsychopharmacology, 11,* 395–398.

Kaas, J. H. (1991). Plasticity of sensory and motor maps in adult mammals. *Annual Review of Neuroscience, 14,* 137–167.

Kagan, J. (1997). Temperament and the reactions to unfamiliarity. *Child Development, 68,* 139–143.

Kahneman, D., Krueger, A. B., Schkade, D. A., Schwarz, N., & Stone, A. A. (2004). A survey method for characterizing daily life experience: The day reconstruction method. *Science, 306,* 1776–1780.

Kahneman, D., & Tversky, A. (1973). On the psychology of prediction. *Psychological Review, 80,* 237–251.

Kahneman, D., & Tversky, A. (1979). Prospect theory: An analysis of decision under risk. *Econometrica, 47,* 263–291.

Kamil, A. C., & Jones, J. E. (1997). The seed-storing corvid Clark's nutcracker learns geometric relationships among landmarks. *Nature, 390,* 276–279.

Kamiya, J. (1969). Operant control of the EEG alpha rhythm and some of its reported effects on consciousness. In C. S. Tart (Ed.), *Altered states of consciousness* (pp. 519–529). Garden City, NY: Anchor Books.

Kan, P. F., & Kohnert, K. (2008). Fast mapping by bilingual preschool children. *Journal of Child Language, 35,* 495–514.

Kandel, E. R. (2000). Nerve cells and behavior. In E. R. Kandel, G. H. Schwartz, & T. M. Jessell (Eds.), *Principles of neural science* (pp. 19–35). New York: McGraw-Hill.

Kandel, E. R. (2006). *In search of memory: The emergence of a new science of mind.* New York: Norton.

Kanner, A. D., Coyne, J. C., Schaefer, C., & Lazarus, R. S. (1981). Comparison of two modes of stress management: Daily hassles and uplifts versus major life events. *Journal of Behavioral Medicine, 4,* 1–39.

Kanwisher, N. (2000). Domain specificity in face perception. *Nature Neuroscience, 3,* 759–763.

Kanwisher, N., McDermott, J., & Chun, M. M. (1997). The fusiform face area: A module in human extrastriate cortex specialized for face perception. *The Journal of Neuroscience, 17,* 4302–4311.

Kanwisher, N., & Yovel, G. (2006). The fusiform face area: A cortical region specialized for the perception of faces. *Philosophical Transactions of the Royal Society (B), 361,* 2109–2128.

Kapur, S., Craik, F. I. M., Tulving, E., Wilson, A. A., Houle, S., & Brown, G. M. (1994). Neuroanatomical correlates of encoding in episodic memory: Levels of processing effects. *Proceedings of the National Academy of Sciences, USA, 91,* 2008–2011.

Karlins, M., Coffman, T. L., & Walters, G. (1969). On the fading of social stereotypes: Studies in three generations of college students. *Journal of Personality and Social Psychology, 13,* 1–16.

Karney, B. R., & Bradbury, T. N. (1995). The longitudinal course of marital quality and stability: A review of theory, methods, and research. *Psychological Bulletin, 118,* 3–34.

Karno, M., & Golding, J. M. (1991). Obsessive-compulsive disorder. In L. N. Robins & D. A. Regier (Eds.), *Psychiatric disorders in America: The epidemiologic catchment area study.* New York: Free Press.

Karow, A., Pajonk, F. G., Reimer, J., Hirdes, F., Osterwald, C., Naber, D., et al. (2007). The dilemma of insight into illness in schizophrenia: Self- and expert-rated insight and quality of life. *European Archives of Psychiatry and Clinical Neuroscience, 258,* 152–159.

Karpicke, J. D., & Roediger, H. L., III (2008). The critical importance of retrieval for learning. *Science, 319,* 966–968.

Kassam, K. S., Gilbert, D. T., Swencionis, J. K., & Wilson, T. D. (2009). Misconceptions of memory: The Scooter Libby effect. *Psychological Science, 20,* 551–552.

Kasser, T., & Sharma, Y. S. (1999). Reproductive freedom, educational equality, and females' preference for resource-acquisition characteristics in mates. *Psychological Science, 10,* 374–377.

Katon, W. (1994). Primary care—psychiatry panic disorder management. In B. E. Wolfe & J. D. Maser (Eds.), *Treatment of panic disorder: A consensus development conference* (pp. 41–56). Washington, DC: American Psychiatric Press.

Katz, D., & Braly, K. (1933). Racial stereotypes of one hundred college students. *Journal of Abnormal and Social Psychology, 28,* 280–290.

Kaufman, A. S. (2001). WAIS-III IQs, Horn's theory, and generational changes from young adulthood to old age. *Intelligence, 29,* 131–167.

Kaufman, L. (2009, January 30). Utilities turn their customers green, with envy. *New York Times.*

Kawakami, K., Dovidio, J. F., Moll, J., Hermsen, S., & Russin, A. (2000). Just say no (to stereotyping): Effects of training in the negation of stereotypic associations on stereotype activation. *Journal of Personality and Social Psychology, 78,* 871–888.

Keefe, F. J., Abernathy, A. P., & Campbell, L. C. (2005). Psychological approaches to understanding and treating disease-related pain. *Annual Review of Psychology, 56,* 601–630.

Keefe, F. J., Lumley, M., Anderson, T., Lynch, T., & Carson, K. L. (2001). Pain and emotion: New research directions. *Journal of Clinical Psychology, 57,* 587–607.

Keisler, D. J. (1999). *Beyond the disease model of mental disorders.* New York: Praeger.

Keller, M. B., Klein, D. N., Hirschfeld, R. M., Kocsis, J. H., McCullough, J. P., Miller, I., et al. (1995). Results of the *DSM-IV* mood disorders field trial. *American Journal of Psychiatry, 152,* 843–849.

Kelley, H. H. (1967). Attribution theory in social psychology. In D. Levine (Ed.), *Nebraska Symposium on Motivation* (Vol. 15, pp. 192–238). Lincoln: University of Nebraska Press.

Kelley, H. H. (1983). Love and commitment. In H. H. Kelley, E. Berscheid, A. Christensen, & J. H. Harvey (Eds.), *Close relationships* (pp. 265–314). New York: Freeman.

Kelley, W. M., Macrae, C. N., Wyland, C. L., Caglar, S., Inati, S., & Heatherton, T. F. (2002). Finding the self? An event-related fMRI study. *Journal of Cognitive Neuroscience, 14,* 785–794.

Kellman, P. J., & Spelke, E. S. (1983). Perception of partly occluded objects in infancy. *Cognitive Psychology, 15,* 483–524.

Kelly, C., & McCreadie, R. (2000). Cigarette smoking and schizophrenia. *Advances in Psychiatric Treatment, 6,* 327–331.

Kelly, G. (1955). *The psychology of personal constructs.* New York: Norton.

Keltner, D. (1995). Signs of appeasement: Evidence for the distinct displays of embarrassment, amusement, and shame. *Journal of Personality and Social Psychology, 68,* 441–454.

Keltner, D., & Buswell, B. N. (1996). Evidence for the distinctness of embarrassment, shame, and guilt: A study of recalled antecedents and facial expressions of emotion. *Cognition and Emotion, 10,* 155–171.

Keltner, D., & Haidt, J. (1999). Social functions of emotions at four levels of analysis. *Cognition and Emotion, 13,* 505–521.

Keltner, D., & Harker, L. A. (1998). The forms and functions of the nonverbal signal of shame. In P. Gilbert & B. Andrews (Eds.), *Shame: Interpersonal behavior, psychopathology, and culture* (pp. 78–98). New York: Oxford University Press.

Keltner, D., & Shiota, M. N. (2003). New displays and new emotions: A commentary on Rozin and Cohen (2003). *Emotion, 3,* 86–91.

Kemmis, L., Hall, J. K., Kingston, R., & Morgan, M. J. (2007). Impaired fear recognition in regular recreational cocaine users. *Psychopharmacology, 194,* 151–159.

Kendler, K. S., Myers, J., & Prescott, C. A. (2002). The etiology of phobias: An evaluation of the stress-diathesis model. *Archives of General Psychiatry, 59,* 242–248.

Kendler, K. S., Neale, M., Kessler, R. C., & Heath, A. (1992). Generalized anxiety disorder in women: A population-based twin study. *Archives of General Psychiatry, 49,* 267–272.

Kendler, K. S., Walters, E. E., Neale, M. C., Kessler, R. C., Heath, A. C., & Eaves, L. J. (1995). The structure of the genetic and environmental risk factors for six major psychiatric disorders in women: Phobia, generalized anxiety disorder, panic disorder, bulimia, major depression, and alcoholism. *Archives of General Psychiatry, 52,* 374–383.

Kenrick, D. T., Sadalla, E. K., Groth, G., & Trost, M. R. (1990). Evolution, traits, and the stages of human courtship: Qualifying the parental investment model. *Journal of Personality, 58,* 97–116.

Kensinger, E. A., Clarke, R. J., & Corkin, S. (2003). What neural correlates underlie successful encoding and retrieval? A functional magnetic resonance imaging study using a divided attention paradigm. *The Journal of Neuroscience, 23,* 2407–2415.

Kensinger, E. A., & Schacter, D. L. (2005). Emotional content and reality monitoring ability: fMRI evidence for the influence of encoding processes. *Neuropsychologia, 43,* 1429–1443.

Kensinger, E. A., & Schacter, D. L. (2006). Amygdala activity is associated with the successful encoding of item, but not source, information for positive and negative stimuli. *The Journal of Neuroscience, 26,* 2564–2570.

Kephart, W. M. (1967). Some correlates of romantic love. *Journal of Marriage and the Family, 29,* 470–474.

Kershaw, T. C., & Ohlsson, S. (2004). Multiple causes of difficulty in insight: The case of the nine-dot problem. *Journal of Experimental Psychology: Learning, Memory, & Cognition, 30,* 3–13.

Kessler, R. C., Berglund, P., Demler, M. A., Jin, R., Merikangas, K. R., & Walters, E. E. (2005). Lifetime prevalence and age-of-onset distributions of *DSM-IV* disorders in the National Comorbidity Survey replication. *Archives of General Psychiatry, 62,* 593–602.

Kessler, R. C., Chiu, W. T., Jin, R., Ruscio, A. M., Shear, K., & Walters, E. E. (2006). The epidemiology of panic attacks, panic disorder, and agoraphobia in the National Comorbidity Survey Replication. *Archives of General Psychiatry, 63,* 415–424.

Kessler, R. C., McGonagle, K. A., Zhao, S., Nelson, C. B., Hughes, M., Eshleman, S., et al. (1994). Lifetime and 12-month prevalence of *DSM-III-R* psychiatric disorders in the United States: Results from the National Comorbidity Study. *Archives of General Psychiatry, 51,* 8–19.

Kessler, R. C., Nelson, C. B., McGonagle, K. A., Liu, J., Swartz, M., & Blazer, D. (1996). Comorbidity of *DSM-III-R* major depressive disorder in the general population: Results from the U.S. national comorbidity survey. *British Journal of Psychiatry, 168,* 17–30.

Kessler, R. C., Sonnega, A., Bromet, E., Hughes, M., & Nelson, C. B. (1995). Posttraumatic stress disorder in the National Comorbidity Survey. *Archives of General Psychiatry, 52,* 1048–1060.

Kessler, R. C., Soukup, J., Davis, R. B., Foster, D. F., Wilkey, S. A., Van Rompay, M. I., et al. (2001). The use of complementary and alternative therapies to treat anxiety and depression in the United States. *American Journal of Psychiatry, 158,* 289–294.

Kessler, R. C., & Wang, P. S. (2008). The descriptive epidemiology of commonly occurring mental disorders in the United States. *Annual Reviews of Public Health, 29,* 115–129.

Kety, S. S. (1990). Genetic factors in suicide: Family, twin, and adoption studies. In S. J. Blumenthal & D. J. Kupfer (Eds.), *Suicide over the life cycle: Risk factors, assessment, and treatment of suicidal patients* (pp. 127–133). Washington, DC: American Psychiatric Press.

Keuler, D. J., & Safer, M. A. (1998). Memory bias in the assessment and recall of pre-exam anxiety: How anxious was I? *Applied Cognitive Psychology, 12,* S127–S137.

Khalid, R. (1991). Personality and academic achievement: A thematic apperception perspective. *British Journal of Projective Psychology, 36,* 25–34.

Khan, A., Khan, S., Kolts, R., & Brown, W. A. (2003). Suicide rates in clinical trials of SSRIs, other antidepressants, and placebo: Analysis of FDA reports. *American Journal of Psychiatry, 160,* 790–792.

Kiecolt-Glaser, J. K., Garner, W., Speicher, C., Penn, G., & Glaser, R. (1984). Psychosocial modifiers of immunocompetence in medical students. *Psychosomatic Medicine, 46,* 7–14.

Kiefer, H. M. (2004). Americans unruffled by animal testing. Retrieved August 8, 2009, from http://www.gallup.com/poll/11767/Americans-Unruffled-Animal-Testing.aspx

Kiefer, M., Schuch, S., Schenk, W., & Fiedler, K. (2007). Mood states modulate activity in semantic brain areas during emotional word encoding. *Cerebral Cortex, 17,* 1516–1530.

Kiehl, K. A., Smith, A. M., Hare, R. D., Mendrek, A., Forster, B. B., Brink, J., et al. (2001). Limbic abnormalities in affective processing by criminal psychopaths as revealed by functional magnetic resonance imaging. *Biological Psychiatry, 50,* 677–684.

Kihlstrom, J. F. (1985). Hypnosis. *Annual Review of Psychology, 36,* 385–418.

Kihlstrom, J. F. (1987). The cognitive unconscious. *Science, 237,* 1445–1452.

Kihlstrom, J. F. (2005). Dissociative disorders. *Annual Review of Clinical Psychology, 1,* 227–253.

Kihlstrom, J. F., Beer, J. S., & Klein, S. B. (2002). Self and identity as memory. In M. R. Leary & J. P. Tangney (Eds.), *Handbook of self and identity* (pp. 68–90). New York: Guilford Press.

Kim, G., Walden, T. A., & Knieps, L. J. (2010). Impact and characteristics of positive and fearful emotional messages during infant social referencing. *Infant Behavior and Development, 33,* 189–195.

Kim, K., & Smith, P. K. (1998). Childhood stress, behavioural symptoms and mother-daughter pubertal development. *Journal of Adolescence, 21,* 231–240.

Kim, U. K., Jorgenson, E., Coon, H., Leppert, M., Risch, N., & Drayna, D. (2003). Positional cloning of the human quantaitive trait locus underlying taste sensitivity to phenylthiocarbamide. *Science, 299,* 1221–1225.

King, C. A. (1997). Suicidal behavior in adolescence. In R. W. Maris, M. M. Silverman, & S. S. Canetton (Eds.), *Review of suicidology, 1997* (pp. 61–95). New York: Guilford Press.

Kinney, D. A. (1993). From nerds to normals—the recovery of identity among adolescents from middle school to high school. *Sociology of Education, 66,* 21–40.

Kinnish, K., Strassberg, D., & Turner, C. (2005). Sex differences in the flexibility of sexual orientation: A multidimensional retrospective assessment. *Archives of Sexual Behavior, 34*(2), 173–183.

Kirchner, W. H., & Towne, W. F. (1994). The sensory basis of the honeybee's dance language. *Scientific American, 270*(6), 74–80.

Kirsch, I., & Sapirstein, G. (1998). Listening to Prozac but hearing placebo: A meta-analysis of antidepressant medication. *Prevention and Treatment, 1,* Article 0002. Retrieved May 18, 2007, from www.journals.apa.org/pt/prevention/volume1/pre0010002a.html

Kirwan, C. B., Bayley, P. J., Galvan, V. V., & Squire, L. R. (2008). Detailed recollection of remote autobiographical memory after damage to the medial temporal lobe. *Proceedings of the National Academy of Sciences, USA, 105,* 2676–2680.

Klein, S. B. (2004). The cognitive neuroscience of knowing one's self. In M. Gazzaniga (Ed.), *The cognitive neurosciences* (3rd ed.). Cambridge, MA: The MIT Press.

Kleinman, A. M. (1986). *Social origins of distress and disease: Depression, neurasthenia and pain in modern China.* New Haven, CT: Yale University Press.

Kleinman, A. M. (1988). *Rethinking psychiatry: From cultural category to personal experience.* New York: Free Press.

Kleinschmidt, A., & Cohen, L. (2006). The neural bases of prosopagnosia and pure alexia: Recent insights from functional neuroimaging. *Current Opinion in Neurology, 19,* 386–391.

Klinger, E. (1975). Consequences of commitment to and disengagement from incentives. *Psychological Review, 82,* 1–25.

Klinger, E. (1977). *Meaning and void.* Minneapolis: University of Minnesota Press.

Kluft, R. P. (1991). Multiple personality disorder. In A. Tasman & S. M. Goldfinger (Eds.), *American Psychiatric Press review of psychiatry* (Vol. 10, pp. 161–188). Washington, DC: American Psychiatric Press.

Klüver, H. (1951). Functional differences between the occipital and temporal lobes with special reference to the interrelations of behavior and extracerebral mechanisms. In L. A. Jeffress (Ed.), *Cerebral mechanisms in behavior* (pp. 147–199). New York: Wiley.

Klüver, H., & Bucy, P. C. (1937). "Psychic blindness" and other symptoms following bilateral temporary lobectomy in rhesus monkeys. *American Journal of Physiology, 119,* 352–353.

Klüver, H., & Bucy, P. C. (1939). Preliminary analysis of functions of the temporal lobes in monkeys. *Archives of Neurology and Psychiatry, 42,* 979–1000.

Knowlton, B. J., Ramus, S. J., & Squire, L. R. (1992). Intact artificial grammar learning in amnesia: Dissociation of classification learning and explicit memory for specific instances. *Psychological Science, 3,* 173–179.

Knutson, B., Adams, C. M., Fong, G. W., & Hommer, D. (2001). Anticipation of increasing monetary reward selectively recruits nucleus accumbens. *The Journal of Neuroscience, 21,* 159.

Knutson, B., Wolkowitz, O. M., Cole, S. W., Chan, T., Moore, E. A., Johnson, R. C., et al. (1998). Selective alteration of personality and social behavior by serotonergic intervention. *American Journal of Psychiatry, 155,* 373–379.

Kobasa, S. (1979). Stressful life events, personality, and health: An inquiry into hardiness. *Journal of Personality and Social Psychology, 37,* 1–11.

Koenigs, M., Huey, E. D., Calamia, M., Raymont, V., Tranel, D., & Grafman, J. (2008). Distinct regions of prefrontal cortex mediate resistance and vulnerability to depression. *Journal of Neuroscience, 28,* 12341–12348.

Koenigs, M., Young, L., Adolphs, R., Tranel, D., Cushman, F., Hauser, M., et al. (2007). Damage to the prefrontal cortex increases utilitarian moral judgements. *Nature, 446,* 908–911.

Koffka, K. (1935). *Principles of Gestalt psychology.* New York: Harcourt, Brace and World.

Kohlberg, L. (1963). Development of children's orientation towards a moral order (Part I). Sequencing in the development of moral thought. *Vita Humana, 6,* 11–36.

Kohlberg, L. (1986). A current statement on some theoretical issues. In S. Modgil & C. Modgil (Eds.), *Lawrence Kohlberg*. Philadelphia: Falmer.

Kohler, P. K., Manhart, L. E., & Lafferty, E. (2008). Abstinence-only and comprehensive sex education and the initiation of sexual activity and teen pregnancy. *Journal of Adolescent Health, 42,* 344–351.

Kolb, B., & Whishaw, I. Q. (2003). *Fundamentals of human neuropsychology* (5th ed.). New York: Worth Publishers.

Kolbert, E. (2009, July 20). XXXL. *The New Yorker,* pp. 73–77.

Kolotkin, R. L., Meter, K., & Williams, G. R. (2001). Quality of life and obesity. *Obesity Reviews, 2,* 219–229.

Komiya, N., Good, G. E., & Sherrod, N. B. (2000). Emotional openness as a predictor of college students' attitudes toward seeking psychological help. *Journal of Counseling Psychology, 47,* 138–143.

Komter, A. (2010). The evolutionary origins of human generosity. *International Sociology, 25*(3), 443–464.

Konen, C. S., & Kastner, S. (2008). Two hierarchically organized neural systems for object information in human visual cortex. *Nature Neuroscience, 11,* 224–231.

Koole, S. L., Dijksterhuis, A., & van Knippenberg, A. (2001). What's in a name: Implicit self-esteem and the automatic self. *Journal of Personality and Social Psychology, 80,* 669–685.

Koss, M. P. (1990). The women's mental health research agenda: Violence against women. *American Psychologist, 45,* 374–380.

Kosslyn, S. M., Alpert, N. M., Thompson, W. L., Chabris, C. F., Rauch, S. L., & Anderson, A. K. (1993). Visual mental imagery activates topographically organized visual cortex: PET investigations. *Journal of Cognitive Neuroscience, 5,* 263–287.

Kosslyn, S. M., Pascual-Leone, A., Felician, O., Camposano, S., Keenan, J. P., Thompson, W. L., et al. (1999). The role of area 17 in visual imagery: Convergent evidence from PET and rTMS. *Science, 284,* 167–170.

Kounios, J., & Beeman, M. (2009). The Aha! moment. *Current Directions in Psychological Science, 18,* 210–216.

Kounios, J., Fleck, J. L., Green, D. L., Payne, L., Stevenson, J. L., Bowden, E. M., & Jung-Beeman, M. (2008). The origins of insight in resting-state brain activity. *Neuropsychologia, 46,* 281–291.

Kounios, J., Frymiare, J. L., Bowden, E. M., Fleck, J. I., Subramaniam, K., Parrish, T. B., & Jung-Beeman, M. (2006). The prepared mind: Neural activity prior to problem presentation predicts subsequent solution by sudden insight. *Psychological Science, 17,* 882–890.

Kraepelin, E. (1899). *Psychiatrie.* Leipzig, Germany: Barth.

Kramer, M. S., Aboud, F., Mironova, E., Vanilovich, I., Platt, R. W., Matush, L., et al. (2008). Breastfeeding and child cognitive development: New evidence from a large randomized trial. *Archives of General Psychiatry, 65,* 578–584.

Kramer, P. D. (1993). *Listening to Prozac.* New York: Viking.

Krantz, D. S., & McCeney, M. K. (2002). Effects of psychological and social factors on organic disease: A critical assessment of research on coronary heart disease. *Annual Review of Psychology, 53,* 341–369.

Krebs, J. R., & Davies, N. B. (1991). *Behavioural ecology: An evolutionary approach* (3rd ed.). Sutherland, MA: Sinauer Associates.

Kreider, R. M., & Fields, J. M. (2002). *Number, timing, and duration of marriages and divorces: 1996.* Washington, DC: U.S. Census Bureau, Current Population Reports.

Kringelbach, M. L., O'Doherty, J., Rolls, E. T., & Andrews, C. (2003). Activation of the human orbitofrontal cortex to a liquid food stimulus is correlated with its subjective pleasantness. *Cerebral Cortex, 13,* 1064–1071.

Krings, T., Topper, R., Foltys, H., Erberich, S., Sparing, R., Willmes, K., et al. (2000). Cortical activation patterns during complex motor tasks in piano players and control subjects. A functional magnetic resonance imaging study. *Neuroscience Letters, 278,* 189–193.

Kristensen, P., & Bjerkedal, T. (2007). Explaining the relation between birth order and intelligence. *Science, 316,* 1717.

Kroenke, K. (2007). Efficacy of treatment for somatoform disorders: A review of randomized controlled trials. *Psychosomatic Medicine, 69,* 881–888.

Kroeze, W. K., & Roth, B. L. (1998). The molecular biology of serotonin receptors: Therapeutic implications for the interface of mood and psychosis. *Biological Psychiatry, 44,* 1128–1142.

Kruk, M. R., Halasz, J., Meelis, W., & Haller, J. (2004). Fast positive feedback between the adrenocortical stress response and a brain mechanism involved in aggressive behavior. *Behavioral Neuroscience, 118,* 1062–1070.

Kubovy, M. (1981). Concurrent-pitch segregation and the theory of indispensable attributes. In M. Kubovy & J. R. Pomerantz (Eds.), *Perceptual organization* (pp. 55–96). Hillsdale, NJ: Lawrence Erlbaum.

Kuffler, S. W. (1953). Discharge patterns and function organization of mammalian retina. *Journal of Neurophysiology, 16,* 37–68.

Kuhl, B. A., Dudukovic, N. M., Kahn, I., & Wagner, A. D. (2007). Decreased demands on cognitive control reveal the neural processing benefits of forgetting. *Nature Neuroscience, 10,* 908–917.

Kuhl, P., & Rivera-Gaxiola, M. (2008). Neural substrates of language acquisition. *Annual Review of Neuroscience, 31,* 511–534.

Kunda, Z., & Oleson, K. C. (1997). When exceptions prove the rule: How extremity of deviance determines the impact of deviant examples on stereotypes. *Journal of Personality and Social Psychology, 72,* 965–979.

Kunugi, H., Urushibara, T., Murray, R. M., Nanko, S., & Hirose, T. (2003). Prenatal underdevelopment and schizophrenia: A case report of monozygotic twins. *Psychiatry and Clinical Neurosciences, 57,* 271–274.

Kunz, P. R., & Woolcott, M. (1976). Season's greetings: From my status to yours. *Social Science Research, 5,* 269–278.

Kurtzman, T. L., Otsuka, K. N., & Wahl, R. A. (2001). Inhalant abuse by adolescents. *Journal of Adolescent Health, 28,* 170–180.

Kutchins, H., & Kirk, S. A. (1997). *Making us crazy:* DSM: *The psychiatric bible and the creation of mental disorders.* New York: Free Press.

Kvavilashvil, L., Mirani, J., Schlagman, S., Foley, K., & Kornbrot, D. E. (2009). Consistency of flashbulb memories of September 11 over long delays: Implications for consolidation and wrong time slice hypotheses. *Journal of Memory and Language, 61,* 556–572.

Kwan, V. S. Y., John, O. P., Robins, R. W., & Kuang, L. L. (2008). Conceptualizing and assessing self-enhancement bias: A componential approach. *Journal of Personality and Social Psychology, 94*(6), 1062–1077.

LaBar, K. S., & Phelps, E. A. (1998). Arousal-mediated memory consolidation: Role of the medial temporal lobe in humans. *Psychological Science, 9,* 490–493.

Lachman, R., Lachman, J. L., & Butterfield, E. C. (1979). *Cognitive psychology and information processing: An introduction.* Hillsdale, NJ: Lawrence Erlbaum.

Lackner, J. R., & DiZio, P. (2005). Vestibular, proprioceptive, and haptic contributions to spatial orientation. *Annual Review of Psychology, 56,* 115–147.

LaFraniere, S. (2007, July 4). In Mauritania, seeking to end an overfed ideal. *New York Times.*

Lai, Y., & Siegal, J. (1999). Muscle atonia in REM sleep. In B. Mallick & S. Inoue (Eds.), *Rapid eye movement sleep* (pp. 69–90). New Delhi, India: Narosa Publishing House.

Lake, J. (2009). Natural products used to treat depressed mood as monotherapies and adjuvants to antidepressants: A review of the evidence. *Psychiatric Times, 26,* 1–6.

Lalonde, J. K., Hudson, J. I., Gigante, R. A., & Pope, H. G., Jr. (2001). Canadian and American psychiatrists' attitudes toward dissociative disorders diagnoses. *Canadian Journal of Psychiatry, 46,* 407–412.

Lamb, M. E., Sternberg, K. J., & Prodromidis, M. (1992). Nonmaternal care and the security of infant/mother attachment: A reanalysis of the data. *Infant Behavior & Development, 15,* 71–83.

Lamb, M. E., Thompson, R. A., Gardner, W., & Charnov, E. L. (1985). *Infant-mother attachment: The origins and developmental significance of individual differences in strange situation behavior.* Hillsdale, NJ: Lawrence Erlbaum.

Landauer, T. K., & Bjork, R. A. (1978). Optimum rehearsal patterns and name learning. In M. M. Gruneberg, P. E. Morris, & R. N. Sykes (Eds.), *Practical aspects of memory* (pp. 625–632). New York: Academic Press.

Lang, F. R., & Carstensen, L. L. (1994). Close emotional relationships in late life: Further support for proactive aging in the social domain. *Psychology and Aging, 9,* 315–324.

Langer, E. J., & Abelson, R. P. (1974). A patient by any other name.... Clinician group difference in labeling bias. *Journal of Consulting and Clinical Psychology, 42,* 4–9.

Langleben, D. D., Loughead, J. W., Bilker, W. B., Ruparel, K., Childress, A. R., Busch, S. I., et al. (2005). Telling truth from lie in individual subjects with fast event-related fMRI. *Human Brain Mapping, 26,* 262–272.

Langlois, J. H., Kalakanis, L., Rubenstein, A. J., Larson, A., Hallam, M., & Smoot, M. (2000). Maxims or myths of beauty? A meta-analytic and theoretical review. *Psychological Bulletin, 126,* 390–423.

Langlois, J. H., Ritter, J. M., Casey, R. J., & Sawin, D. B. (1995). Infant attractiveness predicts maternal behaviors and attitudes. *Developmental Psychology, 31,* 464–472.

Langlois, J. H., & Roggman, L. A. (1990). Attractive faces are only average. *Psychological Science, 1,* 115–121.

Langlois, J. H., Roggman, L. A., & Musselman, L. (1994). What is average and what is not average about attractive faces? *Psychological Science, 5,* 214–220.

Langlois, J. H., Roggman, L. A., & Rieser-Danner, L. A. (1990). Infants' differential social responses to attractive and unattractive faces. *Developmental Psychology, 26,* 153–159.

Langston, J. W. (1995). *The case of the frozen addicts.* New York: Pantheon.

Lareau, A. (2003). *Unequal childhoods: Class, race, and family life.* Berkeley: University of California Press.

Larsen, S. F. (1992). Potential flashbulbs: Memories of ordinary news as baseline. In E. Winograd & U. Neisser (Eds.), *Affect and accuracy in recall: Studies of "flashbulb memories"* (pp. 32–64). New York: Cambridge University Press.

Larson, R., & Richards, M. H. (1991). Daily companionship in late childhood and early adolescence—changing developmental contexts. *Child Development, 62,* 284–300.

Lashley, K. S. (1960). In search of the engram. In F. A. Beach, D. O. Hebb, C. T. Morgan, & H. W. Nissen (Eds.), *The neuropsychology of Lashley.* New York: McGraw-Hill.

Laupa, M., & Turiel, E. (1986). Children's conceptions of adult and peer authority. *Child Development, 57,* 405–412.

Laurence, J., & Perry, C. (1983). Hypnotically created memory among high hypnotizable subjects. *Science, 222,* 523–524.

Laureys, S., Giacino, J. T., Schiff, N. D., Schabus, M., & Owen, A. M. (2006). How should functional imaging of patients with disorders of consciousness contribute to their clinical rehabilitation needs? *Current Opinion in Neurology, 19,* 520–527.

Lavie, P. (2001). Sleep-wake as a biological rhythm. *Annual Review of Psychology, 52,* 277–303.

Lavori, P. W., Klerman, G. L., Keller, M. B., Reich, T., Rice, J., & Endicott, J. (1987). Age-period-cohort analysis of secular trends in onset of major depression: Findings in siblings of patients with major affective disorder. *Journal of Psychiatric Researchers, 21,* 23–25.

Lawrence, N. S., Jollant, F., O'Daly, O., Zelaya, F., & Phillips, M. L. (2009). Distinct roles of prefrontal cortical subregions in the Iowa Gambling Task. *Cerebral Cortex, 19,* 1134–1143.

Lawton, M. P., Kleban, M. H., Rajagopal, D., & Dean, J. (1992). The dimensions of affective experience in three age groups. *Psychology and Aging, 7,* 171–184.

Lazarus, R. S. (1984). On the primacy of cognition. *American Psychologist, 39,* 124–129.

Lazarus, R. S., & Alfert, E. (1964). Short-circuiting of threat by experimentally altering cognitive appraisal. *Journal of Abnormal and Social Psychology, 69,* 195–205.

Lazarus, R. S., & Folkman, S. (1984). *Stress, appraisal, and coping.* New York: Springer.

Leader, T., Mullen, B., & Abrams, D. (2007). Without mercy: The immediate impact of group size on lynch mob atrocity. *Personality and Social Psychology Bulletin, 33*(10), 1340–1352.

Leary, M. R. (1990). Responses to social exclusion: Social anxiety, jealousy, loneliness, depression, and low self-esteem. *Journal of Social and Clinical Psychology, 9,* 221–229.

Leary, M. R. (2010). Affiliation, acceptance, and belonging: The pursuit of interpersonal connection. In S. T. Fiske, D. T. Gilbert, & G. Lindzey (Eds.), *The handbook of social psychology* (5th ed., Vol. 2). New York: Wiley.

Leary, M. R., & Baumeister, R. F. (2000). The nature and function of self-esteem: Sociometer theory. In M. P. Zanna (Ed.), *Advances in experimental social psychology* (Vol. 32, pp. 1–62). San Diego: Academic Press.

Leary, M. R., Britt, T. W., Cutlip, W. D., & Templeton, J. L. (1992). Social blushing. *Psychological Bulletin, 112,* 446–460.

Leary, M. R., Cox, C. B., Shah, J. Y., & Gardner, W. L. (2008). Belongingness motivation: A mainspring of social action. In *Handbook of motivation science* (pp. 27–40). New York: Guilford Press.

Lecky, P. (1945). *Self-consistency: A theory of personality.* New York: Island Press.

Lecrubier, Y., Clerc, G., Didi, R., & Kieser, M. (2002). Efficacy of St. John's wort extract WS 5570 in major depression: A double-blind, placebo-controlled trial. *American Journal of Psychiatry, 159,* 1361–1366.

Lederman, S. J., & Klatzky, R. L. (2009). Haptic perception: A tutorial. *Attention, Perception, & Psychophysics, 71,* 1439–1459.

LeDoux, J. E. (1992). Brain mechanisms of emotion and emotional learning. *Current Opinion in Neurobiology, 2,* 191–197.

LeDoux, J. E. (2000). Emotion circuits in the brain. *Annual Review of Neuroscience, 23,* 155–184.

LeDoux, J. E. (2002). *The synaptic self: How our brains become who we are.* New York: Viking.

LeDoux, J. E., Iwata, J., Cicchetti, P., & Reis, D. J. (1988). Different projections of the central amygdaloid nucleus mediate autonomic and behavioral correlates of conditioned fear. *Journal of Neuroscience, 8,* 2517–2529.

Lee, D. N., & Aronson, E. (1974). Visual proprioceptive control of standing in human infants. *Perception & Psychophysics, 15,* 529–532.

Lee, I., Hunsaker, M. R., & Kesner, R. P. (2005). The role of hippocampal subregions in detecting spatial novelty. *Behavioral Neuroscience, 119,* 145–153.

Lee, L., Loewenstein, G., Ariely, D., Hong, J., & Young, J. (2008). If I'm not hot, are you hot or not? Physical-attractiveness evaluations and dating preferences as a function of one's own attractiveness. *Psychological Science, 19*, 669–677.

Lefcourt, H. M. (1982). *Locus of control: Current trends in theory and research* (2nd ed.). Hillsdale, NJ: Lawrence Erlbaum.

Lefkowitz, E. S., & Zeldow, P. B. (2006). Masculinity and femininity predict optimal mental health: A belated test of the androgyny hypothesis. *Journal of Personality Assessment, 87*, 95–101.

Lehrer, J. (2007). *Proust was a neuroscientist.* New York: Houghton Mifflin Harcourt.

Lempert, D. (2007). *Women's increasing wage penalties from being overweight and obese:* Washington, DC: U.S. Bureau of Labor Statistics.

Lenoir, M., Serre, F., Chantin, L., & Ahmed, S. H. (2007). Intense sweetness surpasses cocaine reward. *PLoS ONE, 2*, e698.

Lentz, M. J., Landis, C. A., Rothermel, J., & Shaver, J. L. (1999). Effects of selective slow wave sleep disruption on musculoskeletal pain and fatigue in middle aged women. *Journal of Rheumatology, 26*, 1586–1592.

Leon, D. A., Lawlor, D. A., Clark, H., Batty, G. D., & Macintyre, S. (2009). The association of childhood intelligence with mortality risk from adolescence to middle age: Findings from the Aberdeen children of the 1950s cohort study. *Intelligence, 37*(6), 520–528.

Lepage, M., Ghaffar, O., Nyberg, L., & Tulving, E. (2000). Prefrontal cortex and episodic memory retrieval mode. *Proceedings of the National Academy of Sciences, USA, 97*, 506–511.

Lepper, M. R., & Greene, D. (1976). *The hidden costs of reward.* Hillsdale, NJ: Lawrence Erlbaum.

Lepper, M. R., Greene, D., & Nisbett, R. E. (1973). Undermining children's intrinsic interest with extrinsic rewards: A test of the "overjustification" hypothesis. *Journal of Personality and Social Psychology, 28*, 129–137.

Lerman, D. (2006). Consumer politeness and complaining behavior. *Journal of Services Marketing, 20*, 92–100.

Levenson, R. W., Cartensen, L. L., Friesen, W. V., & Ekman, P. (1991). Emotion physiology, and expression in old age. *Psychology and Aging, 6*, 28–35.

Levenson, R. W., Ekman, P., & Friesen, W. V. (1990). Voluntary facial action generates emotion-specific autonomic nervous system activity. *Psychophysiology, 27*, 363–384.

Levenson, R. W., Ekman, P., Heider, K., & Friesen, W. V. (1992). Emotion and automatic nervous system activity in the Minangkabau of West Sumatra. *Journal of Personality and Social Psychology, 62*, 972–988.

Levin, D. T., & Simons, D. J. (1997). Failure to detect changes to attended objects in motion pictures. *Psychonomic Bulletin & Review, 4*, 501–506.

Levin, R., & Nielsen, T. (2009). Nightmares, bad dreams, and emotion dysregulation: A review and new neurocognitive model of dreaming. *Current Directions in Psychological Science, 18*, 84–88.

Levine, M. (1981). *History and politics of community mental health.* New York: Oxford University Press.

Levine, R. V., Norenzayan, A., & Philbrick, K. (2001). Cross-cultural differences in helping strangers. *Journal of Cross-Cultural Psychology, 32*, 543–560.

Levy, J., Trevarthen, C., & Sperry, R. W. (1972). Perception of bilateral chimeric figures following hemispheric disconnection. *Brain, 95*, 61–78.

Lewin, K. (1936). *Principles of topological psychology.* New York: McGraw-Hill.

Lewin, K. (1951). Behavior and development as a function of the total situation. In K. Lewin, *Field theory in social science: Selected theoretical papers* (pp. 791–843). New York: Harper & Row.

Lewis, M., & Brooks-Gunn, J. (1979). *Social cognition and the acquisition of self.* New York: Plenum Press.

Lewontin, R., Rose, S., & Kamin, L. J. (1984). *Not in our genes.* New York: Pantheon.

Li, F., & Tsien, J. Z. (2009). Memory and the NMDA receptors. *New England Journal of Medicine, 361*, 302–303.

Li, W., Lexenberg, E., Parrish, T., & Gottfried, J. A. (2006). Learning to smell the roses: Experience-dependent neural plasticity in human piriform and orbitofrontal cortices. *Neuron, 52*, 1097–1108.

Li, W., & Zinbarg, R. E. (2007). Anxiety sensitivity and panic attacks. *Behavior Modification, 31*, 145–161.

Libet, B. (1985). Unconscious cerebral initiative and the role of conscious will in voluntary action. *Behavioral and Brain Sciences, 8*, 529–566.

Liebenluft, E. (1996). Women with bipolar illness: Clinical and research issues. *American Journal of Psychiatry, 153*, 163–173.

Lieberman, M. D., & Rosenthal, R. (2001). Why introverts can't always tell who likes them: Multitasking and nonverbal decoding. *Journal of Personality and Social Psychology, 80*, 294–310.

Liebowitz, M. R., Gorman, J. M., Fyer, A. J., Levitt, M., Dillon, D., Levy, G., et al. (1985). Lactate provocation of panic attacks: II. Biochemical and physiological findings. *Archives of General Psychiatry, 42*, 709–719.

Lilienfeld, S. O., Lynn, S. J., & Lohr, J. M. (Eds.). (2003). *Science and pseudoscience in clinical psychology.* New York: Guilford Press.

Lilienfeld, S. O., Wood, J. M., & Garb, H. N. (2000). The scientific status of projective techniques. *Psychological Science in the Public Interest, 1*, 27–66.

Lillard, L. A., & Waite, L. J. (1995). 'Til death do us part: Marital disruption and mortality. *American Journal of Sociology, 100*, 1131–1156.

Lindenberger, U., & Baltes, P. B. (1997). Intellectual functioning in old and very old age: Cross-sectional results from the Berling aging study. *Psychology and Aging, 12*, 410–432.

Lindquist, K., & Barrett, L. F. (2008). Constructing emotion: The experience of fear as a conceptual act. *Psychological Science, 19*, 898–903.

Lindstrom, M. (2005). *Brand sense: How to build powerful brands through touch, taste, smell, sight and sound.* London: Kogan Page.

Linszen, D. H., Dingemans, P. M., Nugter, M. A., Van der Does, A. J., Scholte, W. F., & Lenoir, M. A. (1997). Patient attributes and expressed emotion as risk factors for psychotic relapse. *Schizophrenia Bulletin, 23*, 119–130.

Little, B. R. (1983). Personal projects: A rationale and method for investigation. *Environment and Behavior, 15*, 273–309.

Little, B. R. (1993). Personal projects and the distributed self: Aspects of a conative psychology. In J. R. Suls (Ed.), *Psychological perspectives on the self* (Vol. 4, pp. 157–185). Hillsdale, NJ: Lawrence Erlbaum.

Liu, D., Wellman, H. M., Tardif, T., & Sabbagh, M. A. (2008). Theory of mind development in Chinese children: A meta-analysis of false-belief understanding across cultures and languages. *Developmental Psychology 44*, 523–531.

Livingstone, M., & Hubel, D. (1988). Segregation of form, color, movement, and depth: Anatomy, physiology, and perception. *Science, 240*, 740–749.

Locksley, A., Ortiz, V., & Hepburn, C. (1980). Social categorization and discriminatory behavior: Extinguishing the minimal intergroup discrimination effect. *Journal of Personality and Social Psychology, 39*, 773–783.

Loehlin, J. C. (1973). Blood group genes and Negro-White ability differences. *Behavior Genetics, 3*(3), 263–270.

Loehlin, J. C. (1992). *Genes and environment in personality development.* Newbury Park, CA: Sage.

Loewenstein, R. J. (2007). Dissociative identity disorder: Issues in the iatrogenisis controversy. In E. Vermetten, M. J. Dorahy, & D. Speigel

(Eds.), *Traumatic dissociation: Neurobiology and treatment* (pp. 275–300). Arlington, VA: American Psychiatric Association.

Loftus, E. F. (1975). Leading questions and eyewitness report. *Cognitive Psychology, 7,* 560–572.

Loftus, E. F. (1993). The reality of repressed memories. *American Psychologist, 48,* 518–537.

Loftus, E. F. (2003). Make-believe memories. *American Psychologist, 58,* 867–873.

Loftus, E. F., & Davis, D. (2006). Recovered memories. *Annual Review of Clinical Psychology, 2,* 469–498.

Loftus, E. F., & Ketchum, K. (1994). *The myth of repressed memory.* New York: St. Martin's Press.

Loftus, E. F., & Klinger, M. R. (1992). Is the unconscious smart or dumb? *American Psychologist, 17,* 761–765.

Loftus, E. F., Miller, D. G., & Burns, H. J. (1978). Semantic integration of verbal information into a visual memory. *Journal of Experimental Psychology: Human Learning and Memory, 4,* 19–31.

Loftus, E. F., & Pickrell, J. E. (1995). The formation of false memories. *Psychiatric Annals, 25,* 720–725.

Lopes, P. N., Grewal, D., Kadis, J., Gall, M., & Salovey, P. (2006). Emotional intelligence and positive work outcomes. *Psichothema, 18,* 132.

Lorenz, K. (1952). *King Solomon's ring.* New York: Crowell.

Lozano, B. E., & Johnson, S. L. (2001). Can personality traits predict increases in manic and depressive symptoms? *Journal of Affective Disorders, 63,* 103–111.

Lubinski, D., Webb, R. M., Morelock, M. J., & Benbow, C. P. (2001). Top 1 in 10,000: A 10-year follow-up of the profoundly gifted. *Journal of Applied Psychology, 86,* 718–729.

Luborsky, L., Rosenthal, R., Diguer, L., Andrusyna, T. P., Berman, J. S., Levitt, J. T., et al. (2002). The dodo bird verdict is alive and well—mostly. *Clinical Psychology: Science and Practice, 9,* 2–12.

Luborsky, L., & Singer, B. (1975). Comparative studies of psychotherapies: Is it true that "everyone has won and all must have prizes"? *Archives of General Psychiatry, 32*(8), 995–1008.

Lucas, R. E., Clark, A. E., Georgellis, Y., & Diener, E. (2003). Reexamining adaptation and the set point model of happiness: Reactions to changes in marital status. *Journal of Personality and Social Psychology, 84,* 527–539.

Luders, E., Narr, K. L., Thompson, P. M., & Toga, A. W. (2009). Neuroanatomical correlates of intelligence. *Intelligence, 37*(2), 156–163.

Ludwig, A. M. (1966). Altered states of consciousness. *Archives of General Psychiatry, 15,* 225–234.

Lustman, P. J., Caudle, M. L., & Clouse, R. E. (2002). Case study: Nondysphoric depression in a man with type 2 diabetes. *Clinical Diabetes, 20,* 122–123.

Lykken, D. T. (1995). *The antisocial personalities.* Hillsdale, NJ: Lawrence Erlbaum.

Lykken, D. T., & Tellegen, A. (1996). Happiness is a stochastic phenomenon. *Psychological Science, 7,* 186–189.

Lynn, M., & Shurgot, B. A. (1984). Responses to lonely hearts advertisements: Effects of reported physical attractiveness, physique, and coloration. *Personality and Social Psychology Bulletin, 10,* 349–357.

Lynn, R. (2009). What has caused the Flynn effect? Secular increases in the development quotients of infants. *Intelligence, 37*(1), 16–24.

Lynn, R., Harvey, J., & Nyborg, H. (2009). Average intelligence predicts atheism rates across 137 nations. *Intelligence, 37*(1), 11–15.

Lynn, R., & Vanhanen, T. (2002). *IQ and the wealth of nations.* Westport, CT: Praeger/Greenwood.

Lynn, S. J., Rhue, J. W., & Weekes, J. R. (1990). Hypnotic involuntariness: A social cognitive analysis. *Psychological Review, 97,* 169–184.

Lyubomirsky, S. (2008). *The how of happiness: A scientific approach to getting the life you want.* New York: Penguin.

Lyubomirsky, S., & Lepper, H. S. (1999). A measure of subjective happiness: Preliminary reliability and construct validation. *Social Indicators Research, 46,* 137–155.

MacDonald, S., Uesiliana, K., & Hayne, H. (2000). Cross-cultural and gender differences in childhood amnesia. *Memory, 8,* 365–376.

MacGregor, J. N., Ormerod, T. C., & Chronicle, E. P. (2001). Information processing and insight: A process model of performance on the nine-dot and related problems. *Journal of Experimental Psychology: Learning, Memory, & Cognition, 27,* 176–201.

Mack, A. H., Franklin, J. E., Jr., & Frances, R. J. (2003). Substance use disorders. In R. E. Hales & S. C. Yudofsky (Eds.), *The American Psychiatric Publishing textbook of clinical psychiatry* (4th ed., pp. 309–377). Washington, DC: American Psychiatric Publishing.

Maclean, P. D. (1970). The triune brain, emotion, and scientific bias. In F. O. Schmitt (Ed.), *The neurosciences: A second study program* (pp. 336–349). New York: Rockefeller University Press.

MacLeod, M. D. (2002). Retrieval-induced forgetting in eyewitness memory: Forgetting as a consequence of remembering. *Applied Cognitive Psychology, 16,* 135–149.

MacLeod, M. D., & Saunders, J. (2008). Retrieval inhibition and memory distortion: Negative consequences of an adaptive process. *Current Directions in Psychological Science, 17,* 26–30.

Macmillan, M. (2000). *An odd kind of fame: Stories of Phineas Gage.* Cambridge, MA: The MIT Press.

Macmillan, N. A., & Creelman, C. D. (2005). *Detection theory.* Mahwah, NJ: Lawrence Erlbaum.

Macrae, C. N., Bodenhausen, G. V., Milne, A. B., & Jetten, J. (1994). Out of mind but back in sight: Stereotypes on the rebound. *Journal of Personality and Social Psychology, 67,* 808–817.

Macrae, C. N., Moran, J. M., Heatherton, T. F., Banfield, J. F., & Kelley, W. M. (2004). Medial prefrontal activity predicts memory for self. *Cerebral Cortex, 14,* 647–654.

Madden, D. J., Turkington, T. G., Provenzale, J. M., Denny, L. L., Hawk, T. C., Gottlob, L. R., & Coleman, R. E. (1999). Adult age differences in functional neuroanatomy of verbal recognition memory. *Human Brain Mapping, 7,* 115–135.

Maddi, S. R., Harvey, R. H., Khoshaba, D. M., Fazel, M., & Resurreccion, N. (2009). Hardiness training facilitates performance in college. *The Journal of Positive Psychology, 4,* 566–577.

Maddi, S. R., Kahn, S., & Maddi, K. L. (1998). The effectiveness of hardiness training. *Consulting Psychology Journal: Practice and Research, 50,* 78–86.

Maddux, W. W., Mullen, E., & Galinsky, A. D. (2008). Chameleons bake bigger pies and take bigger pieces: Strategic behavioral mimicry facilitates negotiation outcomes. *Journal of Experimental Social Psychology, 44,* 461–468.

Maes, M. (1995). Evidence for an immune response in major depression: A review and hypothesis. *Progress in Neuro-Psychopharmacology and Biological Psychiatry, 19,* 11–38.

Magee, W. J., Eaton, W. W., Wittchen, H.-U., McGonagle, K. A., & Kessler, R. C. (1996). Agoraphobia, simple phobia, and social phobia in the National Comorbidity Survey. *Archives of General Psychiatry, 53,* 159–168.

Maguire, E. A., Woollett, K., & Spiers, H. J. (2006). London taxi drivers and bus drivers: A structural MRI and neuropsychological analysis. *Hippocampus, 16,* 1091–1101.

Mah, K., & Binik, Y. M. (2002). Do all orgasms feel alike? Evaluating a two-dimensional model of the orgasm experience across gender and sexual context. *Journal of Sex Research, 39,* 104–113.

Mahon, B. Z., Anzellotti, S., Schwarzbach, J., Zampini, M., & Caramazza, A. (2009). Category-specific organization in the human brain does not require visual experience. *Neuron, 63,* 397–405.

Mahowald, M., & Schenck, C. (2000). REM sleep parasomnias. In M. Kryger, T. Roth, & W. Dement (Eds.), *Principles and practices of sleep medicine* (3rd ed., pp. 724–741). Philadelphia, PA: Saunders.

Maier, S. F., & Watkins, L. R. (1998). Cytokines for psychologists: Implications of bidirectional immune-to-brain communication for understanding behavior, mood, and cognition. *Psychological Review, 105,* 83–107.

Maier, S. F., & Watkins, L. R. (2000). The immune system as a sensory system: Implications for psychology. *Current Directions in Psychological Science, 9,* 98–102.

Makin, J. E., Fried, P. A., & Watkinson, B. (1991). A comparison of active and passive smoking during pregnancy: Long-term effects. *Neurotoxicology and Teratology, 16,* 5–12.

Makris, N., Gasic, G. P., Seidman, L. J., Goldstein, J. M., Gastfriend, D. R., et al. (2004). Decreased absolute amygdala volume in cocaine addicts. *Neuron, 44,* 729–740.

Maldonado, J. R., & Butler, L. D. (1998). *Treatments for dissociative disorders.* New York: Oxford University Press.

Malina, R. M., Bouchard, C., & Beunen, G. (1988). Human growth: Selected aspects of current research on well-nourished children. *Annual Review of Anthropology, 17,* 187–219.

Mampe, B., Friederici, A. D., Christophe, A., & Wermke, K. (2009). Newborns' cry melody is shaped by their native language. *Current Biology, 19,* 1–4.

Mandel, D. R., & Lehman, D. R. (1998). Integration of contingency information in judgments of cause, covariation, and probability. *Journal of Experimental Psychology: General, 127,* 269–285.

Mandle, C. L., Jacobs, S. C., Arcari, P. M., & Domar, A. D. (1996). The efficacy of relaxation response interventions with adult patients: A review of the literature. *Journal of Cardiovascular Nursing, 10,* 4–26.

Mandler, G. (1967). Organization and memory. In K. W. Spence & J. T. Spence (Eds.), *The psychology of learning and motivation* (Vol. 1, pp. 327–372). New York: Academic Press.

Mankiw, N. G., & Weinzierl, M. (2010). The optimal taxation of height: A case study of utilitarian income redistribution. *American Economic Journal: Economic Policy, 2,* 155–176.

Mann, J. J. (2005). The medical management of depression. *New England Journal of Medicine, 353,* 1819–1834.

Mann, J. J., Waternaux, C., Haas, G. L., & Malone, K. M. (1999). Toward a clinical model of suicidal behavior in psychiatric patients. *American Journal of Psychiatry, 156,* 181–189.

Marangell, L. B., Silver, J. M., Goff, D. M., & Yudofsky, S. C. (2003). Psychopharmacology and electroconvulsive therapy. In R. E. Hales & S. C. Yudofsky (Eds.), *The American Psychiatric Publishing textbook of clinical psychiatry* (4th ed., pp. 1047–1149). Washington, DC: American Psychiatric Publishing.

March of Dimes. (2010). Smoking during pregnancy. Retrieved July 15, 2010, from http://www.marchofdimes.com/professionals/14332_1171.asp

Marcus, G. B. (1986). Stability and change in political attitudes: Observe, recall, and "explain." *Political Behavior, 8,* 21–44.

Marian, V., & Neisser, U. (2000). Language-dependent recall of autobiographical memories. *Journal of Experimental Psychology, 129,* 361–368.

Markus, H. (1977). Self-schemata and processing information about the self. *Journal of Personality and Social Psychology, 35,* 63–78.

Marlatt, G. A. (Ed.). (1998). *Harm reduction: Pragmatic strategies for managing high-risk behaviors.* New York: Guilford Press.

Marlatt, G. A., Larimer, M. E., Baer, J. S., & Quigley, L. A. (1993). Harm reduction for alcohol problems: Moving beyond the controlled drinking controversy. *Behavior Therapy, 24,* 461–504.

Marlatt, G. A., & Rohsenow, D. (1980). Cognitive processes in alcohol use: Expectancy and the balanced placebo design. In N. K. Mello (Ed.), *Advances in substance abuse: Behavioral and biological research* (pp. 159–199). Greenwich, CT: JAI Press.

Marmot, M. G., Stansfeld, S., Patel, C., North, F., Head, J., White, L., et al. (1991). Health inequalities among British civil servants: The Whitehall II study. *Lancet, 337,* 1387–1393.

Marr, D., & Nishihara, H. K. (1978). Representation and recognition of the spatial organization of three-dimensional shapes. *Proceedings of the Royal Society B: Biological Sciences, 200,* 269–294.

Marsolek, C. J. (1995). Abstract visual-form representations in the left cerebral hemispheres. *Journal of Experimental Psychology: Human Perception and Performance, 21,* 375–386.

Martin, A. (2007). The representation of object concepts in the brain. *Annual Review of Psychology, 58,* 25–45.

Martin, A., & Caramazza, A. (2003). Neuropsychological and neuroimaging perspectives on conceptual knowledge: An introduction. *Cognitive Neuropsychology, 20,* 195–212.

Martin, A., & Chao, L. L. (2001). Semantic memory and the brain: Structure and processes. *Current Opinion in Neurobiology, 11,* 194–201.

Martin, G., & Koo, L. (1997). Celebrity suicide: Did the death of Kurt Cobain influence young suicides in Australia? *Archives of Suicide Research, 3,* 187–198.

Martin, N. G., Eaves, L. J., Geath, A. R., Jarding, R., Feingold, L. M., & Eysenck, H. J. (1986). Transmission of social attitudes. *Proceedings of the National Academy of Sciences, USA, 83,* 4364–4368.

Marucha, P. T., Kiecolt-Glaser, J. K., & Favagehi, M. (1998). Mucosal wound healing is impaired by examination stress. *Psychosomatic Medicine, 60,* 362–365.

Masand, P. S., & Gupta, S. (2002). Long-term side effects of newer-generation antidepressants: SSRIs, venlafaxine, nefazodone, bupropion, and mirtazipine. *Annals of Clinical Psychiatry, 14,* 175–182.

Maslach, C. (2003). Job burnout: New directions in research and intervention. *Current Directions in Psychological Science, 12,* 189–192.

Maslow, A. H. (1937). Dominance-feeling, behavior, and status. In R. J. Lowry (Ed.), *Dominance, self-esteem, self-actualization: Germinal papers by A. H. Maslow.* Monterey, CA: Brooks-Cole.

Maslow, A. H. (1954). *Motivation and personality.* New York: Harper & Row.

Maslow, A. H. (1962). *Toward a psychology of being.* New York: Van Nostrand Reinhold.

Maslow, A. H. (1970). *Motivation and personality* (2nd ed.). New York: Harper & Row.

Mason, M. F., Norton, M. I., Van Horn, J. D., Wegner, D. M., Grafton, S. T., & Macrae, C. N. (2007). Wandering minds: The default network and stimulus-independent thought. *Science, 3154,* 393–395.

Masserman, J. H. (1961). *Principles of dynamic psychiatry* (2nd ed.). Philadelphia: W. B. Saunders.

Masten, A. S. (2004). Family therapy as a treatment for children: A critical review of outcome research. *Family Process, 18,* 323–335.

Masters, W. H., & Johnson, V. E. (1966). *Human sexual response.* Boston: Little, Brown.

Mather, M., Canli, T., English, T., Whitfield, S., Wais, P., Ochsner, K., et al. (2004). Amygdala responses to emotionally valenced stimuli in older and younger adults. *Psychological Science, 15,* 259–263.

Mather, M., & Carstensen, L. L. (2003). Aging and attentional biases for emotional faces. *Psychological Science, 14,* 409–415.

Mather, M., & Carstensen, L. L. (2005). Aging and motivated cognition: The positivity effect in attention and memory. *Trends in Cognitive Sciences, 9*(10), 496–502.

Mathis, J. L. (1964). A sophisticated version of voodoo death. *Psychosomatic Medicine, 26,* 104–107.

Matsumoto, D., & Willingham, B. (2009). Spontaneous facial expressions of emotion of congenitally and noncongenitally blind individuals. *Journal of Personality and Social Psychology, 96,* 1–10.

Mattar, A. A. G., & Gribble, P. L. (2005). Motor learning by observing. *Neuron, 46,* 153–160.

Matthews, G., & Gilliland, K. (1999). The personality theories of H. J. Eysenck and J. A. Gray: A comparative review. *Personality and Individual Differences, 26,* 583–626.

Mattingly, J. B. (2009). Attention, automaticity, and awareness in synesthesia. *Annals of the New York Academy of Sciences, 1156,* 141–167.

Matzel, L. D., Han, Y. R., Grossman, H., Karnik, M. S., Patel, D., Scott, N., et al. (2003). Individual differences in the expression of a general learning ability in mice. *Journal of Neuroscience, 23*(16), 6423–6433.

Maudsley, H. (1886). *Natural causes and supernatural seemings.* London: Kegan Paul, Trench.

Max, A. (2006, September 16). Dutch reach new heights. *USA Today.*

May, R. (1983). *The discovery of being: Writings in existential psychology.* New York: Norton.

Mayberg, H., Lozano, A., Voon, V., McNeely, H., Seminowicz, D., Hamani, C., et al. (2005). Deep brain stimulation for treatment-resistant depresssion. *Neuron, 45,* 651–660.

Mayer, J. D., Caruso, D. R., & Salovey, P. (1999). Emotional intelligence meets traditional standards for an intelligence. *Intelligence, 27,* 267.

Mayer, J. D., Roberts, R. D., & Barsade, S. G. (2008). Human abilities: Emotional intelligence. *Annual Review of Psychology, 59,* 507–536.

Maynard-Smith, J. (1965). The evolution of alarm calls. *American Naturalist, 100,* 637–650.

McAdams, D. (1993). *The stories we live by: Personal myths and the making of the self.* New York: Morrow.

McCabe, S. E., Knight, J. R., Teter, C. J., & Wechsler, H. (2005). Nonmedical use of prescription stimulants among U.S. college students: Prevalence and correlates from a national survey. *Addiction, 100,* 96–106.

McCann, I. L., & Holmes, D. S. (1984). Influence of aerobic exercise on depression. *Journal of Personality and Social Psychology, 46,* 1142–1147.

McClelland, D. C., Atkinson, J. W., Clark, R. A., & Lowell, E. L. (1953). *The achievement motive.* New York: Appleton-Century-Crofts.

McCloskey, M., & Zaragoza, M. (1985). Misleading postevent information and memory for events: Arguments and evidence against memory impairment hypotheses. *Journal of Experimental Psychology: General, 114,* 1–16.

McClure, S. M., Li, J., Tomlin, D., Cypert, K. S., Montague, L. M., & Montague, P. R. (2004). Neural correlates of behavioral preference for culturally familiar drinks. *Neuron, 44,* 379–387.

McConkey, K. M., Barnier, A. J., & Sheehan, P. W. (1998). Hypnosis and pseudomemory: Understanding the findings and their implications. In S. J. Lynn & K. M. McConkey (Eds.), *Truth in memory* (pp. 227–259). New York: Guilford Press.

McCrae, R. R., & Costa, P. T. (1990). *Personality in adulthood.* New York: Guilford Press.

McCrae, R. R., & Costa, P. T. (1999). A five-factor theory of personality. In L. A. Pervin & O. P. John (Eds.), *Handbook of personality: Theory and research.* New York: Guilford Press.

McCrea, S. M., Buxbaum, L. J., & Coslett, H. B. (2006). Illusory conjunctions in simultanagnosia: Coarse coding of visual feature location? *Neuropsychologia, 44,* 1724–1736.

McDannald, M., & Schoenbaum, G. (2009). Toward a model of impaired reality testing in rats. *Schizophrenia Bulletin, 35,* 664–667.

McDougall, W. (1930). The hormic psychology. In C. Murchison (Ed.), *Psychologies of 1930* (pp. 3–36). Worcester, MA: Clark University Press.

McEvoy, S. P., Stevenson, M. R., McCartt, A. T., Woodward, M., Haworth, C., Palamara, P., et al. (2005). Role of mobile phones in motor vehicle crashes resulting in hospital attendance: A case-crossover study. *British Medical Journal, 331,* 428–430.

McFall, R. M., & Treat, T. A. (1999). Quantifying the information value of clinical assessments with signal detection theory. *Annual Review of Psychology, 50,* 215–241.

McFarlane, A. H., Norman, G. R., Streiner, D. L., Roy, R., & Scott, D. J. (1980). A longitudinal study of the influence of the psychosocial environment on health status: A preliminary report. *Journal of Health and Social Behavior, 21,* 124–133.

McGarty, C., & Turner, J. C. (1992). The effects of categorization on social judgement. *British Journal of Social Psychology, 31,* 253–268.

McGaugh, J. L. (2000). Memory: A century of consolidation. *Science, 287,* 248–251.

McGaugh, J. L. (2006). Make mild moments memorable: Add a little arousal. *Trends in Cognitive Sciences, 10,* 345–347.

McGlinchey-Berroth, R., Carrillo, M. C., Gabrieli, J. D., Brawn, C. M., & Disterhoft, J. F. (1997). Impaired trace eyeblink conditioning in bilateral, medial-temporal lobe amnesia. *Behavioral Neuroscience, 111,* 873–882.

McGrath, J., Saha, S., Chant, D., & Welham, J. (2008). Schizophrenia: A concise overview of incidence, prevalence, and mortality. *Epidemiologic Reviews, 30,* 67–76.

McGue, M., & Bouchard, T. J. (1998). Genetic and environmental influences on human behavioral differences. *Annual Review of Neuroscience, 21,* 1–24.

McGuire, P. K., Shah, G. M., & Murray, R. M. (1993). Increased blood flow in Broca's area during auditory hallucinations in schizophrenia. *Lancet, 342,* 703–706.

McHugh, P. R., Lief, H. I., Freyd, P. P., & Fetkewicz, J. M. (2004). From refusal to recollection: Family relationships after an accusation based on recovered memories. *Journal of Nervous and Mental Disease, 192,* 525–532.

McKetin, R., McLaren, J., Lubman, D. I., & Hides, L. (2006). The prevalence of psychotic symptoms among methamphetamine users. *Addiction, 101,* 1473–1478.

McKetin, R., Ward, P. B., Catts, S. V., Mattick, R. P., & Bell, J. R. (1999). Changes in auditory selective attention and event-related potentials following oral administration of D-amphetamine in humans. *Neuropsychopharmacology, 21,* 380–390.

McKinney, C. H., Antoni, M. H., Kumar, M., Tims, F. C., & McCabe, P. M. (1997). Effects of guided imagery and music (GIM) therapy on mood and cortisol in healthy adults. *Health Psychology, 16,* 390–400.

McLean, K. C. (2008). The emergence of narrative identity. *Social and Personality Psychology Compass, 2*(4), 1685–1702.

McNally, R. J. (2003). *Remembering trauma.* Cambridge, MA: Belknap Press of Harvard University Press.

McNally, R. J., & Geraerts, E. (2009). A new solution to the recovered memory debate. *Perspective on Psychological Science, 4,* 126–134.

McNally, R. J., & Steketee, G. S. (1985). Etiology and maintenance of severe animal phobias. *Behavioral Research and Therapy, 23,* 431–435.

McNeilly, A. S., Robinson, I. C., Houston, M. J., & Howie, P. W. (1983). Release of oxytocin and prolactin in response to suckling. *British Medical Journal, 286,* 257–259.

McRae, C., Cherin, E., Yamazaki, G., Diem, G., Vo, A. H., Russell, D., et al. (2004). Effects of perceived treatment on quality of life and medical outcomes in a double-blind placebo surgery trial. *Archives of General Psychiatry, 61,* 412–420.

McWilliams, N. (1994). *Psychoanalytic diagnosis: Understanding personality structure in the clinical process.* New York: Guilford Press.

McWilliams, P. (1993). *Ain't nobody's business if you do: The absurdity of consensual crimes in a free society.* Los Angeles: Prelude Press.

Mead, G. H. (1934). *Mind, self, and society.* Chicago: University of Chicago Press.

Mead, M. (1968). *Sex and temperament in three primitive societies.* New York: Dell. (Original work published 1935)

Mechelli, A., Crinion, J. T., Noppeney, U., O'Doherty, J., Ashburner, J., Frackowiak, R. S., et al. (2004). Neurolinguistics: Structural plasticity in the bilingual brain. *Nature, 431,* 757.

Mecklenburg, S. H., Bailey, P. J., & Larsen, M. R. (2008). The Illinois field study: A significant contribution to understanding real world witness identification issues. *Law and Human Behavior, 32,* 22–27.

Medin, D. L., & Schaffer, M. M. (1978). Context theory of classification learning. *Psychological Review, 85,* 207–238.

Medvec, V. H., Madey, S. F., & Gilovich, T. (1995). When less is more: Counterfactual thinking and satisfaction among Olympic medalists. *Journal of Personality and Social Psychology, 69,* 603–610.

Meeren, H. K. M., van Heijnsbergen, C. C. R. J., & de Gelder, B. (2005). Rapid perceptual integration of facial expression and emotional body language. *Proceedings of the National Academy of Sciences, USA, 102*(45), 16518–16523.

Mehl, M. R., Vazire, S., Ramirez-Esparza, N., Slatcher, R. B., & Pennebaker, J. W. (2009). Are women really more talkative than men? *Science, 317,* 82.

Meins, E. (2003). Emotional development and attachment relationships. In A. Slater & G. Bremner (Eds.), *An introduction to developmental psychology* (pp. 141–164). Malden, MA: Blackwell.

Meins, E., Fernyhough, C., Fradley, E., & Tuckey, M. (2001). Rethinking maternal sensitivity: Mothers' comments on infants' mental processes predict security of attachment at 12 months. *Journal of Child Psychology & Psychiatry & Allied Disciplines, 42,* 637–648.

Meisel, S. R., Dayan, K. I., Pauzner, H., Chetboun, I., Arbel, Y., David, D., et al. (1991). Effect of Iraqi missile war on incidence of acute myocardial infarction and sudden death in Israeli citizens. *Lancet, 338,* 660–661.

Mekel-Bobrov, N., Gilbert, S. L., Evans, P. D., Vallender, E. J., Anderson, J. R., Hudson, R. R., et al. (2005). Ongoing adaptive evolution of ASPM, a brain size determinant in *Homo sapiens. Science, 309,* 1720–1722.

Mellon, R. C. (2009). Superstitious perception: Response-independent reinforcement and punishment as determinants of recurring eccentric interpretations. *Behaviour Research and Therapy, 47,* 868–875.

Meltzoff, A. N. (1995). Understanding the intentions of others: Re-enactment of intended acts by 18-month-old children. *Developmental Psychology, 31,* 838–850.

Meltzoff, A. N., Kuhl, P. K., Movellan, J., & Sejnowski, T. J. (2009). Foundations for a new science of learning. *Science, 325,* 284–288.

Meltzoff, A. N., & Moore, M. K. (1977). Imitation of facial and manual gestures by human neonates. *Science, 198,* 75–78.

Melzack, R., & Wall, P. D. (1965). Pain mechanisms: A new theory. *Science, 150,* 971–979.

Mendes, W. B., Blascovich, J., Hunter, S. B., Lickel, B., & Jost, J. T. (2007). Threatened by the unexpected: Physiological responses during social interactions with expectancy-violating partners. *Journal of Personality and Social Psychology, 92,* 698–716.

Mendes, W. B., Blascovich, J., Lickel, B., & Hunter, S. (2002). Challenge and threat during social interaction with White and Black men. *Personality & Social Psychology Bulletin, 28,* 939–952.

Mendle, J., Turkheimer, E., & Emery, R. E. (2007). Detrimental psychological outcomes associated with early pubertal timing in adolescent girls. *Developmental Review, 27,* 151–171.

Mennella, J. A., Johnson, A., & Beauchamp, G. K. (1995). Garlic ingestion by pregnant women alters the odor of amniotic fluid. *Chemical Senses, 20,* 207–209.

Merikangas, K. R., Wicki, W., & Angst, J. (1994). Heterogeneity of depression: Classification of depressive subtype by longitudinal course. *British Journal of Psychiatry, 164,* 342–348.

Mervis, C. B., & Bertrand, J. (1994). Acquisition of the "Novel Name" Nameless Category (N3C) principle. *Child Development, 65,* 1646–1662.

Merzenich, M. M., Recanzone, G. H., Jenkins, W. M., & Grajski, K. A. (1990). Adaptive mechanisms in cortical networks underlying cortical contributions to learning and nondeclarative memory. *Cold Spring Harbor Symposia on Quantitative Biology, 55,* 873–887.

Messick, D. M., & Cook, K. S. (1983). *Equity theory: Psychological and sociological perspectives.* New York: Praeger.

Meston, C. M., & Buss, D. M. (2007). Why humans have sex. *Archives of Sexual Behavior, 36,* 477–507.

Mestre, J. M., Guil, R., Lopes, P. N., Salovey, P., & Gil-Olarte, P. (2006). Emotional intelligence and social and academic adaptation to school. *Psicothema, 18,* 112.

Metcalfe, J. (2009). Metacognitive judgments and control of study. *Current Directions in Psychological Science, 18,* 159–163.

Metcalfe, J., & Finn, B. (2008). Evidence that judgments of learning are causally related to study choice. *Psychonomic Bulletin & Review, 15,* 174–179.

Metcalfe, J., & Wiebe, D. (1987). Intuition in insight and noninsight problem solving. *Memory & Cognition, 15,* 238–246.

Meyer-Bahlberg, H. F. L., Ehrhardt, A. A., Rosen, L. R., & Gruen, R. S. (1995). Prenatal estrogens and the development of homosexual orientation. *Developmental Psychology, 31,* 12–21.

Michaela, R., Florian, S., Gert, G. W., & Ulman, L. (2009). Seeking pleasure and seeking pain: Differences in prohedonic and contrahedonic motivation from adolescence to old age. *Psychological Science, 20*(12), 1529–1535.

Michelson, D., Pollack, M., Lydiard, R. D., Tamura, R., Tepner, R., & Tollefson, G. (1999). Continuing treatment of panic disorder after acute responses: Randomized, placebo-controlled trail with fluoxetine. The Fluoxitine Panic Disorder Study Group. *British Journal of Psychiatry, 174,* 213–218.

Michotte, A. (1963). *The perception of causality.* New York: Basic Books.

Miklowitz, D. J., Goldstein, M. J., Nuechterlein, K. H., Snyder, K. S., & Mintz, J. (1988). Family factors and the course of bipolar affective disorder. *Archives of General Psychiatry, 45,* 225–231.

Milgram, S. (1963). Behavioral study of obedience. *Journal of Abnormal and Social Psychology, 67,* 371–378.

Milgram, S. (1974). *Obedience to authority.* New York: Harper & Row.

Milgram, S., Bickman, L., & Berkowitz, O. (1969). Note on the drawing power of crowds of different size. *Journal of Personality and Social Psychology, 13,* 79–82.

Miller, A. J. (1986). *The obedience experiments: A case study of controversy in social science.* New York: Praeger.

Miller, D. T., & Prentice, D. A. (1996). The construction of social norms and standards. In E. T. Higgins & A. W. Kruglanski (Ed.), *Social psychology: Handbook of basic principles* (pp. 799–829). New York: Guilford Press.

Miller, D. T., & Ratner, R. K. (1998). The disparity between the actual and assumed power of self-interest. *Journal of Personality and Social Psychology, 74*, 53–62.

Miller, D. T., & Ross, M. (1975). Self-serving biases in the attribution of causality: Fact or fiction? *Psychological Bulletin, 82*, 213–225.

Miller, G. A. (1956). The magical number seven, plus or minus two: Some limits on our capacity for processing information. *Psychological Review, 63*, 81–96.

Miller, K. F., Smith, C. M., & Zhu, J. (1995). Preschool origins of cross-national differences in mathematical competence: The role of number-naming systems. *Psychological Science, 6*, 56–60.

Miller, N. E. (1960). Motivational effects of brain stimulation and drugs. *Federation Proceedings, 19*, 846–854.

Miller, T. W. (Ed.). (1996). *Theory and assessment of stressful life events.* Madison, CT: International Universities Press.

Mills, P. J., & Dimsdale, J. E. (1991). Cardiovascular reactivity to psychosocial stressors. A review of the effects of beta-blockade. *Psychosomatics, 32*, 209–220.

Milne, E., & Grafman, J. (2001). Ventromedial prefrontal cortex lesions in humans eliminate implicit gender stereotyping. *Journal of Neuroscience, 21*, 1–6.

Milner, A. D., & Goodale, M. A. (1995). *The visual brain in action.* Oxford, England: Oxford University Press.

Milner, B. (1962). Laterality effects in audition. In V. B. Mountcastle (Ed.), *Interhemispheric relations and cerebral dominance* (pp. 177–195). Baltimore: Johns Hopkins University Press.

Mineka, S., & Cook, M. (1988). Social learning and the acquisition of snake fear in monkeys. In T. Zentall & B. G. Galef, Jr. (Eds.), *Social learning* (pp. 51–73). Hillsdale, NJ: Lawrence Erlbaum.

Mineka, S., & Ohman, A. (2002). Born to fear: Non-associative vs. associative factors in the etiology of phobia. *Behaviour Research and Therapy, 40*, 173–184.

Mingroni, M. A. (2007). Resolving the IQ paradox: Heterosis as a cause of the Flynn effect and other trends. *Psychological Review, 114*, 806–829.

Minsky, M. (1986). *The society of mind.* New York: Simon & Schuster.

Mischel, W. (1968). *Personality and assessment.* New York: Wiley.

Mischel, W. (2004). Toward an integrative science of the person. *Annual Review of Psychology, 55*, 1–22.

Mischel, W., Ayduk, O., Baumeister, R. F., & Vohs, K. D. (2004). Willpower in a cognitive-affective processing system: The dynamics of delay of gratification. In *Handbook of self-regulation: Research, theory, and applications* (pp. 99–129). New York: Guilford Press.

Mischel, W., & Shoda, Y. (1999). Integrating dispositions and processing dynamics within a unified theory of personality: The cognitive-affective personality system. In L. A. Pervin & O. P. John (Eds.), *Handbook of personality: Theory and research.* New York: Guilford Press.

Mischel, W., Shoda, Y., & Rodriguez, M. L. (1989). Delay of gratification in children. *Science, 244*, 933–938.

Mita, T. H., Dermer, M., & Knight, J. (1977). Reversed facial images and the mere-exposure hypothesis. *Journal of Personality and Social Psychology, 35*, 597–601.

Mitchell, D. B. (2006). Nonconscious priming after 17 years. *Psychological Science, 17*, 925–929.

Mitchell, J. P. (2006). Mentalizing and Marr: An information processing approach to the study of social cognition. *Brain Research, 1079*, 66–75.

Mitchell, J. P., Heatherton, T. F., & Macrae, C. N. (2002). Distinct neural systems subserve person and object knowledge. *Proceedings of the National Academy of Sciences, USA, 99*, 15238–15243.

Mitchell, K. J., & Johnson, M. K. (2009). Source monitoring 15 years later: What have we learned from fMRI about the neural mechanisms of source memory? *Psychological Bulletin, 135*, 638–677.

Miura, I. T., Okamoto, Y., Kim, C. C., & Chang, C. M. (1994). Comparisons of children's cognitive representation of number: China, France, Japan, Korea, Sweden and the United States. *International Journal of Behavioral Development, 17*, 401–411.

Moffitt, T. E. (1993). Adolescence-limited and life-course-persistent antisocial behavior: A developmental taxonomy. *Psychological Review, 100*, 674–701.

Moffitt, T. E. (2005). Genetic and environmental influences on antisocial behaviors: Evidence from behavioral-genetic research. *Advances in Genetics, 55*, 41–104.

Moghaddam, B., & Bunney, B. S. (1989). Differential effect of cocaine on extracellular dopamine levels in rat medial prefrontal cortex and nucleus accumbens: Comparison to amphetamine. *Synapse, 4*, 156–161.

Molden, D., Lee, A. Y., & Higgins, E. T. (2009). Motivations for promotion and prevention. In J. Shah & W. Gardner (Eds.), *Handbook of motivation science* (pp. 169–187). New York: Guilford Press.

Monahan, J. (1992). Mental disorder and violent behavior: Perceptions and evidence. *American Psychologist, 47*, 511–521.

Monahan, J. L., Murphy, S. T., & Zajonc, R. B. (2000). Subliminal mere exposure: Specific, general, and diffuse effects. *Psychological Science, 11*, 462–466.

Moncrieff, J. (2009). A critique of the dopamine hypothesis of schizophrenia and psychosis. *Harvard Review of Psychiatry, 17*, 214–225.

Monroe, S. M., & Reid, M. W. (2009). Life stress and major depression. *Current Directions in Psychological Science, 18*, 68–72.

Montague, C. T., Farooqi, I. S., Whitehead, J. P., Soos, M. A., Rau, H., Wareham, N. J., et al. (1997). Congenital leptin deficiency is associated with severe early-onset obesity in humans. *Nature, 387*(6636), 903–908.

Monti, M. M., Coleman, M. R., & Owen, A. M. (2009). Neuroimaging and the vegetative state: Resolving the behavioral assessment dilemma? *Annals of the New York Academy of Sciences, 1157*, 81–89.

Monti, M. M., Vanhaudenhuyse, A., Coleman, M. R., Boly, M., Pickard, J. D., Tshibanda, L., et al. (2010). Willful modulation of brain activity in disorders of consciousness. *New England Journal of Medicine, 362*, 579–589.

Mook, D. G. (1983). In defense of external invalidity. *American Psychologist, 38*, 379–387.

Moore, D. W. (2003). Public lukewarm on animal rights. Retrieved June 22, 2010, from http://www.gallup.com/poll/8461/public-lukewarm-animal-rights.aspx

Moore, E. G. J. (1986). Family socialization and the IQ test performance of traditionally and transracially adopted Black children. *Developmental Psychology, 22*, 317–326.

Moore, K. L. (1977). *The developing human* (2nd ed.). Philadelphia: Saunders.

Moray, N. (1959). Attention in dichotic listening: Affective cues and the influence of instructions. *Quarterly Journal of Experimental Psychology, 11*, 56–60.

Morewedge, C. K., & Norton, M. I. (2009). When dreaming is believing: The (motivated) interpretation of dreams. *Journal of Personality and Social Psychology, 96*, 249–264.

Morgan, H. (1990). Dostoevsky's epilepsy: A case report and comparison. *Surgical Neurology, 33*, 413–416.

Morgenstern, J., Labouvie, E., McCrady, B. S., Kahler, C. W., & Frey, R. M. (1997). Affiliation with Alcoholics Anonymous after treatment: A study of its therapeutic effects and mechanisms of action. *Journal of Consulting and Clinical Psychology, 65*, 768–777.

Morin, A. (2002). Right hemisphere self-awareness: A critical assessment. *Consciousness & Cognition, 11*, 396–401.

Morin, A. (2005). Levels of consciousness and self-awareness: A comparison of various neurocognitive views. *Consciousness & Cognition, 15,* 358–371.

Morris, C. D., Bransford, J. D., & Franks, J. J. (1977). Levels of processing versus transfer-appropriate processing. *Journal of Verbal Learning and Verbal Behavior, 16,* 519–533.

Morris, R. G., Anderson, E., Lynch, G. S., & Baudry, M. (1986). Selective impairment of learning and blockade of long-term potentiation by an *N*-methyl-D-aspartate receptor antagonist, AP5. *Nature, 319,* 774–776.

Morris, T. L. (2001). Social phobia. In M. W. Vasey & M. R. Dadds (Eds.), *The developmental psychopathology of anxiety* (pp. 435–458). New York: Oxford University Press.

Morrow, D., Leirer, V., Altiteri, P., & Fitzsimmons, C. (1994). When expertise reduces age differences in performance. *Psychology and Aging, 9,* 134–148.

Moruzzi, G., & Magoun, H. W. (1949). Brain stem reticular formation and activation of the EEG. *Electroencephalography and Clinical Neurophysiology, 1,* 455–473.

Moscovitch, M. (1994). Memory and working-with-memory: Evaluation of a component process model and comparisons with other models. In D. L. Schacter & E. Tulving (Eds.), *Memory systems 1994* (pp. 269–310). Cambridge, MA: The MIT Press.

Moscovitch, M., Nadel, L., Winocur, G., Gilboa, A., & Rosenbaum, R. S. (2006). The cognitive neuroscience of remote episodic, semantic and spatial memory. *Current Opinion in Neurobiology, 16,* 179–190.

Moss, D., McGrady, A., Davies, T., & Wickramasekera, I. (2002). *Handbook of mind-body medicine for primary care.* Newbury Park, CA: Sage.

Motley, M. T., & Baars, B. J. (1979). Effects of cognitive set upon laboratory induced verbal (Freudian) slips. *Journal of Speech & Hearing Research, 22,* 421–432.

Moulin, C. J. A., Conway, M. A., Thompson, R. G., James, N., & Jones, R. W. (2005). Disordered memory awareness: Recollective confabulation in two cases of persistent déjà vecu. *Neuropsychologia, 43,* 1362–1378.

Moura, A. C. A. de, & Lee, P. C. (2004). Capuchin stone tool use in Caatinga dry forest. *Science, 306,* 1909.

Mroczek, D. K., & Spiro, A. (2005). Change in life satisfaction during adulthood: Findings from the Veterans Affairs Normative Aging Study. *Journal of Personality and Social Psychology, 88,* 189.

Mueller, T. E., Gavin, L. E., & Kulkarni, A. (2008). The association between sex education and youth's engagement in sexual intercourse, age at first intercourse, and birth control use at first sex. *The Journal of Adolescent Health, 42*(1), 89–96.

Mueller, T. I., Leon, A. C., Keller, M. B., Solomon, D. A., Endicott, J., Coryell, W., et al. (1999). Recurrence after recovery from major depressive disorder during 15 years of observational follow-up. *American Journal of Psychiatry, 156,* 1000–1006.

Muenter, M. D., & Tyce, G. M. (1971). L-dopa therapy of Parkinson's disease: Plasma L-dopa concentration, therapeutic response, and side effects. *Mayo Clinic Proceedings, 46,* 231–239.

Muggleton, N., Tsakanikos, E., Walsh, V., & Ward, J. (2007). Disruption of synesthesia following TMS of the right parietal cortex. *Neuropsychologia, 45,* 1582–1585.

Mukherjee, S., Sackeim, H. A., & Schnur, D. B. (1994). Electroconvulsive therapy of acute manic episodes: A review of 50 years' experience. *American Journal of Psychiatry, 151,* 169–176.

Mullen, M. K. (1994). Earliest recollections of childhood: A demographic analysis. *Cognition, 52,* 55–79.

Muller, M. N., & Wrangham, R. W. (2004). Dominance, aggression and testosterone in wild chimpanzees: A test of the "challenge hypothesis." *Animal Behaviour, 67,* 113–123.

Multhaup, K. S., Johnson, M. D., & Tetirick, J. C. (2005). The wane of childhood amnesia for autobiographical and public event memories. *Memory, 13,* 161–173.

Munsey, C. (2008, February). Prescriptive authority in the states. *Monitor on Psychology, 39,* 60.

Murphy, N. A., Hall, J. A., & Colvin, C. R. (2003). Accurate intelligence assessments in social interactions: Mediators and gender effects. *Journal of Personality, 71,* 465–493.

Murray, C. (2002). *IQ and income inequality in a sample of sibling pairs from advantaged family backgrounds.* Paper presented at the 114th Annual Meeting of the American Economic Association.

Murray, H. A. (1943). *Thematic Apperception Test manual.* Cambridge, MA: Harvard University Press.

Murray, H. A., & Kluckhohn, C. (1953). Outline of a conception of personality. In C. Kluckhohn, H. A. Murray, & D. M. Schneider (Eds.), *Personality in nature, society, and culture* (2nd ed., pp. 3–52). New York: Knopf.

Myers, D. G., & Diener, E. (1995). Who is happy? *Psychological Science, 6,* 10–19.

Nadasdy, A. (1995). Phonetics, phonology, and applied linguistics. *Annual Review of Applied Linguistics, 15,* 68–77.

Nader, K., & Hardt, O. (2009). A single standard for memory: The case of reconsolidation. *Nature Reviews Neuroscience, 10,* 224–234.

Nader, K., Shafe, G., & LeDoux, J. E. (2000). Fear memories require protein synthesis in the amygdala for reconsolidation after retrieval. *Nature, 406,* 722–726.

Nagasako, E. M., Oaklander, A. L., & Dworkin, R. H. (2003). Congenital insensitivity to pain: An update. *Pain, 101,* 213–219.

Nagell, K., Olguin, R. S., & Tomasello, M. (1993). Processes of social learning in the tool use of chimpanzees (*Pan troglodytes*) and human children (*Homo sapiens*). *Journal of Comparative Psychology, 107,* 174–186.

Nahemow, L., & Lawton, M. P. (1975). Similarity and propinquity in friendship formation. *Journal of Personality and Social Psychology, 32,* 205–213.

Nairne, J. S., & Pandeirada, J. N. S. (2008). Adaptive memory: Remembering with a stone age brain. *Current Directions in Psychological Science, 17,* 239–243.

Nairne, J. S., Pandeirada, J. N. S., & Thompson, S. R. (2008). Adaptive memory: The comparative value of survival processing. *Psychological Science, 19,* 176–180.

Nairne, J. S., Thompson, S. R., & Pandeirada, J. N. S. (2007). Adaptive memory: Survival processing enhances retention. *Journal of Experimental Psychology: Learning, Memory, & Cognition, 33,* 263–273.

Nakazato, M., Murakami, N., Date, Y., Kojima, M., Matsuo, H., Kangawa, K., et al. (2001). A role for ghrelin in the central regulation of feeding. *Nature, 409,* 194–198.

Naqvi, N., Shiv, B., & Bechara, A. (2006). The role of emotion in decision making: A cognitive neuroscience perspective. *Current Directions in Psychological Science, 15,* 260–264.

Narrow, W. E., Rae, D. S., Robins, L. N., & Regier, D. A. (2002). Revised prevalence estimates of mental disorders in the United States: Using a clinical significance criterion to reconcile 2 surveys' estimates. *Archives of General Psychiatry, 59,* 115–123.

Nash, M. (1987). What, if anything, is regressed about hypnotic age regression? A review of the empirical literature. *Psychological Bulletin, 102,* 42–52.

Nathan, P. E., & Gorman, J. M. (2007). *A guide to treatments that work* (3rd ed.). New York: Oxford University Press.

Nathan, P. E., & Lagenbucher, J. W. (1999). Psychopathology: Description and classification. *Annual Review of Psychology, 50*, 79–107.

Nathanson, C., Paulhus, D. L., & Williams, K. M. (2006). Personality and misconduct correlates of body modification and other cultural deviance markers. *Journal of Research in Personality, 40*, 779–802.

National Center for Health Statistics. (2004). *Health, United States, 2004, with chartbook on trends in the health of Americans.* Hyattsville, MD: Author.

National Center for Health Statistics. (2008). *Health, United States.* Retrieved January 25, 2010, from http://www.cdc.gov/nchs/hus.htm

National Research Council. (2003). *The polygraph and lie detection.* Washington, DC: National Academies Press.

National Science Board. (2008). *Science and engineering indicators 2008.* Two volumes. Arlington, VA: National Science Foundation (Vol. 1, NSB 08-01; Vol. 2, NSB 08-01A).

Naumann, L. P., Vazire, S., Rentfrow, P. J., & Gosling, S. D. (2009). Personality judgments based on physical appearance. *Personality & Social Psychology Bulletin, 35*, 1661–1671.

Neihart, M. (1999). The impact of giftedness on psychological well-being: What does the empirical literature say? *Roeper Review, 22*(1), 10.

Neimark, J. (2004, July/August). The power of coincidence. *Psychology Today*, pp. 47–52.

Neimeyer, R. A., & Mitchell, K. A. (1988). Similarity and attraction: A longitudinal study. *Journal of Social and Personal Relationships, 5*, 131–148.

Neisser, U. (1967). *Cognitive psychology.* New York: Appleton-Century-Crofts.

Neisser, U. (Ed.). (1998). *The rising curve: Long-term gains in IQ and related measures.* Washington, DC: American Psychological Association.

Neisser, U., & Becklen, R. (1975). Selective looking: Attending to visually significant events. *Cognitive Psychology, 7*, 480–494.

Neisser, U., Boodoo, G., Bouchard, T. J., Jr., Boykin, A. W., Brody, N., Ceci, S. J., et al. (1996). Intelligence: Knowns and unknowns. *American Psychologist, 51*, 77–101.

Neisser, U., & Harsch, N. (1992). Phantom flashbulbs: False recollections of hearing the news about Challenger. In E. Winograd & U. Neisser (Eds.), *Affect and accuracy in recall: Studies of "flashbulb memories"* (pp. 9–31). Cambridge, England: Cambridge University Press.

Nelson, C. A., Zeanah, C. H., Fox, N. A., Marshall, P. J., Smyke, A. T., & Guthrie, D. (2007). Cognitive recovery in socially deprived young children: The Bucharest early intervention project. *Science, 318*, 1937–1940.

Nemeth, C., & Chiles, C. (1988). Modelling courage: The role of dissent in fostering independence. *European Journal of Social Psychology, 18*, 275–280.

Netherlands Ministry of Justice. (1999). Fact sheet: Dutch drugs policy. Utrecht: Trimbos Institute, Netherlands Institute of Mental Health and Addiction.

Nettleback, T., & Lally, M. (1976). Inspection time and measured intelligence. *British Journal of Psychology, 67*, 17–22.

Neubauer, A. C., & Fink, A. (2009). Intelligence and neural efficiency: Measures of brain activation versus measures of functional connectivity in the brain. *Intelligence, 37*(2), 223–229.

Neuberg, S. L., Kenrick, D. T., & Schaller, M. (2010). Evolutionary social psychology. In S. T. Fiske, D. T. Gilbert, & G. Lindzey (Eds.), *The handbook of social psychology* (5th ed., Vol. 2). New York: Wiley.

Neugebauer, R., Hoek, H. W., & Susser, E. (1999). Prenatal exposure to wartime famine and development of antisocial personality in early adulthood. *Journal of the American Medical Association, 282*, 455–462.

Newberg, A., Alavi, A., Baime, M., Pourdehnad, M., Santanna, J., & d'Aquili, E. (2001). The measurement of regional cerebral blood flow during the complex cognitive task of meditation: A preliminary SPECT study. *Psychiatry Research: Neuroimaging, 106*, 113–122.

Newell, A., Shaw, J. C., & Simon, H. A. (1958). Elements of a theory of human problem solving. *Psychological Review, 65*, 151–166.

Newman, A. J., Bavelier, D., Corina, D., Jezzard, P., & Neville, H. J. (2002). A critical period for right hemisphere recruitment in American Sign Language processing. *Nature Neuroscience, 5*, 76–80.

Newman, L. S., Baumeister, R. F., & Duff, K. J. (1995). A new look at defensive projection: Thought suppression, accessibility, and biased person perception. *Journal of Personality and Social Psychology, 72*, 980–1001.

Newman, M. G., & Stone, A. A. (1996). Does humor moderate the effects of experimentally induced stress? *Annals of Behavioral Medicine, 18*, 101–109.

Newsome, W. T., & Paré, E. B. (1988). A selective impairment of motion perception following lesions of the middle temporal visual area (MT). *Journal of Neuroscience, 8*, 2201–2211.

Neylan, T. C., Metzler, T. J., Best, S. R., Weiss, D. S., Fagan, J. A., Libermans, A., et al. (2002). Critical incident exposure and sleep quality in police officers. *Psychosomatic Medicine, 64*, 345–352.

Niaura, R., Todaro, J. F., Stroud, L., Spiro, A. III, Ward, K. D., Weiss, S., et al. (2002). Hostility, the metabolic syndrome, and incident coronary heart disease. *Health Psychology, 21*, 588–593.

Nicoladis, E., & Genesee, F. (1997). Language development in preschool bilingual children. *Journal of Speech-Language Pathology & Audiology, 21*, 258–270.

Niedenthal, P. M., Barsalou, L. W., Winkielman, P., Krauth-Gruber, S., & Ric, F. (2005). Embodiment in attitudes, social perception, and emotion. *Personality and Social Psychology Review, 9*(3), 184–211.

Nikles, C. D., II, Brecht, D. L., Klinger, E., & Bursell, A. L. (1998). The effects of current concern- and nonconcern-related waking suggestions on nocturnal dream content. *Journal of Personality and Social Psychology, 75*, 242–255.

Nikula, R., Klinger, E., & Larson-Gutman, M. K. (1993). Current concerns and electrodermal reactivity: Responses to words and thoughts. *Journal of Personality, 61*, 63–84.

Nisbett, R. E. (2009). *Intelligence and how to get it.* New York: Norton.

Nisbett, R. E., Caputo, C., Legant, P., & Maracek, J. (1973). Behavior as seen by the actor and as seen by the observer. *Journal of Personality and Social Psychology, 27*, 154–164.

Nisbett, R. E., & Cohen, D. (1996). *Culture of honor: The psychology of violence in the South.* Boulder, CO: Westview Press.

Nishino, S., Mignot, E., & Dement, W. C. (1995). Sedative-hypnotics. In A. F. Schatzberg & C. B. Nemeroff (Eds.), *American Psychiatric Press textbook of psychopharmacology* (pp. 405–416). Washington, DC: American Psychiatric Press.

Nissen, M. J., & Bullemer, P. (1987). Attentional requirements of learning: Evidence from performance measures. *Cognitive Psychology, 19*, 1–32.

Nolen-Hoeksema, S. (2008). Gender differences in coping with depression across the lifespan. *Depression, 3*, 81–90.

Norcross, J. C., Hedges, M., & Castle, P. H. (2002). Psychologists conducting psychotherapy in 2001: A study of the Division 29 membership. *Psychotherapy: Theory/Research/Practice/Training, 39*, 97–102.

Norrholm, S. D., & Ressler, K. J. (2009). Genetics of anxiety and trauma-related disorders. *Neuroscience, 164*, 272–287.

North, R. J., & Swann, W. B., Jr. (2009). Self-verification 360°: Illuminating the light and dark sides. *Self and Identity, 8*(2–3), 131–146.

Nosanchuk, T. A., & Lightstone, J. (1974). Canned laughter and public and private conformity. *Journal of Personality and Social Psychology, 29*, 153–156.

Nowak, M. A. (2006). Five rules for the evolution of cooperation. *Science, 314*, 1560–1563.

Noyes, R., Jr., Stuart, S. P., & Watson, D. B. (2008). A reconceptualization of the somatoform disorders. *Psychosomatics, 49*, 14–22.

Nunn, J. A., Gregory, L. J., & Brammer, M. (2002). Functional magnetic resonance imaging of synesthesia: Activation of V4/V8 by spoken words. *Nature Neuroscience, 5*, 371–375.

Nuttin, J. M. (1985). Narcissism beyond Gestalt and awareness: The name letter effect. *European Journal of Social Psychology, 15*, 353–361.

Nyborg, H., & Jensen, A. R. (2001). Occupation and income related to psychometric *g. Intelligence, 29*, 45–55.

O'Connor, T. G., & Rutter, M. (2000). Attachment disorder following early severe deprivation: Extension and longitudinal follow-up. *Journal of the American Academy of Child and Adolescent Psychiatry, 39*, 703–712.

O'Laughlin, M. J., & Malle, B. F. (2002). How people explain actions performed by groups and individuals. *Journal of Personality and Social Psychology, 82*, 33–48.

O'Sullivan, L. F., & Allegeier, E. R. (1998). Feigning sexual desire: Consenting to unwanted sexual activity in heterosexual dating relationships. *Journal of Sex Research, 35*, 234–243.

Oakes, L. M., & Cohen, L. B. (1990). Infant perception of a causal event. *Cognitive Development, 5*, 193–207.

Oately, K., Keltner, D., & Jenkins, J. M. (2006). *Understanding emotions* (2nd ed.). Malden, MA: Blackwell.

Ochsner, K. N. (2000). Are affective events richly recollected or simply familiar? The experience and process of recognizing feelings past. *Journal of Experimental Psychology: General, 129*, 242–261.

Ochsner, K. N., Bunge, S. A., Gross, J. J., & Gabrieli, J. D. E. (2002). Rethinking feelings: An fMRI study of the cognitive regulation of emotion. *Journal of Cognitive Neuroscience, 14*, 1215–1229.

Ochsner, K. N., Ray, R. R., Hughes, B., McRae, K., Cooper, J. C., Weber, J., et al. (2009). Bottom-up and top-down processes in emotion generation: Common and distinct neural mechanisms. *Psychological Science, 20*, 1322–1331.

Ofshe, R. J. (1992). Inadvertent hypnosis during interrogation: False confession due to dissociative state, misidentified multiple personality, and the satanic cult hypothesis. *International Journal of Clinical and Experimental Hypnosis, 40*, 125–126.

Ofshe, R., & Watters, E. (1994). *Making monsters: False memories, psychotherapy, and sexual hysteria*. New York: Scribner/Macmillan.

Öhman, A. (1996). Preferential preattentive processing of threat in anxiety: Preparedness and attentional biases. In R. M. Rapee (Ed.), *Current controversies in the anxiety disorders*. New York: Guilford Press.

Öhman, A., Dimberg, U., & Öst, L. G. (1985). Animal and social phobias: Biological constraints on learned fear responses. In S. Reiss & R. Bootzin (Eds.), *Theoretical issues in behavior therapy* (pp. 123–175). New York: Academic Press.

Okagaki, L., & Sternberg, R. J. (1993). Parental beliefs and children's school performance. *Child Development, 64*, 36–56.

Okuda, J., Fujii, T., Ohtake, H., Tsukiura, T., Tanji, K., Suzuki, K., Kawashima, R., Fukuda, H., Ioh, M., & Yamadori, A. (2003). Thinking of the future and the past: The roles of the frontal pole and the medial temporal lobes. *Neuroimage, 19*, 1369–1380.

Olausson, P. O., Haglund, B., Weitoft, G. R., & Cnattingius, S. (2001). Teenage child-bearing and long-term socioeconomic consequences: A case study in Sweden. *Family Planning Perspectives, 33*, 70–74.

Oldham, J. M., Skodol, A. E., & Bender, D. S. (2005). *The American Psychiatric Publishing textbook of personality disorders*. Washington, DC: American Psychiatric Publishing.

Olds, J. (1956, October). Pleasure center in the brain. *Scientific American, 195*, 105–116.

Olds, J., & Fobes, J. I. (1981). The central basis of motivation: Intracranial self-stimulation studies. *Annual Review of Psychology, 32*, 523–574.

Olds, J., & Milner, P. (1954). Positive reinforcement produced by electrical stimulation of septal areas and other regions of rat brains. *Journal of Comparative and Physiological Psychology, 47*, 419–427.

Ollers, D. K., & Eilers, R. E. (1988). The role of audition in infant babbling. *Child Development, 59*, 441–449.

Olsson, A., & Phelps, E. A. (2007). Social learning of fear. *Nature Neuroscience, 10*, 1095–1102.

Oltmanns, T. F., Neale, J. M., & Davison, G. C. (1991). *Case studies in abnormal psychology* (3rd ed.). New York: Wiley.

Oltmanns, T. F., & Turkheimer, E. (2006). Perceptions of self and others regarding pathological personality traits. In R. Kreuger & J. Tackett (Eds.), *Personality and psychopathology* (pp. 71–111). New York: Guilford Press.

Olton, D. S., & Samuelson, R. J. (1976). Remembrance of places passed: Spatial memory in rats. *Journal of Experimental Psychology: Animal Behavior Processes, 2*, 97–116.

Onishi, K. H., & Baillargeon, R. (2005). Do 15-month-old infants understand false beliefs? *Science, 308*, 255–258.

Ono, K. (1987). Superstitious behavior in humans. *Journal of the Experimental Analysis of Behavior, 47*, 261–271.

Ophir, E., Nass, C., & Wagner, A. D. (2009). Cognitive montrol in media multitaskers. *Proceedings of the National Academy of Sciences, USA, 106*, 15583–15587.

Oppenheimer, M. (2008, May 4). The queen of the new age. *New York Times*.

Orban, G. A., Van Essen, D., & Vanduffel, W. (2004). Comparative mapping of higher visual areas in monkeys and humans. *Trends in Cognitive Sciences, 8*, 315–324.

Orban, P., Lungu, O., & Doyon, J. (2008). Motor sequence learning and developmental dyslexia. *Annals of the New York Academy of Sciences, 1145*, 151–172.

Orne, M. T., & Evans, F. J. (1965). Social control in the psychological experiment: Antisocial behavior and hypnosis. *Journal of Personality and Social Psychology, 1*, 189–200.

Oswald, L., Taylor, A. M., & Triesman, M. (1960). Discriminative responses to stimulation during human sleep. *Brain, 83*, 440–453.

Owen, A. M., Coleman, M. R., Boly, M., Davis, M. H., Laureys, S., & Pickard, J. D. (2006). Detecting awareness in the vegetative state. *Science, 313*, 1402.

Owens, W. A. (1966). Age and mental abilities: A second adult follow-up. *Journal of Educational Psychology, 57*, 311–325.

Oztekin, I., Curtis, C. E., & McElree, B. (2009). The medial temporal lobe and left inferior prefrontal cortex jointly support interference resolution in verbal working memory. *Journal of Cognitive Neuroscience, 21*, 1967–1979.

Pagnin, D., de Queiroz, V., Pini, S., & Cassano, G. B. (2008). Efficacy of ECT in depression: A meta-analytic review. *Focus, 6*, 155–162.

Paivio, A. (1969). Mental imagery in associative learning and memory. *Psychological Review, 76*, 241–263.

Paivio, A. (1971). *Imagery and verbal processes*. New York: Holt, Rinehart and Winston.

Paivio, A. (1986). *Mental representations: A dual coding approach*. New York: Oxford University Press.

Palmieri, R. M., Ingersoll, C. D., & Stone, M. B. (2002). Center-of-pressure parameters used in the assessment of postural control. *Journal of Sport Rehabilitation, 11*, 51–66.

Papez, J. W. (1937). A proposed mechanism of emotion. *Archives of Neurology and Pathology, 38,* 725–743.

Parker, E. S., Cahill, L. S., & McGaugh, J. L. (2006). A case of unusual autobiographical remembering. *Neurocase, 12,* 35–49.

Parker, H. A., & McNally, R. J. (2008). Repressive coping, emotional adjustment, and cognition in people who have lost loved ones to suicide. *Suicide and Life-Threatening Behavior, 38,* 676–687.

Parkinson, B., & Totterdell, P. (1999). Classifying affect-regulation strategies. *Cognition and Emotion, 13,* 277–303.

Parrott, A. C. (2001). Human psychopharmacology of Ecstasy (MDMA): A review of 15 years of empirical research. *Human Psychopharmacology, 16,* 557–577.

Parrott, A. C., Morinan, A., Moss, M., & Scholey, A. (2004). *Understanding drugs and behavior.* Chichester, England: Wiley.

Parrott, W. G. (1993). Beyond hedonism: Motives for inhibiting good moods and for maintaining bad moods. In D. M. Wegner & J. W. Pennebaker (Eds.), *Handbook of mental control* (pp. 278–308). Englewood Cliffs, NJ: Prentice Hall.

Parsons, T. (1975). The sick role and the role of the physician reconsidered. *Milbank Memorial Fund Quarterly, Health and Society, 53*(3), 257–278.

Partinen, M. (1994). Epidemiology of sleep disorders. In M. H. Kryger, T. Roth, & W. C. Dement (Eds.), *Principles and practice of sleep medicine* (2nd ed.). Philadelphia: Saunders.

Pascoe, E. A., & Richman, L. S. (2009). Perceived discrimination and health: A meta-analytic review. *Psychological Bulletin, 135,* 531–554.

Pascual-Leone, A., Amedi, A., Fregni, F., & Merabet, L. B. (2005). The plastic human brain cortex. *Annual Review of Neuroscience, 28,* 377–401.

Pascual-Leone, A., Houser, C. M., Reese, K., Shotland, L. I., Grafman, J., Sato, S., et al. (1993). Safety of rapid-rate transcranial magnetic stimulation in normal volunteers. *Electroencephalography and Clinical Neurophysiology, 89,* 120–130.

Passini, F. T., & Norman, W. T. (1966). A universal conception of personality structure? *Journal of Personality and Social Psychology, 4,* 44–49.

Patrick, C. J., Cuthbert, B. N., & Lang, P. J. (1994). Emotion in the criminal psychopath: Fear image processing. *Journal of Abnormal Psychology, 103,* 523–534.

Patterson, C. J. (1995). Lesbian mothers, gay fathers, and their children. In A. R. D'Augelli & C. J. Patterson (Eds.), *Lesbian, gay and bisexual identities across the lifespan: Psychological perspectives* (pp. 262–290). New York: Oxford University Press.

Paul, A. M. (2004). *The cult of personality testing.* New York: Free Press.

Pavlidis, I., Eberhardt, N. L., & Levine, J. A. (2002). Human behaviour: Seeing through the face of deception. *Nature, 415,* 35.

Pavlidou, E. V., Williams, J. M., & Kelly, L. M. (2009). Artificial grammar learning in primary school children with and without developmental dyslexia. *Annals of Dyslexia, 59,* 55–77.

Pavlov, I. P. (1923a). New researches on conditioned reflexes. *Science, 58,* 359–361.

Pavlov, I. P. (1923b, July 23). Pavloff. *Time, 1*(21), 20–21.

Pavlov, I. P. (1927). *Conditioned reflexes.* Oxford, England: Oxford University Press.

Pawlowski, B., Dunbar, R. I. M., & Lipowicz, A. (2000). Tall men have more reproductive success. *Nature, 362,* 156.

Payne, J. D., Schacter, D. L., Propper, R., Huang, L., Wamsley, E., Tucker, M. A., et al. (2009). The role of sleep in false memory formation. *Neurobiology of Learning and Memory, 92,* 327–334.

Payne, J. D., Stickgold, R., Swanberg, K., & Kensinger, E. A. (2008). Sleep preferentially enhances memory for emotional components of scenes. *Psychological Science, 19,* 781–788.

Pearce, J. M. (1987). A model of stimulus generalization for Pavlovian conditioning. *Psychological Review, 84,* 61–73.

Peck, J., & Shu, S. B. (2009). The effect of mere touch on perceived ownership. *Journal of Consumer Research, 36,* 434–447.

Peelen, M. V., & Kastner, S. (2009). A nonvisual look at the functional organization of visual cortex. *Neuron, 63,* 284–286.

Peissig, J. J., & Tarr, M. J. (2007). Visual object recognition: Do we know more now than we did 20 years ago? *Annual Review of Psychology, 58,* 75–96.

Pelham, B. W. (1985). Self-investment and self-esteem: Evidence for a Jamesian model of self-worth. *Journal of Personality and Social Psychology, 69,* 1141–1150.

Pelham, B. W., Carvallo, M., & Jones, J. T. (2005). Implicit egotism. *Current Directions in Psychological Science, 14,* 106–110.

Pelham, B. W., Mirenberg, M. C., & Jones, J. T. (2002). Why Susie sells seashells by the seashore: Implicit egotism and major life decisions. *Journal of Personality and Social Psychology, 82,* 469–487.

Pendergrast, M. (1995). *Victims of memory: Incest accusations and shattered lives.* Hinesburg, VT: Upper Access.

Penfield, W., & Rasmussen, T. (1950). *The cerebral cortex of man: A clinical study of localization of function.* New York: Macmillan.

Pennebaker, J. W. (1980). Perceptual and environmental determinants of coughing. *Basic and Applied Social Psychology, 1,* 83–91.

Pennebaker, J. W. (1989). Confession, inhibition, and disease. *Advances in Experimental Social Psychology, 22,* 211–244.

Pennebaker, J. W., & Chung, C. K. (2007). Expressive writing, emotional upheavals, and health. In H. Friedman & R. Silver (Eds.), *Handbook of health psychology* (pp. 263–284). New York: Oxford University Press.

Pennebaker, J. W., Kiecolt-Glaser, J. K., & Glaser, R. (1988). Disclosure of traumas and immune function: Health implications for psychotherapy. *Journal of Consulting and Clinical Psychology, 56,* 239–245.

Pennebaker, J. W., & Sanders, D. Y. (1976). American graffiti: Effects of authority and reactance arousal. *Personality and Social Psychology Bulletin, 2,* 264–267.

Perenin, M.-T., & Vighetto, A. (1988). Optic ataxia: A specific disruption in visuomotor mechanisms. I. Different aspects of the deficit in reaching for objects. *Brain, 111,* 643–674.

Perkins, D. N., & Grotzer, T. A. (1997). Teaching intelligence. *American Psychologist, 52,* 1125–1133.

Perlmutter, J. S., & Mink, J. W. (2006). Deep brain stimulation. *Annual Review of Neuroscience, 29,* 229–257.

Perloff, L. S., & Fetzer, B. K. (1986). Self-other judgments and perceived vulnerability to victimization. *Journal of Personality and Social Psychology, 50,* 502–510.

Perls, F. S., Hefferkine, R., & Goodman, P. (1951). *Gestalt therapy: Excitement and growth in the human personality.* New York: Julian Press.

Perrett, D. I., Burt, D. M., Penton-Voak, I. S., Lee, K. J., Rowland, D. A., & Edwards, R. (1999). Symmetry and human facial attractiveness. *Evolution and Human Behavior, 20,* 295–307.

Perrett, D. I., Rolls, E. T., & Caan, W. (1982). Visual neurones responsive to faces in the monkey temporal cortex. *Experimental Brain Research, 47,* 329–342.

Persons, J. B. (1986). The advantages of studying psychological phenomena rather than psychiatric diagnoses. *American Psychologist, 41,* 1252–1260.

Petersen, A. C. (1985). Pubertal development as a cause of disturbance—myths, realities, and unanswered questions. *Genetic Social and General Psychology Monographs, 111,* 205–232.

Petersen, A. C., & Grockett, L. (1985). Pubertal timing and grade effects on adjustment. *Journal of Youth and Adolescence, 14,* 191–206.

Peterson, C., & Seligman, M. E. P. (2004). *Character strengths and virtues: A handbook and classification.* Washington, DC: American Psychological Association.

Peterson, C., & Siegal, M. (1999). Representing inner worlds: Theory of mind in autistic, deaf and normal hearing children. *Psychological Science, 10,* 126–129.

Peterson, G. B. (2004). A day of great illumination: B. F. Skinner's discovery of shaping. *Journal of the Experimental Analysis of Behavior, 82,* 317–328.

Peterson, L. R., & Peterson, M. J. (1959). Short-term retention of individual verbal items. *Journal of Experimental Psychology, 58,* 193–198.

Peterson, S. E., Fox, P. T., Posner, M. I., Mintun, M. A., & Raichle, M. E. (1989). Positron emission tomographic studies of the processing of single words. *Journal of Cognitive Neuroscience, 1,* 154–170.

Petersson, K. M., Forkstam, C., & Ingvar, M. (2004). Artificial syntactic violations activate Broca's region. *Cognitive Science, 28,* 383–407.

Petitto, L. A., & Marentette, P. F. (1991). Babbling in the manual mode: Evidence for the ontogeny of language. *Science, 251,* 1493–1496.

Petrie, K. P., Booth, R. J., & Pennebaker, J. W. (1998). The immunological effects of thought suppression. *Journal of Personality and Social Psychology, 75,* 1264–1272.

Petty, R. E., & Cacioppo, J. T. (1986). The elaboration likelihood model of persuasion. In L. Berkowitz (Ed.), *Advances in experimental social psychology* (Vol. 19, pp. 123–205). New York: Academic Press.

Petty, R. E., Cacioppo, J. T., & Goldman, R. (1981). Personal involvement as a determinant of argument-based persuasion. *Journal of Personality and Social Psychology, 41,* 847–855.

Petty, R. E., & Wegener, D. T. (1998). Attitude change: Multiple roles for persuasion variables. In D. T. Gilbert, S. T. Fiske, & G. Lindzey (Eds.), *The handbook of social psychology* (4th ed., Vol. 1, pp. 323–390). Boston: McGraw-Hill.

Pew Hispanic Center. (2009). Between two worlds: How young Latinos come of age in America. Retrieved April 22, 2010, from http://pewhispanic.org/reports/report.php?ReportID=117

Pew Research Center for People & the Press. (1997). *Motherhood today: A tougher job, less ably done.* Pew Research Center: Author.

Pew Research Center for People & the Press. (2006). Attitudes toward homosexuality in African countries. Pew Research Center: Author.

Pew Research Center for People & the Press. (2009a). Growing old in America: Expectations vs. reality. Retrieved May 3, 2010, from http://pewsocialtrends.org/pubs/736/getting-old-in-america

Pew Research Center for People & the Press. (2009b). Majority continues to support civil unions: Most still oppose same-sex marriage. Retrieved March 20, 2010, from http://people-press.org/report/553/same-sex-marriage

Phelan, J., Link, B., Stueve, A., & Pescosolido, B. (1997). *Public conceptions of mental illness in 1950 in 1996: Has sophistication increased? Has stigma declined?* Paper presented at the American Sociological Association, Toronto, Ontario.

Phelps, E. A. (2006). Emotion and cognition: Insights from studies of the human amygdala. *Annual Review of Psychology, 24,* 27–53.

Phelps, E. A., & LeDoux, J. L. (2005). Contributions of the amygdala to emotion processing: From animal models to human behavior. *Neuron, 48,* 175–187.

Phillips, D. P., & Carstensen, L. L. (1986). Clustering of teenage suicides after television news stories about suicide. *New England Journal of Medicine, 315,* 685–689.

Phillips, F. (2002, January 24). Jump in cigarette sales tied to Sept. 11 attacks. *Boston Globe,* p. B1.

Piaget, J. (1954). *The child's conception of number.* New York: Norton.

Piaget, J. (1965). *The moral judgment of the child.* New York: Free Press. (Originally published 1932)

Piaget, J. (1977). The first year of life of the child. In H. E. Gruber & J. J. Voneche (Eds.), *The essential Piaget: An interpretative reference and guide* (pp. 198–214). New York: Basic Books. (Originally published 1927)

Piaget, J., & Inhelder, B. (1969). *The psychology of the child* (H. Weaver, Trans.). New York: Basic Books.

Pinel, J. P. J., Assanand, S., & Lehman, D. R. (2000). Hunger, eating, and ill health. *American Psychologist, 55,* 1105–1116.

Pines, A. M. (1993). Burnout: An existential perspective. In W. B. Schaufeli, C. Maslach, & T. Marek (Eds.), *Professional burnout: Recent developments in theory and research* (pp. 33–51). Washington, DC: Taylor & Francis.

Pines, A., M., & Aronson, E. (1988). *Career burnout: Causes and cures* (2nd ed.). New York: Free Press.

Pinker, S. (1994). *The language instinct.* New York: Morrow.

Pinker, S. (1997). Evolutionary psychology: An exchange. *New York Review of Books, 44,* 55–58.

Pinker, S. (2003). *The blank slate: The modern denial of human nature.* New York: Viking.

Pinker, S. (2007). A history of violence. *The New Republic Online.* March 19.

Pinker, S., & Bloom, P. (1990). Natural language and natural selection. *Behavioral & Brain Sciences, 13,* 707–784.

Piper, A., & Merskey, H. (2004). The persistence of folly: A critical examination of dissociative identity disorder. Part I. The excesses of an improbable concept. *Canadian Journal of Psychiatry, 49*(9), 592–600.

Pitcher, D., Garrido, L., Walsh, V., & Duchaine, B. C. (2008). Transcranial magnetic stimulation disrupts the perception and embodiment of facial expressions. *Journal of Neuroscience, 28*(36), 8929–8933.

Planty, M., Hussar, W., Snyder, T., Provasnik, S., Kena, G., Dinkes, R., Kewal Ramani, A., & Kemp, J. (2008). *The condition of education 2008* (NCES 2008-031). National Center for Education Statistics, Institute of Education Sciences, U.S. Department of Education, Washington, DC.

Plassman, H., O'Doherty, J., Shiv, B., & Rangel, A. (2008). Marketing actions can modulate neural representations of experienced pleasantness. *Proceedings of the National Academy of Sciences, USA, 105,* 1050–1054.

Platek, S. M., Critton, S. R., Myers, T. E., & Gallup, G. G., Jr. (2003). Contagious yawning: The role of self-awareness and mental state attribution. *Cognitive Brain Research, 17,* 223–227.

Plato. (trans. 1956). *Protagoras* (O. Jowett, Trans.). New York: Prentice Hall. (Original work from ca. 380 BC)

Pleis, J. R., Lucas, J. W., & Ward, B. W. (2009). Summary of health statistics for U.S. adults: National health interview survey, 2008, *Vital Health Stat 10*(242). National Center for Health Statistics.

Plomin, R., & Caspi, A. (1999). Behavioral genetics and personality. In L. A. Pervin & O. P. John (Eds.), *Handbook of personality: Theory and research* (Vol. 2, pp. 251–276). New York: Guilford Press.

Plomin, R., DeFries, J. C., McClearn, G. E., & Rutter, M. (1997). *Behavioral genetics* (3rd ed.). New York: Freeman.

Plomin, R., DeFries, J. C., McClearn, G. E., & McGuffin, P. (2001a). *Behavioral genetics* (4th ed.). New York: Freeman.

Plomin, R., Hill, L., Craig, I. W., McGuffin, P., Purcell, S., Sham, P., et al. (2001b). A genome-wide scan of 1842 DNA markers for allelic associations with general cognitive ability: A five-stage design using DNA pooling and extreme selected groups. *Behavior Genetics, 31,* 497–509.

Plomin, R., Scheier, M. F., Bergeman, C. S., Pedersen, N. L., Nesselroade, J. R., & McClearn, G. E. (1992). Optimism, pessimism, and mental health: A twin/adoption analysis. *Personality and Individual Differences, 13,* 921–930.

Plomin, R., & Spinath, F. M. (2004). Intelligence: Genetics, genes, and genomics. *Journal of Personality and Social Psychology, 86*, 112–129.

Plotnik, J. M., de Waal, F. B. M., & Reiss, D. (2006). Self-recognition in an Asian elephant. *Proceedings of the National Academy of Sciences, USA, 103*, 17053–17057.

Poliak, S., & Pelas, E. (2003). The local differentiation of myelinated axons at nodes of Ranvier. *Nature Reviews Neuroscience, 4*, 968–980.

Polivy, J., & Herman, C. P. (1992). Undieting: A program to help people stop dieting. *International Journal of Eating Disorders, 11*, 261–268.

Polivy, J., & Herman, C. P. (2002). If at first you don't succeed. False hopes of self-change. *American Psychologist, 57*, 677–689.

Poole, D. A., Lindsay, S. D., Memon, A., & Bull, R. (1995). Psychotherapy and the recovery of memories of childhood sexual abuse: U.S. and British practitioners' opinions, practices, and experiences. *Journal of Consulting and Clinical Psychology, 63*, 426–487.

Pope, A. W., & Bierman, K. L. (1999). Predicting adolescent peer problems and antisocial activities: The relative roles of aggression and dysregulation. *Developmental Psychology, 35*, 335–346.

Porter, S., & ten Brinke, L. (2008). Reading between the lies: Identifying concealed and falsified emotions in universal facial expressions. *Psychological Science, 19*, 508–514.

Portocarrero, J. S., Burright, R. G., & Donovick, P. J. (2007). Vocabulary and verbal fluency of bilingual and monolingual college students. *Archives of Clinical Neuropsychology, 22*, 415–422.

Posey, T. B., & Losch, M. E. (1983). Auditory hallucinations of hearing voices in 375 normal subjects. *Imagination, Cognition and Personality, 3*, 99–113.

Posner, M. I., & Raichle, M. E. (1994). *Images of mind.* New York: Freeman.

Post, R. M., Frye, M. A., Denicoff, G. S., Leverich, G. S., Dunn, R. T., Osuch, E. A., et al. (2008). Emerging trends in the treatment of rapid cycling bipolar disorder: A selected review. *Bipolar Disorders, 2*, 305–315.

Posthuma, D., & de Geus, E. J. C. (2006). Progress in the molecular-genetic study of intelligence. *Current Directions in Psychological Science, 15*, 151–155.

Postman, L., & Underwood, B. J. (1973). Critical issues in interference theory. *Memory & Cognition, 1*, 19–40.

Postmes, T., & Spears, R. (1998). Deindividuation and anti-normative behavior: A meta-analysis. *Psychological Bulletin, 123*, 238–259.

Power, M. L., & Schulkin, J. (2009). *The evolution of obesity.* Baltimore, MD: Johns Hopkins University Press.

Powers, M. B., & Emmelkamp, P. M. (2008). Virtual reality exposure therapy for anxiety disorders: A meta-analysis. *Journal of Anxiety Disorders, 22*, 561–569.

Prasada, S., & Pinker, S. (1993). Generalizations of regular and irregular morphology. *Language and Cognitive Processes, 8*, 1–56.

Pratkanis, A. R. (1992). The cargo-cult science of subliminal persuasion. *Skeptical Inquirer, 16*, 260–272.

Pressman, S. D., Cohen, S., Miller, G. E., Barkin, A., Rabin, B. S., & Treanor, J. J. (2005). Loneliness, social network size, and immune response to influenza vaccination in college freshmen. *Health Psychology, 24*, 297–306.

Price, J. L., & Davis, B. (2008). *The woman who can't forget: The extraordinary story of living with the most remarkable memory known to science.* New York: Free Press.

Prior, H., Schwartz, A., & Güntürkün, O. (2008). Mirror-induced behavior in the magpie (*Pica pica*): Evidence of self-recognition. *PLoS Biology, 6*, e202.

Prochaska, J. J., & Sallis, J. F. (2004). A randomized controlled trial of single versus multiple health behavior change: Promoting physical activity and nutrition among adolescents. *Health Psychology, 23*, 314–318.

Procopio, M., & Marriott, P. (2007). Intrauterine hormonal environment and risk of developing anorexia nervosa. *Archives of General Psychiatry, 64*(12), 1402–1407.

Provine, R. R. (2000). *Laughter: A scientific investigation.* New York: Viking.

Pruitt, D. G. (1998). Social conflict. In D. T. Gilbert, S. T. Fiske, & G. Lindzey (Eds.), *The handbook of social psychology* (4th ed., Vol. 2, pp. 470–503). New York: McGraw-Hill.

Putnam, F. W., Guroff, J. J., Silberman, E. K., Barban, L., & Post, R. M. (1986). The clinical phenomenology of multiple personality disorder: Review of 100 recent cases. *Journal of Clinical Psychiatry, 47*, 285–293.

Pyers, J. E., & Senghas, A. (2009). Language promotes false-belief understanding: Evidence from learners of a new sign language. *Psychological Science, 20*(7), 805–812.

Pyszczynski, T., Holt, J., & Greenberg, J. (1987). Depression, self-focused attention, and expectancy for positive and negative future life events for self and others. *Journal of Personality and Social Psychology, 52*, 994–1001.

Quattrone, G. A. (1982). Behavioral consequences of attributional bias. *Social Cognition, 1*, 358–378.

Querleu, D., Lefebvre, C., Titran, M., Renard, X., Morillon, M., & Crepin, G. (1984). Réactivité de nouveau-né de moins de deux heures de vie á la voix maternelle. *Journal de Gynecologie Obstetrique et de Biologie de la Reproduction, 13*, 125–134.

Quiroga, R. Q., Reddy, L., Kreiman, G., Koch, C., & Fried, I. (2005). Invariant visual representation by single neurons in the human brain. *Nature, 435*, 1102–1107.

Rabbitt, P., Diggle, P., Holland, F., & McInnes, L. (2004). Practice and drop-out effects during a 17-year longitudinal study of cognitive aging. *Journal of Gerontology: Psychological Sciences and Social Sciences, 59*(2), 84–97.

Raby, C. R., Alexis, D. M., Dickinson, A., & Clayton, N. S. (2007). Planning for the future by western scrub-jays. *Nature, 445*, 919–921.

Rachman, S. J., & DeSilva, P. (1978). Abnormal and normal obsessions. *Behavioral Research and Therapy, 16*, 223–248.

Radford, E., & Radford, M. A. (1949). *Encyclopedia of superstitions.* New York: Philosophical Library.

Rahe, R. H., Meyer, M., Smith, M., Klaes, G., & Holmes, T. H. (1964). Social stress and illness onset. *Journal of Psychosomatic Research, 8*, 35–44.

Raichle, M. E., & Mintun, M. A. (2006). Brain work and brain imaging. *Annual Review of Neuroscience, 29*, 449–476.

Ramachandran, V. S., & Altschuler, E. L. (2009). The use of visual feedback, in particular mirror visual feedback, in restoring brain function. *Brain, 132*, 1693–1710.

Ramachandran, V. S., & Blakeslee, S. (1998). *Phantoms in the brain: Probing the mysteries of the human mind.* New York: Morrow.

Ramachandran, V. S., & Hubbard, E. M. (2003). Hearing colors, tasting shapes. *Scientific American, 288*, 52–59.

Ramachandran, V. S., Rodgers-Ramachandran, D., & Stewart, M. (1992). Perceptual correlates of massive cortical reorganization. *Science, 258*, 1159–1160.

Ramirez-Esparza, N., Gosling, S. D., Benet-Martinezm, V., & Potter, J. P. (2004). Do bilinguals have two personalities? A special case of cultural frame-switching. *Journal of Research in Personality, 40*, 99–120.

Rapaport, D. (1946). *Diagnostic psychological testing: The theory, statistical evaluation, and diagnostic application of a battery of tests.* Chicago: Year Book Publishers.

Rapoport, J., Chavez, A., Greenstein, D., Addington, A., & Gogtay, N. (2009). Autism-spectrum disorders and childhood onset schizophrenia:

Clinical and biological contributions to a relationship revisited. *Journal of the American Academy of Child and Adolescent Psychiatry, 48,* 10–18.

Rappoport, J. L. (1990). Obsessive compulsive disorder and basal ganglia dysfunction. *Psychological Medicine, 20,* 465–469.

Rapport, R. (2005). *Nerve endings: The discovery of the synapse.* New York: Norton.

Raskin, N. J., & Rogers, C. R. (2000). Person-centered therapy. In R. J. Corsini & D. Wedding (Eds.), *Current psychotherapies* (6th ed., pp. 133–167). Itasca, IL: Peacock.

Rauschecker, J. P., & Scott, S. K. (2009). Maps and streams in the auditory cortex: Nonhuman primates illuminate human speech processing. *Nature Neuroscience, 12,* 718–724.

Raz, N. (2000). Aging of the brain and its impact on cognitive performance: Integration of structural and functional findings. In F. I. M. Craik & T. A. Salthouse (Eds.), *The handbook of aging and cognition* (pp. 1–90). Mahwah, NJ: Lawrence Erlbaum.

Read, K. E. (1965). *The high valley.* London: Allen and Unwin.

Reason, J., & Mycielska, K. (1982). *Absent-minded?: The psychology of mental lapses and everyday errors.* Englewood Cliffs: Prentice-Hall.

Reber, A. S. (1967). Implicit learning of artificial grammars. *Journal of Verbal Learning and Verbal Behavior, 6,* 855–863.

Reber, A. S. (1996). *Implicit learning and tacit knowledge: An essay on the cognitive unconscious.* New York: Oxford University Press.

Reber, A. S., & Allen, R. (2000). Individual differences in implicit learning. In R. G. Kunzendorf & B. Wallace (Eds.), *Individual differences in conscious experience.* Philadelphia: John Benjamins.

Reber, A. S., Walkenfeld, F. F., & Hernstadt, R. (1991). Implicit learning: Individual differences and IQ. *Journal of Experimental Psychology: Learning, Memory, and Cognition, 17,* 888–896.

Reber, P. J., Gitelman, D. R., Parrish, T. B., & Mesulam, M. M. (2003). Dissociating explicit and implicit category knowledge with fMRI. *Journal of Cognitive Neuroscience, 15,* 574–583.

Recanzone, G. H., & Sutter, M. L. (2008). The biological basis of audition. *Annual Review of Psychology, 59,* 119–142.

Rechsthaffen, A., Gilliland, M. A., Bergmann, B. M., & Winter, J. B. (1983). Physiological correlates of prolonged sleep deprivation in rats. *Science, 221,* 182–184.

Reed, C. L., Klatzky, R. L., & Halgren, E. (2005). What vs. where in touch: An fMRI study. *NeuroImage, 25,* 718–726.

Reed, D. R. (2008). Birth of a new breed of supertaster. *Chemical Senses, 33,* 489–491.

Reed, G. (1988). *The psychology of anomalous experience* (rev. ed.). Buffalo, NY: Prometheus Books.

Reeve, C. L., Heggestad, E. D., & Lievens, F. (2009). Modeling the impact of test anxiety and test familiarity on the criterion-related validity of cognitive ability tests. *Intelligence, 37*(1), 34–41.

Regan, P. C. (1998). What if you can't get what you want? Willingness to compromise ideal mate selection standards as a function of sex, mate value, and relationship context. *Personality and Social Psychology Bulletin, 24,* 1294–1303.

Regier, D. A., Narrow, W. E., Rae, D. S., Manderscheid, R. W., Locke, B. Z., & Goodwin, F. K. (1993). The de facto U.S. mental and addictive disorders service system: Epidemiologic Catchment Area prospective 1-year prevalence rates of disorders and services. *Archives of General Psychiatry, 41,* 934–941.

Regier, T., & Kay, P. (2009). Language, thought, and color: Whorf was half right. *Trends in Cognitive Sciences, 13,* 439–446.

Reinarman, C., Cohen, P. D. A., & Kaal, H. L. (2004). The limited relevance of drug policy: Cannabis in Amsterdam and San Francisco. *American Journal of Public Health, 94,* 836–842.

Reis, H. T., & Aron, A. (2008). Love: What is it, why does it matter, and how does it operate? *Perspectives on Psychological Science, 3,* 80–86.

Reiss, D., & Marino, L. (2001). Mirror self-recognition in the bottlenose dolphin: A case of cognitive convergence. *Proceedings of the National Academy of Sciences, USA, 98,* 5937–5942.

Reissland, N. (1988). Neonatal imitation in the first hour of life: Observations in rural Nepal. *Developmental Psychology, 24,* 464–469.

Reiter, E. O., & Lee, P. A. (2001). Have the onset and tempo of puberty changed? *Archives of Pediatrics and Adolescent Medicine, 155,* 988–989.

Renner, M. J., & Mackin, R. (1998). A life stress instrument for classroom use. *Teaching of Psychology, 25,* 46–48.

Rensink, R. A. (2002). Change detection. *Annual Review of Psychology, 53,* 245–277.

Rensink, R. A., O'Regan, J. K., & Clark, J. J. (1997). To see or not to see: The need for attention to perceive changes in scenes. *Psychological Science, 8,* 368–373.

Rentfrow, P. J., & Gosling, S. D. (2003). The do re mi's of everyday life: The structure and personality correlates of music preferences. *Journal of Personality and Social Psychology, 84,* 1236–1256.

Repacholi, B. M., & Gopnik, A. (1997). Early reasoning about desires: Evidence from 14- and 18-month-olds. *Developmental Psychology, 33,* 12–21.

Rescorla, R. A. (1966). Predictability and number of pairings in Pavlovian fear conditioning. *Psychonomic Science, 4,* 383–384.

Rescorla, R. A. (1988). Classical conditioning: It's not what you think it is. *American Psychologist, 43,* 151–160.

Rescorla, R. A. (2006). Stimulus generalization of excitation and inhibition. *Quarterly Journal of Experimental Psychology, 59,* 53–67.

Rescorla, R. A., & Wagner, A. R. (1972). A theory of Pavlovian conditioning: Variations in effectiveness of reinforcement and nonreinforcement. In A. Black & W. F. Prokasky, Jr. (Eds.), *Classical conditioning II.* New York: Appleton-Century-Crofts.

Ressler, K. J., & Nemeroff, C. B. (1999). Role of norepinephrine in the pathophysiology and treatment of mood disorders. *Biological Psychiatry, 46,* 1219–1233.

Revkin, A. C., & Seelye, K. Q. (2003, June 19). Report by EPA leaves out data on climate change. *New York Times.*

Rhode, D. L. (2010). *The beauty bias: The injustice of appearance in life and law.* Oxford, England: Oxford University Press.

Richards, M., Black, S., Mishra, G., Gale, C. R., Deary, I. J., & Batty, D. G. (2009). IQ in childhood and the metabolic syndrome in middle age: Extended follow-up of the 1946 British birth cohort study. *Intelligence, 37*(6), 567–572.

Richards, M. H., Crowe, P. A., Larson, R., & Swarr, A. (1998). Developmental patterns and gender differences in the experience of peer companionship during adolescence. *Child Development, 69,* 154–163.

Richert, E. S. (1997). Excellence with equity in identification and programming. In N. Colangelo & G. A. Davis (Eds.), *Handbook of gifted education* (2nd ed., pp. 75–88). Boston: Allyn & Bacon.

Richters, J., de Visser, R., Rissel, C., & Smith, A. (2006). Sexual practices at last heterosexual encounter and occurrence of orgasm in a national survey. *Journal of Sex Research, 43,* 217–226.

Rieber, R. W. (Ed.). (1980). *Wilhelm Wundt and the making of scientific psychology.* New York: Plenum Press.

Riefer, D. M., Kevari, M. K., & Kramer, D. L. F. (1995). Name that tune: Eliciting the tip-of-the-tongue experience using auditory stimuli. *Psychological Reports, 77,* 1379–1390.

Ringach, D. L., & Jentsch, J. D. (2009). We must face the threats. *The Journal of Neuroscience, 29,* 11417–11418.

Risman, J. E., Coyle, J. T., Green, R. W., Javitt, D. C., Benes, F. M., Heckers, S., et al. (2008). Circuit-based framework for understanding neurotransmitter and risk gene interactions in schizophrenia. *Trends in Neurosciences, 31,* 234–242.

Rizzolatti, G. (2004). The mirror-neuron system and imitation. In S. Hurley & N. Chater (Eds.), *Perspectives on imitation: From mirror neurons to memes* (pp. 55–76). Cambridge, MA: The MIT Press.

Rizzolatti, G., & Craighero, L. (2004). The mirror-neuron system. *Annual Review of Neuroscience, 27,* 169–192.

Rizzolatti, G., Fabbri-Destro, M., & Cattaneo, L. (2009). Mirror neurons and their clinical relevance. *Nature Clinical Practice Neurology, 5,* 24–34.

Roberson, D., Davidoff, J., Davies, I. R. L., & Shapiro, L. R. (2004). The development of color categories in two languages: A longitudinal study. *Journal of Experimental Psychology: General, 133,* 554–571.

Roberts, B. W., & Mroczek, D. (2008). Personality trait change in adulthood. *Current Directions in Psychological Science, 17,* 31–35.

Roberts, G. A. (1991). Delusional belief and meaning in life: A preferred reality? *British Journal of Psychiatry, 159,* 20–29.

Roberts, G. A., & McGrady, A. (1996). Racial and gender effects on the relaxation response: Implications for the development of hypertension. *Biofeedback and Self-Regulation, 21,* 51–62.

Robertson, L. C. (1999). What can spatial deficits teach us about feature binding and spatial maps? *Visual Cognition, 6,* 409–430.

Robertson, L. C. (2003). Binding, spatial attention and perceptual awareness. *Nature Reviews Neuroscience, 4,* 93–102.

Robins, L. N., Helzer, J. E., Hesselbrock, M., & Wish, E. (1980). Vietnam veterans three years after Vietnam. In L. Brill & C. Winick (Eds.), *The yearbook of substance use and abuse* (Vol. 11). New York: Human Sciences Press.

Robins, R. W., Fraley, R. C., & Krueger, R. F. (Eds.). (2007). *Handbook of research methods in personality psychology.* New York: Guilford Press.

Robinson, A., & Clinkenbeard, P. R. (1998). Giftedness: An exceptionality examined. *Annual Review of Psychology, 49,* 117–139.

Robinson, D. N. (1995). *An intellectual history of psychology.* Madison: University of Wisconsin Press.

Robinson, R. G., & Downhill, J. E. (1995). Lateralization of psychopathology in response to focal brain injury. In R. J. Davidson & K. Hugdahl (Eds.), *Brain asymmetry* (pp. 693–711). Cambridge, MA: The MIT Press.

Rochlen, A. B., Zack, J. S., & Speyer, C. (2004). Online therapy: Review of relevant definitions, debates, and current empirical support. *Journal of Clinical Psychology, 60,* 269–283.

Rodgers, A., Ezzati, M., Vander Hoorn, S., Lopez, A. D., Lin, B., Murray, C. J., et al. (2004). Distribution of major health risks: Findings from the Global Burden of Disease study. *PLoS Med, 1*(1), e27.

Rodieck, R. W. (1998). *The first steps in seeing.* Sunderland, MA: Sinauer.

Roediger, H. L., III. (2000). Why retrieval is the key process to understanding human memory. In E. Tulving (Ed.), *Memory, consciousness, and the brain: The Tallinn conference* (pp. 52–75). Philadelphia: Psychology Press.

Roediger, H. L., III, & Karpicke, J. D. (2006). Test-enhanced learning: Taking memory tests improves long-term retention. *Psychological Science, 17,* 249–255.

Roediger, H. L., III, & McDermott, K. B. (1995). Creating false memories: Remembering words not presented in lists. *Journal of Experimental Psychology: Learning, Memory, and Cognition, 21,* 803–814.

Roediger, H. L., III, & McDermott, K. B. (2000). Tricks of memory. *Current Directions in Psychological Science, 9,* 123–127.

Roediger, H. L., III, Weldon, M. S., & Challis, B. H. (1989). Explaining dissociations between implicit and explicit measures of retention: A processing account. In H. L. I. Roediger & F. I. M. Craik (Eds.), *Varieties of memory and consciousness: Essays in honor of Endel Tulving* (pp. 3–41). Hillsdale, NJ: Lawrence Erlbaum.

Rogers, C. R. (1951). *Client-centered therapy: Its current practice, implications, and theory.* Boston: Houghton Mifflin.

Rogers, T. B., Kuiper, N. A., & Kirker, W. S. (1977). Self-reference and the encoding of personal information. *Journal of Personality and Social Psychology, 35,* 677–688.

Romero-Corral, A., Montori, V. M., Somers, V. K., Korinek, J., Thomas, R. J., Allison, T. G., et al. (2006). Association of body weight with total mortality and with cardiovascular events in coronary artery disease: A systematic review of cohort studies. *Lancet, 368*(9536), 666–678.

Rosch, E. H. (1973). Natural categories. *Cognitive Psychology, 4,* 328–350.

Rosch, E. H. (1975). Cognitive representations of semantic categories. *Journal of Experimental Psychology: General, 104,* 192–233.

Rosch, E. H., & Mervis, C. B. (1975). Family resemblances: Studies in the internal structure of categories. *Cognitive Psychology, 7,* 573–605.

Rose, S. P. R. (2002). Smart drugs: Do they work? Are they ethical? Will they be legal? *Nature Reviews Neuroscience, 3,* 975–979.

Roseman, I. J. (1984). Cognitive determinants of emotion: A structural theory. *Review of Personality and Social Psychology, 5,* 11–36.

Roseman, I. J., & Smith, C. A. (2001). Appraisal theory: Overview, assumptions, varieties and controversies. In K. R. Scherer, A. Schorr, & T. Johnstone (Eds.), *Appraisal processes in emotion: Theory, methods, research* (pp. 3–19). New York: Oxford University Press.

Rosenbaum, J. E. (2009). Patient teenagers? A comparison of the sexual behavior of virginity pledgers and matched nonpledgers. *Pediatrics, 123*(1), e110–e120.

Rosenberg, M. (1965). *Society and the adolescent self-image.* Princeton, NJ: Princeton University Press.

Rosenhan, D. (1973). On being sane in insane places. *Science, 179,* 250–258.

Rosenkranz, K., Williamon, A., & Rothwell, J. C. (2007). Motorcortical excitability and synaptic plasticity is enhanced in professional musicians. *The Journal of Neuroscience, 27,* 5200–5206.

Rosenstein, M. J., Milazzo-Sayre, L. J., & Manderscheid, R. W. (1990). Characteristics of persons using specifically inpatient, outpatient, and partial care programs in 1986. In M. A. Sonnenschein (Ed.), *Mental health in the United States* (pp. 139–172). Washington, DC: U.S. Government Printing Office.

Rosenthal, R., & Fode, K. L. (1963). The effect of experimenter bias on the performance of the albino rat. *Behavioral Science, 8,* 183–189.

Ross, D. F., Ceci, S. J., Dunning, D., & Toglia, M. P. (1994). Unconscious transference and mistaken identity: When a witness misidentifies a familiar but innocent person. *Journal of Applied Psychology, 79,* 918–930.

Ross, L. (1977). The intuitive psychologist and his shortcomings: Distortions in the attribution process. *Advances in Experimental Social Psychology, 10,* 173–220.

Ross, L., Amabile, T. M., & Steinmetz, J. L. (1977). Social roles, social control, and biases in social-perception processes. *Journal of Personality and Social Psychology, 35,* 485–494.

Ross, L., & Nisbett, R. E. (1991). *The person and the situation.* New York: McGraw-Hill.

Roth, H. P., & Caron, H. S. (1978). Accuracy of doctors' estimates and patients' statements on adherence to a drug regimen. *Clinical Pharmacology and Therapeutics, 23,* 361–370.

Rothbart, M. K., & Bates, J. E. (1998). Temperament. In W. Damon (Series Ed.) & N. Eisenberg (Vol. Ed.), *Handbook of child psychology: Vol. 3. Social, emotional and personality development* (5th ed., pp. 105–176). New York: Wiley.

Rothbaum, B. O., Hodges, L., Watson, B. A., Kessler, G. D., & Opdyke, D. (1996). Virtual reality exposure therapy in the treatment of fear of flying: A case report. *Behaviour Research and Therapy, 34,* 477–481.

Rothbaum, B. O., & Schwartz, A. C. (2002). Exposure therapy for post-traumatic stress disorder. *American Journal of Psychotherapy, 56,* 59–75.

Rotstein, A. H. (2006, November 11). Despite 2–1 defeat on Election Day, backer of $1 million voter lottery still likes the idea. *Associated Press.*

Rotter, J. B. (1966). Generalized expectancies for internal versus external locus of control of reinforcement. *Psychological Monographs: General and Applied, 80,* 1–28.

Rotton, L. (1992). Trait humor and longevity: Do comics have the last laugh? *Health Psychology, 11,* 262–266.

Rouw, R., & Scholte, H. S. (2007). Increased structural connectivity in grapheme-color synesthesia. *Nature Neuroscience, 10,* 792–797.

Rowa, K., Antony, M. M., Brar, S., Summerfeldt, L. J., & Swinson, R. P. (2000). Treatment histories of patients with three anxiety disorders. *Depression and Anxiety, 12,* 92–98.

Rowland, L. W. (1939). Will hypnotized persons try to harm themselves or others? *Journal of Abnormal and Social Psychology, 34,* 114–117.

Roy-Byrne, P. P., & Cowley, D. (1998). *Pharmacological treatment of panic, generalized anxiety, and phobic disorders.* New York: Oxford University Press.

Roy-Byrne, P. P., & Cowley, D. S. (2002). Pharmacological treatments for panic disorder, generalized anxiety disorder, specific phobia, and social anxiety disorder. In P. E. Nathan & J. M. Gorman (Eds.), *A guide to treatments that work* (2nd ed., pp. 337–365). New York: Oxford University Press.

Rozin, P. (1968). Are carbohydrate and protein intakes separately regulated? *Journal of Comparative and Physiological Psychology, 65,* 23–29.

Rozin, P., Bauer, R., & Catanese, D. (2003). Food and life, pleasure and worry, among American college students: Gender differences and regional similarities. *Journal of Personality and Social Psychology, 85,* 132–141.

Rozin, P., Dow, S., Moscovitch, M., & Rajaram, S. (1998). What causes humans to begin and end a meal? A role for memory for what has been eaten, as evidenced by a study of multiple meal eating in amnesic patients. *Psychological Science, 9,* 392–396.

Rozin, P., & Kalat, J. W. (1971). Specific hungers and poison avoidance as adaptive specializations of learning. *Psychological Review, 78,* 459–486.

Rozin, P., Trachtenberg, S., & Cohen, A. B. (2001). Stability of body image and body image dissatisfaction in American college students over about the last 15 years. *Appetite, 37,* 245–248.

Rubenstein, A. J., Kalakanis, L., & Langlois, J. H. (1999). Infant preferences for attractive faces: A cognitive explanation. *Developmental Psychology, 35,* 848–855.

Rubin, B. D., & Katz, L. C. (1999). Optical imaging of odorant representations in the mammalian olfactory bulb. *Neuron, 23,* 499–511.

Rubin, Z. (1973). *Liking and loving.* New York: Holt, Rinehart and Winston.

Rudman, L. A., Ashmore, R. D., & Gary, M. L. (2001). "Unlearning" automatic biases: The malleability of implicit prejudice and stereotypes. *Journal of Personality and Social Psychology, 81,* 856–868.

Rusbult, C. E. (1983). A longitudinal test of the investment model: The development (and deterioration) of satisfaction and commitment in heterosexual involvements. *Journal of Personality and Social Psychology, 45,* 101–117.

Rusbult, C. E., & Van Lange, P. A. M. (2003). Interdependence, interaction and relationships. *Annual Review of Psychology, 54,* 351–375.

Rusbult, C. E., Verette, J., Whitney, G. A., & Slovik, L. F. (1991). Accommodation processes in close relationships: Theory and preliminary empirical evidence. *Journal of Personality and Social Psychology, 60,* 53–78.

Rushton, J. P. (1995). Asian achievement, brain size, and evolution: Comment on A. H. Yee. *Educational Psychology Review, 7,* 373–380.

Rushton, J. P., & Templer, D. I. (2009). National differences in intelligence, crime, income, and skin color. *Intelligence, 37*(4), 341–346.

Russell, B. (1945). *A history of Western philosophy.* New York: Simon & Schuster.

Russell, J. A. (1980). A circumplex model of affect. *Journal of Personality and Social Psychology, 39,* 1161–1178.

Rutter, M., O'Connor, T. G., & the English and Romanian Adoptees Study Team. (2004). Are there biological programming effects for psychological development? Findings from a study of Romanian adoptees. *Developmental Psychology, 40,* 81–94.

Rutter, M., & Silberg, J. (2002). Gene-environment interplay in relation to emotional and behavioral disturbance. *Annual Review of Psychology, 53,* 463–490.

Ryan, R. M., & Deci, E. L. (2000). Self-determination theory and the facilitation of intrinsic motivation, social development, and well-being. *American Psychologist, 55,* 68–78.

Sachs, J. S. (1967). Recognition of semantic, syntactic, and lexical changes in sentences. *Psychonomic Bulletin & Review, 1,* 17–18.

Sackeim, H. A., & Devanand, D. P. (1991). Dissociative disorders. In M. Hersen & S. M. Turner (Eds.), *Adult psychopathology and diagnosis* (2nd ed., pp. 279–322). New York: Wiley.

Sacks, O. (1995). *An anthropologist on Mars.* New York: Knopf.

Sacks, O. (1996). *An anthropologist on Mars* (ppbk). Visalia, CA: Vintage.

Saffran, J. R., Aslin, R. N., & Newport, E. I. (1996). Statistical learning by 8-month-old infants. *Science, 274,* 1926–1928.

Sagiv, N., Heer, J., & Robertson, L. (2006). Does binding of synesthetic color to the evoking grapheme require attention? *Cortex, 42,* 232–242.

Sahakian, B., & Morein-Zamir, S. (2007). Professor's little helper. *Nature, 450*(7173), 1157–1159.

Salmon, D. P., & Bondi, M. W. (2009). Neuropsychological assessment of dementia. *Annual Review of Psychology, 60,* 257–282.

Salovey, P., & Grewal, D. (2005). The science of emotional intelligence. *Current Directions in Psychological Science, 14*(6), 281–285.

Salthouse, T. A. (1984). Effects of age and skill in typing. *Journal of Experimental Psychology: General, 113,* 345–371.

Salthouse, T. A. (1987). Age, experience, and compensation. In C. Schooler & K. W. Schaie (Eds.), *Cognitive functioning and social structure over the life course* (pp. 142–150). New York: Ablex.

Salthouse, T. A. (1996a). General and specific mediation of adult age differences in memory. *Journal of Gerontology: Series B: Psychological Sciences and Social Sciences, 51B,* P30–P42.

Salthouse, T. A. (1996b). The processing-speed theory of adult age differences in cognition. *Psychological Review, 103,* 403–428.

Salthouse, T. A. (2000). Pressing issues in cognitive aging. In D. Park & N. Schwartz (Eds.), *Cognitive aging: A primer.* Philadelphia: Psychology Press.

Salthouse, T. A. (2001). Structural models of the relations between age and measures of cognitive functioning. *Intelligence, 29,* 93–115.

Salthouse, T. A. (2006). Mental exercise and mental aging. *Perspectives on Psychological Science, 1*(1), 68–87.

Sampson, R. J., & Laub, J. H. (1995). Understanding variability in lives through time: Contributions of life-course criminology. *Studies of Crime Prevention, 4,* 143–158.

Sandin, R. H., Enlund, G., Samuelsson, P., & Lenmarken, C. (2000). Awareness during anesthesia: A prospective case study. *Lancet, 355,* 707–711.

Sapolsky, R. M., & Share, L. J. (2004). A pacific culture among wild baboons: Its emergence and transmission. *PLoS Biology, 2,* e106.

Sara, S. J. (2000). Retrieval and reconsolidation: Toward a neurobiology of remembering. *Learning and Memory, 7,* 73–84.

Sarris, V. (1989). Max Wertheimer on seen motion: Theory and evidence. *Psychological Research, 51,* 58–68.

Sarter, M. (2006). Preclinical research into cognition enhancers. *Trends in Pharmacological Sciences, 27,* 602–608.

Satcher, D. (2001). *The Surgeon General's call to action to promote sexual health and responsible sexual behavior.* Washington, DC: U.S. Government Printing Office.

Sato, S. (2001). Autonomy and relatedness in psychopathology and treatment: A cross-cultural formulation. *Genetic, Social, and General Psychology Monographs, 127,* 89–127.

Savage, C. R., Deckersbach, T., Heckers, S., Wagner, A. D., Schacter, D. L., Alpert, N. M., et al. (2001). Prefrontal regions supporting spontaneous and directed application of verbal learning strategies: Evidence from PET. *Brain, 124,* 219–231.

Savage-Rumbaugh, S., & Lewin, R. (1996). *Kanzi: The ape on the brink of the human mind.* New York: Wiley.

Savage-Rumbaugh, S., Shanker, S. G., & Taylor, T. J. (1998). *Apes, language, and the human mind.* Oxford, England: Oxford University Press.

Saver, J. L., & Rabin, J. (1997). The neural substrates of religious experience. *Journal of Neuropsychiatry and Clinical Neurosciences, 9,* 498–510.

Savic, I., Berglund, H., & Lindstrom, P. (2005). Brain response to putative pheromones in homosexual men. *Proceedings of the National Academy of Sciences, USA, 102,* 7356–7361.

Savic, I., & Lindstrom, P. (2008). PET and MRI show differences in cerebral asymmetry and functional connectivity between homo- and heterosexual subjects. *Proceedings of the National Academy of Sciences, USA, 105*(27), 9403–9408.

Savin-Williams, R. C. (1998). Disclosure to families of same-sex attraction by lesbian, gay and bisexual youth. *Journal of Research on Adolescence, 8,* 49–68.

Sawa, A., & Snyder, S. H. (2002). Schizophrenia: Diverse approaches to a complex disease. *Science, 295,* 692–695.

Sawyer, T. F. (2000). Francis Cecil Sumner: His views and influence on African American higher education. *History of Psychology, 3*(2), 122–141.

Sayette, M. A., Reichle, E. D., & Schooler, J. W. (2009). Lost in the sauce: The effects of alcohol on mind wandering. *Psychological Science, 20,* 747–752.

Scarborough, E., & Furumoto, L. (1987). *Untold lives: The first generation of American women psychologists.* New York: Columbia University Press.

Scarr, S., Pakstis, A. J., Katz, S. H., & Barker, W. B. (1977). Absence of a relationship between degree of White ancestry and intellectual skills within a Black population. *Human Genetics, 39*(1), 69–86.

Schachter, S. (1982). Recidivism and self-cure of smoking and obesity. *American Psychologist, 37,* 436–444.

Schachter, S., & Gross, L. P. (1968). Manipulated time and eating behavior. *Journal of Personality and Social Psychology, 10,* 98–106.

Schachter, S., & Singer, J. E. (1962). Cognitive, social, and psychological determinants of emotional state. *Physiological Review, 69,* 379–399.

Schacter, D. L. (1987). Implicit memory: History and current status. *Journal of Experimental Psychology: Learning, Memory, and Cognition, 13,* 501–518.

Schacter, D. L. (1996). *Searching for memory: The brain, the mind, and the past.* New York: Basic Books.

Schacter, D. L. (1999). The seven sins of memory: Insights from psychology and cognitive neuroscience. *American Psychologist, 54*(3), 182–203.

Schacter, D. L. (2001a). *Forgotten ideas, neglected pioneers: Richard Semon and the story of memory.* Philadelphia: Psychology Press.

Schacter, D. L. (2001b). *The seven sins of memory: How the mind forgets and remembers.* Boston: Houghton Mifflin.

Schacter, D. L., & Addis, D. R. (2007). The cognitive neuroscience of constructive memory: Remembering the past and imagining the future. *Philosophical Transactions of the Royal Society of London. Series B: Biological Sciences, 362,* 773–786.

Schacter, D. L., Addis, D. R., & Buckner, R. L. (2007). Remembering the past to imagine the future: The prospective brain. *Nature Reviews Neuroscience, 8,* 657–661.

Schacter, D. L., Addis, D. R., & Buckner, R. L. (2008). Episodic simulation of future events: Concepts, data, and applications. *Annals of the New York Academy of Sciences, 1124,* 39–60.

Schacter, D. L., Alpert, N. M., Savage, C. R., Rauch, S. L., & Albert, M. S. (1996a). Conscious recollection and the human hippocampal formation: Evidence from positron emission tomography. *Proceedings of the National Academy of Sciences, USA, 93,* 321–325.

Schacter, D. L., & Curran, T. (2000). Memory without remembering and remembering without memory: Implicit and false memories. In M. S. Gazzaniga (Ed.), *The new cognitive neurosciences* (2nd ed.). Cambridge, MA: The MIT Press.

Schacter, D. L., Dawes, R., Jacoby, L. L., Kahneman, D., Lempert, R., Roediger, H. L., & Rosenthal, R. (2008). Studying eyewitness investigations in the field. *Law and Human Behavior, 32,* 3–5.

Schacter, D. L., Dobbins, I. G., & Schnyer, D. M. (2004). Specificity of priming: A cognitive neuroscience perspective. *Nature Reviews Neuroscience, 5,* 853–862.

Schacter, D. L., Harbluk, J. L., & McLachlan, D. R. (1984). Retrieval without recollection: An experimental analysis of source amnesia. *Journal of Verbal Learning and Verbal Behavior, 23,* 593–611.

Schacter, D. L., Israel, L., & Racine, C. A. (1999). Suppressing false recognition in younger and older adults: The distinctiveness heuristic. *Journal of Memory and Language, 40,* 1–24.

Schacter, D. L., Reiman, E., Curran, T., Yun, L. S., Bandy, D., McDermott, K. B., et al. (1996b). Neuroanatomical correlates of veridical and illusory recognition memory: Evidence from positron emission tomography. *Neuron, 17,* 267–274.

Schacter, D. L., & Tulving, E. (1994). *Memory systems 1994.* Cambridge, MA: The MIT Press.

Schacter, D. L., Wagner, A. D., & Buckner, R. L. (2000). Memory systems of 1999. In E. Tulving & F. I. M. Craik (Eds.), *The Oxford handbook of memory.* New York: Oxford University Press.

Schacter, D. L., Wig, G. S., & Stevens, W. D. (2007). Reductions in cortical activity during priming. *Current Opinion in Neurobiology, 17,* 171–176.

Schaeffer, M. A., McKinnon, W., Baum, A., Reynolds, C. P., Rikli, P., & Davidson, L. M. (1985). Immune status as a function of chronic stress at Three-Mile Island [Abstract]. *Psychosomatic Medicine, 47,* 85.

Schafer, R. B., & Keith, P. M. (1980). Equity and depression among married couples. *Social Psychology Quarterly, 43,* 430–435.

Schaie, K. W. (1996). *Intellectual development in adulthood: The Seattle Longitudinal Study.* New York: Cambridge University Press.

Schaie, K. W. (2005). *Developmental influences on adult intelligence: The Seattle Longitudinal Study.* New York: Oxford University Press.

Schapira, A. H. V., Emre, M., Jenner, P., & Poewe, W. (2009). Levodopa in the treatment of Parkinson's disease. *European Journal of Neurology, 16,* 982–989.

Schatzberg, A. F., Cole, J. O., & DeBattista, C. (2003). *Manual of clinical psychopharmacology* (4th ed.). Washington, DC: American Psychiatric Publishing.

Scheier, M. F., Matthews, K. A., Owens, J. F., Schulz, R., Bridges, M. W., Magovern, G. J., Sr., et al. (1999). Optimism and rehospitalization after coronary artery bypass graft surgery. *Archives of Internal Medicine, 159,* 829–835.

Schenk, T., Ellison, A., Rice, N., & Milner, A. D. (2005). The role of V5/MT+ in the control of catching movements: An rTMS study. *Neuropsychologia, 43*, 189–198.

Scherer, K. R. (1999). Appraisal theory. In T. Dalgleish & M. Power (Eds.), *Handbook of cognition and emotion* (pp. 637–663). New York: Wiley.

Scherer, K. R. (2001). The nature and study of appraisal: A review of the issues. In K. R. Scherer, A. Schorr, & T. Johnstone (Eds.), *Appraisal processes in emotion: Theory, methods, research* (pp. 369–391). New York: Oxford University Press.

Schiff, M., Duyme, M., Stewart, J., Tomkiewicz, S., & Feingold, J. (1978). Intellectual status of working class children adopted early in upper middle class families. *Science, 200*, 1503–1504.

Schildkraut, J. J. (1965). The catecholamine hypothesis of affective disorders: A review of supporting evidence. *American Journal of Psychiatry, 122*, 509–522.

Schiller, D., Monfils, M. H., Raio, C. M., Johnson, D. C., LeDoux, J. E., & Phelps, E. A. (2010). Preventing the return of fear in humans using reconsolidation update mechanisms. *Nature, 463*, 49–54.

Schlegel, A., & Barry, H., III. (1991). *Adolescence: An anthropological inquiry*. New York: Free Press.

Schmader, T., Johns, M., & Forbes, C. (2008). An integrated process model of stereotype threat effects on performance. *Psychological Review, 115*, 336–356.

Schmidt, F. L., & Hunter, J. E. (1998). The validity and utility of selection methods in personnel psychology: Practical and theoretical implications of 85 years of research findings. *Psychological Bulletin, 124*, 262–274.

Schnapf, J. L., Kraft, T. W., & Baylor, D. A. (1987). Spectral sensitivity of human cone photoreceptors. *Nature, 325*, 439–441.

Schneider, B. H., Atkinson, L., & Tardif, C. (2001). Child-parent attachment and children's peer relations: A quantitative review. *Developmental Psychology, 37*, 86–100.

Schneider, M. (2001). Toward a reconceptualization of the coming-out process for adolescent females. In A. R. D'Augelli & C. J. Patterson (Eds.), *Lesbian, gay and bisexual identities and youth: Psychological perspectives* (pp. 71–96). New York: Oxford University Press.

Schneier, F., Johnson, J., Hornig, C. D., Liebowitz, M. R., & Weissman, M. M. (1992). Social phobia: Comorbidity and morbidity in an epidemiologic sample. *Archives of General Psychiatry, 49*, 282–288.

Schnorr, J. A., & Atkinson, R. C. (1969). Repetition versus imagery instructions in the short- and long-term retention of paired associates. *Psychonomic Science, 15*, 183–184.

Schoenemann, P. T., Sheenan, M. J., & Glotzer, L. D. (2005). Prefrontal white matter volume is disproportionately larger in humans than in other primates. *Nature Neuroscience, 8*, 242–252.

Schooler, J. W., Bendiksen, M., & Ambadar, Z. (1997). Taking the middle line: Can we accommodate both fabricated and recovered memories of sexual abuse? In M. A. Conway (Ed.), *Recovered memories and false memories* (pp. 251–292). Oxford, England: Oxford University Press.

Schooler, J. W., Reichle, E. D., & Halpern, D. V. (2005). Zoning out during reading: Evidence for dissociations between experience and meta-consciousness. In D. T. Levin (Ed.), *Thinking and seeing: Visual metacognition in adults and children* (pp. 204–226). Cambridge, MA: The MIT Press.

Schott, B. J., Henson, R. N., Richardson-Klavehn, A., Becker, C., Thoma, V., Heinze, H. J., & Duzel, E. (2005). Redefining implicit and explicit memory: The functional neuroanatomy of priming, remembering, and control of retrieval. *Proceedings of the National Academy of Sciences, USA, 102*, 1257–1262.

Schouwenburg, H. C. (1995). Academic procrastination: Theoretical notions, measurement, and research. In J. R. Ferrari, J. L. Johnson, & W. G. McCown (Eds.), *Procrastination and task avoidance: Theory, research, and treatment*. New York: Plenum Press.

Schreiner, C. E., Read, H. L., & Sutter, M. L. (2000). Modular organization of frequency integration in primary auditory cortex. *Annual Review of Neuroscience, 23*, 501–529.

Schreiner, C. E., & Winer, J. A. (2007). Auditory cortex mapmaking: Principles, projections, and plasticity. *Neuron, 56*, 356–365.

Schubert, T. W., & Koole, S. L. (2009). The embodied self: Making a fist enhances men's power-related self-conceptions. *Journal of Experimental Social Psychology, 45*, 828–834.

Schultz, D., Izard, C. E., & Bear, G. (2004). Children's emotion processing: Relations to emotionality and aggression. *Development and Psychopathology, 16*(2), 371–387.

Schultz, D. P., & Schultz, S. E. (1987). *A history of modern psychology* (4th ed.). San Diego: Harcourt Brace Jovanovich.

Schultz, W. (2006). Behavioral theories and the neurophysiology of reward. *Annual Review of Psychology, 57*, 87–115.

Schultz, W. (2007). Behavioral dopamine signals. *Trends in Neurosciences, 30*, 203–210.

Schwartz, B. L. (2002). *Tip-of-the-tongue states: Phenomenology, mechanisms, and lexical retrieval*. Mahwah, NJ: Lawrence Erlbaum.

Schwartz, C. E., Wright, C. I., Shin, L. M., Kagan, J., & Rauch, S. L. (2003). Inhibited and uninhibited infants "grown up": Adult amygdalar response to novelty. *Science, 300*, 1952–1953.

Schwartz, J. H., & Westbrook, G. L. (2000). The cytology of neurons. In E. R. Kandel, G. H. Schwartz, & T. M. Jessell (Eds.), *Principles of neural science* (pp. 67–104). New York: McGraw-Hill.

Schwartz, S., & Maquet, P. (2002). Sleep imaging and the neuropsychological assessment of dreams. *Trends in Cognitive Sciences, 6*, 23–30.

Schwartzman, A. E., Gold, D., & Andres, D. (1987). Stability of intelligence: A 40-year follow-up. *Canadian Journal of Psychology, 41*, 244–256.

Schwarz, N., & Clore, G. L. (1983). Mood, misattribution, and judgments of well-being: Informative and directive functions of affective states. *Journal of Personality and Social Psychology, 45*, 513–523.

Schwarz, N., Mannheim, Z., & Clore, G. L. (1988). How do I feel about it? The informative function of affective states. In K. Fiedler & J. Forgas (Eds.), *Affect cognition and social behavior: New evidence and integrative attempts* (pp. 44–62). Toronto: C. J. Hogrefe.

Scoville, W. B., & Milner, B. (1957). Loss of recent memory after bilateral hippocampal lesions. *Journal of Neurology, Neurosurgery, and Psychiatry, 20*, 11–21.

Scribner, S. (1975). Recall of classical syllogisms: A cross-cultural investigation of errors on logical problems. In R. J. Falmagne (Ed.), *Reasoning: Representation and process in children and adults*. Hillsdale, NJ: Lawrence Erlbaum.

Scribner, S. (1984). Studying working intelligence. In B. Rogoff & J. Lave (Eds.), *Everyday cognition: Its development in social context* (pp. 9–40). Cambridge, MA: Harvard University Press.

Sedikides, C., & Gregg, A. P. (2008). Self-enhancement: Food for thought. *Perspectives on Psychological Science, 3*(2), 102–116.

Segall, M. H., Campbell, D. T., & Herskovits, M. J. (1963). Cultural differences in the perception of geometric illusions. *Science, 139*, 769–771.

Segall, M. H., Lonner, W. J., & Berry, J. W. (1998). Cross-cultural psychology as a scholarly discipline: On the flowering of culture in behavioral research. *American Psychologist, 53*(10), 1101–1110.

Segerstrom, S. C. (2005). Optimism and immunity: Do positive thoughts always lead to positive effects? *Brain, Behavior, and Immunity, 19*, 195–200.

Seitler, B. (2008). Once the wheels are in motion: Involuntary hospitalization and forced medicating. *Ethical Human Psychology and Psychiatry, 10*, 31–42.

Seligman, M. E. P. (1971). Phobias and preparedness. *Behavior Therapy, 2,* 307–320.

Seligman, M. E. P. (1995). The effectiveness of psychotherapy: The consumer reports study. *American Psychologist, 48,* 966–971.

Selikoff, I. J., Robitzek, E. H., & Ornstein, G. G. (1952). Toxicity of hydrazine derivatives of isonicotinic acid in the chemotherapy of human tuberculosis. *Quarterly Bulletin of SeaView Hospital, 13,* 17–26.

Selye, H., & Fortier, C. (1950). Adaptive reaction to stress. *Psychosomatic Medicine, 12,* 149–157.

Semenza, C. (2009). The neuropsychology of proper names. *Mind & Language, 24,* 347–369.

Semenza, C., & Zettin, M. (1989). Evidence from aphasia from proper names as pure referring expressions. *Nature, 342,* 678–679.

Senghas, A., Kita, S., & Ozyurck, A. (2004). Children create core properties of language: Evidence from an emerging sign language in Nicaragua. *Science, 305,* 1782.

Senju, A., Maeda, M., Kikuchi, Y., Hasegawa, T., Tojo, Y., & Osanai, H. (2007). Absence of contagious yawning in children with autism spectrum disorder. *Biology Letters, 3*(6), 706–708.

Senju, A., Southgate, V., White, S., & Frith, U. (2009). Mindblind eyes: An absence of spontaneous theory of mind in Asperger syndrome. *Science, 325,* 883–885.

Serpell, R. (1974). Aspects of intelligence in a developing country. *African Social Research, 17,* 578–596.

Seymour, K., Clifford, C. W. G., Logothetis, N. K., & Bartels, A. (2010). Coding and binding of color and form in visual cortex. *Cerebral Cortex.* doi:10.1093/cercor/bhp265

Shafran, R., Clark, D. M., Fairburn, C. G., Arntz, A., Barlow, D. H., Ehlers, A., et al. (2009). Mind the gap: Improving the dissemination of CBT. *Behaviour Research and Therapy, 47,* 902–909.

Shafritz, K. M., Gore, J. C., & Marois, R. (2002). The role of the parietal cortex in visual feature binding. *Proceedings of the National Academy of Sciences, USA, 99,* 10917–10922.

Shah, J. Y., & Gardner, W. L. (Eds.). (2008). *Handbook of motivation science.* New York: Guilford Press.

Shah, J. Y., Higgins, E. T., & Friedman, R. S. (1998). Performance incentives and means: How regulatory focus influences goal attainment. *Journal of Personality and Social Psychology, 74,* 285–293.

Shallice, T., Fletcher, P., Frith, C. D., Grasby, P., Frackowiak, R. S. J., & Dolan, R. J. (1994). Brain regions associated with acquisition and retrieval of verbal episodic memory. *Nature, 368,* 633–635.

Shapiro, N. (2005, October 5–11). The day care scare. *Seattle Weekly.*

Shaw, J. S., Bjork, R. A., & Handal, A. (1995). Retrieval-induced forgetting in an eyewitness paradigm. *Psychonomic Bulletin & Review, 13,* 1023–1027.

Shedler, J. (2010). The efficacy of psychodynamic psychotherapy. *American Psychologist, 65,* 98–109.

Shedler, J., & Block, J. (1990). Adolescent drug use and psychological health: A longitudinal inquiry. *American Psychologist, 45,* 612–630.

Sheehan, P. (1979). Hypnosis and the process of imagination. In E. Fromm & R. S. Shor (Eds.), *Hypnosis: Developments in research and new perspectives.* Chicago: Aldine.

Sheese, B. E., & Graziano, W. G. (2005). Deciding to defect: The effects of video-game violence on cooperative behavior. *Psychological Science, 16,* 354–357.

Sheingold, K., & Tenney, Y. J. (1982). Memory for a salient childhood event. In U. Neisser (Ed.), *Memory observed* (pp. 201–212). New York: Freeman.

Shenton, M. E., Dickey, C. C., Frumin, M., & McCarley, R. W. (2001). A review of MRI findings in schizophrenia. *Schizophrenia Research, 49,* 1–52.

Shepherd, G. M. (1988). *Neurobiology.* New York: Oxford University Press.

Shepperd, J., Malone, W., & Sweeny, K. (2008). Exploring the causes of the self-serving bias. *Social and Personality Psychology Compass, 2*(2), 895–908.

Sherrod, D. (1974). Crowding, perceived control, and behavioral aftereffects. *Journal of Applied Social Psychology, 4,* 171–186.

Sherry, D. F., & Schacter, D. L. (1987). The evolution of multiple memory systems. *Psychological Review, 94,* 439–454.

Shettleworth, S. J. (1995). Memory in food-storing birds: From the field to the Skinner box. In E. Alleva, A. Fasolo, H. P. Lipp, L. Nadel, & L. Ricceri (Eds.), *Behavioural brain research in naturalistic and seminaturalistic settings* (pp. 159–192). Boston: Kluwer Academic Publishers.

Shiffman, S., Gnys, M., Richards, T. J., Paty, J. A., & Hickcox, M. (1996). Temptations to smoke after quitting: A comparison of lapsers and maintainers. *Health Psychology, 15,* 455–461.

Shih, M., Pittinsky, T. L., & Ambady, N. (1999). Stereotype susceptibility: Identity salience and shifts in quantitative performance. *Psychological Science, 10,* 80–83.

Shimamura, A. P., & Squire, L. R. (1987). A neuropsychological study of fact memory and source amnesia. *Journal of Experimental Psychology: Learning, Memory, and Cognition, 13,* 464–473.

Shinskey, J. L., & Munakata, Y. (2005). Familiarity breeds searching. *Psychological Science, 16*(8), 596–600.

Shiv, B., Loewenstein, G., Bechara, A., Damasio, H., & Damasio, A. R. (2005). Investment behavior and the negative side of emotion. *Psychological Science, 16,* 435–439.

Shomstein, S., & Yantis, S. (2004). Control of attention shifts between vision and audition in human cortex. *Journal of Neuroscience, 24,* 10702–10706.

Shore, C. (1986). Combinatorial play: Conceptual development and early multiword speech. *Developmental Psychology, 22,* 184–190.

Shweder, R. A. (1991). *Thinking through cultures: Expeditions in cultural psychology.* Cambridge, MA: Harvard University Press.

Shweder, R. A., & Sullivan, M. A. (1993). Cultural psychology: Who needs it? *Annual Review of Psychology, 44,* 497–523.

Siegel, A., Roeling, T. A. P., Gregg, T. R., & Kruk, M. R. (1999). Neuropharmacology of brain-stimulation-evoked aggression. *Neuroscience and Biobehavioral Reviews, 23,* 359–389.

Siegel, B. (1988, October 30). Can evil beget good? Nazi data: A dilemma for science. *Los Angeles Times.*

Siegel, S. (1976). Morphine analgesia tolerance: Its situational specificity supports a Pavlovian conditioning model. *Science, 193,* 323–325.

Siegel, S. (1984). Pavlovian conditioning and heroin overdose: Reports by overdose victims. *Bulletin of the Psychonomic Society, 22,* 428–430.

Siegel, S. (2005). Drug tolerance, drug addiction, and drug anticipation. *Current Directions in Psychological Science, 14,* 296–300.

Siegel, S., Baptista, M. A. S., Kim, J. A., McDonald, R. V., & Weise-Kelly, L. (2000). Pavlovian psychopharmacology: The associative basis of tolerance. *Experimental and Clinical Psychopharmacology, 8,* 276–293.

Sigl, J. C., & Chamoun, N. (1994). An introduction to bispectral analysis for the electroencephalogram. *Journal of Clinical Monitoring, 10,* 392–404.

Sigurdsson, T., Doyere, V., Cain, C. K., & LeDoux, J. E. (2007). Long-term potentiation in the amygdala: A cellular mechanism of fear learning and memory. *Neuropharmacology, 52,* 215–227.

Silver, R. L., Boon, C., & Stones, M. H. (1983). Searching for meaning in misfortune: Making sense of incest. *Journal of Social Issues, 39,* 81–102.

Simon, L. (1998). *Genuine reality: A life of William James.* New York: Harcourt Brace.

Simons, D. J., & Chabris, C. F. (1999). Gorillas in our midst: Sustained inattentional blindness for dynamic events. *Perception, 28,* 1059–1074.

Simons, D. J., & Levin, D. T. (1998). Failure to detect changes to people during a real-world interaction. *Psychonomic Bulletin & Review, 5,* 644–649.

Simons, D. J., & Rensink, R. A. (2005). Change blindness: Past, present, and future. *Trends in Cognitive Sciences, 9,* 16–20.

Simonton, D. K. (2000). Methodological and theoretical orientation and the long-term disciplinary impact of 54 eminent psychologists. *Review of General Psychology, 4,* 13–24.

Simonton, D. K. (2002). *Great psychologists and their times: Scientific insights into psychology's history.* Washington: APA Press.

Simonton, D. K., & Song, A. V. (2009). Eminence, IQ, physical and mental health, and achievement domain: Cox's 282 geniuses revisited. *Psychological Science, 20,* 429–434.

Simpson, E. L. (1974). Moral development research: A case study of scientific cultural bias. *Human Development, 17,* 81–106.

Simpson, J. A., Campbell, B., & Berscheid, E. (1986). The association between romantic love and marriage: Kephart (1967) twice revisited. *Personality and Social Psychology Bulletin, 12,* 363–372.

Singer, P. (1975). *Animal liberation: A new ethics for our treatment of animals.* New York: Random House.

Singer, T., Seymour, B., O'Doherty, J., Kaube, H., Dolan, R. J., & Frith, C. D. (2004). Empathy for pain involves the affective but not sensory components of pain. *Science, 303,* 1157–1162.

Singh, D. (1993). Adaptive significance of female physical attractiveness: Role of waist-to-hip ratio. *Journal of Personality and Social Psychology, 65,* 293–307.

Skinner, B. F. (1938). *The behavior of organisms: An experimental analysis.* New York: Appleton-Century-Crofts.

Skinner, B. F. (1948). "Superstition" in the pigeon. *Journal of Experimental Psychology, 38,* 168–172.

Skinner, B. F. (1950). Are theories of learning necessary? *Psychological Review, 57,* 193–216.

Skinner, B. F. (1953). *Science and human behavior.* New York: Macmillan.

Skinner, B. F. (1957). *Verbal behavior.* New York: Appleton-Century-Crofts.

Skinner, B. F. (1958). Teaching machines. *Science, 129,* 969–977.

Skinner, B. F. (1971). *Beyond freedom and dignity.* New York: Bantam Books.

Skinner, B. F. (1972). The operational analysis of psychological terms. In B. F. Skinner, *Cumulative record* (3rd ed., pp. 370–384). New York: Appleton-Century-Crofts. (Original work published 1945.)

Skinner, B. F. (1979). *The shaping of a behaviorist: Part two of an autobiography.* New York: Knopf.

Slater, A., Morison, V., & Somers, M. (1988). Orientation discrimination and cortical function in the human newborn. *Perception, 17,* 597–602.

Slotnick, S. D., & Schacter, D. L. (2004). A sensory signature that distinguished true from false memories. *Nature Neuroscience, 7,* 664–672.

Smallwood, J., & Schooler, J. W. (2006). The restless mind. *Psychological Bulletin, 132,* 946–959.

Smetacek, V. (2002). Balance: Mind-grasping gravity. *Nature, 415,* 481.

Smetana, J. G. (1981). Preschool children's conceptions of moral and social rules. *Child Development, 52,* 1333–1336.

Smetana, J. G., & Braeges, J. L. (1990). The development of toddlers' moral and conventional judgments. *Merrill-Palmer Quarterly, 36,* 329–346.

Smith, A. R., Seid, M. A., Jimanez, L. C., & Wcislo, W. T. (2010). Socially induced brain development in a facultatively eusocial sweat bee *Megalopta genalis* (Halictidae). *Proceedings of the Royal Society B: Biological Sciences.*

Smith, E. E., & Jonides, J. (1997). Working memory: A view from neuroimaging. *Cognitive Psychology, 33,* 5–42.

Smith, M. L., Glass, G. V., & Miller, T. I. (1980). *The benefits of psychotherapy.* Baltimore: Johns Hopkins University Press.

Smith, N., & Tsimpli, I.-M. (1995). *The mind of a savant.* Oxford, England: Oxford University Press.

Snedeker, J., Geren, J., & Shafto, C. (2007). Starting over: International adoption as a natural experiment in language development. *Psychological Science, 18,* 79–87.

Snyder, C. R., & Lopez, S. J. (Eds.). (2009). *Oxford handbook of positive psychology* (2nd ed.). New York: Oxford University Press.

Solomon, J., & George, C. (1999). The measurement of attachment security in infancy and childhood. In J. Cassidy & P. R. Shaver (Eds.), *Handbook of attachment: Theory, research and clinical applications* (pp. 287–316). New York: Guilford Press.

Solomon, S., Greenberg, J., & Pyszczynski, T. (1991). A terror management theory of social behavior: The psychological functions of self-esteem and cultural worldviews. In M. P. Zanna (Ed.), *Advances in experimental social psychology* (Vol. 24, pp. 93–159). New York: Academic Press.

Solomon, S., Greenberg, J., Pyszczynski, T., Greenberg, J., Koole, S. L., & Pyszczynski, T. (2004). The cultural animal: Twenty years of terror management theory and research. In *Handbook of experimental existential psychology* (pp. 13–34). New York: Guilford Press.

Somers, J. M., Goldner, E. M., Waraich, P., & Hsu, L. (2006). Prevalence and incidence studies of anxiety disorders: A systematic review of the literature. *Canadian Journal of Psychiatry, 51,* 100–113.

Son, L. K., & Metcalfe, J. (2000). Metacognitive and control strategies in study-time allocation. *Journal of Experimental Psychology: Learning, Memory, and Cognition, 26,* 204–221.

Sonnby-Borgstrom, M., Jonsson, P., & Svensson, O. (2003). Emotional empathy as related to mimicry reactions at different levels of information processing. *Journal of Nonverbal Behavior, 27,* 3–23.

Southgate, V., Senju, A., & Csibra, G. (2007). Action anticipation through attribution of false belief by two-year-olds. *Psychological Science, 18,* 587–592.

Spanos, N. P. (1994). Multiple identity enactments and multiple personality disorder: A sociocognitive perspective. *Psychological Bulletin, 116,* 143–165.

Spearman, C. (1904). "General intelligence," objectively determined and measured. *American Journal of Psychology, 15,* 201–293.

Speisman, J. C., Lazarus, R. S., Moddkoff, A., & Davison, L. (1964). Experimental reduction of stress based on ego-defense theory. *Journal of Abnormal and Social Psychology, 68,* 367–380.

Spellman, B. A. (1996). Acting as intuitive scientists: Contingency judgments are made while controlling for alternative potential causes. *Psychological Science, 7,* 337–342.

Sperling, G. (1960). The information available in brief visual presentations. *Psychological Monographs, 74* (Whole No. 48).

Sperry, R. W. (1964). The great cerebral commissure. *Scientific American, 210,* 42–52.

Spinoza, B. (1982). *The ethics and selected letters* (S. Feldman, Ed., & S. Shirley, Trans.). Indianapolis, IN: Hackett. (Original work published 1677)

Spiro, H. M., McCrea Curnan, M. G., Peschel, E., & St. James, D. (1994). *Empathy and the practice of medicine: Beyond pills and the scalpel.* New Haven, CT: Yale University Press.

Spitz, R. A. (1949). Motherless infants. *Child Development, 20,* 145–155.

Spitzer, R. L. (2003). Can some gay men and lesbians change their sexual orientation? 200 participants reporting a change from homosexual to heterosexual orientation. *Archives of Sexual Behavior, 32*(5), 403–417.

Spitzer, R. L., Gibbon, M., Skodol, A. E., Williams, J. B. W., & First, M. B. (1994). *DSM-IV casebook: A learning companion to the Diagnostic & Statistical Manual of Mental Disorders* (4th ed.). Washington, DC: American Psychiatric Press.

Sprecher, S. (1999). "I love you more today than yesterday": Romantic partners' perceptions of changes in love and related affect over time. *Journal of Personality and Social Psychology, 76*, 46–53.

Squire, L. R. (1992). Memory and the hippocampus: A synthesis from findings with rats, monkeys, and humans. *Psychological Review, 99*, 195–231.

Squire, L. R. (2009). The legacy of patient HM for neuroscience. *Neuron, 61*, 6–9.

Squire, L. R., & Kandel, E. R. (1999). *Memory: From mind to molecules.* New York: Scientific American Library.

Squire, L. R., Knowlton, B., & Musen, G. (1993). The structure and organization of memory. *Annual Review of Psychology, 44*, 453–495.

Srivistava, S., John, O. P., Gosling, S. D., & Potter, J. (2003). Development of personality in early and middle adulthood: Set like plaster or persistent change? *Journal of Personality and Social Psychology, 84*, 1041–1053.

Sroufe, L. A., Egeland, B., & Kreutzer, T. (1990). The fate of early experience following developmental change: Longitudinal approaches to individual adaptation in childhood. *Child Development, 61*, 1363–1373.

Staddon, J. E. R., & Simmelhag, V. L. (1971). The "superstition" experiment: A reexamination of its implications for the principles of adaptive behavior. *Psychological Review, 78*, 3–43.

Stankov, L. (2009). Conservatism and cognitive ability. *Intelligence, 37*, 294–304.

Stanovich, K. E. (2009). *What intelligence tests miss: The psychology of rational thought.* New Haven, CT: Yale University Press.

Starkey, P., Spelke, E. S., & Gelman, R. (1983). Detection of intermodal numerical correspondences by human infants. *Science, 222*, 179–181.

Starkey, P., Spelke, E. S., & Gelman, R. (1990). Numerical abstraction by human infants. *Cognition, 36*, 97–127.

Staw, B. M., & Hoang, H. (1995). Sunk costs in the NBA: Why draft order affects playing time and survival in professional basketball. *Administrative Science Quarterly, 40*, 474–494.

Steele, C. M., & Aronson, J. (1995). Stereotype threat and the intellectual test performance of African Americans. *Journal of Personality and Social Psychology, 69*, 797–811.

Steele, C. M., & Josephs, R. A. (1990). Alcohol myopia: Its prized and dangerous effects. *American Psychologist, 45*, 921–933.

Steele, H. (2008). Day care and attachment re-visited. *Attachment & Human Development, 10*, 223.

Steele, H., Steele, M., Croft, C., & Fonagy, P. (1999). Infant-mother attachment at one year predicts children's understanding of mixed emotions at six years. *Social Development, 8*, 161–178.

Stein, D. J., Phillips, K. A., Bolton, D., Fulford, K. W. M., Sadler, J. Z., & Kendler, K. S. (2010). What is a mental/psychiatric disorder? From DSM-IV to DMW-V. *Psychological Medicine.*

Stein, M., Federspiel, A., Koenig, T., Wirth, M., Lehmann, C., Wiest, R., Strik, W., Brandeis, D., & Dierks, T. (2009). Reduced frontal activation with increasing second language proficiency. *Neuropsychologia, 47*, 2712–2720.

Stein, M. B. (1998). Neurobiological perspectives on social phobia: From affiliation to zoology. *Biological Psychiatry, 44*, 1277–1285.

Stein, M. B., Chavira, D. A., & Jang, K. L. (2001). Bringing up bashful baby: Developmental pathways to social phobia. *Psychiatric Clinics of North America, 24*, 661–675.

Stein, M. B., Koverola, C., Hanna, C., Torchia, M. G., & McClarty, B. (1997). Hippocampal volume in women victimized by childhood sexual abuse. *Psychological Medicine, 27*, 951–959.

Stein, Z., Susser, M., Saenger, G., & Marolla, F. (1975). *Famine and development: The Dutch hunger winter of 1944–1945.* Oxford, England: Oxford University Press.

Steinbaum, E. A., & Miller, N. E. (1965). Obesity from eating elicited by daily stimulation of hypothalamus. *American Journal of Physiology, 208*, 1–5.

Steinberg, L. (1999). *Adolescence* (5th ed.). Boston: McGraw-Hill.

Steinberg, L., & Monahan, K. C. (2007). Age differences in resistance to peer influence. *Developmental Psychology, 43*, 1531–1543.

Steinberg, L., & Morris, A. S. (2001). Adolescent development. *Annual Review of Psychology, 52*, 83–110.

Steiner, F. (1986). Differentiating smiles. In E. Branniger-Huber & F. Steiner (Eds.), *FACS in psychotherapy research* (pp. 139–148). Zurich: Department of Clinical Psychology, Universität Zürich.

Steiner, J. E. (1973). The gustofacial response: Observation on normal and anencephalic newborn infants. In J. F. Bosma (Ed.), *Fourth symposium on oral sensation and perception: Development in the fetus and infant* (pp. 254–278). Bethesda, MD: U.S. Department of Heath, Education, and Welfare (DHEW 73-546).

Steiner, J. E. (1979). Human facial expressions in response to taste and smell stimulation. *Advances in Child Development and Behavior, 13*, 257–295.

Stellar, J. R., Kelley, A. E., & Corbett, D. (1983). Effects of peripheral and central dopamine blockade on lateral hypothalamic self-stimulation: Evidence for both reward and motor deficits. *Pharmacology, Biochemistry, and Behavior, 18*, 433–442.

Stellar, J. R., & Stellar, E. (1985). *The neurobiology of motivation and reward.* New York: Springer-Verlag.

Stelmack, R. M. (1990). Biological bases of extraversion: Psychophysiological evidence. *Journal of Personality, 58*, 293–311.

Stephens, R. S. (1999). Cannabis and hallucinogens. In B. S. McCrady & E. E. Epstein (Eds.), *Addictions: A comprehensive guidebook.* New York: Oxford University Press.

Sterelny, K., & Griffiths, P. E. (1999). *Sex and death: An introduction to philosophy of biology.* Chicago: University of Chicago Press.

Stern, J. A., Brown, M., Ulett, A., & Sletten, I. (1977). A comparison of hypnosis, acupuncture, morphine, Valium, aspirin, and placebo in the management of experimentally induced pain. In W. E. Edmonston (Ed.), *Conceptual and investigative approaches to hypnosis and hypnotic phenomena* (Vol. 296, pp. 175–193). New York: Annals of the New York Academy of Sciences.

Stern, W. (1914). *The psychological methods of testing intelligence* (G. M. Whipple, Trans.). Baltimore: Warwick & York.

Sternberg, R. J. (1986). A triangular theory of love. *Psychological Review, 93*, 119–135.

Stevens, G., & Gardner, S. (1982). *The women of psychology* (Vol. 1). Rochester: Schenkman Books.

Stevens, J. (1988). An activity approach to practical memory. In M. M. Gruneberg, P. E. Morris, & R. N. Sykes (Eds.), *Practical aspects of memory: Current research and issues* (Vol. 1, pp. 335–341). New York: Wiley.

Stevens, L. A. (1971). *Explorers of the brain.* New York: Knopf.

Stewart-Williams, S. (2004). The placebo puzzle: Putting together the pieces. *Health Psychology, 23*, 198–206.

Stickgold, R., Hobson, J. A., Fosse, R., & Fosse, M. (2001). Sleep, learning, and dreams: Off-line memory reprocessing. *Science, 294*, 1052–1057.

Stickgold, R., Malia, A., Maguire, D., Roddenberry, D., & O'Connor, M. (2000). Replaying the game: Hypnagogic images in normals and anmesics. *Science, 290,* 350–353.

Stigler, J. W., Shweder, R., & Herdt, G. (Eds.). (1990). *Cultural psychology: Essays on comparative human development.* Cambridge, England: Cambridge University Press.

Stone, A. A., Schwarts, J. E., Broderick, J. E., & Deaton, A. (2010). A snapshot of the age distribution of psychological well-being in the United States. *Proceedings of the National Academy of Sciences, USA, 107,* 9985–9990.

Stone, J., Perry, Z. W., & Darley, J. M. (1997). "White men can't jump": Evidence for the perceptual confirmation of racial stereotypes following a basketball game. *Basic and Applied Social Psychology, 19,* 291–306.

Stoodley, C. J., Ray, N., J., Jack, A., & Stein, J. F. (2008). Implicit learning in control, dyslexic, and garden-variety poor readers. *Annals of the New York Academy of Sciences, 1145,* 173–183.

Storm, B. C., Bjork, E. L., Bjork, R. A., & Nestojko, J. F. (2006). Is retrieval success a necessary condition for retrieval-induced forgetting? *Psychonomic Bulletin & Review, 2,* 249–253.

Storms, M. D. (1973). Videotape and the attribution process: Reversing actors' and observers' points of view. *Journal of Personality and Social Psychology, 27,* 165–175.

Strack, F., Martin, L. L., & Stepper, S. (1988). Inhibiting and facilitating conditions of the human smile: A nonobtrusive test of the facial feedback hypothesis. *Journal of Personality and Social Psychology, 54,* 768–777.

Strahan, E. J., Spencer, S. J., & Zanna, M. P. (2002). Subliminal priming and persuasion: Striking while the iron is hot. *Journal of Experimental Social Psychology, 38,* 556–568.

Strayer, D. L., Drews, F. A., & Johnston, W. A. (2003). Cell phone induced failures of visual attention during simulated driving. *Journal of Experimental Psychology: Applied, 9,* 23–32.

Streissguth, A. P., Barr, H. M., Bookstein, F. L., Sampson, P. D., & Carmichael Olson, H. (1999). The long-term neurocognitive consequences of prenatal alcohol exposure: A 14-year study. *Psychological Science, 10,* 186–190.

Striano, T., & Reid, V. M. (2006). Social cognition in the first year. *Trends in Cognitive Sciences, 10*(10), 471–476.

Strickland, L. H. (1991). Russian and Soviet social psychology. *Canadian Psychology, 32,* 580–595.

Striegel-Moore, R. H., & Bulik, C. M. (2007). Risk factors for eating disorders. *American Psychologist, 62,* 181–198.

Strohmetz, D. B., Rind, B., Fisher, R., & Lynn, M. (2002). Sweetening the till: The use of candy to increase restaurant tipping. *Journal of Applied Social Psychology, 32,* 300–309.

Strueber, D., Lueck, M., & Roth, G. (2006). The violent brain. *Scientific American Mind, 17.*

Stuss, D. T., & Benson, D. F. (1986). *The frontal lobes.* New York: Raven Press.

Suarez-Morales, L., & Lopez, B. (2009). The impact of acculturative stress and daily hassles on pre-adolescent psychological adjustment: Examining anxiety symptoms. *Journal of Primary Prevention, 30,* 335–349.

Subramaniam, K., Kounios, J., Parrish, T. B., & Jung-Beeman, M. (2009). A brain mechanism for facilitation of insight by positive affect. *Journal of Cognitive Neuroscience, 21,* 415–432.

Substance Abuse and Mental Health Services Administration. (2005). *Suicide warning signs.* Washington, DC: U.S. Department of Health and Human Services.

Suchman, A. L., Markakis, K., Beckman, H. B., & Frankel, R. (1997). A model of empathic communication in the medical interview. *Journal of the American Medical Association, 277,* 678–682.

Suddendorf, T., & Corballis, M. C. (2007). The evolution of foresight: What is mental time travel and is it unique to humans? *Behavioral and Brain Sciences, 30,* 299–313.

Suler, J. (2004). The online disinhibition effect. *Cyberpsychology and Behavior, 7,* 321–326.

Sulloway, F. J. (1992). *Freud, biologist of the mind.* Cambridge, MA: Harvard University Press.

Sulloway, F. J. (2007). Birth order and intelligence. *Science, 317,* 1711–1712.

Sundet, J. M., Eriksen, W., & Tambs, K. (2008). Intelligence correlations between brothers decrease with increasing age difference: Evidence for shared environmental effects in young adults. *Psychological Science, 19,* 843–847.

Susman, S., Dent, C., McAdams, L., Stacy, A., Burton, D., & Flay, B. (1994). Group self-identification and adolescent cigarette smoking: A 1-year prospective study. *Journal of Abnormal Psychology, 103,* 576–580.

Susser, E. B., Brown, A., & Matte, T. D. (1999). Prenatal factors and adult mental and physical health. *Canadian Journal of Psychiatry, 44*(4), 326–334.

Sussman, L. K., Robins, L. N., & Earls, F. (1987). Treatment-seeking for depression by Black and White Americans. *Social Science and Medicine, 24,* 187–196.

Suzuki, L. A., & Valencia, R. R. (1997). Race-ethnicity and measured intelligence: Educational implications. *American Psychologist, 52,* 1103–1114.

Swann, W. B., Jr. (1983). Self-verification: Bringing social reality into harmony with the self. In J. M. Suls & A. G. Greenwald (Ed.), *Psychological perspectives on the self* (Vol. 2, pp. 33–66). Hillsdale, NJ: Lawrence Erlbaum.

Swann, W. B., Jr. (in press). Self-verification theory. In A. W. Kruglanski, E. T. Higgins, & P. A. M. Lange (Eds.), *Handbook of theories of social psychology.* London: Sage.

Swann, W. B., Jr., & Rentfrow, P. J. (2001). Blirtatiousness: Cognitive, behavioral, and physiological consequences of rapid responding. *Journal of Personality and Social Psychology, 181*(6), 1160–1175.

Swann, W. B., Jr., Rentfrow, P. J., Guinn, J. S., Leary, M. R., & Tangney, J. P. (2003). Self-verification: The search for coherence. In *Handbook of self and identity* (pp. 367–383). New York: Guilford Press.

Swayze II, V. W. (1995). Frontal leukotomy and related psychosurgical procedures before antipsychotics (1935–1954): A historical overview. *American Journal of Psychiatry, 152,* 505–515.

Swednsen, J., Hammen, C., Heller, T., & Gitlin, M. (1995). Correlates of stress reactivity in patients with bipolar disorder. *American Journal of Psychiatry, 152,* 795–797.

Swets, J. A., Dawes, R. M., & Monahan, J. (2000). Psychological science can improve diagnostic decisions. *Psychological Science in the Public Interest, 1,* 1–26.

Swinkels, A. (2003). An effective exercise for teaching cognitive heuristics. *Teaching of Psychology, 30,* 120–122.

Szasz, T. S. (1987). *Insanity.* New York: Wiley.

Szechtman, H., & Woody, E. Z. (2006). Obsessive-compulsive disorder as a disturbance of security motivation: Constraints on comorbidity. *Neurotoxicity Research, 10,* 103–112.

Szechtman, H., Woody, E., Bowers, K. S., & Nahmias, C. (1998). Where the imaginal appears real: A positron emission tomography study of auditory hallucinations. *Proceedings of the National Academy of Sciences, USA, 95,* 1956–1960.

Szpunar, K. K., Watson, J. M., & McDermott, K. B. (2007). Neural substrates of envisioning the future. *Proceedings of the National Academy of Sciences, USA, 104,* 642–647.

Tajfel, H. (1970). Experiments in intergroup discrimination. *Scientific American, 223*, 96–102.

Tajfel, H., Billig, M. G., Bundy, R. P., & Flament, C. (1971). Social categorization and intergroup behaviour. *European Journal of Social Psychology, 1*, 149–178.

Tajfel, H., & Turner, J. C. (1986). The social identity theory of intergroup behavior. In S. Worchel & W. G. Austin (Eds.), *Psychology of intergroup relations* (pp. 7–24). Chicago: Nelson.

Tajfel, H., & Wilkes, A. L. (1963). Classification and quantitative judgement. *British Journal of Psychology, 54*, 101–114.

Takahashi, K. (1986). Examining the strange-situation procedure with Japanese mothers and 12-month-old infants. *Developmental Psychlogy, 22*, 265–270.

Tamis-LeMonda, C. S., Adolph, K. E., Lobo, S. A., Karasik, L. B., Ishak, S., & Dimitropoulou, K. A. (2008). When infants take mothers' advice: 18-month-olds integrate perceptual and social information to guide motor action. *Developmental Psychology, 44*, 734–746.

Tamminga, C. A., Nemeroff, C. B., Blakely, R. D., Brady, L., Carter, C. S., Davis, K. I., Dingledine, R., et al. (2002). Developing novel treatments for mood disorders: Accelerating discovery. *Biological Psychiatry, 52*, 589–609.

Tanaka, F., Cicourel, A., & Movellan, J. R. (2007). Socialization between toddlers and robots at an early childhood education center. *Proceedings of the National Academy of Sciences, USA, 104*(46), 17954–17958.

Tanaka, K. (1996). Inferotemporal cortex and object vision. *Annual Review of Neuroscience, 19*, 109–139.

Tang, T. Z., DeRubeis, R., Hollon, S. D., Amsterdam, J., Shelton, R., & Schalet, B. (2009). Personality change during depression treatment: A placebo-controlled trial. *Archives of General Psychiatry, 66*, 1322–1330.

Tang, Y.-P., Shimizu, E., Dube, G. R., Rampon, C., Kerchner, G. A., Zhuo, M., et al. (1999). Genetic enhancement of learning and memory in mice. *Nature, 401*, 63–69.

Tanner, L. (2002, February 7). Woman gives birth after pre-pregnancy test is used to screen for early Alzheimer's gene. *Associated Press.*

Tarr, M. J., & Vuong, Q. C. (2002). Visual object recognition. In S. Yantis & H. Pashler (Eds.), *Stevens' handbook of experimental psychology: Vol. 1. Sensation and perception* (3rd ed., pp. 287–314). New York: Wiley.

Tart, C. T. (Ed.). (1969). *Altered states of consciousness*. New York: Wiley.

Task Force on Promotion and Dissemination of Psychological Procedures. (1995). Training in and dissemination of empirically-validated psychological treatments: Report and recommendations. *Clinical Psychologist, 48*, 3–23.

Taylor, D., & Lambert, W. (1990). *Language and culture in the lives of immigrants and refugees*. Austin, TX: Hogg Foundation for Mental Health.

Taylor, E. (2001). *William James on consciousness beyond the margin*. Princeton, NJ: Princeton University Press.

Taylor, S. E. (1986). *Health psychology*. New York: Random House.

Taylor, S. E. (1989). *Positive illusions*. New York: Basic Books.

Taylor, S. E. (2002). *The tending instinct: How nurturing is essential to who we are and how we live*. New York: Times Books.

Taylor, S. E., & Brown, J. D. (1988). Illusion and well-being: A social psychological perspective on mental health. *Psychological Bulletin, 103*, 193–210.

Taylor, S. E., & Fiske, S. T. (1978). Salience, attention, and attribution: Top of the head phenomena. In L. Berkowitz (Ed.), *Advances in experimental social psychology* (Vol. 11, pp. 249–288). New York: Academic Press.

Teasdale, J. D., Segal, Z. V., & Williams, J. M. G. (2000). Prevention of relapse/recurrence in major depression by mindfulness-based cognitive therapy. *Journal of Consulting and Clinical Psychology, 68*, 615–623.

Tejada-Vera, B., & Sutton, P. D. (2009). Births, marriages, divorces, and deaths: Provisional data for 2008. *National Vital Statistics Reports, 57.*

Telch, M. J., Lucas, J. A., & Nelson, P. (1989). Non-clinical panic in college students: An investigation of prevalence and symptomology. *Journal of Abnormal Psychology, 98*, 300–306.

Tellegen, A., & Atkinson, G. (1974). Openness to absorbing and self-altering experiences ("absorption"), a trait related to hypnotic susceptibility. *Journal of Abnormal Psychology, 83*, 268–277.

Tellegen, A., Lykken, D. T., Bouchard, T. J., Wilcox, K., Segal, N., & Rich, A. (1988). Personality similarity in twins reared together and apart. *Journal of Personality and Social Psychology, 54*, 1031–1039.

Temerlin, M. K., & Trousdale, W. W. (1969). The social psychology of clinical diagnosis. *Psychotherapy: Theory, Research & Practice, 6*, 24–29.

Tempini, M. L., Price, C. J., Josephs, O., Vandenberghe, R., Cappa, S. F., Kapur, N., et al. (1998). The neural systems sustaining face and proper-name processing. *Brain, 121*, 2103–2118.

Terman, L. M. (1916). *The measurement of intelligence*. Boston: Houghton Mifflin.

Terman, L. M., & Oden, M. H. (1959). *Genetic studies of genius: Vol. 5. The gifted group at mid-life*. Stanford, CA: Stanford University Press.

Terman, M., Terman, J. S., Quitkin, F. M., McGrath, P. J., Stewart, J. W., & Rafferty, B. (1989). Light therapy for seasonal affective disorder. A review of efficacy. *Neuropsychopharmacology, 2*, 1–22.

Tesser, A. (1991). Emotion in social comparison and reflection processes. In J. Suls & T. A. Wills (Ed.), *Social comparison: Contemporary theory and research* (pp. 117–148). Hillsdale, NJ: Lawrence Erlbaum.

Tesser, A. (1993). The importance of heritability in psychological research: The case of attitudes. *Psychological Review, 100*, 129–142.

Teyler, T. J., & DiScenna, P. (1986). The hippocampal memory indexing theory. *Behavioral Neuroscience, 100*, 147–154.

Thaker, G. K. (2002). Current progress in schizophrenia research. Search for genes of schizophrenia: Back to defining valid phenes. *Journal of Nervous and Mental Disease, 190*, 411–412.

Thaler, R. H. (1988). The ultimatum game. *Journal of Economic Perspectives, 2*, 195–206.

Thase, M. E., & Howland, R. H. (1995). Biological processes in depression: An updated review and integration. In E. E. Beckham & W. R. Leber (Eds.), *Handbook of depression* (2nd ed., pp. 213–279). New York: Guilford Press.

The State of the Nation's Housing. (2009). Cambridge, MA: Joint Center for Housing Studies of Harvard University.

The World Bank. (2009). *World development report 2009: Reshaping economic geography*. Washington DC: Quebecor World.

Thelen, E., Corbetta, D., Kamm, K., Spencer, J. P., Schneider, K., & Zernicke, R. F. (1993). The transition to reaching: Mapping intention and intrinsic dynamics. *Child Development, 64*, 1058–1098.

Thibaut, J. W., & Kelley, H. H. (1959). *The social psychology of groups*. New Brunswick, NJ: Transaction Publishers.

Thoma, S. J., Narvaez, D., Rest, J., & Derryberry, P. (1999). Does moral judgment development reduce to political attitudes or verbal ability? Evidence using the defining issues test. *Educational Psychology Review*, 325–341.

Thomaes, S., Bushman, B. J., Stegge, H., & Olthof, T. (2008). Trumping shame by blasts of noise: Narcissism, self-esteem, shame, and aggression in young adolescents. *Child Development, 79*(6), 1792–1801.

Thomas, A., & Chess, S. (1977). *Temperament and development*. New York: Brunner/Mazel.

Thompson, B., Coronado, G., Chen, L., Thompson, L. A., Halperin, A., Jaffe, R., et al. (2007). Prevalence and characteristics of smokers at 30 Pacific Northwest colleges and universities. *Nicotine & Tobacco Research, 9*, 429–438.

Thompson, C. P., Skowronski, J., Larsen, S. F., & Betz, A. (1996). *Autobiographical memory: Remembering what and remembering when.* Mahwah, NJ: Lawrence Erlbaum.

Thompson, P. M., Giedd, J. N., Woods, R. P., MacDonald, D., Evans, A. C., & Toga, A. W. (2000). Growth patterns in the developing brain detected by using continuum mechanical tensor maps. *Nature, 404*, 190–193.

Thompson, P. M., Vidal, C., Giedd, J. N., Gochman, P., Blumenthal, J., Nicolson, R., et al. (2001). Accelerated gray matter loss in very early-onset schizophrenia. *Proceedings of the National Academy of Sciences, USA, 98*, 11650–11655.

Thompson, R. F. (2005). In search of memory traces. *Annual Review of Psychology, 56*, 1–23.

Thompson, S. C., Schlehofer, M. l. M., Shah, J. Y., & Gardner, W. L. (2008). The many sides of control motivation: Motives for high, low, and illusory control. In *Handbook of motivation science* (pp. 41–56). New York: Guilford Press.

Thomson, D. M. (1988). Context and false recognition. In G. M. Davies & D. M. Thomson (Eds.), *Memory in context: Context in memory* (pp. 285–304). Chichester, England: Wiley.

Thorndike, E. L. (1898). Animal intelligence: An experimental study of associative processes in animals. *Psychological Review Monograph Supplements, 2*, 4–160.

Thornhill, R., & Gangestad, S. W. (1993). Human facial beauty: Averageness, symmetry, and parasite resistance. *Human Nature, 4*, 237–269.

Thornhill, R., & Gangestad, S. W. (1999). The scent of symmetry: A human sex pheromone that signals fitness? *Evolution and Human Behavior, 20*, 175–201.

Thurber, J. (1956). *Further fables of our time.* New York: Simon & Schuster.

Thurstone, L. L. (1938). *Primary mental abilities.* Chicago: University of Chicago Press.

Tice, D. M., & Baumeister, R. F. (1997). Longitudinal study of procrastination, performance, stress, and health: The costs and benefits of dawdling. *Psychological Science, 8*(6), 454–458.

Tickle, J. J., Sargent, J. D., Dalton, M. A., Beach, M. L., & Heatherton, T. F. (2001). Favourite movie stars, their tobacco use in contemporary movies, and its association with adolescent smoking. *Tobacco Control, 10*, 16–22.

Tienari, P., Wynne, L. C., Sorri, A., Lahti, I., Läksy, K., Moring, J., et al. (2004). Genotype-environment interaction in schizophrenia-spectrum disorder: Long-term follow-up study of Finnish adoptees. *British Journal of Psychiatry, 184*, 216–222.

Time poll. (2005, January 17). Just how happy are we? *Time*, p. A4.

Timmerman, T. A. (2007). "It was a thought pitch": Personal, situational, and target influences on hit-by-pitch events across time. *Journal of Applied Psychology, 92*, 876–884.

Tittle, P. (Ed.). (2004). *Should parents be licensed?: Debating the issues.* New York: Prometheus Books.

Todd, J. T., & Morris, E. K. (1992). Case histories in the great power of steady misrepresentation. *American Psychologist, 47*(11), 1441–1453.

Tolman, E. C., & Honzik, C. H. (1930a). "Insight" in rats. *University of California Publications in Psychology, 4*, 215–232.

Tolman, E. C., & Honzik, C. H. (1930b). Introduction and removal of reward and maze performance in rats. *University of California Publications in Psychology, 4*, 257–275.

Tolman, E. C., Ritchie, B. F., & Kalish, D. (1946). Studies in spatial learning: I: Orientation and short cut. *Journal of Experimental Psychology, 36*, 13–24.

Tomarken, A. J., Simien, C., & Garber, J. (1994). Retesting frontal brain asymmetry discriminates adolescent children of depressed mothers from low-risk controls. *Psychophysiology, 31*, 97–98.

Tomasello, M., & Call, J. (2004). The role of humans in the cognitive development of apes revisited. *Animal Cognition, 7*, 213–215.

Tomasello, M., Davis-Dasilva, M., Camak, L., & Bard, K. (1987). Observational learning of tool use by young chimpanzees. *Human Evolution, 2*, 175–183.

Tomasello, M., Savage-Rumbaugh, S., & Kruger, A. C. (1993). Imitative learning of actions on objects by children, chimpanzees, and enculturated chimpanzees. *Child Development, 64*, 1688–1705.

Tomkins, S. S. (1981). The role of facial response in the experience of emotion. *Journal of Personality and Social Psychology, 40*, 351–357.

Tooby, J., & Cosmides, L. (2000). Mapping the evolved functional organization of mind and brain. In M. S. Gazzaniga (Ed.), *The cognitive neurosciences* (pp. 1185–1198). Cambridge, MA: The MIT Press.

Tootell, R. B. H., Reppas, J. B., Dale, A. M., Look, R. B., Sereno, M. I., Malach, R., et al. (1995). Visual-motion aftereffect in human cortical area MT revealed by functional magnetic resonance imaging. *Nature, 375*, 139–141.

Torgensen, S. (1983). Genetic factors in anxiety disorders. *Archives of General Psychiatry, 40*, 1085–1089.

Torgensen, S. (1986). Childhood and family characteristics in panic and generalized anxiety disorder. *American Journal of Psychiatry, 143*, 630–639.

Torrey, E. F., Bower, A. E., Taylor, E. H., & Gottesman, I. I. (1994). *Schizophrenia and manic-depressive disorder: The biological roots of mental illness as revealed by the landmark study of identical twins.* New York: Basic Books.

Trebach, A. S., & Zeese, K. B. (Eds.). (1992). *Friedman and Szasz on liberty and drugs: Essays on the free market and prohibition.* Washington, DC: Drug Policy Foundation Press.

Treede, R. D., Kenshalo, D. R., Gracely, R. H., & Jones, A. K. (1999). The cortical representation of pain. *Pain, 79*, 105–111.

Treisman, A. (1998). Feature binding, attention and object perception. *Philosophical Transactions of the Royal Society (B), 353*, 1295–1306.

Treisman, A. (2006). How the deployment of attention determines what we see. *Visual Cognition, 14*, 411–443.

Treisman, A., & Gelade, G. (1980). A feature integration theory of attention. *Cognitive Psychology, 12*, 97–136.

Treisman, A., & Schmidt, H. (1982). Illusory conjunctions in the perception of objects. *Cognitive Psychology, 14*, 107–141.

Trimble, M. R. (2007). *The soul in the brain: The cerebral basis of language, art, and belief.* Baltimore, MD: Johns Hopkins University Press.

Trivers, R. L. (1972). Parental investment and sexual selection. In B. Campbell (Ed.), *Sexual selection and the descent of man, 1871–1971* (pp. 139–179). Chicago: Aldine.

Trull, T. J., & Durrett, C. A. (2005). Categorical and dimensional models of personality disorder. *Annual Review of Clinical Psychology, 1*, 355–380.

Tucker, E. (2003, June 25). Move over, Fido! Chickens are becoming hip suburban pets. *USA Today.*

Tuerlinckx, F., De Boeck, P., & Lens, W. (2002). Measuring needs with the Thematic Apperception Test: A psychometric study. *Journal of Personality and Social Psychology, 82*, 448–461.

Tulving, E. (1972). Episodic and semantic memory. In E. Tulving & W. Donaldson (Eds.), *Organization of memory* (pp. 381–403). New York: Academic Press.

Tulving, E. (1983). *Elements of episodic memory.* Oxford, England: Clarendon Press.

Tulving, E. (1985). Memory and consciousness. *Canadian Psychologist, 25*, 1–12.

Tulving, E. (1998). Neurocognitive processes of human memory. In C. von Euler, I. Lundberg, & R. Llins (Eds.), *Basic mechanisms in cognition and language* (pp. 261–281). Amsterdam: Elsevier.

Tulving, E., Kapur, S., Craik, F. I. M., Moscovitch, M., & Houle, S. (1994). Hemispheric encoding/retrieval asymmetry in episodic memory: Positron emission tomography findings. *Proceedings of the National Academy of Sciences, USA, 91*, 2016–2020.

Tulving, E., & Pearlstone, Z. (1966). Availability versus accessibility of information in memory for words. *Journal of Verbal Learning and Verbal Behavior, 5*, 381–391.

Tulving, E., & Schacter, D. L. (1990). Priming and human memory systems. *Science, 247*, 301–306.

Tulving, E., Schacter, D. L., & Stark, H. (1982). Priming effects in word-fragment completion are independent of recognition memory. *Journal of Experimental Psychology: Learning, Memory, and Cognition, 8*, 336–342.

Tulving, E., & Thompson, D. M. (1973). Encoding specificity and retrieval processes in episodic memory. *Psychological Review, 80*, 352–373.

Turiel, E. (1998). The development of morality. In N. Eisenberg (Ed.), *Handbook of child psychology: Vol. 3. Social, emotional and personality development* (pp. 863–932). New York: Wiley.

Turiel, E. (2006). Thought, emotions, and social interactional processes in moral development. In M. Killen & J. G. Smetana (Eds.), *Handbook of moral development* (pp. 7–35). Mahwah, NJ: Lawrence Erlbaum.

Turkheimer, E. (2000). Three laws of behavior genetics and what they mean. *Current Directions in Psychological Science, 9*, 160–164.

Turkheimer, E., Haley, A., Waldron, M., D'Onofrio, B., & Gottesman, I. I. (2003). Socioeconomic status modifies heritability of IQ in young children. *Psychological Science, 14*, 623–628.

Turkheimer, E., & Waldron, M. (2000). Nonshared environment: A theoretical, methodological, and quantitative review. *Psychological Bulletin, 126*, 78–108.

Turner, D. C., Robbins, T. W., Clark, L., Aron, A. R., Dowson, J., & Sahakian, B. J. (2003). Cognitive enhancing effects of modafinil in healthy volunteers. *Psychopharmacology, 165*, 260–269.

Turner, D. C., & Sahakian, B. J. (2006). Neuroethics of cognitive enhancement. *BioSocieties, 1*, 113–123.

Turtle, J., Read, J. D., Lindsay, D. S., & Brimacombe, C. A. E. (2008). Toward a more informative psychological science of eyewitness evidence. *Applied Cognitive Psychology, 22*, 769–778.

Tversky, A., & Kahneman, D. (1973). Availability: A heuristic for judging frequency and probability. *Cognitive Psychology, 5*, 207–232.

Tversky, A., & Kahneman, D. (1974). Judgment under uncertainty: Heuristics and biases. *Science, 185*, 1124–1131.

Tversky, A., & Kahneman, D. (1981). The framing of decisions and the psychology of choice. *Science, 211*, 453–458.

Tversky, A., & Kahneman, D. (1983). Extensional versus intuitive reasoning: The conjunction fallacy in probability judgment. *Psychological Review, 90*, 293–315.

Tversky, A., & Kahneman, D. (1992). Advances in prospect theory: Cumulative representation of uncertainty. *Journal of Risk and Uncertainty, 5*, 297–323.

Twenge, J. M., Campbell, W. K., & Foster, C. A. (2003). Parenthood and marital satisfaction: A meta-analytic review. *Journal of Marriage and Family, 65*, 574–583.

Tyler, T. R. (1990). *Why people obey the law.* New Haven, CT: Yale University Press.

Umberson, D., Williams, K., Powers, D. A., Liu, H., & Needham, B. (2006). You make me sick: Marital quality and health over the life course. *Journal of Health and Social Behavior, 47*, 1–16.

Uncapher, M. R., & Rugg, M. D. (2008). Fractionation of the component processes underlying successful episodic encoding: A combined fMRI and divided-attention study. *Journal of Cognitive Neuroscience, 20*, 240–254.

Ungerleider, L. G., & Mishkin, M. (1982). Two cortical visual systems. In D. J. Ingle, M. A. Goodale, & R. J. W. Mansfield (Eds.), *Analysis of visual behavior* (pp. 549–586). Cambridge, MA: The MIT Press.

Ursano, R. J., & Silberman, E. K. (2003). Psychoanalysis, psychoanalytic psychotherapy, and supportive psychotherapy. In R. E. Hales & S. C. Yudofsky (Eds.), *The American Psychiatric Publishing textbook of clinical psychiatry* (4th ed., pp. 1177–1203). Washington, DC: American Psychiatric Publishing.

U.S. Department of State. (2009). Total adoptions to the United States. Retrieved March 23, 2010, from http://adoption.state.gov/news/total_chart.html

U.S. Department of Transportation. (2008). Traffic safety facts 2006: Alcohol-impaired driving [Electronic version]. Retrieved December 2, 2008, from http://www.nrd.nhtsa.dot.gov/Pubs/810801.PDF

Usher, J. A., & Neisser, U. (1993). Childhood amnesia and the beginnings of memory for four early life events. *Journal of Experimental Psychology: General, 122*, 155–165.

Valentine, T., Brennen, T., & Brédart, S. (1996). *The cognitive psychology of proper names: On the importance of being Ernest.* London: Routledge.

Valins, S. (1966). Cognitive effects of false heart-rate feedback. *Journal of Personality and Social Psychology, 4*, 400–408.

Vallacher, R. R., & Wegner, D. M. (1985). *A theory of action identification.* Hillsdale, NJ: Lawrence Erlbaum.

Vallacher, R. R., & Wegner, D. M. (1987). What do people think they're doing? Action identification and human behavior. *Psychological Review, 94*, 3–15.

Vallender, E. J., Mekel-Bobrov, N., & Lahn, B. T. (2008). Genetic basis of human brain evolution. *Trends in Neurosciences, 31*, 637–644.

van den Boon, D. C. (1994). The influence of temperament and mothering on attachment and exploration: An experimental manipulation of sensitive responsiveness among lower-class mothers with irritable infants. *Child Development, 65*, 1457–1477.

van den Boon, D. C. (1995). Do first year intervention effects endure? Follow-up during toddlerhood of a sample of Dutch irritable infants. *Child Development, 66*, 1798–1816.

Van Der Werf, Y. D., Van Der Helm, W., Schoonheim, M., Ridderikhoff, A., & Van Smeren, E. J. W. (2009). Learning by observation requires an early sleep window. *Proceedings of the National Academy of Sciences, USA, 106*, 18926–18930.

van Dis, I., Kromhout, D., Geleijnse, J. M., Boer, J. M. A., & Verschuren, W. M. M. (2009). Body mass index and waist circumference predict both 10-year nonfatal and fatal cardiovascular disease risk: Study conducted in 20,000 Dutch men and women aged 20–65 years. *European Journal of Cardiovascular Prevention & Rehabilitation, 16*(6), 729–734.

Van Essen, D. C., Anderson, C. H., & Felleman, D. J. (1992). Information processing in the primate visual system: An integrated systems perspective. *Science, 255*, 419–423.

van Honk, J., & Schutter, D. J. L. G. (2007). Testosterone reduces conscious detection of signals serving social correction: Implications for antisocial behavior. *Psychological Science, 18*, 663–667.

van Ijzendoorn, M. H. (1995). Adult attachment representations, parental responsiveness, and infant attachment: A meta-analysis on the predictive validity of the Adult Attachment Interview. *Psychological Bulletin, 117,* 387–403.

van Ijzendoorn, M. H., & Kroonenberg, P. M. (1988). Cross-cultural patterns of attachment: A meta-analysis of the strange situation. *Child Development, 59,* 147–156.

van Ijzendoorn, M. H., Juffer, F., & Klein Poelhuis, C. W. (2005). Adoption and cognitive development: A meta-analytic comparison of adopted and nonadopted children's IQ and school performance. *Psychological Bulletin, 131,* 301–316.

van Ijzendoorn, M. H., & Sagi, A. (1999). Cross-cultural patterns of attachment: Universal and contextual dimensions. In J. Cassidy & P. R. Shaver (Eds.), *Handbook of attachment: Theory, research and clinical applications* (pp. 713–734). New York: Guilford Press.

van Praag, H. (2009). Exercise and the brain: Something to chew on. *Trends in Neuroscience, 32,* 283–290.

van Stegeren, A. H., Everaerd, W., Cahill, L., McGaugh, J. L., & Gooren, L. J. G. (1998). Memory for emotional events: Differential effects of centrally versus peripherally acting blocking agents. *Psychopharmacology, 138,* 305–310.

Van Velzen, C. J. M., & Emmelkamp, P. M. G. (1996). The assessment of personality disorders: Implications for cognitive and behavior therapy. *Behaviour Research and Therapy, 34,* 655–668.

Vance, E. B., & Wagner, N. N. (1976). Written descriptions of orgasm: A study of sex differences. *Archives of Sexual Behavior, 5,* 87–98.

Vargha-Khadem, F., Gadian, D. G., Copp, A., & Mishkin, M. (2005). FOXP2 and the neuroanatomy of speech and language. *Nature Reviews Neuroscience, 6,* 131–138.

Vargha-Khadem, F., Gadian, D. G., Watkins, K. E., Connelly, A., Van Paesschen, W., & Mishkin, M. (1997). Differential effects of early hippocampal pathology on episodic and semantic memory. *Science, 277,* 376–380.

Varona, J., Perales, F. J., & Arellano, D. (2008). Generation and visualization of emotional states in virtual characters. *Computer Animation and Virtual Worlds, 19,* 259–270.

Vazire, S., & Mehl, M. R. (2008). Knowing me, knowing you: The relative accuracy and unique predictive validity of self-ratings and other-ratings of daily behavior. *Journal of Personality and Social Psychology, 95,* 1202–1216.

Vinter, A., & Perruchet, P. (2002). Implicit motor learning through observational training in adults and children. *Memory & Cognition, 30,* 256–261.

Vitkus, J. (1996). *Casebook in abnormal psychology* (3rd ed.). New York: McGraw-Hill.

Vitkus, J. (1999). *Casebook in abnormal psychology* (4th ed.). New York: McGraw-Hill.

Von Frisch, K. (1974). Decoding the language of the bee. *Science, 185,* 663–668.

Vondra, J. I., Shaw, D. S., Swearingen, L., Cohen, M., & Owens, E. B. (2001). Attachment stability and emotional and behavioral regulation from infancy to preschool age. *Development and Psychopathology, 13,* 13–33.

Vortac, O. U., Edwards, M. B., & Manning, C. A. (1995). Functions of external cues in prospective memory. *Memory, 3,* 201–219.

Vygotsky, L. S. (1978). *Mind in society: The development of higher psychological processes.* Cambridge, MA: Harvard University Press.

Wade, N. J. (2005). *Perception and illusion: Historical perspectives.* New York: Springer.

Wadhwa, P. D., Sandman, C. A., & Garite, T. J. (2001). The neurobiology of stress in human pregnancy: Implications for prematurity and development of the fetal central nervous system. *Progress in Brain Research, 133,* 131–142.

Wager, T. D., Rilling, J., K., Smith, E. E., Sokolik, A., Casey, K. L., Davidson, R. J., et al. (2004). Placebo-induced changes in fMRI in the anticipation and experience of pain. *Science, 303,* 1162–1167.

Wagner, A. D., Schacter, D. L., Rotte, M., Koutstaal, W., Maril, A., Dale, A. M., et al. (1998). Remembering and forgetting of verbal experiences as predicted by brain activity. *Science, 281,* 1188–1190.

Wagner, G., & Morris, E. (1987). Superstitious behavior in children. *Psychological Record, 37,* 471–488.

Wahba, M. A., & Bridwell, L. G. (1976). Maslow reconsidered: A review of research on the need hierarchy theory. *Organizational Behavior & Human Performance, 15,* 212–240.

Wahl, O. F. (1976). Monozygotic twins discordant for schizophrenia: A review. *Psychological Bulletin, 83,* 91–106.

Waite, L. J. (1995). Does marriage matter? *Demography, 32,* 483–507.

Waiter, G. D., Deary, I. J., Staff, R. T., Murray, A. D., Fox, H. C., Starr, J. M., et al. (2009). Exploring possible neural mechanisms of intelligence differences using processing speed and working memory tasks: An fMRI study. *Intelligence, 37*(2), 199–206.

Walden, T. A., & Ogan, T. A. (1988). The development of social referencing. *Child Development, 59,* 1230–1240.

Waldfogel, S. (1948). The frequency and affective character of childhood memories. *Psychological Monographs, 62* (Whole No. 291).

Waldmann, M. R. (2000). Competition among causes but not effects in predictive and diagnostic learning. *Journal of Experimental Psychology: Learning, Memory, and Cognition, 26,* 53–76.

Walker, C. (1977). Some variations in marital satisfaction. In R. C. J. Peel (Ed.), *Equalities and inequalities in family life* (pp. 127–139). London: Academic Press.

Walker, L. J. (1988). The development of moral reasoning. *Annals of Child Development, 55,* 677–691.

Walker, M. P., & Stickgold, R. (2006). Sleep, memory, and plasticity. *Annual Review of Psychology, 57,* 139–166.

Wallace, J., Schnieder, T., & McGuffin, P. (2002). Genetics of depression. In I. H. Gottlieb & C. L. Hammen (Eds.), *Handbook of depression* (pp. 169–191). New York: Guilford Press.

Wallbott, H. G. (1998). Bodily expression of emotion. *European Journal of Social Psychology, 28,* 879–896.

Walster, E., Aronson, V., Abrahams, D., & Rottmann, L. (1966). Importance of physical attractiveness in dating behavior. *Journal of Personality and Social Psychology, 4,* 508–516.

Walster, E., Walster, G. W., & Berscheid, E. (1978). *Equity: Theory and research.* Boston: Allyn & Bacon.

Walton, D. N. (1990). What is reasoning? What is an argument? *Journal of Philosophy, 87,* 399–419.

Walton, G. M., & Spencer, S. J. (2009). Latent ability: Grades and test scores systematically underestimate the intellectual ability of negatively stereotyped students. *Psychological Science, 20,* 1132–1139.

Waltzman, S. B. (2006). Cochlear implants: Current status. *Expert Review of Medical Devices, 3,* 647–655.

Wang, L. H., McCarthy, G., Song, A. W., & LaBar, K. S. (2005). Amygdala activation to sad pictures during high-field (4 tesla) functional magnetic resonance imaging. *Emotion, 5,* 12–22.

Wang, S.-H., & Baillargeon, R. (2008). Detecting impossible changes in infancy: A three-system account. *Trends in Cognitive Sciences, 12*(1), 17–23.

Wansink, B., & Linder, L. R. (2003). Interactions between forms of fat consumption and restaurant bread consumption. *International Journal of Obesity, 27,* 866–868.

Wansink, B., Painter, J. E., & North, J. (2005). Bottomless bowls: Why visual cues of portion size may influence intake. *Obesity Research, 13,* 93–100.

Wansink, B., & Wansink, C. S. (2010). The largest last supper: Depictions of food portions and plate size increased over the millennium. *International Journal of Obesity, 34*, 943–944.

Ward, J., Parkin, A. J., Powell, G., Squires, E. J., Townshend, J., & Bradley, V. (1999). False recognition of unfamiliar people: "Seeing film stars everywhere." *Cognitive Neuropsychology, 16*, 293–315.

Warneken, F., & Tomasello, M. (2009). Varieties of altruism in children and chimpanzees. *Trends in Cognitive Sciences, 13*, 397–402.

Warnock, M. (2003). *Making babies: Is there a right to have children?* Oxford, England: Oxford University Press.

Warren, K. R., & Hewitt, B. G. (2009). Fetal alcohol spectrum disorders: When science, medicine, public policy, and laws collide. *Developmental Disabilities Research Reviews, 15*, 170–175.

Warrington, E. K., & McCarthy, R. A. (1983). Category specific access dysphasia. *Brain, 106*, 859–878.

Warrington, E. K., & Shallice, T. (1984). Category specific semantic impairments. *Brain, 107*, 829–854.

Watanabe, S., Sakamoto, J., & Wakita, M. (1995). Pigeons' discrimination of painting by Monet and Picasso. *Journal of the Experimental Analysis of Behavior, 63*, 165–174.

Watkins, L. R., & Maier, S. F. (2005). Immune regulation of central nervous system functions: From sickness responses to pathological pain. *Journal of Internal Medicine, 257*, 139–155.

Watson, D., & Pennebaker, J. W. (1989). Health complaints, stress, and distress: Exploring the central role of negative affectivity. *Psychological Review, 96*, 234–254.

Watson, D., & Tellegen, A. (1985). Toward a consensual structure of mood. *Psychological Bulletin, 98*, 219–235.

Watson, J. B. (1913). Psychology as the behaviorist views it. *Psychological Review, 20*, 158–177.

Watson, J. B. (1924). *Behaviorism.* New York: People's Institute.

Watson, J. B. (1928). *Psychological care of infant and child.* New York: Norton.

Watson, J. B., & Rayner, R. (1920). Conditioned emotional reactions. *Journal of Experimental Psychology, 3*, 1–14.

Watson, R. I. (1978). *The great psychologists.* New York: Lippincott.

Watt, H. J. (1905). Experimentelle Beitraege zu einer Theorie des Denkens [Experimental contributions to a theory of thinking]. *Archiv fuer die gesamte Psychologie, 4*, 289–436.

Watzlawick, P., Beavin, J., & Jackson, D. D. (1967). *Pragmatics of human communication: A study of interactional patterns, pathologies, and paradoxes.* New York: Norton.

Weber, R., & Crocker, J. (1983). Cognitive processes in the revision of stereotypic beliefs. *Journal of Personality and Social Psychology, 45*, 961–977.

Webster Marketon, J. I., & Glaser, R. (2008). Stress hormones and immune function. *Cellular Immunology, 252*, 16–26.

Wechsler, H., Davenport, A., Dowdall, G., Moeykens, B., & Castillo, S. (1994). Health and behavioral consequences of binge drinking in college: A national survey of students at 140 campuses. *Journal of the American Medical Association, 272*, 1672–1677.

Wegner, D. M. (1989). *White bears and other unwanted thoughts.* New York: Viking.

Wegner, D. M. (1994a). Ironic processes of mental control. *Psychological Review, 101*, 34–52.

Wegner, D. M. (1994b). *White bears and other unwanted thoughts: Suppression, obsession, and the psychology of mental control.* New York: Guilford Press.

Wegner, D. M. (1997). Why the mind wanders. In J. D. Cohen & J. W. Schooler (Eds.), *Scientific approaches to consciousness* (pp. 295–315). Mahwah, NJ: Lawrence Erlbaum.

Wegner, D. M. (2002). *The illusion of conscious will.* Cambridge, MA: The MIT Press.

Wegner, D. M. (2009). How to think, say, or do precisely the worst thing for any occasion. *Science, 325*, 48–51.

Wegner, D. M., Ansfield, M., & Pilloff, D. (1998). The putt and the pendulum: Ironic effects of the mental control of action. *Psychological Science, 9*, 196–199.

Wegner, D. M., Broome, A., & Blumberg, S. J. (1997). Ironic effects of trying to relax under stress. *Behavior Research and Therapy, 35*, 11–21.

Wegner, D. M., Erber, R. E., & Zanakos, S. (1993). Ironic processes in the mental control of mood and mood-related thought. *Journal of Personality and Social Psychology, 65*, 1093–1104.

Wegner, D. M., & Gilbert, D. T. (2000). Social psychology: The science of human experience. In H. Bless & J. Forgas (Eds.), *The message within: Subjective experience in social cognition and behavior* (pp. 1–9). Philadelphia: Psychology Press.

Wegner, D. M., Schneider, D. J., Carter, S. R., & White, T. L. (1987). Paradoxical effects of thought suppression. *Journal of Personality and Social Psychology, 53*, 5–13.

Wegner, D. M., Vallacher, R. R., Macomber, G., Wood, R., & Arps, K. (1984). The emergence of action. *Journal of Personality and Social Psychology, 46*, 269–279.

Wegner, D. M., & Wenzlaff, R. M. (1996). Mental control. In E. T. Higgins & A. Kruglanski (Eds.), *Social psychology: Handbook of basic mechanisms and processes* (pp. 466–492). New York: Guilford Press.

Wegner, D. M., Wenzlaff, R. M., & Kozak, M. (2004). Dream rebound: The return of suppressed thoughts in dreams. *Psychological Science, 15*, 232–236.

Wegner, D. M., & Zanakos, S. (1994). Chronic thought suppression. *Journal of Personality, 62*, 615–640.

Weinstock, S., Berman, S., & Cates, W., Jr. (2004). Sexually transmitted diseases among American youth: Incidence and prevalence estimates, 2000. *Perspectives on Social and Reproductive Health, 36*, 6–10.

Weir, C., Toland, C., King, R. A., & Martin, L. M. (2005). Infant contingency/extinction performance after observing partial reinforcement. *Infancy, 8*, 63–80.

Weisfeld, G. (1999). *Evolutionary principles of human adolescence.* New York: Basic Books.

Weiss, J. (2010, May 1). The new female villain. *The Boston Globe.*

Weiss, P. H., Zilles, K., & Fink, G. R. (2005). When visual perception causes feeling: Enhanced cross-modal processing in grapheme-color synesthesia. *Neuroimage, 28*, 859–868.

Weissenborn, R. (2000). State-dependent effects of alcohol on explicit memory: The role of semantic associations. *Psychopharmacology, 149*, 98–106.

Weissman, M. M., Bland, R. C., Canino, G. J., Faravelli, C., Greenwald, S., Hwu, H. G., et al. (1997). The cross-national epidemiology of panic disorder. *Archives of General Psychiatry, 54*, 305–309.

Weissman, M. M., Markowitz, J. C., & Klerman, G. L. (2000). *Comprehensive guide to interpersonal psychotherapy.* New York: Basic Books.

Wells, G. L., Malpass, R. S., Lindsay, R. C. L., Fisher, R. P., Turtle, J. W., & Fulero, S. M. (2000). From the lab to the police station: A successful application of eyewitness research. *American Psychologist, 55*, 581–598.

Wells, G. L., Small, M., Penrod, S., Malpass, R. S., Fulero, S. M., & Brimacombe, C. A. E. (1998). Eyewitness identification procedures: Recommendations for lineups and photospreads. *Law and Human Behavior, 22*, 603–647.

Wenner, L. A. (2004). On the ethics of product placement in media entertainment. In M. L. Galacian (Ed.), *Handbook of product placement in the mass media* (pp. 101–132). Binghamton, NY: Haworth Press.

Wenzlaff, R. M. (2005). Seeking solace but finding despair: The persistence of intrusive thoughts in depression. In D. A. Clark (Ed.), *Intrusive thoughts in clinical disorders: Theory, research, and treatment* (pp. 54–85). New York: Guilford Press.

Wenzlaff, R. M., & Bates, D. E. (1998). Unmasking a cognitive vulnerability to depression: How lapses in mental control reveal depressive thinking. *Journal of Personality and Social Psychology, 75,* 1559–1571.

Wenzlaff, R. M., & Eisenberg, A. R. (2001). Mental control after dysphoria: Evidence of a suppressed, depressive bias. *Behavior Therapy, 32,* 27–45.

Wenzlaff, R. M., & Grozier, S. A. (1988). Depression and the magnification of failure. *Journal of Abnormal Psychology, 97,* 90–93.

Wenzlaff, R. M., & Wegner, D. M. (2000). Thought suppression. In S. T. Fiske (Ed.), *Annual review of psychology* (Vol. 51, pp. 51–91). Palo Alto, CA: Annual Reviews.

Wernicke, K. (1874). *Der Aphasische Symptomenkomplex.* Breslau: Cohn and Weigart.

Wertheimer, M. (1982). *Productive thinking.* Chicago: University of Chicago Press. (Originally published 1945)

Wesch, N. N., Law, B., & Hall, C. R. (2007). The use of observational learning by athletes. *Journal of Sport Behavior, 30,* 219–231.

Westrin, A., & Lam, R. W. (2007). Seasonal affective disorder: A clinical update. *Journal of Clinical Psychiatry, 19,* 239–246.

Wexler, K. (1999). Maturation and growth of grammar. In W. C. Ritchie & T. K. Bhatia (Eds.), *Handbook of child language acquisition* (pp. 55–110). San Diego: Academic Press.

Whalen, P. J., Rauch, S. L., Etcoff, N. L., McInerney, S. C., Lee, M. B., & Jenike, M. A. (1998). Masked presentations of emotional facial expressions modulate amygdala activity without explicit knowledge. *The Journal of Neuroscience, 18,* 411–418.

Whalley, L. J., & Deary, I. J. (2001). Longitudinal cohort study of childhood IQ and survival up to age 76. *British Medical Journal, 322,* 1–5.

Wheatley, T., & Haidt, J. (2005). Hypnotic disgust makes moral judgments more severe. *Psychological Science, 16,* 780–784.

Wheeler, M. A., Petersen, S. E., & Buckner, R. L. (2000). Memory's echo: Vivid recollection activates modality-specific cortex. *Proceedings of the National Academy of Sciences, USA, 97,* 11125–11129.

White, B. L., & Held, R. (1966). Plasticity of motor development in the human infant. In J. F. Rosenblith & W. Allinsmith (Eds.), *The cause of behavior* (pp. 60–70). Boston: Allyn & Bacon.

White, F. J. (1996). Synaptic regulation of mesocorticolimbic dopamine neurons. *Annual Review of Neuroscience, 19,* 405–436.

White, G. M., & Kirkpatrick, J. (Eds.). (1985). *Person, self, and experience: Exploring pacific ethnopsychologies.* Berkeley: University of California Press.

White, N. M., & Milner, P. M. (1992). The psychobiology of reinforcers. *Annual Review of Psychology, 41,* 443–471.

Whitney, D., Ellison, A., Rice, N. J., Arnold, D., Goodale, M., Walsh, V., & Milner, D. (2007). Visually guided reaching depends on motion area MT+. *Cerebral Cortex, 17,* 2644–2649.

Whorf, B. (1956). *Language, thought, and reality.* Cambridge, MA: The MIT Press.

Whybrow, P. C. (1997). *A mood apart.* New York: Basic Books.

Wicker, B., Keysers, C., Plailly, J., Royet, J.-P., Gallese, V., & Rizzolatti, G. (2003). Both of us disgusted in *my* insula: The common neural basis of seeing and feeling disgust. *Neuron, 40,* 655–664.

Wicklund, R. (1975). Objective self-awareness. In L. Berkowitz (Ed.), *Advances in experimental social psychology* (Vol. 8, pp. 233–275). New York: Academic Press.

Widiger, T. A. (2001). The best and the worst of us? *Clinical Psychology: Science and Practice, 8,* 374–377.

Wiederman, M. W. (1997). Pretending orgasm during sexual intercourse: Correlates in a sample of young adult women. *Journal of Sex & Marital Therapy, 23,* 131–139.

Wiener, D. N. (1996). *B. F. Skinner: Benign anarchist.* Boston: Allyn & Bacon.

Wig, G. S., Buckner, R. L., & Schacter, D. L. (2009). Repetition priming influences distinct brain systems: Evidence from task-evoked data and resting-state correlations. *Journal of Neurophysiology, 101,* 2632–2648.

Wiggs, C. L., & Martin, A. (1998). Properties and mechanisms of perceptual priming. *Current Opinion in Neurobiology, 8,* 227–233.

Wilcoxon, H. C., Dragoin, W. B., & Kral, P. A. (1971). Illness-induced aversions in rats and quail: Relative salience of visual and gustatory cues. *Science, 171,* 826–828.

Wiley, J. L. (1999). Cannabis: Discrimination of "internal bliss"? *Pharmacology, Biochemistry, & Behavior, 64,* 257–260.

Wilkinson, L., Teo, J. T., Obeso, I., Rothwell, J. C., & Jahanshahi, M. (2010). The contribution of primary motor cortex is essential for probabilistic implicit sequence learning: Evidence from theta burst magnetic stimulation. *Journal of Cognitive Neuroscience, 22,* 427–436.

Williams, A. C. (2002). Facial expression of pain: An evolutionary account. *Behavioral and Brain Sciences, 25,* 439–488.

Williams, C. M., & Kirkham, T. C. (1999). Anandamide induces overeating: Mediation by central cannabinoid (CB1) receptors. *Psychopharmacology, 143,* 315–317.

Wilson, T. D. (2002). *Strangers to ourselves: Discovering the adaptive unconscious.* Cambridge, MA: Harvard University Press.

Wilson, T. D., & Lassiter, G. D. (1982). Increasing intrinsic interest with superfluous extrinsic constraints. *Journal of Personality and Social Psychology, 42,* 811–819.

Wilson, T. D., Meyers, J., & Gilbert, D. T. (2003). "How happy was I, anyway?" A retrospective impact bias. *Social Cognition, 21,* 421–446.

Wimber, M., Rutschmann, R. N., Greenlee, M. W., & Bauml, K.-H. (2009). Retrieval from episodic memory: Neural mechanisms of interference resolution. *Journal of Cognitive Neuroscience, 21,* 538–549.

Wimmer, H., & Perner, J. (1983). Beliefs about beliefs: Representations and constraining function of wrong beliefs in young children's understanding of deception. *Cognition, 13,* 103–128.

Winawer, J., Witthoft, N., Frank, M. C., Wu, L., Wade, A. R., & Boroditsky, L. (2009). Russian blues reveal effects of language on color discrimination. *Proceedings of the National Academy of Sciences, USA, 104,* 7780–7785.

Windeler, J., & Kobberling, J. (1986). Empirische Untersuchung zur Einschatzung diagnostischer Verfahren am Beispiel des Haemoccult-Tests [An empirical study of the value of diagnostic procedures using the example of the hemoccult test]. *Klinische Wochenscrhrift, 64,* 1106–1112.

Windham, G. C., Eaton, A., & Hopkins, B. (1999). Evidence for an association between environmental tobacco smoke exposure and birthweight: A meta-analysis and new data. *Pediatrics and Perinatal Epidemiology, 13,* 35–57.

Winner, E. (2000). The origins and ends of giftedness. *American Psychologist, 55,* 159–169.

Winter, L., & Uleman, J. S. (1984). When are social judgments made? Evidence for the spontaneousness of trait inferences. *Journal of Personality and Social Psychology, 47,* 237–252.

Winterer, G., & Weinberger, D. R. (2004). Genes, dopamine and cortical signal-to-noise ratio in schizophrenia. *Trends in Neuroscience, 27,* 683–690.

Wise, R. A. (1989). Brain dopamine and reward. *Annual Review of Psychology, 40,* 191–225.

Wise, R. A. (2005). Forebrain substrates of reward and motivation. *Journal of Comparative Neurology, 493*, 115–121.

Wittchen, H., Knauper, B., & Kessler, R. C. (1994). Lifetime risk of depression. *British Journal of Psychiatry, 165*, 16–22.

Wittgenstein, L. (1999). *Philosophical investigations.* Upper Saddle River, NJ: Prentice Hall. (Originally published 1953)

Wixted, J. T., & Ebbescn, E. (1991). On the form of forgetting. *Psychological Science, 2*, 409–415.

Wolf, J. (2003, May 18). Through the looking glass. *The New York Times Magazine,* p. 120.

Wolf, J. R., Arkes, H. R., & Muhanna, W. A. (2008). The power of touch: An examination of the effect of duration of physical contact on the valuation of objects. *Judgment and Decision Making, 3*, 476–482.

Wolpe, J. (1958). *Psychotherapy by reciprocal inhibition.* Stanford, CA: Stanford University Press.

Wong, D. T., Bymaster, F. P., & Engleman, E. A. (1995). Prozac (fluoxetine, Lilly 110140), the first selective serotonin uptake inhibitor and an antidepressant drug: Twenty years since its first publication. *Life Sciences, 57*, 411 411.

Wood, J. M., & Bootzin, R. R. (1990). Prevalence of nightmares and their independence from anxiety. *Journal of Abnormal Psychology, 99*, 64–68.

Wood, J. M., Bootzin, R. R., Rosenhan, D., Nolen-Hoeksema, S., & Jourden, F. (1992). Effects of the 1989 San Francisco earthquake on frequency and content of nightmares. *Journal of Abnormal Psychology, 101*, 219–224.

Wood, J. M., Nezworski, M. T., Lilienfeld, S. O., & Garb, H. N. (2003). *What's wrong with the Rorschach? Science confronts the controversial inkblot test.* New York: Wiley.

Woods, E. R., Lin, Y. G., Middleman, A., Beckford, P., Chase, L., & DuRant, R. H. (1997). The associations of suicide attempts in adolescents. *Pediatrics, 99*, 791–796.

Woods, S. C., Seeley, R. J., Porte, D., Jr., & Schwartz, M. W. (1998). Signals that regulate food intake and energy homeostasis. *Science, 280*, 1378–1383.

Woods, S. M., Natterson, J., & Silverman, J. (1966). Medical students' disease: Hypochondriasis in medical education. *Journal of Medical Education, 41*, 785–790.

Woody, S. R., & Nosen, E. (2008). Psychological models of phobic disorders and panic. In M. M. Anthony & M. B. Stein (Eds.), *Oxford handbook of anxiety and related disorders* (pp. 209–224). New York: Oxford University Press.

Woody, S. R., & Sanderson, W. C. (1998). Manuals for empirically supported treatments: 1998 update. *Clinical Psychologist, 51*, 17–21.

Wrangham, R., & Peterson, D. (1997). *Demonic males: Apes and the origin of human violence.* New York: Mariner.

Wren, A. M., Seal, L. J., Cohen, M. A., Brynes, A. E., Frost, G. S., Murphy, K. G., et al. (2001). Ghrelin enhances appetite and increases food intake in humans. *Journal of Clinical Endocrinology and Metabolism, 86*, 5992–5995.

Wrenn, C. C., Turchi, J. N., Schlosser, S., Dreiling, J. L., Stephenson, D. A., & Crawley, J. N. (2006). Performance of galanin transgenic mice in the 5-choice serial reaction time attentional task. *Pharmacology Biochemistry and Behavior, 83*, 428–440.

Wright, L. (1994). *Remembering Satan: A case of recovered memory and the shattering of an American family.* New York: Knopf.

Wulf, S. (1994, March 14). Err Jordan. *Sports Illustrated.*

Wundt, W. (1900–20). *Völkerpsychologie. Eine untersuchung der entwicklungsgesetze von sprache, mythos und sitte* [Völkerpsychologie: An examination of the developmental laws of language, myth, and custom]. Leipzig, Germany: Engelmann & Kroner.

Xiaohe, X., & Whyte, K. J. (1990). Love matches and arranged marriages: A Chinese replication. *Journal of Marriage and the Family, 52*, 709–722.

Yamaguchi, S. (1998). Basic properties of umami and its effects in humans. *Physiology and Behavior, 49*, 833–841.

Yang, S., & Sternberg, R. J. (1997). Conceptions of intelligence in ancient Chinese philosophy. *Journal of Theoretical and Philosophical Psychology, 17*, 101–119.

Yelsma, P., & Athappilly, K. (1988). Marital satisfaction and communication practices: Comparisons among Indian and American couples. *Journal of Comparative Family Studies, 19*, 37–53.

Yin, R. K. (1970). Face recognition by brain-injured patients: A dissociable ability. *Neuropsychologia, 8*, 395–402.

Young, A. S., Klap, R., Sherbourne, C. D., & Wells, K. B. (2001). The quality of care for depressive and anxiety disorders in the United States. *Archives of General Psychiatry, 58*, 55–61.

Young, P. C. (1948). Antisocial uses of hypnosis. In L. M. LeCron (Ed.), *Experimental hypnosis* (pp. 376–409). New York: Macmillan

Young, R. M. (1990). *Mind, brain, and adaptation in the nineteenth century: Cerebral localization and its biological context from Gall to Ferrier.* New York: Oxford University Press.

Yucha, C., & Gilbert, C. D. (2004). *Evidence-based practice in biofeedback and neurofeedback.* Colorado Springs, CO: Association for Applied Psychophysiology and Biofeedback.

Yuill, N., & Perner, J. (1988). Intentionality and knowledge in children's judgments of actor's responsibility and recipient's emotional reaction. *Developmental Psychology, 24*, 358–365.

Yzerbyt, V., & Demoulin, S. (2010). Intergroup relations. In S. T. Fiske, D. T. Gilbert, & G. Lindzey (Eds.), *The handbook of social psychology* (5th ed., Vol. 2). New York: Wiley.

Zahn-Waxler, C., Radke-Yarrow, M., Wagner, E., & Chapman, M. (1992). Development of concern for others. *Developmental Psychology, 28*, 126–136.

Zajonc, R. B. (1968). Attitudinal effects of mere exposure. *Journal of Personality and Social Psychology, 9*, 1–27.

Zajonc, R. B. (1989). Feeling the facial efference: Implications of the vascular theory of emotion. *Psychological Review, 96*, 395–416.

Zajonc, R. B. (1997). Birth order: Reconciling conflicting effects. *American Psychologist, 52*, 685–699.

Zajonc, R. B. (2001). The family dynamic of intellectual development. *American Psychologist, 56*, 490–496.

Zebrowitz, L. A., Hall, J. A., Murphy, N. A., & Rhodes, G. (2002). Looking smart and looking good: Facial cues to intelligence and their origins. *Personality and Social Psychology Bulletin, 28*, 238–249.

Zebrowitz, L. A., & Montepare, J. M. (1992). Impressions of baby-faced individuals across the life span. *Developmental Psychology, 28*, 1143–1152.

Zeki, S. (1993). *A vision of the brain.* London: Blackwell Scientific Publications.

Zeki, S. (2001). Localization and globalization in conscious vision. *Annual Review of Neuroscience, 24*, 57–86.

Zentall, T. R., Sutton, J. E., & Sherburne, L. M. (1996). True imitative learning in pigeons. *Psychological Science, 7*, 343–346.

Zhang, T. Y., & Meaney, M. J. (2010). Epigenetics and the environmental regulation of the genome and its function. *Annual Review of Psychology, 61*, 439–466.

Zihl, J., von Cramon, D., & Mai, N. (1983). Selective disturbance of movement vision after bilateral brain damage. *Brain, 106*, 313–340.

Zillmann, D., Katcher, A. H., & Milavsky, B. (1972). Excitation transfer from physical exercise to subsequent aggressive behavior. *Journal of Experimental Psychology, 8,* 247–259.

Zimprich, D., & Martin, M. (2002). Can longitudinal changes in processing speed explain longitudinal age changes in fluid intelligence? *Psychology and Aging, 17,* 690–695.

Zola, S. M., & Squire, L. R. (2000). The medial temporal lobe and the hippocampus. In E. Tulving & F. I. M. Craik (Eds.), *The Oxford handbook of memory* (pp. 485–500). New York: Oxford University Press.

Zuckerman, M., DePaulo, B. M., & Rosenthal, R. (1981). Verbal and nonverbal communication of deception. In L. Berkowitz (Ed.), *Advances in experimental social psychology* (Vol. 14, pp. 1–59). New York: Academic Press.

Zuckerman, M., & Driver, R. E. (1985). Telling lies: Verbal and nonverbal correlates of deception. In W. Seigman & S. Feldstein (Eds.), *Multichannel integrations of nonverbal behavior* (pp. 129–147). Hillsdale, NJ: Lawrence Erlbaum.

Zuckerman, M., Kolin, E. A., Price, L., & Zoob, I. (1964). Development of a sensation-seeking scale. *Journal of Consulting Psychology, 28,* 477–482.

Name Index

A

Aarts, H., 188, 340
Abbott, J. M., 621
Abel, T., 231
Abelson, J., 615
Abelson, R. P., 557
Abernathy, A. P., 164
Abrams, D., 513
Abrams, M., 301
Abramson, L. Y., 567
Abromov, I., 140
Acevedo, B. P., 522
Acevedo-Garcia, D., 416
Achter, J. A., 418
Acocella, J., 567, 572, 620
Acton, G. S., 396
Adams, H. E., 482
Addis, D. R., 106, 241, 256
Adelmann, P. K., 320
Adelson, E. H., 154
Adler, A., 14, 596, 597
Adolph, K. E., 429
Adolphs, R., 99, 321
Adorno, T. W., 473
Aggleton, J., 99
Agin, D., 72
Aharon, I., 290
Ainslie, G., 202
Ainsworth, M. D. S., 440, 442
Aksglaede, L., 449
Albarracín, D., 532
Albee, E., 549
Albert, Prince of England, 210
Aleman, A., 614
Alfert, E., 316
al-Haytham, I., 41
Alicke, M. D., 498
Allegeier, E. R., 336
Allen, C. A., 387
Allen, R., 300
Allison, D. B., 330, 332
Alloway, T. P., 227
Alloy, L. B., 567
Allport, G. W., 28, 472–473,
    475, 536
Almond, P., 465
Alt, K. W., 606
Altschuler, E. L., 103
Alvarez, L., 63, 635
Amabile, T. M., 280, 543
Ambadar, Z., 573
Ambady, N., 319, 321, 416
Ames, A., 153
Ames, M. A., 452

Amsler, S., 337
Anand, S., 118
Andersen, H. C., 646
Andersen, S. M., 596
Anderson, C. A., 56, 507, 509
Anderson, C. H., 141
Anderson, J., 508
Anderson, J. R., 256
Anderson, J. W., 410, 411
Anderson, M. C., 235, 237, 482
Anderson, R. C., 234
Anderson, T., 505
Andres, D., 409
Andrewes, D., 111
Andrews, I., 359
Andrews-Hanna, J. R., 535
Angelone, B., 155
Angst, J., 566
Ansfield, M., 186, 195
Ansuini, C. G., 453
Antoni, M. H., 650
Antony, M. M., 563, 590
Apicella, C. L., 520
Apperly, I. A., 434
Apted, M., 465
Archibold, R. C., 343
Arellano, D., 319
Ariely, D., 387
Aristotle, 5, 6, 326, 327
Ariyasu, H., 330
Arkes, H. R., 163
Arlow, J. A., 596
Armstrong, D. M., 181
Arndt, J., 337
Arnold, M. B., 313
Arnold, S. E., 579
Aron, A. P., 312, 517, 522, 523
Aronson, E., 165, 339, 521, 534,
    636
Aronson, J., 415, 539
Asch, S. E., 27, 28, 529
Aschoff, J., 191
Aserinsky, E., 192
Ashby, F. G., 366
Ashcraft, M. H., 23
Asher, S. J., 63
Ashmore, R. D., 541
Aslin, R. N., 300
Asmundson, G. J. G., 600
Assanand, S., 651
Astington, J. W., 434, 435
Athappilly, K., 523
Atkinson, G., 209
Atkinson, J. W., 340

Atkinson, L., 443
Atkinson, R. C., 222
Aurelius, M., 316
Avery, D., 614
Aviezer, H., 320
Avolio, A. M., 429
Avolio, B. J., 409
Axel, R., 167
Axelrod, R., 510
Ayduk, O., 338
Ayres, C. E., 327
Azuma, H., 403

B

Baars, B. J., 19, 187
Bachman, J., 450
Back, K., 516
Back, M. D., 476, 517
Backman, C. W., 521
Bäckman, L., 458
Baddeley, A. D., 227, 234
Baer, L., 563, 615
Bagby, R. M., 475
Bahrick, H. P., 228, 244, 254
Bai, D. L., 165
Bailey, J. M., 452
Bailey, P. J., 250
Bailey, R., 419
Baillargeon, R., 431, 432,
    434, 436
Baird, J., 435
Baker, T. B., 206, 619
Baldwin, M. W., 497
Baler, R. D., 87
Baltes, P. B., 409, 412
Banaji, M. R., 540
Bandura, A., 293, 294, 305, 489
Banks, M. S., 428
Banse, R., 318
Barazani, A., 330
Barbee, A. P., 520
Bard, P., 311
Bargh, J. A., 189, 320, 340, 525
Barker, A. T., 118
Barkow, J., 497
Barlow, D. H., 558, 612, 613
Barnard, P. J., 244
Barnes, C. D., 508
Barnier, A. J., 252, 637
Baron-Cohen, S., 435
Barondes, S., 606
Barrett, L. F., 312
Barrientos, R. M., 633
Barry 3rd, H., 450

Barsade, S. G., 403
Barston, J. L., 383
Bartlett, F. C., 20–21, 244
Bartol, C. R., 479
Bartoshuk, L. M., 169, 170, 171
Basquiat, J.-M., 493
Bates, D. E., 568
Bates, E., 354
Bates, J. E., 442
Bateson, G., 29
Bateson, M., 512
Batson, C. D., 514
Batty, G. D., 395, 396
Bauer, R., 330, 651
Baumeister, R. F., 35, 335, 453, 482,
    496, 498, 508, 526, 642, 651
Baxter, L. R., 564
Bayley, P. J., 229, 301
Baylor, D. A., 140
Bear, G., 403
Beauchamp, G. K., 169, 426
Beavin, J., 603
Bechara, A., 374, 375
Beck, A. T., 567, 599
Becker, J. B., 450
Beckers, G., 118
Becklen, R., 180
Beek, M. R., 155
Beeman, M., 379
Beer, J. S., 495
Beevers, C. G., 569
Bekerian, D. A., 244
Békésy, G. von, 160
Bekinschtein, T. A., 273
Bell, A. P., 452
Bellotto, B., 179
Belsky, J., 441
Bem, S. L., 478
Benbow, C. P., 418
Bender, D. S., 581
Bendiksen, M., 573
Benedetti, F., 645
Bennett, I. J., 301
Benoit, S. C., 333
Benson, D. F., 102, 315
Benson, H., 640
Bereczkei, T., 385
Bergen, J. R., 154
Berger, H., 191
Berger, S. A., 254
Berglund, H., 169
Bering, J., 296, 297
Berk, J. S., 596
Berkerian, D. A., 251

Subject Index

Note: Page numbers followed by f indicate figures; those followed by t indicate tables.

A

AA. *See* Alcoholics Anonymous
Absentmindedness, 4–5, 244–246, 256
Absolute threshold, 129t, 129–130, 130f
Absolutism, 29–30
Abstract thought, frontal lobe and, 102
Abuse, in childhood, dissociative identity disorder caused by, 572
ACC. *See* Anterior cingulate cortex
Acceptance, as motive for social influence, 526–531
Accommodation, in cognitive development, 430
Accuracy, as motive for social influence, 531–535
Acetylcholine (ACh), 87
Achievement, need for, 340
Acquired immunodeficiency syndrome, 650
    avoiding, 652
Acquisition, in classical conditioning, 266–267, 268f
ACTH. *See* Adrenocorticotropic hormone
Action potential, 84f, 84–85, 85f
    neurotransmitter release and, 86, 86f
Activation-synthesis model of dreaming, 198–199
Actor-observer effect, 544
Actuarial method, for personality assessment, 470
Adaptation
    food aversions and, 274–275
    sensory, 133
Adaptiveness, of psychological processes, 3
Adderall, as cognitive enhancer, 417
Addiction, 201–203, 652. *See also* Alcohol use/abuse
Additive color mixing, 140, 140f
A-delta fibers, 163
Adjustment disorders, 553t
Adolescence, 448–456, 449f
    brain development during, 448–449, 449f
    emotions during, 450–451
    Erikson's developmental tasks of, 454t
    parent-child relationships during, 454t, 454–455
    peers during, 455
    pregnancy during, 454, 454f
    protraction of, 449–451, 450f
    puberty and, 448
    schizophrenia in, 580f
    sexuality during, 451–454, 451f–454f
    smoking in, smoking in movies and, 653

Adoption, of children who do not know English prior to adoption, 354
Adrenal glands, 99
    threat and, 631, 631f
Adrenaline
    memory and, 255
    stress and, 642
Adrenocorticotropic hormone
    release of, 98–99
    threat and, 631, 631f
Adulthood, 456f, 456–463
    age-related decline in intelligence and, 409
    changing abilities in, 456–458, 458f, 459f
    changing goals in, 459–461, 459f–461f
    changing roles in, 461–462, 462f
    definition of, 456
    Erikson's developmental tasks of, 454t
    marriage in, 461, 462f, 522, 523
    parenting and, 463
    sleep needs in, 193
Advertising
    informational influence in, 531
    product placement and, 171
    sensory branding and, 171
    subliminal perception and, 188–189
Advice, parental, in infancy, 438
Aerobic exercise, for stress management, 641
African Americans
    in American Psychological Association, 33
    intelligence of, 416–418
    puberty among, 449
    stereotyping and. *See* Stereotyping
    Tuskegee Experiment and, 69
Afterimages, color, 140, 141f
Age. *See also* Adolescence; Adulthood; Childhood; Infancy
    age-related decline in intelligence and, 409
    attraction and, 520
    mental, 391
    sleep needs and, 193
Aggression, 507–509, 507f–509f. *See also* Hostility; Violence
    biology and, 507–508, 508f, 509
    culture and, 508–509, 509f
    definition of, 507
    frustration-aggression hypothesis and, 507
Agnosia, visual-form, 143f, 143–144
Agonists, 88, 88f, 89
Agoraphobia, 562
Agreeableness, 474–475, 475t, 476
AIDS, 650
    avoiding, 652
Air-crib, 18
Al-Anon, 604

Alarm phase of general adaptation syndrome, 631
Alcohol myopia, 204–205
Alcohol use/abuse, 203t, 204–205
    Alcoholics Anonymous and, 604, 605
    benzodiazepines combined with, 608
    mindwandering and, 182
    teratogenic effects of, 426–427
Alcoholics Anonymous, 604, 605
Algorithms, 370
Alpha waves, 191, 192f
    meditation and, 213
Alprazolam, 608
Altered states of consciousness. *See also* Dream(s); Hypnosis; Sleep; Substance abuse
    definition of, 190
    meditation and religious experiences, 212–214
Altruism, 514
    reciprocal, 514
Alzheimer's disease, acetylcholine and, 87
Ambien, 609
Ambivalent attachment style, 440
American Journal of Psychology, founding of, 12
American Psychological Association, 30–31, 33
    criteria for psychotherapy effectiveness published by, 619
    Ethical Principles of Psychologists and Codes of Conduct of, 69–70
    ethical treatment standards of, 620
    women and minorities in, 32, 34
American Psychological Society, 31
American Sign Language
    babbling in, 352
    brain areas and learning of, 25
    nonhuman primate learning of, 358, 360
Ames room, 153, 153f
Amitriptyline, 609
Amnesia, 553t
    anterograde, 228
    childhood (infantile), 257–258
    dissociative, 573
    posthypnotic, 211
    retrograde, 228–229
Ampakines, as cognitive enhancers, 417
Amphetamines. *See also* Adderall; Methamphetamine
    neurotransmitters and, 89
    overdose of, 89
    use/abuse of, 203t, 205–206
Amplitude
    of light waves, 134, 134t
    of sound waves, 157, 157t